PHILOSOPHY

PHILOSOPHY

AN INTRODUCTION TO THE LABOR OF REASON

◆

GARY PERCESEPE
Cedarville College

MACMILLAN PUBLISHING COMPANY
New York
COLLIER MACMILLAN CANADA
Toronto

Editor: Helen McInnis
Production Supervisor: York Production Services
Production Manager: Aliza Greenblatt
Cover Designer: Natasha Sylvester
Cover illustration: Reginald Wickham

This book was set in Janson by TSI Graphics, and
printed and bound by Book Press.
The cover was printed by Lehigh Press.

Macmillan Publishing Company
866 Third Avenue, New York, New York 10022

Collier Macmillan Canada, Inc.
1200 Eglinton Avenue East
Suite 200
Don Mills, Ontario M3C 3N1

Library of Congress Cataloging-in-Publication Data

Percesepe, Gary John.
    Philosophy : an introduction to the labor of reason / Gary J.
Percesepe.
        p.   cm.
    Includes index.
    ISBN 0-02-393981-8 (case)
    1. Philosophy—Introductions.   2. Philosophy—History.   I. Title.
BD21.P42   1991
100—dc20   90-41894
                              CIP

Printing: 1 2 3 4 5 6 7   Year: 1 2 3 4 5 6 7

FOR ARNOLD AND ROSALIA PERCESEPE
(MY FIRST TEACHERS),
AND FOR JAE AND VINNY PERCESEPE
WHO CONTINUE TO TEACH ME.

PREFACE

Philosophy: An Introduction to the Labor of Reason has grown out of my experiences over the years in the classroom. It is intended primarily for the introduction to philosophy course with a secondary application for the history of philosophy course. In putting this text together I have been guided by four principles:

1. *Philosophy is best introduced through the use of primary sources, both classical and contemporary.* Wherever possible, contemporary philosophers ought to be allowed to "talk back" to their philosophical predecessors; similarly, reading selections from the past should be shown to anticipate later philosophical developments.

2. *An anthology of primary sources needs to be supplemented by an "orientation" to both the subject matter and the lives of the various philosophers who have written on the subject.* A textbook must make every effort to provide a full range of "services" to the reader.

3. *A bridge must be built between the topical and historical study of philosophy.* To paraphrase Kant, a historical analysis of philosophical topics is blind; historical study without topical focus tends to be empty.

4. *A bridge must be built between the various philosophical traditions: Analytic, American, and Continental voices must all be given a hearing.* Russell, Dewey, and Heidegger all have a wisdom to share with us, as do Ryle, Peirce, and Foucault. Allan Bloom can be put in dialogue with Nietzsche and postmodern thinkers in a way that goes beyond trivial stereotyping and name-calling. All deserve to be heard.

In order to achieve these aims, primary source readings have been collected, organized topically, and placed in historical order in ten parts. Each part includes a detailed "Orientation" section, biographical sketches of the authors, and a discussion of each selection. A "Contemporary Perspectives" section at the end of each part features two contemporary readings, demonstrating the way the topic has "rotated" on its historical axis, admitting new points of view and carrying the conversation forward into the new century. Thus, in Part 1 the Contemporary Perspectives section addresses the topic of "Philosophy and the University" and features Richard Rorty and Allan Bloom on the status of philosophy at the university today; Part 3 features Nietzsche and Foucault on "The Politics of Truth," while phenomenology and feminist philosophy are featured in Part 5. Part 10 features an unusual pairing in aesthetics: the philosopher and novelist William H. Gass and the poet Elizabeth Bishop on the topic of "The Artist and Society."

With seventy-seven reading selections drawn from three traditions arranged historically on ten basic topics in philosophy, this is clearly a comprehensive textbook that can be used in a multitude of ways. Some instructors will be drawn to its topical format, while others will choose to move historically through the text, traversing chapters and topics. Two tables of contents are provided for these purposes, one topical, one historical. All parts conclude with a glossary of terms and suggestions for further reading. A separate study guide offers questions designed to stimulate classroom discussion.

I am somewhat uncomfortable making large claims about this textbook—my colleagues and, of course, our students must be the judge of how useful this volume is or is not. Still, I offer it in the sincere hope that it will help generate excitement and enthusiasm for a subject that I love. I am solely responsible for its flaws and indebted to a host of students and colleagues for whatever virtues it may possess. I am particularly grateful to my student assistant Dwight Davidson who worked diligently on the permissions, helped write study questions, prepared the indexes, provided the proverbial "student perspective" on the project, and served as general assistant. My colleague Doug Anderson reviewed the text carefully, making helpful suggestions and providing invaluable assistance, especially in the area of American philosophy. His willingness to take a phone call from a frantic author (day or night) has made this a better book. Naturally, I am indebted to all my teachers in philosophy, especially my first, James Grier, Jere Surber, and Frank Seeberger at the University of Denver, and James Collins, James Marsh, and Richard Blackwell from my years at Saint Louis University. I also wish to thank my editor, Helen McInnis, who believed in this project from the beginning and has helped make it a reality. Finally, special thanks are due to my wife, Suzanne, who managed to remain gracious as the printer spit out the pages of the manuscript long into the night; my parents, who taught me the value of education and how to question; and to my children, Jae and Vinny, whose childlike wonder about "the making of a book" has both delighted and inspired me.

Gary J. Percesepe

CONTENTS

CONTENTS

HISTORICAL CONTENTS

(Selection number appears in parentheses)

PART ONE

◆

On the Nature
and Possibility of Philosophy

For it is owing to their wonder that
men both now begin and first began to philosphize.

ARISTOTLE

ORIENTATION

o-ri-ent (or' e-ent). To set so as to face the East; to place in a definite direction to the points of the compass or other fixed or known directions; to acquaint (someone, oneself) with the present position relative to known point(s), or (fig.) with the details of the situation.

Taking a course in philosophy is a little like taking a long journey to a distant and foreign land: Everything is unfamiliar, the language sounds strange and exotic (even incomprehensible), and the natives that you meet seem ready to take advantage of you.

Travelers to foreign lands often feel compelled to consult a map, to compare the relative positions of where they are and where they want to go, so that they can see at a glance *the exact point in the world where they are.* Sometimes they buy tour books in an attempt to orient themselves to the new territory they will be exploring.

You may think of this textbook as a special kind of tour book, designed to acquaint you with the realm of philosophy. You needn't explore the world of philosophy by yourself—at least not at first. The course you are taking comes equipped with an instructor (your general tour guide) and maps (the Orientations to each chapter), as well as letters of introduction to the local tour guides (the authors of the reading selections that comprise this text). Instructor, Orientations, tour guides—all this is designed to make your journey into philosophy less forbidding.

The word *orient* is itself a geographical word. It means east. The ancient Eastern traditions (including the Biblical tradition) give a precise meaning to the east. The east symbolizes the point of departure, the direction of the rising sun. In the Bible, Abraham came searching from the east, as did the magi upon seeing a great star in the eastern sky. In our own early morining experience, as we set out on a journey or quest, it is the sun that greets us in the east. The east is the direction of beginnings, the point of orientation, the starting point. To "orient ourselves" thus means to face in the direction of beginnings, that we might know our way.

However, we do not remain fixed at the starting point; we leave. And so here we find ourselves, fellow travelers in this text-land called philosophy, poised at the beginning, Part One, ready to make a start. Yet perhaps this territory is neither as strange nor as alien as we suppose.

THE MEANING(S) OF PHILOSOPHY

DEFINITIONS

As you pick up this book, maybe for the first time, perhaps it is in hope of finding an answer to the nagging but perennial question, "Just what exactly *is* philosophy?" Be assured that many before you have made this query and have looked for a few words to fill in the blank at the end of the question, just as we have here:

Philosophy is _____.

This is certainly a straightforward approach, and one that may turn up a good many responses, some more helpful than others. Here a few of the standard ones:

1. Philosophy is the love of wisdom. (This is the very popular **etymological** approach.)

2. Philosophy is both the seeking of wisdom and the wisdom sought. (A more expansive approach, stressing both the *process* of philosophizing as well as the *product*.)

3. Philosophy is the logical analysis of language, clarifying the meaning of words and concepts. (An approach stressing the **analytic** nature of philosophy.)

4. Philosophy is that department of knowledge dealing with ultimate reality, or with the most general causes and principles of things (*Shorter Oxford Dictionary*).

5. Philosophy is a process of reflecting on and criticizing our most deeply held concepts and beliefs (Harold Titus, *Living Issues in Philosophy*).

6. Philosophy is a bunch of head games (an anonymous student).

Each of these formulations has its value, and each could be explored at greater length. Let us concentrate for a moment on the sixth approach. Suppose that we were to ask this question: "What does this formula, 'philosophy is a bunch of head games,' *mean*, and what understanding of philosophy does it reveal?"

One of the things it might mean is that philosophy is essentially playful, a kind of game. But what is a game? Organized play. But this is no ordinary game; it is said to be a "head game," which suggests that there is something intellectual about this game.

If we were to continue in this way, we might uncover a deeper set of understanding. For instance:

a. The idea of a game also suggests that there must be rules to follow and penalties for not following the rules. A person not knowing the rules will find it difficult to play the game.

b. Every game employs its own peculiar vocabulary, because the pieces or parts of the game must be named. Often games that at first seem strange and complicated come to be familiar with practice.

c. Over the course of time, the rules of the game may change, adapting to changing circumstances or social conditions. New ways to play games are constantly emerging.

Pushing deeper (admittedly deeper than this anonymous student may have dreamed of going), the idea of intellectual "head" labor may conjure up images of the University, as the appropriate arena for head games as practiced by academic specialists (a.k.a. Professors), persons who are acquainted with the game, knowledgable of the rules, and skilled at playing. It may also suggest that this specialist is the one most apt to teach the rules of the games to others so that they in turn may play.

What does all of this prove? One thing is that even popular, humorous definitions of philosophy harbor a certain understanding of what philosophy is all about. Even misconceptions about philosophy are still *conceptions*, and therefore instructive for discovering what ordinary people actually understand about philosophy, even when they may expressly claim that they understand nothing of philosophy and actually hold it in contempt. Blaise Pascal, a seventeenth century philosopher and mathematician, put it this way: "To ridicule philosophy is really to philosophize."

This leads us to a very significant observation. *We come to know what philosophy is when we ourselves try to philosophize.* Every attempt to answer the question "What is philosophy?" therefore harbors a pre-understanding of what philosophy is—at least enough of an understanding to make the question meaningful, to provide a base of understanding upon which we build. When we arrive at the point where the question is at least not nonsensical, then we are on the way to understanding the question itself, as well as the candidates for an answer. *Every attempt to "define" philosophy is itself an attempt, however awkward or humorous, to philosophize.* Like the person who wishes to learn to swim while refusing to enter the water, it is unreasonable to try to learn what philosophy is without philosophizing for yourself.

COMMON MEANINGS OF PHILOSOPHY (PHILOSOPHY-AS-ACTUALITY)

Reflecting further on the nature of philosophy, we soon encounter some common, well-publicized and "ready-made" meanings for philosophy. Like old friends, these are the meanings of philosophy that exist in actuality in our world.

Certainly there are many images of the philosopher in the public imagination, but they all seem to resolve themselves into the two opposing categories of lightness and weight. Put another way, it seems that our society cannot decide whether philosophy is a weighty matter deserving of utmost seriousness or the very lightest matter of all.

For some, the notion of the philosopher conjures up images of an old man with a long, flowing beard, propounding mysterious doctrines about "The Meaning of Life." A weighty matter.

To others, philosophy is a joke. Recalling again the sixth definition, perhaps we can uncover yet another meaning for the statement, "Philosophy is a bunch of head games." There is reason to believe that what this formula is really saying is that philosophy is at best a useless passion, mere mental or verbal gymnastics that may exercise the mind but have little relation to life. In this view, philosophy is perceived as an enterprise wherein whatever you say cannot be wrong, therefore anything (and everything) goes. There are no answers in philosophy. Since there are no answers, the questions of the philosopher are devalued as well, being regarded as the lightest of all, frivolous, unconnected to "real life."

There is an unmistakable tension here. It seems that we are both attracted and repelled by philosophy, an ambivalence that is quite striking. Our inability to decide whether philosophy is the weightiest affair imaginable or the silliest (lighter than air) ought to make us pause. Such ambiguity is instructive, arresting our attention and calling for further thought. What is it about philosophy that causes us to halt between images of lightness and weight?

This ambivalance in the public mind toward philosophy is nothing new. In fact, it is quite ancient, having a long history in Western civilization. As early as the fifth century B.C., Plato was joking about one of his predecessors, a Thracian named Thales (often presented in textbooks as the "first philospher").[1] It seems that Thales was studying the stars one night, deep in thought, when he tumbled down a well! Unfortunately for Thales, this misadventure was observed by a Thracian maid with a sharp wit, who scoffed at him for being so eager to know what was happening in the sky that he could not see what lay at his feet! To this Plato adds, in good editorial fashion, "Anyone who gives his life to philosophy is open to such mockery."[2]

Yet the image of the guru exists along with the mocking tone, and for good reason. Philosophy does seem to restore to things their weight, by taking seriously the problems and paradoxes that have bewildered men and women since the beginning. And we seem to have needed that weight, especially in the modern world, where everything seems weightless and insecure, and we seem compelled to view ourselves as unremarkable specks coasting in a universe of chance. After all these centuries, despite an explosion in knowledge unprecedented in human history, philosophy lives on, because of the peculiar and extraordinary desire we have to give our lives weight, addressing the "big questions," the questions that seem to mock us, yet also shape us and make us distinct from every other form of life.

Lightness and weight are the two poles of our existence. The ability to laugh, even at ourselves, sets us apart from every other creature known in the universe. Man is the laughing animal—and also the animal that gives himself weight. Along with art and religion, philosophy holds out the promise of calming the dreary

---

[1]Thrace was an ancient Greek city in Ionia, at the eastern end of the Aegean Sea.
[2]You may read this delightful story for yourself in one of the selections from Plato that follow.

technological frenzy of our lives, humanizing us, and making us more open to the problems and questions of human existence.

Lightness or weight? How shall we regard philosophy in its common meaning? The answer seems to be plural. Let us regard it with both humor and profound seriousness, befitting a matter of such lightness and weight.

PHILOSOPHY IS . . . (PHILOSOPHY-AS-POSSIBILITY)

Suppose that we drop the "fill in the blank" approach to the meaning of philosophy, leaving behind the realm of actuality and entering the realm of possibility. Suppose that we focus on the two words before us, *philosophy is* . . . What then?

When we do so, the meaning of philosophy becomes an undetermined possibility, *a yet to be*. The ellipsis (. . .) symbolizes a certain hesitancy to close on any *one* meaning of philosophy as the *only* meaning. In this reading, the meanings of philosophy are plural and in flux, not singular and static. No single meaning prevails. Philosophy is not simply identical with its own history, otherwise there would be no room in it for us. Nor is it completely unrelated to its history, otherwise there would be no point in reading the works of previous philosophers.

Simply put, philosophy has other possibilities that have yet to be realized (or actualized) in its history, and that is where *you* come in. Because philosophy belongs to all of us, not merely *some* of us, we can all have a say in what it shall come to mean in the future. Because philosophy is a public affair as well as a private concern, it continues to be socially available to all those for whom its possible meanings are an issue.

The meanings of philosophy are therefore directed toward the future. As we contemplate what philosophy is, we are already pointing at what philosophy might possibly become. We contemplate our own future as well as philosophy's future, and the points of intersection between the two. We put ourselves in question. As we question what philosophy is, philosophy questions us.

In asking ourselves "What is philosophy?" and responding "Philosophy is . . ." we *enact* the future, by refusing to restrict philosophy's possibilities, choosing instead to create room within ourselves for philosophy's future. Thus anyone attempting to write or say what philosophy is will be writing or saying the future: the future of philosophy as well as the philosophy of the future.

The readings in this book attempt to address these concerns by exhibiting texts from philosophy's past alongside texts drawn from its present—a present already proceeding into the future. These readings are quite literally "works" of philosophy, systematic yet loving evidence of the labor of reason in history. The Contemporary Perspectives sections in particular are intended to project us in the direction of our common future.

THE PROBLEMS OF PHILOSOPHY

THE PHILOSOPHER AS PROBLEM SOLVER

Philosophy is traditionally thought of as the discipline that discusses and attempts to resolve problems. When one thinks of a "philosophical problem," the image of weight naturally recurs. The problems of philosophy are perceived as weighty or "heavy" problems. This is appropriate but can be somewhat misleading. Without care, we may fall victim to thinking that philosophical problems are abstract, useless, and unrelated to life. Nothing could be further from the truth. The problems of philosophy are merely the problems that arise when we wonder about our life situations, or, as the twentieth century philosopher Martin Heidegger put it, our *being-in-the-world*. When you simply wonder about the world that has presented you with some problem, philosophy is born.

Any subject, provided it is pursued far enough, will reveal philosophical problems. Philosophical problems are merely extensions of our everyday problems, heightened and focused by our sense of wonder, and invariably posed in the form of the question.

The transition whereby we move from problem to question is best illustrated by an example. Suppose that a love affair goes hopelessly wrong (maybe not for the first time), or a trusted friend betrays you. You may be led to wonder why you seem to always be disappointed in love, or why people who care about you most are most capable of hurting you. If sometime after this event you learn that your parents are getting a divorce because of problems in their marriage they were unable to resolve, your sense of wonder may lead you to ask the questions "What is true love, and can it fail?" or "What is real friendship?"

As you listen to news reports of famine and terrorism, environmental pollution and violent crime, you may may be led to wonder why anyone would want to bring human life into this world. As you reflect on this at length, a problem may begin to emerge that can be captured by the following question: "Do we have responsibilities to future generations, and if so, why?"

If you are a religious person who has been taught to believe in the essential goodness and wisdom of God, you may someday be disturbed to learn of some tragic death that befalls another seemingly innocent religious person. Perhaps it will be a fatal disease, or the violent death of a loved one that will lead you ask a series of questions like these: Why did God allow this innocent person to suffer when God was powerful enough to stop it, especially when so many cruel and unkind people seem to prosper? Can belief in a loving and wise God be reconciled with the existence of physical and moral evil in the world? Must the reality of evil in the world cause us to give up traditional belief in God?

Let's say that you are hungry and learn that you will be forced to miss your regular dinner hour due to unexpected circumstances. It may occur to you that although you "understand with your mind" why you must miss your meal, your body can be quite demanding. As you ponder this dilemma (accompanied by the growling of your stomach), you may wonder whether your mind and body lead separate lives. Your body, which appears to be a physical object, may seem to you to be quite different from your mind, which is . . . . Well, what exactly *is* a mind? How would you describe one? What beings have one? What about animals? How does your mind differ from your body? Is there a distinction between brain and mind, or are they identical?

Perhaps you have gazed at the sky late at night, wondering about the universe. Has it always existed like this, or did it have a beginning in time? (Like others before you, you may get sidetracked here. What is time, anyway?) How can we ever know which of these two options is true? What is our place in the universe? How are humans different from other living or nonliving things? (Consider this briefly: Perhaps *thinking* is what makes us different from other beings. But what is thinking? Is it the performance of high level intellectual operations? If so, do computers think, while human infants do not? Now you find yourself deep in philosophical problems.)

By now you may have noticed several things that each of these "problem-experiences" has in common:

1. They all arise when we reflect at length on the meaning of our average every-day existence.

2. It is possible to identify and isolate each of these problems (although a relat-edness among problems can also be detected).

3. The way we identify a problem is by formulating a question that seems to capture the heart of the problem by stating its essential characteristics.

4. There does not seem to be any obvious or standard way to answer these questions.

This last point is especially important. Neither **common sense** nor **scientific method** (our usual problem-solving allies), provide us with an assured way of solving these problems or answering these questions. These problems seem to resist common sense or scientific resolution, since common sense reports to us an incredible variety of opinions (some contradictory to each other), while science (the chief problem-solver of the modern age) seemingly has no way of making these questions scientifically meaningful.[3] Because these questions seem to lack *scientific* meaning, they have been said to possess *philosophical* meaning. (Whether this is flattering or demeaning to philosophy is a matter of some dispute and is itself an example of a philosophical question.) What is clear is that problems such

---

[3]The famous scientist Albert Einstein once remarked, "Common sense is the sum total of all prejudices formed by the age of eighteen!"

as these properly belong to the world of philosophy, a world that is very near to us, being an extension of our everyday experience. It is also clear that philosophy must have some special method for addressing these questions and resolving these problems.

Problems such as these may irritate and disturb us, making us feel uncomfortable. Acting as an irritant, they prod us to think, feel, and question. By gently uncovering our ignorance, they point us in the direction of personal growth, demanding inquiry and study. By arousing our natural sense of wonder, they project us on an adventurous pathway of questioning that we trust will lead us to some answers.

At times we may wish that these problems would go away. In moments of frustration we may come to wish we had never heard of them! We are always free *not* to think of philosophical problems. Of course, ignoring a problem is not the same thing as solving it, nor is it as intellectually satisfying. And it is worth noting that moments of frustration are often the prelude to moments of great breakthrough.

THE PHILOSOPHER AS PHYSICIAN

Because philosophy is concerned with such daunting questions, treating them with utmost care, some people get impatient, expecting instant answers. Of course, it is true that some questions, being relatively simple and of a factual nature, may be answered simply and factually; for example, "What time is it?," or "Where in Denver is Mile High Stadium?" But philosophical questions are not simple; they are complex. They deserve to be taken seriously, in accordance with the weight we choose to assign to the meaning of our experience.

Identifying, clarifying, classifying, and analyzing problems have long been regarded as the tasks of philosophy. Like a doctor treating a problematic disease, the philosopher carefully observes a problem, noting its symptoms and distinguishing it from other problems. Ultimately, the philosopher attempts to treat (or solve) the problem. Just as it is unreasonable to blame a physician for causing a disease, it is a mistake to believe that philosophers are the causes of the problems they treat. Like physicians, philosophers play an important role in our society by identifying the ills that afflict us and educating us to treat ourselves.

NAMING PHILOSOPHICAL PROBLEMS

Sometimes honorific names are given to those problems that seem to recur again and again in the philosophic tradition from one generation to the next. For example, questions about the nature of mind and body have been organized around the honorific title, the "Mind-Body Problem," while questions about God and about evil are grouped under the heading, "The Problem of Evil."

Perennial problems are those stubborn problems of human experience that are difficult to resolve. Each of the problems mentioned in the preceding pages (and many others) may be regarded as perennial problems. Requiring individual treatment in each successive generation, perennial problems often adapt to changing social conditions, shifting the axis of philosophical discussion. It is instructive to follow the historical evolution of perennial problems such as the Mind-Body Problem and the Problem of Evil, noting the variation in philosophical treatment in accordance with the demands of each age. In this book, we attempt to do just that.

FROM PROBLEM TO CRISIS

It is possible for a problem to escalate into a crisis, both at the personal level and the social level. The word "crisis" is derived from a Greek word that means "to sift or separate." A crisis is a time of great danger or trouble in which the sifting of our character will determine whether bad consequences will follow. Popular culture has taken note of the heightened awareness that a crisis creates, often describing a person's reaction to adversity in his or her personal life as "being philosophical."

When a parent or grandparent dies, we are reminded of our own mortality. The reality of our own impending death may free us to see things in a new light, often heightening our sense of urgency in life and stimulating us to seek a life with more meaning. Psychologists, members of the clergy, and others in the helping professions are assigned the task of analyzing and treating these crises. In every case it is meaning we are after.

But there is also a sense in which a society may perceive that it is in crisis. Edmund Husserl, a twentieth century German philosopher and the founder of a movement in philosophy known as **phenomenology,** spoke of "the crisis of the European sciences."[4] By this he meant the fateful prospect of a society whose science had become so highly developed and abstract that it has lost contact with what Husserl called "the life world"—that is, the world of everyday existence. More recently, some philosophers have warned of the dangers of scientific and technological development apart from a corresponding rebirth in the sphere of human values and the life of the spirit. Others have sensed a crisis in philosophy itself, wondering aloud about "the end of philosophy" and employing the language of crisis.

---

[4]For Husserl, the adjective "European" meant the ideological identity that extends beyond geographical Europe (to America, for instance), among those who are the heirs of Greek philosophy.

Philosophizing from a sense of crisis, then, involves the cultivation of a heightened awareness of a problem or network of problems as leading to a loss of meaning. "Crisis philosophy" is that attempt to recover lost meaning, both for oneself and for one's culture.

THE QUESTIONS OF PHILOSOPHY

THE QUESTION OF THE QUESTION

Asking questions is undeniably part of the human condition. All of us have been asking questions for as long as we can remember. Question-asking seems to return us to our childhood by creating in us a sense of wondrous expectation and vulnerability that we frequently lose as we enter adulthood. Czech novelist Milan Kundera has brilliantly captured the childlike aspect behind questioning when he writes of Tereza, one of his memorable characters:

> These are the questions that have been going through Tereza's head since she was a child. Indeed, the only truly serious questions are the ones that even a child can formulate. Only the most naive of quesitons are truly serious.[5]

Although it is fairly obvious that questioning is an important part of what makes us truly human, exactly what a question is may not be so obvious. Suppose that we were to "question the question itself" by asking, "What are the essential conditions that must be present in order to have or to ask a question?" Three conditions seem to be crucial.

1. The very first requirement for asking a question is experience. Questioning is a natural outgrowth of our experience. Our living in the world seems to somehow compel us to question that experience. We do not question unless we have first experienced something. The question is always an inquiry into the depths of this experience. When we ask, "What is it that I am experiencing" (a question which frequently lies beneath the surface of our conscious life), we are asking for both the *cause* as well as the *meaning* of our experience.

2. Questioning involves a certain kind of ignorance about our experience. Confronted by an experience we do not fully understand, we desire to know more about that experience. Genuine questions arise when we respond to some inner

---

[5]Milan Kundera, *The Unbearable Lightness of Being* (New York: Harper & Row, 1984). p. 139.

drive to dispel ignorance, replacing it with knowledge. We question simply in order to know what we do not know. All of us naturally desire to know the "why" of our experience. The philosopher is simply the last person to stop asking why.

3.   Questioning also requires that something be known about our experience. This is the most profound aspect of the question and may seem **paradoxical** at first. Reflection reveals that every question is guided beforehand by what is sought in the question. As questioners, we must somehow know that we do not know (for why else would we be led to question?) and we must have a vague sense of what we are looking for. Of course, this knowledge is what we might call "background knowledge" and may remain vague and imprecise. Yet it is important, for without it we would have no reason to formulate a question, nor would we be capable of recognizing whether or not the question had been answered.

To review, our questions must meet three conditions:

1. We must experience something that alerts us to the incompleteness of our experience.
2. We must be aware of our ignorance, desiring to dispel it and replace it with knowledge.
3. We must be vaguely aware of what it is we do not know yet diligently seek.

We can illustrate the fulfillment of these three conditions by taking a simple example from our common experience. Suppose that a young child has for the first time in her life experience the freezing of a pond. A former liquid has now become a solid, as water has become ice. If the ice were thick enough, the child might even be able to walk across the pond, a decidedly new experience. Naturally, she would be puzzled by this experience, wondering what has happened. If you look closely at her, in her wonder and ignorance (as well as her natural desire to dispel that ignorance), her lips will begin to form a question.

It should be clear that when the child asks a question about her experience she is *not* questioning the fact of her recent experience—she has no doubt that this new smooth solid under her feet is there. Rather, she is questioning the *meaning* of her experience, and perhaps its *value* as well. She is perfectly aware of the fact that she is experiencing something new, yet it is also clear to her that there is something in this new experience that is eluding her, and it is that elusive something that has led her to question. Her question points to the direction of future knowledge that promises to complete the partiality of this experience, rendering it whole and complete. The question stands as a bridge between present ignorance and future knowledge.

ABOUT ANSWERS

In academic settings (particularly in philosophy classes) one sometimes gets the impression that questions are to be celebrated, while answers are not so important. Although it is true that a pathbreaking question diligently pursued is more exciting than a "pat answer" to a tired question, we should not allow ourselves to leap to the conclusion that answers are trivial and unimportant. There is a real sense in which questions cannot be thought apart from answers. Questions and answers are correlative—that is to say, they both need each other and apart from one another both are rendered ineffectual. Every authentic question has an answer (although the answer may not currently be known), and every answer is a response to some previously asked question.

An answer is simply the knowledge sought in the question. We know we have an answer when the ignorance that led us to question has been dispelled. If questions are like journeys, then answers are most like home. Questions are like long wanderings in the woods, excursions always fraught with the possibility of being lost, yet holding out the prospect of the security that comes with the end of a journey. When we find our answer, we know that we have safely arrived home, and we experience a sense of wholeness and satisfaction. Yet we also know that we live in the world, a condition that requires us to leave the safety and security of our homes for the uncertainty of crossing the boundaries again into a new world of knowledge. Risking being lost, we follow our questions into new, unexplored territories. Just as it seems unreasonable to think that we would have ever set out on a journey without the prospect of arriving home, so it seems unlikely for there to be questions that have no answers.

This does not mean, however, that philosophy can answer all of our questions. Some questions have answers that are humanly unknowable. How many fish are in Lake Superior? It seems doubtful that anyone knows the answer, yet this does not invalidate the question, nor does it prevent us from attempting to give a *response*. In a similar way, the philosopher, when confronted with a particularly complex and difficult question, may tentatively offer a response, or a series of responses. The question may be taken before the collective judgment of the philosophic community (through seminars, books, articles, and conferences), where all stakeholders in the question may extend, correct, and refine the question, projecting their responses in the direction of an answer. That answer may withstand the demands of an age, only to be reassessed by other individuals in another age. In such ways does science progress. Philosophical questions are the questions that set the limits of human possibilities and describe the boundaries of human existence.

Some answers are more complete than others. If someone asks, "What is that in the field," and we reply, "Something gray," or "An animal," we have not really answered the question if the object in question is a horse. Since the horse is gray, and most certainly is an animal, we have a partial answer, not a complete one. It is not yet a complete answer because it fails to dispel the ignorance that framed the question. In the same way philosophers give perspectives on the question, tendering responses that attempt to "fill up" the measure of the question, until a complete answer is within reach. Yet it seems unlikely that we shall dispel all of our ignorance on every question; hence, while complete answers to factual questions are possible, a total answer to a philosophical question may exist only as an ideal. Our reach in these matters always exceeds our grasp.

THE PSEUDO-QUESTION

If it is true that a question always involves ignorance as well as a recognition of that ignorance, then to question what is already known must be a false question, or a pseudo-question. Although the pseudo-question resembles the authentic question in every detail, it is a question in appearance only. We often refer to such questions as *rhetorical questions*, since they are employed almost exclusively by public speakers or writers (frequently teachers) in order to emphasize a point they wish to make. Rhetorical questions serve a useful function in society but this does not make them authentic questions, as we have been using that term.

Although rhetorical questions are socially useful, it is hard to see the usefulness of questions asked by other persons (not rhetoriticians) who already know the answer to the question they pose. Most of us have on occasion witnessed a classmate who asked a teacher a question, not to dispel some ignorance but to see if the teacher could be stumped, or to proudly display some knowledge. Such self-serving behavior is unfortunate, and perhaps reveals more about the "questioner" than it does about the question.

THE METHOD OF PHILOSOPHY

SOCRATIC DIALECTIC

We have seen that philosophy originates in wonder about the problem of life, a wonder that leads us to question. Philosophical questions are those heightened expressions of our curiosity about ourselves and our world. But how does philosophy go about answering all of these questions?

Philosophy answers questions through a method known as **dialectic.** Dialectic may be thought of as the art of disciplined conversation. The use of dialectic can be traced back to Socrates, perhaps the best known of the early Greek philosophers. Since Socrates wrote nothing, we have come to learn of his "Socratic method" largely through the writings of his most famous student, Plato. Plato used the dialogue as his favorite form of writing, developing a style that proved to be highly conducive to dialectical reasoning.

Dialectical reasoning is disarmingly simple and may be practiced by anyone, although like most skills it is perfected through practice. The idea is to clarify the meaning of some basic question (for example, "What is justice?") by exchanging reasoned arguments and views on the subject with other interested persons, in what we might call a "community of inquirers." As Socrates practiced the method, the asking of the initial question would elicit intense self-examination, as each member of the group was challenged to ponder the *reasons* behind a given response and gently prodded to relinquish any position that was found to be groundless or contrary to reason. No one was allowed to "philosophize from on high"—that is, appeals to authority, tradition, or social convention were rejected as inadequate in themselves. For Socrates and his dialogical companions, the only sure foundation of knowledge was that which could withstand relentless criticism; thus, they boldly followed the question wherever it led. As the leader of the conversation, Socrates played the role of the gadfly, stinging and cajoling his companions until it became clear that the "first offerings" of positions were confused ideas—unclear and untrue. Undaunted, Socrates and his partners would begin again, perpetual philosophical beginners, building on the new knowledge of their ignorance time and time again, until gradually their conversation began to converge on the true.

Three things are noteworthy about the Platonic/Socratic treatment of dialectic:

1. Platonic dialectic assumes that truth exists and is accessible to us through diligent practice of the method. According to Plato, dialectic is the pathway to the Good, the True, and the Beautiful.

2. Platonic dialectic assumes that language mirrors reality in such a way that careful attention to language and definition will reveal the way things really are in the world.

3. Platonic dialectic cherishes the public pronoun "we," believing that philosophy is best practiced in a community. Although individually each of us may only possess an **opinion,** (our own private belief), together, in common conversation, we can correct each other in the direction of truth, as the private "I" becomes the social "we." This "publicness of knowledge," a hallmark of all

science, provides an **objectivity** that distinguishes real knowledge from mere subjective opinion.[6]

OBSTACLES TO THE METHOD

The greatest obstacles to the success of this methodology are intellectual conceit and uncritical dogmatism. It appears that one of Socrates' objectives in dialectic was to draw out the inconsistencies, errors, and absurdities of a person's original confident assertions about justice, beauty, piety, or whatever happened to be the topic under consideration. The aim was to demonstrate the need for **justifying** one's **assertions** through sustained argument. Any claim that is put forward without evidence is a mere assertion—a free-floating sentence detached from any supporting evidence. As Socrates repeatedly showed, anything that is arbitrarily asserted can be rationally questioned or denied. *Providing sound arguments to justify our assertions can be thought of as the main business of philosophy.* Hence, Socrates' relentless questioning was designed to demonstrate to his companions (and to himself) the poverty of their thought. Whereas they thought they were rich in knowledge, the dialectical conversation had shown them to be poor indeed. This sense of poverty, or *intellectual humility*, is our greatest asset in the quest for truth and is an essential condition of real learning. As Socrates and Martin Heidegger realized, the best teachers (not to be confused with the most famous Professors) are those who succeed in modeling how learning happens, by their willingness to learn themselves. Heidegger expressed it this way:

Teaching is even more difficult than learning. We know that; but we rarely think about it. And why is teaching more difficult than learning? Not because the teacher must have a larger store of information, and have it always ready. Teaching is more difficult than learning because what teaching calls for is this: to let learn. The real teacher, in fact, lets nothing else be learned than— learning. . . The teacher is ahead of his apprentices in this alone, that he has still more to learn than they—he has to learn to let them learn. The teacher must be capable of being more teachable than the apprentices. The teacher is far less assured of his ground than those who learn are of theirs.[7]

[6]Although Platonic/Socratic dialectic has been emphasized in this section, it is important to realize that other philosophers have stressed the importance of dialectic as well, each highlighting different aspects of these three characteristics, and in some cases challenging or refining them. Philosophers who stress the importance of dialectic besides Plato and Socrates include Aristotle, Kierkegaard, Hegel, Nietzsche, Marx, Merleau-Ponty, and Adorno.

[7]Martin Heidegger, *What Is Called Thinking*, trans. J. Glenn Gray (New York: Harper & Row, 1968), p. 15.

There is no room in philosophy for the know-it-all, be it teacher or student. Once humility has been established and every pretense to knowledge given up, the serious task of establishing secure rational grounds for belief begin. The method is the same as before—the question/answer dialectical process—but now it has been enriched by a genuine sense of intellectual and personal *need* that energizes the process in a continual quest for truth, with insistent demands for better arguments, more thoughtful analysis, and more critical self-examination. Taking this method seriously, nothing shall be left unquestioned, least of all we ourselves. As Socrates observed, "The unexamined life is not worth living."[8]

THE PHILOSOPHIC COMMUNITY

Of course, the philosophy class you are enrolled in is itself a philosophical community. As such, it is a natural place to practice Socratic dialectic. As you become comfortable with the method, you may find it spilling out of the four walls of the classroom to the dining hall or student union, or even to your living room. You may even find yourself in the position of a Socratic gadfly, challenging received opinion in the pursuit of the true. Should this occur, try to remember that for Socrates, the conversation was never far from some basis in morality. That is, it aimed at the the edification and betterment of each person, not at the destruction or censoring of a person.

THE BRANCHES OF PHILOSOPHY

Historically, philosophers have identified four main branches of their discipline: **logic, metaphysics, epistemology,** and **axiology.** These branches of philosophy are clusters of problems and questions that arise for thought. The next few pages are intended to give you a sampling of the kinds of problems and questions that arise in these areas.

---

[8]The youthful Karl Marx once wrote a remarkable letter to his friend Arnold Ruge in which he dedicated himself to, "A Ruthless Criticism of Everything Existing." This is very much in the spirit of dialectic! There is some question, however, of whether this ideal can be realized. Some philosophers have argued that the best of us have certain "blind spots," immune from criticism, which we jealously protect in order to further our own designs. One question that emerges is this: Can there be an "assumption-free" or presuppositionless philosophy? Or is it the case that every philosophy is laden with certain biases that militate against the very ideals of objectivity and self-criticism that they claim to embrace? If the latter is the case, (and it seems likely it is) then it would seem that there can be no such thing as a "self-grounding philosophy," and every attempt to propogate one should be greeted with suspicion.

LOGIC: WHAT IS GOOD THINKING?

Our English word *logic* is derived from the Greek word *logos*, which means "reasoned discourse." You may have noticed derivatives from this word in the *logy* ending into certain words, such as these naming academic disciplines—biology, sociology, theology, and anthropology. These disciplines are reasoned discourses on life, society, God, and man.

But what kind of reasoned discourse is logic? Clearly it is not the same category as any of the aforementioned, since it is not about any *thing*. That is, logic is concerned with thought itself, rather than thought about any particular kind of object in the world. In this sense, logic is a *formal* discipline, not a *factual* discipline. Logic is abstract, and therefore empty of content other than thought itself. The study of logic involves thought scrutinizing and classifying its own patterns and processes, and enumerating rules of correct thinking.

Because logic is an abstract, or general, science, it has a great variety of applications. As "the science of the sciences," it is indispensible to the other branches of philosophy and indeed to any endeavor where truth and conceptual clarity are prized. All of use reason every day. Logic is a powerful tool for evaluating whether or not we are thinking correctly.

Logic may be defined as the science of evaluating arguments. An **argument,** as the word is used in logic, is simply a group of statements containing one or more statements (the **premises**) that are claimed to provide support for one of the other statements (called the **conclusion**). An **inference** is a conclusion that has been derived from one of two sources: from other general premises **(deduction)** or from factual evidence **(induction).** Arguments whose premises fail to establish their conclusion are said to be unsound (or bad) arguments, while arguments whose premises succeed in establishing their conclusion are called sound (or good) arguments. The purpose of logic, then, is to assist us in recognizing and employing good arguments, while avoiding fallacies (defects in arguments).

EPISTEMOLOGY: WHAT MAY BE KNOWN?

The term **epistemology** is derived from the Greek word *episteme*, meaning knowledge. Broadly speaking, epistemology is the branch of philosophy that studies the nature, sources, validity, and limits of knowledge. There are four fundamental questions that concern epistemologists:

1. What is the nature of knowledge? Is it mere opinion or belief, or must belief be **justified**—that is, must it be supported by evidence? If the latter, then how much evidence do we need in order to justify our beliefs? How can we know that we know? How can we be sure that there is a real world outside of our minds?

2.   What are the sources of knowledge? That is, where does our knowledge come from? Does it come from sense experience, or from pure reason, apart from any use of the five senses? What about claims that appear to be self-evident? Are intuition and authority legitimate sources of knowledge?

3.   Is our knowledge valid? What do we mean by truth, and how do we distinguish it from error? Is there a reliable way to test truth, to verify that we have it?

4.   What is science? What is scientific method? What is technology? Can science tell us everything we want to know, or are there limits to the objective methods of scientific explanation? What is the relationship between science, technology, and human values?

As philosophers have wrestled with these questions through the years, two schools of thought have emerged: **rationalism** and **empiricism.** Rationalists believe that pure reason alone, unaided by the senses, is sufficient for obtaining reliable knowledge. (Some rationalists, like Plato, go so far as to argue that sense experience contributes nothing to genuine knowledge.) Empiricists claim that all knowledge is ultimately derived from sense experience; hence, our knowledge of the world is restricted to what we can actually experience. (Some empiricists, such as the eighteenth century British philosopher David Hume, argue that speculation beyond what is directly experienced via sense perception is bound to lead us into error and metaphysical foolishness.)

Of course, our view of reality will affect our view of what may be known. Conversely, our theory of knowledge depends on our understanding of the self and its relation to the world. Hence, metaphysics and epistemology are closely linked with one another.

METAPHYSICS: WHAT IS REAL?

The branch of philosophy that deals with the nature of reality is called **meta-physics.** For Aristotle (Plato's most famous student, and the author of many important treatises in philosophy), the term metaphysics meant "first philosophy," a discipline that discusses the most universal principles and causes of things. There is reason to believe that the treatise Aristotle wrote on this subject was entitled *Metaphysics* simply because it came after *(meta)* his treatise on physics. However, the term metaphysics eventually came to be understood as the science that deals with reality beyond the physical world, or beyond nature *(meta-physikon)*. Philosophers generally subdivide metaphysics into three main divisions: **ontology** (or the science of Being), **philosophical anthropology** (e.g., philosophy of mind), and **philosophy of religion.**

Metaphysics is the branch of philosophy that many students find hardest to understand. Metaphysics attempts to construct a comprehensive view of all reality. It is concerned with some of the most challenging and perplexing questions you will face in your study of philosophy—the origin and nature of space and time, the nature of change and causality, the nature of the human person, freedom and determinism, the existence of God, and the problem of evil. Parts 5 through 7 of this textbook deal with some of these metaphysical problems and the questions they engender.

Some philosophers, attracted by a scientific model emphasizing sense perception and nonspeculative objective methods, are skeptical about the value of practicing metaphysical thinking in the modern age. Doubting that a comprehensive view of all reality is possible, they choose to restrict their efforts in this area to clarifying what is meant by metaphysical questions, analyzing the language of metaphysics even while admitting the "closure" of metaphysics as a viable source of philosophic knowledge. On this view, metaphysics is an outdated mode of philosophy that aims merely at edification, not scientific knowledge. Other philosophers disagree, continuing to see value in traditional approaches to metaphysics and looking for new ways to make its problems and questions meaningful in a skeptical age. These philosophers believe that part of what it means to be human is a desire to push beyond the limits of the natural order, led by questions about transcendent reality.

AXIOLOGY: WHAT IS OF VALUE?

Axiology is the branch of philosophy that deals with value theory. It has traditionally been subdivided into **ethics, social and political philosophy,** and **aesthetics.**

Ethics is the discipline that attempts to establish rational grounds for right conduct. It is a normative discipline as opposed to a descriptive discipline. This is a crucial distinction, deserving a few words of explanation.

By now you may have noticed that statements can be roughly divided into two types: descriptive and normative. Descriptive statements are those that simply assert a fact, without making any kind of evaluation. Normative statements, on the other hand, make value judgments, asserting that something is right or wrong, good or bad. Consider the following sets of statements, and ask yourself which are descriptive statements and which are normative.

A	B
1. Dana Smith was born in 1954.	1. Dana Smith is a good person.
2. Handguns have killed many people.	2. Handguns are bad things to have.
3. Some people break promises.	3. Promise breaking is immoral.
4. Suicide rates among teens are rising.	4. Suicide is wrong.

When we compare these groups of statements, it is clear that Group A is merely describing states of affairs in the world, while Group B is evaluating those same states from a moral point of view. Type-A statements describe *the world as it is*, while Type-B statements pass judgment on *how the world ought to be*. The language of "moral oughtness" is the language of ethics.

Social and political philosophy examines the value judgments operative in the state and society. The central problem concerns the relation of the individual to the state. What does a person really owe to the state? Is the state justified in limiting human liberties? Is there a distinction between legal and moral justice? How ought we to act when we believe the law of the land to be unjust? Is civil disobedience ever justified? These are examples of questions that arise in this domain of value theory.

Finally, aesthetics is the philosophy of art and beauty. When we pass judgment on a work of art, we are expressing our sense of artistic value. At first, likes and dislikes in the realm of art are apt to seem quite subjective. A very important problem in aesthetics is the question of criteria. What are the criteria of good work of art? Is there a set of objective criteria grounding normative claims about good and bad art or is this all merely relative, "a matter of taste"? Do we have an obligation to "educate our taste" in art? Is it possible that the wide varieties of aesthetic response reflect varying degrees of preparation on the part of viewers? Finally, what is the role of artists in society?

The Value of Philosophy

It is fitting that we should conclude this section with a series of questions about value. A very large question that you may have on your mind at this point may well be, "What is the value of philosophy?" In large part, the readings that follow are designed to answer this question, from a variety of perspectives. Philosophers as different as Bertrand Russell and Martin Heidegger will address this question *for you* and *with you*. But in the end, this is a question that you must answer for yourself. The way that you answer will reveal quite a bit about what is most important to you—what *you* value. For instance, will you join those who criticize philosophy because it "bakes no bread"—that is, it does not *seem* to be materially profitable to study philosophy? Or will you reveal yourself to be a person that values ideas and a life of reflection and reasonableness? How will you respond to Martin Heidegger's challenge in the pages that follow when he acknowledges the old complaint that one cannot *do* anything with philosophy but then shifts the question to ask "What can philosophy do with us?" There is an answer to this question, but you must supply it, beginning now.

CHAPTER 1

PLATO

THE MYTH OF THE CAVE AND THE STORY OF THALES

Plato (427–347 B.C.), born in Athens into an aristocratic family, was one of the great lights of Western culture. He had originally planned to enter politics but was profoundly affected by the trial and execution of his beloved teacher, Socrates. After the death of Socrates, he left Athens and traveled extensively, returning in 387 to found a school, known as the Academy, where he taught for the next forth years.

Plato's writings, elegantly written and profound, are distinctive for their dialogue form, often featuring Socrates as the principal figure. In the later dialogues, the character Socrates is a mouthpiece for Plato's own philosophical explorations and positions. His best known writings, *Apology*, *Crito*, and *Phaedo*, deal with Socrates' trial and his last visits with his friends. The *Republic*, arguably Plato's greatest work, concerns justice in the individual and in the State. Other classic Platonic dialogues include *Euthyphro*, which discusses piety; *Theatetus*, which is concerned with the theory of knowledge; and the *Symposium*, on the nature of love and beauty.

Our first selection is taken from Plato's *Republic* and is in the form of a parable, or **myth**.[1] A myth is a story or legend of often forgotten origin, that offers poetic insight into the nature of reality. In this myth, Plato likens the human race to prisoners in a cave, trapped since birth. The bonds are the chains of ignorance that

---

[1]From Plato, *The Republic*, translated by Benjamin Jowett (Oxford: Oxford University Press, 1892).

bind us all, keeping us in darkness, dwellers in unreality. Philosophy is presented as the ascension of the soul out of the cave and into the sunshine of full reality. (The sun in Plato's writings is a symbol of the Good.) Philosophy is thus understood as waking up the soul to reality.

The second selection is a brief passage from *Theatetus*, featuring Plato's humorous and poignaint commentary on his philosophical predecessor, Thales.[2] The theme of lightness and weight is unmistakable.

THE MYTH OF THE CAVE

Next, said I, compare our nature in respect of education and its lack to such an experience as this. Picture men dwelling in a sort of subterranean cavern with a long entrance open to the light on its entire width. Conceive them as having their legs and necks fettered from childhood, so that they remain in the same spot, able to look forward only, and prevented by the fetters from turning their heads. Picture further the light from a fire burning higher up and at a distance behind them, and between the fire and the prisoners and above them a road along which a low wall has been built, as the exhibitors of puppet shows have partitions before the men themselves, above which they show the puppets.

All that I see, he said.

See also, then, men carrying past the wall implements of all kinds that rise above the wall, and human images and shapes of animals as well, wrought in stone and wood and every material, some of these bearers presumably speaking and others silent.

A strange image you speak of, he said, and strange prisoners.

Like to us, I said. For, to begin with, tell me do you think that these men would have seen anything of themselves or of one another except the shadows cast from the fire on the wall of the cave that fronted them?

How could they, he said, if they were compelled to hold their heads unmoved through life?

And again, would not the same be true of the objects carried past them?

Surely.

If then they were able to talk to one another, do you not think that they would suppose that in naming the things that they saw they were naming the passing objects?

Necessarily.

And if their prison had an echo from the wall opposite them, when one of the passers-by uttered a sound, do you think that they would suppose anything else than the passing shadow to be the speaker?

By Zeus, I do not, said he.

Then in every way such prisoners would deem reality to be nothing else than the shadows of the artificial objects.

Quite inevitably, he said.

[2]This portion of Plato's dialogue *Theatetus* is taken from *The Collected Dialogues of Plato*, edited by Edith Hamilton and Huntington Cairn. Bollingen Series 71. Copyright 1961, © 1989 renewed by Princeton University Press. Excerpt, pp. 747–750, 878–880. Reprinted by permission of Princeton University Press.

Consider, then, what would be the manner of the release and healing from these bonds and this folly if in the course of nature something of this sort should happen to them. When one was freed from his fetters and compelled to stand up suddenly and turn his head around and walk and to lift up his eyes to the light, and in doing all this felt pain and, because of the dazzle and glitter of the light, was unable to discern the objects whose shadows he formerly saw, what do you suppose would be his answer if someone told him that what he had seen before was all a cheat and an illusion, but that now, being nearer to reality and turned toward more real things, he saw more truly? And if also one should point out to him each of the passing objects and constrain him by questions to say what it is, do you not think that he would be at a loss and that he would regard what he formerly saw as more real than the things now pointed out to him?

Far more real, he said.

And if he were compelled to look at the light itself, would not that pain his eyes, and would he not turn away and flee to those things which he is able to discern and regard them as in very deed more clear and exact than the objects pointed out?

It is so, he said.

And if, said I, someone should drag him thence by force up the ascent which is rough and steep, and not let him go before he had drawn him out into the light of the sun, do you not think that he would find it painful to be so haled along, and would chafe at it, and when he came out into the light, that his eyes would be filled with its beams so that he would not be able to see even one of the things that we call real?

Why, no, not immediately, he said.

Then there would be need of habituation, I take it, to enable him to see the things higher up. And at first he would most easily discern the shadows and, after that, the likenesses or reflections in water of men and other things, and later, the things themselves, and from these he would go on to contemplate the appearances in the heavens and heaven itself, more easily by night, looking at the light of the stars and the moon, than by day the sun and the sun's light.

Of course.

And so, finally, I suppose, he would be able to look upon the sun itself and see its true nature, not by reflections in water or phantasms of it in an alien setting, but in and by itself in its own place.

Necessarily, he said.

And at this point he would infer and conclude that this it is that provides the seasons and the courses of the year and presides over all things in the visible region, and is in some sort the cause of all these things that they had seen.

Obviously, he said, that would be the next step.

Well then, if he recalled to mind his first habitation and what passed for wisdom there, and his fellow bondsmen, do you not think that he would count himself happy in the change and pity them?

He would indeed.

And if there had been honors and commendations among them which they bestowed on one another and prizes for the man who is quickest to make out the shadows as they pass and best able to remember their customary precedences, sequences, and coexistences, and so most successful in guessing at what was to come, do you think he would be very keen about such rewards, and that he would envy and emulate those who were honored by these prisoners and lorded it among them, or that he would feel with Homer and greatly prefer while living on earth to be serf of another, a landless man, and endure anything rather than opine with them and live that life?

Yes, he said, I think that he would choose to

endure anything rather than such a life.

And consider this also, said I. If such a one should go down again and take his old place would he not get his eyes full of darkness, thus suddenly coming out of the sunlight?

He would indeed.

Now if he should be required to contend with these perpetual prisoners in 'evaluating' these shadows while his vision was still dim and before his eyes were accustomed to the dark— and this time required for habituation would not be very short—would he not provoke laughter, and would it not be said of him that he had returned from his journey aloft with his eyes ruined and that it was not worth while even to attempt the ascent? And if it were possible to lay hands on and to kill the man who tried to release them and lead them up, would they not kill him?

They certainly would, he said.

This image then, dear Glaucon, we must apply as a whole to all that has been said, likening the region revealed through sight to the habitation of the prison, and the light of the fire in it to the power of the sun. And if you assume that the ascent and the contemplation of the things above is the soul's ascension to the intelligible region, you will not miss my surmise, since that is what you desire to hear. But Gods knows whether it is true. But, at any rate, my dream as it appears to me is that in the region of the known the last thing to be seen and hardly seen is the idea of good, and that when seen it must needs point us to the conclusion that this is indeed the cause for all things of all that is right and beautiful, giving birth in the visible world to light, and the author of light and itself in the intelligible world being the authentic source of truth and reason, and that anyone who is to act wisely in private or public must have caught sight of this.

I concur, he said, so far as I am able.

Come then, I said, and join me in this further thought, and do not be surprised that those who have attained to this height are not willing to occupy themselves with the affairs of men, but their souls ever feel the upward urge and the yearning for that sojourn above. For this, I take it, is likely if in this point too the likeness of our image holds.

Yes, it is likely.

And again, do you think it at all strange, said I, if a man returning from divine contemplations to the petty miseries of men cuts a sorry figure and appears most ridiculous, if, while still blinking through the gloom, and before he has become sufficiently accustomed to the environing darkness, he is compelled in courtrooms or elsewhere to contend about the shadows of justice or the images that cast the shadows and to wrangle in debate about the notions of these things in the minds of those who have never seen justice itself?

It would be by no means strange, he said.

But a sensible man, I said, would remember that there are two distinct disturbances of the eyes arising from two causes, according as the shift is from light to darkness or from darkness to light, and, believing that the same thing happens to the soul too, whenever he saw a soul perturbed and unable to discern something, he would not laugh unthinkingly, but would observe whether coming from a brighter life its vision was obscured by the unfamiliar darkness, or whether the passage from the deeper dark of ignorance into a more luminous world and the greater brightness had dazzled its vision. And so he would deem the one happy in its experience and way of life and pity the other, and if it pleased him to laugh at it, his laughter would be less laughable than that at the expense of the soul that had come down from the light above.

That is a very fair statement, he said.

25

THE STORY OF THALES

THEODORUS: Well, Socrates, we have time at our disposal.

SOCRATES: Evidently. And it strikes me now, as often before, how natural it is that men who have spent much time in philosophical studies should look ridiculous when they appear as speakers in a court of law.

THEODORUS: How do you mean?

SOCRATES: When you compare men who have knocked about from their youth up in law courts and such places with others bred in philosophical pursuits, the one set seem to have been trained as slaves, the others as free men.

THEODORUS: In what way?

SOCRATES: In the way you spoke of. The free man always has time at his disposal to converse in peace at his leisure. He will pass, as we are doing now, from one argument to another—we have just reached the third. Like us, he will leave the old for a fresh one which takes his fancy more, and he does not care how long or short the discussion may be, if only it attains the truth. The orator is always talking against time, hurried on by the clock; there is no space to enlarge upon any subject he chooses, but the adversary stands over him ready to recite a schedule of the points to which he must confine himself. He is a slave disputing about a fellow slave before a master sitting in judgment with some definite plea in his hand, and the issue is never indifferent, but his personal concerns are always at stake, sometimes even his life. Hence he acquires a tense and bitter shrewdness; he knows how to flatter his master and earn his good graces, but his mind is narrow and crooked. An apprenticeship in slavery has dwarfed and twisted his growth and robbed him of his free spirit, driving him into devious ways, threatening him with fears and dangers which the tenderness of youth could not face with truth

and honesty; so, turning from the first to lies and the requital of wrong with wrong, warped and stunted, he passes from youth to manhood with no soundness in him and turns out, in the end, a man of formidable intellect—as he imagines.

So much for the orator, Theodorus. Shall I now describe the philosophical choir to which we belong, or would you rather leave that and go back to our discussion? We must not abuse that freedom we claimed of ranging from one subject to another.

THEODORUS: No, Socrates, let us have your description first. As you said quite rightly, we are not the servants of the argument, which must stand and wait for the moment when we choose to pursue this or that topic to a conclusion. We are not in a court under the judge's eye, not in the theater with an audience to criticize our philosophical evolutions.

SOCRATES: Then, if that is your wish, let us speak of the leaders in philosophy, for the weaker members may be neglected. From their youth up they have never known the way to market place or law court or Council Chamber or any other place of public assembly; they never hear a decree read out or look at the text of a law. To take any interest in the rivalries of political cliques, in meetings, dinners, and merrymakings with flute girls, never occurs to them even in dreams. Whether any fellow citizen is well- or ill-born or has inherited some defect from his ancestors on either side, the philosopher knows no more than how many pints of water there are in the sea. He is not even aware that he knows nothing of all this, for if he holds aloof, it is not for reputation's sake, but because it is really only his body that sojourns in the city, while his thought, disdaining all such things as worthless, takes wings, as Pindar says, 'beyond the sky, beneath the earth,' searching the heavens and measuring the plains, everywhere seeking the true nature of everything as a whole, never sinking to what lies close at hand.

THEODORUS: What do you mean, Socrates?

SOCRATES: The same thing as the story about the Thracian maidservant who exercised her wit at the expense of Thales, when he was looking up to study the stars and tumbled down a well. She scoffed at him for being so eager to know what was happening in the sky that he could not see what lay at his feet. Anyone who gives his life to philosophy is open to such mockery. It is true that he is unaware what his next-door neighbor is doing, hardly knows, indeed, whether the creature is a man at all; he spends all his pains on the question, what man is, and what powers and properties distinguish such a nature from any other. You see what I mean, Theodorus?

THEODORUS: Yes, and it is true.

SOCRATES: And so, my friend, as I said at first, on a public occasion or in private company, in a law court or anywhere else, when he is forced to talk about what lies at his feet or is before his eyes, the whole rabble will join the maidservants in laughing at him, as from inexperience he walks blindly and stumbles into every pitfall. His terrible clumsiness makes him seem so stupid. He cannot engage in an exchange of abuse, for, never having made a study of anyone's peculiar weaknesses, he has no personal scandals to bring up; so in his helplessness he looks a fool. When people vaunt their own or other men's merits, his unaffected laughter makes him conspicuous and they think he is frivolous. When a despot or king is eulogized, he fancies he is hearing some keeper of swine or sheep or cows being congratulated on the quantity of milk he has squeezed out of his flock; only he reflects that the animal that princes tend and milk is more given than sheep or cows to nurse a sullen grievance, and that a herdsman of this sort, penned up in his castle, is doomed by sheer press of work to be as rude and uncultivated as the shepherd in his mountain fold. He hears of the marvelous wealth of some landlord who owns ten thousand acres or more, but that seems a small matter to one accustomed to think of the earth as a whole. When they harp upon birth—some gentleman who can point to seven generations of wealthy ancestors—he thinks that such commendation must come from men of purblind vision, too uneducated to keep their eyes fixed on the whole or to reflect that any man has had countless myriads of ancestors and among them any number of rich men and beggars, kings and slaves, Greeks and barbarians. To pride oneself on a catalogue of twenty-five progenitors going back to Heracles, son of Amphitryon, strikes him as showing a strange pettiness of outlook. He laughs at a man who cannot rid his mind of foolish vanity by reckoning that before Amphitryon there was a twenty-fifth ancestor, and before him a fiftieth, whose fortunes were as luck would have it. But in all these matters the world has the laugh of the philosopher, partly because he seems arrogant, partly because of his helpless ignorance in matters of daily life.

THEODORUS: Yes, Socrates, that is exactly what happens.

SOCRATES: On the other hand, my friend, when the philosopher drags the other upward to a height at which he may consent to drop the question, 'What injustice have I done to you or you to me?' and to think about justice and injustice in themselves, what each is, and how they differ from one another and from anything else, or to stop quoting poetry about the happiness of kings or of men with gold in store and think about the meaning of kingship and the whole question of human happiness and misery, what their nature is, and how humanity can gain the one and escape the other—in all this field, when that small, shrewd, legal mind has to render an account, then the situation is reversed. Now it is he who is dizzy from hanging at such an unaccustomed height and looking down from mid-air. Lost and dismayed and stammering, he will be laughted at, not by maidservants or the uneducated—they will not see what is happening—but by everyone whose breeding has been the antithesis of a slave's.

Such are the two characters, Theodorus. The one is nursed in freedom and leisure, the philosopher, as you call him. He may be excused if he looks foolish or useless when faced with some menial task, if he cannot tie up bedclothes into a neat bundle or flavor a dish with spices and a speech with flattery. The other is smart in the dispatch of all such services, but has not learned to wear his cloak like a gentleman, or caught the accent of discourse that will rightly celebrate the true life of happiness for gods and men.

CHAPTER 2

ARISTOTLE

THE PURSUIT OF WISDOM

Aristotle (384–322 B.C.), scientist, philosopher, and educator, was one of the most influential thinkers the world has ever known. Born in northern Greece, the son of the court physician to the King of Macedonia, he entered Plato's Academy at the age of eighteen, working closely with Plato for twenty years. After Plato's death, Aristotle was employed as a tutor to the thirteen-year-old son of Philip of Macedon, Alexander (later to become known as Alexander the Great). Aristotle eventually returned to Athens to found his own school, the Lyceum. Here, Aristotle and his colleagues carried on research and teaching in virtually every field of human knowledge. When Alexander died in 323 B.C., Athens was longer a hospitible place for the Macedonian-born Aristotle. Remembering the death of Socrates, Aristotle left Athens, "lest they sin twice against philosophy." He moved to his country estate in Chalcis, where he died the next year at the age of sixty-three.

Aristotle's wide-ranging scientific interests included physics, biology, astronomy, zoology, and medicine. He was the first to devise systematic criteria for analyzing and evaluating arguments, earning him the title the "Father of Logic." His classification of knowledge into the theoretical, the practical, and the productive is still recognized today. Although there is some crossover in his writings, theoretical knowledge is best represented by his *Metaphysics*, the practical by his *Nichomachean Ethics* and *Politics*, and the productive by his *Poetics*. As the medieval poet Dante put it, Aristotle was "il maestro di color che sanna"—that is, the master of them that know.

In this selection from his *Metaphysics*,[1] Aristotle reflects on the nature of philosophy as the pursuit of wisdom. He argues that the most authoritative science is the one that seeks the first principles and causes of all that can be known. Such a science is not a science of *production* (the Greek word is *techné*, from which we derive the English word *technology*), which seeks knowledge for some utilitarian end. It is rather the pursuit of knowledge for its own sake, a most divine science—the kind of science most fitting for a God to have. This science that investigates being as being is distinguished from every other science and is named "first philosophy," or metaphysics. Aristotle regards it as the only free science, for it alone exists for its own sake, and for the sake of nothing else.

THE PURSUIT OF WISDOM

Book A (1)

1. All men by nature desire to know. An indication of this is the delight we take in our senses; for even apart from their usefulness they are loved for themselves; and above all others the sense of sight. For not only with a view to action, but even when we are not going to do anything, we prefer seeing (one might say) to everything else. The reason is that this, most of all the senses, makes us know and brings to light many differences between things.

By nature animals are born with the faculty of sensation, and from sensation memory is produced in some of them, though not in others. And therefore the former are more intelligent and apt at learning than those which cannot remember; those which are incapable of hearing sounds are intelligent though they cannot be taught, e.g. the bee, and any other race of animals that may be like it; and those which besides memory have this sense of hearing can be taught.

The animals other than man live by appearances and memories, and have but little of connected experience; but the human race lives also by art and reasonings. Now from memory experience is produced in men; for the several memories of the same thing produce finally the capacity for a single experience. And experience seems pretty much like science and art, but really science and art come to men *through* experience; for 'experience made art', as Polus says, 'but inexperience luck'. Now art arises when from many notions gained by experience one universal judgement about a class of objects is produced. For to have a judgement that when Callias was ill of this disease this did him good, and similarly in the case of Socrates and in many individual cases, is a matter of experience; but to judge that it has done good to all persons of a certain constitution, marked off in one class, when they were ill of this disease, e.g. to phlegmatic or bilious people when burning with fever—this is a matter of art.

With a view to action experience seems in no

---

[1]Reprinted from *The Oxford Translation of Aristotle*, edited by W.D. Ross, Vol. 8 (1928) by permission of Oxford University Press.

respect inferior to art, and men of experience succeed even better than those who have theory without experience. (The reason is that experience is knowledge of individuals, art of universals, and actions and productions are all concerned with the individual; for the physician does not cure *man*, except in an incidental way, but Callias or Socrates or some other called by some such individual name, who happens to be a man. If, then, a man has the theory without the experience, and recognizes the universal but does not know the individual included in this, he will often fail to cure; for it is the individual that is to be cured.) But yet we think that *knowledge* and *understanding* belong to art rather than to experience, and we suppose artists to be wiser than men of experience (which implies that Wisdom depends in all cases rather on knowledge): and this because the former know the cause, but the latter do not. For men of experience know that the thing is so, but do not know why, while the others know the 'why' and the cause. Hence we think also that the master-workers in each craft are more honourable and know in a truer sense and are wiser than the manual workers, because they know the causes of the things that are done (we think the manual workers are like certain lifeless things which act indeed, but act without knowing what they do, as fire burns— but while the lifeless things perform each of their functions by a natural tendency, the labourers perform them through habit); thus we view them as being wiser not in virtue of being able to act, but of having the theory for themselves and knowing the causes. And in general it is a sign of the man who knows and of the man who does not know, that the former can teach, and therefore we think art more truly knowledge than experience is; for artists can teach, and men of mere experience cannot.

Again, we do not regard any of the senses as Wisdom; yet surely these give the most authoritative knowledge of particulars. But they do not tell us the 'why' of anything—e.g. why fire is hot; they only say *that* it is hot.

At first he who invented any art whatever that went beyond the common perceptions of man was naturally admired by men, not only because there was something useful in the inventions, but because he was thought wise and superior to the rest. But as more arts were invented, and some were directed to the necessities of life, others to recreation, the inventors of the latter were naturally always regarded as wiser than the inventors of the former, because their branches of knowledge did not aim at utility. Hence when all such inventions were already established, the sciences which do not aim at giving pleasure or at the necessities of life were discovered, and first in the places where men first began to have leisure. This is why the mathematical arts were founded in Egypt; for there the priestly caste was allowed to be at leisure.

We have said in the *Ethics* what the difference is between art and science and the other kindred faculties; but the point of our present discussion is this, that all men suppose what is called Wisdom to deal with the first causes and the principles of things; so that, as has been said before, the man of experience is thought to be wiser than the possessors of any sense-perception whatever, the artist wiser than the men of experience, the master-worker than the mechanic, and the theoretical kinds of knowledge to be more of the nature of Wisdom than the productive. Clearly then Wisdom is knowledge about certain principles and causes.

2.   Since we are seeking this knowledge, we must inquire of what kind are the causes and the principles, the knowledge of which is Wisdom. If one were to take the notions we have about the wise man, this might perhaps make the answer more evident. We suppose first, then, that the wise man knows all things, as far as possible,

although he has not knowledge of each of them in detail; secondly, that he who can learn things that are difficult, and not easy for man to know, is wise (sense-perception is common to all, and therefore easy and no mark of Wisdom); again, that he who is more exact and more capable of teaching the causes is wiser, in every branch of knowledge; and that of the sciences, also, that which is desirable on its own account and for the sake of knowing it is more of the nature of Wisdom than that which is desirable on account of its results, and the superior science is more of the nature of Wisdom than the ancillary; for the wise man must not be ordered but must order, and he must not obey another, but the less wise must obey *him*.

Such and so many are the notions, then, which we have about Wisdom and the wise. Now of these characteristics that of knowing all things must belong to him who has in the highest degree universal knowledge; for he knows in a sense all the instances that fall under the universal. And these things, the most universal, are on the whole the hardest for men to know; for they are farthest from the senses. And the most exact of the sciences are those which deal most with first principles; for those which involve fewer principles are more exact than those which involve additional principles, e.g. arithmetic than geometry. But the science which investigates causes is also *instructive*, in a higher degree, for the people who instruct us are those who tell the causes of each thing. And understanding and knowledge pursued for their own sake are found most in the knowledge of that which is most knowable (for he who chooses to know for the sake of knowing will choose most readily that which is most truly knowledge, and such is the knowledge of that which is most knowable); and the first principles and the causes are most knowable; for by reason of these, and from these, all other things come to be known, and not these by means of the things subordinate to them. And the science which knows to what end each thing must be done is the most authoritative of the sciences, and more authoritative than any ancillary science; and this end is the good of that thing, and in general the supreme good in the whole of nature. Judged by all the tests we have mentioned, then, the name in question falls to the same science; this must be a science that investigates the first principles and causes; for the good, i.e. the end, is one of the causes.

That it is not a science of production is clear even from the history of the earliest philosophers. For it is owing to their wonder that men both now begin and at first began to philosophize; they wondered originally at the obvious difficulties, then advanced little by little and stated difficulties about the greater matters, e.g. about the phenomena of the moon and those of the sun and of the stars, and about the genesis of the universe. And a man who is puzzled and wonders thinks himself ignorant (whence even the lover of myth is in a sense a lover of Wisdom, for the myth is composed of wonders); therefore since they philosophized in order to escape from ignorance, evidently they were pursuing science in order to know, and not for any utilitarian end. And this is confirmed by the facts; for it was when almost all the necessities of life and the things that make for comfort and recreation had been secured, that such knowledge began to be sought. Evidently then we do not seek it for the sake of any other advantage; but as the man is free, we say, who exists for his own sake and not for another's, so we pursue this as the only free science, for it alone exists for its own sake.

Hence also the possession of it might be justly regarded as beyond human power; for in many ways human nature is in bondage, so that according to Simonides 'God alone can have this privilege', and it is unfitting that man should not be content to seek the knowledge that is suited to him. If, then, there is something in what the poets say, and jealousy is natural to the divine power, it would probably occur in this case above all, and all who excelled in this knowledge would be unfortunate. But the divine power cannot be jealous (nay, according to the proverb, 'bards tell many a lie'), nor should any other science be thought more honourable than one of this sort. For the most divine science is also most honourable; and this science alone must be, in two ways, most divine. For the science which it would be most meet for God to have is a divine science, and so is any science that deals with divine objects; and this science alone has both these qualities; for (1) God is thought to be among the causes of all things and to be a first principle, and (2) such a science either God alone can have, or God above all others. All the sciences, indeed, are more necessary than this, but none is better.

Yet the acquisition of it must in a sense end in something which is the opposite of our original inquiries. For all men begin, as we said, by wondering that things are as they are, as they do about self-moving marionettes, or about the solstices or the incommensurability of the diagonal of a square with the side; for it seems wonderful to all who have not yet seen the reason, that there is a thing which cannot be measured even by the smallest unit. But we must end in the contrary and, according to the proverb, the better state, as is the case in these instances too when men learn the cause; for there is nothing which would surprise a geometer so much as if the diagonal turned out to be commensurable.

We have stated, then, what is the nature of the science we are searching for, and what is the mark which our search and our whole investigation must reach.

Book Γ (IV)

1. There is a science which investigates being as being and the attributes which belong to this in virtue of its own nature. Now this is not the same as any of the so-called special sciences; for none of these others treats universally of being as being. They cut off a part of being and investigate the attribute of this part; this is what the mathematical sciences for instance do. Now since we are seeking the first principles and the highest causes, clearly there must be something to which these belong in virtue of its own nature. If then those who sought the elements of existing things were seeking these same principles, it is necessary that the elements must be elements of being not by accident but just because it *is* being. Therefore is is of being as being that we also must grasp the first causes.

2. There are many senses in which a thing may be said to 'be', but all that 'is' is related to one central point, one definite kind of thing, and is not said to 'be' by a mere ambiguity. Everything which is healthy is related to health, one thing in the sense that it preserves health, another in the sense that it produces it, another in the sense that it is a symptom of health, another because it is capable of it. And that which is medical is relative to the medical art, one thing being called medical because it possesses it, another because it is naturally adapted to it, another because it is a function of the medical art. And we shall find other words used similarly to these. So, too, there are many senses in which a thing is said to be, but all refer to one starting-point; some things are said to be because they are substances, others because they are affections of substance, others because they are a process towards substance, or destructions or privations or qualities of substance, or productive or generative of substance, or of things which are relative to sub-

stance, or negations of one of these things or of substance itself. It is for this reason that we say even of non-being that it *is* non-being. As, then, there is one science which deals with all healthy things, the same applies in the other cases also. For not only in the case of things which have one common notion does the investigation belong to one science, but also in the case of things which are related to one common nature; for even these in a sense have one common notion. It is clear then that it is the work of one science also to study the things that are, *qua* being.—But everywhere science deals chiefly with that which is primary, and on which the other things depend, and in virtue of which they get their names. If, then, this is substance, it will be of substances that the philosopher must grasp the principles and the causes.

Now for each one class of things, as there is one perception, so there is one science, as for instance grammar, being one science, investigates all articulate sounds. Hence to investigate all the species of being *qua* being is the work of a science which is generically one, and to investigate the several species is the work of the specific parts of the science.

If, now, being and unity are the same and are one thing in the sense that they are implied in one another as principle and cause are, not in the sense that they are explained by the same definition (though it makes no difference even if we suppose them to be like that—in fact this would even strengthen our case); for 'one man' and 'man' are the same thing, and so are 'existent man' and 'man', and the doubling of the words in 'one man and one *existent* man' does not express anything different (it is clear that the two things are not separated either in coming to be or in ceasing to be); and similarly '*one* existent man' adds nothing to 'existent man', so that it is obvious that the addition in these cases means the same thing, and unity is nothing apart from being; and if, further,

the substance of each thing is one in no merely accidental way, and similary is from its very nature something that *is*:—all this being so, there must be exactly as many species of being as of unity. And to investigate the essence of these is the work of a science which is generically one—I mean, for instance, the discussion of the same and the similar and the other concepts of this sort; and nearly all contraries may be referred to this origin; let us take them as having been investigated in the 'Selection of Contraries'.

And there are as many parts of philosophy as there are kinds of substance, so that there must necessarily be among them a first philosophy and one which follow this. For being falls immediately into genera; for which reason the sciences too will correspond to these genera. For the philosopher is like the mathematician, as that word is used; for mathematics also has parts, and there is a first and a second science and other successive ones within the sphere of mathematics.

Now since it is the work of one science to investigate opposites, and plurality is opposed to unity—and it belongs to one science to investigate the negation and the privation because in both cases we are really investigating the one thing of which the negation or the privation is a negation or privation (for we either say simply that that thing is not present, or that it is not present in some particular class; in the latter case difference is present over and above what is implied in negation; for negation means just the absence of the thing in question, while in privation there is also employed an underlying nature of which the privation is asserted): —in view of all these facts, the contraries of the concepts we named above, the other and the dissimilar and the unequal, and everything else which is derived either from these or from plurality and unity, must fall within the province of the science above named. And contrariety is one of these concepts; for contrariety is a kind of difference, and difference is a kind of otherness. Therefore, since there are many senses in which a thing is said to be one, these terms also will have many senses, but yet it belongs to one science to know them all; for a term belongs to different sciences not if it has different senses, but if it has not one meaning and its definitions cannot be referred to one central meaning. And since all things are referred to that which is primary, as for instance all things which are called one are referred to the primary one, we must say that this holds good also of the same and the other and of contraries in general; so that after distinguishing the various senses of each, we must then explain by reference to what is primary in the case of each of the predicates in question, saying how they are related to it; for some will be called what they are called because they posses it, others because they produce it, and others in other such ways.

It is evident, then, that it belongs to one science to be able to give an account of these concepts as well as of substance (this was one of the questions in our book of problems), and that it is the function of the philosopher to be able to investigate all things. For if it is not the function of the philosopher, who is it who will inquire whether Socrates and Socrates seated are the same thing, or whether one thing has one contrary, or what contrariety is, or how many meanings it has? And similarly with all other such questions. Since, then, these are essential modifications of unity *qua* unity and of being *qua* being, not *qua* numbers or lines or fire, it is clear that it belongs to this science to investigate both the essence of these concepts and their properties. And those who study these properties err not by leaving the sphere of philosophy, but by forgetting that substance, of which they have no correct idea, is prior to these other things. For number *qua* number has peculiar attributes, such as oddness and evenness, commensurability and equality, excess and defect, and these belong to

numbers either in themselves or in relation to one another. And similarly the solid and the motionless and that which is in motion and the weightless and that which has weight have other peculiar properties. So too there are certain properties peculiar to being as such, and it is about these that the philosopher has to investigate the truth.—An indication of this may be mentioned:—dialecticians and sophists assume the same guise as the philosopher, for sophistic is Wisdom which exists only in semblance, and dialecticians embrace all things in their dialectic, and being is common to all things; but evidently their dialectic embraces these subjects because these are proper to philosophy.—For sophistic and dialectic turn on the same class of things as philosophy, but this differs from dialectic in the nature of the faculty required and from sophistic in respect of the purpose of the philosophic life. Dialectic is merely critical where philosophy claims to know, and sophistic is what appears to be philosophy but is not.

Again, in the list of contraries one of the two columns is privative, and all contraries are reducible to being and non-being, and to unity and plurality, as for instance rest belongs to unity and movement to plurality. And nearly all thinkers agree that being and substance are composed of contraries; at least all name contraries as their first principles—some name odd and even, some hot and cold, some limit and the unlimited, some love and stife. And all the others as well are evidently reducible to unity and plurality (this reduction we must take for granted), and the principles stated by other thinkers fall entirely under these as their genera. It is obvious then from these considerations too that it belongs to one science to examine being *qua* being. For all things are either contraries or composed of contraries, and unity and plurality are the starting-points of all contraries. and these belong to one science, whether they have or have not one single meaning. Probably the truth is that they have not; yet even if 'one' has several meanings, the other meanings will be related to the primary meaning (and similarly in the case of the contraries), even if being or unity is not a universal and the same in every instance or is not separable from the particular instances (as in fact it probably is not; the unity is in some cases that of common reference, in some cases that of serial succession). And for this reason it does not belong to the geometer to inquire what is contrariety or completeness or unity or being or the same or the other, but only to presuppose these concepts and reason from this starting-point.—Obviously then it is the work of one science to examine being *qua* being, and the attributes which belong to it *qua* being, and the same science will examine not only substances but also their attributes, both those above named and the concepts 'prior' and 'posterior', 'genus' and 'species', 'whole' and 'part', and the others of this sort.

CHAPTER 3

G. W. F. HEGEL

ON THE UNINTELLIGIBILITY OF PHILOSOPHY

G. W. F. Hegel (1770–1831) was a German philosopher born in Stuttgart, who spent his entire adulthood in academic life. He was a student at the famous Theological Institute at Tübingen, where he and his youthful friends welcomed the French Revolution with the singing of the "Marseillaise." Teaching successively at the universities in Jena, Heidelberg, and Berlin, he exercised a large influence on the direction philosophy was to take during his era. After his death, Hegel's devoted students compiled and edited his lecture notes, producing four books: lectures on the history of philosophy, the philosophy of history, the philosophy of religion, and the philosophy of art.

Hegel was an **idealist,** meaning that he believed that thought is the essence of the universe, and nature is simply the unfolding of mind or spirit *(geist)* in the world. Hegel believed that the laws of thought (logic) and the laws of reality (nature) correspond with one another, such that "the real is the rational, and the rational is the real." Hence, the world was "objective thought," the historical process of spirit manifesting itself in the world.

Hegel is perhaps most famous for his logic, or dialectical method, which involved the surmounting of initial opposition or contradiction in order to create new synthetic meanings. Hegel's dialectic became fixed in the popular imagination as thesis–*anti*thesis–*syn*thesis, a triadic structure that fired the imagination of Karl Marx. Marx, rejecting Hegel's idealist metaphysics, took over his dialectic, and applied it to social conditions in his now famous analysis of class conflict.

Hegel's important philosophical writings include the *Phenomenology of Spirit* (1807), *Science of Logic* (1812), *Encyclopedia of the Philosophical Sciences* (1817), and *Philosophy of Right* (1821).

In this selection from the *Encyclopedia of the Philosophical Sciences*,[1] Hegel describes the process wherein our original, common sense acquaintance with objects is revealed to be inadequate. This dissatisfaction is the impulse for thought to become philosophy, "the thinking study of things." His discussion of the "unintelligibility of philosophy" is not without irony, since Hegel is regarded by some as being the best example of an unintelligible philosopher! Hegel's comparison of philosophy to the craft of shoemaking is intended to instruct all those who are ready, at a moment's notice, to criticize philosophy.

ON THE UNINTELLIGIBILITY OF PHILOSOPHY

Philosophy misses an advantage enjoyed by the other sciences. It cannot like them rest the existence of its objects on the natural admissions of consciousness, nor can it assume that its method of cognition, either for starting or continuing, is one already accepted. The objects of philosophy, it is true, are upon the whole the same as those of religion. In both the object is Truth, in that supreme sense in which God and God only is the Truth. Both in like manner go on to treat of the finite worlds of Nature and the human Mind, with their relation to each other and to their truth in God. Some *acquaintance* with its objects, therefore, philosophy may and even must presume, that and a certain interest in them to boot, were it for no other reason than this: that in point of time the mind makes general *images* of objects, long before it makes *notions* of them, and that it is only through these mental images, and by recourse to them, that the thinking mind rises to know and comprehend *thinkingly*.

But with the rise of this thinking study of things, it soon becomes evident that thought will be satisfied with nothing short of showing the *necessity* of facts, of demonstrating the existence of its objects, as well as their nature and qualities. Our original acquaintance with them is thus discovered to be inadequate. We can assume nothing and assert nothing dogmatically; nor can we accept the assertions and assumptions of others. And yet we must make a beginning: and a beginning, as primary and underived, makes an assumption, or rather is an assumption. It seems as if it were impossible to make a beginning at all.

This *thinking study of things* may serve, in a general way, as a description of philosophy. But the description is too wide. If it be correct to say, that thought makes the distinction between man and the lower animals, then everything human is human, for the sole and simple reason that it is due to the operation of thought. Philosophy, on the other hand, is a peculiar mode of thinking— a mode in which thinking becomes knowledge, and knowledge through notions. However great

---

[1]G.W.F. Hegel. *Hegel's Logic: Being Part One of the Encyclopedia of the Philosophical Sciences*, trans. William Wallace (Oxford: Clarendon Press, 1975), p. 3–8.

therefore may be the identity and essential unity of the two modes of thought, the philosophic mode gets to be different from the general thought which acts in all that is human, in all that gives humanity its distinctive character. And this difference connects itself with the fact that the strictly human and thought-induced phenomena of consciousness do not originally appear in the form of a thought, but as a feeling, a perception, or mental image—all of which aspects must be distinguished from the form of thought proper. . .

The several modes of feeling, perception, desire, and will, so far as we are *aware* of them, are in general called ideas (mental representations): and it may be roughly said that philosophy puts thoughts, categories, or, in more precise language, adequate *notions*, in the place of the generalized images we ordinarily call ideas. Mental impressions such as these may be regarded as the metaphors of thoughts and notions. But to have these figurate conceptions does not imply that we appreciate their intellectual significance, the thoughts and rational notions to which they correspond. Conversely, it is one thing to have thoughts and intelligent notions, and another to know what impressions, perceptions, and feelings correspond to them.

This difference will to some extent explain what people call the unintelligibility of philosophy. Their difficulty lies partly in an incapacity—which in itself is nothing but want of habit—for abstract thinking; i.e. in an inability to get hold of pure thoughts and move around in them. In our ordinary state of mind, the thoughts are clothed upon and made one with the sensuous or spiritual material of the hour; and in reflection, meditation, and general reasoning, we introduce a blend of thoughts into feelings, percepts, and mental images. (Thus, in propositions where the subject-matter is due to the sense— e.g. 'This leaf is green'—we have such categories introduced, as being and individuality.) But it is a very different thing to make the thoughts pure and simple our object.

But their complaint that philosophy is unintelligible is as much due to another reason; and that is an impatient wish to have before them as a mental picture that which is in the mind as a thought or notion. When people are asked to apprehend some notion, they often complain that they do not know what they have to think. But the fact is that there is nothing further to be thought than the notion itself. What the phrase reveals is a hankering after an image with which we are already familiar. The mind, denied the use of its familiar ideas, feels the ground where it once stood firm and at home taken away from beneath it, and when transported into the region of pure thought, cannot tell where in the world it is. . .

Nature has given every one a faculty of thought. But thought is all that philosophy claims as the form proper to her business. . . . In other words, this science must often submit to the slight of hearing even people who have never taken any trouble with it talking as if they thoroughly understood all about it. With no preparation beyond an ordinary education they do not hesitate, especially under the influence of religious sentiment, to philosophize and to criticize philosophy. Everybody allows that to make a shoe you must have learned and practiced the craft of the shoemaker, though every man has a model in his own foot, and possesses in his hands the natural endowments for the operations required. For philosophy alone, it seems to be imagined, such study, care, and application are not in the least requisite. . .

CHAPTER 4

BERTRAND RUSSELL

THE VALUE OF PHILOSOPHY AND TEN COMMANDMENTS FOR BEGINNING PHILOSOPHERS

Bertrand Russell (1872–1970) was born in Wales, the grandson of Lord John Russell, a Prime Minister under Queen Victoria. Russell is one of the best known twentieth century philosophers, having written on a great variety of topics. Russell's *Principia Mathematica* (written with Alfred North Whitehead) attracted a good deal of attention in the early part of this century, arguing that mathematics is reducible to logic, and uncovering a paradox of class membership, appropriately known as "Russell's paradox."

Russell was Lecturer in Philosophy at Trinity College, Cambridge, from 1910 to 1916, when he was dismissed from his position because of his pacifist activities. He was later imprisoned for six months for his steadfast opposition to World War I. In the 1930s and 1940s he was a controversial champion for an array of causes, including greater sexual freedom. In 1961, at the age of 89, he was imprisoned for one week in connection with his campaign for nuclear disarmament. He was outspoken in his opposition to the Vietnam War.

Among the many honors he received in his long life were the Order of Merit in 1949 and the Nobel Prize for Literature in 1950. In making the latter award, the Nobel Committee described Russell as "one of our time's most brilliant spokesmen of rationality and humanity, and a fearless champion of free speech and free thought in the West."

Our first selection is taken from Russell's *The Problems of Philosophy*[1]. Russell argues that although it is true that philosophy often deals with questions that have uncertain answers, this is a virtue and not a vice. Contemplation of large questions helps us escape a life of narrow self-interest. The so-called "practical person" who scorns philosophy actually does have a philosophy—a philosophy that is hopelessly inadequate to the intellectual needs of the human person.

The second selection is taken from an article that Russell wrote for *The Independent*, in 1965. These "Ten Commandments" are designed to teach the virtue of intellectual independence. In emphasizing this virtue, Russell sees himself in solidarity with Socrates, who was executed for his questioning of the "conventional wisdom" and "morality" of his day. In the place of majority opinion and uncritical acceptance of tradition, Socrates and Bertrand Russell sought to substitute the authority of reason.

THE VALUE OF PHILOSOPHY

Having now come to the end of our brief and very incomplete review of the problems of philosophy, it will be well to consider, in conclusion, what is the value of philosophy and why it ought to be studied. It is the more necessary to consider this question, in view of the fact that many men, under the influence of science or of practical affairs, are inclined to doubt whether philosophy is anything better than innocent but useless trifling, hair-splitting distinctions, and controversies on matters concerning which knowledge is impossible.

This view of philosophy appears to result, partly from a wrong conception of the ends of life, partly from a wrong conception of the kind of goods which philosophy strives to achieve. Physical science, through the medium of inventions, is useful to innumerable people who are wholly ignorant of it; thus the study of physical science is to be recommended, not only, or primarily, because of the effect on mankind in general. This utility does not belong to philosophy. If the study of philosophy has any value at all for others than students of philosophy, it must be only indirectly, through its effects upon the lives of those who study it. It is in these effects, therefore, if anywhere, that the value of philosophy must be primarily sought.

But further, if we are not to fail in our endeavour to determine the value of philosophy, we must first free our minds from the prejudices of what are wrongly called "practical" men. The "practical" man, as this word is often used, is one who recognizes only material needs, who realizes that men must have food for the body, but is oblivious of the necessity of providing food for the mind. If all men were well off, if poverty and disease had been reduced to their lowest possible

[1]Reprinted from *The Problems of Philosophy* by Bertrand Russell (1912) by permission of Oxford University Press.

point, there would still remain much to be done to produce a valuable society; and even in the existing world the goods of the mind are at least as important as the goods of the body. It is exclusively among the goods of the mind that the value of philosophy is to be found; and only those who are not indifferent to these goods can be persuaded that the study of philosophy is not a waste of time.

Philosophy, like all other studies, aims primarily at knowledge. The knowledge it aims at is the kind of knowledge which gives unity and system to the body of the sciences, and the kind which results from a critical examination of the grounds of our convictions, prejudices, and beliefs. But it cannot be maintained that philosophy has had any very great measure of success in its attempts to provide definite answers to its questions. If you ask a mathematician, a mineralogist, a historian, or any other man of learning, what definite body of truths has been ascertained by his science, his answer will last as long as you are willing to listen. But if you put the same question to a philosopher, he will, if he is candid, have to confess that his study has not achieved positive results such as have been achieved by other sciences. It is true that this is partly accounted for by the fact that, as soon as definite knowledge concerning any subject becomes possible, this subject ceases to be called philosophy, and becomes a separate science. The whole study of the heavens, which now belongs to astronomy, was once included in philosophy; Newton's great work was called "the mathematical principles of natural philosophy." Similarly, the study of the human mind, which was, until very lately, a part of philosophy, has now been separated from philosophy and has become the science of psychology. Thus, to a great extent, the uncertainty of philosophy is more apparent than real: those questions which are already capable of definite answers are placed in the sciences, while those

only to which, at present, no definite answer can be given, remain to form the residue which is called philosophy.

This is, however, only a part of the truth concerning the uncertainty of philosophy. There are many questions—and among them those that are of the profoundest interest to our spiritual life—which, so far as we can see, must remain insoluble to the human intellect unless its powers become of quite a different order from what they are now. Has the universe any unity of plan or purpose, or is it a fortuitous concourse of atoms? Is consciousness a permanent part of the universe, giving hope of indefinite growth in wisdom, or is it a transitory accident on a small planet on which life must ultimately become impossible? Are good and evil of importance to the universe or only to man? Such questions are asked by philosophy, and variously answered by various philosophers. But it would seem that, whether answers be otherwise discoverable or not, the answers suggested by philosophy are none of them demonstrably true. Yet, however slight may be the hope of discovering an answer, it is part of the business of philosophy to continue the consideration of such questions, to make us aware of their importance, to examine all the approaches to them, and to keep alive that speculative interest in the universe which is apt to be killed by confining ourselves to definitely ascertainable knowledge.

Many philosophers, it is true, have held that philosophy could establish the truth of certain answers to such fundamental questions. They have supposed that what is of most importance in religious beliefs could be proved by strict demonstration to be true. In order to judge of such attempts, it is necessary to take a survey of human knowledge, and to form an opinion as to its methods and its limitations. On such a subject it would be unwise to pronounce dogmatically; but if the investigations of our previous chapters have not led us astray, we shall be compelled to renounce the hope of finding philosophical proofs of religious beliefs. We cannot, therefore, include as part of the value of philosophy any definite set of answers to such questions. Hence, once more, the value of philosophy must not depend upon any supposed body of definitely ascertainable knowledge to be acquired by those who study it.

The value of philosophy is, in fact, to be sought largely in its very uncertainty. The man who has no tincture of philosophy goes through life imprisoned in the prejudices derived from common sense, from the habitual beliefs of his age or his nation, and from convictions which have grown up in his mind without the co-operation or consent of his deliberate reason. To such a man the world tends to become definite, finite, obvious; common objects rouse no questions, and unfamiliar possibilities are contemptuously rejected. As soon as we begin to philosophize, on the contrary, we find, as we saw in our opening chapters, that even the most everyday things lead to problems to which only very incomplete answers can be given. Philosophy, though unable to tell us with certainty what is the true answer to the doubts which it raises, is able to suggest many possibilities which enlarge our thoughts and free them from the tyranny of custom. Thus, while diminishing our feeling of certainty as to what things are, it greatly increases our knowledge as to what they may be; it removes the somewhat arrogant dogmatism of those who have never travelled into the region of liberating doubt, and it keeps alive our sense of wonder by showing familiar things in an unfamiliar aspect.

Apart from its utility in showing unsuspected possibilities, philosophy has a value—perhaps its chief value—through the greatness of the objects which it contemplates, and the freedom from narrow and personal aims resulting from this contemplation. The life of the instinctive man is shut up within the circle of his private interests: family and friends may be included, but the outer world is not regarded except as it may help or hinder what comes within the circle of instinctive wishes. In such a life there is something feverish and confined, in comparison with which the philosophic life is calm and free. The private world of instinctive interests is a small one, set in the midst of a great and powerful world which must, sooner or later, lay our private world in ruins. Unless we can so enlarge our interests as to include the whole outer world, we remain like a garrison in a beleaguered fortress, knowing that the enemy prevents escape and that ultimate surrender is inevitable. In such a life there is no peace, but a constant strife between the insistence of desire and the powerlessness of will. In one way or another, if our life is to be great and free, we must escape this prison and this strife.

One way of escape is by philosophic contemplation. Philosophic contemplation does not, in its widest survey, divide the universe into two hostile camps—friends and foes, helpful and hostile, good and bad—it views the whole impartially. Philosophic contemplation, when it is unalloyed, does not aim at proving that the rest of the universe is akin to man. All acquisition of knowledge is an enlargement of the Self, but this enlargement is best attained when it is not directly sought. It is obtained when the desire for knowledge is alone operative, by a study which does not wish in advance that its objects should have this or that character, but adapts the Self to the characters which it finds in its objects. This enlargement of Self is not obtained when, taking the Self as it is, we try to show that the world is so similar to this Self that knowledge of it is possible without any admission of what seems alien. The desire to prove this is a form of self-assertion, and like all self-assertion, it is an obstacle to the growth of Self which it desires, and of which the Self knows that it is capable. Self-assertion, in philosophic speculation as elsewhere, views the world as a means to its own ends; thus its makes the world of less account than Self, and the Self sets bounds to the greatness of its goods. In contemplation, on the contrary, we start from the not-Self, and through its greatness the boundaries of Self are enlarged; through the infinity of the universe the mind which contemplates it achieves some share in infinity.

For this reason greatness of soul is not fostered by those philosophies which assimilate the universe to Man. Knowledge is a form of union of Self and not-Self; like all union, it is impaired by dominion, and therefore by any attempt to force the universe into conformity with what we find in ourselves. There is a widespred philosophical tendency towards the view which tells us that man is the measure of all things, that truth is man-made, that space and time and the world of universals are properties of the mind, and that, if there be anything not created by the mind, it is unknowable and of no account for us. This view, if our previous discussions were correct, is untrue; but in addition to being untrue, it has the effect of robbing philosophic contemplation of all that gives it value, since it fetters contemplation to Self. What it calls knowledge is not a union with the not-Self, but a set of prejudices, habits, and desires, making an impenetrable veil between us and the world beyond. The man who finds pleasure in such a theory of knowledge is like the man who never leaves the domestic circle for fear his word might not be law.

The true philosophic contemplation, on the contrary, finds its satisfaction in every enlargement of the not-Self, in everything that magnifies the objects contemplated, and thereby the subject contemplating. Everything, in contemplation, that is personal or private, everything that depends upon habit, self-interest, or desire, distorts the object, and hence impairs the union which the intellect seeks. By thus making a barrier between subject and object, such personal and private things become a prison to the intellect. The free intellect will see as God might see, without a *here* and *now*, without hopes and fears, without the trammels of customary beliefs and traditional prejudices, calmly, dispassionately, in the sole and exclusive desire of knowledge— knowledge as impersonal, as purely contemplative, as it is possible for man to attain. Hence also the free intellect will value more the abstract and universal knowledge into which the accidents of private history do not enter, than the knowledge brought by the senses, and dependent, as such knowledge must be, upon an exclusive and personal point of view and a body whose sense-organs distort as much as they reveal.

The mind which has become accustomed to the freedom and impartiality of philosophic contemplation will preserve something of the same freedom and impartiality in the world of action and emotion. It will view its purposes and desires as parts of the whole, with the absence of insistence that results from seeing them as infinitesimal fragments in a world of which all the rest is unaffected by any one man's deeds. The impartiality which, in contemplation, is the unalloyed desire for truth, is the very same quality of mind which, in action, is justice, and in emotion is that universal love which can be given to all, and not only to those who are judged useful or admirable. Thus contemplation enlarges not only the objects of our thoughts, but also the objects of our actions and our affections: it makes us citizens of the universe, not only of one walled city at war with all the rest. In this citizenship of the universe consists man's true freedom, and his liberation from the thraldom of narrow hopes and fears.

Thus, to sum up our discussion of the value of philosophy: Philosophy is to be studied, not for the sake of any definite answers to its questions, since no definite answers can, as a rule, be known to be true, but rather for the sake of the questions themselves; because these questions enlarge our conception of what is possible, enrich our intellectual imagination, and diminish the dogmatic assurance which closes the mind against specula-tion; but above all because, through the greatness of the universe which philosophy contemplates, the mind also is rendered great, and becomes capable of that union with the universe which constitutes its highest good.

TEN COMMANDMENTS FOR BEGINNING PHILOSOPHERS

1. Do not feel certain of anything.

2. Do not think it worthwhile to produce belief by concealing evidence, for the evidence is sure to come to light.

3. Never try to discourage thinking, for you are sure to succeed.

4. When met with opposition, even if it should be from your husband or children, endeavour to overcome it by argument and not by authority, for a victory dependent upon authority is unreal and illusory.

5. Have no respect for the authority of others, for there are always contrary authorities to be found.

6. Do not use power to suppress opinions you think pernicious, for if you do the opinions will suppress you.

7. Do not fear to be eccentric in opinion, for every opinion now accepted was once eccentric.

8. Find more pleasure in intelligent dissents than in passive agreement, for, if you value intelligence as you should, the former implies a deeper agreement than the latter.

9. Be scrupulously truthful, even when truth is inconvenient, for it is more inconvenient when you try to conceal it.

10. Do not feel envious of the happiness of those who live in a fool's paradise, for only a fool will think that it is happiness.

CHAPTER 5

MARTIN HEIDEGGER

TWO MISINTERPRETATIONS OF PHILOSOPHY

Martin Heidegger (1889–1976), born in Baden, Germany, is one of the most important and influential twentieth century European philosophers. He studied at the University of Freiburg with Edmund Husserl, the founder of phenomenology, then a new movement in philosophy. After teaching at the University of Marburg, he returned to Freiburg to succeed Husserl.

The rise of the Nazi movement in Germany saw Heidegger disavow his allegiance to the Jewish Husserl; in 1933 Heidegger became rector at the University of Freiburg. His inaugural lecture, "The Role of the University in the New Reich," celebrated the National Socialist movement as the advent of a new and glorious Germany—inaugurating as well a nationalistic strain in his philosophy that came to haunt him in later years, as he tried to cover and re-write his past. In 1934 Heidegger resigned as rector, but his relationship to the Nazi party continues to be debated even today.

Every great thinker, Heidegger claimed, thinks but one thought. It seems it was given to Heidegger to thoughtfully reopen in the twentieth century *die frage nach dem Sinn von Sein* (the question of the meaning of Being). This he did in his greatest and most systematic work, *Being and Time* (1927). Among his numerous later writings is the *Introduction to Metaphysics* (1953).

This selection from the *Introduction to Metaphysics* reveals Heidegger's insight into philosophy as an essentially "untimely activity" that never makes things easier, only more difficult, as it reveals new areas that have been hidden from thought. As one of humankind's creative possibilities, philosophy is often plagued by certain misinterpretations (often perpetuated by philosophy professors) about its role and usefulness in society. Heidegger sought to correct these misinterpretations, concluding with Nietzsche (a nineteenth century German philosopher whose thought intrigued Heidegger all his life) that philosophy is an extra-ordinary inquiry into the extra-ordinary—"a voluntary living amid the ice and mountain heights." This poetic rendering is characteristic of the later Heidegger, who insisted that poetic thinking is vital to recovering a lost sense of relatedness to Being in the troubled age of Modernity.

Two Misinterpretations of Philosophy

It would not serve our purpose to begin our discussion with a detailed report on philosophy. But there are a few things that all must know who wish to concern themselves with philosophy. They can be briefly stated.

All essential philosophical questioning is necessarily untimely. This is so because philosophy is always projected far in advance of its time, or because it connects the present with its antecedent, with what *initially* was. Philosophy always remains a knowledge which not only cannot be adjusted to a given epoch but on the contrary imposes its measure upon its epoch.

Philosophy is essentially untimely because it is one of those few things that can never find an immediate echo in the present. When such an echo seems to occur, when a philosophy becomes fashionable, either it is no real philosophy or it has been misinterpreted and misused for ephemeral and extraneous purposes.

Accordingly, philosophy cannot be directly learned like manual and technical skills; it cannot be directly applied, or judged by its usefulness in the manner of economic or other professional knowledge.

But what is useless can still be a force, perhaps the only real force. What has no immediate echo in everyday life can be intimately bound up with a nation's profound historical development, and can even anticipate it. What is untimely will have its own times. This is true of philosophy. Consequently there is no way of determining once and for all what the task of philosophy is, and accordingly what must be expected of it. Every stage and every beginning of its development bears within it its own law. All that can be said is what philosophy cannot be and cannot accomplish. . .

Every essential form of spiritual life is marked by ambiguity. The less commensurate it is with other forms, the more it is misinterpreted.

Philosophy is one of the few autonomous creative possibilities and at times necessities of man's historical being-there. The current misinterpretations of philosophy, all of which have some truth about them, are legion. Here we shall

[1]From Martin Heidegger, *Introduction to Metaphysics*, translated by Ralph Manheim (New Haven: Yale University Press, 1959), p. 8–13. Reprinted by permission of the publisher.

mention only two, which are important because of the light they throw on the present and future situation of philosophy. The first misinterpretation asks too much of philosophy. The second distorts its function.

Roughly speaking, philosophy always aims at the first and last grounds of the essent, with particular emphasis on man himself and on the meaning and goals of human being-there. This might suggest that philosophy can and must provide a foundation on which a nation will build its historical life and culture. But this is beyond the power of philosophy. As a rule such excessive demands take the form of a belittling of philosophy. It is said, for example: Because metaphysics did nothing to pave the way for the revolution it should be rejected. This is no cleverer than saying that because the carpenter's bench is useless for flying it should be abolished. Philosophy can never *directly* supply the energies and create the opportunities and methods that bring about a historical change; for one thing, because philosophy is always the concern of the few. Which few? The creators, those who initiate profound transformations. It spreads only indirectly, by devious paths that can never be laid out in advance, until at last, at some future date, it sinks to the level of a commonplace; but by then it has long been forgotten as original philosophy.

What philosophy essentially can and must be is this: a thinking that breaks the paths and opens the perspectives of the knowledge that sets the norms and hierarchies, of the knowledge in which and by which a people fulfills itself historically and culturally, the knowledge that kindles and necessitates all inquiries and thereby threatens all values.

The second misinterpretation involves a distortion of the function of philosophy. Even if philosophy can provide no foundation for a culture, the argument goes, it is nevertheless a cultural force, whether because it gives us an over-

all, systematic view of what is, supplying a useful chart by which we may find our way amid the various possible things and realms of things, or because it relieves the sciences of their work by reflecting on their premises, basic concepts, and principles. Philosophy is expected to promote and even to accelerate—to make easier as it were—the practical and technical business of culture.

But—it is in the very nature of philosophy never to make things easier but only more difficult. And this not merely because its language strikes the everyday understanding as strange if not insane. Rather, it is the authentic function of philosophy to challenge historical being-there and hence, in the last analysis, being pure and simple. It restores to things, to the essents, their weight (being). How so? Because the challenge is one of the essential prerequisites for the birth of all greatness, and in speaking of greatness we are referring to the works and destinies of nations. We can speak of historical destiny only where an authentic knowledge of things dominates man's being-there. And it is philosophy that opens up the paths and perspectives of such knowledge.

The misinterpretations with which philosophy is perpetually beset are promoted most of all by people of our kind, that is, by professors of philosophy. It is our customary business—which may be said to be justified and even useful—to transmit a certain knowledge of the philosophy of the past, as part of a general education. Many people suppose that this is philosophy itself, whereas at best it is the technique of philosophy.

In correcting these two misinterpretations I cannot hope to give you at one stroke a clear conception of philosophy. But I do hope that you will be on your guard when the most current judgements and even supposed observations assail you unawares. Such judgments are often disarming, precisely because they seem so natural. You hear remarks such as "Philosophy leads to nothing," "You can't do anything with philosophy," and readily imagine that they confirm an experience of your own. There is no denying the soundness of these two phrases, particularly common among scientists and teachers of science. Any attempt to refute them by proving that after all it does "lead to something," merely strengthens the prevailing misinterpretation to the effect that the everyday standards by which we judge bicycles or sulphur baths are applicable to philosophy.

It is absolutely correct and proper to say that "You can't do anything with philosophy." It is only wrong to suppose that this is the last word on philosophy. For the rejoinder imposes itself: granted that *we* cannot do anything with philosophy, might not philosophy, if we concern ourselves with it, do something *with us?* So much for what philosophy is not.

At the outset we stated a question: "Why are there essents rather than nothing?" We have maintained that to ask this question is to philosophize. When in our thinking we open our minds to this question, we first of all cease to dwell in any of the familiar realms. We set aside everything that is on the order of the day. Our question goes beyond the familiar and the things that have their place in everyday life. Nietzsche once said (*Werke*, 7,269): "A philosopher is a man who never ceases to experience, see, hear, suspect, hope, and dream extraordinary things . . ."

To philosophize is to inquire into the *extra-ordinary*. But because, as we have just suggested, this questioning recoils upon itself, not only what is asked after is extraordinary but also the asking itself. In other words: this questioning does not lie along the way so that we bump into it one day unexpectedly. Nor is it a part of everyday life: there is no requirement or regulation that forces us into it; it gratifies no urgent or prevailing need. The questioning itself is "out of order." It is entirely voluntary, based wholly and uniquely on the mystery of freedom, on what we have called the leap. The same Nietzsche said: "Philosophy . . . is a voluntary living amid ice and mountain heights" (*Werke*, 15,2). To philosophize, we may now say, is an extra-ordinary inquiry into the extra-ordinary. . . .

CONTEMPORARY PERSPECTIVES: PHILOSOPHY AT THE UNIVERSITY

Where is philosophy today at the university?

This question may be interpreted in at least two different ways: spatially and metaphorically. These two interpretations are not as unrelated as they might seem.

1.   Where is philosophy—that is, where may it be found at the university? The answer is as individual as each institution. Hence, it may be appropriate to answer that it is to be found somewhere in the College of Arts and Sciences, or in the Humanities Division; or that philosophy is a department of the university,

with a specific geographical location on campus, complete with offices, lounge, faculty, etc. Such a question would not be difficult to answer, provided one had some rudimentary knowledge of one's college or university, or a reliable campus map.

2.   But what map do we have for the metaphorical interpretation of our question? Is the place that philosophy occupies at the university a prominent one, a place of importance and esteem? What place does philosophy have in the curriculum? Is philosophy placed at the "core" of the liberal education that the university purports to offer? Is philosophy a "mainstream" academic experience, or is it a "marginal" concern at the university, the concern of the few? *Where is philosophy today at the university?*

It is this second, more explicitly philosophical interpretation of the question that concerns us in this Contemporary Perspectives section (although you may be interested in exploring with your instructor and classmates the relationship between the *status* of philosophy and the *space/location* philosophy occupies at your university or college, debating this formula: space = power).

There is good reason to believe that the status of philosophy at the university is in a state of decline. Once regarded as the foundation of the university and its *raison d'être* (reason to be), philosophy now finds itself living a marginal, fugitive existence, its role decreasing in visibility and power, and its voice diminished. It was not always so.

Let us begin again.

How was it that philosophy came to reside at the university in the first place? Who (or what) determined that philosophy should take up residence there, when seemingly it can live anywhere—anywhere, that is, where problems provoke wonder and questions are seriously valued and pursued. How was it that the university itself came into existence? We are not asking a simple historical question; we are asking a question about the foundations of the university. Why did it come to be?

To wonder why there is a university is to ask for its *raison d'être, a reason that is none other than reason itself.* The university is in the service of reason. The idea that gave rise to the university some eight centuries ago in Europe (where the university was founded and erected) was the thought of a community of thinkers gathered in the name of reason to assemble the whole of knowledge. This advanced school, or *university*, according to its founding ideal, would be dedicated to the oneness of knowledge yet organized into principal disciplines of knowing (the origins of modern day academic departments). Immanuel Kant, in a collection of essays entitled *The Conflict of the Faculties*, makes it clear that the university receives its legitimate authorization from an outside authority—that is, from the state. Thus authorized, the university is invested with the power to create titles and confer degrees.

And what place was philosophy to have? Kant, speaking in the same tradition as Aristotle before him, makes it clear that philosophy's concern is with the true, and must have freedom to pursue the truth without restraint. This freedom is identical with philosophical reason itself, since philosophy has always understood itself as that discipline that prescribes its own law, namely truth itself. Thinking back to Aristotle's *Metaphysics* (Part One), recall that the wisdom philosophy seeks is not sought for the sake of anything other than itself, but rather for its own sake, meaning it alone is free. The holder of this theoretical knowledge, the philosopher, is according to Aristotle positioned above the manual laborer *who acts without knowing*. The "practical person" does not know the causes, the "reasons" of things. The knower of causes is for Aristotle the true teacher, able to lead and to command. Above all, the philosopher answers only to reason, to the principle of reason, which is the first principle, the principle of principles. This is why philosophy, from its origins in ancient Greece right on through the Enlightenment has not hesitated to order, prescribe, and lay down the law, in society as well as in the university, reason's home. *Without a faculty of philosophy, there can be no university.* As Jacques Derrida points out, *the concept of the university is always more than the concept of a teaching or research institute, it is the concept of reason itself.*[1] The department of philosophy is founded upon reason, answers to reason, and is a necessary condition for the existence of the university itself. The philosophy faculty are assigned the task of overseeing all other faculties in matters of truth. The collective teaching of Western philosophy from Aristotle to the Age of Modernity teaches this same thing.

Yet where are we today? The "founding" act of reason itself at the university is now in question. Suppose one were to question the university's founding upon reason. What then? *We cannot demand a reason for reasonableness itself.* As Derrida points out, a founding act cannot be simply included in the logic of what it founds, just as the foundation of a law is not itself a juridical or legal event. Put simply, the foundation of the university is not itself an academic founding because the origin of the principle of reason *is not in itself rational*. The university today is currently engaged in seeking new acts of founding. It appears, then, that the university is precariously founded (with a small change in type suggesting that the university *founders*).

The foundering of the university is the anthem of today. One may hear this anthem in scores of new books and periodicals. The two selections that follow provide a forum for reflecting on the founding/foundering of the university and on the future(s) of philosophy. The first is taken from Richard Rorty's controversial book, *Philosophy and the Mirror of Nature*. Rorty argues that the old Kantian idea of philosophy as the "foundational tribunal of reason" that exercises hegemonic

---

[1]Jacques Derrida, "The Principle of Reason: The University in the Eyes of its Pupils", *Diacritics*, vol. XIX (1983), pp. 3–20.

authority over all of life and culture is at an end. An admitted "anti-foundation-alist," Rorty is clearly speaking back to Kant and the entire Enlightenment tradition when he states that the three most important philosophers of the twentieth century (in his opinion they are Ludwig Wittgenstein, Martin Heidegger, and John Dewey) all attempted to set aside Kant's excessively formal, ahistorical concept of philosophy. *Philosophy, like everything else in human culture, is historically situated and socially constructed.* Hence, Kant's Enlightenment foundationalism is itself a historical product of a set of assumptions governed by what Rorty calls "the metaphor of the mind as the mirror of nature." Rorty contends that contemporary Analytic philosophy is the successor to Enlightenment philosophy, and is very much in need of deconstruction. Against the very Analytic model of philosophy in which Rorty himself was trained, he insists that philosophy should abandon its vision of itself as lawgiving profession in order to recover its more fundamental (and Socratic) meaning of *conversation*. In this view, the philosopher will no longer be viewed as the knowledgable professional presiding *ex officio* over all of culture, but rather as but one (nonpriviliged) voice in the ongoing conversation of life.

Rorty's depiction of philosophy as a rhetorical enterprise, precariously perched on a pile of unstable and historically shifting metaphors, has made philosophers and educators like Allan Bloom very nervous—some think that Rorty's relativism spells the demise of American higher education. In our second selection, taken from the concluding chapter of the surprising bestseller *The Closing of the American Mind*, Bloom claims that the foundering of the university and the marginalization of philosophy have led to a crisis in society. His argument in this book (stated in myriad ways) is that American higher education has lapsed into a "democratic relativism," where no one knows what is right or best, and there is no consensus as to what is important for a student to study. This "democracy of the disciplines" has proven to be bewildering to students; as each discipline competes with other disciplines to attract students, all offer a narrow, specialized course of study, but none offers a unifying vision of the whole of knowledge. Academic departments market their "majors" like street vendors hawking their wares, each promising the ultimate in a "bottom line" society: a job upon graduation.

The three segments of the university—*the natural sciences, social sciences, and humanities*—are islands unto themselves, each leading separate lives. Bloom contends that the humanities are especially adrift. Philosophy has been vastly scaled down from what it once was; its role has been reduced and its voice diminished in the clamour of university life.

The disagreements between Rorty and Bloom are philosophical in nature, and reflect many of the tensions in higher education today. One thing seems clear: the role of philosophy at the university, and in society, is little understood today. In the closing years of the twentieth century we are experiencing a loss of certainty about the mission and role of the university in society. "Reassessment" is the byword, as colleges and universities review their programs and expenditures to position themselves for the next century. In such an atmosphere, there is an increasing tendency among administrators, faculty, and students to regard philosophy as a nonessential "luxury." Far from being a "luxury," philosophy historically has been viewed as the *core* of a liberal education, fostering critical thinking, interdisciplinary perspectives, intellectual history, examination of world views, and the development of writing skills and effective communication. Furthermore, historically philosophy has attempted to provide a unique and systematic approach to normative issues through such courses as ethics, social and political philosophy, philosophy of law, and aesthetics. Although other disciplines treat these same concerns, none of them devotes the sustained critical scrutiny to these issues that philosophy does. Whether philosophy will continue to play an important role in the life of the university or in society itself—whether it deserves to— are questions to ponder as you read these two selections.

CHAPTER 6

RICHARD RORTY

PHILOSOPHY AND THE MIRROR OF NATURE

Richard Rorty (1931–   ) is Kenan Professor of Humanities at the University of Virginia. He taught previously at Wellesley College and from 1961 to 1982 at Princeton University where he was Stuart Professor of Philosophy. A past President of the American Philosophical Association, Rorty is the author of *Philosophy and the Mirror of Nature* (1979), *Consequences of Pragmatism* (1982), and *Contingency, Irony, and Solidarity* (1989).

PHILOSOPHY AND THE MIRROR OF NATURE[1]

Philosophers usually think of their discipline as one which discusses perennial, eternal problems—problems which arise as soon as one reflects. Some of these concern the difference between human beings and other beings, and are crystallized in questions concerning the relation between the mind and the body. Other problems concern the legitimation of claims to know, and are crystallized in questions concerning the "foundations" of knowledge. To discover these foundations is to discover something about the mind, and conversely. Philosophy as a discipline thus sees itself as the attempt to underwrite or debunk claims to knowledge made by science, morality, art, or religion. It purports to do this on

[1]From Richard Rorty, *Philosophy and the Mirror of Nature.* Copyright © 1979 Princeton University Press. Excerpt, pp. 3–10, 11–13, 389–394. Reprinted with permission of Princeton University Press.

the basis of its special understanding of the nature of knowledge and of mind. Philosophy can be foundational in respect to the rest of culture because culture is the assemblage of claims to knowledge, and philosophy adjudicates such claims. It can do so because it understands the foundations of knowledge, and it finds these foundations in a study of man-as-knower, of the "mental processes" or the "activity of representation" which make knowledge possible. To know is to represent accurately what is outside the mind; so to understand the possibility and nature of knowledge is to understand the way in which the mind is able to construct such representations. Philosophy's central concern is to be a general theory of representation, a theory which will divide culture up into the areas which represent reality well, those which represent it less well, and those which do not represent it at all (despite their pretense of doing so).

We owe the notion of a "theory of knowledge" based on an understanding of "mental processes" to the seventeenth century, and especially to Locke. We owe the notion of "the mind" as a separate entity in which "processes" occur to the same period, and especially to Descartes. We owe the notion of philosophy as a tribunal of pure reason, upholding or denying the claims of the rest of culture, to the eighteenth century and especially to Kant, but this Kantian notion presupposed general assent to Lockean notions of mental processes and Cartesian notions of mental substance. In the nineteenth century, the notion of philosophy as a foundational discipline which "grounds" knowledge-claims was consolidated in the writings of the neo-Kantians. Occasional protests against this conception of culture as in need of "grounding" and against the pretensions of a theory of knowledge to perform this task (in, for example, Nietzsche and William James) went largely unheard. "Philosophy" became, for the intellectuals, a substitute for religion. It was the area of culture where one touched bottom, where one found the vocabulary and the convictions which permitted one to explain and justify one's activity *as* an intellectual, and thus to discover the significance of one's life.

At the beginning of our century, this claim was reaffirmed by philosophers (notably Russell and Husserl) who were concerned to keep philosophy "rigorous" and "scientific." But there was a note of desperation in their voices, for by this time the triumph of the secular over the claims of religion was almost complete. Thus the philosopher could no longer see himself as in the intellectual avant-garde, or as protecting men against the forces of superstition.[2] Further, in the course of the nineteenth century, a new form of culture had arisen—the culture of the man of letters, the intellectual who wrote poems and novels and political treatises, and criticisms of other people's poems and novels and treatises. Descartes, Locke, and Kant had written in a period in which the secularization of culture was being made possible by the success of natural science. But by the early twentieth century the scientists had become as remote from most intellectuals as had the theologians. Poets and novelists had taken the place of both preachers and philosophers as the moral teachers of the youth. The result was that the more "scientific" and "rigorous" philosophy became, the less it had to do with the rest of culture and the more absurd its traditional pretensions seemed. The attempts of both analytic philosophers and phenomenologists to "ground" this and "criticize" that were shrugged off by those whose activities were purportedly being grounded or criticized. Philosophy as a whole was shrugged off by those who wanted an ideology or a self-image.

[2] Terms such as "himself" and "men" should, throughout this book [reading], be taken as abbreviations for "himself or herself," "men and women," and so on.

It is against this background that we should see the work of the three most important philosophers of our century—Wittgenstein, Heidegger, and Dewey. Each tried, in his early years, to find a new way of making philosophy "foundational"—a new way of formulating an ultimate context for thought. Wittgenstein tried to construct a new theory of representation which would have nothing to do with mentalism, Heidegger to construct a new set of philosophical categories which would have nothing to do with science, epistemology, or the Cartesian quest for certainty, and Dewey to construct a naturalized version of Hegel's vision of history. Each of the three came to see his earlier effort as self-deceptive, as an attempt to retain a certain conception of philosophy after the notions needed to flesh out that conception (the seventeenth-century notions of knowledge and mind) had been discarded. Each of the three, in his later work, broke free of the Kantian conception of philosophy as foundational, and spent his time warning us against those very temptations to which he himself had once succumbed. Thus their later work is therapeutic rather than constructive, edifying rather than systematic, designed to make the reader question his own motives for philosophizing rather than to supply him with a new philosophical program.

Wittgenstein, Heidegger, and Dewey are in agreement that the notion of knowledge as accurate representation, made possible by special mental processes, and intelligible through a general theory of representation, needs to be abandoned. For all three, the notions of "foundations of knowledge" and of philosophy as revolving around the Cartesian attempt to answer the epistemological skeptic are set aside. Further, they set aside the notion of "the mind" common to Descartes, Locke, and Kant—as a special subject of study, located in inner space, containing elements or processes which make knowledge possible. This is not to say that they have *alternative* "theories of knowledge" or "philosophies of mind." They set aside epistemology and metaphysics as possible disciplines. I say "set aside" rather than "argue against" because their attitude toward the traditional problematic is like the attitude of seventeenth century philosophers toward the scholastic problematic. They do not devote themselves to discovering false propositions or bad arguments in the works of their predecessors (though they occasionally do that too). Rather, they glimpse the possibility of a form of intellectual life in which the vocabulary of philosophical reflection inherited from the seventeenth century would seem as pointless as the thirteenth-century philosophical vocabulary had seemed to the Enlightenment. To assert the possibility of a post-Kantian culture, one in which there is no all-encompassing discipline which legitimizes or grounds the others, is not necessarily to argue against any particular Kantian doctrine, any more than to glimpse the possibility of a culture in which religion either did not exist, or had no connection with science or politics, was necessarily to argue against Aquinas's claim that God's existence can be proved by natural reason. Wittgenstein, Heidegger, and Dewey have brought us into a period of "revolutionary" philosophy (in the sense of Kuhn's "revolutionary" science) by introducing new maps of the terrain (viz., of the whole panorama of human activities) which simply do not include those features which previously seemed to dominate.

This book is a survey of some recent developments in philosophy, especially analytic philosophy, from the point of view of the anti-Cartesian and anti-Kantian revolution which I have just described. The aim of the book is to undermine the reader's confidence in "the mind" as something about which one should have a "philosophical" view, in "knowledge" as something about which there ought to be a "theory" and which has foundations," and in "philosophy" as it has been conceived since Kant. Thus the reader in search of a new theory on any of the subjects discussed will be disappointed. Although I discuss "solutions to the mind-body problem" this is not in order to propose one but to illustrate why I do not think there is a problem. Again, although I discuss "theories of reference" I do not offer one, but offer only suggestions about why the search for such a theory is misguided. The book, like the writings of the philosophers I most admire, is therapeutic rather than constructive. The therapy offered is, nevertheless, parasitic upon the constructive efforts of the very analytic philosophers whose frame of reference I am trying to put in question. Thus most of the particular criticisms of the tradition which I offer are borrowed from such systematic philosophers as Sellars, Quine, Davidson, Ryle, Malcolm, Kuhn, and Putnam.

I am as much indebted to these philosophers for the means I employ as I am to Wittgenstein, Heidegger, and Dewey for the ends to which these means are put. I hope to convince the reader that the dialectic within analytic philosophy, which has carried philosophy of mind from Broad to Smart, philosophy of language from Frege to Davidson, epistemology from Russell to Sellars, and philosophy of science from Carnap to Kuhn, needs to be carried a few steps further. These additional steps will, I think, put us in a position to criticize the very notion of "analytic philosophy," and indeed of "philosophy" itself as it has been understood since the time of Kant.

From the standpoint I am adopting, indeed, the difference between "analytic" and other sorts of philosophy is relatively unimportant—a matter of style and tradition rather than a difference of "method" or of first principles. The reason why the book is largely written in the vocabulary of

contemporary analytic philosophers, and with reference to problems discussed in the analytic literature, is merely autobiographical. They are the vocabulary and the literature with which I am most familiar, and to which I owe what grasp I have of philosophical issues. Had I been equally familiar with other contemporary modes of writing philosophy, this would have been a better and more useful book, although an even longer one. As I see it, the kind of philosophy which stems from Russell and Frege is, like classical Husserlian phenomenology, simply one more attempt to put philosophy in the position which Kant wished it to have—that of judging other areas of culture on the basis of its special knowledge of the "foundations" of these areas. "Analytic" philosophy is one more variant of Kantian philosophy, a variant marked principally by thinking of representation as linguistic rather than mental, and of philosophy of language rather than "transcendental critique," or psychology, as the discipline which exhibits the "foundations of knowledge." This emphasis on language, I shall be arguing in chapters four and six, does not essentially change the Cartesian-Kantian problematic, and thus does not really give philosophy a new self-image. For analytic philosophy is still committed to the construction of a permanent, neutral framework for inquiry, and thus for all of culture.

It is the notion that human activity (and inquiry, the search for knowledge, in particular) takes place within a framework which can be isolated prior to the conclusion of inquiry—a set of presuppositions discoverable a priori—which links contemporary philosophy to the Descartes-Locke-Kant tradition. For the notion that there is such a framework only makes sense if we think of this framework as imposed by the nature of the knowing subject, by the nature of his faculties or by the nature of the medium within which he works. The very idea of "philosophy" as something distinct from "science" would make little sense without the Cartesian claim that by turning inward we could find ineluctable truth, and the Kantian claim that this truth imposes limits on the possible results of empirical inquiry. The notion that there could be such a thing as "foundations of knowledge" (*all* knowledge—in every field, past, present, and future) or a "theory of representation" (*all* representation, in familiar vocabularies and those not yet dreamed of) depends on the assumption that there is some such a priori constraint. If we have a Deweyan conception of knowledge, as what we are justified in believing, then we will not imagine that there are enduring constraints on what can count as knowledge, since we will see "justification" as a social phenomenon rather than a transaction between "the knowing subject" and "reality." If we have a Wittgensteinian notion of language as tool rather than mirror, we will not look for necessary conditions of the possibility of linguistic representation. If we have a Heideggerian conception of philosophy, we will see the attempt to make the nature of the knowing subject a source of necessary truths as one more self-deceptive attempt to substitute a "technical" and determinate question for that openness to strangeness which initially tempted us to begin thinking.

One way to see how analytic philosophy fits within the traditional Cartesian-Kantian pattern is to see traditional philosophy as an attempt to escape from history—an attempt to find nonhistorical conditions of any possible historical development. From this perspective, the common message of Wittgenstein, Dewey, and Heidegger is a historicist one. Each of the three reminds us that investigations of the foundations of knowledge or morality or language or society may be simply apologetics, attempts to eternalize a certain contemporary language-game, social practice, or self-image. The moral of this book is also historicist, and the three parts into which it is divided are intended to put the notions of "mind," of "knowledge," and of "philosophy," respectively, in historical perspective. . . . I present Wittgenstein, Heidegger, and Dewey as philosophers whose aim is to edify—to help their readers, or society as a whole, break free from outworn vocabularies and attitudes, rather than to provide "grounding" for the intuitions and customs of the present.

I hope that what I have been saying has made clear why I chose "Philosophy and the Mirror of Nature" as a title. It is pictures rather than propositions, metaphors rather than statements, which determine most of our philosophical convictions. The picture which holds traditional philosophy captive is that of the mind as a great mirror, containing various representations—some accurate, some not—and capable of being studied by pure, nonempirical methods. Without the notion of the mind as mirror, the notion of knowledge as accuracy of representation would not have suggested itself. Without this latter notion, the strategy common to Descartes and Kant—getting more accurate representations by inspecting, repairing, and polishing the mirror, so to speak—would not have made sense. Without this strategy in mind, recent claims that philosophy could consist of "conceptual analysis" or "phenomenological analysis" or "explication of meanings" or examination of "the logic of our language" or of "the structure of the constituting activity of consciousness" would not have made sense. It was such claims as these which Wittgenstein mocked in the *Philosophical Investigations*, and it is by following Wittgenstein's lead that analytic philosophy has progressed toward the "postpositivistic" stance it presently occupies. But Wittgenstein's flair for deconstructing captivating pictures needs to be supplemented by historical awareness—awareness of the source of all this mirror-imagery—and that seems to me Heidegger's greatest contribution. Heidegger's way of recounting history of philosophy lets us see the beginnings of the Cartesian imagery in the Greeks and the metamorphoses of this imagery during the last three centuries. He thus lets us "distance" ourselves from the tradition. Yet neither Heidegger nor Wittgenstein lets us see the historical phenomenon of mirror-imagery, the story of the domination of the mind of the West by ocular metaphors, within a social perspective. Both men are concerned with the rarely favored individual rather than with society—with the chances of keeping oneself apart from the banal self-deception typical of the latter days of a decaying tradition. Dewey, on the other hand, though he had neither Wittgenstein's dialectical acuity nor Heidegger's historical learning, wrote his polemics against traditional mirror-imagery out of a vision of a new kind of society. In his ideal society, culture is no longer dominated by the ideal of objective cognition but by that of aesthetic enhancement. In that culture, as he said, the arts and the sciences would be "the unforced flowers of life." I would hope that we are now in a position to see the charges of "relativism" and "irrationalism" once leveled against Dewey as merely the mindless defensive reflexes of the philosophical tradition which he attacked. Such charges have no weight if one takes seriously the criticisms of mirror-imagery which he, Wittgenstein, and Heidegger make. This book has little to add to these criticisms, but I hope that it presents some of them in a way which will help pierce through that crust of philosophical convention which Dewey vainly hoped to shatter.

PHILOSOPHY IN THE CONVERSATION OF MANKIND

I end this book with an allusion to Oakeshott's famous title,[3] because it catches the tone in which, I think, philosophy should be discussed.

Much of what I have said about epistemology and its possible successors is an attempt to draw some corollaries from Sellar's doctrine that

> in characterizing an episode or a state as that of *knowing*, we are not giving an empirical description of that episode or state; we are placing it in the logical space of reasons, of justifying and being able to justify what one says.[4]

If we see knowing not as having an essence, to be described by scientists or philosophers, but rather as a right, by current standards, to believe, then we are well on the way to seeing *conversation* as the ultimate context within which knowledge is to be understood. Our focus shifts from the relation between human beings and the objects of their inquiry to the relation between alternative standards of justification, and from there to the actual changes in those standards which make up intellectual history. This brings us to appreciate Sellars's own description of his mythical hero Jones, the man who invented the Mirror of Nature and thereby made modern philosophy possible:

> Does the reader not recognize Jones as Man himself in the middle of his journey from the grunts and groans of the cave to the subtle and polydimensional discourse of the drawing room, the laboratory, and the study, the language of Henry and William James, of Einstein and of the philosophers who, in their efforts to break out of the discourse to an ἀρχή beyond discourse, have provided the most curious dimension of all? (p. 196)

[3]Cf. Michael Oakeshott, "The Voice of Poetry in the Conversation of Mankind," in his *Rationalism and Politics* (New York, 1975).
[4]Wilfrid Sellars, *Science, Perception and Reality* (London and New York, 1963), p. 169.

In this book I have offered a sort of prolegomenon to a history of epistemology-centered philosophy as an episode in the history of European culture. Such philosophy goes back to the Greeks, and goes sideways into all sorts of non-philosophical disciplines which have, at one time or another, proposed themselves as substitutes for epistemology, and thus for philosophy. So the episode in question cannot simply be identified with "modern philosophy," in the sense of the standard textbook sequence of great philosophers from Descartes to Russell and Husserl. But that sequence is, nevertheless, where the search for foundations for knowledge is most explicit. So most of my attempts to deconstruct the image of the Mirror of Nature have concerned these philosophers. I have tried to show how their urge to break out into an ἀρχή beyond discourse is rooted in the urge to see social practices of justification as more than just such practices. I have, however, focused mainly on the expressions of this urge in the recent literature of analytical philosophy. The result is thus no more than a prolegomenon. A proper historical treatment would require both learning and skills which I do not possess. But I would hope that the prolegomenon has been sufficient to let one see contemporary issues in philosophy as events in a certain stage of a conversation—a conversation which once knew nothing of these issues and may know nothing of them again.

The fact that we can continue the conversation Plato began without discussing the topics Plato wanted discussed, illustrates the difference between treating philosophy as a voice in a conversation and treating it as a subject, a *Fach*, a field of professional inquiry. The conversation Plato began has been enlarged by more voices than Plato would have dreamed possible, and thus by topics he knew nothing of. A "subject"—astrology, physics, classical philosophy, furniture design—may undergo revolutions, but it gets its self-image from its present state, and its history is necessarily written "Whiggishly" as an account of its gradual maturation. This is the most frequent way of writing the history of philosophy, and I cannot claim to have avoided such Whiggery entirely in sketching the sort of history which needs to be written. But I hope that I have shown how we can see the issues with which philosophers are presently concerned, and with which they Whiggishly see philosophy as having always (perhaps unwittingly) been concerned, as results of historical accident, as turns the conversation has taken. It has taken this turn for a long time, but it might turn in another direction without human beings thereby losing their reason, or losing touch with "the real problems."

The conversational interest of philosophy as a subject, or of some individual philosopher of genius, has varied and will continue to vary in unpredictable ways depending upon contingencies. These contingencies will range from what happens in physics to what happens in politics. The lines between disciplines will blur and shift, and new disciplines will arise, in the ways illustrated by Galileo's successful attempt to create "purely scientific questions" in the seventeenth century. The notions of "philosophical significance" and of "purely philosophical question," as they are currently used, gained sense only around the time of Kant. Our post-Kantian sense that epistemology or some successor subject is at the center of philosophy (and that moral philosophy, aesthetics, and social philosophy, for example, are somehow derivative) is a reflection of the fact that the professional philosopher's self-image depends upon his professional preoccupation with the image of the Mirror of Nature. Without the Kantian assumption that the philosopher can decide *quaestiones juris* concerning the claims of the rest of culture, this self-image collapses. That assumption depends on the notion that there is such a thing as understanding the essence of knowledge—doing what Sellars tells us we cannot do.

To drop the notion of the philosopher as knowing something about knowing which nobody else knows so well would be to drop the notion that his voice always has an overriding claim on the attention of the other participants in the conversation. It would also be to drop the notion that there is something called "philosophical method" or "philosophical technique" or "the philosophical point of view" which enables the professional philosopher, *ex officio*, to have interesting views about, say, the respectability of psychoanalysis, the legitimacy of certain dubious laws, the resolution of moral dilemmas, the "soundness" of schools of historiography or literary criticism, and the like. Philosophers often do have interesting views upon such questions, and their professional training as philosophers is often a necessary condition for their having the views they do. But this is not to say that philosophers have a special kind of knowledge about knowledge (or anything else) from which they draw relevant corollaries. The useful kibitzing they can provide on the various topics I just mentioned is made possible by their familiarity with the historical background of arguments on similar topics, and, most importantly, by the fact that arguments on such topics are punctuated by stale philosophical clichés which the other participants have stumbled across in their reading, but about which professional philosophers know the pros and cons by heart.

The neo-Kantian image of philosophy as a profession, then, is involved with the image of the "mind" or "language" as mirroring nature. So it might seem that epistemological behaviorism and the consequent rejection of mirror-imagery entail the claim that there can or should be no such profession. But this does not follow. Professions can survive the paradigms which gave them birth. In any case, the need for teachers who

have read the great dead philosophers is quite enough to insure that there will be philosophy departments as long as there are universities. The actual result of a widespread loss of faith in mirror-imagery would be merely an "encapsulation" of the problems created by this imagery within a historical period. I do not know whether we are in fact at the end of an era. This will depend, I suspect, on whether Dewey, Wittgenstein, and Heidegger are taken to heart. It may be that mirror-imagery and "mainstream," systematic philosophy will be revitalized once again by some revolutionary of genius. Or it may be that the image of the philosopher which Kant offered is about to go the way of the medieval image of the priest. If that happens, even the philosophers themselves will no longer take seriously the notion of philosophy as providing "foundations" or "justifications" for the rest of culture, or as adjudicating *quaestiones juris* about the proper domains of other disciplines.

Whichever happens, however, there is no danger of philosophy's "coming to an end." Religion did not come to an end in the Enlightenment, nor painting in Impressionism. Even if the period from Plato to Nietzsche is encapsulated and "distanced" in the way Heidegger suggests, and even if twentieth-century philosophy comes to seem a stage of awkward transitional backing and filling (as sixteenth-century philosophy now seems to us), there will be something called "philosophy" on the other side of the transition. For even if problems about representation look as obsolete to our descendants as problems about hylomorphism look to us, people will still read Plato, Aristotle, Descartes, Kant, Hegel, Wittgenstein, and Heidegger. What roles these men will play in our descendants' conversation, no one knows. Whether the distinction between systematic and edifying philosophy will carry over, no one knows either. Perhaps philosophy will become purely edifying, so that one's self-identification as a philosopher will be purely in terms of the books one reads and discusses, rather than in terms of the problems one wishes to solve. Perhaps a new form of systematic philosophy will be found which has nothing whatever to do with epistemology but which nevertheless makes normal philosophical inquiry possible. These speculations are idle, and nothing I have been saying makes one more plausible than another. The only point on which I would insist is that philosophers' moral concern should be with continuing the conversation of the West, rather than with insisting upon a place for the traditional problems of modern philosophy within that conversation.

CHAPTER 7

ALLAN BLOOM

THE CLOSING OF THE AMERICAN MIND

Allan Bloom (1930–   ) was educated at the University of Chicago, where he is currently Professor of Social Thought. He has been a visiting professor at the University of Tel Aviv and has taught at Cornell University and the University of Toronto. The author of *Shakespeare's Politics*, he has translated selected writings of Plato and Jean Jacques Rousseau. Professor Bloom's book, *The Closing of the American Mind: How Higher Education Has Failed Democracy and Impoverished the Souls of Today's Students*, was a landmark event in the academic world upon its publication in 1987, remaining on The *New York Times* best-seller list for months. His analysis of the condition of the modern American university has provoked anxiety, controversy, and debate, forcing educators to reopen questions of academic mission, curriculum, cultural pluralism, and social change.

THE CLOSING OF THE AMERICAN MIND[1]

Liberal Education

What image does a first-rank college or university present today to a teen-ager leaving home for the first time, off to the adventure of a liberal education? He has four years of freedom to discover himself—a space between the intellectual wasteland he has left behind and the inevitable dreary professional training that awaits him after the baccalaureate. In this short time he must learn that there is a great world beyond the little one he knows, experience the exhilaration of it and digest enough of it to sustain himself in the intellectual deserts he is destined to traverse. He must do this, that is, if he is to have any hope of a higher life. These are the charmed years when he can, if he so chooses, become anything he wishes and when he has the opportunity to survey his alternatives, not merely those current in his time or provided by careers, but those available to him as a human being. The importance of these years for an American cannot be overestimated. They are civilization's only chance to get to him.

In looking at him we are forced to reflect on what he should learn if he is to be called educated; we must speculate on what the human potential to be fulfilled is. In the specialities we can avoid such speculation, and the avoidance of them is one of specialization's charms. But here it is a simple duty. What are we to teach this person? The answer may not be evident, but to attempt to answer the question is already to philosophize and to begin to educate. Such a concern in itself poses the question of the unity of man and the unity of the sciences. It is childishness to say, as some do, that everyone must be allowed to develop freely, that it is authoritarian to impose a point of view on the student. In that case, why have a university? If the response is "to provide an atmosphere for learning," we come back to our original questions at the second remove. Which atmosphere? Choices and reflection on the reasons for those choices are unavoidable. The university has to stand for something. The practical effects of unwillingness to think positively about the contents of a liberal education are, on the one hand, to ensure that all the vulgarities of the world outside the university will flourish within it, and, on the other, to impose a much harsher and more illiberal necessity on the student—the one given by the the imperial and imperious demands of the specialized disciplines unfiltered by unifying thought.

The university now offers no distinctive visage to the young person. He finds a democracy of the disciplines—which are there either because they are autochthonous or because they wandered in recently to perform some job that was demanded of the university. This democracy is really an anarchy, because there are no recognized rules for citizenship and no legitimate titles to rule. In short there is no vision, nor is there a set of competing visions, of what an educated human being is. The question has disappeared, for to pose it would be a threat to the peace. There is no organization of the sciences, no tree of knowledge. Out of chaos emerges dispiritedness, because it is impossible to make a reasonable choice. Better to give up on liberal education and get on with a specialty in which there is at least a prescribed curriculum and a prospective career. On the way the student can pick up in elective courses a little of whatever is thought to make one cultured. The student gets no intimation that great mysteries might be revealed to him, that new and higher motives of action might be discovered within him, that a different and more human way of life can be harmoniously constructed by what he is going to learn.

Simply, the university is not distinctive. Equality for us seems to culminate in the unwillingness and incapacity to make claims of superiority, particularly in the domains in which such claims have always been made—art, religion and philosophy. . . .

Thus, when a student arrives at the university, he finds a bewildering variety of departments and a bewildering variety of courses. And there is no official guidance, no university-wide agreement, about what he *should* study. Nor does he usually find readily available examples, either among students or professors, of a unified use of the university's resources. It is easiest simply to make a career choice and go about getting prepared for that career. The programs designed for those having made such a choice render their students immune to charms that might lead them out of the conventionally respectable. The sirens sing *sotto voce* these days, and the young already have enough wax in their ears to pass them by without danger. These specialties can provide enough courses to take up most of their time for four years in preparation for the inevitable graduate study. With the few remaining courses they can do what they please, taking a bit of this and a bit of that. No public career these days—not doctor nor lawyer nor politician nor journalist nor businessman nor entertainer—has much to do with humane learning. An education, other than purely professional or technical, can even seem to be an impediment. That is why a countervailing atmosphere in the university would be necessary for the students to gain a taste for intellectual pleasures and learn that they are viable.

The real problem is those students who come hoping to find out what career they want to have, or are simply looking for an adventure with themselves. There are plenty of things for them to do—courses and disciplines enough to spend many a lifetime on. Each department or great division of the university makes a pitch for itself, and each offers a course of study that will make the student an initiate. But how to choose among them? How do they relate to one another? The fact is they do not address one another. They are competing and contradictory, without being aware of it. The problem of the whole is urgently indicated by the very existence of the specialties, but it is never systematically posed. The net effect of the student's encounter with the college catalogue is bewilderment and very often demoralization. It is just a matter of chance whether he finds one or two professors who can give him an insight into one of the great visions of education that have been the distinguishing part of every civilized nation. Most professors are specialists,

concerned only with their own fields, interested in the advancement of those fields in their own terms, or in their own personal advancement in a world where all the rewards are on the side of professional distinction. They have been entirely emancipated from the old structure of the university, which at least helped to indicate that they are incomplete, only parts of an unexamined and undiscovered whole. So the student must navigate among a collection of carnival barkers, each trying to lure him into a particular sideshow. This undecided student is an embarrassment to most universities, because he seems to be saying, "I am a whole human being. Help me to form myself in my wholeness and let me develop my real potential," and he is the one to whom they have nothing to say.

The Disciplines

How are they today, the big three that rule the academic roost and determine what is knowledge? Natural science is doing just fine. Living alone, but happily, running along like a well-wound clock, successful and useful as ever. There have been great things lately, physicists with their black holes and biologists with their genetic code. Its objects and methods are agreed upon. It offers exciting lives to persons of very high intelligence and provides immeasurable benefits to mankind at large. Our way of life is utterly dependent on the natural scientists, and they have more than fulfilled their every promise. Only at the margins are there questions that might threaten their theoretical equanimity— doubts about whether America produces synoptic scientific geniuses, doubts about the use of the results of science, such as nuclear weapons, doubts that lead to biology's need for "ethicists" in its experiments and its applications when, as scientists, they know that there are no such knowers as ethicists. In general, however, all is well.

But where natural science ends, trouble begins. It ends at man, the one being outside of its purview, or to be exact, it ends at that part or aspect of man that is not body, whatever that may be. Scientists as scientists can be grasped only under that aspect, as is the case with politicians, artists and prophets. All that is human, all that is of concern to us, lies outside of natural science. That should be a problem for natural science, but it is not. It is certainly a problem for us that we do not know what this thing is, that we cannot even agree on a name for this irreducible bit of man that is not body. Somehow this fugitive thing or aspect is the cause of science and society and culture and politics and economics and poetry and music. We know what these latter are. But can we really, if we do not know their cause, know what its status is, whether it even exists?

The difficulty is reflected in the fact that for the study of this one theme, man, or this *je ne sais quoi* pertaining to man, and his activities and products, there are two great divisions of the university—humanities and social science—while for bodies there is only natural science. This would all be very well if the division of labor were founded on an agreement about the subject matter and reflected a natural articulation within it, as do the divisions between physics, chemistry and biology, leading to mutual respect and cooperation. It could be believed and is sometimes actually said, mostly in commencement speeches, that social science treats man's social life, and humanities his creative life—the great works of art, etc. And, although there is something to this kind of distinction, it really will not do. This fact comes to light in a variety of ways. While both social science and humanities are more or less willingly awed by natural science, they have a mutual contempt for one another, the former

looking down on the latter as unscientific, the latter regarding the former as philistine. They do not cooperate. And most important, they occupy much of the same ground. Many of the classic books now part of the humanities talk about the same things as do social scientists but use different methods and draw different conclusions; and each of the social sciences in one way or another attempts to explain the activities of the various kinds of artists in ways that are contrary to the way they are treated in humanities. The difference comes down to the fact that social science really wants to be predictive, meaning that man is predictable, while the humanities say that he is not. The divisions between the two camps resemble truce lines rather than scientific distinctions. They disguise old and unresolved struggles about the being of man.

The social sciences and the humanities represent the two responses to the crisis caused by the definitive ejection of man—or of the residue of man extracted from, or superfluous to, body—from nature, and hence from the purview of natural science or natural philosophy, toward the end of the eighteenth century. One route led toward valiant efforts to assimilate man to the new natural sciences, to make the science of man the next rung in the ladder down from biology. The other took over the territory newly opened up by Kant, that of freedom as opposed to nature, separate but equal, not requiring the aping of the methods of natural science, taking spirituality at least as seriously as body. Neither challenged the champion, natural science, newly emancipated from philosophy: social science tried humbly to find a place at court, humanities proudly to set up shop next door. The result has been two continuous and ill-assorted strands of thought about man, one tending to treat him essentially as another of the brutes, without spirituality, soul, self, consciousness, or what have you; the other acting as though he is not an animal or does not have a body. There is no junction of these two roads. One must choose between them, and they end up in very different places. . .

Neither of these solutions has fully succeeded. Social science receives no recognition form natural science.[2] It is an imitation, not a part. And the humanities shop has turned out to be selling diverse and ill-assorted antiques, decaying and ever dustier, while business gets worse and worse. Social science has proved more robust, more in harmony with the world dominated by natural science, and, while losing its inspiration and evangelical fervor, has proved useful to different aspects of modern life, as the mere mention of economics and psychology indicates. Humanities languish, but this proves only that they do not suit the modern world. It may very well be the indication of what is wrong with modernity. Moreover the language that in an unscholarly way influences life so powerfully today emerged from investigations undertaken in the realm of freedom. Social science comes more out of the school founded by Locke; humanities out of that founded by Rousseau. But social science, while looking to natural science, has actu-

ally received a large part of its impulse in recent times from the nether world. One need only think of Weber, although Marx and Freud are similar cases. It cannot be avowed, but *man*, to be grasped, needs something the natural sciences cannot provide. Man is the problem, and we live with various stratagems for not facing it. The strange relations between the three divisions of knowledge in the present university tell us all about it.

The third island of the university is the almost submerged old Atlantis, the humanities. In it there is no semblance of order, no serious account of what should and should not belong, or of what its disciplines are trying to accomplish or how. It is somehow the repair of man or of humanity, the place to go to find ourselves now that everyone else has given up. But where to look in this heap or jumble? It is difficult enough for those who already know what to look for to get any satisfaction here. For students it requires a powerful instinct and a lot of luck. The analogies tumble uncontrollably from my pen. The humanities are like the great old Paris Flea Market where, amidst masses of junk, people with a good eye found castaway treasures that made them rich. Or they are like a refugee camp where all the geniuses driven out of their jobs and countries by unfriendly regimes are idling, either unemployed or performing menial tasks. The other two divisions of the university have no use for the past, are forward-looking and not inclined toward ancestor worship.

The problem of the humanities, and therefore of the unity of knowledge, is perhaps best represented by the fact that if Galileo, Kepler and Newton exist anywhere in the university now it is in the humanities, as part of one kind of history or another—history of science, history of ideas, history of culture. In order to have a place, they have to be understood as something other than what they were—great contempla-

---

[2]Natural science simply does not care. There is no hostility (unless it is attacked) to anything that is going on elsewhere. It is really self-sufficient, or almost so. If some other discipline proved itself, satisfied natural science's standards of rigor and proof, it would be automatically admitted. Natural science does not boast, is not snobbish. It is genuine. As Swift pointed out, its only habitual and apparently necessary sortie from its own proper domain is into politics. This is where it itself, if only in confused fashion, recognizes that it is a part of a larger project, and that it is dependent on that project, which is not a product of methods. Lowly, despised politics points toward the need for philosophy, as Socrates originally said, in such a way that even scientists have to admit it. Natural scientists have no respect for political science as a science, but they have a passionate concern for politics. This is a beginning point for rethinking everything. Is the danger of nuclear war or the imprisonment of Sakharov just an accident?

tors of the whole of nature who understood themselves to be of interest only to the extent that they told the truth about it. If they were wrong or have been completely surpassed, then they themselves would say that they are of no interest. To put them in the humanities is the equivalent of naming a street after them or setting up a statue in a corner of a park. They are effectively dead. Plato, Bacon, Machiavelli and Montesquieu are in the same condition, except for that little enclave in political sciene. The humanities are the repository for *all* of the classics now—but much of the classic literature claimed to be about the order of the whole of nature and man's place in it, to legislate for that whole and to tell the truth about it. If such claims are denied, these writers and their books cannot be read seriously, and their neglect elsewhere is justified. They have been saved only on the condition of being mummified. The humanities' willingness to receive them has taken them off the backs of the natural and social sciences, where they constituted a challenge that no longer has to be met. On the portal of the humanities is written in many ways and many tongues, "There is no truth—at least here."

The humanities are the specialty that now exclusively possesses the books that are not specialized, that insist upon asking the questions about the whole that are excluded from the rest of the university, which is dominated by real specialties, as resistant to self-examination as they were in Socrates' day and now rid of the gadfly. The humanities have not had the vigor to fight it out with triumphant natural science, and want to act as though it were just a specialty. But, as I have said over and over again, however much the humane disciplines would like to forget about their essential conflict with natural science as now practiced and understood, they are gradually undermined by it. Whether it is old philosophic texts that raise now inadmissible questions, or

old works of literature that presuppose the being of the noble and the beautiful, materialism, determinism, reductionism, homogenization—however one describes modern natural science—deny their importance and their very possibility. Natural science asserts that it is metaphysically neutral, and hence has no need for philosophy, and that imagination is not a faculty that in any way intuits the real—hence art has nothing to do with truth. The kinds of questions children ask: Is there a God? Is there freedom? Is there punishment for evil deeds? Is there certain knowledge? What is a good society? were once also the questions addressed by science and philosophy. But now the grownups are too busy at work, and the children are left in a day-care center called the humanities, in which the discussions have no echo in the adult world. Moreover, students whose nature draws them to such questions and to the books that appear to investigate them are very quickly rebuffed by the fact that their humanities teachers do not want or are unable to use the books to respond to their needs.

This problem of the old books is not new. In Swift's *Battle of the Books* one finds Bentley, the premier Greek scholar of the eighteenth century, on the side of the moderns. He accepted the superiority of modern thought to Greek thought. So why study Greek books? This question remains unanswered in classics departments. There are all sorts of dodges, ranging from pure philological analysis to using these books to show the relation between thought and economic conditions. But practically no one even tries to read them as they were once read—for the sake of finding out whether they are true. Aristotle's *Ethics* teaches us not what a good man is but what the Greeks thought about morality. But who really cares very much about that? Not any normal person who wants to lead a serious life.

All the things I have said about books in our

time help to characterize the situation of the humanities, which are the really exposed part of the university. They have been buffeted more severely by historicism and relativism than the other parts. They suffer most from democratic society's lack of respect for tradition and its emphasis on utility. To the extent that the humanities are supposed to treat of creativity, professors' lack of creativity becomes a handicap. The humanities are embarrassed by the political content of many of the literary works belonging to them. They have had to alter their contents for the sake of openness to other cultures. And when the old university habits were changed, they found themselves least able to answer the question "Why?," least able to force students to meet standards, or to attract them with any clear account of what they would learn. One need only glance at the situation of the natural sciences in all these respects to see the gravity of the problem faced by the humanities. Natural science is sovereignly indifferent to the fact that there were and are other kinds of explanations of natural phenomena in other ages or cultures. The relation between Einstein and Buddha is purely for educational TV, in programs put together by humanists. Whatever its practitioners may say, they are sure its explanations are true, or truth. They do not have to give reasons "why," because the answer seems all too evident.

The natural sciences are able to assert that they are pursuing the important truth, and the humanities are not able to make any such assertion. That is always the critical point. Without this, no study can remain alive. Vague insistence that without the humanities we will no longer be civilized rings very hollow when no one can say what "civilized" means, when there are said to be many civilizations that are all equal. The claim of "the classic" loses all legitimacy when the classic cannot be believed to tell the truth. The truth question is most pressing and acutely embarrass-

ing for those who deal with the philosophic texts, but also creates problems for those treating purely literary works. There is an enormous difference between saying, as teachers once did, "You must learn to see the world as Homer or Shakespeare did," and saying, as teachers now do, "Homer and Shakespeare had some of the same concerns you do and can enrich your vision of the world." In the former approach students are challenged to discover new experiences and reassess old; in the latter, they are free to use the books in any way they please. . .

Most interesting of all, lost amidst this collection of disciplines, modestly sits philosophy. It has been dethroned by political and theoretical democracy, bereft of the passion or the capacity to rule. Its story defines in itself our whole problem. Philosophy once proudly proclaimed that it was the best way of life, and it dared to survey the whole, to seek the first causes of all things, and not only dictated its rules to the special sciences but constituted and ordered them. The classic philosophic books are philosophy in action, doing precisely these things. But this was all impossible, *hybris*, say their impoverished heirs. Real science did not need them, and the rest is ideology or myth. Now they are just books on a shelf. Democracy took away philosophy's privileges, and philosophy could not decide whether to fade away or to take a job. Philosophy was architectonic, had the plans for the whole building, and the carpenters, masons and plumbers were its subordinates and had no meaning without its plan. Philosophy founded the university, but it could no longer do so. We live off its legacy. When people speak vaguely about generalists vs. specialists, they must mean by the generalist the philosopher, for he is the only kind of knower who embraces, or once embraced, all the specialties, possessing a subject matter, necessary to the specialties, which was real—being or the good—and not just a collection of the matters of the specialties. Philosophy is no longer a way of life, and it is no longer a sovereign science. Its situation in our universities has something to do with the desperate condition of philosophy in the world today, and something to do with its peculiar history as a discipline in America. With respect to the former, although reason is gravely threatened, Nietzsche and Heidegger were genuine philosophers and able to face up to and face down both natural science and historicism, the two great contemporary opponents of philosophy. Philosophy is still possible. And on the Continent even now, schoolchildren are taught philosophy, and it seems to be something real. An American high school student knows only the word "philosophy," and it does not appear to be any more serious a life choice than yoga. In America, anyhow, everybody has a philosophy. Philosophy was not ever a very powerful presence in universities, although there were important exceptions. We began with a public philosophy that sufficed for us, and we thought that it was common sense. In America, Tocqueville said, everyone is a Cartesian although no one has read Descartes. We were almost entirely importers of philosophy, with the exception of Pragmatism. One need not have read a line of philosophy to be considered educated in this country. It is easily equated with hot air, much more so than any of the other humane disciplines. So it always had an uphill fight. Students who did seek it could, however, find some refreshment at its source.

But it has succumbed and probably could disappear without being much noticed. It has a scientific component, logic, which is attached to the sciences and could easily be detached from philosophy. This is serious, practiced by competent specialists, and responds to none of the permanent philosophic questions. History of philosophy, the compendium of dead philosophies that was always most lively for the students, has been neglected, and students find it better treated in a variety of other disciplines. Positivism and ordinary language analysis have long dominated, although they are on the decline and evidently being replaced by nothing. These are simply methods of a sort, and they repel students who come with the humanizing questions. Professors of these schools simply would not and could not talk about anything important, and they themselves do not represent a philosophic life for the students. In some places existentialism and phenomenology have gained a foothold, and they are much more attractive to students than positivism or ordinary language analysis. Catholic universities have always kept some contact with medieval philosophy, and hence, Aristotle. But, in sum, the philosophy landscape is largely bleak. That is why so much of the philosophic instinct in America used to lead toward the new social sciences and is now veering off toward certain branches of literature and literary criticism. As it stands, philosophy is just another humanities subject, rather contentless, without a thought of trying to take command in the crisis of the university. Actually it contains less of the exhilarating presence of the tradition in philosophy than do the other humanities disciplines, and one finds its professors least active of the humanists in attempts to revitalize liberal education. Although there was a certain modesty about ordinary language analysis—"We just help to give you clarity about what you are already doing"—there was also smugness: "We know what was wrong with the whole tradition, and we don't need it anymore." Therefore the tradition disappeared from philosophy's confines.

CONCLUSION

These are the shadows cast by the peaks of the university over the entering undergraduate. Together they represent what the university has to say about man and his education, and they do not project a coherent image. The differences and the indifferences are too great. It is difficult to imagine that there is either the wherewithal or the energy within the university to constitute or reconstitute the idea of an educated human being and establish a liberal education again.

However, the contemplation of this scene is in itself a proper philosophic activity. The university's evident lack of wholeness in an enterprise that clearly demands it cannot help troubling some of its members. The questions are all there. They only need to be addressed continuously and seriously for liberal learning to exist; for it does not consist so much in answers as in the permanent dialogue. It is in such perplexed professors that at least the idea might persevere and help to guide some of the needy young persons at our doorstep. The matter is still present in the university; it is the form that has vanished. One cannot and should not hope for a general reform. The hope is that the embers do not die out.

Men may live more truly and fully in reading Plato and Shakespeare than at any other time, because then they are participating in essential being and are forgetting their accidental lives. The fact that this kind of humanity exists or existed, and that we can somehow still touch it with the tips of our outstretched fingers, makes our imperfect humanity, which we can no longer bear, tolerable. The books in their objective beauty are still there, and we must help protect and cultivate the delicate tendrils reaching out toward them through the unfriendly soil of students' souls. Human nature, it seems, remains the same in our very altered circumstances because we still face the same problems, if in different guises, and have the distinctively human need to solve them, even though our awareness and forces have become enfeebled.

After a reading of the *Symposium* a serious student came with deep melancholy and said it was impossible to imagine that magic Athenian atmosphere reproduced, in which friendly men, educated, lively, on a footing of equality, civilized but natural, came together and told wonderful stories about the meaing of their longing. But such experiences are always accessible. Actually, this playful discussion took place in the midst of a terrible war that Athens was destined to lose, and Aristophanes and Socrates at least could foresee that this meant the decline of Greek civilization. But they were not given to culture despair, and in these terrible political circumstances, their abandon to the joy of nature proved the viability of what is best in man, independent of accidents, of circumstance. We feel ourselves too dependent on history and culture. This student did not have Socrates, but he had Plato's book about him, which might even be better; he had brains, friends and a country happily free enough to let them gather and speak as they will. What is essential about that dialogue, or any of the Platonic dialogues, is reproducible in almost all times and places. He and his friends can think together. It requires much thought to learn that this thinking might be what it is all for. That's where we are beginning to fail. But it is right under our noses, improbable but always present.

Throughout this book I have referred to Plato's *Republic*, which is for me *the* book on education, because it really explains to me what I experience as a man and a teacher, and I have almost always used it to point out what we should not hope for, as a teaching of moderation and resignation. But all its impossibilities act as a filter to leave the residue of the highest and non-illusory possibility. The real community of man, in the midst of all the self-contradictory simulacra of community, is the community of those who seek the truth, of the potential knowers, that is, in principle, of all men to the extent they desire to know. But in fact this includes only a few, the true friends, as Plato was to Aristotle at the very moment they were disagreeing about the nature of the good. Their common concern for the good linked them; their disagreement about it proved they needed one another to understand it. They were absolutely one soul as they looked at the problem. This, according to Plato, is the only real friendship, the only real common good. It is here that the contact people so desperately seek is to be found. The other kinds of relatedness are only imperfect reflections of this one trying to be self-subsisting, gaining their only justification from their ultimate relation to this one. This is the meaning of the riddle of the improbable philosopher-kings. They have a true community that is exemplary for all other communities.

This is a radical teaching but perhaps one appropriate to our own radical time, in which proximate attachments have become so questionable and we know of no others. This age is not utterly insalubrious for philosophy. Our problems are so great and their sources so deep that to understand them we need philosophy more than ever, if we do not despair of it, and it faces the challenges on which it flourishes. I still believe that universities, rightly understood, are where community and friendship can exist in our times. Our thought and our politics have become inextricably bound up with the universities, and they have served us well, human things being what they are. But for all that, and even though they deserve our strenuous efforts, one should never forget that Socrates was not a professor, that he was put to death, and that the love of wisdom survived, partly because of his *individual* example. This is what really counts, and we must remember it in order to know how to defend the university.

This is the American moment in world history, the one for which we shall forever be judged. Just as in politics the responsibility for the fate of freedom in the world has devolved upon our regime, so the fate of philosophy in the world has devolved upon our universities, and the two are related as they have never been before. The gravity of our given task is great, and it is very much in doubt how the future will judge our stewardship.

GLOSSARY

AESTHETICS   That branch of philosophy that studies the nature of art and beauty.

ARGUMENT   A group of statements containing one or more statements (the premises) that are claimed to provide support for one of the other statements (called the conclusion).

ANALYSIS   The process of uncovering the meaning of a statement or of a system of belief.

ANALYTIC PHILOSOPHY   A twentieth century philosophic movement centered in Great Britain and the United States, specializing in the analysis of statements or concepts.

ANSWER   The knowledge sought in a question.

ASSERTION   A claim that is unsupported by evidence.

AXIOLOGY   The study of values. One of the main branches of philosophy, it is subdivided into ethics, social and political philosophy, and aesthetics.

COMMON SENSE   A general trust in the senses and in commonly received knowledge.

CONCLUSION   A statement inferred from the premises of an argument.

DEDUCTION   An inference necessarily derived from general premises.

DESCRIPTIVE STATEMENT   A statement that merely describes a fact or set of facts, making no evaluation.

DIALECTIC   A method of reasoning where opposing points of view are exchanged and relentlessly criticized, producing a new point of view that incorporates whatever truth was found in the original formulations.

EMPIRICISM   In epistemology, the view that the origin of knowledge is experience; in opposition to *rationalism*.

EPISTEMOLOGY   A theory of knowledge; a main branch of philosophy that studies the nature, origins, and validity of knowledge.

ETHICS   That branch of axiology that attempts to establish rational grounds for right conduct; in its *normative* sense, ethics prescribes what human beings ought and ought not to do.

ETYMOLOGY   The study of words and their origins.

INDUCTION   An inference derived from factual evidence, yielding probability.

INFERENCE   A conclusion derived either from general premises (deduction) or factual evidence (induction).

JUSTIFICATION   An argued defense offered as sufficient grounds for believing an assertion to be true.

LOGIC   A main branch of philosophy that evaluates arguments and formulates rules for good thinking.

METAPHYSICS   A main branch of philosophy that questions the nature of reality; subdivided onto ontology, philosophical anthropology, and philosophy of religion.

MYTH   A story of often forgotten origin that offers poetic insight into reality.

NORMATIVE STATEMENT   A statement about what is good or what ought to be done.

OBJECTIVITY   A scientific postulate that requires investigators to be impartial with regard to data, eliminating insofar as possible all subjective or personal elements and arranging for facts to be experienced in the same way by normal observers.

ONTOLOGY   A subdivision of metaphysics that studies the essential characteristics of Being apart from the study of individually existing things.

OPINION   A belief, often lacking supporting evidence, based on personal or subjective factors.

PARADOX   An apparent contradiction.

PHENOMENOLOGY   A twentieth century movement in philosophy founded by Edmund Husserl (1859–1938); a descriptive science of pure consciousness.

PREMISE   A sentence in an argument used to support a conclusion.

RATIONALISM   A view in epistemology that emphasizes the mind's ability to know truth apart from sense experience; in opposition to *empiricism*.

SCIENCE   A body of knowledge obtained through observation and experimentation; a method of obtaining knowledge.

FOR FURTHER STUDY

Edwards, Paul, ed. *The Encyclopedia of Philosophy*. 8 vols. New York: Macmillan and Free Press, 1967.

A useful encyclopedia containing articles on a wide variety of philosophical topics, each written by an expert in the field. Many of the entries are written from the standpoint of analytic philosophy.

Ewing, A.C. *The Fundamental Questions of Philosophy*. London: Routledge and Kegan Paul, 1951.

As the title suggests, this book deals with the leading questions of philosophy, in a clear and readable fashion.

Heidegger, Martin. *Introduction to Metaphysics*. Translated by Ralph Manheim, New Haven: Yale University Press, 1959.

Heidegger's clearest statement of the task of philosophy, tracking the shifts in the way philosophy has understood itself since the days of early Greek philosophy.

Jones, W.T.A. *A History of Western Philosophy*. 2d ed. New York: Harcourt Brace & World, 1969, 1975.

This five-volume history of philosophy is superbly written; it consistently explores the relation between philosophy and general culture.

Taylor, Richard. *Metaphysics*. 3d ed. Englewood Cliffs, N.J.: Prentice-Hall, 1983.

A well-written account of the major problems of metaphysics.

PART TWO

◆

DOUBT AND BELIEF: THE PHILOSOPHICAL USES OF UNCERTAINTY

A doubt that doubted everything would not be a doubt.

LUDWIG WITTGENSTEIN

ORIENTATION

Part 2 is the first of four parts dealing with the branch of philosophy known as epistemology. Broadly defined as the theory of knowledge, epistemology is concerned with the nature, sources, validity, and limits of knowledge. These concerns translate into three fundamental groupings of questions, to be discussed in Parts 2, 3, and 4 of this book:

1. What is the nature of knowledge; how is knowledge possible?
2. What are the sources of knowledge; how is truth tested?
3. What is science; what are the limits of science?

BELIEF

Belief is a habit of mind, a disposition to respond in a particular way to the demands of the world. To believe that the Los Angeles Lakers won the NBA championship in 1987 and 1988 is to be disposed to respond "yes" when asked if this is the case. To believe that Vail is the best ski resort in Colorado is to be disposed to go there when circumstances allow.

The duration of a belief may be short or long. Some beliefs, like the belief that John F. Kennedy was the thirty-fifth president of the United States, we are apt to retain as long as we live. Others, like the belief that Vail is the best ski resort in Colorado, may be abandoned if we discover evidence to the contrary. Should this occur, the disposition to believe has been replaced by a disposition to disbelieve, which is still a case of belief.

The disposition to believe, disbelieve, or not believe at all are three natural responses to the world. Of these three, not believing is the most rare, involving a disposition to suspend judgment in the absence of sufficient evidence. If someone asks me whether the number of fish in Lake Superior is an even number, I am disposed not to believe, rather than disbelieve. For all I know, maybe there is an even number, but I cannot be certain, so the wisest course of action is to remain neutral on this question, suspending judgment.

KNOWLEDGE

Knowing is a special kind of believing. The class of things that we believe is always larger than the class of things that we know. Part of the reason for this is that we are disposed to believe all kinds of things in the course of a day, many of which may be inconsequential. We may believe that the road is wet, or that an egg is undercooked, or that a bird just perched on the feeder outside. As we turn our attention elsewhere, the disposition to believe these things may disappear.

Knowing, on the other hand, takes more effort. It requires a stronger disposition. One can believe without knowing. Believing something does not count as knowing unless what is believed is in fact certain. Knowing requires certainty. *Mere* beliefs may turn out to be *false* beliefs. False beliefs are not only possible, they are quite common, since humans are **fallible** creatures. (After all, it was not all that long ago that respected thinkers believed that the earth was flat, a belief we now recognize as being decidedly false.) Yet no one would want to equate false beliefs with knowledge.

JUSTIFICATION

So we would want to say that knowledge consists of beliefs that are certain. But what conditions must be met in order for a belief to be certain? Philosophers have argued that terms such as "certain," "evident," and "reasonable" are all terms of epistemic appraisal that have to do with **justification.** When applied to beliefs, the term "justify" acts very much like a judge or magistrate, positively attributing right standing to a belief, and negatively, making the belief in question free from blame or reproach. It is safe to say that most of us, if not all of us, wish to do our best to improve our set of beliefs. The Socratic method outlined in the previous chapter requires that we lead lives of self-examination, meaning we must be willing to examine our beliefs, replacing unjustified beliefs with ones that are justified. It also means that we must be willing to replace beliefs having lesser justification with those having a greater degree of justification.

A person may be said to be justified in believing a proposition when that proposition is evident beyond reasonable doubt. A proposition is beyond reasonable doubt for a subject when that subject is more justified in believing the proposition than in not believing it. This can be illustrated by the proposition that my car will not blow up when I turn the ignition key. This proposition is such that believing it is more justified than not believing it (although the situation might be different if I had reason to suspect that international terrorists were stalking me).

How does one justify belief and attain certainty? By acquiring sufficient evidence to dispel reasonable doubt. Perhaps this is best illustrated by example.

Suppose that you are soundly asleep in your house when you are awakened by the sound of a car engine, the slamming of a door, and a general commotion in the next room. You may believe that your roommate Fred has arrived home and is in the next room. But can you properly be said to know that Fred is in the next room?

No. After all, couldn't it be the case that the car you heard belonged to someone else, or has pulled into another driveway, and that the noise next door is being caused by someone (or something) other than Fred? Clearly, the belief that Fred is in the next room has yet to be justified.

Question: What would it take to justify your belief that Fred is in the next room? Answer: More evidence.

Suppose that you get out of bed and go to the front window. In the driveway you see what appears to be Fred's car. Is this enough evidence to justify your belief that Fred is next door? No. After all, it is possible that someone has borrowed Fred's car and has now returned it. Perhaps the person who drove the car and the person making the commotion next door (assuming for a moment that it is a *person*) are different persons, neither of them Fred.

Suppose that you knock on the door of the room next door. A voice calls out in response. It sounds very much like Fred's voice. Has your belief now been justified? There is good reason to once again answer no. How can you be certain that the voice you heard is not that of someone impersonating Fred in order to deceive you, or someone playing a practical joke?

Suppose that you open the door and enter the room. There on the bed you recognize the familiar features of Fred. Have we reached bedrock now? Some philosophers would argue that we have now arrived at a belief that is beyond reasonable doubt, in no need of further justification. The fact that you see a person with the voice and features of Fred constitutes sufficient evidence for you to state confidently, "I know that Fred is in the room."

SKEPTICISM

Nevertheless, it is possible that someone might object to our confident statement about Fred, claiming that we have not eliminated all of the **counterpossibilities.** In other words, in asserting that we are certain (we know) that Fred is in the room, we have not ruled out every possible state of affairs that might conceivably count against this belief. Critics making this argument (known as skeptics) would object that our belief is not yet justified. One can easily see how such an approach could be expanded in scope to apply to all knowledge claims. Without being restricted to our experience of Fred in the next room, one could generalize about all purported knowledge claims, denying the very possibility of epistemic justification. The philosophical position that holds that no beliefs can ever be justified because of the failure to eliminate counterpossibilities, or because specific counterpossibilities create irremovable doubt, is known as **skepticism.**

The word *skeptic* is derived from the Greek word *skeptikos*, meaning "inquirer." Skepticism in its broadest sense is an expression of inquisitive doubt or disbelief.

In its narrowest, most extreme sense, it is the position that knowledge is impossible and truth is in vain. The Sophist Gorgias (c. 483–376 B.C.) was expressing this extreme sense of skepticism when he asserted that nothing exists; and that if it did, we could not know it; and that even if we did come to know anything, we could not communicate it. It should be clear that endorsing the mild skepticism contained in the broad definition does not commit one to the extreme skepticism of a Gorgias. To see why this is the case, we shall have to examine skepticism more carefully.

THE LOGIC OF SKEPTICISM

Skeptics typically argue that any proposition that can be presented for belief can be **counterbalanced** through its negation. If a proposition on a given subject p is counterbalanced, it would mean that a person would be equally justified in believing p or the negation of p. The strategy here is to balance opposing evidence or arguments against one another, with the dismaying result that one is at least as justified in not believing p as in believing p. This seems to have been the strategy adopted by an early Greek skeptic, Pyrrho of Elis (c. 365–275 B.C.)

Pyrrho's strategy is important, for it points to a crucial question that epistemologists must decide: Must we be more concerned with knowing the truth, or in avoiding error? The American philosopher William James posed the question in this way:

> There are two ways of looking at our duty in the matter of opinion—ways entirely different, and yet ways about whose difference the theory of knowledge seems hitherto to have shown little concern. We *must know* the truth; and we *must avoid error*—these are our first and great commandments as would-be knowers; but they are not two ways of stating an identical commandment, they are two separable laws.[1]

We may paraphrases James' question and ask, "Is it more reasonable to try to reach the truth or to try to avoid error?" It should be clear that skeptics must opt for the latter choice; those who desire to refute skepticism will adopt the former approach.

It is difficult to overestimate just how important this choice has been in the history of philosophy. Skeptics have always regarded it as more important to avoid error than to arrive at truth. They tend to stress "good epistemic

---

[1]William James, *The Will to Believe and Other Essays in Popular Philosophy* (New York: David McKay, 1911), 17. For a more detailed discussion of this passage in James emphasizing antiskeptical principles, see Roderick Chisholm, *Theory of Knowledge*, 3d ed. (Englewood Cliffs, N.J.: Prentice Hall, 1989), 13–14.

hygeine"—that is, keeping oneself pure from the taint of error or mistake. It bothers skeptics to think that they have at times given intellectual assent to propositions, thinking them correct, only to find out at a later date that they were hopelessly wrong. Most of us can think of cases like this in our own lives. Perhaps you have raised your hand to answer a question in class, convinced that you had the right answer. Your feeling of exhilaration at having the correct answer turns into acute embarrassment as the teacher shakes her head "no" at your response. You are wrong! But you were sure that you knew that answer. How do you respond to this experience?

If you obey the first of James' commandments—"know the truth"—you will be inclined to risk being wrong in order to pursue the truth. In other words, you accept the risk of being wrong as one of the natural hazards of truth-making. Although momentarily embarrassed, you will not be dissuaded from volunteering another answer at some point in the future.

If, however, you are obedient to James' second commandment—"avoid error"—you will view things very differently. Playing it safe rather than taking chances may appeal to you as being the more reasonable course of action. Since the only foolproof way to avoid error is to withhold judgment, you may resolve never to risk being wrong again, even if it means sacrificing all traditional claims to "knowledge." This, then, is the logic of skepticism: risking loss of knowledge for fear of error. (In "The Will to Believe," one of the readings that follow, James makes it clear that embracing the first commandment entails being willing to risk error for fear of losing the truth.)

Skepticism may be thought of as a systematic attempt to protect ourselves from error by refusing to claim knowledge in the absence of certainty. In order to hold this position, it is necessary to demonstrate that certainty is impossible. Here, at least three strategies are possible for the skeptic. First, we can argue that there are perfectly good everyday reasons for supposing that we cannot know the kinds of things that people ordinarily claim to know. In support of this contention we can cite an impressive number of examples from experience, like the one mentioned earlier—you thought you had the right answer in class when, in fact, you did not. Human fallibility is generally recognized to be widespread. Nevertheless, this strategy can be effectively rebutted when we consider that we can be aware of human fallibility; that is to say, we can know of it and take it into account when constructing a theory of knowledge. If I can know that I am fallible, subject to error, at least there is *something* that I can know. In being aware of my fallibility, I learn something positive about the world. This strategy is therefore not very promising for the extreme version of skepticism.

Second, we can pursue the previously mentioned strategy of counterbalancing, finding arguments that work against justification of belief. This strategy seems much more promising for the extreme skeptic. Think back to our example of knowing that Fred was in the room. Suppose someone were absolutely committed to continue doubting that Fred was in the room, even in the face of massive evidence to the contrary. Each time new evidence was submitted to justify the belief that Fred was present, a counterbalancing new reason for not believing it would be introduced. For instance, it is possible that what you are naively calling "Fred" is actually a film image, the result of a masterful "special effects" camera and sound technology. If you say that you can go up to Fred and actually touch him, proving he is more than a camera image, then the skeptic can respond that it is possible that someone has performed plastic surgery in order to create an individual that looks remarkably like Fred. Or perhaps this person in Fred's bed is some kind of human replicant designed by someone who wishes to deceive you into falsely believing that it is Fred, because she enjoys witnessing your foolish claims to epistemic justification. It should be clear by now that there is no "protection" against this kind of counterbalancing technique. Theoretically, it could go on forever, with the skeptic drawing upon more and more imaginative counterarguments.

The third strategy often adopted by skeptics is a special kind of counterpossibility argument that is sufficient in itself to cast doubt on all of our most ordinary beliefs. In the history of philosophy several ingenious arguments have been offered that catch us up short like this, causing us to question our uncritical attitudes. The philosopher best known for this kind of strategy was the seventeenth century philosopher and mathematician René Descartes (1596–1650), who in his *Meditations on First Philosophy* employed a variety of devices, involving dreamers, evil demons, and madmen to achieve his purpose.[2] His famous "dream argument" is quite simple. Have you ever had a dream in which you dreamed you were awake and going about your daily business? If so, then you know the power of dreams to exist right alongside wakeful life, mimicking it, and at times being confused with it. How can you be sure that you are not dreaming right now? For me, it seems perfectly certain that I am dressed and sitting in a chair punching keys on my word processor right now, but if this is all a dream then I'm probably still undressed and lying in bed, not sitting in a chair. The fact that I have mistaken dreams for waking life in the past makes me wonder how I can be sure that I am not dreaming now. Once I admit the bare possibility that I *might* be dreaming, this casts doubt on every knowledge claim I might have, including such allegedly "obvious" things such as the fact I am dressed, or sitting at a desk in an office. If I pinch my arm to try to convince myself that I am not dreaming, then I recall that I have sometimes had dreams within dreams, and there do not seem to be any criteria to distinguish the *inside* of a dream from the *outside*. Admit the possibility that you are inside a dream and it becomes difficult if not impossible to get outside

[2]See Harry Frankfurt's masterful study of Descartes' *Meditations* (which has one of the more delightful titles in philosophical literature), *Demons, Dreamers, and Madmen: The Defense of Reason in Descartes' Meditations* (Indianapolis: Bobbs-Merrill, 1970).

it. Hence, dreams represent for Descartes one example of skeptical counterpossibility.

Descartes went on to postulate the existence of a powerful but malevolent being whose sinister intent was to deceive us into thinking things that were clearly false. If such a being were to exist (and how can we know that this being doesn't?) wouldn't he or she be capable of causing us to believe that $2 + 2 = 4$ even if the "correct" answer were 5, or 6, or 784? As preposterous as this sounds, we are obliged to confess that if such beings existed they would be powerful enough to cause us to go wrong even in areas that seem to us to be the most certain. It is conceivable that our belief-forming mechanism might therefore be deficient, rendering suspect everything that we currently believe, as well as everything that we may come to believe in the future. Hence nothing would be certain, everything would be doubtful, and we would be in the uncomfortable position of not knowing anything about anything.

More recently Peter Unger has updated Descartes' gambit. In an article included in the Contemporary Perspectives section of this part, he asks us to consider the possibility that an evil scientist has implanted electrodes in our heads, which cause us to falsely believe that we know all kinds of things, and then laughs at our preposterous claims to know. Yet another variation on this theme is played by Hilary Putnam:

> Imagine that a human being (you can imagine this to be yourself) has been subjected to an operation by an evil scientist. The person's brain, (your brain) has been removed from the body and placed in a vat of nutrients which keeps the brain alive. The nerve endings have been connected to a super-scientific computer which causes the person whose brain it is to have the illusion that everything is perfectly normal. There seem to be people, objects, the sky, etc; but really all the person (you) is experiencing is the result of electronic impulses traveling from the computer to the nerve endings.[3]

The skeptic now argues that because it is logically possible (however unlikely) that such a situation currently exists, you cannot be justified in believing that you exist outside the vat of nutrients. Of course, the skeptic is not saying that your brain is actually in the vat, or that you are justified in believing that you are in the vat. The point is simply that you cannot be justified in saying that you are *not* in the vat. Of course, if you cannot know that you are not in the vat, then you cannot be justified in believing anything else about people, objects in the world, etc., since these experiences are the result of the evil scientist doing devious things to your brain.

[3]Hilary Putnam, *Reason, Truth and History* (Cambridge, England: Cambridge University Press, 1981), 5–6. For a critical response to this argument, see Chisholm's *Theory of Knowledge*, pp. 2–4.

The beauty (or terror!) of this line of argument is that it is always available for skeptics to employ after one has constructed a theory of knowledge believed to be immune from skeptical assault. After we have done our work, constructing a defense of knowledge, they can do their work, tearing it down. For this reason, many philosophers have concluded that skepticism cannot be refuted.

Some philosophers have argued that although skepticism may be logically faultless, it is from a practical standpoint virtually useless. These philosophers point out that even skeptics must live ordinary lives, in which they sit in chairs (even though they cannot *know* that the chair will support their weight) and open doors (even though they cannot *know* that the opening of the door will trigger a high explosive device). Even the Scottish philosopher David Hume (1711–1776), one of the most famous skeptics of the modern era, wrote that his skeptical worries seemed to disappear as soon as he left his study to play a game of backgammon. Doesn't this refute skepticism?

In a word, no. The problem with this view is that it assumes that skepticism ceases to be compelling when it is focused on affairs of everyday life. In fact, just the opposite is true: Nowhere is skepticism more compelling than when it causes us to doubt ordinary sense perceptions and everyday beliefs, which is what happens when we consider Putnam's evil scientist argument. The fact that skeptics, like the rest of us, do not go around in a perpetual state of questioning every single belief or event is not sufficient to refute skepticism. It merely heightens the realization that things we take for granted as certain and beyond doubt in ordinary experience may not be the case at all. As soon as we accuse the skeptics of violating their skeptical principles by sitting in a chair, we invite back the evil scientist argument with a vengeance, and wind up losing the chair, the world, and ourselves, with our dogmatism adrift in a sea of skeptical doubt.

RELIGIOUS ALTERNATIVES

Recognizing the severe challenge that skepticism presents to religious belief, some thinkers have chosen to emphasize the need for extra-philosophical aid. Believing that human reason is insufficient to overcome its own limitations, some have suggested that God's revelation is our only source of certainty. This view is called **fideism**—the view that truth is founded on faith, not on reason, since faith is superior to reason as a source of knowledge.

The sixteenth century philosopher Michel de Montaigne (c. 1550–1623) argued that all criteria used to support judgments are themselves open to questions and doubt, unless God gives us some indubitable first principles and makes our intellectual faculties reliable.[4] Apart from divine grace, Montaigne taught, even

[4]See Richard H. Popkin's helpful article "Scepticism," which includes a detailed history of the subject, in *The Encyclopedia of Philosophy*, vol. 7, ed. Paul Edwards, (New York: Macmillan, 1967), 449–61.

the most remarkable human achievements sink into the abyss of doubt. The best we can hope for is to follow the principle of Pyrrho's suspension of judgment, and accept whatever God chooses to reveal to us.

The French mathematician and philosopher Blaise Pascal (1623–1662), in a selection included in this chapter, stated the case for skepticism as eloquently as it has ever been stated, but he concluded that since man is "a sink of uncertainty and error," the solution lies in turning to God and divine revelation, not to any philosophy.

As attractive as fideism has been to its followers, it has been severely criticized, even by religious thinkers, who are not so willing to separate faith and reason. Even if it is not possible finally to refute skepticism, is it not possible to present an argument showing the reasonableness of justified belief, and to do so without resorting to fideistic strategies? Current efforts in philosophy are being made to do just that, emphasizing the *rationality* rather than the *certainty* of belief, and stressing the necessary linkage of doubt and belief.

DOUBT

The history of skepticism is a long one. As we have seen, it can be traced back to Pyrrho and his followers in the third century B.C., yet its roots go back as far as Gorgias and the Sophists of the fifth century B.C. (The Sophists were itinerant teachers who denied knowledge of any ultimate reality beyond our sensations.) It is interesting to note that epistemology began in the context of a general skepticism on the part of the Sophists about knowledge, a skepticism that the early Greek philosophers (including Socrates and Plato) felt compelled to answer. It is both ironic and instructive that this should be the case: ironic that skepticism and doubt should have led to such epistemological activity, and instructive, because the enduring questions of skepticism continue to have the same effect today.

The irony was heightened when Descartes came on the scene in the early seventeenth century, another period of intense skeptical doubt, featuring such skeptical philosophers as Montaigue and Pierre Gassendi. The genius of Descartes is that he realized that only doubt can save knowledge from doubt. Descartes proposed to beat the skeptics at their own game by taking doubt seriously—so seriously, in fact, that he proposed it as his method. Descartes was firmly convinced that indubitable truth and a secure foundation for all knowledge and science could be achieved only if we apply the skeptical method more thoroughly than the skeptics. In his pioneering philosophy, Descartes launched what historians have come to call the "modern era" of philosophy. This modern era saw epistemology become central to the philosophical task, as philosophy turned away from the **scholastism** of the Middle Ages.

Descartes began a revolution in philosophy by discovering what we might call "the therapeutic value of doubt." Rather than thinking of doubt as a negative, troubling, or debilitating characteristic of human life, Descartes thought of it as a positive and healthy characteristic. He realized that we must make our peace with doubt, embracing it as a friend rather than treating it as an enemy. The irony is that when we view doubt in this way, skepticism's power is weakened. Of course, the notion that skepticism can be weakened by doubt sounds strange. Let's explore this idea a bit further by returning to our example of "Fred."

Think back to the experience of waking up, hearing a commotion, getting up to investigate, and opening the door to the room. In each step of this example, what was it that caused you to try to obtain better evidence that Fred was home? In a word, it was doubt—doubt that your belief was true, as well as doubt that you had enough evidence to justify your belief. Doubt in this case functioned as an irritant, prodding you to investigate your belief, to scrutinize each piece of evidence, spurring you on to acquire more. It was doubt that led you to get out of bed; doubt that led you to look for the car in the driveway; doubt that led you to knock on the door; doubt that led you to open the door, and doubt that required you to get a good look at the person in the room.

Your doubt was quite useful in leading you to form a justified belief. Another way to think about the relationship between belief and doubt is to say that doubt is the engine that drives our belief-forming mechanism. Doubtful uncertainty is a powerful tool to promote investigation, a fact that is well known in the sciences. Ask yourself this question: What sense could we make of a scientist who refused to doubt? Such a person would be so convinced of the certainty of a hypothesis that the door to testing for confirmation or disconfirmation would be closed. Would such an individual still be practicing science? Or, imagine a situation where your chemistry professor walks into your chemistry lab and announces: "Chemistry, as of this moment, is officially over. The scientific community of chemists has met this morning and determined that there is no longer any reason to continue this science, being convinced that there is nothing further to be learned in this area." You would be quite correct to be skeptical of such a pronouncement. The prospect of a "closed science" is as absurd as a world free from uncertainty. Uncertainty and doubt are useful machines for driving science forward. To cancel doubt is to cancel the prospect for further inquiry leading to knowledge. If we are to believe, we must maintain the ability to doubt. But the converse holds as well: if we are to doubt, we must also believe.

The great American philosopher Charles Sanders Peirce (1839–1914) placed doubt and belief on a continuum, arguing in "The Fixation of Belief" (included in a reading in this part) that every genuine doubt is targeted on belief. This being the case, one cannot have a case of doubt apart from a case of belief. The psychology of belief is such that doubt, which is an uncomfortable, irritating state of mind, is always looking to resolve itself in belief. When doubt comes to understand itself authentically, it acts to rid itself of the irritation it has presented itself with, arriving at the peaceful shore of belief. Doubt needs beliefs in order to perform its "irritant role" as doubt, and beliefs are subject to doubts.

The twentieth century Austrian philosopher Ludwig Wittgenstein (1889–1951) had this thought in mind when he wrote, "A doubt that doubted everything would not be a doubt." In another place Wittgenstein argued that doubt itself can only rest on that which is beyond doubt—in other words, belief.[5]

Skepticism may be thought of as an excess of doubt. Ask yourself, is it ever possible to doubt too much? In other words, are there occasions when doubt functions as an impediment to belief rather than as a prod to belief? There is reason to believe that this is the case with skepticism. What is noteworthy in Descartes, Peirce, and Wittgenstein is the refusal to engage in "doubt for the sake of doubt." Doubt must always be kept in the larger context of belief. We doubt in order that we may believe.

"BEING SKEPTICAL" AND "SKEPTICISM"

The trouble with skepticism as a philosophical position is that it winds up killing doubt, not nurturing it. Philosophical positions may be thought of as fluid expressions of ideas, poured into a mold. Often the best way to ruin an otherwise acceptable philosophical position is to allow it to set and harden in the mold. When philosophical positions lose their flexibility and fluidity, they begin to harden and congeal, like bacon grease in a refrigerator. Being skeptical of beliefs is a healthy condition, creating in us a fluid and flexible response to beliefs and the world. In its broadest sense, skepticism implies being skeptical—that is, rigorously questioning any belief, conclusion, or assumption in good Socratic fashion. Being skeptical involves admitting that our senses and our reason are frequently unreliable and that even "experts" studying the same issue can come to different conclusions. Being skeptical is, therefore, a natural philosophical attitude, a constant reminder to avoid hasty judgment and to be aware of the ever present danger of uncritical dogmatism. Such an attitude is our only defense against error, prejudice, and superstition; setting itself in opposition to the know-it-all, it clears the way for scientific progress.

We have good reason, then, to be skeptical of skepticism. An extreme, thoroughgoing skepticism (adopted as a philosophical position) would have to be skeptical of itself, but can it be? In denying that knowledge is possible, do we not make a claim to knowledge? If nothing can be known, how can the skeptic know that this is a valid position? In affirming their own position, skeptics are forced into

5See Ludwig Wittgenstein, *On Certainty* (New York: Harper & Row, 1972).

distinguishing between the false (the view that there is knowledge) and the true (the view that there can be no knowledge), a logical contradition that admits of no easy answers. The only way for skeptics to avoid this contradiction would be to deny that they were affirming a position, relinquishing any claim to validity. But in employing arguments (such as the evil scientist argument and others), we must adhere to a certain model of intelligibility that presupposes a world of knowledge, complete with distinctions between valid and invalid forms of argument. The very attempt to present skeptical arguments involves the nonskeptical appeal to principles of reasoning, and we do not escape this **performative contradiction** by denying the principles if we must invoke them in order to deny them.

In the end, extreme skepticism refuses to allow doubt to remain genuine, putting in its place "doubt for the sake of doubt," which is no doubt at all. And for what? Rejecting knowledge for fear of error, skepticism is a room without a view, looking out over nothing. If true, it would mean the death of philosophy.

SKEPTICISM AND DIALECTIC

Although we have offered reasons for rejecting skepticism, we have not claimed to refute it. This does not mean that skepticism is a correct philosophical position, merely that it is impossible to demonstrate conclusively that it is incorrect. Contemporary philosophers still argue its viability today, thousands of years after it was initially formulated. What can this mean?

1.   One of the things it means is that the labor of reason in history is often labor against itself, as reason tries to set the limits of its own capacity. Thinking about skepticism throws us up against the boundaries of human thought, causing us to wonder whether our model of rationality is itself acceptable, or whether it can be modified in ways that challenge traditional thought. Must skeptics be considered "irrational" in challenging the prevailing model of rationality, or is their challenge itself evidence that alternative rational paradigms exist? Many contemporary philosophers have tried to "push out the envelope" on just this question, including the German thinker of the last century, Friedrich Nietzsche (1844–1900), and the contemporary postmodern French thinkers Jacques Derrida, Jean-François Lyotard, and Michel Foucault. We will explore this question more fully in Part 4, as we consider "The Question of Truth."

2.   The stubbornness of skepticism means that the philosophical conversation, begun so long ago, continues on to this day. When the skeptic relentlessly asks for more evidence, resisting the justification of belief, the only way that we can respond is Socratically, establishing again the dialectical nature of philosophy. W.K. Clifford and William James, arguing about the role of skepticism with respect to religious belief, demonstrate one important way this discussion might

take shape; Peter Unger and John Hospers, in the Contemporary Perspectives selections, demonstrate another. As your own conversation about epistemology and skepticism continues beyond the classroom, you will be demonstrating still another.

THE VALUE OF SKEPTICISM

Skepticism is valuable because it keeps philosophy honest. As Richard Popkin put it:

> From Greek times onward, skepticism has functioned as a gadfly to dogmatic philosophy and as a challenge to keep it honest. The skeptical critique has thrived on the desire to find a coherent and consistent account of our knowledge and beliefs about the world. Had there never been disillusionment about what was accepted as true, skepticism would probably not have arisen. Nevertheless, skepticism has led to continual re-examination of philosophical claims and to new dogmatic systems trying to avoid difficulties in others. This in turn has led to new skeptical attacks and ingenious new criticisms or new versions of criticism. Thus skepticism has been a major dynamic force in intellectual history.[6]

What is remarkable about skepticism is the way it has thrived right alongside philosophy for all these years, suggesting that it is parasitical upon our desire for complete and total understanding. You may think of it as a guard against the possibility of the total—total insight, total understanding, total vision of ourselves and the way our world should be ordered. Thinking of it in this way will help you to understand why totalitarian political regimes or authoritarian religious establishments cannot tolerate the skeptical impulse to question or doubt, for fear that their pronouncements will not withstand the light that reason shines on all our folly.

Finally, going a round or two with skepticism will make you appreciate whatever beliefs survive its fire. As Lord Shaftesbury put it, (after living with the ferocious skeptic Pierre Bayle for a while), any view that could survive the continuous skeptical assault should be valued as highly as the purest gold.[7] The same can be said of our beliefs: They have value only to the extent that they have endured the skeptical challenge.

[6]Richard H. Popkin, "Scepticism," in *The Encyclopedia of Philosophy*, vol. 7, ed. Paul Edwards (New York: Macmillan and Free Press, 1967), 449–61.
[7]Quoted in Popkin, 460.

CHAPTER 8

PLATO

SOCRATES' DEFENSE (APOLOGY)

The title of our selection comes from one of Plato's early dialogues, the *Apology*. (see Chapter 1 for a biography of Plato)[1] The Greek word *apologia* does not mean "excuse," as the word is commonly used today but rather "defense." Socrates had been accused of "corrupting the minds of the young, and of believing in deities of his own invention instead of the gods recognized by the state." The *Apology* thus contains Socrates' detailed defense of the way he lived and the convictions he held. It is clear that he is prepared to die for these convictions, and in fact he is convicted by the jury and sentenced to death. Weeks later, he is finally executed, having willingly accepted the fatal poison from the prison guard. The story of his last days is told in the *Crito* and the *Phaedo*.

The *Apology* consists of three separate speeches: Socrates' defense, his counterproposal for the penalty, and a final address to the court. The selection below is taken from his opening speech, where he tells his audience of his friend Chaerephon's visit to the oracle at Delphi. The oracle disclosed that there was no man wiser than Socrates. But what can this mean? Socrates' response to the oracle, packed with irony, is one of the most eloquent passages in all of Western literature, beautifully illustrating "the philosophical uses of uncertainty."

[1]This selection is taken from Plato, "The Apology," in *The Dialogues of Plato*, translated by Benjamin Jowett (Oxford: Oxford University Press, 1920).

SOCRATES' DEFENSE (APOLOGY)

I am sure someone will ask the question, "Why is this, Socrates, and what is the origin of these accusations of you: for there must have been something strange which you have been doing? All this great fame and talk about you would never have come up if you had been like other men. Tell us then, why this is, as we should be sorry to judge you too quickly."

I regard this as a fair challenge, and I will try to explain to you the origin of this name of "wise," and of this evil fame. Please attend then and although some of you may think I am joking, I declare I will tell you the entire truth. Men of Athens, this reputation of mine has come from a certain kind of wisdom which I possess. If you ask me what kind of wisdom, I reply, such wisdom as is attainable by man, for to that extent I am inclined to believe I am wise. Whereas, the persons of whom I was speaking have a superhuman wisdom which I may fail to describe, because I do not have it. He who says I have, speaks false, and slanders me.

O men of Athens, I must beg you not to interrupt me, even if I seem to say something extravagant. For the word which I will speak is not mine. I will refer you to a wisdom which is worthy of credit, and will tell you about my wisdom—whether I have any, and of what sort—and that witness shall be the god of Delphi. You must have known Chaerephon. He was a friend of mine and also a friend of yours, for he shared in the exile of the people and returned with you. Well, Chaerephon, as you know, was very impetuous in all his doings, and he went to Delphi and boldly asked the oracle to tell him whether—as I said, I must beg you not to interrupt—he asked the oracle to tell him whether there was anyone wiser than I was. The Pythian prophetess answered, there was no man wiser. Chaerephon is

dead himself but his brother, who is in court, will confirm the truth of this story.

Why do I mention this? Because I am going to explain to you why I have such an evil name. When I heard the answer, I said to myself, "What can the god mean and what is the interpretation of this riddle? I know I have no wisdom, great or small. What can he mean when he says I am the wisest of men? And yet he is a god, and cannot lie; that would be against his nature." After long consideration, I at last thought of a method of answering the question.

I reflected if I could only find a man wiser than myself then I might go to the god with a refutation in my hand. I would say to him, "Here is a man who is wiser than I am, but you said I was the wisest." Accordingly I went to one who had the reputation of wisdom, and observed him—his name I need not mention; he was a politician whom I selected for examination. When I began to talk with him I could not help thinking he was not really wise, although he was thought wise by many, and wiser still by himself. I tried to explain to him that he thought himself wise, but was not really wise. The result was he hated me and his hatred was shared by several who were present who heard me. So I left him, saying to myself, as I went away: "Well, although I do not suppose either of us knows anything really beautiful and good, I am better off than he is,—for he knows nothing and thinks that he knows. I neither know nor think that I know. In this latter, then, I seem to have an advantage over him." Then I went to another who had still higher philosophical pretensions and my conclusion was exactly the same. I made another enemy of him and of many others besides him.

After this I went to one man after another, being aware of the anger which I provoked and I lamented and feared this, but necessity was laid upon me. The word of the god, I thought, ought to be considered first. And I said to myself, "I must go to all who appear to know, and find out the meaning of the oracle." And I swear to you Athenians, by the dog, I swear!, the result of my mission was this: I found the men with the highest reputations were all nearly the most foolish and some inferior men were really wiser and better.

I will tell you the tale of my wanderings and of the Herculean labors, as I may call them, which I endured only to find at last the oracle was right. When I left the politicians, I went to the poets: tragic, dithyrambic, and all sorts. There, I said to myself, you will be detected. Now you will find out you are more ignorant than they are. Accordingly, I took them some of the most elaborate passages in their own writings, and asked what was the meaning of them— thinking the poets would teach me something. Will you believe me? I am almost ashamed to say this, but I must say there is hardly a person present who would not have talked better about their poetry than the poets did themselves. That quickly showed me poets do not write poetry by wisdom, but by a sort of inspiration. They are like soothsayers who also say many fine things, but do not understand the meaning of what they say. The poets appeared to me to be much the same and I further observed that upon the strength of their poetry they believed themselves to be the wisest of men in other things in which they were not wise. So I departed, conceiving myself to be superior to them for the same reason I was superior to the politicians.

At last I went to the artisans, because I was conscious I knew nothing at all and I was sure they knew many fine things. In this I was not mistaken, for they did know many things of which I was ignorant, and in this they certainly were wiser than I was. But I observed even the good artisans fell into the same error as the poets. Because they were good workmen, they thought they also knew all sorts of high matters and this defect in them overshadowed their wisdom. Therefore, I asked myself on behalf of the oracle whether I would like to be as I was, having neither their knowledge nor their ignorance, or like them in both. I answered myself and the oracle that I was better off as I was.

This investigation led to my having many enemies of the worst and most dangerous kind and has given rise also to many falsehoods. I am called wise because my listeners always imagine I possess the wisdom which I do not find in others. The truth is, O men of Athens, the gods only are wise and in this oracle they mean to say wisdom of men is little or nothing. They are not speaking of Socrates, only using my name as an illustration, as if they said, "He, O men, is the wisest who, like Socrates, knows his wisdom is in truth worth nothing." And so I go my way, obedient to the gods, and seek wisdom of anyone, whether citizen or stranger, who appears to be wise. If he is not wise, then in support of the oracle I show him he is not wise. This occupation quite absorbs me, and I have no time to give either to any public matter of interest or to any concern of my own, but I am in utter poverty by reason of my devotion to the gods.

CHAPTER 9

RENÉ DESCARTES

MEDITATIONS ON FIRST PHILOSOPHY

René Descartes (1596–1650), French philosopher, mathematician, and scientist, was educated by the Jesuits, a religious order founded in opposition to the Protestant Reformation. A rationalist, he emphasized human reason as the primary source of knowledge. Descartes is customarily known as the "father of modern philosophy" and is the single most important philosophical figure in the transition from the Middle Ages to the Renaissance. The founder of analytic geometry and a pioneer of the seventeenth century revolution in science, Descartes' philosophical beliefs were patterned on the methods of geometry.

After having a series of lucid dreams in 1619, alerting him to the necessity of unifying science through a new method, Descartes set out to provide all of the sciences with a secure metaphysical foundation. In 1628 Descartes left Paris for the quiet of Holland, where he remained for twenty years. It was here that he wrote his famous *Meditations on First Philosophy*, using doubt in methodical fashion to overcome the skepticism that threatened the foundations of knowledge. In 1634, frightened by the Church's censure of his friend Galileo and recognizing the threat that the Copernican revolution represented to outmoded scientific views (which the Church, unfortunately, embraced) Descartes withdrew the publication of *Le Monde*, his treatise on astronomy. After this, he allowed his writings to be circulated privately and was cautious and diplomatic, working to gain acceptance of his work by the religious authorities. He wrote the *Discourse of Method* (1637) in French rather than the scholarly Latin, in order to appeal to persons of "good sense," sharing his method with those outside of academic life. This was typical of Descartes, who never lost sight of his vision that science should lead to the widest possible benefits for all people.

In 1649 Descartes reluctantly went to Sweden at the request of Queen Christina, who was developing a great center of learning at her court in Stockholm. He died the following year of pneumonia, his health broken by the harsh climate and the rigorous academic schedule of the Queen.

Descartes wrote the *Meditations on First Philosophy* in Latin during the period from 1638 to 1640, when he was living in North Holland.[1] This work, his philosophical masterpiece, is a vivid and dramatic attempt to "raze the foundations" of human knowledge, eliminating preconceived opinions and prejudice in an attempt to establish a secure foundation for knowledge. From geometry Descartes had gained a very definite idea of what the structure of human knowledge must resemble; it was his intent to apply the method of geometry to the task of constructing a system of absolutely certain truths. Descartes makes it clear in the preface that the book is intended to be read as a set of mental exercises that each reader must enact personally, not as a static set of philosophical doctrines. As he puts it, "I would not urge anyone to read this book except those who are able and willing to meditate seriously along with me." This accounts for the use of the "artful I" in the *Meditations*, as we are encouraged to become co-inquirers along with Descartes.

Descartes' tool for razing the foundations of knowledge in the search for new foundational truth is doubt. The only way to discover metaphysically certain truths is to subject every candidate for belief to the full range of radical doubt, retaining only those beliefs that survive the process. We can illustrate this process with an example. A man has a bushel of apples. How can he be sure that each of the apples in the basket is a sound one, free from worms and rottenness? He could establish a procedure whereby each apple is taken from the basket, examined, and replaced only if it is sound. The problem with this procedure is that he might miss an apple lying near the bottom, which could endanger otherwise sound apples. A better procedure would be to completely empty the basket of *all* apples at once, returning to the basket only those apples that were demonstrably sound. The latter is Descartes' procedure. He proposes "once in the course of his life" to empty all the apples; that is, to divest himself of all beliefs that he may have held.

In the first meditation Descartes searches for reasons to doubt his beliefs. Rather than requiring a reason for doubting each individual belief, he looks for reasons to doubt large classes of beliefs. This strategy enables him to invalidate everything believed through sense perception, since sense experience has been shown to be deceptive. Other skeptical counterpossibilities, which we discussed

[1]From René Descartes, *Meditations on First Philosophy*, translated by Donald A. Cress (Indianapolis: Hackett Publishing, 1979). Reprinted with permission.

earlier in the Orientation, are put into play, including dreamers, madmen, and demons. The Meditation concludes with Descartes stubbornly insisting on his method even with the prospect of his entire system of belief suspended, or "put out of play." This is his only defense against the cunning of the "malicious demon."

Having dismissed as doubtful virtually everything we would have previously believed, Descartes searches in the second meditation for something that can be known with absolute certainty—something so certain it could withstand even the evil devices of a powerful demonic deceiver. By the third paragraph of this extraordinary meditation, he claims to have found it. Having reached bedrock he proceeds to attempt to recover all his other beliefs by attempting to prove the existence of God in the third Meditation, believing that the existence of an all powerful nondeceiver gives us immunity from the skeptical doubts of the first meditation. Although we still make mistakes, he argues, God has not constructed us such that error is the best we can do. Consequently, we recover much of the knowledge that was lost in the first mediation, having been chastened by our encounter with skepticism.

MEDITATIONS ON FIRST PHILOSOPHY

Meditation One: Concerning Those Things That Can Be Called into Doubt

Several years have now passed since I first realized how many were the false opinions that in my youth I took to be true, and thus how doubtful were all the things that I subsequently built upon these opinions. From the time I became aware of this, I realized that for once I had to raze everything in my life, down to the very bottom, so as to begin again from the first foundations, if I wanted to establish anything firm and lasting in the sciences. But the task seemed so enormous that I waited for a point in my life that was so ripe that no more suitable a time for laying hold of these disciplines would come to pass. For this reason, I have delayed so long that I would be at fault were I to waste on deliberation the time that is left for action.

Therefore, now that I have freed my mind from all cares, and I have secured for myself some leisurely and carefree time, I withdraw in solitude. I will, in short, apply myself earnestly and openly to the general destruction of my former opinions.

Yet to this end it will not be necessary that I show that all my opinions are false, which perhaps I could never accomplish anyway. But because reason now persuades me that I should withhold my assent no less carefully from things which are not plainly certain and indubitable than I would to what is patently false, it will be sufficient justification for rejecting them all, if I find a reason for doubting even the least of them. Nor therefore need one survey each opinion one after the other, a task of endless proportion. Rather—because undermining the foundations will cause whatever has been built upon them to

94

fall down of its own accord—I will at once attack those principles which supported everything that I once believed.

Whatever I had admitted until now as most true I took in either from the senses or through the senses; however, I noticed that they sometimes deceived me. And it is a mark of prudence never to trust wholly in those things which have once deceived us.

But perhaps, although the senses sometimes deceive us when it is a question of very small and distant things, still there are many other matters which one certainly cannot doubt, although they are derived from the very same senses: that I am sitting here before the fireplace wearing my dressing gown, that I feel this sheet of paper in my hands, and so on. But how could one deny that these hands and that my whole body exist? Unless perhaps I should compare myself to insane people whose brains are so impaired by a stubborn vapor from a black bile that they continually insist that they are kings when they are in utter poverty, or that they are wearing purple robes when they are naked, or that they have a head made of clay, or that they are gourds, or that they are made of glass. But they are all demented, and I would appear no less demented if I were to take their conduct as a model for myself.

All of this would be well and good, were I not a man who is accustomed to sleeping at night, and to undergoing in my sleep the very same things—or now and then even less likely ones—as do these insane people when they are awake. How often has my evening slumber persuaded me of such customary things as these: that I am here, clothed in my dressing gown, seated at the fireplace, when in fact I am lying undressed between the blankets! But right now I certainly am gazing upon this piece of paper with eyes wide awake. This head which I am moving is not heavy with sleep. I extend this hand consciously and deliberately and I feel it. These things would not be so distinct for one who is asleep. But this all seems as if I do not recall having been deceived by similar thoughts on other occasions in my dreams. As I consider these cases more intently, I see so plainly that there are no definite signs to distinguish being awake from being asleep that I am quite astonished, and this astonishment almost convinces me that I am sleeping.

Let us say, then, for the sake of argument, that we are sleeping and that such particulars as these are not true: that we open our eyes, move our heads, extend our hands. Perhaps we do not even have these hands, or any such body at all. Nevertheless, it really must be admitted that things seen in sleep are, as it were, like painted images, which could have been produced only in the likeness of true things. Therefore at least these general things (eyes, head, hands, the whole body) are not imaginary things, but are true and exist. For indeed when painters wish to represent sirens and satyrs by means of bizarre and unusual forms, they surely cannot ascribe utterly new natures to these creatures. Rather, they simply intermingle the members of various animals. And even if they concoct something so utterly novel that its likes have never been seen before (being utterly fictitious and false), certainly at the very minimum the colors from which the painters compose the thing ought to be true. And for the same reason, although even these general things (eyes, head, hands, and the like) can be imaginary, still one must necessarily admit that at least other things that are even more simple and universal are true, from which, as from true colors, all these things—be they true or false—which in our thought are images of things, are constructed.

To this class seems to belong corporeal nature in general, together with its extension; likewise the shape of extended things, their quantity or size, their number; as well as the place where they exist, the time of their duration, and other such things.

Hence perhaps we do not conclude improperly that physics, astronomy, medicine, and all the other disciplines that are dependent upon the consideration of composite things are all doubtful. But arithmetic, geometry, and other such disciplines—which treat of nothing but the simplest and most general things and which are indifferent as to whether these composite things do or do not exist—contain something certain and indubitable. For whether I be awake or asleep, two plus three makes five, and a square does not have more than four sides; nor does it seem possible that such obvious truths can fall under the suspicion of falsity.

All the same, a certain opinion of long standing has been fixed in my mind, namely that there exists a God who is able to do anything and by whom I, such as I am, have been created. How do I know that he did not bring it about that there be no earth at all, no heavens, no extended thing, no figure, no size, no place, and yet all these things should seem to me to exist precisely as they appear to do now? Moreover—as I judge that others sometimes make mistakes in matters that they believe they know most perfectly— how do I know that I am not deceived every time I add two and three or count the sides of a square or perform an even simpler operation, if such can be imagined? But perhaps God has not willed that I be thus deceived, for it is said that he is supremely good. Nonetheless, if it were repugnant to his goodness that he should have created me such that I be deceived all the time, it would seem, form this same consideration, to be foreign to him to permit me to be deceived occasionally. But we cannot make this last assertion.

Perhaps there are some who would rather deny such a powerful God, than believe that all other matters are uncertain. Let us not put these people off just yet; rather, let us grant that everything said here about God is fictitious. Now they suppose that I came to be what I am either by fate or by chance or by a continuous series of events or by some other way. But because being deceived and being mistaken seem to be imperfections, the less powerful they take the author of my being to be, the more probable it will be that I would be so imperfect as to be deceived perpetually. I have nothing to say in response to these arguments. At length I am forced to admit that there is nothing, among the things I once believed to be true, which it is not permissible to doubt—not for reasons of frivolity or a lack of forethought, but because of valid and considered arguments. Thus I must carefully withhold assent no less from these things than from the patently false, if I wish to find anything certain.

But it is not enough simply to have made a note of this; I must take care to keep it before my mind. For long-standing opinions keep coming back again and again, almost against my will; they seize upon my credulity, as if it were bound over to them by long use and the claims of intimacy. Nor will I get out of the habit of assenting to them and believing in them, so long as I take them to be exactly what they are, namely, in some respects doubtful as by now is obvious, but nevertheless highly probable, so that it is much more consonant with reason to believe them than to deny them. Hence, it seems to me, I would do well to turn my will in the opposite direction, to deceive myself and pretend for a considerable period that they are wholly false and imaginary, until finally, as if with equal weight of prejudice[1] on both sides, no bad habit should turn my judgment from the correct perception of things. For indeed I know that no dan-

---

[1] A "prejudice" is a prejudgment, that is, an adjudication of an issue without having first reviewed the appropriate evidence.

ger or error will follow and that it is impossible for me to indulge in too much distrust, since I now am concentrating only on knowledge, not on action.

Thus I will suppose not a supremely good God, the source of truth, but rather an evil genius, as clever and deceitful as he is powerful, who has directed his entire effort to misleading me. I will regard the heavens, the air, the earth, colors, shapes, sounds, and all external things as nothing but the deceptive games of my dreams, with which he lays snares for my credulity. I will regard myself as having no hands, no eyes, no flesh, no blood, no senses, but as nevertheless falsely believing that I possess all these things. I will remain resolutely fixed in this meditation, and, even if it be out of my power to know anything true, certainly it is within my power to take care resolutely to withhold my assent to what is false, lest this deceiver, powerful and clever as he is, have an effect on me. But this undertaking is arduous, and laziness brings me back to my customary way of living. I am not unlike a prisoner who might enjoy an imaginary freedom in his sleep. When he later begins to suspect that he is sleeping, he fears being awakened and conspires slowly with these pleasant illusions. In just this way, I spontaneously fall back into my old beliefs, and dread being awakened, lest the toilsome wakefulness which follows upon a peaceful rest, have to be spent thenceforward not in the light but among the inextricable shadows of the difficulties now brought forward.

Meditation Two: Concerning the Nature of the Human Mind: That the Mind is More Known Than the Body

Yesterday's meditation filled my mind with so many doubts that I can no longer forget about them—nor yet do I see how they are to be resolved. But, as if I had suddenly fallen into a deep whirlpool, I am so disturbed that I can neither touch my foot to the bottom, nor swim up to the top. Nevertheless I will work my way up, and I will follow the same path I took yesterday, putting aside everything which admits of the least doubt, as if I had discovered it to be absolutely false. I will go forward until I know something certain—or, if nothing else, until I at least know for certain that nothing is certain. Archimedes sought only a firm and immovable point in order to move the entire earth from one place to another. Surely great things are to be hoped for if I am lucky enough to find at least one thing that is certain and indubitable.

Therefore I will suppose that all I see is false. I will believe that none of those things that my deceitful memory brings before my eyes ever existed. I thus have no senses: body, shape, extension, movement, and place are all figments of my imagination. What then will count as true? Perhaps only this one thing: that nothing is certain.

But on what grounds do I know that there is nothing over and above all those which I have just reviewed, concerning which there is not even the least cause for doubt? Is there not a God (or whatever name I might call him) who instills these thoughts in me? But why should I think that, since perhaps I myself could be the author of these things? Therefore am I not at least something? But I have already denied that I have any senses and any body. Still, I hesitate; for what follows from that? Am I so tied to the body and to the senses that I cannot exist without them? But I have persuaded myself that there is nothing at all in the world: no heaven, no earth, no minds, no bodies. Is it not then true that I do not exist? But certainly I should exist, if I were to persuade myself of something. But there is a deceiver (I know not who he is) powerful and sly in the highest degree, who is always purposely deceiving me. Then there is no doubt that I exist, if he deceives me. And deceive me as he will, he can never bring it about that I am nothing so long as I shall think that I am something. Thus it must be granted that, after weighing everything carefully and sufficiently, one must come to the considered judgement that the statement "I am, I exist" is necessarily true every time it is uttered by me or conceived in my mind.

But I do not yet understand well enough who I am—I, who now necessarily exist. And from this point on, I must take care lest I imprudently substitute something else in place of myself; and thus be mistaken even in that knowledge which I claim to be the most certain and evident of all. To this end, I shall meditate once more on what I once believed myself to be before having embarked upon these deliberations. For this reason, then, I will set aside whatever can be refuted even to a slight degree by the arguments brought forward, so that at length there shall remain precisely nothing but what is certain and unshaken.

What therefore did I formerly think I was? A man, of course. But what is a man? Might I not say a rational animal? No, because then one would have to inquire what an "animal" is and what "rational" means. And then from only one question we slide into many more difficult ones. Nor do I now have enough free time that I want to waste it on subtleties of this sort. But rather here I pay attention to what spontaneously and at nature's lead came into my thought beforehand whenever I pondered what I was. Namely, it occurred to me first that I have a face, hands, arms, and this entire mechanism of bodily members, the very same as are discerned in a corpse—which I referred to by the name "body." It also occurred to me that I eat, walk, feel and think; these actions I used to assign to the soul as their cause. But what this soul was I either did not think about or I imagined it was something terribly insubstantial—after the fashion of a wind,

fire, or ether—which has been poured into my coarser parts. I truly was not in doubt regarding the body; rather I believed that I distinctly knew its nature, which, were I perhaps tempted to describe it such as I mentally conceived it, I would explain it thus: by "body," I understand all that is suitable for being bounded by some shape, for being enclosed in some place, and thus for filling up space, so that it excludes every other body from that space; for being perceived by touch, sight, hearing, taste, or smell; for being moved in several ways, not surely by itself, but by whatever else that touches it. For I judged that the power of self-motion, and likewise of sensing or of thinking, in no way pertains to the nature of the body. Nonetheless, I used to marvel especially that such faculties were found in certain bodies.

But now what am I, when I suppose that some deceiver—omnipotent and, if I may be allowed to say it, malicious—takes all the pains he can in order to deceive me? Can I not affirm that I possess at least a small measure of all those traits which I already have said pertain to the nature of the body? I pay attention, I think, I deliberate—but nothing happens. I am wearied of repeating this in vain. But which of these am I to ascribe to the soul? How about eating or walking? These are surely nothing but illusions, because I do not have a body. How about sensing? Again, this also does not happen without a body, and I judge that I really did not sense those many things I seemed to have sensed in my dreams. How about thinking? Here I discover that thought is an attribute that really does belong to me. This alone cannot be detached from me. I am; I exist; this is certain. But for how long? For as long as I think. Because perhaps it could also come to pass that if I should cease from all thinking I would then utterly cease to exist. I now admit nothing that is not necessarily true. I am therefore precisely only a thing that thinks; that is, a mind, or soul, or intellect, or reason—words the meaning of which I was ignorant before. Now, I am a true thing, and truly existing; but what kind of thing? I have said it already: a thing that thinks.

What then? I will set my imagination going to see if I am not something more. I am not that connection of members which is called the human body. Neither am I some subtle air infused into these members, not a wind, not a fire, not a vapor, not a breath—nothing that I imagine to myself, for I have supposed all these to be nothing. The assertion stands: the fact still remains that I am something. But perhaps it is the case that nevertheless, these very things which I take to be nothing (because I am ignorant of them) in reality do not differ from that self which I know. This I do not know. I shall not quarrel about it right now; I can make a judgement only regarding things which are known to me. I know that I exist; I ask now who is this "I" whom I know. Most certainly the knowledge of this matter, thus precisely understood, does not depend upon things that I do not yet know to exist. Therefore, it is not dependent upon any of those things that I feign in my imagination. But this word "feign" warns me of my error. For I would be feigning if I should "imagine" that I am something, because imagining is merely the contemplation of the shape or image of a corporeal thing. But I know now with certainty that I am, and at the same time it could happen that all these images—and, generally, everything that pertains to the nature of the body—are nothing but dreams. When these things are taken into account, I would speak no less foolishly were I to say: "I will imagine so that I might recognize more distinctly who I am," than were I to say: "Now I surely am awake, and I see something true, but because I do not yet see it with sufficient evidence, I will take the trouble of going to sleep so that my dreams might show this to me more truly and more evi-

dently." Thus I know that none of what I can comprehend by means of the imagination pertains to this understanding that I have of myself. Moreover, I know that I must be most diligent about withdrawing my mind from these things so that it can perceive its nature as distinctly as possible.

But what then am I? A thing that thinks. What is that? A thing that doubts, understands, affirms, denies, wills, refuses, and which also imagines and senses.

It is truly no small matter if all of these things pertain to me. But why should they not pertain to me? Is it not I who now doubt almost everything, I who nevertheless understand something, I who affirm that this one thing is true, I who deny other things, I who desire to know more things, I who wish not to be deceived, I who imagine many things against my will, I who take note of many things as if coming from the senses? Is there anything in all of this which is not just as true as it is that I am, even if I am always dreaming or even if the one who created me tries as hard as possible to delude me? Are any of these attributes distinct from my thought? What can be said to be separate from myself? For it is so obvious that it is I who doubt, I who understand, I who will, that there is nothing through which it could be more evidently explicated. But indeed I am also the same one who imagines; for, although perhaps as I supposed before, no imagined thing would be wholly true, the very power of imagining does really exist, and constitutes a part of my thought. Finally, I am the same one who senses or who takes note of bodily things as if through the senses. For example, I now see a light, I hear a noise, I feel heat. These are false, since I am asleep. But I certainly seem to see, hear, and feel. This cannot be false: properly speaking, this is what is called "sensing" in me. But this is, to speak precisely, nothing other than thinking.

From these considerations I began to know a little better who I am. But it still seems that I cannot hold back from believing that bodily things—whose images are formed by thought, and which the senses themselves examine—are much more distinctly known than this unknown aspect of myself which does not come under the imagination. And yet it would be quite strange if the very things which I consider to be doubtful, unknown, and foreign to me are comprehended by me more distinctly than what is true, what is known—than, in fine, myself. But I see what is happening: my mind loves to wander and does not allow itself to be restricted to the confines of truth. Let it be that way then: let us allow it the freest rein in every respect, so that, when we pull in the reins at the right time a little later, the mind may suffer itself to be ruled more easily.

Let us consider those things which are commonly believed to be the most distinctly comprehended of all: namely the bodies which we touch and see. But not bodies in general, for these generic perceptions are often somewhat more confused; rather let us consider one body in particular. Let us take, for instance, this piece of wax. It has very recently been taken from the honeycombs; it has not as yet lost all the flavor of its honey. It retains some of the smell of the flowers from which it was collected. Its color, shape, and size are obvious. It is hard and cold. It can easily be touched, and if you rap on it with a knuckle it makes a sound. In short, everything is present in it that appears to be needed in order that a body can be known as distinctly as possible. But notice that while I am speaking, it is brought close to the fire; the remaining traces of the honey flavor are purged; the odor vanishes; the color is changed; the original shape disappears. Its magnitude increases, it becomes liquid and hot, and can hardly be touched; and now, when you knock on it, it does not emit any sound. Up to this point, does the same wax

remain? One must confess that it does: no one denies it; no one thinks otherwise. What was there then in the wax that was so distinctly comprehended? Certainly none of the things that I reached by means of the senses. For whatever cam under taste or smell or sight or touch or hearing by now has changed, yet the wax remains.

Perhaps the wax was what I now think it is: namely that it really never was the sweetness of the honey or the fragrance of the flowers, not this whiteness, not a figure, not a sound, but a body which a little earlier manifested itself to me in these ways, and now does so in other ways. But just what precisely is this thing which I imagine thus? Let us direct our attention to this and see what remains after we have removed everything which does not belong to the wax: only that it is something extended, flexible, and subject to change. What is this flexible and mutable thing? Is it not the fact that I imagine that this wax can change from a round to a square shape, or from the latter to a rectangular shape? Not at all: for I comprehend that the wax is capable of innumerable changes, yet I cannot survey these innumerable changes by imagining them. Therefore this comprehension is not accomplished by the faculty of imagination. What is this extended thing? Is this thing's extension also unknown? For it becomes larger in wax that is beginning to liquify, greater in boiling wax, and greater still as the heat is increased. And I would not judge rightly what the wax is if I did not believe that this wax can take on even more varieties of extension than I could ever have grasped by the imagination. It remains then for me to concede that I in no way imagine what this wax is, but perceive it by the mind only. I am speaking about this piece of wax in particular, for it is clearer in the case of wax in general. But what is this wax which is perceived only by the mind? It is the same that I see, touch, and imagine; in short it is the same as I took it to be from the very beginning. But we must take note of the fact that the perception of the wax is neither by sight, nor touch, not imagination, nor was it ever so (although it seemed so before), but rather an inspection on the part of the mind alone. This inspection can be imperfect and confused, as it was before, or clear and distinct, as it is now, according to whether I pay greater or less attention to those things of which the wax consists.

But meanwhile I marvel at how prone my mind is to errors; for although I am considering these things within myself silently and without words, nevertheless I latch onto words themselves and I am very nearly deceived by the ways in which people speak. For we say that we see the wax itself, if it is present, and not that we judge it to be present from its color or shape. Whence I might conclude at once: the wax is therefore known by eyesight, and not by an inspection on the part of the mind alone, unless I perhaps now might have looked out the window at the men crossing the street whom I say I am no less wont to see than the wax. But what do I see over and above the hats and clothing? Could not robots be concealed under these things? But I judge them to be men; thus what I believed I had seen with my eyes, I actually comprehend with nothing but the faculty of judgment which is in my mind.

But a person who seeks to know more than the common crowd should be ashamed of himself if he has come upon doubts as a result of an encounter with the forms of speech devised by the common crowd. Let us then go forward, paying attention to the following question: did I perceive more perfectly and evidently what the wax was when I first saw it and believed I had known it by the external sense—or at least by the common sense, as they say, that is, the imaginative power—than I know it now, after having examined more diligently both what the wax is and how it is known. Surely it is absurd to doubt this

matter. For what was there in the first perception that was distinct? What was there that any animal could not have seemed capable of possessing? But when I distiguish the wax from its external forms, as if having taken off its clothes, as it were, I look at the naked wax, even though at this point there can be an error in my judgment; nevertheless I could not perceive it without a human mind.

But what am I to say about this mind, or about myself? For as yet I admit nothing else to be in me over and above my mind. What, I say, am I who seem to perceive this wax so distinctly? Do I not know myself not only much more truly and with more certainty, but also much more distinctly and evidently? For if I judge that the wax exists form the fact that I see it, certainly it follows much more evidently that I myself exist, from the fact that I see the wax. For it could happen that what I see is not truly wax. It could happen that I have no eyes with which to see anything. But it could not happen that, while I see or think I see (I do not now distinguish these two), I who think am not something. Likewise, if I judge that the wax exists from the fact that I touch it, the same thing will again follow: I exist. If from the fact that I imagine, or from whatever other cause, the same thing readily follows. But what I noted regarding the wax applies to all the other things that are external to me. Furthermore, if the perception of the wax seemed more distinct after it became known to me not only from sight or touch, but from many causes, how much more distinctly I must be known to myself; for there are no considerations that can aid in the perception of the wax or any other body without these considerations demonstrating even better the nature of my mind. But there are still so many other things in my mind from which one can draw a more distinct knowledge of the mind, so that those things which emanate from a body seem hardly worth enumerating.

But lo and behold, I have arrived on my own at the place I wanted. Since I know that bodies are not, properly speaking, perceived by the senses or by the faculty of imagination, but only by the intellect, and since, moreover, I know that they are not perceived by being touched or seen, but only insofar as they are expressly understood, nothing can be more easily and more evidently perceived by me than my mind. But because an established habit of belief cannot be put aside so quickly, it is appropriate to stop here, so that by the length of my meditation this new knowledge may be more deeply impressed on my memory.

CHAPTER 10

BLAISE PASCAL

PENSÉES

Blaise Pascal (1623–1662)—mathematician, physicist, inventor, philosopher, and theologian—was born in south central France. It soon became evident that he was a mathematical prodigy, for at the age of twelve, without any training or instruction, he worked out by himself the principles of geometry. By the age of sixteen he had written a major text in mathematics. In 1642, at age nineteen, he invented the calculating machine. This device is considered to be the forerunner of the modern-day computer. It is no accident that one of the important computer languages of our day is called PASCAL. Pascal kept up his mathematical research throughout his life, making important contributions to probability theory and number theory, as well as geometry.

On November 23, 1654, while crossing a bridge in Paris during a storm, Pascal had an overwhelming religious experience. He wrote down all that he could recall of it in a statement that he called the "Memorial." In it he recorded that he had felt himself in the very presence of the God of Abraham, Isaac, and Jacob, not the god of the philosophers. He resolved to dedicate whatever life he had left to the service of this God. He had the "Memorial" sewn into his clothes as a constant reminder of this experience, and it was found shortly after his death.

The most famous statement of Pascal's philosophy and theology appears in the *Pensées*, an unfinished collection of Pascal's thoughts that purport to demonstrate that the problem of knowledge is essentially a religious problem. Pascal insistently leads his readers to the conclusion that reason apart from divine revelation shipwrecks on extreme skepticism. From this shipwreck they can be saved only by God, not by Descartes' rationalism. The *Pensées* contain the famous "wager argument," where Pascal presents theistic belief as a reasonable gamble, and disbelief an infinitely unreasonable risk. This argument was taken up and modified by William James in his classic essay, "The Will to Believe."

In 1659 Pascal gave a lecture in which he mentioned a major work he was writing, which he described as an **apology** for the Christian religion. (An apology, remember, is a "reasoned defense.") This work we now know as the *Pensées*, one of the classics of philosophy and religion, and masterpiece of French literature.[1]

The *Pensées* opens by endeavoring to make people uneasy about their lives by exposing the vanity and futility of human goals and values. (Solomon had effectively used this argument in the Old Testament Book of Ecclesiastes.) No matter what we do, we always seem to come face to face with our own emptiness. Even those who try to distract themselves by "fame, diversion, and the thought of the future" dry up with weariness when their diversions are played out. Their fortunes cease to satisfy them—"They feel then their nothingness without knowing it; for it is indeed to be in insufferable sadness as soon as we are reduced to thinking of self, and have no diversion." For many, especially those who reject Pascal's fideistic solutions, these passages in the *Pensées* that deal with the frailty and futility of the human predicament are the most valuable, for they retain their power to speak to the modern condition.

The consideration of why we cannot find what we seek naturally leads Pascal to discuss the state of human knowledge. Well acquainted with the philosophies of Montaigne and Descartes, Pascal extends and deepens their treatments of extreme skepticism. Our "first principles," provided by nature, may or may not be true. They are not established by rational demonstration but by intuition; by the heart, not the head. As Pascal puts it, "The heart has its reasons that the reason knows not of." The only thing that saves us from extreme skepticism (or **Pyrrhonism**) is that nature itself cannot sustain it, and *forces* us to believe a variety of things. As we have seen in the Orientation, this "natural blockage" does not, however, *refute* skepticism; it merely permits us to retain our sanity. The result is that "nature confounds the Pyrrhonists and reason confounds the dogmatists." For Pascal, the only way out of this dilemma is to abandon the attempt to find an answer through human reason and to "hear from your master your real state which you do not know." The problem of knowledge admits of no human answer. "It is the heart which experiences God, and not the reason. This, then, is faith; God felt by the heart, not by reason." The sum of Pascal's advice, then, is to "Hear God!"

In Pascal's famous pensée of the wager, Pascal argues that God either exists or he does not exist. All of us must choose which belief we will hold. Looking at this

---

[1]Reprinted with permission of Macmillan Publishing Company from Blaise Pascal, "Pensées," in *Pascal Selections*, edited by Richard H. Popkins. Copyright © 1989 by Macmillan Publishing Company.

from the perspective of a gambler, Pascal insists that the prudent person must bet on the religious possibility. Careful readers of Pascal will want to compare his text with that of William James, keeping in mind the "uses of uncertainty" in overcoming skepticism

PENSÉES

109. *Against skepticism.* It is, then, a strange fact that we cannot define these things without obscuring them, while we speak of them with all assurance. We assume that all conceive of them in the same way; but we assume it quite gratuitously, for we have no proof of it. I see, in truth, that the same words are applied on the same occasions, and that every time two men see a body change its place, they both express their view of this same fact by the same word, both saying that it is moved; and from this conformity of application we derive a strong conformity of ideas. But this is not absolutely or finally convincing, though there is enough to support a bet on the affirmative, since we know that we often draw the same conclusions from different premises.

This is enough, at least, to obscure the matter; not that it completely extinguishes the natural light which assures us of these things. The Academic skeptics [the skeptics in Plato's Academy like Arcesilaus and Carneades] would have won. But this dulls it, and troubles the dogmatists to the glory of the skeptical crowd, which consists in this doubtful ambiguity, and in a certain doubtful dimness from which our doubts cannot take away all the clearness, nor our own natural lights chase away all the darkness. (392)

110. We know the truth, not only by the reason, but also by the heart, and it is in this last way that we know first principles; and reason, which has no part in it, tries in vain to impugn them. The skeptics, who have only this for their object, labor to no purpose. We know that we do not dream, and however impossible it is for us to prove it by reason, this inability demonstrates only the weakness of our reason, but not, as they affirm, the uncertainty of all our knowledge. For the knowledge of first principles, as space, time, motion, number, is as sure as any of those which we get from reasoning. And reason must trust these intuitions of the heart, and must base them on every argument. (We have intuitive knowledge of the tri-dimensional nature of space, and of the infinity of number, and reason then shows that there are no two square numbers one of which is double to the other. Principles are intuited, propositions are inferred, all with certainty, though in different ways.) And it is as useless and is absurd for reason to demand from the heart proofs of her first principles, before admitting them, as it would be for the heart to demand from reason an intuition of all demonstrated propositions before accepting them.

This inability ought, then, to serve only to humble reason, which would judge all, but not to impugn our certainty, as if only reason were capable of instructing us. Would to God, on the contrary, that we had never need of it, and that we knew everything by instinct and intuition! But nature has refused us this boon. On the contrary she has given us but very little knowledge of this kind, and all the rest can be acquired only by reasoning.

There, those to whom God has imparted reli-

105

gion by intuition are very fortunate and justly convinced. But to those who do not have it, we can give it only by reasoning, waiting for God to give them spiritual insight, without which faith is only human, and useless for salvation. (282)

119.   Let man now know his value. Let him love himself, for there is in him a nature capable of good; but let him not for this reason love the vileness which is in him. Let him despise himself, for this capacity is barren; but let him not therefore despise this natural capacity. Let him hate himself, let him love himself; he has within him the capacity of knowing the truth and of being happy, but he possesses no truth either constant or satisfactory.

I would then lead man to the desire of finding truth; to be free from passions, and ready to follow it where he may find it, knowing how much his knowledge is obscured by the passions. I would indeed that he should hate in himself the lust which determined his will by itself, so that it may not blind him in making his choice, and may not hinder him when he has chosen. (423)

121.   It is a danger to make man see too clearly his equality with the brutes without showing him his greatness. It is also dangerous to make him see his greatness too clearly, apart from his vileness. It is still more dangerous to leave him in ignorance of both. But is is very advantageous to show him both. Man must not think that he is on a level either with the brutes or with the angels, nor must he be ignorant of both sides of his nature; but he must know both. (418)

122.   Wretchedness being deduced from greatness, and greatness from wretchedness, some have inferred man's wretchedness all the more because they have taken his greatness as a proof of it, and others have inferred his greatness with all the more force, because they have inferred it from his very wretchedness. All that

the one party has been able to say in proof of his greatness has only served as an argument of his wretchedness to the others, because the greater our fall, the more wretched we are, and *vice versa.* The one party is brought back to the other in an endless circle, it being certain that in proportion as men possess light they discover both the greatness and the wretchedness of man. In a word man knows that he is wretched. He is therefore wretched because he is so; but he is really great because he knows it. (416)

125.   What are our natural principles but principles of custom? In children they are those that they have received from the habits of their fathers, as hunting in animals. A different custom will cause different natural principles. This is seen in experience; and if there are some natural principles ineradicable by custom, there are also some customs opposed to nature, ineradicable by nature, or by a second custom. This depends on disposition. (92)

127.   The nature of man may be viewed in two ways: the one according to its end, and then he is great and incomparable; the other according to the multitude, just as we judge of the nature of the horse and the dog, popularly, by seeing its fleetness; and then man is abject and vile. These are two ways which make us judge of him differently, and which occasion such disputes among philosophers. The one denies the assumption of the other. One says, "He is not born for this end, for all of his actions are repugnant to it." The other says, "He forsakes his end, when he does these base actions." (415)

128.   Two things instruct man about his whole nature; instinct and experience. (396)

130.   If he exalt him, I humble him; if he humbles himself, I exalt him, and I always contradict him, till he understands that he is an incomprehensible monster. (420)

131.   The chief argument of the skeptics—I pass over the lesser ones—are that we have no certainty of the truth of these principles apart from faith and revelation, except in so far as we naturally perceive them in ourselves. Now this natural intuition is not a convincing proof of their truth; since, having no certainty, apart from faith, whether man was created by a good God, or by a wicked demon, or by chance, it is doubtful whether these principles given to us are true, or false or uncertain, according to our origin. Again no person is certain, apart from faith, whether he is awake or sleeps, seeing that during sleep we believe that we are awake as firmly as we do when we are awake; we believe that we see space, figure and motion; we are aware of the passage of time, we measure it; and in fact we act as if we were awake. So that half of our life being passed in sleep, we have on our own admission no idea of truth, whatever we may imagine. As all our intuitions are then illusions, who knows whether the other half of our life, in which we think we are awake, is not another sleep a little different from the former, from which we awake when we suppose ourselves asleep?

And who doubts that, if we dreamt in company, and the dreams chanced to agree, which is common enough, and if we were always alone when awake, we should believe that matters were reversed? In short, as we often dream that we dream, heaping dream upon dream, may it not be that this half of our life, wherein we think ourselves awake, is itself only a dream on which the others are grafted, from which we wake at death, during which we have as few principles of truth and good as during natural sleep, these different thoughts which disturb us being perhaps only illusions like the flight of time and the vain fancies of our dreams?

These are the chief arguments on one side and the other.

I omit minor ones, such as the skeptical talk against the impressions of custom, education, manners, country, and the like. Though these influence the majority of common folk, who dogmatize only on shallow foundations, they are upset by the least breath of the skeptics. We have only to see their books if we are not sufficiently convinced of this, and we shall very quickly become so, perhaps too much.

I notice the only strong point of the dogmatists, namely that, speaking in good faith and sincerely, we cannot doubt natural principles. Against this the skeptics set up in one word the uncertainty of our origin, which includes that of our nature. The dogmatists have been trying to answer this objection ever since the world began.

So there is an open war among men, in which each must take a part, and side either with dogmatism or skepticism. For he who thinks to remain neutral is above all a skeptic. This neutrality is the essence of the sect; he who is against them is essentially for them. In this appear their advantage. They are not for themselves; they are neutral, indifferent, in suspense as to all things, even themselves being no exception.

What then shall man do in this state? Shall he doubt everything? Shall he doubt whether he is awake, whether he is being pinched, or whether he is being burned? Shall he doubt whether he doubts? Shall he doubt whether he exists? We cannot go as far as that; and I lay it down as a fact that there never has been a real complete skeptic. Nature sustains our feeble reason, and prevents it raving to that extent.

Shall he then say, on the contrary, that he certainly possesses truth—he who when pressed ever so little, can show no title to it, and is forced to let go his hold?

What a chimera then is man! What a novelty! What a monster, what a chaos, what a contradiction, what a prodigy! Judge of all things, imbecile worm of the earth; depositary of truth, a sink of uncertainty and error; the pride and refuse of the universe!

Who will unravel this tangle? Nature confutes the skeptics, and reason confutes the dogmatists. What then will you become, O men! who try to find out by your natural reason what is your true condition? You cannot avoid one of these sects, nor adhere to one of them.

Know then, proud man, what a paradox you are to yourself. Humble yourself, weak reason; be silent foolish nature; learn that man infinitely transcends man, and learn from your Master your true condition, of which you are ignorant. Hear God.

For in fact, if man had never been corrupt, he would enjoy in his innocence both truth and happiness with assurance; and if man had always been corrupt, he would have no idea of truth or bliss. But, wretched as we are, and more so than if there were no greatness in our condition, we have an idea of happiness, and cannot reach it. We perceive an image of truth, and possess only a lie. Incapable of absolute ignorance and of certain knowledge, we have been manifestly in a degree of perfection from which we have unhappily fallen.

It is, however, an astonishing thing that the mystery furthest removed from our knowledge, namely that of the transmission of sin, should be a fact without which we can have no knowledge of ourselves. For it is beyond doubt that there is nothing which more shocks our reason than to say that the sin of the first man has rendered guilty those, who, being so removed from this source, seem incapable of participation in it. This transmission does not only seem to us impossible, it seems also very unjust. For what is more contrary to the rules of our miserable justice than to damn eternally an infant incapable of will, for a sin wherein he seems to have so little a share, that it was committed six thousand years before he was in existence? Certainly nothing offends us more rudely than this doctrine, and yet, without this mystery, the most incomprehensible of all, we are incomprehensible to ourselves. The knot of our condition takes its twists and turns in this abyss, so that man is more inconceivable without this mystery than this mystery is inconceivable to man.

Whence it seems that God, willing to render the difficulty of our existence unintelligble to ourselves, has concealed the knot so high, or, better speaking, so low, that we are quite incapable of reaching it; so that it is not by the proud exertions of our reason, but by the simple submissions of reason, that we can truly know ourselves.

These foundations, solidly established on the inviolable authority of religion, makes us know that there are two truths of faith equally certain; the one, that man, in the state of creation, or in that of grace, is raised above all nature, made like unto God and sharing in His divinity; the other, that, in the state of corruption and sin, he is fallen from this state and made like unto the beasts.

These two propositions are equally sound and certain. Scripture manifestly declares this to us, when it says in some places: *My delights were with the sons of men*, Proverbs 8:31; and in other places, *I will pour out my spirit upon all flesh*, Joel 2:28. *Ye are gods*, Psalms 82:6; and in other places, *All flesh is grass*, Isaiah 11:6. *Man is like the beasts that perish*, Psalms 49:12. *I said in my heart concerning the state of the sons of men*, Ecclesiastes 3:18.

Whence it clearly seems that man by grace is made like unto God, and a partaker in His divinity, and that without grace he is like unto the brute beasts. (434)

CHAPTER 11

CHARLES SANDERS PEIRCE

SOME CONSEQUENCES OF FOUR INCAPACITIES AND THE FIXATION OF BELIEF

Charles Sanders Peirce (1839–1914), the founder of pragmatism and thought by many to be America's greatest philosopher, was born in Cambridge, Massachusetts, where his father was a mathematician at Harvard University. His father, recognizing his son's intellectual gifts, imposed upon Charles a rigorous educational program emphasizing science. Peirce's graduate degree was in chemistry, not philosophy, and at times he would refer to himself as a chemist who had been born into a scientific laboratory.

After obtaining his degree from Harvard in 1859, desiring direct experience with the methods of natural science, he was employed by the United States Coast Guard Survey, at that time the premier government scientific agency. In 1865 he made his academic debut with a series of lectures at Harvard entitled "On the Logic of Science." In 1867 he performed astronomical work at Harvard that eventually culminated in a pioneering attempt to chart the Milky Way galaxy. During the 1870s and early 1880s he traveled extensively throughout the United States and Europe, conducting gravity surveys, which he summarized in a report in 1891 upon his resignation from the Coast Guard. In the late 1870s he designed a pendulum that became the standard instrument for mathematical physicists in geodesy. Besides his astronomical, geodetic, and metrological research, Peirce also played an important role in the creation of modern symbolic logic. This extensive background in science helps explain why Peirce could say in 1895 that, "My philosophy may be described as the attempt of a physicist to make such conjecture as to the constitution of the universe as the methods of science may permit with the aid of all that has been done by previous philosophers."

From 1879 to 1884 Peirce was a lecturer in logic at Johns Hopkins University in Baltimore. He later retired to a farmhouse in Milford, Pennsylvania, where he lived with his wife in relative isolation, poor health, and poverty. During his life he published little, but since his death his papers have been collected and published, most notably by Harvard University Press, causing interest in his philosophy to steadily increase. Indiana University Press is in the process of publishing a twenty-volume chronological edition of his writings.

Our first selection is the first few pages of a much longer manuscript that Peirce published in 1868.[1] Peirce is critical of Descartes and his followers for believing that complete doubt is possible. Peirce not only argues that such a thing is impossible, he questions whether such a procedure even understands the nature of doubt. He makes a distinction between what we might call "methodological doubt" and "existential doubt" when he states: "Let us not pretend to doubt in philosophy what we do not doubt in our hearts."

"The Fixation of Belief," published in 1877, presents Peirce's "psychology of belief" as an alternative to Descartes' account of doubt. Peirce thinks of doubt and belief as a continuum. Every genuine doubt is targeted on belief. Peirce, a **pragmatist** like James, thinks of belief as that which we are willing to act on. The important question for Peirce is this: how does one arrive at, or "fix" belief, not only in the individual, but also in society? Is there some method which is better than others?

The term "fixation of belief" refers to those habits of mind that determine our conduct. Peirce considers three "pre-scientific" habits of the mind: tenacity, authority, and "a priori fashions." All three of these methods have their problems, because all three fail to resolve doubt satisfactorily. (Peirce is especially critical of the "a priori method," practiced by rationalists like Plato and Descartes, because it provides no "reality check," leaving reason free to speculate on whatever suits a person's fancy, no matter if it conforms to the facts of experience.) Although the other three methods have their good features in building character, social institutions, and new perspectives, they are completely unreliable for settling conflict and resolving doubt. Only scientific method proves to be satisfactory in this regard, because its self-correcting nature produces experimental results subject to future revision. Scientific method is best suited to the fallible nature of human beings, and least dangerous to society.

---

[1]The selection that follows is from Charles Sanders Peirce, "Some Consequences of Four Incapacites," *The Journal of Speculative Philosophy*, 2 (1868): 140–141; the second selection is from Charles Sanders Peirce, "The Fixation of Belief." *Popular Science Monthly* (November 1877).

SOME CONSEQUENCES OF FOUR INCAPACITIES

Descartes is the father of modern philosophy, and the spirit of Cartesianism—that which principally distinguishes it from the scholasticism which it displaced—may be compendiously stated as follows:

1. It teaches that philosophy must begin with universal doubt, whereas scholasticism had never questioned fundamentals.

2. It teaches that the ultimate test of certainty is to be found in the individual consciousness; whereas scholaticism had rested on the testimony of sages and of the Catholic Church.

3. The multiform argumentation of the middle ages is replaced by a single thread of inference depending often upon inconspicuous premises.

4. Scholasticism had its mysteries of faith, but undertook to explain all created things. But there are many facts which Cartesianism not only does not explain, but renders absolutely inexplicable, unless to say that "God makes them so" is to be regarded as an explanation.

In some, or all of these respects, most modern philosophers have been, in effect, Cartesians. Now without wishing to return to scholasticism, it seems to be that modern science and modern logic require us to stand upon a very different platform from this.

1. We cannot begin with complete doubt. We must begin with all the prejudices which we actually have when we enter upon the study of philosophy. These prejudices are not to be dispelled by a maxim, for they are things which it does not occur to us *can* be questioned. Hence this initial scepticism will be a mere self-decep-

tion, and not real doubt; and no one who follows the Cartesian method will ever be satisfied until he has formally recovered all those beliefs which in form he has given up. It is, therefore, as useless a preliminary as going to the North Pole would be in order to get to Constantinople by coming down regularly upon a meridian. A person may, it is true, in the course of his studies, find reason to doubt what he began by believing; but in that case he doubts because he has a positive reason for it, and not on account of the Cartesian maxim. Let us not pretend to doubt in philosophy what we do not doubt in our hearts.

2. The same formalism appears in the Cartesian criterion, which amounts to this: "Whatever I am clearly convinced of, is true." If I were really convinced, I should have done with reasoning, and should require no test of certainty. But thus to make single individuals absolute judges of truth is most pernicious. The result is that metaphysicians will all agree that metaphysics has reached a pitch of certainty far beyond that of the physical sciences;—only they can agree upon nothing else. In sciences in which men come to agreement, when a theory has been broached, it is considered to be on probation until this agreement is reached. After it is reached, the question of certainty becomes an idle one, because there is no one left who doubts it. We individually cannot reasonably hope to attain the ultimate philosophy which we pursue; we can only seek it, therefore, for the *community* of philosophers. Hence, if disciplined and candid minds carefully examine a theory and refuse to accept it, this ought to create doubts in the mind of the author of the theory himself.

3. Philosophy ought to imitate the successful sciences in its methods, so far as to proceed

only from tangible premises which can be subjected to careful scrutiny, and to trust rather to the multitude and variety of its arguments than to the conclusiveness of any one. Its reasoning should not form a chain which is no stronger than its weakest link, but a cable whose fibres may be ever so slender, provided they are sufficiently numerous and intimately connected.

4. Every unidealistic philosophy supposes some absolutely inexplicable, unanalyzable ultimate; in short, something resulting from mediation itself not susceptible of mediation. Now that anything is thus inexplicable can only be known by reasoning from signs. But the only justification of an inference from signs is that the conclusion explains the fact. To suppose the fact absolutely inexplicable, is not to explain it, and hence this supposition is never allowable.

THE FIXATION OF BELIEF

We generally know when we wish to ask a question and when we wish to pronounce a judgment, for there is a dissimilarity between the sensation of doubting and that of believing.

But this is not all which distinguishes doubt from belief. There is a practical difference. Our beliefs guide our desires and shape our actions. The Assassins, or followers of the Old Man of the Mountain,[1] used to rush into death at his least command, because they believed that obedience to him would insure everlasting felicity. Had they doubted this, they would not have acted as they did. So it is with every belief, according to its degree. The feeling of believing is a more or less sure indication of there being established in our nature some habit which will determine our actions. Doubt never has such an effect.

Nor must we overlook a third point of difference. Doubt is an uneasy and dissatisfied state from which we struggle to free ourselves and pass into the state of belief; while the latter is a calm and satisfactory state which we do not wish to avoid, or to change to a belief in anything else.

On the contrary, we cling tenaciously, not merely to believing, but to believing just what we do believe.

Thus, both doubt and belief have positive effects upon us, though very different ones. Belief does not make us act at once, but puts us into such a condition that we shall behave in a certain way, when the occasion arises. Doubt has not the least effect of this sort, but stimulates us to action until it is destroyed. This reminds us of the irritation of a nerve and the reflex action produced thereby; while for the analogue of belief, in the nervous system, we must look to what are called nervous associations—for example, to that habit of the nerves in consequence of which the smell of a peach will make the mouth water.

The irritation of doubt causes a struggle to attain a state of belief. I shall term this struggle *inquiry*, though it must be admitted that this is sometimes not a very apt designation.

The irritation of doubt is the only immediate motive for the struggle to attain belief. It is certainly best for us that our beliefs should be such as may truly guide our actions so as to satisfy our desires; and this reflection will make us reject any belief which does not seem to have been so

[1]Members of a cult.—Ed.

formed as to insure this result. But it will only do so by creating a doubt in the place of that belief. With the doubt, therefore, the struggle begins, and with the cessation of doubt it ends. Hence, the sole object of inquiry is the settlement of opinion. We may fancy that this is not enough for us, and that we seek not merely an opinion, but a true opinion. But put this fancy to the test, and it proves groundless; for as soon as a firm belief is reached we are entirely satisfied, whether the belief be false or true. And it is clear that nothing out of the sphere of our knowledge can be our object, for nothing which does not affect the mind can be a motive for a mental effort. The most that can be maintained is, that we seek for a belief that we shall *think* to be true. But we think each one of our beliefs to be true, and, indeed, it is mere tautology to say so.

That the settlement of opinion is the sole end of inquiry is a very important proposition It sweeps away, at once, various vague and errone-ous conceptions of proof. A few of these may be noticed here.

1.   Some philosophers have imagined that to start an inquiry it was only necessary to utter a question or set it down on paper, and have even recommended us to begin our studies with ques-tioning everything! But the mere putting of a proposition into the interrogative form does not stimulate the mind to any struggle after belief. There must be a real and living doubt, and with-out this all discussion is idle.

2.   It is a very common idea that a demon-stration must rest on some ultimate and absolute-ly indubitable propositions. These, according to one school, are first principles of a general nature; according to another, are first sensations. But in point of fact, an inquiry, to have that com-pletely satisfactory result called demonstration, has only to start with propositions perfectly free

from all actual doubt. If the premises are not in fact doubted at all, they cannot be more satisfac-tory than they are.

3.   Some people seem to love to argue a point after all thw world is fully convinced of it. But no further advance can be made. When doubt ceases, mental action on the subject comes to an end; and if it did go on, it would be without a purpose.

1. The Method of Tenacity

If the settlement of opinion is the sole object of inquiry, and if belief is of the nature of a habit, why should we not attain the desired end by tak-ing any answer to a question which we may fancy and constantly reiterating it to ourselves, dwell-ing on all which may conduce to that belief and learning to turn with contempt and hatred from anything which might disturb it? This simple and direct method is really pursued by many men. I remember once being entreated not to read a certain newspaper lest it might change my opin-ion upon free trade. "Lest I might be entrapped by its fallacies and misstatements," was the form of expression. "You are not," my friend said, "a special student of political economy. You might, therefore, easily be deceived by fallacious argu-ments upon the subject. You might, then, if you read this paper, be led to believe in protection But you admit that free trade is the true doctrine; and you do not wish to believe what is not true." I have often known this system to be deliberately adopted. Still oftener, the instinctive dislike of an undecided state of mind, exaggerated into a vague dread of doubt, makes men cling spasmod-ically to the views they have already taken. The man feels that, if he only holds to his belief with-out wavering, it will be entirely satisfactory. Nor can it be denied that a steady and immovable faith yields great peace of mind. It may, indeed, give rise to inconveniences, as if a man should resolutely continuue to believe that fire would not burn him, or that he would be eternally damned if he received his *ingesta* otherwise than through a stomach pump. But then the man who adopts this method will not allow that its inconveniences are greater than its advantages. He will say, "I hold steadfastly to the truth and the truth is always wholesome." And in many cases it may very well be that the pleasure he derives from his calm faith overbalances any inconveniences resulting from its deceptive character. Thus, if it be true that death is annihilation, then the man who believes that he will certainly go straight to heaven when he dies, provided he has fulfilled certain simple observances in this life, has a cheap pleasure which will not be followed by the least disappointment. A similar consideration seems to have weight with many persons in religious topics, for we frequently hear it said, "Oh, I could not believe so-and-so, because I should be wretched if I did." When an ostrich buries its head in the sand as danger approaches, it very likely takes the happiest course. It hides the danger, and then calmly says there is no danger; and if it feels perfectly sure there is none, why should it raise its head to see? A man may go through life systematically keeping out of view all that might cause change in his opinions, and if he only succeeds—basing his method, as he does, on two fundamental psychological laws—I do not see what can be said against his doing so. It would be an egotistical impertinence to object that his procedure is irrational, for that only amounts to saying that his method of settling belief is not ours. He does not propose to himself to be rational, and indeed, will often talk with scorn of man's weak and illusive reason. So let him think as he pleases.

But this method of fixing belief, which may be called the method of tenacity, will be unable to hold its ground in practice. The social impulse is against it. The man who adopts it will find that other men think differently from him, and it will be apt to occur to him in some saner moment that their opinions are quite as good as his own, and this will shake his confidence in belief. This conception, that another man's thought or sentiment may be equivalent to one's own, is a distinctly new step, and a highly important one. It arises from an impulse too strong in man to be suppressed without danger of destroying the human species. Unless we make ourselves hermits, we shall necessarily influence each other's opinions; so that the problem becomes how to fix belief, not in the individual merely, but in the community.

2. THE METHOD OF AUTHORITY

Let the will of the state act, then, instead of that of the individual. Let an institution be created which shall have for its object to keep correct doctrines before the attention of the people, to reiterate them perpetually, and to teach them to the young; having at the same time power to prevent contrary doctrines from being taught, advocated, or expressed. Let all possible causes of a change of mind be removed from men's apprehensions. Let them be kept ignorant, lest they should learn of some reason to think otherwise than they do. Let their passions be enlisted, so that they may regard private and unusual opinions with hatred and horror. Then let all men who reject the established belief be terrified into silence. Let the people turn out and tar-and-feather such men, or let inquisitions be made into the manner of thinking of suspected persons, and when they are found guilty of forbidden beliefs, let them be subjected to some signal punishment. When complete agreement could not otherwise be reached, a general massacre of all who have not thought in a certain way has proved a very effective means of settling opinions in a country. If the power to do this be wanting, let a list of opinions be drawn up, to which no man of the least independence of thought can assent, and let the faithful be required to accept all these propositions, in order to segregate them as radically as possible from the influence of the rest of the world.

This method has, from the earliest times, been one of the chief means of upholding correct theological and political doctrines, and of preserving their universal or catholic character. In Rome, especially, it has been practiced from the days of Numa Pompilius to those of Pius Nonus. This is the most perfect example in history; but wherever there is a priesthood—and no religion has been without one—this method has been more or less made use of. Wherever there is aristocracy, or a guild, or any association of a class of men whose interests depend or are supposed to depend on certain propositions, there will inevitably be found some traces of this natural product of social feeling. Cruelties always accompany this system; and when it is consistently carried out, they become atrocities of the most horrible kind in the eyes of any rational man. Nor should this occasion surprise, for the officer of a society does not feel justified in surrendering the interests of that society for the sake of mercy, as he might his own private interests. It is natural, therefore, that sympathy and fellowship should thus produce a most ruthless power.

In judging this method of fixing belief, which may be called the method of authority, we must, in the first place, allow its immeasurable mental and moral superiority to the method of tenacity. Its success is proportionally greater; and in fact it has over and over again worked the most majestic results. The mere structures of stone which it has caused to be put together, in Siam, for example, in Egypt, and in Europe—have many of them a sublimity hardly more than rivaled by the greatest works of Nature. And, except the geological epochs, there are no periods of time so vast as those which are measured by some of these organized faiths. If we scrutinize the matter closely, we shall find that there has not been one of their creeds which has remained always the same; yet the change is so slow as to be imperceptible during one person's life, so that individual belief remains sensibly fixed. For the mass of mankind, then, there is perhaps no better method than this. If it is their highest impulse to be intellectual slaves, then slaves they ought to remain.

3. THE A PRIORI METHOD

But no institution can undertake to regulate opinions upon every subject. Only the most important ones can be attended to, and on the rest men's minds must be left to the action of natural causes. This imperfection will be no source of weakness so long as men are in such a state of culture that one opinion does not influence another—that is, so long as they cannot put two and two together. But in the most priestridden states some individuals will be found who are raised above that condition. These men possess a wider sort of social feeling; they see that men in other countries and in other ages have held to very different doctrines from those which they themselves have been brought up to believe; and they cannot help seeing that it is the mere accident of their having been taught as they have, and of their having been surrounded with the manners and associations they have, that has caused them to believe as they do and not far differently. And their candor cannot resist the reflection that there is no reason to rate their own views at a higher value than those of other nations and other centuries; and this gives rise to doubts in their minds.

They will further perceive that such doubts as these must exist in their minds with reference to every belief which seems to be determined by the caprice either of themselves or of those who originated the popular opinions. The willful adherence to a belief, and the arbitrary forcing of it upon others, must, therefore, both be given up and a new method of settling opinions must be adopted, which shall not only produce an impulse to believe, but shall also decide what proposition it is which is to be believed. Let the action of natural preferences be unimpeded, then, and under their influence let men conversing together and regarding matters in different lights gradually develop beliefs in harmony with natural causes. This method resembles that by which conceptions of art have been brought to maturity. The most perfect example of it is to be found in the history of metaphysical philosophy. Systems of this sort have not usually rested upon observed facts, at least not in any great degree. They have been chiefly adopted because their fundamental propositions seemed "agreeable to reason." This is an apt expression; it does not mean that which agrees with experience, but that which we find ourselves inclined to believe. Plato, for example, finds it agreeable to reason that the distances of the celestial spheres from one another should be proportional to the different lengths of strings which produce harmonious chords. Many philosophers have been led to their main conclusions by considerations like this; but this is the lowest and least developed form which the method takes, for it is clear that another man might find Kepler's (earlier) theory, that the celestial spheres are proportional to the inscribed and circumscribed spheres of the different regular solids, more agreeable to *his* reason. But the shock of opinions will soon lead men to rest on preferences of a far more universal nature. Take, for example, the doctrine that man only acts selfishly—that is, from the consideration that acting in one way will afford him more pleasure than acting in another. This rests on no

fact in the world, but it has had a wide acceptance as being the only reasonable theory.

This method is far more intellectual and respectable from the point of view of reason than either of the others which we have noticed. But its failure has been the most manifest. It makes of inquiry something similar to the development of taste; but taste, unfortunately, is always more or less a matter of fashion, and accordingly, metaphysicians have never come to any fixed agreement, but the pendulum has swung backward and forward between a more material and a more spiritual philosophy, from the earliest times to the latest. And so from this, which has been called the *a priori* method, we are driven, in Lord Bacon's phrase, to a true induction. We have examined into this *a priori* method as something which promised to deliver our opinions from their accidental and capricious element. But development, while it is a process which eliminated the effect of some casual circumstances, only magnifies that of others. This method, therefore, does not differ in a very essential way from that of authority. The government may not have lifted its finger to influence my convictions; I may have been left outwardly quite free to choose, we will say, between monogamy and polygamy, and appealing to my conscience only, I may have concluded that the latter practice is in itself licentious. But when I come to see that the chief obstacle to the spread of Christianity among a people of a high culture as the Hindoos has been a conviction of the immorality of our way of treating women, I cannot help seeing that, though governments do not interfere, sentiments in their development will be very greatly determined by accidental causes. Now, there are some people, among whom I must suppose that my reader is to be found, who, when they see that any belief of theirs is determined by any circumstance extraneous to the facts, will from that moment not merely admit in words that that belief is doubtful, but will experience a real doubt of it, so that it ceases to be a belief.

4. The Method of Science

To satisfy our doubts, therefore, it is necessary that a method should be found by which our beliefs may be caused by nothing human, but by some external permanency—by something upon which our thinking has no effect. Some mystics imagine that they have such a method in a private inspiration from on high. But that is only a form of the method of tenacity, in which the conception of truth as something public is not yet developed. Our external permanency would not be external, in our sense, if it was restricted in its influence to one individual. It must be something which affects, or might affect, every man. And, though these affections are necessarily as various as are individual conditions, yet the method must be such that the ultimate conclusion of every man shall be the same. Such is the method of science. Its fundamental hypothesis, restated in more familiar language, is this: There are real things, whose characters are entirely independent of our opinions about them; those realities affect our senses according to regular laws, and, though our sensations are as different as our relations to the objects, yet, by taking advantage of the laws of perception, we can ascertain by reasoning how things really are, and any man, if he has sufficient experience and reason enough about it, will be led to the one true conclusion. The new conception here involved is that of reality. It may be asked how I know that there are any realities. If this hypothesis is the sole support of my method of inquiry, my method of inquiry must not be used to support my hypothesis. The reply is this: (1) If investigation cannot be regarded as proving that there are real things, it at least does not lead to a contrary con-

clusion; but the method and the conception on which it is based remain ever in harmony. No doubts of the method, therefore, necessarily arise from its practice, as is the case with all the others. (2) The feeling which gives rise to any method of fixing belief is a dissatisfaction at two repugnant propositions. But here already is a vague concession that there is some *one* thing to which a proposition should conform. Nobody, therefore, can really doubt that there are realities, or if he did, doubt would not be a source of dissatisfaction. The hypothesis, therefore, is one which every mind admits. So the social impulse does not cause me to doubt it. (3) Everybody uses the scientific method about a great many things, and only ceases to use it when he does not know how to apply it. (4) Experience of the method has not led me to doubt it, but, on the contrary, scientific investigation has had the most wonderful triumphs in the way of settling opinion. These afford the explanation of my not doubting the method or the hypothesis which it supposes; and not having any doubt, nor believing that anybody else whom I could influence has, it would be the merest babble for me to say more about it. If there be anybody with a living doubt upon the subject, let him consider it. . . .

At present I have only room to notice some points of contrast between the method of scientific investigation and other methods of fixing belief.

This is the only one of the four methods which presents any distinction of a right and a wrong way. If I adopt the method of tenacity and shut myself out from all influences, whatever I think necessary to doing this is necessary eaccording to that method. So with the method of authority: The state may try to put down heresy by means which, from a scientific point of view, seem very ill-calculated to accomplish its purposes; but the only test *on that method* is what the state thinks, so that it cannot pursue the method wrongly. So with the *a priori* method. The very essence of it is to think as one is inclined to think. . . . But with the scientific method the case is different. I may start with known and observed facts to proceed to the unknown; and yet the rules which I follow in doing so may not be such as investigation would approve. The test of whether I am truly following the method is not an immediate appeal to my feelings and purposes, but, on the contrary, itself involves the application of the method. Hence it is that bad reasoning as well as good reasoning is possible; and this fact is the foundation of the practical side of logic. . . .

It is not to be supposed that the first three methods of settling opinion present no advantage whatever over the scientific method. On the contrary, each has some peculiar convenience of its own. The *a priori* method is distinguished for its comfortable conclusions. It is the nature of the process to adopt whatever belief we are inclined to, and there are certain flatteries to one's vanities which we all believe by nature, until we are awakened from our pleasing dream by rough facts. The method of authority will always govern the mass of mankind; and those who wield the various forms of organized force in the state will never be convinced that dangerous reasoning ought not to be suppressed in some way. If liberty of speech is to be untrammeled by the grosser forms of constraint, then uniformity of opinion will be secured by a moral terrorism to which the respectability of society will give its thorough approval. Following the method of authority is the path of peace. Certain nonconformities are permitted; certain others (considered unsafe) are forbidden. These are different in different countries and in different ages; but wherever you are let it be known that you seriously hold a tabooed belief, and you may be perfectly sure of being treated with a cruelty no less brutal but more refined than hunting you like a wolf. Thus, the greatest intellectual benefactors of mankind have never dared, and dare not now, to utter the whole of their thought; and thus a shade of *prima facie* doubt is cast upon every proposition which is considered essential to the security of society. Singularly enough, the persecution does not all come from without; but a man torments himself and is oftentimes most distressed at finding himself believing propositions which he has brought up to regard with aversion. The peaceful and sympathetic man will, therefore, find it hard to resist the temptation to submit his opinions to authority. But most of all I admire the method of tenacity for its strength, simplicity, and directness. Men who pursue it are distinguished for their decision of character, which becomes very easy with such a mental rule. They do not waste time in trying to make up their minds to what they want, but, fastening like lightning upon whatever alternative comes first, they hold to it to the end, whatever happens, without an instant's irresolution. This is one of the splendid qualities which generally accompany brilliant, unlasting success. It is impossible not to envy the man who can dismiss reason, although we know how it must turn out at last.

Such are the advantages which the other methods of settling opinions have over scientific investigation. A man should consider well all of them; and then he should consider that, after all, he wishes his opinions to coincide with the fact, and that there is no reason why the results of these three methods should do so. To bring about this effect is the preogative of the method of science. Upon such considerations he has to make his choice—a choice which is far more than the adoption of any intellectual opinion, which is one of the ruling decisions of his life, to which when once made he is bound to adhere. The force of habit will sometimes cause a man to hold on to old beliefs, after he is in a condition to see that they have no sound basis. But reflection upon the state of the case will overcome these habits, and he ought to allow reflection full weight. People sometimes shrink from doing this, having an idea that beliefs are wholesome which they cannot help feeling rest on nothing. But let such persons suppose an analogous though different case from their own. Let them ask themselves what they would say to a reformed Mussulman[2] who should hesitate to give up his old notions in regard to the relations of the sexes; or to a reformed Catholic who should still shrink from the Bible. Would they not say that these persons ought to consider the matter fully, and clearly understand the new doctrine, and then ought to embrace it in its entirety? But, above all, let it be considered that what is more wholesome than any particular belief is integrity of belief; and that to avoid looking into the support of any belief from a fear that it may turn out rotten is quite as immoral as it is disadvantageous. The person who confesses that there is such a thing as truth, which is distinguished from falsehood simply by this, that if acted on it will carry us to the point we aim at and not astray, and then though convinced of this, dares not know the truth and seeks to avoid it, is in a sorry state of mind, indeed.

Yes, the other methods do have their merits: a clear logical conscience does cost something—just as any virtue, just as all that we cherish, costs us dear. But we should not desire it to be otherwise. The genius of a man's logical method should be loved and reverenced as his bride, whom he has chosen from all the world. He need not condemn the others; on the contrary, he may honor them deeply, and in doing so he only honors her the more. But she is the one that he has chosen, and he knows that he was right in making that choice. And having made it, he will work and fight for her, and will not complain that there are blows to take, hoping that there may be as many and as hard to give, and will strive to be the worthy knight and championof her from the blaze of whose splendors he draws his inspiration and his courage.

[2]Muslim.—Ed.

CHAPTER 12

WILLIAM KINGDON CLIFFORD

THE ETHICS OF BELIEF

William Kingdon Clifford (1845–1879), English mathematician and philosopher, was educated at Trinity College, Cambridge, where he distinguished himself in mathematics, publishing several papers during his first year of study. In his early undergraduate years he seems to have been quite interested in religious questions, for he studied the work of the great Christian philosopher Thomas Aquinas and actively supported Catholic positions. He later became an **agnostic** and turned against religion. Charles Darwin became an important influence upon his thought, and Clifford tried to work out a theory of scientific epistemology, conceiving of knowledge as a biological response to the world.

In 1870 he was appointed professor of applied mathematics at University College, London. He was in demand as a public lecturer, and most of his published work is derived from his lectures. He contracted tuberculosis and died in 1879. Several of his friends collected his philosophical and mathematical papers, which are published under the titles *Lectures and Essays* (1879) and *Mathematical Papers* (1882).

The selection presented here may be read as a sustained plea for integrity of belief.[1] It is not enough that I have a belief I think to be true; the *origin* of belief must be taken into account as well. He uses the example of a shipowner who,

---

[1] From Part I of "The Ethics of Belief," *Contemporary Review* (January 1877), reprinted in W.K. Clifford, *Lectures and Essays* (1879).

through suppressing his doubts about the seaworthiness of his ship, arrived at a belief that the ship was safe. When the ship went down in middle of the ocean, he collected his insurance money and told no tales.

What is wrong with the shipowner's behavior? It seems obvious that he did something wrong, but what? Clifford argues that his crime consisted of believing on insufficient evidence. The shipowner did not have the right to believe that the ship was seaworthy, because he misused doubt. As Clifford expresses it, "he had acquired his belief not by honestly earning it in patient investigation, but by stifling his doubts." Extending the example, Clifford contends that even if the ship proved to be sound, making many future journeys, it would not diminish the guilt of the shipowner one bit, because it is always immoral to believe when we have no right to believe—that is, when our evidence is insufficient.

Clifford stresses in this reading the social nature of beliefs. Whatever I choose to believe affects not only me but all humanity. The credulous person, trained to fear doubt and to recoil in horror from its use, actually endangers all mankind.

By insisting on such a high evidence standard, and by making the origin of belief part of the process of justification, Clifford recognizes that many beliefs will have to be abandoned. So be it, he would say. Morality demands it. Careful readers, alert to the arguments of Pascal and James, will wonder where this leaves us with respect to skepticism. Can religious belief (which has always linked itself to morality) survive this strong an evidence condition?

THE ETHICS OF BELIEF

A ship-owner was about to send to sea an emigrant-ship. He knew that she was old, and not over-well built at the first; that she had seen many seas and climes, and often had needed repairs. Doubts had been suggested to him that possibly she was not seaworthy. These doubts preyed upon his mind and made him unhappy; he thought that perhaps he ought to have her thoroughly overhauled and refitted, even though this should put him to great expense. Before the ship sailed, however, he succeeded in overcoming these melancholy reflections. He said to himself that she had gone safely through so many voyages and weathered so many storms that it was idle to suppose she would not come safely home from this trip also. He would put his trust in Providence, which could hardly fail to protect all these unhappy families that were leaving their father-land to seek for better times elsewhere. He would dismiss from his mind all ungenerous suspicions about the honesty of builders and contractors. In such ways he acquired a sincere and comfortable conviction that his vessel was thoroughly safe and seaworthy; he watched her departure with a light heart, and benevolent wishes for the success of the exiles in their strange new home that was to be; and he got his insurance money when she went down in mid-ocean and told no tales.

[1.] What shall we say of him? Surely this, that he was verily guilty of the death of those men. It is admitted that he did sincerely believe

121

in the soundness of his ship; but the sincerity of his conviction can in no wise help him, because *he had no right to believe on such evidence as was before him.* He had acquired his belief not by honestly earning it in patient investigation, but by stifling his doubts. And although in the end he may have felt so sure about it that he could not think otherwise, yet inasmuch as he had knowingly and willingly worked himself into that frame of mind, he must be held responsible for it.

[2.] Let us alter the case a little, and suppose that the ship was not unsound after all; that she made her voyage safely, and many others after it. Will that diminish the guilt of her owner? Not one jot. When an action is once done, it is right or wrong forever; no accidental failure of its good or evil fruits can possibly alter that. The man would not have been innocent, he would only have been not found out. The question of right or wrong has to do with the origin of his belief, not the matter of it; not what it was, but how he got it; not whether it turned out to be true or false, but whether he had a right to believe on such evidence as was before him.

[1, 2 cont.] There was once an island in which some of the inhabitants professed a religion teaching neither the doctrine of original sin nor that of eternal punishment. A suspicion got abroad that the professors of this religion had made use of unfair means to get their doctrines taught to children. They were accused of wresting the laws of their country in such a way as to remove children from the care of their natural and legal guardians; and even of stealing them away and keeping them concealed from their friends and relations. A certain number of men formed themselves into a society for the purpose of agitating the public about this matter. They published grave accusations against individual citizens of the highest position and character, and did all in their power to injure those citizens in the exercise of their profession. So great was

the noise they made, that a Commission was appointed to investigate the facts; but after the Commission had carefully inquired into all the evidence that could be got, it appeared that the accused were innocent. Not only had they been accused on insufficient evidence, but the evidence of their innocence was such as the agitators might easily have obtained, if they had attempted a fair inquiry. After these disclosures the inhabitants of that country looked upon the members of the agitating society, not only as persons whose judgment was to be distrusted, but also as no longer to be counted honorable men. For although they had sincerely and conscientiously believed in the charges they had made, *yet they had no right to believe on such evidence as was before them.* Their sincere convictions, instead of being honestly earned by patient inquiring, were stolen by listening to the voice of prejudice and passion.

Let us vary this case also, and suppose, other things remaining as before, that a still more accurate investigation proved the accused to have been really guilty. Would this make any difference in the guilt of the accusers? Clearly not; the question is not whether their belief was true or false, but whether they entertained it on wrong grounds. They would no doubt say, "Now you see that we were right after all; next time perhaps you will believe us." And they might be believed, but they would not thereby become honorable men. They would not be innocent, they would only be not found out. Every one of them, if he chose to examine himself *in foro conscientiae,*[1] would know that he had acquired and nourished a belief, when he had no right to believe on such evidence as was before him; and therein he would know that he had done a wrong thing.

It may be said, however, that in both of these supposed cases it is not the belief which is judged

---

[1] In the forum of his conscience. —Ed.

to be wrong, but the action following upon it. The shipowner might say, "I am perfectly certain that my ship is sound, but still I feel it my duty to have her examined, before trusting the lives of so many people to her." And it might be said to the agitator, "However convinced you were of the justice of your cause and the truth of your convictions, you ought not to have made a public attack upon any man's character until you had examined the evidence on both sides with the utmost patience and care."

In the first place, let us admit that, so far as it goes, this view of the case is right and necessary; right, because even when a man's belief is so fixed that he cannot think otherwise, he still has a choice in regard to the action suggested by it, and so cannot escape the duty of investigating on the ground of the strength of his convictions; and necessary, because those who are not yet capable of controlling their feelings and thoughts must have a plain rule dealing with overt acts.

But this being premised as necessary, it becomes clear that it is not sufficient, and that our previous judgment is required to supplement it. For it is not possible so to sever the belief from the action it suggests as to condemn the one without condemning the other. No man holding a strong belief on one side of a question, or even wishing to hold a belief on one side, can investigate it with such fairness and completeness as if he were really in doubt and unbiased; so that the existence of a belief not founded on fair inquiry unfits a man for the performance of this necessary duty.

[3.] Nor is that truly a belief at all which has not some influence upon the actions of him who holds it. He who truly believes that which prompts him to an action has looked upon the action to lust after it, he has committed it already in his heart. If a belief is not realized immediately in open deeds, it is stored up for the guidance of

the future. It goes to make a part of that aggregate of beliefs which is the link between sensation and action at every moment of all our lives, and which is so organized and compacted together that no part of it can be isolated from the rest, but every new addition modifies the structure of the whole. No real belief, however trifling and fragmentary it may seem, is ever truly insignificant; it prepares us to receive more of its like, confirms those which resembled it before, and weakens others; and so gradually it lays a stealthy train in our inmost thoughts, which may some day explode into overt action, and leave its stamp upon our character forever.

[4.] And no one man's belief is in any case a private matter which concerns himself alone. Our lives are guided by that general conception of the course of things which has been created by society for social purposes. Our words, our phrases, our forms and processes and modes of thought, are common property, fashioned and perfected from age to age; an heirloom which every succeeding generation inherits as a precious deposit and a sacred trust to be handed on to the next one, not unchanged but enlarged and purified, with some clear marks of its proper handiwork. Into this, for good or ill, is woven every belief of every man who has speech of his fellows. An awful privilege, and an awful responsibility, that we should help to create the world in which posterity will live.

In the two supposed cases which have been considered, it has been judged wrong to believe on insufficient evidence, or to nourish belief by suppressing doubts and avoiding investigation. The reason of this judgment is not far to seek: It is that in both these cases the belief held by one man was of great importance to other men. But for as much as no belief held by one man, however seemingly trivial the belief, and however obscure the believer, is ever actually insignificant or without its effect on the fate of mankind, we have no choice but to extend our judgment to all cases of belief whatever. Belief, that sacred faculty which prompts the decisions of our will, and knits into harmonious working all the compacted energies of our being, is ours not for ourselves, but for humanity. It is rightly used on truths which have been established by long experience and waiting toil, and which have stood in the fierce light of free and fearless questioning. Then it helps to bind men together, and to strengthen and direct their common action. It is desecrated when given to unproved and unquestioned statements, for the solace and private pleasure of the believer; to add a tinsel splendor to the plain straight road of our life and display a bright mirage beyond it; or even to drown the common sorrows of our kind by a self-deception which allows them not only to cast down but also to degrade us. Whoso would deserve well of his fellows in this matter will guard the purity of his belief with a very fanaticism of jealous care, lest at any time it should rest on an unworthy object and catch a stain which can never be wiped away.

It is not only the leader of men, statesman, philosopher, or poet, that owes this bounden duty to mankind. Every rustic who delivers in the village alehouse his slow, infrequent sentences may help to kill or keep alive the fatal superstitions which clog his race. Every hard-worked wife of an artisan may transmit to her children beliefs which shall knit society together, or rend it in pieces. No simplicity of mind, no obscurity of station can escape the duty of questioning all that we believe.

It is true that this duty is a hard one, and the doubt which comes out of it is often a very bitter thing. It leaves us bare and powerless where we thought that we were safe and strong. To know all about anything is to know how to deal with it under all circumstances. We feel much happier and more secure when we think we know pre-

cisely what to do, no matter what happens, than when we have lost our way and do not know where to turn. And if we have supposed ourselves to know all about anything, and to be capable of doing what is fit in regard to it, we naturally do not like to find that we are really ignorant and powerless, that we have to begin again at the beginning, and try to learn what the thing is and how it is to be dealt with—if indeed anything can be learned about it. It is the sense of power attached to a sense of knowledge that makes men desirous of believing, and afraid of doubting.

This sense of power is the highest and best of pleasures when the belief on which it is founded is a true belief, and has been fairly earned by investigation. For then we may justly feel that it is common property, and holds good for others as well as for ourselves. Then we may be glad, not that *I* have learned secrets by which I am safer and stronger, but that *we men* have got mastery over more of the world; and we shall be strong, not for ourselves, but in the name of Man and in his strength. But if the belief has been accepted on insufficient evidence, the pleasure is a stolen one. Not only does it deceive ourselves by giving us a sense of power which we do not really possess, but it is sinful, because it is stolen in defiance of our duty to mankind. That duty is to guard ourselves from such beliefs as from a pestilence, which may shortly master our own body and then spread to the rest of the town. What would be thought of one who, for the sake of a sweet fruit, should deliberately run the risk of bringing a plague upon his family and his neighbors?

[5.] And, as in other such cases, it is not the risk only which has to be considered; for a bad action is always bad at the time when it is done, no matter what happens afterwards. Every time we let ourselves believe for unworthy reasons, we weaken our powers of self-control, of doubting, of judicially and fairly weighing evidence. We all suffer severely enough from the maintenance and support of false beliefs and the fatally wrong actions which they lead to, and the evil born when one such belief is entertained is great and wide. But a greater and wider evil arises when the credulous character is maintained and supported, when a habit of believing for unworthy reasons is fostered and made permanent. If I steal money from any person, there may be no harm done by the mere transfer of possession; he may not feel the loss, or it may prevent him from using the money badly. But I cannot help doing this great wrong toward Man, that I make myself dishonest. Wht hurts society is not that it should lose its property, but that is should become a den of thieves; for then it must cease to be society. This is why we ought not to do evil that good may come; for at any rate this great evil has come, that we have done evil and are made wicked thereby. In like manner, if I let myself believe anything on insufficient evidence, there may be no great harm done by the mere belief; it may be true after all, or I may never have occasion to exhibit it in outward acts. But I cannot help doing this great wrong toward Man, that I make myself credulous. The danger to society is not merely that it should believe wrong things, though that is great enough, but that it should become credulous, and lose the habit of testing things and inquiring into them; for then it must sink back into savagery.

The harm which is done by credulity in a man is not confined to the fostering of a credulous character in others, and consequent support of false beliefs. Habitual want of care about what I believe leads to habitual want of care in others about the truth of what is told to me. Men speak the truth to one another when each reveres the truth in his own mind and in the other's mind; but how shall my friend revere the truth in my mind when I myself am careless about it, when I believe things because I want to believe them, and because they are comforting and pleasant? Will he not learn to cry "Peace" to me, when there is no peace? By such a course I shall surround myself with a thick atmosphere of falsehood and fraud, and in that I must live. It may matter little to me, in my cloud-castle of sweet illusions and darling lies; but it matters much to Man that I have made my neighbors ready to deceive. The credulous man is father to the liar and the cheat; he lives in the bosom of this his family, and it is no marvel if he should become even as they are. So closely are our duties knit together, that whoso shall keep the whole law, and yet offend in one point, he is guilty of all.

To sum up: It is wrong always, everywhere, and for any one to believe anything upon insufficient evidence. . . .

"But," says one, "I am a busy man; I have no time for the long course of study which would be necessary to make me in any degree a competent judge of certain questions, or even able to understand the nature of the arguments." Then he should have no time to believe.

CHAPTER 13

WILLIAM JAMES

THE WILL TO BELIEVE[1]

William James (1842–1910), brother of the famous novelist Henry James, is an important figure in the history of American intellectual life. Born in New York City in a family that fostered free-thinking, his father was a friend and confidant of such men as Ralph Waldo Emerson, Nathaniel Hawthorne, and Henry David Thoreau. James was a brilliant writer who made lasting contributions in psychology as well as philosophy. A popularizer of Charles Sanders Peirce's pragmatism, James believed that truth is something that happens to an idea, meaning that an idea becomes or is made true by events. In his writings James anticipated many of the directions of modern physics, art, religion, and psychology.

In his role as metaphysician, James was opposed to all forms of determinism, describing reality as pluralistic, incapable of being grasped in its entirety, and shot through with chance. He stressed the view that reality does not come "ready made," but rather is malleable, "waiting for its final touches at our hand." In his epistemology James was a "radical empiricist" who stressed the creative aspect of life, thinking of science as process rather than product. He was an antifoundationalist, meaning that he opposed the efforts of Descartes and others to put philosophy on a secure footing, as if philosophical certainty could rival mathematical certainty.

---

[1]From William James, *The Will to Believe and Other Essays*, 1897.

James had a lifelong interest in religion, and wrote the definitive work on religious experience, *Varieties of Religious Experience* (1902). His other writings include *The Principles of Psychology* (1890); *Pragmatism* (1907); *The Meaning of Truth* and *A Pluralisitic Universe* (1909); and *Some Problems in Philosophy* (1911) and *Essays in Radical Empiricism* (1912), published after his death.

"The Will to Believe" is William James' best known, and most controversial essay. Unfortunately, it is also the most misunderstood. James is *not* arguing that if we believe strongly enough, the belief will come true. He is arguing that belief enables us to realize hypotheses otherwise out of our ordinary experience. The point of the essay is to encourage us to risk belief in new hypotheses that are often laughed at or ridiculed by those held captive by the requirements of common sense or (what passes for) scientific method. Our very willingness to risk belief often opens up new horizons of experience. James believes that this is the case with religious belief.

W.K. Clifford's name surfaces in the essay as a representative of those who argue (on the basis of "a duty to mankind") that fear of error justifies restraining our belief-forming mechanism: we shouldn't risk error by believing on insufficient evidence. James' response is quite simple: Skepticism is as much a risk as the religious hypothesis, since the religious hypothesis is a "living, forced, momentous option." As James puts it, "To preach skepticism as a duty until 'sufficient evidence' for religion be found is tantamount therefore to telling us, when in the presence of the religious hypothesis, that to yield to our fear of its being error is wiser and better than to yield to our hope that it may be true." To extinguish "the will to believe," cheating us of all our possibilities, is "the queerest idol ever manufactured in the philosophic cave."

THE WILL TO BELIEVE

. . . Let us give the name of *hypothesis* to anything that may be proposed to our belief; and just as the electricians speak of live and dead wires, let us speak of any hypothesis as either *live* or *dead*. A live hypothesis is one which appeals as a real possibility to him to whom it is proposed. If I ask you to believe in the Mahdi,[1] the notion makes no electric connection with your nature—it refuses to scintillate with any credibility at all. As

an hypothesis it is completely dead. To an Arab, however (even if he be not one of the Mahdi's followers), the hypothesis is among the mind's possibilities: It is alive. This shows that deadness and liveness in an hypothesis are not intrinsic properties, but relations to the individual thinker. They are measured by his willingness to act. The maximum of liveness in an hypothesis means willingness to act irrevocably. Practically, that means belief; but there is some believing tendency wherever there is willingness to act at all.

Next, let us call the decision between two

[1] In Mohammedism, an expected spiritual and temporal ruler.—Ed.

127

hypotheses an *option*. Options may be of several kinds. They may be (1) *living* or *dead*, (2) *forced* or *avoidable*, (3) *momentous* or *trivial*; and for our purposes we may call an option a *genuine* option when it is of the forced, living, and momentous kind.

1.   A living option is one in which both hypotheses are live ones. If I say to you, "Be a theosophist[2] or be a Mohammedan," it is probably a dead option, because for you neither hypothesis is likely to be alive. But if I say, "Be an agnostic or be a Christian," it is otherwise: Trained as you are, each hypothesis makes some appeal, however small, to your belief.

2.   Next, if I say to you, "Choose between going out with your umbrella or without it," I do not offer you a genuine option, for it is not forced. You can easily avoid it by not going out at all. Similarly, if I say, "Either love me or hate me," "Either call my theory true or call it false," your option is avoidable. You may remain indifferent to me, neither loving nor hating, and you may decline to offer any judgment as to my theory. But if I say, "Either accept this truth or go without it." I put on you a forced option, for there is no standing place outside of the alternative. Every dilemma based on a complete logical disjunction, with no possibility of not choosing, is an option of this forced kind.

3.   Finally, if I were Dr. Nansen[3] and proposed to you to join my North Pole expedition, your option would be momentous; for this would probably be your only similar opportunity, and your choice now would either exclude you from the North Pole sort of immortality altogether or put at least the chance of it into your hands. He who refuses to embrace a unique opportunity

loses the prize as surely as if he tried and failed. *Per contra*,[4] the option is trivial when the opportunity is not unique, when the stake is insignificant, or when the decision is reversible if it later prove unwise. Such trivial options abound in the scientific life. A chemist finds an hypothesis live enough to spend a year in its verification: He believes in it to that extent. But if his experiments prove inconclusive either way, he is quit for his loss of time, no vital harm being done.

It will facilitate our discussion if we keep all these distinctions well in mind. . . .

The thesis I defend is, briefly stated, this: *Our passional nature not only lawfully may, but must, decide an option between propositions, whenever it is a genuine option that cannot by its nature be decided on intellectual grounds; for to say, under such circumstances, "Do not decide, but leave the question open," is itself a passional decision—just like deciding yes or no—and is attended with the same risk of losing the truth. . . .*

Wherever the option between losing truth and gaining it is not momentous, we can throw the chance of *gaining truth* away, and at any rate save ourselves from any chance of *believing falsehood*, by not making up our minds at all till objective evidence has come. In scientific questions, this is almost always the case; and even in human affairs in general, the need of acting is seldom so urgent that a false belief to act on is better than no belief at all. Law courts, indeed, have to decide on the best evidence attainable for the moment, because a judge's duty is to make law as well as to ascertain it, and (as a learned judge once said to me) few cases are worth spending much time over: The great thing is to have them decided on *any* acceptable principle and gotten out of the way. But in our dealings with objective nature we obviously are recorders, not makers, of the truth; and decisions for the mere sake of

[2]Practitioner of a system of religious belief based largely on certain Eastern traditions, such as Buddhism.—Ed.
[3]An explorer, a contemporary of James.—Ed.

[4]By contrast.—Ed.

deciding promptly and getting on to the next business would be wholly out of place. Throughout the breadth of physical nature facts are what they are quite independently of us, and seldom is there any such hurry about them that the risks of being duped by believing a premature theory need be faced. The questions here are always trivial options; the hypotheses are hardly living (at any rate not living for us spectators); the choice between believing truth or falsehood is seldom forced. The attitude of skeptical balance is therefore the absolutely wise one if we would escape mistakes. What difference, indeed, does it make to most of us whether we have or have not a theory of the Röntgen rays,[5] whether we believe or not in mind-stuff, or have a conviction about the causality of conscious states? It makes no difference. Such options are not forced on us. On every account it is better not to make them, but still keep weighing reasons *pro et contra*[6] with an indifferent hand.

I speak, of course, here of the purely judging mind. For purposes of discovery such indifference is to be less highly recommended, and science would be far less advanced than she is if the passionate desires of individuals to get their own faiths confirmed had been kept out of the game. . . . On the other hand, if you want an absolute duffer in an investigation, you must, after all, take the man who has no interest whatever in its results: He is the warranted incapable, the positive fool. The most useful investigator, because the most sensitive observer, is always he whose eager interest in one side of the question is balanced by an equally keen nervousness lest he become deceived. Science has organized this nervousness into a regular *technique*, her so-called method of verification; and she has fallen so deeply in love with the method that one may

even say she has ceased to care for truth by itself at all. It is only truth as technically verified that interests her. The truth of truths might come in merely affirmative form, and she would decline to touch it. Such truth as that, she might repeat with Clifford, would be stolen in defiance of her duty to mankind. Human passions, however, are stronger than technical rules. "Le coeur a ses raisons," as Pascal says, "que la raison ne connaît pas"[7]: and however indifferent to all but the bare rules of the game the umpire, the abstract intellect, may be, the concrete players who furnish him the materials to judge of are usually, each one of them, in love with some pet "live hypothesis" of his own. Let us agree, however, that wherever there is no forced option, the dispassionately judicial intellect with no pet hypothesis, saving us, as it does, from dupery at any rate, ought to be our ideal.

The question next arises, Are there not somewhere forced options in our speculative questions, and can we (as men who may be interested at least as much in positively gaining truth as in merely escaping dupery) always wait with impunity till the coercive evidence shall have arrived? It seems *a priori* improbable that the truth should be so nicely adjusted to our needs and powers as that. In the great boarding-house of nature, the cakes and the butter and the syrup seldom come out so even and leave the plates so clean. Indeed, we should view them with scientific suspicion if they did.

Moral questions immediately present themselves as questions whose solution cannot wait for sensible proof. A moral question is a question not of what sensibly exists, but of what is good, or would be good if it did exist. Science can tell us what exists; but to compare the *worths*, both of what exists and of what does not exist, we must

---

[5]X rays.—Ed.
[6]Pro and con.—Ed.

[7]The heart has its reasons that reason does not know. —Ed.

consult, not science, but what Pascal calls our heart. Science herself consults her heart when she lays it down that the infinite ascertainment of fact and correction of false belief are the supreme goods for man. Challenge the statement, and science can only repeat it oracularly, or else prove it by showing that such ascertainment and correction bring man all sorts of other goods which man's heart in turn declares. The question of having moral beliefs at all or not having them is decided by our will. Are our moral preferences true or false, or are they only odd biological phenomena, making things good or bad for *us*, but in themselves indifferent? How can your pure intellect decide? If your heart does not *want* a world of moral reality, your head will assuredly never make you believe in one. . . .

Turn now from these wide questions of good to a certain class of questions of fact, questions concerning personal relations, states of mind between one man and another. *Do you like me or not?*—for example. Whether you do or not depends, in countless instances, on whether I meet you halfway, am willing to assume that you must like me, and show you trust and expectation. The previous faith on my part in your liking's existence is in such cases what makes your liking come. But if I stand aloof, and refuse to budge an inch until I have objective evidence, until you shall have done something apt, as the absolutists say, *ad extorquendum assensum meum,*[8] ten to one your liking never comes. How many women's hearts are vanquished by the mere sanguine insistence of some man that they *must* love him! He will not consent to the hypothesis that they cannot. The desire for a certain kind of truth here brings about that special truth's existence; and so it is in innumerable cases of other sorts. Who gains promotions, boons, appointments but the man in whose life they are seen to play the part

[8]For forcing my agreement.—Ed.

of live hypotheses, who discounts them, sacrifices other things for their sake before they have come, and takes risks for them in advance? His faith acts on the powers above him as a claim, and creates its own verification.

A social organism of any sort whatever, large or small, is what it is because each member proceeds to his own duty with a trust that the other members will simultaneously do theirs. Wherever a desired result is achieved by the cooperation of many independent persons, its existence as a fact is a pure consequence of the precursive faith in one another of those immediately concerned. A government, an army, a commercial system, a ship, a college, an athletic team, all exist on this condition, without which not only is nothing achieved, but nothing is even attempted. A whole train of passengers (individually brave enough) will be looted by a few highwaymen, simply because the latter can count on one another, while each passenger fears that if he makes a movement of resistance, he will be shot before anyone else backs him up. If we believed that the whole car-full would rise at once with us, we should each severally rise, and train-robbing would never even be attempted. There are, then, cases where a fact cannot come at all unless a preliminary faith exists in its coming. *And where faith in a fact can help create the fact,* that would be an insane logic which should say that faith running ahead of scientific evidence is the "lowest kind of immorality" into which a thinking being can fall. Yet such is the logic by which our scientific absolutists pretend to regulate our lives!

In truths dependent on our personal action, then, faith based on desire is certainly a lawful and possibly an indispensable thing.

But now, it will be said, these are all childish human cases, and have nothing to do with great cosmic matters, like the question of religious faith. Let us then pass on to that. Religions differ so much in their accidents that in discussing the religious question we must make it very generic and broad. What then do we now mean by the religious hypothesis? Science says things are; morality says some things are better than other things; and religion says essentially two things.

First, she says that the best things are the more eternal things, the overlapping things, the things in the universe that throw the last stone, so to speak, and say the final word. . . .

The second affirmation of religion is that we are better off even now if we believe her first affirmation to be true.

Now, let us consider what the logical elements of this situation are *in case the religious hypothesis in both its branches be really true*. . . . So proceeding, we see, first, that religion offers itself as a *momentous* option. We are supposed to gain, even now, by our belief, and to lose by our non-belief, a certain vital good. Secondly, religion is a *forced* option, so far as that good goes. We cannot escape the issue by remaining skeptical and waiting for more light, because, although we do avoid error in that way *if religion be untrue*, we lose the good, *if it be true*, just as certainly as if we positively chose to disbelieve.   Skepticism, then, is not avoidance of option; it is option of a certain particular kind of risk. *Better risk loss of truth than chance of error*—that is your faith-vetoer's exact position. He is actively playing his stake as much as the believer is; he is backing the field against the religious hypothesis, just as the believer is backing the religious hypothesis against the field. To preach skepticism to us as a duty until "sufficient evidence" for religion be found is tantamount therefore to telling us, when in presence of the religious hypothesis, that to yield to our fear of its being error is wiser and better than to yield to our hope that it may be true. It is not intellect against all passions, then; it is only intellect with one passion laying down its law. And by what, forsooth, is the supreme wisdom of this passion warranted? Dupery for dupery, what

proof is there that dupery through hope is so much worse than dupery through fear? I, for one, can see no proof; and I simply refuse obedience to the scientist's command to imitate his kind of option, in a case where my own stake is important enough to give me the right to choose my own form of risk. If religion be true and the evidence for it be still insufficient, I do not wish, by putting your extinguisher upon my nature (which feels to me as if it had after all some business in this matter), to forfeit my sole chance in life of getting upon the winning side—that chance depending, of course, on my willingness to run the risk of acting as if my passional need of taking the world religiously might be prophetic and right.

All this is on the supposition that it really may be prophetic and right, and that, even to us who are discussing the matter, religion is a live hypothesis which may be true. Now, to most of us religion comes in a still further way that makes a veto on our active faith even more illogical. The more perfect and more eternal aspect of the universe is represented in our religions as having personal form. The universe is no longer a mere *It* to us, but a *Thou*, if we are religious; and any relation that may be possible from person to person might be possible here. For instance, although in one sense we are passive portions of the universe, in another we show a curious autonomy, as if we were small, active centres on our own account. We feel, too, as if the appeal of religion to us were made to our own active good-will, as if evidence might be forever withheld from us unless we met the hypothesis half-way. To take a trivial illustration: Just as a man who in a company of gentlemen made no advances, asked a warrant for every concession, and believed in no one's word without proof would cut himself off by such churlishness from all the social rewards that a more trusting spirit would earn, so here, one who should shut himself up in snarling logicality and try to make the gods extort his recognition willy-nilly, or not get it at all, might cut himself off forever from his only opportunity of making the gods' acquaintance. This feeling, forced on us we know not whence, that by obstinately believing that there are gods (although not to do so would be so easy both for our logic and our life) we are doing the universe the deepest service we can, seems part of the living essence of the religious hypothesis. If the hypothesis *were* true in all its parts, including this one, then pure intellectualism, with its veto on our making willing advances, would be an absurdity; and some participation of our sympathetic nature would be logically required. I, therefore, for one, cannot see my way to accepting the agnostic rules for truth-seeking, or wilfully agree to keep my willing nature out of the game. I cannot do so for this plain reason that *a rule of thinking which would absolutely prevent me from acknowledging certain kinds of truth if those kinds of truth were really there, would be an irrational rule.* That for me is the long and short of the formal logic of the situation, no matter what the kinds of truth might materially be.

I confess I do not see how this logic can be escaped. But sad experience makes me fear that some of you may still shrink from radically saying with me, *in abstracto,* that we have the right to believe at our own risk any hypothesis that is live enough to tempt our will. I suspect, however, that if this is so, it is because you have got away from the abstract logical point of view altogether, and are thinking (perhaps without realizing it) of some particular religious hypothesis which for you is dead. The freedom to "believe what we will" you apply to the case of some patent superstition; and the faith you think of is the faith defined by the schoolboy when he said, "Faith is when you believe something that you know ain't true." I can only repeat that this is misapprehen-

sion. *In concreto,* the freedom to believe can only cover living options which the intellect of the individual cannot by itself resolve; and living options never seem absurdities to him who has them to consider. When I look at the religious question as it really puts itself to concrete men, and when I think of all the possibilities which both practically and theoretically it involves, then this command that we shall put a stopper on our heart, instincts and courage, and *wait*—acting of course meanwhile more or less as if religion were *not* true—till doomsday, or till such time as our intellect and sense working together may have raked in evidence enough—this command, I say, seems to me the queerest idol ever manufactured in the philosophic cave. Were we scholastic absolutists, there might be more excuse. If we had an infallible intellect with its objective certitudes, we might feel ourselves disloyal to such a perfect organ of knowledge in not trusting to it exclusively, in not waiting for its releasing word. But if we are empiricists, if we believe that no bell in us tolls to let us know for certain when truth is in our grasp, then it seems a piece of idle fantasticality to preach so solemnly our duty of waiting for the bell. Indeed we *may* wait if we will—I hope you do not think that I am denying that—but if we do so, we do so at our peril as much as if we believed. In either case we *act,* taking our life in our hands. No one of us ought to issue vetoes to the other, nor should we bandy words of abuse. We ought, on the contrary, delicately and profoundly to respect one another's mental freedom—then only shall we bring about the intellectual republic; then only shall we have that spirit of inner tolerance without which all our outer tolerance is soulless, and which is empiricism's glory; then only shall we live and let live, in speculative as well as in practical things.

CHAPTER 14

EDMUND HUSSERL

CARTESIAN MEDITATIONS

Edmund Husserl (1859–1938), German philosopher and founder of the philosophical movement known as phenomenology, began his academic career in mathematics. Upon moving to Vienna, he came under the influence of the philosopher Franz Brentano and decided to devote himself to philosophy. He taught for many years at the University of Freiburg, where one of his students was the young Martin Heidegger. The last years of his life were difficult ones, as his Jewish ancestry exposed him to social and political pressures erupting in Germany.

Husserl was quite passionate about philosophy in general, and about phenomenology in particular, which he thought of as both a method and a philosophy. As a method, (what Husserl called the transcendental phenomenological reduction, or epoché), it details the steps that must be taken to arrive at pure essences, stripped clean of metaphysical entanglements: the "things themselves." Phenomenology itself is a descriptive science of pure essences, concerned with describing all possible objects of consciousness, as well as the various ways these objects are presented to consciousness.

Like Descartes, Husserl was a foundationalist, seeking the essential truths upon which all human knowledge rests. His *Cartesian Meditations* (1931), based on lectures that he gave in France, are an attempt to affirm Descartes' insistence on beginning with the human subject, or consciousness, while denying all of the "metaphysical baggage" that Descartes' system carried with it. A "perpetual philosophical beginner," his last work, *The Crisis of the European Sciences and Transcendental Phenomenology* (1954), examined the differences between the world as known to science, and the "lifeworld," which grounds it. His other works include *Logical Investigations* (1900–1901), *The Idea of Phenomenology* (1906–1907), and *Ideas: General Introduction to Phenomenology* (1913 and 1952).

It is impossible to overestimate the importance of Descartes' *Meditations on First Philosophy*. This slim volume was the decisive work that launched the modern era in philosophy. Descartes was the first to attempt to methodically ground philosophy in the human subject. This turn to the "philosophy of the subject" is what fascinated Husserl, and is the reason he so admired Descartes. Descartes refused to naively accept the "received knowledge" of the day, including a host of scholastic assumptions about the knowability of the world and of God. As Husserl stated, "Descartes had the serious will to free himself radically from prejudice." In attempting to free himself, he was attempting to free philosophy as well. Unfortunately, says Husserl, he failed.

Many scholars have pointed out the many unclarified prejudices that remained in Descartes' *Meditations*, including medieval conceptions of substance, the idea of God, and an uncritical admiration of mathematical natural science, which led in the end to an unacceptable mind-body dualism.[1]

Despite this failure, in the introduction to the *Cartesian Meditations* Husserl begins his argument in the spirit of Descartes.[2] What remains useful in the Cartesian project is the methodological *attempt to doubt*, for it requires the philosopher to turn inward, making philosophy answerable only to the self. "Philosophy—wisdom— . . . is the philosophizer's quite personal affair. It must arise as *his* wisdom, as his self-acquired knowledge tending towards universality, a knowledge for which he can answer from the beginning, and at each step, by virtue of his own absolute insights."

Husserl views Descartes as his own forerunner, as well as the forerunner of the new science, phenomenology. In the attempt to doubt radically, Descartes unlocked the secret that Husserl's phenomenology must explore more fully: the strategic importance of consciousness. Rejecting Descartes' metaphysics, Husserl aims to recover his spirit of "radical self-responsibility."

[1]We will examine Descartes' mind-body dualism in Part 6.
[2]From *Cartesian Meditations: An Introduction to Phenomenology*, translated by Dorien Cairns (The Hague: Martinus Nijhoff, 1977). Reprinted by permission of Kluwer Academic Publishers.

CARTESIAN MEDITATIONS

Introduction

§1. DESCARTES' MEDITATIONS AS THE PROTOTYPE OF PHILOSOPHICAL REFLECTION

Every beginner in philosophy knows the remarkable train of thoughts contained in the *Meditations*. Let us recall its guiding idea. The aim of the *Meditations* is a complete reforming of philosophy into a science grounded on an absolute foundation. That implies for Descartes a corresponding reformation of all the sciences, because in his opinion they are only non-selfsufficient members of the one all-inclusive science, and this is philosophy. Only within the systematic unity of philosophy can they develop into genuine sciences. As they have developed historically, on the other hand, they lack that scientific genuineness which would consist in their complete and ultimate grounding on the basis of absolute insights, insights behind which one cannot go back any further. Hence the need for a radical rebuilding that satisfies the idea of philosophy as the all-inclusive unity of the sciences, within the unity of such an absolutely rational grounding. With Descartes this demand gives rise to a philosophy turned toward the subject himself. The turn to the subject is made at two significant levels.

First, anyone who seriously intends to become a philosopher must "once in his life" withdraw into himself and attempt, within himself, to overthrow and build anew all the sciences that, up to then, he has been accepting. Philosophy—wisdom—is the philosophizer's quite personal affair. It must arise as *his* wisdom, as his self-acquired knowledge tending toward universality, a knowledge for which he can answer from the beginning, and at each step, by virtue of his own

absolute insights. If I have decided to live with this as my aim—the decision that alone can start me on the course of a philosophical development—I have thereby chosen to begin in absolute poverty, with an absolute lack of knowledge. Beginning thus, obviously one of the first things I ought to do is reflect on how I might find a method for going on, a method that promises to lead to genuine knowing. Accordingly the Cartesian *Meditations* are not intended to be a merely private concern of the philosopher Descartes, to say nothing of their being merely an impressive literary form in which to present the foundations of his philosophy. Rather they draw the prototype for any beginning philosopher's necessary meditations, the meditations out of which alone a philosophy can grow originally.

When we turn to the content of the *Meditations*, so strange to us men of today, we find a regress to the philosophizing ego in a second and deeper sense: the ego as subject of his pure *cogitationes*. The meditator executes this regress by the famous and very remarkable method of doubt. Aiming with radical consistency at absolute knowledge, he refuses to let himself accept anything as existent unless it is secured against every conceivable possibility of becoming doubtful. Everything that is certain, in his natural experiencing and thinking life, he therefore subjects to methodical criticism with respect to the conceivability of a doubt about it; and, by excluding everything that leaves open any possibility of doubt, he seeks to obtain a stock of things that are absolutely evident. When this method is followed, the certainty of sensuous experience, the certainty with which the world is given in natural living, does not withstand criticism; accordingly the being of the world must remain unaccepted at this initial stage. The meditator keeps only himself, qua pure ego of his *cogitationes*, as having an absolutely indubitable existence, as something that cannot be done away with, something that would exist even though this world were non-existent. Thus reduced, the ego carries on a kind of solipsistic philosophizing. He seeks apodictically certain ways by which, within his own pure inwardness, an Objective outwardness can be deduced. The course of the argument is well known: First God's existence and veracity are deduced and then, by means of them, Objective Nature, the duality of finite substances—in short, the Objective field of metaphysics and the positive sciences, and these disciplines themselves. All the various inferences proceed, as they must, according to guiding principles that are immanent, or "innate", in the pure ego.

§ 2. THE NECESSITY OF A RADICAL NEW BEGINNING OF PHILOSOPHY

Thus far, Descartes. We ask now: It is really worth while to hunt for an eternal significance belonging to these thoughts or to some clarifiable core that may be contained in them? Are they still such thoughts as might infuse our times with living forces?

Doubt is raised at least by the fact that the positive sciences, which were to experience an absolutely rational grounding by these meditations, have paid so little attention to them. To be sure, the positive sciences, after three centuries of brilliant development, are now feeling themselves greatly hampered by obscurities in their foundations, in their fundamental concepts and methods. But, when they attempt to give those foundations a new form, they do not think of turning back to resume Cartesian meditations. On the other hand, great weight must be given to the consideration that, in philosophy, the

Meditations were epoch-making in a quite unique sense, and precisely because of their going back to the pure *ego cogito*. Descartes, in fact, inaugurates an entirely new kind of philosophy. Changing its total style, philosophy takes a radical turn: from naïve Objectivism to transcendental subjectivism—which, with its ever new but always inadequate attempts, seems to be striving toward some necessary final form, wherein its true sense and that of the radical transmutation itself might become disclosed. Should not this continuing tendency imply an eternal significance and, for us, a task imposed by history itself, a great task in which we are all summoned to collaborate?

The splintering of present-day philosophy, with its perplexed activity, sets us thinking. When we attempt to view western philosophy as a unitary science, its decline since the middle of the nineteenth century is unmistakable. The comparative unity that it had in previous ages, in its aims, its problems and methods, has been lost. When, with the beginning of modern times, religious belief was becoming more and more externalized as a lifeless convention, men of intellect were lifted by a new belief, their great belief in an autonomous philosophy and science. The whole of human culture was to be guided and illuminated by scientific insights and thus reformed, as new and autonomous.

But meanwhile this belief too has begun to languish. Not without reason. Instead of a unitary living philosophy, we have a philosophical literature growing beyond all bounds and almost without coherence. Instead of a serious discussion among conflicting theories that, in their very conflict, demonstrate the intimacy with which they belong together, the commonness of their underlying convictions, and an unswerving belief in a true philosophy, we have a pseudo-reporting and a pseudo-criticizing, a mere semblance of philosophizing seriously with and for one another. This hardly attests a mutual study carried on with a consciousness of responsibility, in the spirit that caracterizes serious / collaboration and an intention to produce Objectively valid results. "Objectively valid results"—the phrase, after all, signifies nothing but results that have been refined by mutual criticism and that now withstand every criticism. But how could actual study and actual collaboration be possible, where there are so many philosophers and almost equally many philosophies? To be sure, we still have philosophical congresses. The philosophers meet but, unfortunately, not the philosophies. The philosophies lack the unity of a mental space in which they might exist for and act on one another. It may be that, within each of the many different "schools" or "lines of thought", the situation is somewhat better. Still, with the existence of these in isolation, the total philosophical present is essentially as we have described it.

In this unhappy present, is not our situation similar to the one encountered by Descartes in his youth? If so, then is not this a fitting time to renew his radicalness, the radicalness of the beginning philosopher: to subject to a Cartesian overthrow the immense philosophical literature with its medley of great traditions, of comparatively serious new beginnings, of stylish literary activity (which accounts on "making an effect" but not on being studied), and to begin with new *meditationes de prima philosophia?* Cannot the disconsolateness of our philosophical position be traced back ultimately to the fact that the driving forces emanating from the *Meditations* of Descartes have lost their original vitality—lost it because the spirit that characterizes radicalness of philosophical self-responsibility has been lost? Must not the demand for a philosophy aiming at the ultimate conceivable freedom from prejudice, shaping itself with actual autonomy according to ultimate evidences it has itself produced, and therefore absolutely self-responsible—must not this demand, instead of being excessive, be part of

the fundamental sense of genuine philosophy? In recent times the longing for a fully alive philosophy has led to many a renaissance. Must not the only fruitful renaissance be the one that reawakens the impulse of the Cartesian *Meditations:* not to adopt their content but, in *not* doing so, to renew with greater intensity the radicalness of their spirit, the radicalness of self-responsibility, to make that radicalness true for the first time by enhancing it to the last degree, to uncover thereby for the first time the genuine sense of the necessary regress to the ego, and consequently to overcome the hidden but already felt naïveté of earlier philosophizing?

In any case, the question indicates one of the ways that has led to transcendental phenomenology.

Along that way we now intend to walk together. In a quasi-Cartesian fashion we intend, as radically beginning philosophers, to carry out meditations with the utmost critical precaution and a readiness for any—even the most far-reaching—transformation of the old-Cartesian meditations. Seductive aberrations, into which Descartes and later thinkers strayed, will have to be clarified and avoided as we pursue our course.

First Meditation: The Way to the Transcendental Ego

§ 3. THE CARTESIAN OVERTHROW AND THE GUIDING FINAL IDEA OF AN ABSOLUTE GROUNDING OF SCIENCE

And so we make a new beginning, each for himself and in himself, with the decision of philosophers who begin radically: that at first we shall put out of action all the convictions we have been accepting up to now, including all our sciences. Let the idea guiding our meditations be at first the Cartesian idea of a science that shall be established as radically genuine, ultimately an all-embracing science.

But, now that we no longer have at our disposal any already-given science as an example of radically genuine science (after all, we are not accepting any given science), what about the indubitability of that idea itself, the idea namely of a science that shall be grounded absolutely? Is it a legitimate final idea, the possible aim of some possible practice? Obviously that too is something we must not presuppose, to say nothing of taking any norms as already established for testing such possibilities—or perchance a whole system of norms in which the style proper to genuine science is allegedly prescribed. That would mean presupposing a whole logic as a theory of science; whereas logic must be included among the sciences overthrown in overthrowing all science. Descartes himself presupposed an ideal of science, the ideal approximated by geometry and mathematical natural science. As a fateful prejudice this ideal determines philosophies for centuries and hiddenly determines the *Meditations* themselves. Obviously it was, for Descartes, a truism from the start that the all-embracing science must have the form of a deductive system, in which the whole structure rests, *ordine geometrico*, on an axiomatic foundation that grounds the deduction absolutely. For him a role similar to that of geometrical axioms in geometry is played in the all-embracing science by the axiom of the ego's absolute certainty of himself, along with the axiomatic principles innate in the ego—only this axiomatic foundation lies even deeper than that of geometry and is called on to participate in the ultimate grounding even of geometrical knowledge.

None of that shall determine our thinking. As beginning philosophers we do not as yet accept any normative ideal of science; and only so far as we produce one newly for ourselves can we ever have such an ideal.

But this does not imply that we renounce the general aim of grounding science absolutely. That aim shall indeed continually motivate the course of our meditations, as it motivated the course of the Cartesian meditations; and gradually, in our meditations, it shall become determined concretely. Only we must be careful about how we make an absolute grounding of science our aim. At first we must not presuppose even its possibility. How then are we to find the legitimate manner in which to make it our aim? How are we to make our aim perfectly assured, and thus assured as a practical possibility? How are we then to differentiate the possibility, into which at first we have a general insight, and thereby mark out the determinate methodical course of a genuine philosophy, a radical philosophy that begins with what is intrinsically first?

Naturally we get the general idea of science from the sciences that are factually given. If they have become for us, in our radical critical attitude, merely alleged sciences, then, according to what has already been said, their general final idea has become, in a like sense, a mere supposition. Thus we do not yet know whether that idea is at all capable of becoming actualized. Nevertheless we do have it in this form, and in a state of indeterminate fluid generality; accordingly we have also the idea of philosophy: as an idea about which we do not know whether or how it can be actualized. We take the general idea of science, therefore, as a precursory presumption, which we allow ourselves tentatively, by which we tentatively allow ourselves to be guided in our meditations. We consider how it might be thought out as a possibility and then consider whether and how it might be given determinate actualization. To be sure, we get into what are, at first, rather strange circumstantialities—but how can they be avoided, if our radicalness is not to remain an empty gesture but is to become an actual deed? Let us go on then with patience. . . .

CONTEMPORARY PERSPECTIVES: SKEPTICISM RE-VISITED

The history of skepticism is as long as the history of philosophy itself. What is knowledge, and how is it possible? Skepticism as a philosophical position emerges from honestly probing the question of the nature of knowledge.

One of the traditional responses to the question, "What is knowledge," has been to say that knowledge is *justified true belief*. Plato, in the *Theatetus*, was the first to offer this definition of knowledge, and philosophers have been playing variations on it ever since.

The idea of knowledge as true belief seems simple enough (although this has been challenged as well), but how can we know that a belief is justified? A typical response is to say that a belief is justified when made evident. But how much evidence is necessary to transform mere belief into knowledge? Shall we insist on an "adequate evidence" condition? But how do we know if our evidence is adequate? Couldn't someone always demand more evidence before being willing to grant that a belief is justified? Is there any way to limit the amount of evidence necessary to justify belief?

One way to limit the amount of evidence is to argue that a belief is justified when it is evident beyond reasonable doubt. This is the evidence requirement that juries are assigned by judges in criminal law cases. My belief in a defendent's innocence means that I am more justified in believing in the defendant's innocence than I am in not believing in it.

But suppose someone rejects "beyond reasonable doubt" as an unsatisfactory evidence condition, insisting that we need to be more rigorous. What if someone were to insist on a "perfect evidence" condition? This would mean that if I ever wanted to make claim to knowledge (justify a belief), I would be required to have total and complete evidence. But how can I be expected to have complete evidence when human experience is always incomplete? For example, although I can offer a good bit of evidence in support of the proposition "All crows are black," I have to admit that I haven't actually seen every crow on the face of the earth, nor can I imagine any way in which I could. Even if I had, there is no guarantee that a yellow crow will not show up tomorrow in Afghanistan, or that someone is not hoarding all of the purple crows in the universe on a space satellite somewhere. On the face of it, this strong an evidence condition seems to make impossible demands on us. Although it surely seems unreasonable, what if someone insisted on it? Would it not be possible to define knowledge right out of existence?

Of course, this is precisely the strategy of the skeptic. It is important to realize that in insisting on this evidence condition the skeptic is not introducing some bizarre notion that has no place in human reasoning—as we have seen, skepticism naturally arises for thought when one simply reflects on the requirements for knowledge.

The philosophical conversation about skepticism has gone on for thousands of years, and continues today. Whatever else we may say about it, one thing is clear: The only way to respond to the skeptical challenge is to cling to the method of philosophy, and respond dialectically. Now is not the time to resort to prejudice, tradition, or power in order to kill the question. Like a latter-day Socrates, we must be willing to follow the question wherever it leads, patiently examining the skeptic's requirements and making our response, point by painstaking point.

In the two selections that follow, you will have an opportunity to read a defense of skepticism by Peter Unger as well as a critique of skepticism by John Hospers. In the first main section of his article, Unger offers an update on Descartes' argument from counterpossibility, substituting an evil scientist for Descartes' evil demon. His argument is quite simple, having two premises and a conclusion. It is also logically valid. The conclusion of the argument, however, is startling: We cannot know anything whatsoever about the external world! Can you accept this argument? More importantly, can you think of a way to respond to Unger?

The second section of Unger's article addresses one of the standard ways to refute a philosophical argument: trying to reverse it. Unger claims that G.E. Moore, an outstanding British philosopher, was unsuccessful in his attempt to reverse this kind of "classical argument" for skepticism.

Finally, in the third section Unger considers "ordinary cases," much less exotic than the evil scientist argument, yet no less effective in reminding us of human fallibility and the need for extreme caution when making a claim to knowledge.

In our second selection, John Hospers begins by making a standard distinction among three types of knowledge: knowing by acquaintance, knowing how to, and knowledge of propositions. He makes it clear that this third sense of knowing, "knowing that," is the one he wishes to analyze.

Hospers identifies three conditions for "knowing that," explaining each at length, then focusing on the third condition. In the course of his discussion of the third condition (the "evidence condition"), he makes a useful distinction between *strong* and *weak* senses of the word 'know.' He then discusses various test cases, enacting an imaginary dialogue with a skeptic. As you read, the applications of his arguments to Unger's article should become apparent. You will need to decide for yourself whether the "antiskeptical ammunition" that Hospers provides is sufficient to demolish Unger's argument, or whether skepticism will survive to live another day.

CHAPTER 15

PETER UNGER

A CASE FOR SKEPTICISM

Peter Unger (1942–   ) taught philosophy at the University of Wisconsin, Madison, for seven years and is currently professor of philosophy at New York University, having taught there since 1971. His book, *Ignorance: A Case for Skepticism* (1975) did much to revive contemporary interest in skepticism. He is also the author of *Philosophical Relativism* (1984).

A DEFENSE OF SKEPTICISM[1]

In these pages, I try to argue compellingly for skepticism. . . . The type of skepticism for which I first argue is perhaps the most traditional one: skepticism about knowledge. This is the thesis that no one ever *knows* anything about anything. . . .[2]

I. A Classical Form of Skeptical Argument

There are certain arguments for skepticism which conform to a familiar . . . pattern or form. These arguments rely, at least for their psychological power, on vivid descriptions of exotic *contrast cases*. The following is one such rough argument, this one in support of skepticism regarding any alleged *knowledge of an external world*.[3] The

---

[1]From Peter Unger, *Ignorance: A Case for Skeptism.* © 1975 by Oxford University Press. Reprinted by permission of Oxford University Press.

[2]In this selection, Unger does not argue for this extreme thesis. Rather, he argues that: No one can know anything about an *external world*. See Section I, first paragraph. —Ed.

[3]The external world consists of objects which exist independently of being perceived, for example, chairs, rocks, etc. It is external to our minds. —Ed.

exotic contrast case here concerns an evil scientist, and is described to be in line with the most up to date developments of science, or science fiction. We begin by arbitrarily choosing something concerning an external world which might conceivably, we suppose, be *known*, in one way or another, e.g., that there are rocks or, as we will understand it, that there is at least one rock.

[*Argument*] Now, first, *if* someone, anyone *knows* that there are rocks, then the person *can know* the following quite exotic thing: There is *no* evil scientist deceiving him into *falsely* believing that there are rocks. This scientist use electrodes to induce experiences and thus carries out his deceptions, concerning the existence of rocks and anything else. He first drills hole painlessly in the variously colored skulls, or shells, of his subjects and implants his electrodes into the appropriate parts of their brains, or protoplasm, or systems. He sends patterns of electrical impulses into them through the electrodes, which are themselves connected by wires to a laboratory console on which he plays, punching various keys and buttons in accordance with his ideas of how the whole thing works and with his deceptive designs. The scientist's delight is intense, and it is caused not so much be his exercising his scientific and intellectual gifts as by the thought that he is deceiving various subjects about all sorts of things. Part of that delight is caused, on this supposition, by his thought that he is deceiving a certain person, perhaps yourself, into falsely believing that there are rocks. He is, then, an evil scientist, and he lives in a world which is entirely bereft of rocks.

[*Argument continued*] Now, as we have agreed, [1] *if you know* that there are rocks, then you *can know* that there is no such scientist doing this to you, [i.e., deceiving you to falsely believe that ther are rocks.] But [2] no one *can* ever *know* that this exotic situation does *not obtain*[4]; no one can

⁴Obtain: to occur or be prevalent in occurring.—Ed.

ever *know* that there is *no* evil scientist who is, by means of electrodes, deceiving him into falsely believing there to be rocks. That is our second premise, and it is also very difficult to deny. So, thirdly, as a consequence of these two premises, we have our skeptical conclusion: [3] You never *know* that there are rocks. But of course we have chosen our person, and the matter of there being rocks, quite arbitrarily, and this argument, it surely seems, may be generalized to cover any external matter at all. From this, we may conclude, finally, that [4] nobody ever *knows* anything about the external world.

[*Comments*] This argument is the same in form as the "evil demon" argument in Descartes' *Meditations*⁵; it is but a more modern, scientific counterpart, with its domain of application confined to matters concerning the external world.⁶ Taking the *Meditations* as our source of the most compelling skeptical argument the philosophical literature has to offer, we may call any argument of this form *the classical argument* for skepticism. . . .

These arguments are exceedingly compelling. They tend to make skeptics of us all if only for a brief while. Anyone who would try to further skepticism, as I will try to do, will do well to link his own ideas to these arguments. For then, the very notable feelings and intuitions which they arouse may serve as support for the theses he would advance. . . .

II. On Trying to Reverse This Argument: Exotic Cases and Feelings of Irrationality

Our skeptical conclusion would not be welcome to many philosophers. Indeed, most philoso-

⁵Descartes was a seventeenth century philosopher. Unger's argument is an up-to-date version of Descartes'.—Ed.
⁶René Descartes, *Meditations on First Philosophy*, 2nd ed., 1642, in *The Philosophical Works of Descartes*, trans. E. S. Haldane and G. R. T. Ross (Cambridge, 1972), vol. 1, Meditation I, pp. 144–149. The crux of what I take to be the main argument occurs near the end of Meditation I.

phers would be inclined to try to reverse the argument, perhaps in the manner made popular by G. E. Moore.[7] They would not, I think, wish to deny the first premise, which in any case seems quite unobjectionable, at least in essential thrust. But even in its early formulation, they would be most happy to deny the second premise, which is the more substantive one.

[*Reverse Argument*] The Moorean attempt to reverse our argument will proceed like this: [1.] According to your argument, nobody ever *knows* that there are rocks. [2.] But I *do* know that there are rocks. This is something concerning the external world, and I do know it. Hence, [3.] somebody *does know* something about the external world. Mindful of our first premise, the reversal continues: I can reason at least moderately well and thereby come to know things which I see to be entailed by things I already know. Before reflecting on classical arguments such as this, I may have never realized or even had the idea that from there being rocks it follows that there is *no* evil scientist who is deceiving me into *falsely* believing there to be rocks. But, having been presented with such arguments, I of course *now know* that this last *follows* from what I know. And so, while I might not have known *before* that there is no such scientist, at least [4.] I *now* do know that there is no evil scientist who is deceiving me into falsely believing that there are rocks. So far has the skeptical argument failed to challenge my knowledge successfully that it seems actually to have occasioned an increase in what I know about things.

[*Comments*] While the robust character of this reply has a definite appeal, it also seems quite daring. Indeed, the more one thinks on it, the more it seems to be somewhat foolhardy and

even dogmatic. One cannot help but think that for all this philosopher really can *know*, he might have all his experience artificially induced by electrodes, these being operated by a terribly evil scientist who, having an idea of what his "protege" is saying to himself, chuckles accordingly. One thinks as well that for all *one can know oneself,* there really is no Moore or any other thinker with whose works one has actually had any contact. The belief that one has may, for all one really can *know,* be due to experiences induced by just such a chuckling operator. For all one can *know,* then, there may not really be any rocks. Positive assertions to the contrary, even on one's own part, seem quite out of place and even dogmatic.

[*Counter Argument*] Suppose that you yourself have just positively made an attempt to reverse; you try to be a Moore [and claim to know that there is no scientist who implanted electrodes and is deceiving you.] Now, [*case 1*] we may suppose that electrodes are removed, that your experiences are now brought about through your perception of actual surroundings, and you are, so to speak, forced to encounter your deceptive tormentor. Wouldn't you be made to feel quite *foolish,* even *embarrassed,* by your claims to *know*? Indeed, you would seem to be exposed quite clearly as having been, not only wrong, but rather irrational and even dogmatic. And [*case 2*] if there *aren't* ever any experiences of electrodes and so on, that happy fact can't mean that you are any *less* irrational and dogmatic in saying or thinking that you know. In thinking that you *know,* you will be equally and notably irrational and dogmatic. And, for at least *that* reason, in thinking yourself to *know* there is no such scientist, you will be *wrong* in *either* case. So it appears that one doesn't ever really *know* that there is no such scientist doing this thing.

[*Extension and Qualification*] Now, if you think or say to yourself that you are *certain* or *sure* that there is no scientist doing this, you may be dou-

[7]See several of Moore's most famous papers. But most especially, I suggest, see his "Four Forms of Scepticism" in his *Philosophical Papers* (New York, 1959) p. 226. [Moore was a twentieth century philosopher in England who claimed to know with certainty that an external world exists.—Ed.]

bly right, but even that does not seem to make matters much better for you. You may be right on *one* count because you may, I will suppose, *be* certain that there is no such scientist, and so be right *in what* you *think*. And in the second place, there may be no evil scientist deceiving you, so that you may be right *in that of which you are certain*. But, even if doubly right here, it seems just as dogmatic and irrational for you ever sincerely to profess this certainty. Thus it seems that, even if you *are* certain of the thing, and even if there *is no* scientist, you *shouldn't be certain* of it. It seems that your are *wrong*, then, and *not* right on a third count, namely, *in being certain* of the thing. It seems much better, perhaps perfectly all right, if you are instead only *confident* that there is no such scientist. It seems perfectly all right for you to *believe* there to be no evil scientist doing this. If you say, not only that you believe it, but that you have some *reason* to believe this thing, what you say *may* seem somewhat suspect, at least on reasoned reflection, but it doesn't have any obvious tint of dogmatism or irrationality to it. Finally, you may simply *assert*, perhaps to yourself, *that there is no evil scientist who is deceiving me into falsely believing that there are rocks*. Perhaps strangely, this seems at least pretty nearly as foolhardy and dogmatic as asserting, or as thinking, *that you know the thing*. . . .

[*Comments*] This idea, that claims to *know* about external things are at least somewhat foolhardy and dogmatic, applies in all possible situations, even the most exotic cases. Suppose, for example, that you actually *do* have a sequence of experience which seems to indicate that an evil scientist was deceiving you into falsely believing that there are rocks. You seem to be confronting an exotic scientist who shows you electrodes, points out places of insertion on your skull or shell, and explains in detail how the whole thing works. And you seem to see no rocks outside the window of this scientist's laboratory. The scien-

tist assures you that there really are no such things as rocks, that he only created an impression of such things by stimulating certain groups of cells in your brain. After enough of this sort of thing dominates your experiences, you *might* suppose that you *know* that there *is* an evil scientist who deceived you in the past, but he now does not. And you may also come to suppose that you *know* that there were *never any* rocks at all. But *should* you think you *know*? These latter experiences might *themselves* find no basis in reality, for all you really might *know*. For all you can *know*, it may be that all the time your experiences are induced by electrodes which are operated by *no* scientist, and it may be that there are no scientists at all, and plenty of rocks. Whether or not this is the case, you may always have new experience to the effect that it is. Is the new experience part of an encounter with *reality*, or is it *too* only part of an induced stream, or perhaps even a random sequence of experience? No matter how involved the going gets, it may always get still more involved. And each new turn may make any previously developed claim to *know* seem quite irrational and dogmatic, if not downright embarrassing. No matter what turns one's experience takes, the statement that one *knows* there to be no scientist *may* be wrong for the reason that there is a scientist. But it *will always* be wrong, it seems, for the reason of dogmatism and irrationality, however this last is to be explained. . . .

III. Ordinary Cases

Largely because it is so exotic and bizarre, the case of a deceiving scientist lets one feel acutely the apparent irrationality in thinking oneself to *know*. But the exotic cases have no monopoly on generating feelings of irrationality.

[*Ordinary Cases*] [1.] If you are planning a

philosophical book and trying to estimate the energy you will spend on each of the several chapters, you might think that you *know* that it will not take much to write the *third* chapter. For the argument *there* may seem *already* so *clearly* outlined in your head. But experience may later seem to show that this argument is far from clear. And much time and effort may become absorbed with no clear fruits to show for it. In that case, you will, I suggest, feel somewhat embarrassed and foolish, even if there is no other person to whom your idea that you *knew* was ever communicated. If you just *believed,* or even if you were quite *confident* that this chapter would not take much effort to write, then, I suggest, you would not feel nearly so foolish or embarrassed, oftentimes not at all.

[2.] Again, you may think you *know* that a certain city is the capital of a certain state, and you may feel quite content in this thought while watching another looking the matter up in the library. You will feel quite foolish, however, if the person announces the result to be *another* city, and if subsequent experience seems to show that announcement to be right. This will occur, I suggest, even if you are just an anonymous, disinterested bystander who happens to hear the question posed and the answer later announced. This is true even if the reference was a newspaper, *The Times,* and the capital was changed only yesterday. But these feelings will be very much less apparent, or will not occur at all, if you only feel very confident, at the outset, that the city is thus-and-such, which later is not announced. You might of course feel that you shouldn't be quite so confident of such things, or that you should watch out in the future. But you probably *wouldn't* feel, I suggest, that you were *irrational* to be confident of that thing at that time. Much less would you feel that you were *dogmatic* in so being.

[3.] Finally, if you *positively asserted* something to another in a conversation, as though reporting

a *known fact,* later contrary experiences might well cause you to feel that you had overstepped the bounds of good sense and rationality. The feeling is that you have manifested a trait of a dogmatic personality. If you happen to be right, your extremely positive approach is not likely to be questioned. In case subsequent events seem to indicate you are wrong about the matter, then you come in for a severe judgement, whether or not this judgement is ever made out loud. This is a rather familiar social experience. (As I say this, even in trying to make my style a little less cautious, to be readable, I leave myself open to just such a judgement by putting the matter in such a positive, unqualified way.) I suggest that such feelings *ought* to be far *more* familiar, occurring even where you are *right* about the matter. They *should not* just occur where you are in fact wrong about things. Accordingly, we should avoid making these claims in *any* case, whether we be right or whether wrong in the matter, e.g., of which city is the capital of that state.

It is hard for us to think that there is any important similarity between such common cases as these and the case of someone thinking himself to *know* that *there are rocks.* Exotic contrast cases, like the case of the evil scientist, help one to appreciate that these cases are really essentially the same. By means of contrast cases, we encourage thinking of all sorts of new sequences of experience, sequences which people would never begin to imagine in the normal course of affairs. How would you react to such developments as *these,* no matter *how* exotic or unlikely? It appears the the proper reaction is to feel as irrational about claiming knowledge of rocks as you felt before, where, e.g., one was apparently caught in thought by the library reference to the state's capital. Who would have thought so, before thinking of contrast cases? Those cases help you see, I suggest, that in *either* case, no matter whether you are in fact right in the matter or whether wrong, thinking that you *know* manifests an attitude of dogmatism. Bizarre experiential sequences help show that there is no essential difference between any two external matters; the apparently most certain ones, like that of rocks, and the ones where thinking about *knowing* appears, even without the most exotic skeptical aids, *not* the way to think.

CHAPTER 16

JOHN HOSPERS

A CRITIQUE OF SKEPTICISM

John Hospers (1918–) received his Ph.D. in philosophy from Columbia University in 1944. He has taught philosophy at numerous universities, including Columbia, the University of Minnesota, and the University of California at Los Angeles. He is the editor of *The Monist*, an important philosophical journal. Among his many books are *Meaning and Truth in the Arts* (1946). *Introduction to Philosophical Analysis* (1967, third edition, 1988), and *Libertarianism A Political Philosophy for Tomorrow* (1971).

A CRITIQUE OF SKEPTICISM[1]

I. Requirements for Knowing

The word "know" is slippery. It is not always used in the same way. Here are some of its principal uses:

[1]From John Hospers, *An Introduction to Philosophical Analysis*, 2d ed. © 1967, pp. 143–145, 146–155. Reprinted by permission of Prentice-Hall, Inc., Englewood Cliffs, New Jersey.

[*Senses of "know"*] 1. Sometimes when we talk about knowing, we are referring to *acquaintance* of some kind. For example, "Do you know Richard Smith?" means approximately the same as "Are you acquainted with Richard Smith? (have you met him? etc.). . ."

2. Sometimes we speak of knowing *how*: Do you know how to ride a horse, do you know how to use a soldering iron? We even use a colloquial

noun, "know-how," in talking about this. Knowing how is an *ability*—we know how to ride a horse if we have the ability to ride a horse, and the test of whether we have the ability is whether in the appropriate situation we can perform the activity in question. . . .

3.   But by far the most frequent use of the word "know"—and the one with which we shall be primarily concerned—is the *propositional* sense: "I know that . . ." where the word "that" is followed by a proposition: "I know that I am now reading a book," "I know that I am an American citizen," and so on. There is some relation between this last sense of "know" and the earlier ones. We cannot be acquainted with Smith without knowing some things about him (without knowing *that* certain propositions about him are true), and it is difficult to see how one can know *how* to swim without knowing some true propositions about swimming, concerning what you must do with your arms and legs when in the water. (But the dog knows how to swim, though presumably he knows no propositions about swimming.). . .

[*Conditions for knowing that*] Now, what is required for us to know in this third and most important sense? Taking the letter *p* to stand for any proposition, what requirements must be met in order for one to assert truly that he knows *p*? There are, after all, many people who claim to know something when they don't; so how can one separate the rightful claims to know from the mistaken ones?

a. p must be true. The moment you have some reason to believe that a proposition is not true, this immediately negates a person's claim to know it: You can't know *p* if *p* isn't true. If I say, "I know *p*, but *p* is not true," my statement is self-contradictory, for part of what is involved in knowing *p* is that *p* is true. Similarly, if I say, "He knows *p*, but *p* is not true," this too is self-contradictory. It may be that I thought I knew *p*; but if *p*

is false, I didn't really know it. I only thought I did. If I nevertheless claim to know *p*, while admitting that *p* is false, my hearers may rightly conclude that I have not yet learned how to use the word "know." This is already implicit in our previous discussion, for what is it that you know about *p* when you know *p*? You know *that p is true*, of course; the very formulation gives away the case: Knowing *p* is knowing that *p* is true. . . .

But the truth-requirement, though necessary, is not sufficient. There are plenty of true propositions, for example in nuclear physics, that you and I do not know to be true unless we happen to be specialists in that area. But the fact that they are true does not imply that we know them to be true. . . .

b. Not only must p be true: We must believe that p is true. This may be called the "subjective requirement": We must have a certain attitude toward *p*—not merely that of wondering or speculating about *p*, but positively *believing* that *p* is true. "I know that *p* is true, but I don't believe that it is" would not only be a very peculiar thing to say, it would entitle our hearers to conclude that we had not learned in what circumstances to use the word "know." There may be numerous statements that you believe but do not know to be true, but there can be none which you know to be true but don't believe, since believing is a part (a defining characteristic) of knowing.

"I know *p*" implies "I believe *p*," and "He knows *p*" implies "He believes *p*," for believing is a defining characteristic of knowing. But believing *p* is *not* a defining characteristic of *p*'s being true: *p* can be true even though neither he nor I nor anyone else believes it. (The earth was round even before anyone believed that it was.) There is no contradiction whatever in saying, "He believed *p* (that is, believed it to be true), but *p* is not true." Indeed, we say things of this kind all the time: "He believes that people are persecuting him, but of course it isn't true." . . .

We have now discussed two requirements for knowing, an "objective" one (*p* must be true) and a "subjective" one (one must believe *p*). Are these sufficient? Can you be said to know something if you believe it and if what you believe is true? If so, we can simply define knowledge as true belief, and that will be the end of the matter.

Unfortunately, however, the situation is not so simple. True belief is not yet knowledge. A proposition may be true, and you may believe it to be true, and yet you may not *know* it to be true. Suppose you believe that there are sentient beings on Mars, and suppose that in the course of time, after space-travelers from the earth have landed there, your belief turns out to be true. The statement was true at the time you uttered it, and you also believed it at the time you uttered it—but did you *know* it to be true at the time you uttered it? Certainly not, we would be inclined to say; you were not in a position to know. It was a lucky guess. Even if you had *some* evidence that it was true, you didn't *know* that it was true at the time you said it. Some further condition, therefore, is required to prevent a lucky guess from passing as knowledge. . . .

c. You must have evidence for p (reason to believe p). When you guessed which tosses of the coin would be heads, you had no reason to believe that your guesses would be correct, so you did not *know*. But after you watched all the tosses and carefully observed which way the coin tossed each time, then you knew. You had the evidence of your senses—as well as of people around you, and photographs if you wished to take them— that this throw was heads, that one tails, and so on. Similarly, when you predict on the basis of tonight's red sunset that tomorrow's weather will be fair, you don't yet *know* that your prediction will be borne out by the facts; you have some reason (perhaps) to believe it, but you cannot be sure. But tomorrow when you go outdoors and see for yourself what the weather is like, you do know for sure; when tomorrow comes you have the full evidence before you, which you do not yet have tonight. Tomorrow "the evidence is in"; tonight, it is not knowledge but only an "educated guess."

[*Problem*] This, then, is our third requirement—evidence. But at this point our troubles begin. How much evidence must there be? "Some evidence" won't suffice as an answer: there may be *some* evidence that tomorrow will be sunny, but you don't yet know it. How about "all the evidence that is available"? But this won't do either; all the evidence that is now available may not be enough. All the evidence that is now available is far from sufficient to enable us to know whether there are conscious beings on other planets. We just don't know, even after we have examined all the evidence at our disposal.

How about "enough evidence to give us *good reason* to believe it"? But how much evidence is this? I may have known someone for years and found him to be scrupulously honest during all that time; by virtually any criterion, this would constitute good evidence that he will be honest the next time—and yet he may not be; suppose that the next time he steals someone's wallet. I had good reason to believe that he would remain honest, but nevertheless I didn't *know* that he would remain honest, for it was not true. We are all familiar with cases in which someone had good reason to believe a proposition that nevertheless turned to be false.

What then *is* sufficient? We are now tempted to say, "Complete evidence—all the evidence there could ever be—the works, everything." But if we say this, let us notice at once that there are very few propositions whose truth we can claim to know. Most of those propositions that in daily life we claim to know without the slightest hesitation we would *not* know according to this criterion. For example, we say, "I know that if I were to let go of this pencil, it would fall," and we don't have the slightest hesitation about it; but although we may have excellent evidence (pencils and other objects have always fallen when let go), we don't have *complete* evidence, for we have not yet observed the outcome of letting go of it *this* time. To take an even more obvious case, we say, "I know that there is a book before me now," but we have not engaged in every possible observation that would be relevant to determining the truth of this statement: We have not examined the object (the one we take to be a book) from *all* angles (and since there are an infinite number of angles, who could?), and even if we have looked at it steadily for half an hour, we have not done so for a hundred hours, or a million; and yet it would *seem* (though some have disputed this, as we shall see) that if one observation provides evidence, a thousand observations should provide more evidence—and when could the accumulation of evidence end? . . .

We might, nevertheless, stick to our definition and say that we really do *not* know most of the propositions that in daily life we claim to know: Perhaps I don't *know* that this is a book before me, that I am now indoors and not outdoors, that I am now reading sentences written in the English language, or that there are any other people in the world. But this is a rather astounding claim and needs to be justified. We are all convinced that we know these things: We act on them every day of our lives, and if we were asked outside a philosophy classroom whether we knew them, we would say "yes" without hesitation. Surely we cannot accept a definition of "know" that would practically define knowledge out of existence? But if not, what alternative have we?

"Perhaps we don't have to go so far as to say 'all the evidence,' 'complete evidence,' and so on. All we have to say is that we must have *adequate* evidence." But when is the evidence adequate? Is anything less than "all the evidence there could

ever be" adequate? "Well, adequate for enabling us to know." But this little addition to our definition lands us in a circle. We are trying to define "know," and we cannot in doing so employ the convenient phrase "enough to enable us to know"—for the last word in this definition is the very one we are trying to define. But once we have dropped the phrase "to know," we are left with our problem once more: How much evidence is adequate evidence? Is it adequate when anything less than *all* the evidence is in? If not all the evidence is in, but only 99.99 percent of it, couldn't that .01 per cent go contrary to the rest of it and require us to conclude that the proposition might not be true after all, and that therefore we didn't know it? Surely it has happened often enough that a statement that we thought we knew, perhaps even would have staked our live on, turned out in the end to be false, or just doubtful. But in that case we didn't really *know* it after all: The evidence was good, even overwhelming, but yet not good enough, not really adequate, for it was not enough to guarantee the truth of the proposition. Can we know p with anything less than *all* the evidence there ever could be for p?

II. Strong and Weak Senses of "Know"

[*Disputes About Knowing*] In daily life we say we know—not just believe or surmise, but *know*—that heavier-than-air objects fall, that snow is white, that we can read and write, and countless other things. If someone denies this, and no fact cited by the one disputant suffices to convince the other, we may well suspect that there is a verbal issue involved: in this case, that they are operating on two different meanings of "know," because they construe the third requirement—the evidence requirement—differently.

[*Case 1*] Suppose I say, "There is a bookcase in my office," and someone challenges this assertion. I reply, "I *know* that there is a bookcase in my office. I put it there myself, and I've seen it there for years. In fact, I saw it there just two minutes ago when I took a book out of it and left the office to go into the classroom." Now suppose we both go to my office, take a look, and there is the bookcase, exactly as before. "See, I *knew* it was here," I say. "Oh no," he replies, "you *believed with good reason* that it was still there, because you had seen it there often before and you didn't see or hear anyone removing it. But you didn't *know* it was there when you said it, for at that moment you were in the classroom and not in your office.

At this point, I may reply, "But I did know it was there, even when I said it. I knew it because (1) *I believed it*, (2) *I had good grounds on which to base the belief*, and (3) *the belief was true*. And I would call it knowledge whenever these three conditions are fulfilled. This is the way we use the word 'know' every day of our lives. One knows those true propositions that one believes with good reason. And when I said the bookcase was still in my office, I was uttering one of those propositions."

But now my opponent may reply, "But you still didn't know it. You had good reason to say it, I admit, for you had not seen or heard anyone removing it. You had good reason, but not *sufficient* reason. The evidence you gave was still compatible with your statement being false—and if it was false, you of course did not *know* that it was true. [*Case* 2] Suppose that you had made your claim to knowledge, and I had denied your claim, and we had both gone into your office, and to your great surprise (and mine too) the bookcase was no longer there. Could you *then* have claimed to know that it was still there?"

"Of course not. The falsity of a statement always invalidates the claim to know it. If the bookcase had not been there, I would not have been entitled to say that I knew it was there; my

claim would have been mistaken."

"Right—it would have been mistaken. But now please note that the only difference between the two cases is that in the first case the bookcase was there and in the second case it wasn't. *The evidence in the two cases was exactly the same.* You had exactly the same reason for saying that the bookcase was still there in the *second* case (when we found it missing) that you did in the *first* case (when we found it still there). And since you—as you yourself admit—didn't know it in the second case, you couldn't have known it in the first case either. You believed it with good reason, but you didn't *know* it."

[*Solution*] Here my opponent may have scored an important point; he may have convinced me that since I admittedly didn't know in the second case I couldn't have known in the first case either. But here I may make an important point in return: "My belief was the same in the two cases; the evidence was the same in the two cases (I had seen the bookcase two minutes before, had heard or seen no one removing it). The only difference was that in the first case the bookcase was there and in the second case it wasn't (*p* was true in the first case, false in the second). But *this doesn't show that I didn't know* in the first case. What it does show is that *although I might have been mistaken, I wasn't mistaken*. Had the bookcase not been there, I couldn't have claimed to know that it was; but since the bookcase in fact *was* still there, I *did* know, although (on the basis of the evidence I had) I *might* have been mistaken."

"Yes, it turned out to be true—you were lucky. But as we both agree, a lucky guess isn't the same as knowledge."

"But this wasn't just a lucky guess. I had excellent reasons for believing that the bookcase was still there. So the evidence requirement was fulfilled."

"No, it wasn't. You had good reason, excellent reason, but not *sufficient* reason—both times—for believing that the bookcase was still there. But in the second case it wasn't there, so you didn't know; therefore, in the first case where your evidence was *exactly the same,* you didn't know either; you just believed it with good reason, but that wasn't enough: your reason wasn't sufficient, and so you didn't *know*."

Now the difference in the criterion of knowing between the two disputants begins to emerge. According to me, I did know *p* in the first case because my belief was based on excellent evidence and was also true. According to my opponent, I did not know *p* in the first case because my evidence was still less than complete—I wasn't in the room seeing or touching the bookcase when I made the statement. It seems, then, that I am operating with a less demanding definition of "know" than he is. I am using "know" in the *weak* sense, in which I know a proposition when I believe it, have good reason for believing it, and it is true. But he is using "know" in a more demanding sense: He is using it in the *strong* sense, which requires that in order to know a proposition, it must be true, I must believe it, and I must have absolutely *conclusive* evidence in favor of it.

[*Examples*] Let us contrast these two cases:

Suppose that after a routine medical examination the excited doctor reports to me that the X-ray photographs show that I have no heart. I should tell him to get a new machine. I should be inclined to say that the fact that I have a heart is one of the few things that I can count on as absolutely certain. I can feel it beat. I know it's there. Furthermore, how could my blood circulate if I didn't have one? Suppose that later on I suffer a chest injury and undergo a surgical operation. Afterwards the astonished surgeons solemnly declare that they searched my chest cavity and found

no heart, and that they made incisions and looked about in other likely places but found it not. They are convinced that I am without a heart. They are unable to understand how circulation can occur or what accounts for the thumping in my chest. But they are in agreement and obviously sincere, and they have clear photographs of my interior spaces. What would be my attitude? Would it be to insist that they were all mistaken? I think not. I believe that I should eventually accept their testimony and the evidence of the photographs. I should consider to be false what I now regard as an absolute certainty. [When I say I know I have a heart, I know it in the weak sense.]

Suppose that as I write this paper someone in the next room were to call out to me, "I can't find an ink-bottle; is there one in the house?" I should reply, "Here is an ink-bottle." If he said in a doubtful tone, "Are you sure? I looked there before," I should reply, "Yes, I know there is; come and get it."

Now could it turn out to be false that there is an ink-bottle directly in front of me on this desk? Many philosophers have thought so. They would say that many things could happen of such a nature that if they did happen it would be proved that I am deceived. I agree that many extraordinary things could happen, in the sense that there is no logical absurdity in the supposition. It could happen that when I next reach for this ink-bottle my hand should seem to pass *through* it and I should not feel the contact of any object. It could happen that in the next moment the ink-bottle will suddenly vanish from sight; or that I should find myself under a tree in the garden with no ink-bottle about; or that one or more persons should enter this room and declare with apparent sincerity that they see no ink-bottle on this desk; or that a photograph taken now of the top of the desk should clearly show all of the objects on it except the ink-bottle. Having admitted that these things *could happen*, am I compelled to admit that if they did happen, then it would be proved that there is no ink-bottle here *now?* Not at all. I could say that when my hand seemed to pass through the ink-bottle I should *then* be suffering from hallucination; that if the ink-bottle suddenly vanished, it would have miraculously ceased to exist; that the other persons were conspiring to drive me mad, or were themselves victims of remarkable concurrent hallucinations; that the camera possessed some strange flaw or that there was trickery in developing the negative: . . . Not only do I not *have* to admit that those extraordinary occurrences would be evidence that there is no ink-bottle here; the fact is that I *do not admit* it. There is nothing whatever that could happen in the next moment or the next year that would by me be called *evidence* that there is not an ink-bottle here now. No future experience or investigation could prove to me that I am mistaken. Therefore, if I were to say, "I know that there is a ink-bottle here," I should be using "know" in the strong sense.[2]

It is in the weak sense that we use the word "know" in daily life, as when I say I know that I have a heart, that if I let go of this piece of chalk it will fall, that the sun will rise tomorrow, and so on. I have excellent reason (evidence) to believe all these things, evidence so strong that (so we say) it amounts to certainty. And yet there are events that could conceivably occur which, if they did occur, would cast doubt on the beliefs or even show them to be false. . . .

[2]Norman Malcolm, "Knowledge and Belief," in *Knowledge and Certainty*, pp. 66–68.

III. Argument Against Skepticism

[*Skepticism*] But the philosopher is apt to be more concerned with "know" in the strong sense. He wants to inquire whether there are any propositions that we can know without the shadow of a doubt will never be proved false, or even rendered dubious to the smallest degree. "You can say," he will argue, "and I admit that it would be good English usage to say, that you know that you have a heart and that the sun is more than 90 million miles from the earth. But you don't know it until you have absolutely conclusive evidence, and you must admit that the evidence you have, while very strong, is not conclusive. So I shall say, using 'know' in the strong sense, that you do not know these propositions. I want then to ask what propositions can be known in the strong sense, the sense that puts the proposition forever past the possibility of doubt."

And on this point many philosophers have been quite skeptical; they have granted few if any propositions whose truth we could know in the strong sense. . . . Such a person is a *skeptic*. We claim (he says) to know many things about the world, but in fact none of these propositions can be known for certain. What are we to say of the skeptic's position?

[*Criticism*] Let us first note that in the phrase "know for certain" the "for certain" is redundant—how can we know except for certain? If it is less than certain, how can it be knowledge? We do, however, use the word "certain" ambiguously: (1) Sometimes we say "I am certain," which just means that I have a feeling of certainty about it—"I feel certain that I locked the door of the apartment"—and of course the feeling of certainty is no guarantee that the statement is true. People have very strong feelings of certainty about many propositions that they have no evidence for at all, particularly if they want to believe them or are consoled by believing them. The phrase "feeling certain," then, refers simply to a psychological state, whose existence in no way guarantees that what the person feels certain about is true. But (2) sometimes when we say "I am certain" we mean that it *is* certain—in other words, that we *do* know the proposition in question to be true. This, of course, is the sense of "certain" that is of interest to philosophers (the first sense is of more interest to psychiatrists in dealing with patients). Thus we could reformulate our question, "Is anything certain?" or "Are any propositions certain?"

"I can well understand," one might argue, "how you could question some statements, even most statements. But if you carry on this merry game until you have covered *all* statements, you are simply mistaken, and I think I can show you why. You may see someone in a fog or in a bad light and not know (not be certain) whether he has a right hand. But don't you know that *you* have a right hand? There it is! Suppose I now raise my hand and say, 'Here is a hand.' Now you say to me, 'I doubt that there's a hand.' But what evidence do you want? What does your doubt consist of? You don't believe your eyes, perhaps? Very well, then come up and touch the hand. You still aren't satisfied? Then keep on looking at it steadily and touching it, photograph it, call in other people for testimony if you like. If after all this you still say it isn't certain, what more do you want? Under what conditions would you admit that it *is* certain, that you *do* know it? I can understand your doubt when there is some condition left unfulfilled, some test left uncompleted. At the beginning, perhaps you doubted that *if* you tried to touch my hand you would find anything there to touch; but then you did touch, and so you resolved *that* doubt. You resolved further doubts by calling in other people and so on. You performed all the relevant tests, and they turned out favorably. So now, at the end of the process, what is it that you doubt? Oh, I know what you

say: 'I still doubt that that's a hand.' But isn't this saying 'I doubt' now an empty formula? I can no longer attach any content to that so-called doubt, for there is nothing left to doubt; you yourself *cannot specify any further test that, if performed, would resolve your doubt.* 'Doubt' now becomes an empty word. You're not doubting now that *if* you raised your hand to touch mine, you would touch it, or that *if* Smith and others were brought in, they would also testify that this is a hand—we've already gone through all that. So what is it specifically that you doubt? What possible test is there the negative result of which you fear? I submit that there isn't any. You are confusing a situation in which doubt is understandable (*before* you made the tests) with the later situation in which it isn't, for it has all been dispelled. . . .

"But your so-called doubt becomes meaningless when there is nothing left to doubt—when the tests have been carried out and their results are all favorable. Suppose a physician examines a patient and says, 'It's probable that you have an inflamed appendix.' Here one can still doubt, for the signs may be misleading. So the physician operates on the patient, finds an inflamed appendix and removes it, and the patient recovers. *Now* what would be the sense of the physician's saying, 'It's *probable* that he had an inflamed appendix'? If seeing it and removing it made it only *probable*, what would make it certain? Or you are driving along and you hear a rapid regular thumping sound and you say, 'It's probable that I have a flat tire.' So far you're right; it's only probable—the thumping might be caused by something else. So you go out and have a look, and there is the tire, flat. You find a nail embedded in it, change the tire, and then resume your ride with no more thumping. Are you *now* going to say, 'It's merely *probable* that the car had a flat tire'? But if given all those conditions it would be merely probable, what in the world would make it certain? Can you describe to me the circumstances in which you would say it's certain? If you can't, then the phrase 'being certain' has no meaning as you are using it. You are simply using it in such a special way that it has no application at all, and there is no reason at all why anyone else should follow your usage. In daily life we have a very convenient and useful distinction between the application of the words 'probable' and 'certain.' We say appendicitis is probable *before* the operation, but when the physician has the patient's appendix visible before him on the operating table, now it's certain—that's just the kind of situation in which we apply the word 'certain,' as opposed to 'probable.' Now you, for some reason, are so fond of the word 'probable' that you want to use it for everything—you use it to describe *both* the preoperative and postoperative situations, and the word 'certain' is left

without any application at all. But this is nothing but a *verbal manipulation* on your part. You have changed nothing; you have only taken, as it were, two bottles with different contents, and instead of labeling them differently ('probable' and 'certain'), as the rest of us do, you put the same label ('probable') on both of them! What possible advantage is there in this? It's just verbal contrariness. And since you have pre-empted the word 'probable' to cover *both* the situations, we now have to devise a *different* pair of words to mark the perfectly obvious distinction between the situation *before* the surgery and the situation *during* the surgery—the same difference we previously marked by the words 'probable' and 'certain' until you used the word 'probable' to apply to both of them. What gain is there in this verbal manipulation of yours?". . .

GLOSSARY

APRIORI   Knowledge that is logically prior or independent of experience; usually opposed to a *a posteriori*, which applies to knowledge derived from our experience of the world.

AGNOSTICISM   A profession of ignorance, in particular the claim that it is impossible to conclusively demonstrate either God's existence or nonexistence.

APOLOGY   A defense.

CARTESIAN   An adjective describing Descartes' philosophy or that of his followers.

COUNTERBALANCING   A technique used by skeptics to negate a belief by balancing arguments or evidence against one another; a counterbalanced proposition means that one is justified in believing either the proposition or its negation.

COUNTERPOSSIBILITY   Any possible state of affairs that might count against a belief; a favorite technique of skeptics.

EPISTEMOLOGY   A theory of knowledge; that branch of philosophy dealing with the nature, sources, validity and limits of knowledge.

ESSENCE   That which makes a thing what it is; often contrasted with existence.

EVIDENCE   Proof or fact; that which is used to prove or support something. Often employed as a condition of knowledge.

FALLIBILITY   The making of mistakes.

FIDEISM   The view that truth is founded on faith, not on human reason.

JUSTIFICATION   To attribute right standing to a belief; negatively, to make a belief free from reproach.

PERFORMATIVE CONTRADICTION A contradiction between a stated philosophical position and an act that does not follow from it; in skepticism, the practice of assuming rational categories while denying them (either implicitly or explicitly) in argument.

PRAGMATISM The name originally assigned by Charles Sanders Peirce for a view of philosophy that holds that experience is that which brings satisfactory results; for pragmatists, truth is that which has practical value in our experience of life.

PYRRHONISM An adjective describing the Greek skeptic Pyrrho's practice of counterbalancing propositions.

SCHOLASTICISM Often used historically to refer to the entire medieval Christian movement in Western philosophy, dominated by various "schools" of thought; often characterized by the attempt to create a systematic defense of Christian belief.

SKEPTICISM\ The extreme philosophical position that we cannot know anything about anything; a more limited skepticism ("being skeptical") emphasizes human fallibility, and the usefulness of doubt in arriving at belief.

FOR FURTHER STUDY

Ayer, A.J. *The Problem of Knowledge*. London: Macmillan & Co., 1956.
Besides dealing in detail with the question of skepticism and certainty, Ayer examines the problems of perception, memory, and knowledge of other minds.

Chisholm, Roderick. *Theory of Knowledge*. 3d ed. Englewood Cliffs, N.J.: Prentice-Hall, 1989.
A brief, lucid presentation by the dean of American epistemologists. The first two chapters argue explicitly against skepticism.

Hamlyn, D.W. *The Theory of Knowledge*. Garden City, N.J.: Doubleday, 1970.
A comprehensive treatment exploring the origin and nature of all knowledge.

Hospers, John. *An Introduction to Philosophical Analysis*. Englewood Cliffs, N.J.: Prentice-Hall, 1967.
Students frequently remark that Hospers writes clearly and is easy to understand. This book covers all the basic issues.

Husserl, Edmund. *Cartesian Meditations: An Introduction to Phenomenology*. Translated by Doren Cairns. The Hague: Martinus Nijhoff, 1960.
Husserl returns philosophy to the *Meditations* of Descartes but with the agenda of phenomenology. This important book includes reflections on the significance of Descartes' project, as well as a phenomenological treatment of the problem of evidence and judgment.

Polanyi, M. *Personal Knowledge: Towards a Post-Critical Philosophy*. Chicago: University of Chicago Press, 1958.
Polyani argues that every act of knowing, including scientific knowing, requires a personal element, fusing the objective and the personal.

Unger, Peter. *Ignorance: A Case for Skepticism*. Oxford: Oxford University Press, 1975.
An influential defense of skepticism by a contemporary philosopher.

PART THREE

◆

SOURCES OF KNOWLEDGE AND TESTS OF TRUTH

Anyone who conducts an argument by appealing to
authority is not using his intelligence; he is just using
his memory."

LEONARDO DA VINCI

What are man's truths ultimately?
Merely his *irrefutable* errors.

FRIEDRICH NIETZSCHE

ORIENTATION

Having addressed in the previous chapter the question, "What is knowledge and how is it possible?" we turn now to the important questions of the sources of knowledge and the tests for truth. Where does genuine knowledge come from? Traditionally, philosophers in the Western tradition have claimed that there are at least four different sources of knowledge. Each has a special role to play in epistemology, but two have emerged as primary: empiricism and rationalism.

The question of the tests of truth is a question of validity: How can I know what beliefs are true? Traditionally, philosophers have relied on three tests of truth: correspondence, coherence, and utility. Each of these has something valuable to contribute, and may be thought of as complementary rather than as mutually exclusive.

The relationship between the sources of knowledge and the tests of truth is a close one. Empiricists have been apt to employ the correspondence test of truth, while rationalists have generally preferred the coherence test. Because the analysis of the sources of knowledge has implications for the way truth is tested, these two questions have been combined in this chapter.

THE SOURCES OF KNOWLEDGE

AUTHORITY AS A SOURCE OF KNOWLEDGE

Have you ever stopped to consider who "they" are? "They" show up in casual conversation, on television news programs, and in the daily newspaper. A friend may ask, "Have you heard what *they* are saying now about the dangerous effects of caffeine?" Someone else may state, "*They* advised me to take these three classes so I can be on track for graduation." Still another person may wonder what *they* are projecting will happen in Soviet-American relations. In each case, "they" is a reference to some **authority.**

Authorities are those presumed to have reliable knowledge in a given field. Thus scientists who study the effects of caffeine on the human body, your faculty advisor, and members of a prestigious international "think tank" may all qualify as authorities.

One of the most common ways to gain knowledge is to rely on the testimony of some expert authority. After all, who has the time to verify every single fact of life? Should I be required to run the caffeine tests myself? How would I go about doing such a thing, and what if I don't have the time? Have I studied the history of Soviet-American relations enough to be able to make an informed judgment? Am I confident that I know enough about graduation requirements to do without the guidance of my faculty advisors? It is obvious that we depend heavily on the knowledge accumulated in the various sciences, and upon the men and women (often unknown to us personally) whose experience is greater than our own. If we were required to verify everything we believe on our own, without benefit of the labor of others, it is clear that we would not get much of anything accomplished. This social aspect of knowledge underscores our dependence upon authorities, raising this fundamental question: Is it legitimate to accept the word of an acknowledged authority?

The answer to this question is yes—with certain important qualifications. Because of our personal and social limitations, we are dependent on the authority of others *when there is no other way to obtain the knowledge for ourselves.* For instance, you accept the word of your doctor when she gives a diagnosis of your illness, realizing that her special training has enabled her to make an informed judgment about your condition. For you to duplicate that special training in order to "know for yourself" is not only unnecessary, it may be impossible. For the same reason, on your own you may never be able to know what it is like to hit a game-winning home run in the ninth inning of a World Series game. However, it is possible to acquire such knowledge by listening to a television interview with Kirk Gibson, an "authority" who accomplished this feat in 1988.

For these reasons, authority can be a legitimate source of knowledge. But knowledge by authority has its dangers as well. We need to be sure that the person whose word we are accepting as authoritative is really an acknowledged authority in that particular field. It is relatively easy to check Kirk Gibson's credentials to testify about World Series experiences, but what if you heard him delivering a commercial "pitch" on the merits of Buick's automobile technology? Furthermore, how do you evaluate people debating health issues on a talk show? In these cases, can you be sure that "they" are persons of integrity, who are in a position to know more than you, having used the best research methods to arrive at their conclusions? Wouldn't we be wrong to accept the word of someone merely because of a television appearance?

In situations like this it is important that we do not give up our right to exercise independent judgment. One way to know that an authority is genuine is when the person does not object to an honest inquiry into her credentials. (If your doctor begins to get nervous when you inspect a degree certificate on the wall, you may have cause to get nervous as well!) Often when guest speakers are introduced to an audience, an impressive list of accomplishments is read off by another authority figure, lending credibility to the presentation that follows. Thus the testimony of others whose judgment we respect, as well as the agreement of other authorities, is grounds for accepting a person as an authority.

It is instructive to ask, "From what source did our authority gain her knowledge?" Asking this question helps us realize that authority is a secondary or col-

159

laborative source of knowledge. This is because the authority herself must have acquired her knowledge using a source other than authority, such as experience or reason. For instance, would you accept as your brain surgeon a person familiar with surgical procedures and capable of quoting famous surgeons, but who had never performed an operation? Obviously not. Appeals to authority, while valuable, must ultimately be supplemented by independent judgment sustained through reason or experience. If we surrender our own judgment to the "they" completely, we lose the ability to check spurious authorities, making ourselves victims.

SENSE EXPERIENCE AS A SOURCE OF KNOWLEDGE: EMPIRICISM

The word *empiricism* is derived from the Greek word *empeiria*, the Latin translation of which is *experiencia*, from which we get our English word *experience*. In its simplest formulation, empiricism is the theory that our sense experience—seeing, touching, hearing, smelling, tasting—provides us with reliable knowledge of the world. Philosophers who stress the importance of sense experience as a primary source of knowledge are called empiricists. Important empiricists in the history of philosophy include the British thinkers John Locke (1632–1704), George Berkeley (1685–1753), and David Hume (1711–1776).

Ask yourself: how do you know that water will freeze, forming ice? Surely it is because of your experience of seeing this happen, or the memory of its having happened in the past. Hence, your knowledge is the product of your sensory organs operating in conjunction with your memory.

In the history of philosophy, empiricism has been formulated in a number of different ways, some more extreme than others. For example, some empiricists have insisted that *all* knowledge, except for certain logical truths and mathematical principles, comes from experience. The British empiricist John Locke, generally considered the father of modern empiricism, held that the mind is a blank slate (*tabula rasa*), formed only by experience. In another famous image, Locke argued that the mind is like a piece of wax: in the same way that wax retains the impression of whatever is forced against it, so the mind registers images of the world.

Other empiricists, more radical still, have held that even the truths of mathematics (such as $2 + 2 = 4$) are merely highly confirmed generalizations drawn from experience. Concerned with the refutation of rationalism, the British philosophers John Stuart Mill (1806–1873) and A.J. Ayer (1910–), have argued this extreme position, but they have not had many followers.

Modern science, of course, is an empirical enterprise. The word *science*, from the Latin word *scire*, meaning "to know," may be thought of as an elaboration and refinement of our common perceptual knowledge. Stressing the importance of particular facts and the systematic arrangement of those facts, scientists methodically attempt to describe and explain our world. Key components of modern science include observation, hypothesis-making, and experimentation. American elementary and secondary education, built largely on the assumptions of **realism,** has tended to stress empirical science as being critically important. Consequently you may find yourself feeling more comfortable with empiricism as a source of knowledge than with rationalism, which will be discussed next. In Part 4 we will explore the nature and task of science and scientific methods, focusing on strengths as well as limitations.

Because knowledge from experience seems basic to a sound theory of knowledge, empiricism has been recognized by all but the most extreme rationalists to be a primary source of knowledge. A word of caution is in order, however. In and of themselves, facts are quite meaningless. They exhibit no pattern or relationship. A mere collection of facts is no more a science than a collection of stones is a house. It is the systematic arrangement of facts, or theories, that is important. Once we admit this, we must also be willing to admit that prejudice, emotion, personal expectations, and even gender differences may interfere with scientific objectivity, causing us to see in facts what we wish to see. This being the case, is it possible for empiricists to construct "theory-neutral" ways of knowing? Most philosophers would say no.

REASON AS A SOURCE OF KNOWLEDGE: RATIONALISM

Rationalism is the view that the human mind is sufficient in itself to discover truth by apprehending relations of ideas. Philosophers who stress the importance of reason or thought as the primary source of knowledge are called rationalists. Important rationalists in the history of philosophy include Plato (427–347 B.C.) and the "Continental rationalists," Descartes (1596–1650), Spinoza (1632–1677), and Leibniz (1646–1716).

In order to understand the rationalist position, it may be helpful to return to the theories of Descartes, highlighted in Part 2. As you might expect from someone whose dream it was to create a unified system of science derived from logical and mathematical principles, Descartes was more attracted by reason as a source of knowledge than he was by sense experience. This can be seen clearly in the second meditation in his *Meditations on First Philosophy*, where he performed what we might call a "thought experiment." Unlike empirical scientific experiments, which stress observation and facts, Descartes' thought experiment was merely a device for exploring the logical relationships between ideas. Thus, in his famous "experiment" with the wax, Descartes demonstrates that the "true wax" is *not* that which I can see, touch, taste, or smell, since when I place the wax near a fire all of these **secondary qualities** are not present. What are present are the **primary**

qualities of the wax, namely its extension, flexibility, and movability. *Thus the "real piece of wax" is not apprehended by the senses, but by reason alone.*

In its most extreme form, rationalism claims that we can know reality completely independent of sense experience, in an irrefutable way. (Long before Descartes, Plato had advanced this argument in the *Phaedo*.) This is in stark contrast to the British empiricists, who argue that reason could do no more than sort out and rearrange the raw sense materials provided by perception. The argument between the Continental rationalists and the British empiricists has continued for some 400 years, raising important questions along the way.

Digression: A priori Knowledge and the Analytic-Synthetic Distinction

One of these questions concerns a term we have previously encountered, *a priori* knowledge. Is there knowledge that is apprehended independently of experience? Following Plato and Descartes, rationalists have said yes, citing logical and mathematical truths that are not matters of fact but rather relations of ideas. For instance, philosophers are in general agreement that three laws of thinking are fundamental: the Principle of Identity (All A is A); the Principle of Noncontradiction (Not both A and not-A); and the Principle of Excluded Middle (Either A or Not-A). Aren't these laws evidence that the mind can know something apart from sense experience?

Empiricists respond that *a priori* knowledge of the kind found in logic and mathematics is purely formal and abstract. In technical terms, it is **analytic** rather than **synthetic.** Analytic truths do not extend our knowledge of the world, whereas synthetic truths do. Thus *a priori* knowledge, while valuable and important, has no real bearing on the nature of the world. Because logic is a purely formal science (as opposed to a factual science, like biology), it has nothing to do with the world in which we live. It is concerned with universal concepts, not particular facts. For this reason, logical truths do not extend our knowledge of the world; that is, they are not synthetic.

In the history of philosophy the analytic/synthetic distinction was to become very important, particularly in the work of the Prussian philosopher Immanuel Kant (1724–1804). Kant agreed with the empiricists that many *a priori* judgments were analytic, including mathematical and logical principles. For Kant, an analytic statement was one that merely spells out (or "unpacks") the subject of the statement. For example, the proposition "All triangles have three angles" merely analyzes or unpacks the concept of the subject term, *triangle*. Synthetic propositions, on the other hand, *add something* to what is contained in the concept of the subject term of the proposition. Thus, whereas "All bachelors are unmarried" is an analytic statement (since being unmarried is part of what it means to be a bachelor), "All bachelors are neurotic" is synthetic, since being neurotic is clearly *not* part of what we mean by bachelor. (Fortunately, this particular synthetic proposition is also false!)

The consequences of this for rationalism as a source of knowledge are profound. Accepting many of the legitimate insights of the empiricists (especially those of Hume, whose writing "awakened him from his dogmatic slumber"), Kant was highly critical of the rationalism that he himself had formerly held. It is certainly possible, he reasoned, to construct a rationalistic system of beliefs that is internally consistent, noncontradictory, *and completely unrelated to the world we live in!* The danger of extreme rationalism is that we shall do just that, precisely because correspondence to experience was not one of the criteria of system-building. In the history of philosophy, many such systems were constructed, often in opposition to one another. Obviously, not all of them can be correct. For instance, medieval philosophers, following Aristotle, theorized that the planets must have circular motions since (it was assumed) perfect motion is circular motion. These theorists built elaborate metaphysical systems, internally consistent, but built on false assumptions. Galileo and Johannes Kepler, working from sound scientific principles, discovered the laws of motion that proved them wrong. Such is the danger of rationalist deductive systems, constructed without an "experience check." Metaphysics, Kant argued, was doomed to go around in circles like this forever unless someone could set it on a different course. Kant saw himself as that person.

What if someone could discover *a priori* knowledge that *did* extend our knowledge of the world? This is precisely what Kant set out to show: the possibility of a **synthetic a priori** type of knowledge. In *The Critique of Pure Reason* (1781), Kant's guiding thesis is that the synthetic *a priori* judgment is not only possible, it is necessary if we are to escape the errors of both the British empiricists (whose conclusions had dead-ended in Hume's skepticism) and the Continental rationalists (whose conclusions resulted in speculative flights of fancy and the worst kind of dogmatism). In working out his famous "merger" of the best of empiricism with the best of rationalism, Kant set metaphysics on a totally different course, launching the equivalent of a "Copernican Revolution" in philosophy.

INTUITION AS A SOURCE OF KNOWLEDGE

"We hold these truths to be self-evident. . . ." Most Americans recognize these words from the opening to the Declaration of Independence, but few have ever thought of them as a philosophical statement as well as a political one. You may recall from Part Two that justifying beliefs requires evidence. Producing evidence in support of our beliefs is one of the most important acts we can do, whether it is in the courtroom, the classroom, or the boardroom. So what does it mean for a belief to be **self-evident?** Can some beliefs "carry with them their own justification," that is, supply their own evidence? Can you think of a belief that seemed self-evident to you?

Have you ever felt that you had "fallen in love at first sight?" Or perhaps, on meeting someone for the first time, you sensed that this person would become a trusted friend? How could you know these things? Reflecting on this question, you might respond that these experiences are not the kind that you really had to think about, "you just know them." Often when people speak of "just knowing something," they are referring to something they believe to be self-evident. They are appealing to **intuition** as a legitimate source of knowledge. Is it? Not surprisingly, philosophers have responded to this difficult question in a number of different ways; some are more enthusiastic about intuition than others. Before we look at some of these ways, let's be sure we know what intuition means.

Intuition, from the Latin word *inteuri* ("to look on"), may be defined as the ability to have direct, immediate knowledge of something without relying on the conscious use of reason or sense perception. In its most general sense, it may simply mean a direct, unmediated, privileged knowledge of one's own personhood. In its strongest sense intuition can mean a type of mystical experience that gives a person direct access to a higher way of knowledge.

There is good reason to believe that an element of intuition is present in all forms of knowledge. Since all knowledge is ultimately knowledge of and for someone, there is a personal element in all that we know. Perhaps this is best illustrated in the way we are aware of our own bodies. Have you ever attempted to walk through a door that someone else has opened, just before it was about to close? How did you know that you could fit through the ever-narrowing gap? You didn't stop to do a thought experiment to deduce the likelihood of your making it through the gap, and it is absurd to think that you would have to get out a yardstick to measure whether your body would fit! Your knowledge of your own body is direct and immediate, not requiring conscious thought or perceptual measurements. The French phenomenologist Merleau-Ponty (1908–1961) spoke of experiences like this as an awareness of one's "lived body." Your "lived body" is not just another object that exists in the world; it is rather that through which the world presents itself to you. You can misplace your pen, but you cannot misplace your body! Knowledge of your own body appears to be intuitional, since it is experienced as permanent presence, an "absolute here" that (contrary to Descartes, as we shall see in Part 5) cannot be distinguished from yourself.

The experience of the lived body is one manifestation of the broad, general sense of intuition, as the word is commonly used. Another example would be the kind of rapid insight that specialists often display in their field. One may think of intuition as a kind of "intellectual shortcut," available only to those who are expert in their field. Thus poets, scientists, and musicians frequently astound us with what appears to be a flash of insight that often leads to a work of genius. Mozart constantly amazed his friends with the frequency of these kinds of intuitions, as did Albert Einstein, with his tremendous powers of concentration.

Some philosophers have argued in favor of a stronger, more specific sense of intuition, claiming that there is an intuitional element present in artistic and religious experiences, and in our knowledge of good and evil as well. Religious people have often reported a "sense of the holy," the awe-ful and mysterious experience of God, which filled them with blank wonder and astonishment.[1] Similar experiences are reported by those who have been struck by the "feeling of the sublime," as they contemplated a work of art. (We will return to this theme in Part 10.) Perhaps you have listened to someone like Elie Wiesel, a surviver of the Nazi holocaust. Many who have listened to Wiesel find themselves silently aware of the reality of evil in the world, an intuition that comes as they contemplate what occurred in the death camps; others sense that, with Wiesel, they are in the presence of someone overwhelmingly good.

The French philosopher Henri Bergson (1859–1941) claimed that intuition was a separate and distinct kind of knowledge in which we advance beyond the need of symbols, grasping the heart of reality itself. Bergson attempted to construct a philosophical method for apprehending this reality, which he said presented itself as an ever changing stream or duration.[2]

Like authority, intuition is a secondary source of knowledge, valid when it is guided and checked by reason and sense experience. Apart from these checkpoints, intuition is apt to land us in a mystical nowhere-land, cut off from rational categories of explanation and incapable of expressing itself. Human intelligence seems to be constructed in such a way that intuitional experiences allow us access to hidden meanings which might otherwise be closed off to us, yet force us to adopt rational or empirical ways of explaining those same experiences. The solution is not to carelessly reject the use of intuition, but rather to make use of the insights it yields. To do this, intuition must align itself finally with reason and sense experience, resisting its urge to be complete in itself.

THE TESTS OF TRUTH

Pilate saith unto him, What is truth?
And when he had said this, he went out again . . .

John 18:38

---

[1]See Rudolph Otto's classic *The Idea of the Holy*, translated by John W. Harvey (London: Oxford University Press, 1923). See also William James', *Varieties of Religious Experience* (New York: Penguin Books, 1982).
[2]See Henri Bergson, *An Introduction to Metaphysics* (Boston: J.W. Luce & Co., 1912).

Like most politicians, Pilate was a busy man. He didn't have time to waste discussing questions of truth with an itinerant Jewish preacher. His comment to Jesus was a dismissive one, as he turned on his heel and went to attend to government business. He failed to take the question of truth seriously. Unlike Pilate, the philosopher must take the question seriously.

The problem of truth has always been central to philosophy. The ancient pre-Socratic philosophers tried to discover the real nature of things behind appearances. Plato, learning from them, divided the "True World" from the world of appearances. The British empiricists and the Continental rationalists, divided though they were on many issues, were in agreement that there was such a thing as truth, and that their preferred method of philosophy could secure it.

More recently, the question of truth has shifted, becoming more explicitly epistemological and less metaphysical. Why are certain beliefs true? How can we know which ones are true and which ones are false? Rejecting tradition, feeling, instinct, and bare intuition as unreliable guides to the true, philosophers have set forth various theories of truth. We will now examine the three most prominent theories, briefly weighing the strengths and weaknesses of each. Later, you may read representative selections from each of these perspectives, as well as a Contemporary Perspectives section that addresses "the politics of truth."

THE CORRESPONDENCE THEORY OF TRUTH

The correspondence theory is the view that truth is a function of our language such that it is present when our statements and beliefs correspond with actual facts, and false when they fail to correspond. This view purports to be very close to what the word *truth* means in everyday language. For instance, if I say "The cat is on the mat," my statement is true if and only if the cat is actually on the mat. If no cat is there, my statement must be false. According to this theory, when we say that a person has acquired truth, we mean that the person's beliefs match up with the facts of the situation. A person is in error when his or her beliefs fail to match the facts of the case.

Suppose I were to say, "the Hudson River flows from north to south," or "Yonkers is north of New York City." According to the correspondence theory, these statements would be true not because they might happen to agree with previous statements I have made, or because they lead to good results when I believe them; they are true purely because they correspond with the physical geography of New York state, which exists independently of any beliefs or persons who hold beliefs!

The view that objects of sense experience exist independently of our minds is called realism. This position contrasts sharply with **idealism,** which holds that reality is mind-dependent. Whereas most idealists hold to some version of the coherence theory, realists tend to be correspondence theorists. This is because they believe that our beliefs are irrelevant when assessing the truthfulness of propositions. To a realist, it makes no difference whether I am inclined to believe or disbelieve the proposition "Yonkers is north of New York City." It is still a true statement; my belief in it cannot make it more true, nor can my disbelief make it false.

Critics of the correspondence theory point out that there are serious problems in comparing our ideas with reality. For instance, suppose that I really believe that my pen is black. I express this belief in a proposition, "My pen is black." According to the correspondence theory, in order for me to know that this proposition is true, I would have to somehow check it against reality, which is impossible, since all I can know is the world of my own experience. How can I step outside of my own consciousness to verify the color of the pen, since the pen's color depends in some way on my consciousness?

Furthermore, critics point out, the correspondence theory naively assumes that our sense perceptions are perfectly reliable, showing the world exactly as it is. Is this the case? Or is it that our perceptions are modified by our network of beliefs, such that we always see what we wish to see? Imagine Ptolemy and Copernicus together on a hill watching the dawn. Ptolemy, of course believed that the earth was stationary, while Copernicus believed the sun to be stationary and the earth in motion. Do Ptolemy and Copernicus see the same thing? The impossibility of knowing objects apart from our perceptions of those objects has led some to consider the coherence theory of truth.

THE COHERENCE THEORY OF TRUTH

The coherence theory, abandoning the attempt to compare beliefs with reality, embraces consistency or harmony as its basic principle. A judgment is said to be true if and only if it is consistent with other judgments accepted as true. True judgments are those that comport well with other judgments; those not logically consistent are said to be false.

Coherence theorists have tended to be idealists. Some idealists, such as Plato, Hegel, and Bradley, have enlarged the theory of coherence to claim that a statement cannot properly be called true unless it fits with the one comprehensive system of all reality.

Defenders of the coherence theory argue that it is the only theory capable of accounting for "degrees of truth." Thinking back to our example of Ptolemy and Copernicus, we might ask, "How can a belief be accepted as true in one era and found to be false in another?" The coherence theorist is able to answer this question by making a distinction between partial and complete truth. Because only the system as a whole is absolutely true, an individual judgment separated from the system can be only partly true. Thus Ptolemy was partly right, from the perspective or his partial understanding of the system, and partly wrong. Copernicus, with his richer, more complete understanding of the system, was right as well. Yet even Copernicus, with his more complex, more richly funded understanding of the world, did not have a totally true view. Nor do we. The mark of the truth is its expansiveness and all-inclusiveness.

The coherence theory provides a strong sense of unity and consistency. Certainly we would not want to hold a belief that is inconsistent with other well-supported beliefs. Yet critics such as Bertrand Russell have pointed out that it is possible to construct false coherent systems as well as true ones. Why should we suppose that there is only one true, coherent body of belief in the universe? Furthermore, mathematicians, dreamers, and novelists can construct internally consistent worlds of belief that are completely unrelated to the world in which we live. In J.R.R. Tolkien's fantasy world dragons, orcs, wizards, hobbits, elves, and dwarves dwell together in a place called Middle Earth. Shall we say that Tolkien's tale is true? Simply because a judgment fits nicely with other judgments does not mean that it is true. Must we not at some point come back to the bedrock demand that our beliefs correspond to facts? Or is there an alternative theory that is more successful than either correspondence or coherence?

THE PRAGMATIC THEORY

Let us review what we have seen so far. Truth cannot simply be correspondence with reality, because our view of reality depends on our experience. On the other hand, the coherence theory seems unable to provide the "reality check" necessary to judge everyday experiences. Recognizing the difficulty of saying "the last word" on ultimate questions of reality, **pragmatism** suggests that we make the test of truth utility or workability. Does a given idea lead to satisfactory consequences?

Charles Sanders Peirce argued that the traditional discussions of truth were absurd because they left out those concrete situations that led to our being concerned with truth in the first place. Truth is neither a function between sentences and the world, nor is it a logical relationship between sentences. Rather, truth is the answer to the questions that we ask whenever uncertainty and doubt irritate us. Truth grows; in a word, truth is what would be eventually agreed to by a free, uncoerced community of inquirers. As Peirce put it, "The opinion which is fated to be ultimately agreed to by all who investigate, is what we mean by the truth."

William James suggested that the best test of truth is to merely ask yourself, "What would be the effect on my life if this idea were true?" In other words, what is the "cash value" of your belief? Truth is that upon which we are prepared to act. Truth is very much a product of this world, socially adjusted to the demands of human life. As James explains in a selection that follows, "True ideas are those we can assimilate, validate, corroborate, and verify. False ideas are those that we can not."

The American philosopher and educator John Dewey (1859–1952) stressed the need for truth to be demonstrated experimentally; believing truly leads to confirmation in the laboratory of life. This stress on action as opposed to static contemplation leads him to prefer the adverb *truly* to the noun *truth*, or the adjective *true*. This passage from Dewey's *Reconstruction in Philosophy* states clearly the pragmatic conception of truth:

> By their fruits shall *ye know* them. That which guides truly is true—demonstrated capacity for such guidance is precisely what is meant by truth. The adverb "truly" is more fundamental than either the adjective, true, or the noun, truth. An adverb expresses a way, a mode of acting. Now an idea or conception is a claim or injunction or plan to act in a certain way as the way to arrive at the clearing up of a specific situation. When the claim or pretension or plan is acted upon *it guides us truly or falsely;* it leads us to our end or away from it. Its active, dynamic function is the all-important thing about it, and in the quality of activity induced by it lies all its truth and falsity. The hypothesis that works is the *true* one; and *truth* is an abstract noun applied to the collection of cases, actual, foreseen, and desired, that receive confirmation in their works and consequences.[3]

Critics of pragmatism, however, point out that the test of "workability" is dangerous, since many false theories have worked successfully for hundreds of years. Ptolemy's geocentric theory is a case of point. As a hypothesis, it worked brilliantly for many years. Was it therefore true? If we call it "true for its age," have we not slipped into a dangerous form of **relativism** that poses serious problems? Although it may be the case that true beliefs tend to work in the long haul, is it necessarily the case that a belief that works must be true? Furthermore, if we believed things merely because of their beneficial consequences for us, wouldn't we wind up believing all kinds of fanciful things that had no sound basis in fact?

SUMMARY

Each of these theories of truth has able defenders, and each has particular applications; yet each seems to have limitations as well. The correspondence test has a wide range of applications in the sciences as well as in everyday life, but

---

[3]John Dewey, *Reconstruction in Philosophy* (Boston: Beacon Press, 1948), 156–157.

there are cases where it is difficult to know how to apply it. The coherence test and the pragmatic test have their uses as well. After reading the selections that follow, noting the strengths and weaknesses of each, you may emerge from your reading as a champion of one against the others. Or you may come to the conclusion that no one theory by itself can hope to exhaust the richness of the concept of truth. Perhaps the three tests of truth may be used together to supplement each other somehow. Can you think of ways to do this?

CHAPTER 17

PLATO

KNOWLEDGE AS THE SOUL'S RATIONAL ACTIVITY

In the history of philosophy those philosophers who have stressed the role of reason as the primary source of knowledge have been called rationalists. Common to all rationalists is a de-valuing of sense experience. René Descartes, whose *Meditations on First Philosophy* was featured in the previous chapter, is the best known rationalist of the modern era.

Although Descartes was a highly original thinker, we can trace his perspective on the theory of knowledge back to Plato (see Chapter 1 for a brief biography). Plato was a dualist, who made a sharp distinction between the soul and the body, and the activities of each. For Plato, the soul is pure, eternal and unchanging, the seat of intelligence and personhood. The body, on the contrary, he views as unintellectual and temporal, subject to change and corruption. Although the soul desires to know, it is hindered in its proper intellectual activity by the body, which attempts to distract soul by dragging it into the realm of "appearances," where sense perception is mistaken for knowledge. (Although Descartes replaced Plato's concept of soul with the more modern term *mind*, he retained Plato's rigid division of intellect and body, thus engendering the modern mind-body problem, which is the topic of Part 5.)

In this brief selection from the *Phaedo*,[1] an early dialogue recounting the last days of Socrates, Plato lays out his distinction between the unseen world and the

[1]From Plato, *Phaedo*, in *Dialogues of Plato*, 3d ed. translated by Benjamin Jowett (Oxford: Oxford Unversity Press, 1896).

seen world, and the relationship of soul and body to each. When the soul uses the body as an instrument of sense perception, it is subjected to a world characterized by change and flux. Because sense perception belongs to the metaphysically inferior realm of the seen and is characterized by change and flux, it can contribute nothing to genuine knowledge. The primary source of knowledge is the pure activity of reason, the soul addressing itself to the unchanging truths of the unseen world. The *Phaedo* established a rationalist tradition of devaluing sense experience that Aristotle and modern empiricists were later to reject.

KNOWLEDGE AS THE SOUL'S RATIONAL ACTIVITY

And were we not saying long ago that the soul when using the body as an instrument of perception, that is to say, when using the sense of sight or hearing or some other sense (for the meaning of perceiving through the body is perceiving through the senses)—were we not saying that the soul too is then dragged by the body into the region of the changeable, and wanders and is confused; the world spins round her, and she is like a drunkard, when she touches change?

Very true.

But when returning into herself she reflects, then she passes into the other world, the region of purity, and eternity, and immortality, and unchangeableness, which are her kindred, and with them she ever lives, when she is by herself and is not let or hindered; then she ceases from her erring ways, and being in communion with the unchanging is unchanging. And this state of the soul is called wisdom?

That is well and truly said, Socrates, he replied.

And to which class is the soul more nearly alike and akin, as far as may be inferred from this argument, as well as from the preceding one?

I think, Socrates, that, in the opinion of everyone who follows the argument, the soul will be infinitely more like the unchangeable—even the most stupid person will not deny that.

And the body is more like the changing?

Yes.

Yet once more consider the matter in another light: When the soul and the body are united, then nature orders the soul to rule and govern, and the body to obey and serve. Now which of these two functions is akin to the divine? and which to the mortal? Does not the divine appear to you to be that which naturally orders and rules, and the mortal to be that which is subject and servant?

True.

And which does the soul resemble?

The soul resembles the divine, and the body the mortal—there can be no doubt of that, Socrates.

Then reflect, Cebes: of all which has been said is not this the conclusion?—that the soul is in the very likeness of the divine, and immortal, and intellectual, and uniform, and indissoluble, and unchangeable; and that the body is in the very likeness of the human, and mortal, and unintellectual, and multiform, and dissoluble, and changeable. Can this, my dear Cebes, be denied?

It cannot.

But if it be true, then is not the body liable to speedy dissolution? and is not the soul almost or altogether indissoluble?

Certainly.

Must we not, said Socrates, ask ourselves what that is which, as we imagine, is liable to be scattered, and about which we fear? and what again is that about which we have no fear? And then we may proceed further to inquire whether that which suffers dispersion is or is not of the nature of soul—our hopes and fears as to our own souls will turn upon the answers to these questions.

Very true, he said.

Now the compound or composite may be supposed to be naturally capable, as of being compounded, so also of being dissolved; but that which is uncompounded, and that only, must be, if anything is, indissoluble.

Yes; I should imagine so, said Cebes.

And the uncompounded may be assumed to be the same and unchanging, whereas the compound is always changing and never the same.

I agree, he said.

Then now let us return to the previous discussion. Is that idea or essence, which in the dialectical process we define as essence or true existence—whether essence of equality, beauty, or anything else—are these essences, I say, liable at times to some degree of change? or are they each of them always what they are, having the same simple self-existent and unchanging forms, not admitting of variation at all, or in any way, or at any time?

They must be always the same, Socrates, replied Cebes.

And what would you say of the many beautiful—whether men or horses or garments or any other things which are named by the same names and may be called equal or beautiful,—are they all unchanging and the same always, or quite the reverse? May they not rather be described as almost always changing and hardly ever the same, either with themselves or with one another?

The latter, replied Cebes; they are always in a state of change.

And these you can touch and see and perceive with the senses, but the unchanging things you can only perceive with the mind—they are invisible and are not seen?

That is very true, he said.

Well then, added Socrates, let us suppose that there are two sorts of existences—one seen, the other unseen.

Let us suppose them.

The seen is the changing, and the unseen is the unchanging?

That may be also supposed.

And, further, is not one part of us body, another part soul?

To be sure.

And to which class is the body more alike and akin?

Clearly to the seen—no one can doubt that.

And is the soul seen or not seen?

Not by man, Socrates.

And what we mean by 'seen' and 'not seen' is that which is or is not visible to the eye of man?

Yes, to the eye of man.

And is the soul seen or not seen?

Not seen.

Unseen then?

Yes.

Then the soul is more like to the unseen, and the body to the seen?

That follows necessarily, Socrates.

CHAPTER 18

JOHN LOCKE

KNOWLEDGE AS SENSE EXPERIENCE

John Locke (1632–1704), British empiricist and moral and political philosopher, lived during a turbulent period in English history. His father, an attorney, fought on the parliamentary side during the rebellion against Charles I. Locke attended Oxford University and later taught philosophy and classics there. While at Oxford, Locke became acquainted with many of the important figures in the developing new sciences, including Robert Boyle, from whom he learned much about empirical methods, and Thomas Sydenham, who sparked his interest in medicine.

Locke was more than a thinker about issues in politics, science, medicine, and religion; he was a man of action as well. He held numerous government posts, and eventually became secretary and personal physician to Lord Shaftesbury. When Shaftesbury became leader of the opposition to the Stuarts, Locke came under suspicion of treason and was forced to flee to Holland in 1682. While there, he worked on a plan to set William of Orange on the throne of England. Locke also wrote his *Essay Concerning Human Understanding*, which became one of the most influential works ever written in epistemology. In the fall of 1688 the Glorious Revolution was accomplished, and Locke returned to England the following year, escorting the princess of Orange, who later became Queen Mary.

All of Locke's writings came as responses to the events going on around him. His *Two Treatises of Government*, forged during the heat of the struggle against the monarchy, provided the philosophic rationale for revolution that Thomas Jefferson and the American revolutionaries would later rely on.

174

In addition to the *Essay* and the *Two Treatises*, both published in 1690, Locke also wrote *Some Thoughts Concerning Education* (1693) and *The Reasonableness of Christianity* (1695), published anonymously. After being in poor health for several years, he died on October 28, 1704, while a friend was reading the Psalms to him. This same friend would later write of Locke, "His death was like his life, truly pious, yet natural, easy and unaffected."

The *Essay Concerning Human Understanding* had its origin in a remarkable conversation Locke had with some of his friends, wherein they determined that before they could reasonably hope to make much progress in complex metaphysical topics, they must first inquire into what the understanding can know, and what it cannot hope to know.[1] Locke viewed the *Essay* as a restoration of common sense in philosophy. Rejecting Descartes' deductive method along with his dream of unified sciences founded on clear and distinct ideas known only to reason, Locke insisted on an inductive method which stressed generalizations drawn from experience. This emphasis on the limits of human knowledge, modesty in philosophical endeavors, and the need for common sense became hallmarks of modern empiricism.

The *Essay* is built on a single premise: All knowledge is ultimately derived from sense experience. Speaking back to Plato as well as to Descartes, Locke argued that there are no innate ideas, born into the mind. Locke rejected the Platonic notion of an idea as a timeless, eternal archetype or form, of which existing things are imperfect copies. Similarly, he rejected Descartes' claim that the ideas of God, self, and matter can be known by reason directly, without any appeal to experience. Instead, ideas are simply objects of the understanding, "the immediate object of perception, thought, or understanding."

Following this negative argument, Locke presented his positive argument on the origin of ideas. There are two sources for our ideas: sensation, which furnishes the mind with sense data; and reflection, which furnishes the mind with ideas of its own operation. In a famous image, he described the mind itself as "white paper, void of all characters, without any ideas." The "furnishings of the mind," then, all come from experience.

Knowledge as Sense Experience

Introduction

1. Since it is the *understanding* that sets man above the rest of sensible beings, and gives him all the advantage and dominion which he has over them, it is certainly a subject, even for its nobleness, worth our labour to inquire into. The understanding, like the eye, whilst it makes us see and perceive all other things, takes no notice of itself; and it requires art and pains to set it at a

[1]From John Locke, *An Essay Concerning Human Understanding* (London: E. Holt, 1689).

distance and make it its own object. But whatever be the difficulties that lie in the way of this inquiry, whatever it be that keeps us so much in the dark to ourselves, sure I am that all the light we can let in upon our minds, all the acquaintance we can make with our own understandings, will not only be very pleasant, but bring us great advantage in directing our thoughts in the search of other things.

2. This, therefore, being my purpose—to inquire into the original, certainty, and extent of *human knowledge,* together with the grounds and degrees of *belief, opinion,* and *assent*—I shall not at present meddle with the physical consideration of the mind, or trouble myself to examine wherein its essence consists, or by what motions of our spirits or alterations of our bodies we come to have any *sensation* by our organs, or any *ideas* in our understandings, and whether those ideas do in their formation, any or all of them, depend on matter or not. These are speculations which, however curious and entertaining, I shall decline, as lying out of my way in the design I am now upon. It shall suffice to my present purpose to consider the discerning faculties of a man, as they are employed about the objects which they have to do with. And I shall imagine I have not wholly misemployed myself in the thoughts I shall have on this occasion, if, in this historical, plain method, I can give any account of the ways whereby our understandings come to attain those notions of things we have, and can set down any measures of the certainty of our knowledge, or the grounds of those persuasions which are to be found amongst men, so various, different, and wholly contradictory and yet asserted somewhere or other with such assurance and confidence that he that shall take a view of the opinions of mankind, observe their opposition, and at the same time consider the fondness and devotion wherewith they are embraced, the

resolution and eagerness wherewith they are maintained may perhaps have reason to suspect that either there is no such thing as truth at all, or that mankind hath no sufficient means to attain a certain knowledge of it.

3. It is therefore worthwhile to search out the bounds between opinion and knowledge; and examine by what measures, in things whereof we have no certain knowledge, we ought to regulate our assent and moderate our persuasion. In order whereunto I shall pursue this following method:—

First, I shall inquire into the original of those *ideas,* notions, or whatever else you please to call them, which a man observes, and is conscious to himself he has in his mind; and the ways whereby the understanding comes to be furnished with them.

Secondly, I shall endeavour to show what *knowledge* the understanding hath by those ideas; and the certainty, evidence, and extent of it.

Thirdly, I shall make some inquiry into the nature and grounds of *faith* or *opinion:* whereby I mean that assent which we give to any proposition as true, of whose truth yet we have not certain knowledge. And here we shall have occasion to examine the reasons and degrees of *assent.*

4. If by this inquiry into the nature of the understanding, I can discover the powers thereof; how far they reach; to what things they are in any degree proportionate; and where they fail us, I suppose it may be of use to prevail with the busy mind of man to be more cautious in meddling with things exceeding its comprehension; to stop when it is at the utmost extent of its tether; and to sit down in a quiet ignorance of those things which, upon examination, are found to be beyond the reach of our capacities. We should not then perhaps be so forward, out of an affectation of an universal knowledge, to raise questions, and perplex ourselves and others with dis-

putes about things to which our understandings are not suited, and of which we cannot frame in our minds any clear or distinct perceptions, or whereof (as it has perhaps too often happened) we have not any notions at all. If we can find out how far the understanding can extend its view; how far it has faculties to attain certainty, and in what cases it can only judge and guess, we may learn to content ourselves with what is attainable by us in this state.

5.   For though the comprehension of our understandings comes exceeding short of the vast extent of things, yet we shall have cause enough to magnify the bountiful Author of our being for that proportion and degree of knowledge he has bestowed on us, so far above all the rest of the inhabitants of this our mansion. Men have reason to be well satisfied with what God hath thought fit for them, since he hath given them . . . whatsoever is necessary for the conveniences of life and information of virtue; and has put within the reach of their discovery the comfortable provision for this life, and the way that leads to a better. How short soever their knowledge may come of an universal or perfect comprehension of whatsoever is, it yet secures their great concernments that they have light enough to lead them to the knowledge of their Maker and the sight of their own duties. Men may find matter sufficient to busy their heads and employ their hands with variety, delight, and satisfaction, if they will not boldly quarrel with their own constitution, and throw away the blessings their hands are filled with because they are not big enough to grasp everything. We shall not have much reason to complain of the narrowness of our minds if we will but employ them about what may be of use to us, for of that they are very capable. And it will be an unpardonable, as well as childish, peevishness if we undervalue the advantages of our knowledge, and neglect to improve it to the ends for which it was given us because there are some things that are set out of the reach of it. It will be no excuse to an idle and untoward servant who would not attend his business by candle light to plead that he had not broad sunshine. The Candle that is set up in us shines bright enough for all our purposes. The discoveries we can make with this ought to satisfy us; and we shall then use our understandings right, when we entertain all objects in that way and proportion that they are suited to our faculties, and upon those grounds they are capable of being proposed to us; and not peremptorily or intemperately require demonstration, and demand certainty, where probability only is to be had, and which is sufficient to govern all our concernments. If we will disbelieve everything, because we cannot certainly know all things, we shall do much what as wisely as he who would not use his legs, but sit still and perish, because he had no wings to fly.

6.   When we know our own strength, we shall the better know what to undertake with hopes of success; and when we have well surveyed the *powers* of our own minds, and made some estimate what we may expect from them, we shall not be inclined either to sit still, and not set our thoughts on work at all, in despair of knowing anything; nor on the other side, question everything, and disclaim all knowledge, because some things are not to be understood. It is of great use to the sailor to know the length of his line, though he cannot with it fathom all the depths of the ocean. It is well he knows that it is long enough to reach the bottom at such places as are necessary to direct his voyage, and caution him against running upon shoals that may ruin him. Our business here is not to know all things, but those which concern our conduct. If we can find out those measures, whereby a rational creature, put in that state in which man is in this

world, may and ought to govern his opinions, and actions depending thereon, we need not to be troubled that some other things escape our knowledge.

7.   This was that which gave the first rise to this *Essay* concerning the understanding. For I thought that the first step towards satisfying several inquiries the mind of man was very apt to run into was to take a survey of our own understandings, examine our own powers, and see to what things they were adapted. Till that was done I suspected we began at the wrong end, and in vain sought for satisfaction in a quiet and sure possession of truths that most concerned us, whilst we let loose our thoughts into the vast ocean of Being; as if all that boundless extent were the natural and undoubted possession of our understandings wherein there was nothing exempt from its decisions, or that escaped its comprehension. Thus men, extending their inquiries beyond their capacities, and letting their thoughts wander into those depths where they can find no sure footing, it is no wonder that they raise questions and multiply disputes, which, never coming to any clear resolution, are proper only to continue and increase their doubts, and to confirm them at last in perfect scepticism. Whereas, were the capacities of our understandings well considered, the extent of our knowledge once discovered, and the horizon found which sets the bounds between the enlightened and dark parts of things, between what is and what is not comprehensible by us, men would perhaps with less scruple acquiesce in the avowed ignorance of the one, and employ their thoughts and discourse with more advantage and satisfaction in the other.

8.   Thus much I thought necessary to say concerning the occasion of this Inquiry into human Understanding. But, before I proceed on to what I have thought on this subject, I must here

in the entrance beg pardon of my reader for the frequent use of the word *idea*, which he will find in the following treatise. It being that term which, I think, serves best to stand for whatsoever is the *object* of the understanding when a man thinks, I have used it to express whatever is meant by *phantasm, notion, species,* or *whatever it is which the mind can be employed about in thinking,* and I could not avoid frequently using it.

I presume it will be easily granted me, that there are such *ideas* in men's minds: everyone is conscious of them in himself; and men's words and actions will satisfy him that they are in others.

Our first inquiry then shall be how they come into the mind.

No Innate Speculative Principles

1.   It is an established opinion amongst some men, that there are in the understanding certain *innate principles;* some primary notions, characters, as it were stamped upon the mind of man, which the soul receives in its very first being, and brings into the world with it. It would be sufficient to convince unprejudiced readers of the falseness of this supposition, if I should only show (as I hope I shall in the following parts of this Discourse) how men, barely by the use of their natural faculties, may attain to all the knowledge they have, without the help of any innate impressions; and may arrive at certainty, without any such original notions or principles. For I imagine any one will easily grant that it would be impertinent to suppose the ideas of colours innate in a creature to whom God hath given sight, and a power to receive them by the eyes from external objects: and no less unreasonable would it be to attribute several truths to the impressions of nature, and innate characters, when we may observe in ourselves faculties fit to

attain as easy and certain knowledge of them as if they were originally imprinted on the mind.

But because a man is not permitted without censure to follow his own thoughts in the search of truth when they lead him ever so little out of the common road, I shall set down the reasons that made me doubt of the truth of that opinion, as an excuse for my mistake, if I be in one, which I leave to be considered by those who, with me, dispose themselves to embrace truth wherever they find it.

2. There is nothing more commonly taken for granted than that there are certain *principles*, both *speculative* and *practical*, (for they speak of both), universally agreed upon by all mankind: which therefore, they argue, must needs be the constant impressions which the souls of men receive in their first beings, and which they bring into the world with them, as necessarily and really as they do any of their inherent faculties.

3. This argument, drawn from universal consent, has this misfortune in it, that if it were true in matter of fact that there were certain truths wherein all mankind agreed, it would not prove them innate, if there can be any other way shown how men may come to that universal agreement in the things they do consent in, which I presume may be done.

4. But, which is worse, this argument of universal consent, which is made use of to prove innate principles, seems to me a demonstration that there are none such: because there are none to which all mankind give an universal assent. I shall begin with the speculative, and instance in those magnified principles of demonstration, 'Whatsoever is, is,' and 'It is impossible for the same thing to be and not to be', which, of all others, I think have the most allowed title to innate. These have so settled a reputation of maxims universally received that it will no doubt be thought strange if any one should seem to question it. But yet I take liberty to say, that these propositions are so far from having an universal assent, that there are a great part of mankind to whom they are not so much as known.

5. For, first, it is evident, that all children and idiots have not the least apprehension or thought of them. And the want of that is enough to destroy that universal assent which must needs be the necessary concomitant of all innate truths: it seeming to me near a contradiction to say, that there are truths imprinted on the soul which it perceives or understands not: imprinting, if it signify anything, being nothing else but the making certain truths to be perceived. For to imprint anything on the mind without the mind's perceiving it seems to me hardly intelligible. If therefore children and idiots have souls, have minds, with those impressions upon them, *they must unavoidably perceive them, and necessarily know and assent to these truths;* which since they do not, it is evident that there are no such impressions. For if they are not notions naturally imprinted, how can they be innate? and if they are notions imprinted, how can they be unknown? To say a notion is imprinted on the mind, and yet at the same time to say, that the mind is ignorant of it, and never yet took notice of it, is to make this impression nothing. No proposition can be said to be in the mind which it never yet knew, which it was never yet conscious of. For if any one may, then, by the same reason, all propositions that are true, and the mind is capable ever of assenting to, may be said to be in the mind, and to be imprinted: since, if any one can be said to be in the mind, which it never yet knew, it must be only because it is capable of knowing it; and so the mind is of all truths it ever shall know. Nay, thus truths may be imprinted on the mind which it never did, nor ever shall know; for a man may live long, and die at last in ignorance of many truths which his

mind was capable of knowing, and that with certainty. So that if the capacity of knowing be the natural impression contended for, all the truths a man ever comes to know will, by this account, be every one of them innate; and this great point will amount to no more, but only to a very improper way of speaking; which, whilst it pretends to assert the contrary, says nothing different from those who deny innate principles. For nobody, I think, ever denied that the mind was capable of knowing several truths. The capacity, they say, is innate; the knowledge acquired. But then to what end such contest for certain innate maxims? If truths can be imprinted on the understanding without being perceived, I can see no difference there can be between any truths the mind is *capable* of knowing in respect of their original: they must all be innate or all adventitious: in vain shall a man go about to distinguish them. He therefore that talks of innate notions in the understanding cannot (if he intend thereby any distinct sort of truths) mean such truths to be in the understanding as it never perceived, and is yet wholly ignorant of. For if these words 'to be in the understanding' have any propriety, they signify to be understood. So that to be in the understanding, and not to be understood, to be in the mind and never to be perceived, is all one as to say anything is and is not in the mind or understanding. If therefore these two propositions, 'Whatsoever is, is,' and 'It is impossible for the same thing to be and not to be,' are by nature imprinted, children cannot be ignorant of them: infants, and all that have souls, must necessarily have them in their understandings, know the truth of them, and assent to it.

6.   To avoid this it is usually answered that all men know and assent to them *when they come to the use of reason,* and this is enough to prove them innate. I answer:

7.   Doubtful expressions, that have scarce any significance, go for clear reasons to those who, being prepossessed, take not the pains to examine even what they themselves say. For, to apply this answer with any tolerable sense to our present purpose, it must signify one of these two things: either that as soon as men come to the use of reason these supposed native inscriptions come to be known and observed by them, or else, that the use and exercise of men's reason assists them in the discovery of these principles, and certainly makes them known to them.

8.   If they mean that by the use of reason men may discover these principles, and that this is sufficient to prove them innate, their way of arguing will stand thus, viz. that whatever truths reason can certainly discover to us, and make us firmly assent to, those are all naturally imprinted on the mind, since that universal assent, which is made the mark of them amounts to no more but this—that by the use of reason we are capable to come to a certain knowledge of and assent to them, and, by this means, there will be no difference between the maxims of the mathematicians and theorems they deduce from them: all must be equally allowed innate; they being all discoveries made by the use of reason, and truths that a rational creature may certainly come to know, if he apply his thoughts rightly that way.

9.   But how can these men think the use of reason necessary to discover principles that are supposed innate, when reason (if we may believe them) is nothing else but the faculty of deducing unknown truths from principles of propositions that are already known? That certainly can never be thought innate which we have need of reason to discover, unless as I have said, we will have all the certain truths that reason ever teaches us to be innate. We may as well think the use of reason necessary to make our eyes discover visible objects, as that there should be need of reason, or

the exercise thereof, to make the understanding see what is originally engraven on it, and cannot be in the understanding before it be perceived by it. So that to make reason discover those truths thus imprinted is to say that the use of reason discovers to a man what he knew before: and if men have those innate impressed truths originally, and before the use of reason, and yet are always ignorant of them till they come to the use of reason, it is in effect to say that men know and know them not at the same time.

10.   It will here perhaps be said that mathematical demonstrations, and other truths that are not innate, are not assented to as soon as proposed, wherein they are distinguished from these maxims and other innate truths. I shall have occasion to speak of assent upon the first proposing more particularly by and by. I shall here only, and that very readily, allow that these maxims and mathematical demonstrations are in this different: that the one have need of reason, using of proofs, to make them out and to gain our assent; but the other, as soon as understood, are, without any the least reasoning, embraced and assented to. But I withal beg leave to observe, that it lays open the weakness of this subterfuge, which requires the use of reason for the discovery of these general truths: since it must be confessed that in their discovery there is no use made of reasoning at all. And I think those who give this answer will not be forward to affirm that the knowledge of this maxim, 'That it is impossible for the same thing to be and not to be,' is a deduction of our reason. For this would be to destroy that bounty of nature they seem so fond of, whilst they make the knowledge of those principles to depend on the labour of our thoughts. For all reasoning is search, and casting about, and requires pains and application. And how can it with any tolerable sense be supposed, that what was imprinted by nature, as the foundation and guide of our reason, should need the use of reason to discover it?

11.   Those who will take the pains to reflect with a little attention on the operations of the understanding will find that this ready assent of the mind to some truths depends not either on native inscription or the use of reason, but on a faculty of the mind quite distinct from both of them, as we shall see hereafter. Reason, therefore, having nothing to do in procuring our assent to these maxims, if by saying, that 'men know and assent to them when they come to the use of reason,' be meant, that the use of reason assists us in the knowledge of these maxims, it is utterly false; and were it true, would prove them not to be innate.

12.   If by knowing and assenting to them 'when we come to the use of reason,' be meant, that this is the time when they come to be taken notice of by the mind, and that as soon as children come to the use of reason they come also to know and assent to these maxims, this also is false and frivolous. First, it is false because it is evident these maxims are not in the mind so early as the use of reason; and therefore the coming to the use of reason is falsely assigned as the time of their discovery. How many instances of the use of reason may we observe in children a long time before they have any knowledge of this maxim, 'That it is impossible for the same thing to be and not to be'? And a great part of illiterate people and savages pass many years, even of their rational age, without ever thinking on this and the like general propositions. I grant, men come not to the knowledge of these general and more abstract truths, which are thought innate, till they come to the use of reason; and I add, nor then neither. Which is so because till after they come to the use of reason, those general abstract ideas are not framed in the mind, about which those general maxims are, which are mistaken for

innate principles, but are indeed discoveries made and verities introduced and brought into the mind by the same way, and discovered by the same steps, as several other propositions, which nobody was ever so extravagant as to suppose innate. This I hope to make plain in the sequel of this Discourse. I allow therefore, a necessity that men should come to the use of reason before they get the knowledge of those general truths; but deny that men's coming to the use of reason is the time of their discovery.

13.   In the mean time it is observable, that this saying, that men know and assent to these maxims 'when they come to the use of reason,' amounts in reality of fact to no more but this— that they are never known nor taken notice of before the use of reason, but may possibly be assented to some time after, during a man's life; but when is uncertain. And so may all other knowable truths, as well as these; which therefore have no advantage nor distinction from others by this note of being known when we come to the use of reason; nor are thereby proved to be innate, but quite the contrary.

14.   But, secondly, were it true that the precise time of their being known and assented to were when men come to the use of reason, neither would that prove them innate. This way of arguing is as frivolous as the supposition itself is false. For, by what kind of logic will it appear that any notion is originally by nature imprinted in the mind in its first constitution, because it comes first to be observed and assented to when a faculty of the mind, which has quite a distinct province, begins to exert itself? And therefore the coming to the use of speech, if it were supposed the time that these maxims are first assented to, (which it may be with as much truth as the time when men come to the use of reason) would be as good a proof that they were innate, as to say they are innate because men assent to

them when they come to the use of reason. I agree then with these men of innate principles, that there is no knowledge of these general and self-evident maxims in the mind, till it comes to the exercise of reason: but I deny that the coming to the use of reason is the precise time when they are first taken notice of; and if that were the precise time, I deny that it would prove them innate. All that can with any truth be meant by this proposition, that men 'assent to them when they come to the use of reason,' is no more but this— that the making of general abstract ideas and the understanding of general names being a concomitant of the rational faculty, and growing up with it, children commonly get not those general ideas, nor learn the names that stand for them, till, having for a good while exercised their reason about familiar and more particular ideas, they are, by their ordinary discourse and actions with others, acknowledged to be capable of rational conversation. If assenting to these maxims, when men come to the use of reason, can be true in any other sense, I desire it may be shown; or at least, how in this, or any other sense, it proves them innate.

15.   The senses at first let in *particular* ideas, and furnish the yet empty cabinet, and the mind by degrees growing familiar with some of them, they are lodged in the memory, and names got to them. Afterwards, the mind proceeding further, abstracts them, and by degrees learns the use of general names. In this manner the mind comes to be furnished with ideas and language, the *materials* about which to exercise its discursive faculty. And the use of reason becomes daily more visible, as these materials that give it employment increase. But though the having of general ideas and the use of general words and reason usually grow together, yet I see not how this any way proves them innate. The knowledge of some truths, I confess, is very early in the mind; but in a way that shows them not to be innate. For, if

we will observe, we shall find it still to be about ideas, not innate, but acquired; it being about those first which are imprinted by external things, with which infants have earliest to do, which make the most frequent impressions on their senses. In ideas thus got, the mind discovers that some agree and others differ, probably as soon as it has any use of memory; as soon as it is able to retain and perceive distinct ideas. But whether it be then or no, this is certain, it does so long before it has the use of words; or comes to that which we commonly call 'the use of reason.' For a child knows as certainly before it can speak the difference between the ideas of sweet and bitter (i.e. that sweet is not bitter), as it knows afterwards (when it comes to speak) that wormwood and sugarplums are not the same thing. . . .

Of Ideas in General, and Their Origin

1.   Every man being conscious to himself that he thinks, and that which his mind is applied about whilst thinking being the *ideas* that are there, it is past doubt that men have in their minds several ideas—such as are those expressed by the words *whiteness, hardness, sweetness, thinking, motion, man, elephant, army, drunkenness*, and others: it is in the first place then to be inquired, *How he comes by them?*

I know it is a received doctrine that men have native ideas and original characters stamped upon their minds in their very first being. This opinion I have at large examined already, and I suppose what I have said in the foregoing Book will be much more easily admitted when I have shown whence the understanding may get all the ideas it has; and by what ways and degrees they may come into the mind—for which I shall appeal to every one's own observation and experience.

2.   Let us then suppose the mind to be, as we say, white paper, void of all characters, without any ideas—How comes it to be furnished? Whence comes it by that vast store which the busy and boundless fancy of man has painted on it with an almost endless variety? Whence has it all the *materials* of reason and knowledge? To this I answer, in one word, from *experience*. In that all our knowledge is founded; and from that it ultimately derives itself. Our observation employed either about external sensible objects or about the internal operations of our minds perceived and reflected on by ourselves, is that which supplies our understandings with all the *materials* of thinking. These two are the fountains of knowledge from whence all the ideas we have, or can naturally have, do spring.

3.   First, our Senses, conversant about particular sensible objects, do convey into the mind several distinct perceptions of things, according to those various ways wherein those objects do affect them. And thus we come by those *ideas* we have of *yellow, white, heat, cold, soft, hard, bitter, sweet*, and all those which we call sensible qualities; which when I say the senses convey into the mind, I mean, they from external objects convey into the mind what produces there those perceptions. This great source of most of the ideas we have, depending wholly upon our senses, and derived by them to the understanding, I call *sensation*.

4.   Secondly, the other fountain from which experience furnisheth the understanding with ideas is the perception of the operations of our own mind within us, as it is employed about the ideas it has got which operations, when the soul comes to reflect on and consider, do furnish the understanding with another set of ideas, which could not be had from things without. And such are *perception, thinking, doubting, believing, reasoning, knowing, willing*, and all the different actings of our

own minds—which we being conscious of, and observing in ourselves, do from these receive into our understandings as distinct ideas as we do from bodies affecting our senses. This source of ideas every man has wholly in himself; and though it be not sense, as having nothing to do with external objects, yet it is very like it, and might properly enough be called *internal* sense. But as I call the other Sensation, so I call this *reflection*, the ideas it affords being such only as the mind gets by reflecting on its own operations within itself. By reflection then, in the following part of this discourse, I would be understood to mean, that notice which the mind takes of its own operations, and the manner or not; and the operations of our minds will not let us be without, at least, some obscure notions of them. No man can be wholly ignorant of what he does when he thinks. These simple ideas, when offered to the mind, the understanding can no more refuse to have, nor alter when they are imprinted, nor blot them out and make new ones itself, than a mirror can refuse, alter or obliterate the images or ideas which the objects set before it do therein produce. As the bodies that surround us do diversely affect our organs, the mind is forced to receive the impressions, and cannot avoid the perception of those ideas that are annexed to them.

Of Simple Ideas

1.   The better to understand the nature, manner, and extent of our knowledge, one thing is carefully to be observed concerning the ideas we have, and that is, that some of them are *simple* and some *complex.*

Though the qualities that affect our senses are, in the things themselves, so united and blended that there is no separation, no distance between them, yet it is plain that the ideas they produce in the mind enter by the senses simple and unmixed. For, though the sight and touch often take in from the same object, at the same time, different ideas—as a man sees at once motion and colour [and] the hand feels softness and warmth in the same piece of wax—yet the simple ideas thus united in the same subject are as perfectly distinct as those that come in by different senses. The coldness and hardness which a man feels in a piece of ice being as distinct ideas in the mind as the smell and whiteness of a lily, or as the taste of sugar and smell of a rose. And there is nothing can be plainer to a man than the clear and distinct perception he has of those simple ideas; which, being each in itself uncompounded, contains in it nothing but *one uniform appearance or conception in the mind,* and is not distinguishable into different ideas.

2.   These simple ideas, the materials of all our knowledge, are suggested and furnished to the mind only by those two ways above mentioned, viz. sensation and reflection. When the understanding is once stored with these simple ideas, it has the power to repeat, compare, and unite them, even to an almost infinite variety, and so can make at pleasure new complex ideas. But it is not in the power of the most exalted wit, or enlarged understanding, by any quickness or variety of thought, to *invent* or *frame* one new simple idea in the mind, not taken in by the ways before mentioned: nor can any force of the understanding *destroy* those that are there. The dominion of man, in this little world of his own understanding being much what the same as it is in the great world of visible things, wherein his power, however managed by art and skill, reaches no farther than to compound and divide the materials that are made to his hand, but can do nothing towards the making the least particle of new matter, or destroying one atom of what is already in being. The same inability will every one find in himself, who shall go about to fashion

in his understanding one simple idea, not received in by his senses from external objects, or by reflection from the operations of his own mind about them. I would have any one try to fancy any taste which had never affected his palate, or frame the idea of a scent he had never smelt: and when he can do this, I will also conclude that a blind man hath ideas of colours, and a deaf man true distinct notions of sounds.

3. This is the reason why—though we cannot believe it impossible to God to make a creature with other organs, and more ways to convey into the understanding the notice of corporeal things than those five, as they are usually counted, which he has given to man—yet I think it is not possible for any *man* to imagine any other qualities in bodies, howsoever constituted, whereby they can be taken notice of, besides sounds, tastes, smells, visible and tangible qualities. And had mankind been made but with four senses, the qualities then which are the objects of the fifth sense had been as far from our notice,

imagination, and conception, as now any belonging to a sixth, seventh, or eighth sense can possibly be—which, whether yet some other creatures, in some other parts of this vast and stupendous universe, may not have, will be a great presumption to deny. He that will not set himself proudly at the top of all things, but will consider the immensity of this fabric, and the great variety that is to be found in this little and inconsiderable part of it which he has to do with, may be apt to think that, in other mansions of it, there may be other and different intelligent beings of whose faculties he has as little knowledge or apprehension as a worm shut up in one drawer of a cabinet hath of the senses or understanding of a man; such variety and excellency being suitable to the wisdom and power of the Maker. I have here followed the common opinion of man's having but five senses, though, perhaps, there may be justly counted more—but either supposition serves equally to my present purpose.

CHAPTER 19

IMMANUEL KANT

KNOWLEDGE AS A SYNTHESIS OF REASON AND EXPERIENCE

Immanuel Kant (1724–1804) was born in Königsberg, a small city in East Prussia. Although frail in body, his genius was enormous, and he is regarded by some as the greatest philosopher since Plato and Aristotle. For thirty-four years, he was a professor of philosophy at the University of Königsberg, where he led a quiet, unassuming academic life, never venturing beyond his native Prussia. Although there were few outward events of much significance in Kant's life (for his life was one of inward development and ideas), his thinking spawned a revolution in modern thought that continues to this day. One of Kant's former students had this to say: "He was indifferent to nothing worth knowing. No cabal, no sect, no prejudice, no desire for fame could ever tempt him in the slightest way from broadening and illuminating the truth. He incited and gently forced others to think for themselves; despotism was foreign to his mind. This man, whom I name with the greatest gratitude and respect, was Immanuel Kant."

In his lectures on *Logic*, Kant said that philosophy addressed four questions:

1. What can I know?
2. What ought I to do?
3. What may I hope?
4. What is man?

His response to the first question was to construct a theory of knowledge whose revolutionary consequences were compared to the Copernican Revolution in science, and may be found in his *Critique of Pure Reason* (1781). His response to the second question was to work out a system of ethics based on duty, contained in his *Critique of Practical Reason* (1788). Kant's third critique, *Critique of Judgment* (1790), contains his aesthetic theory.

In 1782, thinking back to a time some ten years before, Kant wrote these words: "I openly confess that a reminder by David Hume was the very thing which many years ago first interrupted my dogmatic slumber." This "reminder" that Kant referred to was Hume's disturbing discovery that the idea of causality (or "necessary connection") was neither a logical truth (like the law of noncontradiction) nor was it intuitively certain. Hume had argued that we have no way of knowing that the future will resemble the past, or indeed whether there is any connection between them at all. Causality was merely a subjective expectation that future events would repeat past events. Consequently, Hume restricted human knowledge to what we could directly perceive or remember—a very tiny portion of what we think we know. This was an extremely important development in epistemology. If Hume was right, the empiricist experiment in philosophy begun by Locke had reached the dead-end of skepticism, and natural science as well as philosophy was threatened.

To save scientific knowledge from Hume's skepticism now became Kant's philosophical quest. Perhaps it was at this time that he remembered a statement of the rationalist Leibniz. Trying to find some common ground with Locke's empiricism, Leibniz had written, "There is nothing in the intellect which was not first in the senses," but then added: "except the intellect itself." Soon Kant had his solution, the basis of the famous "Copernican Revolution" in philosophy, and a bold synthesis of empiricism and rationalism. The content of knowledge, he freely admitted, must come from experience *(a posteriori)*. But the formal structures and rules of knowledge reside in the mind *a priori*, and the content conforms to the structures and rules, not the reverse, as the empiricists presumed.

Kant worked out his revolution in the pages of the *Critique of Pure Reason*, arguing that synthetic *a priori* knowledge was possible.[1] Synthetic *a priori* judgments are those judgments that make meaningful statements about reality, yet are known independently of experience. Such knowledge was merely the knowledge of our own rules when we constitute reality. Thus space and time for Kant were not features of external reality; they were structures of the mind itself, the "irremovable glasses" through which we view the world. Similarly, causality was itself a category of the understanding, something the mind brings to experience—this explains why Hume had been unable to locate it *in* experience. The sentence, "Every event is caused" is, according to Kant, a synthetic *a priori* judgment.

[1]From Immanuel Kant, *Critique of Pure Reason*, translated by Norman Kemp Smith (London: Macmillan, 1929). Reprinted with permission of Macmillan, London and Basingstoke.

KNOWLEDGE AS A SYNTHESIS OF REASON AND EXPERIENCE

There can be no doubt that all our knowledge begins with experience. For how should our faculty of knowledge be awakened into action did not objects affecting our senses partly of themselves produce representations, partly arouse the activity of our understanding to compare these representations, and, by combining or separating them, work up the raw material of the sensible impressions into that knowledge of objects which is entitled experience? In the order of time, therefore, we have no knowledge antecedent to experience, and with experience all our knowledge begins.

But though all our knowledge begins with experience, it does not follow that it all arises out of experience. For it may well be that even our empirical knowledge is made up of what we receive through impressions and of what our own faculty of knowledge (sensible impressions serving merely as the occasion) supplies from itself. If our faculty of knowledge makes any such addition, it may be that we are not in a position to distinguish it from the raw material, until with long practice of attention we have become skilled in separating it.

This, then, is a question which at least calls for closer examination, and does not allow of any off-hand answer:—whether there is any knowledge that is thus independent of experience and even of all impressions of the senses. Such knowledge is entitled *a priori*, and distinguished from the *empirical*, which has its sources *a posteriori*, that is, in experience.

The expression '*a priori*' does not, however, indicate with sufficient precision the full meaning of our question. For it has been customary to say, even of much knowledge that is derived from empirical sources, that we have it or are capable of having it *a priori*, meaning thereby that we do not derive it immediately from experience, but from a universal rule—a rule which is itself, however, borrowed by us from experience. Thus we would say of a man who undermined the foundations of his house, that he might have known *a priori* that it would fall, that is, that he need not have waited for the experience of its actual falling. But still he could not know this completely *a priori*. For he had first to learn through experience that bodies are heavy, and therefore fall when their supports are withdrawn.

In what follows, therefore, we shall understand by *a priori* knowledge, not knowledge independent of this or that experience, but knowledge absolutely independent of all experience. Opposed to it is empirical knowledge, which is knowledge possible only *a posteriori*, that is, through experience. *A priori* modes of knowledge are entitled pure when there is no admixture of anything empirical. Thus, for instance, the proposition, 'every alteration has its cause,' while an *a priori* proposition, is not a pure proposition, because alteration is a concept which can be derived only from experience.

We Are in Possession of Certain Modes of *A Priori* Knowledge, and Even the Common Understanding Is Never Without Them

What we here require is a criterion by which to distinguish with certainty between pure and empirical knowledge. Experience teaches us that a thing is so and so, but not that it cannot be otherwise. First, then, if we have a proposition which in being thought is thought as *necessary*, it is an *a priori* judgment; and if, besides, it is not derived from any proposition except one which also has the validity of a necessary judgment, it is an absolutely *a priori* judgment. Secondly, experience never confers on its judgments true or strict, but only assumed and comparative *universality*, through induction. We can properly only say, therefore, that, so far as we have hitherto observed, there is no exception to this or that rule. If, then, a judgment is thought with strict universality, that is, in such manner that no exception is allowed as possible, it is not derived from experience, but is valid absolutely *a priori*. Empirical universality is only an arbitrary extension of a validity holding in most cases to one which holds in all, for instance, in the proposition, 'all bodies are heavy.' When, on the other hand, strict universality is essential to a judgment, this indicates a special source of knowledge, namely, a faculty of *a priori* knowledge. Necessity and strict universality are thus sure criteria of *a priori* knowledge, and are inseparable from one another. But since in the employment of these criteria the contingency of judgments is sometimes more easily shown than their empirical limitation, or, as sometimes also happens, their unlimited universality can be more convincingly proved than their necessity, it is advisable to use the two criteria separately, each by itself being infallible.

Now it is easy to show that there actually are in human knowledge judgments which are necessary and in the strictest sense universal, and which are therefore pure *a priori* judgments. If an example from the sciences be desired, we have only to look to any of the propositions of mathematics; if we seek an example from the understanding in its quite ordinary employment, the proposition, 'every alteration must have a cause', will serve our purpose. In the latter case, indeed, the very concept of a cause so manifestly contains the concept of a necessity of connection with an effect and of the strict universality of the rule, that the concept would be altogether lost if we attempted to derive it, as Hume has done, from a repeated association of that which happens with that which precedes, and from a custom of connecting representations, a custom originating in this repeated association, and constituting therefore a merely subjective necessity. Even without appealing to such examples, it is possible to show that pure *a priori* principles are indispensable for the possibility of experience, and so to prove their existence *a priori*. For whence could experience derive its certainty, if all the rules, according to which it proceeds, were always themselves empirical, and therefore contingent? Such rules could hardly be regarded as first principles. At present, however, we may be content to have established the fact that our faculty of knowledge does have a pure employment, and to have shown what are the criteria of such an employment.

Such *a priori* origin is manifest in certain concepts, no less than in judgments. If we remove from our empirical concept of a body, one by one, every feature in it which is [merely] empirical, the colour, the hardness or softness, the weight, even the impenetrability, there still remains the space which the body (now entirely vanished) occupied, and this cannot be removed. Again, if we remove from our empirical concept of any object, corporeal or incorporeal, all properties which experience has taught us, we yet cannot take away that property through which the object is thought as substance or as inhering in a substance (although this concept of substance is more determinate than that of an object in general). Owing, therefore, to the necessity with which this concept of substance forces itself upon us, we have no option save to admit that it has its seat in our faculty of *a priori* knowledge.

The Distinction Between Analytic and Synthetic Judgments

In all judgments in which the relation of a subject to the predicate is thought (I take into consideration affirmative judgments only, the subsequent application to negative judgments being easily made), this relation is possible in two different ways. Either the predicate B belongs to the subject A, as something which is (covertly) contained in this concept A; or B lies outside the concept A, although it does indeed stand in connection with it. In the one case I entitle the judgment analytic, in the other synthetic. Analytic judgments (affirmative) are therefore those in which the connection of the predicate with the subject is thought through identity; those in which this connection is thought without identity should be entitled synthetic. The former, as adding nothing through the predicate to the concept of the subject, but merely breaking it up into those constituent concepts that have all along been thought in it, although confusedly, can also be entitled explicative. The latter, on the other hand, add to the concept of the subject a predicate which has not been in any wise thought in it, and which no analysis could possibly extract from it; and they may therefore be entitled ampliative. If I say, for instance, 'All bodies are extended,' this is an analytic judgment. For I do not require to go beyond the concept which I connect with 'body' in order to find extension as bound up with it. To meet with this predicate, I have merely to analyze the concept, that is, to become conscious to myself of the manifold which I always think in that concept. The judgment is therefore analytic. But when I say, 'All bodies are heavy,' the predicate is something quite different from anything that I think in the mere concept of body in general; and the addition of such a predicate therefore yields a synthetic judgment.

Judgments of experience, as such, are one and all synthetic. For it would be absurd to found an analytic judgment on experience. Since, in framing the judgment, I must not go outside my concept, there is no need to appeal to the testimony of experience in its support. That a body is extended is a proposition that holds *a priori* and is not empirical. For, before appealing to experience, I have already in the concept of body all the conditions required for my judgment. I have only to extract from it, in accordance with the principle of contradiction, the required predicate, and in so doing can at the same time become conscious of the necessity of the judgment—and that is what experience could never have taught me. On the other hand, though I do not include in the concept of a body in general the predicate 'weight,' none the less this concept indicates an object of experience through one of its parts, and I can add to that part other parts of this same experience, as in this way belonging together with the concept. From the start I can apprehend the concept of body analytically through the characters of extension, impenetrability, figure, etc., all of which are thought in the concept. Now, however, looking back on the experience from which I have derived this concept of body, and finding weight to be invariably connected with the above characters, I attach it as a predicate to the concept; and in doing so I attach it synthetically, and am therefore extending my knowledge. The possibility of the synthesis of the predicate 'weight' with the concept of 'body' thus rests upon experience. While the one concept is not contained in the other, they yet belong to one another, though only contingently, as parts of a whole, namely, of an experience which is itself a synthetic combination of intuitions.

But in *a priori* synthetic judgments this help is entirely lacking: [I do not here have the advantage of looking around in the field of experience.] Upon what, then, am I to rely, when I seek to go beyond the concept A, and to know that another concept B is connected with it? Through what is the synthesis made possible? Let us take the proposition, 'Everything which happens has its cause.' In the concept of 'something which happens,' I do indeed think an existence which is preceded by a time, etc., and from this concept analytic judgments may be obtained. But the concept of a 'cause' lies entirely outside the other concept, and signifies something different from 'that which happens,' and is not therefore in any way contained in this latter representation. How come I then to predicate of that which happens something quite different, and to apprehend that the concept of cause, though not contained in it, yet belongs, and indeed necessarily belongs, to it? What is here the unknown — X which gives support to the understanding when it believes that it can discover outside the concept A a predicate B foreign to this concept, which it yet at the same time considers to be connected with it? It cannot be experience, because the suggested principle has connected the second representation with the first, not only with greater universality, but also with the character of necessity, and therefore completely *a priori* and on the basis of mere concepts. Upon such synthetic, that is, ampliative principles, all our *a priori* speculative knowledge must ultimately rest; analytic judgments are very important, and indeed necessary, but only for obtaining that clearness in the concepts which is requisite for such a sure and wide synthesis as will lead to a genuinely new addition to all previous knowledge.

The Highest Principle of All Analytic Judgments

The universal, though merely negative, condition of all our judgments in general, whatever be the content of our knowledge, and however it

may relate to the object is that they be not self-contradictory; for if self-contradictory, these judgments are in themselves, even without reference to the object, null and void. But even if our judgment contains no contradiction, it may connect concepts in a manner not borne out by the object, or else in a manner for which no ground is given, either *a priori* or *a posteriori*, sufficient to justify such judgment, and so may still, in spite of being free from all inner contradiction, be either false or groundless.

The proposition that no predicate contradictory of a thing can belong to it, is entitled the principle of contradiction, and is a universal, though merely negative, criterion of all truth. For this reason it belongs only to logic. It holds of knowledge, merely as knowledge in general, irrespective of content; and asserts that the contradiction completely cancels and invalidates it.

But it also allows of a positive employment, not merely, that is, to dispel falsehood and error (so far as they rest on contradiction), but also for the knowing of truth. For, *if the judgment is analytic*, whether negative or affirmative, its truth can always be adequately known in accordance with the principle of contradiction. The reverse of that which as concept is contained and is thought in the knowledge of the object, is always rightly denied. But since the opposite of the concept would contradict the object, the concept itself must necessarily be affirmed of it.

The principle of contradiction must therefore be recognized as being the universal and completely sufficient *principle of all analytic knowledge*; but beyond the sphere of analytic knowledge it has, as a *sufficient* criterion of truth, no authority and no field of application. The fact that no knowledge can be contrary to it without self-nullification, makes this principle a *conditio sine qua non*, but not a determining ground, of the truth of our [non-analytic] knowledge. Now in our critical enquiry it is only with the synthetic portion of our knowledge that we are concerned; and in regard to the truth of this kind of knowledge we can never look to the above principle for any positive information, though, of course, since it is inviolable, we must always be careful to conform to it.

Although this famous principle is thus without content and merely formal, it has sometimes been carelessly formulated in a manner which involves the quite unnecessary admixture of a synthetic element. The formula runs: It is impossible that something should *at one and the same time* both be and not be. Apart from the fact that the apodeictic certainty, expressed through the word 'impossible', is superfluously added—since it is evident of itself from the [very nature of the] proposition—the proposition is modified by the condition of time. It then, as it were, asserts: A thing = A, which is something = B, cannot at the same time be not-B, but may very well in succession be both B and not-B. For instance, a man who is young cannot at the same time be old, but may very well at one time be young and at another time not-young, that is, old. The principle of contradiction, however, as a merely logical principle, must not in any way limit its assertions to time-relations. The above formula is therefore completely contrary to the intention of the principle. The misunderstanding results from our first of all separating a predicate of a thing from the concept of that thing, and afterwards connecting this predicate with its opposite—a procedure which never occasions a contradiction with the subject but only with the predicate which has been synthetically connected with that subject, and even then only when both predicates are affirmed at one and the same time. If I say that a man who is unlearned is not learned, the condition, *at one and the same time*, must be added; for he who is at one time unlearned can very well at another be learned. But if I say, no unlearned man is learned, the proposition is analytic, since the property, unlearnedness, now goes to make up the concept of the subject, and the truth of the negative judgment then becomes evident as an immediate consequence of the principle of contradiction, without requiring the supplementary condition, *at one and the same time.* This, then, is the reason why I have altered its formulation, namely, in order that the nature of an analytic proposition be clearly expressed through it.

CHAPTER 20

BERTRAND RUSSELL

THE CORRESPONDENCE THEORY OF TRUTH

Russell begins by identifying three requirements that he believes a satisfactory theory of truth must possess (see Chapter 4 for a brief biography of Bertrand Russell). His discussion of the third requirement in particular leads him to set the view that "truth consists in some form of correspondence between belief and fact." He then discusses Bradley's coherence theory, enumerating two important objections, and restating his own three requirements. The remainder of the passage is an "unpacking" of these requirements. Russell defines "fact" more precisely, and analyzes the nature of the correspondence that must obtain between beliefs and facts in order for a belief to be true.[1]

THE CORRESPONDENCE THEORY OF TRUTH

Our knowledge of truths, unlike our knowledge of things, has an opposite, namely *error*. So far as things are concerned, we may know them or not know them, but there is no positive state of mind which can be described as erroneous knowledge of things, so long, at any rate, as we confine ourselves to knowledge by acquaintance. Whatever we are acquainted with must be something: we

---

[1]Reprinted with permission from *The Problems of Philosophy* by Bertrand Russell (1912) by permission of Oxford University Press.

may draw wrong inference from our acquaintance, but the acquaintance itself cannot be deceptive. Thus there is no dualism as regards acquaintance. But as regards knowledge of truths, there is a dualism. We may believe what is false as well as what is true. We know that on very many subjects different people hold different and incompatible opinions: hence some beliefs must be erroneous. Since erroneous beliefs are often held just as strongly as true beliefs, it becomes a difficult question how they are to be distinguished from true beliefs. How are we to know, in a given case, that our belief is not erroneous? That is a question of the very greatest difficulty, to which no completely satisfactory answer is possible. There is, however, a preliminary question which is rather less difficult, and that is: What do we *mean* by truth and falsehood? It is this preliminary question which is to be considered in this chapter.

. . . We are not asking how we can know whether a belief is true or false: we are asking what is meant by the question whether a belief is true or false. It is to be hoped that a clear answer to this question may help us to obtain an answer to the question what beliefs are true, but for the present we ask only "What is truth?" and "What is falsehood?" not "What beliefs are true?" and "What beliefs are false?" It is very important to keep these different questions entirely separate, since any confusion between them is sure to produce an answer which is not really applicable to either.

There are three points to observe in the attempt to discover the nature of truth, three requisites which any theory must fulfill.

. (1) Our theory of truth must be such as to admit of its opposite, falsehood. A good many philosophers have failed adequately to satisfy this condition: they have constructed theories according to which all our thinking ought to have been true, and have then had the greatest

difficulty in finding a place for falsehood. In this respect our theory of belief must differ from our theory of acquaintance, since in the case of acquaintance it was not necessary to take account of any opposite.

(2) It seems fairly evident that if there were no beliefs there could be no falsehood, and no truth either, in the sense in which truth is correlative to falsehood. If we imagine a world of mere matter, there would be no room for falsehood in such a world, and although it would contain what may be called "facts," it would not contain any truths, in the sense in which truths are things of the same kind as falsehoods. In fact, truth and falsehood are properties of beliefs and statements: hence a world of mere matter, since it would contain no beliefs or statements, would also contain no truth or falsehood.

(3) But, as against what we have just said, it is to be observed that the truth or falsehood of a belief always depends upon something which lies outside the belief itself. If I believe that Charles I died on the scaffold, I believe truly, not because of any intrinsic quality of my belief, which could be discovered by merely examining the belief, but because of an historical event which happened two and a half centuries ago. If I believe that Charles I died in his bed, I believe falsely: no degree of vividness in my belief, or of care in arriving at it, prevents it from being false, again because of what happened long ago, and not because of any intrinsic property of my belief. Hence, although truth and falsehood are properties of beliefs, they are properties dependent upon the relations of the beliefs to other things, not upon any internal quality of the beliefs.

The third of the above requisites leads us to adopt the view—which has on the whole been commonest among philosophers—that truth consists in some form of correspondence between belief and fact. It is, however, by no means an easy matter to discover a form of correspondence to which there are no irrefutable objections. By this partly—and partly by the feeling that, if truth consists in a correspondence of thought with something outside thought, thought can never know when truth has been attained—many philosophers have been led to try to find some definition of truth which shall not consist in relation to something wholly outside belief. The most important attempt at a definition of this sort is the theory that truth consists in *coherence.* It is said that the mark of falsehood is failure to cohere in the body of our beliefs, and that it is the essence of a truth to form part of the completely rounded system which is The Truth.

There is, however, a great difficulty in this view, or rather two great difficulties. The first is that there is no reason to support that only *one* coherent body of beliefs is possible. It may be that, with sufficient imagination, a novelist might invent a past for the world that would perfectly fit on to what we know, and yet be quite different from the real past. In more scientific matters, it is certain that there are often two or more hypotheses which account for all the known facts on some subject, and although, in such cases, men of science endeavor to find facts which will rule out all the hypotheses except one, there is no reason why they should always succeed.

In philosophy, again, it seems not uncommon for two rival hypotheses to be both able to account for all the facts. Thus, for example, it is possible that life is one long dream, and that the outer world has only that degree of reality that the objects of dreams have; but although such a view does not seem inconsistent with known facts, there is no reason to prefer it to the common-sense view, according to which other people and things do really exist. Thus coherence as the definition of truth fails because there is no proof that there can be only one coherent system.

The other objection to this definition of truth is that it assumes the meaning of "coherence" known, whereas, in fact, "coherence" presupposes the truth of the laws of logic. Two propositions are coherent when both may be true, and are incoherent when one at least must be false. Now in order to know whether two propositions can both be true, we must know such truths as the law of contradiction. For example, the two propositions "this tree is a beech" and "this tree is not a beech," are not coherent, because of the law of contradiction. But if the law of contradiction itself were subjected to the test of coherence, we should find that, if we choose to suppose it false, nothing will any longer be incoherent with anything else. Thus the laws of logic supply the skeleton or framework within which the test of coherence applies, and they themselves cannot be established by this test.

For the above two reasons, coherence cannot be accepted as giving the *meaning* of truth, though it is often a most important *test* of truth after a certain amount of truth has become known.

Hence we are driven back to *correspondence with fact* as constituting the nature of truth. It remains to define precisely what we mean by "fact," and what is the nature of the correspondence which must subsist between belief and fact, in order that belief may be true.

In accordance with our three requisites, we have to seek a theory of truth which (1) allows truth to have an opposite, namely falsehood, (2) makes truth a property of beliefs, but (3) makes it a property wholly dependent upon the relation of the beliefs to outside things.

The necessity of allowing for falsehood makes it impossible to regard belief as a relation of the mind to a single object, which could be said to be what is believed. If belief were so regarded, we should find that, like acquaintance, it would not admit of the opposition of truth and falsehood, but would have to be always true. This

195

may be made clear by examples. Othello believes falsely that Desdemona loves Cassio. We cannot say that this belief consists in a relation to a single object, "Desdemona's love for Cassio," for if there were such an object, the belief would be true. There is in fact no such object, and therefore Othello cannot have any relation to such an object. Hence his belief cannot possibly consist in a relation to this object.

It might be said that his belief is a relation to a different object, namely "that Desdemona loves Cassio"; but it is almost as difficult to suppose that there is such an object as this, when Desdemona does not love Cassio, as it was to suppose that there is "Desdemona's love for Cassio." Hence it will be better to seek for a theory of belief which does not make it consist in a relation of the mind to a single object.

It is common to think of relations as though they always held between *two* terms, but in fact this is not always the case. Some relations demand three terms, some four, and so on. Take, for instance, the relation "between." So long as only two terms come in, the relation "between" is impossible: three terms are the smallest number that render it possible. York is between London and Edinburgh; but if London and Edinburgh were the only places in the world, there could be nothing which was between one place and another. Similarly *jealousy* requires three people: there can be no such relation that does not involve three at least. Such a proposition as "A wishes B to promote C's marriage with D" involves a relation of four terms; that is to say, A and B and C and D all come in, and the relation involved cannot be expressed otherwise than in a form involving all four. Instances might be multiplied indefinitely, but enough has been said to show that there are relations which require more than two terms before they can occur.

The relation involved in *judging* or *believing* must, if falsehood is to be duly allowed for, be taken to be a relation between several terms, not between two. When Othello believes that Desdemona loves Cassio, he must not have before his mind a single object, "Desdemona's love for Cassio," or "that Desdemona loves Cassio," for that would require that there should be objective falsehoods, which subsist independently of any minds; and this, though not logically refutable, is a theory to be avoided if possible. Thus it is easier to account for falsehood if we take judgment to be a relation in which the mind and the various objects concerned all occur severally; that is to say, Desdemona and loving and Cassio must all be terms in the relation which subsists when Othello believes that Desdemona loves Cassio. This relation, therefore, is a relation of four terms, since Othello also is one of the terms of the relation. When we say that it is a relation of four terms, we do not mean that Othello has a certain relation to Desdemona, and has the same relation to loving and also to Cassio. This may be true of some other relation than believing; but believing, plainly, is not a relation which Othello has to *each* of the three terms concerned, but to *all* of them together: there is only one example of the relation of believing involved, but this one example knits together four terms. Thus the actual occurrence, at the moment when Othello is entertaining his belief, is that the relation called "believing" is knitting together into one complex whole the four terms Othello, Desdemona, loving, and Cassio. What is called belief or judgment is nothing but this relation of believing or judging, which relates a mind to several things other than itself. An *act* of belief or of judgment is the occurrence between certain terms at some particular time, of the relation of believing or judging.

We are now in a position to understand what it is that distinguishes a true judgment from a false one. For this purpose we will adopt certain definitions. In every act of judgment there is a mind which judges, and there are terms concerning which it judges. We will call the mind the *subject* in the judgment, and the remaining terms the *objects*. Thus, when Othello judges that Desdemona loves Cassio, Othello is the subject, while the objects are Desdemona and loving and Cassio. The subject and the objects together are called the *constituents* of the judgment. It will be observed that the relation of judging has what is called a "sense" or "direction." We may say, metaphorically, that it puts its objects in a certain *order*, which we may indicate by means of the order of the words in the sentence. (In an inflected language, the same thing will be indicated by inflections, e.g., by the difference between nominative and accusative.) Othello's judgment that Cassio loves Desdemona differs from his judgment that Desdemona loves Cassio, in spite of the fact that it consists of the same constituents, because the relation of judging places the constituents in a different order in the two cases. Similarly, if Cassio judges that Desdemona loves Othello, the constituents of the judgment are still the same, but their order is different. This property of having a "sense" or "direction" is one which the relation of judging shares with all other relations. The "sense" of relations is the ultimate source of order and series and a host of mathematical concepts; but we need not concern ourselves further with this aspect.

We spoke of the relation called "judging" or "believing" as knitting together into one complex whole the subject and the objects. In this respect, judging is exactly like every other relation. Whenever a relation holds between two or more terms, it unites the terms into a complex whole. If Othello loves Desdemona, there is such a complex whole as "Othello's love for Desdemona." The terms united by the relation may be themselves complex, or may be simple, but the whole which results from their being united must be complex. Wherever there is a relation which

relates certain terms, there is a complex object formed of the union of those terms; and conversely, wherever there is a complex object, there is a relation which relates its constituents. When an act of believing occurs, there is a complex, in which "believing" is the uniting relation, and subject and objects are arranged in a certain order by the "sense" of the relation of believing. Among the objects, as we saw in considering "Othello believes that Desdemona loves Cassio," one must be a relation—in this instance, the relation "loving." But this relation, as it occurs in the act of believing, is not the relation which creates the unity of the complex whole consisting of the subject and the objects. The relation "loving," as it occurs in the act of believing, is one of the objects—it is a brick in the structure, not the cement. The cement is the relation "believing." When the belief is *true*, there is another complex unity, in which the relation which was one of the objects of the belief relates the other objects. Thus, e.g., if Othello believes *truly* that Desdemona loves Cassio, then there is a complex unity, "Desdemona's love for Cassio," which is composed exclusively of the *objects* of the belief, in the same order as they had in the belief, with the relation which was one of the objects occurring now as the cement that binds together the other objects of the belief. On the other hand, when a belief is *false*, there is no such complex unity composed only of the objects of the belief. If Othello believes *falsely* that Desdemona loves Cassio, then there is no such complex unity as "Desdemona's love for Cassio."

Thus a belief is *true* when it *corresponds* to a certain associated complex, and *false* when it does not. Assuming, for the sake of definiteness, that the objects of the belief are two terms and a relation, the terms being put in a certain order by the "sense" of the believing, then if the two terms in that order are united by the relation into a complex, the belief is true; if not, it is false. This constitutes the definition of truth and falsehood that we were in search of. Judging or believing is a certain complex unity of which a mind is a constituent; if the remaining constituents, taken in the order which they have in the belief, form a complex unity, then the belief is true; if not, it is false.

Thus although truth and falsehood are properties of beliefs, yet they are in a sense extrinsic properties, for the condition of the truth of a belief is something not involving beliefs, or (in general) any mind at all, but only the *objects* of the belief. A mind, which believes, believes truly when there is a *corresponding* complex not involving the mind, but only its objects. This correspondence ensures truth, and its absence entails falsehood. Hence we account simultaneously for the two facts that beliefs (a) depend on minds for their *existence*, (b) do not depend on minds for their *truth*.

We may restate our theory as follows: If we take such a belief as "Othello believes that Desdemona loves Cassio," we will call Desdemona and Cassio the *object-terms*, and loving the *object-relation*. If there is a complex unity "Desdemona's love for Cassio," consisting of the object-terms related by the object-relation in the same order as they have in the belief, then this complex unity is called the *fact corresponding to the belief.* Thus a belief is true when there is a corresponding fact, and is false when there is no corresponding fact.

. . . Minds do not *create* truth or falsehood. They create beliefs, but when once the beliefs are created, the mind cannot make them true or false, except in the special case where they concern future things which are within the power of the person believing, such as catching trains. What makes a belief true is a *fact*, and this fact does not (except in exceptional cases) in any way involve the mind of the person who has the belief.

CHAPTER 21

FRANCIS HERBERT BRADLEY

THE COHERENCE THEORY OF TRUTH

Francis Herbert Bradley (1846–1924) was a British idealist best known for his book *Appearance and Reality* (1893), which defends a very strong version of the coherence theory of truth. Educated at Oxford University, he was elected to a fellowship there that enabled him to devote himself completely to philosophical writing, without teaching responsibilities.

An admirer of Hegel, Bradley was a controversial writer whose work influenced Bertrand Russell and William James, among others. Russell's version of the correspondence theory of truth was formulated in response to Bradley's coherence theory. Bradley's literary style was admired by many, including the poet T.S. Eliot, who wrote a thesis on Bradley's work while a student at Harvard.

In this selection, Bradley begins by stressing the necessity of employing a test of truth that functions as a system, rather than one built on cases of fact, perception, and memory.[1] Against the correspondence theory, he argues that our judgments are not like the physical objects to which they refer; hence, we cannot know the "reality" to which our beliefs are supposed to correspond. Truth is "an ideal expression of the universe," and perfect truth must take the form of a systematic whole.

---

[1]From Francis Herbert Bradley, *Essays on Truth and Reality* (Oxford: Oxford University Press, 1914).

THE COHERENCE THEORY OF TRUTH

. . . What I maintain is that in the case of facts of perception and memory the test [of truth] which we do apply, and which we must apply, is that of system. I contend that this test works satisfactorily, and that no other test will work. And I argue in consequence that there are no judgements of sense which are in principle infallible. . . .

The reason for maintaining independent facts and infallible judgements, as I understand it, is twofold. (1) Such data, it may be said, can be actually shown. And (2) in any case they must exist, since without them the intelligence cannot work. . . .

(1) I doubt my ability to do justice to the position of the man who claims to show ultimate given facts exempt from all possible error. In the case of any datum of sensation or feeling, to prove that we have this wholly unmodified by what is called 'apperception' seems a hopeless undertaking. And how far it is supposed that such a negative can be proved I do not know. What, however, is meant must be this, that we somehow and somewhere have verifiable facts of perception and memory, and also judgements, free from all chance of error.

I will begin hereby recalling a truth familiar but often forgotten. . . . In your search for independent facts and for infallible truths you may go so low that, when you have descended beyond the level of error, you find yourself below the level of any fact or of any truth which you can use. What you seek is particular facts of perception or memory, but what you get may be something not answering to that character. I will go on to give instances of what I mean, and I think that in every case we shall do well to ask this question, 'What on the strength of our ultimate fact are we able to contradict?'

(a) If we take the instance of simple unrelated sensations or feelings, a, b, c—supposing that there are such things—what judgement would such a fact enable us to deny? We could on the strength of this fact deny the denial that a, b and c exist in any way, manner or sense. But surely this is not the kind of independent fact of which we are in search.

(b) From this let us pass to the case of a complex feeling containing, at once and together, both a and b. On the ground of this we can deny the statement that a and b cannot or do not ever anyhow co-exist in feeling. This is an advance, but it surely leaves us far short of our goal.

(c) What we want, I presume, is something that at once is infallible and that also can be called a particular fact of perception or memory. And we want, in the case of perception, something that would be called a fact for observation. We do not seem to reach this fact until we arrive somewhere about the level of 'I am here and now having a sensation or complex of sensations of such or such a kind.' The goal is reached; but at this point, unfortunately, the judgement has become fallible, so far at least as it really states particular truth.

(α) In such a judgement it is in the first place hard to say what is meant by the 'I.' If, however, we go beyond feeling far enough to mean a self with such or such a real existence in time, then memory is involved, and the judgement at once, I should urge, becomes fallible. . . . Thus the statement made in the judgement is liable to error, or else the statement does not convey particular truth.

(β) And this fatal dilemma holds good when applied to the 'now' and 'here.' If these words mean a certain special place in a certain special series or order, they are liable to mistake. But, if they fall short of this meaning, then they fail to state individual fact. My feeling is, I agree, not subject to error in the proper sense of that term, but on the other side my feeling does not of itself deliver truth. And the process which gets from it a deliverance as to individual fact is fallible.

Everywhere such fact depends on construction. And we have here to face not only the possibility of what would commonly be called mistaken interpretation. We have in addition the chance of actual sense-hallucination. And, worse than this, we have the far-reaching influence of abnormal suggestion and morbid fixed idea. This influence may stop short of hallucination, and yet may vitiate the memory and the judgement to such an extent that there remains no practical difference between idea and perceived fact. And, in the face of these possibilities, it seems idle to speak of perceptions and memories secure from all chance of error. Or on the other side banish the chance of error, and with what are you left? You then have something which (as we have seen) goes no further than to warrant the assertion that such and such elements can and do co-exist—somehow and somewhere, or again that such or such a judgement happens—without any regard to its truth and without any specification of its psychical context. And no one surely will contend that with this we have particular fact.

The doctrine that perception gives us infallible truth rests on a foundation which in part is sound and in part fatally defective. That what is felt is felt, and cannot, so far as felt, be mistaken—so much as this must be accepted. But the view that, when I say 'this,' 'now,' 'here,' or 'my,' what I feel, when so speaking, is carried over intact into my judgement, and that my judgement in consequence is exempt from error, seems wholly indefensible. It survives, I venture to think, only because it never has understood its

complete refutation. That which I designate is not and cannot be carried over into my judgement. The judgement may in a sense answer to that which I feel, but none the less it fails to contain and to convey my feeling. And on the other hand, so far as it succeeds in expressing my meaning, the judgement does this in a way which makes it liable to error. Or, to put it otherwise, the perceived truth, to be of any use, must be particularized. So far as it is stated in a general form, it contains not only that which you meant to say but also, and just as much, the opposite of that which you meant. And to contend for the infallibility of such a truth seems futile. On the other side so far as your truth really is individualized, so far as it is placed in a special construction and vitally related to its context, to the same extent the element of interpretation or implication is added. And, with this element obviously comes the possibility of mistake. And we have seen above that, viewed psychologically, particular judgements of perception immune from all chance of error seem hardly tenable.

(2) I pass now to the second reason for accepting infallible data of perception. Even if we cannot show these (it is urged) we are bound to assume them. For in their absence our knowledge has nothing on which to stand, and this want of support results in total scepticism.

It is possible of course here to embrace both premises and conclusion, and to argue that scepticism is to be preferred to an untrue assumption. And such a position I would press on the notice of those who uphold infallible judgements of sense and memory. But personally I am hardly concerned in this issue, for I reject both the conclusion and the premises together. Such infallible and incorrigible judgements are really not required for our knowledge, and, since they cannot be shown, we must not say that they exist. . . .

I agree that we depend vitally on the sense-world, that our material comes from it, and that apart from it knowledge could not begin. To this world, I agree, we have for ever to return, not only to gain new matter but to confirm and maintain the old. I agree that to impose order from without on sheer disorder would be wholly impracticable, and that, if my sense-world were disorderly beyond a certain point, my intelligence would not exist. And further I agree that we cannot suppose it possible that *all* the judgements of perception and memory which for me come first, could in fact for me be corrected. I cannot, that is, imagine the world of my experience to be so modified that in the end none of these accepted facts should be left standing. But so far, I hasten to add, we have not yet come to the real issue. There is still a chasm between such admissions and the conclusion that there are judgements of sense which possess truth absolute and infallible.

We meet here a false doctrine largely due to a misleading metaphor. My known world is taken to be a construction built upon such and such foundations. It is argued, therefore, to be in principle a superstructure which rests upon these supports. You can go on adding to it no doubt, but only so long as the supports remain; and, unless they remain, the whole building comes down. But the doctrine, I have to contend, is untenable, and the metaphor ruinously inapplicable. The foundation in truth is provisional merely. In order to begin my construction I take the foundation as absolute—so much certainly is true. But that my construction continues to rest on the beginnings of my knowledge is a conclusion which does not follow. It does not follow that, if these are allowed to be fallible, the whole building collapses. For it is in another sense that my world rests upon the data of perception.

My experience is solid, not so far as it is a superstructure but so far as in short it is a system. My object is to have a world as comprehensive

and coherent as possible, and, in order to attain this object, I have not only to reflect but perpetually to have recourse to the materials of sense. I must go to this source both to verify the matter which is old and also to increase it by what is new. And in this way I must depend upon the judgements of perception. Now it is agreed that, if I am to have an orderly world, I cannot possibly accept all 'facts.' Some of these must be relegated, as they are, to the world of error, whether we succeed or fail in modifying and correcting them. And the view which I advocate takes them all as in principle fallible. On the other hand, that view denies that there is any necessity for absolute facts of sense. Facts for it are true, we may say, just so far as they work, just so far as they contribute to the order of experience. If by taking certain judgements of perception as true, I can get more system into my world, then these 'facts' are so far true, and if by taking certain 'facts' as errors I can order my experience better, then so far these 'facts' are errors. And there is no 'fact' which possesses an absolute right. Certainly there are truths with which I begin and which I personally never have to discard, and which therefore remain in fact as members of my known world. And of some of these certainly it may be said that without them I should not know how to order my knowledge. But it is quite another thing to maintain that every single one of these judgements is in principle infallible. The absolute indispensable fact is in my view the mere creature of false theory. Facts are valid so far as, when taken otherwise than as 'real,' they bring disorder into my world. And there are today for me facts such that, if I take them as mistakes, my known world is damaged and, it is possible, ruined. But how does it follow that I cannot tomorrow on the strength of new facts gain a wider order in which these old facts can take a place as errors? The supposition may be improbable, but what you have got to show is that it is in principle impossible. A foundation used at the beginning does not in short mean something fundamental at the end, and there is no single 'fact' which in the end can be called fundamental absolutely. It is all a question of relative contribution to my known world-order.

'Then no judgement of perception will be more than probable?' Certainly that is my contention. 'Facts' are justified because and as far as, while taking them as real, I am better able to deal with the incoming new 'facts' and in general to make my world wider and more harmonious. The higher and wider my structure, and the more that any particular fact or set of facts is implied in that structure, the more certain are the structure and the facts. And, if we could reach an all-embracing ordered whole, then our certainty would be absolute. But, since we cannot do this, we have to remain content with relative probability. Why is this or that fact of observation taken as practically certain? It is so taken just so far as it is *not* taken in its own right. (i) Its validity is due to such and such a person perceiving it under such and such conditions. This means that a certain intellectual order in the person is necessary as a basis, and again that nothing in the way of sensible or mental distortion intervenes between this order and what is given. And (ii) the observed fact must agree with our world as already arranged, or at least must not upset this. If the fact is too much contrary to our arranged world we provisionally reject it. We eventually accept the fact only when after confirmation the hypothesis of its error becomes still more ruinous. We are forced then more or less to rearrange our world, and more or less perhaps to reject some previous 'facts.' The question throughout is as to what is better or worse for our order as a whole.

Why again to me is a remembered fact certain, supposing that it is so? Assuredly not because it is infallibly delivered by the faculty of Memory, but because I do not see how to recon-

cile the fact of its error with my accepted world. Unless I go on the principle of trusting my memory, apart from any special reason to the contrary, I cannot order my world so well, if indeed I can order it at all. The principle here again is system. . . .

The same account holds with regard to the facts of history. For instance, the guillotining of Louis XVI is practically certain because to take this as error would entail too much disturbance of my world. Error is possible here of course. Fresh facts conceivably might come before me such as would compel me to modify in part my knowledge as so far arranged. And in this modified arrangement the execution of Louis would find its place as an error. But the reason for such a modification would have to be considerable, while, as things are, no reason exists. . . . To take memory as in general trustworthy, where I have no special reason for doubt, and to take the testimony of those persons, whom I suppose to view the world as I view it, as being true, apart from special reason on the other side—these are principles by which I construct my ordered world, such as it is. And because by any other method the result is worse, therefore for me these principles are true. On the other hand to suppose that any 'fact' or perception or memory is so certain that no possible experience could justify me in taking it as error seems to me injurious if not ruinous. On such a principle my world of knowledge would be ordered worse, if indeed it could be ordered at all. For to accept all the 'facts,' as they offer themselves, seems obviously impossible; and, if it is we who have to decide as to which facts are infallible, then I ask how we are to decide. The ground of validity, I maintain, consists in successful contribution. That is a principle of order, while any other principle, so far as I see, leads to chaos.

'But,' it may still be objected, 'my fancy is unlimited. I can therefore invent an imaginary world even more orderly than my known world. And further this fanciful arrangement might possibly be made so wide that the world of perception would become for me in comparison small and inconsiderable. Hence, my perceived world, so far as not supporting my fancied arrangement, might be included within it as *error*. Such a consequence would or might lead to confusion in theory and to disaster in practice. And yet the result follows from your view inevitably, unless after all you fall back upon the certainty of perception.'

To this possible objection, I should reply first, that it has probably failed to understand rightly the criterion which I defend. The aspect of comprehensiveness has not received here its due emphasis. The idea of system demands the inclusion of all possible material. Not only must you include everything to be gained from immediate experience and perception, but you must also be ready to act on the same principle with regard to fancy. But this means that you cannot confine yourself within the limits of this or that fancied world, as suits your pleasure or private convenience. You are bound also, so far as is possible, to recognize and to include the opposite fancy.

This consideration to my mind ruins the above hypothesis on which the objection was based. The fancied arrangement not only has opposed to it the world of perception. It also has against it any opposite arrangement and any contrary fact which I can fancy. And, so far as I can judge, these contrary fancies will balance the first. Nothing, therefore, will be left to outweigh the world as perceived, and the imaginary hypothesis will be condemned by our criterion.

. . . I may state the view which has commended itself to my mind. Truth is an ideal expression of the Universe, at once coherent and comprehensive. It must not conflict with itself, and there must be no suggestion which fails to fall inside it. Perfect truth in short must realize the idea of a systematic whole. And such a whole . . . possesses essentially the two characters of coherence and comprehensiveness.

CHAPTER 22

WILLIAM JAMES

THE PRAGMATIC THEORY OF TRUTH

The selection opens with James' often quoted "stages of a theory's career," and closes with his response to the most frequent criticism of his theory.[1] In between, with his customary eloquence, James presents the case for a pragmatic theory of truth (see Chapter 13 for a brief biography of James). Central to his argument is the idea that truths are made in the course of experience. Rather than being a stagnant property, an unobtainable "copy of reality," truth happens to an idea as it is made true by events. As James puts it, "The true is the name of whatever proves itself to be good in the way of belief." The test of truth is utility, workability, and the emergence of satisfactory consequences.

THE PRAGMATIC THEORY OF TRUTH

. . . I fully expect to see the pragmatist view of truth run through the classic stages of a theory's career. First, you know, a new theory is attacked as absurd; then it is admitted to be true, but obvious and insignificant; finally it is seen to be so important that its adversaries claim that they themselves discovered it. Our doctrine of truth is at present in the first of these three stages, with symptoms of the second stage having begun in certain quarters. I wish that this lecture might

---

[1]The selection that follows is from William James, *Pragmatism* (New York: Longmans, Green & Co., 1907).

help it beyond the first stage in the eyes of many of you.

Truth, as any dictionary will tell you, is a property of certain of our ideas. It means their "agreement," as falsity means their disagreement, with "reality." Pragmatists and intellectualists both accept this definition as a matter of course. They begin to quarrel only after the question is raised as to what may precisely be meant by the term "agreement," and what by the term "reality," when reality is taken as something for our ideas to agree with.

In answering these questions the pragmatists are more analytic and painstaking, the intellectualists more offhand and irreflective. The popular notion is that a true idea must copy its reality. Like other popular views, this one follows the analogy of the most usual experience. Our true ideas of sensible things do indeed copy them. Shut your eyes and think of yonder clock on the wall, and you get just such a true picture or copy of its dial. But your idea of its "works" (unless you are a clock-maker) is much less of a copy, yet it passes muster, for it in no way clashes with the reality. Even though it should shrink to the mere word "works," that word still serves you truly; and when you speak of the 'time-keeping function" of the clock, or of its spring's "elasticity," it is hard to see exactly what your ideas can copy.

You perceive that there is a problem here. Where our ideas cannot copy definitely their object, what does agreement with that object mean? Some idealists seem to say that they are true whenever they are what God means that we ought to think about that object. Others hold the copy-view all through, and speak as if our ideas possessed truth just in proportion as they approach to being copies of the Absolute's eternal way of thinking.

These views, you see, invite pragmatistic discussion. But the great assumption of the intellectualists is that truth means essentially an inert

static relation. When you've got your true idea of anything, there's an end of the matter. You're in possession; you *know*; you have fulfilled your thinking destiny. You are where you ought to be mentally; you have obeyed your categorical imperative; and nothing more need follow on that climax of your rational destiny. Epistemologically you are in stable equilibrium.

Pragmatism, on the other hand, asks its usual question. "Grant an idea or belief to be true," it says, "what concrete difference will its being true make in anyone's actual life? How will the truth be realized? What experiences will be different from those which would obtain if the belief were false? What, in short, is the truth's cash-value in experiential terms?"

The moment pragmatism asks this question, it sees the answer. *True ideas are those that we can assimilate, validate, corroborate and verify. False ideas are those that we cannot.* That is the practical difference it makes to us to have true ideas; that, therefore, is the meaning of truth, for it is all that truth is known as.

This thesis is what I have to defend. The truth of an idea is not a stagnant property inherent in it. Truth *happens* to an idea. It *becomes* true, is *made* true by events. Its verity *is* in fact an event, a process: the process namely of its verifying itself, its veri-*fication*. Its validity is the process of its valid-*ation*.

But what do the words verification and validation themselves pragmatically mean? They again signify certain practical consequences of the verified and validated idea. It is hard to find any one phrase that characterized these consequences better than the ordinary agreement-formula—just such consequences being what we have in mind whenever we say that our ideas "agree" with reality. They lead us, namely, through the acts and other ideas which they instigate, into or up to, or towards, other parts of experience with which we feel all the while—

such feeling being among our potentialities—that the original ideas remain in agreement. The connections and transitions come to us from point to point as being progressive, harmonious, satisfactory. This function of agreeable leading is what we mean by an idea's verification. . . .

. . . The possession of true thoughts means everywhere the possession of invaluable instruments of action; and . . . our duty to gain truth, so far from being a blank command from out of the blue, or a "stunt" self-imposed by our intellect, can account for itself by excellent practical reasons.

The importance to human life of having true beliefs about matters of fact is a thing too notorious. We live in a world of realities that can be infinitely useful or infinitely harmful. Ideas that tell us which of them to expect count as the true ideas in all this primary sphere of verification, and the pursuit of such ideas is a primary human duty. The possession of truth, so far from being here an end in itself, is only a preliminary means towards other vital satisfactions. If I am lost in the woods and starved, and find what looks like a cow-path, it is of the utmost importance that I should think of a human habitation at the end of it, for if I do so and follow it, I save myself. The true thought is useful here because the house which is its object is useful. The practical value of true ideas is thus primarily derived from the practical importance of their objects to us. Their objects are, indeed, not important at all times. I may on another occasion have no use for the house; and then my idea of it, however verifiable, will be practically irrelevant, and had better remain latent. Yet since almost any object may some day become temporarily important, the advantage of having a general stock of *extra* truths, of ideas that shall be true of merely possible situations, is obvious. We store such extra truths away in our memories, and with the overflow we fill our books of reference. Whenever such an extra truth becomes practically relevant to one of our emergencies, it passes from cold-storage to do work in the world and our belief in it grows active. You can say of it then either that "it is useful because it is true" or that "it is true because it is useful." Both these phrases mean exactly the same thing, namely that here is an idea that gets fulfilled and can be verified. True is the name for whatever idea starts the verification-process, useful is the name for its completed function in experience. True ideas would never have been singled out as such, would never have acquired a class-name, least of all a name suggesting value, unless they had been useful from the outset in this way.

From this simple cue pragmatism gets her general notion of truth as something essentially bound up with the way in which one moment in our experience may lead us towards other moments which it will be worthwhile to have been led to. Primarily, and on the common-sense level, the truth of a state of mind means this function of *a leading that is worthwhile*. When a moment in our experience, of any kind whatever, inspires us with a thought that is true, that means that sooner or later we dip by that thought's guidance into the particulars of experience again and make advantageous connection with them. This is a vague enough statement, but I beg you to retain it, for it is essential.

Our experience meanwhile is all shot through with regularities. One bit of it can warn us to get ready for another bit, can "intend" or be "significant of" that remoter object. The object's advent is the significance's verification. Truth, in these cases, meaning nothing but eventual verification, is manifestly incompatible with waywardness on our part. Woe to him whose beliefs play fast and loose with the order which realities follow in his experience; they will lead him nowhere or else make false connections.

By "realities" or "objects" here, we mean

either things of common sense, sensibly present, or else common-sense relations, such as dates, places, distances, kinds, activities. Following our mental image of a house along the cow-path, we actually come to see the house; we get the image's full verification. *Such simply and fully verified leadings are certainly the originals and prototypes of the truth-process.* Experience offers indeed other forms of truth-process, but they are all conceivable as being primary verifications arrested, multiplied or substituted one for another.

Take, for instance, yonder object on the wall. You and I consider it to be a "clock," altho no one of us has seen the hidden works that make it one. We let our notion pass for true without attempting to verify. If truths mean verification-process essentially, ought we then to call such unverified truths as this abortive? No, for they form the overwhelmingly large number of the truths we live by. Indirect as well as direct verifications pass muster. Where circumstantial evidence is sufficient, we can go without eye-witnessing. Just as we here assume Japan to exist without ever having been there, because it *works* to do so, everything we know conspiring with the belief, and nothing interfering, so we assume that thing to be a clock. We *use* it as a clock, regulating the length of our lecture by it. The verification of the assumption here means its leading to no frustration or contradiction. Verif*ability* of wheels and weights and pendulum is as good as verification. For one truth-process completed there are a million in our lives that function in this state of nascency. They turn us *towards* direct verification; lead us into the *surroundings* of the objects they envisage; and then, if everything runs on harmoniously, we are so sure that verification is possible that we omit it, and are usually justified by all that happens.

Truth lives, in fact, for the most part on a credit system. Our thoughts and beliefs "pass," so long as nothing challenges them, just as bank-

notes pass so long as nobody refuses them. But this all points to direct face-to-face verifications somewhere, without which the fabric of truth collapses like a financial system with no cash-basis whatever. You accept my verification of one thing, I yours of another. We trade on each other's truth. But beliefs verified concretely by *somebody* are the posts of the whole superstructure.

Another great reason—beside economy of time—for waiving complete verification in the usual business of life is that all things exist in kinds and not singly. Our world is found once for all to have that peculiarity. So that when we have once directly verified our ideas about one specimen of a kind, we consider ourselves free to apply them to other specimens without verification. A mind that habitually discerns the kind of thing before it, and acts by the law of the kind immediately, without pausing to verify, will be a "true" mind in ninety-nine out of a hundred emergencies, proved so by its conduct fitting everything it meets, and getting no refutation.

Indirectly or only potentially verifying processes may thus be true as well as full verification-processes. They work as true processes would work, give us the same advantages, and claim our recognition for the same reasons. . . .

II

Our account of truth is an account of truths in the plural, of processes of leading, realized *in rebus,*[1] and having only this quality in common, that they *pay.* They pay by guiding us into or towards some part of a system that dips at numerous points into sensepercepts, which we may copy mentally or not, but with which at any rate we are now in the kind of commerce vaguely

[1] In things. [ED.]

designated as verification. Truth for us is simply a collective name for verification-processes, just as health, wealth, strength, etc., are names for other processes connected with life, and also pursued because it pays to pursue them. Truth is *made*, just as health, wealth and strength are made, in the course of experience.

Here rationalism is instantaneously up in arms against us. I can imagine a rationalist to talk as follows:

"Truth is not made," he will say; "it absolutely obtains, being a unique relation that does not wait upon any process, but shoots straight over the head of experience, and hits its reality every time. Our belief that yon thing on the wall is a clock is true already, altho no one in the whole history of the world should verify it. The bare quality of standing in that transcendent relation is what makes any thought true that possesses it, whether or not there be verification. You pragmatists put the cart before the horse in making truth's being reside in verification-processes. These are merely signs of its being, merely our lame ways of ascertaining after the fact which of our ideas already has possessed the wondrous quality. The quality itself is timeless, like all essences and natures. Thoughts partake of it directly, as they partake of falsity or of irrelevancy. It can't be analyzed away into pragmatic consequences."

The whole plausibility of this rationalist tirade is due to the fact to which we have already paid so much attention. In our world, namely, abounding as it does in things of similar kinds and similarly associated, one verification serves for others of its kind, and one great use of knowing things is to be led not so much to them as to their associates, especially to human talk about them. The quality of truth, obtaining *ante rem*,[2] pragmatically means, then, the fact that in such a world innumerable ideas work better by their indirect or possible than by their direct and actual verification. Truth *ante rem* means only verifiability, then; or else it is a case of the stock rationalist trick of treating the *name* of a concrete phenomenal reality as an independent prior entity, and placing it behind the reality as its explanation. . . .

In the case of "wealth" we all see the fallacy. We know that wealth is but a name for concrete processes that certain men's lives play a part in, and not a natural excellence found in Messrs. Rockefeller and Carnegie, but not in the rest of us.

Like wealth, health also lives *in rebus*. It is a name for processes, as digestion, circulation, sleep, etc., that go on happily, tho in this instance we are more inclined to think of it as a principle and to say the man digests and sleeps so well *because* he is so healthy.

With "strength" we are, I think, more rationalistic still, and decidedly inclined to treat it as an excellence pre-existing in the man and explanatory of the herculean performances of his muscles.

With "truth" most people go over the border entirely, and treat the rationalistic account as self-evident. But really all these words in *th* are exactly similar. Truth exists *ante rem* just as much and as little as the other things do.

The scholastics, following Aristotle, made much of the distinction between habit and act. Health *in actu*[3] means, among other things, good sleeping and digesting. But a healthy man need not always be sleeping, or always digesting, any more than a wealthy man need be always handling money, or a strong man always lifting weights. All such qualities sink to the status of "habits" between their times of exercise; and similarly truth becomes a habit of certain of our

[2]Before the thing. [ED.]

[3]In actuality. [ED.]

ideas and beliefs in their intervals of rest from their verifying activities. But those activities are the root of the whole matter, and the condition of there being any habit to exist in the intervals.

"The true," to put it very briefly, *is only the expedient in the way of our thinking, just as "the right" is only the expedient in the way of our behaving.* Expedient in almost any fashion; and expedient in the long run and on the whole of course; for what meets expediently all the experience in sight won't necessarily meet all farther experiences equally satisfactorily. Experience, as we know, has ways of *boiling over,* and making us correct our present formulas.

The "absolutely" true, meaning what no farther experience will ever alter, is that ideal vanishing-point towards which we imagine that all our temporary truths will some day converge. It runs on all fours with the perfectly wise man, and with the absolutely complete experience; and, if these ideals are ever realized, they will all be realized together. Meanwhile we have to live today by what truth we can get today, and be ready tomorrow to call it falsehood. Ptolemaic astronomy, Euclidean space, Aristotelian logic, scholastic metaphysics, were expedient for centuries, but human experience has boiled over those limits, and we now call these things only relatively true, or true within those borders of experience. "Absolutely" they are false; for we know that those limits were casual, and might have been transcended by past theorists just as they are by present thinkers. . . .

III

. . . Truth is *one species of good,* and not, as is usually supposed, a category distinct from good, and coordinate with it. *The true is the name of whatever proves itself to be good in the way of belief, and good, too,* *for definite, assignable reasons.* Surely you must admit this, that if there were *no* good for life in true ideas, or if the knowledge of them were positively disadvantageous and false ideas the only useful ones, then the current notion that truth is divine and precious, and its pursuit a duty, could never have grown up or become a dogma. In a world like that, our duty would be to *shun* truth, rather. But in this world, just as certain foods are not only agreeable to our taste, but good for our teeth, our stomach, and our tissues; so certain ideas are not only agreeable to think about, or agreeable as supporting other ideas that we are fond of, but they are also helpful in life's practical struggles. If there be any life that it is really better we should lead, and if there be any idea which, if believed in, would help us to lead that life, then it would be really *better for us* to believe in that idea, *unless, indeed, belief in it incidentally clashed with other greater vital benefits.*

"What would be better for us to believe!" This sounds very like a definition of truth. It comes very near to saying "what we *ought* to believe:" and in *that* definition none of you would find any oddity. Ought we ever not to believe what it is *better for us* to believe? And can we then keep the notion of what is better for us, and what is true for us, permanently apart?

Pragmatism says no, and I fully agree with her. Probably you also agree, so far as the abstract statement goes, but with a suspicion that if we practically did believe everything that made for good in our own personal lives, we should be found indulging all kinds of fancies about this world's affairs, and all kinds of sentimental superstitions about a world hereafter. Your suspicion here is undoubtedly well founded, and it is evident that something happens when you pass from the abstract to the concrete that complicates the situation.

I said just now that what is better for us to believe is true *unless the belief incidentally clashes with* some other vital benefit. Now in real life what vital benefits is any particular belief of ours most liable to clash with? What indeed except the vital benefits yielded by *other beliefs* when these *prove* incompatible with the first ones? In other words, the greatest enemy of any one of our truths may be the rest of our truths. Truths have once for all this desperate instinct of self-preservation and of desire to extinguish whatever contradicts them. . . .

CONTEMPORARY PERSPECTIVES: THE POLITICS OF TRUTH

The last two centuries have witnessed a dramatic shift in the concept of truth. It has not yet been 200 years since Hegel gave us his monumental *Phenomenology of Spirit*. Hastily finished in 1806, just as the conquering Napoleon was entering the college town of Jena, Germany, Hegel's *Phenomenology* captured the excitement, tension, and anxiety of his day. It also introduced to the cultured public a comprehensive system of thought and reality that was striking in its claims to finality, totality, and completeness. For instance, Hegel often spoke of his philosophical system as "the end of the history of the concept." By this, he did not mean that history as a temporal flow of events would end, nor did he mean that all philosophical activity would cease. What he meant was that his philosophy had comprehended its own historical epoch in thought; it was an encyclopedic cultural form that contained the true spirit of the age and its people.

For today's philosophy student, aware of the great diversity of philosophic thought and the cultural pluralism that pervades America, and indeed, the world, Hegel's "encyclopedic approach" to philosophy will seem quaintly outdated. We may very well be amused at many of the outrageous claims that Hegel made for his system until we realize that in rejecting Hegel's vision of a unified absolute system of thought and reality, we are rejecting as well his claim that truth is one. If it is true that ideas have consequences, then we shall have to reckon with the meaning of our disavowal of the oneness of truth in favor of a plurality of truths. The turning away from Hegel's system may well be the most significant cultural event in the past 200 years.

Yet the turn did not happen all at once, nor was it the result of only one person's thought. The crisis that thought entered after Hegel gave rise to a family of new philosophical movements. Karl Marx (1818–1883), Søren Kierkegaard (1813–1855), and Friedrich Nietzsche (1844–1900), the three most prominent post-Hegelians of the nineteenth century, vigorously and at times bitterly criticized Hegel as they attempted to redirect philosophy. In Marx's case, philosophy was redirected away from Hegelian abstractions toward economic and political concerns. Vowing that philosophy must go beyond *interpreting* the world to actually *changing* the world, Marx put Hegel's dialectical method to work exploring the history of class struggle. The Danish thinker Kierkegaard launched the philosophical movement called **existentialism** with his claim that Hegel's philosophy had paid attention to everything except the one thing that really mattered—the solitary existing individual. Ridiculing Hegel's grandiose system as a glorious mansion whose proprietor lives in a shack next door, Kierkegaard made a passionate plea for a philosophy that originated in the anxious lived-experience of real individuals. And then there was Nietzsche.

Calling himself an "immoralist," Nietzsche's central philosophic task was revolutionary: the creation of values. He attacked Christianity along with modern formulations of morality as "slave moralities," binding people like cattle into duty-bound obedience—a herd motivated out of cowardice. Since no human "nature" was the same, each individual had to create a personal set of values, leading to different moralities for different persons. Each person had to be his own creator. As Nietzsche put it: "What does your conscience say? 'You should become him who you are.'" Values are never final; at any given moment they must be recreated anew if we are to live authentically. Nietzsche was aware that his style of philosophizing put his culture on the brink of a historic shift in history. He anticipated the coming of the "overman," who would have the courage to enact a **transvaluation** of all values.

And what of truth? Nietzsche's radical views on this subject grew from the soil of morality. *Every belief takes itself as true.* The only criterion of truth is the "strength of evidence" on the part of those who will to have truth. Hence, truth is a power-enhancing operation. Truth functions as the validation of our individual desires, conceived in the will. From this denial of "objective, universal truth" comes the doctrine of **perspectivism:** all truth is relative to the will to power of the individual, the drive of the organism toward self-affirmation. The idea of powerless truth is an illusion; what we call truth is merely our irrefutable errors.

Far more important than what things are is the question of what things are called. Realizing this, we learn to cast a suspicious eye on the things that are called true. The traditional epistemic question has always been "Why are certain things true and others false?" Nietzsche, on the other hand, taught us to ask a different question, namely: "Whose interests are served in calling this truth?" The implications of this new question are staggering. When white landowners told black slaves that blacks were inferior by nature, and endorsed this view by quoting the "truth" of holy scripture, whose interests were served by this truth? Clearly not the interests of the slaves! The language of religion and morality often acts as a mask, deceitfully disguising self-interest.

Clearly truth can be quite useful. The "utility of truth" has proved to be an enduring theme in the twentieth century. Contemporary philosophical movements as diverse as pragmatism, phenomenology, existentialism, critical theory, feminism, and deconstruction have all grown out of the attempt to come to grips with the turn from Hegel to Nietzsche. Although each of these movements has its own hallmarks, the question of truth, as Nietzsche taught us to ask the question, is a central concern in all of them.

More recently, a cultural phenomenon frequently called **postmodernism** has come on the scene. The postmodern bears the marks of Nietzsche in its insistence on antisystematic ways of thought; an emphasis on the importance of aesthetics; and a suspicion of totality, whether expressed politically, morally, philosophically, or artistically. Important postmodern thinkers include Michel Foucault (1926–1984), Jacques Derrida (1930–   ), and Jean-François Lyotard (1924–   ).

Foucault's linkage of knowledge, truth, and power is very reminiscent of Nietzsche. Foucault argues that power is always relational, never substantial. That is to say, "power-in itself" does not exist; power is nothing more than a clustering of relations in society. Power relations govern every aspect of societal life, including labor, production, government, family, kinship, and sexuality. (Not even love is immune from power relations, as veterans of the "wars of love" can attest. Relations of power in love and marriage were the constant theme of the English novelist D.H. Lawrence.) Power is everywhere, not because it embraces everything, but because it comes from everywhere.

Relations of power produce discourses of truth. Because truth always induces regular effects of power, truth is manufactured and circulated in society. Every society has its "truth regime" (what George Orwell in his book *1984* called "The Ministry of Truth") presiding over a "general politics of truth." Certain types of discourse (for example, legal, religious, moral, educational, sexual) are decreed as true, and then circulated widely. In this way, it is not necessary to put a policeman on every corner to ensure obedience to power. The people will police themselves, citing each other for truth-violations and enforcing the penalties. Truth is therefore a machine for autocolonization, ensuring that people regulate themselves.

Foucault, as a postmodern thinker, is concerned about resisting oppressive relations of power. If power is everywhere, so is resistance to power. Like power, resistance to power is relational and plural. Foucault expressed it in this way:

> [T]here is so single locus of great Refusal, no soul of revolt, source of all rebellions, or pure law of revolutionary. Instead, there is a plurality of resistances, each of them a special case: resistances that are possible, necessary, improbable; others that are spontaneous, savage, solitary, concerted, rampant, or even violent; still others that are quick to compromise, interested, or sacrificial; by definition, they can only exist in the strategic field of power relations.[1]

---

[1]See Michel Foucault, in "An Introduction." *History of Sexuality*, vol. 1, trans. Robert Hurley (New York: Vintage Books, 1978), 95–96.

Foucault is describing a counterpolitics of truth, advocating a textual and political strategy of poking around in the "official truth discourses," finding and exposing the seams and weak spots in the fabric of society. Jacques Derrida is the founder of a textual strategy of this sort, which he calls **deconstruction.** Deconstruction involves the undoing of a text through careful teasing out of warring meanings; the deconstructor is alert to places and times where the text seems to differ from itself, revealing an undecidability of meaning. A deconstructive reading of a text is a reading that analyzes the text's critical difference from itself. Derrida has made it clear that deconstruction must be understood as a vigilant political practice, opposed to every form of totalitarianism (whether political or ideological) that claims to possess "total truth," or a "final interpretation." Jean-François Lyotard, in the conclusion to his essay "What Is Postmodernism?" stresses this significance of the postmodern as a resistance to totality when he states: "Let us wage a war on totality; let us be witnesses to the unpresentable; let us activate the differences and save the honor of the name."[2]

It would seem that Hegel's dream of an absolute encyclopedic system of philosophy with a unified account of truth has been lost in the nightmarish age of postmodernity. Or has it? Defenders of Hegel, joined by those who are dismayed at the directions postmodern thought has taken, point out that if indeed philosophy is the universal expression of the culture in which it is rooted, then we ought to expect the discontents, discontinuities, and anxieties of the age to be reflected in its philosophy. Postmodern thinkers, following Nietzsche, are merely philosophizing on the basis of their experience in a troubled and violent century. It may well be that postmodern thought is but a "negative moment" in the cunning labor of reason. The German critical theorist Jürgen Habermas theorizes that postmodern thought represents the exhaustion of the subject-oriented philosophy of modernity that has dominated philosophy since Descartes and advocates a new Enlightenment.[3] Others point out that the perspectivism of Foucault and Nietzsche encounters logical problems. If all truth is perspectival will to power, then what about the statement "all truth is perspectival?" Either this statement is nonperspectival and consequently self-contradictory or it is itself perspectival, merely a personal opinion. Presumably, Nietzsche would claim that the latter is the case, making the doctrine of the will to power merely his own fruitful fiction. Yet his writings at times seem to argue otherwise, making Nietzsche at odds with himself, guilty of a performative contradiction.

[2]Jean-François Lyotard, *The Postmodern Condition*, trans. Geoff Bennington and Brian Massumi (Minneapolis: University of Minnesota Press, 1984), 82.
[3]Jürgen Habermas, *The Philosophical Discourse of Modernity*, trans. Frederick Lawrence (Cambridge: M.I.T. Press, 1987).

In any case, the thought of Nietzsche and the postmoderns have generated an excitement that has spilled over into many areas outside philosophy, most notably in art, architecture, film, and education. They have been lauded and cursed. (Allan Bloom, in *The Closing of the American Mind*, blames Nietzsche and the postmoderns for much of what has gone wrong with American higher education in this century!) In the reading selections that follow, you are invited to see for yourself what all the fuss is about.

CHAPTER 23

FRIEDRICH NIETZSCHE

ON THE UTILITY OF TRUTH[1]

Friedrich Nietzsche (1844–1900), German philosopher, classicist, philologist, and poet, is one of the most influential thinkers of the modern age. Indeed, it is difficult to overestimate the extent of Nietzsche's influence. The great psychoanalyst Sigmund Freud on several occasions said of Nietzsche, "he had a more penetrating knowledge of himself than any other man who ever lived or is ever likely to live."

Nietzsche's father, a Lutheran minister, died at an early age. Friedrich was brought up by his mother, sister, grandmother, and two aunts. He was a precocious student, and his academic career was stunning. He was appointed associate professor at the University of Basel at the age of twenty-four. Two years later he became a full professor. Throughout his life he suffered from poor health, and was afflicted with severe migraine headaches, which often deprived him of sleep. After teaching at Basel for ten years, he retired due to ill health, devoting himself to writing. In January 1889, Nietzsche collapsed in the street, suffering a complete mental breakdown from which he never recovered. His mother lovingly cared for him during the last eleven years of his life, his once brilliant mind completely darkened.

Nietzsche was an enemy of traditional morality, which he called "slave morality," suggesting it was suitable only for the weak and timid. Demanding honesty and exposing moral hypocrisy, he demonstrated how traditional morality is often a mask to cover self-interest and self-advancement. He was also an avowed enemy of Christianity, viewing it as a profound misunderstanding of the historic Jesus, characterized by resentment and fear. Asserting that "God is dead," he celebrated the *übermensch* (overman) as a life-affirming person who lives creatively and courageously without resentment. His analysis of power has had a tremendous influence upon postmodern thinkers, including Michel Foucault.

Unlike most philosophers' writings, Nietzsche's writings are not typically characterized by extended arguments. Instead, they often take the form of a series of aphorisms—terse, pithy (frequently humorous) pronouncements. Although his style is frequently imitated, no one has used this style as wittily and poignantly as Nietzsche. His writings include *The Birth of Tragedy* (1872), *Thus Spake Zarathustra* (1883–84, 1891), *Beyond Good and Evil* (1886), *Toward a Genealogy of Morals* (1887), and *The Will to Power* (1901), published after his death.

ON THE UTILITY OF TRUTH

The different languages placed side by side show that with words truth or adequate expression matters little: for otherwise there would not be so many languages.

What therefore is truth? A mobile army of metaphors, metonymics, anthropomorphisms: in short a sum of human relations which became poetically and rhetorically intensified, metamorphosed, adorned, and after long usage seem to a nation fixed, canonic and binding; truths are illusions of which one has forgotten that they *are* illusions; worn-out metaphors which have become powerless to affect the senses. . . .

Man builds "with the . . . delicate material of ideas, which he must first manufacture within himself. He is very much to be admired here—but not on account of his impulse for truth, his bent for pure cognition of things. If somebody hides a thing behind a bush, seeks it again and finds it in the self-same place, then there is not much to boast of, respecting this seeking and finding; thus, however, matters stand with the seeking and finding of 'truth' within the realm of reason. If I make the definition of the mammal and then declare after inspecting a camel, 'Behold a mammal,' then no doubt a truth is brought to light thereby, but it is of very limited value, I mean it is anthropocentric through and through, and does not contain one single point which is 'true-in-itself,' real and universally valid, apart from man. The seeker after such truths seeks at the bottom only the metamorphosis of the world in man, he strives for an understanding of the world as a human-like thing, and by his battling gains at best the feeling of an assimilation. . . . Such a seeker contemplates the whole world as related to man, as the infinitely protracted echo of an original sound: man; as the multiplied copy of one arch-type: man. His procedure is to apply man as the measure of all things, whereby he starts from the error of believing that he has these things immediately before him as pure objects. He therefore forgets that the original metaphors of perception *are* metaphors, and takes them for the things themselves."

As we say, it is *language* which has worked

217

originally at the construction of ideas; in later times it is *science*. Just as the bee works at the same time at the cells and fills them with honey, thus science works irresistibly at that great columbarium of ideas, the cemetary of perceptions, builds ever newer and higher storeys; supports, purifies, renews the old cells, and endeavours above all to fill that gigantic framework and to arrange within it the whole of the empirical world, i.e., the anthropocentric world.

ONLY AS CREATORS!

This has given me the greatest trouble and still does: to realize that what things *are called* is incomparably more important than what they are. The reputation, name, and appearance, the usual measure and weight of a thing, what it counts for—originally almost always wrong and arbitrary, thrown over things like a dress and altogether foreign to their nature and even to their skin—all this grows from generation unto generation, merely because people believe in it, until it gradually grows to be part of the thing and turns into its very body. What at first was appearance becomes in the end, almost invariably, the essence and is effective as such. How foolish it would be to suppose that one only needs to point out this origin and this misty shroud of delusion in order to *destroy* the world that counts for real, so-called *"reality."* We can destroy only as creators—But let us not forget this either; it is enough to create new names and estimations and probabilities in order to create in the long run new "things."

ORIGIN OF KNOWLEDGE

Over immense periods of time the intellect produced nothing but errors. A few of these proved to be useful and helped to preserve the species: those who hit upon or inherited these had better luck in their struggle for themselves and their progeny. Such erroneous articles of faith, which were continually inherited, until they became almost part of the basic endowment of the species, include the following: that there are enduring things; that there are equal things; that there are things, substances, bodies; that a *thing is what it appears to be; that our will is free; that what is good for me is also good in itself.* It was only very late that such propositions were denied and doubted; it was only very late that truth emerged—as the weakest form of knowledge. It seemed that one was unable to live with it: our organism was prepared for the opposite; all its higher functions, sense perception and every kind of sensation worked with those basic errors which had been incorporated since time immemorial. Indeed, even in the realm of knowledge these propositions became the norms according to which "true" and "untrue" were determined—down to the most remote regions of logic.

Thus the *strength* of knowledge does not depend on its degree of truth but on its age, on the degree to which it has been incorporated, on its character as a condition of life. Where life and knowledge seemed to be at odds there was never any real fight, but denial and doubt were simply considered madness. Those exceptional thinkers, like the Eleatics, who nevertheless posited and clung to the opposites of the natural errors, believed that it was possible to *live* in accordance with these opposites: they invented the sage as the man who was unchangeable and impersonal, the man of the universality of intuition who was One and All at the same time, with a special capacity for his inverted knowledge: they had the faith that their knowledge was also the principle of *life*. But in order to claim all of this, they had to *deceive* themselves about their own state: they had to attribute to themselves, fictitiously, impersonality and changeless duration; they had to misapprehend the nature of the knower; they had to deny the role of the impulses in knowledge; and quite generally they had to conceive of reason as a completely free and spontaneous activity. They shut their eyes to the fact that they, too, had arrived at their propositions through opposition to common sense, or owing to a desire for tranquility, for sole possession, or for dominion. The subtler development of honesty and skepticism eventually made these people, too, impossible; their ways of living and judging were seen to be also dependent upon the primeval impulses and basic errors of all sentient existence.

This subtler honesty and skepticism came into being wherever two contradictory sentences appeared to be *applicable* to life because *both* were compatible with the basic errors, and it was therefore possible to argue about the higher or lower degree of *utility* for life; also wherever new propositions, though not useful for life, were also evidently not harmful to life: in such cases there was room for the expression of an intellectual play impulse, and honesty and skepticism were innocent and happy like all play. Gradually, the human brain became full of such judgments and convictions, and a ferment, struggle, and lust for power developed in this tangle. Not only utility and delight but every kind of impulse took sides in this fight about "truths." The intellectual fight became an occupation, an attraction, a profession, a duty, something dignified—and eventually knowledge and the striving for the true found their place as a need among other needs. Henceforth not only faith and conviction but also scrutiny, denial, mistrust, and contradiction became a *power*; all "evil" instincts were subordinated to knowledge, employed in her service, and acquired the splendor of what is permitted, honored, and useful—and eventually even the eye and innocence of the *good*.

Thus knowledge became a piece of life itself, and hence a continually growing power—until eventually knowledge collided with those primeval basic errors: two lives, two power, both in the same human being. A thinker is now that being in whom the impulse for truth and those life-preserving errors clash for their first fight, after the impulse for truth has proved to be also a life-preserving power. Compared to the significance of this fight, everything else is a matter of indifference: the ultimate question about the conditions of life has been posed here, and we confront the first attempt to answer this question by experiment. To what extent can truth endure incorporation?

ORIGIN OF THE LOGICAL

How did logic come into existence in man's head? Certainly out of illogic, whose realm originally must have been immense. Innumerable beings who made inferences in a way different from ours perished: for all that, their ways might have been truer. Those, for example, who did not know how to find often enough what is "equal" as regards both nourishment and hostile animals—those, in other words, who subsumed things too slowly and cautiously—were favored with a lesser probability of survival than those who guessed immediately upon encountering similar instances that they must be equal. The dominant tendency, however, to treat as equal what is merely similar—an illogical tendency, for nothing is really equal—is what first created any basis for logic.

In order that the concept of substance could originate—which is indispensable for logic although in the strictest sense nothing real corresponds to it—it was likewise necessary that for a long time one did not see nor perceive the changes in things. The beings that did not see so precisely had an advantage over those that saw everything "in flux." At bottom, every high degree of caution in making inferences and every skeptical tendency constitute a great danger for life. No living beings would have survived if the opposite tendency—to affirm rather than suspend judgement, to err and *make up* things rather than wait, to assent rather than negate, to pass judgement rather than be just—had not been bred to the point where it became extraordinarily strong.

The course of logical ideas and inferences in our brain today corresponds to a process and a struggle among impulses that are, taken singly, very illogical and unjust. We generally experience only the result of this struggle because this primeval mechanism now runs its course so quickly and is so well concealed.

CAUSE AND EFFECT

"Explanation" is what we call it, but it is "description" that distinguishes us from older stages of knowledge and science. Our descriptions are better—we do not explain any more than our predecessors. We have uncovered a manifold one-after-another where the naive man and inquirer of older cultures saw only two seperate things. "Cause" and "effect" is what one says; but we have merely perfected the image of becoming without reaching beyond the image or behind it. In every case the series of "causes" confronts us much more completely, and we infer: first, this and that has to precede in order that this or that may then follow—but this does not involve any *comprehension*. In every chemical process, for example, quality appears as a "miracle," as ever; also, every locomotion; nobody has "explained" a push. But how could we possibly explain anything? We operate only with things that do not exist: lines, planes, bodies, atoms, divisible time spans, divisible spaces. How should explanations be at all possible when we first turn everything into an *image*, our image!

It will do to consider science as an attempt to humanize things as faithfully as possible; as we describe things and their one-after-another, we learn how to describe ourselves more and more

precisely. Cause and effect: such a duality probably never exists; in truth we are confronted by a continuum out of which we isolate a couple of pieces, just as we perceive motion only as isolated points and then infer it without ever actually seeing it. The suddenness with which many effects stand out misleads us; actually, it is sudden only for us. In this moment of suddenness there is an infinite number of processes that elude us. An intellect that could see cause and effect as a continuum and a flux and not, as we do, in terms of an arbitrary division and dismemberment, would repudiate the concept of cause and effect and deny all conditionality.

LIFE NO ARGUMENT

We have arranged for ourselves a world in which we can live—by positing bodies, lines, planes, causes and effects, motion and rest, form and content; without these articles of faith nobody now could endure life. But that does not prove them. Life is no argument. The conditions of life might include error.

ULTIMATE SKEPSIS

What are man's truths ultimately? Merely his *irrefutable* errors.

HOW WE, TOO, ARE STILL PIOUS

In science convictions have no rights of citizenship, as one says with good reason. Only when they decide to descend to the modesty of hypotheses, of a provisional experimental point of view, of a regulative fiction, they may be granted admission and even a certain value in the realm of knowledge—though always with the restriction that they remain under police supervision, under the police of mistrust.—But does this not mean, if you consider it more precisely, that a conviction may obtain admission to science only

220

when it *ceases* to be a conviction? Would it not be the first step in the discipline of the scientific spirit that one would not permit oneself any more convictions?

Probably this is so; only we still have to ask: *To make it possible for this discipline to begin,* must there not be some prior conviction—even one that is so commanding and unconditional that it sacrifices all other convictions to itself? We see that science also rests on a faith; there simply is no science "without presuppositions." The question whether *truth* is needed must not only have been affirmed in advance, but affirmed to such a degree that the principle, the faith, the conviction finds expression: *"Nothing* is needed *more* than truth, and in relation to it everything else has only second-rate value."

This unconditional will to truth—what is it? Is it the will *not to allow oneself to be deceived?* Or is it the will *not to deceive?* For the will to truth could be interpreted in the second way, too—if only the special case "I do not want to deceive myself" is subsumed under the generalization "I do not want to deceive." But why not deceive? But why not allow oneself to be deceived?

Note that the reasons for the former principle belong to an altogether different realm from those for the second. One does not want to allow oneself to be deceived because one assumes that it is harmful, dangerous, calamitous to be deceived. In this sense, science would be a long-range prudence, a caution, a utility; but one could object in all fairness: How is that? Is wanting not to allow oneself to be deceived really less harmful, less dangerous, less calamitous? What do you know in advance of the character of existence to be able to decide whether the greater advantage is on the side of the unconditionally mistrustful or of the unconditionally trusting? But if both should be required much trust *as well as* much mistrust, from where would science then be permitted to take its unconditional faith or conviction on which it rests, that truth is more important than any other thing, including every other conviction? Precisely this conviction could never have come into being if both truth and untruth constantly proved to be useful, which is the case. Thus—the faith in science, which after all exists undeniably, cannot owe its origin to such a calculus of utility; it must have originated *in spite of* the fact that the disutility and dangerousness of "the will to truth," of "truth at any price" is proved to it constantly. "At any price": how well we understand these words once we have offered and slaughtered one faith after another on this altar!

Consequently, "will to truth" does *not* mean "I will not allow myself to be deceived" but—there is no alternative—"I will not deceive, not even myself"; *and with that we stand on moral ground.* For you only have to ask yourself carefully, "Why do you not want to deceive?" especially if it should seem—and it does seem!—as if life aimed as semblance, meaning error, deception, simulation, delusion, self-delusion, and when the great sweep of life has actually always shown itself to be on the side of the most unscrupulous *polytropoi.*[2] Charitably interpreted, such a resolve might perhaps be a quixotism,[3] a minor slightly mad enthusiasm; but it might also be something more serious, namely, a principle that is hostile to life and destructive.—"Will to truth"—that might be a concealed will to death.

Thus the question "Why science?" leads back to the moral problem: *Why have morality at all* when life, nature, and history are "not moral"? No doubt, those who are truthful in that audacious and ultimate sense that is presupposed by the faith in science *thus affirm another world* than the

---

[2] *Polytropoi* is a learned borrowing from the Greek meaning a "multiplicity of meanings."

[3] A "quixotism" is a quixotic, that is, a highly romantic or impractical idea.

world of life, nature, and history: and insofar as they affirm this "other world"—look, must they not by the same token negate its counterpart, this world, *our* world?—But you will have gathered what I am driving at, namely, that it is still a *metaphysical faith* upon which our faith in science rests—that even we seekers after knowledge today, we godless anti-metaphysicians still take our fire, too, from the flame lit by a faith that is thousands of years old, that Christian faith which was also the faith of Plato, that God is the truth, that truth is divine.—But what if this should become more and more incredible, if nothing should prove to be divine any more unless it were error, blindness, the life—if God himself should prove to be our most enduring lie?—

Now, if you are willing to listen to my answer and the perhaps extravagant surmise that it involves, it seems to me as if the subtlety and strength of consciousness always were proportionate to a man's (or animal's) *capacity for communication,* and as if this capacity in turn were proportionate to the *need for communication.* But this last point is not to be understood as if the individual human being who happens to be a master in communicating and making understandable his needs must also be most dependent on others in his needs. But it does seem to me as if it were that way when we consider whole races and chains of generations: Where need and distress have forced men for a long time to communicate and to understand each other quickly and subtly, the ultimate result is an excess of this strength and art of communication—as it were, a capacity that has gradually been accumulated and now waits for an heir who might squander it. (Those who are called artists are these heirs; so are orators, preachers, writers—all of them people who always come at the end of a long chain, "late born" every one of them in the best sense of that word and, as I have said, by their nature squanderers.)

Supposing that this observation is correct, I may now proceed to the surmise that *consciousness has developed only under the pressure of the need for communication;* that from the start it was needed and useful only between human beings (particularly between those who commanded and those who obeyed); and that it also developed only in proportion to the degree of this utility. Consciousness is really only a net of communication between human beings; it is only as such that it had to develop; a solitary human being who lived like a beast of prey would not have needed it. That our actions, thoughts, feelings, and movements enter our own consciousness—at least a part of them—that is the result of a "must" that for a terribly long time lorded it over man. As the most endangered animal, he *needed* help and protection, he needed his peers, he had to learn to express his distress and to make himself understood; and for all of this he needed "consciousness" first of all, he needed to "know" himself what distressed him, he needed to know how he felt, he needed to "know" what he thought. For, to say it once more: Man, like every living being, thinks continually without knowing it; the thinking that rises to *consciousness* is only the smallest part of all this—the most superficial and worst part—for only this conscious thinking *takes the form of words, which is to say signs of communication,* and the fact uncovers the origin of consciousness.

In brief, the development of language and the development of consciousness (*not* of reason but merely of the way reason enters consciousness) go hand in hand. Add to this that not only language serves as a bridge between human beings but also a mien, a pressure, a gesture. The emergence of our sense impressions into our own consciousness, the ability to fix them and, as it were, exhibit them externally, increased proportionately with the need to communicate them to *others* by means of signs. The human being inventing signs is at the same time the human being who becomes ever more keenly conscious of himself. It was only as a social animal that man acquired self-consciousness—which he is still in the process of doing, more and more.

My idea is, as you see, that consciousness does not really belong to man's individual existence but rather to his social or herd nature; that, as follows from this, it has developed subtlety only insofar as this is required by social or herd utility. Consequently given the best will in the world to understand ourselves as individually as possible, "to know ourselves," each of us will always succeed in becoming conscious only of what is not individual but "average." Our thoughts themselves are continually governed by the character of consciousness—by the "genius of the species" that commands it—and translated back into the perspective of the herd. Fundamentally, all our actions are altogether incomparably personal, unique, and infinitely individual; there is no doubt of that. But as soon as we translate them into consciousness *they no longer seem to be.*

This is the essence of phenomenalism and perspectivism as I understand them: Owing to the nature of *animal consciousness,* the world of which we can become conscious is only a surface-and sign-world, a world that is made common and meaner; whatever becomes conscious *becomes* by the same token shallow, thin, relatively stupid, general, sign, herd signal; all becoming conscious involves a great and thorough corruption, falsification, reduction to superficialities, and generalization. Ultimately, the growth of consciousness becomes a danger; and anyone who lives among the most conscious Europeans even knows that it is a disease.

You will guess that it is not the opposition of subject and object that concerns me here: This distinction I leave to the epistemologists who have become entangled in the snares of grammar (the metaphysics of the people). It is even less

the opposition of "thing-in-itself" and appearance; for we do not "know" nearly enough to be entitled to any such distinction. We simply lack any organ for knowledge, for "truth": we "know" (or believe or imagine) just as much as may be *useful* in the interests of the human herd, the species; and even what is here called "utility" is ultimately also a mere belief, something imaginary, and perhaps precisely that most calamitous stupidity of which we shall perish some day.

What is it that the common people take for knowledge? What do they want when they want "knowledge"? Nothing more than this: Something strange is to be reduced to something *familiar.* And we philosophers—have we really meant *more* than this when we have spoken of knowledge? What is familar means what we are used to so that we no longer marvel at it, our everyday, some rule in which we are stuck, anything at all in which we feel at home. Look, isn't our need for knowledge precisely this need for the familiar, the will to uncover under everything strange, unusual, and questionable something that no longer disturbs us? Is it not the *instinct of fear* that bids us to know? And is the jubilation of those who attain knowledge not the jubilation over the restoration of a sense of security?

Behind all logic and its seeming sovereignty of movement . . . there stand valuations or, more clearly, physiological demands for the preservation of a certain type of life.

And we are fundamentally inclined to claim . . . that without accepting the fictions of logic, without measuring reality against the purely invented world of the unconditional and self-identical, without a constant falsification of the world by means of numbers, man could not live—that renouncing false judgements would mean renouncing life and a denial of life.

There are still harmless self-observers who believe that there are 'immediate certainties'; for example, 'I think,' or as the superstition of Schopenhauer put it, 'I will'; as though knowledge here got hold of its object purely and nakedly as 'the thing in itself,' without any falsification on the part of either the subject or the object. But that 'immediate certainty,' as well as 'absolute knowledge' and the 'thing in itself,' involve a *contradiction in adjecto*. I shall repeat a hundred times; we really ought to free ourselves from the seduction of words!

Let the people suppose that knowledge means knowing things entirely; the philosopher must say to himself: When I analyze the process that is expressed in the sentence, 'I think,' I find a whole series of daring assertions that would be difficult, perhaps impossible, to prove; for example, that it is *I* who think, that there must necessarily be something that thinks, that thinking is an activity and operation on the part of a being who is thought of as a cause, that there is an 'ego,' and, finally, that it is already determined what is to be designated by thinking—that I *know* what thinking is. . . . In short, the assertion 'I think' assumes that I *compare* my state at the present moment with other states of myself which I know, in order to determine what it is; on account of this retrospective connection with further 'knowledge,' it has, at any rate, no immediate certainty for me.

In place of the 'immediate certainty' in which the people may believe in the case at hand, the philosopher thus finds a series of metaphysical questions presented to him. . . . Whoever ventures to answer these metaphysical questions at once by an appeal to a sort of *intuitive* perception . . . will encounter a smile and two question marks from a philosopher nowadays.

But precisely because we seek knowledge, let us not be ungrateful to such resolute reversals of accustomed perspectives and valuations which the spirit has, with apparent mischievousness and futility, raged against itself for so long: to see differently in this way for once, to *want* to see

differently, is no small discipline and preparation of the intellect for its future 'objectivity'—the latter understood not as 'contemplation without interest' (which is a nonsensical absurdity), but as the ability to *control* one's Pro and Con and to dispose of them, so that one knows how to employ a *variety* of perspectives and affective interpretations in the service of knowledge.

Henceforth, my dear philosophers, let us be on guard against the dangerous old conceptual fiction that posited a 'pure, will-less, painless, timeless knowing subject'; let us guard against the snares of such contradictory concepts as 'pure reason,' 'absolute spirituality,' 'knowledge in itself': these always demand that we should think of an eye that is completely unthinkable, an eye turned in no particular direction, in which the active and interpreting forces, through which alone seeing becomes seeing *something*, are supposed to be lacking; these always demand of the eye an absurdity and a nonsense. There is *only* a perspective seeing, *only* a perspective 'knowing'; and the *more* affects we allow to speak about one thing, the *more* eyes, different eyes, we can use to observe one thing, the more complete will our 'concept' of this thing, our 'objectivity,' more complete will our 'concept' of this thing our 'objectivity,' be.

Philosophers . . . have trusted in concepts as completely as they have mistrusted the senses: they have not stopped to consider that concepts and words are our inheritance from ages in which thinking was very modest and unclear. . . .

Hitherto one has generally trusted one's concepts as if they were a wonderful dowry from some sort of wonderland: but they are, after all, the inheritance from our most remote, most foolish as well as most intelligent ancestors. This piety toward what we find in us is perhaps part of the moral element in knowledge. What is needed above all is an absolute skepticism toward all inherited concepts. . . .

How is truth proved? By the feeling of enhanced power—by utility—by indispensability—in short, by advantages (namely, presuppositions concerning what truth *ought* to be like for us to recognize it). But that is a prejudice: a sign that truth is not involved at all—

The presupposition that things are, at bottom, ordered so morally that human reason must be justified—is an ingenuous presupposition and a piece of naivete, the after-effect of belief in God's veracity. . . .

The intellect cannot criticize itself, simply because . . . in order to criticize the intellect we should have to be a higher being with 'absolute knowledge.' This presupposes that, distinct from every perspective kind of outlook or sensual-spiritual appropriation, something exists, an 'in-itself.'—But the psychologic derivation of the belief in things forbids us to speak of 'things-in-themselves.'

There exists neither 'spirit,' nor reason, nor thinking, nor consciousness, nor soul, nor will, nor truth: all are fictions that are of no use. There is no question of 'subject and object,' but of a particular species of animal that can prosper only through a certain *relative rightness*; above all, regularity of its perceptions (so that it can accumulate experience)—

Knowledge works as a tool of power. Hence it is plain that it increases with every increase of power.

The meaning of 'knowledge': here, as in the case of 'good' or 'beautiful,' the concept is to be regarded in a strict and narrow anthropocentric and biological sense. In order for a particular species to maintain itself and increase its power, its conception of reality must comprehend enough of the calculable and constant for it to base a scheme of behavior on it. The utility of preservation—not some abstract-theoretical need not to be deceived—stands as the motive behind the development of the organs of knowledge—they develop in such a way that their observations suffice for our preservation. In other words . . . : a species grasps a certain amount of reality in order to become master of it, in order to press it into service.

Against positivism, which halts at phenomena—'There are only *facts*'—I would say: **No, facts is precisely what there is not, only interpretations.** We cannot establish any fact 'in itself': perhaps it is folly to want to do such a thing.

'Everything is subjective,' you say; but even this is interpretation. The 'subject' is not something given, it is something added and invented and projected behind what there is.—Finally, is it necessary to posit an interpreter behind the interpretation? Even this is invention, hypothesis. . . .

It is our needs that interpret the world; our drives and their For and Against.

In so far as the word 'knowledge' has any meaning, the world is knowable; but it is *interpretable* otherwise, it has no meaning behind it, but countless meanings.—'Perspectivism'

'There is thinking: therefore there is something that thinks': this is the upshot of all Descartes' argumentation. But that means positing as 'true *a priori*' our belief in the concept of substance—that when there is thought there has to be something 'that thinks' is simply a formulation of our grammatical custom that adds a doer to every deed. In short, this is not merely the substantiation of a fact but a logical-metaphysical postulate—Along the lines followed by Descartes one does not come upon something absolutely certain but only upon the fact of a very strong belief.

Truth is the kind of error without which a certain species of life could not live. The value of *life* is ultimately decisive.

It is improbable that our 'knowledge' should extend further than is strictly necessary for the preservation of life. Morphology shows us how the senses and the nerves, as well as the brain, develop in proportion to the difficulty of finding nourishment.

Our perceptions, as we understand them: i.e., the sum of all those perceptions the becoming-conscious of which was useful and essential to us and to the entire organic process—therefore not all perceptions in general. . . ; this means: we have senses only for a selection of perceptions—those with which we have to concern ourselves in order to preserve ourselves. *Consciousness is present only to the extent that consciousness is* useful. It cannot be doubted that *all sense perceptions are permeated with value judgements* (useful and harmful—consequently, pleasant or unpleasant).

First *images*—to explain how images arise in the spirit. Then *words*, applied to images. Finally *concepts*, possible only when there are words—the collecting together of many images in something nonvisible but audible (word). The tiny amount of emotion to which the 'word' gives rise, as we contemplate similar images for which *one* word exists—this weak emotion is the common element, the basis of the concept. That weak sensations are regarded as alike, sensed as being the same, is the fundamental fact.

Not 'to know' but to schematize—to impose upon chaos as much regularity and form as our practical needs require.

In the formation of reason, logic, the categories, it was *need* that was authoritative: the need, not to 'know,' but to subsume, to schematize, for the purpose of intelligibility and calculation—(The development of reason is adjustment, invention, with the aim of making similar, equal—the same process that every sense impression goes through!) No pre-existing 'idea' was here at work, but the utilitarian fact that only when we see things coarsely and made equal do they become calculable and usable to us—Finality in reason is an effect, not a cause: life miscarries

with any other kinds of reason, to which there is a continual impulse—it becomes difficult to survey—too unequal—

The categories are 'truths' only in the sense that they are conditions of life for us: as Euclidean space is a conditional 'truth.' (Between ourselves: since no one would maintain that there is any necessity for men to exist, reason, as well as Euclidean space, is a mere idiosyncracy of a certain species of animal, and one among many—)

The subjective compulsion not to contradict here is a biological compulsion: the instinct for the utility of inferring as we do infer is part of us, we almost *are* this instinct—But what naivete to extract from this a proof that we are there with in possession of a 'truth in itself'!—Not being able to contradict is proof of an incapacity, not of 'truth.'

We believe in reason: this, however, is the philosophy of gray *concepts*. Language depends on the most naive prejudices.

Now we read disharmonies and problems into things because we think only in the form of language—and thus believe in the 'eternal truth' of 'reason' (e.g., subject, attribute, etc.)

We cease to think when we refuse to do so under the constraint of language; we barely reach the doubt that sees this limitation as a limitation.

Rational thought is interpretation according to a scheme that we cannot throw off.

"No matter how strongly a thing may be believed, strength of belief is no criterion of truth." But what is truth? Perhaps a kind of belief that has become a condition of life: In that case, to be sure, strength could be a criterion; e.g., in regard to causality.

The criterion of truth resides in the enhancement of the feeling of power.

'Truth': this, according to my way of thinking, does not necessarily denote the antithesis of error, but in the most fundamental cases only the posture of various errors in relation to one another. Perhaps one is older, more profound than another, even ineradicable, in so far as an organic entity of our species could not live without it; while other errors do not tyranize over us in this way as conditions of life, but on the contrary when compared with such 'tyrants' can be set aside and 'refuted.'

An assumption that is irrefutable—why should it for that reason be 'true'? This proposition may perhaps outrage logicians, who posit *their* limitations as the limitations of things: but I long ago declared war on this optimism of logicians.

CHAPTER 24

MICHEL FOUCAULT

POWER/KNOWLEDGE

Michel Foucault (1926–1984), one of the most influential thinkers in the contemporary world, was born in Poitier, France. He lectured in many universities throughout the world, serving as director of the Institut Français in Hamburg and the Institut de Philosophie at the Faculté des Lettres in the University of Clermont-Ferrand. Before his untimely death in 1984, he taught at France's most prestigious institution, the Collège de France.

The goal of Foucault's work, which is receiving an enormous amount of attention in various fields, is to create a history of the different modes by which, in our culture, human beings are made subjects. His explorations as "archeologist" and "genealogist" led him to examine closely the phenomena of madness, medicine, law, power, and sexuality. A prolific writer, Foucault is the author of *Madness and Civilization* (1965), *The Order of Things* (1970), *The Archaeology of Knowledge* (1972), *The Birth of the Clinic* (1973), *Discipline and Punish: The Birth of the Prison* (1977), and *The History of Sexuality, Volume 1: An Introduction* (1978); Volume 2: *The Use of Pleasure* (1985); and Volume 3: *The Care of the Self* (1988).

POWER/KNOWLEDGE[1]

The course of study that I have been following until now . . . has been concerned with the *how* of power. I have tried, that is, to relate its mechanisms to two points of reference, two limits: on the one hand, to the rules of right that provide a formal delimitation of power; on the other, to the effects of truth that this power produces and transmits, and which in their turn reproduce this power. Hence we have a triangle: power, right, truth.

[1]From Michel Foucault, *Power/Knowledge: Selected Interviews and Other Writings, 1972–1977*. Text copyright © 1977 by Michel Foucault. Reprinted by permission of Pantheon Books, a division of Random House, Inc.

Schematically, we can formulate the traditional question of political philosophy in the following terms: how is the discourse of truth, or quite simply, philosophy as that discourse which *par excellence* is concerned with truth, able to fix limits to the rights of power? That is the traditional question. The one I would prefer to pose is rather different. Compared to the traditional, noble and philosophic question it is much more down to earth and concrete. My problem is rather this: what rules of right are implemented by the relations of power in the production of discourses of truth? Or alternatively, what type of power is susceptible of producing discourses of truth that in a society such as ours are endowed with such potent effects? What I mean is this: in a society such as ours, but basically in any society, there are manifold relations of power which permeate, characterise and constitute the social body, and these relations of power cannot themselves be established, consolidated nor implemented without the production, accumulation, circulation and functioning of a discourse. There can be no possible exercise of power without a certain economy of discourses of truth which operates through and on the basis of this association. (We are subjected to the production of truth through power and we cannot exercise power except through the production of truth.) This is the case for every society, but I believe that in ours the relationship between power, right and truth is organised in a highly specific fashion. If I were to characterise, not its mechanism itself, but its intensity and constancy, I would say that we are forced to produce the truth of power that our society demands, of which it has need, in order to function: we *must* speak the truth; we are constrained or condemned to confess or to discover the truth. Power never ceases its interrogation, its inquisition, its registration of truth: it institutionalises, professionalises and rewards its pursuit. In the last analysis, we must

produce truth as we must produce wealth, indeed we must produce truth in order to produce wealth in the first place. In another way, we are also subjected to truth in the sense in which it is truth that makes the laws, that produces the true discourse which, at least partially, decides, transmits and itself extends upon the effects of power. In the end, we are judged, condemned, classified, determined in our undertakings, destined to a certain mode of living or dying, as a function of the true discourses which are the bearers of the specific effects of power.

So, it is the rules of right, the mechanisms of power, the effects of truth or if you like, the rules of power and the powers of true discourses, that can be said more or less to have formed the general terrain of my concern, even if, as I know full well, I have traversed it only partially and in a very zig-zag fashion. I should like to speak briefly about this course of research, about what I have considered as being its guiding principle and about the methodological imperatives and precautions which I have sought to adopt. As regards the general principle involved in a study of the relations between right and power, it seems to me that in Western societies since Medieval times it has been royal power that has provided the essential focus around which legal thought has been elaborated. It is in response to the demands of royal power, for its profit and to serve as its instrument or justification, that the juridical edifice of our own society has been developed. Right in the West is the King's right. Naturally everyone is familiar with the famous, celebrated, repeatedly emphasised role of the jurists in the organisation of royal power. We must not forget that the re-vitalisation of Roman Law in the twelfth century was the major event around which, and on whose basis, the juridical edifice which had collapsed after the fall of the Roman Empire was reconstructed. This resurrection of Roman Law had in effect a technical and constitutive role to play in the establishment of the authoritarian, administrative, and, in the final analysis, absolute power of the monarchy. And when this legal edifice escapes in later centuries from the control of the monarch, when, more accurately, it is turned against that control, it is always the limits of this sovereign power that are put in question, its prerogatives that are challenged. In other words, I believe that the King remains the central personage in the whole legal edifice of the West. When it comes to the general organisation of the legal system in the West, it is essentially with the King, his rights, his power and its eventual limitations, that one is dealing. Whether the jurists were the King's henchmen or his adversaries, it is of royal power that we are speaking in every case when we speak of these grandiose edifices of legal thought and knowledge.

There are two ways in which we do so speak. Either we do so in order to show the nature of the juridical armoury that invested royal power, to reveal the monarch as the effective embodiment of sovereignty, to demonstrate that his power, for all that it was absolute, was exactly that which befitted his fundamental right. Or, by contrast, we do so in order to show the necessity of imposing limits upon this sovereign power, of submitting it to certain rules of right, within whose confines it had to be exercised in order for it to remain legitimate. The essential role of the theory of right, from medieval times onwards, was to fix the legitimacy of power; that is the major problem around which the whole theory of right and sovereignty is organised.

When we say that sovereignty is the central problem of right in Western societies, what we mean basically is that the essential function of the discourse and techniques of right has been to efface the domination intrinsic to power in order to present the latter at the level of appearance under two different aspects: on the one hand, as

the legitimate rights of sovereignty, and on the other, as the legal obligation to obey it. The system of right is centered entirely upon the King, and it is therefore designed to eliminate the fact of domination and its consequences.

My general project over the past few years has been, in essence, to reverse the mode of analysis followed by the entire discourse of right from the time of the Middle Ages. My aim, therefore, was to invert it, to give due weight, that is, to the fact of domination, to expose both its latent nature and its brutality. I then wanted to show not only how right is, in a general way, the instrument of this domination—which scarcely needs saying—but also to show the extent to which, and the forms in which, right (not simply the laws but the whole complex of apparatuses, institutions and regulations responsible for their application) transmits and puts in motion relations that are not relations of sovereignty, but of domination. Moreover, in speaking of domination I do not have in mind that solid and global kind of domination that one person exercises over others, or one group over another, but the manifold forms of domination that can be exercised within society. Not the domination of the King in his central position, therefore, but that of his subjects in their mutual relations: not the uniform edifice of sovereignty, but the multiple forms of subjugation that have a place and function within the social organism.

The system of right, the domain of the law, are permanent agents of these relations of domination, these polymorphous techniques of subjugation. Right should be viewed, I believe, not in terms of a legitimacy to be established, but in terms of the methods of subjugation that it instigates.

The problem for me is how to avoid this question, central to the theme of right, regarding sovereignty and the obedience of individual subjects in order that I may substitute the problem of domination and subjugation for that of sovereignty and obedience. Given that this was to be the general line of my analysis, there were a certain number of methodological precautions that seemed requisite to its pursuit. In the very first place, it seemed important to accept that the analysis in question should not concern itself with the regulated and legitimate forms of power in their central locations, with the general mechanisms through which they operate, and the continual effects of these. On the contrary, it should be concerned with power at its extremities, in its ultimate destinations, with those points where it becomes capillary, that is, in its more regional and local forms and institutions. Its paramount concern, in fact, should be with the point where power surmounts the rules of right which organise and delimit it and extends itself beyond them, invests itself in institutions, becomes embodied in techniques, and equips itself with instruments and eventually even violent means of material intervention. To give an example: rather than try to discover where and how the right of punishment is founded on sovereignty, how it is presented in the theory of monarchical right or in that of democratic right, I have tried to see in what ways punishment and the power of punishment are effectively embodied in a certain number of local, regional, material institutions, which are concerned with torture or imprisonment, and to place these in the climate—at once institutional and physical, regulated and violent—of the effective apparatuses of punishment. In other words, one should try to locate power at the extreme points of its exercise, where it is always less legal in character.

A second methodological precaution urged that the analysis should not concern itself with power at the level of conscious intention or decision; that it should not attempt to consider power from its internal point of view and that it should refrain from posing the labyrinthine and unanswerable question: 'Who then has power and what has he in mind? What is the aim of someone who possesses power?' Instead, it is a case of studying power at the point where its intention, if it has one, is completely invested in its real and effective practices. What is needed is a study of power in its external visage, at the point where it is in direct and immediate relationship with that which we can provisionally call its object, its target, its field of application, there—that is to say—where it installs itself and produces its real effects.

Let us not, therefore, ask why certain people want to dominate, what they seek, what is their overall strategy. Let us ask, instead, how things work at the level of on-going subjugation, at the level of those continuous and uninterrupted processes which subject our bodies, govern our gestures, dictate our behaviours etc. In other words, rather than ask ourselves how the sovereign appears to us in his lofty isolation, we should try to discover how it is that subjects are gradually, progressively, really and materially constituted through a multiplicity of organisms, forces, energies, materials, desires, thoughts etc. We should try to grasp subjection in its material instance as a constitution of subjects. This would be the exact opposite of Hobbes' project in *Leviathan*, and of that, I believe, of all jurists for whom the problem is the distillation of a single will—or rather, the constitution of a unitary, singular body animated by the spirit of sovereignty—from the particular wills of a multiplicity of individuals. Think of the scheme of Leviathan: insofar as he is a fabricated man, Leviathan is no other than the amalgamation of a certain number of separate individualities, who find themselves reunited by the complex of elements that go to compose the State; but at the heart of the State, or rather, at its head, there exists something which constitutes it as such, and this is sovereignty, which Hobbes says is precisely the spirit of Leviathan. Well, rather than worry about the problem of the central spirit, I believe that we must attempt to study the myriad of bodies which are constituted as peripheral *subjects* as a result of the effects of power.

A third methodological precaution relates to the fact that power is not to be taken to be a phenomenon of one individual's consolidated and homogeneous domination over others, or that of one group or class over others. What, by contrast, should always be kept in mind is that power, if we do not take too distant a view of it, is not that which makes the difference between those who exclusively possess and retain it, and those who do not have it and submit to it. Power must be analysed as something which circulates, or rather as something which only functions in the form of a chain. It is never localised here or there, never in anybody's hands, never appropriated as a commodity or piece of wealth. Power is employed and exercised through a net-like organisation. And not only do individuals circulate between its threads; they are always in the position of simultaneously undergoing and exercising this power. They are not only its inert or consenting target; they are always also the elements of its articulation. In other words, individuals are the vehicles of power, not its points of application.

The individual is not to be conceived as a sort of elementary nucleus, a primitive atom, a multiple and inert material on which power comes to fasten or against which it happens to strike, and in so doing subdues or crushes individuals. In fact, it is already one of the prime effects of power that certain bodies, certain gestures, certain discourses, certain desires, come to be identified and constituted as individuals. The individual, that is, is not the *vis-à-vis* of power; it is, I believe, one of its prime effects. The individual is an effect of power, and at the same time, or precisely to the extent to which it is that effect, it is the element of its articulation. The individual

which power has constituted is at the same time its vehicle.

• • •

The important thing here, I believe, is that truth isn't outside power, or lacking in power: contrary to a myth whose history and functions would repay further study, truth isn't the reward of free spirits, the child of protracted solitude, nor the privilege of those who have succeeded in liberating themselves. Truth is a thing of this world: it is produced only by virtue of multiple forms of constraint. And it induces regular effects of power. Each society has its regime of truth, its 'general politics' of truth: that is, the types of discourse which it accepts and makes function as true; the mechanisms and instances which enable one to distinguish true and false statements, the means by which each is sanctioned; the techniques and procedures accorded value in the acquisition of truth; the status of those who are charged with saying what counts as true.

In societies like ours, the 'political economy' of truth is characterised by five important traits. 'Truth' is centred on the form of scientific discourse and the institutions which produce it; it is subject to constant economic and political incitement (the demand for truth, as much for economic production as for political power); it is the object, under diverse forms, of immense diffusion and consumption (circulating through apparatuses of education and information whose extent is relatively broad in the social body, not withstanding certain strict limitations); it is produced and transmitted under the control, dominant if not exclusive, of a few great political and economic apparatuses (university, army, writing, media); lastly, it is the issue of a whole political debate and social confrontation ('ideological' struggles).

It seems to me that what must now be taken into account in the intellectual is not the 'bearer of universal values.' Rather, it's the person occupying a specific position—but whose specificity is linked, in a society like ours, to the general functioning of an apparatus of truth. In other words, the intellectual has a three-fold specificity: that of his class position (whether as petty-bourgeois in the service of capitalism or 'organic' intellectual of the proletariat); that of his conditions of life and work, linked to his condition as an intellectual (his field of research, his place in a laboratory, the political and economic demands to which he submits or against which he rebels, in the university, the hospital, etc.); lastly, the specificity of the politics of truth in our societies. And it's with this last factor that his position can take on a general significance and that his local, specific struggle can have effects and implications which are not simply professional or sectoral. The intellectual can operate and struggle at the general level of that régime of truth which is so essential to the structure and functioning of our society. There is a battle, 'for truth', or at least 'around truth'—it being understood once again that by truth I do not meant 'the ensemble of truths which are to be discovered and accepted', but rather 'the ensemble of rules according to which the true and the false are separated and specific effects of power attached to the true', it being understood also that it's not a matter of a battle 'on behalf' of the truth, but of a battle about the status of truth and the economic and political role it plays. It is necessary to think of the political problems of intellectuals not in terms of 'science' and 'ideology', but in terms of 'truth' and 'power'. And thus the question of the professionalisation of intellectuals and the division between intellectual and manual labour can be envisaged in a new way.

All this must seem very confused and uncertain. Uncertain indeed, and what I am saying here is above all to be taken as a hypothesis. In order for it to be a little less confused, however, I would like to put forward a few 'propositions'—not firm assertions, but simply suggestions to be further tested and evaluated.

'Truth' is to be understood as a system of ordered procedures for the production, regulation, distribution, circulation and operation of statements.

'Truth' is linked in a circular relation with systems of power which produce and sustain it, and to effects of power which it induces and which extend it. A 'régime' of truth.

This régime is not merely ideological or superstructural; it was a condition of the formation and development of capitalism. And it's this same régime which, subject to certain modifications, operates in the socialist countries. . .

The essential political problem for the intellectual is not to criticise the ideological contents supposedly linked to science, or to ensure that his own scientific practice is accompanied by a correct ideology, but that of ascertaining the possibility of constituting a new politics of truth. The problem is not changing people's consciousnesses—or what's in their heads—but the political, economic, institutional régime of the production of truth.

It's not a matter of emancipating truth from every system of power (which would be a chimera, for truth is already power) but of detaching the power of truth from the forms of hegemony, social, economic and cultural, within which it operates at the present time.

The political question, to sum up, is not error, illusion, alienated consciousness or ideology; it is truth itself. Hence the importance of Nietzsche.

GLOSSARY

ANALYTIC TRUTH   According to Kant, a judgment where what has been thought in the predicate has already been thought in the subject. Example: "All bachelors are unmarried adult males."

AUTHORITARIANISM   The view that endorses uncritical obedience to some authority, who is viewed as being beyond question; a negative sense of authority.

AUTHORITY   In its positive sense, an individual or group of individuals considered to have reliable knowledge; a valid source of knowledge in the absence of any other way of knowing.

DECONSTRUCTION   A textual strategy initiated by Jacques Derrida; deconstructive readings of texts call attention to moments of undecidability, where the text differs from itself.

EXISTENTIALISM   An outlook in philosophy, religion, and the arts that stresses the anxious nature of the human predicament. Important existentialists include Kierkegaard, Nietzsche, and Sartre.

IDEALISM   The theory that reality is mind-dependent.

INTUITION   Direct, immediate knowledge of something, without reliance on reason or sense perception.

PERSPECTIVISM   Nietzsche's view that truth is relative to the will to power of the individual.

POSTMODERNISM   A contemporary movement in philosophy and the arts, characterized by its anti-foundationalism and by a resistance to all forms of totality.

PRAGMATISM   An American philosophical movement founded by Charles Sanders Peirce, and popularized by William James and John Dewey. Its central thesis is the idea that truth is determined by what has practical value in our lives.

PRIMARY QUALITIES   Qualities such as motion, rest, size, shape, and number, which are believed to be inherent properties of matter itself, not dependent on mind for their existence.

REALISM   The theory that objects of our senses exist independently of the mind, that reality is not mind-dependent.

RELATIVISM   The view that truth or values vary from context to context, depending on culture, language, and social conditioning.

SECONDARY QUALITIES   Sensed qualities such as taste, color, smell, and sound, believed by John Locke and others to depend upon mind for their existence.

SELF-EVIDENT BELIEF   A belief that is obvious, without proof or argument.

SYNTHETIC TRUTH   According to Kant, a judgment where what is thought in the predicate has not been thought in the subject. Example: "Elephants are heavy."

SYNTHETIC A PRIORI   According to Kant, knowledge that is prior to the experience of something, by which that experience is structured and made possible. Example: "Every event has a cause."

TRANSVALUATION   According to Nietzsche, the radical reappraisal of the traditional values of a given society.

FOR FURTHER STUDY

Aaron, R. I. *Knowing and the Function of Reason*. Oxford: Clarendon Press, 1971.

This excellent analysis of knowing, thought, and reason makes room for intuition as a source of knowledge.

Bunge, M. *Intuition and Science*, Englewood Cliffs, N.J.: Prentice Hall, 1962.

A critical evaluation of intuition in philosophy, mathematics, and science.

Blanshard, Brand. *The Nature of Thought*. London: Allen and Unwin, 1948.

A well-reasoned defense of the coherence theory or truth.

Dewey, John. *Reconstruction in Philosophy*. Boston: Beacon Press, 1948.

A modern classic. Dewey defends the position that the modern role of philosophy is to interpret the conclusions of science with respect to their consequences for human values and purposes. The sixth chapter lays out the pragmatic test of truth.

Ewing, A.C. *The Fundamental Questions of Philosophy*. London: Routledge & Kegan Paul, 1959.

See especially the chapter on truth, where Ewing explores the criteria of truth.

Gadamer, Hans-Georg. *Truth and Method*. New York: Seabury Press, 1975.

A former student of Heidegger, Gadamer is suspicious of all method in philosophy. He argues that philosophy should stress the shared understandings we have with one another rather than the quest for certainty.

Rorty, Richard. *Philosophy and the Mirror of Nature*. Princeton: Princeton University Press, 1979.

A controversial book. Rorty argues that the traditional view of a correspondence between thought, language and the world must be given up. There are serious implications for truth.

White, A. R. *Truth*. Garden City: Doubleday (Anchor Books), 1970.

A small paperback that carefully analyzes the different meanings of truth and discusses important theories of truth.

PART FOUR

◆

SCIENCE, TECHNOLOGY, AND HUMAN VALUES

It is true that the whole scientific inquiry starts from
the familiar world and in the end it must return to
the familiar world; but the part of the journey over
which the physicist has charge is in foreign territory.

SIR ARTHUR EDDINGTON

All the sciences have leapt from the womb of
philosophy, in a twofold manner. The sciences came
out of philosophy, because they have to part with
her. And now that they are so apart they can never
again, by their own power as sciences, make the leap
back into the source from which they have sprung.
Henceforth they are remanded to a realm of being
where only thinking can find them.

MARTIN HEIDEGGER

ORIENTATION

Most of the first philosophers thought that principles in the form of matter were the only principles of all things. . . But as to the number and form of this sort of principle, they do not all agree. Thales, the founder of this kind of philosophy, says that it is water.

Aristotle, *Metaphysics*

Two things in this passage from Aristotle seem strange. First, it seems odd that Thales, usually cited as "the first western philosopher," should be interested in matter. Isn't matter a topic that one considers in science classes, not philosophy classes? It may come as a surprise to learn that in ancient Greece there was no real distinction between philosophy and science, as there is today. Thales, who had a reputation as an inventor and engineer, was also given to philosophizing. Aristotle, famous for his philosophical writings, also wrote important works in physics, biology, and astronomy.

Far more surprising, however, is the startling claim by Thales that "all things are water." At first glance this seems to be an unpromising beginning to the history of western science and philosophy. Yet one must remember that at this stage in western civilization the concepts of matter, physics, science, and philosophy had yet to be discovered. In Thales' day, whatever explanations there were for the natural world took the form of mythology and superstition. Wind, for example, was "explained" by referring to a god who puffed out his cheeks and blew, in much the same way as we do. What we know as planets were viewed then as "travelers" who wandered the skies. As Thales thought about the nature of the universe, asking himself what the world was really like, he was asking a new kind of question. What is remarkable about Thales is not his claim that water is the fundamental principle of all reality (a theory that would soon be abandoned, replaced by the more sophisticated accounts of his students), but rather that he attempted such a theory in the first place. Unsatisfied by the common sense wisdom and mythology of his time, Thales insisted on his scientific/philosophical question. Scientists and philosophers have followed his example for the past 2,500 years.

In the spirit of Thales, this chapter attempts to put philosophy and science in dialogue with one another. For a variety of reasons, science has been allowed to become detached from philosophy in the public imagination. Although still officially linked together in the language of the university—perhaps you are taking a philosophy course in a "college of arts and sciences"—philosophy and science often appear to lead separate lives at the university. This "compartmentalization of knowledge" is an unfortunate development, since both have much to learn from one another. Science has given philosophy much to think about, and philosophy still has the power to shed light on the scientific project.

The twentieth century has produced an explosion of knowledge unprecedented in human history; yet there is reason to believe that this knowledge has not made us wiser. Knowledge resulting from scientific investigations is put to use in new technologies, shaping the way we live and the way we view ourselves and our world; yet there is widespread anxiety about the role of technology in the modern world. Science and technology are critically important in our society, yet they are little understood.

Because science plays such a large role in the way we understand our world, philosophers have studied the nature, aims, methods, concepts, and limitations of science. These philosophical studies have resulted in an important area of philosophy known as **philosophy of science.** The questions asked in philosophy of science, highly evolved from Thales' original question, include the following. What is science, and how does it differ from nonscience? What are the methods of science, and what are the limitations of those methods? What are scientific models and paradigms? What role do they play in the way scientific theories gain acceptance in the scientific community? Has modern science become an ideology from which society must be protected? Does science have anything to say about values, or is it value-neutral? In the pages that follow we shall explore these questions at some length. The Contemporary Perspectives section, "The Technological Society," focuses on the nature of technology as well as its role in society.

THE NATURE OF SCIENCE

The English word **science** is derived from the Latin word *scire*, meaning "to know." Like the attempt to define philosophy, defining science is no easy task. Perhaps it is easiest to look at three ways the word is commonly used. First, the term *science* may be used to refer collectively to a *product*—the various sciences, such as biology, physics, astronomy. Second, the term is used to refer to a *process* or method of obtaining knowledge that is objective and verifiable or falsifiable. Finally, the term is often used to mean *a body of systematic knowledge* compiled through observation and experimentation, having a valid theoretical base. We shall be employing all three of these senses in the present chapter.

CLASSIFICATION OF THE SCIENCES

Taking the first usage of the term *science*, it is possible to classify the various special sciences. Since Aristotle, it has been customary to classify the sciences according to the type of knowledge pursued. In our first reading selection Aristotle suggests the division of knowledge into three parts: the theoretical, the practical, and the productive. Today it is more common to collapse Aristotle's three classes into two: **pure science** and **applied science.**

Pure science, corresponding to Aristotle's theoretical knowing, is objective knowledge for its own sake, without consideration for practical applications. (There is much debate today whether any of the sciences can be considered pure today, since the findings of the sciences are applied in numerous ways by a wide range of disciplines.) Among the so-called pure sciences, further distinctions can be made between (a) formal sciences, such as logic and mathematics; and (b) factual or empirical sciences. The latter are further subdivided into (b1) natural sciences (including the physical sciences, physics, chemistry) as well as the life sciences (biology, botany, zoology); and (b2) the human sciences, such as sociology, anthropology, psychology, and economics.

The applied sciences (sometimes referred to as "technological sciences"), refer to knowledge put to practical use. They include medicine, agriculture, engineering, aeronautics, and the like. The term **technology** is frequently used to mean applied science.

SCIENCE AND NONSCIENCE

One of the central problems in the philosophy of science is the problem of **demarcation.** There are two aspects to this problem. First, how do we distinguish between science and common sense knowledge? Second, how do we distinguish between scientific theories and nonscientific theories?

Science has been called by some "organized common sense." While there is some value in this formulation, we must be careful. Although organization or system is important to science, equally important to the scientist is sound explanation based on the facts. Many people can bake a loaf of bread but few can give an explanation of why bread rises. Ernest Nagel points out that many of the sciences did grow out of the practical concerns of daily living. Geometry grew out of problems of measuring and surveying fields; biology out of health problems; economics out of problems of household and government management, and so on. Nevertheless, there are important differences between common sense and science. Common sense suffers from a serious incompleteness. Because it rests on custom and tradition, common sense becomes ineffectual when new situations arise that go beyond common experience. Thus, a community of farmers may habitually spread manure on their fields, acting on the traditional common sense rule that this preserves the fertility of the soil, unaware that this rule does not always apply. If the rule is unconnected to principles of biology and soil chemistry it will be followed blindly, even when the deterioration of the soil creates conditions that manure will not help. Systematic science, going beyond common sense, seeks explanations that are factually based. As Nagel puts it, "It is the desire for explanations which are at once systematic and controllable by factual evidence that generates science; and it is the organization and classification of knowledge on the basis of explanatory principle that is the distinctive goal of the sciences."[1]

If explanation, facticity, and organization demarcate science from common sense, what is the demarcation between a scientific theory and a nonscientific one? This is a far more difficult question. In Chapter 26 Karl Popper argues that what makes a theory scientific is its **falsifiability.** To say that a theory is falsifiable is not the same as saying it is falsified. Falsifiability means that a theory *could possibly be falsified* if there were some circumstance or state of affairs that, if obtained, would count against the theory. Popper defends falsifiability (or refutability) as a more adequate criterion of science than verifiability, the principle that a theory justifies belief if it is confirmed by experience. The problem with verifiability, Popper argues, is that all kinds of absurd things have been "verified" by the "true believers" in a theory. True believers tend to see confirming instances of their theories everywhere. One gets suspicious when everything counts *for* theory but nothing can be found to count *against* it. Where is the risk of failure that seems so much a part of the scientific enterprise? Rather than merely chalking up a number of confirming instances, why not require a theory to run the risks of being shown false in order to be worthy of the name "scientific?" In support of his criterion of demarcation, Popper compares Einstein's theory of gravitation with theories he considers to be nonscientific.

Popper's work has spawned many other attempts to demarcate science from nonscience. Imre Lakatos, in Chapter 27, criticizes Popper's criterion of falsifiability as being too simplistic, since theories are embedded in complex "research programs" that shield them from easy refutation. The mark of a degenerating research program is when it can no longer predict new factual developments; progressive research programs have the power to explain new facts. W. V. Quine and J. S. Ullian, in Chapter 28, provide a set of five "virtues" scientific hypotheses should have that is more extensive than the criteria of Popper or Lakatos. A scientific **hypothesis** must explain past and predict the future. Hypotheses are more likely to perform these two functions if they possess conservatism, modesty, simplicity, generality, and refutability. Scientific preference for and acceptance of a given hypothesis is due to the degree to which it possesses these five virtues.

SCIENTIFIC METHOD

There is no one universally agreed upon scientific method. Some sciences, such as astronomy, rely heavily upon observation and mathematical calculations based on those observations. Other sciences, such as chemistry, biology, and

---

[1] Ernest Nagel, *The Structure of Science* (New York: Harcourt, Brace and World, 1961), 4.

physics, stress controlled experimentation. Still others, especially the human sciences, employ trial and error, statistics, and random sampling. The method used depends upon the nature of the problem to be solved.

OBSERVATION

Our English word **observation** is derived from the Latin word *observare*, meaning "to save or keep." Observation in science means employing the five senses to systematically notice and record features, facts, and occurrences concerning the object of study. As a science matures, it builds an ever expanding observational base from which conclusions can be drawn. Some sciences, such as botany, are very dependent on careful observation. Other sciences, such as physics, have become increasingly abstract and less directly dependent upon observation.

The British philosopher John Stuart Mill (1806–1873) identified five inductive methods. One of these, the **method of agreement,** is an observational method for identifying a causal connection between phenomena. The method consists of recognizing some single factor that is present in a number of different occurrences in which the effect is also present. Here is an example:

> After eating lunch at the same restaurant, five individuals became ill with hepatitis. Inspectors from the Health Department learned that while the five individuals had eaten different foods, they all had tomatoes in their salad. Furthermore, this was the only food that all five had eaten. The inspectors concluded that the disease had been transmitted by the tomatoes.[2]

TRIAL AND ERROR

Trial and error is a method frequently employed by psychologists who study the behavior of animals and human beings when solving problems. A rat uses trial and error when trying to get out of a maze. (This is also the method used by parents when trying to assemble a child's bicycle!) Trial and error is successfully employed by scientists as they try out different hypotheses.

EXPERIMENTATION

Although observation and trial and error have been widely used in the sciences, they have limitations. Under normal circumstances, it is difficult to control

---

[2]This example is taken from Patrick J. Hurley, *A Concise Introduction to Logic* (Belmont, Calif.: Wadsworth Publishing, 1988), 421.

events in the world—things just happen. In an experiment, however, a researcher can control and manipulate the environmental conditions of a given study. Mill's **method of difference,** sometimes called the laboratory method, is widely used in science to discover causal connections under carefully controlled conditions. The method consists of varying one factor at a time while the other factors are kept constant. The investigator then records the results of this difference. Here is an example:

> Two identical white mice in a controlled experiment were given identical amounts of four different foods. In addition, one of the mice was fed a certain drug. A short time later the mouse that was fed the drug became nervous and agitated. The researchers concluded that the drug caused the nervousness.[3]

It is possible to identify a causal connection between two conditions by matching variations in one condition with variations in another. Mill's **method of concomitant variation** is useful when it is impossible for a condition to be either wholly present of wholly absent. Many conditions are of this kind—for instance, the price of gold, the temperature in Vermont in September, or a person's blood pressure. If some kind of correlation can be detected between variations in two conditions, then the method of concomitant variation asserts that the two are causally connected. For example:

> In attempting to diagnose Mrs. Thompson's high blood pressure, doctors discovered a correlation between fluctuations in blood pressure and certain brain waves. As the blood pressure increased and decreased, so did the intensity of the brain waves. The doctors concluded that the two conditions were causally related.[4]

STATISTICAL METHOD

A statistic is simply an item of information expressed numerically. **Statistics** is an applied mathematical science that collects, classifies, and interprets numerical data. Statistical methods were originally developed by rulers interested in collecting information about population, wealth, births, deaths, taxes, and so on. Now greatly refined, statistical methods are routinely employed in business, finance, marketing, economics, politics, psychology, and many other areas. Statistics help to determine the probability of given events, enabling us to explain, predict, and compare.

[3]Hurley, p. 427.
[4]Hurley, p. 432.

SAMPLING

Much of the statistical evidence gathered by researchers in support of conclusions is attained from analyzing samples. When a sample (or specimen) is found to possess a given characteristic, it is argued that the group as a whole possesses that characteristic. If a researcher is studying material that is the same throughout, a single random sample may accurately reflect the whole. Samples that are not representative are said to be biased.

If the subject of the study is heterogeneous, it is especially important that the sample be representative. Numerous differences come into play, including age, sex, occupation, education, religion, and economic status. A classic example of a biased sample occurred in 1936, when the *Literary Digest* conducted a survey to predict the outcome of the Presidential election. The sample consisted of a large number of the magazine's subscribers, plus a number of others selected from the telephone book. The Republican candidate, Alf Landon, received a significant majority in the poll, yet Franklin D. Roosevelt won the election in a landslide. What happened? The incorrect prediction was the result of a biased sample, since in 1936 America was in the middle of the Great Depression, when few people could afford magazines or telephones. These were the people overlooked in the poll, and they were also the ones who voted for Roosevelt!

MODELS AND PARADIGMS

MODELS

Models are pictorial, theoretical, mechanical, or physical representations of things in the universe that act as tools to guide scientific practices. Thinking back to your elementary school days, perhaps you can remember a teacher exhibiting a scale model of the solar system, which demonstrated how the nine planets orbited the sun. This kind of mechanical and physical model was useful for demonstrating **observables,** objects like the sun and plancts. Often, however, models are representations of **unobservables,** objects not actually seen by scientists. Scientific terms used to describe unobservable entities or properties are called theoretical terms, as opposed to observation terms. Examples of theoretical terms used to describe unobservable entities and properties include the electron, quark, valence, and Hamiltonian function. Most of us are familiar with the model of the atom that we observed in science class, complete with visual representations of protons, neutrons, and electrons. This is an example of a **theoretical model.** Theoretical models guide scientific practices, allowing scientists to formulate hypotheses and make predictions about unobservable entities.

PARADIGMS

In 1962 Thomas S. Kuhn, a historian and philosopher of science, wrote a book called *The Structure of Scientific Revolutions*. In this important book Kuhn argued that science is not guided simply by models; it is guided largely by the conditions of its own practice. Kuhn argued that science under normal conditions ("normal science") accepts the past accomplishments of the scientific community as supplying the foundations for its further practice. A coherent set of scientific beliefs and practices guide normal science by establishing "traditions of research." These traditions are often named after their founder (for example, Copernican astronomy, Newtonian physics). Kuhn gives the name **paradigm** to those background traditions that govern the way scientists view the world, select their subjects and methods, analyze their data, and publish their findings. It is impossible to interpret the world without some general context of interpretation. Paradigms provide the world-picture accepted by the community of scientists, providing the necessary context for interpretation.

Kuhn views normal science as a puzzle-solving activity. Occasionally, problems arise that cannot be solved by the existing paradigm. The seventeenth century was such a time. The astronomical world-picture of Aristotle and Ptolemy held sway. In this world-picture, the earth was at the center, with the rest of the universe encased in concentric spheres. Like a theater in the round, everything in the universe revolved around the human drama center stage on earth. Officially endorsed by the most influential institution of the Middle Ages, the Catholic church, this world-picture was entrenched in society. Only a revolution could change it. And that is precisely what occurred when Copernicus and Galileo began experimenting with a new scientific paradigm. The old paradigm began to break down, unable to account for new discoveries concerning planetary orbits. Stubbornly, it hung on, its defenders insisting that the moon's orbit around the earth was conclusive evidence that the earth, not the sun, was the center. The final deathblow was dealt when Galileo discovered that the planet Jupiter had three moons. Kuhn, in his book *The Copernican Revolution*, cites this as a classic example of a revolutionary shift in paradigms, as scientists worked diligently to solve the puzzle.

Kuhn's paradigm thesis has been severely criticized by some, who find his concept of paradigm flawed, even incoherent. Others object to the idea that the scientific community's acceptance of a paradigm might be less than rational, a mere question of preference. Is adherence to a paradigm ultimately a question of faith, not science? To use the language of William James, does science "consult her heart" when it accepts one paradigm over another? If this is the case, can there be genuine progress in science, or is the history of science simply a history of preferences? Is science steadily progressing in its accumulation of knowledge, or are there discontinuities and "leaps" as science shifts paradigms? The debate that Kuhn started has continued to this day.

245

LIMITATIONS OF SCIENTIFIC METHODS

Science is one of the noblest, most remarkable achievements of the human mind. Unfortunately, it has often been misused by those who do not understand the limitations of its methods. Carried away by their enthusiasm for science, some have claimed that the factual knowledge gained by objective scientific methods is the only real knowledge one can attain. This reductionistic view, known as scientism, asks more of science than its methods can deliver, and is not itself scientific. Jürgen Habermas points out that scientism means science's belief in itself—"the conviction that we can no longer understand science as one form of possible knowledge, but rather must identify knowledge with science."[5] There are areas of human experience that remain opaque to traditional scientific methods. This section is not intended to keep science out of these areas; rather, it points out the boundaries and limitations that science, by its very nature, encounters. Here are a few things to keep in mind.

1.   *Objective scientific methods can turn up only that which can be stated objectively*. If your scientific research leads you to investigate the physical or chemical properties of an object, your findings will be limited to what can be stated in physical or chemical terms. This presents an interesting situation when science attempts to reflect on itself. Can we hope to understand the nature of science through purely objective scientific techniques? Using mathematical formulae, can we hope to discover the essence of mathematics? Obviously not. Consequently, science cannot explore its own theoretical underpinnings except through "nonscientific" means. Martin Heidegger calls this limitation of scientific method "one track thinking."

2.   *Scientific instruments are quite useful for measurement until we encounter something that cannot be measured*. A set of scales can tell you the weight of an engagement ring, but can it measure its value? Sophisticated machines can measure your brain waves, but can such a measurment pick up what you feel when you taste chocolate, hug your dog, or "ace" a philosophy exam?

3.   *Remaining faithful to the methods of science requires either keeping silent when encountering realms of experience outside their range or adapting them to fit the new experience*. Adapting scientific methods to explore new territories is precisely what Edmund Husserl and Sigmund Freud set out to do when they founded phenomenology and psychoanalysis, respectively. Husserl thought of phenomenology as philosophical science, a descriptive science of pure consciousness. As a science, phenomenology was to yield objectively valid knowledge. Yet it was clear that the methods of the natural sciences were unsuited to a science of subjectivity. Hence,

---

[5]Jürgen Habermas, *Knowledge and Human Interests*, trans. Jeremy J. Shapiro (Boston: Beacon Press, 1971), 4.

Husserl devised a method suitable for exploring the intentional structures of human consciousness. Sigmund Freud (1856–1939), a contemporary of Husserl, attempted the same thing with respect to the unconscious. This is not the place to discuss their methods, which have proved to be enormously influential. What is notable about Husserl and Freud is that both men claimed to be practicing science even though their methods were often criticized by scientists. We should keep them in mind when we listen to scientists who claim, on the basis of purely physiological investigations, to have never found things such as thoughts, feelings, or acts of the will. Can we reasonably expect to find thoughts, intentions, or feelings if our methods are unsuited to their discovery?

4. *All observations and theory is done in connection with human interests.* If "objective truth" as our scientific goal was really taken seriously, we would devote all our intellectual energy to studying interstellar dust, and only a fraction of a second studying ourselves, since, objectively speaking, human beings are of little cosmic significance in the order of things. Obviously this would be unsatisfactory. Why? Because we do not want, and are incapable of, the kind of objectivity that is not overwhelmingly interested in us! What we seek are truths that are interesting, useful, and valuable to us. There is a sense in which every method or technique masks a prejudice on the part of the observer or theorist, making complete or total objectivity impossible. Complete and total objectivity would mean the death of the human subject, and therefore the death of science itself. Some try to escape this insight by insisting that objectivity is only an "ideal." Of course, this is true, but we must not forget that the prejudice against prejudice is itself a prejudice! Methods that attempt to mask human interests in the name of "objectivity" are increasingly coming under suspicion.

5. *The scientist as scientist cannot prescribe values.* Science is a descriptive enterprise, not a prescriptive one. This is illustrated by reflecting on the dual meaning of the word "law." In daily life we most often use the word law in a prescriptive sense. A law is a rule of behavior imposed by a legislative body and enforced by the legal machinery of the state. But in natural science, law is used to describe the way nature works. *Laws of nature do not prescribe anything.* For instance, Kepler's laws of planetary motion do not dictate to the planets that they move in a certain way, with penalties if they get out of line. (To imagine the absurdity of such a thing, picture trying to lecture Saturn on the immorality of bad orbiting!) Rather than prescribing behavior, Kepler's laws simply describe how the planets actually do move.

Because science is descriptive, it is limited to the vocabulary of "the world of is," not "the world of what ought to be." "What ought to be" is the domain of values, the traditional concern of philosophers. Therefore when scientists prescribe values, as they must in the course of their investigations, they are no longer restricting themselves to scientific methods—they have entered the domain of philosophy, the womb that gave birth to science. Of course, this is perfectly natural and acceptable, and it is proof that a rigid separation of facts and values betrays human experience. As we said at the outset of this part, philosophy and science need each other. The relationship between science and values is the topic of the next section.

6. *Science, by overvaluing its methods, may become ideology.* In Chapter 29, Paul Feyerabend claims that he wishes to defend society from all ideologies, including science. He argues "against method" and "against results," likening science to fairytales that have lots of interesting things to say but contain wicked lies as well. More could be said about Feyerabend's controversial views, but it is best if you investigate his claims for yourself.

SCIENCE AND VALUES

There has been a long tradition of value-neutrality in science. The view that science must insist on objectivity and objective methods to the exclusion of subjective features such as value and purpose can be traced back to the seventeenth century. The separation of fact and value, a concept foreign to ancient Greek philosophy, came to be one of the hallmarks of modern science in the west. Galileo, Descartes, and Newton were the chief architects of a new, mechanical world-picture, where nature was a vast machine governed by quantitative laws. Descartes expressed the new world-picture philosophically, with his vision of the universality of science in the shape of mathematics; Galileo gave the world-picture its scientific expression, viewing nature itself as a mathematical code. In a famous passage Galileo wrote these words:

> Philosophy is written in this grand book, the universe, which stands continually open to our gaze. But the book cannot be understood unless one first learns to comprehend the language and read the letters in which it is composed. It is written in the language of mathematics, and its characters are triangles, circles, and other geometric figures without which it is humanly impossible to understand a single word of it; without these, one wanders about in a dark labyrinth.[6]

For Galileo and Descartes, it is the objective features of the world that are important: matter, motion, and physical magnitude. These essential features of the world—primary qualities, as they were called—formed the nuts and bolts of the machine, along with the laws that governed them. (It was left to Newton to refine Galileo's laws of motion and to discover the universal law of gravitation.)

---

[6]From "The Assayer," in *Discoveries and Opinions of Galileo*, trans. Stillman Drake (Garden City, N.J.: Doubleday Anchor Books, 1957), 237–238.

Since mathematics is the only language of nature, rational comprehension of the real nature of the universe came only through quantification and measurement. All other features of the world—for example, color, values, purposes—were viewed as "secondary qualities," second class citizens because they were not objective. The centrality of the ideal of objectivity meant that the methods of science must not be tainted by subjectivity. Hence, value considerations were out of bounds to scientists. Eventually, modern versions of materialism such as behaviorism reduced secondary qualities as well to objective features, as we shall see in Part 5.

The "mathematitization of nature" resulted in a false notion of objectivity. As modern science has developed within this perspective, there has been a movement toward greater and greater abstraction, eventually resulting in a formalization of meaning that mistakes the formulas of science and technology for the original thinking that gave rise to them. As a result, the formulas themselves are taken for the total truth—what Alfred North Whitehead called a "fallacy of misplaced concreteness."

The relationship between science and values has in recent years become an important topic in the philosophy of science. As powerful new technologies have been developed, both scientists and philosophers have become uncomfortable with the idea of a strict separation of fact and value. Attention has been focused on the nature of science itself: Does the scientist *as* a scientist make value judgments? Because the discussion of values often conjures up images of morality, religion, or aesthetics—areas not known for their objectivity—many scientists have tended to say "no." And yet the scientific search for knowledge is itself an expression of value. If this were not the case, it would not be possible to distinguish between reliable and unreliable knowledge claims, or good and bad scientific methods. The project of demarcation would be impossible as well: demarcating science from astrology, occultism, psychoanalysis, and creationism certainly involves value judgments. Nicholas Rescher has argued that ethical questions arise in connection with scientific work at seven crucial junctures:

1. The choice of research goals
2. The staffing of research activities
3. The selection of research methods
4. The specification of standards of proof
5. The dissemination of research findings
6. The control of scientific misinformation
7. The allocation of credit for research accomplishments[7]

[7]Nicholas Rescher, "The Ethical Dimensions of Scientific Research," in *Beyond the Edge of Certainty*, ed. Robert G. Colodny, (Englewood Cliffs, N.J.: Prentice-Hall, 1965) 261–76.

Richard Rudner, in an article entitled "The Scientist *Qua* Scientist Makes Value Judgments," points out that since no scientific hypothesis is ever completely verified, in choosing to accept or reject hypotheses scientists must make value judgments—they are deciding whether the evidence is *sufficiently* strong or the probability *sufficiently* high to justify scientific acceptance.[8] Such a decision does not take place in a moral vacuum: It is a personal, social, and perhaps political barometer, indicating the importance of a hypothesis to some individual, or to some group of people. Rudner raises the interesting question of how sure we need to be before we accept a hypothesis. He concludes that this depends on how serious a mistake would be. Applying this standard to the "Manhattan Project," an American program of scientific research that led to the making of the atom bomb and the eventual destruction of two Japanese cities in 1945, we begin to sense the centrality of value decisions in scientific work. We sense also the importance of the question concerning technology, the topic of our Contemporary Perspective section.

[8]Richard Rudner, "The Scientist *Qua* Scientist Makes Value Judgment," *Philosophy of Science*, XX (1953): 1–6.

CHAPTER 25

ARISTOTLE

THE CLASSIFICATION OF THE SCIENCES

Aristotle divides the sciences into the theoretical, the practical, and the productive (see chapter 2 for a biography of Aristotle). The immediate purpose of each kind is to know. Each gives rise to a certain wisdom. The theoretical sciences aim at knowledge for its own sake; the practical aim at knowledge for the sake of conduct; and the productive aim at knowledge used in making something useful or beautiful. Elsewhere in his writings Aristotle identifies ethics and especially politics as the supreme practical, social sciences. Practical wisdom is the power of good deliberation, "a true disposition towards action, by the aid of a rule, with regard to things good and bad for men." Art—*techne* is the Greek word Aristotle uses—is "the disposition by which we *make* things by the aid of a true rule." Art and technology are subordinate to practical and theoretical wisdom.

In this brief passage from the *Metaphysics*, Aristotle subdivides the theoretical sciences into "theology" (or metaphysics), physics, and mathematics.[1] Physics deals with things that have a separate existence but are not unchangeable (for example, bodies found in nature, capable of motion and rest). Mathematics deals with things that are unchangeable but have no separate existence (numbers and spatial figures, for example). Theology deals with things that have both a separate existence and are unchangeable (i.e. nonmaterial substances, such as God).

---

[1]Reprinted from *The Oxford Translation of Aristotle*, edited by W.D. Ross, Vol. 8 (1928) by permission of Oxford University Press.

The Classification of the Sciences

Book E (VI)

We are seeking the principles and the causes of the things that are, and obviously of them *qua* being. For, while there is a cause of health and of good condition, and the objects of mathematics have first principles and elements and causes, and in general every science which is ratiocinative or at all involves reasoning deals with causes and principles, more or less precise, all these sciences mark off some particular being—some genus, and inquire into this, but not into being simply nor *qua* being, nor do they offer any discussion of the essence of the things of which they treat; but starting from the essence—some making it plain to the senses, others assuming it as a hypothesis—they then demonstrate, more or less cogently, the essential attributes of the genus with which they deal. It is obvious, therefore, that such an induction yields no demonstration of substance or of the essence, but some other way of exhibiting it. And similarly the sciences omit the question whether the genus with which they deal exists or does not exist, because it belongs to the same kind of thinking to show what it is and that it is.

And since natural science, like other sciences, is in fact about one class of being, i.e. to that sort of substance which has the principle of its movement and rest present in itself, evidently it is neither practical nor productive. For in the case of things made the principle is in the maker—it is either reason or art or some faculty, while in the case of things done it is in the doer—viz. will, for that which is done and that which is willed are the same. Therefore, if all thought is either practical or productive or theoretical, physics must be a theoretical science, but it will theorize about such being as admits of being moved, and about

substance-as-defined for the most part only as not separable from matter. Now, we must not fail to notice the mode of being of the essence and of its definition, for, without this, inquiry is but idle. Of things defined, i. e. of 'whats', some are like 'snub', and some like 'concave'. And these differ because 'snub' is bound up with matter (for what is snub is a concave *nose*), while concavity is independent of perceptible matter. If then all natural things are analogous to the snub in their nature—e. g. nose, eye, face, flesh, bone, and, in general, animal; leaf, root, bark, and, in general, plant (for none of these can be defined without reference to movement—they always have matter), it is clear how we must seek and define the 'what' in the case of natural objects, and also that it belongs to the student of nature to study even soul in a certain sense, i. e. so much of it as is not independent of matter.

That physics, then, is a theoretical science, is plain from these considerations. Mathematics also, however, is theoretical; but whether its objects are immovable and separable from matter, is not at present clear; still, it is clear that *some* mathematical theorems *consider* them *qua* immovable and *qua* separable from matter. But if there is something which is eternal and immovable and separable, clearly the knowledge of it belongs to a theoretical science—not, however, to physics (for physics deals with certain movable things) nor to mathematics, but to a science prior to both. For physics deals with things which exist separately but are not immovable, and some parts of mathematics deal with things which are immovable but presumably do not exist separately, but as embodied in matter; while the first science deals with things which both exist separately and are immovable. Now all causes must be eternal, but especially these; for they are the causes that operate on so much of the divine as appears to us. There must, then, be three theoretical philosophies, mathematics, physics, and what we may call theology, since it is obvious that if the divine is present anywhere, it is present in things of this sort. And the highest science must deal with the highest genus. Thus, while the theoretical sciences are more to be desired than the other sciences, this is more to be desired than the other theoretical sciences. For one might raise the question whether first philosophy is universal, or deals with one genus, i. e. some one kind of being; for not even the mathematical sciences are all alike in this respect—geometry and astronomy deal with a certain particular kind of thing, while universal mathematics applies alike to all. We answer that if there is no substance other than those which are formed by nature, natural science will be the first science; but if there is an immovable substance, the science of this must be prior and must be first philosophy, and universal in this way, because it is first. And it will belong to this to consider being *qua* being—both what it is and the attributes which belong to it *qua* being.

CHAPTER 26

KARL POPPER

SCIENCE: CONJECTURES AND REFUTATIONS

Karl Popper (1902–   ), Austrian philosopher of science, was born in Vienna. He studied mathematics, physics, and philosophy at the University of Vienna. He was senior lecturer at Canterbury University in New Zealand from 1937 to 1945. Since 1949, he has been professor of logic and scientific method at London School of Economics. He was knighted in 1964.

Best known for his work on the demarcation of science from pseudoscience and metaphysics, Popper is the author of *The Logic of Scientific Discovery* (1959). In *The Open Society and Its Enemies* (1945) and *The Poverty of Historicism* (1957), he applied his theory of knowledge to an attack on historicism, the doctrine that there are general laws of historical development that make history predictable and inevitable. His main targets in these books are Plato, Hegel, and Marx. A collection of his essays, *Conjectures and Refutations: The Growth of Scientific Knowledge*, was published in 1963.

Popper's claim that falsifiability demarcates science from nonscience, first proposed in 1933, must be seen in historical context. In the 1920s a philosophical movement known as a logical positivism arose in Vienna, which was destined to dominate the philosophy of science for almost thirty years. Although he shared many philosophical interests with the group, Popper's break with the positivists on the issue of demarcation proved to be a decisive event. Philosophy of science has been in a state of turmoil ever since.

Logical positivists such as Rudolph Carnap had established "the principle of verifiability." The strong version of this principle claimed that a statement is *meaningful* if and only if it is empirically verified. Popper rejected empirical verifiability as the criterion for distinguishing meaningful discourse from nonmeaningful discourse, believing the verifiability principle to be arbitrary and unsound. More importantly, he was convinced that the logical positivists had ignored the real task, which was to distinguish empirical science from other modes of discourse commonly confused with it, including various "pseudosciences" such as Freudian psychoanalysis and the Marxist theory of history.

For Popper, the line between science and pseudoscience (or "myth," as Popper sometimes called it) is a thin one, and it is conceivable that in time what is now regarded as myth may develop critically and become science. After all, the history of human knowledge may be read as the history of a transformation of myth into science. In the meantime, however, scientists ought to be concerned with attempting to refute, or falsify hypotheses, for this is the activity that gives science its singular identity. Hypotheses are never conclusively established. If a hypothesis survives ongoing attempts to falsify it, then it has proved its value and should be provisionally accepted.[1]

SCIENCE: CONJECTURES AND REFUTATIONS

Mr. Turnbull had predicted evil consequences, . . . and was now doing the best in his power to bring about the verification of his own prophecies.

Anthony Trollope

I

When I received the list of participants in this course and realized that I had been asked to speak to philosophical colleagues I thought, after some hesitation and consultation, that you would probably prefer me to speak about those problems which interest me most, and about those developments with which I am most intimately acquainted. I therefore decided to do what I have never done before: to give you a report on my own work in the philosophy of science, since the autumn of 1919 when I first began to grapple with the problem, *"When should a theory be ranked as scientific?"* or *"Is there a criterion for the scientific character or status of a theory?"*

The problem which troubled me at the time was neither, "When is a theory true?" nor, "When is a theory acceptable?" My problem was different. I *wished to distinguish between science and pseudo-science*, knowing very well that science often errs, and that pseudo-science may happen to stumble on the truth.

I knew, of course, the most widely accepted answer to my problem: that science is distinguished from pseudo-science—or from "**metaphysics**"— by its **empirical** method, which is

[1]The reading that follows was originally presented as a lecture at Peterhouse, Cambridge, in 1953. It is contained in Karl Popper, *Conjectures and Refutations*, 5th Edition (London: Routledge & Kegan Paul, 1989).

essentially *inductive,* proceeding from observation or experiment. But this did not satisfy me. On the contrary, I often formulated my problem as one of distinguishing between a genuinely empirical method and a non-empirical or even a pseudo-empirical method—that is to say, a method which, although it appeals to observation and experiment, nevertheless does not come up to scientific standards. The latter method may be exemplified by astrology, with its stupendous mass of empirical evidence based on observation—on horoscopes and on biographies.

But as it was not the example of astrology which led me to my problem I should perhaps briefly describe the atmosphere in which my problem arose and the examples by which it was stimulated. After the collapse of the Austrian Empire there had been a revolution in Austria: the air was full of revolutionary slogans and ideas, and new and often wild theories. Among the theories which interested me Einstein's theory of relativity was no doubt by far the most important. Three others were Marx's theory of history, Freud's psychoanalysis, and Alfred Adler's so-called "individual psychology."

There was a lot of popular nonsense talked about these theories, and especially about relativity (as still happens even today), but I was fortunate in those who introduced me to the study of this theory. We all—the small circle of students to which I belonged—were thrilled with the result of Eddington's eclipse observations which in 1919 brought the first important confirmation of Einstein's theory of gravitation. It was a great experience for us, and one which had a lasting influence on my intellectual development.

The three other theories I have mentioned were also widely discussed among students at that time. I myself happened to come into personal contact with Alfred Adler, and even to cooperate with him in his social work among the children and young people in the working-class districts of Vienna where he had established social guidance clinics.

It was during the summer of 1919 that I began to feel more and more dissatisfied with these three theories—the Marxist theory of history, psychoanalysis, and individual psychology; and I began to feel dubious about their claims to scientific status. My problem perhaps first took the simple form, "What is wrong with Marxism, psychoanalysis, and individual psychology? Why are they so different from physical theories, from Newton's theory, and especially from the theory of relativity?"

To make this contrast clear I should explain that few of us at the time would have said that we believed in the *truth* of Einstein's theory of gravitation. This shows that it was not my doubting the *truth* of those other three theories which bothered me, but something else. Yet neither was it that I merely felt mathematical physics to be more *exact* than the sociological or psychological type of theory. Thus what worried me was neither the problem of truth, at that stage at least, nor the problem of exactness or measurability. It was rather that I felt that these other three theories, though posing as sciences, had in fact more in common with primitive myths than with science; that they resembled astrology rather than astronomy.

I found that those of my friends who were admirers of Marx, Freud, and Adler, were impressed by a number of points common to these theories, and especially by their apparent *explanatory power.* These theories appeared to be able to explain practically everything that happened within the fields to which they referred. The study of any of them seemed to have the effect of an intellectual conversion or revelation, opening your eyes to a new truth hidden from those not yet initiated. Once your eyes were thus opened you saw confirming instances everywhere: the world was full of *verifications* of the theory. Whatever happened always confirmed it. Thus its truth appeared manifest; and unbelievers were clearly people who did not want to see the manifest truth; who refused to see it, either because it was against their class interest, or because of their repressions which were still "unanalyzed" and crying aloud for treatment.

The most characteristic element in this situation seemed to me the incessant stream of confirmations, of observations which "verified" the theories in question; and this point was constantly emphasized by their adherents. A Marxist could not open a newspaper without finding on every page confirming evidence for his interpretation of history; not only in the news, but also in its presentation—which revealed the class bias of the paper—and especially of course in what the paper did *not* say. The Freudian analysts emphasized that their theories were constantly verified by their "clinical observations." As for Adler, I was much impressed by a personal experience. Once, in 1919, I reported to him a case which to me did not seem particularly Adlerian, but which he found no difficulty in analyzing in terms of his theory of inferiority feelings, although he had not even seen the child. Slightly shocked, I asked him how he could be so sure. "Because of my thousandfold experience," he replied; whereupon I could not help saying: "And with this new case, I suppose, your experience has become thousand-and-one-fold."

What I had in mind was that his previous observations may not have been much sounder than this new one; that each in its turn had been interpreted in the light of "previous experience," and at the same time counted as additional confirmation. What, I asked myself, did it confirm? No more than that a case could be interpreted in the light of the theory. But this meant very little, I reflected, since every conceivable case could be interpreted in the light of Adler's theory, or

equally of Freud's. I may illustrate this by two very different examples of human behavior: that of a man who pushes a child into the water with the intention of drowning it; and that of a man who sacrifices his life in an attempt to save the child. Each of these two cases can be explained with equal ease in Freudian and in Adlerian terms. According to Freud the first man suffered from repression (say, of some component of his Oedipus complex), while the second man had achieved sublimation. According to Adler the first man suffered from feelings of inferiority (producing perhaps the need to prove to himself that he dared to commit some crime), and so did the second man (whose need was to prove to himself that he dared to rescue the child). I could not think of any human behavior which could not be interpreted in terms of either theory. It was precisely this fact—that they always fitted, that they were always confirmed—which in the eyes of their admirers constituted the strongest argument in favor of these theories. It began to dawn on me that this apparent strength was in fact their weakness.

With Einstein's theory the situation was strikingly different. Take one typical instance— Einstein's prediction, just then confirmed by the findings of Eddington's expedition. Einstein's gravitational theory had led to the result that light must be attracted by heavy bodies (such as the sun), precisely as material bodies were attracted. As a consequence it could be calculated that light from a distant fixed star whose apparent position was close to the sun would reach the earth from such a direction that the star would seem to be slightly shifted away from the sun; or, in other words, that stars close to the sun would look as if they had moved a little away from the sun, and from one another. This is a thing which cannot normally be observed since such stars are rendered invisible in daytime by the sun's overwhelming brightness; but during an eclipse it is possible to take photographs of them. If the same constellation is photographed at night one can measure the distances on the two photographs, and check the predicted effect.

Now the impressive thing about this case is the *risk* involved in a prediction of this kind. If observation shows that the predicted effect is definitely absent, then the theory is simply refuted. The theory is *incompatible with certain possible results of observation*—in fact with results which everybody before Einstein would have expected.[1] This is quite different from the situation I have previously described, when it turned out that the theories in question were compatible with the most divergent human behavior, so that it was practically impossible to describe any human behavior that might not be claimed to be a verification of these theories.

These considerations led me in the winter of 1919–20 to conclusions which I may now reformulate as follows:

1. It is easy to obtain confirmations, or verifications, for nearly every theory—if we look for confirmations.

2. Confirmations should count only if they are the result of *risky predictions*; that is to say, if, unenlightened by the theory in question, we should have expected an event which was incompatible with the theory—an event which would have refuted the theory.

3. Every "good" scientific theory is a prohibition: it forbids certain things to happen. The more a theory forbids, the better it is.

4. A theory which is not refutable by any conceivable event is nonscientific. Irrefutability is not a virtue of a theory (as people often think) but a vice.

5. Every genuine *test* of a theory is an attempt to falsify it, or to refute it. Testability is falsifiability; but there are degrees of testability:

some theories are more testable, more exposed to refutation, than others; they take, as it were, greater risks.

6. Confirming evidence should not count *except when it is the result of a genuine test of the theory*; and this means that it can be presented as a serious but unsuccessful attempt to falsify the theory. (I now speak in such cases of "corroborating evidence.")

7. Some genuinely testable theories, when found to be false, are still upheld by their admirers—for example by introducing **ad hoc** some auxiliary assumption, or by reinterpreting the theory *ad hoc* in such a way that it escapes refutation. Such a procedure is always possible, but it rescues the theory from refutation only at the price of destroying, or at least lowering, its scientific status. (I later described such a rescuing operation as a *"conventionalist twist"* or a *'"conventionalist stratagem."*)

One can sum up all of this by saying that *the criterion of the scientific status of a theory is its falsifiability, or refutability, or testability.*

II

I may perhaps exemplify this with the help of the various theories so far mentioned. Einstein's theory of gravitation clearly satisfied the criterion of falsifiability. Even if our measuring instruments at the time did not allow us to pronounce on the results of the tests with complete assurance, there was clearly a possibility of refuting the theory.

Astrology did not pass the test. Astrologers were greatly impressed, and misled, by what they believed to be confirming evidence—so much so that they were quite unimpressed by any unfavorable evidence. Moreover, by making their interpretations and prophecies sufficiently vague they were able to explain away anything that might have been a refutation of the theory had the theory and the prophecies been more precise. In order to escape falsification they destroyed the testability of their theory. It is a typical soothsayer's trick to predict things so vaguely that the predictions can hardly fail: that they become irrefutable.

The Marxist theory of history, in spite of the serious efforts of some of its founders and followers, ultimately adopted this soothsaying practice. In some of its earlier formulations (for example in Marx's analysis of the character of the "coming social revolution") their predictions were testable, and in fact falsified.[2] Yet instead of accepting the refutations the followers of Marx reinterpreted both the theory and the evidence in order to make them agree. In this way they rescued the theory from refutation; but they did so at the price of adopting a device which made it irrefutable. They thus gave a "conventionalist twist" to the theory; and by this stratagem they destroyed its much advertised claim to scientific status.

The two psychoanalytic theories were in a different class. They were simply non-testable, irrefutable. There was no conceivable human behavior which could contradict them. This does not mean that Freud and Adler were not seeing certain things correctly: I personally do not doubt that much of what they say is of considerable importance, and may well play its part one day in a psychological science which is testable. But it does mean that those "clinical observations" which analysts naively believe confirm their theory cannot do this any more than the daily confirmations which astrologers find in their practice.[3] And as for Freud's epic of the Ego, the Super-ego, and the Id, no substantially stronger claim to scientific status can be made for it than for Homer's collected stories from Olympus. These theories describe some facts, but in the manner of myths. They contain most interesting psychological suggestions, but not in a testable form.

At the same time I realized that such myths may be developed, and become testable; that historically speaking all—or very nearly all—scientific theories originate from myths, and that a myth may contain important anticipations of scientific theories. Examples are Empedocles' theory of evolution by trial and error, or Parmenides' myth of the unchanging block universe in which nothing ever happens and which, if we add another dimension, becomes Einstein's block universe (in which, too, nothing ever happens, since everything is, four-dimensionally speaking, determined and laid down from the beginning). I thus felt that if a theory is found to be non-scientific, . . . it is not thereby found to be unimportant, or insignificant, or "meaningless," or "nonsensical."[4] But it cannot claim to be backed by empirical evidence in the scientific sense—although it may easily be, in some genetic sense, the "result of observation."

(There were a great many other theories of this pre-scientific or pseudoscientific character, some of them, unfortunately, as influential as the Marxist interpretation of history; for example, the racialist interpretation of history—another of those impressive and all-explanatory theories which act upon weak minds like revelations.)

Thus the problem which I tried to solve by proposing the criterion of falsifiability was neither a problem of meaningfulness or significance, nor a problem of truth or acceptability. It was the problem of drawing a line (as well as this can be done) between the statements, or systems of statements, of the empirical sciences, and all other statements. . . . Years later—it must have been in 1928 or 1929—I called this first problem of mine the *"problem of demarcation."* The criterion of falsifiability is a solution to this problem of demarcation, for it says that statements or systems of statements, in order to be ranked as scientific, must be capable of conflicting with possible, or conceivable, observations. . . .

Notes

1. This is a slight oversimplification, for about half of the Einstein effect may be derived from the classical theory, provided we assume a ballistic theory of light.

2. See, for example, my *Open Society and Its Enemies*, ch. 15, section iii, and notes 13–14.

3. "Clinical observations," like all other observations, are *interpretations in the light of theories*; and for this reason alone they are apt to seem to support those theories in the light of which they were interpreted. But real support can be obtained only from observations undertaken as tests (by "attempted refutations"); and for this purpose *criteria of refutation* have to be laid down beforehand: it must be agreed which observable situations, if actually observed, mean that the theory is refuted. But what kind of clinical responses would refute to the satisfaction of the analyst not merely a particular analytic diagnosis but psychoanalysis itself? And have such criteria ever been discussed or agreed upon by analysts? Is there not, on the contrary, a whole family of analytic concepts, such as "ambivalence" (I do not suggest that there is no such thing as ambivalence), which would make it difficult, if not impossible, to agree upon such criteria? Moreover, how much headway has been made in investigating the question of the extent to which the (conscious or unconscious) expectations and theories held by the analyst influence the "clinical responses" of the patient? (To say nothing about the conscious attempts to influence the patient by proposing interpreta-

tions to him, etc.) Years ago I introduced the term *"Oedipus effect"* to describe the influence of a theory or expectation or prediction *upon the event which it predicts* or describes: it will be remembered that the causal chain leading to Oedipus' parricide was started by the oracle's prediction of this event. This is a characteristic and recurrent theme of such myths, but one which seems to have failed to attract the interest of the analysts, perhaps not accidentally. (The problem of confirmatory dreams suggested by the analyst is discussed by Freud, for example in *Gesammelte Schriften, III*, 1925, where he says on p. 314: "If anybody asserts that most of the dreams which can be utilized in an analysis . . . owe their origin to the analyst's suggestion, then no objection can be made from the point of view of analytic theory. Yet there is nothing in this fact," he surprisingly adds, "which would detract from the reliability of our results.")

4. The case of astrology, nowadays a typical pseudoscience, may illustrate this point. It was attacked, by Aristotelians and other rationalists, down to Newton's day, for the wrong reason—for its now accepted assertion that the planets had an "influence" upon terrestrial ("sublunar") events. In fact Newton's theory of gravity, and especially the lunar theory of the tides, was historically speaking an offspring of astrological lore. Newton, it seems, was most reluctant to adopt a theory which came from the same stable as for example the theory that "influenza" epidemics are due to an astral "influence." And Galileo, no doubt for the same reason, actually rejected the lunar theory of the tides; and his misgivings about Kepler may easily be explained by his misgivings about astrology.

CHAPTER 27

IMRE LAKATOS

SCIENCE AND PSEUDOSCIENCE

Imre Lakatos (1922–1974) was, with Thomas S. Kuhn, a major figure in the recent revolution in the philosophy of science. He is the author of a number of books and articles in the philosophy of mathematics and the philosophy of science, including *Proofs and Refutations: The Logic of Mathematical Discovery* (1976), *The Methodology of Scientific Research Programmes* (1977), from which the following selection was taken, and *Mathematics, Science, and Epistemology* (1978).

Lakatos argues that Popper's falsification criterion is not the solution for demarcating science from pseudoscience. Taking his cues from Thomas Kuhn's *The Structure of Scientific Revolutions*, Lakatos theorizes that scientists do not normally abandon a theory just because facts contradict it. Instead, they invent a "rescue hypothesis" to explain "recalcitrant instances," or what Kuhn calls **anomalies.** But Lakatos does not wish to follow Kuhn much further than this. Believing that Kuhn has given up all attempts at demarcation, abandoning traditional notions of scientific progress and rationality, Lakatos proposes a middle way between Popper and Kuhn.

In the following selection Lakatos places scientific theories in the larger context of research programs.[1] He then suggests criteria for evaluating the quality of

[1]From Imre Lakatos, "The Methodology of Scientific Research," in *Philosophical Papers*, Vol. 1, edited by I. Lakatos, J. Worrall, and G. Currie. (New York: Cambridge University Press, 1977), 1–7. Reprinted with the permission of Cambridge University Press.

research programs on rational and objective grounds. Rejecting the "myths" of Popper's "crucial experiment," and Kuhn's "scientific revolution," Lakatos explains how it is that one program eventually displaces another.

SCIENCE AND PSEUDOSCIENCE

Man's respect for knowledge is one of his most peculiar characteristics. Knowledge in Latin is *scientia*, and science came to be the name of the most respectable kind of knowledge. But what distinguishes knowledge from superstition, ideology or pseudoscience? The Catholic Church excommunicated Copernicans, the Communist Party persecuted Mendelians on the ground that their doctrines were pseudoscientific. The demarcation between science and pseudoscience is not merely a problem of armchair philosophy: it is of vital social and political relevance.

Many philosophers have tried to solve the problem of demarcation in the following terms: a statement constitutes knowledge if sufficiently many people believe it sufficiently strongly. But the history of thought shows us that many people were totally committed to absurd beliefs. If the strength of beliefs were a hallmark of knowledge, we should have to rank some tales about demons, angels, devils, and of heaven and hell as knowledge. Scientists, on the other hand, are very sceptical even of their best theories. Newton's is the most powerful theory science has yet produced, but Newton himself never believed that bodies attract each other at a distance. So no degree of commitment to beliefs makes them knowledge. Indeed, the hallmark of scientific behavior is a certain scepticism even towards one's most cherished theories. Blind commitment to a theory is not an intellectual virtue: it is an intellectual crime.

Thus a statement may be pseudoscientific even if it is eminently "plausible" and everybody believes in it, and it may be scientifically valuable even if it is unbelievable and nobody believes in it. A theory may even be of supreme scientific value even if no one understands it, let alone believes it.

The cognitive value of a theory has nothing to do with its psychological influence on people's minds. Belief, commitment, understanding are states of the human mind. But the objective, scientific value of a theory is independent of the human mind which creates it or understands it. Its scientific value depends only on what objective support these conjectures have in facts. As Hume said:

> If we take in our hand any volume; of divinity, or school metaphysics, for instance; let us ask, does it contain any abstract reasoning concerning quantity or number? No. Does it contain any experimental reasoning concerning matter of fact and existence? No. Commit it then to the flames. For it can contain nothing but sophistry and illusion.

But what is "experimental" reasoning? If we look at the vast seventeenth-century literature on witchcraft, it is full of reports of careful observations and sworn evidence—even of experiments. Glanvill, the house philosopher of the early Royal Society, regarded witchcraft as the paradigm of experimental reasoning. We have to define experimental reasoning before we start Humean book burning.

In scientific reasoning, theories are confronted with facts; and one of the central conditions of scientific reasoning is that theories must be supported by facts. Now how exactly can facts support theory?

Several different answers have been proposed. Newton himself thought that he proved his laws from facts. He was proud of not uttering mere hypotheses: he only published theories proven from facts. In particular, he claimed that he deduced his laws from the "phenomena" provided by Kepler. But his boast was nonsense, since according to Kepler, planets move in ellipses, but according to Newton's theory, planets would move in ellipses only if the planets did not disturb each other in their motion. But they do. This is why Newton had to devise a perturbation theory from which it follows that no planet moves in an ellipse.

One can today easily demonstrate that there can be no valid derivation of a law of nature from any finite number of facts; but we still keep reading about scientific theories being proved from facts. Why this stubborn resistance to elementary logic?

There is a very plausible explanation. Scientists want to make their theories respectable, deserving of the title "science," that is, genuine knowledge. Now the most relevant knowledge in the seventeenth century, when science was born, concerned God, the Devil, Heaven and Hell. If one got one's conjectures about matters of divinity wrong, the consequence of one's mistake was eternal damnation. Theological knowledge cannot be fallible: it must be beyond doubt. Now the Enlightenment thought that we were fallible and ignorant about matters theological. There is no scientific theology and, therefore, no theological knowledge. Knowledge can only be about Nature, but this new type of knowledge had to be judged by the standards they took over straight from theology: it had to be proven beyond doubt. Science had to achieve the very certainty

which had escaped theology. A scientist, worthy of the name, was not allowed to guess: he had to prove each sentence he uttered from facts. This was the criterion of scientific honesty. Theories unproven from facts were regarded as sinful pseudoscience, heresy in the scientific community.

It was only the downfall of Newtonian theory in this century which made scientists realize that their standards of honesty had been utopian. Before Einstein most scientists thought that Newton had deciphered God's ultimate laws by proving them from the facts. Ampère, in the early nineteenth century, felt he had to call his book on his speculations concerning electromagnetism: *Mathematical Theory of Electrodynamic Phenomena Unequivocally Deduced from Experiment.* But at the end of the volume he casually confesses that some of the experiments were never performed and even that the necessary instruments had not been constructed!

If all scientific theories are equally unprovable, what distinguishes scientific knowledge from ignorance, science from pseudoscience?

One answer to this question was provided in the twentieth century by "**inductive** logicians." Inductive logic set out to define the probabilities of different theories according to the available total evidence. If the mathematical probability of a theory is high, it qualifies as scientific; if it is low or even zero, it is not scientific. Thus the hallmark of scientific honesty would be never to say anything that is not at least highly probable. **Probabilism** has an attractive feature: instead of simply providing a black-and-white distinction between science and pseudoscience, it provides a continuous scale from poor theories with low probability to good theories with high probability. But, in 1934, Karl Popper, one of the most influential philosophers of our time, argued that the mathematical probability of all theories, scientific or pseudoscientific, given *any* amount of evidence is zero. If Popper is right, scientific theories are not only equally unprovable but also equally improbable. A new demarcation criterion was needed and Popper proposed a rather stunning one. A theory may be scientific even if there is not a shred of evidence in its favor, and it may be pseudoscientific even if all the available evidence is in its favor. That is, the scientific or nonscientific character of a theory can be determined independently of the facts. A theory is "scientific" if one is prepared to specify in advance a crucial experiment (or observation) which can falsify it, and it is pseudoscientific if one refuses to specify such a "potential falsifier." But if so, we do not demarcate scientific theories from pseudoscientific ones, but rather scientific method from non-scientific method. Marxism, for a Popperian, is scientific if the Marxists are prepared to specify facts which, if observed, make them give up Marxism. If they refuse to do so, Marxism becomes a pseudoscience. It is always interesting to ask a Marxist, what conceivable event would make him abandon his Marxism. If he is committed to Marxism, he is bound to find it immoral to specify a state of affairs which can falsify it. Thus a proposition may petrify into pseudoscientific dogma or become genuine knowledge, depending on whether we are prepared to state observable conditions which would refute it.

Is, then, Popper's falsifiability criterion the solution to the problem of demarcating science from pseudoscience? No. For Popper's criterion ignores the remarkable tenacity of scientific theories. Scientists have thick skins. They do not abandon a theory merely because facts contradict it. They normally either invent some rescue hypothesis to explain what they then call a mere **anomaly** or, if they cannot explain the anomaly, they ignore it, and direct their attention to other problems. Note that scientists talk about anomalies, recalcitrant instances, not refutations. History of science, of course, is full of accounts of how

crucial experiments allegedly killed theories. But such accounts are fabricated long after the theory had been abandoned. Had Popper ever asked a Newtonian scientist under what experimental conditions he would abandon Newtonian theory, some Newtonian scientists would have been exactly as nonplussed as are some Marxists.

What, then, is the hallmark of science? Do we have to capitulate and agree that a scientific revolution is just an irrational change in commitment, that it is a religious conversion? Tom Kuhn, a distinguished American philosopher of science, arrived at this conclusion after discovering the naïvety of Popper's falsificationism. But if Kuhn is right, then there is no explicit demarcation between science and pseudoscience, no distinction between scientific progress and intellectual decay, there is no objective standard of honesty. But what criteria can he then offer to demarcate scientific progress from intellectual degeneration?

In the last few years I have been advocating a methodology of scientific research programs, which solves some of the problems which both Popper and Kuhn failed to solve.

First, I claim that the typical descriptive unit of great scientific achievements is not an isolated hypothesis but rather a research program. Science is not simply trial and error, a series of conjectures and refutations. "All swans are white" may be falsified by the discovery of one black swan. But such trivial trial and error does not rank as science. Newtonian science, for instance, is not simply a set of four conjectures—the three laws of mechanics and the law of gravitation. These four laws constitute only the "hard core" of the Newtonian program. But this hard core is tenaciously protected from refutation by a vast "protective belt" of auxiliary hypotheses. And, even more importantly, the research program also has a "heuristic," that is, a powerful problem-solving machinery, which, with the help of sophisticated mathematical techniques, digests anomalies and even turns them into positive evidence. For instance, if a planet does not move exactly as it should, the Newtonian scientist checks his conjectures concerning atmospheric refraction, concerning propagation of light in magnetic storms, and hundreds of other conjectures which are all part of the program. He may even invent a hitherto unknown planet and calculate its position, mass and velocity in order to explain the anomaly.

Now, Newton's theory of gravitation, Einstein's relativity theory, quantum mechanics, Marxism, Freudianism, are all research programs, each with a characteristic hard core stubbornly defended, each with its more flexible protective belt and each with its elaborate problem-solving machinery. Each of them, at any stage of its development, has unsolved problems and undigested anomalies. All theories, in this sense, are born refuted and die refuted. But are they equally good? Until now I have been describing what research programs are like. But how can one distinguish a scientific or progressive program from a pseudoscientific or degenerating one?

Contrary to Popper, the difference cannot be that some are still unrefuted, while others are already refuted. When Newton published his *Principia*, it was common knowledge that it could not properly explain even the motion of the moon; in fact, lunar motion refuted Newton. Kaufmann, a distinguished physicist, refuted Einstein's relativity theory in the very year it was published. But all the research programs I admire have one characteristic in common. They all predict novel facts, facts which had been either undreamt of, or have indeed been contradicted by previous or rival programs. In 1686, when Newton published his theory of gravitation, there were, for instance, two current theories concerning comets. The more popular one regarded comets as a signal from an angry God

warning that He will strike and bring disaster. A little known theory of Kepler's held that comets were celestial bodies moving along straight lines. Now according to Newtonian theory, some of them moved in hyperbolas or parabolas never to return; others moved in ordinary ellipses. Halley, working in Newton's program, calculated on the basis of observing a brief stretch of a comet's path that it would return in seventy-two years' time; he calculated to the minute when it would be seen again at a well-defined point of the sky. This was incredible. But seventy-two years later, when both Newton and Halley were long dead, Halley's comet returned exactly as Halley predicted. Similarly, Newtonian scientists predicted the existence and exact motion of small planets which had never been observed before. Or let us take Einstein's program. This program made the stunning prediction that if one measures the distance between two stars in the night and if one measures the distance between them during the day (when they are visible during an eclipse of the sun), the two measurements will be different. Nobody had thought to make such an observation before Einstein's program. Thus, in a progressive research program, theory leads to the discovery of hitherto unknown novel facts. In degenerating programs, however, theories are fabricated only in order to accommodate known facts. Has, for instance, Marxism ever predicted a stunning novel fact successfully? Never! It has some famous unsuccessful predictions. It predicted the absolute impoverishment of the working class. It predicted that the first socialist revolution would take place in the industrially most developed society. It predicted that socialist societies would be free of revolutions. It predicted that there will be no conflict of interests between socialist countries. Thus the early predictions of Marxism were bold and stunning but they failed. Marxists explained all their failures: they explained the rising living standards of the working class by devising a theory of imperialism; they even explained why the first socialist revolution occurred in industrially backward Russia. They "explained" Berlin 1953, Budapest 1956, Prague 1968. They "explained" the Russian–Chinese conflict. But their auxiliary hypotheses were all cooked up after the event to protect Marxian theory from the facts. The Newtonian program led to novel facts; the Marxian lagged behind the facts and has been running fast to catch up with them.

To sum up. The hallmark of empirical progress is not trivial verifications: Popper is right that there are millions of them. It is no success for Newtonian theory that stones, when dropped, fall towards the earth, no matter how often this is repeated. But so-called "refutations" are not the hallmark of empirical failure, as Popper has preached, since all programs grow in a permanent ocean of anomalies. What really count are dramatic, unexpected, stunning predictions: a few of them are enough to tilt the balance; where theory lags behind the facts, we are dealing with miserable degenerating research programs.

Now, how do scientific revolutions come about? If we have two rival research programs, and one is progressing while the other is degenerating, scientists tend to join the progressive program. This is the rationale of scientific revolutions. But while it is a matter of intellectual honesty to keep the record public, it is not dishonest to stick to a degenerating program and try to turn it into a progressive one.

As opposed to Popper the methodology of scientific research programs does not offer instant rationality. One must treat budding programs leniently: programs may take decades before they get off the ground and become empirically progressive. Criticism is not a Popperian quick kill, by refutation. Important criticism is always constructive: there is no refutation without a better theory. Kuhn is wrong in thinking that scientific revolutions are sudden, irrational changes in vision. The history of science refutes both Popper and Kuhn: on close inspection both Popperian crucial experiments and Kuhnian revolutions turn out to be myths: what normally happens is that progressive research programs replace degenerating ones.

The problem of demarcation between science and pseudoscience has grave implications also for the institutionalization of criticism. Copernicus's theory was banned by the Catholic Church in 1616 because it was said to be pseudoscientific. It was taken off the index in 1820 because by that time the Church deemed that facts had proved it and therefore it became scientific. The Central Committee of the Soviet Communist Party in 1949 declared Mendelian genetics pseudoscientific and had its advocates, like Academician Vavilov, killed in concentration camps; after Vavilov's murder Mendalian genetics was rehabilitated; but the Party's right to decide what is science and publishable and what is pseudoscience and punishable was upheld. The new liberal Establishment of the West also exercises the right to deny freedom of speech to what it regards as pseudoscience, as we have seen in the case of the debate concerning race and intelligence. All these judgments were inevitably based on some sort of demarcation criterion. This is why the problem of demarcation between science and pseudoscience is not a pseudo-problem of armchair philosophers: it has grave ethical and political implications.

CHAPTER 28

WILLARD VAN ORMAN QUINE AND J.S. ULLIAN

HYPOTHESIS

Willard Van Orman Quine (1908–   ), Edgar Pierce professor of philosophy at Harvard University, is one of America's foremost philosophers. He has made important contributions in logic, metaphysics, epistemology, philosophy of science, and philosophy of language. Graduating from Oberlin College with an undergraduate degree in mathematics, he received his Ph.D. from Harvard two years later. Among his numerous books are *From A Logical Point of View* (1953), and *Word and Object* (1960).

J.S. Ullian (1930–   ) was graduated in mathematics and philosophy at Harvard and also received his Ph.D. in philosophy from Harvard. He has held teaching positions at Harvard, Stanford, Johns Hopkins, the University of Pennsylvania, the University of Chicago, and the University of California. He is currently professor of philosophy at Washington University, where he has taught since 1965. He has published extensively in philosophy and computer science. He is the co-author, with Quine, of an introductory philosophy text, *The Web of Belief*.

In clear, straightforward fashion Quine and Ullian describe the virtues that a scientific hypothesis should have if it is to be successful at performing its proper functions: explaining the past and predicting the future.[1] The authors identify five

[1]From W.V. Quine and J.S. Ullian, *The Web of Belief*, 2d ed. (New York: McGraw-Hill Publishing Company, 1978), pp. 64–82. Reprinted with permission.

virtues: conservativism, modesty, simplicity, generality, and refutability. These virtues are consistent with the requirements that Lakatos sets forth, yet they are more extensive.

None of these virtues should be thought of as "all or nothing." Each may be present in varying degrees. At times trade-offs may be necessary, as the scientist sacrifices some degree of virtue in one area for an enormous gain in virtue in another. Preference of one hypothesis over another must be determined in light of all five virtues.

HYPOTHESIS

Some philosophers once held that whatever was true could in principle be proved from self-evident beginnings by self-evident steps. The trait of absolute demonstrability, which we attributed to the truths of logic in a narrow sense and to relatively little else, was believed by those philosophers to pervade all truth. They thought that but for our intellectual limitations we could find proofs for any truths, and so, in particular, predict the future to any desired extent. These philosophers were the rationalists. Other philosophers, a little less sanguine, had it that whatever was true could be proved by self-evident steps from two-fold beginnings: self-evident truths and observations. Philosophers of both schools, the rationalists and the somewhat less sanguine ones as well, strained toward their ideals by construing self-evidence every bit as broadly as they in conscience might, or somewhat more so.

Actually even the truths of elementary number theory are presumably not in general derivable, we noted, by self-evident steps from self-evident truths. We owe this insight to Godel's theorem, which was not known to the old-time philosophers.

What then of the truths of nature? Might these be derivable still by self-evident steps from self-evident truths together with observations? Surely not. Take the humblest generalization from observation: that giraffes are mute, that sea water tastes of salt. We infer these from our observations of giraffes and sea water because we expect instinctively that what is true of all observed samples is true of the rest. The principle involved here, far from being self-evident, does not always lead to true generalizations. It worked for the giraffes and the sea water, but it would have let us down if we had inferred from a hundred observations of swans that all swans are white.

Such generalizations already exceed what can be proved from observations and self-evident truths by self-evident steps. Yet such generalizations are still only a small part of natural science. Theories of molecules and atoms are not related to any observations in the direct way in which the generalizations about giraffes and sea water are related to observations of mute giraffes and salty sea water.

It is now recognized that deduction from self-evident truths and observation is not the sole avenue to truth nor even to reasonable belief. A dominant further factor, in solid science as in daily life, is *hypothesis*. In a word, hypothesis is guesswork; but it can be enlightened guesswork.

It is the part of scientific rigor to recognize hypothesis as hypothesis and then to make the most of it. Having accepted the fact that our observations and our self-evident truths do not together suffice to predict the future, we frame hypotheses to make up the shortage.

Calling a belief a hypothesis says nothing as to what the belief is about, how firmly it is held, or how well founded it is. Calling it a hypothesis suggests rather what sort of reason we have for adopting or entertaining it. People adopt or entertain a hypothesis because it would explain, if it were true, some things that they already believe. Its evidence is seen in its consequences. For example, consider again the detective thriller in Chapter II. We were concerned in those pages with change of belief on the strength of new evidence. But how should we have regarded, in the first place, the belief which the new evidence led us to abandon? It was a hypothesis. It was the belief that Cabot committed the murder, and it was, for a while, the best hypothesis we could devise to explain such circumstances as the killing, the undisturbed state of the victim's effects, the record of Abbott in the hotel register, and the testimony of Babbitt's brother-in-law. And then, when Cabot was discovered on television, what we did was to try to devise a plausible new hypothesis that would explain the enlarged array of circumstances.

Hypothesis, where successful, is a two-way street, extending back to explain the past and forward to predict the future. What we try to do in framing hypotheses is to explain some otherwise unexplained happenings by inventing a plausible story, a plausible description or history of relevant portions of the world. What counts in favor of a hypothesis is a question not to be lightly answered. We may note five virtues that a hypothesis may enjoy in varying degrees.

Virtue I is *conservatism*. In order to explain the happenings that we are inventing it to explain, the hypothesis may have to conflict with some of our previous beliefs; but the fewer the better. Acceptance of a hypothesis is of course like acceptance of any belief in that it demands rejection of whatever conflicts with it. The less rejection of prior beliefs required, the more plausible the hypothesis—other things being equal.

Often some hypothesis is available that conflicts with no prior beliefs. Thus we may attribute a click at the door to arrival of mail through the slot. Conservatism usually prevails in such a case; one is not apt to be tempted by a hypothesis that upsets prior beliefs when there is no need to resort to one. When the virtue of conservatism deserves notice, rather, is when something happens that cannot evidently be reconciled with our prior beliefs.

There could be such a case when our friend the amateur magician tells us what card we have drawn. How did he do it? Perhaps by luck, one chance in fifty-two; but this conflicts with our reasonable belief, if all unstated, that he would not have volunteered a performance that depended on that kind of luck. Perhaps the cards were marked; but this conflicts with our belief that he had had no access to them, they being ours. Perhaps he peeked or pushed, with help of a sleight-of-hand; but this conflicts with our belief in our perceptiveness. Perhaps he resorted to telepathy or clairvoyance; but this would wreak havoc with our whole web of belief. The counsel of conservatism is the sleight-of-hand.

Conservatism is rather effortless on the whole, having inertia in its favor. But it is sound strategy too, since at each step it sacrifices as little as possible of the evidential support, whatever that may have been, that our overall system of beliefs has hitherto been enjoying. The truth may indeed be radically remote from our present system of beliefs, so that we may need a long series of conservative steps to attain what might have been attained in one rash leap. The longer the leap, however, the more serious an angular error in the direction. For a leap in the dark the likelihood of a happy landing is severely limited.

Conservatism holds out the advantages of limited liability and a maximum of live options for each next move.

Virtue II, closely akin to conservatism, is *modesty*. One hypothesis is more modest than another if it is weaker in a logical sense: if it is implied by the other, without implying it. A hypothesis *A* is more modest than *A* and *B* as a joint hypothesis. Also, one hypothesis is more modest than another if it is more humdrum: that is, if the events that it assumes to have happened are of a more usual and familiar sort, hence more to be expected.

Thus suppose a man rings our telephone and ends by apologizing for dialing the wrong number. We will guess that he slipped, rather than that he was a burglar checking to see if anyone was home. It is the more modest of the two hypotheses, butterfingers being rife. We could be wrong, for crime is rife too. But still the butterfingers hypothesis scores better on modesty than the burglar hypothesis, butterfingers being rifer.

We habitually practice modesty, all unawares, when we identify recurrent objects. Unhesitating we recognize our car off there where we parked it, though it may have been towed away and another car of the same model may have happened to pull in at that spot. Ours is the more modest hypothesis, because staying put is a more usual and familiar phenomenon than the alternative combination.

It tends to be the counsel of modesty that the lazy world is the likely world. We are to assume as little activity as will suffice to account for appearances. This is not all there is to modesty. It does not apply to the preferred hypothesis in the telephone example, since Mr. Butterfingers is not assumed to be a less active man than one who might have plotted burglary. Modesty figured there merely in keeping the assumptions down, rather than in actually assuming inactivity. In the example of the parked car, however, the modest hypothesis does expressly assume there to be less activity than otherwise. This is a policy that guides science as well as common sense. It is even erected into an explicit principle of mechanics under the name of the law of least action.

Between modesty and conservatism there is no call to draw a sharp line. But by Virtue I we meant conservatism only in a literal sense—conservation of past beliefs. Thus there remain grades of modesty still to choose among even when Virtue I—compatibility with previous beliefs—is achieved to perfection; for both a slight hypothesis and an extravagant one might be compatible with all previous beliefs.

Modesty grades off in turn into Virtue III, *simplicity*. Where simplicity considerations become especially vivid is in drawing curves through plotted points on a graph. Consider the familiar practice of plotting measurements. Distance up the page represents altitude above sea level, for instance, and distance across represents the temperature of boiling water. We plot our measurements on the graph, one dot for each pair. However many points we plot, there remain infinitely many curves that may be drawn through them. Whatever curve we draw represents our generalization from the data, our prediction of what boiling temperatures would be found at altitudes as yet untested. And the curve we will choose to draw is the simplest curve that passes through or reasonably close to all the plotted points.

There is a premium on simplicity in any hypothesis, but the highest premium is on simplicity in the giant joint hypothesis that is science, or the particular science, as a whole. We cheerfully sacrifice simplicity of a part for greater simplicity of the whole when we see a way of doing so. Thus consider gravity. Heavy objects tend downward: here is an exceedingly simple hypothesis, or even a mere definition. However, we complicate matters by accepting rather the hypothesis that the heavy objects around us are slightly attracted also by one another, and by the neighboring mountains, and by the moon, and that all these competing forces detract slightly from the downward one. Newton propounded this more complicated hypothesis even though, aside from tidal effects of the moon, he had no means of detecting the competing forces; for it meant a great gain in the simplicity of physics as a whole. His hypothesis of universal gravitation, which has each body attracting each in proportion to mass and inversely as the square of the distance, was what enabled him to make a single neat system of celestial and terrestrial mechanics.

A modest hypothesis that was long supported both by theoretical considerations and by observation is that the trajectory of a projectile is a parabola. A contrary hypothesis is that the trajectory deviates imperceptibly from a parabola, constituting rather one end of an ellipse whose other end extends beyond the center of the earth. This hypothesis is less modest, but again it conduces to a higher simplicity: Newton's laws of motion and, again, of gravitation. The trajectories are brought into harmony with Kepler's law of the elliptical orbits of the planets.

Another famous triumph of this kind was achieved by Count Rumford and later physicists when they showed how the relation of gas pressure to temperature could be accounted for by the impact of oscillating particles, for in this way they reduced the theory of gases to the general laws of motion. Such was the kinetic theory of gases. In order to achieve it they had to add the hypothesis, by no means a modest one, that gas consists of oscillating particles or molecules; but the addition is made up for, and much more, by the gain in simplicity accruing to physics as a whole.

What is simplicity? For curves we can make good sense of it in geometrical terms. A simple curve is continuous, and among continuous curves the simplest are perhaps those whose curvature changes most gradually from point to point. When scientific laws are expressed in equations, as they so often are, we can make good sense of simplicity in terms of what mathematicians call the degree of an equation, or the order of a differential equation. This line was taken by Sir Harold Jeffreys. The lower the degree, the lower the order, and the fewer the terms, the simpler the equation. Such simplicity ratings of equations agree with the simplicity ratings of curves when the equations are plotted as in analytical geometry.

Simplicity is harder to define when we turn away from curves and equations. Sometimes in such cases it is not to be distinguished from modesty. Commonly a hypothesis A will count as simpler than A and B together; thus far simplicity and modesty coincide. On the other hand the simplicity gained by Newton's hypothesis of universal gravitation was not modesty, in the sense that we have assigned to that term; for the hypothesis was not logically implied by its predecessors, nor was it more humdrum in respect of the events that it assumed. Newton's hypothesis was simpler than its predecessors in that it covered in a brief unified story what had previously been covered only by two unrelated accounts. Similar remarks apply to the kinetic theory of gases.

In the notion of simplicity there is a nagging subjectivity. What makes for a brief unified story depends on the structure of our language, after all, and on our available vocabulary, which need not reflect the structure of nature. This subjectivity of simplicity is puzzling, if simplicity in hypotheses is to make for plausibility. Why should the subjectively simpler of two hypotheses stand a better chance of predicting objective events? Why should we expect nature to submit to our subjective standards of simplicity?

That would be too much to expect. Physicists and others are continually finding that they have to complicate their theories to accommodate new data. At each stage, however, when choosing a hypothesis subject to subsequent correction, it is still best to choose the simplest that is not yet excluded. This strategy recommends itself on much the same grounds as the strategies of conservatism and modesty. The longer the leap, we reflected, the more and wilder ways of going wrong. But likewise, the more complex the hypothesis, the more and wilder ways of going wrong; for how can we tell which complexities to adopt? Simplicity, like conservatism and modesty, limits liability. Conservatism can be good strategy even though one's present theory be ever so far from the truth, and simplicity can be good strategy even though the world be ever so complicated. Our steps toward the complicated truth can usually be laid out most dependably if the simplest hypothesis that is still tenable is chosen at each step. It has even been argued that this policy will lead us at least asymptotically toward a theory that is true.

There is more, however, to be said for simplicity: the simplest hypothesis often just is the likeliest, apparently, quite apart from questions of cagy strategy. Why should this be? There is a partial explanation in our ways of keeping score on predictions. The predictions based on the simpler hypotheses tend to be scored more leniently. Thus consider curves, where simplicity comparisons are so clear. If a curve is kinky and complex, and if some measurement predicted from the curve turns out to miss the mark by a distance as sizable as some of the kinks of the curve itself, we will count the prediction a failure. We will feel that so kinky a curve, if correct, would have had a kink to catch this wayward point. On the other hand, a miss of the same magnitude might be excused if the curve were smooth and simple. It might be excused as due to inaccuracy of measurement or to some unexplained local interference. This cynical doctrine of selective leniency is very plausible in the case of the curves. And we may reasonably expect a somewhat similar but less easily pictured selectivity to be at work in the interest of the simple hypotheses where curves are not concerned.

Considering how subjective our standards of simplicity are, we wondered why we should expect nature to submit to them. Our first answer was that we need not expect it; the strategy of favoring the simple at each step is good anyway. Now we have noted further that some of nature's seeming simplicity is an effect of our bookkeeping. Are we to conclude that the favoring of simplicity is entirely our doing, and that nature is neutral in the matter? Not quite. Darwin's theory of natural selection offers a causal connection between subjective simplicity and objective truth in the following way. Innate subjective standards of simplicity that make people prefer some hypotheses to others will have survival value insofar as they favor successful prediction. Those who predict best are likeliest to survive and reproduce their kind, in a state of nature anyway, and so their innate standards of simplicity are handed down. Such standards will also change in the light of experience, becoming still better adapted to the growing body of science in the course of the individual's lifetime. (But these improvements do not get handed down genetically.)

Virtue IV is *generality*. The wider the range of application of a hypothesis, the more general it is. When we find electricity conducted by a piece of copper wire, we leap to the hypothesis that all copper, not just long thin copper, conducts electricity.

The plausibility of a hypothesis depends largely on how compatible the hypothesis is with our being observers placed at random in the world. Funny coincidences often occur, but they are not the stuff that plausible hypotheses are made of. The more general the hypothesis is by which we account for our present observation, the less of a coincidence it is that our present observation should fall under it. Hence, in part, the power of the Virtue IV to confer plausibility.

The possibility of testing a hypothesis by repeatable experiment presupposes that the hypothesis has at least some share of Virtue IV. For in a repetition of an experiment the test situation can never be exactly what it was for the earlier run of the experiment; and so, if both runs are to be relevant to the hypothesis, the hypothesis must be at least general enough to apply to both test situations. One would of course like to have it much more general still.

Virtues I, II, and III made for plausibility. So does Virtue IV to some degree, we see, but that is not its main claim; indeed generality conflicts with modesty. But generality is desirable in that it makes a hypothesis interesting and important if true.

We lately noted a celebrated example of generality in Newton's hypothesis of universal gravitation, and another in the kinetic theory of gases. It is no accident that the same illustrations should serve for both simplicity and generality. Generality without simplicity is cold comfort. Thus take celestial mechanics with its elliptical orbits, and take also terrestrial mechanics with its parabolic trajectories, just take them in tandem as a bipartite theory of motion. If the two together cover everything covered by Newton's unified laws of motion, then generality is no ground for preferring Newton's theory to the two taken together. But Virtue III, simplicity, is. When a way is seen of gaining great generality with little loss of simplicity, or great simplicity with no loss of generality, then conservatism and modesty give way to scientific revolution.

The aftermath of the famous Michelson-Morley experiment of 1887 is a case in point. The purpose of this delicate and ingenious experiment was to measure the speed with which the earth travels through the ether. For two centuries, from Newton onward, it had been a well entrenched tenet that something called the ether pervaded all of what we think of as empty space. The great physicist Lorentz (1853–1928) had hypothesized that the ether itself was stationary. What the experiment revealed was that the method that was expected to enable measurement of the earth's speed through the ether was totally inadequate to that task. Supplementary hypotheses multiplied in an attempt to explain the failure without seriously disrupting the accepted physics. Lorentz, in an effort to save the hypothesis of stationary ether, shifted to a new and more complicated set of formulas in his mathematical physics. Einstein soon cut through all this, propounding what is called the special theory of relativity.

This was a simplification of physical theory. Not that Einstein's theory is as simple as Newton's had been; but Newton's physics had been shown untenable by the Michelson-Morley experiment. The point is that Einstein's theory is simpler than Newton's as corrected and supplemented and complicated by Lorentz and others. It was a glorious case of gaining simplicity at the sacrifice of conservatism; for the time-honored ether went by the board, and far older and more fundamental tenets went by the board too. Drastic changes were made in our conception of the very structure of space and time, as noted in Chapter V.

Yet let the glory not blind us to Virtue I. When our estrangement from the past is excessive, the imagination boggles; genius is needed to devise the new theory, and high talent is needed to find one's way about in it. Even Einstein's revolution, moreover, had its conservative strain; Virtue I was not wholly sacrificed. The old phys-

273

ics of Newton's classical mechanics is, in a way, preserved after all. For the situation in which the old and the new theories would predict contrary observations are situations that we are not apt to encounter without sophisticated experiment—because of their dependence on exorbitant velocities or exorbitant distances. This is why classical mechanics held the field so long. Whenever, even having switched to Einstein's relativity theory, we dismiss those exorbitant velocities and distances for the purpose of some practical problem, promptly the discrepancy between Einstein's theory and Newton's becomes too small to matter. Looked at from this angle, Einstein's theory takes on the aspect not of a simplification but a generalization. We might say that the sphere of applicability of Newtonian mechanics in its original simplicity was shown, by the Michelson-Morley experiment and related results, to be less than universal; and then Einstein's theory comes as a generalization, presumed to hold universally. Within its newly limited sphere, Newtonian mechanics retains its old utility. What is more, the evidence of past centuries for Newtonian mechanics even carries over, within these limits, as evidence for Einstein's physics; for, as far as it goes, it fits both.

What is thus illustrated by Einstein's relativity is more modestly exemplified elsewhere, and generally aspired to: the retention, in some sense, of old theories in new ones. If the new theory can be so fashioned as to diverge from the old only in ways that are undetectable in most ordinary circumstances, then it inherits the evidence of the old theory rather than having to overcome it. Such is the force of conservatism even in the context of revolution.

Virtues I through IV may be further illustrated by considering Neptune. That Neptune is among the planets is readily checked by anyone with reference material; indeed it passes as common knowledge, and there is for most of us no need to check it. But only through extensive application of optics and geometry was it possible to determine, in the first instance, that the body we call Neptune exists, and that it revolves around the sun. This required not only much accumulated science and mathematics, but also powerful telescopes and cooperation among scientists.

In fact it happens that Neptune's existence and planethood were strongly suspected even before that planet was observed. Physical theory made possible the calculation of what the orbit of the planet Uranus should be, but Uranus' path differed measurably from its calculated course. Now the theory on which the calculations were based was, like all theories, open to revision or refutation. But here conservatism operates: one is loath to revise extensively a well established set of beliefs, especially a set so deeply entrenched as a basic portion of physics. And one is even more loath to abandon as spurious immense numbers of observation reports made by serious scientists. Given that Uranus had been observed to be as much as two minutes of arc from its calculated position, what was sought was a discovery that would render this deviation explicable within the framework of accepted theory. Then the theory and its generality would be unimpaired, and the new complexity would be minimal.

It would have been possible in principle to speculate that some special characteristic of Uranus exempted that planet from the physical laws that are followed by other planets. If such a hypothesis had been resorted to, Neptune would not have been discovered; not then, at any rate. There was a reason, however, for not resorting to such a hypothesis. It would have been what is called an *ad hoc hypothesis*, and ad hoc hypotheses are bad air; for they are wanting in Virtues III and IV. Ad hoc hypotheses are hypotheses that purport to account for some particular observations by supposing some very special forces to be at work in the particular cases at hand, and not generalizing sufficiently beyond those cases. The vice of an ad hoc hypothesis admits of degrees. The extreme case is where the hypothesis covers only the observations it was invented to account for, so that it is totally useless in prediction. Then also it is insusceptible of confirmation, which would come of our verifying its predictions.

Another example that has something of the implausibility of an ad hoc hypothesis is the water-diviner's belief that a willow wand held above the ground can be attracted by underground water. The force alleged is too special. One feels, most decidedly, the lack of an intelligible mechanism to explain the attraction. And what counts as intelligible mechanism? A hypothesis strikes us as giving an intelligible mechanism when the hypothesis rates well in familiarity, generality, simplicity. We attain the ultimate in intelligibility of mechanism, no doubt, when we see how to explain something in terms of physical impact, or the familiar and general laws of motion.

There is an especially notorious sort of hypothesis which, whether or not properly classified also as ad hoc, shares the traits of insusceptibility of confirmation and uselessness in prediction. This is the sort of hypothesis that seeks to save some other hypothesis from refutation by systematically excusing the failures of its predictions. When the Voice from Beyond is silent despite the incantations of the medium, we may be urged to suppose that "someone in the room is interfering with the communication." In an effort to save the prior hypothesis that certain incantations will summon forth the Voice, the auxiliary hypothesis that untoward thoughts can thwart audible signals is advanced. This auxiliary hypothesis is no wilder than the hypothesis that it was invoked to save, and thus an uncritical person may find the newly wrinkled theory no harder to accept than its predecessor had been. On the other hand the critical observer sees that evidence has ceased altogether to figure. Experi-

mental failure is being milked to fatten up theory.

These reflections bring a fifth virtue to the fore: *refutability*, Virtue V. It seems faint praise of a hypothesis to call it refutable. But the point, we have now seen, is approximately this: some imaginable event, recognizable if it occurs, must suffice to refute the hypothesis. Otherwise the hypothesis predicts nothing, is confirmed by nothing, and confers upon us no earthly good beyond perhaps a mistaken peace of mind.

This is too simple a statement of the matter. Just about any hypothesis, after all, can be held unrefuted no matter what, by making enough adjustments in other beliefs—though sometimes doing so requires madness. We think loosely of a hypothesis as implying predictions when, strictly speaking, the implying is done by the hypothesis together with a supporting chorus of ill-distinguished background beliefs. It is done by the whole relevant theory taken together.

Properly viewed, therefore, Virtue V is a matter of degree, as are its four predecessors. The degree to which a hypothesis partakes of Virtue V is measured by the cost of retaining the hypothesis in the face of imaginable events. The degree is measured by how dearly we cherish the previous beliefs that would have to be sacrificed to save the hypothesis. The greater the sacrifice, the more refutable the hypothesis.

A prime example of deficiency in respect of Virtue V is astrology. Astrologers can so hedge their predictions that they are devoid of genuine content. We may be told that a person will "tend to be creative" or "tend to be outgoing," where the evasiveness of a verb and the fuzziness of adjectives serve to insulate the claim from repudiation. But even if a prediction should be regarded as a failure, astrological devotees can go on believing that the stars rule our destinies; for there is always some item of information, perhaps as to a planet's location at a long gone time, that may be alleged to have been overlooked.

Conflict with other beliefs thus need not arise.

All our contemplating of special virtues of hypotheses will not, we trust, becloud the fact that the heart of the matter is observation. Virtues I through V are guides to the framing of hypotheses that, besides conforming to past observations, may plausibly be expected to conform to future ones. When they fail on the latter score, questions are reopened. Thus it was that the Michelson-Morley experiment led to modifications, however inelegant, of Newton's physics at the hands of Lorentz. When Einstein came out with a simpler way of accommodating past observations, moreover, his theory was no mere reformulation of the Newton-Lorentz system; it was yet a third theory, different in some of its predicted observations and answerable to them. Its superior simplicity brought plausibility to its distinctive consequences.

Hypotheses were to serve two purposes: to explain the past and predict the future. Roughly and elliptically speaking, the hypothesis serves these purposes by implying the past events that it was supposed to explain, and by implying future ones. More accurately speaking, as we saw, what does the implying is the whole relevant theory taken together, as newly revised by adoption of the hypothesis in question. Moreover, the predictions that are implied are mostly not just simple predictions of future observations or other events; more often they are conditional predictions. The hypothesis will imply that we will make these further observations if we look in such and such a place, or take other feasible steps. If the predictions come out right, we can win bets or gain other practical advantages. Also, when they come out right, we gain confirmatory evidence for our hypotheses. When they come out wrong, we go back and tinker with our hypotheses and try to make them better.

What we called limiting principles in Chapter IV are, when intelligible, best seen as hypotheses—some good, some bad. Similarly, of course, for scientific laws generally. And similarly for laws of geometry, set theory, and other parts of mathematics. All these laws—those of physics and those of mathematics equally—are among the component hypotheses that fit together to constitute our inclusive scientific theory of the world. The most general hypotheses tend to be the least answerable to any particular observation, since subsidiary hypotheses can commonly be juggled and adjusted to accommodate conflicts; and on this score of aloofness there is no clear boundary between theoretical physics and mathematics. Of course hypotheses in various fields of inquiry may tend to receive their confirmation from different kinds of investigation, but this should in no way conflict with our seeing them all as hypotheses.

We talk of framing hypotheses. Actually we inherit the main ones, growing up as we do in a going culture. The continuity of belief is due to the retention, at each particular time, of most beliefs. In this retentiveness science even at its most progressive is notably conservative. Virtue I looms large. A reasonable person will look upon some of his or her retained beliefs as self-evident, on others as common knowledge though not self-evident, on others as vouched for by authority in varying degree, and on others as hypotheses that have worked all right so far.

But the going culture goes on, and each of us participates in adding and dropping hypotheses. Continuity makes the changes manageable. Disruptions that are at all sizable are the work of scientists, but we all modify the fabric in our small way, as when we conclude on indirect evidence that the schools will be closed and the planes grounded so that an umbrella thought to have been forgotten by one person was really forgotten by another.

CHAPTER 29

PAUL FEYERABEND

HOW TO DEFEND SOCIETY AGAINST SCIENCE

Paul Feyerabend (1924–   ) is Professor of philosophy at the University of California at Berkeley. He is the author of numerous articles in the philosophy of science, including the controversial book *Against Method* (1977).

This selection is a revised version of a paper that Feyerabend delivered to the Philosophy Society at Sussex University in 1974.[1] It is highly controversial in that it equates science with ideology, fairytale, and myth. In support of his ideas Feyerabend offers two arguments: one very general (contained in the section "Fairytales") and one specific.

His general argument is that there is nothing *inherently* liberating in any ideology, science included. Although the science of the seventeenth and eighteenth centuries did liberate and enlighten people, it does not follow that science will *continue* to liberate and enlighten. Science in our day has wrapped itself in the mantle of "truth" and reigns in our society, alone, supreme, and unchallenged. It has become the mainstream ideology, marginalizing all other myths and ideologies. As Feyerabend expresses it, using the language of democracy and resistance, "A truth that reigns without checks and balances is a tyrant who must be overthrown, and any falsehood that can aid us in the overthrow of this tyrant is to be welcomed."

The second part of the article (beginning with the section titled "Against Method") is Feyerabend's response to an argument he anticipates will be made by

[1]From *Radical Philosophy* 2 (Summer, 1975): 4–8.

his critics. According to this argument, (1) science has finally found the correct *method* for achieving results; and (2) there are many *results* to prove the excellence of the method. Feyerabend vigorously argues against these two points, venting his critisms of Popper, Kuhn, and Lakatos along the way. Surprisingly, he embraces (lukewarmly!) Christian fundamentalists in California who succeeded in removing "a dogmatic formulation of the theory of evolution" from textbooks. He concludes with some provocative reflections in the section titled "Education and Myth."

HOW TO DEFEND SOCIETY AGAINST SCIENCE

Practitioners of a strange trade, friends, enemies, ladies and gentlemen: Before starting with my talk, let me explain to you, how it came into existence.

About a year ago I was short of funds. So I accepted an invitation to contribute to a book dealing with the relation between science and religion. To make the book sell I thought I should make my contribution a provocative one and the most provocative statement one can make about the relation between science and religion is that science is a religion. Having made the statement the core of my article I discovered that lots of reasons, lots of excellent reasons, could be found for it. I enumerated the reasons, finished my article, and got paid. That was stage one.

Next I was invited to a Conference for the Defense of Culture. I accepted the invitation because it paid for my flight to Europe. I also must admit that I was rather curious. When I arrived in Nice I had no idea what I would say. Then while the conference was taking its course I discovered that everyone thought very highly of science and that everyone was very serious. So I decided to explain how one could defend culture from science. All the reasons collected in my article would apply here as well and there was no need to invent new things. I gave my talk, was

rewarded with an outcry about my "dangerous and ill considered ideas," collected my ticket and went on to Vienna. That was stage number two.

Now I am supposed to address you. I have a hunch that in some respect you are very different from my audience in Nice. For one, you look much younger. My audience in Nice was full of professors, businessmen, and television executives, and the average age was about 58½. Then I am quite sure that most of you are considerably to the left of some of the people in Nice. As a matter of fact, speaking somewhat superficially I might say that you are a leftist audience while my audience in Nice was a rightist audience. Yet despite all these differences you have some things in common. Both of you, I assume, respect science and knowledge. Science, of course, must be reformed and must be made less authoritarian. But once the reforms are carried out, it is a valuable source of knowledge that must not be contaminated by ideologies of a different kind. Secondly, both of you are serious people. Knowledge is a serious matter, for the Right as well as for the Left, and it must be pursued in a serious spirit. Frivolity is out, dedication and earnest application to the task at hand is in. These similarities are all I need for repeating my Nice talk to you with hardly any change. So, here it is.

Fairytales

I want to defend society and its inhabitants from all ideologies, science included. All ideologies must be seen in perspective. One must not take them too seriously. One must read them like fairytales which have lots of interesting things to say but which also contain wicked lies, or like ethical prescriptions which may be useful rules of thumb but which are deadly when followed to the letter.

Now—is this not a strange and ridiculous attitude? Science, surely, was always in the forefront of the fight against authoritarianism and superstition. It is to science that we owe our increased intellectual freedom vis-à-vis religious beliefs; it is to science that we owe the liberation of mankind from ancient and rigid forms of thought. Today these forms of thought are nothing but bad dreams—and this we learned from science. Science and enlightenment are one and the same thing—even the most radical critics of society believe this. Kropotkin wants to overthrow all traditional institutions and forms of belief, with the exception of science. Ibsen criticises the most intimate ramifications of nineteenth century bourgeois ideology, but he leaves science untouched. Levi-Strauss has made us realize that Western Thought is not the lonely peak of human achievement it was once believed to be, but he excludes science from his relativization of ideologies. Marx and Engels were convinced that science would aid the workers in their quest for mental and social liberation. Are all these people deceived? Are they all mistaken about the role of science? Are they all the victims of a chimaera?

To these questions my answer is a firm *Yes and No.*

Now, let me explain my answer.

My explanation consists of two parts, one more general, one more specific.

The general explanation is simple. Any ideology that breaks the hold a comprehensive system of thought has on the minds of men contributes to the liberation of man. Any ideology that makes man question inherited beliefs is an aid to enlightenment. A truth that reigns without checks and balances is a tyrant who must be overthrown and any falsehood that can aid us in the overthrow of this tyrant is to be welcomed. It follows that seventeenth and eighteenth century science indeed *was* an instrument of liberation and enlightenment. It does not follow that science is bound to *remain* such an instrument. There is nothing inherent in science or in any other ideology that makes it *essentially* liberating. Ideologies can deteriorate and become stupid religions. Look at Marxism. And that the science of today is very different from the science of 1650 is evident at the most superficial glance.

For example, consider the role science now plays in education. Scientific "facts" are taught at a very early age and in the very same manner in which religious "facts" were taught only a century ago. There is no attempt to waken the critical abilities of the pupil so that he may be able to see things in perspective. At the universities the situation is even worse, for indoctrination is here carried out in a much more systematic manner. Criticism is not entirely absent. Society, for example, and its institutions, are criticised most severely and often most unfairly and this already at the elementary school level. But science is excepted from the criticism. In society at large the judgement of bishops and cardinals was accepted not too long ago. The move towards "demythologization," for example, is largely motivated by the wish to avoid any clash between Christianity and scientific ideas. If such a clash occurs, then science is certainly right and Christianity wrong. Pursue this investigation further and you will see that science has now become as oppressive as the ideologies it had once to fight.

Do not be misled by the fact that today hardly anyone gets killed for joining a scientific heresy. This has nothing to do with science. It has something to do with the general quality of our civilization. Heretics in science are still made to suffer from the *most severe* sanctions this relatively tolerant civilization has to offer.

But—is this description not utterly unfair? Have I not presented the matter in a very distorted light by using tendentious and distorting terminology? Must we not describe the situation in a very different way? I have said that science has become *rigid*, that it has ceased to be an instrument of *change* and *liberation* without adding that it has found the *truth*, or a large part thereof. Considering this additional fact we realise, so the objection goes, that the rigidity of science is not due to human willfulness. It lies in the nature of things. For once we have discovered the truth—what else can we do but follow it?

This trite reply is anything but original. It is used whenever an ideology wants to reinforce the faith of its followers. "Truth" is such a nicely neutral word. Nobody would deny that it is commendable to speak the truth and wicked to tell lies. Nobody would deny that—and yet nobody knows what such an attitude amounts to. So it is easy to twist matters and to change allegiance to truth in one's everyday affairs into allegiance to the Truth of ideology which is nothing but the dogmatic defence of that ideology. And it is of course *not* true that we *have* to follow the truth. Human life is guided by many ideas. Truth is one of them. Freedom and mental independence are others. If Truth, as conceived by some ideologists, conflicts with freedom then we have a *choice*. We may abandon freedom. But we may also abandon Truth. (Alternatively, we may adopt a more sophisticated idea of truth that no longer contradicts freedom; that was Hegel's solution.) My criticism of modern science is that it inhibits freedom of thought. If the reason is that

it has found the truth and now follows it then I would say that there are better things than first finding, and then following such a monster.

This finishes the general part of my explanation.

There exists a more specific argument to defend the exceptional position science has in society today. Put in a nutshell the argument says (1) that science has finally found the correct *method* for achieving results and (2) that there are many *results* to prove the excellence of the method. The argument is mistaken—but most attempts to show this lead into a dead end. Methodology has by now become so crowded with empty sophistication that it is extremely difficult to perceive the simple errors at the basis. It is like fighting the hydra—cut off one ugly head, and eight formalizations take its place. In this situation the only answer is superficiality: when sophistication loses content then the only way of keeping in touch with reality is to be crude and superficial. This is what I intend to be.

Against Method

There is a method, says part (1) of the argument. What is it? How does it work?

One answer which is no longer as popular as it used to be is that science works by collecting facts and inferring theories from them. The answer is unsatisfactory as theories never *follow* from facts in the strict logical sense. To say that they may yet be *supported* by facts assumes a notion of support that (a) does now show this defect and is (b) sufficiently sophisticated to permit us to say to what extent, say, the theory of relativity is supported by the facts. No such notion exists today nor is it likely that it will ever be found (one of the problems is that we need a notion of support in which grey ravens can be said to support "All Ravens are Black"). This was realised by conventionalists and transcendental idealists who pointed out that theories *shape* and *order* facts and can therefore be retained come what may. They can be retained because the human mind either consciously or unconsciously carried out its ordering function. The trouble with these views is that they assume for the mind what they want to explain for the world, viz. that it works in a regular fashion. There is only one view which overcomes all these difficulties. It was invented twice in the nineteenth century, by Mill, in his immortal essay *On Liberty*, and by some Darwinists who extended Darwinism to the battle of ideas. This view takes the bull by the horns: theories cannot be justified and their excellence cannot be shown without reference to other theories. We may explain the *success* of a theory by reference to a more comprehensive theory (we explain the success of Newton's theory by using the general theory of relativity), and we may explain our *preference* for it by comparing it with other theories. Such a comparison does not establish the intrinsic excellence of the theory we have chosen. As a matter of fact, the theory we have chosen may be pretty lousy. It may contain contradictions, it may conflict with well-known facts, it may be cumbersome, unclear, ad hoc in decisive places and so on. But it may still be better than any other theory that is available at the time. It may in fact be the best lousy theory there is. Nor are the standards of judgement chosen in an absolute manner. Our sophistication increases with every choice we make, and so do our standards. Standards compete just as theories compete and we choose the standards most appropriate to the historical situation in which the choice occurs. The rejected alternatives (theories; standards; "facts") are not eliminated. They serve as correctives (after all, we may have made the wrong choice) and they also explain the content of the preferred views (we understand relativity better when we understand the structure of its competitors; we know the full meaning of freedom only when we have an idea of life in a totalitarian state, of its advantages—and there are many advantages—as well as of its disadvantages). Knowledge so conceived is an ocean of alternatives channelled and subdivided by an ocean of standards. It forces our mind to make imaginative choices and thus makes it grow. It makes our mind capable of choosing, imagining, criticising.

Today this view is often connected with the name of Karl Popper. But there are some very decisive differences between Popper and Mill. To start with, Popper developed his view to solve a special problem of epistemology—he wanted to solve "Hume's problem." Mill, on the other hand, is interested in conditions favourable to human growth. His epistemology is the result of a certain theory of man, and not the other way around. Also Popper, being influenced by the Vienna Circle, improves on the logical form of a theory before discussing it while Mill uses every theory in the form in which it occurs in science. Thirdly, Popper's standards of comparison are rigid and fixed while Mill's standards are permitted to change with the historical situation. Finally, Popper's standards eliminate competitors once and for all: theories that are either not falsifiable, or falsifiable and falsified have no place in science. Popper's criteria are clear, unambiguous, precisely formulated; Mill's criteria are not. This would be an advantage if science itself were clear, unambiguous, and precisely formulated. Fortunately, it is not.

To start with, no new and revolutionary scientific theory is ever formulated in a manner that permits us to say under what circumstances we must regard it as endangered: many revolutionary theories are unfalsifiable. Falsifiable versions do exist, but they are hardly ever in agreement with accepted basic statements: every moderately interesting theory is falsified. Moreover, theories have formal flaws, many of them contain contradictions, ad hoc adjustments, and so on and so forth. Applied resolutely, Popperian criteria would eliminate science without replacing it by anything comparable. They are useless as an aid to science.

In the past decade this has been realised by various thinkers, Kuhn and Lakatos among them. Kuhn's ideas are interesting but, alas, they are much too vague to give rise to anything but lots of hot air. If you don't believe me, look at the literature. Never before has the literature on the philosophy of science been invaded by so many creeps and incompetents. Kuhn encourages people who have no idea why a stone falls to the ground to talk with assurance about scientific method. Now I have no objection to incompetence but I do object when incompetence is accompanied by boredom and self-righteousness. And this is exactly what happens. We do not get interesting false ideas, we get boring ideas or words connected with no ideas at all. Secondly, wherever one tries to make Kuhn's ideas more definite one finds that they are *false.* Was there ever a period of normal science in the history of thought? No—and I challenge anyone to prove the contrary.

Lakatos is immeasurably more sophisticated than Kuhn. Instead of theories he considers research programmes which are sequences of theories connected by methods of modification, so-called heuristics. Each theory in the sequence may be full of faults. It may be beset by anomalies, contradictions, ambiguities. What counts is not the shape of the single theories, but the tendency exhibited by the sequence. We judge historical developments, achievements over a period of time, rather than the situation at a particular time. History and methodology are combined into a single enterprise. A research programme is said to progress if the sequence of theories leads to novel predictions. It is said to

degenerate if it is reduced to absorbing facts that have been discovered without its help. A decisive feature of Lakatos's methodology is that such evaluations are no longer tied to methodological rules which tell the scientist to either retain or to abandon a research programme. Scientists may stick to a degenerating programme, they may even succeed in making the programme overtake its rivals and they therefore proceed rationally with whatever they are doing (provided they continue calling degenerating programmes degenerating and progressive programmes progressive). This means that Lakatos offers *words* which *sound* like the elements of a methodology; he does not offer a methodology. This is no method according to the most advanced and sophisticated methodology in existence today. This finishes my reply to part (1) of the specific argument.

Against Rules

According to part (2), science deserves a special position because it has produced *results.* This is an argument only if it can be taken for granted that nothing else has ever produced results. Now it may be admitted that almost everyone who discusses the matter makes such an assumption. It may also be admitted that it is not easy to show that the assumption is false. Forms of life different from science have either disappeared or have degenerated to an extent that makes a fair comparison impossible. Still, the situation is not as hopeless as it was only a decade ago. We have become acquainted with methods of medical diagnosis and therapy which are effective (and perhaps even more effective then the corresponding parts of Western medicine) and which are yet based on an ideology that is radically different from the ideology of Western science. We have learned that there are phenomena such as telepathy and telekinesis which are obliterated by a scientific approach and which could be used to do research in an entirely novel way (earlier thinkers such as Agrippa of Nettesheim, John Dee, and even Bacon were aware of these phenomena). And then—is it not the case that the Church saved souls while science often does the very opposite? Of course, nobody now believes in the ontology that underlies this judgement. Why? Because of ideological pressures identical with those which today make us listen to science to the exclusion of everything else. It is also true that phenomena such as telekinesis and acupuncture may eventually be absorbed into the body of science and may therefore be called "scientific." But note that this happens only *after* a long period of resistance during which a science *not yet* containing the phenomena wants to get the upper hand over forms of life that contain them. And this leads to a further objection against part (2) of the specific argument. The fact that science has results counts in its favour only if these results were achieved by science alone, and without any outside help. A look at history shows that science hardly ever gets its results in this way. When Copernicus introduced a new view of the universe, he did not consult *scientific* predecessors, he consulted a crazy Pythagorean such as Philolaos. He adopted his ideas and he maintained them in the face of all sound rules of scientific method. Mechanics and optics owe a lot to artisans, medicine to midwives and witches. And in our own day we have seen how the interference of the state can advance science; when the Chinese Communists refused to be intimidated by the judgement of experts and ordered traditional medicine back into universities and hospitals there was an outcry all over the world that science would now be ruined in China. The very opposite occurred: Chinese science advanced and Western science learned from it. Wherever we look we see that great scientific advances are due to outside interference which is made to prevail in the face of the most basic and most "rational" methodological rules. The lesson is plain: there does not exist a single argument that could be used to support the exceptional role which science today plays in society. Science has done many things, but so have other ideologies. Science often proceeds systematically, but so do other ideologies (just consult the records of the many doctrinal debates that took place in the Church) and, besides, there are no overriding rules which are adhered to under any circumstances; there is no "scientific methodology" that can be used to separate science from the rest. *Science is just one of the many ideologies that propel society and it should be treated as such* (this statement applies even to the most progressive and most dialectical sections of science). What consequences can we draw from this result?

The most important consequence is that there must be a *formal separation between state and science* just as there is now a formal separation between state and church. Science may influence society but only to the extent to which any political or other pressure group is permitted to influence society. Scientists may be consulted on important projects but the final judgement must be left to the democratically elected consulting bodies. These bodies will consist mainly of laymen. Will the laymen be able to come to a correct judgement? Most certainly, for the competence, the complications and the successes of science are vastly exaggerated. One of the most exhilarating experiences is to see how a lawyer, who is a layman, can find holes in the testimony, the technical testimony of the most advanced expert and thus prepare the jury for its verdict. Science is not a closed book that is understood only after years of training. It is an intellectual discipline that can be examined and criticised by anyone who is interested and that looks difficult and profound only because of a systematic campaign of obfuscation carried out by many scientists (though, I am happy to say, not by all). Organs of the state should never hesitate to reject the judgement of scientists when they have reason for doing so. Such rejection will educate the general public, will make it more confident and it may even lead to improvement. Considering the sizeable chauvinism of the scientific establishment we can say: the more Lysenko affairs the better (it is not the *interference* of the state that is objectionable in the case of Lysenko, but the *totalitarian* interference which kills the opponent rather than just neglecting his advice). Three cheers to the fundamentalists in California who succeeded in having a dogmatic formulation of the theory of evolution removed from the text books and an account of Genesis included (but I know that they would become as chauvinistic and totalitarian as scientists are today when given the chance to run society all by themselves. Ideologies are marvelous when used in the company of other ideologies. They become boring and doctrinaire as soon as their merits lead to the removal of their opponents). The most important change, however, will have to occur in the field of *education*.

Education and Myth

The purpose of education, so one would think, is to introduce the young into life, and that means: into the *society* where they are born and into the *physical universe* that surrounds the society. The method of education often consists in the teaching of some *basic myth*. The myth is available in various versions. More advanced versions may be taught by initiation rites which firmly implant them into the mind. Knowing the myth the grown-up can explain almost everything (or else he can turn to experts for more detailed information). He is the master of Nature and of Society. He understands them both and he knows how to interact with them. However, *he is not the master of the myth that guides his understanding.*

Such further mastery was aimed at, and was partly achieved, by the Pre-Socratics. The Pre-Socratics not only tried to understand the *world*. They also tried to understand, and thus to become the masters of, the *means of understanding the world*. Instead of being content with a single myth they developed many and so diminished the power which a well-told story has over the minds of men. The Sophists introduced still further methods for reducing the debilitating effect of interesting, coherent, "empirically adequate" etc. etc. tales. The achievements of these thinkers were not appreciated and they certainly are not understood today. When teaching a myth we want to increase the chance that it will be understood (i.e. no puzzlement about any feature of the myth), believed, *and accepted*. This does not do any harm when the myth is counterbalanced by other myths: even the most dedicated (i.e. totalitarian) instructor in a certain version of Christianity cannot prevent his pupils from getting in touch with Buddhists, Jews and other disreputable people. It is very different in the case of science, or of rationalism where the field is almost completely dominated by the believers. In this case it is of paramount importance to strengthen the minds of the young and "strengthening the minds of the young" means strengthening them *against* any easy acceptance of comprehensive views. What we need here is an education that makes people *contrary, counter-suggestive without* making them incapable of devoting themselves to the elaboration of any single view. How can this aim be achieved?

It can be achieved by protecting the tremendous imagination which children possess and by developing to the full the spirit of contradiction that exists in them. On the whole children are much more intelligent than their teachers. They succumb, and give up their intelligence because they are bullied, or because their teachers get the better of them by emotional means. Children can learn, understand, and keep separate two to three different languages ("children" and by this I mean three to five year olds, *not* eight year olds who were experimented upon quite recently and did not come out too well; why? because they were already loused up by incompetent teaching at an earlier age). Of course, the languages must be introduced in a more interesting way than is usually done. There are marvellous writers in all languages who have told marvellous stories—let us begin our language teaching with *them* and not with "der Hund hat einen Schwanz" and similar inanities. Using stories we may of course also introduce "scientific" accounts, say, of the origin of the world and thus make the children acquainted with science as well. But science must not be given any special position except for pointing out that there are lots of people who believe in it. Later on the stories which have been told will be supplemented with "reasons," where by reasons I mean further accounts of the kind found in the tradition to which the story belongs. And, of course, there will also be contrary reasons. Both reasons and contrary reasons will be told by the experts in the fields and so the young generation becomes acquainted with all kinds of sermons and all types of wayfarers. It becomes acquainted with them, it becomes acquainted with their stories, and every individual can make up his mind which way to go. By now everyone knows that you can earn a lot of money and respect and perhaps even a Nobel Prize by becoming a scientist, so many will become scientists. They will *become* scientists *without having been taken in by the ideology of science,* they will *be* scientists *because they have made a free choice.* But has not much time been wasted on unscientific subjects and will this not detract from their competence once they have become scientists? Not at all! The progress of science, of good science depends on

novel ideas and on intellectual freedom: science has very often been advanced by outsiders (remember that Bohr and Einstein regarded themselves as outsiders). Will not many people make the wrong choice and end up in a dead end? Well, that depends on what you mean by a "dead end." Most scientists today are devoid of ideas, full of fear, intent on producing some paltry result so that they can add to the flood of inane papers that now constitutes "scientific progress" in many areas. And, besides, what is more important? To lead a life which one has chosen with open eyes, or to spend one's time in the nervous attempt of avoiding what some not so intelligent people call "dead ends"? Will not the number of scientists decrease so that in the end there is nobody to run our precious laboratories? I do not think so. Given a choice many people may choose science, for a science that is run by free agents looks much more attractive than the science of today which is run by slaves, slaves of institutions and slaves of "reason." And if there is a temporary shortage of scientists the situation may always be remedied by various kinds of incentives. Of course, scientists will not play any predominant role in the society I envisage. They will be more than balanced by magicians, or priests, or astrologers. Such a situation is unbearable for many people, old and young, right and left. Almost all of you have the firm belief that at least *some* kind of truth has been found, that it must be preserved, and that the method of teaching I advocate and the form of society I defend will dilute it and make it finally disappear. You have this firm belief; many of you may even have reasons. *But what you have to consider is that the absence of good contrary reasons is due to a historical accident; it does not lie in the nature of things.* Build up the kind of society I recommend and the views you now despise (without knowing them, to be sure) will return in such splendour that you will have to work hard to maintain your own position and will perhaps be entirely unable to do so. You do not believe me? Then look at history. Scientific astronomy was firmly founded on Ptolemy and Aristotle, two of the greatest minds in the history of Western Thought. Who upset their well-argued, empirically adequate and precisely formulated system? Philolaos the mad and antediluvian Pythagorean. How was it that Philolaos could stage such a comeback? Because he found an able defender: Copernicus. Of course, you may follow your intuitions as I am following mine. But remember that your intuitions are the result of your "scientific" training where by science I also mean the science of Karl Marx. My training, or, rather, my non-training, is that of a journalist who is interested in strange and bizarre events. Finally, is it not utterly irresponsible, in the present world situation, with millions of people starving, others enslaved, downtrodden, in abject misery of body and mind, to think luxurious thoughts such as these? Is not freedom of choice a luxury under such circumstances? Is not the flippancy and the humour I want to see combined with the freedom of choice a luxury under such circumstances? Must we not give up self-indulgence and *act*? Join together, and *act*? This is the most important objection which today is raised against an approach such as the one recommended by me. It has tremendous appeal, it has the appeal of unselfish dedication. Unselfish dedication—to what? Let us see!

We are supposed to give up our selfish inclinations and dedicate ourselves to the liberation of the oppressed. And selfish inclinations are what? They are our wish for maximum liberty of thought in the society in which we live *now*, maximum liberty not only of an abstract kind, but expressed in appropriate institutions and methods of teaching. This wish for concrete intellectual and physical liberty in our own surroundings is to be put aside, for the time being. This

assumes, first, that we do not need this liberty for our task. It assumes that we can carry out our task with a mind that is firmly closed to some alternatives. It assumes that the correct way of liberating others *has always been found* and that all that is needed is to carry it out. I am sorry, I cannot accept such doctrinaire self-assurance in such extremely important matters. Does this mean that we cannot act at all? It does not. But it means that *while acting we have to try to realise as much of the freedom I have recommended so that our actions may be corrected in the light of the ideas we get while increasing our freedom.* This will slow us down, no doubt, but are we supposed to charge ahead simply because some people tell us that they have found an explanation for all the misery and an excellent way out of it? Also we want to liberate people not to make them succumb to a new kind of slavery, *but to make them realise their own wishes*, however different these wishes may be from our own. Self-righteous and narrow-minded liberators cannot do this. As a rule they soon impose a slavery that is worse, because more systematic, than the very sloppy slavery they have removed. And as regards humour and flippancy the answer should be obvious. Why would anyone want to liberate anyone else? Surely not because of some *abstract* advantage of liberty but because liberty is the best way to free development *and thus to happiness.* We want to liberate people so that *they can smile.* Shall we be able to do this if we ourselves have forgotten how to smile and are frowning on those who still remember? Shall we then not spread another disease, comparable to the one we want to remove, the disease of puritanical self-righteousness? Do not object that dedication and humour do not go together—Socrates is an excellent example to the contrary. *The hardest task needs the lightest hand or else its completion will not lead to freedom but to a tyranny much worse than the one it replaces.*

CONTEMPORARY PERSPECTIVES: THE TECHNOLOGICAL SOCIETY

Mary Shelley was only nineteen and in the grip of what she called "a waking dream" when she wrote the novel *Frankenstein*. The book tells the frightening story of Dr. Victor Frankenstein, scientific genuis and mad doctor, who wanted to do good but created a monster. With this one book, Shelley joined the ranks of history's great myth-makers, giving voice to fears about science and technology that many share today.

What "monsters" haunt us today? Since 1945, the world has been aware of a monstrous presence in its midst. Nuclear weapons, created secretly by physicists working for the U.S. Government, have given us much to think about. In a speech given in Hiroshima in February 1981, Pope Paul II said:

> In the past, it was possible to destroy a village, a town, a region, even a country. Now it is the whole planet that has come under threat. This fact should fully compel everyone to face a basic moral consideration: from now on, it is only through conscious choice and then deliberate policy that humanity can survive.[1]

Nuclear weapons are not the only things that have caused anxiety. There are also chemical weapons, toxic waste from nuclear power plants, widespread pollution, and the carcinogenic effects of new petrochemicals and other products of science-based industry, sophisticated electronic devices used for surveillance, computer data banks compiled by market researchers that threaten our privacy, prospects for genetic engineering, and the list goes on.

Historians and social scientists often define modern technology as the application of power machinery to production, dating its origins to the eighteenth-century Industrial Revolution in England. Although historically accurate as far as it goes, this is inadequate philosophically, since it might lead us to identify technology with the machine. In reality, techniques and technology predate the machine by thousands of years, making the machine dependent upon technique, not vice versa. Our English words *technique* and *technology* are derived from the Greek word *techne*, meaning "art, skill, or craft; a system or method of making something." Humans have always been makers. The ancient Greeks included a variety of sciences and arts under the heading of *techne*, including the fine arts, the

---

[1] Quoted by Jonathon Schell, *The New Yorker* (January 2, 1984): 36.

industrial-vocational arts, medicine, and all the applied sciences, such as engineering.

Remembering Aristotle's threefold classification of theoretical, practical, and productive sciences, we might say that humans are knowers, doers, and makers. Yet the Greeks considered productive wisdom or *techne* as inferior to practical and theoretical wisdom. For Aristotle, the ideal life was a life of contemplation. Of course, a large population of slaves in Athens provided the labor that freed aristocrats like Aristotle to have time for contemplation! Even so, *techne* remained important in Greek culture, but it was balanced by practical and theoretical wisdom in pursuit of the Greek ideals of harmony, moderation, and self-control.

As Jacques Ellul points out, this harmony of knowing, doing, and making was shattered as history progressed, and *techne* became more and more dominant in society.[2] By the twentieth century, Ellul believes, technology had established itself as the defining characteristic of the age, an end-in-itself. Ellul's dark vision of "the technological society" is one in which an autonomous technology subverts and controls every human value to the point where humans are themselves cogs in a wheel, indifferent nonpersonal units in a dreary, monolithic world culture. In the technological society, technology is the real metaphysics of the age, and the university is reduced to producing unthinking technicians to operate the machines that increasingly enslave them.

Our first reading, "Two Tables," is written by Sir Arthur Eddington, a twentieth century astronomer and popularizer of science.[3] Eddington begins innocently enough, using his table to contrast the scientific world with the common sense world. Before long, Eddington has the reader thinking about the significance of the atomic model in modern physics, a model that seems to run counter to common sense. By the end of the article the reader must make a decision. Is Eddington arguing that the scientific and common sense descriptions of the world are merely different descriptions of the same thing? (If so, perhaps there is hope that the ancient Greek harmony of knowing, doing, and making can be recovered.) Or is he arguing the more radical thesis that the scientific and common sense descriptions are incompatible, and one of them must be rejected? If he is arguing the latter, what are the implications for ordinary citizens, who are not specially trained as scientists? Remembering that knowledge is power, and that no scientific work is value-free, we might ask the following questions: Whose values dictate what kind of technologies result from scientific knowledge? Are members of a society communally responsible for whatever good or evil comes of their technology? If scientific knowledge is the concern of a powerful elite in society, then how

[2]See Jacques Ellul, *The Technological Society*, trans. John Wilkinson (New York: Vintage Books, 1964).
[3]Sir Arthur Eddington, *The Nature of the Physical World*, (Cambridge: Cambridge University Press, 1928).

can a culture choose its technological advances?

The second reading is taken from Jacques Ellul's article, "The Ethics of Non-power." For Ellul, "technique" is a pervasive and systematic force that has over-powered us and has become the center of society. In *The Technological Society*, he defines technique as "the totality of methods rationally arrived at and having absolute efficiency in every field of human activity." According to Ellul, science and technology have come to be dominated by false ideals of rationality, values, and objectivity. When dislodged from religious moorings, or when attached to a social or political system officially indifferent to morality, the technological max-im takes on a life of its own—that is, it becomes a self-sustaining and self-regu-lating system of rational choice and action. In other words, whatever is techno-logically feasible is right.

Wanting to develop an ethics for technological society, Ellul postulates a new system of "nonpower ethics," where humans would agree to set limits to the use of technique. This new ethical system would liberate humankind from its slavery to technique, opposing the uniformity and conformity required by technique. Ellul is calling for nothing less than a new ethics that would repudiate completely the current role of technique in contemporary society.

Critics of Ellul counter that his critique is "romanticist." According to Jean Jacques Rousseau and other Romantic thinkers, the sciences are grounded in human vanity, pride, idle curiosity, and egoism. They are the products of a cor-rupt and morally decadent civilization in which simpler, nobler virtues—such as family, religion, and a simple life—are stifled so that human life is distorted beyond recognition. Such romantic conceptions idealize "nontechnological" forms of life and are hopelessly naive. These critics contend that there is nothing intrin-sically evil, dehumanizing, or alienating about knowledge, science, or technology. Tools or machines are morally neutral and thus indifferent to human ends and purposes. All is not lost as long as humans act responsibly, controlling the use of technology and directing it toward moral ends. In the face of all these develop-ments, it is important to not allow our fears to overwhelm us. Romantic miscon-ceptions of technology as inherently evil must be laid aside. In itself, technology is neither praiseworthy nor blameworthy; it reflects human values and human choices.

Perhaps there is a middle path between Ellul and his critics. After all, the question of technology is not a new question; it has always been with us. Know-ing, making, and doing are inseparable components of human life; we dare not emphasize one to the exclusion of another. What is new, and what we must face up to, is the bewildering array of potential applications for scientific knowledge and the increasing shift in the decision-making process that determines which of these applications become reality. Unfortunately, the decision-making process has shifted away from ordinary citizens towards specialized interests, producing a sense of helplessness in the general public. This helplessness can be overcome only by democratizing the decision-making process, as we educate ourselves about the nature of technology and its relation to human values. That is the purpose of this Contemporary Perspectives section.

CHAPTER 30

ARTHUR EDDINGTON

TWO TABLES

Arthur Eddington (1882–1944), English astronomer and popularizer of science, was educated at Cambridge University, where he was professor of astronomy from 1913 to 1944. He was elected a fellow of the Royal Society in 1914 and knighted in 1930. A brilliant scientific theoretician, he is the author of *The Mathematical Theory of Relativity* (1923), *Nature of the Physical World* (1928), and *New Pathways in Science* (1935).

TWO TABLES[1]

I have settled down to the task of writing these lectures and have drawn up my chairs to my two tables. Two tables! Yes; there are duplicates of every object about me—two tables, two chairs, two pens.

This is not a very profound beginning to a course which ought to reach transcendent levels of scientific philosophy. But we cannot touch bedrock immediately; we must scratch a bit at the surface of things first. And whenever I begin to scratch; the first thing I strike is—my two tables.

One of them has been familiar to me from earliest years. It is a commonplace object of that environment which I call the world. How shall I describe it? It has extension; it is comparatively

[1]From Sir Arthur Eddington, *The Nature of the Physical World* (Cambridge: Cambridge University Press, 1978). Reprinted by permission of Cambridge University Press.

permanent; it is colored; above all it is *substantial*. By substantial I do not merely mean that it does not collapse when I lean up on it; I mean that it is constituted of "substance," and by that word I am trying to convey to you some conception of its intrinsic nature. It is a *thing*; not like space, which is a mere negation; nor like time, which is— Heaven knows what! But that will not help you to my meaning because it is the distinctive characteristic of a "thing" to have this substantiality, and I do not think substantiality can be described better than by saying that it is the kind of nature exemplified by an ordinary table. And so we go round in circles. After all if you are a plain commonsense man, not too much worried with scientific scruples, you will be confident that you understand the nature of an ordinary table. I have even heard of plain men who had the idea that they could better understand the mystery of their own nature if scientists would discover a way of explaining it in terms of the easily comprehensible nature of a table.

Table no. 2 is my scientific table. It is a more recent acquaintance and I do not feel so familiar with it. It does not belong to the world previously mentioned—that world which spontaneously appears around me when I open my eyes, though how much of it is objective and how much subjective I do not here consider. It is part of a world which in more devious ways has forced itself on my attention. My scientific table is mostly emptiness. Sparsely scattered in that emptiness are numerous electric charges rushing about with great speed; but their combined bulk amounts to less than a billionth of the bulk of the table itself. Notwithstanding its strange construction it turns out to be an entirely efficient table. It supports my writing paper as satisfactorily as table no. 1; for when I lay the paper on it the little electric particles with their headlong speed keep on hitting the underside, so that the paper is maintained in shuttlecock fashion at a nearly steady level. If I lean upon this table I shall not go through; or, to be strictly accurate, the chance of my scientific elbow going through my scientific table is so excessively small that it can be neglected in practical life. Reviewing their properties one by one, there seems to be nothing to choose between the two tables for ordinary purposes; but when abnormal circumstances befall, then my scientific table shows to advantage. If the house catches fire my scientific table will dissolve quite naturally into scientific smoke, whereas my familiar table undergoes a metamorphosis of its substantial nature which I can only regard as miraculous.

There is nothing *substantial* about my second table. It is nearly all empty space—space pervaded, it is true, by fields of force, but these are assigned to the category of "influences," not of "things." Even in the minute part which is not empty we must not transfer the old notion of substance. In dissecting matter into electric charges we have travelled far from that picture of it which first gave rise to the conception of substance, and the meaning of that conception—if it ever had any—has been lost by the way. The whole trend of modern scientific views is to break down the separate categories of "things," "influences," "forms," etc., and to substitute a common background of all experience. Whether we are studying a material object, a magnetic field, a geometrical figure, or a duration of time, our scientific information is summed up in measures; neither the apparatus of measurement nor the mode of using it suggests that there is anything essentially different in these problems. The measures themselves afford no ground for a classification by categories. We feel it necessary to concede some background to the measures—an external world; but the attributes of this world, except insofar as they are reflected in the measures, are outside scientific scrutiny. Science has at last revolted against attaching the exact knowledge contained in these measurements to a traditional picture-gallery of conceptions which convey no authentic information of the background and obtrude irrelevancies into the scheme of knowledge.

I will not here stress further the nonsubstantiality of electrons, since it is scarcely necessary to the present line of thought. Conceive them as substantially as you will, there is a vast difference between my scientific table with its substance (if any) thinly scattered in specks in a region mostly empty and the table of everyday conception which we regard as the type of solid reality—an incarnate protest against Berkeleian subjectivism.[2] It makes all the difference in the world whether the paper before me is poised as it were on a swarm of flies and sustained in shuttlecock fashion by a series of tiny blows from the swarm underneath, or whether it is supported because there is substance below it, it being the intrinsic nature of substance to occupy space to the exclusion of other substance; all the difference in conception at least, but no difference to my practical task of writing on the paper.

I need not tell you that modern physics has by delicate test and remorseless logic assured me that my second scientific table is the only one which is really there—wherever "there" may be. On the other hand I need not tell you that modern physics will never succeed in exorcising that first table—strange compound of external nature, mental imagery, and inherited prejudice—which lies visible to my eyes and tangible to my grasp. We must bid good-bye to it for the present, for we are about to turn from the familiar world to the scientific world revealed by physics.

[2]Bishop Berkeley thought that tables were sets of ideas. —Ed.

This is, or is intended to be, a wholly external world.

"You speak paradoxically of two worlds. Are they not really two aspects or two interpretations of one and the same world?"

Yes, no doubt they are ultimately to be identified after some fashion. But the process by which the external world of physics is transformed into a world of familiar acquaintance in human consciousness is outside the scope of physics. And so the world studied according to the methods of physics remains detached from the world familiar to consciousness, until after the physicist has finished his labors upon it. Provisionally, therefore, we regard the table which is the subject of physical research as altogether separate from the familiar table, without prejudging the question of their ultimate identification. It is true that the whole scientific inquiry starts from the familiar world and in the end it must return to the familiar world; but the part of the journeys over which the physicist has charge is in foreign territory.

Until recently there was a much closer linkage; the physicist used to borrow the raw material of his world from the familiar world, but he does so no longer. His raw materials are ether, electrons, quanta, potentials, Hamiltonian functions, etc., and he is nowadays scrupulously careful to guard these from contamination by conceptions borrowed from the other world. There is a familiar table parallel to the scientific table, but there is no familiar electron, quantum, or potential parallel to the scientific electron, quantum, or potential. We do not even desire to manufacture a familiar counterpart to these things or, as we should commonly say, to "explain" the electron. After the physicist has quite finished his world-building a linkage or identification is allowed; but premature attempts at linkage have been found to be entirely mischievous.

CHAPTER 31

JACQUES ELLUL

THE ETHICS OF NONPOWER

Jacques Ellul (1912–   ), French intellectual, theologian, and social critic, was educated at the University of Bordeaux and the University of Paris. Since 1947, he has been professor of the history of law at the University of Bordeaux. A prolific writer, he was one of the first to focus on the role of technology in modern society. His book, *La Technique: ou L'Enjeu du siecle.* translated into English as *The Technological Society* (1964), is a searing and pessimistic critique of technical civilization. Some of his other important books are *Propaganda: The Formation of Men's Attitudes* (1965), *The Meaning of the City* (1970), and *The Ethics of Freedom* (1976).

THE ETHICS OF NONPOWER[1]

Technique itself has become a value. Technical progress appears to the average Western person as the guarantee of the future good and happiness, and technology assures him of the necessity of the kind of behavior favorable to this progress. Technique carries our hopes (thanks to technical progress, cancer will be conquered). Here it gives life a meaning. And the usual attitude, whenever there appear to be drawbacks in the use of technique, consists in declaring that it is not technique that is to be blamed, but rather

[1]From Jacques Ellul, "The Ethics of Nonpower" in *Ethics in an Age of Pervasive Technology*, edited by Melvin Kranzbery (Boulder, CO: Westview Press, 1980), 204–12. Reprinted with permission.

man, who does not know how to use it. This means, by implication, that it is man who produces evil and that technique therefore stands for good. It is a desirable value and worth man's sacrificing himself for it (the martyrs of science).

A complete system of values is built on this premise—Georges Fourastie *(La Morale Prospective)* and Gabriel Monod *(Le Hasard et la Necessite)* tried to show how science might imply a certain virtue on the part of man and how, on the basis of this virtue, henceforth scientifically founded (since it is on itself that science is based), the whole of ethics can be rebuilt. This virtue is that of intellectual honesty. But as far as technique is concerned, there is no systematic intellectual structure of a scale of values. What does exist is spontaneous creation, which corresponds to the working of the system. Normalcy, efficiency, success, work, professional conscience, devotion to collective work—these are the principal values of the technical ethics on the basis of which all conduct is judged in our society.

All these values converge in the one direction of man's total adaptation to machines, instruments, and procedures on the one hand, and to his technical environment on the other. This adaptation, obtained by various psychological techniques, plays its part as far as attitudes in production, in consumption, and toward technical organisms are concerned. Socially nonadapted man is the exact counterpart of the old "immoral" man in traditional society. The only good perspective that is open and being extolled is that of adaptation; for example, the couple "man-machine," or the creation of the Kybert (cybernetic mechanism).

Society, though, continues to assert traditional morals. For Karen Horney this is the cause of the "neurotic personality of our time," i.e., the antagonism between the principles, values, and morals expounded to children and the actual conduct demanded of the adult, who thus finds himself in a state of contradiction. As Ivan Illich has pointed out (in *Tools for Conviviality* [New York, Harper & Row, 1969]), "The Churches are preaching humility, charity, poverty, while financing programs of industrial development. The Socialists have become unscrupulous defenders of industrial monopoly." This fundamental discordance, though, tends to become obliterated by the creation of technical morality.

Technical morality tends to devaluate other kinds of behavior (games, waste, laziness), other values, and other virtues (humor, faithfulness, goodness, etc.). It drives back into the spheres of futility and ineffectiveness that which might give meaning to human life. It does not tolerate any other meaning than itself. It is totalitarian and exclusive. It never has been formulated, though, in this authoritarian way, for it is not systematic. This at least is our impression, since technical morality was not formulated by a philosopher or moralist. It is effectively formulated, though, not as a set of morals, but as the imperative of behavior for a whole body of technolators (worshippers of technology such as B. F. Skinner and others).

Under these circumstances one cannot consider a conciliation, one cannot "split the difference" between the two morals. Morals based on the behavior required by technique are dominant. Those who mean to support another ethical direction are forced to enter into conflict, not directly with technique, but rather with the ideology of technique, with technical beliefs and morals.

The totality of problems raised by technique eventually may be summed up as a matter of power. It is because man is able to do practically everything that problems come up such as, for example, the exhaustion of world resources or exponential demographic growth or the boundlessly murderous character of wars. Each one of these problems of fact presents a purely technical as well as an ethical aspect. This is typical of all these difficulties we are so well acquainted with.

But power itself has a dual character. First of all, it is extrinsic. It is not part of man; it is not embodied in him. It is a power that rests in the new human environment. Second, it concerns the means only; it is the excessiveness of means that eventually precipitates the crisis.

Ethical thought therefore must be situated on the level of access to power. What we have here, though, is the first basic factor, i.e., the contradiction between power and values. Any increase of power is always paid for by the questioning, the regression, or the surrender of values. Of course, this proposition cannot be demonstrated objectively and scientifically. Its nature is pragmatic and experimental. When a state accepts judicial limitations and a constitutional framework where values are laid down, it is because it either is not very powerful or agrees not to be so, or because it agrees not to use all the power it might use. When a state becomes in effect all-powerful, values are no longer respected. It is an utter illusion to maintain that power can be made to serve values and that with the increase of power values will be defended better. This is completely idealistic and unrealistic. The increase of power, in fact, does away with values.

But if there are no longer any values that are widely believed and accepted, there are henceforth neither limits nor guideposts. The result of the destruction of values is, first, that man becomes incapable of effectively judging and appraising his actions. At this point the rule that imposes itself comes to be: "All that can be done must be done." Why not resort to torture or the concentration camp? There exists no predetermined limit whatsoever. Power implies an "Always more"—"Always further and beyond." At

what moment must one stop? One encounters no internal limit, no objective limit. What is involved, every time, is just one more step. This is the permanent simultaneous escalation of power and of demoralization. And since the previous step has been taken, why not this one? In order to judge one's actions, to impose limits and a meaning, one also needs a body of values that is irrefutable and irrefragable. If one agrees with the ideology of power one must of course proclaim firmly at the same time that ethical problems no longer exist, and even that ethics no longer exist and that man is no longer in need of them. But we also must know what we are doing. Specifically, the question must be asked whether man will be satisfied when nothing at all has meaning anymore and when nothing can serve to give meaning to what one is doing.

And this research on ethics then may refer only to the nature of means. We may put aside the "end-means" problems, since more and more thinkers seem to be agreed that it is impossible to dissociate the two at the present time. There no longer exist good ends that may be reached by just any means. The end is already contained in the means that technique puts at our disposal. Evil means thoroughly corrupt all ends, however excellent they be. The power and the scope of present technical means completely dominate the sphere of our thought and life, and leave no space for extratechnical means. It is in this context that we have to state the ethical problem and to search for an adequate way of behavior.

As a function of the preceding pronouncements, one might state that ethics for a technical society must be of such a nature that they can be only nonpower ethics, ethics of freedom, of conflicts, and of transgression. . . . In each case it is a matter of reducing power, of discovering what is essential for man to live in this universe; and in each case, what is involved is a moral quality that requires not making full use of all the means at one's disposal. Man is called upon to grow in the moral sense while appraising his means.

These ethics of nonpower: the heart of the matter is of course that man will agree not to do all he is capable of. But there is no longer any progress, there are no values, reasons, no divine law that might be opposed from the outside. One therefore has to attack from the inside and assert the impossibility of living together, and probably even of living at all, if the ethics of nonpower are not put into practice. This is the basic option. As long as man is motivated by the spirit of power and the acquisition of power, nothing is possible. What would be called for is a systematic and voluntary search for nonpower. (This of course does not mean the acceptance of fate, passivity, etc.—although it is not this danger that is threatening us!)

These ethics of nonpower extend to all levels of human action and can be clearly and specifically indicated: in the *nonuse* of technical means (not to try to overtake others, not to be the first, not to drive one's car to the maximum of its power, not to have one's transistor radio howl, etc.) as well as in the avoidance of certain institutions. Those that tend to develop power by basing social organization on competition are to be rejected. The matter must be addressed in arenas ranging from certain pedagogical methods through the Olympic Games to the economic system of free competition. In every one of these cases, it is efficiency that has had to be proved, thereby cultivating power in the technical system and devaluating all morals. In the very field of scientific research the ethics of nonpower (for example, what Illich calls radical research) have to establish criteria allowing one to set the nuisance threshhold of a tool, and to invent tools optimizing the amenity of life. The ethics of nonpower must be practiced in politics as well (penalization of the powerful, protection of the weak and of those exploited a priori, etc.).

Nonpower ethics imply the setting of limits. . . . The setting of limits always is constitutive of society and culture. No human group can exist as such if no limits are set, whatever these may be (absolute regimentation as well as the complete absence of regimentation, for example). The setting of limits (which correspond to what formerly was "sacred") is the specific characteristic of freedom. When man learned to be free he became capable of limiting himself.

It is evident that these characteristics of nonpower ethics constitute the basic roots, leaving wide open the question of the possibility of the "how" of this conversion to nonpower.

The second aspect of this system of ethics for a technical society is that of freedom. Power over means assures man of no freedom whatsoever. There is no freedom for man in a technical society (though I am perfectly familiar with all the discourses about freedom from primary wants, from danger, from illness, from natural environment; of freedom of choice, of consumption, of movement, etc.). The freedoms just mentioned are but superficial. Fundamentally, man is alienated within the technical system that substituted technical fatality for the former fatality of nature.

Man is increasingly called upon to liberate himself from that which constrains and determines him. But where he formerly was determined by natural factors (and he used science and technique to liberate himself from these) he now is alienated by the very means of his earlier liberation. Liberation can occur only to the extent that one aims at the present factors of alienation, on the one hand, and is able, on the other hand, either to reject them, to use them, or to divert them. Technique as a system nowadays represents for man the world of necessity he finds himself in, and it claims it spares him the ethical problem itself because it is situated outside the field of choices and ethical positions. We have shown that in the present state no mastery seems to be possible over the technical system. Liberation, then, only can be brought about by rejecting it, or by driving it back into an even-narrower sphere.

But here we find ourselves back in the sphere of nonpower ethics, since we stated that it will be by the setting of limits that freedom will be practiced. If, on the other hand, choice is the ethical situation *par excellence,* and if it is in and by choice that freedom expresses itself, the basic choice before us is indeed one concerned with the increase or decrease of power. In comparison, all freedom to choose the color of one's car or the make of one's computer is perfectly vain and superficial!

The ethics of nonpower and freedom create tensions and conflicts. Here we are witnessing an essential characteristic of ethics in a technical society: Technique tends to promote conformity and unity. This doing away with conflicts is presented as a virtue. But it is known that human groups where tensions and conflicts have disappeared are groups suffering from a kind of sclerosis, losing their ability to change, to resist aggression, and to evolve.

Here we are facing a basic question, viz., the substitution of technical progress (with its uniform and linear mode) for the earlier kind of human progress (which always was made by way of conflict). Technical progress, though, is disastrous for the human group as such, because the effect of sclerosis (or still entropy) necessarily continues to make itself felt.

If we want human groups to go on existing and man to have a specific way of acting freely in a human environment, we have to call on the ethics of conflict and we have to call into question the universality of the huge units and huge organizations produced by and necessary for technical progress. The element of conflict is a survival value for the whole of humanity.

What is referred to here is of course a negotiated, controlled form of conflict, not one that aims at the destruction of the group. Nor is it nihilistic; rather it is the result of calculated tensions within human groups so that they cannot close up or shut themselves off and regard themselves as having reached their goals (any society that considers itself fulfilled in this sense is dead), but will instead regain the aptitude to evolve by themselves, without depending upon technique.

Finally (though we do not presume to exhaust here the contents of this type of ethics), another characteristic of ethics in a technical society would be transgression. This may seem to contradict the notion of the ethics of limitation that are the expression of freedom. Not at all—for what is involved here is not the transgressing of limits that do not yet exist (so as to enter the sphere of that which is limitless), but the transgression of rules and limits produced by technique, which entails alienation.

It is essential not to be mistaken about the direction of this transgression. When we refer to this nowadays, what we have in mind first of all are the principles and the taboos of thirteenth-century society. To enter the sphere of the limitless byway of the use of drugs, the transgression of sexual taboos, the transgression of traditional family relationships, of paternal or marital authority, of politeness or honesty, does not constitute an act of genuine transgression, for it means going precisely in the direction of technique. Eroticism, for example, pretends to be transgressing that which technique has already shaken, and sometimes destroyed. Any enterprise of destruction of so-called taboos actually is the mere translation of technical reality.

Transgression must address itself to reality.

This reality is technique itself. It therefore will take the form either of destruction of the myth of technique, or of challenging the imperatives of action based on technique, or of questioning the conditions imposed on man and the group in order that technique may develop.

Transgression against technique will consist in destroying man's belief in it and in reducing technique to nothing but the production of aleatory and insignificant objects. It therefore will imply the search for an external meaning in the name of which transgression takes place and which, by this very act, does away with the very significance of technique.

GLOSSARY

APPLIED SCIENCE   Scientific knowledge put to practical use; contrasted with *pure science*, or objective knowledge pursued for its own sake, not for the sake of any particular application.

ANOMALY   An experimental result or observation found to be not in accordance with theoretical predictions. Anomalous findings are generally not enough to overthrow a theory; rather, they are treated by scientists as a problem to be solved within the existing theory.

DEMARCATION   In philosophy of science, marking the boundaries between science and nonscience.

FALSIFIABILITY   According to Karl Popper, a criterion of genuine science; a theory is falsifiable if there are events or discoveries that would clearly show it to be false.

HYPOTHESIS   A conjecture or "educated guess" entertained or accepted because it would explain, if it were true, some things already believed; evidence for a hypothesis is seen in its consequences.

METHOD OF AGREEMENT   A method for identifying a causal connection between an effect and a necessary condition.

METHOD OF CONCOMITANT VARIATION   A method for identifying a causal connection between two conditions by matching variations in one condition with variations in another.

METHOD OF DIFFERENCE   A method for identifying an effect and a sufficient condition present in a specific occurence.

OBSERVABLES   Those items of reality derived from observation, especially sense perception. *Nonobservables* are items of reality, such as photons, that cannot be observed in priniciple or at present but which may have observable effects.

PARADIGM   A way of looking at something; according to Thomas Kuhn, the background set of conditions and traditions within which normal science takes place.

PHILOSOPHY OF SCIENCE   A second order discipline, studying the meaning, methods, and consequences of scientific knowledge.

PROBABALISM   The view that observation and experimental evidence support scientific theories, not by demonstrating their truth, but by making their truth probable. The more supporting evidence, the greater the probability that the theory is true.

SCIENCE   (1) A term used collectively to denote the various formal, factual, and applied sciences; (2) an objective method of obtaining knowledge; (3) a body of systematic knowledge built up through experimentation and observation, and having a valid theoretical base.

TECHNOLOGY   A body of knowledge useful for making or doing things; the sphere of applied sciences, such as engineering, aeronautics, and so on.

FOR FURTHER STUDY

Ellul, Jacques. *The Technological Society*. Translated by John Wilkinson. New York: Vintage Books, 1964.
A penetrating critique of the ever-expanding role of technique in modern society.

Feyerabend, Paul. *Realism, Rationalism and Scientific Method. 2 vols.* Cambridge: Cambridge University Press, 1981.
The author, an important contemporary philosopher of science, identifies three key ideas that have shaped the history of science, philosophy, and civilization: criticism, proliferation, and reality.

Hempel, Carl. *The Philosophy of Natural Science*. Englewood Cliffs, N.J.: Prentice-Hall, 1966.
Readable and wide-ranging.

Kuhn, Thomas S. *The Copernican Revolution*. Cambridge: Harvard University Press, 1957.
A masterful treatment. Read it along with *The Structure of Scientific Revolutions* (Chicago: University of Chicago Press, 1962) to understand the importance of the history of science and its role in the formation of paradigms.

Russell, Bertrand. *The Impact of Science on Society*. New York: Simon & Schuster, 1953.
Lectures that Russell gave in the United States and Great Britain, exploring the relationship of science to such topics as tradition, war, and values.

Whitehead, A. N. *Science and the Modern World*. New York: Macmillan, 1925.
A classic discussion of the origins of science and its impact on philosophy, religion, and culture; highly recommended.

PART FIVE

◆

THE SELF AS MIND, BODY, AND MACHINE

All real life is meeting.

MARTIN BUBER

ORIENTATION

Parts 2, 3, and 4 were concerned with questions arising in that branch of philosophy known as epistemology. From this view of the theory of knowledge, we now shift our attention to metaphysics, asking questions about the nature of reality. Parts 5 and 6 are both concerned with the philosophy of the human being. Part 5 asks: "What is the self, and is it best understood as mind, body, or machine?" Part 6 asks: "Is the self free or determined?" Part 7 explores questions about religion, God, and evil.

THE SELF

The concept of self is an elusive concept, resisting simple one-sentence formulations. Attempts at describing and defining it seem somehow to distort it. *Who am I?* This simple, childlike question plunges us into the deepest philosophical waters. In her poem, "In the Waiting Room," Elizabeth Bishop describes her childhood fascination with what philosophers would call "the question of personal identity." Recalling a winter day in 1918 spent waiting for her aunt in a dentist's waiting room, she describes the precise moment when she became aware of herself *as a self*.

I said to myself: three days
 and you'll be seven years old.
I was saying it to stop
the sensation of falling off
the round, turning world
into cold, blue-black space.
But I felt: you are an *I*,
you are an *Elizabeth*,
you are one of *them*.
Why should you be one, too?
I scarcely dared to look
to see what it was I was.
I gave a sidelong glance
—I couldn't see any higher—
at shadowy gray knees,
trousers and skirts and boots
and different pairs of hands
lying under the lamps.

I knew that nothing stranger
had ever happened, that nothing
stranger could ever happen.
Why should I be my aunt,
or me, or anyone?
What similarities—
boots, hands, the family voice
I felt in my throat . . .
held us all together
or made us all just one?[1]

The experience of Elizabeth Bishop is the experience of us all. Looking at this remarkable passage, three things stand out as marks of the self: **personal identity, self-transcendence,** and **privacy.**

PERSONAL IDENTITY

It is evident that Elizabeth Bishop's experience of her self is direct and intuitive: she has captured poetically that moment when she perceived herself as a subject at the center of experience, separate and distinct from the external objects around her—trousers, skirts, boots, and different pairs of hands. All of these objects are experienced only in relation to a centering person or self who supplies the unity for experience. Without the centering self, there is nothing to differentiate us from "the cold blue-black space" of the round turning world. The self as a center of subjectivity gives me a vantage point in the world, a place from which to view things. Like Elizabeth, I am conscious of myself *as a self*—that is, I am self-conscious. It is **self-consciousness** that permits me to say "I" or "me," that produces awe and wonder as I name myself. The wonder of a self is that there is some agency that remains constant through the passage of time, unifying experiences, enabling me to identify memories, ideas, dreams, decisions, and feelings as mine and not another's, whether they are experienced as past, present, or future. I look at a faded photograph or a ticket stub from my first date and I remember my self, the self that I was, that I am, that I carry into the future. I look at my hands, feel "the family voice" in my throat, and am reminded both of the similarities and differences that I share with others. Like the seven-year-old Elizabeth Bishop, our "essential selves" will remain unchanged through time and circumstance, a unique combination of thoughts, intentions, wishes, feelings, memories, and desires.

---

[1]Elizabeth Bishop, "In The Waiting Room," in *Elizabeth Bishop: The Complete Poems, 1927–1979* (New York: Farrar, Straus & Giroux, 1983), 159–161. Reprinted by permission.

SELF-TRANSCENDENCE

The relation of the self to time is one of the most profound problems of human existence. Although we are finite beings materially locked in the sequence of time, we are nevertheless able to rise above or "transcend" it, so that we perceive ourselves at the subjective intersection of past and future. Human self-transcendence is experienced in many ways, including memory, love, and having children.

We keep the past alive through memory. Even the dead retain an identity, spark in us a remembrance, still speak to us of their experiences. Works of art are one way we seek to preserve our relation to the past. "In the Waiting Room" records one artist's momentary transcendence of time, and the inevitable re-entry into the "now." The poem concludes with these words:

> The waiting room was bright
>   and too hot. It was sliding
>   beneath a big black wave,
>   another, and another.
>
> Then I was back in it.
>   The War was on. Outside,
>   in Worcester, Massachusetts,
>   were night and slush and cold,
>   and it was still the fifth
>   of February, 1918.

Like Bishop's poem, the Vietnam memorial in Washington D.C. is a powerful repository of feelings and memories. We build such monuments in the hope of preserving some link to the past; lifting ourselves out of the mundane present, we hope for a better future.

In a similar way, experiencing love or having children can be understood as acts of self-transcendence. Human beings are made for community, capable of shared understandings that meld a collection of *I*'s into the social *We*. Love may be understood as a union of wills, as persons are brought into solidarity by willing the same object or the same destiny. When I love another, I do not lose my self; rather, I share it by willingly becoming part of a larger social unit, giving up my exclusive claims to my objects, my destiny, and so on. The human capacity for self-transcendence likewise manifests itself in having children, through whom we hope to both shape the future and preserve some memory of ourselves.

PRIVACY

It is instructive to reflect on the etymology of the word "person." The word is derived from two Latin words: *sonare*, which means "to give a sound;" and *per*, which means "through." Thus a person is one who "sounds or speaks through." The word was used to refer to *personae*, actors in Greek theatre who wore masks to disguise their identity so that their parts might be played with greater realism. As the performer's voice sounded forth from an opening in the mask, the inner character of the actor remained hidden. As a person using language to communicate my self to the world, I am destined to both succeed and fail, for language half reveals and half conceals the self within. I never quite succeed in communicating the full depth of my self. Something of my inner person will be disclosed, but something remains hidden and private as well.

Although humans are social beings made for community, they frequently experience loneliness. This is because in the deepest recesses of our personhood we are incommunicable. There is a real sense in which we are fundamentally alone in the world. Even in the midst of a crowd, I am alone. My knowledge of my self is intimate and personal, a privileged relationship that no one else can know in quite the same way. Because I cannot actually enter into the world of another, I can never completely know what another person is thinking or feeling. In reading Elizabeth Bishop's poems or letters, I can comport myself with understanding toward her, even to the point of visualizing myself along with her in the waiting room, but I cannot enter her consciousness. Although I can sympathize, understand, and even empathize, I cannot feel another person's pain, nor can I face death for them. I can give another person an eye, some blood, or a kidney, but I cannot give them my consciousness of my self.

Using the language of objectivity, we frequently express the publicness of observations, meaning that the object or event can be seen by everyone, everywhere, at any time. It is clear however that when we speak of the self, the language of objectivity breaks down, for we cannot substitute another person's consciousness for our own. The presence of the self is not a public event that can be measured or detected through objective methods; we simply cannot verify the presence or absence of a self in the same way that we can a rock or a table. The self is clearly not that kind of thing. We should not therefore be surprised that sense perception does not detect any "self," or when scientists insist that if there is a self, it must be reducible to that which can be stated objectively or behavioristically. The limitations of scientific method, discussed in Part 4, make the self in its subjectivity appear to be invisible.

Summarizing, we can say that the self is found wherever there is an awareness of identity across time, a sense of transcendence or privacy, or an intuition of our specialness. With a few notable exceptions, most philosophers have believed that personhood means more than simply matter in motion, collections of perceptions, behavioral responses, or bodies in space. It is to these notable exceptions that we now turn our attention.

DENIALS OF SELF

BUDDHISM

Siddhartha Gautama, the Buddha, founded the Buddhist tradition in Asia some five hundred years before the Christian era. Known as the Enlightened One, he taught the doctrines of the Middle Way, promising similar enlightenment to a number of his followers if they followed this Way. Buddhism denies the permanent existence of anything like a "soul" or "self," postulating instead an *an-atta* (no self) comprised of bodily sensation, perception, feeling, mental conception, and consciousness. The aim of all Buddhist teaching is the extinction of the self. Those desiring enlightenment must rid themselves of the false enchantment of separate personal identity.

DAVID HUME

The existence of a separate, private, individual self is one of the watershed issues dividing eastern and western approaches to philosophy. But not every western philosopher has believed in the existence of the self. The British empiricist David Hume argued, against Descartes, that the self was not some kind of substance but rather a bundle of transient perceptions. In his classic *A Treatise of Human Nature*, Hume attempted to track down this elusive idea of self as permanent personal identity. He concluded that the idea of self, like the idea of substance, could not be found among the vast variety of sense perceptions.

> When I enter most intimately into what I call *myself*, I always stumble on some particular perception or other, of heat or cold, light or shade, love or hatred, pain or pleasure. I never can catch *myself* at any time without a perception, and never can observe any thing but the perceptions.[2]

Hume's "bundle theory of the mind" views mind as a mere stage for bundles of sense perceptions. According to his view, no permanent self-identity is necessary to hold the shifting contents of experience together.

[2]David Hume, *A Treatise of Human Nature*, vol. 1, ed. T.H. Green. (London: Longmans, Green, 1874), 534.

PSCHOLOGICAL BEHAVIORISM

Among the many contemporary social scientists who have taken up Hume's denial of the self, the psychologist B.F. Skinner is perhaps the best known. For Skinner, no concept of self is necessary when analyzing human behavior. The concept of the self can be reduced to a device for representing an observable system of responses to stimuli. The "science" of human behavior studies the responses of humans to their environment. Mental behavior, in the end, is no more than bodily behavior. Because science has no way of observing or measuring alleged mental events such as motives, ideas, intentions, or feelings, these events lack the dimension of scientific events and can be discounted. Behavioral science need not take account of them.

While Buddhism represents an important religious conception of human nature, Hume's bundle theory and Skinner's psychological behaviorism pose more direct challenges to western thinkers. We shall return to these two theories of mind in a later section.

THE NATURE OF MIND AND BODY

When we want to learn the nature of a thing, it is often helpful to examine the language used to describe it. How do humans describe themselves? The nature of human beings is typically described in two very different ways. On the one hand, humans can be described in terms of length, weight, or spatial location. These descriptions might apply equally well to physical objects, since they also have length, weight, and take up space. Since they share these characteristics with inanimate physical objects, we can call these types of statements about humans physicalistic statements. On the other hand, humans can also be described as thinking, hoping, wishing, feeling, expecting, purposing, remembering, feeling pain, and so on. Clearly these are not the kinds of activities we would attribute to physical objects. If I hit my desk, it feels no pain, and my pen has no list of wishes. Because these are descriptions of experiences normally associated only with conscious beings such as humans and (in some cases) animals, let us call them mentalistic statements.

Taking our clues from the language we use to describe ourselves, it seems perfectly natural to think of ourselves as somehow composed of two sorts of things: a body whose nature is purely material, and a mind, which is not material but is conscious. The view that human nature is a composite of material body and **immaterial** mind (or soul) is as old as philosophy itself. Plato and Descartes both held this dual view of human nature, giving rise to the term **dualism.** Plato made a sharp distinction between body and soul, claiming that the soul existed before the

[margin note: No where is language more important then in Philosophy.]

307

body and would survive its death. Descartes thought of the human person as composed of two separate substances: the mind, an immaterial substance whose essential nature is to think, and the body, whose essential nature is to be material ("extended") and nonthinking. Christianity and other religions teach the immortality of the soul, the belief that the immaterial conscious self will survive the death of the material body.

Why proceed further? If the dual nature view matches up with common sense and has significant philosophical and religious support, why not drop the matter right here?

The serious philosopher cannot stop here. As always, doing philosophy requires a critical examination of our beliefs. When we seriously examine what is involved in the belief that we are composed of two different, utterly opposite sorts of things, some difficult questions arise. Is the distinction between mind and body valid? How exactly are these two different, opposite parts of us connected? Do they interact with each other? If so, how? Can we make sense of the idea of an immaterial thing, let alone the idea that this immaterial thing somehow interacts with a material thing? Taking our cues from modern science, can we account for the alleged "mental events" reported by mentalistic statements without resorting to some conception of an immaterial mind?

Put together, these are the questions that have been traditionally grouped under the heading of the mind-body problem. In the history of philosophy, virtually every conceivable response has been suggested as the answer to the above questions. It is not our intention to catalogue exhaustively every solution ever proposed to the mind-body problem. Instead, we will discuss several general strategies for resolving the problem. Because the problem is so complex, let us begin by examining various theories of the mind before we take up the question of the mind's relation to body.

THEORIES OF MIND

The numerous theories of mind that have been developed in the history of philosophy can be classified in five general groups: (1) mind as immaterial substance, (2) mind as a principle of organization, (3) mind as a bundle of sense perceptions, (4) mind as behavior, and (5) mind as machine.

MIND AS SUBSTANCE: PLATO AND DESCARTES

The term *substance* has had a long and interesting history in philosophy. Typically, it has been taken to mean some underlying reality in which various qualities reside; that upon which everything else depends for its existence. For example, was possesses the qualities of color, plasticity, and so on. Substance is the "underlying something" that is left once these qualities are removed.

Plato used the term *psyche*, or soul, to mean a simple, disembodied, eternal, incorruptible spiritual substance, the source of all that is good. The soul existed before its imprisonment in the body and will be released from its bodily residence at death, providing it wards off the body's corrupting influences. The soul originated in the eternal world of the Forms, that world of eternal truth and unchanging reality that contrasts sharply with the world of Becoming, which is a realm of fleeting, changing sense experience. The rational part of human nature, desiring knowledge of the eternal Forms, is in constant war with the lawless bodily appetites and desires. Philosophers must be lovers of wisdom, not lovers of body, since it is the body that hampers soul from performing its rational function.

Plato's "two worlds" view had an enormous influence on the thinking of neo-Platonists such as Plotinus (204–269) and Saint Augustine (354–430), and through them, the Christian church. But it was left to Descartes to develop a systematic theory of the substantial nature of the mind and its relation to body.

It is important to remember the historical context in which Descartes formulated his theory of mind and body. The seventeenth revolution in science (discussed in Part 4) had introduced a mechanical world picture that emphasized matter and motion as the most important features of the universe. It was clear to Descartes that the principles of mechanics must govern all bodies everywhere, including human bodies. The human body, after all, is part of the world of matter and therefore subject to its laws. How then shall we understand mind? (Note the shift in terms. The term *soul*, with its religious connotations, is replaced by the more neutral term *mind*.) For Descartes, attempting to preserve something of the *psychic*, nonmaterial aspect of human nature, mind must be everything that body is not. The primary characteristic of body is that it is nonthinking, extended substance. Hence, mind must be thinking, nonextended substance.

Descartes' split or "bifurcation" of human nature into separate and opposite substances is the modern origin of the mind-body problem. For Plato and Aristotle, the relation between mind and body was not problematic, since soul and body were in intimate relation with each other. While Cartesian dualism of mind and body enabled us to interpret the external world in mechanical and quantitative terms, it also required that these terms be privileged, and mentalistic terms deprivileged. The metaphysical shelter that Descartes built for mind turned out to be unstable. It would not be long before mentalistic aspects of existence were interpreted in quantitive, mechanistic terms as well.

MIND AS A PRINCIPLE OF ORGANIZATION: ARISTOTLE AND KANT

Aristotle studied with Plato for twenty years, yet his own philosophy represents a clear movement away from the mental substance theory in its rejection of the Platonic theory of Forms. For Plato, the Forms had been archetypes that existed in a separate realm, providing the pattern for the physical copies in the world of Becoming. Physical objects imitated or copied the Forms, and were thus metaphysically inferior. Aristotle insisted that the forms existed *in* things, *in this world*. Form is but one aspect of reality, not the whole, and it is to be found in the shaping, organizing, and order given to matter.

The implications of this view for mind and body are profound. Aristotle asks us to think of soul in terms of its activities. Soul is the life principle: the sum of all life processes as well as the organizing principle for all of these processes. This process or functional view is a clear movement away from Plato's substance view.

The mental-substance theory came under heavy attack in the Enlightenment. Empirically minded philosophers had little use for the idea of substance. John Locke wrote that it was a "confused idea," little better than the idea of "a some-thing-I-know-not-what, which acts in some-way-I-know-not-how." Hume argued that the concept was unintelligible and unnecessary. Immanuel Kant argued that the concept is the result of confusing logical requirements with metaphysical spec-ulations.

For Kant, the mind was active, forming a system of knowledge from the raw materials of the senses and the concepts of the understanding. Because percepts without concepts are blind, and concepts without percepts are empty, the mind is simply that unifying agency (a "trancendental unity of apperception") that joins experience to structure, making knowledge possible. This unity we call the self, the center of morality as well as knowledge.

MIND AS A BUNDLE OF SENSE PERCEPTIONS

Taking empiricism to its logical conclusion, David Hume asserted that ideas are only meaningful if they can be traced back to some originating sense impres-sion. Impressions are our most simple and forceful sense experiences, of which ideas are faint copies. Using this criterion, it is obvious that the complex ideas of substance and personal identity do not qualify. Ever the skeptic, Hume insisted that these ideas can be tossed on the scrap heap of metaphysics!

When we engage in introspection, hoping to locate the idea of self or perma-nent substance, we find nothing but fleeting impressions. The mind is "nothing but a bundle or collection of sense perceptions, which succeed each other with an inconceivable rapidity, and are in a perpetual flux and movement."

Of course, the problem here is to give a satisfactory account of how "bundles of mental experiences" are related to one another. Hume's atomistic account rules out the possibility of any organizing principle to relate or distinguish one bundle from another, since there is no unifying personal "agent" or self. Hume's denial of the self did not prevent him from using the full range of personal pronouns in his writing. Must we not affirm the concept of a self in order to deny it; otherwise, how is denial possible? The bundle theory has failed to withstand these criticisms.

MIND AS BEHAVIOR

Theories of this sort fall into two separate categories: psychological behaviorism and logical behaviorism.

Psychological behaviorists, such as John B. Watson and B.F. Skinner, believe that talk about mental states and processes can be eliminated in favor of a set of causal correlations between environmental stimuli and the responses to those stimuli. Believing that the concept of self is not essential to any analysis of behavior, behaviorists offer the following argument: as long as there is a rigid causal sequence of stimulus, internal event, and response, from a logical and scientific point of view it makes no difference whether the internal event is physical or psychical. Since these events cannot be scientifically observed, and since they do not make any difference in terms of response, they play no role in the scientific story. Why not simply study human behavior scientifically, ridding ourselves of alleged unobservable metaphysical entities such as "mind" that serve no function and should not be given theoretical existence?

As a methodology in psychology, behaviorism was a dominant force in America for many years. As Skinner admits, the impulse towards behaviorism was a desire to reconcile psychology with the theory of evolution.[3] In recent years, however, behaviorism has been displaced by other paradigms. Although it worked fairly well for lower animals, the theory had difficulty explaining a wide range of human behavior. The "environment" that behaviorists like to talk about is always an environment *interpreted* by human beings; we respond to an environment in terms of its meaning for us. But interpretation is a mental process. Consequently, the behavioral responses observed by behaviorists are always determined by the intentions and purposes of human beings, not simply by a set of physicalistic circumstances. With the demise of behaviorism, psychology has looked toward phenomenology in an attempt to reintroduce into its theoretical framework intentional mental processes that behaviorists had eliminated.

Logical behaviorism is essentially a theory about the meaning and use of mentalistic language. Defenders of this view, such as Gilbert Ryle, argue that all references to mental events and processes can be replaced by references to behavior or behavioral dispositions. The strategy here is to argue that statements about mental events reduce to statements about human behavior or behavioral disposi-

---

[3]See B.F. Skinner, "Behaviorism at Fifty," in *Behaviorism and Phenomenology*, ed. T.W. Wann (Chicago: University of Chicago Press, 1964), 79–108.

tions. This type of strategy is typical of all forms of **materialism.** According to logical behaviorism, to say that a person is angry is *not* to say that the immaterial part of that person is in the state called anger. It simply means that the person is behaving or is disposed to behave in certain ways—clenching her fists, raising her voice, making wild gestures, saying things like, "I'm so angry!" and so on.

Ryle found support for this view in the way that mental terms are learned. For instance, we did not learn the meaning of the term anger by having someone point to an inner state. We learned it by simply observing people in situations—for example, in traffic jams—that typically evoke angry behavior.

Critics of logical behaviorism point out that emotional states such as anger or grief seem to include an inner feeling that goes along with the behavior associated with it. When we are grieving because of the death of a loved one, for example, we experience an inner feeling of loss or emptiness that belongs to the emotion of grief as much as the resulting behavior.

MIND AS MACHINE

Cognitive science is an interdisciplinary field that includes cognitive psychology, computer science, linguistics, psychobiology, anthropology, and philosophy. Cognitive scientists view the mind as a complex computational or information-processing *function*. Jerry Foder is a leading philosophical proponent of functionalism, a theory that has attracted significant attention in recent years. Functionalism seeks to define mental states and processes by their causal, functional roles. The mind is, in effect, a function of the patterns of neurological activity in the brain.

Artificial intelligence (AI) is the name given to a branch of cognitive science that attempts to program digital computers to produce intelligent behavior. Recent developments in this field have sparked a heated debate among scientists and philosophers over the potential of computing machines, and the value of thinking of the human mind as a machine. Proponents of AI argue that if the mental can be duplicated by a digital computer, then our understanding of how the computer functions could become the key that unlocks the mysteries of human thought. By creating the functional, machine-equivalent of intelligent behavior, we could have at our fingertips a map of the human cognitive process.

Some philosophers believe that AI provides a way to finally resolve the mind-body problem. If the mental life of humans could be explained in terms of the manipulation of physical symbols in the brain, then the mind-body problem would be reduced to the "software-hardware" problem in digital computers (a much less daunting problem!).

Critics of AI do not believe that digital computers will ever be capable of anything matching human intelligence. Some, like Herbert Dreyfuss in *What*

Computers Can't Do,[4] take an empirical approach, arguing that AI research is approaching its natural limits since the computer is restricted in the kind of input it can handle, and the way that input is processed. Others, such as John Searle, argue that even if digital computers were able to simulate the behavior of human beings, they would still not possess human understanding, beliefs, or knowledge. Searle's influential article, "Minds, Brains, and Programs," is the reading selection in Chapter 36; it provides insight into the complexities of this important, ongoing debate.

THE RELATION OF MIND TO BODY

Although the question of the relationship of mind to body has challenged thinkers for centuries, it took on a new urgency in the seventeenth century, due to the growing influence of science, and scientists' description of the world in increasingly quantitative and mechanical terms.

Interpretations of the meaning of the mind-body problem and proposed solutions to it are numerous and vary widely. Again, it is not our intent to make an exhaustive survey of the field. Instead, we will classify two general strategies for understanding and resolving the mind-body problem, **dualism** and **monism,** with historical examples of how philosophers have pursued each strategy.

DUALISM

Earlier, we identified dualism as the view that human nature is comprised of a material body and an immaterial mind. According to this view, mentalistic and physicalistic statements differ not only in meaning but in reference as well—they "pick out" different entities or substances. This is the common sense view that is widely accepted by most people. As we hinted earlier, however, it does have its problems. Once we accept the essential difference between separate and opposite entities or substances, how do we explain the relation between them? Various dualistic theories have been offered to explain the relation of mind and body. The two most prominent theories are interactionism and parallelism.

INTERACTIONISM

By far the most common form of dualism is interactionism. Interactionism is the thesis that mental events can sometimes cause bodily events, and bodily events can sometimes cause mental events. Descartes gave interactionism its classic for-

[4]See Hubert Dreyfus, *What Computers Can't Do.* (New York: Harper & Row, 1979).

mulation, claiming that the human being is a composite of two substances: thinking, nonextended substance (mind), and extended, nonthinking substance (body). These two substances are intimately combined, so that events in the mind may cause bodily changes, and bodily changes may produce mental effects. Therefore, the human being is a single system of mutually interacting substances.

One does not have to accept Descartes' overall philosophy or even his substance-formulation to be an interactionist. Many people who know nothing of Descartes have been impressed by the way physical conditioning (or the lack of it) can affect mental outlook. It is evident that we think more clearly when we are well rested. Likewise, the effects of drugs and alcohol on mental processes have been well documented. Hearing a piece of music may trigger emotions and memories. Scientists have discovered that electrical brain stimulations can cause a person to have certain thoughts.

Similarly, interactionists argue that mental events can affect bodily processes. As examples, they cite pain that causes a person to wince, fear that causes the heart to pound, and feelings of awe that cause a person to tremble.

The major objection to interactionism is that it fails to account adequately for causation. If the mind is nonphysical, it has no position in physical space. How can it then cause a physical change that has a position in space? It is simply inconceivable to think that a nonphysical mind could move a physical body, or that a change in brain cells could produce a thought. Furthermore, how can a nonphysical event give rise to a physical event without violating the laws of the conservation of matter and energy and of momentum? It doesn't take long to see that common sense is not entirely on the side of dualism.

PARALLELISM

The difficulties of accounting for causal interaction led to the theory of parallelism. On this view, there is no interaction or causal connection between mind and body. Like two trains moving on parallel tracks, mind and body operate according to separate systems yet constantly accompany one another.

How is such a noncausal constant correlation possible? The German philosopher Gottfried Leibniz (1646–1716) believed that it was due to a preestablished harmony set up by God at the beginning of the separate careers of mind and body. Like two clocks keeping perfect time due to the skill of their creator, mind and body are perfect mechanisms synchronized by God at their origin, remaining in phase with each other without the need of further intervention.

Unlike interactionism, parallelism has never enjoyed widespread support, for it seems to divide the universe in two and to run counter to common experiences. The idea of the mind as a separate isolated system runs into difficulty when we try to explain why radio waves give rise to a pleasant sensation. Furthermore, for the two-clock analogy to apply, there must be a one-to-one correspondence such that *every* physical event corresponded with a mental event. But this is clearly not true of our experience, for there are deep sleeps and comas where no mental events occur.

MONISM

Whereas dualistic mind-body theories admit there are two things to be related, and offer accounts of that relationship, monism adopts the strategy of denying that there are two things to be related. Thinking back to our earlier distinction between physicalistic and mentalistic statements, one sees that monists are interested in denying or "explaining away" one set of statements. There are two possibilities here. (1) We can attempt to translate or reduce mentalistic statements to physicalistic statements. This strategy has a long philosophical tradition and is known as materialism. (2) We can attempt to translate or reduce physicalistic statements to mentalistic ones. This is known as **idealism.**

SUBJECTIVE IDEALISM

Bishop George Berkeley (1685–1753), an Irish philosopher and a bishop in the Anglican church, developed one of the most provocative theories in modern philosophy. **Subjective idealism** is the view that there are no material substances, nor are there any physical objects. Minds and the perceptions of those minds are the only things that really exist: to be is to be perceived, or to be a perceiver. Therefore, physicalistic statements are meaningful only if they are taken as statements about the perceptions of perceivers. To account for objects that exist unperceived (the proverbial tree that falls in the forest with no one present), Berkeley appealed to a supreme perceiver, God.

Berkeley arrived at this surprising and unusual position by carrying John Locke's empiricism to its logical end. If we can have no clear idea of what substance is, and if all knowledge of the world (except for knowledge of God and of one's own existence) must be based upon experience, then why should we think that there is anything other than our experiences? Locke had argued that our experiences were somehow caused by physical objects. But clearly this claim cannot itself be justified by experience. Thus we have no knowledge of physical objects themselves; we can know only their effects, that is, the ideas they cause in us.

It is intriguing to look at the world from Berkeley's perspective, but in the end subjective idealism is most improbable, reducing the physical world to nothing but an illusion, and making simple statements about furniture in the next room equivalent in meaning to theological statements about God's perceptions. No wonder Berkeley's idealism failed to attract many supporters.

MATERIALISM

Historically, materialism is the oldest mind-body theory. There have been many versions of materialism in the history of philosophy, some more extreme than others. Materialism is the view that matter is the fundamental reality in the world, and whatever else exists is dependent upon matter. In its most extreme form, materialism holds that whatever exists is physical. According to this view, mentalistic statements are either meaningless, or else synonymous with statements describing physical events and processes. As we have seen, both psychological and logical behaviorism are variations on the materialist theme.

One problem materialism faces is that it requires us to think of matter as thinking. Richard Taylor discusses this in one of the reading selections, arguing that dualistic assumptions are at fault: once these assumptions are given up, the problem evaporates. A more serious difficulty with materialism comes when one attempts to *translate* certain types of mentalistic statements into purely physical terms. For example, it does not appear to be the case that mental events such as pain or grief reduce simply, without remainder, to physical events. Attempts to provide a translation schema for a simple mentalistic statement like "I have a pain" have failed miserably. It is clear that when you tell me you have a pain you are telling me what you *feel*, not merely exhibiting behavior. It strains credibility to insist that all humans (including oneself) are devoid of mental events. For this reason, milder versions of materialism such as the identity theory, have emerged.

IDENTITY THEORY

As the name suggests, identity theory is the view that mental states and processes are literally identical to states and processes of the brain. Identity theory, sometimes referred to as reductive materialism, has in recent years become quite popular as researchers discover more about the neurochemistry of the brain. Identity theorists such as J.J.C. Smart and Herbert Feigl have argued that physicalistic and mentalistic statements may presently connote different things, but will, in time, turn out as a matter of empirical fact to denote one and the same thing, namely physical phenomena. It is important to stress that the type of identity being identified here is one that is discovered later, a *de facto* (after the fact) identity. Examples of this kind of identity are the morning star and evening star, H_2O

and water, or lightning and a kind of electrical discharge. In all of these cases the discovery of identity rested on later empirical discoveries that replaced the conventional wisdom of the day. Similarly, it is argued, we will one day be able to trace all thoughts and feelings back to electrochemical events, thus achieving the goal of a unified science.

Although many scientists are quite committed to identity theory, using it as a guide to their research, there are reasons to be cautious. Is a strict identification of mind and brain possible? By matching up electrical and chemical data with the introspective reports of experimental subjects, scientists are turning up a good deal of information about which region of the brain controls which types of conscious thought. But there is no experiment that would show that these two objects, brain and conscious thought, are identical.

Another crucial objection to the identity theory is that it fails to account for an essential feature of the mental, namely the privileged position of the subject with respect to his or her own mental life. This "first-person perspective" suggests that mental events are not ordinary physical events.

DOUBLE-ASPECT THEORY

Double-aspect theory is the view that the mental and the physical are simply different aspects of something that is itself neither mental nor physical. Both mind and matter are expressions of some underlying reality that appears as mind when viewed subjectively (from the "inside") and as body when viewed objectively (from the "outside").

Problems arise when one attempts to state the nature of the underlying unity that presents two aspects. Benedict de Spinoza (1632–1677) identified the underlying unity as "God or Nature," while the contemporary philosopher P.F. Strawson suggests "person." Spinoza's formulation takes us back to the problems encountered in substance metaphysics, while Strawson's has been criticized for its circularity and failure to improve our understanding of the mind-body relationship.

SUMMARY

Just as psychologists differ in their interpretations of mind, so philosophers differ when theorizing about the mind-body relationship. Given the complexity of human life, it is safe to say that any single interpretation is inadequate. The reading selections are designed to give you a firsthand look at philosophical strategies for resolving the problem. The selection from Aristotle illustrates the early

317

origins of functional approaches to mind, before a mechanistic world picture alienated mind from body. Selections are included from Descartes, representing dualism (interactionism) and Richard Taylor, representing monism (materialism). Gilbert Ryle critiques Descartes' view at some length and defends logical behaviorism, while John Searle discusses and critiques artificial intelligence. Taken together, these selections show the paths philosophers have traveled in their quest to reach self-understanding.

The Contemporary Perspectives selections ask us to take a new look at the old paths. The phenomenologist Maurice Merleau-Ponty and the feminist philosopher Elizabeth V. Spelman are critical of the ways philosophers have treated the body. Merleau-Ponty argues (against Descartes) that the body is more than an object for natural science—it is lived body. Spelman offers an alternative interpretation to any presented in these pages, showing how philosophical accounts of the mind-body relation have been systematically influenced by unacknowledged social, political, and gender views.

CHAPTER 32

ARISTOTLE

FUNCTIONS OF THE SOUL

This selection is from Aristotle's *De Anima*, a treatise on the soul or *psyche*, the Greek root of the word *psychology*.[1] He begins by describing the difficulties in any theorizing about the soul: the problem of finding uncontested facts from which to begin, problems of method and classification, and the complications resulting from an unclear view of the relation between mind and body. He points out that while most people agree on movement and sensation as two essential attributes of the soul, there is widespread disagreement about the nature of the soul, with some views likening it to fire, and others to minute particles ("motes") in the air. Aristotle, as is his custom, discusses some of the views of his predecessors before offering his own analysis. A crucial area of controversy concerns the question of whether the soul should be identified with the mind—that is, with the faculty of thinking and attaining truth.

Aristotle's own approach is to think about the soul in terms of its characteristic activities. He aims to define the soul by enumerating an integrated set of activities that soul performs. Soul is as soul does. It should be noted that Aristotle rejects the possibility of a disembodied soul. Such a being, he argues, could not perform the activities that have been enumerated. Descartes, in the next selection, defends such a possibility.

[1]Reprinted from *The Oxford Translation of Aristotle*, edited by W.D. Ross, by permission of Oxford University Press.

FUNCTIONS OF THE SOUL

1. Holding as we do that, while knowledge of any kind is a thing to be honoured and prized, one kind of it may, either by reason of its greater exactness or of a higher dignity and greater wonderfulness in its objects, be more honourable and precious than another, on both accounts we should naturally be led to place in the front rank the study of the soul. The knowledge of the soul admittedly contributes greatly to the advance of truth in general, and, above all, to our understanding of Nature, for the soul is in some sense the principle of animal life. Our aim is to grasp and understand, first its essential nature, and secondly its properties; of these some are thought to be affections proper to the soul itself, while others are considered to attach to the animal[1] owing to the presence within it of soul.

To attain any assured knowledge about the soul is one of the most difficult things in the world. As the form of question which here presents itself, viz. the question 'What is it?', recurs in other fields, it might be supposed that there was some single method of inquiry applicable to all objects whose essential nature we are endeavouring to ascertain (as there *is* for derived properties the single method of demonstration); in that case what we should have to seek for would be this unique method. But if there is no such single and general method for solving the question of essence, our task becomes still more difficult; in the case of each different subject we shall have to determine the appropriate process of investigation. If to this there be a clear answer, e.g. that the process is demonstration or division, or some other known method, difficulties and hesitations still beset us—with what facts shall we begin the inquiry? For the facts which form the starting-points in different subjects must be different, as e.g. in the case of numbers and surfaces.

First, no doubt, it is necessary to determine in which of the *summa genera* soul lies, what it *is*; is it 'a this-somewhat', a substance, or is it a quale or a quantum, or some other of the remaining kinds of predicates which we have distinguished?[2]

Further, does soul belong to the class of potential existents, or is it not rather an actuality? Our answer to this question is of the greatest importance.

We must consider also whether soul is divisible or is without parts, and whether it is everywhere homogeneous or not; and if not homogeneous, whether its various forms are different specifically or generically: up to the present time those who have discussed and investigated soul seem to have confined themselves to the human soul. We must be careful not to ignore the question whether soul can be defined in a single unambiguous formula, as is the case with animal, or whether we must not give a separate formula for each sort of it, as we do for horse, dog, man, god (in the latter case the 'universal' animal— and so too every other 'common predicate'— being treated either as nothing at all or as a later product[3]). Further, if what exists is not a plurality of souls, but a plurality of parts of one soul, which ought we to investigate first, the whole soul or its parts? (It is also a difficult problem to decide which of these parts are in nature distinct from one another.) Again, which ought we to investigate first, these parts or their functions, mind or thinking, the faculty or the act of sensa-

[1] i.e. the complex of soul and body.—TRANS.

[2] That is, is the soul a thing, like a dog or a house, or a property, like redness or baldness?

[3] i.e. as presupposing the various sorts instead of being presupposed by them—TRANS.

tion, and so on? If the investigation of the functions precedes that of the parts, the further question suggests itself: ought we not before either to consider the correlative objects, e.g. of sense or thought? It seems not only useful for the discovery of the causes of the derived properties of substances to be acquainted with the essential nature of those substances (as in mathematics it is useful for the understanding of the property of the equality of the interior angles of a triangle to two right angles to know the essential nature of the straight and the curved or of the line and the plane) but also conversely, for the knowledge of the essential nature of a substance is largely promoted by an acquaintance with its properties: for, when we are able to give an account conformable to experience of all or most of the properties of a substance, we shall be in the most favourable position to say something worth saying about the essential nature of that subject; in all demonstration a definition of the essence is required as a starting-point, so that definitions which do not enable us to discover the derived properties, or which fail to facilitate even a conjecture about them, must obviously, one and all, be dialectical and futile.

A further problem presented by the affections of soul is this: are they all affections of the complex of body and soul, or is there any one among them peculiar to the soul by itself? To determine this is indispensable but difficult. If we consider the majority of them, there seems to be no case in which the soul can act or be acted upon without involving the body; e.g. anger, courage, appetite, and sensation generally. Thinking seems the most probable exception; but if this too proves to be a form of imagination or to be impossible without imagination, it too requires a body as a condition of its existence. If there is any way of acting or being acted upon proper to soul, soul will be capable of separate existence; if there is none, its separate existence is impossible. In the latter case, it will be like what is straight, which has many properties arising from the straightness in it, e.g. that of touching a bronze sphere at a point, though straightness divorced from the other constituents of the straight thing cannot touch it in this way; it cannot be so divorced at all, since it is always found in a body. It therefore seems that all the affections of soul involve a body—passion, gentleness, fear, pity, courage, joy, loving, and hating; in all these there is a concurrent affection of the body. In support of this we may point to the fact that, while sometimes on the occasion of violent and striking occurrences there is no excitement or fear felt, on others faint and feeble stimulations produce these emotions, viz. when the body is already in a state of tension resembling its condition when we are angry. Here is a still clearer case: in the absence of any external cause of terror we find ourselves experiencing the feelings of a man in terror. From all this it is obvious that the affections of soul are enmattered formulable essences.

Consequently their definitions ought to correspond, e.g. anger should be defined as a certain mode of movement of such and such a body (or part or faculty of a body) by this or that cause and for this or that end. That is precisely why the study of the soul must fall within the science of Nature, at least so far as in its affections it manifests this double character. Hence a physicist would define an affection of soul differently from a dialectician; the latter would define e.g. anger as the appetite for returning pain for pain, or something like that, while the former would define it as a boiling of the blood or warm substance surrounding the heart. The latter assigns the material conditions, the former the form or formulable essence; for what he states is the formulable essence of the fact, though for its actual existence there must be embodiment of it in a material such as is described by the other. Thus the essence of a house is assigned in such a formula as 'a shelter against destruction by wind, rain, and heat'; the physicist would describe it as 'stones, bricks, and timbers'; but there is a third possible description which would say that it was that form in that material with that purpose or end.[4] Which, then, among these is entitled to be regarded as the genuine physicist? The one who confines himself to the material, or the one who restricts himself to the formulable essence alone? Is it not rather the one who combines both in a single formula? If this is so, how are we to characterize the other two? Must we not say that there is no type of thinker who concerns himself with those qualities or attributes of the material which are in fact inseparable from the material, and without attempting even in thought to separate them? The physicist is he who concerns himself with all the properties active and passive of bodies or materials thus or thus defined; attributes not considered as being of this character he leaves to others, in certain cases it may be to a specialist, e.g. a carpenter or a physician, in others (a) where they are inseparable in fact, but are separable from any particular kind of body by an effort of abstraction, to the mathematician, (b) where they are separate both in fact and in thought from body altogether, to the First Philosopher or metaphysician. But we must return from this digression, and repeat that the affections of soul are inseparable from the material substratum of animal life, to which we have seen that such affections, e.g. passion and fear, attach, and have not the same mode of being as a line or a plane.

2. For our study of soul it is necessary, while formulating the problems of which in our further advance we are to find the solutions, to call into council the views of those of our predecessors who have declared any opinion on this subject, in order that we may profit by whatever is sound in their suggestions and avoid their errors.

The starting-point of our inquiry is an exposition of those characteristics which have chiefly been held to belong to soul in its very nature. Two characteristic marks have above all others been recognized as distinguishing that which has soul in it from that which has not—movement and sensation. It may be said that these two are what our predecessors have fixed upon as characteristic of soul.

Some say that what originates movement is both pre-eminently and primarily soul; believing that what is not itself moved cannot originate movement in another, they arrived at the view that soul belongs to the class of things in movement. This is what led Democritus to say that soul is a sort of fire or hot substance; his 'forms' or atoms are infinite in number; those which are spherical he calls fire and soul, and compares them to the motes in the air which we see in shafts of light coming through windows; the mixture of seeds of all sorts he calls the elements of the whole of Nature (Leucippus gives a similar account); the spherical atoms are identified with soul because atoms of that shape are most adapted to permeate everywhere, and to set all the others moving by being themselves in movement. This implies the view that soul is identical with what produces movement in animals. That is why, further, they regard respiration as the characteristic mark of life; as the environment compresses the bodies of animals, and tends to extrude those atoms which impart movement to them, because they themselves are never at rest, there must be a reinforcement of these by similar atoms coming in from without in the act of respiration; for they prevent the extrusion of those which are already within by counteracting the compressing and consolidating force of the environment; and animals continue to live only as

---

[4]That is, a shelter against destruction by wind, rain, and heat out of stones, bricks, and timbers.

long as they are able to maintain this resistance.

The doctrine of the Pythagoreans seems to rest upon the same ideas; some of them declared the motes in air, others what moved them, to be soul. These motes were referred to because they are seen always in movement, even in a complete calm.

The same tendency is shown by those who define soul as that which moves itself; all seem to hold the view that movement is what is closest to the nature of soul, and that while all else is moved by soul, it alone moves itself. This belief arises from their never seeing anything originating movement which is not first itself moved.

Similarly also Anaxagoras (and whoever agrees with him in saying that mind set the whole in movement) declares the moving cause of things to be soul. His position must, however, be distinguished from that of Democritus. Democritus roundly identifies soul and mind, for he identifies what appears with what is true—that is why he commends Homer for the phrase 'Hector lay with thought distraught'; he does not employ mind as a special faculty dealing with truth, but identifies soul and mind. What Anaxagoras says about them is more obscure; in many places he tells us that the cause of beauty and order is mind, elsewhere that it is soul; it is found, he says, in all animals, great and small, high and low, but mind (in the sense of intelligence) appears not to belong alike to all animals, and indeed not even to all human beings.

All those, then, who had special regard to the fact that what has soul in it is moved, adopted the view that soul is to be identified with what is eminently originative of movement. All, on the other hand, who looked to the fact that what has soul in it knows or perceives what is, identify soul with the principle or principles of Nature, according as they admit several such principles or one only. Thus Empedocles declares that it is

formed out of all his elements, each of them also being soul; his words are:

> For 'tis by Earth we see Earth, by Water Water,
> By Ether Ether divine, by Fire destructive Fire,
> By Love Love, and Hate by cruel Hate.

In the same way Plato in the *Timaeus*[5] fashions the soul out of his elements; for like, he holds, is known by like, and things are formed out of the principles or elements, so that soul must be so too. Similarly also in his lectures 'On Philosophy' it was set forth that the Animal-itself is compounded of the Idea itself of the One together with the primary length, breadth, and depth, everything else, the objects of its perception, being similarly constituted. Again he puts his view in yet other terms: Mind is the monad, science or knowledge the dyad (because[6] it goes undeviatingly from one point to another), opinion the number of the plane,[7] sensation the number of the solid[8]; the numbers are by him expressly identified with the Forms themselves or principles, and are formed out of the elements; now things are apprehended either by mind or science or opinion or sensation, and these same numbers are the Forms of things.

Some thinkers, accepting both premises, viz. that the soul is both originative of movement and cognitive, have compounded it of both and declared the soul to be a self-moving number.

As to the nature and number of the first principles opinions differ. The difference is greatest between those who regard them as corporeal and

---

[5] 35 A ff.—TRANS.
[6] Like the straight line, whose number is the dyad. —TRANS.
[7] The triad.—TRANS.
[8] The tetrad.—TRANS.

those who regard them as incorporeal, and from both dissent those who make a blend and draw their principles from both sources. The number of principles is also in dispute; some admit one only, others assert several. There is a consequent diversity in their several accounts of soul; they assume, naturally enough, that what is in its own nature originative of movement must be among what is primordial. That has led some to regard it as fire, for fire is the subtlest of the elements and nearest to incorporeality; further, in the most primary sense, fire both is moved and originates movement in all the others.

Democritus has expressed himself more ingeniously than the rest on the grounds for ascribing each of these two characters to soul; soul and mind are, he says, one and the same thing, and this thing must be one of the primary and indivisible bodies, and its power of originating movement must be due to its fineness of grain and the shape of its atoms; he says that of all the shapes the spherical is the most mobile, and that this is the shape of the particles of both fire and mind.

Anaxagoras, as we said above, seems to distinguish between soul and mind, but in practice he treats them as a single substance, except that it is mind that he specially posits as the principle of all things; at any rate what he says is that mind alone of all that is is simple, unmixed, and pure. He assigns both characteristics, knowing and origination of movement, to the same principle, when he says that it was mind that set the whole in movement.

Thales, too, to judge from what is recorded about him, seems to have held soul to be a motive force, since he said that the magnet has a soul in it because it moves the iron.

Diogenes (and others) held the soul to be air because he believed air to be finest in grain and a first principle; therein lay the grounds of the soul's powers of knowing and originating move-

ment. As the priordial principle from which all other things are derived, it is cognitive; as finest in grain, it has the power to originate movement.

Heraclitus too says that the first principle—the 'warm exhalation' of which, according to him, everything else is composed—is soul; further, that this exhalation is most incorporeal and in ceaseless flux; that what is in movement requires that what knows it should be in movement; and that all that is has its being essentially in movement (herein agreeing with the majority).

Alcmaeon also seems to have held a similar view about soul; he says that it is immortal because it resembles 'the immortals', and that this immortality belongs to it in virtue of its ceaseless movement; for all the 'things divine', moon, sun, the planets, and the whole heavens, are in perpetual movement.

Of more superficial writers, some, e.g. Hippo, have pronounced it to be water; they seem to have argued from the fact that the seed of all animals is fluid, for Hippo tries to refute those who say that the soul is blood, on the ground that the seed, which is the primordial soul, is not blood.

Another group (Critias, for example) did hold it to be blood; they take perception to be the most characteristic attribute of soul, and hold that perceptiveness is due to the nature of blood.

Each of the elements has thus found its partisan, except earth—earth has found no supporter unless we count as such those who have declared soul to be, or to be compounded of, *all* the elements. All, then, it may be said, characterize the soul by three marks, Movement, Sensation, Incorporeality, and each of these is traced back to the first principles. That is why (with one exception) all those who define the soul by its power of knowing make it either an element or construct it out of the elements. The language they all use is similar; like, they say, is known by like; as the soul knows everything, they construct it out of all the principles. Hence all those who admit but one cause or element, make the soul also one (e.g. fire or air), while those who admit a multiplicity of principles make the soul also multiple. The exception is Anaxagoras; he alone says that mind is impassible and has nothing in common with anything else. But, if this is so, how or in virtue of what cause can it know? That Anaxagoras has not explained, nor can any answer be inferred from his words. All who acknowledge pairs of opposites among their principles, construct the soul also out of these contraries, while those who admit as principles only one contrary of each pair, e.g. either hot or cold, likewise make the soul some one of these. That is why, also, they allow themselves to be guided by the names; those who identify soul with the hot argue that *zen* (to live) is derived from *zein* (to boil), while those who identify it with the cold say that soul (*psyche*) is so called from the process of respiration and refrigeration (*katapsyxis*).

Such are the traditional opinions concerning soul, together with the grounds on which they are maintained.

3. We must begin our examination with movement; for, doubtless, not only is it false that the essence of soul is correctly described by those who say that it is what moves (or is capable of moving) itself, but it is an impossibility that movement should be even an attribute of it.

We have already pointed out that there is no necessity that what originates movement should itself be moved. There are two senses in which anything may be moved—either (a) indirectly, owing to something other than itself, or (b) directly, owing to itself. Things are 'indirectly moved' which are moved as being contained in something which is moved, e.g. sailors in a ship, for they are moved in a different sense from that

in which the ship is moved; the ship is 'directly moved', they are 'indirectly moved', because they are in a moving vessel. This is clear if we consider their limbs; the movement proper to the legs (and so to man) is walking, and in this case the sailors are not walking. Recognizing the double sense of 'being moved', what we have to consider now is whether the soul is 'directly moved' and participates in such direct movement.

There are four species of movement—locomotion, alteration, diminution, growth; consequently if the soul is moved, it must be moved with one or several or all of these species of movement. Now if its movement is not incidental, there must be a movement natural to it, and, if so, as all the species enumerated involve place, place must be natural to it. But if the essence of soul be to move itself, its being moved cannot be incidental to it, as it is to what is white or three cubits long; they too can be moved, but only incidentally—what is moved is that of which 'white' and 'three cubits long' are the attributes, the body in which they inhere; hence *they* have no place: but if the soul naturally partakes in movement, it follows that it must have a place.

Further, if there be a movement natural to the soul, there must be a countermovement unnatural to it, and conversely. The same applies to rest as well as to movement; for the *terminus ad quem* of a thing's natural movement is the place of its natural rest, and similarly the *terminus ad quem* of its enforced movement is the place of its enforced rest. But what meaning can be attached to enforced movements or rests of the soul, it is difficult even to imagine.

Further, if the natural movement of the soul be upward, the soul must be fire; if downward, it must be earth; for upward and downward movements are the definitory characteristics of these bodies. The same reasoning applies to the intermediate movements, *termini*, and bodies. Further, since the soul is observed to originate movement

325

in the body, it is reasonable to suppose that it transmits to the body the movements by which it itself is moved, and so, reversing the order, we may infer from the movements of the body back to similar movements of the soul. Now the body is moved from place to place with movements of locomotion. Hence it would follow that the soul too must in accordance with the body change either its place as a whole or the relative places of its parts. This carries with it the possibility that the soul might even quit its body and re-enter it, and with this would be involved the possibility of a resurrection of animals from the dead. But, it may be contended, the soul can be moved indirectly by something else; for an animal can be pushed out of its course. Yes, but that to whose *essence* belongs the power of being moved by itself, cannot be moved by something else except incidentally,[9] just as what is good by or in itself cannot owe its goodness to something external to it or to some end to which it is a means.

If the soul *is* moved, the most probable view is that what moves it is sensible things.[10]

We must note also that, if the soul moves itself, it must be the mover itself that is moved, so that it follows that if movement is in every case a displacement of that which is in movement, in that respect in which it is said to be moved, the movement of the soul must be departure from its essential nature, at least if its self-movement is essential to it, not incidental.

Some go so far as to hold that the movements which the soul imparts to the body in which it is are the same in kind as those with which it itself is moved. An example of this is Democritus, who uses language like that of the comic dramatist

Philippus, who accounts for the movements that Daedalus imparted to his wooden Aphrodite by saying that he poured quicksilver into it; similarly Democritus says that the spherical atoms which according to him constitute soul, owing to their own ceaseless movements draw the whole body after them and so produce its movements. We must urge the question whether it is these very same atoms which produce rest also—how they could do so, it is difficult and even impossible to say. And, in general, we may object that it is not in this way that the soul appears to originate movement in animals—it is through intention or process of thinking.

It is in the same fashion that the *Timaeus* also tries to give a physical account of how the soul moves its body; the soul, it is here said, is in movement, and so owing to their mutual implication moves the body also. After compounding the soul-substance out of the elements and dividing it in accordance with the harmonic numbers, in order that it may possess a connate sensibility for 'harmony' and that the whole may move in movements well attuned, the Demiurge bent the straight line into a circle; this single circle he divided into two circles united at two common points; one of these he subdivided into seven circles. All this implies that the movements of the soul are identified with the local movements of the heavens.

Now, in the first place, it is a mistake to say that the soul is a spatial magnitude. It is evident that Plato means the soul of the whole to be like the sort of soul which is called mind—not like the sensitive or the desiderative soul, for the movements of neither of these are circular. Now mind is one and continuous in the sense in which the process of thinking is so, and thinking is identical with the thoughts which are its parts; these have a serial unity like that of number, not a unity like that of a spatial magnitude. Hence mind cannot have that kind of unity either; mind

---

[9]i.e. so that what is moved is not it but something which 'goes along with it', e.g. a vehicle in which it is contained. —TRANS.

[10]sc. in which case the movement can only be 'incidental'; for, as we shall see later, is is really the bodily organ of sensation that then is 'moved'. —TRANS.

is either without parts or is continuous in some other way than that which characterizes a spatial magnitude. How, indeed, if it were a spatial magnitude, could mind possibly think? Will it think with any one indifferently of its parts? In this case, the 'part' must be understood either in the sense of a spatial magnitude or in the sense of a point (if a point *can* be called a part of a spatial magnitude). If we accept the latter alternative, the points being infinite in number, obviously the mind can never exhaustively traverse them; if the former, the mind must think the same thing over and over again, indeed an infinite number of times (whereas it is manifestly possible to think a thing once only). If contact of any part whatsoever of itself with the object is all that is required, why need mind move in a circle, or indeed possess magnitude at all? On the other hand, if contact with the whole circle is necessary, what meaning can be given to the contact of the parts? Further, how could what has no parts think what has parts, or what has parts think what has none?[11] We must identify the circle referred to with mind; for it is mind whose movement is thinking, and it is the circle whose movement is revolution, so that if thinking is a movement of revolution, the circle which has this characteristic movement must be mind.

If the circular movement is eternal, there must be something which mind is always thinking—what *can* this be? For all practical processes of thinking have limits—they all go on for the sake of something outside the process, and all theoretical processes come to a close in the same way as the phrases in speech which express processes and results of thinking. Every such linguistic phrase is either definitory or demonstrative. Demonstration has both a starting point and may be said to end in a conclusion or inferred result; even if the process never reaches final comple-

tion, at any rate it never returns upon itself again to its starting point, it goes on assuming a fresh middle term or a fresh extreme, and moves straight forward, but circular movement returns to its starting point. Definitions, too, are closed groups of terms.

Further, if the same revolution is repeated, mind must repeatedly think the same object.

Further, thinking has more resemblance to a coming to rest or arrest than to a movement; the same may be said of inferring.

It might also be urged that what is difficult and enforced is incompatible with blessedness; if the movement of the soul is not of its essence, movement of the soul must be contrary to its nature. It must also be painful for the soul to be inextricably bound up with the body; nay more, if, as is frequently said and widely accepted, it is better for mind not to be embodied, the union must be for it undesirable.

Further, the cause of the revolution of the heavens is left obscure. It is not the essence of soul which is the cause of this circular movement—that movement is only incidental to soul—nor is, *a fortiori*, the body its cause. Again, it is not even asserted that it is better that soul should be so moved; and yet the reason for which God caused the soul to move in a circle can only have been that movement was better for it than rest, and movement of this kind better than any other. But since this sort of consideration is more appropriate to another field of speculation, let us dismiss it for the present.

The view we have just been examining, in company with most theories about the soul, involves the following absurdity: they all join the soul to a body, or place it in a body, without adding any specification of the reason of their union, or of the bodily conditions required for it. Yet such explanation can scarcely be omitted; for some community of nature is presupposed by the fact that the one acts and the other is acted upon,

[11]*sc.* but mind in fact or cognizes both.—TRANS.

327

the one moves and the other is moved; interaction always implies a *special* nature in the two interagents. All, however, that these thinkers do is to describe the specific characteristics of the soul; they do not try to determine anything about the body which is to contain it, as if it were possible, as in the Pythagorean myths, that any soul could be clothed upon with any body—an absurd view, for each body seems to have a form and shape of its own. It is as absurd as to say that the art of carpentry could embody itself in flutes; each art must use its tools, each soul its body.

CHAPTER 33

RENÉ DESCARTES

MIND-BODY DUALISM

Descartes' general project in his *Meditations on First Philosophy*, explained in Part 2, is to show how we are capable of having certain knowledge.[1] By the sixth meditation, Descartes believes he has shown that we can know with certainty that we exist as minds, since a benevolent God exists and would not allow us to be deceived about things we believe with certainty. He now takes up the question of how we can know that we have bodies as well as minds. He argues that all of our ordinary experience attests to us having a body, and God would not allow our experience to completely mislead us. We can also know that the mind is a distinct entity from body, with a completely different nature. Whereas mind is conscious and nonextended, body is extended and not conscious. The "separate careers" of mind and body in the *Meditations* has been evident from the first meditation, where Descartes showed how one could be certain of the existence of oneself as a thinking thing while being in complete doubt about the existence of bodies. Although he states that mind and body are conjoined in a relation more intimate than that between a captain and ship, Descartes offers no clear suggestions as to how we may understand this relation.

---

[1]From René Descartes, *Meditations on First Philosophy*, translated by Donald A. Cress (Indianapolis: Hackett Publishing Co., 1979). Reprinted with permission.

MIND-BODY DUALISM

Meditation Six: Concerning the Existence of Material Things, and the Real Distinction of the Mind from the Body

It remains for me to examine whether material things exist. Indeed I now know that they can exist, at least insofar as they are the object of pure mathematics, because I clearly and distinctly perceive them. For no doubt God is capable of bringing about everything that I am thus capable of perceiving. And I have never judged that God was incapable of something, except when it was incompatible with being perceived by me distinctly. Moreover, from the faculty of imagination, which I observe that I use while I am engaged in dealing with these material things, it seems to follow that they exist; to someone paying very close attention to what imagination is, it appears to be nothing else but an application of the knowing faculty to a body intimately present to it—hence, a body that exists.

And to make this very clear, I first examine the difference between imagination and pure intellection. So, for example, when I imagine a triangle, I not only understand that it is a figure bounded by three lines, but at the same time I also intuit by my powers of discernment these three lines as present—this is what I call "imagining." But if I want to think about a chiliagon, I certainly understand just as well that it is a figure consisting of a thousand sides, and that a triangle is a figure consisting of three lines; but I do not imagine those thousand sides in the same way, that is, I do not intuit them as being present. Albeit that when I think of a chiliagon I may perchance represent to myself some figure confusedly—because whenever I think about some-

thing corporeal, I always, out of force of habit, imagine something—nevertheless it is evident that it is not a chiliagon. This is so because it is not really different from the figure I would represent to myself if I were to think of a myriagon or any other figure with a large number of sides. Nor is imagination of any help in knowing the properties that differentiate the chiliagon from other polygons. But if it is a question of a pentagon, I surely can understand its form, just as was the case with the chiliagon, without the help of my imagination. But I can also imagine it, that is, by applying the powers of discernment both to its five sides and, at the same time, to the area bounded by those sides; clearly I am aware at this point that I need a peculiar sort of effort on the part of the mind in order to imagine, one that I do not employ in order to understand. This new effort on the part of the mind clearly shows the difference between imagination and pure intellection.

Besides, I believe that this power of imagining that is in me, insofar as it differs from the power of understanding, is not a necessary element of my essence, that is, of the essence of my mind; for although I might lack this power, nonetheless I would undoubtedly remain the same person as I am now. Thus it seems to follow that the power of imagining depends upon something different from me. And I readily understand that were a body to exist to which a mind is so joined that it might direct itself to look at it anytime it wishes, it could happen that by means of this body I intuit corporeal things. The result would be that this mode of thinking differs from pure intellection only in the fact that the mind, when it understands, in a sense turns itself toward itself and gazes upon one of the ideas that are in it. But when it imagines, it turns itself toward the body, and intuits something in the body similar to an idea either understood by the mind or perceived by sense. I say I easily understand that the imagination can function in this way, provided a body does exist. But this is only a probability; although I may investigate everything carefully, nevertheless, I do not yet see how, from the distinct idea of corporeal nature that I find in my imagination, I can draw up an argument that necessarily concludes that some body exists.

But I am in the habit of imagining many other things—over and above the corporeal nature that is the object of pure mathematics—such as colors, sounds, tastes, pain, and so on, but not so distinctly. Inasmuch as I perceive these things better with those senses from which, with the aid of the memory, they seem to have come to the imagination, the same trouble should also be taken concerning the senses, so that I might deal with them more appropriately. It must be seen whether I can obtain any certain argument for the existence of corporeal things from those things that are perceived by the way of thinking that I call "sense."

First I will repeat to myself here what those things were that I believed to be true because I had perceived them by means of the senses and what the grounds were for so believing. Next I will assess the reasons why I called them into doubt. Finally, I will consider what I must now believe concerning these things.

So, first, I sensed that I have a head, hands, feet, and other members that composed this body; I viewed it as a part of me, or perhaps even as the whole of me. I sensed that this body is frequently amid many other bodies, and that these bodies can affect my body in pleasant and unpleasant ways; I gauged what was pleasant by a certain sense of pleasure, and what was unpleasant by a sense of pain. In addition to pain and pleasure, I also sensed in me hunger, thirst, and other such appetites, as well as certain corporeal tendencies to mirth, sadness, anger, and other such feelings. But, as for things external to me—besides the extension, shapes, and motions of bodies—I also sensed their roughness, heat, and other tactile qualities; I sensed, too, the light, colors, odors, tastes, and sounds from whose variety I distinguished the heavens, the earth, the seas, and the other bodies one from the other. Indeed, because of the ideas of all these qualities that presented themselves to my thought and that alone I properly and immediately sensed, it was not wholly without reason that I believed that I sensed things clearly different from my thought, namely, the bodies from which these ideas might proceed. For I knew by experience that they come upon me without my consent, to the extent that, wish as I may, I cannot sense any object unless it be present to the organ of sense, and I cannot fail to sense it when it is present. Since the ideas perceived by sense are much more vivid and clear-cut, and even, in their own way, more "distinct," than any of those that I willingly and knowingly formed by meditation or those that I found impressed on my memory, it seems impossible that they come from myself. Therefore, it remained that they came from other things. Since I had no knowledge of such things except from these ideas themselves, I could not help entertaining the view that these things were similar to those ideas. Also, because I recalled that I had used my senses earlier than my reason, and I saw that the ideas that I myself constructed were not as clear-cut as those that I perceived by means of the senses, I saw that these former ideas were for the most part composed of parts of these latter ideas; I easily convinced myself that I plainly have no idea in the intellect that I did not have beforehand in the sense. Not without reason did I judge that this body, which by a special right I called "mine," belongs more to me than to any other thing, for I could never be separated from it in the same way as I could be from the rest. I sensed all appetites and feelings in it and for it. Finally, I have noticed pain and pleasurable excitement in its parts, but not in other bodies external to it. But why a certain sadness of spirit arises from one feeling of pain or another, and why a certain elation arises from a feeling of excitement, or why some sort of twitching of the stomach, which I call hunger, should warn me to take in nourishment, or why dryness of throat should warn me to take something to drink, and so on—for all these I plainly had no explanation other than that I have been taught so by nature. For there is clearly no affinity, at least none I am aware of, between the twitching of the stomach and the will to take in nourishment, or between the sense of something that causes pain and the thought of the sadness arising from this sense. But nature seems to have taught me everything else that I judged concerning the objects of the senses, because I convinced myself—even before having spent time on any of the arguments that might prove it—that things were this way.

But afterwards many experiences gradually caused all faith that I had in the senses to totter; occasionally towers, which had seemed round from afar, appeared square at close quarters; very large statues, standing on their pinnacles, did not seem large to someone looking at them from ground level; in countless other such things I detected that judgments of the external senses deceived me—not just the external senses, but also the internal senses. What can be more intimate than pain? But I had once heard it said by people whose leg or arm had been amputated that it seems to them that they occasionally sense pain in the very limb that they lacked. Therefore, even in me, it did not seem to be clearly certain that some part of my body was causing me pain, although I did sense pain in it. To these causes of doubt I recently added two quite general ones: first, I believed I never sensed anything while I was awake that I could not believe I also sometimes perceive while asleep. Since I do not believe that what I seem to sense in my dreams comes to me from things external to me, I did not see any reason why I should have these beliefs about things that I seem to sense while I am awake. The second cause of doubt was that, since I was ignorant of the cause of my coming into being (or at least pretended that I was ignorant of it), I saw that nothing prevented my having been so constituted by nature that I should be deceived about even what appeared to me most true. As to the arguments by which I formerly convinced myself of the truth of sensible things, I found no difficulty in responding to them. Since I seemed driven by nature toward many things opposed to reason, I did not think what was taught by nature deserved much credence. Although the perceptions of the senses did not depend on my will, I did not think that we must therefore conclude that they came from things external to me, because perhaps there is in me some faculty, as yet unknown to me, that produces these perceptions.

However, now, after having begun to know better the cause of my coming to be, I believe that I must not rashly admit everything that I seem to derive from the senses. But, then, neither should I call everything into doubt.

First, because I know that all the things that I clearly and distinctly understand can be made by God exactly as I understand them, it is enough that I can clearly and distinctly understand one thing without the other in order for me to be certain that the one thing is different from the other, because at least God can establish them separately. The question of the power by which this takes place is not relevant to their being thought to be different. For this reason, from the fact that I know that I exist, and that meanwhile I judge that nothing else clearly belongs to my nature or essence except that I am a thing that thinks, I rightly conclude that my essence conie. Bird Ramp

sists in this alone: that I am a thing that thinks. Although perhaps (or rather, as I shall soon say, to be sure) I have a body that is very closely joined to me, nevertheless, because on the one hand I have a clear and distinct idea of myself—insofar as I am a thing that thinks and not an extended thing—and because on the other hand I have a distinct idea of a body—insofar as it is merely an extended thing, and not a thing that thinks—it is therefore certain that I am truly distinct from my body, and that I can exist without it.

Moreover, I find in myself faculties endowed with certain special modes of thinking—namely the faculties of imagining and sensing—without which I can clearly and distinctly understand myself in my entirety, but not vice versa: I cannot understand them clearly and distinctly without me, that is, without the knowing substance to which they are attached. For in their formal concept they include an act of understanding; thus I perceive that they are distinguished from me just as modes are to be distinguished from the thing of which they are modes. I also recognize certain other faculties—like those of moving from one place to another, of taking on various shapes, and so on—that surely no more can be understood without the substance to which they are attached than those preceding faculties; for that reason they cannot exist without the substance to which they are attached. But it is clear that these faculties, if in fact they exist, must be attached to corporeal or extended substances, but not to a knowing substance, because extension—but certainly not understanding—is contained in a clear and distinct concept of them. But now there surely is in me a passive faculty of sensing, that is, of receiving and knowing the ideas of sensible things; but I cannot use it unless there also exists, either in me or in something else, a certain active faculty of producing or bringing about these ideas. This faculty surely cannot be in me, since

it clearly presupposes no intellection, and these ideas are produced without my cooperation and often against my will. Because this faculty is in a substance other than myself, in which ought to be contained—formally or eminently—all the reality that is objectively in the ideas produced by this faculty (as I have just now taken notice), it thus remains that either this substance is a body (or corporeal nature) in which is contained formally all that is contained in ideas objectively or it is God—or some other creature more noble than a body—in which it is all contained eminently. But, since God is not a deceiver, it is absolutely clear that he sends me these ideas neither directly and immediately—nor even through the mediation of any creature, in which the objective reality of these ideas is contained not formally but only eminently. Since he clearly gave me no faculty for making this discrimination—rather, he gave me a great inclination to believe that these ideas proceeded from things—I fail to see why God cannot be understood to be a deceiver, if they proceeded from a source other than corporeal things. For this reason, corporeal things exist. Be that as it may, perhaps not all bodies exist exactly as I grasp them by sense, because this grasp by the senses is in many cases very obscure and confused. But at least everything is in these bodies that I clearly and distinctly understand—that is, everything, considered in a general sense, that is encompassed in the object of pure mathematics.

But as to how this point relates to the other remaining matters that are either merely particular—as, for example, that the sun is of such and such a size or shape, and so on—or less clearly understood—as, for example, light, sound, pain, and so on—although they are very doubtful and uncertain, still, because God is not a deceiver, and no falsity can be found in my opinions, unless there is also in me a faculty given me by God for the purpose of rectifying this falsity, these features provide me with a certain hope of reaching the truth in them. And plainly it cannot be doubted that whatever I am taught by nature has some truth to it; for by "nature," taken generally, I understand only God himself or the coordination, instituted by God, of created things. I understand nothing else by my nature in particular than the totality of all the things bestowed on me by God.

There is nothing that this nature teaches me in a more clear-cut way than that I have a body that is ill-disposed when I feel pain, that it needs food and drink when I suffer hunger or thirst, and so on. Therefore, I ought not to doubt that there is some truth in this.

By means of these feelings of pain, hunger, thirst and so on, nature also teaches that I am present to my body not merely in the way a seaman is present to his ship, but that I am tightly joined and, so to speak, mingled together with it, so much so that I make up one single thing with it. For otherwise, when the body is wounded, I, who am nothing but a thing that thinks, would not then sense the pain. Rather, I would perceive the wound by means of the pure intellect, just as a seaman perceives by means of sight whether anything in the ship is broken. When the body lacks food or drink, I would understand this in a clear-cut fashion; I would not have confused feelings of hunger and thirst. For certainly these feelings of thirst, hunger, pain, and so on are nothing but confused modes of thinking arising from the union and, as it were, the mingling of the mind with the body.

Now, first, I realize at this point that there is a great difference between a mind and a body, because the body, by its very nature, is something divisible, whereas the mind is plainly indivisible. Obviously, when I consider the mind, that is, myself insofar as I am only a thing that thinks, I cannot distinguish any parts in me; rather, I take myself to be one complete thing.

Although the whole mind seems to be united to the whole body, nevertheless, were a foot or an arm or any other bodily part amputated, I know that nothing would be taken away from the mind; nor can the faculties of willing, sensing, understanding, and so on be called its "parts," because it is one and the same mind that wills, senses, and understands. On the other hand, no corporeal or extended thing can be thought by me that I did not easily in thought divide into parts; in this way I know that it is divisible. If I did not yet know it from any other source, this consideration alone would suffice to teach me that the mind is wholly different from the body.

Next, I observe that my mind is not immediately affected by all the parts of the body, but merely by the brain, or perhaps even by just one small part of the brain—namely, by that part in which the "common sense" is said to be found. As often as it is disposed in the same manner, it presents the same thing to the mind, although the other parts of the body can meanwhile orient themselves now this way, now that way, as countless experiments show—none of which need be reviewed here.

I also notice that the nature of the body is such that none of its parts can be moved by another part a short distance away, unless it is also moved in the same direction by any of the parts that stand between them, even though this more distant part does nothing. For example, in the cord ABCD, if the final part D is pulled, the first part A would be moved in exactly the same direction as it could be moved if one of the intermediate parts, B or C, were pulled and the last part D remained motionless. Just so, when I sense pain in the foot, physics teaches me that this feeling took place because of nerves scattered throughout the foot. These nerves, like cords, are extended from that point all the way to the brain; when they are pulled in the foot, they also pull on the inner parts of the brain to which they are stretched, and produce a certain motion in these parts of the brain. This motion has been constituted by nature so as to affect the mind with a feeling of pain, as if it existed in the foot. But because these nerves need to pass through the tibea, thigh, loins, back, and neck, with the result that they extend from the foot to the brain, it can happen that the part that is in the foot is not stretched; rather, one of the intermediate parts is thus stretched, and obviously the same movement will occur in the brain that happens when the foot was badly affected. The necessary result is that the mind feels the same pain. And we must believe the same regarding any other sense.

Finally, I observe that, since each of the motions occurring in that part of the brain that immediately affects the mind occasions only one sensation in it, there is no better way to think about this than that it occasions the sensation that, of all that could be occasioned by it, is most especially and most often conducive to the maintenance of a healthy man. Moreover, experience shows that such are all the senses bestowed on us by nature; therefore, clearly nothing is to be found in them that does not bear witness to God's power and goodness. Thus, for example, when the nerves in the foot are violently and unusually agitated, their motion, which extends through the marrow of the spine to the inner reaches of the brain, gives the mind at that point a sign to feel something—namely, the pain as if existing in the foot. This pain provokes it to do its utmost to move away from the cause, since it is harmful to the foot. But the nature of man could have been so constituted by God that this same motion in the brain might have displayed something else to the mind: either the motion itself as it is in the brain, or as it is in the foot, or in some place in between—or somewhere else entirely different. But nothing else serves so well the maintenance of the body. Similarly, when we need a drink, a certain dryness arises in the throat that moves its nerves, and, by means of them, the inner recesses of the brain. This motion affects the mind with a feeling of thirst, because in this situation nothing is more useful for us to know than that we need a drink to sustain our health; the same holds for the other matters.

From these considerations it is totally clear that, notwithstanding the immense goodness of God, the nature of man—insofar as it is composed of mind and body, cannot help but sometimes be deceived. For if some cause, not in the foot but in some other part through which the nerves are stretched from the foot to the brain—or perhaps even in the brain itself—were to produce the same motion that would normally be produced by a badly affected foot, then the pain will be felt as if it were in the foot, and the senses will naturally be deceived, because it is reasonable that the motion should always show the pain to the mind as something belonging to the foot rather than to some other part, since an identical motion in the brain can bring about only the identical effect and this motion more frequently is wont to arise from a cause that harms the foot than from something existing elsewhere. And if the dryness of the throat does not, as is the custom, arise from the fact that drink aids in the health of the body, but from a contrary cause—as happens in the case of the person with dropsy—then it is far better that it should deceive, than if, on the contrary, it were always deceptive when the body is well constituted. The same goes for the other cases.

This consideration is most helpful, not only for noticing all the errors to which my nature is liable, but also for easily being able to correct or avoid them. To be sure, I know that every sense more frequently indicates what is true than what is false regarding those things that concern the advantage of the body, and I can almost always use more than one sense in order to examine the same thing. Furthermore, I can use memory, which connects present things with preceding ones, plus the intellect, which now has examined all the causes of error. I should no longer fear lest those things that are daily shown me by the senses, are false; rather, the hyperbolic doubts of the last few days ought to be rejected as worthy of derision—especially the principal doubt regarding sleep, which I did not distinguish from being awake. For I now notice that a very great difference exists between these two; dreams are never joined with all the other actions of life by the memory, as is the case with those actions that occur when one is awake. For surely, if someone, while I am awake, suddenly appears to me, and then immediately disappears, as happens in dreams, so that I see neither where he came from or where he went, it is not without reason that I would judge him to be a ghost or a phantom conjured up in my brain, rather than a true man.

But when these things happen, regarding which I notice distinctly where they come from, where they are now, and when they come to me, and I connect the perception of them without any interruption with the rest of my life, obviously I am certain that these perceptions have occurred not in sleep but in a waking state. Nor ought I to have even a little doubt regarding the truth of these things, if, having mustered all the senses, memory, and intellect in order to examine them, nothing is announced to me by one of these sources that conflicts with the others. For from the fact that God is no deceiver, it follows that I am in no way deceived in these matters. But because the need to get things done does not always give us the leisure time for such a careful inquiry, one must believe that the life of man is vulnerable to errors regarding particular things, and we must acknowledge the infirmity of our nature.

CHAPTER 34

GILBERT RYLE

DESCARTES' MYTH

Gilbert Ryle (1900–1976) was Waynfleet Professor of Metaphysical Philosophy at Oxford University. For many years the editor of the philosophy journal *Mind*, he wrote extensively on a wide range of philosophical topics, including Plato's philosophy. He is best known, however, for contributions to the philosophy of mind contained in his most important book, *The Concept of Mind* (1949). This book, a defense of the position that came to be known as "logical behaviorism," set the stage for decades of renewed debate on the mind-body problem.

In this lively and provocative selection, the first chapter of *The Concept of Mind*, Ryle contends that the "official doctrine" about the nature and place of minds, derived from Descartes, is unsound.[1] In its simplest form, the official doctrine holds that every human being has both a mind and a body, that these two are somehow "harnessed together," but at death the mind will continue to exist and function.

The official doctrine leads to serious difficulties, since the contrast between the public character of the body and the private character of the mind require us to treat the workings of the body as "external," and those of the mind as "internal." From here it is but one short step to conclude that the mind is in the body, closed off from other minds, a mysterious, solitary, ghostly Robinson Crusoe.

---

[1] From Gilbert Ryle, *The Concept of Mind*. (New York: Harper & Row, 1949). Reprinted with the permission of Hertford College, Oxford, England.

Ryle criticizes the official doctrine, which he calls "the dogma of the ghost in the machine," as being one huge mistake, which he calls a "category-mistake." To illustrate what he means by category-mistake, Ryle asks us to think of a foreigner visiting Oxford University for the first time. After viewing the various playing fields, museums, laboratories, and colleges, the visitor asks, "But where is the University?" This misguided question mistakenly places the University into the wrong category, assuming that the University is yet another entity or institution that can be seen alongside the others. The category-mistake is at bottom an inability to use language correctly. Similarly, the official doctrine is a category-mistake that originates from the attempt to invest mind with its own nonmechanical causal status, possessing a separate career from that of the mechanical body. Just as the visitor expected the University to be yet another thing, so Descartes and his followers treated minds as additional, special, causal centers.

In opposition to the official doctrine, Ryle's logical behaviorism asserts that in describing the workings of a person's mind we are not describing a second set of operations to those of the body. Rather, we are describing the person's one career: the ways in which her conduct is managed. To say that a person is intelligent, for example, is not to make an assertion about some private events in her mind; it is simply our knowledge of her public performance. In Ryle's words, "It is being maintained throughout this book that when we characterize people by mental predicates, we are not making untestable inferences to any ghostly processes occurring in streams of consciousness that we are debarred from visiting; we are describing the ways in which those people conduct parts of their predominantly public behavior."

DESCARTES' MYTH

(1) The Official Doctrine

There is a doctrine about the nature and place of minds which is so prevalent among theorists and even among laymen that it deserves to be described as the official theory. Most philosophers, psychologists and religious teachers subscribe, with minor reservations, to its main articles and, although they admit certain theoretical difficulties in it, they tend to assume that these can be overcome without serious modifications being made to the architecture of the theory. It will be argued here that the central principles of the doctrine are unsound and conflict with the whole body of what we know about minds when we are not speculating about them.

The official doctrine, which hails chiefly from Descartes, is something like this. With the doubtful exceptions of idiots and infants in arms every human being has both a body and a mind. Some would prefer to say that every human being is both a body and a mind. His body and his mind are ordinarily harnessed together, but after the death of the body his mind may continue to exist and function.

Human bodies are in space and are subject to

the mechanical laws which govern all other bodies in space. Bodily processes and states can be inspected by external observers. So a man's bodily life is as much a public affair as are the lives of animals and reptiles and even as the careers of trees, crystals and planets.

But minds are not in space, nor are their operations subject to mechanical laws. The workings of one mind are not witnessable by other observers; its career is private. Only I can take direct cognisance of the states and processes of my own mind. A person therefore lives through two collateral histories, one consisting of what happens in and to his body, the other consisting of what happens in and to his mind. The first is public, the second private. The events in the first history are events in the physical world, those in the second are events in the mental world.

It has been disputed whether a person does or can directly monitor all or only some of the episodes of his own private history; but, according to the official doctrine, of at least some of these episodes he has direct and unchallengeable cognisance. In consciousness, self-consciousness and introspection he is directly and authentically apprised of the present states and operations of his mind. He may have great or small uncertainties about concurrent and adjacent episodes in the physical world, but he can have none about at least part of what is momentarily occupying his mind.

It is customary to express this bifurcation of his two lives and of his two worlds by saying that the things and events which belong to the physical world, including his own body, are external, while the workings of his own mind are internal. This antithesis of outer and inner is of course meant to be construed as a metaphor, since minds, not being in space, could not be described as being spatially inside anything else, or as having things going on spatially inside themselves. But relapses from this good intention are common and theorists are found speculating how stimuli, the physical sources of which are yards or miles outside a person's skin, can generate mental responses inside his skull, or how decisions framed inside his cranium can set going movements of his extremities.

Even when "inner" and "outer" are construed as metaphors, the problem how a person's mind and body influence one another is notoriously charged with theoretical difficulties. What the mind wills, the legs, arms and the tongue execute; what affects the ear and the eye has something to do with what the mind perceives; grimaces and smiles betray the mind's moods and bodily castigations lead, it is hoped, to moral improvement. But the actual transactions between the episodes of the private history and those of the public history remain mysterious, since by definition they can belong to neither series. They could not be reported among the happenings described in a person's autobiography of his inner life, but nor could they be reported among those described in some one else's biography of that person's overt career. They can be inspected neither by introspection nor by laboratory experiment. They are theoretical shuttlecocks which are forever being bandied from the physiologist back to the psychologist and from the psychologist back to the physiologist.

Underlying this partly metaphorical representation of the bifurcation of a person's two lives there is a seemingly more profound and philosophical assumption. It is assumed that there are two different kinds of existence or status. What exists or happens may have the status of physical existence, or it may have the status of mental existence. Somewhat as the faces of coins are either heads or tails, or somewhat as living creatures are either male or female, so, it is supposed, some existing is physical existing, other existing is mental existing. It is a necessary feature of what has physical existence that it is in space and time, it is a necessary feature of what has mental existence that it is in time but not in space. What has physical existence is composed of matter, or else is a function of matter; what has mental existence consists of consciousness, or else is a function of consciousness.

There is thus a polar opposition between mind and matter, an opposition which is often brought out as follows. Material objects are situated in a common field, known as "space", and what happens to one body in one part of space is mechanically connected with what happens to other bodies in other parts of space. But mental happenings occur in insulated fields, known as "minds", and there is, apart maybe from telepathy, no direct causal connection between what happens in one mind and what happens in another. Only through the medium of the public physical world can the mind of one person make a difference to the mind of another. The mind is its own place and in his inner life each of us lives the life of a ghostly Robinson Crusoe. People can see, hear and jolt one another's bodies, but they are irremediably blind and deaf to the workings of one another's minds and inoperative upon them.

What sort of knowledge can be secured of the workings of a mind? On the one side, according to the official theory, a person has direct knowledge of the best imaginable kind of the workings of his own mind. Mental states and processes are (or are normally) conscious states and processes, and the consciousness which irradiates them can engender no illusions and leaves the door open for no doubts. A person's present thinkings, feelings and willings, his perceivings, rememberings and imaginings are intrinsically "phosphorescent"; their existence and their nature are inevitably betrayed to their owner. The inner life is a stream of consciousness of such a sort that it would be absurd to suggest that the mind whose life is that stream might be unaware of what is passing down it.

True, the evidence adduced recently by Freud seems to show that there exist channels tributary to this stream, which run hidden from their owner. People are actuated by impulses the existence of which they vigorously disavow; some of their thoughts differ from the thoughts which they acknowledge; and some of the actions which they think they will to perform they do not really will. They are thoroughly gulled by some of their own hypocrisies and they successfully ignore facts about their mental lives which on the official theory ought to be patent to them. Holders of the official theory tend, however, to maintain that anyhow in normal circumstances a person must be directly and authentically seized of the present state and workings of his own mind.

Besides being currently supplied with these alleged immediate data of consciousness, a person is also generally supposed to be able to exercise from time to time a special kind of perception, namely inner perception, or introspection. He can take a (non-optical) "look" at what is passing in his mind. Not only can he view and scrutinize a flower through his sense of sight and listen to and discriminate the notes of a bell through his sense of hearing; he can also reflectively or introspectively watch, without any bodily organ of sense, the current episodes of his inner life. This self-observation is also commonly supposed to be immune from illusion, confusion or doubt. A mind's reports of its own affairs have a certainty superior to the best that is possessed by its reports of matters in the physical world. Sense-perceptions can, but consciousness and introspection cannot, be mistaken or confused.

On the other side, one person has no direct access of any sort to the events of the inner life of another. He cannot do better than make problematic inferences from the observed behaviour of the other person's body to the states of mind which, by analogy from his own conduct, he supposes to be signalised by that behaviour. Direct access to the workings of a mind is the privilege of that mind itself; in default of such privileged access, the workings of one mind are inevitably occult to everyone else. For the supposed arguments from bodily movements similar to their own to mental workings similar to their own would lack any possibility of observational corroboration. Not unnaturally, therefore, an adherent of the official theory finds it difficult to resist this consequence of his premises, that he has no good reason to believe that there do exist minds other than his own. Even if he prefers to believe that to other human bodies there are harnessed minds not unlike his own, he cannot claim to be able to discover their individual characteristics, or the particular things that they undergo and do. Absolute solitude is on this showing the ineluctable destiny of the soul. Only our bodies can meet.

As a necessary corollary of this general scheme there is implicitly prescribed a special way of construing our ordinary concepts of mental powers and operations. The verbs, nouns and adjectives, with which in ordinary life we describe the wits, characters and higher-grade performances of the people with whom we have do, are required to be construed as signifying special episodes in their secret histories, or else as signifying tendencies for such episodes to occur. When someone is described as knowing, believing or guessing something, as hoping, dreading, intending or shirking something, as designing this or being amused at that, these verbs are supposed to denote the occurrence of specific modifications in his (to us) occult stream of consciousness. Only his own privileged access to this stream in direct awareness and introspection could provide authentic testimony that these mental-conduct verbs were correctly or incorrectly applied. The onlooker, be he teacher, critic, biographer or friend, can never assure himself that his comments have any vestige of truth. Yet it was just because we do in fact all know how to make such comments, make them with general correctness and correct them when they turn out to be confused or mistaken, that philosophers found it necessary to construct their theories of the nature and place of minds. Finding mental-conduct concepts being regularly and effectively used, they properly sought to fix their logical geography. But the logical geography officially recommended would entail that there could be no regular or effective use of these mental-conduct concepts in our descriptions of, and prescriptions for, other people's minds.

(2) The Absurdity of the Official Doctrine

Such in outline is the official theory. I shall often speak of it, with deliberate abusiveness, as "the dogma of the Ghost in the Machine". I hope to prove that it is entirely false, and false not in detail but in principle. It is not merely an assemblage of particular mistakes. It is one big mistake and a mistake of a special kind. It is, namely, a category-mistake. It represents the facts of mental life as if they belonged to one logical type or category (or range of types or categories), when they actually belong to another. The dogma is therefore a philosopher's myth. In attempting to explode the myth I shall probably be taken to be denying well-known facts about the mental life of human beings, and my plea that I aim at doing nothing more than rectify the logic of mental-conduct concepts will probably be disallowed as mere subterfuge.

I must first indicate what is meant by the phrase "Category-mistake". This I do in a series of illustrations.

A foreigner visiting Oxford or Cambridge for the first time is shown a number of colleges, libraries, playing fields, museums, scientific departments and administrative offices. He then asks "But where is the University? I have seen where the members of the Colleges live, where the Registrar works, where the scientists experiment and the rest. But I have not yet seen the University in which reside and work the members of your University." It has then to be explained to him that the University is not another collateral institution, some ulterior counterpart to the colleges, laboratories and offices which he has seen. The University is just the way in which all that he has already seen is organized. When they are seen and when their co-ordination is understood, the University has been seen. His mistake lay in his innocent assumption that it was correct to speak of Christ Church, the Bodleian Library, The Ashmolean Museum *and* the University, to speak, that is, as if "the University" stood for an extra member of the class of which these other units are members. He was mistakenly allocating the University to the same category as that to which the other institutions belong.

The same mistake would be made by a child witnessing the march-past of a division, who, having had pointed out to him such and such battalions, batteries, squadrons, etc., asked when the division was going to appear. He would be supposing that a division was counterpart to the units already seen, partly similar to them and partly unlike them. He would be shown his mistake by being told that in watching the battalions, batteries and squadrons marching past he had been watching the division marking past. The march-past was not a parade of battalions, batteries, squadrons *and* a division; it was a parade of the battalions, batteries and squadrons *of* a division.

One more illustration. A foreigner watching his first game of cricket learns what are the functions of the bowlers, the batsmen, the fielders, the umpires and the scorers. He than says "But there is no one left on the field to contribute the famous element of team-spirit. I see who does the bowling, the batting and the wicket-keeping; but I do not see whose role it is to exercise *esprit de corps*." Once more, it would have to be explained that he was looking for the wrong type of thing. Team-spirit is not another cricketing-operation supplementary to all of the other special tasks. It is, roughly, the keenness with which each of the special tasks is performed, and performing a task keenly is not performing two tasks. Certainly exhibiting team-spirit is not the same thing as bowling or catching, but nor is it a third thing such that we can say that the bowler first bowls *and* then exhibits team-spirit or that a fielder is at a given moment *either* catching *or* displaying *esprit de corps*.

These illustrations of category-mistakes have a common feature which must be noticed. The mistakes were made by people who did not know how to wield the concepts *University, division* and *team-spirit*. Their puzzles arose from inability to use certain items in the English vocabulary.

The theoretically interesting category-mistakes are those made by people who are perfectly competent to apply concepts, at least in the situations with which they are familiar, but are still liable in their abstract thinking to allocate those concepts to logical types to which they do not belong. An instance of a mistake of this sort would be the following story. A student of politics has learned the main differences between the British, the French and the American Constitutions, and has learned also the differences and connections between the Cabinet, Parliament, the various Ministries, the Judicature and the Church of England. But he still becomes embarrassed when asked questions about the connections between the Church of England, the Home Office and the British Constitution. For while the

Church and the Home Office are institutions, the British Constitution is not another institution in the same sense of that noun. So inter-institutional relations which can be asserted or denied to hold between the Church and the Home Office cannot be asserted or denied to hold between either of them and the British Constitution. "The British Constitution" is not a term of the same logical type as "the Home Office" and "the Church of England". In a partially similar way, John Doe may be a relative, a friend, an enemy or a stranger to Richard Roe; but he cannot be any of these things to the Average Taxpayer. He knows how to talk sense in certain sorts of discussions about the Average Taxpayer, but he is baffled to say why he could not come across him in the street as he can come across Richard Roe.

It is pertinent to our main subject to notice that, so long as the student of politics continues to think of the British Constitution as a counterpart to the other institutions, he will tend to describe it as a mysteriously occult institution; and so long as John Doe continues to think of the Average Taxpayer as a fellow-citizen, he will tend to think of him as an elusive insubstantial man, a ghost who is everywhere yet nowhere.

My destructive purpose is to show that a family of radical category-mistakes is the source of the double life theory. The representation of a person as a ghost mysteriously ensconced in a machine derives from this argument. Because, as is true, a person's thinking, feeling and purposive doing cannot be described solely in the idioms of physics, chemistry and physiology, therefore they must be described in counterpart idioms. As the human body is a complex organised unit, so the human mind must be another complex organised unit, though one made of a different sort of stuff and with a different sort of structure. Or, again, as the human body, like any other parcel of matter, is a field of causes and effects, so the mind must be another field of causes and effects, though not (Heaven be praised) mechanical causes and effects.

(3) The Origin of the Category-Mistake

One of the chief intellectual origins of what I have yet to prove to be the Cartesian category-mistake seems to be this. When Galileo showed that his methods of scientific discovery were competent to provide a mechanical theory which should cover every occupant of space, Descartes found in himself two conflicting motives. As a man of scientific genius he could not but endorse the claims of mechanics, yet as a religious and moral man he could not accept, as Hobbes accepted, the discouraging rider to those claims, namely that human nature differs only in degree of complexity from clockwork. The mental could not be just a variety of the mechanical.

He and subsequent philosophers naturally but erroneously availed themselves of the following escape-route. Since mental-conduct words are not to be construed as signifying the occurrence of mechanical processes, they must be construed as signifying the occurrence of nonmechanical processes; since mechanical laws explain movements in space as the effects of other movements in space, other laws must explain some of the nonspatial workings of minds as the effects of other non-spatial working of minds. The difference between the human behaviours which we describe as intelligent and those which we describe as unintelligent must be a difference in their causation; so, while some movements of human tongues and limbs are the effects of mechanical causes, others must be the effects of nonmechanical causes, i.e. some issue from movements of particles of matter, others from workings of the mind.

The differences between the physical and the

mental were thus represented as differences inside the common framework of the categories of "thing", "stuff", "attribute", "stage", "process", "change", "cause" and "effect". Minds are things, but different sorts of things from bodies; mental processes are causes and effects but different sorts of causes and effects from bodily movements. And so on. Somewhat as the foreigner expected the University to be an extra edifice, rather like a college but also considerably different, so the repudiators of mechanism represented minds as extra centers of causal processes, rather like machines but also considerably different from them. Their theory was a paramechanical hypothesis.

That this assumption was at the heart of the doctrine is shown by the fact that there was from the beginning felt to be a major theoretical difficulty in explaining how minds can influence and be influenced by bodies. How can a mental process, such as willing, cause spatial movements like the movements of the tongue? How can a physical change in the optic nerve have among its effects a mind's perception of a flash of light? This notorious crux by itself shows the logical mould into which Descartes pressed his theory of the mind. It was the self-same mould into which he and Galileo set their mechanics. Still unwittingly adhering to the grammar of mechanics, he tried to avert disaster by describing minds in what was merely an obverse vocabulary. The workings of minds had to be described by the mere negatives of the specific descriptions given to bodies; they are not in space, they are not motions, they are not modifications of matter, they are not accessible to public observation. Minds are not bits of clockwork, they are just bits of not-clockwork.

As thus represented, minds are not merely ghosts harnessed to machines, they are themselves just spectral machines. Though the human body is an engine, it is not quite an ordinary engine, since some of its workings are governed by another engine inside it—this interior governor-engine being one of a very special sort. It is invisible, inaudible and it has no size or weight. It cannot be taken to bits and the laws it obeys are not those known to ordinary engineers. Nothing is known of how it governs the bodily engine.

A second major crux points the same moral. Since, according to the doctrine, minds belong to the same category as bodies and since bodies are rigidly governed by mechanical laws, it seemed to many theorists to follow that minds must be similarly governed by rigid non-mechanical laws. The physical world is a deterministic system, so the mental world must be a deterministic system. Bodies cannot help the modifications that they undergo, so minds cannot help pursuing the careers fixed for them. *Responsibility, choice, merit* and *demerit* are therefore inapplicable concepts—unless the compromise solution is adopted of saying that the laws governing mental processes, unlike those governing physical processes, have the congenial attribute of being only rather rigid. The problem of the Freedom of the Will was the problem how to reconcile the hypothesis that minds are to be described in terms drawn from the categories of mechanics with the knowledge that higher-grade human conduct is not of a piece with the behavior of machines.

It is an historical curiosity that it was not noticed that the entire argument was broken-backed. Theorists correctly assumed that any sane man could already recognise the differences between, say, rational and non-rational utterances or between purposive and automatic behaviour. Else there would have been nothing requiring to be salved from mechanism. Yet the explanation given presupposed that one person could in principle never recognise the difference between the rational and the irrational utterances issuing from other human bodies, since he could never get access to the postulated immaterial causes of some of their utterances. Save for the doubtful exception of himself, he could never tell the difference between a man and a Robot. It would have to be conceded, for example, that, for all that we can tell, the inner lives of persons who are classed as idiots or lunatics are as rational as those of anyone else. Perhaps only their overt behaviour is disappointing; that is to say, perhaps "idiots" are not really idiotic, or "lunatics" lunatic. Perhaps, too, some of those who are classed as sane are really idiots. According to the theory, external observers could never know how the overt behaviour of others is correlated with their mental powers and processes and so they could never know or even plausibly conjuncture whether their applications of mental-conduct concepts to these other people were correct or incorrect. It would then be hazardous or impossible for a man to claim sanity or logical consistency even for himself, since he would be debarred from comparing his own performances with those of others. In short, our characterisations of persons and their performances as intelligent, prudent and virtuous or as stupid, hypocritical and cowardly could never have been made, so the problem of providing a special causal hypothesis to serve as the basis of such diagnoses would never have arisen. The question, "How do persons differ from machines?" arose just because everyone already knew how to apply mental-conduct concepts before the new causal hypothesis was introduced. This causal hypothesis could not therefore be the source of the criteria used in those applications. Nor, of course, has the causal hypothesis in any degree improved our handling of those criteria. We still distinguish good from bad arithmetic, politic from impolitic conduct and fertile from infertile imaginations in the ways in which Descartes himself distinguished them before and after he speculated how the applicability of these criteria

was compatible with the principle of mechanical causation.

He had mistaken the logic of his problem. Instead of asking by what criteria intelligent behaviour is actually distinguished from non-intelligent behaviour, he asked "Given that the principle of mechanical causation does not tell us the difference, what other causal principle will tell it us?" He realised that the problem was not one of mechanics and assumed that it must therefore be one of some counterpart to mechanics. Not unnaturally psychology is often cast for just this role.

When two terms belong to the same category, it is proper to construct conjunctive propositions embodying them. Thus a purchaser may say that he bought a left-hand glove and a right-hand glove, but not that he bought a left-hand glove, a right-hand glove and a pair of gloves. "She came home in a flood of tears and a sedan-chair" is a well-known joke based on the absurdity of conjoining terms of different types. It would have been equally ridiculous to construct the disjunction "She came home either in a flood of tears or else in a sedan-chair". Now the dogma of the Ghost in the Machine does just this. It maintains that there exist both bodies and minds; that there occur physical processes and mental processes; that there are mechanical causes of corporeal movements and mental causes of corporeal movements. I shall argue that these and other analogous conjunctions are absurd; but, it must be noticed, the argument will not show that either of the illegitimately conjoined propositions is absurd in itself. I am not, for example, denying that there occur mental processes. Doing long division is a mental process and so is making a joke. But I am saying that the phrase "there occur mental processes" does not mean the same sort of thing as "there occur physical processes", and, therefore, that it makes no sense to conjoin or disjoin the two.

345

If my argument is successful, there will follow some interesting consequences. First, the hallowed contrast between Mind and Matter will be dissipated, but dissipated not by either of the equally hallowed absorptions of Mind by Matter or of Matter by Mind, but in quite a different way. For the seeming contrast of the two will be shown to be as illegitimate as would be the contrast of "she came home in a flood of tears" and "she came home in a sedan-chair". The belief that there is a polar opposition between Mind and Matter is the belief that they are terms of the same logical type.

It will also follow that both Idealism and Materialism are answers to an improper question. The "reduction" of the material world to mental states and processes, as well as the "reduction" of mental states and processes to physical states and processes, presuppose the legitimacy of the disjunction "Either there exist minds or there exist bodies (but not both)". It would be like saying, "Either she bought a left-hand and a right-hand glove or she bought a pair of gloves (but not both)".

It is perfectly proper to say, in one logical tone of voice, that there exist minds and to say, in another logical tone of voice, that there exist bodies. But these expressions do not indicate two different species of existence, for "existence" is not a generic word like "coloured" or "sexed". They indicate two different senses of "exist", somewhat as "rising" has different senses in "the tide is rising", "hopes are rising", and "the average age of death is rising". A man would be thought to be making a poor joke who said that three things are now rising, namely the tide, hopes and the average age of death. It would be just as good or bad a joke to say that there exist prime numbers and Wednesdays and public opinions and navies; or that there exist both minds and bodies. . . .

(4) Historical Note

It would not be true to say that the official theory derives solely from Descartes's theories, or even from a more widespread anxiety about the implications of seventeenth century mechanics. Scholastic and Reformation theology had schooled the intellects of the scientists as well as of the laymen, philosophers and clerics of that age. Stoic-Augustinian theories of the will were embedded in the Calvinist doctrines of sin and grace; Platonic and Aristotelian theories of the intellect shaped the orthodox doctrines of the immortality of the soul. Descartes was reformulating already prevalent theological doctrines of the soul in the new syntax of Galileo. The theologian's privacy of conscience became the philosopher's privacy of consciousness, and what had been the bogy of Predestination reappeared as the bogy of Determinism.

It would also not be true to say that the two-worlds myth did no theoretical good. Myths often do a lot of theoretical good, while they are still one benefit bestowed by the para-mechanical myth was that it partly superannuated the then prevalent para-political myth. Minds and their Faculties had previously been described by analogies with political superiors and political subordinates. The idioms used were those of ruling, obeying, collaborating and rebelling. They survived and still survive in many ethical and some epistemological discussions. As, in physics, the new myth of occult Forces was a scientific improvement on the old myth of Final Causes, so, in anthropological and psychological theory, the new myth of hidden operations, impulses and agencies was an improvement on the old myth of dictations, deferrences and disobediences.

CHAPTER 35

RICHARD TAYLOR

HOW TO BURY THE MIND-BODY PROBLEM

Richard Taylor (1919–   ), professor of philosophy at the University of Roches-ter, is the author of several highly acclaimed books and articles, including the influential *Metaphysics* (1963). His original contribution to the debate on the free-dom of the will can be found in his *Action and Purpose* (1965). He is also the author of *Good and Evil* (1960), *Freedom, Anarchy, and the Law* (1973), and *With Heart and Mind* (1973).

Materialism is the monistic view that everything that exists is physical, or completely dependent on the physical for its existence. Against all forms of dual-ism, philosophical materialists maintain that there is only one basic kind of reality, the physical. Human beings, therefore, are not composites of material bodies and immaterial souls; they are fundamentally bodily in nature.

As a philosophical materialist, Richard Taylor believes there are no mind-body problems because there are no such things as minds in the first place![1] His strategy is not to deny the existence of minds—he believes that philosophical arguments are incapable of proving that something exists or does not exist. He merely denies the contention of "mentalism" that mind is best understood as immaterial soul, rather than as matter. In arguing for his position, Taylor realizes he shall have to convince his readers that there is no good reason to believe the "grand presupposition" of mentalism—namely, that matter cannot think. In good

[1]From Richard Taylor, "How to Bury the Mind-Body Problem," *American Philosophical Quarterly* 6 (April 1969): 136–43. Reprinted by permission.

dialectical fashion he presents four arguments for the mentalistic thesis, replying to each one. He concludes by returning to the question of how matter can think. Even if one admits that the idea of bodies thinking, imagining, and planning is baffling, he argues, it is no less baffling to imagine something other than body doing these things. Hence, materialism is at least as plausible as mentalism and has the virtue of being theoretically simpler.

HOW TO BURY THE MIND-BODY PROBLEM

The mind-body problem, in all its variants, is a philosophical fabrication resting on no genuine data at all. It has arisen from certain presuppositions about matter and human nature familiar to philosophy from the time of the Pythagoreans, presuppositions which have persisted just to the extent that they have been left unexamined. And they have not been questioned very much simply because they are so familiar.

There are vexing, unsolved problems of psychology and problems of mental health, but there are no mind-body problems. And there are problems of "philosophical psychology," as they are sometimes called today—problems of perception, sensation, the analysis of deliberation, of purposeful behavior, and so on—but there are no mind-body problems.

The reason why there are no mind-body problems is the most straightforward imaginable: It is because there are no such things as *minds* in the first place. There being no minds, there are in strictness no mental states or events; there are only certain familiar states, capacities, and abilities which are conventionally but misleadingly called "mental." They are so-called, partly in deference to certain philosophical presuppositions, and partly as a reflection of our lack of understanding of them, that is of our ignorance.

Men and women are not minds, nor do they "have" minds. It is not merely that they do not "have" minds the way they have arms and legs; they do not have minds in any proper sense at all. And just as no man or woman has or ever has had any mind, so also are cats, dogs, frogs, vegetables, and the rest of living creation without minds—though philosophers of the highest rank, such as Aristotle, have felt driven to say that all living things, vegetables included, must have souls (else how could they be *living* things?) just as others of similar eminence, like Descartes, have thought that men must have minds, else how could they be *thinking* things? Today, when philosophers talk about mind-body problems, and advance various claims concerning the possible relationships between "mental" and "physical" states and events, they are, of course, talking about men. But they might as well be talking about frogs, because the presuppositions that give rise to these theories apply to other animals as well as to men.

I. Philosophical Arguments for the Existence or Nonexistence of Things

There cannot be any philosophical argument proving that something does or does not exist, so long as the description or definition of it is self-consistent. Thus there cannot be a philosophical argument proving that men do or do not, as some medieval thinkers believed, have an indestructible bone in their bodies. One can only say that such a bone has never been found (which is not a philosophical argument) and then exhibit the groundlessness or falsity of the presuppositions that gave rise to the belief in the first place. (In this case it was certain presuppositions concerning the requirements of the resurrection of the body.) Similarly, there can be no philosophical argument proving that men do or do not have souls, spirits, or minds, or that there are not *sui generis* mental states or events, assuming that these can be described in a self-consistent way. One can only note that such things have never been found in any man, living or dead, and then exhibit the arbitrariness and apparent falsity of the presuppositions that give rise to these opinions in the first place. Now of course, as far as *finding* them goes, many philosophers claim to find them all the time, *within themselves.* They are alleged to be *private* things, deeply hidden, discernible only by their possessors. All they really "find," however, are the most commonplace facts about themselves that are perfectly well known to anyone who knows anything at all—but of this, more later.

II. The Grand Presupposition of the Mind-Body Problem

What I must do now, then, is consider the presupposition that has given birth to the so-called "mind-body" problem, and show that there is nothing in it at all that anyone needs to believe; that, on the contrary, we have good evidence that it is false.

The presupposition can be tersely expressed by saying: *Matter cannot think.* That is the way a Cartesian would put it, but philosophers now spell it out a little better. Thus, we are apt to be told that thinking, choosing, deliberating, reasoning, perceiving, and even feeling, are not concepts of physics and chemistry, so that these terms have no application to bodies. Since, however, men do think, choose, deliberate, reason, perceive and feel, it follows that men are not "mere bodies." They are instead minds or souls or, as it is more common to say today "selves" or "persons," and such terms as "is thinking," "is choosing," "is perceiving," etc., are not physical or bodily but *personal* predications. A man may be in one clear sense a physical object, having arms and legs and so on, but a person is not just that visible and palpable object; there is more to a self or person than this. For it is the self or person that thinks, chooses, deliberates, feels, and so on, and not his body or some part of it.

Again—and this is really only another way of expressing the same presupposition—we are apt to be told that thoughts, choices, reasons, feelings, etc., are not physical things. It makes no sense to ask how large a thought is, whether it is soluble in alcohol, and so on. Yet these things do exist—any man can be aware of them, "within himself." Hence, that "self" within which such things occur must be something more than or other than the body. It might be just the totality of all those nonphysical ("mental") things, but in any case it is mental in nature, so a self or person is not the same thing as his body.

Or again, in case one boggles at calling thoughts, feelings, and the like, "things," at least (it is said) no one can deny that they are events or states. But they are not events or states that occur or obtain in the laboratories of physicists and chemists—except in the sense that they sometimes occur in physicists and chemists themselves, who sometimes happen to be in laboratories. No one could ever truly represent whatever might be happening in a test tube or vacuum tube as the transpiring of a thought or feeling. These things just do not—indeed, obviously could not—happen in test tubes or vacuum tubes, because they are not the *kind* of event involving changes of matter. They are a kind of "mental" event. And since these things do, obviously, happen in men, then things happen in men which are nonphysical, "mental," in nature. . . .

III. "Selves" or "Persons" as Minds and Bodies

The word "self" and the plural "selves" are fairly common items of contemporary philosophical vocabulary. These words never occur outside of philosophy, except as suffixes to personal pronouns, but in philosophical contexts they are sometimes taken to denote rather extraordinary things. Selves are, indeed, about the strangest inhabitants of nature that one can imagine—except that, as sometimes described in philosophy, they are not even imaginable in the first place, being quite nonphysical. You cannot poke a self with a stick; the nearest you can come to that is to poke his body. The self that has that body is not supposed to be quite the same thing as his body—that is a (mere) physical object, a possible subject matter for physics and chemistry. *That* is not what thinks, reasons, deliberates, and so on; it is the self that does things like this.

At the same time, selves are never doubted to be the same things as *persons*, and persons are thought to be the same things as people, as men. And there is no doubt at all that men are visible, palpable objects, having arms and legs and so on: That they are in short, physical objects. So the thing becomes highly ambiguous. We do not, in contexts in which it would seem silly or embarrassing to do so, have to say that selves (men) are spirit beings (minds) which in some sense or other happen to "have" bodies. Clearly men are visible and palpable things, that is, are bodies. We can say that all right. But at the same time we need not say—indeed, *must* not say—that men are just (mere) bodies. There is, after all, a difference between a man's body, and that which thinks, perceives, feels, deliberates, and so on; and those are things that men (selves) do, not things that bodies do. Or again, there is, after all, a difference between bodily predicates (weighs 160 pounds, falls, is warm, etc.) and personal predicates (chooses, believes, loves his country, etc.). The former can be predicated of a man's body, just like any other body, but it would "make no sense" to predicate the latter of any (mere) body, and hence of any man's body. They are only predicated of persons. So even though selves are persons and persons are men and men are visible, palpable beings, we must not think that they are just nothing but physical beings. They are physical bodies with minds, or, as some would prefer, minds with physical bodies or, as most writers on this subject want to say, they are somehow *both*.

So the "mental" is discriminated from the (merely) "physical," and the mind-body problem emerges at once: What is the *connection* between them? What is the relationship between men's minds and their bodies? Or between mental and physical events? Or between personal and physical predicates? Anyone who raises this question—for these all amount to one and the same question—can see at once that it is going to be extremely difficult to answer. And this means that it is capable of nourishing a vast amount of philosophy. It has, in fact, kept philosophers on scattered continents busy for hundreds of years, and even today claims much of the time of philosophical faculties and their proteges. It seems a conceit to undertake to put an end to all this, but that is what I propose now to do.

IV. Mentalism and Materialism

Consider the following two theses:

(I) A person is not something that has, possesses, utilizes, or contains a mind. That is, a person is not one thing and his mind another thing. A person or self and his mind are one and the same thing.

(II) A person is not something that has, possesses, utilizes, or occupies a body. That is, a person is not one thing and his body another thing. A person or self and his body are one and the same thing.

We can call these two theses "mentalism" and "materialism" respectively, since the first asserts that men are minds and not bodies, and the second that they are bodies and not minds.

Now the first thing to note about these two rather crudely stated theses is that both of them cannot be true, since each asserts what the other denies. They could, of course, both be false, since a person might be identical neither with his body nor with his mind (though it is hard to think of any other candidate for the title of "person"), or a person might somehow be identical with the two of them at once. These two simple theses are, nevertheless, a good starting point for discussion, and I am going to maintain that (II), the materialist thesis, is absolutely true.

Philosophers have tended to regard (I), or some more sophisticated version of it, as correct, and to dismiss (II) as unworthy of consideration. In fact, however—and it is hard to see how this could have been so generally overlooked—*any* philosophical argument in favor of (I) against (II) is just as good an argument for (II) against (I). This I shall illustrate shortly.

In the meantime, let us give what is due to the humble fact that there are considerations drawn from common sense, indeed from the common knowledge of mankind, which favor, without proving, (II). It is common knowledge that there are such things as human bodies, that there are men and women in the world. There is also one such body which everyone customarily, and without the least suggestion of absurdity, refers to as himself; he sees himself in the mirror, dresses himself, scratches himself, and so on. This is known, absolutely as well as anything can be known, and if any man were to profess doubt about it—if he doubted, for example, that there are such physical objects in the world as men and women, and therefore doubted the reality of his own body—then that man would have to be considered *totally* ignorant. For there is nothing more obvious than this. A man would be ignorant indeed if he did not know that there are such things as the sun, moon, earth, rivers, and lakes. I have never met anyone so ignorant as that. But a man who did not even know that there are men and women in the world, and that he—his body—was one of them, would be totally ignorant.

Now there is no such common knowledge of the existence of minds or souls. No one has ever found such a thing anywhere. Belief in such things rests either on religious persuasion or on philosophical arguments, sometimes on nothing but the connotations of familiar words. Such beliefs are opinions, easily doubted, and nothing that anyone knows. If a man denies that such things exist, as many have, then he exhibits no ignorance; he expresses only scepticism or doubt concerning certain religious or philosophical presuppositions or arguments.

If, accordingly, we are seeking some sort of thing with which to identify persons, then this is a *prima facie* consideration in favor of identifying them with their bodies, with things we know to be real, rather than with things postulated to suit the requirements of philosophical arguments or religious faith. This does not prove that men are nothing but bodies, of course, but it is enough to show that, since we know there are such things as persons, and we know there are such things as men (living human bodies), we had better regard these as the very same things *unless* there are some facts which would prohibit our doing so. And I shall maintain that there are no such facts. There are only philosophical arguments, not one of which proves anything.

THE ARGUMENTS FOR MENTALISM

I shall now consider the arguments I know, already adumbrated, in favor of what I have called mentalism. Of course not all philosophers who take seriously the mind-body problem subscribe to this simple thesis as I have formulated it, but the more sophisticated versions can be considered as we go along, and it will be seen that the arguments for these are equally inconclusive.

The First Argument

There are certain predicates that undoubtedly apply to persons, but not to their bodies. Persons and their bodies cannot, therefore, be the same. One can sometimes truly say of a person, for example, that he is intelligent, sentimental, that he loves his country, believes in God, holds strange theories on the doctrine of universals, and so on. But it would sound very odd—indeed, not even make sense—to assert any such things of any physical object whatever and hence of any man's body. It would at best be a confusion of categories to say that a certain man's *body* loves its country, for example.

Reply

If the foregoing is considered a good argument for the nonidentity of persons and bodies, then the following is obviously just as good an argument for not identifying them with their

minds: There are certain predicates that undoubtedly apply to persons, but not to their minds. A person and his mind cannot, therefore, be the same. One can sometimes truly say of a person, for example, that he is walking, ran into a post, is feverish, or that he fell down. But it would sound very odd—indeed not even make sense—to assert such things of any mind whatever. It would at best be a confusion of categories to say, for instance, that a certain man's *mind* ran into a post.

Considerations such as these have led many philosophers to affirm that a person or the "true self" is neither a mind, nor a body. Hence, a person must be either (*a*) something else altogether or, as some would prefer to say, the term "person" must express a "primitive" concept or (*b*) both mind and body; i.e., a person must be something having both mental and physical properties.

The former of these alternatives is simply evasive. Persons are real beings, so there must be existing things which are persons. If when we bump into a man we are not bumping into a person, and if at the same time we are not referring to a person when we say of someone that he is thinking, then it is quite impossible to see what is left to fill the role of a person. The word "person" may indeed be a primitive one, but this, I think, only means that such arguments as the two just cited are equally good and equally bad.

The second alternative that persons are beings having both mental and physical properties, is obviously only as good as the claim that there are such things as "mental properties" to begin with. Indeed, it is not even that good, for just as a physical property can be nothing but a property of a physical thing, i.e., a body, so also a mental property can be nothing but the property of a mental thing, i.e., a mind. For something to count as a physical property of something it is sufficient, and necessary, that the thing in question is a physical object. By the same token, for something to count as a mental property it is sufficient, and necessary, that it be the property that some mind possesses. Any property whatsoever that can be truly claimed to be the property of some body, animate or inanimate, is a physical property; the assertion that some body possesses a nonphysical property is simply a contradiction. This second alternative, that persons are beings possessing both physical and mental properties, therefore amounts to saying that a person is at one and the same time *two* utterly different things—a body with its physical properties and a mind with its mental properties. These are not supposed to be two things in the same sense that a family, for instance, is a plurality of beings consisting of husband, wife, and perhaps one or more children, but two wholly disparate kinds of beings having, as Descartes put it, nothing in common. Now this is no resolution of the antithesis between what I have called mentalism and materialism. It is only a reformulation of that issue. For now we can surely ask: Which of these two is the person, the true self? The body which has a mind, or the mind which has a body? And we are then back where we started.

The Second Argument

This argument consists of pointing out the rather remarkable things that a person can do but which, it is alleged, no physical object, of whatever complexity, can do, from which it of course follows that a person is not a physical object and hence not identical with his own body. A person, for example, can reason, deliberate about ends and means, plan for the future, draw inferences from evidence, speculate, and so on. No physical objects do such things, and even complicated machines can at best only simulate these activities. Indeed, it would not even make sense to say that a man's body was, for example, speculating on the outcome of an election, though this would not be an absurd description of some person. A

person, therefore, is not the same thing as his body, and can only be described in terms of certain concepts of mind.

Reply

This argument is not very different from the first; it only substitutes activities for properties which are baptized "mental." And one reply to it is the same as to the first argument; namely, that since persons often do things that no mind could do—for instance, they run races, go fishing, raise families, and so on—then it follows that persons are not minds.

A far better reply, however, and one that is not so question-begging as it looks, is to note that since men do reason, deliberate, plan, speculate, draw inferences, run races, go fishing, raise families, and so on, and since the men that do all such things are the visible, palpable beings that we see around us all the time, then it follows that *some* physical objects—namely, men—do all these things. All are, accordingly, the activities of physical objects; they are not activities divided between a physical object, the visible man, on the one hand, and some invisible thing, his mind, on the other.

Consider the statement: "I saw George yesterday; he was trying to figure out the best way to get from Albany to Montpelier." Now this statement obviously refers, in a normal context, to a person, and it is perfectly clear that the name "George" and the pronoun "he" refer to *one and the same* being, that person. And what they both refer to is something that was seen, a certain man's body; they do not refer to some unseen thing, of which that body is some sort of visible manifestation. If that were so, then the statement would not really be true. And in any case, it would be embarrassingly silly to suppose that a more accurate rendition of the thought expressed in this statement might be: "I saw George's body yesterday. His mind was trying to figure out how to get (how to get what?) from Albany to Montpelier." It is, accordingly, one and the same thing which (a) is seen, and (b) figures and plans, and that thing is undoubtedly the physical object George. Now if conventions incline us to describe figuring out something as a "mental" activity, then we shall have to say that some purely physical objects—namely, living men—engage in mental activities. But this is simply misleading, if not contradictory, for it suggests that we are ascribing to a physical object an activity of something that is not physical, but mental. It would, therefore, be far better to say that some physical objects, namely, men or persons, sometimes perform physical activities such as figuring and planning which are quite unlike those we are accustomed to finding in certain other physical objects such as machines and the like.

The Third Argument

This argument, the commonest of all, is to the effect that while there may or may not be such things as "minds" (whatever that might mean), there are indisputably certain nonphysical things which are quite properly called "mental," as anyone can verify within himself. Indeed, it is sometimes claimed that nothing, not even the reality of our own bodies, is as certain as the existence of these mental things, which are perceived "directly."

Reply

What are here referred to as mental entities are, of course, such things as thoughts, mental images, after-images, sensations, feelings, and so on. Pains are frequently mentioned in this context, being, presumably, things whose existence no one would question. Having got to this point then the next step, of course, is to speculate on the connection between these mental things and certain "physical" states of the body. They evidently are not the same, and yet it is hard to see

what the connection could be. Speculation also extends to such questions as whether two or more men might have "the same" pain, or why it is impossible that they should, in view of the fact that they can hold common possession of ordinary "physical" things like clocks and books. Again, curiosity is aroused by the fact that a mental image, for instance, seems to have color, and yet it somehow can be perceived only by one person, its owner. Again, images sometimes seem to have shape—enough so that a perceiver can distinguish one from another, for instance—and yet no assignable size. Here, really, is a gold mine for philosophical speculation, and such speculations have filled, as they still fill, volumes.

Now surely there is a *better* way to express all that is known to be true in all this, and it is a way that does not even permit these odd theories to get started. What we know is true, and all we know is true, is that men think, sense, imagine, feel, etc. It is sheer redundancy to say that men think things called "thoughts," sense things called "sensations," imagine "images," and feel "feelings." There are no such things. And to say there are no such things is *not* to deny that men think, sense, imagine, and feel.

What, for instance, does it mean to say a man feels a pain in his foot? Absolutely nothing, except that his foot hurts. But this hurting, what sort of thing is it? It is not a thing at all; not a thing felt, and certainly not a mental thing that is felt *in his foot*. It is a state, and in no sense a state of his mind, but a straightforward state of his foot. But can that be a *physical* state? Well, it is assuredly a state of his foot, and that is a physical object; there is nothing else—no spirit foot, no spirit being, no spirit mind—that it can be a state of. Why, then, cannot other people have that same state? Why cannot other people feel the same pain I feel in my foot? And if it is a physical state, why cannot we open the foot and *see* it there? Or make some straightforward test of its presence in another man's foot?

To ask questions like these is just not to understand what is meant by describing an object as being in a certain state. Consider a piece of molten lead. Now this molten state, what sort of thing is it? The answer is that it is not a thing at all; it is a state or condition of a thing. Is it a physical state? Well, it is a state of the lead, and that is a physical object; there is nothing else for it to be a state of. Why, then, cannot another piece of lead have that same state? Why cannot something else have the molten state of this piece of lead? Of course something else can, in the only meaningful sense that can be attached to such a question; that is, another piece of lead, or some things which are not lead can melt the same way this piece of lead melted. To ask why another piece of lead cannot have the molten state of this piece of lead is, of course, unintelligible, unless it is interpreted the way just suggested, in which case the answer is that it can. But similarly, to ask why another man cannot have the pain that this man is feeling is also unintelligible, unless construed as the question why other men cannot suffer pain, in which case its presupposition is wrong—they can. And if the piece of lead's being melted is a "physical" state, why can we not separate the lead into drops and see that state? Simply because it is a state of the lead, and not some other thing contained in the lead. Indeed, to separate it into drops *is* to see, not its meltedness (there is no such thing), but that it is melted—that is just the test. We do not have to *ask* the lead whether it is melted, and rely upon its testimony; we can tell by its behavior. And in the same way we can sometimes—admittedly not always—see that a man is suffering, without having to ask him. That we sometimes go wrong here does not result from the fact that

his suffering is something quite hidden within him, which he alone can find and then report; there is nothing hidden, and nothing for him to find. Still, there is a straightforward way of testing whether a piece of lead is melted, and there is no similarly straightforward way of testing whether a man's foot hurts—he may only be pretending it does. Does this indicate that there might be a pain, which he has found in his foot but might conceal, as he might conceal the contents of his wallet? Surely not; it shows only that men, unlike pieces of lead, are capable of dissimulating. No philosophy was needed to unearth that commonplace fact. It is easier to test for the presence of some states of properties than others, and this is true not only of the states of men's bodies, but of everything under the sun. But things that are hard to establish do not, just by virtue of that, warrant the title of "mental."

Similar remarks can be made about images, which are frequent candidates for the role of mental entities. When queried about their mental imagery, people often will describe it in colorful detail and even with pride, not unlike the regard one might have for a precious gem accessible only to himself. It turns out, though, that all one thereby describes is his power of imagination, which is, of course, sometimes quite great. To say that one has a lively imagination, even great powers of imagination, does not mean that he can create within his mind . . . things called "images" and composed of some mental, nonphysical, spiritual material. There is no material that is nonmaterial, and there are no images composed of this or anything else—except, of course, those physical objects (pictures, etc.) visible to anyone who can see, which are rightly called images of things. When someone *sees* something, there is (*i*) the man who sees, and (*ii*) the thing seen; for instance, some building or scene. There is not, between these, a third thing called the appearance of what is seen; philosophers are pretty much agreed on this. But similarly, when someone *imagines* something or, as it is misleadingly put, "forms an image" of it, there is (*i*) the man who imagines, and (*ii*) sometimes, but not always, something that he imagines; for instance, some building or scene, which might or might not be real. There is not, between these, a third thing called the image of what is imagined. There is just the imagining of the thing in question. And to say that a man is imagining something is to say what he is doing, or perhaps to refer to some state he is in; it is not to refer to some inner thing that he creates and, while it lasts, exclusively possesses.

It is enough, it seems to me, to point this out; that is, to point out that we can say all we want to say about men's powers of imagination without ever introducing the substantive "an image." Philosophy is robbed of nothing by the disposal of these, and there is absolutely no fact about human nature which requires us to affirm their existence. But if one does insist upon the reality of mental images, and professes, for instance, to find them right in his own mind by introspecting—and it is astonishing how eager students of philosophy seem to be to make this claim—then we can ask some very embarrassing questions. Suppose, for instance, one professes to be able to form a very clear image of, say, the campus library—he can bring it before his mind, hold it there, perhaps even turn it bottom side up, and banish it at will. We ask him, then, to hold it before his mind and count the number of steps in the image, the number of windows, the number and disposition of pigeons on the roof, and so on. He could do these things if he had a photograph of the thing before him. But he cannot do them with the image, in spite of the fact that it is supposed to be right there "before his mind," easily and "directly" inspectable. He can tell how many steps there are only if he has sometime counted

the steps on the building itself (or in a photograph of it) and now *remembers*—but that is not counting the steps in the image. Or he can *imagine* that it has, say, 30 steps, and then *say* "30"—but that is not counting anything either; it is only a performance. The image he professes to "have" there, so clearly and with such detail, does not even exist. He claims to have produced in his mind an image of the library; but all he has actually done is imagine the library.

What, then, is imagining something? Is it an activity, a state, or what? It does not really matter here how we answer that; it is only *not* the producing of an entity called a "mental image." Let us suppose for this context, then, that to be imagining something is to be in a certain *state.* Is it, then, a *physical* state? Well, it is a state of a man, just as drunkenness, sleep, perspiration, obesity, etc., are sometimes states of this man or that. What is meant by asking whether these are "physical" states, other than asking whether they are states of a physical object? What shall we say of being in a state of sleep, for instance? It is the state of a man, and a man is a physical—that is, a visible and palpable—being. You cannot poke a man's state of imagining something with a stick; all you can do is poke him. That is true. But you cannot poke his somnolence with a stick either. There is nothing to poke; there is only the man sleeping, or the man imagining, or the man becoming drunk, or whatever.

How then can a man, if he is nothing but a (mere) physical object, be in such a state as this, that is, of imagining something? If he is only a body and can do this, why cannot sticks and stones be in such a state, for are they not bodies too? The answer is: For just the same reason that sticks and stones cannot be drunken, asleep, perspiring, obese, or hungry; namely, that they are sticks and stones and not men. The reason is not that they lack minds. Even if they had them, they still could not be drunken, asleep, perspiring, obese or hungry, for they would still be sticks and stones and not men.

The Fourth (and last) Argument

It is fairly common for people, including philosophers, to say that they can perfectly well imagine surviving the death of their bodies, which would be quite impossible for anyone who supposed that he and his body were one and the same thing. Admittedly no one knows whether there is any survival of death, but it is at least not necessarily false. The doctrine of metempsychosis,[1] for example, though there may be no reason for believing it, cannot be shown to be impossible just on philosophical grounds. It would be impossible, however, if a person and his body were identical, and so would any other form of survival. We know the fate of the body: dust. If I am the same as my body, then it is logically impossible that I should not share that fate.

Reply

All this argument shows is that not everyone, perhaps even no one, *knows* that he and his body are one and the same thing. It does not in the least show that, in fact, they are not. Some things, like the Evening Star and the Morning Star, which some are accustomed to thinking of and describing as different things, nevertheless do turn out to be the same.

Suppose a god were to promise me a life after death—promising, perhaps, to have me (the very person that I am) reborn elsewhere with a different body. Now such a promise might quicken a real hope in me, provided I am capable (as everyone is) of thinking of myself as being something different from my body. But the fact that I can think such a distinction does not show that there is one, and in case there is not—in case I happen to be identical with my body—then of course no god could fulfill such a promise. Con-

sider this analogy: If an enemy of our country did not know that Albany is (the same thing as) the capital of New York, then he might be very interested in a proposal to bomb the one but to spare the other. It would nevertheless be a proposal that no one could carry out. The fact that someone who is ignorant of this identity can entertain the possibility of its being carried out does not show that it is possible; it shows only that he does not know that it is not.

V. The Soul as Life and the Soul as Thought

It is useful in concluding, I think, to compare the philosophical conception of the mind with what was once the philosophical conception of life. It was once pretty much taken for granted that men and other animals *possess* something which inanimate things lack, namely, life, and that it is *because* they possess this that they can do all sorts of things that inanimate things cannot do, such as move themselves, assimilate nourishment, reproduce their kind, and so on. Aristotle classified the souls of living things according to the abilities they imparted to their owners, and thought that even vegetables had souls. Indeed, an animal's *life* and *soul* were generally thought to be one and the same thing. The very word "animal" has its origin in this belief. Socrates, according to Plato, was even able to convince himself of his own immortality on the basis of this notion for, he thought, if it is only because he has a life or soul to begin with that he is a living man, then it is idle to fear the death of that very soul. Life seemed to him identical with his soul, but accidental to his body, indeed even foreign to such a thing of clay. A similar model was at work in Descartes' philosophy when he declared that the soul could never stop thinking. Thought seemed to him identical

---

[1]The passing of the soul at death into another body. [ED.]

with his soul, but positively foreign to his body.

Now of course we still talk of life that way, but we no longer take such common modes of speech as descriptive of any reality. We speak of a man "losing" his life, of a man "taking" another's life, of the "gift" of life, and even of the "breath" of life which God is supposed to infuse into an otherwise *lifeless* body. But these are plainly metaphors. No one supposes that a man or animal moves, assimilates nourishment, reproduces, and so on *because* it is possessed of life. We no longer think of life as something added to an animal body, some separable thing that quickens matter. To distinguish something as a living animal is only to call attention to the very complicated way the matter of its body is organized and to a large class of capacities which result from such organization. A living body is simply one in which certain processes, some of them frightfully complex and ill understood, take place. A living body, in short, differs from a nonliving one, not in what it possesses, but in what it does, and these are facts about it that can be verified in a straightforward way.

I have been urging a similar way of speaking of the mind; not as something mysteriously *embodied* here and there, and something that is supposed to *account* for the more or less intelligent thought and action differs from one lacking such capacities, not in something it possesses, but precisely in what it does. And this, incidentally, explains why a man tends to regard it as a deep insult to be told that he has no mind. It is not because he is thus divested in our eyes of some possession dearly prized, but rather, because such a remark is quite rightly taken to mean that he lacks certain important and distinctively human abilities and capacities. If a man is assured that his possession of certain more or less intellectual abilities is in no way in question, he feels divested of nothing upon learning that among his parts or possessions there is none that is properly denoted "a mind."

VI. Does Matter Think?

Probably every philosopher has felt more or less acutely at one time or another a profound puzzlement in the idea of (mere) matter doing those various things rightly ascribable only to persons. How, it is wondered, can a body think, deliberate, imagine things, figure and plan, and so on?

This is really no proper source of bafflement, however. No one can say, *a priori*, what the highly organized material systems of one's body are or are not capable of. It was once thought incredible that matter, unquickened by any soul, could be alive, for matter seemed to inquirers to be inert or lifeless by its very nature. Yet we see around us all the time specimens of living matter—in the merest insects, for instance—so philosophical prejudice has had to yield to the fact. Similarly, I submit, we see around us all the time specimens of thinking matter; that is, material beings which deliberate, imagine, plan, and so on. For men do in fact do these things, and when we see a man, we are seeing a material being—a dreadfully complex and highly organized one, to be sure, but no less a visible and palpable object for that. In any case, the seeming mystery or incredibility that may attach to the idea of matter exercising intellectual capacities is hardly dissolved by postulating something *else* to exercise those capacities. If there is a difficulty in comprehending how a body can do such things, there is surely no less difficulty in seeing how something which is not a body can do them any better.

CHAPTER 36

JOHN SEARLE

MINDS, BRAINS, AND PROGRAMS

John Searle (1932–   ) is a professor of philosophy at the University of California, Berkeley. The proponent of "speech-act theory" in the philosophy of language, he has recently become involved in the debate over artificial intelligence. Among Searle's many published works are *Speech Acts* (1969), *The Philosophy of Language* (1971), and *Minds, Brains and Science* (1984).

In the selection that follows, Searle responded to the claim that certain mental properties can be attributed to computers on the basis of what they can do.[1] Searle contends that if we examine the way computers work, we will see that this claim is nonsense. Digital computers are capable of performing only formal operations on symbols; these are insufficient to produce a mental state or process. Although computers may be programmed to perform certain tasks as well as humans, they do not employ the mental properties of understanding or intentionality that humans typically use to accomplish these tasks. Searle's argument is built around his famous "Chinese room" thought experiment, wherein he imagines himself locked in a room following mechanical rules that, unknown to him, result in his writing suitable Chinese answers to Chinese questions, even though he does not know a word of Chinese. In this case, Searle argues, his ability to write out suitable Chinese answers would not mean that he understood Chinese. Similarly,

---

[1]From "Minds, Brains, and Programs," in *The Behavioral and Brain Sciences* vol. 3.(New York: Cambridge University Press, 1980). Reprinted with the permission of Cambridge University Press.

it is a mistake to attribute mental properties to computers on the basis of the operations they perform. What distinguishes humans from computers must be certain nonformal properties, to which the computer in principle has no access.

MINDS, BRAINS, AND PROGRAMS

What psychological and philosophical significance should we attach to recent efforts at computer simulations of human cognitive capacities? In answering this question, I find it useful to distinguish what I will call "strong" AI from "weak" or "cautious" AI (Artificial Intelligence). According to weak AI, the principal value of the computer in the study of the mind is that it gives us a very powerful tool. For example, it enables us to formulate and test hypotheses in a more rigorous and precise fashion. But according to strong AI, the computer is not merely a tool in the study of the mind; rather, the appropriately programmed computer really *is* a mind, in the sense that computers given the right programs can be literally said to *understand* and have other cognitive states. In strong AI, because the programmed computer has cognitive states, the programs are not mere tools that enable us to test psychological explanations; rather, the programs are themselves the explanations.

I have no objection to the claims of weak AI, at least as far as this article is concerned. My discussion here will be directed at the claims I have defined as those of strong AI, specifically the claim that the appropriately programmed computer literally has cognitive states and that the programs thereby explain human cognition. When I hereafter refer to AI, I have in mind the strong version, as expressed by these two claims.

I will consider the work of Roger Schank and his colleagues at Yale, because I am more familiar with it than I am with any other similar claims,

and because it provides a very clear example of the sort of work I wish to examine. But nothing that follows depends upon the details of Schank's programs. The same arguments would apply to Winograd's SHRDLU, Weizenbaum's ELIZA, and indeed any **Turing machine** simulation of human mental phenomena.

Very briefly, and leaving out the various details, one can describe Schank's program as follows: the aim of the program is to simulate the human ability to understand stories. It is characteristic of human beings' story-understanding capacity that they can answer questions about the story even though the information that they give was never explicitly stated in the story. Thus, for example, suppose you are given the following story: "A man went into a restaurant and ordered a hamburger. When the hamburger arrived it was burned to a crisp, and the man stormed out of the restaurant angrily, without paying for the hamburger or leaving a tip." Now, if you are asked "Did the man eat the hamburger?" you will presumably answer, "No, he did not." Similarly, if you are given the following story: "A man went into a restaurant and ordered a hamburger; when the hamburger came he was very pleased with it; and as he left the restaurant he gave the waitress a large tip before paying his bill," and you are asked the question, "Did the man eat the hamburger?," you will presumably answer, "Yes, he ate the hamburger." Now Schank's machines can similarly answer questions about restaurants in this fashion. To do this, they have a "representation" of the sort of information that human beings have about restaurants, which enables them to answer such questions as those above, given these sorts of stories. When the machine is given the story and then asked the question, the machine will print out answers of the sort that we would expect human beings to give if told similar stories. Partisans of strong AI claim that in this question and answer sequence the machine is not only simulating a human ability but also

1. that the machine can literally be said to *understand* the story and provide the answers to questions, and

2. that what the machine and its program do *explains* the human ability to understand the story and answer questions about it.

Both claims seem to me to be totally unsupported by Schank's[1] work, as I will attempt to show in what follows.

One way to test any theory of the mind is to ask oneself what it would be like if my mind actually worked on the principles that the theory says all minds work on. Let us apply this test to the Schank program with the following *Gedankenexperiment*. Suppose that I'm locked in a room and given a large batch of Chinese writing. Suppose furthermore (as is indeed the case) that I know no Chinese, either written or spoken, and that I'm not even confident that I could recognize Chinese writing as Chinese writing distinct from, say, Japanese writing or meaningless squiggles. To me, Chinese writing is just so many meaningless squiggles. Now suppose further that after this first batch of Chinese writing I am given a second batch of Chinese script together with a set of rules for correlating the second batch with the first batch. The rules are in English, and I understand these rules as well as any other native speaker of English. They enable me to correlate one set of formal symbols with another set of formal symbols, and all that "formal" means here is that I can identify the symbols entirely by their shapes. Now suppose also that I am given a third

batch of Chinese symbols together with some instructions, again in English, that enable me to correlate elements of this third batch with the first two batches, and these rules instruct me how to give back certain Chinese symbols with certain sorts of shapes in response to certain sorts of shapes given me in the third batch. Unknown to me, the people who are giving me all of these symbols call the first batch "a script," they call the second batch a "story," and they call the third batch "questions." Furthermore, they call the symbols I give them back in response to the third batch "answers to the questions," and the set of rules in English that they gave me, they call "the program." Now just to complicate the story a little, imagine that these people also give me stories in English, which I understand, and they then ask me questions in English about these stories, and I give them back answers in English. Suppose also that after a while I get so good at following the instructions for manipulating the Chinese symbols and the programmers get so good at writing the programs that from the external point of view—that is, from the point of view of somebody outside the room in which I am locked—my answers to the questions are absolutely indistinguishable from those of native Chinese speakers. Nobody just looking at my answers can tell that I don't speak a word of Chinese. Let us also suppose that my answers to the English questions are, as they no doubt would be, indistinguishable from those of other native English speakers, for the simple reason that I am a native English speaker. From the external point of view—from the point of view of someone reading my "answers"—the answers to the Chinese questions and the English questions are equally good. But in the Chinese case, unlike the English case, I produce the answers by manipulating uninterpreted formal symbols. As far as the Chinese is concerned, I simply behave like a computer; I perform computational operations on formally specified elements. For the purposes of the Chinese, I am simply an instantiation of the computer program.

Now the claims made by strong AI are that the programmed computer understands the stories and that the program in some sense explains human understanding. But we are now in a position to examine these claims in light of our thought experiment.

1. As regards the first claim, it seems to me quite obvious in the example that I do not understand a word of the Chinese stories. I have inputs and outputs that are indistinguishable from those of the native Chinese speaker, and I can have any formal program you like, but I still understand nothing. For the same reasons, Schank's computer understands nothing of any stories, whether in Chinese, English, or whatever, since in the Chinese case the computer is me, and in cases where the computer is not me, the computer has nothing more than I have in the case where I understand nothing.

2. As regards the second claim, that the program explains human understanding, we can see that the computer and its program do not provide sufficient conditions of understanding since the computer and the program are functioning, and there is no understanding. But does it even provide a necessary condition or a significant contribution to understanding? One of the claims made by the supporters of strong AI is that when I understand a story in English, what I am doing is exactly the same—or perhaps more of the same—as what I was doing in manipulating the Chinese symbols. It is simply more formal symbol manipulation that distinguishes the case in English, where I do understand, from the case in Chinese, where I don't. I have not demonstrated that this claim is false, but it would certainly appear an incredible claim in the example. Such plausibility as the claim has derives from the supposition that we can construct a program that

will have the same inputs and outputs as native speakers, and in addition we assume that speakers have some level of description where they are also instantiations of a program. On the basis of these two assumptions we assume that even if Schank's program isn't the whole story about understanding, it may be part of the story. Well, I suppose that is an empirical possibility, but not the slightest reason has so far been given to believe that it is true, since what is suggested—though certainly not demonstrated—by the example is that the computer program is simply irrelevant to my understanding of the story. In the Chinese case I have everything that artificial intelligence can put into me by way of a program, and I understand nothing; in the English case I understand everything, and there is so far no reason at all to suppose that my understanding has anything to do with computer programs, that is, with computational operations on purely formally specified elements. As long as the program is defined in terms of computational operations on purely formally defined elements, what the example suggests is that these by themselves have no interesting connection with understanding. They are certainly not **sufficient conditions**, and not the slightest reason has been given to suppose that they are **necessary conditions** or even that they make a significant contribution to understanding. Notice that the force of the argument is not simply that different machines can have the same input and output while operating on different formal principles—that is not the point at all. Rather, whatever purely formal principles you put into the computer, they will not be sufficient for understanding, since a human will be able to follow the formal principles without understanding anything. No reason whatever has been offered to suppose that such principles are necessary or even contributory, since no reason has been given to suppose that when I understand English I am operating with any formal program at all.

Well, then, what is it that I have in the case of the English sentences that I do not have in the case of the Chinese sentences? The obvious answer is that I know what the former mean, while I haven't the faintest idea what the latter mean. But in what does this consist and why couldn't we give it to a machine, whatever it is? I will return to this question later, but first I want to continue with the example.

I have had the occasions to present this example to several workers in artificial intelligence, and, interestingly, they do not seem to agree on what the proper reply to it is. I get a surprising variety of replies, and in what follows I will consider the most common of these (specified along with their geographic origins).

But first I want to block some common misunderstandings about "understanding": in many of these discussions one finds a lot of fancy footwork about the word "understanding." My critics point out that there are many different degrees of understanding; that "understanding" is not a simple two-place predicate; that there are even different kinds and levels of understanding, and often the law of excluded middle doesn't even apply in a straightforward way to statements of the form "x understands y"; that in many cases it is a matter for decision and not a simple matter of fact whether x understands y; and so on. To all of these points I want to say: of course, of course. But they have nothing to do with the points at issue. There are clear cases in which "understanding" literally applies and clear cases in which it does not apply; and these two sorts of cases are all I need for this argument.[2] I understand stories in English; to a lesser degree I can understand stories in French; to a still lesser degree, stories in German; and in Chinese, not at all. My car and my adding machine, on the other hand, understand nothing: they are not in that line of business. We often attribute "understanding" and

other cognitive predicates by metaphor and analogy to cars, adding machines, and other artifacts, but nothing is proved by such attributions. We say, "The door *knows* when to open because of its photoelectric cell," "The adding machine *knows how (understands how, is able)* to do addition and subtraction but not division," and "The thermostat *perceives* changes in the temperature." The reason we make these attributions is quite interesting, and it has to do with the fact that in artifacts we extend our own intentionality;[3] our tools are extensions of our purposes, and so we find it natural to make metaphorical attributions of intentionality to them; but I take it no philosophical ice is cut by such examples. The sense in which an automatic door "understands instructions" from its photoelectric cell is not at all the sense in which I understand English. If the sense in which Schank's programmed computers understand stories is supposed to be the metaphorical sense in which the door understands, and not the sense in which I understand English, the issue would not be worth discussing. But Newell and Simon write that the kind of cognition they claim for computers is exactly the same as for human beings. I like the straightforwardness of this claim, and it is the sort of claim I will be considering. I will argue that in the literal sense the programmed computer understands what the car and the adding machine understand, namely, exactly nothing. The computer understanding is not just (like my understanding of German) partial or incomplete; it is zero.

Now to the replies:

1. The Systems Reply (Berkeley)

"While it is true that the individual person who is locked in the room does not understand the story, the fact is that he is merely part of a whole system, and the system does understand the story. The person has a large ledger in front of him in which are written the rules, he has a lot of scratch paper and pencils for doing calculations, he has 'data banks' of sets of Chinese symbols. Now, understanding is not being ascribed to the mere individual; rather it is being ascribed to this whole system of which he is a part."

My response to the systems theory is quite simple: let the individual internalize all of these elements of the system. He memorizes the rules in the ledger and the data banks of Chinese symbols, and he does all the calculations in his head. The individual then incorporates the entire system. There isn't anything at all to the system that he does not encompass. We can even get rid of the room and suppose he works outdoors. All the same, he understands nothing of the Chinese, and a fortiori neither does the system, because there isn't anything in the system that isn't in him. If he doesn't understand, then there is no way the system could understand because the system is just a part of him.

Actually I feel somewhat embarrassed to give even this answer to the systems theory because the theory seems to me so unplausible to start with. The idea is that while a person doesn't understand Chinese, somehow the *conjuction* of that person and bits of paper might understand Chinese. It is not easy for me to imagine how someone who was not in the grip of an ideology would find the idea at all plausible. Still, I think many people who are committed to the ideology of strong AI will in the end be inclined to say something very much like this; so let us pursue it a bit further. According to one version of this view, while the man in the internalized systems example doesn't understand Chinese in the sense that a native Chinese speaker does (because, for example, he doesn't know that the story refers to restaurants and hamburgers, etc.), still "the man as a formal symbol manipulation system" *really*

does understand Chinese. The subsystem of the man that is the formal symbol manipulation system for Chinese should not be confused with the subsystem for English.

So there are really two subsystems in the man; one understands English, the other Chinese, and "it's just that the two systems have little to do with each other." But, I want to reply, not only do they have little to do with each other, they are not even remotely alike. The subsystem that understands English (assuming we allow ourselves to talk in this jargon of "subsystems" for a moment) knows that the stories are about restaurants and eating hamburgers, he knows that he is being asked questions about restaurants and that he is answering questions as best he can by making various inferences from the content of the story, and so on. But the Chinese system knows none of this. Whereas the English subsystem knows that "hamburgers" refers to hamburgers, the Chinese subsystem knows only that "squiggle squiggle" is followed by "squoggle squoggle." All he knows is that various formal symbols are being introduced at one end and manipulated according to rules written in English, and other symbols are going out at the other end. The whole point of the original example was to argue that such symbol manipulation by itself couldn't be sufficient for understanding Chinese in any literal sense because the man could write "squoggle squoggle" after "squiggle squiggle" without understanding anything in Chinese. And it doesn't meet that argument to postulate subsystems within the man, because the subsystems are no better off than the man was in the first place; they still don't have anything even remotely like what the English-speaking man (or subsystem) has. Indeed, in the case as described, the Chinese subsystem is simply a part of the English subsystem, a part that engages in meaningless symbol manipulation according to rules in English.

Let us ask ourselves what is supposed to motivate the systems reply in the first place; that is, what *independent* grounds are there supposed to be for saying that the agent must have a subsystem within him that literally understands stories in Chinese? As far as I can tell the only grounds are that in the example I have the same input and output as native Chinese speakers and a program that goes from one to the other. But the whole point of the examples has been to try to show that that couldn't be sufficient for understanding, in the sense in which I understand stories in English, because a person, and hence the set of systems that go to make up a person, could have the right combination of input, output, and program and still not understand anything in the relevant literal sense in which I understand English. The only motivation for saying there *must* be a subsystem in me that understands Chinese is that I have a program and I can pass the Turing test; I can fool native Chinese speakers. But precisely one of the points at issue is the adequacy of the Turing test. The example shows that there could be two "systems," both of which pass the Turing test, but only one of which understands; and it is no argument against this point to say that since they both pass the Turing test they must both understand, since this claim fails to meet the argument that the system in me that understands English has a great deal more than the system that merely processes Chinese. In short, the systems reply simply begs the question by insisting without argument that the system must understand Chinese.

Furthermore, the systems reply would appear to lead to consequences that are independently absurd. If we are to conclude that there must be cognition in me on the grounds that I have a certain sort of input and output and a program in between, then it looks like all sorts of noncognitive subsystems are going to turn out to be cognitive. For example, there is a level of description at which my stomach does information processing, and it instantiates any number of computer programs, but I take it we do not want to say that it has any understanding. But if we accept the systems reply, then it is hard to see how we avoid saying that stomach, heart, liver, and so on, are all understanding subsystems, since there is no principled way to distinguish the motivation for saying the Chinese subsystem understands from [the motivation for] saying that the stomach understands. It is, by the way, not an answer to this point to say that the Chinese system has information as input and output and the stomach has food and food products as input and output, since from the point of view of the agent, from my point of view, there is no information in either the food or the Chinese—the Chinese is just so many meaningless squiggles. The information in the Chinese case is solely in the eyes of the programmers and the interpreters, and there is nothing to prevent them from treating the input and output of my digestive organs as information if they so desire.

This last point bears on some independent problems in strong AI, and it is worth digressing for a moment to explain it. If strong AI is to be a branch of psychology, then it must be able to distinguish those systems that are genuinely mental from those that are not. It must be able to distinguish the principles on which the mind works from those on which nonmental systems work; otherwise it will offer us no explanations of what is specifically mental about the mental. And the mental-nonmental distinction cannot be just in the eye of the beholder but it must be intrinsic to the systems; otherwise it would be up to any beholder to treat people as nonmental and, for example, hurricanes as mental if he likes. But quite often in the AI literature the distinction is blurred in ways that would in the long run prove disastrous to the claim that AI is a cognitive inquiry. McCarthy, for example, writes, "Machines as simple as thermostats can be said to have beliefs, and having beliefs seems to be a characteristic of most machines capable of problem solving performance." Anyone who thinks strong AI has a chance as a theory of the mind ought to ponder the implications of that remark. We are asked to accept it as a discovery of strong AI that the hunk of metal on the wall that we use to regulate the temperature has beliefs in exactly the same sense that we, our spouses, and our children have beliefs, and furthermore that "most" of the other machines in the room—telephone, tape recorder, adding machine, electric light switch—also have beliefs in this literal sense. It is not the aim of this article to argue against McCarthy's point, so I will simply assert the following without argument. The study of the mind starts with such facts as that humans have beliefs, while thermostats, telephones, and adding machines don't. If you get a theory that denies this point you have produced a counter-example to the theory and the theory is false. One gets the impression that people in AI who write this sort of thing think they can get away with it because they don't really take it seriously, and they don't think anyone else will either. I propose, for a moment at least, to take it seriously. Think hard for one minute about what would be necessary to establish that that hunk of metal on the wall over there had real beliefs, beliefs with direction of fit, propositional content, and conditions of satisfaction; beliefs that had the possibility of being strong beliefs or weak beliefs; nervous, anxious, or secure beliefs; dogmatic, rational, or superstitious beliefs; blind faiths or hesitant cogitations; any kind of beliefs. The thermostat is not a candidate. Neither is stomach, liver, adding machine, or telephone. However, since we are taking the idea seriously, notice that its truth would be fatal to strong AI's claim to be a science of the mind. For now the mind is everywhere. What we wanted to know is what distinguishes the mind

from thermostats and livers. And if McCarthy were right, strong AI wouldn't have a hope of telling us that.

II. The Robot Reply (Yale)

"Suppose we wrote a different kind of program from Schank's program. Suppose we put a computer inside a robot, and this computer would not just take in formal symbols as input and give out formal symbols as output, but rather would actually operate the robot in such a way that the robot does something very much like perceiving, walking, moving about, hammering nails, eating, drinking—anything you like. The robot would, for example, have a television camera attached to it that enabled it to 'see,' it would have arms and legs that enabled it to 'act,' and all of this would be controlled by its computer 'brain.' Such a robot would, unlike Schank's computer, have genuine understanding and other mental states."

The first thing to notice about the robot reply is that it tacitly concedes that cognition is not solely a matter of formal symbol manipulation, since this reply adds a set of causal relation[s] with the outside world. But the answer to the robot reply is that the addition of such "perceptual" and "motor" capacities adds nothing by way of understanding, in particular, or intentionality, in general, to Schank's original program. To see this, notice that the same thought experiment applies to the robot case. Suppose that instead of the computer inside the robot, you put me inside the room and, as in the original Chinese case, you give me more Chinese symbols with more instructions in English for matching Chinese symbols to Chinese symbols and feeding back Chinese symbols to the outside. Suppose, unknown to me, some of the Chinese symbols that come to me come from a television camera attached to the robot and other Chinese symbols that I am giving out serve to make the motors inside the robot move the robot's legs or arms. It is important to emphasize that all I am doing is manipulating formal symbols: I know none of these other facts. I am receiving "information" from the robot's "perceptual" apparatus, and I am giving out "instructions" to its motor apparatus without knowing either of these facts. I am the robot's **homunculus**, but unlike the traditional homunculus, I don't know what's going on. I don't understand anything except the rules for symbol manipulation. Now in this case I want to say that the robot has no intentional states at all; it is simply moving about as a result of its electrical wiring and its program. And furthermore, by instantiating the program I have no intentional states of the relevant type. All I do is follow formal instructions about manipulating formal symbols.

III. The Brain Simulator Reply (Berkeley and M.I.T.)

"Suppose we design a program that doesn't represent information that we have about the world, such as the information in Schank's scripts, but simulates the actual sequence of neuron firings at the synapses of the brain of a native Chinese speaker when he understands stories in Chinese and gives answers to them. The machine takes in Chinese stories and questions about them as input, it simulates the formal structure of actual Chinese brains in processing these stories, and it gives out Chinese answers as outputs. We can even imagine that the machine operates, not with a single serial program, but with a whole set of programs operating in parallel, in the manner that actual human brains presumably operate when they process natural language. Now surely in such a case we would have to say that the

machine understood the stories; and if we refuse to say that, wouldn't we also have to deny that native Chinese speakers understood the stories? At the level of the synapses, what would or could be different about the program of the computer and the program of the Chinese brain?"

Before countering this reply I want to digress to note that it is an odd reply for any partisan of artificial intelligence (or functionalism, etc.) to make: I thought the whole idea of strong AI is that we don't need to know how the brain works to know how the mind works. The basic hypothesis, or so I had supposed, was that there is a level of mental operations consisting of computational processes over formal elements that constitute the essence of the mental and can be realized in all sorts of different brain processes, in the same way that any computer program can be realized in different computer hardwares: on the assumptions of strong AI, the mind is to the brain as the program is to the hardware, and thus we can understand the mind without doing neurophysiology. If we had to know how the brain worked to do AI, we wouldn't bother with AI. However, even getting this close to the operation of the brain is still not sufficient to produce understanding. To see this, imagine that instead of a monolingual man in a room shuffling symbols we have the man operate an elaborate set of water pipes with valves connecting them. When the man receives the Chinese symbols, he looks up in the program, written in English, which valves he has to turn on and off. Each water connection corresponds to a synapse in the Chinese brain, and the whole system is rigged up so that after doing all the right firings, that is after turning on all the right faucets, the Chinese answers pop out at the output end of the series of pipes.

Now where is the understanding in this system? It takes Chinese as input, it simulates the formal structure of the synapses of the Chinese brain, and it gives Chinese as output. But the man certainly doesn't understand Chinese, and neither do the water pipes, and if we are tempted to adopt what I think is the absurd view that somehow the *conjunction* of man *and* water pipes understands, remember that in principle the man can internalize the formal structure of the water pipes and do all the "neuron firings" in his imagination. The problem with the brain simulator is that it is simulating the wrong things about the brain. As long as it simulates only the formal structure of the sequence of neuron firings at the synapses, it won't have simulated what matters about the brain, namely its causal properties, its ability to produce intentional states. And that the formal properties are not sufficient for the causal properties is shown by the water pipe example: we can have all the formal properties carved off from the relevant neurobiological causal properties.

IV. The Combination Reply (Berkeley and Stanford)

"While each of the previous three replies might not be completely convincing by itself as a refutation of the Chinese room counterexample, if you take all three together they are collectively much more convincing and even decisive. Imagine a robot with a brain-shaped computer lodged in its cranial cavity, imagine the computer programmed with all the synapses of a human brain, imagine the whole behavior of the robot is indistinguishable from human behavior, and now think of the whole thing as a unified system and not just as a computer with inputs and outputs. Surely in such a case we would have to ascribe intentionality to the system."

I entirely agree that in such a case we would find it rational and indeed irresistible to accept the hypothesis that the robot had intentionality, as long as we knew nothing more about it. Indeed, besides appearance and behavior, the other elements of the combination are really irrelevant. If we could build a robot whose behavior was indistinguishable over a large range from human behavior, we would attribute intentionality to it, pending some reason not to. We wouldn't need to know in advance that its computer brain was a formal analogue of the human brain.

But I really don't see that this is any help to the claims of strong AI; and here's why: According to strong AI, instantiating a formal program with the right input and output is a sufficient condition of, indeed is constitutive of, intentionality. As Newell puts it, the essence of the mental is the operation of a physical symbol system. But the attributions of intentionality that we make to the robot in this example have nothing to do with formal programs. They are simply based on the assumption that if the robot looks and behaves sufficiently like us, then we would suppose, until proven otherwise, that it must have mental states like ours that cause and are expressed by its behavior, and it must have an inner mechanism capable of producing such mental states. If we knew independently how to account for its behavior without such assumptions we would not attribute intentionality to it, especially if we knew it had a formal program. And this is precisely the point of my earlier reply to objection II.

Suppose we knew that the robot's behavior was entirely accounted for by the fact that a man inside it was receiving uninterpreted formal symbols from the robot's sensory receptors and sending out uninterpreted formal symbols to its motor mechanisms, and the man was doing this symbol manipulation in accordance with a bunch of rules. Furthermore, suppose the man knows none of these facts about the robot, all he knows is which operations to perform on which meaningless symbols. In such a case we would regard the robot as an ingenious mechanical dummy.

The hypothesis that the dummy has a mind would now be unwarranted and unnecessary, for there is now no longer any reason to ascribe intentionality in manipulating the symbols. The formal symbol manipulations go on, the input and output are correctly matched, but the only real locus of intentionality is the man, and he doesn't [have] any of the relevant intentional states; he doesn't, for example, *see* what comes into the robot's eyes, he doesn't *intend* to move the robot's arm, and he doesn't *understand* any of the remarks made to or by the robot. Nor, for the reasons stated earlier, does the system of which man and robot are a part.

To see this point, contrast this case with cases in which we find it completely natural to ascribe intentionality to members of certain other primate species such as apes and monkeys and to domestic animals such as dogs. The reasons we find it natural are, roughly, two: we can't make sense of the animal's behavior without the ascription of intentionality, and we can see that the beasts are made of similar stuff to ourselves—that is an eye, that a nose, this is its skin, and so on. Given the coherence of the animal's behavior and the assumption of the same causal stuff underlying it, we assume both that the animal must have mental states underlying its behavior, and that the mental states must be produced by mechanisms made out of the stuff that is like our stuff. We would certainly make similar assumptions about the robot unless we had some reason not to, but as soon as we knew that the behavior was the result of a formal program, and that the actual causal properties of the physical substance were irrelevant we would abandon the assumption of intentionality.

There are two other responses to my example that come up frequently (and so are worth discussing) but really miss the point.

V. The Other Minds Reply (Yale)

"How do you know that other people understand Chinese or anything else? Only by their behavior. Now the computer can pass the behavioral tests as well as they can (in principle), so if you are going to attribute cognition to other people you must in principle also attribute it to computers."

This objection really is only worth a short reply. The problem in this discussion is not about how I know that other people have cognitive states, but rather what it is that I am attributing to them when I attribute cognitive states to them. The thrust of the argument is that it couldn't be just computational processes and their output because the computational processes and their output can exist without the cognitive state. It is no answer to this argument to feign anesthesia. In "cognitive sciences" one presupposes the reality and knowability of the mental in the same way that in physical sciences one has to presuppose the reality and knowability of physical objects.

VI. The Many Mansions Reply (Berkeley)

"Your whole argument presupposes that AI is only about analogue and digital computers. But that just happens to be the present state of technology. Whatever these causal processes are that you say are essential for intentionality (assuming you are right), eventually we will be able to build devices that have these causal processes, and that will be artificial intelligence. So your arguments are in no way directed at the ability of artificial intelligence to produce and explain cognition."

I really have no objection to this reply save to say that it in effect trivializes the project of strong AI by redefining it as whatever artificially produces and explains cognition. The interest of the original claim made on behalf of artificial intelligence is that it was a precise, well defined thesis: mental processes are computational processes over formally defined elements. I have been concerned to challenge that thesis. If the claim is redefined so that it is no longer that thesis, my objections no longer apply because there is no longer a testable hypothesis for them to apply to.

Let us now return to the question I promised I would try to answer: granted that in my original example I understand the English and I do not understand the Chinese, and granted therefore that the machine doesn't understand either English or Chinese, still there must be something about me that makes it the case that I understand English and a corresponding something lacking in me that makes it the case that I fail to understand Chinese. Now why couldn't we give those somethings, whatever they are, to a machine?

I see no reason in principle why we couldn't give a machine the capacity to understand English or Chinese, since in an important sense our bodies with our brains are precisely such machines. But I do see very strong arguments for saying that we could not give such a thing to a machine where the operation of the machine is defined solely in terms of computational processes over formally defined elements; that is, where the operation of the machine is defined as an instantiation of a computer program. It is not because I am the instantiation of a computer program that I am able to understand English and have other forms of intentionality (I am, I suppose, the instantiation of any number of computer programs), but as far as we know it is because I am a certain sort of organism with a certain biological (i.e. chemical and physical) structure, and this structure, under certain conditions, is causally capable of producing perception, action, un-

derstanding, learning, and other intentional phenomena. And part of the point of the present argument is that only something that had those causal powers could have that intentionality. Perhaps other physical and chemical processes could produce exactly these effects; perhaps, for example, Martians also have intentionality but their brains are made of different stuff. That is an empirical question, rather like the question whether photosynthesis can be done by something with a chemistry different from that of chlorophyll.

But the main point of the present argument is that no purely formal model will ever be sufficient by itself for intentionality because the formal properties are not by themselves constitutive of intentionality, and they have by themselves no causal powers except the power, when instantiated, to produce the next stage of the formalism when the machine is running. And any other causal properties that particular realizations of the formal model have are irrelevant to the formal model because we can always put the same formal model in a different realization where those causal properties are obviously absent. Even if, by some miracle, Chinese speakers exactly realize Schank's program, we can put the same program in English speakers, water pipes, or computers, none of which understand Chinese, the program notwithstanding.

What matters about brain operations is not the formal shadow cast by the sequence of synapses but rather the actual properties of the sequences. All the arguments for the strong version of artificial intelligence that I have seen insist on drawing an outline around the shadows cast by cognition and then claiming that the shadows are the real thing.

By way of concluding I want to try to state some of the general philosophical points implicit in the argument. For clarity I will try to do it in a question and answer fashion, and I begin with that old chestnut of a question:

"Could a machine think?"

The answer is, obviously, yes. We are precisely such machines.

"Yes, but could an artifact, a man-made machine, think?"

Assuming it is possible to produce artificially a machine with a nervous system, neurons with axons and dendrites, and all the rest of it, sufficiently like ours, again the answer to the question seems to be obviously, yes. If you can exactly duplicate the causes, you could duplicate the effects. And indeed it might be possible to produce consciousness, intentionality, and all the rest of it using some other sorts of chemical principles than those that human beings use. It is, as I said, an empirical question.

"OK, but could a digital computer think?"

If by "digital computer" we mean anything at all that has a level of description where it can correctly be described as the instantiation of a computer program, then again the answer is, of course, yes, since we are the instantiations of any number of computer programs, and we can think.

"But could something think, understand, and so on *solely* in virtue of being a computer with the right sort of program? Could instantiating a program, the right program of course, by itself be a sufficient condition of understanding?"

This I think is the right question to ask, though it is usually confused with one or more of the earlier questions, and the answer to it is no.

"Why not?"

Because the formal symbol manipulations by themselves don't have any intentionality; they are quite meaningless; they aren't even *symbol* manipulations, since the symbols don't symbolize anything. In the linguistic jargon, they have only a syntax but no semantics. Such intention-

ality as computers appear to have is solely in the minds of those who program them and those who use them, those who send in the input and those who interpret the output.

The aim of the Chinese room example was to try to show this by showing that as soon as we put something into the system that really does have intentionality (a man), and we program him with the formal program, you can see that the formal program carries no additional intentionality. It adds nothing, for example, to a man's ability to understand Chinese.

Precisely that feature of AI that seemed so appealing—the distinction between the program and the realization—proves fatal to the claim that simulation could be duplication. The distinction between the program and its realization in the hardware seems to be parallel to the distinction between the level of mental operations and the level of brain operations. And if we could describe the level of mental operations as a formal program, then it seems we could describe what was essential about the mind without doing either introspective psychology or neurophysiology of the brain. But the equation, "mind is to brain as program is to hardware" breaks down at several points, among them the following three:

First, the distinction between program and realization has the consequence that the same program could have all sorts of crazy realizations that had no form of intentionality. Weizenbaum, for example, shows in detail how to construct a computer using a roll of toilet paper and a pile of small stones. Similarly, the Chinese story understanding program can be programmed into a sequence of water pipes, a set of wind machines, or a monolingual English speaker, none of which thereby acquires an understanding of Chinese. Stones, toilet paper, wind, and water pipes are the wrong kind of stuff to have intentionality in the first place—only something that has the same causal powers as brains can have intentionality—and though the English speaker has the right kind of stuff for intentionality you can easily see that he doesn't get any extra intentionality by memorizing the program, since memorizing it won't teach him Chinese.

Second, the program is purely formal, but the intentional states are not in that way formal. They are defined in terms of their content, not their form. The belief that it is raining, for example, is not defined as a certain formal shape, but as a certain mental content with conditions of satisfaction, a direction of fit, and the like. Indeed the belief as such hasn't even got a formal shape in this syntactic sense, since one and the same belief can be given an indefinite number of different syntactic expressions in different linguistic systems.

Third, as I mentioned before, mental states and events are literally a product of the operation of the brain, but the program is not in that way a product of the computer.

"Well if programs are in no way constitutive of mental processes, why have so many people believed the converse? That at least needs some explanation."

I don't really know the answer to that one. The idea that computer simulations could be the real thing ought to have seemed suspicious in the first place because the computer isn't confined to simulating mental operations, by any means. No one supposes that computer simulations of a five-alarm fire will burn the neighborhood down or that a computer simulation of a rainstorm will leave us all drenched. Why on earth would anyone suppose that a computer simulation of understanding actually understood anything? It is sometimes said that it would be frightfully hard to get computers to feel pain or fall in love, but love and pain are neither harder nor easier than cognition or anything else. For simulation, all

you need is the right input and output and a program in the middle that transforms the former into the latter. That is all the computer has for anything it does. To confuse simulation with duplication is the same mistake, whether it is pain, love, cognition, fires, or rainstorms.

Still, there are several reasons why AI must have seemed—and to many people perhaps still does seem—in some way to reproduce and thereby explain mental phenomena, and I believe we will not succeed in removing these illusions until we have fully exposed the reasons that give rise to them.

First, and perhaps most important, is a confusion about the notion of "information processing": many people in cognitive science believe that the human brain, with its mind, does something called "information processing," and analogously the computer with its program does information processing, but fires and rainstorms, on the other hand, don't do information processing at all. Thus, though the computer can simulate the formal features of any process whatever, it stands in a special relation to the mind and brain because when the computer is properly programmed, ideally with the same program as the brain, the information processing is identical in the two cases, and this information processing is really the essence of the mental. But the trouble with this argument is that it rests on an ambiguity in the notion of "information." In the sense in which people "process information" when they reflect, say, on problems in arithmetic or when they read and answer questions about stories, the programmed computer does not do "information processing." Rather, what it does is manipulate formal symbols. The fact that the programmer and the interpreter of the computer output use the symbols to stand for objects in the world is totally beyond the scope of the computer. The computer, to repeat, has a syntax but no semantics. Thus, if you type into the computer "2 plus 2 equals?" it will type out "4." But it has no idea that "4" means 4 or that it means anything at all. And the point is not that it lacks some second-order information about the interpretation of its first-order symbols, but rather that its first-order symbols don't have any interpretations as far as the computer is concerned. All the computer has is more symbols. The introduction of the notion of "information processing" therefore produces a dilemma: either we construe the notion of "information processing" in such a way that it implies intentionality as part of the process or we don't. If the former, then the programmed computer does not do information processing, it only manipulates formal symbols. If the latter, then, though the computer does information processing, it is only doing so in the sense in which adding machines, typewriters, stomachs, thermostats, rainstorms, and hurricanes do information processing; namely, they have a level of description at which we can describe them as taking information in at one end, transforming it, and producing information as output. But in this case it is up to outside observers to interpret the input and output as information in the ordinary sense. And no similarity is established between the computer and the brain in terms of any similarity of information processing.

Second, in much of AI there is a residual behaviorism or operationalism. Since appropriately programmed computers can have input-output patterns similar to those of human beings, we are tempted to postulate mental states in the computer similar to human mental states. But once we see that it is both conceptually and empirically possible for a system to have human capacities in some realm without having any intentionality at all, we should be able to overcome this impulse. My desk adding machine has calculating capacities, but no intentionality, and in this paper I have tried to show that a system could have input and output capabilities that duplicated those of a native Chinese speaker and still not understand Chinese, regardless of how it was programmed. The Turing test is typical of the tradition in being unashamedly behavioristic and operationalistic, and I believe that if AI workers totally repudiated behaviorism and operationalism much of the confusion between simulation and duplication would be eliminated.

Third, this residual operationalism is joined to a residual form of dualism; indeed strong AI only makes sense given the dualistic assumption that, where the mind is concerned, the brain doesn't matter. In strong AI (and in functionalism, as well) what matters are programs, and programs are independent of their realization in machines; indeed, as far as AI is concerned, the same program could be realized by an electronic machine, a Cartesian mental substance, or a Hegelian world spirit. The single most surprising discovery that I have made in discussing these issues is that many AI workers are quite shocked by my idea that actual human mental phenomena might be dependent on actual physical-chemical properties of actual human brains. But if you think about it a minute you can see that I should not have been surprised; for unless you accept some form of dualism, the strong AI project hasn't got a chance. The project is to reproduce and explain the mental by designing programs, but unless the mind is not only conceptually but empirically independent of the brain you couldn't carry out the project, for the program is completely independent of any realization. Unless you believe that the mind is separable from the brain both conceptually and empirically— dualism in a strong form—you cannot hope to reproduce the mental by writing and running programs since programs must be independent of brains or any other particular forms of instantiation. If mental operations consist in computational operations on formal symbols, then it follows that they have no interesting connection with the brain; the only connection would be that the brain just happens to be one of the indefinitely many types of machines capable of instantiating the program. This form of dualism is not the traditional Cartesian variety that claims there are two sorts of *substances*, but it is Cartesian in the sense that it insists that what is specifically mental about the mind has no intrinsic connection with the actual properties of the brain. This underlying dualism is masked from us by the fact that AI literature contains frequent fulminations against "dualism"; what the authors seem to be unaware of is that their position presupposes a strong version of dualism.

"Could a machine think?" My own view is that *only* a machine could think, and indeed only very special kinds of machines, namely brains and machines that had the same causal powers as brains. And that is the main reason strong AI has had little to tell us about thinking, since it has nothing to tell us about machines. By its own definition, it is about programs, and programs are not machines. Whatever else intentionality is, it is a biological phenomenon, and it is as likely to be as causally dependent on the specific biochemistry of its origins as lactation, photosynthesis, or any other biological phenomena. No one would suppose that we could produce milk and sugar by running a computer simulation of the formal sequences in lactation and photosynthesis, but where the mind is concerned many people are willing to believe in such a miracle because of a deep and abiding dualism: the mind they suppose is a matter of formal processes and is independent of quite specific material causes in the way that milk and sugar are not.

In defense of this dualism the hope is often expressed that the brain is a digital computer (early computers, by the way, were often called "electronic brains"). But that is no help. Of course the brain is a digital computer. Since everything is a digital computer, brains are too. The point is that the brain's causal capacity to produce intentionality cannot consist in its instantiating a computer program, since for any program you like it is possible for something to instantiate that program and still not have any mental states. Whatever it is that the brain does to produce intentionality, it cannot consist in instantiating a program since no program, by itself, is sufficient for intentionality.

Acknowledgments

I am indebted to a rather large number of people for discussion of these matters and for their patient attempts to overcome my ignorance of artificial intelligence. I would especially like to thank Ned Block, Hubert Dreyfus, John Haugeland, Roger Schank, Robert Wilensky, and Terry Winograd.

Notes

1. I am not, of course, saying that Schank himself is committed to these claims.

2. Also, "understanding" implies both the possession of mental (intentional) states and the truth (validity, success) of these states. For the purposes of this discussion we are concerned only with the possession of the states.

3. Intentionality is by definition that feature of certain mental states by which they are directed at or about objects and states of affairs in the world. Thus,

beliefs, desires, and intentions are intentional states; undirected forms of anxiety and depression are not.

CONTEMPORARY PERSPECTIVES: PHENOMENOLOGY AND FEMINISM

Phenomenology is opposed to those pseudo-problems that parade themselves as 'problems,' often for generations at a time.

Martin Heidegger

Founded by Edmund Husserl near the turn of the century, phenomenology is a way of philosophizing that attempts to describe the essential structures of consciousness and experience. Consciousness and mind are not synonymous terms. Phenomenologists think of consciousness as an activity, *a minding*. Consciousness is an awareness of a relation between a perceiving individual (the knowing subject) and some object of attention (the known object).

According to Husserl, consciousness is characterized by **intentionality,** meaning it is always aiming at something beyond itself. Whatever is present in experience has "meaning" or "sense." The meaning or sense of an object is nothing but the way in which the object is "present to" or "intended by" consciousness. In Husserl's words, "consciousness is always consciousness of something." For example, as you read this page you are conscious of philosophy, or the mind-body problem; you are intending the words on the page with some meaning. Or perhaps you are conscious of something else going on in the hall outside. If so, you may close the book and investigate. In that case, your consciousness is aiming at some object in the hall, or the hall itself. The task of phenomenology is to describe both the *intended* objects of consciousness and the various acts of *intending*.

How do these phenomenological reflections shed light on the mind-body problem? To many phenomenologists, like Martin Heidegger and Maurice Merleau-Ponty, the mind-body problem is a clear example of a false or "pseudo" problem. The "problem" became a problem as a result of a failure to investigate thoroughly "the phenomena themselves" grouped under the headings "mind" and "body." Ignoring the intentional structure of consciousness as well as the peculiar way consciousness is always conscious of body, the modern philosophic tradition since Descartes has succeeded in alienating mind from body. Putting phenomenology to work on the mind-body problem requires that we stop abstracting the meaning of "body" from our lived experience. How, concretely, do I experience my body? Put another way, how am I conscious of my body?

As Maurice Merleau-Ponty asks these questions of body, it becomes clear that Descartes' understanding of body is wholly inadequate. Violating the very first rule of his own method, Descartes hastily accepted the prejudices of the newly emerging seventeenth century mechanistic world picture. He concluded that natural science with its mathematical interpretation of nature was an adequate description of all bodies everywhere, including his own body! Under the spell of "objective" natural science, Descartes banished from matter all of the biological considerations that Aristotle considered important, with the result that matter became completely alien to mind, two separate, distinct substances that led independent lives. This is the historical origin of the modern mind-body problem. Having separated in his philosophy mind from body, Descartes was hard-pressed to get them back together again. His interactionism, which proposed the pineal gland as "switchhouse" where mind and body got recoupled, was a failure, and philosophers have struggled with the legacy of Descartes' problems ever since.

mistake made!

Merleau-Ponty sought to return philosophy to the perceptual questions, "What is it that I am experiencing when I experience my body, and how do I experience it?" He argues that Descartes' interpretation of *body-as-object* ignores the *body-as-subject*, or what he calls the "lived body." To perceive a table in a room is to be intentionally aware of oneself as an embodied perceiver. I do not perceive my body as just another object in the world; rather, it is that through which I am present to the world. I can misplace my pen, but I cannot misplace my body. I do not merely have a body, I *am* my body, a perceptual insight that shatters the subject/object bifurcation that has plagued modern philosophy since Descartes. To reduce the meaning of body to "body-as-object-for-natural-science," as Descartes did, is to ignore the "body-as-lived," as well as the "body-as-perceiving-subject."

Like phenomenology, feminist philosophy calls into question the very process of addressing philosophical problems. In her article "Woman As Body," Elizabeth V. Spelman continues the interrogation of the philosophic tradition on the question of body. Historically, philosophy has had little to say about women. What little has been said has not been flattering. Feminism has given voice to many gifted philosophers who are asking thoughtful questions, not only of philosophy's past but of its future as well.

Given the association of women with body that has been a part of the philosophic tradition since Plato (a tradition not noted for its celebration of the body!), Spelman wonders what connection there might be between attitudes toward the body and attitudes toward women. In alerting us to the social and political implications of the mind-body distinction, Spelman illustrates the liberating dimension of feminist philosophizing.

CHAPTER 37

MAURICE MERLEAU-PONTY

THE LIVED BODY

Maurice Merleau-Ponty (1908–1961), French phenomenologist, studied at the prestigious Ecole Normale Supérieure in Paris, and subsequently taught there. After serving as an officer in World War II, he taught philosophy at the University of Lyon, the Sorbonne, and the College de France.

It was Jean-Paul Sartre who first introduced Merleau-Ponty to the writings of Edmund Husserl, the founder of phenomenology. Merleau-Ponty accepted Husserl's general understanding of phenomenology as a descriptive account of consciousness, but he rejected the idea of a complete phenomenological reduction, or *epoché*. The phenomenological reduction (the attempt to describe human experience without prejudice or presupposition) reveals only an embodied subject who experiences the world from a particular point of view. In stressing the primacy of perception and the role of ambiguity in philosophy, Merleau-Ponty insisted that all scientific description and explanation presupposed the perceptual "life world." The life world disclosed by perception is the pretheoretical lived context in which all human projects take place; it is the foundation of all rationality, value, and existence. Since meaning is always grounded in perception, and perceptual experience is always ambiguous, the philosophic ideal of total clarity and certitude is a myth that must be rejected.

Merleau-Ponty's principal works translated into English include *Phenomenology of Perception* (1962), *Sense and Nonsense* (1964), and *The Primacy of Perception* (1964).

THE LIVED BODY[1]

1. Introduction

What is phenomenology? . . . Phenomenology is the study of essences; and according to it, all problems amount to finding definitions of essences: the essence of perception, or the essence of consciousness, for example. But phenomenology is also a philosophy which puts essences back into existence, and does not expect to arrive at an understanding of man and the world from any starting point other than that of their 'facticity'. It is a transcendental philosophy which places in abeyance the assertions arising out of the natural attitude, the better to understand them; but it is also a philosophy for which the world is always 'already there' before reflection begins—as an inalienable presence; and all its efforts are concentrated upon re-achieving a direct and primitive contact with the world, and endowing that contact with a philosophical status. It is the search for a philosophy which shall be a 'rigorous science', but it also offers an account of space, time and the world as we 'live' them. It tries to give a direct description of our experience as it is, without taking account of its psychological origin and the causal explanations which the scientist, the historian or the sociologist may be able to provide.

It is a matter of describing, not of explaining or analysing. Husserl's first directive to phenomenology, in its early stages, to be a 'descriptive psychology', or to return to the 'things themselves', is from the start a rejection of science. I am not the outcome or the meeting-point of numerous causal agencies which determine my bodily or psychological make-up. I cannot conceive myself as nothing but a bit of the world, a mere object of biological, psychological or sociological investigation. I cannot shut myself up

within the realm of science. All my knowledge of the world, even my scientific knowledge, is gained from my own particular point of view, or from some experience of the world without which the symbols of science would be meaningless. The whole universe of science is built upon the world as directly experienced, and if we want to subject science itself to rigorous scrutiny and arrive at a precise assessment of its meaning and scope, we must begin by reawakening the basic experience of the world of which science is the second-order expression. Science has not and never will have, by its nature, the same significance *qua* form of being as the world which we perceive, for the simple reason that it is a rationale or explanation of that world. I am, not a 'living creature' nor even a 'man', nor again even 'a consciousness' endowed with all the characteristics which zoology, social anatomy or inductive psychology recognize in these various products of the natural or historical process—I am the absolute source, my existence does not stem from my antecedents, from my physical and social environment; instead it moves out towards them and sustains them, for I alone bring into being for myself (and therefore into being in the only sense that the word can have for me) the tradition which I elect to carry on, or the horizon whose distance from me would be abolished—since that distance is not one of its properties—if I were not there to scan it with my gaze. Scientific points of view, according to which my existence is a moment of the world's, are always both naïve and at the same time dishonest, because

---

[1]From Maurice Merleau-Ponty, *Phenomenology of Perception*, translated by Colin Smith (New York: Humanities Press, 1962). Reprinted with the permission of Humanities Press International, Inc., Atlantic Highlands, N.J.

they take for granted, without explicitly mentioning it, the other point of view, namely that of consciousness, through which from the outset a world forms itself round me and begins to exist for me. To return to things themselves is to return to that world which precedes knowledge, of which knowledge always *speaks*, and in relation to which every scientific schematization is an abstract and derivative sign-language, as is geography in relation to the countryside in which we have learnt beforehand what a forest, a prairie or a river is.

This move is absolutely distinct from the idealist return to consciousness, and the demand for a pure description excludes equally the procedure of analytical reflection on the one hand, and that of scientific explanation on the other. Descartes and particularly Kant *detached* the subject, or consciousness, by showing that I could not possibly apprehend anything as existing unless I first of all experienced myself as existing in the act of apprehending it. They presented consciousness, the absolute certainty of my existence for myself, as the condition of there being anything at all; and the act of relating as the basis of relatedness. It is true that the act of relating is nothing if divorced from the spectacle of the world in which relations are found; the unity of consciousness in Kant is achieved simultaneously with that of the world. And in Descartes methodical doubt does not deprive us of anything, since the whole world, at least in so far as we experience it, is reinstated in the *Cogito*, enjoying equal certainty, and simply labelled 'thought about . . .'. But the relations between subject and world are not strictly bilateral: if they were, the certainty of the world would, in Descartes, be immediately given with that of the *Cogito*, and Kant would not have talked about his 'Copernican revolution'. Analytical reflection starts from our experience of the world and goes back to the subject as to a condition of possibility distinct from that experi-ence, revealing the all-embracing synthesis as that without which there would be no world. To this extent it ceases to remain part of our experience and offers, in place of an account, a reconstruction. It is understandable, in view of this, that Husserl, having accused Kant of adopting a 'faculty psychologism', should have urged, in place of a noetic analysis which bases the world on the synthesizing activity of the subject, his own *'noematic reflection'* which remains within the object and, instead of begetting it, brings to light its fundamental unity.

The world is there before any possible analysis of mine, and it would be artificial to make it the outcome of a series of syntheses which link, in the first place sensations, then aspects of the object corresponding to different perspectives, when both are nothing but products of analysis, with no sort of prior reality. Analytical reflection believes that it can trace back the course followed by a prior constituting act and arrive, in the 'inner man'—to use Saint Augustine's expression—at a constituting power which has always been identical with that inner self. Thus reflection itself is carried away and transplanted in an impregnable subjectivity, as yet untouched by being and time. But this is very ingenuous, or at least it is an incomplete form of reflection which loses sight of its own beginning. When I begin to reflect my reflection bears upon an unreflective experience; moreover my reflection cannot be unaware of itself as an event, and so it appears to itself in the light of a truly creative act, of a changed structure of consciousness, and yet it has to recognize, as having priority over its own operations, the world which is given to the subject, because the subject is given to himself. The real has to be described, not constructed or formed. Which means that I cannot put perception into the same category as the syntheses represented by judgements, acts or predications. My field of perception is constantly filled with a play of colors, noises and fleeting tactile sensations which I cannot relate precisely to the context of my clearly perceived world, yet which I nevertheless immediately 'place' in the world, without ever confusing them with my daydreams. Equally constantly I weave dreams round things. I imagine people and things whose presence is not incompatible with the context, yet who are not in fact involved in it: they are ahead of reality, in the realm of the imaginary. If the reality of my perception were based solely on the intrinsic coherence of 'representations', it ought to be for ever hesitant and, being wrapped up in my conjectures on probabilities, I ought to be ceaselessly taking apart misleading syntheses, and reinstating in reality stray phenomena which I had excluded in the first place. But this does not happen. The real is a closely woven fabric. It does not await our judgement before incorporating the most surprising phenomena, or before rejecting the most plausible figments of our imagination. Perception is not a science of the world, it is not even an act, a deliberate taking up of a position; it is the background from which all acts stand out, and is presupposed by them. The world is not an object such that I have in my possession the law of its making; it is the natural setting of, and field for, all my thoughts and all my explicit perceptions. Truth does not 'inhabit' only 'the inner man',[2] or more accurately, there is no inner man, man is in the world, and only in the world does he know himself. When I return to myself from an excursion into the realm of dogmatic common sense or of science, I find, not a source of intrinsic truth, but a subject destined to be in the world.

2. The Experience of the Body and Classical Psychology

In its descriptions of the body from the point of view of the self, classical psychology was already wont to attribute to it 'characteristics' incompatible with the status of an object. In the first place it was stated that my body is distinguishable from the table or the lamp in that I can turn away from the latter whereas my body is constantly perceived. It is therefore an object which does not leave me. But in that case is it still an object? If the object is an invariable structure, it is not one *in spite of* the changes of perspective, but *in* that change or *through* it. It is not the case that ever-renewed perspectives simply provide it with opportunities of displaying its permanence, and with contingent ways of presenting itself to us. It is an object, which means that it is standing in front of us, only because it is observable: situated, that is to say, directly under our hand or gaze, indivisibly overthrown and re-integrated with every movement they make. Otherwise it would be true like an idea and not present like a thing. It is particularly true that an object is an object only in so far as it can be moved away from me, and ultimately disappear from my field of vision. Its presence is such that it entails a possible absence. Now the permanence of my own body is entirely different in kind: it is not at the extremity of some indefinite exploration; it defies exploration and is always presented to me from the same angle. Its permanence is not a permanence in the world, but a permanence from my point of view. To say that it is always near me, always there for me, is to say that it is never really in front of me, that I cannot array it before my eyes, that it remains marginal to all my perceptions, that it is *with* me. It is true that external objects too never turn one of their sides to me without hiding the rest, but I can at least freely choose the side which they are to present to me. They could not appear otherwise than in perspective, but the particular perspective which I acquire at each moment is the outcome of no more than physical necessity, that is to say, of a necessity which I can use and which is not a prison for me: from my window only the tower of the church is visible, but this limitation simultaneously holds out the promise that from elsewhere the whole church could be seen. It is true, moreover, that if I am a prisoner the church will be restricted, for me, to a truncated steeple. If I did not take off my clothes I could never see the inside of them, and it will in fact be seen that my clothes may become appendages of my body. But this fact does not prove that the presence of my body is to be compared to the *de facto* permanence of certain objects, or the organ compared to a tool which is always available. It shows that conversely those actions in which I habitually engage incorporate their instruments into themselves and make them play a part in the original structure of my own body. As for the latter, it is my basic habit, the one which conditions all the others, and by means of which they are mutually comprehensible. Its permanence near to me, its unvarying perspective are not a *de facto* necessity, since such necessity presupposes them: in order that my window may impose upon me a point of view of the church, it is necessary in the first place that my body should impose upon me one of the world; and the first necessity can be merely physical only in virtue of the fact that the second is metaphysical; in short, I am accessible to factual situations only if my nature is such that there are factual situations for me. In other words, I observe external objects with my body, I handle them, examine them, walk round them, but my body itself is a thing which I do not observe: in order to be able to do so, I should need the use of a second body which itself would be unobservable. When I say that my body is always perceived by me, these words are not to be taken in a purely statistical sense, for there must be, in the way my own body presents itself, something which makes its absence or its variation inconceivable. What can it be? My head is presented to my sight only to the extent of my nose end and the boundaries of my eye-sockets. I can see my eyes in three mirrors, but they are the eyes of someone observing, and I have the utmost difficulty in catching my living glance when a mirror in the street unexpectedly reflects my image back at me. My body in the mirror never stops following my intentions like their shadow, and if observation consists in varying the point of view while keeping the object fixed, then it escapes observation and is given to me as a simulacrum of my tactile body since it imitates the body's actions instead of responding to them by a free unfolding of perspectives. My visual body is certainly an object as far as its parts far removed from my head are concerned, but as we come nearer to the eyes, it becomes divorced from objects, and reserves among them a quasi-space to which they have no access, and when I try to fill this void by recourse to the image in the mirror, it refers me back to an original of the body which is not out there among things, but in my own province, on this side of all things seen. It is no different, in spite of what may appear to be the case, with my tactile body, for if I can, with my left hand, feel my right hand as it touches an object, the right hand as an object is not the right hand as it touches: the first is a system of bones, muscles and flesh brought down at a point of space, the second shoots through space like a rocket to reveal the external object in its place. In so far as it sees or touches the world, my body can therefore be neither seen nor touched. What prevents its ever being an object, ever being 'completely constituted is that it is that by which there are objects. It is neither tangible nor visible in so far as it is that which sees and touches. The body therefore is not the nondescript one among external objects and simply having the peculiarity of always being there. If it is permanent, the permanence is absolute and is the ground for the relative permanence of disappearing objects, real objects. The presence and absence of external objects are only variations within a field of primordial presence, a perceptual domain over which my body exercises power. Not only is the permanence of my body not a particular case of the permanence of external objects in the world, but the second cannot be understood except through the first: not only is the perspective of my body not a particular case of that of objects, but furthermore the presentation of objects in perspective cannot be understood except through the resistance of my body to all variation of perspective. If objects may never show me more than one of their facets, this is because I am myself in a certain place from which I see them and which I cannot see. If nevertheless I believe in the existence of their hidden sides and equally in a world which embraces them all and co-exists with them, I do so in so far as my body, always present for me, and yet involved with them in so many objective relationships, sustains their co-existence with it and communicates to them all the pulse of its duration. Thus the permanence of one's own body, if only classical psychology had analysed it, might have led it to the body no longer conceived as an object of the world, but as our means of communication with it, to the world no longer conceived as a collection of determinate objects, but as the horizon latent in all our experience and itself ever-present and anterior to every determining thought.

The other 'characteristics' whereby one's own body were defined were no less interesting, and for the same reasons. My body, it was said, is recognized by its power to give me 'double sensations': when I touch my right hand with my left, my right hand, as an object, has the strange property of being able to feel too. We have just seen that the two hands are never simultaneously in the relationship of touched and touching to each other. When I press my two hands together, it is not a matter of two sensations felt together as one perceives two objects placed side by side, but of an ambiguous set-up in which both hands can alternate the rôles of 'touching' and being 'touched'. What was meant by talking about 'double sensations' is that, in passing from one rôle to the other, I can identify the hand touched as the same one which will in a moment be touching. In other words, in this bundle of bones and muscles which my right hand presents to my left, I can anticipate for an instant the integument or incarnation of that other right hand, alive and mobile, which I thrust towards things in order to explore them. The body catches itself from the outside engaged in a cognitive process; it tries to touch itself while being touched, and initiates 'a kind of reflection' which is sufficient to distinguish it from objects, of which I can indeed say that they 'touch' my body, but only when it is inert, and therefore without ever catching it unawares in its exploratory function.

It was also said that the body is an affective object, whereas external things are from my point of view merely represented. This amounted to stating a third time the problem of the status of my own body. For if I say that my foot hurts, I do not simply mean that it is a cause of pain in the same way as the nail which is cutting into it, differing only in being nearer to me; I do not mean that it is the last of the objects in the external world, after which a more intimate kind of pain should begin, an unlocalized awareness of pain in itself, related to the foot only by some causal connection and within the closed system of experience. I mean that the pain reveals itself as localized, that it is constitutive of a 'pain-infested space'. 'My foot hurts' means not: 'I think that my foot is the cause of this pain'. This is shown clearly by the 'primitive voluminousness of pain' formerly spoken of by psychologists. It was therefore recognized that my body does not present itself as the objects of external impressions do, and that perhaps even these latter objects do no more than stand out against the affective background which in the first place throws consciousness outside itself.

Finally when the psychologists tried to confine 'kinaesthetic sensations' to one's own body, arguing that these sensations present the body's movements to us globally, whereas they attributed the movements of external objects to a mediating perception and to a comparison between successive positions, it could have been objected that movement, expressing a relationship, cannot be felt, but demands a mental operation. This objection, however, would merely have been an indictment of their language. What they were expressing, badly it is true, by 'kinaesthetic sensation', was the originality of the movements which I perform with my body: they directly anticipate the final situation, for my intention initiates a movement through space merely to attain the objective initially given at the starting point; there is as it were a germ of movement which only secondarily develops into an objective movement. I move external objects with the aid of my body, which takes hold of them in one place and shifts them to another. But my body itself I move directly, I do not find it at one point of objective space and transfer it to another, I have no need to look for it, it is already with me—I do not need to lead it towards the movement's completion, it is in contact with it from the start and propels itself towards that end. The relationships between my decision and my body are, in movement, magic ones.

If the description of my own body given by classical psychology already offered all that is necessary to distinguish it from objects, how does it come about that psychologists have not made this distinction or that they have in any case seen no philosophical consequence flowing from it? The reason is that, taking a step natural to them, they chose the position of impersonal thought to which science has been committed as long as it believed in the possibility of separating, in observation, on the one hand what belongs to the situation of the observer and on the other the properties of the absolute object. For the living subject his own body might well be different from all external objects; the fact remains that for the unsituated thought of the psychologist the experience of the living subject became itself an object and, far from requiring a fresh definition of being, took its place in universal being. It was the life of the 'psyche' which stood in opposition to the real, but which was treated as a second reality, as an object of scientific investigation to be brought under a set of laws. It was postulated that our experience, already besieged by physics and biology, was destined to be completely absorbed into objective knowledge, with the consummation of the system of the sciences. Thenceforth the experience of the body degenerated into a 'representation' of the body; it was not a phenomenon but a fact of the psyche. In the matter of living appearance, my visual body includes a large gap at the level of the head, but biology was there ready to fill that gap, to explain it through the structure of the eyes, to instruct me in what the body really is, showing that I have a retina and a brain like other men and like the corpses which I dissect, and that, in short, the surgeon's instrument could infallibly bring to light in this indeterminate zone of my head the exact replica of plates illustrating the human anatomy. I apprehend my body as a subject-object, as capable of 'seeing' and 'suffering', but these confused representations were so many psychological oddities, samples of a magical variety of thought the laws of which are studied by psychology and sociology and which has its place assigned to it by them, in the system of the real world, as an object of scientific investigation. This imperfect picture of my body, its marginal presentation, and its equivocal status as touching and touched, could not therefore be *structural* characteristics of the body itself; they did not affect the idea of it; they became 'distinctive characteristics' of those *contents* of consciousness which make up our representation of the body: these contents are consistent, affective and strangely duplicated in 'double sensations', but apart from this the representation of the body is a representation like any other and correspondingly the body is an object like any other. Psychologists did not realize that in treating the experience of the body in this way they were simply, in accordance with the scientific approach, shelving a problem which ultimately could not be burked. The inadequacy of my perception was taken as a *de facto* inadequacy resulting from the organization of my sensory apparatus; the presence of my body was taken as a *de facto presence* springing from its constant action on my receptive nervous system; finally the union of soul and body, which was presupposed by these two explanations, was understood, in Cartesian fashion, as a *de facto union* whose *de jure* possibility need not be established, because the fact, as the starting point of knowledge, was eliminated from the final result. Now the psychologist could imitate the scientist and, for a moment at least, see his body as others saw it, and conversely see the bodies of others as mechanical things with no inner life. The contribution made from the experiences of others had the effect of dimming the structure of his own, and conversely, having lost contact with himself he became blind to the behaviour of others. He thus saw everything from the point of view of universal thought which abolished equally his experience of others and his experience of himself. But as a psychologist he was engaged in a task which by nature pulled him back into himself, and he could not allow himself to remain unaware to this extent. For whereas neither the physicist nor the chemist are the objects of their own investigation, the psychologist *was himself*, in the nature of the case, the fact which exercised him. This representa-

tion of the body, this magical experience, which he approached in a detached frame of mind, was himself; he lived it as he thought it. It is true that, as has been shown, it was not enough for him to be a psyche in order to know this, for this knowledge, like other knowledge, is acquired only through our relations with other people. It does not emerge from any recourse to an ideal of introspective psychology, and between himself and others no less than between himself and himself, the psychologist was able and obliged to rediscover a pre-objective relationship. But as a psyche speaking of the psyche, he *was* all that he was *talking* about. This history of the psyche which he was elaborating in adopting the objective attitude was one whose outcome he already possessed within himself, or rather he was, in his existence, its contracted outcome and latent memory. The union of soul and body had not been brought about once and for all in a remote realm; it came into being afresh at every moment beneath the psychologist's thinking, not as a repetitive event which each time takes the psyche by surprise, but as a necessity that the psychologist knew to be in the depths of his being as he became aware of it as a piece of knowledge. The birth of perception from the 'sense-data' to the 'world' was supposed to be renewed with each act of perception, otherwise the sense-data would have lost the meaning they owed to this development. Hence the 'psyche' was not an object like others: it had done everything that one was about to say of it before it could be said; the psychologist's being knew more about itself than he did; nothing that had happened or was happening according to science was completely alien to it. Applied to the psyche, the notion of fact, therefore, underwent a transformation. The *de facto* psyche, with its 'peculiarities', was no longer an event in objective time and in the external world, but an event with which we were in internal contact, of which we were ourselves the ceaseless accomplishment or upsurge, and which continually gathered within itself its past, its body and its world. Before being an objective fact, the union of soul and body had to be, then, a possibility of consciousness itself and the question arose as to what the perceiving subject is and whether he must be able to experience a body as his own. There was no longer a fact passively submitted to, but one assumed. To be a consciousness or rather *to be an experience* is to hold inner communication with the world, the body and other people, to be with them instead of being beside them. To concern oneself with psychology is necessarily to encounter, beneath objective thought which moves among ready-made things, a first opening upon things without which there would be no objective knowledge. The psychologist could not fail to rediscover himself as experience, which means as an immediate presence to the past, to the world, to the body and to others at the very moment when he was trying to see himself as an object among objects. Let us then return to the 'characteristics' of one's own body and resume the study of it where we left off. By doing so we shall trace the progress of modern psychology and thereby contrive along with it the return to experience.

3. The Body as Expression and Speech

The analysis of speech and expression brings home to us the enigmatic nature of our own body even more effectively than did our remarks on bodily space and unity. It is not a collection of particles, each one remaining in itself, nor yet a network of processes defined once and for all—it is not where it is, nor what it is—since we see it secreting in itself a 'significance' which comes to it from nowhere, projecting that significance upon its material surrounding, and communicating it to other embodied subjects. It has always

been observed that speech or gesture transfigure the body, but no more was said on the subject than that they develop or disclose another power, that of thought or soul. The fact was overlooked that, in order to express it, the body must in the last analysis become the thought or intention that it signifies for us. It is the body which points out, and which speaks; so much we have learnt in this chapter. Cézanne used to say of a portrait: 'If I paint in all the little blue and brown touches, I make him gaze as he does gaze. . . . Never mind if they suspect how, by bringing together a green of various shades and a red, we sadden a mouth or bring a smile to a cheek.' This disclosure of an immanent or incipient significance in the living body extends, as we shall see, to the whole sensible world, and our gaze, prompted by the experience of our own body, will discover in all other 'objects' the miracle of expression. In his *Peau de Chagrin* Balzac describes a 'white tablecloth, like a covering of snow newly fallen, from which rose symmetrically the plates and napkins crowned with light-coloured rolls'. 'Throughout my youth,' Cézanne said, 'I wanted to paint that table-cloth like freshly fallen snow. . . . I know now that one must try to paint only: "the plates and napkins rose symmetrically", and "the light-coloured rolls". If I paint: "crowned", I'm finished, you see. And if I really balance and shade my napkins and rolls as they really are, you may be sure that the crowning, the snow and all the rest of it will be there.' The problem of the world, and, to begin with, that of one's own body, consists in the fact that *it is all there*.

We have become accustomed, through the influence of the Cartesian tradition, to jettison the subject: the reflective attitude simultaneously purifies the common notions of body and soul by defining the body as the sum of its parts with no interior, and the soul as a being wholly present to itself without distance. These definitions make matters perfectly clear both within and outside ourselves: we have the transparency of an object with no secret recesses, the transparency of a subject which is nothing but what it thinks it is. The object is an object through and through, and consciousness a consciousness through and through. There are two senses, and two only, of the word 'exist': one exists as a thing or else one exists as a consciousness. The experience of our own body, on the other hand, reveals to us an ambiguous mode of existing. If I try to think of it as a cluster of third person processes—'sight', 'motility', 'sexuality'—I observe that these 'functions' cannot be interrelated, and related to the external world, by causal connections, they are all obscurely drawn together and mutually implied in a unique drama. Therefore the body is not an object. For the same reason, my awareness of it is not a thought, that is to say, I cannot take it to pieces and reform it to make a clear idea. Its unity is always implicit and vague. It is always something other than what it is, always sexuality and at the same time freedom, rooted in nature at the very moment when it is transformed by cultural influences, never hermetically sealed and never left behind. Whether it is a question of another's body or my own, I have no means of knowing the human body other than that of living it, which means taking up on my own account the drama which is being played out in it, and losing myself in it. I am my body, at least wholly to the extent that I possess experience, and yet at the same time my body is as it were a 'natural' subject, a provisional sketch of my total being. Thus experience of one's own body runs counter to the reflective procedure which detaches subject and object from each other, and which gives us only the thought about the body, or the body as an idea, and not the experience of the body or the body in reality. Descartes was well aware of this, since a famous letter of his to Elizabeth draws the distinction between the body as it is conceived through use in living and the body as it is conceived by the understanding.[2] But in Descartes this peculiar knowledge of our body, which we enjoy from the mere fact that we are a body, remains subordinated to our knowledge of it through the medium of ideas, because, behind man as he in fact is, stands God as the rational author of our *de facto* situation. On the basis of this transcendent guarantee, Descartes can blandly accept our irrational condition: it is not we who are required to bear the responsibility for reason and, once we have recognized it at the basis of things, it remains for us only to act and think in the world.[3] But if our union with the body is substantial, how is it possible for us to experience in ourselves a pure soul from which to accede to an absolute Spirit? Before asking this question, let us look closely at what is implied in the rediscovery of our own body. It is not merely one object among the rest which has the peculiarity of resisting reflection and remaining, so to speak, stuck to the subject. Obscurity spreads to the perceived world in its entirety.

[2] To Elizabeth, 28th June 1643, AT, T. III, p. 690.
[3] 'Finally, as I consider that it is very necessary to have understood, once in one's lifetime, the principles of metaphysics, since they are what provide us with knowledge of God and our soul, I think too, however, that it would be extremely harmful to occupy our mind often in meditating upon them, since it could not then attend so effectively to the work of imagination and the senses; but that the best course is merely to retain in memory and belief conclusions once arrived at, and thenceforth to employ the rest of the time one can devote to study to thoughts in which the understanding acts along with the imagination and the senses.' Ibid.

CHAPTER 38

ELIZABETH V. SPELMAN

WOMAN AS BODY

Elizabeth V. Spelman (1945–) received her Ph.D. in philosophy from Johns Hopkins University in 1974. Since 1982, she has taught philosophy at Smith College. She is the author of *Inessential Woman: Problems of Exclusion in Feminist Thought* (1988).

WOMAN AS BODY[1]

and what pure happiness to know all our high-toned questions breed in a lively animal.

Adrienne Rich, from "Two Songs"

What philosophers have had to say about women typically has been nasty, brutish, and short. A page or two of quotations from those considered among the great philosophers (Aristotle, Hume, and Nietzsche, for example) constitutes a veritable litany of contempt. Because phi-losophers have not said much about women, and, when they have, it has usually been in short essays or chatty addenda which have not been considered to be part of the central body of their work, it is tempting to regard their expressed views about women as asystemic: their remarks

[1]This article is reprinted from FEMINIST STUDIES, Volume 8, number 1 (Spring 1982):109–131, by permission of the publisher FEMINIST STUDIES, Inc., c/o Women's Studies Program, University of Maryland, College Park, MD 20742.

on women are unofficial asides which are unrelated to the heart of their philosophical doctrines. After all, it might be thought, how could one's views about something as unimportant as women have anything to do with one's views about something as important as the nature of knowledge, truth, reality, freedom? Moreover—and this is the philosopher's move par excellence—wouldn't it be charitable to consider those opinions about women as coming merely from the *heart*, which all too easily responds to the tenor of the times, while philosophy "proper" comes from the *mind*, which resonates not with the times but with the truth?

Part of the intellectual legacy from philosophy "proper," that is, the issues that philosophers have addressed which are thought to be the serious province of philosophy, it the soul/body or mind/body distinction (differences among the various formulations are not crucial to this essay). However, this part of philosophy might have not merely accidental connections to attitudes about women. For when one recalls that the Western philosophical tradition has not been noted for its celebration of the body, and that women's nature and women's lives have long been associated with the body and bodily functions, then a question is suggested. What connection might there be between attitudes toward the body and attitudes toward women? . . .

Plato's Lessons about the Soul and the Body

Plato's dialogues are filled with lessons about knowledge, reality, and goodness, and most of the lessons carry with them strong praise for the soul and strong indictments against the body. According to Plato, the body, with its deceptive senses, keeps us from real knowledge; it rivets us in a world of material things which is far removed from the world of reality; and it tempts us away from the virtuous life. It is in and through the soul, if at all, that we shall have knowledge, be in touch with reality, and lead a life of virtue. Only the soul can truly know, for only the soul can ascend to the real world, the world of the Forms or Ideas. That world is the perfect model to which imperfect, particular things, we find in matter merely approximate. It is a world which, like the soul, is invisible, unchanging, not subject to decay, eternal. To be good, one's soul must know the Good, that is, the Form of Goodness, and this is impossible while one is dragged down by the demands and temptations of bodily life. Hence, bodily death is nothing to be feared: immortality of the soul not only is possible, but greatly to be desired, because when one is released from the body one finally can get down to the real business of life, for this real business of life is the business of the soul. Indeed, Socrates describes his own commitment, while still on earth, to encouraging his fellow Athenians to pay attention to the real business of life:

> [I have spent] all my time going about trying to persuade you, young and old, to make your first and chief concern not for your bodies nor for your possessions, but for the highest welfare of your souls.

Plato also tells us about the nature of beauty. Beauty has nothing essentially to do with the body or with the world of material things. *Real* beauty cannot "take the form of a face, or of hands, or of anything that is of the flesh." Yes, there are beautiful things, but they only are entitled to be described that way because they "partake in" the form of Beauty, which itself is not found in the material world. Real beauty has characteristics which merely beautiful *things* cannot have; real beauty is an everlasting loveliness which neither comes nor goes, which neither flowers nor fades, for such beauty is the same on every hand, the same then as now, here as there, this way as that way, the same to every worshipper as it is to every other.

Because it is only the soul that can know the Forms, those eternal and unchanging denizens of Reality, only the soul can know real Beauty; our changing, decaying bodies only can put us in touch with changing, decaying pieces of the material world.

Plato also examines love. His famous discussion of love in the *Symposium* ends up being a celebration of the soul over the body. Attraction to and appreciation for the beauty of another's body is but a vulgar fixation unless one can use such appreciation as a stepping stone to understanding Beauty itself. One can begin to learn about Beauty, while one is still embodied, when one notices that this body is beautiful, that that body is beautiful, and so on, and then one begins to realize that Beauty itself is something beyond any particular beautiful body or thing. The kind of love between people that is to be valued is not the attraction of one body for another, but the attraction of one soul for another. There is procreation of the spirit as well as of the flesh. All that bodies in unison can create are more bodies—the children women bear—which are mortal, subject to change and decay. But souls in unison can create "something lovelier and less mortal than human seed," for spiritual lovers "conceive and bear the things of the spirit," that is, "wisdom and all her sister virtues." Hence, spiritual love between men is preferable to physical love between men and women. At the same time, physical love between men is ruled out, on the grounds that "enjoyment of flesh by flesh" is "wanton shame," while desire of soul for soul is at the heart of a relationship that "reverences, aye

and worships, chastity and manhood, greatness and wisdom." The potential for harm in sexual relations is very great—harm not so much to one's body or physique, but to one's soul. Young men especially shouldn't get caught up with older men in affairs that threaten their "spiritual development," for such development is "assuredly and ever will be of supreme value in the sight of gods and men alike."

So, then, one has no hope of understanding the nature of knowledge, reality, goodness, love, or beauty unless one recognizes the distinction between soul and body; and one has no hope of attaining any of these unless one works hard on freeing the soul from the lazy, vulgar, beguiling body. A philosopher is someone who is committed to doing just that, and that is why philosophers go willingly unto death; it is, after all, only the death of their bodies, and finally, once their souls are released from their bodies, these philosophical desiderata are within reach. . . .

The division among parts of the soul is intimately tied to one other central and famous aspect of Plato's philosophy that hasn't been mentioned so far: Plato's political views. His discussion of the parts of the soul and their proper relation to one another is integral to his view about the best way to set up a state. The rational part of the soul ought to rule the soul and ought to be attended by the spirited part in keeping watch over the unruly appetitive part; just so, there ought to be rulers of the state (the small minority in whom reason is dominant), who, with the aid of high-spirited guardians of order, watch over the multitudes (whose appetites need to be kept under control).

What we learn from Plato, then, about knowledge, reality, goodness, beauty, love, and statehood, is phrased in terms of a distinction between soul and body, or alternatively and roughly equivalently, in terms of a distinction between the rational and irrational. And the body, or the irrational part of the soul, is seen as an enormous and annoying obstacle to the possession of these desiderata. If the body gets the upper hand over the soul, or if the irrational part of the soul overpowers the rational part, one can't have knowledge, one can't see beauty, one will be far from the highest form of love, and the state will be in utter chaos. So the soul/body distinction, or the distinction between the rational and irrational parts of the soul, is a highly charged distinction. An inquiry into the distinction is no mild metaphysical musing. It is quite clear that the distinction is heavily value-laden. Even if Plato hadn't told us outright that the soul is more valuable than the body, and the rational part of the soul is more important than the irrational part, that message rings out in page after page of his dialogues. The soul/body distinction, then, is integral to the rest of Plato's views, and the higher worth of the soul is integral to that distinction.

Plato's View of the Soul and Body, and His Attitude Toward Women

Plato, and anyone else who conceives of the soul as something unobservable, cannot of course speak as if we could point to the soul, or hold it up for direct observation. At one point, Plato says no mere mortal can really understand the nature of the soul, but one perhaps could tell what it resembles. So it is not surprising to find Plato using many metaphors and analogies to describe what the soul is *like*, in order to describe relations between the soul and the body or relations between parts of the soul. For example, thinking, a function of the soul, is described by analogy to talking. The parts of the soul are likened to a team of harnessed, winged horses and their charioteer. The body's relation to the soul is such that we are to think of the body vis-à-vis the

soul as a tomb, a grave or prison, or as barnacles or rocks holding down the soul. Plato compares the lowest or bodylike part of the soul to a brood of beasts.

But Plato's task is not only to tell us what the soul is like, not only to provide us with ways of getting a fix on the differences between souls and bodies, or differences between parts of the soul. As we've seen, he also wants to convince us that the soul is much more important than the body, and that it is to our peril that we let ourselves be beckoned by the rumblings of the body at the expense of harkening to the call of the soul. And he means to convince us of this by holding up for our inspection the silly and sordid lives of those who pay too much attention to their bodies and do not care enough for their souls; he wants to remind us of how unruly, how without direction, are the lives of those in whom the lower part of the soul holds sway over the higher part. Because he can't *point* to an adulterated soul, he points instead to those embodied beings whose lives are in such bad shape that we can be sure that their souls are adulterated. And whose lives exemplify the proper soul/body relationship gone haywire? The lives of women (or sometimes the lives of children, slaves, and brutes).

For example, how are we to know when the body has the upper hand over the soul, or when the lower part of the soul has managed to smother the higher part? We presumably can't see such conflict, so what do such conflicts translate into, in terms of actual human lives? Well, says Plato, look at the lives of women. It is women who get hysterical at the thought of death; obviously, their emotions have overpowered their reason, and they can't control themselves. The worst possible model for young men could be "a woman, young or old or wrangling with her husband, defying heaven, loudly boasting, fortunate in her own conceit, or involved in misfortune or possessed by grief and lamentation—still less a woman that is sick, in love, or in labor". . . .

Moreover, Plato on many occasions points to women to illustrate the improper way to pursue the things for which philosophers are constantly to be searching. For example, Plato wants to explain how important and also how difficult the attainment of real knowledge is. He wants us to realize that not just anyone can have knowledge, there is a vital distinction between those who really have knowledge and those who merely think they do. Think, for example, about the question of health. If we don't make a distinction between those who know what health is, and those who merely have unfounded and confused opinions about what health is, then "in the matter of good or bad health . . . any woman or child— or animal, for that matter—knows what is wholesome for it and is capable of curing itself." The implication is clear: if any old opinion were to count as real knowledge, then we'd have to say that women, children, and maybe even animals have knowledge. But surely *they* don't have knowledge! And why not? For one thing, because they don't recognize the difference between the material, changing world of appearance, and the invisible, eternal world of Reality. In matters of beauty, for example, they are so taken by the physical aspects of things that they assume that they can see and touch what is beautiful; they don't realize that what one knows when one has knowledge of real Beauty cannot be something that is seen or touched. Plato offers us, then, as an example of the failure to distinguish between Beauty itself, on the one hand, and beautiful things, on the other, "boys and women when they see bright-colored things." They don't realize that it is not through one's senses that one knows about beauty or anything else, for real beauty is eternal and invisible and unchangeable and can only be known through the soul.

So the message is that in matters of knowledge, reality, and beauty, don't follow the example of women. They are mistaken about those things. In matters of love, women's lives serve as negative examples also. Those men who are drawn by "vulgar" love, that is, love of body for body, "turn to women as the object of their love, and raise a family"; those men drawn by a more "heavenly" kind of love, that is, love of soul for soul, turn to other men. But there are strong sanctions against physical love between men: such physical unions, especially between older and younger men, are "unmanly." The older man isn't strong enough to resist his lust (as in woman, the irrational part of the soul has overtaken the rational part), and the younger man, "the impersonator of the female," is reproached for this "likeness to the model." The problem with physical love between men, then, is that men are acting like women.

To summarize the argument so far: the soul/body distinction is integral to the rest of Plato's views; integral to the soul/body distinction is the higher worth and importance of the soul in comparison to the body; finally, Plato tries to persuade his readers that it is to one's peril that one does not pay proper attention to one's soul—for if one doesn't, one will end up acting and living as if one were a woman. We know, Plato says, about lives dictated by the demands and needs and inducements of the body instead of the soul. Such lives surely are not good models for those who want to understand and undertake a life devoted to the nurturance of the best part of us: our souls.

To anyone at all familiar with Plato's official and oft-reported views about women, the above recitation of misogynistic remarks may be quite surprising. Accounts of Plato's views about women usually are based on what he says in book 5 of the *Republic*. In that dialogue, Plato startled his contemporaries, when as part of his proposal for the constitution of an ideal state, he suggested that there is no pursuit of the administrators of a state that belongs to woman because she is a woman or to a man because he is a man. But the natural capacities are distributed alike among both creatures, and women naturally share in all pursuits and men in all. . . .

Well now, what are we to make of this apparent double message in Plato about women? What are we to do with the fact that on the one hand, when Plato explicitly confronts the question of women's nature, in the *Republic*, he seems to affirm the equality of men and women; while on the other hand, the dialogues are riddled with misogynistic remarks? . . .

So the contradictory sides of Plato's views about women are tied to the distinction he makes between soul and body and the lessons he hopes to teach his readers about their relative values. When preaching about the overwhelming importance of the soul, he can't but regard the kind of body one has as of no final significance, so there is no way for him to assess differentially the lives of women and men; but when making gloomy pronouncements about the worth of the body, he points an accusing finger at a class of people with a certain kind of body—women— because he regards them, as a class, as embodying the very traits he wishes no one to have. In this way, women constitute a deviant class in Plato's philosophy, in the sense that he points to their lives as the kinds of lives that are not acceptable philosophically: they are just the kind of lives no one, especially philosophers, ought to live. . . .

In summary, Plato does not merely embrace a distinction between soul and body; for all the good and hopeful and desirable possibilities for human life (now and in an afterlife) are aligned with the soul, while the rather seedy and undesirable liabilities of human life are aligned with the body (alternatively, the alignment is with the higher or lower parts of the soul). There is a highly polished moral gloss to the soul/body distinction in Plato. One of his favorite devices for bringing this moral gloss to a high luster is holding up, for our contempt and ridicule, the lives of women. This is one of ways he tries to make clear that it makes no small difference whether you lead a soul-directed or a bodily directed life.

Feminism and "Somatophobia"

There are a number of reasons why feminists should be aware of the legacy of the soul/body distinction. It is not just that the distinction has been wound up with the depreciation and degradation of women, although, as has just been shown, examining a philosopher's view of the distinction may give us a direct route to his views about women.

First of all, as the soul or mind or reason is extolled, and the body or passion is denounced by comparison, it is not just women who are both relegated to the bodily or passionate sphere of existence and then chastised for belonging to that sphere. Slaves, free laborers, children, and animals are put in "their place" on almost the same grounds as women are. The images of women, slaves, laborers, children, and animals are almost interchangeable. For example, we find Plato holding that the best born and best educated should have control over "children, women and slaves . . . and the base rabble of those who are free in name," because it is in these groups that we find "the mob of motley appetites and pleasures and pains." As we saw above, Plato lumps together women, children, and animals as ignoramuses. (For Aristotle, there is little difference between a slave and an animal, because both "with their bodies attend to the needs of life." A common way of denigrating a member of any one of these groups is to compare that member to a member of one of the other groups—

women are thought to have slavish or childish appetites, slaves are said to be brutish. Recall too, that Plato's way of ridiculing male homosexuals was to say that they imitated women. It is no wonder that the images and insults are almost interchangeable, for there is a central descriptive thread holding together the images of all these groups. The members of these groups lack, for all intents and purposes, mind or the power of reason; even the humans among them are not considered fully human.

It is important for feminists to see to what extent the images and arguments used to denigrate women are similar to those used to denigrate one group of men vis-à-vis another, children vis-à-vis adults, animals vis-à-vis humans, and even—though I have not discussed it here—the natural world vis-à-vis man's will (yes, man's will). For to see this is part of understanding how the oppression of women occurs in the context of, and is related to, other forms of oppression or exploitation.

There is a second reason why feminists should be aware of the legacy of the soul/body distinction. Some feminists have quite happily adopted both the soul/body distinction and relative value attached to soul and to body. But in doing so, they may be adopting a position inimical to what on a more conscious level they are arguing for.

For all her magisterial insight into the way in which the image of woman as body has been foisted upon and used against us, Simone de Beauvoir can't resist the temptation to say that woman's emancipation will come when woman, like man, is freed from this association with—according to the male wisdom of the centuries—the less important aspect of human existence. According to *The Second Sex*, women's demand is "not that they be exalted in their femininity; they wish that in themselves, as in humanity in general, transcendence may prevail over immanence."

But in de Beauvoir's own terms, for "transcendence" to prevail over "immanence" is for spirit or mind to prevail over matter or body, for reason to prevail over passion and desire. This means not only that the old images of women as mired in the world of "immanence"—the world of nature and physical existence—will go away. It will also happen that women won't lead lives given over mainly to their "natural" functions: "the pain of childbirth is on the way out"; "artificial insemination is on the way in." Although de Beauvoir doesn't explicitly say it, her directions for women are to find means of leaving the world of immanence and joining the men in the realm of transcendence. Men have said, de Beauvoir reminds us, that to be human is to have mind prevail over body; and no matter what disagreements she has elsewhere with men's perceptions and priorities, de Beauvoir here seems to agree with them. . . .

. . . can we as a species sustain negative attitudes and negative ideologies about the bodily aspects of our existence and yet keep those attitudes and ideologies from working in behalf of one group of people as it attempts to oppress other groups?

. . . in *The Feminist Mystique*, [Betty] Friedan remarks on the absence, in women's lives, of "the world of thought and ideas, the life of the mind and spirit." She wants women to be "culturally" as well as "biologically" creative—she wants us to think about spending our lives "mastering the secrets of the atoms, or the stars, composing symphonies, pioneering a new concept in government or society." And she associates "mental activity" with the "professions of highest value to society." Friedan thus seems to believe that men have done the more important things, the mental things; women have been relegated in the past to the less important human tasks involving bodily functions, and their liberation will come when they are allowed and encouraged to do the more important things in life.

393

Friedan's analysis relies on our old friend, the mind/body distinction, and Friedan, no less than Plato or de Beauvoir, quite happily assumes that mental activities are more valuable than bodily ones. Her solution to what she referred to as the "problem that has no name" is for women to leave (though not entirely) women's sphere and "ascend" into man's. Certainly there is much pleasure and value in the "mental activities" she extolls. But we can see the residue of her own negative attitude about tasks associated with the body: the bodily aspects of our existence must be attended to, but the "liberated" woman, who is on the ascendant, can't be bothered with them. There is yet another group of people to whom these tasks will devolve: servants. Woman's liberation—and of course it is no secret that by "woman," Friedan could only have meant middle-class white women—seems to require woman's dissociation and separation from those who will perform the bodily tasks which the liberated woman has left behind in pursuit of "higher," mental activity. So we find Friedan quoting, without comment, Elizabeth Cady Stanton:

> I now understood the practical difficulties most women had to contend with in the isolated household and the impossibility of women's best development if in contact the chief part of her life with servants and children. . .

Friedan at times seems to chide those women who could afford to have servants but don't: the women pretend there's a "servant problem" when there isn't, or insist on doing their own menial work. The implication is that women could find servants to do the "menial work," if they wanted to, and that it would be desirable for them to do so. But what difference is there between the place assigned to women by men and the place assigned to some women (or men) by Friedan herself? . . .

What I have tried to do here is bring attention to the fact that various versions of women's liberation may themselves rest on the very same assumptions that have informed the deprecation and degradation of women, and other groups which, of course, include women. Those assumptions are that we must distinguish between soul and body, and that the physical part of our existence is to be devalued in comparison to the mental. Of course, these two assumptions alone don't mean that women or other groups have to be degraded; it's these two assumptions, along with the further assumption that woman is body, or is bound to her body, or is meant to take care of the bodily aspects of life, that have so deeply contributed to the degradation and oppression of women. And so perhaps feminists would like to keep the first two assumptions (about the difference between mind and body, and the relative worth of each of them) and somehow or other get rid of the last—in fact, that is what most of the feminists previously discussed have tried to do. Nothing that has been said so far has amounted to an argument against those first two assumptions: it hasn't been shown that there is no foundation for the assumptions that the mind and body are distinct and that the body is to be valued less than the mind.

There is a feminist thinker, however, who has taken it upon herself to chip away directly at the second assumption and to a certain extent at the first. Both in her poetry, and explicitly in her recent book, *Of Woman Born*, Adrienne Rich has begun to show us why use of the mind/body distinction does not give us appropriate descriptions of human experience; and she has begun to remind us of the distance we keep from ourselves when we try to keep a distance from our bodies. She does this in the process of trying to redefine the dimensions of the experience of childbirth, as she tries to show us why childbirth and motherhood need not mean what they have meant under patriarchy.

We are reminded by Rich that it is possible to be alienated from our bodies not only by pretending or wishing they weren't there, but also by being "incarcerated" in them. The institution of motherhood has done the latter in its insistence on seeing woman only or mainly as a reproductive machine. Defined as flesh by flesh-loathers, woman enters the most "fleshly" of her experiences with that same attitude of flesh-loathing—surely "physical self-hatred and suspicion of one's own body is scarcely a favorable emotion with which to enter an intense physical experience.

But Rich insists that we don't have to experience childbirth in that way—we don't have to experience it as "torture rack", but neither do we have to mystify it as a "peak experience." The experience of childbirth can be viewed as a way of recognizing the integrity of our experience, because pain itself is not usefully catalogued as something just our minds or just our bodies experience. . . . The point of "natural childbirth" should be thought of not as enduring pain, but as having an active physical experience—a distinction we recognize as crucial for understanding, for example, the pleasure in athletics.

Rich recognizes that feminists have not wanted to accept patriarchal versions of female biology, of what having a female body means. It has seemed to feminists, she implies, that we must either accept that view of being female, which is, essentially, to be a body, or deny that view and insist that we are "disembodied spirits." It perhaps is natural to see our alternatives that way:

We have been perceived for too many centuries as pure Nature, exploited and raped

like the earth and the solar system; small wonder if we not try to become Culture: pure spirit, mind.

But we don't *have* to do that, Rich reminds us; we can appeal to the physical without denying what is called "mind." We can come to regard our physicality as "resource, rather than a destiny":

In order to live a fully human life we require not only *control* of our bodies (though control is a prerequisite); we must touch the unity and resonance of our physicality, our bond with the natural order, the corporeal ground of our intelligence.

Rich doesn't deny that we will have to start thinking about our lives in new ways; she even implies that we'll have to start thinking about thinking in new ways. Maybe it will give such a project a small boost to point out that philosophers for their part still squabble about mind/body dualism; the legacy of dualism is strong, but not unchallenged by any means. And in any event, . . . one can hardly put the blame for sexism (or any other form of oppression) on dualism itself. Indeed, the mind/body distinction can be put to progressive political ends, for example, to assert equality between human beings in the face of physical differences between them. There is nothing intrinsically sexist or otherwise oppressive about dualism, that is, about the belief that there are minds and there are bodies and that they are distinct kinds of things. But historically, the story dualists tell often ends up being a highly politicized one: although the story may be different at different historical moments, often it is said not only that there are minds (or souls) and bodies, but also that one is meant to rule and control the other. And the stage is thereby set for the soul/body distinction, now highly politicized and hierarchically ordered, to be used in a variety of ways in connection with repressive theories of the self, as well as oppressive theories of social and political relations. Among the tasks facing feminists is to think about the criteria for an adequate theory of self. Part of the value of Rich's work is that it points to the necessity of such an undertaking, and it is no criticism of her to say that she does no more than remind us of some of the questions that need to be raised.

A Final Note about the Significance of Somatophobia in Feminist Theory

In the history of political philosophy, the grounds given for the inferiority of women to men often are quite similar to those given for the inferiority of slaves to masters, children to fathers, animals to humans. In Plato, for example, all such subordinate groups are guilty by association with one another and each group is guilty by association with the bodily. In their eagerness to end the stereotypical association of woman and body, feminists such as de Beauvoir, Friedan, Firestone, and Daly have overlooked the significance of the connections—in theory and in practice—between the derogation and oppression of women on the basis of our sexual identity and the derogation and oppression of other groups on the basis of, for example, skin color and class membership. It is as if in their eagerness to assign women a new place in the scheme of things, these feminist theorists have by implication wanted to dissociate women from other subordinate groups. One problem with this, of course, is that those other subordinate groups include women.

What is especially significant about Rich's recent work is that in contrast to these other theorists she both challenges the received tradition about the insignificance and indignity of bodily life and bodily tasks and explicitly focuses on racism as well as sexism as essential factors in women's oppression. I believe that it is not merely a coincidence that someone who attends to the first also attends to the second. Rich pauses not just to recognize the significance attached to the female body, but also to reevaluate that significance. "Flesh-loathing" is loathing of flesh by some particular group under some particular circumstances—the loathing of women's flesh by men, but also the loathing of black flesh by whites. (Here I begin to extrapolate from Rich, but I believe with some warrant.) After all, bodies are always particular bodies—they are male or female bodies (our deep confusion when we can't categorize a body in either way supports and does not belie the general point); but they are black or brown or biscuit or yellow or red bodies as well. We cannot seriously attend to the social significance attached to embodiment without recognizing this. I believe that it is Rich's recognition of this that distinguishes her work in crucial ways from that of most other major white feminists. Although the topic of feminism, sexism, and racism deserves a much fuller treatment, it is important to point out in the context of the present paper that not only does Rich challenge an assumption about the nature of the bodily that has been used to oppress women, but, unlike other feminists who do not challenge this assumption, she takes on the question of the ways in which sexism and racism interlock. Somatophobia historically has been symptomatic not only of sexism, but also of racism, so it is perhaps not surprising that someone who has examined that connection between flesh-loathing and sexism would undertake an examination of racism.

GLOSSARY

BUNDLE THEORY   Hume's theory that the mind is not a mental substance but merely a bundle of different perceptions; the entire collection is named "mind" or "self."

COGNITIVE SCIENCE   An interdisciplinary field including cognitive psychology, computer science, linguistics, psychobiology, anthropology, and philosophy.

CONSCIOUSNESS   An awareness of one's own existence; an awareness of a relation between oneself as a subject and some object of knowledge.

DUALISM   The view that human nature is comprised of a material mind and an immaterial mind or soul.

FORMAL OPERATIONS   Processes defined solely in terms of the nonsemantic properties of the things they operate on.

IMMATERIAL   Not consisting of matter; synonyms include incorporeal, spiritual, nonmaterial, nonphysical.

INTENTIONALITY   The ability of consciousness to refer or point to some object beyond itself; a key doctrine of phenomenology.

MATERIALISM   In its extreme form, the belief that nothing but matter in motion exists. A milder version is the belief that mind does exist, but is caused by material changes.

MONISM   The view that all things can be reduced to, or explained in terms of, one fundamental principle. For materialists, that principle is matter; for idealists, it is mind.

PERSONAL IDENTITY   Sameness of self; an awareness that I am the same conscious unity at different times and places.

PRIVACY   An immediate knowledge of the self that is personal and cannot be completely reduced to objective, scientific terms.

SELF   A conscious unity that endures throughout change; a person as an individual, characterized by personal identity, transcendence, and privacy.

SELF-CONSCIOUSNESS   To be aware of one's own state of awareness; the ability to treat one's own consciousness as an object of knowledge.

SELF-TRANSCENDENCE   The view that the self has an awareness of itself that goes beyond any of its particular states, acts, or processes; the ability of the self to rise above time limitations to become part of a larger whole, merging past, present, and future.

SUBJECTIVE IDEALISM   The view, held by Bishop George Berkeley, that reality is comprised of minds and the perceptions of those minds; all reality is mind-dependent.

FOR FURTHER STUDY

Buber, Martin. *I and Thou.* New York: Scribner's, 1958.
A beautifully written existential view of the self. Buber makes his famous distinction between the I-Thou and the I-It relationship in this book.

Dreyfus, Hubert. *What Computers Can't Do.* New York: Harper & Row, 1979.
The title says it all. Written by a respected phenomenologist who has been influenced by Heidegger and Merleau-Ponty.

Foder, Jerry. *Representations*. Cambridge: M.I.T. Press, 1981.

A functionalist account of the mind-body relation.

Hofstadter, D.R. *Gödel, Escher, Bach: An Eternal Golden Braid*. New York: Vintage Books, 1980.

An attempt to synthesize elements of philosophy, artificial intelligence, and neuroscience, written by a Pulitzer-prize winning author.

Hook, Sidney, ed. *Dimensions of Mind: A Symposium*. New York: Collier Books, 1961.

A useful collection of essays representing a wide variety of views.

Johnstone, Henry W. *The Problem of the Self*. University Park, Pa.: The Pennsylvania State University Press, 1970.

Stressing the uniqueness of human beings, Johnstone makes helpful distinctions between persons, selves, and computers.

Lloyd, Genevieve. *The Man of Reason: "Male" and "Female" in Western Philosophy*. Minneapolis: University of Minnesota Press, 1984.

A feminist reading of the history of philosophy. The third chapter deals with Descartes, the mind-body relation, and the exclusion of women from Reason.

Ryle, Gilbert. *The Concept of Mind*. New York: Harper & Row, 1949.

A systematic presentation of logical behaviorism. Historically, a very important book in the philosophy of mind.

Shaffer, Jerome. *Philosophy of Mind*. Englewood Cliffs, N.J.: Prentice Hall, 1968.

Includes an important critique of identity theory.

PART SIX

◆

FREEDOM, DETERMINISM, AND RESPONSIBILITY

Freedom is the ethical aspect of hope

JACQUES ELLUL

ORIENTATION

Are human actions free or are they universally determined by forces over which humans have no control? Perhaps no philosophical question has more practical implications than this one, for it affects the way we think about ourselves in relation to the external world, the future, the law, morality, God, and eternity. For example, if all events in the universe, including human events, are determined by rigid laws and forces described by science and completely beyond our control, what would be the point of making plans for the future? From a legal standpoint, could we hold a person responsible for some crime if her actions were merely the result of impersonal mechanical forces? How could the legal machinery of the state punish individuals if there were no freedom of choice? If human beings are not free, is ethical behavior possible? How do we account for the fact that we often "feel free," even in the face of an impressive amount of scientific evidence that suggests that the universe is an ironclad system of cause and effect that has no room in it for freedom? Is "felt freedom" enough to offset the deterministic thesis of the sciences, or is it merely an illusion? Must we resign ourselves to view the world from two very different sets of assumptions: one theoretical, where we accept the scientific doctrine of **hard determinism,** and the other practical, where we act as if we were free?

This barrage of questions provides an introduction to the ancient problem of free will versus determinism. In the history of philosophy, three strategies for resolving the problem have been employed. This Orientation is designed to acquaint you with these three theoretical approaches: (1) the denial of freedom (fatalism, predestination, hard determinism); (2) the affirmation of freedom (indeterminism); and the attempt to reconcile freedom with determinism (compatibilism and self-determinism). The Contemporary Perspectives section focuses on the important issues of crime and punishment.

DENIALS OF FREEDOM: FATALISM, PREDESTINATION, HARD DETERMINISM

Although fatalism, predestination, and hard determinism are often combined in the popular mind, in fact they are logically distinct. Since hard determinism is the most popular denial of freedom today, we shall devote most of our attention to it. It is interesting to note the historical shift in emphasis away from fatalism and predestination toward hard determinism. This shift took place in the transition from the Middle Ages to the Renaissance, reflecting the displacement of religion and the rise of science as the major cultural force in the West.

FATALISM

Fatalism is the view that events in the universe are predetermined: what will happen and what will not happen have already been decided, and nothing we do can alter our fate. This belief is often expressed by a series of popular expressions, clichés that people reach for when facing difficult circumstances. Thus the soldier going into combat may say, "If there is a bullet with my name on it, I'll get it." Family members faced with the sudden loss of a loved one may sigh with resignation, "When your number comes up, there is nothing you can do about it." A popular song in the 1950s captured the spirit of fatalism perfectly with these words: "Que sera, sera. Whatever will be, will be. The future's not ours to see. Que sera, sera."

The emotional attitude that goes along with these expressions is frequently described as "being philosophical," or "being stoical." Stoicism was a philosophy founded in Cyprus during the fourth century B.C. by Zeno of Citium (c. 336–c. 264 B.C.). Zeno and his disciples were probably called "Stoics" because Zeno lectured from a "stoa," or roofed porch. The Stoics believed that we should not attempt to fight against fate. Instead, we should adopt a stance of indifference toward the world, emotionally accepting whatever life brings. Because "being philosophical" has come to be identified with this stoical restraint of emotion when facing the worst that life can bring, many people assume that philosophers must be fatalists. In fact, nothing could be further from the truth. Very few philosophers are fatalists.

The concept of fate was prominent in ancient Greece and Rome. Sometimes it is identified with the will of Zeus or Jupiter. It is a recurrent theme in the ancient Greek plays, particularly the tragedies of Sophocles (496–406 B.C.). In Sophocles' great play, *Oedipus the King*, Oedipus knows long before his tragedy occurs that he will kill his father and marry his mother, having been warned by a prophecy. To escape his fate, he leaves home, changes his identity, and takes all the precautions that he can. Nothing helps—the prophecy tragically unfolds in an ironic way that holds audiences spellbound to this day. The Romans embraced the mythology of the Greeks, introducing the concept of Fortune. Wealth, prosperity, death, calamity—all depend on the turning of Fortune's wheel.

It was Sir Francis Bacon and René Descartes who broke with this historical fatalism. Near the end of his *Discourse on Method*, Descartes speaks of a practical science that would make humans "masters and possessors of nature." Bacon, pointedly speaking back to Roman times, revived the saying, "Man is the architect of his fortune," even as he mapped out an ambitious program for scientific advance. By the time of the Enlightenment, this confident attitude of self-reliance and human control (what the historian Peter Gay calls "a recovery of nerve"[1]) had

[1]See Peter Gay, *The Enlightenment: An Interpretation* (New York: W.W. Norton, 1969), 3–8.

replaced the fearful helplessness of fatalism. As the Enlightenment ideals of progress and scientific mastery became dominant in Western civilization, fatalism became increasingly unpopular.

Even so, are there any reasons to think that fatalism might be true? Aristotle explored one argument that seems to support fatalism from a logical point of view. When we consider any state of affairs, either in the present or in the past, it is obvious that statements describing them must either be true or false. For instance, either it is raining now or it is not raining. It is either Tuesday or it is not Tuesday. The same pattern holds true for past events: either Napoleon won the battle of Jena in 1807 or he did not win. But now consider statements about the future. To use Aristotle's example, either there will be a sea battle tomorrow, or there will not be a sea battle tomorrow. Or, to use a more contemporary example, either Mario Cuomo will be president of the United States in 1996 or he will not be. Suppose it is true that Mario Cuomo will be president in 1996; *in that case, it is true right now that he will be president in 1996.* If you take the opposite supposition—that Mario Cuomo will not be president in 1996—you do not avoid the fatalistic conclusion. If Mario Cuomo will not be president in 1996, then it is true right now that he will not be president in 1996.

Of course, it is possible to avoid fatalism by not making truth claims about future events. But if we choose to speak truthfully only about present or past events, excluding future events, haven't we restricted the application of logic? If the past and the present are logical, isn't the future logical as well? After all, except for our "fatalism problem," the laws of logic work perfectly well in the future. Wouldn't it be arbitrary to restrict the use of logic simply because its use in certain cases produces a metaphysical problem? Shouldn't philosophers just concentrate on trying to solve the problem? Aristotle's "sea battle" has inspired many ingenious attempts in this regard.

PREDESTINATION

Predestination is a theological doctrine, primarily associated with **Calvinism,** which holds that from eternity God has decreed every event that is to take place, including the final salvation of men and women. The doctrine is a logical consequence of another doctrine, the **omniscience** of God. If God knows everything, then God knows the future; the history of humankind is merely the working out of the sovereign will of God on earth. The Westminster Confession of Faith provides the classic Calvinist expression of the doctrine:

God from all eternity did by the most wise and holy counsel of his own will, freely and unchangeably ordain whatsoever comes to pass: yet so as thereby neither is God the author of sin, nor is violence offered to the will of the creatures, nor is the liberty or contingency of second causes taken away, but rather established.[2]

Although the doctrine of predestination is found in Judaism and Islam, it is most prominent in Christianity. There is a historical line of development of the doctrine in Christianity, from the New Testament writings of Paul through Saint Augustine to Martin Luther, John Calvin, and the other leaders of the Reformation. The doctrine finds its most complete expression in the writings of John Calvin (1509–1564) and the Puritan theologian Jonathan Edwards (1703–1758), who taught that salvation is not the product of any human work, but solely of the grace of God.

Predestination raises a series of thorny questions. If God has decreed all things, including what choices we will make in life, what role is there for the human will? Furthermore, many of these human choices are clearly evil. Is God then the author of evil? Because the idea of God as the author of evil is so repugnant, Saint Augustine proposed that the free will of humans is the cause of evil. Careful study of the Westminster statement reveals that Calvinists have followed Saint Augustine, believing that the sovereignty of God and the free will of humans can be reconciled through the doctrine of "secondary causes," meaning humans are free to act within the prior environment of God's sovereign will. The carefully worded statement has two aims: to establish the real freedom of humans and to clear God of any responsibility for evil. There is considerable debate over whether it succeeds in either of its two aims. The problem of evil, one of the central problems in the philosophy of religion, will be discussed at greater length in Part 7 of this book.

HARD DETERMINISM

Hard determinism is the theory that everything in the universe, including human action, is entirely governed by causal laws. Every event has a sufficient natural cause; nothing is left to chance. The same laws of causality that govern nature govern human actions as well.

It is important to not confuse determinism with either fatalism or predestination. The Greek tragedy of Oedipus is fatalistic because the outcome is inevitable. It makes no difference what Oedipus decides to do because he is fated to kill his father and marry his mother. Determinism, on the other hand, does not claim that human actions are inevitable; it merely claims that *if* certain antecedent conditions exist, *then* certain events will occur as a necessary consequence. For example, if you drop your pen, then it will fall to the floor. Determinism differs from pre-

[2]*Baker's Dictionary of Theology* (Grand Rapids: Baker Book House, 1960), 416.

destination in that it claims that natural causes, not God, are sufficient to explain all events in the universe. In a sense, determinism replaced predestination's causal activity of God with the sufficiency of natural causes.

Historically, determinism has been associated with the rise of modern science and the mechanistic world picture that science has produced. Thus the determinist thesis flourished as a consequence of Newton's discovery that the world was a great machine that operated according to fixed, scientific laws. The French astronomer Pierre-Simon Laplace had such confidence in the Newtonian system that he claimed that if some superhuman intelligence knew all the facts of the universe and the laws governing those facts, it would be possible to deduce all the facts about the past and to know everything about the future as well!

The appeal of determinist reasoning is easy to see. We are accustomed to think that all events have natural causes. Two examples from medicine serve to remind us how widespread this assumption is. Doctors, by law, must list the cause of death on death certificates. Sometimes—for example, when a person has been dead for a long time—it may be impossible to determine the exact cause of death. But what would we make of a doctor who wrote on the death certificate, "There is no cause of death!" Or suppose that you are feeling ill. Not recognizing any of your symptoms, you go to see a doctor. After a careful examination, your doctor tells you that you are suffering from a mysterious disease *that has no cause*. A moment's reflection reveals how bizarre these experiences would be.

Determinism appeals to scientists and philosophers who wish to construct a science of human behavior. Indeed, one of the trends of the twentieth century has been to model the social sciences on the natural sciences. This is the strategy of psychological behaviorism. Dismissing the hypothesis that humans are free as being "prescientific," behaviorists such as B.F. Skinner believe that through conditioning, humans learn which activities lead to pleasure and which lead to pain. Using positive reinforcement to reward desirable behavior, and negative reinforcement to punish undesirable behavior, humans can be trained to do what is morally appropriate.

In a similar way, psychoanalytic theory can be put to deterministic uses, serving as causal explanations of human behavior. Freud demonstrated how psychoanalysis could be employed to explain every piece of human behavior, from the most ordinary (slips of the tongue) to the most bizarre (violent psychotic episodes). John Hospers, in an article entitled "Meaning and Free Will," demonstrated how the concepts of psychoanalysis can be used to show that people's unconscious desires and urges are as rigidly determined as the law of gravity; like any machine, nature frequently turns out "lemons," in this case "psychological lemons," who go astray.

We all agree that machines turn out "lemons," we all agree that nature turns out misfits in the realm of biology—the blind, the crippled, the diseased; but we hesitate to include the realm of the personality, for here, it seems, is the last retreat of our dignity as human beings. . . . But may not precisely the same analysis be made here also? Nature turns out psychological "lemons" too, in far greater quantities than any other kind; and indeed all of us are "lemons" in some respect or other, the difference being one of degree. Some of us are lucky enough not to have a gambling-neurosis or criminotic tendencies or masochistic mother-attachment. . . but most of our actions, those usually considered the most important, are unconsciously dominated just the same.[3]

The great trial lawyer Clarence Darrow was a master of this line of argument in the courtroom. In the famous Leopold and Loeb case in 1924, Darrow defended two boys from wealthy families who had kidnapped and murdered another boy, Bobby Franks, arguing that the act was determined.

Why did they kill little Bobby Franks? Not for money, not for spite, not for hate. They killed him as they might kill a spider or a fly, for the experience. They killed him because they were made that way. . . . Intelligent people now know that every human being is the product of the endless heredity back of him and the infinite environment around him. . . . it is just as often a great misfortune to be the child of the rich as it is to be the child of the poor.[4]

Those who reject determinism find the approaches of Skinner, Hospers, and Darrow to be unsatisfactory. Some argue that if behaviorism were true, societal institutions would have to be completely overhauled. Criminals would not be at fault for their actions. They would simply need to be placed in different environments and retrained. How could they be found "guilty" or at fault in any way if their actions are merely the result of operant conditioning? If this were really true, wouldn't traditional legal and moral concepts be stood on their heads? Criminals would become victims of ineffectual conditioning, and society (the environment that determined their behavior) would become guilty. Don't behaviorism and deterministic uses of psychoanalysis remove all sense of responsibility for one's action?

Others argue that behaviorists are guilty of a performative contradiction. On the one hand, in claiming that morality is the result of environmental conditioning, behaviorists adopt a stance that is itself the product of environmental forces. How are we to know that the morality of the conditioners is the right morality, unless we examine the view of those who have conditioned them? On the other hand, if the behaviorist claims that his or her own behavior and beliefs are unconditioned, this contradicts the theory's central claim.

[3]See John Hospers, "Meaning and Free Will," *Philosophy and Phenomenological Research* 10 no. 3 (March 1950): 307–27.

[4]Clarence Darrow, *Attorney for the Damned* (New York: Simon and Schuster, 1957), 35, 56, 59.

Furthermore, how can determinism account for the fact that we *feel* ourselves to be free, responsible moral agents? Believing that determinism cannot offer an adequate account of moral responsibility and that it contradicts the experience of "felt freedom," some philosophers have championed indeterminism.

AFFIRMATION OF FREEDOM: INDETERMINISM

Indeterminism is the thesis that some events in the universe are not determined because they have no antecedent, sufficient cause. This theory attempts to make room for human freedom, arguing that human actions are among the events in the universe that are not determined by strict causal law.

Indeterminists defend their position by arguing that nothing is more certain than our immediate experience. As I drive home from work, several different routes are available to me, and I am under no compulsion to choose one rather than the others. I feel free to choose whatever route I wish, or no route at all—maybe I will go to a friend's house, or a ball game, or a restaurant. My experience of freedom is more basic than any complicated theory of causality.

In his essay, "The Dilemma of Determinism," William James rejected determinism because he believed the world to be more *open* than *closed*. In a closed universe there could be no genuine novelty, spontaneity, or creativity. In a closed universe, no surprises await us in the future. In an open universe, not all of the parts are causally connected; there are "loose ends" and the future is a plurality of possibilities. In an open universe, the possibilities are greater than the actualities. Just as you may choose from a plurality of possibilities in going home, the universe is open to possible futures, and it has not been determined which future will be actualized. James defended the ideas of chance, novelty, and spontaneity, arguing that if we accept them as real, our world is no less consistent than the world of the determinist.

James also pointed out the difficulty that determinists have accounting for judgments of regret, and evil events like murder. On the determinist thesis, wouldn't an act of murder be fully determined in the overall workings of the universe? If so, then any sentiment of regret seems foolish, or at the least, inappropriate. I cannot understand the belief that an act like murder is bad without feeling regret; but I cannot understand regret without the admission of real, genuine possibilities in the world. Hence freedom is required to make sense of moral judgments.

Similarly, indeterminists argue that freedom is required to make sense of our feeling of responsibility. The French existentialist philosopher Jean-Paul Sartre (1905–1980) offered a provocative, radical analysis of freedom and responsibility.

According to Sartre, human consciousness is free because it experiences itself as *other than the world,* uncoupled to any causal chain that it discerns in the world. In the face of this freedom, we may adopt two very different attitudes. On the one hand, we may choose to conceal our freedom from ourselves. This is precisely what determinists do when they deny what their conscious experience is reporting to them. All of these efforts are doomed to failure, Sartre argues, because humans can conceal their freedom only to the extent that they recognize it. This state of denial Sartre calls "bad faith." On the other hand, we may choose to accept our freedom, recognizing that we are the absolute origins of our own acts. Radically free, we have no essence other than that which we create for ourselves. "Condemned to be free," with no God to supply us with an essence, we choose to make ourselves every day, through each of our decisions. This is what Sartre means by his famous motto, "existence precedes essence." This dazzling freedom also means, however, that we are completely responsible for the essence we choose to create.

For Sartre, what makes human existence significant is the ability of human beings to choose goals. This unique ability enables us to construct a future that in turn supplies the present with real meaning. We are responsible not only for all our decisions and actions but for our situation as well. Since we all are, in a sense, the makers of the world, we are all responsible for the world that we make. Refusing to take responsibility for the life situation I find myself in (my personal situation), or the troubled, unjust world I live in (my social situation), is "bad faith." Acknowledging responsibility for my situation means being committed to changing the world—for instance, making those choices that contribute to a more just, peaceful world. This is what Sartre means when he states that man "is responsible for the world and for himself as a way of being."

Ironically, in recent years the indeterminist thesis has received something of a boost from science. One of the most important discoveries of modern physics is the **Heisenberg Uncertainty Principle.** Named after Werner Heisenberg, the physicist who discovered it, the principle states that we cannot simultaneously know both the position and the momentum of a subatomic particle. If the position is known, then a determination of its motion will be impossible; when its motion is known, then the determination of its position will be uncertain. Heisenberg and Sir Arthur Eddington have used this principle to defend the indeterminist concepts of uncaused events and free will. Many scientists now agree that the concept of "cause" does not apply to certain subatomic particles.

Defenders of determinism point out that physicists are not in agreement in the complex area of quantum theory; no one has yet shown that quantum theory is actually incompatible with Newton's theories. In any case, determinism is of primary importance to us as a theory explaining visible bodies, not subatomic particles. Furthermore, they argue, even if one makes a convincing case for indeterminism in the universe, that is not the same as freedom.

RECONCILING FREEDOM AND DETERMINISM: COMPATIBILISM, SELF-DETERMINISM, AND PHENOMENOLOGY

We have seen that some philosophers have been impressed by the scientific evidence for determinism. According to this view, freedom and personal choice are illusory. Other philosophers have been impressed with the evidence supporting freedom of choice, arguing that determinism is inadequate to explain the human experiences of freedom and responsibility. There is a third alternative. One can argue that both determinism and indeterminism are inadequate in themselves. Rather than adopting an "either-or" position on the issue, some philosophers see determinism and freedom as a "both-and" situation. These philosophers believe it is possible to have human freedom in a deterministic universe. On the one hand, they accept the determinist thesis as it applies to the world, but, on the other, they refuse to give up notions of human freedom and responsibility. **Compatibilism** and **self-determinism** are two theoretical strategies of reconciliation.

There have been numerous versions of compatibilism in the history of philosophy. Important compatibilists include John Stuart Mill (1806–1873), W.T. Stace (1886–1967), and the contemporary Australian philosopher J. J. C. Smart. In order to gain some historical context, we will briefly discuss the contributions of Immanuel Kant before turning to Mill's compatibilism.

Although, strictly speaking, he was not a compatibilist, Kant nevertheless made an important contribution to the determinism-indeterminism debate. Kant appreciated, perhaps more than anyone before or since, the importance of unqualified freedom for human responsibility. But his keen understanding of Newton gave him an appreciation for the need for natural science to operate on the assumption of universal causation in the universe. How could he both defend universal determination on the basis of natural causes *and* human freedom? Kant's synthesis recognized the importance of determinism as a necessary postulate of science, and freedom as a necessary postulate of human action.

Kant believed that the principle of universal causation, the heart of the determinist thesis, was a necessary rule of all human experience. Determinism is true of every possible event in nature, and it is also true of every object of human knowledge. But *knowledge* differs greatly from *action*. Consequently, one must adopt two different standpoints toward the world: one *theoretical*, and one *practical*. Insofar as we wish to know something, we must adopt the scientific standpoint of hard determinism. But when we decide to act, we shift to the practical standpoint. Since the idea of freedom is a practical idea, not a theoretical idea, freedom does not have to be established as a metaphysical fact. Instead, freedom functions as a postulate of the practical life. In other words, the practical idea of freedom is what makes human action possible. In order to act at all, we have to think of ourselves as free, and to have to think of ourselves as free means that we are free.

John Stuart Mill defended a form of compatiblism that William James labelled **soft determinism.** Once again, Mill accepts the determinist idea that all human actions are necessary and inevitable, given their causes. But he argued that these causes are themselves within human control. Unlike rocks and trees, we are not merely part of the natural environment; we are creators of it as well. It is possible to alter the causes of events, just as it is possible to alter our own character. Our actions are as predictable as any other events in the natural world; but predictability is not incompatible with freedom, according to Mill, since freedom simply means acting in accordance with our own character.

More recently, Richard Taylor and the French phenomenologist Paul Ricoeur, from different philosophical traditions, have proposed what some have called "agency theory," or self-determinism. Denying both strict determinism as well as strict indeterminism, Taylor and Ricouer stress the self as a causal agent in its own right, a unity of the voluntary and the involuntary.[5]

Richard Taylor agrees with determinism—to a point. All events *are* caused. However, Taylor agrees with phenomenologists that free action is action that is self-caused, or intentional. Therefore human beings are themselves causal agents in the world, with the power to choose between alternatives. If people are real causes, then strict determinism must be false, since the self causes some things to occur in relation to human purposes.

The phenomenological approach of Ricoeur and James Marsh, a contemporary phenomenologist whose article "The Irony and Ambiguity of Freedom" is included in this section, requires looking more carefully on what actually transpires when we make a decision. Agreeing with Taylor, yet developing his argument differently, Marsh contends that strict determinism and strict indeterminism are both self-refuting. When we reflect on the way we experience our freedom in concrete situations (such as deciding where to vacation), it becomes clear that freedom is an ambiguous unity of opposites, bearing many meanings. All decisions require the constant interplay of determination and indetermination, the involuntary and the voluntary. The error of both determinism and indeterminism is to "absolutize one opposite," and exclude the other.

SUMMARY

In order to support the idea of human freedom, it is not necessary to deny scientific evidence of causal laws operative in the universe. We must recognize that

[5]See Richard Taylor, *Metaphysics* (Englewood Cliffs, N.J.: Prentice-Hall, 1963) and Paul Ricoeur, *The Voluntary and the Involuntary*, translated by Crazim V. Kohak (Evanston, Ill.: Northwestern University Press, 1966).

Key

the self is at times a causal agent. The self is not only acted upon, it acts. If we think of the self as a determining agent in the world, then it is possible to affirm human freedom in a causally determined world. We act on the basis of goals that we choose for ourselves, adjusting the environment around us, to the extent that this is possible, to fulfill our purposes. Being free does not mean we are free from determining causes, or free from natural laws. It does mean that these limitations do not tell the whole story.

He Read this ff

MD

It is true that humans are subject to the same causal determinants as other objects in the world. What makes us different, however, is our ability to rise above these limitations. Beings who are not free cannot control how they behave; the only way they can behave is the way they do behave, making it pointless to say how they *ought* to behave. Beings who are not free cannot be held responsible for their actions, since there was no genuine possibility of acting in any other way. We affirm our freedom when we elect to modify our own behavior by losing weight, giving up cigarettes, or staying with an exercise program. We affirm our freedom when we see others in need and elect to share our resources with them. We affirm our freedom when we ignore the apathy around us and decide that one person can make a difference. Freedom, then, is a necessary postulate of the ethical life. It is also the basis for hope in the world. If we choose wisely, we may yet make the world a better place.

In the reading selections that follow, the first discusses fatalism. Aristotle's famous "sea battle" illustrates the problem of making truthful statements about the future. How can fatalism be avoided? Brand Blanshard presents the case for determinism, while William James and Jean-Paul Sartre state different versions of the case for indeterminism. James Marsh, in the phenomenological tradition, puts phenomenology to work on problem of freedom and determinism.

As we have seen, the concept of freedom is intimately linked to the concepts of responsibility and punishment. The Contemporary Perspectives selections address the issue of crime and punishment. The two selections by Clarence Darrow and C. S. Lewis, drawing out the implications of the freedom-determinism debate, should produce lively discussion.

410

CHAPTER 39

ARISTOTLE

THE SEA BATTLE

Aristotle, the founder of traditional logic, identified three fundamental laws of thought:

1. A thing is what it is and is not another thing (Law of Identity).
2. Something cannot take on a property and its opposite property in the same way at the same time (Law of Contradiction).
3. Either something is the case or it is not the case (Law of Excluded Middle).

A problem arises when we try to apply the Law of Excluded Middle to statements about the future. Some event in the future will either occur or it will not occur. If it occurs, then it is true now that it will occur. If it does not occur, then it is true now that it will not occur. Since these are the only two possibilities, it appears that fatalism is the result. Aristotle illustrates the problem through his famous "sea battle" example.[1] Must the Law of Excluded Middle, intended as a universal principle of human thought, be given up? Or is there some other solution to the problem?

---

[1]Reprinted from *The Oxford Translation of Aristotle*, edited by W.D. Ross, by permission of Oxford University Press.

THE SEA BATTLE

. . . An affirmation is a positive assertion of something about something, a denial a negative assertion. . . .

We will call such a pair of propositions a pair of contradictories. Those positive and negative propositions are said to be contradictory which have the same subject and predicate. The identity of subject and of predicate must not be "**equivocal**." . . .

In the case of that which is or which has taken place, **propositions**, whether positive or negative, must be true or false. . . . When the subject . . . is individual, and that which is predicated of it relates to the future, the case is altered. For if all propositions whether positive or negative are either true or false, then any given predicate must either belong to the subject or not, so that if one man affirms that an event of a given character will take place and another denies it, it is plain that the statement of the one will correspond with reality and that of the other will not. For the predicate cannot both belong and not belong to the subject at one and the same time with regard to the future.

Thus, if it is true to say that a thing is white, it must necessarily be white; if the reverse proposition is true, it will of necessity not be white. Again, if it is white, the proposition stating that it is white was true; if it is not white, the proposition to the opposite effect was true. And if it is not white, the man who states that it is is making a false statement; and if the man who states that it is white is making a false statement, it follows that it is not white. It may therefore be argued that it is necessary that affirmations or denials must be either true or false.

Now if this be so, nothing is or takes place fortuitously, either in the present or in the future, and there are no real alternatives; everything takes place of necessity and is fixed. For either he that affirms that it will take place or he that denies this is in correspondence with fact, whereas if things did not take place of necessity, an event might just as easily not happen as happen; for the meaning of the word "**fortuitous**" with regard to present or future events is that reality is so constituted that it may issue in either of two opposite directions.

Again, if a thing is white now, it was true before to say that it would be white, so that of anything that has taken place it was always true to say "it is" or "it will be." But if it was always true to say that a thing is or will be, it is not possible that it should not be or not be about to be, and when a thing cannot not come to be, it is impossible that it should not come to be, and when it is impossible that it should not come to be, it must come to be. All, then, that is about to be must of necessity take place. It results from this that nothing is uncertain or fortuitous, for if it were fortuitous it would not be necessary.

Again, to say that neither the affirmation nor the denial is true, maintaining, let us say, that an event neither will take place nor will not take place, is to take up a position impossible to defend. In the first place, though facts should prove the one proposition false, the opposite would still be untrue. Secondly, if it was true to say that a thing was both white and large, both these qualities must necessarily belong to it; and if they will belong to it the next day, they must necessarily belong to it the next day. But if an event is neither to take place nor not to take place the next day, the element of chance will be eliminated. For example, it would be necessary that a sea-fight should neither take place nor fail to take place on the next day.

These awkward results and others of the

same kind follow, if it is an irrefragable law that of every pair of contradictory propositions, whether they have regard to universals and are stated as universally applicable, or whether they have regard to individuals, one must be true and the other false, and that there are no real alternatives, but that all that is or takes place is the outcome of necessity. There would be no need to deliberate or to take trouble, on the supposition that if we should adopt a certain course, a certain result would follow, while, if we did not, the result would not follow. For a man may predict an event ten thousand years beforehand, and another may predict the reverse; that which was truly predicted at the moment in the past will of necessity take place in the fullness of time.

Further, it makes no difference whether people have or have not actually made the contradictory statements. For it is manifest that the circumstances are not influenced by the fact of an affirmation or denial on the part of anyone. For events will not take place or fail to take place because it was stated that they would or would not take place, nor is this any more the case if the prediction dates back ten thousand years or any other space of time. Wherefore, if through all time the nature of things was so constituted that a prediction about an event was true, then through all time it was necessary that that prediction should find fulfilment; and with regard to all events, circumstances have always been such that their occurrence is a matter of necessity. For that of which someone has said truly that it will be, cannot fail to take place; and of that which takes place, it was always true to say that it would be.

Yet this view leads to an impossible conclusion; for we see that both deliberation and action are causative with regard to the future, and that, to speak more generally, in those things which are not continuously actual there is a potentiality in either direction. Such things may either be or

not be; events also therefore may either take place or not take place. There are many obvious instances of this. It is possible that this coat may be cut in half, and yet it may not be cut in half, but wear out first. In the same way, it is possible that it should not be cut in half; unless this were so, it would not be possible that it should wear out first. So it is therefore with all other events which possess this kind of potentiality. It is therefore plain that it is not of necessity that everything is or takes place; but in some instances there are real alternatives, in which case the affirmation is no more true and no more false than the denial; while some exhibit a predisposition and general tendency in one direction or the other, and yet can issue in the opposite direction by exception.

Now that which is must needs be when it is, and that which is not must needs not be when it is not. Yet it cannot be said without qualification that all existence and non-existence is the outcome of necessity. For there is a difference between saying that that which is, when it is, must needs be, and simply saying that all that is must needs be, and similarly in the case of that which is not. In the case, also, of two contradictory propositions this holds good. Everything must either be or not be, whether in the present or in the future, but it is not always possible to distinguish and state determinately which of these alternatives must necessarily come about.

Let me illustrate. A sea-fight must either take place tomorrow or not, but it is not necessary that it should take place tomorrow, neither is it necessary that it should not take place, yet it is necessary that it either should or should not take place tomorrow. Since propositions correspond with facts, it is evident that when in future events there is a real alternative, and a potentiality in contrary directions, the corresponding affirmation and denial have the same character.

This is the case with regard to that which is

not always existent or not always non-existent. One of the two propositions in such instances must be true and the other false, but we cannot say determinately that this or that is false, but must leave the alternative undecided. One may indeed be more likely to be true than the other, but it cannot be either actually true or actually false. It is therefore plain that it is not necessary that of an affirmation and a denial one should be true and the other false. For in the case of that which exists potentially, but not actually, the rule which applies to that which exists actually does not hold good. . . .

CHAPTER 40

BRAND BLANSHARD

THE CASE FOR DETERMINISM

Brand Blanshard (1892–   ) is one of America's most important philosophers. He was educated at the University of Michigan, Columbia University, Oxford University, and Harvard University, where he received his Ph.D. in philosophy in one year in 1921. He taught for twenty years at Swarthmore College, and for seventeen years at Yale. His many published works include *The Nature of Thought* (1939), a comprehensive statement of his philosophical position, *Reason and Goodness* (1961), and *Reason and Analysis* (1962).

A common objection to determinism is that it allows no place for human deliberation or ethical behavior. Blanshard argues against that view in this selection.[1] He argues that rational thought is governed by causal laws, as are all mental events. But this does not, in his view, make moral behavior impossible or unintelligible. Taking issue with Kant and the indeterminists, Blanshard paraphrases Saint Paul in the New Testament: "I feel most free . . . precisely when I am most a slave."

[1]Abridged from Brand Blanshard, "The Case for Determinism," in *Determinism and Freedom in the Age of Science*, edited by Sidney Hook (New York: New York University Press, 1958), 19–30. Reprinted by permission.

THE CASE FOR DETERMINISM

I am a determinist. None of the arguments offered on the other side seem of much weight except one form of the moral argument, and that itself is far from decisive. Perhaps the most useful thing I can do in this paper is explain why the commoner arguments for **indeterminism** do not, to my mind, carry conviction. In the course of this explanation the brand of determinism to which I am inclined should become gradually apparent. . . .

By determinism, then, I mean the view that every event A is so connected with a later event B that, given A, B must occur. By indeterminism I mean the view that there is some event B that is not so connected with any previous event A that, given A, it must occur. Now, what is meant here by "must"? We cannot in the end evade that question, but I hope you will not take it as an evasion if at this point I am content to let you fill in the blank in any way you wish. Make it a logical "must," if you care to, or a physical or metaphysical "must," or even the watered-down "must" that means "A is always in fact followed by B." We can discuss the issue usefully though we leave ourselves some latitude on this point.

With these definitions in mind, let us ask what are the most important grounds for indeterminism. This is not the same as asking what commonly moves people to be indeterminists; the answer to that seems to me all too easy. Everyone vaguely knows that to be undetermined is to be free, and everyone wants to be free. My question is rather, When reflective people accept the indeterminist view nowadays, what considerations seem most cogent to them? It seems to me that there are three: first, the stubborn feeling of freedom, which seems to resist all dialectical solvents; second,[1] the conviction that natural sci-

ence itself has now gone over to the indeterminist side; and, third, that determinism would make nonsense of moral responsibility. The third of these seems to me the most important, but I must try to explain why none of them seem to me conclusive.

One of the clearest heads that ever devoted itself to this old issue was Henry Sidgwick. Sidgwick noted that, if at any given moment we stop to think about it, we always feel as if more than one course were open to us, that we could speak or be silent, lift our hand or not lift it. If the determinist is right, this must be an illusion, of course, for whatever we might have done, there must have been a cause, given which we had to do what we did. Now, a mere intuitive assurance about ourselves may be a very weak ground for belief; Freud has shown us that we may be profoundly deceived about how we really feel or why we act as we do. But the curious point is that, though a man who hates his father without knowing it can usually be shown that he does and can often be cured of his feeling, no amount of dialectic seems to shake our feeling of being free to perform either of two proposed acts. By this feeling of being free I do not mean merely the freedom to do what we choose. No one on either side questions that we have that sort of freedom, but it is obviously not the sort of freedom that the indeterminist wants, since it is consistent with determinism of the most rigid sort. The real issue, so far as the will is concerned, is not whether we can do what we choose to do, but whether we can choose our own choice, whether the choice itself issues in accordance with law from some antecedent. And the feeling of freedom that is relevant as evidence is the feeling of an open future as regards the choice itself. After the noise of argument has died down, a sort of intuition stubbornly remains that we can not only lift our hand if we choose, but that the choice itself is open to us. Is this not an impressive fact?

No, I do not think it is. The first reason is that when we are making a choice our faces are always turned toward the future, toward the consequences that one act or the other will bring us, never toward the past with its possible sources of constraint. Hence these sources are not noticed. Hence we remain unaware that we are under constraint at all. Hence we feel free from such constraint. The case is almost as simple as that. When you consider buying a new typewriter your thought is fixed on the pleasure and advantage you would gain from it, or the drain it would make on your budget. You are not delving into the causes that led to your taking pleasure in the prospect of owning a typewriter or to your having a complex about expenditure. You are too much preoccupied with the ends to which the choice would be a means to give any attention to the causes of which your choice may be an effect. But that is no reason for thinking that if you did preoccupy yourself with these causes you would not find them at work. You may remember that Sir Francis Galton was so much impressed with this possibility that for some time he kept account in a notebook of the occasions on which he made important choices with a full measure of this feeling of freedom; then shortly after each choice he turned his eye backward in search of constraints that might have been acting on him stealthily. He found it so easy to bring such constraining factors to light that he surrendered to the determinist view.

But this, you may say, is not enough. Our preoccupation with the future may show why we are not aware of the constraints acting on us, and hence why we do not feel bound by them; it does not explain why our sense of freedom persists after the constraints are disclosed to us. By disclosing the causes of some fear, for example, psychoanalytic therapy can remove the fear, and when these causes are brought to light, the fear commonly does go. How is it, then, that when the causes of our **volition** are brought to light volition continues to feel as free as before? Does this not show that it is really independent of those causes?

No again. The two cases are not parallel. The man with the panic fear of dogs is investing all dogs with the qualities—remembered, though in disguised form—of the monster that frightened him as a child. When this monster and his relation to it are brought to light, so that they can be dissociated from the Fidos and Towsers around him, the fear goes, because its appropriate object has gone. It is quite different with our feeling of freedom. We feel free, it was suggested, because we are not aware of the forces acting on us. Now, in spite of the determinist's conviction that when a choice is made there are always causal influences at work, he does not pretend to reveal the influences at work in our present choice. The chooser's face is always turned forward; his present choice is always unique; and no matter how much he knows about the will and the laws, his present choice always emerges out of deep shadow. The determinist who buys a typewriter is as little interested at the moment in the strings that may be pulling at him from his physiological or subconscious cellars as his indeterminist colleague, and hence feels just as free. Thus, whereas the new knowledge gained through psychoanalysis does remove the grounds of fear, the knowledge gained by the determinist is not at all of the sort that would remove the grounds for the feeling of freedom. To make the persistence of this feeling in the determinist an argument against his case is therefore a confusion.

We come now to the third of the reasons commonly advanced in support of indeterminism. This is that determinism makes a mess of morality. The charge has taken many forms. We are told that determinism makes praise and blame meaningless, punishment brutal, remorse pointless, amendment hopeless, duty a deceit. All these allegations have been effectively answered except the one about duty, where I admit I am not quite satisfied. But none of them are in the form in which determinism most troubles the plain man. What most affronts him, I think, is the suggestion that he is only a machine, a big foolish clock that seems to itself to be acting freely, but whose movements are controlled completely by the wheels and weights inside, a Punch-and-Judy show whose appearance of doing things because they are right or reasonable is a sham because everything is mechanically regulated by wires from below. He has no objections to determinism as applied by physicists to atoms, by himself to machines, or by his doctor to his body. He has an emphatic objection to determinism as applied by anyone to his reflection and his will, for this seems to make him a gigantic mechanical toy, or worse, a sort of Frankenstein monster.

In this objection I think we must agree with the plain man. If anyone were to show me that determinism involved either materialism or mechanism, I would renounce it at once, for that would be equivalent, in my opinion, to reducing it to absurdity. The "**physicalism**" once proposed by Neurath and Carnap as a basis for the scientific study of behavior I could not accept for a moment, because it is so dogmatically antiempirical. To use empirical methods means, for me, not to approach nature with a preconceived notion as to what facts must be like, but to be ready to consider all kinds of alleged facts on their merits. Among these the introspectively observable fact of reflective choice, and the inference to its existence in others, are particularly plain, however different from anything that occurs in the realm of the material or the publicly observable or the mechanically controlled.

Now, what can be meant by saying that such choice, though not determined mechanically, is still determined? Are you suggesting, it will be asked, that in the realm of reflection and choice there operates a different kind of causality from any we know in the realm of bodies? My answer is: Yes, just that. To put it more particularly, I am suggesting (1) that even within the psychical realm there are different causal levels, (2) that a causality of higher level may supervene on one of lower level, and (3) that when causality of the highest level is at work, we have precisely what the indeterminists, without knowing it, want.

1. First, then, as to causal levels. I am assuming that even the indeterminist would admit that most mental events are causally governed. No one would want to deny that his stepping on a tack had something to do with his feeling pain, or that his touching a flame had something to do with his getting burned, or that his later thought of the flame had something to do with his experience of its hotness. A law of association is a causal law of mental events. In one respect it is like a law of physical events: in neither case have we any light as to *why* the consequent follows on the antecedent. Hume was right about the billiard balls. He was right about the flame and the heat; we do not see why something bright and yellow should also be hot. He was right about association; we do not understand how one idea calls up another; we only know that it does. Causality in all such cases means to us little if anything more than a routine of regular sequence.

Is all mental causation like that? Surely not. Consider a musician composing a piece or a logician making a deduction. Let us make our musician a philosopher also, who after adding a bar pauses to ask himself, "Why did I add just that?" Can we believe he would answer, "Because whenever in the past I have had the preceding bars in mind, they have always been followed by this bar"? What makes this suggestion so inept is partly that he may never have thought of the preceding bars before, partly that, if he had, the repetition of an old sequence would be precisely what he would avoid. No, his answer, I think, would be something like this: "I wrote what I did because it seemed the right thing to do. I developed my theme in the manner demanded to carry it through in an aesthetically satisfactory way." In other words, the constraint that was really at work in him was not that of association; it was something that worked distinctly against association; it was the constraint of an aesthetic ideal. And, if so, there is a causality of a different level. It is idle to say that the musician is wholly in the dark about it. He can see not only *that* B succeeded A; as he looks back, he can see in large measure *why* it did.

It is the same with logical inference, only more clearly so. The thinker starts, let us say, with the idea of a regular solid whose faces are squares, and proceeds to develop in thought the further characteristics that such a solid must possess. He constructs it in imagination and then sees that it must have six faces, eight vertices, and twelve edges. Is this association merely? It may be. It is, for example, if he merely does in imagination what a child does when it counts the edges on a lump of sugar. This is not inference and does not feel like it. When a person, starting with the thought of a solid with square faces, deduces that it must have eight vertices, and then asks why he should have thought of that, the natural answer is, Because the first property entails the second. Of course this is not the only condition, but it seems to me contrary to introspectively plain fact to say that it had nothing to do with the movement of thought. It is easy to put this in such a way as to invite attack. If we say that the condition of our thinking of B is the observed necessity between A and B, we are assuming that B is already thought of as a means of explaining how it comes to be thought of. But that is not what I am saying. I am saying that in thinking at its best thought comes under the constraint of necessities in its object, so that the objective fact that A necessitates B partially determines our passing in thought from A to B. Even when the explanation is put in this form, the objection has been raised that necessity is a timeless link between concepts, while causality is a temporal bond between events, and that the two must be kept sharply apart. To which the answer is: Distinct, yes; but always apart, no. A timeless relation may serve perfectly well as the condition of a temporal passage. I hold that in the course of our thinking we can easily verify this fact, and, because I do, I am not put off by pronouncements about what we should and should not be able to see.

2. My second point about the causal levels is that our mental processes seldom move on one level alone. The higher is always supervening on the lower and taking over partial control. Though brokenly and imperfectly rational, rational creatures we still are. It must be admitted that most of our so-called thinking moves by association, and is hardly thinking at all. But even in the dullest of us "bright shoots of everlastingness," strands of necessity, aesthetic or logical, from time to time appear. "The quarto and folio editions of mankind" can follow the argument with fewer lapses than most of us; in the texts of the greatest of all dramas, we are told, there was seldom a blot or erasure; but Ben Jonson added, and no doubt rightly, that there ought to have been a thousand. The effort of both thought and art is to escape the arbitrary, the merely personal, everything that, causal and capricious, is irrelevant, and to keep to lines appointed by the whole that one is constructing. I do not suggest that logical and aesthetic necessity are the same. I do say that they are both to be distinguished from association or habit as representing a different level of control. That control is never complete; all creation in thought or art is successful in degree only. It is successful in the degree to

which it ceases to be an expression of merely personal impulses and becomes the instrument of a necessity lying in its own subject matter.

3. This brings us to our last point. Since moral choice, like thought and art, moves on different causal levels, it achieves freedom, just as they do, only when it is determined by its own appropriate necessity. Most of our so-called choices are so clearly brought about by association, impulse, and feeling that the judicious indeterminist will raise no issue about them. When we decide to get a drink of water, to take another nibble of chocolate, to go to bed at the usual hour, the forces at work are too plain to be denied. It is not acts like these on which the indeterminist takes his stand. It is rather on those where, with habit, impulse, and association prompting us powerfully to do X, we see that we ought to do Y and therefore do it. To suppose that in such cases we are still the puppets of habit and impulse seems to the indeterminist palpably false.

So it does to us. Surely about this the indeterminist is right. Action impelled by the sense of duty, as Kant perceived, is action on a different level from anything mechanical or associative. But Kant was mistaken in supposing that when we were determined by reason we were not determined at all. This supposition seems to me wholly unwarranted. The determination is still there, but, since it is a determination by the moral necessities of the case, it is just what the moral man wants and thus is the equivalent of freedom. For the moral man, like the logician and the artist, is really seeking self-surrender. Through him as through the others an impersonal ideal is working, and to the extent that this ideal takes possession of him and molds him according to its pattern, he feels free and is free.

The logician is most fully himself when the wind gets into his sails and carries him effortlessly along the line of his calculations. Many an artist and musician have left it on record that their best work was done when the whole they were creating took the brush or pen away from them and completed the work itself. It determined them, but they were free, because to be determined by this whole was at once the secret of their craft and the end of their desire. This is the condition of the moral man also. He has caught a vision, dimmer perhaps than that of the logician or the artist, but equally objective and compelling. It is a vision of the good. This good necessitates certain things, not as means to ends merely, for that is not usually a necessary link, but as integral parts of itself. It requires that he should put love above hate, that he should regard his neighbor's good as of like value with his own, that he should repair injuries, and express gratitude, and respect promises, and revere truth. Of course it does not guide him infallibly. On the values of a particular case he may easily be mistaken. But that no more shows that there are no values present to be estimated, and no ideal demanding a special mode of action, than the fact that we make a mistake in adding figures shows that there are no figures to be added, or a right way of adding them. In both instances what we want is control by the objective requirements of the case. The saint, like the thinker and the artist, has often said this in so many words. I feel most free, said St. Paul, precisely when I am most a slave. . . .

CHAPTER 41

WILLIAM JAMES

THE DILEMMA OF DETERMINISM

In this famous article James argues for indeterminism.[1] Going beyond denying determinism with respect to human persons—a model of philosophical consistency—James denies causal determinism in the universe as well. He defends the notion of chance in the universe, giving it a completely negative definition, simply meaning "disconnection"—signalling an event "not controlled, secured, or necessitated by other things in advance of its own actual presence." James concludes by arguing that determinism cannot account for creativity, spontaneity, or morality.

THE DILEMMA OF DETERMINISM

A common opinion prevails that the juice has ages ago been pressed out of the free-will controversy, and that no new champion can do more than warm up stale arguments which everyone has heard. This is a radical mistake. I know of no subject less worn out, or in which inventive genius has a better chance of breaking open new ground,—not, perhaps, of forcing a conclusion or of coercing assent, but of deepening our sense of what the issue between the two parties really is, of what the ideas of fate and of free-will imply. . . . [O]ur first act of freedom, if we are free,

[1]From William James, *Essays on Faith and Morals*, (Cleveland: World Publishing, 1962).

ought in all inward propriety to be to affirm that we are free. . . .

With this much understood at the outset, we can advance. But not without one more point understood as well. The arguments I am about to urge all proceed on two suppositions: first, when we make theories about the world and discuss them with one another, we do so in order to attain a conception of things which shall give us subjective satisfaction; and, second, if there be two conceptions, and the one seems to us, on the whole, more rational than the other, we are entitled to suppose that the more rational one is the truer of the two.

I hope that you are all willing to make these suppositions with me; for I am afraid that if there be any of you here who are not, they will find little edification in the rest of what I have to say. I cannot stop to argue the point; but I myself believe that all the magnificent achievements of mathematical and physical science—our doctrines of evolution, of uniformity of law, and the rest—proceed from our indomitable desire to cast the world into a more rational shape in our minds than the shape into which it is thrown there by the crude order of our experience. The world has shown itself, to a great extent, plastic to this demand of ours for rationality. How much farther it will show itself plastic no one can say. Our only means of finding out is to try; and I, for one, feel as free to try conceptions of moral as of mechanical or of logical rationality. If a certain formula for expressing the nature of the world violates my moral demand, I shall feel as free to throw it overboard, or at least to doubt it, as if it disappointed my demand for uniformity of sequence, for example; the one demand being, so far as I can see, quite as subjective and emotional as the other is. The principle of causality, for example—what is it but a postulate, an empty name covering simply a demand that the sequence of events shall some day manifest a deep-

er kind of belonging of one thing with another than the mere arbitrary juxtaposition which now phenomenally appears? It is as much an altar to an unknown god as the one that Saint Paul found at Athens. All our scientific and philosophic ideals are altars to unknown gods. Uniformity is as much so as is free-will. If this be admitted, we can debate on even terms. But if any one pretends that while freedom and variety are, in the first instance, subjective demands, necessity and uniformity are something altogether different, I do not see how we can debate at all.

To begin, then, I must suppose you acquainted with all the usual arguments on the subject. I cannot stop to take up the old proofs from causation, from statistics, from the certainty with which we can foretell one another's conduct, from the fixity of character, and all the rest. But there are two *words* which usually encumber these classical arguments, and which we must immediately dispose of if we are to make any progress. One is the eulogistic word *freedom*, and the other is the opprobrious word *chance*. The word "chance" I wish to keep, but I wish to get rid of the word "freedom." Its eulogistic associations have so far overshadowed all the rest of its meaning that both parties claim the sole right to use it, and determinists today insist that they alone are freedom's champions. Old-fashioned determinism was what we may call **hard** determinism. It did not shrink from such words as fatality, bondage of the will, necessitation, and the like. Nowadays, we have a **soft** determinism which abhors harsh words, and, repudiating fatality, necessity, and even predetermination, says that its real name is freedom; for freedom is only necessity understood, and bondage to the highest is identical with true freedom. . . .

Now, all this is a quagmire of evasion under which the real issue of fact has been entirely smothered. Freedom in all these senses presents simply no problem at all. No matter what the soft determinist mean by it—whether he mean the acting without external constraint; whether he mean the acting rightly, or whether he mean the acquiescing in the law of the whole—who cannot answer him that sometimes we are free and sometimes we are not? But there *is* a problem, an issue of fact and not of words, an issue of the most momentous importance, which is often decided without discussion in one sentence—nay, in one clause of a sentence—by those very writers who spin out whole chapters in their efforts to show what "true" freedom is; and that is the question of determinism. . . .

Fortunately, no ambiguities hang about this word or about its opposite, **indeterminism**. Both designate an outward way in which things may happen, and their cold and mathematical sound has no sentimental associations that can bribe our partiality either way in advance. Now, evidence of an external kind to decide between determinism and indeterminism is, as I intimated a while back, strictly impossible to find. Let us look at the difference between them and see for ourselves. What does determinism profess?

It professes that those parts of the universe already laid down absolutely appoint and decree what the other parts shall be. The future has no ambiguous possibilities hidden in its womb: the part we call the present is compatible with only one totality. Any other future complement than the one fixed from eternity is impossible. The whole is in each and every part, and welds it with the rest into an absolute unity, an iron block, in which there can be no equivocation or shadow of turning.

> With earth's first clay they did the last
>   man knead,
> And there of the last harvest sowed the
>   seed.
> And the first morning of creation wrote

> What the last dawn of reckoning shall
>   read.

Indeterminism, on the contrary, says that the parts have a certain amount of loose play on one another, so that the laying down of one of them does not necessarily determine what the others shall be. It admits that possibilities may be in excess of actualities, and that things not yet revealed to our knowledge may really in themselves be ambiguous. Of two alternative futures which we conceive, both may now be really possible; and the one become impossible only at the very moment when the other excludes it by becoming real itself. Indeterminism thus denies the world to be one unbending unit of fact. It says there is a certain ultimate pluralism in it; and, so saying, it corroborates our ordinary unsophisticated view of things. To that view, actualities seem to float in a wider sea of possibilities from out of which they are chosen; and, *somewhere*, indeterminism says, such possibilities exist, and form a part of truth.

Determinism, on the contrary, says they exist *nowhere*, and that necessity on the one hand and impossibility on the other are the sole categories of the real. Possibilities that fail to get realized are, for determinism, pure illusions: they never were possibilities at all. There is nothing inchoate, it says, about this universe of ours, all that was or is or shall be actual in it having been from eternity virtually there. . . .

The issue, it will be seen, is a perfectly sharp one, which no eulogistic terminology can smear over or wipe out. The truth *must* lie with one side or the other, and its lying with one side makes the other false.

The question relates solely to the existence of possibilities, in the strict sense of the term, as things that may, but need not, be. Both sides admit that a **volition**, for instance, has occurred. The indeterminists say another volition might have occurred in its place: the determinists swear that nothing could possibly have occurred in its place. Now, can science be called in to tell us which of these two point-blank contradicters of each other is right? Science professes to draw no conclusions but such as are based on matters of fact, things that have actually happened; but how can any amount of assurance that something actually happened give us the least grain of information as to whether another thing might or might not have happened in its place? Only facts can be proved by other facts. With things that are possibilities and not facts, facts have no concern. If we have no other evidence than the evidence of existing facts, the possibility-question must remain a mystery never to be cleared up.

And the truth is that facts practically have hardly anything to do with making us either determinists or indeterminists. Sure enough, we make a flourish of quoting facts this way or that; and if we are determinists, we talk about the infallibility with which we can predict one another's conduct; while if we are indeterminists, we lay great stress on the fact that it is just because we cannot foretell one another's conduct, either in war or statecraft or in any of the great and small intrigues and businesses of men, that life is so intensely anxious and hazardous a game. But who does not see the wretched insufficiency of this so-called objective testimony on both sides? What fills up the gaps in our minds is something not objective, not external. What divides us into possibility men and anti-possibility men is different faiths or postulates—postulates of rationality. To this man the world seems more rational with possibilities in it—to that man more rational with possibilities excluded; and talk as we will about having to yield to evidence, what makes us monists or pluralists, determinists or indeterminists, is at bottom always some sentiment like this.

The stronghold of the deterministic senti-

ment is the antipathy to the idea of chance. As soon as we begin to talk indeterminism to our friends, we find a number of them shaking their heads. This notion of alternative possibility, they say, this admission that any one of several things may come to pass, is, after all, only a roundabout name for chance; and chance is something the notion of which no sane mind can for an instant tolerate in the world. What is it, they ask, but barefaced crazy unreason, the negation of intelligibility and law? And if the slightest particle of it exist anywhere, what is to prevent the whole fabric from falling together, the stars from going out, and chaos from recommencing her topsy-turvy reign?

Remarks of this sort about chance will put an end to discussion as quickly as anything one can find. I have already told you that "chance" was a word I wished to keep and use. Let us then examine exactly what it means, and see whether it ought to be such a terrible bugbear to us. I fancy that squeezing the thistle boldly will rob it of its sting.

The sting of the word "chance" seems to lie in the assumption that it means something positive, and that if anything happens by chance, it must needs be something of an intrinsically irrational and preposterous sort. Now, chance means nothing of the kind. It is a purely negative and relative term, giving us no information about that of which it is predicated, except that it happens to be disconnected with something else—not controlled, secured, or necessitated by other things in advance of its own actual presence. As this point is the most subtile one of the whole lecture, and at the same time the point on which all the rest hinges, I beg you to pay particular attention to it. What I say is that it tells us nothing about what a thing may be in itself to call it "chance." It may be a bad thing, it may be a good thing. It may be lucidity, transparency, fitness incarnate, matching the whole system of other things, when it has once befallen, in an unimaginably perfect way. All you mean by calling it "chance" is that this is not guaranteed, that it may also fall out otherwise. For the system of other things has no positive hold on the chance-thing. Its origin is in a certain fashion negative: it escapes, and says, Hands off! coming, when it comes, as a free gift, or not at all. . . .

Nevertheless, many persons talk as if the minutest dose of disconnectedness of one part with another, the smallest modicum of independence, the faintest tremor of ambiguity about the future, for example, would ruin everything, and turn this goodly universe into a sort of insane sand-heap or nulliverse, no universe at all. Since future human volitions are as a matter of fact the only ambiguous things we are tempted to believe in, let us stop for a moment to make ourselves sure whether their independent and accidental character need be fraught with such direful consequences to the universe as these.

What is meant by saying that my choice of which way to walk home after the lecture is ambiguous and matter of chance as far as the present moment is concerned? It means that both Divinity Avenue and Oxford Street are called; but that only one, and that one *either* one, shall be chosen. Now, I ask you seriously to suppose that this ambiguity of my choice is real; and then to make the impossible hypothesis that the choice is made twice over, and each time falls on a different street. In other words, imagine that I first walk through Divinity Avenue, and then imagine that the powers governing the universe annihilate ten minutes of time with all that it contained, and set me back at the door of this hall just as I was before the choice was made. Imagine then that, everything else being the same, I now make a different choice and traverse Oxford Street. You, as passive spectators, look on and see the two alternative universes—one of them with me walking through Divinity Avenue in it, the other

with the same me walking through Oxford Street. Now, if you are determinists you believe one of these universes to have been from eternity impossible: you believe it to have been impossible because of the intrinsic irrationality or accidentality somewhere involved in it. But looking outwardly at these universes, can you say which is the impossible and accidental one, and which the rational and necessary one? I doubt if the most iron-clad determinist among you could have the slightest glimmer of light on this point. In other words, either universe *after the fact* and once there would, to our means of observation and understanding, appear just as rational as the other. There would be absolutely no criterion by which we might judge one necessary and the other matter of chance. Suppose now we relieve the gods of their hypothetical task and assume my choice, once made, to be made forever. I go through Divinity Avenue for good and all. If, as good determinists, you now begin to affirm, what all good determinists punctually do affirm, that in the nature of things I *couldn't* have gone through Oxford Street—had I done so it would have been chance, irrationality, insanity, a horrid gap in nature—I simply call your attention to this, that your affirmation is . . . a mere conception fulminated as a dogma and based on no insight into details. Before my choice, either street seemed as natural to you as to me. Had I happened to take Oxford Street, Divinity Avenue would have figured in your philosophy as the gap in nature; and you would have so proclaimed it with the best deterministic conscience in the world.

But what a hollow outcry, then, is this against a chance which, if it were present to us, we could by no character whatever distinguish from a rational necessity! I have taken the most trivial of examples, but no possible example could lead to any different result. For what are the alternatives which, in point of fact, offer themselves to human volition? What are those futures that now seem matters of chance? Are they not one and all like the Divinity Avenue and Oxford Street of our example? Are they not all of them *kinds* of things already here and based in the existing frame of nature? Is any one ever tempted to produce an *absolute* accident, something utterly irrelevant to the rest of the world? Do not all the motives that assail us, all the futures that offer themselves to our choice, spring equally from the soil of the past; and would not either one of them, whether realized through chance or through necessity, the moment it was realized, seem to us to fit that past, and in the completest and most continuous manner to interdigitate with the phenomena already there?

And this at last brings us within sight of our subject. We have seen what determinism means: we have seen that indeterminism is rightly described as meaning chance; and we have seen that chance, the very name of which we are urged to shrink from as from a metaphysical pestilence, means only the negative fact that no part of the world, however big, can claim to control absolutely the destinies of the whole. But although, in discussing the word "chance," I may at moments have seemed to be arguing for its real existence, I have not meant to do so yet. We have not yet ascertained whether this be a world of chance or no; at most, we have agreed that it seems so. And I now repeat what I said at the outset, that, from any strict theoretical point of view, the question is insoluble. To deepen our theoretic sense of the *difference* between a world with chances in it and a deterministic world is the most I can hope to do; and this I may now at last begin upon, after all our tedious clearing of the way.

I wish first of all to show you just what the notion that this is a deterministic world implies. The implications I call your attention to are all bound up with the fact that it is a world in which we constantly have to make what I shall, with your permission, call judgments of regret. Hardly an hour passes in which we do not wish that something might be otherwise; and happy indeed are those of us whose hearts have never echoed the wish of Omar Khayam—

> That we might clasp, ere closed, the book
> of fate,
> And make the writer on a fairer leaf
> Inscribe our names, or quite obliterate.

> Ah! Love, could you and I with fate
> conspire
> To mend this sorry scheme of things
> entire,
> Would we not shatter it to bits, and then
> Remould it nearer to the heart's desire?

Now, it is undeniable that most of these regrets are foolish, and quite on a par in point of philosophic value with the criticisms on the universe of that friend of our infancy, the hero of the fable The Atheist and the Acorn,—

> Fool! had that bough a pumpkin bore,
> Thy whimsies would have worked no
> more, etc.

Even from the point of view of our own ends, we should probably make a botch of remodelling the universe. How much more then from the point of view of ends we cannot see! Wise men therefore regret as little as they can. But still some regrets are pretty obstinate and hard to stifle,—regrets for acts of wanton cruelty or treachery, for example, whether performed by others or by ourselves. Hardly any one can remain *entirely* optimistic after reading the confession of the murderer at Brockton the other day: how, to get rid of the wife whose continued existence bored him, he inveigled her into a desert spot, shot her four times, and then, as she lay on the ground and said to him, "You didn't do it on purpose, did you dear?" replied, "No, I didn't do it on purpose," as he raised a rock and smashed her skull. Such an occurrence, with the mild sentence and self-satisfaction of the prisoner, is a field for a crop of regrets, which one need not take up in detail. We feel that, although a perfect mechanical fit to the rest of the universe, it is a bad moral fit, and that something else would really have been better in its place.

But for the deterministic philosophy the murder, the sentence, and the prisoner's optimism were all necessary from eternity; and nothing else for a moment had a ghost of a chance of being put into their place. To admit such a chance, the determinists tell us, would be to make a suicide of reason; so we must steel our hearts against the thought. And here our plot thickens, for we see the first of those difficult implications of determinism and monism which it is my purpose to make you feel. If this Brockton murder was called for by the rest of the universe, if it had to come at its preappointed hour, and if nothing else would have been consistent with the sense of the whole, what are we to think of the universe? Are we stubbornly to stick to our judgment of regret, and say, though it *couldn't* be, yet it *would* have been a better universe with something different from this Brockton murder in it? That, of course, seems the natural and spontaneous thing for us to do; and yet it is nothing short of deliberately espousing a kind of pessimism. The judgment of regret calls the murder bad. Calling a thing bad means, if it mean anything at all, that the thing ought not to be, that something else ought to be in its stead. Determinism, in denying that anything else can be in its stead, virtually defines the universe as a place in which what ought to be is impossible,—in other words, as an organism whose constitution is afflicted with an incurable taint, an irremediable flaw. The pessimism of a Schopenhauer says

no more than this,—that the murder is a symptom; and that it is a vicious symptom because it belongs to a vicious whole, which can express its nature no otherwise than by bringing forth just such a symptom as that at this particular spot. Regret for the murder must transform itself, if we are determinists and wise, into a larger regret. It is absurd to regret the murder alone. Other things being what they are, *it* could not be different. What we should regret is that whole frame of things of which the murder is one member. I see no escape whatever from this pessimistic conclusion, if, being determinists, our judgment of regret is to be allowed to stand at all.

The only deterministic escape from pessimism is everywhere to abandon the judgment of regret. That this can be done, history shows to be not impossible. The devil, *quoad existentiam*, may be good. That is, although he be a *principle* of evil, yet the universe, with such a principle in it, may practically be a better universe than it could have been without. On every hand, in a small way, we find that a certain amount of evil is a condition by which a higher form of good is bought. There is nothing to prevent anybody from generalizing this view, and trusting that if we could but see things in the largest of all ways, even such matters as this Brockton murder would appear to be paid for by the uses that follow in their train. An optimism *quand même*, a systematic and infatuated optimism like that ridiculed by Voltaire in his Candide, is one of the possible ideal ways in which a man may train himself to look on life. Bereft of dogmatic hardness and lit up with the expression of a tender and pathetic hope, such an optimism has been the grace of some of the most religious characters that ever lived.

Throb thine with Nature's throbbing breast,
And all is clear from east to west.

Even cruelty and treachery may be among the absolutely blessed fruits of time, and to quarrel with any of their details may be blasphemy. The only real blasphemy, in short, may be that pessimistic temper of the soul which lets it give way to such things as regrets, remorse, and grief.

Thus, our deterministic pessimism may become a deterministic optimism at the price of extinguishing our judgments of regret.

But does not this immediately bring us into a curious logical predicament? Our determinism leads us to call our judgments of regret wrong, because they are pessimistic in implying that what is impossible yet ought to be. But how then about the judgments of regret themselves? If they are wrong, other judgments, judgments of approval presumably, ought to be in their place. But as they are necessitated, nothing else *can* be in their place; and the universe is just what it was before,—namely, a place in which what ought to be appears impossible. We have got one foot out of the pessimistic bog, but the other one sinks all the deeper. We have rescued our actions from the bonds of evil, but our judgments are now held fast. When murders and treacheries cease to be sins, regrets are theoretic absurdities and errors. The theoretic and the active life thus play a kind of seesaw with each other on the ground of evil. The rise of either sends the other down. Murder and treachery cannot be good without regret being bad: regret cannot be good without treachery and murder being bad. Both, however, are supposed to have been foredoomed: so something must be fatally unreasonable, absurd, and wrong in the world. It must be a place of which either sin or error forms a necessary part. From this dilemma there seems at first sight no escape.

CHAPTER 42

JEAN-PAUL SARTRE

RADICAL FREEDOM

Jean-Paul Sartre (1905–1980), French philosopher, novelist, and playwright, was the dominant figure in the post–World War II existentialist movement. At the outbreak of war in 1939, he entered the French army, and in 1940 was captured by the Germans. He was later active in the Resistance movement.

In 1943 Sartre completed his massive *L'Etre et le néant (Being and Nothingness)*, a work that combined phenomenological analysis with existentialist themes. A co-founder (with Merleau-Ponty and Simone de Beauvoir) of the important journal *Les Temps Moderne*, Sartre was at the center of European intellectual life for fifty years. A staunch defender of human freedom, Sartre refused the Nobel Prize for literature in 1964, because of his political and philosophical commitments. His *Critique of Dialectical Reason* (1960) was an attempt to rethink Marxism along existentialist lines. His novel *Nausea* (1938) and his plays *No Exit* (1947) and *The Flies* (1947) popularized his existentialism, which was set forth most clearly in his famous lecture, *Existentialism and Humanism* (1946).

One of the hallmarks of existentialism is its insistence on human freedom. According to Sartre, human beings are free in all circumstances. Such absolute freedom calls for absolute responsibility. There are no accidents in life. In this famous passage from *Being and Nothingness*, Sartre contends that if I am mobilized in war, "this war is my war; it is in my image and I deserve it. . . . For lack of getting out of it, I have chosen it."[1] Thus I am responsible, even when, in bad faith, I flee my responsibilities.

---

[1]From Jean-Paul Sartre, *Being and Nothingness*. (New York: Philosophical Library, 1956). Reprinted by permission.

RADICAL FREEDOM

I

It is strange that philosophers have been able to argue endlessly about determinism and free-will, to cite examples in favor of one or the other thesis without ever attempting first to make explicit the structures contained in the very idea of *action*. The concept of an act contains, in fact, numerous subordinate notions which we shall have to organize and arrange in a hierarchy: to act is to modify the shape of the world; it is to arrange means in view of an end; it is to produce an organized instrumental complex such that by a series of concatenations and connections the modification effected on one of the links causes modifications throughout the whole series and finally produces an anticipated result. But this is not what is important for us here. We should observe first that an action is on principle *intentional*. The careless smoker who has through negligence caused the explosion of a powder magazine has not *acted*. On the other hand the worker who is charged with dynamiting a quarry and who obeys the given orders has acted when he has produced the expected explosion; he knew what he was doing or, if you prefer, he intentionally realized a conscious project. . . .

. . . Since freedom is identical with my existence, it is the foundation of ends which I shall attempt to attain either by the will or by passionate efforts. Therefore it can not be limited to voluntary acts. **Volitions,** on the contrary, like passions are certain subjective attitudes by which we attempt to attain the ends posited by original freedom. By original freedom, of course, we should not understand a freedom which would be prior to the voluntary or passionate act but rather a foundation which is strictly contempo-

rary with the will or the passion and which these manifest, each in its own way. . . .

If these ends are already posited, then what remains to be decided at each moment is the way in which I shall conduct myself with respect to them; in other words, the attitude which I shall assume. Shall I act by volition or by passion? Who can decide except me? In fact, if we admit that circumstances decide for me (for example, I can act by volition when faced with a minor danger but if the peril increases, I shall fall into passion), we thereby suppress all freedom. It would indeed be absurd to declare that the will is autonomous when it appears but that external circumstances strictly determine the moment of its appearance. . . .

. . . This does not mean that I am free to get up or to sit down, to enter or to go out, to flee or to face danger—if one means by freedom here a pure capricious, unlawful, gratuitous, and incomprehensible contingency. To be sure, each one of my acts, even the most trivial, is entirely free in the sense which we have just defined; but this does not mean that my act can be anything *whatsoever* or even that it is *unforeseeable*. Someone, nevertheless may object and ask how if my act can be understood *neither* in terms of the state of the world nor in terms of the ensemble of my past taken as an irremediable thing, it could possibly be anything but gratuitous. . . .

II

The decisive argument which is employed by common sense against freedom consists in reminding us of our impotence. Far from being able to modify our situation at our whim, we seem to be unable to change ourselves. I am not "free" either to escape the lot of my class, of my nation, of my family, or even to build up my own power or my fortune or to conquer my most insignificant appetites or habits. I am born a worker, a Frenchman, an hereditary syphilitic, or a tubercular. The history of a life, whatever it may be, is the history of a failure. The **coefficient of adversity** of things is such that years of patience are necessary to obtain the feeblest result. Again it is necessary "to obey nature in order to command it"; that is, to insert my action into the network of determinism. Much more than he appears "to make himself," man seems "to be made" by climate and the earth, race and class, language, the history of the collectivity of which he is a part, heredity, the individual circumstances of his childhood, acquired habits, the great and small events of his life.

This argument has never greatly troubled the partisans of human freedom. . . . Many of the facts set forth by the determinists do not actually deserve to enter into our considerations. In particular the coefficient of adversity in things can not be an argument against our freedom, for it is by *us*—*i.e.*, by the preliminary positing of an end—that this coefficient of adversity arises. A particular crag, which manifests a profound resistance if I wish to displace it, will be on the contrary a valuable aid if I want to climb upon it in order to look over the countryside. In itself—if one can even imagine what the crag can be in itself—it is neutral; that is, it waits to be illuminated by an end in order to manifest itself as adverse or helpful. Again it can manifest itself in one or the other way only within an instrumental-complex which is already established. Without picks and piolets, paths already worn, and a technique of climbing, the crag would be neither easy nor difficult to climb; the question would not be posited, it would not support any relation

of any kind with the technique of mountain climbing. Thus although brute things . . . can from the start limit our freedom of action, it is our freedom itself which must first constitute the framework, the technique, and the ends in relation to which they will manifest themselves as limits. Even if the crag is revealed as "too difficult to climb," and if we must give up the ascent, let us note that the crag is revealed as such only because it was originally grasped as "climbable"; it is therefore our freedom which constitutes the limits which it will subsequently encounter. . . .

III

The essential consequence of our earlier remarks is that man being condemned to be free carries the weight of the whole world on his shoulders; he is responsible for the world and for himself as a way of being. We are taking the word "responsibility" in its ordinary sense as "consciousness (of) being the incontestable author of an event or of an object." . . . He must assume the situation with the proud consciousness of being the author of it, for the very worst disadvantages or the worst threats which can endanger my person have meaning only in and through my project; and it is on the ground of the engagement which I am that they appear. It is therefore senseless to think of complaining since nothing foreign has decided what we feel, what we live, or what we are.

Furthermore this absolute responsibility is not resignation; it is simply the logical requirement of the consequences of our freedom. What happens to me happens through me, and I can neither affect myself with it nor revolt against it nor resign myself to it. Moreover everything which happens to me is *mine*. By this we must understand first of all that I am always equal to what happens to me *qua* man, for what happens to a man through other men and through himself can be only human. The most terrible situations of war, the worst tortures do not create a non-human state of things; there is no non-human situation. It is only through fear, flight, and recourse to magical types of conduct that I shall decide on the non-human, but this decision is human, and I shall carry the entire responsibility for it. But in addition the situation is *mine* because it is the image of my free choice of myself, and everything which it presents to me is *mine* in that this represents me and symbolizes me. Is it not I who decide the coefficient of adversity in things and even their unpredictability by deciding myself?

Thus there are no accidents in a life; a community event which suddenly bursts forth and involves me in it does not come from the outside. If I am mobilized in a war, this war is my war; it is in my image and I deserve it. I deserve it first because I could always get out of it by suicide or by desertion; these ultimate possibles are those which must always be present for us when there is a question of envisaging a situation. For lack of getting out of it, I have chosen it. This can be due to inertia, to cowardice in the face of public opinion, or because I prefer certain other values to the value of the refusal to join in the war (the good opinion of my relatives, the honor of my family, etc.). Anyway you look at it, it is a matter of choice. This choice will be repeated later on again and again without a break until the end of the war. . . .

But in addition the war is *mine* because by the sole fact that it arises in a situation which I cause to be and that I can discover it there only by engaging myself for or against it, I can no longer distinguish at present the choice which I make of myself from the choice which I make of the war. To live this war is to choose myself through it and to choose it through my choice of myself. There can be no question of considering it as "four years of vacation" or as a "reprieve," as a "recess," the essential part of my responsibilities being elsewhere in my married, family, or professional life. In this war which I have chosen I choose myself from day to day, and I make it mine by making myself. If it is going to be four empty years, then it is I who bear the responsibility for this. . . .

Yet this responsibility is of a very particular type. Someone will say, "I did not ask to be born." This is a naive way of throwing greater emphasis on our facticity. I am responsible for everything, in fact, except for my very responsibility, for I am not the foundation of my being. Therefore everything takes place as if I were compelled to be responsible. I am *abandoned* in the world, not in the sense that I might remain abandoned and passive in a hostile universe like a board floating on the water, but rather in the sense that I find myself suddenly alone and without help, engaged in a world for which I bear the whole responsibility without being able, whatever I do, to tear myself away from this responsibility for an instant. For I am responsible for my very desire of fleeing responsibilities. To make myself passive in the world, to refuse to act upon things and upon Others is still to choose myself, and suicide is one mode among others of being-in-the-world. . . . That is why I can not ask, "Why was I born?" or curse the day of my birth or declare that I did not ask to be born, for these various attitudes toward my birth—*i.e.*, toward the *fact* that I realize a presence in the world—are absolutely nothing else but ways of assuming this birth in full responsibility and of making it *mine*. . . . The one who realizes in anguish his condition as *being* thrown into a responsibility which extends to his very abandonment has no longer either remorse or regret or excuse; he is no longer anything but a freedom which perfectly reveals itself and whose being resides in this very revelation. But . . . most of the time we flee anguish in bad faith.

432

CHAPTER 43

JAMES MARSH

THE IRONY AND AMBIGUITY OF FREEDOM

James Marsh (1937–) received his Ph.D. in philosophy from Northwestern University in 1971. Having taught at Saint Louis University for fifteen years, he is currently professor of philosophy at Fordham University. He is the author of *Post-Cartesian Meditations* (1988),[1] as well as a number of scholarly articles.

James Marsh and Richard Taylor represent different philosophical traditions, yet their analyses of freedom as self-determination are remarkably similar. Marsh's dialectical analysis reveals that determinism and indeterminism are both self-refuting. Rejecting Blanshard's determinism and Sartre's indeterminism, Marsh follows the phenomenologist Paul Ricouer in insisting on freedom as a unity of opposites, the voluntary and the involuntary. As Marsh puts it, "The experienced reality of freedom is an ambiguous unity of opposites, a unity that itself has several meanings. Both determinism and indeterminism distort this reality by absolutizing one opposite and excluding the other. Only a notion sufficiently nuanced to do justice to freedom in all its paradoxical complexity is an adequate account of freedom. Such is the notion I have advanced and defended. . . . "

THE IRONY AND AMBIGUITY OF FREEDOM

[My] argument . . . has two steps: one, dialectical, the other, descriptive. The first is that neither strict determinism nor strict indeterminism is tenable because each is self-refuting. Determinism and indeterminism, contrary to their original intentions, imply indetermination and determination. The conclusion of the first section is that determination and indetermination, albeit redefined, *must* go together in the sense of implying each other.

That they must go together, however, leaves open the question of *how* they go together. The second section answers this question by describing the actual experience and essential structure of freedom. The two parts of the argument are both necessary, and each complements the other. Without the prior dialectic, there would be the possibility that freedom as we experience it is an illusion. The dialectical moment removes this possibility once for all. Description must also complement dialectic if the affirmation of mutual implication is not to remain empty and abstract. The total argument is phenomenological, but perhaps more in an Hegelian than in an Husserlian sense. Both the dialectical and descriptive moments are essential to an adequate phenomenology of freedom.

As a result, freedom is both ironical and legitimately ambiguous. It is ironical in that attempts to defend as true either strict determinism or strict indeterminism refute themselves and become untrue. Also, the content of each of these extremes implies its opposite; determinism implies indetermination and indeterminism implies determination. This irony manifests itself most fully in the first section.

Freedom is also paradoxical and ambiguous because it is a thoroughgoing unity of indetermination and determination not accurately described by the clear and distinct idea of either determinism or indeterminism. This reciprocity itself has at least four different meanings. Determination and indetermination imply one another. The first section demonstrates the necessity, the second the content, of this ambiguity. The meanings of "determination" and "indetermination" grow out of the dialectic in the first section, and will be fully defined in the second section.

The Dialectic of Determinism and Indeterminism

Determinism

The thesis of strict determinism is that there are no free acts, no acts in which a person could have acted otherwise. Both the necessary and the sufficient conditions for an apparently free act lie in conditions and causes prior to the act. If the antecedents are given, then the consequence necessarily follows. Freedom is an illusion that cannot withstand rational, critical examination.

Yet the problem with determinism as a philosophical position is that it has to justify itself as true. Consequently a contradiction emerges between the content of determinism and the act of affirming it as true. If determinism *is*, then truth and freedom of any kind are impossible. If determinism is *true*, then determinism is false because of the logic of any truth claim.

Such self-refutation, depending on the kind of determinism defended, has three forms. The first involves a contradiction between the conscious form that a truth claim must necessarily take and posited unconscious forces. For example, physiological determinism argues that a person's actions and thoughts have their necessary and sufficient conditions in previous states of the brain. If this claim is true, then it is true of the determinist's claim itself. She holds a certain position not because of reasons or standards of evidence, but because of previous physical states of the brain. If so, then appeal to good reasons or standards of evidence is illusory or irrelevant; what really causes her to hold a position is previous physical states as understood through the laws of physiology. If the physiological determinist is correct, then she cannot defend the truth of a position consistently by appeal to good reasons. If she can defend her position, then she is not physiologically determined.

Another example of this kind of self-refutation is the psychological determinist's saying that human acts are really determined by the unconscious. Yet since the psychological determinist appeals to conscious evidence and reasons to justify his position, he contradicts himself. Consciousness can only announce itself as a dupe before a consciousness that is undeceived and rational.

Ayer objects to this analysis by arguing that a computer can arrive at true results and yet is also clearly determined. My response to this objection is that the results can be true only for a mind, which can evaluate and test them. Short of the presence of a mind, there is no truth, only facts that have resulted from physically determined objects. Such a claim is easily intelligible if one reflects on what occurs when a question arises about the "competence" of a computer and the validity of its results. If it is working well, then that competence will be known by recourse to rational inquiry, checking the machine's results against those of competent mathematicians. If it is not working well, then that fact too will be known through rational inquiry.

A second kind of self-refutation occurs when there is a contradiction between an explicit class-inclusion of all acts and an implicit class-exclusion, leaving out the determinist's act of asserting something as true. For example, if a sociological determinist wishes to argue that all theories are class influenced and consequently false, then either her own theory is included in the class or it is not. If it is, then it is a false theory. If it is not, then not all theories are class based and the initial claim turns out to be false.

A third kind of self-refutation depends on the conscious logic of the truth claim itself. On the side of the object known or proposition asserted, there is the necessary "questionableness" of what is asserted. To say that something is true is to have a good reason for what I assert. But a good reason is known only in the context of its possi-bly "bad," then it cannot be possibly "good" either. In the language game of making truth claims, "good" and "bad," "true" and "false" have meaning only in terms of each other. Because of this logic, holding something to be true implies freedom, in the sense of openness to at least two possibilities.

On the side of the subject considering the proposition, there is a necessary open-mindedness involved in saying that determinism is true. He must have the ability and willingness to look at both sides of the question, to consider alternative evidence, to raise further questions. Such open-mindedness must be present at least as a possibility in saying that anything is true.

Without such questionableness in the object and open-mindedness in the subject, any truth claim becomes indistinguishable from a rigidly held dogma. If Skinner wishes to argue for environmental determinism, then either he has considered both sides of the question or he has not. If he has considered both sides of the question, then he is not determined to hold the position he does and is, therefore, free. Unless the possibility of determinism's being false is a real possibility for Skinner, he cannot argue that his determinism is true. If such falsity is a real possibility, he is free.

On the other hand, if Skinner has not considered both sides of the question, then we cannot and should not take him seriously, any more than we would take seriously the claim of a prisoner brainwashed by the Soviets about the relative merits of capitalism and socialism. It may be that the prisoner is correct, but we could discover that only by a process of critical inquiry that differs from brainwashing.

Thus even a determinist such as Blanshard, arguing that we are determined to believe something by reasons for the belief, convicts himself through self-refutation. Because a reason that literally coerces us to believe in such a way as to

435

exclude its possible falsity is not and cannot be a good reason, Blanshard cannot defend his position as true. If, on the other hand, he does have good reasons for his belief, then he is free. The explicit deterministic content contradicts the implicit, free act of defending it as true.

Determinism is thus ironical in two senses. It is formally self-refuting in the three above senses; the truth of determinism changes into its opposite, untruth. In a second way, determinism is ironical in that defending it as true implies indeterminism or freedom, the ability to consider alternatives. This second meaning of irony is present in the third kind of self-refutation. Such self-refutation applies to all deterministic claims because each gives reasons for itself, reasons that imply freedom.

Indeterminism

Perhaps, since strict determinism does not work, a strict indeterminism is the answer. Since essence does not determine existence, perhaps existence or freedom is the source of essence. I am the freedom to create my own essence. It is not written in the heavens that I am to be reasonable or unreasonable, homosexual or heterosexual, Catholic or Protestant, peaceful or warlike. Because it is not so written, none of these is objectively preferable to another. One person's virtues are another's vices; one person's sacrifices, another's follies. The consequence of Sartre's indeterminism, as of all indeterminism, is an absurd, arbitrary world where nothing is objectively better than anything else.

There are only two alternatives: "Either man is wholly determined (which is inadmissible, especially because a determined consciousness—i.e., a consciousness externally motivated—becomes itself pure exteriority and ceases to be consciousness) or else man is wholly free." An appropriate philosophical method, phenomenology, is necessary to describe consciousness as it actually experiences itself. Phenomenology takes consciousness on its own terms and does not assume that it is a thing or basically similar to things.

What careful phenomenological description reveals is that consciousness is negativity, the internal negation of the external thing. To be aware of a chair is to be aware of my non-identity with the chair. The chair does not exhaust my possibilities of perception because there are other things I could perceive. Because consciousness is this negativity, total identity with the chair would imply unconsciousness, an impossibility.

Consciousness is a lived paradox: it is what it is not and is not what it is. It is aware of possibilities that are not yet realized and in the light of which it distances itself from what it is in the present. The external thing is simply what it is. It is purely positive, not able to question itself or negate itself the way consciousness can. A chair cannot suddenly decide not to be a chair, but I can choose to leave my business for the teaching profession, to desert my wife for another woman, to reject my middle class status for political radicalism.

Consciousness is pure spontaneity from which all positive determination or definition is absent and which is not influenced by anything other than itself. Consciousness is totally free, therefore, not in the sense that it encounters no limits or obstacles, but in the sense that the meaning these have for consciousness comes from consciousness itself. A person climbing a mountain who becomes fatigued is not forced to stop climbing. If my fundamental project, that basic commitment underlying and giving meaning to everything else, is a life of ease, I may cease climbing. But if my fundamental project is a life delighting in hardships and obstacles that test my courage and ability, I may complete the climb at great cost to myself. Freedom is not influenced by motives or reasons; these are simply expressions of the fundamental project. There is no reciprocity between motivation and freedom because motivation is not really other than freedom.

Nonetheless such an affirmation of absolute freedom has its problems. The first is that if existence precedes essence, the world is arbitrary and absurd. If absurdity is total, however, Sartre cannot defend the truth of his position. For he presumably uses phenomenological method to describe freedom because it is better than other methods, and he argues that his account of freedom is superior to other accounts. In a totally absurd world "better" and "superior" and "truer" make no sense. Sartre's recourse to a method and to standards of truth and falsity that are not absurd contradicts his affirmation of absurdity.

A similar tension arises in Sartre's discussion of good and bad faith. Good faith is living according to the nothingness that I am and accepting responsibility for the choices that I make. Bad faith is the attempt to live like a thing, to avoid the anxiety of freedom, and to shift responsibility from myself to some external agent. The former is definitely preferable to the latter because it is more reasonable and more honest. Yet why, we may ask, are reason and honesty more valuable than their opposites in a totally absurd world?

Another tension exists between Sartre's existentialism and his phenomenology. If existence precedes essence, then there should be no universal, necessary essences prior to freedom. Yet the assumption of phenomenological method is that there are such essences, and Sartre spends some six hundred pages of *Being and Nothingness* describing such structures. For example, consciousness is an internal negation of the external thing, is totally lucid, is temporal, is non-thematically aware of itself, projects value and possibility, is present to the world through embodiment, and desires to be God. Such structures, which

limit and define freedom, have not been chosen and are prior to existence. In a sense broader than Sartre intended, I am "condemned to be free."

Freedom, therefore, is not totally empty of content, is not the mere absence of determination. Neither is it totally spontaneous. Even some of the experiences mentioned by Sartre imply receptivity in freedom, experiences such as fatigue, the resistance of external obstacles, the shame before another person catching me in a degrading act. For whether I wish to or not, I experience fatigue in climbing a mountain. Whether I wish to or not, my attention is drawn momentarily to the loud report of an automobile outside my window. Such experiences are not just bare factual events, but inherently meaningful. I do not experience mere noise, but the loud report of an automobile. Certainly I experience this noise in the context of certain projects such as reading a book or writing a letter. These projects determine the value that such an experience may have at the time, irritating, stimulating, or disturbing, but such values presuppose a meaning that I perceive in a receptive manner.

The positing of total spontaneity also is inconsistent with the experienced difference between arbitrary and non-arbitrary interpretations of phenomena, a difference tacitly presupposed by Sartre when he admits that we intuit external things and qualities in things. If I cannot make this orange peel cease being green, then perceiving consciousness to some extent is determined or informed by what is not itself. Such intuition is impossible without a receptivity to meanings in the thing, which are not imposed but discovered.

Sartre's strict indeterminism is ironically self-refuting; in attempting to maintain his position, Sartre has recourse to determination. His freedom turns out to be a freedom that should be reasonable and honest, possesses certain essential structures, has positive content, and is receptive.

Since both strict determinism and strict indeterminism are self-contradictory, determination and indetermination imply one another.

The Description of Determination and Indetermination

We have established the necessary, mutual implication of determination and indetermination. The task now is to indicate the content of this relationship, to show how they go together. In this section, which is heavily indebted to Paul Ricoeur, determination and indetermination signify four kinds of reciprocity: motive and "leap," reflection and choice, essence and existence, and necessity and consent.

We can view decision either as a static whole, in which I prescind from its involvement with the body and personal history, or as a dynamic whole, in which such involvement is crucial. Considered as a static whole, decision is the project, the chosen action to be performed because of certain motives. Motive and "leap" are essentially related moments or aspects of a decision considered in this manner. This project is the whole, and motive and "leap" are parts.

Motives are not causes that compel me to act in a certain way; rather, they incline without compelling. A cause is distinct in its being from that which it causes, whereas a motive fully becomes a motive only in the "leap" of a decision, in the final *fiat* of choice whereby I opt for one course of action rather than another. The leap involved in making a decision is never indifferent to motives or arbitrary; rather, the decision itself is the result of a search for the right motives. "I decide because . . ." is the basic model for a decision. To determine is not to compel, but to legitimize or justify.

It is essential that I know a motive, whereas I could be ignorant of causes influencing me. If I announce that I am going to the grocery store and I am asked why, the answer "I do not know" makes no sense. On the other hand, if I am feeling irritable, the cause of that feeling could be unknown to me at the time. It could be a lack of sleep, inadequate diet, or too much sun the day before.

To decide to do something is not to predict that I will do it; this mistake confuses causal explanation with motivated decision. For example, on the eve of an exam, I say "I will fail tomorrow," which could mean one of two things. If it is a prediction, it means that in spite of all my efforts to pass the exam, I will fail, due to circumstances beyond my control. If it is a decision, the statement means that I intend to fail. In this case, I experience the future action as dependent on me, as within my power to execute. The certitude of the prediction is more or less probable and uncertain, whereas the certitude of the decision is total because trying to fail is both a necessary and a sufficient condition for failure.

Because all decisions have a history, a decision is not only project but process. It can last a few seconds, as when I decide to have a cup of coffee, or several years, as when I decide to marry. When I need to make a decision, I initially appear as a question to myself because I experience a conflict between many possible motives and projects. If I am trying to decide where to take a vacation, for instance, many considerations appear. How much will it cost? How far away is the place? Once I arrive at my destination, are there activities that I will enjoy? Of the two or three possible vacation spots, which would be the most enjoyable and most restful?

The process of making a decision is a unity in multiplicity; the unity is supplied by the question "Where should I take my vacation?" and the multiplicity is the various temporal phases through which I pass in making up my mind. At each stage of the way there is a dynamic unity of past, present, and future as three essentially related aspects of the process. Each present slides back into the past and is retained in consciousness as past; the above question, once asked, becomes a question that *was* asked but nonetheless continues to influence my deliberations. Each consideration, each alternative accepted or rejected, each motive clarified or qualified I automatically retain as a part of the ongoing process of making up my mind. What I intend is also a unity, a resolution of many possible projects and motives into one project and constellation of motives. The one question, asked in the present because of motives deriving from the past, is an anticipation of a future unity.

Motives initially appear involuntarily, and the basic involuntary is the lived body, or body subject. Not all motives are bodily, but awareness of higher values is founded on these motives. I can respond to bodily hunger by eating a hamburger, or I can endure such hunger for the sake of justice or love of God. I can give in to my fear of the enemy in battle, or I can overcome such fear through patriotism. All motives are either bodily or elaborated and constructed in relation to bodily motives.

As I have already shown, I experience my body as subject, not object. It is my incarnate self present to the world, not as something I have but as something I am. At the beginning of the process of making a decision, therefore, I experience myself as an embodied self, hesitant, open to many possible courses of action, confused, unclear. The process of making a decision is the movement from confusion to clarity, multiplicity to unity. What makes such progress possible is the power of attention whereby I sort out motives. Fatigue, financial considerations, desires to see friends, interest in stimulating cultural activities—all are competing in the decision about a vacation. Which can I safely ignore or relegate to secondary status? How much weight should I

give to financial considerations as opposed to need for a rest? Attention enables me to answer these questions.

The attention involved in choice is analogous to perception. When I am looking at a table in this room, I am aware also of my ability to shift my attention, to look at something else, a book, a picture on the wall, another person in the room. When my attention shifts from the table to a book, the table slides into the background, a background of which I am prethematically or implicitly aware.

There is similar freedom of attention operative in choice. I experience my power of controlling the internal debate, of making one motive the theme of my reflections and relegating the others to the background. Because of my desire to see a friend, I may focus on that motive rather than on my fatigue. Because of my desire to witness good theater, I may concentrate on that and minimize financial considerations. Such shifts of attention are themselves not arbitrary, but motivated. If my goal is to have a relaxing vacation, I see that New York in August would not be as relaxing as Canada. Consequently, I shift my attention to Canada.

The considerations of possible motives and projects can be endless. Because the projected action is always uncertain, risky, and imperfect, no possible vacation can be the perfect vacation, and there is no guarantee that it will turn out well. Also the possible motives and projects cannot all be exhaustively tested and probed. Because of the lived body there will always be a darkness and obscurity that are not totally clarified. If I am to make a decision, therefore, something has to bring reflection to an end. It is an act of freedom itself, choosing one project and set of motives to the exclusion of others, that cuts the reflection short.

The act of choice that terminates reflection is both continuous with what preceded it and discontinuous. Choice is continuous in that it is the last judgment in a series of judgments. This judgment is an act of freedom, a fixing of attention on one motive or hierarchy of motives to the exclusion of others. The rationalistic reading of choice, which excludes or minimizes discontinuity, is, therefore, a mistake. At the beginning of a choice, being reasonable is itself a possible motive; I am not compelled to be reasonable. Because attention is free, it can always listen to the irrational and reject reason. Even in a choice that approximates the classical ideal of rational clarity and continuity, the final judgment is always undergirded by an act of freedom.

There is also a novelty or discontinuity in a decision. I move from consideration of a multiplicity of possible projects to one actual project: going to Canada for a vacation. I experience the decision as a "leap," as not compelled by the reasons I have for it. This aspect of decision, emphasized by Sartre, can tempt me to view decision as totally arbitrary. All reasons would be rationalizations or pretexts created by freedom itself.

Such a reading of choice is false for two reasons. First of all, affirmations of a totally spontaneous freedom end up making freedom itself a motive, as we saw in the case of Sartre. Freedom as described by his phenomenological method becomes a reason for choosing in good faith rather than bad faith. Hidden behind the apparently arbitrary act is a reason: namely, to prove oneself as free. Such, for example, is Raskolnikov's murder of the old woman in *Crime and Punishment*.

Second, in any act for which I give pretexts, I am aware of a deeper, truer motivation. I may rationalize my trip to Canada by telling myself I should visit this friend, but my real reason is that I need a rest, some sunbathing or fishing, and a cooler climate.

At each stage of deciding, determination and indetermination are present and require each other. At the beginning certain possible motives and projects appear involuntarily, but because they have not been sorted out and clarified, there is an indetermination of hesitation. I know what I could do or might do, but not what I wish to do or will do. In the course of resolving my doubts, there is the indetermination of attention seeking to be "determined" by the "best" motives.

Finally, in the actual *fiat*, the final act of choice itself, there is the determination of the self by the self in the creative irruption of a project, the fixing of a free act of attention on this project rather than that, on this motive rather than that. Such determination implies the indetermination of attentive freedom because only freedom can stop the internal debate and constitute a motive in the full sense. For a motive to be efficacious implies not only its content, but its actuality, the fact of its being chosen. There is determination of content and indetermination of form because even though I have committed myself to one project, I have the implicit awareness that I could always reopen the debate, that I am not coerced to choose this content. It is always possible for me to consider other motives and projects.

Summarizing my reflections on decision, I conclude that we can view decision as either a static or a temporal whole. Viewed statically, the "leap" or decision is determined by motive, and the motive becomes a motive in the full sense only by being chosen. Viewed as a temporal whole, decision is, first of all, a movement from the indeterminacy of multiplicity to the determination of unity. Second, there is the indetermination of hesitation related to the determination of possible motives. Third, there is the indetermination of attention searching for the best motive and project. Fourth, there is the *fiat* of self-determination, whereby a possible project and motive become actual. Indetermination here is the indetermination of possibility. Fifth, there are a determination of content and an indetermination of form. Content becomes determinate in the full sense only through the indetermination of form, the awareness that I can change my mind.

Such is the first main kind of reciprocity, that between motive and "leap." A second is that between reason and choice. All motives are not rational; there are motives deriving from my body and my passions. Whereas all choices are motivated, all choices are not necessarily guided by reason. Reason is that capacity to distance myself from my life, bring it into question, conceive of possibilities, and criticize them as authentic or inauthentic. It is possible for a person to elect as a matter of policy to live an irrational life. Therefore, the determination of choice by reflection is an "ought"; when there is conflict between the rational and the irrational, one should listen to reflection and prefer it to other sources of motives.

Such an "ought" becomes apparent when the irrationalist tries to defend her position. When Sartre argues for his concept of freedom and for the superiority of good faith over bad faith, he is implicitly presuming the superiority of reason to other sources of motives. If one is to live an authentic life, one has to know the authentic possibilities and be able to distinguish them from inauthentic possibilities. Reflection makes this possible. Freedom without reason becomes dark and destructive. A woman contemplating a serious decision such as marriage must ask herself questions about the genuineness of her love, compatibility with her prospective spouse, and so forth. Not to do so is to invite personal disaster.

Not only is reason necessary for freedom, but freedom is necessary for reason. Even when I am considering theoretical reasons, as we saw when discussing Blanshard's determinism, I must have the requisite distance from two contradictory hypotheses in order to ascertain the evidence for each. If questioning is essential to theoretical reasoning, then such questioning is impossible without freedom. Freedom is also necessary for practical reason to move from possibility to actuality. Without the actual *fiat* by which a possible motive becomes an actual motive, reflection remains a plaything of possibility, a pitiful Hamlet caught up and stifled in a world of speculation, struggling in vain to escape.

A third kind of relationship between determination and indetermination is essence and existence. Freedom is not an airy nothing, but a structured indetermination; freedom has an essence that it does not choose. The essence of a decision is "I decide because. . . ." Freedom is essentially temporal, a dynamic unity of past, present, and future. It is founded on reason and on the body, both as the basic source of motives and as that through which its projects are realized. Making a decision and carrying it out are essentially related to one another as "empty" to "full." Going to Canada is the realization of the decision to go to Canada, and the lived body is the necessary condition of such fullness.

A determinist still might object that I have not looked at the whole picture. Surely a person's bodily constitution, innate talents, and emotional disposition are not results of choice. If a person has a weak heart, there are certain things that he simply cannot do. If a pianist has her hands cut off in an accident, she is determined by circumstances not to be a pianist.

Because of this kind of determination, the determination of necessity, it is necessary to distinguish between decision and consent or revolt. Decision projects a future action dependent on me. Consent accepts or revolt rejects necessity: what existed prior to my freedom occurred independently and cannot be changed by it.

Nonetheless even here there is not an either—or dichotomy between the voluntary and the

441

involuntary, but a reciprocity, in two senses. Necessity is first of all the servant of freedom, the essential basis for its presence to and expression in the world. My temperament is not something I choose; it is the way I can carry out and realize my projects in the world. Braque and Picasso could work from the same still-life model, but their pictures are different because their temperaments are different.

I also do not choose the automatic, necessary functioning of my body, but this enables me, as I have already shown, to realize projects that would otherwise remain abstract possibilities. Also because I do not have to think about my heart rate, circulatory system, or digestion, my mind is freed to think about possible projects such as vacations, political action, or marriage. Necessity is the condition of freedom, and freedom realizes itself only through necessity.

Second, the necessity of the body poses a question to freedom, the question of acceptance or revolt. Do I accept my incarnate situation, with the kind of body, temperament, and unconscious I have, with all my limitations and deficiencies, or do I revolt? Ricoeur suggests that only a religious and metaphysical answer to this question is fully satisfactory, but I think that a limited answer is also possible within the scope of phenomenology.

Since necessity is rooted in the body, revolt would mean revolt against the body. But such a revolt would mean a freedom continually at odds with itself, with the conditions for its possibility. This is the freedom Sartre defends: limited by necessity, yet striving to be unlimited; dependent, yet striving for total independence; recep-

tive, yet yearning for complete spontaneity. A freedom at odds with itself in this way must affirm that both it and the world are absurd, but it cannot do so in a consistent way. If freedom is a good, then the conditions of its possibility are also good and should be affirmed. With such an affirmation freedom becomes one with itself and fully concrete because in a sense it has taken necessity into itself. Necessity ceases to be an alien, brute fact because it has been understood, affirmed, and accepted.

Conclusion

[My] argument . . . is a disjunctive syllogism. Strict determinism or strict indeterminism or a unity of determination and indetermination is true. Since both determinism and indeterminism are self-refuting, we must affirm a unity of determination and indetermination. The first section of this discussion of freedom demonstrates the necessity, and the second section the content, of this unity.

The experienced reality of freedom is an ambiguous unity of opposites, a unity that itself has several meanings. Both determinism and indeterminism distort this reality by absolutizing one opposite and excluding the other. Only a notion sufficiently nuanced to do justice to freedom in all its paradoxical complexity is an adequate account of freedom. Such is the notion I have advanced and defended: the reciprocal, mutual implication of determination and indetermination, the involuntary and the voluntary.

CONTEMPORARY PERSPECTIVES: CRIME AND PUNISHMENT

The concept of freedom is intimately connected to the concepts of responsibility and punishment. Should criminals be punished or rehabilitated? Our perspective on the free will-determinism debate will influence the way we view the controversial area of crime and punishment. Psychoanalytic and behavioristic determinism require us to re-examine traditional theories of punishment. In a deterministic world, where humans are completely the product of their conditioning, wouldn't it be cruel to punish those who, through no fault of their own, have turned to a life of crime? The renowned criminal lawyer Clarence Darrow believed that it would, offering this analysis of crime and punishment:

> Before any progress can be made in dealing with crime the world must first realize that crime is only a part of conduct; that each act, criminal or otherwise, follows a cause; that given the same conditions the same result will follow forever and ever; that all punishment for the purpose of causing suffering, or growing out of hatred, is cruel and anti-social; that however much society may feel the need of confining the criminal, it must first of all understand that the act had an all-sufficient cause for which the individual was in no way responsible, and must find the cause of his conduct, and, so far as possible, remove the cause.

In his "Address Delivered to the Prisoners in the Chicago County Jail," Darrow argues that, since certain factors in our environment cause crime, the elimination of these factors would result in the elimination of crime. According to Darrow, the "cause of criminal conduct" is the unequal distribution of wealth. A more equitable distribution of wealth in society, he believes, would eliminate the desire to commit crimes. Eventually, jails would become completely unnecessary.

C. S. Lewis could not disagree more. In his article, "The Humanitarian Theory of Punishment," Lewis contends that criminals are responsible for their actions and, therefore, deserve to be punished. He argues against those who favor replacing punishment with rehabilitation, as well as those who wish to use punishment to influence a person's future behavior. He believes that the methods used to rehabilitate criminals are harsher and more inhumane than traditional penalties, and that the idea of using punishment merely to influence behavior is seriously flawed.

If you have been reading this chapter serenely indifferent to the outcome of the freedom-determinism debate, believing that nothing important is at stake, it is time to draw up the balance. Ideas always have consequences. This philosophical issue has far-reaching implications that cannot be ignored.

CHAPTER 44

CLARENCE SEWARD DARROW

THE RESPONSIBILITY OF CRIMINALS

Clarence Seward Darrow (1857–1938) was the foremost criminal and trial lawyer of his day. His famous cases include the Leopold and Loeb murder trial, and the Scopes evolution trial in Tennessee. An outspoken opponent of traditional penal practices, he is the author of *Crime and Criminals* (1902) and *Attorney for the Damned* (1957).

THE RESPONSIBILITY OF CRIMINALS[1]

An Address Delivered to the Prisoners in the Chicago County Jail

If I looked at jails and crimes and prisoners in the way the ordinary person does, I should not speak on this subject to you. The reason I talk to you on the question of crime, its cause and cure, is because I really do not in the least believe in crime. There is no such thing as a crime as the word is generally understood. I do not believe there is any sort of distinction between the real moral condition of the people in and out of jail.

One is just as good as the other. The people here can no more help being here than the people outside can avoid being outside. I do not believe that people are in jail because they deserve to be. They are in jail simply because they can not avoid it on account of circumstances which are entirely beyond their control and for which they are in no way responsible.

I suppose a great many people on the outside

[1]From Clarence Darrow, *Crime and Criminals* (Chicago: Charles H. Kerr & Company, 1902).

would say I was doing you harm if they should hear what I say to you this afternoon, but you can not be hurt a great deal anyway, so it will not matter. Good people outside would say that I was really teaching you things that were calculated to injure society, but it's worth while now and then to hear something different from what you ordinarily get from preachers and the like. These will tell you that you should be good and then you will get rich and be happy. Of course we know that people do not get rich by being good, and that is the reason why so many of you people try to get rich some other way, only you do not understand how to do it quite as well as the fellow outside.

There are people who think that everything in this world is an accident. But really there is no such thing as an accident. A great many folks admit that many of the people in jail ought not to be there, and many who are outside ought to be in. I think none of them ought to be here. There ought to be no jails, and if it were not for the fact that the people on the outside are so grasping and heartless in their dealings with the people on the inside, there would be no such institutions as jails.

I do not want you to believe that I think all you people here are angels. I do not think that. You are people of all kinds, all of you doing the best you can, and that is evidently not very well—you are people of all kinds and conditions and under all circumstances. In one sense everybody is equally good and equally bad. We all do the best we can under the circumstances. But as to the exact things for which you are sent here, some of you are guilty and some of you are not guilty. Some of you did the particular act because you needed the money. Some of you did it because you are in the habit of doing it, and some of you because you are born to it, and it comes to be as natural as it does, for instance, for me to be good.

Most of you probably have nothing against me, and most of you would treat me the same as any other person would; probably better than some of the people on the outside would treat me, because you think I believe in you and they know I do not believe in them. While you would not have the least thing against me in the world you might pick my pockets. I do not think all of you would, but I think some of you would. You would not have anything against me, but that's your profession, a few of you. Some of the rest of you, if my doors were unlocked, might come in if you saw anything you wanted—not out of any malice to me, but because that is your trade. There is no doubt there are quite a number of people in this jail who would pick my pockets. And still I know this, that when I get outside pretty nearly everybody picks my pocket. There may be some of you who would hold up a man on the street, if you did not happen to have something else to do, and needed the money; but when I want to light my house or my office the gas company holds me up. They charge me one dollar for something that is worth twenty-five cents, and still all these people are good people; they are pillars of society and support the churches, and they are respectable.

When I ride on the street cars, I am held up—I pay five cents for a ride that is worth two and a half cents, simply because a body of men have bribed the city council and the legislature, so that all the rest of us have to pay tribute to them.

If I do not want to fall into the clutches of the gas trust and choose to burn oil instead of gas, then good Mr. Rockefeller holds me up, and he uses a certain portion of his money to build universities and support churches which are engaged in telling us how to be good.

Some of you are here for obtaining property under false pretenses—yet I pick up a great Sunday paper and read the advertisements of a mer-

445

chant prince—"Shirt waists for 39 cents, marked down from $3.00."

When I read the advertisements in the paper I see they are all lies. When I want to get out and find a place to stand anywhere on the face of the earth, I find that it has all been taken up long ago before I came here, and before you came here, and somebody says, "Get off, swim into the lake, fly into the air; go anywhere, but get off." That is because these people have the police and they have the jails and the judges and the lawyers and the soldiers and all the rest of them to take care of the earth and drive everybody off that comes in their way.

A great many people will tell you that all this is true, but that it does not excuse you. These facts do not excuse some fellow who reaches into my pocket and takes out a five dollar bill; the fact that the gas company bribes the members of the legislature from year to year, and fixes the law, so that all you people are compelled to be "fleeced" whenever you deal with them; the fact that the street car companies and the gas companies have control of the streets and the fact that the landlords own all the earth, they say, has nothing to do with you.

Let us see whether there is any connection between the crimes of the respectable classes and your presence in the jail. Many of you people are in jail because you have really committed burglary. Many of you, because you have stolen something: in the meaning of the law, you have taken some other person's property. Some of you have entered a store and carried off a pair of shoes because you did not have the price. Possibly some of you have committed murder. I can not tell what all of you did. There are a great many people here who have done some of these things who really do not know themselves why they did them. I think I know why you did them—every one of you; you did these things because you were bound to do them. It looked to

you at the time as if you had a chance to do them or not, as you saw fit, but still after all you had no choice. There may be people here who had some money in their pockets and who still went out and got some more money in a way society forbids. Now you may not yourselves see exactly why it was you did this thing, but if you look at the question deeply enough and carefully enough you would see that there were circumstances that drove you to do exactly the thing which you did. You could not help it any more than we outside can help taking the positions that we take. The reformers who tell you to be good and you will be happy, and the people on the outside who have property to protect—they think that the only way to do it is by building jails and locking you up in cells on week-days and praying for you Sundays.

I think that all of this has nothing whatever to do with right conduct. I think it is very easily seen what has to do with right conduct. Some so-called criminals—and I will use this word because it is handy, it means nothing to me—I speak of the criminals who get caught as distinguished from the criminals who catch them—some of these so-called criminals are in jail for the first offenses, but nine-tenths of you are in jail because you did not have a good lawyer and of course you did not have a good lawyer because you did not have enough money to pay a good lawyer. There is no very great danger of a rich man going to jail.

Some of you may be here for the first time. If we would open the doors and let you out, and leave the laws as they are today, some of you would be back tomorrow. This is about as good a place as you can get anyway. There are many people here who are so in the habit of coming that they would not know where else to go. There are people who are born with the tendency to break into jail every chance they get, and they can not avoid it. You can not figure out your life and see why it was, but still there is a reason for it, and if we were all-wise and knew all the facts we could figure it out.

In the first place, there are a good many more people who go to jail in the winter time than in summer. Why is this? Is it because people are more wicked in winter? No, it is because the coal trust begins to get us in its grip in the winter. A few gentlemen take possession of the coal, and unless the people will pay $7 or $8 a ton for something that is worth $3, they will have to freeze. Then there is nothing to do but to break into jail, and so there are many more in jail in the winter than in summer. It costs more for gas in the winter because the nights are longer, and people go to jail to save gas bills. The jails are electric-lighted. You may not know it, but these economic laws are working all the time, whether we know it or do not know it.

There are more people go to jail in hard times than in good times—few people comparatively go to jail except when they are hard up. They go to jail because they have no other place to go. They may not know why, but it is true all the same. People are not more wicked in hard times. That is not the reason. The fact is true all over the world that in hard times more people go to jail than in good times, and in winter more people go to jail than in summer. Of course it is pretty hard times for people who go to jail at any time. The people who go to jail are almost always poor people—people who have no other place to live first and last. When times are hard then you find large numbers of people who go to jail who would not otherwise be in jail.

Long ago, Mr. Buckle, who was a great philosopher and historian, collected facts and he showed that the number of people who are arrested increased just as the price of food increased. When they put up the price of gas ten cents a thousand I do not know who will go to jail, but I do know that a certain number of peo-ple will go. When the meat combine raises the price of beef I do not know who is going to jail, but I know that a large number of people are bound to go. Whenever the Standard Oil Company raises the price of oil, I know that a certain number of girls who are seamstresses, and who work night after night long hours for somebody else, will be compelled to go out on the streets and ply another trade, and I know that Mr. Rockefeller and his associates are responsible and not the poor girls in the jails.

First and last, people are sent to jail because they are poor. Sometimes, as I say, you may not need money at the particular time, but you wish to have thrifty forehanded habits, and do not always wait until you are in absolute want. Some of you people are perhaps plying the trade, the profession, which is called burglary. No man in his right senses will go into a strange house in the dead of night and prowl around with a dark lantern through unfamiliar rooms and take chances of his life if he has plenty of the good things of the world in his own home. You would not take any such chances as that. If a man had clothes in his clothes press and beefsteak in his pantry, and money in a bank, he would not navigate around nights in houses where he knows nothing about the premises whatever. It always requires experience and education for this profession, and people who fit themselves for it are no more to blame than I am for being a lawyer. A man would not hold up another man on the street if he had plenty of money in his own pocket. He might do it if he had one dollar or two dollars, but he wouldn't if he had as much money as Mr. Rockefeller has. Mr. Rockefeller has a great deal better hold-up game than that.

The more that is taken from the poor by the rich, who have the chance to take it, the more poor people there are who are compelled to resort to these means for a livelihood. They may not understand it, they may not think so at once, but after all they are driven into that line of employment.

There is a bill before the legislature of this State to punish kidnaping children, with death. We have wise members of the Legislature. They know the gas trust when they see it and they always see it,—they can furnish light enough to be seen, and this Legislature thinks it is going to stop kidnaping children by making a law punishing kidnapers of children, with death. I don't believe in kidnaping children, but the Legislature is all wrong. Kidnaping children is not a crime, it is a profession. It has been developed with the times. It has been developed with our modern industrial conditions. There are many ways of making money—many new ways that our ancestors knew nothing about. Our ancestors knew nothing about a billion dollar trust; and here comes some poor fellow who has no other trade and he discovers the profession of kidnaping children.

This crime is born, not because people are bad; people don't kidnap other people's children because they want the children or because they are devilish, but because they see a chance to get some money out of it. You cannot cure this crime by passing a law punishing by death kidnapers of children. There is one way to cure it. There is one way to cure all these offenses, and that is to give the people a chance to live. There is no other way, and there never was any other way since the world began, and the world is so blind and stupid that it will not see. If every man and woman and child in the world had a chance to make a decent, fair, honest living, there would be no jails, and no lawyers and no courts. There might be some persons here or there with some peculiar formation of their brain, like Rockefeller, who would do these things simply to be doing them; but they would be very, very few, and those should be sent to a hospital and

treated, and not sent to jail; and they would entirely disappear in the second generation, or at least in the third generation.

I am not talking pure theory. I will just give you two or three illustrations.

The English people once punished criminals by sending them away. They would load them on a ship and export them to Australia. England was owned by lords and nobles and rich people. They owned the whole earth over there, and the other people had to stay in the streets. They could not get a decent living. They used to take their criminals and send them to Australia—I mean the class of criminals who got caught. When these criminals got over there, and nobody else had come, they had the whole continent to run over, and so they could raise sheep and furnish their own meat, which is easier than stealing it; these criminals then became decent, respectable people because they had a chance to live. They did not commit any crimes. They were just like the English people who sent them there, only better. And in the second generation the descendants of those criminals were as good and respectable a class of people as there were on the face of the earth, and then they began building churches and jails themselves.

A portion of this country was settled in the same way, landing prisoners down on the southern coast; but when they got here and had a whole continent to run over and plenty of chances to make a living, they became respectable citizens, making their own living just like any other citizen in the world; but finally these descendants of the English aristocracy, who sent the people over to Australia, found out they were getting rich, and so they went over to get possession of the earth as they always do, and they organized land syndicates and got control of the land and ores, and then they had just as many criminals in Australia as they did in England. It was not because the world had grown bad; it was because the earth had been taken away from the people.

Some of you people have lived in the country. It's prettier than it is here. And if you have ever lived on a farm you understand that if you put a lot of cattle in a field, when the pasture is short they will jump over the fence; but put them in a good field where there is plenty of pasture, and they will be lawabiding cattle to the end of time. The human animal is just like the rest of the animals, only a little more so. The same thing that governs in the one governs in the other.

Everybody makes his living along the lines of least resistance. A wise man who comes into a country early sees a great undeveloped land. For instance, our rich men twenty-five years ago saw that Chicago was small and knew a lot of people would come here and settle, and they readily saw that if they had all the land around here it would be worth a good deal, so they grabbed the land. You can not be a landlord because somebody has got it all. You must find some other calling. In England and Ireland and Scotland less than five per cent own all the land there is, and the people are bound to stay there on any kind of terms the landlords give. They must live the best they can, so they develop all these various professions— burglary, picking pockets and the like.

Again, people find all sorts of ways of getting rich. These are diseases like everything else. You look at people getting rich, organizing trusts, and making a million dollars, and somebody gets the disease and he starts out. He catches it just as a man catches the mumps or the measles; he is not to blame, it is in the air. You will find men speculating beyond their means, because the mania of money-getting is taking possession of them. It is simply a disease; nothing more, nothing less. You can not avoid catching it; but the fellows who have control of the earth have the advantage of

you. See what the law is; when these men get control of things, they make the laws. They do not make the laws to protect anybody; courts are not instruments of justice; when your case gets into court it will make little difference whether you are guilty or innocent; but it's better if you have a smart lawyer. And you can not have a smart lawyer unless you have money. First and last it's a question of money. Those men who own the earth make the laws to protect what they have. They fix up a sort of fence or pen around what they have, and they fix the law so the fellow on the outside can not get in. The laws are really organized for the protection of the men who rule the world. They were never organized or enforced to do justice. We have no system for doing justice, not the slightest in the world.

Let me illustrate: Take the poorest person in this room. If the community had provided a system of doing justice the poorest person in this room would have as good a lawyer as the richest, would he not? When you went into court you would have just as long a trial, and just as fair a trial as the richest person in Chicago. Your case would not be tried in fifteen or twenty minutes, whereas it would take fifteen days to get through with a rich man's case.

Then if you were rich and were beaten, your case would be taken to the Appellate Court. A poor man can not take his case to the Appellate Court; he has not the price; and then to the Supreme Court, and if he were beaten there he might perhaps go to the United States Supreme Court. And he might die of old age before he got into jail. If you are poor, it's a quick job. You are almost known to be guilty, else you would not be there. Why should any one be in the criminal court if he were not guilty? He would not be there if he could be anywhere else. The officials have no time to look after all these cases. The people who are on the outside, who are running banks and building churches and making jails, they have no time to examine 600 or 700 prisoners each year to see whether they are guilty or innocent. If the courts were organized to promote justice the people would elect somebody to defend all these criminals, somebody as smart as the prosecutor—and give him as many detectives and as many assistants to help, and pay as much money to defend you as to prosecute you. We have a very able man for State's Attorney, and he has many assistants, detectives and policemen without end, and judges to hear the case—everything handy.

Most of all our criminal code consists in offenses against property. People are sent to jail because they have committed a crime against property. It is of very little consequence whether one hundred people more or less go to jail who ought not go—you must protect property, because in this world property is of more importance than anything else.

How is it done? These people who have property fix it so they can protect what they have. When somebody commits a crime it does not follow that he had done something that is morally wrong. The man on the outside who has committed no crime may have done something. For instance: to take all the coal in the United States and raise the price two dollars or three dollars when there is no need of it, and thus kill thousands of babies and send thousands of people to the poorhouse and tens of thousands to jail, as is done every year in the United States,—this is a greater crime than all the people in our jails ever committed, but the law does not punish it. Why? Because the fellows who control the earth make the laws. If you and I had the making of the laws, the first thing we would do would be to punish the fellow who gets control of the earth. Nature put this coal in the ground for me as well as for them and nature made the prairies

up here to raise wheat for me as well as for them, and then the great railroad companies came along and fenced it up.

Most all of the crimes for which we are punished are property crimes. There are a few personal crimes, like murder—but they are very few. The crimes committed are mostly those against property. If this punishment is right the criminals must have a lot of property. How much money is there in this crowd? And yet you are all here for crimes against property. The people up and down the Lake Shore have not committed crime, still they have so much property they don't know what to do with it. It is perfectly plain why these people have not committed crimes against property; they make the laws and therefore do not need to break them. And in order for you to get some property you are obliged to break the rules of the game. I don't know but what some of you may have had a very nice chance to get rich by carrying the hod for one dollar a day, twelve hours. Instead of taking that nice, easy profession, you are a burglar. If you had been given a chance to be a banker you would rather follow that. Some of you may have had a chance to work as a switchman on a railroad where you know, according to statistics, that you can not live and keep all your limbs more than seven years, and you can get fifty dollars or seventy-five dollars a month for taking your lives in your hands, and instead of taking that lucrative position you choose to be a sneak thief, or something like that. Some of you made that sort of choice. I don't know which I would take if I was reduced to this choice. I have an easier choice.

I will guarantee to take from this jail, or any jail in the world, five hundred men who have been the worst criminals and law-breakers who ever got into jail, and I will go down to our lowest streets and take five hundred of the most abandoned prostitutes, and go out somewhere

where there is plenty of land, and will give them a chance to make a living, and they will be as good people as the average in the community.

There is a remedy for the sort of condition we see here. The world never finds it out, or when it does find it out it does not enforce it. You may pass a law punishing every person with death for burglary, and it will make no difference. Men will commit it just the same. In England there was a time when one hundred different offenses were punishable with death, and it made no difference. The English people strangely found out that so fast as they repealed the severe penalties and so fast as they did away with punishing men by death, crime decreased instead of increased; that the smaller the penalty the fewer the crimes.

Hanging men in our county jails does not prevent murder. It makes murderers.

And this has been the history of the world. It's easy to see how to do away with what we call crime. It is not so easy to do it. I will tell you how to do it. It can be done by giving the people a chance to live—by destroying special privileges. So long as big criminals can get the coal fields, so long as the big criminals have control of the city council and get the public streets for street cars and gas rights, this is bound to send thousands of poor people to jail. So long as men are allowed to monopolize all the earth, and compel others to live on such terms as these men see fit to make, then you are bound to get into jail.

The only way in the world to abolish crime and criminals is to abolish the big ones and the little ones together. Make fair conditions of life. Give men a chance to live. Abolish the right of the private ownership of land, abolish monopoly, make the world partners in production, partners in the good things of life. Nobody would steal if he could get something of his own some easier way. Nobody will commit burglary when he has a house full. No girl will go out on the streets when she has a comfortable place at home. The man who owns a sweatshop or a department store may not be to blame himself for the condition of his girls, but when he pays them five dollars, three dollars, and two dollars a week, I wonder where he thinks they will get the rest of their money to live. The only way to cure these conditions is by equality. There should be no jails. They do not accomplish what they pretend to accomplish. If you would wipe them out, there would be no more criminals than now. They terrorize nobody. They are a blot upon any civilization, and a jail is an evidence of the lack of charity of the people on the outside who make the jails and fill them with the victims of their greed.

CHAPTER 45

C. S. LEWIS

THE HUMANITARIAN THEORY OF PUNISHMENT

Clive Staples Lewis (1898–1963) was professor of medieval and renaissance English at Cambridge University from 1954 until his death. He is the author of numerous books and articles written in defense of Christianity, including *Mere Christianity*, *The Problem of Pain*, and *The Screwtape Letters*.

THE HUMANITARIAN THEORY OF PUNISHMENT[1]

In England we have lately had a controversy about Capital Punishment. I do not know whether a murderer is more likely to repent and make a good end on the gallows a few weeks after his trial or in the prison infirmary thirty years later. I do not know whether the fear of death is an indispensable deterrent. I need not, for the purpose of this article, decide whether it is a morally permissible deterrent. Those are questions which I propose to leave untouched. My subject is not Capital Punishment in particular, but that theory of punishment in general which the controversy showed to be almost universal among my fellow-countrymen. It may be called the Humanitarian Theory. Those who hold it think that it is mild and merciful. In this I believe that they are seriously mistaken. I believe that the "Humanity" which it claims is a dangerous illusion and disguises the possibility of cruelty and injustice without end. I urge a return to the traditional or

[1]From C. S. Lewis "The Humanitarian Theory of Punishment" from *God in the Dock: Essays on Theology and Ethics* (Grand Rapids: Eerdmans Pub. Co., 1970), 287–300.

Retributive theory not solely, nor even primarily, in the interests of society but in the interests of the criminal.

According to the Humanitarian theory, to punish a man because he deserves it, and as much as he deserves, is mere revenge, and, therefore, barbarous and immoral. It is maintained that the only legitimate motives for punishing are the desire to deter others by example or to mend the criminal. When this theory is combined, as frequently happens, with the belief that all crime is more or less pathological, the idea of mending tails off into that of healing or curing and punishment becomes therapeutic. Thus it appears at first sight that we have passed from the harsh and self-righteous notion of giving the wicked their deserts to the charitable and enlightened one of tending the psychologically sick. What could be more amiable? One little point which is taken for granted in this theory needs, however, to be made explicit. The things done to the criminal, even if they are called cures, will be just as compulsory as they were in the old days when we called them punishments. If a tendency to steal can be cured by psychotherapy, the thief will no doubt be forced to undergo the treatment. Otherwise, society cannot continue.

My contention is that this doctrine, merciful though it appears, really means that each one of us, from the moment he breaks the law, is deprived of the rights of a human being.

The reason is this. The Humanitarian theory removes from Punishment the concept of Desert. But the concept of Desert is the only connecting link between punishment and justice. It is only as deserved or undeserved that a sentence can be just or unjust. I do not here contend that the question "Is it deserved?" is the only one we can reasonably ask about a punishment. We may very properly ask whether it is likely to deter others and to reform the criminal. But neither of these two last questions is a question about justice. There is no sense in talking about a "just deterrent" or a "just cure." We demand of a deterrent not whether it is just but whether it will deter. We demand of a cure not whether it is just but whether it succeeds. Thus when we cease to consider what the criminal deserves and consider only what will cure him or deter others, we have tacitly removed him from the sphere of justice altogether; instead of a person, a subject of rights, we now have a mere object, a patient, a "case."

The distinction will become clearer if we ask who will be qualified to determine sentences when sentences are no longer held to derive their propriety from the criminal's deservings. On the old view the problem of fixing the right sentence was a moral problem. Accordingly, the judge who did it was a person trained in jurisprudence; trained, that is, in a science which deals with rights and duties, and which, in origin at least, was consciously accepting guidance from the Law of Nature, and from Scripture. We must admit that in the actual penal code of most countries at most times these high originals were so much modified by local custom, class interests, and utilitarian concessions, as to be very imperfectly recognizable. But the code was never in principle, and not always in fact, beyond the control of the conscience of the society. And when (say, in Eighteenth Century England) actual punishments conflicted too violently with the moral sense of the community, juries refused to convict and reform was finally brought about. This was possible because, so long as we are thinking in terms of Desert, the propriety of the penal code, being a moral question, is a question on which every man has the right to an opinion, not because he follows this or that profession, but because he is simply a man, a rational animal enjoying the Natural Light. But all this is changed when we drop the concept of Desert. The only two questions we may now ask about a punishment are whether it deters and whether it cures. But these are not questions on which anyone is entitled to have an opinion simply because he is a man. He is not entitled to an opinion even if, in addition to being a man, he should happen also to be a jurist, a Christian, and a moral theologian. For they are not questions about principle but about matter of fact; and for such *cuiquam in sua arte credendum.*[2] Only the expert "penologist" (let barbarous things have barbarous names), in the light of previous experiment, can tell us what is likely to deter: only the psychotherapist can tell us what is likely to cure. It will be in vain for the rest of us, speaking simply as men, to say, "but this punishment is hideously unjust, hideously disproportionate to the criminal's deserts." The experts with perfect logic will reply, "but nobody was talking about deserts. No one was talking about *punishment* in your archaic vindictive sense of the word. Here are the statistics proving that this treatment deters. Here are the statistics proving that this other treatment cures. What is your trouble?"

The Humanitarian theory, then, removes sentences from the hands of jurists whom the public conscience is entitled to criticize and places them in the hands of technical experts whose special sciences do not even employ such categories as Rights or Justice. It might be argued that since this transference results from an abandonment of the old idea of punishment, and, therefore, of all vindictive motives, it will be safe to leave our criminals in such hands. I will not pause to comment on the simple minded view of fallen human nature which such a belief implies. Let us rather remember that the "cure" of criminals is to be compulsory; and let us then watch how the theory actually works in the mind of the Humanitarian. The immediate starting point of this article was a letter I read in one of our Leftist

weeklies. The author was pleading that a certain sin, now treated by our Laws as a crime, should henceforward be treated as a disease. And he complained that under the present system the offender, after a term in gaol, was simply let out to return to his original environment where he would probably relapse. What he complained of was not the shutting up but the letting out. On his remedial veiw of punishment the offender should, of course, be detained until he was cured. And of course the official straighteners are the only people who can say when that is. The first result of the Humanitarian theory is, therefore, to substitute for a definite sentence (reflecting to some extent the community's moral judgment on the degree of ill-desert involved) an indefinite sentence terminable only by the word of those experts—and they are not experts in moral theology nor even in the Law of Nature—who inflict it. Which of us, if he stood in the dock, would not prefer to be tried by the old system?

It may be said that by the continued use of the word Punishment and the use of the verb "inflict" I am misrepresenting the Humanitarians. They are not punishing, not inflicting, only healing. But do not let us be deceived by a name. To be taken without consent from my home and friends; to lose my liberty; to undergo all those assaults on my personality which modern psychotherapy knows how to deliver; to be remade after some pattern of "normality" hatched in a Viennese laboratory to which I never professed allegiance; to know that this process will never end until either my captors have succeeded or I grown wise enough to cheat them with apparent success—who cares whether this is called Punishment or not? That it includes most of the elements for which any punishment is feared—shame, exile, bondage, and years eaten by the locust—is obvious. Only enormous ill-desert could justify it; but ill-desert is the very concep-

[2]"Experts must be believed."—Ed.

tion which the Humanitarian theory has thrown overboard.

If we turn from the curative to the deterrent justification of punishment we shall find the new theory even more alarming. When you punish a man *in terrorem*, make of him an "example" to others, you are admittedly using him as a means to an end; someone else's end. This, in itself, would be a very wicked thing to do. On the classical theory of Punishment it was of course justified on the ground that the man deserved it. That was assumed to be established before any question of "making him an example" arose. You then, as the saying is, killed two birds with one stone; in the process of giving him what he deserved you set an example to others. But take away desert and the whole morality of the punishment disappears. Why, in Heaven's name, am I to be sacrificed to the good of society in this way?—unless, of course, I deserve it.

But that is not the worst. If the justification of exemplary punishment is not to be based on desert but solely on its efficacy as a deterrent, it is not absolutely necessary that the man we punish should even have committed the crime. The deterrent effect demands that the public should draw the moral, "If we do such an act we shall suffer like that man." The punishment of a man actually guilty whom the public think innocent will not have the desired effect; the punishment of a man actually innocent will, provided the public think him guilty. But every modern State has powers which make it easy to fake a trial. When a victim is urgently needed for exemplary purposes and a guilty victim cannot be found, all the purposes of deterrence will be equally served by the punishment (call it "cure" if you prefer) of an innocent victim, provided that the public can be cheated into thinking him guilty. It is no use to ask me why I assume that our rulers will be so wicked. The punishment of an innocent, that is, an undeserving, man is wicked only if we grant

the traditional view that righteous punishment means deserved punishment. Once we have abandoned that criterion, all punishments have to be justified, if at all, on other grounds that have nothing to do with desert. Where the punishment of the innocent can be justified on those grounds (and it could in some cases be justified as a deterrent) it will be no less moral than any other punishment. Any distaste for it on the part of a Humanitarian will be merely a hang-over from the Retributive theory.

It is, indeed, important to notice that my argument so far supposes no evil intentions on the part of the Humanitarian and considers only what is involved in the logic of his position. My contention is that good men (not bad men) consistently acting upon that position would act as cruelly and unjustly as the greatest tyrants. They might in some respects act even worse. Of all tyrannies a tyranny sincerely exercised for the good of its victims may be the most oppressive. It may be better to live under robber barons than under omnipotent moral busybodies. The robber baron's cruelty may sometimes sleep, his cupidity may at some point be satiated; but those who torment us for our own good will torment us without end for they do so with the approval of their own conscience. They may be more likely to go to Heaven yet at the same time likelier to make a Hell of earth. Their very kindness stings with intolerable insult. To be "cured" against one's will and cured of states which we may not regard as disease is to be put on a level with those who have not yet reached the age of reason or those who never will; to be classed with infants, imbeciles, and domestic animals. But to be punished, however severely, because we have deserved it, because we "ought to have known better," is to be treated as a human person made in God's image.

In reality, however, we must face the possibility of bad rulers armed with a Humanitarian theory of punishment. A great many popular blue prints for a Christian society are merely what the Elizabethans called "eggs in moonshine" because they assume that the whole society is Christian or that the Christians are in control. This is not so in most contemporary States. Even if it were, our rulers would still be fallen men, and, therefore, neither very wise nor very good. As it is, they will usually be unbelievers. And since wisdom and virtue are not the only or the commonest qualifications for a place in the government, they will not often be even the best unbelievers. The practical problem of Christian politics is not that of drawing up schemes for a Christian society, but that of living as innocently as we can with unbelieving fellow-subjects under unbelieving rulers who will never be perfectly wise and good and who will sometimes be very wicked and very foolish. And when they are wicked the Humanitarian theory of Punishment will put in their hands a finer instrument of tyranny than wickedness ever had before. For if crime and disease are to be regarded as the same thing, it follows that any state of mind which our masters choose to call "disease" can be treated as crime; and compulsorily cured. It will be vain to plead that states of mind which displease government need not always involve moral turpitude and do not therefore always deserve forfeiture of liberty. For our masters will not be using the concepts of Desert and Punishment but those of disease and cure. We know that one school of psychology already regards religion as a neurosis. When this particular neurosis becomes inconvenient to government what is to hinder government from proceeding to "cure" it? Such "cure" will, of course, be compulsory; but under the Humanitarian theory it will not be called by the shocking name of Persecution. No one will blame us for being Christians, no one will hate us, no one will revile us. The new Nero will approach us with the silky manners of a doctor, and though all will be in fact as compulsory as the *tunica molesta* or Smithfield or Tyburn, all will go on within the unemotional therapeutic sphere where words like "right" and "wrong" or "freedom" and "slavery" are never heard. And thus when the command is given every prominent Christian in the land may vanish overnight into Institutions for the Treatment of the Ideologically Unsound, and it will rest with the expert gaolers to say when (if ever) they are to re-emerge. But it will not be persecution. Even if the treatment is painful, even if it is life-long, even if it is fatal, that will be only a regrettable accident; the intention was purely therapeutic. Even in ordinary medicine there were painful operations and fatal operations; so in this. But because they are "treatment," not punishment, they can be criticized only by fellow-experts and on technical grounds, never by men as men and on grounds of justice.

This is why I think it essential to oppose the Humanitarian theory of Punishment, root and branch, wherever we encounter it. It carries on its front a semblance of Mercy which is wholly false. That is how it can deceive men of good will. The error began, perhaps, with Shelley's statement that the distinction between Mercy and Justice was invented in the courts of tyrants. It sounds noble, and was indeed the error of a noble mind. But the distinction is essential. The older view was that Mercy "tempered" Justice, or (on the highest level of all) that Mercy and Justice had met and kissed. The essential act of Mercy was to pardon; and pardon in its very essence involves the recognition of guilt and ill-desert in the recipient. If crime is only a disease which needs cure, not sin which deserves punishment, it cannot be pardoned. How can you pardon a man for having a gum-boil or a club foot? But the Humanitarian theory wants simply to abolish Justice and substitute Mercy for it. This means that you start being "kind" to people before you have considered their rights, and then force upon them supposed kindnesses which they in fact had a right to refuse, and finally kindnesses which no one but you will recognize as kindnesses and which the recipient will feel as abominable cruelties. You have overshot the mark. Mercy, detached from Justice, grows unmerciful. That is the important paradox. As there are plants which will flourish only in mountain soil, so it appears that Mercy will flower only when it grows in the crannies of the rock of Justice; transplanted to the marshlands of mere Humanitarianism, it becomes a man-eating weed, all the more dangerous because it is still called by the same name as the mountain variety. But we ought long ago to have learned our lesson. We should be too old now to be deceived by those humane pretensions which have served to usher in every cruelty of the revolutionary period in which we live. These are the "precious balms" which will "break our heads."

There is a fine sentence in Bunyan: "It came burning hot into my mind, whatever he said, and however he flattered, when he got me home to his house, he would sell me for a slave." There is a fine couplet, too, in John Ball:

Be ware ere ye be wo
Know your friend from your foe.

One last word. You may ask why I send this to an Australian periodical. The reason is simple and perhaps worth recording; I can get no hearing for it in England.

GLOSSARY

CALVINISM   A system of theology, originated by John Calvin, that teaches the doctrine of *predestination*.

COEFFICIENT OF ADVERSITY   A term appearing in Sartre's philosophy; refers to an impediment that exists with respect to a special human goal or purpose.

COMPATIBILISM   The veiw that it is possible to assert *both* that all events are caused *and* that with respect to some events human beings have free will.

DETERMINISM   *Hard determinism* is the view that every event is caused by antecedent events over which the agent has no control; hence, there can be no room for human freedom. *Soft determinism* is the view that there is a place for human freedom in a world governed totally by causal laws; sometimes this term is used as a synonym for *compatibilism*.

FATALISM   The belief that events are irrevocably fixed so that no human effort can alter them. "Whatever shall be, shall be."

FREEDOM   The state or quality of being free, exemplified by the concepts of self-determination, self-control, self-direction, self-regulation; being compelled by desirable internal motives, ideals, wishes, desires as opposed to external constraints.

HEISENBERG UNCERTAINTY PRINCIPLE   A theory stating that both the exact position and the exact momentum of subatomic particles cannot be known at the same time. Heisenberg and others have used this principle to defend the concepts of uncaused events and free will.

INDETERMINISM   The theory that some events, such as personal choices, are independent of antecedent events and are thus uncaused.

457

Some indeterminsts, such as William James, hold that there are genuine possibilities in the future and that the universe is open to novelty, chance, and spontaneity.

OMNISCIENCE The state or quality of being all-knowing; usually attributed to God, a being who knows all there is to know.

PREDESTINATION A theological doctrine (usually associated with *Calvinism*) that all human events have been decreed or determined from the beginning of time by the sovereign will of God.

RESPONSIBILITY The condition of being answerable or accountable for some act or event presumed to be within a person's control.

SELF-DETERMINISM A position that links determination and freedom, stressing the causal effectiveness of human participation in events. Defended by Richard Taylor and others.

VOLITION The act of making a choice. Determinists argue that volitions are caused: nondeterminists argue that volitions are uncaused or self-caused.

FOR FURTHER STUDY

Beck, Lewis White. *The Actor and the Spectator*. New Haven: Yale University Press, 1975.
A carefully reasoned argument for freedom in human action.

Hook, Sidney, ed. *Determinism and Freedom in the Age of Modern Science*. New York: Collier Books, 1961.
An excellent reference book, including essays by scientists and philosophers.

Ricoeur, Paul. *The Voluntary and the Involuntary*. Translated by Crazin V. Kohak. Evanston, Ill.: Northwestern University Press, 1966.
A brilliant and comprehensive treatment by the renowned French phenomenologist.

Skinner, B. F. *Walden Two*. New York: Macmillan, 1948.
A utopian novel, in which the well-known behaviorist sets forth his deterministic views.

Trusted, Jennifer. *Free Will and Responsibility*. Oxford: Oxford University Press, 1984.
A clearly written book, thorough in its coverage.

Watson, Gary, ed. *Free Will*. New York: Oxford University Press, 1982.
Eleven important essays written by well-known analytic philosophers, including A. J. Ayer, Roderick Chisholm, and Peter Strawson. Highly recommended.

PART SEVEN

◆

RELIGION, GOD, AND EVIL

———————————

God is the fundamental symbol for what concerns us ultimately. . . . Where there is ultimate concern, God can be denied only in the name of God

PAUL TILLICH

ORIENTATION

In every age, philosophers have been intensely interested in the meaning of religion and its role in our personal and social existence. For example, Parmenides' seminal thoughts about Being were cast in the form of a religious revelation, Plato inquired into the relation of religion to morality, and Aristotle's *Metaphysics* culminates in a full blown **theology,** complete with speculation about the nature and activity of God. Christian philosophers of the Middle Ages (such as Augustine, Anselm, and Thomas Aquinas) stressed the compatibility of religious and philosophical insights and viewed philosophy as contributing to the spiritual life. While religion remained important in the writings of the modern philosophers (from the early moderns Descartes, Locke, and Berkeley, to the later Kant and Hegel), an important shift takes place in the modern era. The philosophers of this period approach the study of religion not as "church fathers" or theologians, but as professional philosophers, intent on grasping the human meaning of religion. The de-coupling of philosophy from theology resulted in a freedom to pursue new kinds of religious questions. Sometimes these questions were asked by those who labored to understand the meaning of religion in the modern world, even while they relentlessly criticized religious beliefs. Thus David Hume, who probably did more than any other modern philosopher to raise critical questions about traditional religious beliefs, was a Christian believer in his childhood and always kept in mind his personal experiences of Christian living.[1] In recent years, philosophical interest in religion has grown tremendously, spawning new publications, professional organizations, and conferences devoted to the philosophy of religion.

Remembering the example of Hume, it is important to realize that one need not be religious in order to have an interest in studying religion. In other words, the philosophical study of religion is not restricted to "believing souls," already convinced of the value of religion. It is open to anyone who has a sincere interest in the phenomena of the religious life. One of the ironies of studying religion is that it tends to hide its deeper meanings to those most anxious to claim that they are already religious, while at the same time rewarding self-professed "nonreligious" people with a wealth of insights. Hegel alerts us to this irony when he writes, "The familiar, just because it is familiar, is not really understood." Philosophizing about religion requires that we relearn how to look at the world of religion, by suspending whatever preconceptions or biases that we bring to the subject. It is dangerous to make judgments about religion, pro or con, before we have immersed ourselves in the question of what it means to be religious.[2] As we embark on this study of religion, a word of caution may be in order: Let us pledge

---

[1]See James Collins, *The Emergence of Philosophy of Religion* (New Haven: Yale University Press, 1967) 3.
[2]See Merold Westphal, *God, Guilt, and Death* (Bloomington: Indiana University Press, 1984), 9–15. This question—What does it mean to be religious?—is at the heart of Westphal's remarkable book.

not to be premature in our judgments, lest we be guilty of defending or attacking, building up or tearing down the religious phenomena under consideration before we have achieved some common understanding of the phenomena themselves.

Following Aristotle's lead, philosophers have traditionally treated religion as lying within the province of metaphysics. However, religion is a vast and highly complex subject that can be viewed from a wide variety of perspectives, spilling out beyond the boundaries of philosophy. While it is impossible for us to discuss religion in any exhaustive sense, we shall make an attempt in this part to understand the nature of religion, the nature of God, grounds for belief and disbelief in God, and the problem of evil. Since the problem of evil looms large in the philosophy of religion, the Contemporary Perspectives section is devoted to exploring this issue at some length.

THE NATURE OF RELIGION

RELIGION DEFINED

Psychologists, sociologists, naturalists, anthropologists, political scientists, and literary theorists, to name a few, have all theorized about the nature of religion. Since it can be studied profitably from such different standpoints, religion is notoriously difficult to define. Etymologically, our English word religion is derived from the Latin words *religio*, meaning "reverence for the gods, holiness," and *religare*, meaning "to bind," or "bind together." Taking the latter meaning in its broadest sense, we might define religion as "any pursuit which dominates the lives of men and women, binding them together in a common dedication to an aim." Such a broad definition, however, would include zealous Marxists; it would also include rabid college football fans, who flock to the stadium to attend "the church of sport," participating religiously in a series of rituals (e.g. wearing sacred colors, chanting sacred songs, offering silent prayers for the team in the hour of its need) that have meaning only to the true believers! Because this broad definition seems a bit too inclusive, some prefer to understand religion in its narrower sense as a pursuit that involves worship of a God and a binding desire to do the will of this God. Strictly speaking, however, religion needn't make reference to a God; in some forms of Buddhism, for instance, worship of a God has little or no importance.

For our purposes in this chapter, we shall understand religion as a system of response to the **holy** that offers **salvation** (that is, a transition from an unsatisfactory state of existence to a limitlessly better one) and permeates the whole of life, including elements of feeling, belief, ritual, and organization. In their own way,

461

each of the world's great developed religions speak of the wrong, distorted, or deluded nature of present existence. The common everyday life may be characterized as a fallen life, lived in alienation from God, or as caught in the illusion of maya, or as pervaded by *dukkha*, radical unsatisfactoriness. The good news (or gospel) that a religion proclaims promises deliverance from guilt and death, a deep understanding of the world and our place in it, guidance on the most worthwhile way to live, and a continuation and deepening of this well-being in a blissful after-life. Adopting such an understanding of religion will enable us to classify Buddhism as a religion, while excluding college football.

RELIGION AS A WAY OF RESPONSE TO THE HOLY

There is widespread agreement that religion concerns the sacred, or what Rudolph Otto has called "the numinous," or "the holy."[3] Otto describes the holy as the *mysterium tremendum et fascinans* (the awe-ful and fascinating mystery). Unpacking Otto's famous formula, we can see that our experience of the holy is characterized by two important elements: a consciousness of our own creature-hood, or "deficiency of being," and a sense of anxious ambivalence, Otto's two adjectives, *tremendum* and *fascinans*, are meant to alert us to the mystery of an encounter with something "wholly other"—that is, something completely out of the ordinary, which both attracts and repels us.

As *tremendum*, the holy is absolutely unapproachable and absolutely overpowering; in its presence we experience fear, terror, shuddering, dread, and horror.[4] Filled with wonder and blank astonishment, we are aware that we are in the presence of something more real than ourselves. As *fascinans*, the holy is overwhelmingly attractive, an object of horror and dread, but at the same time something that draws us with a potent charm, offering love, mercy, grace, comfort, and bliss. Putting these two adjectives together, we see that the holy is simultaneously attractive and repulsive. In the believing soul, however, this fundamental ambivalence is overcome by an overwhelming yearning and desire to be "with" the holy. When the believing soul and the holy are joined, there is the most remarkable kind of rapture and exhilaration—a rush of feeling and emotion that makes language seem inadequate. Accounts of such experiences are numerous and are not restricted to any one world religion. William James, in his classic *The Varieties of Religious Experience*, gives a vivid example from the account of an anonymous Christian clergyman:

[3]See Rudolph Otto's classic work, *The Idea of the Holy*, translated by John W. Harvey (New York: Oxford University Press, 1958)
[4]Westphal, p. 38.

I remember the night, and almost the very spot on the hilltop, where my soul opened out, as it were, into the Infinite, and there was a rushing together of the two worlds, the inner and the outer. It was deep calling unto deep . . . I stood alone with Him who had made me . . . I did not seek Him, but felt the perfect unison of my spirit with his. The ordinary sense of things around me faded. . . . The darkness held a presence that was all the more felt because it was not seen. I could not any more have doubted that He was there than that I was. Indeed, *I felt myself to be, if possible, the less real of the two.*[5]

This experience of the holy as awe-ful and overpoweringly real is not limited to the Christian tradition. The essential structure of the experience was the same for Mahatma Gandhi, a Hindu:

But I worship God as Truth only. I have not found him, but I am seeking after him. . . . Often in my progress I have had faint glimpses of the Absolute Truth, God, and daily the conviction is growing upon me that *He alone is real and all else is unreal.*[6]

The experience is the same in the Jewish tradition. Merold Westphal cites a story of a Jewish rabbi who seeks to transmit something of the experience of the holy to his pupil, Moshe, asking "What do we mean by God?" Three times the question is met by silence because, as Moshe explains, "I do not know." "Do you think I know?" asks the rabbi. "But I must say it, for it is so, and therefore I must say it. *He is definitely there, and except for Him nothing is definitely there—and this is He.*"[7]

In summary, we may say that the sense of the holy lies at the very core of the religious life. As Otto puts it, "There is no religion in which it does not live as the real innermost core, and without it no religion would be worthy of the name."[8]

RELIGION AS FEELING

Anyone who has spent time gazing up at a clear sky on a summer's night can well understand the feeling of being "at one with the universe." Such "oceanic feelings" (as Freud called them) seek to remind us that we are part of something

[5]William James, *Varieties of Religious Experience*, (New York: Penguin, 1982), 67. Italics added for emphasis.—Ed.
[6]Mohandas K. Gandhi, *An Autobiography: The Story of My Experiments with Truth*, translated by Mahadev Desai (New York: Dover Publishing Co., 1983), xiv. Italics added for emphasis.—Ed.
[7]Cited in Maurice Friedman, *Touchstones of Reality* (New York: 1972), 16. Italics added for emphasis. —Ed.
[8]Otto, p. 6.

much larger than ourselves, and often result in a sense of bottomless serenity and profound peace.

Not surprisingly, the sense of human nothingness in the presence of the holy has led some to believe that religion is best understood as "a feeling of absolute dependence." The nineteenth century German theologian Friedrich Schleiermacher developed this position at some length, citing biblical passages such as this:

Why, to him nations are but drops from a bucket,
   no more than moisture on the scales;

coasts and islands weigh as light as specks of dust. . . .
   All nations dwindle to nothing before him,

he reckons them as mere nothings, less than nought.[9]

Following Schleiermacher, some have argued that stressing religious feelings rather than beliefs has the advantage of avoiding the delicate question of the justification of religious beliefs. After all, they argue, feelings and emotions are in no need of rational justification. Can the head undo what the heart passionately feels? As Pascal so eloquently put it, "the heart has its reasons, which Reason cannot know." Taken to its logical end (and forced to speak the language of epistemology), "religion as feeling" eventually gets expressed as fideism, the belief that faith and reason are in opposition to one another. (Fideism has been especially popular in the Christian religion, a belief-specific religion where the justification of beliefs is of particular importance.) Others disagree, arguing that feeling by itself is never enough; emotions can lead one astray when unguided by the intellect. One cannot sidestep the question of religious belief indefinitely, for the holy makes demands on the entire human person, calling for intellectual as well as affective response.

RELIGION AS BELIEF

Responding to the Absolute intellectually and conceptually, mature religions gradually develop a theology, that is, a systematic articulation of beliefs about the holy. Positive theologies, such as those found in Christianity, Judaism, and Islam, emphasize the supernatural, transcendent nature of God and God's **transcendence** from the world. Negative theologies, such as those found in Buddhism, emphasize nothingness, silence, and the void. All theologies are hampered by the inadequacy of human language to express the idea of the holy, as if one were

[9]Isaiah 40:15, 17 *(New English Bible)*.

trying to describe a three-dimensional world in the images of two-dimensional creatures.

Religion always presents itself to its adherents as being true, that is, as containing justified beliefs. Religious beliefs are, very simply, the beliefs a person has about highest reality, including beliefs about whether or not there is a God, what properties God has, and what actions God has performed. In religion, the holding of justified beliefs is deemed to be valuable in itself, not merely as a means to something else. This is because religious well-being is taken to be the highest aim or purpose of human life; all other human aims and purposes, even the accumulation of worldly goods, are relative to it. In the Christian religion, Jesus made this point very simply when he said, "What shall it profit a man if he gain the whole world and lose his own soul?" Hegel made the same point in philosophical terms:

> Religion, as something which is occupied with this final object and end, is therefore absolutely free and is its own end; for all other aims converge in this ultimate end, and in the presence of it they vanish and cease to have value of their own. No other aim can hold its ground against this, and here alone all find their fulfillment.[10]

Some religions stress correctness of belief more than others. In those religions where correctness of belief is especially important, a **creed** often develops. From the Latin *credo*, the word simply means "I believe"; in Christianity, it is the first word in the ancient Apostle's Creed and the Nicene Creed. A creed, then, is a theological system consisting of a collection of propositions assented to by the believing soul. Through the creed, a religion offers its picture of the world, shows the dependence of all things upon God, reveals the nature of God's purposes for humans, explains how God has intervened in history to accomplish these divine purposes, and provides guidance as to what actions ought morally to be done if a person is to attain salvation.

One of the ironies of creedal religions like Christianity is that in the course of twenty centuries a more restrictive understanding of what it means to be a Christian believer has developed than existed earlier. In the early centuries adherents had merely to believe that various beliefs were more probable than beliefs in various rival religions. In later centuries they had to believe that various items were each more probable than their negation. Thus, in the course of centuries, Christianity has become more demanding in the beliefs that it requires of its adherents. In the historical evolution of Christianity, particularly in the era of the Crusades, the increase in belief-specificity brought with it a concomitant increase

---

[10]G.W.F. Hegel, *On Art, Religion, and Philosophy*, edited by J. Glenn Gray (New York: Harper & Row, 1970), 129.

in penalties for not believing—thus resulting in bloody wars that were fought because of a perceived lack of correct belief. Similarly, the Protestant Reformation, led by men like Luther, Calvin, and Zwingli, can be directly traced to the Reformers' theological differences with the Church of Rome over such questions as church authority, interpretation of the Bible, and the means of salvation. Because Judaism is less concerned with correctness of belief (**orthodoxy**) than it is with correctness of practice (orthopraxy), some Jews measure their commitment to their religion by the extent to which they are observant of the Jewish customs and rituals, not by what beliefs they may hold about God. Quite the opposite situation exists in Christianity.

RELIGION AS RITUAL

A **ritual** is a set form or rite, publicly observed, for the sake of some higher purpose. Rituals need not be religious. When a U.S. citizen places her hand over her heart and voluntarily recites the pledge of allegiance, or salutes the flag, she enacts an import civic ritual, signifying solidarity with the aims and aspirations of a free people. Carrying the coach off the field after winning a championship football game or cutting down the basketball net have become part of the expected ritual behavior in sports. In our society the adolescent years are full of various "rites of passage" that must be negotiated on the way to adulthood. Ritual acts include the first date, the first kiss, and getting a driver's license. Couples who decide to marry may choose to have a wedding—an elaborate ritual ceremony fraught with religious symbolism. (Marriage in the Roman Catholic church is a sacrament—that is, a means of grace.) Or they may choose to be married by a justice of the peace in a simple civil ceremony. In either case, a ritual will be observed. These events contribute to the making of a person's identity in our culture.

Participation in formal religious observances helps to make a person more conscious of his or her religious beliefs. Prayer, meditation, song, dance, sacrifice, and fasting are important religious rituals. When the believing soul feels the need for purification, forgiveness, or reconciliation, a religion's prescribed activity, such as prayer or confession, provides comfort and reassurance. Religious rituals also provide structure for **worship,** the central religious act of the believing soul. Worship is essentially an act of celebration and adoration, as the believing soul expresses the feelings of awe aroused by proximity to the sacred. In the Jewish religion, when Moses entered into the presence of God, he was told to take off his shoes, for the ground upon which he stood was holy. This is typical of ritual forms of worship, where the concepts of space and time take on new meaning. A "sacred space" is observed, often around an altar. As believing souls feel their spirits soaring, they enter "sacred time" (quite different from "clock time") where the cares and worries of the mundane present begin to melt away.

Perhaps no ritual is as important as the one observed at death. Humans are distinct from other living things in the meaning that they give to their own death. The existentialist philosopher Gabriel Marcel has observed, "As long as death plays no further role than that of providing man with an incentive to evade it, man behaves as a mere living being, not as an existing being." As humans face up to the reality of their own impending death, a struggle often ensues to escape self-deception and secure divine and human forgiveness. At funeral services space and time are religiously altered. Standing at the grave site, we are conscious of a sacred space; contemplating the memory of the person who has died, our relation to time is altered. When a national leader dies, civic and religious rituals are frequently combined. Few who have seen it (in person or on videotape) can forget the funeral of President John F. Kennedy, a memorable and moving display of personal faith and **civil religion.**

RELIGION AS ORGANIZATION

Suppose that a group of citizens, concerned about the homeless in their community, band together to do something about the problem. They determine that their purpose will be the construction of decent, affordable housing. How shall they begin to realize their purpose? Who will secure a building lot? Who will provide building materials? Who will supply the labor? Who will determine who gets to live in the new homes? Whenever people assemble to commit themselves to a common purpose, religious or otherwise, some type of organization is necessary.

Nevertheless, many people feel hostile toward "organized religion." Scratch any "unbeliever" and often as not you will discover underneath a person who has been "burned by organized religion." Perhaps the minister, rabbi, or priest was inattentive to their need, giving simplistic answers to heartfelt questions. Perhaps they have had religion "forced down their throat" by overbearing parents, or maybe they are disgusted by the hypocrisy in the lives of so called "believing souls." Increasingly, many are turned off by the ceaseless demands for money by television evangelists who seem more interested in feathering their own nests than in ministering to those in need. Often, individuals may feel so betrayed by a particular religious "institution" that they abandon religion entirely. Curiously, the same people who abandon religious institutions would not think of abandoning their nation, or giving up their citizenship because a political leader did not measure up to expectations! Yet it is a fact of life that religious institutions are held to a higher standard.

Individuals who feel alienated from organized religion would do well to ask themselves the following questions: Am I angry with religion in general, or with this particular institution? Am I angered by poorly taught and inadequately practiced religion? Am I demanding perfection from a human institution?

467

There are certainly some religious purposes (e.g. prayer and meditation) that may be achieved in solitude, apart from a formal organizational affiliation. Many religious purposes, however, can only be accomplished in community with other people. The selection and training of leaders, the promotion of interpersonal relationships, the education of members, and the continuation of the group beyond its present membership all require minimal amounts of organization. If an organization seems to exist for its own sake, and not for the general welfare of the group, the organization should be criticized; as in any human institution, reform may be necessary.

RELIGION AS LIFE

Religion is more than feeling, belief, ritual, or organization; it is in its essence a way of life. Religion is felt, thought, celebrated, and administered, but at its best it is lived. As Charles Sanders Peirce observed:

> It is absurd to say that religion is a mere belief. You might as well call society a belief, or politics a belief or civilization a belief. Religion is a life, and can be identified with a belief only provided that belief be a living belief—a thing to be lived rather than said or thought.[11]

A religion worthy of the name will seek to not merely interpret the individual and the world, but to change both of them. True religion cannot be compartmentalized into any one sphere; it asks for a unified, integrated person, making demands of the entire person, in every aspect of life. Hegel expressed it this way,

> Now that religion of the simple, godly man is not kept shut off and divided from the rest of his existence and life, but on the contrary, it breathes its influence over all his feelings and actions, and his consciousness brings *all* the aims and objects of his worldly life into relation to God, as to its infinite and ultimate source.[12]

THE NATURE OF GOD

Belief in God is central to most of the world's religions. But what does it mean to believe (or disbelieve) in God? Before we can make much progress in answering

---

[11]Charles Sanders Pierce, *Collected Papers*, vol. 6, edited by C. Hartshorne and P. Weiss, 439.
[12]Hegel, 134.

this question, it is necessary to clarify terminology frequently used when discussing the nature and existence of God.

The terms used for thinking about God are in general derived from *theos*, the Greek word for God, or its Latin equivalent, *deus*. **Theism** is the belief in a personal God who has created the universe, and with whom a person may have a personal relationship. **Monotheism** (one-God-ism) is a form of theism that stresses belief in but one God; it is often used as a synonym for theism. Judaism, Christianity, and Islam are all monotheistic religions. **Polytheism** (many-gods-ism) is the belief, common among the Greeks and Romans in the classical age, that there is a multitude of personal gods, each responsible for a different sphere of life.

Deism, a form of belief popular in the eighteenth century, stresses the remoteness of God from the world; God is likened to an "absentee landlord" who, having created the world and set it in motion, permits it to administer itself according to natural law. Among the most notable deists were Benjamin Franklin, Thomas Jefferson, and Thomas Paine.

Pantheism (God-is-all-ism) is the belief, often expressed poetically, that God is identical with nature; all is God, and God is all. **Panentheism** (everything-in-God-ism) is the belief that everything exists ultimately in God.

Moving to the negative side of the ledger, **agnosticism** (literally "not knowing") is the belief that we do not have sufficient reason to either affirm or deny God's existence. It is the extension of skepticism (discussed in Part 2) into the religious realm. **Atheism** (no-God-ism) is the belief that there is no God at all. Unlike agnosticism, which advocates suspension of belief on the God question, atheism is the positive belief that God does not exist.

Naturalism is the theory that "every aspect of human existence, including the moral and religious life, can be adequately described and accounted for in terms of our existence as gregarious and intelligent animals whose life is organic to our natural environment."[13]

THE ANCIENT GREEK CONCEPT OF GOD

The Classical Age included both religious and philosophical views of God. The former is best represented by Homer's epics, the *Iliad* and *Odyssey*, the latter by Plato and Aristotle. The religious view, held by most people, was polytheistic. Thus Homer depicted a complex hierarchy of gods, headed by Zeus. The Greek gods functioned as guardians of the social order, and the people were expected to participate in public worship as evidence of their loyalty to the state. Such an

[13]John Hick, *Philosophy of Religion*, 4th ed. (Englewood Cliffs, N.J.: Prentice Hall, 1990), 5.

arrangement was hardly satisfactory for more thoughtful individuals, who increasingly turned toward reason to understand the source of all existence.

Plato's search for the unchanging, eternal essences of all things led him to propose that ultimate reality must lie beyond the world of space and time, where sense experience was of no avail. Plato's concept of God was the idea of the Good, an ultimate transcendence of which the universe was a pale reflection.

Aristotle's *Metaphysics* teaches the idea of God as the "Prime Mover," or "Uncaused Cause" of the universe. Aristotle believed in the necessity and existence of such a being, and formulated a method for proving the existence of God (the cosmological argument), which was taken up centuries later by the Christian theologian Thomas Aquinas.

From the Greeks we have inherited the dualistic way of thinking about such fundamental categories as spirit and matter, eternal and temporal, changeless and changing, male and female. Here is an inventory of Greek dualistic terms, with dominant terms listed on the left, and subordinate on the right.

Superior	Inferior
Form	Matter
Active	Passive
Male	Female
Husband	Wife
Eternal	Temporal
Necessity	Contingency
Stability	Change

The importance of the Greek dualistic system to the development of modern Western philosophical thought cannot be overestimated. From this perspective we inherit not only the "negative" terms used to indicate divine transcendence (for example, **infinite**–not finite, **incorporeal**–not material, **immutable**) but also a definite bias in favor of males as superior, rational, active, and females as inferior, emotional, and passive. In recent years feminists have called our attention to the subtle ways that this bias lives on, especially in patriarchal religious structures.[14]

THE JUDAIC-CHRISTIAN CONCEPT OF GOD

The concept of God in Judaic-Christian monotheism is stated succinctly by John Hick: "God is conceived as the infinite, eternal, uncreated, personal reality,

---

[14]See Mary Daly, "The Leap Beyond Patriarchal Religion," *Quest*, 1, no. 4, (Spring 1975).

who has created all that exists and who is revealed to human creatures as holy and loving."[15]

God has unlimited being, an attribute that medieval theologians captured with the term **aseity** (from the Latin, *aseitas*, being from oneself). The self-existence of God means that there is nothing capable of either creating or destroying God. God is the one truly independent being in the universe, an infinite, unconditioned, all-conditioning reality. It follows from this that God is eternal, without beginning or end. (If God had a beginning, there would have to be a prior reality to bring God into being, a God behind God; similarly, for God's existence to be terminated, there would have to be a reality capable of doing this.) Furthermore, the existence of God is qualitatively different from the existence of finite beings, for God is not merely the first among finite beings but the source and ground of all being. Protestant theologian Paul Tillich believed that we should therefore restrict the usage of the term "exists" to the finite realm; strictly speaking, God the Creator does not "exist" in the same way that beings in the created order exist.

> Thus the question of the existence of God can be neither asked nor answered. If asked, it is a question about that which by its very nature is above existence, and therefore the answer—whether negative or affirmative—implicitly denies the nature of God. It is as atheistic to affirm the existence of God as it is to deny it. God is being-itself, not a being.[16]

The Judaic-Christian tradition affirms the doctrine of creation *ex nihilo* (out of nothing), meaning that God did not merely fashion the world from previously present materials, God summoned the world into existence from an absolute void. Because there is an absolute distinction between God and the created order, it is logically impossible for any creature to become God; the created must forever remain created. We have a part in the universe only by the grace of God, not because of some natural right to existence.

There has been much debate regarding the scientific implications of creation. Is the universe eternal, or did it have a beginning in time? Thomas Aquinas (1224–1274) believed that the idea of creation does not necessarily rule out the possibility that the created universe may be eternal. It is philosophically conceivable that God has been creative from all eternity, in which case the universe needn't have had a beginning at some specific moment of time. He also believed, however, that the Bible teaches a beginning; it is on the grounds of **revelation** (not reason) that he rejected the idea of an eternal creation. Augustine took a different approach; arguing that creation did not take place *in* time, but rather, time itself is an aspect

---

[15]Hick, p. 14.
[16]Paul Tillich, *Systematic Theology I* (Chicago: University of Chicago Press, 1951), 237.

of the created order. Commenting on the scientific implications of this, John Hick suggests:

> If this is true it may also be, as relativity theory suggests, that space-time is internally infinite—that is to say, from within the space-time continuum the universe is found to be unbounded both spacially and temporally. It may nevertheless, although internally infinite, depend for its existence and its nature upon the will of a transcendent Creator. . . . Such a doctrine is neutral as between the various rival theories of the origin of the present state of the universe developed in scientific cosmology.[17]

It is Hick's belief that the creation story in the first two chapters of Genesis is to be interpreted mythologically, not as a piece of scientific description. Not all Christians agree. A branch of Protestant conservatives, known as fundamentalists, defend a literal interpretation of the Genesis account, rejecting the Darwinian account of evolution. The fundamentalist-evolutionary controversy peaked in 1925, during the famous Scopes trial in Dayton, Tennessee.[18] Some contemporary fundamentalists defend a view known as creation-science or creationism. Purporting to offer an alternative scientific view to the theory of evolution, creationists regard a literal account of Genesis as a genuine scientific alternative to the theory of evolution, and argue that it should be taught as such in the public schools.

The belief that God is personal should not be understood as an attempt to reduce God to finite proportions; the intent is to stress that God is some*one*, not some*thing*. In the Bible God often speaks in personal terms. For example, in Exodus 3:6: "I am the God of your father, the God of Abraham, the God of Isaac, and the God of Jacob."

The love of God is unconditional and universal. The primary New Testament word for love, *agape* (which is also the Greek word for love), speaks of a love that always seeks the deepest welfare and fulfillment of the human person, without regard to the worthiness of the recipient. When Jesus wished to speak of the love of God, he told the story of the prodigal son, presenting God as a loving parent who persists in loving an errant child, patiently waiting for the wanderer to return home.[19]

The goodness of God raises a significant philosophical problem that can be formulated in the form of two questions: (1) Does morality depend on religion?

---

[17]Hick, pp. 9–10.

[18]See G. Ray, *Six Days or Forever? Tennessee vs. John Thomas Scopes*, (Boston: Beacon, 1958); George Marsden, *Fundamentalism and America, Culture: The Shaping of Twentieth Century Evangelicalism 1870–1925* (Oxford: Oxford University Press, 1980).

[19]Luke 15:11–32.

and (2) Are religious ethics essentially different from "secular" ethics?" Underlying both of these questions is the larger question of whether moral standards somehow depend upon God for their validity, or whether they are autonomous, so that ultimately even God is subject to the moral order. As Plato asks in the *Euthyphro*, "Do the gods love holiness because it is holy, or is it holy because the gods love it?" According to one theory, called the **Divine Command Theory,** ethical principles derive their validity from that fact that God commanded them. On this view, without God there would be no morality. The Russian novelist Dostoyevsky, in *The Brothers Karamazov*, put it this way: "If God doesn't exist, everything is permissible." The opposing view is that ethical values exist independently of God; even God must keep the moral law. Divine Command Theory is discussed and critiqued in Part 8, where you may read an excerpt from the *Euthyphro*.

The holiness of God communicates both the immensity and otherness of God. Both are captured in this passage from Isaiah, recording the Hebrew prophet's vision of God:

> I saw the Lord seated on a throne, high and exalted, and the train of
> his robe filled the temple. Above him were seraphs, each with six
> wings . . . calling to one another:

> "Holy, holy, holy is the LORD
> Almighty;
> the whole earth is full of his glory."

> At the sound of their voices the doorposts and thresholds shook and
> the temple was filled with smoke.

> "Woe to me!" I cried. "I am ruined! For I am a man of unclean lips, and
> I live among a people of unclean lips, and my eyes have seen the King,
> the LORD Almighty."[20]

THE EXISTENCE OF GOD

In this section we shall briefly examine the most important philosophical arguments that have been offered as justification for belief in the existence of God. The reading selections are designed to give you the opportunity to explore these arguments in greater detail. As you read these traditional "theistic proofs," keep two questions in mind. First, does the proof succeed? Although they have survived

---

[20]Isaiah 6:1–5 (*New International Bible*).

hundreds of years of intense philosophical criticism, and numerous revisions, many remain unconvinced. Second, of what value are the theistic proofs?

THE ONTOLOGICAL ARGUMENT

The **ontological argument** for the existence of God was first formulated by Anselm (1033–1109), Archbishop of Canterbury and one of Christianity's most original thinkers. The argument attempts to prove God's existence by moving from a mental concept of God to the actual existence of God; that is to say, it is an *a priori* argument that seeks to establish the reality of God from the mere idea of God.

Anselm masterfully translates the monotheistic concept of God into the logic of perfection, using the formula "a being than which nothing greater can be conceived." By "greater" Anselm means "most perfect," not spatially bigger. If the most perfect conceivable being existed only in the mind, we would be faced with the contradictory thought that it is possible to conceive of a more perfect being, namely one that exists in reality as well as in the mind. In other words, a God who exists *only* as a human idea is inferior to one who exists *both* in the mind and in reality. Hence, God must exist as an idea and in reality.

It is important to realize that Anselm believed it was logically necessary for God to exist. In other words, God must exist because of who God is. Since God by definition is perfect, and nonexistence is clearly an imperfection, God must necessarily exist. Several centuries later, Descartes reformulated Anselm's argument, arguing that existence is a necessary defining characteristic of God. Just as one cannot conceive of a triangle without three angles or a mountain that has no valley, so one cannot conceive of God without existence.

CRITICISMS OF THE ONTOLOGICAL ARGUMENT

The first important critic of Anselm's argument was a French monk named Gaunilon. He attempted to reduce Anselm's argument to absurdity by setting up a parallel argument for the existence of a most perfect island. The mere idea of such an island, "beyond which no greater island can be conceived," does not mean that such an island exists in reality! Anselm's reply to Gaunilon is important: He objected that Gaunilon's island was by definition a dependent entity, not a necessary one, since islands are part of the physical world. There is nothing contradictory about the nonexistence of an island; unlike God, an island needn't necessarily exist.

Immanuel Kant's criticisms of the argument were far more damaging. Addressing Descartes' version of the argument, Kant agreed that the idea of existence belongs analytically to the concept of God, just as having three angles belongs analytically to the idea of a triangle. To conceive of a triangle, yet to reject its three angles *is* self-contradictory. But there is no self-contradiction in rejecting the triangle together with its three angles. In the same way, *if* there is an infinitely perfect being, then that being must have existence. But the argument has failed to demonstrate that there actually is such a being!

More importantly, Kant rejected the basic assumption that existence is a quality (like triangularity) that can add or detract from the perfection of something. In a famous example, Kant pointed out that an imaginary hundred dollars has the same number of dollars as a real hundred dollars, but that will not help much when you attempt to deposit the imaginary hundred at the bank! When we say that *x* exists, we are simply saying that *x* has an instance in the real world, not that *x* has the attribute of existence. Bertand Russell brought this out more clearly when he pointed out that the phrase "cows exist" means "there are *x*'s such that '*x* is a cow' is true." This translation makes it clear that to say that "cows exist" is *not* to attribute the quality of existence to cows; it is merely to assert that there are objects in the world that fit the description of cow. Similarly, to say "unicorns do not exist" is simply to say that there are no known instances of unicorns in the world; unicorn, like God, is a concept that may be thought but has no known instances in the real world.

THE COSMOLOGICAL ARGUMENT

The **cosmological argument** (sometimes known as the "first cause" argument) was formulated by Thomas Aquinas, who drew upon the theology of Aristotle in offering five "Ways" of proving God's existence. Of the five proofs, the ones that have received the most attention are the second and third. The second Way is as follows. Everything that happens has a cause, and this cause in turn has a cause, and so on in a series that is either infinite, or has its starting point in a first cause. Aquinas rules out the possibility of an infinite regress of causes, concluding that there must be a first cause, which we call God.

The third Way is an argument from the contingency of the world. Everything in the world is contingent—that is, each thing might not have existed at all, or might have existed differently, since there was a time when each did not exist at all. But if everything were truly contingent, there would have been a time when nothing existed. If this were the case, nothing could have ever come to exist. But things do exist; therefore there must be something that is not contingent, and this we call God.

CRITICISMS OF THE COSMOLOGICAL ARGUMENT

The obvious weakness of the second Way, as Aquinas himself recognized, is that it fails to eliminate logically the possibility of an infinite series of causes. Furthermore, if every event must have a cause, what was the cause of the first cause? Why must one stop with God?

The third Way presents us with a dilemma: *either* there is a necessary being or the universe is ultimately unintelligible. But has the second alternative been effectively ruled out? Ironically, it would seem to reinforce the position of the skeptic, who views the world as logically inexplicable in the first place. As John Hick explains it, "This inability to exclude the possibility of an unintelligible universe prevents the cosmological argument from operating for the skeptic as a proof of God's existence—and the skeptic is, after all, the only person who needs such a proof."[21]

THE TELEOLOGICAL ARGUMENT

The teleological argument, or argument from design, is perhaps the most popular of the theistic proofs. The most famous formulation of the argument is that of William Paley (1743–1805), summarized as follows:

> Suppose that while walking in a desert place I see a rock lying on the ground and ask myself how this object came to exist. I can properly attribute its presence to chance. . . . However, if I see a watch lying on the ground, I cannot reasonably account for it in a similar way. A watch consists of a complex arrangement of wheels, cogs, axles, springs, and balances, all operating together to provide a regular measurement of the lapse of time. It would be utterly implausible to attribute the formation and assembling of these metal parts into a functioning machine to the chance operation of such factors as wind and rain. We are obliged to postulate an intelligent mind which is responsible for the phenomenon.[22]

CRITICISMS OF THE TELEOLOGICAL ARGUMENT

Ironically, the most devastating criticism of Paley's argument was offered by David Hume in his *Dialogues Concerning Natural Religion*, published some twenty-three years before Paley's book was written! Even so, Paley made no mention of Hume's critique. (It was not the first time a theologian was oblivious to the arguments of philosophers, nor is it likely to be the last!) Hume argued that the teleological argument was based on a weak analogy. All analogies contain dissimilarities as well as similarities; Hume took great care to point out the disorder, chance, and even chaos that is apparent in the world. The argument assumes an order; it does not demonstrate one.

[21]Hick, p. 22.
[22]Hick, p. 23.

Kant argued that, at best, the argument from design points to a designer who is not necessarily the omnipotent creator of the world. Even if it could be proven that order exists, the problem of inferring a Transcendent God (the God of the Bible) remains. Other critics have pointed out that the Darwinian theory of natural selection has weakened the force of the teleological argument.

THE MORAL ARGUMENT

The **moral argument** for belief in God is grounded in the moral nature of the human person. Although it has been formulated in a number of different ways, two forms are predominant.

The first form is a simple logical inference: From objective moral laws we may properly infer a divine lawgiver; from the fact of human conscience and sense of obligation we may infer a moral God. When we feel responsible or ashamed, this implies One that we feel responsible towards, before whom we are ashamed. This One we call God.

The second kind of moral argument is, strictly speaking, not an argument at all. It is claimed by some that anyone seriously committed to respecting moral values must implicitly believe in the reality of a transhuman source for those values, which religion calls God. D.M. Baille puts it this way: "Is it too paradoxical in the modern world to say that faith in God is a very part of our moral consciousness, without which the latter becomes meaningless?. . . . Either our moral values tell us something about the nature and purpose of reality (i.e. give us the germ of religious belief) or they are subjective and therefore meaningless."[23]

CRITICISMS OF THE MORAL ARGUMENT

Critics of the argument point out that moral values could be explained naturalistically, in terms of human needs and desires. Why place the derivation of moral norms outside the natural world if they can be accounted for from within it? Furthermore, even if the argument was moderately successful, in establishing a move in the direction of belief in God as a transcendent moral reality, it does not point all the way to the supremely perfect being of Anselm, or the Judaic-Christian God.

[23]D.M. Baille, *Faith in God and its Christian Consummation* (Edinburgh: T. and T. Clark, 1927), 172–73.

RELIGIOUS REJECTION OF THE THEISTIC ARGUMENTS

Since the time of Descartes, rationalist philosophy has held that "to know is to prove." In his *Meditations*, Descartes argued that we cannot claim to know that the self, the material world, our neighbor, or God exists unless we can support these beliefs with logically compelling proofs.

After four centuries of trying to provide such "knock-down" proofs, most philosophers today would agree that there are and can be no proofs to satisfy the rationalist desire. As we have seen in our examination of skepticism (Part 2), if we were seriously to doubt the reality of the world in which we live, we could never be rescued from such a state of radical doubt by means of philosophical demonstration.

It should therefore not be surprising that the rationalist program should also fail when applied to the question of God's existence. It is notable that the Bible, the primary source book of Western civilization, contains no attempts to prove the existence of God. To the biblical writers, a proof for the existence of God would have seemed as pointless as a proof for the existence of their hands or feet, or the reality of their neighbors; to them, belief in God was basic, a given. Consequently, the theistic arguments that we have examined have been of primary interest to the philosopher rather than the person of faith.

This is not to say that the theistic arguments have no value. On the contrary, to the atheist, they present a philosophical challenge: Find defective premises and demonstrate the failure of the alleged proof. To the theist, the question of value is more complex. To some, they are an unfolding of God's progressive revelation, not intended to convert the atheist but rather to lead the believing soul into a deeper understanding of God. (Some theologians, including Karl Barth (1886–1968), view Anselm's ontological argument in this way.) To others, the most important benefit of the theistic arguments is that they show the reasonableness of belief in God—theists who formulate them demonstrate that their theology and philosophy can be "connected" in an integrated fashion.

Some religious thinkers, however, have been unremittingly hostile to the theistic arguments. Fideism (discussed briefly in Part 2) is the view that objective reason is inappropriate for religious belief. To the fideist, religion is bound to appear absurd when judged by the standards of reason unaided by divine revelation. Some extreme fideists, such as the Danish existentialist Søren Kierkegaard (1813–1855), hold that faith is the highest virtue that a human can attain, higher even than reason. "[I]f God does not exist it would of course be impossible to prove it; and if he does exist it would be folly to attempt it." Thus begins Kierkegaard's fideistic rejection of the rationalist desire for proofs of God's existence. According to Kierkegaard (in one of the reading selections that follow), genuine theistic faith comes only when reason has "shipwrecked" in its quest for wholeness and is at the point of despair—only then will God be revealed as the Absolute Paradox, the Absurd, an offense to reason but the salvation of the soul. In a famous passage, Kierkegaard discusses the meaning of faith as risk:

> Without risk there is no faith. Faith is precisely the contradiction between the infinite passion of the individual's inwardness and the objective uncertainty. If I am capable of grasping God objectively, I do not believe, but precisely because I cannot do this I must believe. If I wish to preserve myself in faith I must constantly be intent upon holding fast the objective uncertainty, so as to remain out upon the deep, over seventy thousand fathoms of water, still preserving my faith.[24]

Faith is the soul's deepest yearnings, a hope beyond hopelessness, which the rational part of us cannot comprehend. As the Apostle Paul put it, "Faith is the substance of things hoped for, the evidence of things not seen." Kierkegaard thinks that there is something fundamentally misguided about trying to base religious faith on the objective evidence of reason. Not only will it not work, it is actually dangerous to faith:

> [F]aith isn't produced through academic investigations. It doesn't come directly at all, but, on the contrary, it is precisely in objective analysis that one loses the infinite personal and passionate concern that is the requisite condition for faith, its ubiquitous ingredient, wherein faith comes into existence.[25]

Critics of fideism, such as Robert Merrihew Adams,[26] point out that Kierkegaard's religious views have more logical structure than is ordinarily supposed, and that it is difficult and undesirable to get away from objective justification, in religion as in every other area of life.

In recent years, followers of the Austrian-born philosopher Ludwig Wittgenstein (1889–1951) have proposed a linguistic version of fideism. There is something unique about religious language; there is no impartial, nonperspectival way of assessing the truth value of religious assertion. Concepts employed by religious persons cannot be grasped by outsiders who are not conversant with the peculiar "language game" of the religious group. Advocates of Wittgensteinian fideism include Norman Malcolm and D.Z. Phillips.[27]

[24]Soren Kierkegaard, *Concluding Unscientific Postscript to the Philosophical Fragments*, trans. David Swenson and Walter Lowrie (Princeton: Princeton University Press, 1969) 182–83.

[25]Kierkegaard, p. 185f.

[26]See Robert Merrihew Adams, "Kierkegaard's Arguments Against Objective Reasoning in Religion, *The Monist*, 60, no. 2 (1977).

[27]See Norman Malcolm, "The Groundlessness of Belief," in *Reason and Religion*, ed. Stuart C. Brown (Ithaca: Cornell University Press, 1977) and D.Z. Phillips, *Religion Without Explanation* (Oxford: Basil Blackwell, 1976).

GROUNDS FOR DISBELIEF IN GOD

Responsible skeptics (whether agnostic or atheistic) do not deny that religious people have had certain experiences that have led them to believe in the reality of God. The skeptic differs from the believing soul, however, in insisting that these experiences can be accounted for on purely naturalistic grounds, without postulating a God. In this section we shall consider several influential naturalistic theories. Additionally, we shall present the traditional problem of evil, considered by many to be the most powerful reason for disbelief in God.

THE SOCIOLOGICAL THEORY OF RELIGION

Developed in the early twentieth century by a group of French sociologists, most notably Emile Durkheim, the sociological theory of religion claims that the gods whom people worship are imaginary beings who are unconsciously constructed by society in order to exercise control over the intellectual and social life of a people. Consequently, when men and women report having an experience of standing before a higher power that urges its will on them as a moral imperative, they are indeed in the presence of a larger reality. Far from being a supernatural being, however, this larger reality is society, which exercises the attributes of God in relation to its members.

What of Otto's "idea of the holy?" It is merely the result of society's absolute demand for loyalty and obedience. In the Australian aboriginal societies where Durkheim's formulation was originally worked out, there was a strong sense that the customs, beliefs, and taboos of the tribe were sovereign and must never be questioned. Collectively, these customs, beliefs, and taboos play a double role, constituting a societal version of "the holy" as that awesome reality that must never be questioned, which ensures unquestioned obedience to that society.

It is, then, society as a greater envisioning reality standing over against the individual, a veritable "ancient of days" existing long before one's little life and destined to persist long after one's disappearance, that constitutes the concrete reality which has been symbolized as God. This theory accounts for the transformation of the natural pressures of society into the felt supernatural presence of God by referring to a universal tendency of the human mind to create mental images and symbols.[28]

---

[28]Hick, p. 31.

CRITICISMS OF THE SOCIOLOGICAL THEORY

H.H. Farmer, in his *Towards Belief in God*,[29] offers the following criticisms of the sociological theory.

In the first place, the theory fails to account for the universality of religious consciousness, which goes beyond the bounds of any specific society in affirming a relation of *all* the world's peoples. For example, if the call of God to love one's neighbor is merely society imposing upon its members what is in the best interest of that particular society, what is the origin of the religiously felt obligation to be concerned equally for all humanity?

Secondly, it is claimed that the sociological theory fails to account for the creativity of the prophetic mind. The moral prophet (an innovator like Jesus or Gandhi who goes beyond established moral codes in summoning us to acknowledge new and far-reaching claims of morality upon our lives) cannot be accounted for if there is no other source of morality than the "closed society" in which a person lives.

Finally, it is claimed that the sociological theory fails to explain the socially detaching power of conscience, which "individuates" by setting a person at variance with the norms of his or her country. How else can one explain an Amos or Jeremiah denouncing his Hebrew countrymen, a Helen Suzman rejecting the privileges of her race in South Africa, or the resistance of Dr. Martin Luther King, Jr. to the Vietnam war?

> If the sociological theory is correct, the sense of divine support should be at a minimum or even altogether absent in such cases. How can the prophet have the support of God against society if God is simply society in disguise? The record shows, however, that the sense of divine backing and support is often at a maximum in such situations. These people are sustained by a vivid sense of the call and leadership of the Eternal. It is striking that in one instance after another the Hebrew prophets express a sense of closeness to God as they are rejected by their own people; yet they belonged to an intensely self-conscious and nationalistic society of the kind that, according to the sociological theory, ought most readily to be best able to impress its will upon its members.[30]

THE FREUDIAN THEORY OF RELIGION

Sigmund Freud (1856–1939) theorized that the origin of religion lies in infantile psychology. The child fears the power of its parents (primarily the father) but

[29]H. H. Farmer, *Towards Belief in God* (London: Students Christian Movement Press Ltd. 1942), Chapter 9.
[30]Hick, p. 32.

also trusts them for protection against the dangers and cruelties of the natural world, such as sickness, disease, storms, earthquakes, and inevitable death. The sense of dependence upon the father lives on into adulthood. Humans invent gods, or accept the gods their culture imposes on them, precisely because they have grown up with such a god in their house! Here is how Freud presents it:

> In this function [of protection] the mother is soon replaced by the stronger father, who retains that position for the rest of childhood. But the child's attitude to its father is coloured by a peculiar ambivalence. The father himself constitutes a danger for the child, perhaps because of its earlier relation to its mother. Thus it fears him no less than it longs for him and admires him. . . . When the growing individual finds that he is destined to remain a child forever, that he can never do without protection against strange superior powers, he lends those powers the features belonging to the figure of his father; he creates for himself the gods whom he dreads, whom he seeks to propitiate, and whom he nevertheless entrusts with his own protection. Thus his longing for a father is a motive identical with his need for protection against the consequences of his human weakness.[31]

Freud thought that he had unmasked the secret of religion—underneath all of the impressive ceremonial trappings and sophisticated theological formulations of belief was a childish illusion. Religious doctrines "are not precipitates of experience or end results of thought; they are illusions, fulfillments of the oldest, strongest, most urgent wishes of mankind; the secret of their strength is the strength of these wishes." The Judaic-Christian religion has simply projected upon an otherwise indifferent universe the buried memory of our father as the great Protecting Power; the face that smiled down at us in the cradle has been magnified to infinity, and now smiles down on us from an illusory heaven, constructed from the wishes of our childish imaginations. Hence, religion is "the universal obsessional neurosis of humanity," a psychological crutch that may be left behind when people learn to face the uncertainties and terrors of the world on their own, relying on scientifically authenticated knowledge.

How does one account for the tremendous emotional intensity of the religious life? In *Totem and Taboo*, Freud applied the concept of the **Oedipus complex** to religion. Like Oedipus, the tragic King in Sophocles' play who unknowingly kills his father and marries his mother, the child has an unconscious jealousy of his father and a desire for his mother. Freud postulates a stage of human prehistory in which the basic unit was a "primal horde," consisting of father, mother, and offspring. The father, as the dominant male, retained to himself exclusive rights

[31]Sigmund Freud, *The Future of an Illusion*, tran. and ed. James Strachey (New York: W.W. Norton, 1961), 24.

over all the females, driving away or killing any of his sons who challenged his position. Realizing that individually they could not defeat the father-leader, the sons eventually banded together to kill the father. This primal crime of patricide has set up tensions in the human psyche that religion and morality seek to ease through legislation. Struck with remorse, the dead father's prohibition takes on a new moral authority as a taboo against incest; the renewal of the Oedipus complex in each male individual accounts for the mysterious authority of God (the Father) in the human mind and the powerful guilt feelings that make people submit to such a fantasy. As Freud observes, religion is thus a "return of the repressed."

MARX, NIETZSCHE, FREUD: THE RELIGIOUS USES OF THE ATHEISM OF SUSPICION

The literature discussing Freud's theory is quite extensive, both pro and con. Summarizing, we may say that the primal horde theory, which Freud borrowed from Charles Darwin and Robertson Smith, is now generally rejected by anthropologists, and the Oedipus complex is no longer regarded (even by Freud's successors in psychoanalysis) as the key to unlocking the mysteries of cognitive, moral, and religious development. Finally, critics such as Karl Popper (see Part 4) have pointed out that Freud's observations lack the element of falsifiability necessary to classify them as scientific; they are dismissed in many circles as being highly speculative and unfounded in fact. It is fair to say that Freud's theory of religion, while highly provocative, is destined to be the least-enduring aspect of his thought.

This is not to say that Freud's critique is without value to the believing soul. Merold Westphal distinguishes between two types of atheism: evidential atheism and the atheism of suspicion.[32] The atheism of Bertrand Russell and Ernest Nagel (whose "The Case for Atheism" is included as a reading in Chapter 50) is evidential, focusing on specific grounds for disbelief in the existence of God. It is best exemplified in Bertrand Russell's famous account of what he would say to God if the two were ever to meet and God were to ask him why he had not been a believer: "I'd say, 'Not enough evidence, God! Not enough evidence!'" The atheism of suspicion (practiced by Marx and Nietzsche as well as Freud) is quite different. It is targeted not on the *truth* of religious beliefs but rather on their *function*. That is, instead of asking whether or not particular religious beliefs are true or false, Marx, Nietzsche, and Freud ask what role religious beliefs play in masking self-interest and legitimizing injustice! As we have seen, for Freud religious beliefs function as a wish-fulfilling illusion that permits a believing soul to

---

[32]See Merold Westphal, "Taking Suspicion Seriously: The Religious Uses of Modern Atheism," in *Faith and Philosophy* 4, no. 1 (January 1987): 26–42.

deal with the senseless anxiety of the human condition by appeasing, flattering, or bribing some superior being. In Marx, religion is an instrument of the ruling class to provide an illusory happiness for an oppressed people. By encouraging people to be religious, the ruling class succeeds in legitimating a false consciousness that passively accepts its sorry situation in life and even embraces its own suffering as a point of honor—religion, in short, is a drug.

> Religion is indeed man's self-consciousness and self-awareness so long as he has not found himself or has lost himself again. But *man* is not an abstract being, squatting outside the world. Man is *the human world*, the state, society. This state, this society, produce religion which is an *inverted world consciousness*, because they are in an *inverted world*. Religion is the general theory of this world, its encyclopedic compendium, its logic in popular form, its spiritual *point d'honneur*, its enthusiasm, its moral sanction, its solemn complement, its general basis of consolation and justification. It is the *fantastic realization* of the human being inasmuch as the *human being* possesses no true reality. The struggle against religion is therefore, indirectly a struggle against *that world* whose spiritual *aroma* is religion.
>
> Religious suffering is at the same time an *expression* of real suffering and a *protest* against real suffering. Religion is the sigh of the oppressed creature, the sentiment of a heartless world, and the soul of a soulless people. It is the *opium* of the people.
>
> The abolition of religion as the *illusory* happiness of men, is a demand for their *real* happiness. The call to abandon their illusions about their condition is a call to abandon a condition which requires illusions. The criticism of religion is, therefore, *the embryonic criticism of this vale of tears* of which religion is the *halo*.[33]

Nietzsche practices an atheism of suspicion that functions in much the same way as that of Marx and Freud, in the sphere of morality. How ironic, Nietzsche observes, that the most splendid virtues, when unmasked, are no more than egoistic vices! Take justice, for example. In an ingenious word play in the German language, Nietzsche makes this suspicious observation: "And when they say, 'I am just,' it always sounds like 'I am just-revenged.' "

Westphal's point is this: Although believing souls may be sorely tempted to disregard or refute the suspicious atheism of Freud, Marx, and Nietzsche, it is far more profitable to take them seriously, by critically examining their own religious practice. All too often, these three "masters of suspicion" have identified instances where piety *has* become inseparable from self-deception. Sadly, religion has fre-

---

[33]Karl Marx, "The Contribution to the Critique of Hegel's Philosophy of Right: Introduction" in *The Marx-Engels Reader*, edited by Robert C. Tucker (New York: W. W. Norton, 1978), 53–54.

quently functioned as a mask to disguise self-interest, authorizing and legitimating oppression, injustice, and delusion. As Westphal observes, the only real refutation of the atheism of suspicion is a practical one, not a theoretical one. Religious believers must take care to practice a virtue or proclaim a belief even when it is manifestly *not* in their self-interest to do so. This is precisely what Jesus taught with reference to the virtue of hospitality when he said, "But when you give a feast, invite the poor, the maimed, the lame, the blind, and you will be blessed, because they cannot repay you."[34]

THE PROBLEM OF EVIL

In this part we look at several arguments that purport to show that God exists. The atheologian (a person who argues against the existence of God) has one very powerful argument for disbelief in God. It is the problem of evil.

For centuries, the existence of evil in the world has been viewed as a major problem for theism. For many who find themselves attracted to various naturalistic interpretations of religion, it is the shocking depth and extent of human suffering in the world that makes the idea of a loving creator seem implausible. Yet, even the most devoutly religious person has difficulty answering the question, "Why do good people suffer?"

Generally, philosophers have distinguished between two types of evil: natural and moral. Moral evil includes all those bad things that human beings do to one another and to animals, for which they are morally responsible. Natural evil includes those terrible events that occur in nature, such as hurricanes, earthquakes, tornadoes, volcano eruptions, natural diseases, and so on, that cause humans and animals to suffer. For our purposes in this part, then, evil may be understood as referring to physical pain, mental suffering, and moral wickedness. The latter is frequently the cause of the first two, for an enormous amount of pain and suffering is the result of people's inhumanity.

As a challenge to theism, the problem of evil has traditionally been put in the form of a dilemma. One of the earliest formulations was by Epicurus (341–270 B.C.). Speaking of God, Epicurus asked, "Is he willing to prevent evil, but not able? Then he is impotent. Is he able, but not willing? Then he is malevolent. Is he both able and willing? Whence then is evil?" One can see that this poses a serious problem for Judaic-Christian religion, which has traditionally affirmed these three propositions:

1. God is all powerful.
2. God is perfectly good.
3. Evil exists.

[34]Luke 14:13 *(Revised Standard Version)*.

Paradox But if God is perfectly good, then God must wish to abolish all evil; if God is all powerful, then God must be able to abolish all evil. But evil exists; therefore God cannot be both omnipotent and perfectly loving.

Many have argued that this paradox, first articulated by Epicurus, is actually a contradiction, since it contains premises that are inconsistent with one another. Their argument is as follows:

4. If God (an all-powerful, all-knowing, all-loving being) exists, there would be no (or no unnecessary) evil in the world.

5. There is evil (or unnecessary evil) in the world.

6. Therefore, God does not exist.

How do theists respond to this powerful challenge? The main defense, going back as far as Saint Augustine (354–430) and receiving modern treatment in the work of John Hick, Richard Swinburne, and Alvin Plantinga, is the free will defense. Consider the following passage from Alvin Plantinga's book, *God, Freedom, and Evil*:[35]

A world containing creatures who are significantly free (and freely perform more good than evil actions) is more valuable, all else being equal, than a world containing no free creatures at all. Now God can create free creatures, but He can't *cause* or *determine* them to do only what is right. For if He does so, then they aren't significantly free after all; they do not do what is right *freely*. To create creatures capable of *moral good*, therefore, He must create creatures capable of moral evil; and He can't give these creatures the freedom to perform evil and at the same time prevent them from doing so. As it turned out, sadly enough, some of the free creatures God created went wrong in the exercise of their freedom; this is the source of moral evil. The fact that free creatures sometimes go wrong, however, counts neither against God's omnipotence nor against His goodness for He could have forestalled the occurrence of moral evil only by removing the possibility of moral good.

Plantinga's free will defense, then, would add a fourth premise to Epicurus's paradox in order to demonstrate that premises 1, 2, and 3 are consistent and noncontradictory:

7. It is logically impossible for God to create free creatures *and* guarantee that they will never do evil.

For advocates of the free will defense from Augustine to Plantinga, all moral evil derives from the freedom of the human will. But how do theists account for

[35]Alvin Plantinga, *God, Freedom and Evil* (New York: Harper & Row, 1974), 30.

natural evil? There are two different strategies here. The first, advocated by Plantinga, is to attribute natural evil, such as earthquakes and hurricanes, to the work of the devil (Satan) and his angels. The second strategy, advocated by Swinburne, is to argue that natural evil is an essential part of the natural order, resulting from a combination of deterministic physical laws that are necessary for consistent human action, freedom, and responsibility.

Before turning to the readings, one further distinction is necessary. Some theists answer the charge of inconsistency by simply showing that there is no formal contradiction in premises 1 through 3. Others, however, wish to go beyond this negative function, and attempt to offer a plausible account of evil. These theists are called theodicists; a **theodicy** is an attempt to justify the ways of God to humankind. One of the most famous theodicists was the German philosopher Gottfried Leibniz (1646–1716), who argued that the fact of evil in no way refutes theism. Answering many of the atheistic objections of David Hume, Leibniz argued that God permitted evil to exist in order to bring about greater good, and that Adam's fall was a *felix culpa* ("happy sin") because it led to the incarnation of Jesus, the Son of God, raising humanity to a higher destiny than would otherwise have been the case. (Leibniz' optimistic view of things, expressed in his view that "this is the best of all possible worlds," was the butt of Voltaire's satire in the book *Candide*.) In the Contemporary Perspectives section you will have an opportunity to read the opposing views of two theists, Richard Swinburne and D.Z. Phillips. Swinburne lays out an elaborate theodicy, attempting to modify and improve Leibniz' position. Phillips, in his criticism of Swinburne, rejects all attempts at formulating a theodicy.

CHAPTER 46

SAINT AUGUSTINE

THE PROBLEM OF EVIL

Saint Augustine (Aurelius Augustinus, 354–430) was born in Thagaste, North Africa, the son of a devout Christian mother. Before his conversion, he had embraced Manichaeism, a dualistic system of religious thought that taught that matter was evil and spirit good. At the age of twenty, after his father died, Augustine turned to teaching to support his family. In 383 he went to Rome, where he became a professor of rhetoric. For three years he was in contact with Saint Ambrose, Bishop of Milan, who encouraged his conversion to Christianity in 386. He was baptised the following year. A short while later he prepared to return to his native Thagaste, where he planned to resume a quiet life of reflection and solitude. His plans changed abruptly when, visiting a church in nearby Hippo, Algeria, the people cried for him to become their priest. Augustine, yielding to their insistence, became a priest, and later the Bishop of Hippo.

The story of Augustine's spiritual journey is recorded in his *Confessions*, written about 400. In one poignant passage, Augustine describes his emotions as he read a passage in Saint Paul's Epistle to the Romans: "I had no wish to read further, and no need. For in that instant, with the very ending of the sentence, it was as though a light of utter confidence shone in all my heart, and all the darkness of uncertainty vanished away."

Augustine's masterful work, *On the Trinity*, borrowed concepts from neo-Platonism, and proved to be a model of Christian thinking. His last great work, *The City of God*, begun in 412 and not completed until about 426, used the sack of

Rome by the Visigoths in 410 to demonstrate the passing nature of temporal power in contrast to the eternal kingdom of God. These and other works have made Saint Augustine one of the strongest influences in Western thought.

The standard traditional Christian response to the problem of evil was formulated by Saint Augustine, and includes philosophical as well as theological elements. Accepting the biblical account of creation, Augustine believes that the universe as it came from the hand of God was a perfect harmony reflecting perfectly the divine intent. There is an ontological hierarchy of greater and lesser, higher and lower, with each good in its proper place. Evil originated in those parts of the universe that involve free will—the free will of angels and of human beings. Angels, like humans, were created good, but some turned from the Supreme good, God, to lesser goods, thereby rebelling against their Creator; the angels in turn tempted the first man and woman to fall into sin. The fall (known theologically as "original sin") of angels and humans was the origin of all moral evil. Natural evils (disease, earthquake, tornado, "nature red in tooth and claw") are the penal consequences of sin; humans, intended by God to be caretakers of the earth, have forfeited their responsibility, so that Nature itself has gone astray. Hence, Augustine could say, "All evil is either sin or a punishment for sin."

The key to Augustine's position is to think of evil as a privation or lack of good (a negative concept). Evil cannot be the work of God, but is rather the result of a good that has become defective. To illustrate this "metaphysical concept of evil," Augustine points to blindness, which is clearly not a "thing." The eye, as created by God, is inherently good; the evil of blindness consists of the lack of a proper functioning of the eye. Thus evil is the result of a "good which has gone astray," or a malfunctioning of the good.

In formulating his theodicy, Augustine sought to clear the Creator from any responsibility for the existence of evil by placing that responsibility solely upon human beings. The misuse of creaturely freedom in human prehistory is viewed as a tragic act of truly cosmic significance that will be corrected only with the second advent of Jesus Christ, the "second Adam," who will correct the mistakes of the first Adam.

In reading Augustine,[1] you might ask yourself a few questions. How is it that a universe which was created exactly as God wished it to be, without any evil whatsoever, has nevertheless managed to go wrong? That is, how can a flawless creation go wrong? If the creation has gone wrong, isn't God, as its Creator, ultimately responsible? (Doesn't "the buck stop with God?" Why pass the blame on to humans?) Finally, wouldn't it have been possible for God, as the ultimately imaginative Being, to have created free beings who would never in fact fall?

---

[1] From *Augustine: Confessions and Enchiridion*, translated and edited by Albert C. Outler (Volume VII: The Library of Christian Classics). Published simultaneously in Great Britain and the United States of America by the S.C.M. Press, Ltd., London, and The Westminster Press, Philadelphia. Used by permission of Westminster/John Knox Press, Louisville, KY.

THE PROBLEM OF EVIL: 1 (FROM CONFESSIONS)

4. But as yet, although I said and was firmly persuaded that thou our Lord, the true God, who madest not only our souls but our bodies as well—and not only our souls and bodies but all creatures and all things—wast free from stain and alteration and in no way mutable, yet I could not readily and clearly understand what was the cause of evil. Whatever it was, I realized that the question must be so analyzed as not to constrain me by any answer to believe that the immutable God was mutable, lest I should myself become the thing that I was seeking out. And so I pursued the search with a quiet mind, now in a confident feeling that what had been said by the Manicheans—and I shrank from them with my whole heart—could not be true. I now realized that when they asked what was the origin of evil their answer was dictated by a wicked pride, which would rather affirm that thy nature is capable of suffering evil than that their own nature is capable of doing it.

5. And I directed my attention to understand what I now was told, that free will is the cause of our doing evil and that thy just judgment is the cause of our having to suffer from its consequences. But I could not see this clearly. So then, trying to draw the eye of my mind up out of that pit, I was plunged back into it again, and trying often was just as often plunged back down. But one thing lifted me up toward thy light: it was that I had come to know that I had a will as certainly as I knew that I had life. When, therefore, I willed or was unwilling to do something, I was utterly certain that it was none but myself who willed or was unwilling—and immediately I realized that there was the cause of my sin. I could see that what I did against my will I suffered rather than did; and I did not regard such

actions as faults, but rather as punishments in which I might quickly confess that I was not unjustly punished, since I believed thee to be most just. Who was it that put this in me, and implanted in me the root of bitterness, in spite of the fact that I was altogether the handiwork of my most sweet God? If the devil is to blame, who made the devil himself? And if he was a good angel who by his own wicked will became the devil, how did there happen to be in him that wicked will by which he became a devil, since a good Creator made him wholly a good angel? By these reflections was I again cast down and stultified. Yet I was not plunged into that hell of error—where no man confesses to thee—where I thought that thou didst suffer evil, rather than that men do it.

6. For in my struggle to solve the rest of my difficulties, I now assumed henceforth as settled truth that the incorruptible must be superior to the corruptible, and I did acknowledge that thou, whatever thou art, art incorruptible. For there never yet was, nor will be, a soul able to conceive of anything better than thee, who art the highest and best good. And since most truly and certainly the incorruptible is to be placed above the corruptible—as I now admit it—it followed that I could rise in my thoughts to something better than my God, if thou wert not incorruptible. When, therefore, I saw that the incorruptible was to be preferred to the corruptible, I saw then where I ought to seek thee, and where I should look for the source of evil: that is, the corruption by which thy substance can in no way be profaned. For it is obvious that corruption in no way injures our God, by no inclination, by no necessity, by no unforeseen chance—because he is our God, and what he wills is good, and he himself is

that good. But to be corrupted is not good. Nor art thou compelled to do anything against thy will, since thy will is not greater than thy power. But it would have to be greater if thou thyself wert greater than thyself—for the will and power of God are God himself. And what can take thee by surprise, since thou knowest all, and there is no sort of nature but thou knowest it? And what more should we say about why that substance which God is cannot be corrupted; because if this were so it could not be God?

7. And I kept seeking for an answer to the question, Whence is evil? And I sought it in an evil way, and I did not see the evil in my very search. I marshaled before the sight of my spirit all creation: all that we see of earth and sea and air and stars and trees and animals; and all that we do not see, the firmament of the sky above and all the angels and all spiritual things, for my imagination arranged these also, as if they were bodies, in this place or that. And I pictured to myself thy creation as one vast mass, composed of various kinds of bodies—some of which were actually bodies, some of those which I imagined spirits were like. I pictured this mass as vast—of course not in its full dimensions, for these I could not know—but as large as I could possibly think, still only finite on every side. But thou, O Lord, I imagined as environing the mass on every side and penetrating it, still infinite in every direction—as if there were a sea everywhere, and everywhere through measureless space nothing but an infinite sea; and it contained within itself some sort of sponge, huge but still finite, so that the sponge would in all its parts be filled from the immeasurable sea.

Thus I conceived thy creation itself to be finite, and filled by thee, the infinite. And I said, "Behold God, and behold what God hath created!" God is good, yea, most mightily and incomparably better than all his works. But yet he who is good has created them good; behold how he encircles and fills them. Where, then, is evil, and whence does it come and how has it crept in? What is its root and what its seed? Has it no being at all? Why, then, do we fear and shun what has no being? Or if we fear it needlessly, then surely that fear is evil by which the heart is unnecessarily stabbed and tortured—and indeed a greater evil since we have nothing real to fear, and yet do fear. Therefore, either that is evil which we fear, or the act of fearing is in itself evil. But, then, whence does it come, since God who is good has made all these things good? Indeed, he is the greatest and chiefest Good, and hath created these lesser goods; but both Creator and created are all good. Whence, then, is evil? Or, again, was there some evil matter out of which he made and formed and ordered it, but left something in his creation that he did not convert into good? But why should this be? Was he powerless to change the whole lump so that no evil would remain in it, if he is the Omnipotent? Finally, why would he make anything at all out of such stuff? Why did he not, rather, annihilate it by his same almighty power? Could evil exist contrary to his will? And if it were from eternity, why did he permit it to be nonexistent for unmeasured intervals of time in the past, and why, then, was he pleased to make something out of it after so long a time? Or, if he wished now all of a sudden to create something, would not an almighty being have chosen to annihilate this evil matter and live by himself—the perfect, true, sovereign, and infinite Good? Of, if it were not good that he who was good should not also be the framer and creator of what was good, then why was that evil matter not removed and brought to nothing, so that he might form good matter, out of which he might then create all things? For he would not be omnipotent if he were not able to create something good without being assisted by that matter which had not been created by himself.

Such perplexities I revolved in my wretched breast, overwhelmed with gnawing cares lest I die before I discovered the truth. And still the faith of thy Christ, our Lord and Saviour, as it was taught me by the Catholic Church, stuck fast in my heart. As yet it was unformed on many points and diverged from the rule of right doctrine, but my mind did not utterly lose it, and every day drank in more and more of it.

18. And it was made clear to me that all things are good even if they are corrupted. They could not be corrupted if they were supremely good; but unless they were good they could not be corrupted. If they were supremely good, they would be incorruptible; if they were not good at all, there would be nothing in them to be corrupted. For corruption harms; but unless it could diminish goodness, it could not harm. Either, then, corruption does not harm—which cannot be—or, as is certain, all that is corrupted is thereby deprived of good. But if they are deprived of all good, they will cease to be. For if they are at all and cannot be at all corrupted, they will become better, because they will remain incorruptible. Now what can be more monstrous than to maintain that by losing all good they have become better? If, then, they are deprived of all good, they will cease to exist. So long as they are, therefore, they are good. Therefore, whatsoever is, is good. Evil, then, the origin of which I had been seeking, has no substance at all; for if it were a substance, it would be good. For either it would be an incorruptible substance and so a supreme good, or a corruptible substance, which could not be corrupted unless it were good. I understood, therefore, and it was made clear to me that thou madest all things good, nor is there any substance at all not made by thee. And because all that thou madest is not equal, each by itself is good, and the sum of all of them is very good, for our God made all things very good.

19. To thee there is no such thing as evil, and even in thy whole creation taken as a whole, there is not; because there is nothing from beyond it that can burst in and destroy the order which thou hast appointed for it. But in the parts of creation, some things, because they do not harmonize with others, are considered evil. Yet those same things harmonize with others and are good, and in themselves are good. And all these things which do not harmonize with each other still harmonize with the inferior part of creation which we call the earth, having its own cloudy and windy sky of like nature with itself. Far be it from me, then, to say, "These things should not be." For if I could see nothing but these, I should indeed desire something better—but still I ought to praise thee, if only for these created things. For that thou art to be praised is shown from the fact that "earth, dragons, and all deeps; fire, and hail, snow and vapors, stormy winds fulfilling thy word; mountains, and all hills, fruitful trees, and all cedars; beasts and all cattle; creeping things, and flying fowl; things of the earth, and all people; princes, and all judges of the earth; both young men and maidens, old men and children," praise thy name! But seeing also that in heaven all thy angels praise thee, O God, praise thee in the heights," and all thy hosts, sun and moon, all stars and light, the heavens of heavens, and the waters that are above the heavens," praise thy name—seeing this, I say, I no longer desire a better world, because my thought ranged over all, and with a sounder judgment I reflected that the things above were better than those below, yet that all creation together was better than the higher things alone.

THE PROBLEM OF EVIL: 2 (FROM ENCHIRIDION)

12. All of nature, therefore, is good, since the Creator of all nature is supremely good. But nature is not supremely and immutably good as is the Creator of it. Thus the good in created things can be diminished and augmented. For good to be diminished is evil; still, however much it is diminished, something must remain of its original nature as long as it exists at all. For no matter what kind or however insignificant a thing may be, the good which is its "nature" cannot be destroyed without the thing itself being destroyed. There is good reason, therefore, to praise an uncorrupted thing, and if it were indeed an incorruptible thing which could not be destroyed, it would doubtless be all the more worthy of praise. When, however, a thing is corrupted, its corruption is an evil because it is, by just so much, a privation of the good. Where there is no privation of the good, there is no evil. Where there is evil, there is a corresponding diminution of the good. As long, then, as a thing is being corrupted, there is good in it of which it is being deprived; and in this process, if something of its being remains that cannot be further corrupted, this will then be an incorruptible entity (natura incorruptibilis), and to this great good it will have come through the process of corruption. But even if the corruption is not arrested, it still does not cease having some good of which it cannot be further deprived. If, however, the corruption comes to be total and entire, there is no good left either, because it is no longer an entity at all. Wherefore corruption cannot consume the good without also consuming the thing itself. Every actual entity [natura] is therefore good; a greater good if it cannot be corrupted, a lesser good if it can be. Yet only the foolish and unknowing can deny that it is still good even when corrupted. Whenever a thing is consumed by corruption, not even the corruption remains, for it is nothing in itself, having no subsistent being in which to exist.

13. From this it follows that there is nothing to be called evil if there is nothing good. A good that wholly lacks an evil aspect is entirely good. Where there is some evil in a thing, its good is defective or defectible. Thus there can be no evil where there is no good. This leads us to a surprising conclusion: that, since every being, in so far as it is a being, is good, if we then say that a defective thing is bad, it would seem to mean that we are saying that what is evil is good, that only what is good is ever evil and that there is no evil apart from something good. This is because every actual entity is good [omnis natura bonum est.] Nothing evil exists in itself, but only as an evil aspect of some actual entity. Therefore, there can be nothing evil except something good. Absurd as this sounds, nevertheless the logical connections of the argument compel us to it as inevitable. At the same time, we must take warning lest we incur the prophetic judgment which reads: "Woe to those who call evil good and good evil: who call darkness light and light darkness; who call the bitter sweet and the sweet bitter." Moreover the Lord himself saith: "An evil man brings forth evil out of the evil treasure of his heart." What, then, is an evil man but an evil entity [natura mala], since man is an entity? Now, if a man is something good because he is an entity, what, then, is a bad man except an evil good? When, however, we distinguish between these two concepts, we find that the bad man is not bad because he is a man, nor is he good because he is

wicked. Rather, he is a good entity in so far as he is a man, evil in so far as he is wicked. Therefore, if anyone says that simply to be a man is evil, or that to be a wicked man is good, he rightly falls under the prophetic judgment: "Woe to him who calls evil good and good evil." For this amount to finding fault with God's work, because man is an entity of God's creation. It also means that we are praising the defects in this particular man *because* he is a wicked person. Thus, every entity, even if it is a defective one, in so far as it is an entity, is good. In so far as it is defective, it is evil.

14. Actually, then, in these two contraries we call evil and good, the rule of the logicians fails to apply. No weather is both dark and bright at the same time; no food or drink is both sweet and sour at the same time; no body is, at the same time and place, both white and black, nor deformed and well-formed at the same time. This principle is found to apply in almost all disjunctions: two contraries cannot coexist in a single thing. Nevertheless, while no one maintains that good and evil are not contraries, they can not only coexist, but the evil cannot exist at all without the good, or in a thing that is not a good. On the other hand, the good can exist without evil. For a man or an angel could exist and yet not be wicked, whereas there cannot be wickedness except in a man or an angel. It is good to be a man, good to be an angel; but evil to be wicked. These two contraries are thus coexistent, so that if there were no good in what is evil, then the evil simply could not be, since it can have no mode in which to exist, nor any source from which corruption springs, unless it be something corruptible. Unless this something is good, it cannot be cor-

rupted, because corruption is nothing more than the deprivation of the good. Evils, therefore, have their source in the good, and unless they are parasitic on something good, they are not anything at all. There is no other source whence an evil thing can come to be. If this is the case, then, in so far as a thing is an entity, it is unquestionably good. If it is an incorruptible entity, it is a great good. But even if it is a corruptible entity, it still has no mode of existence except as an aspect of something that is good. Only by corrupting something good can corruption inflict injury.

15. But when we say that evil has its source in the good, do not suppose that this denies our Lord's judgment: "A good tree cannot bear evil fruit." This cannot be, even as the Truth himself declareth: "Men do not gather grapes from thorns," since thorns cannot bear grapes. Nevertheless, from good soil we can see both vines and thorns spring up. Likewise, just as a bad tree does not grow good fruit, so also an evil will does not produce good deeds. From a human nature, which is good in itself, there can spring forth either a good or an evil will. There was no other place from whence evil could have arisen in the first place except from the nature—good in itself—of an angel or a man. This is what our Lord himself most clearly shows in the passage about the trees and the fruits, for he said: "Make the tree good and the fruits will be good, or make the tree bad and its fruits will be bad." This is warning enough that bad fruit cannot grow on a good tree nor good fruit on a bad one. Yet from that same earth to which he was referring, both sorts of trees can grow.

CHAPTER 47

SAINT ANSELM

THE ONTOLOGICAL ARGUMENT

Anselm (1033–1109), born of a noble family in Aosta, in the Italian Alps, was one of the greatest thinkers of the Middle Ages. As a young man he entered a Benedictine monastery in Bec, Normandy, where he lived as a monk—praying, teaching, writing, and working—for thirty-three years. In 1093 he was called to be Archbishop of Canterbury in England, but when King William refused to recognize the freedom of the church from royal control, Anselm went into exile in Italy in protest. He was later summoned back to England by King Henry I.

As with Augustine, Anselm's main interest was theology; he hoped to satisfy the demands of his intellect by trying to understand the truths he already held by faith. As he puts it in his *Proslogion*, "I desire to understand, if only a little, the truth of Yours which my heart already believes and loves. Indeed I do not seek to understand that I may believe; no, I believe so that I may understand."[1]

Anselm is the originator of the ontological argument for God's existence. His most famous works, the *Monologion* (a soliloquy, written around 1077) and the *Proslogion* (a discourse, written around 1077) were responses to a request he had received from some of his monks to produce a meditation on the meaning of faith. He is also the author of *Cur Deus Homo?* (c. 1099) which treats the doctrines of the incarnation and atonement of Jesus Christ.

---

[1]From *St. Anselm's Proslogion*, translated by M. J. Charlesworth (Oxford: Oxford University Press, 1965). © 1965 Oxford University Press. Reprinted by permission of Oxford University Press.

For Anselm, who was Augustinian in his theology, the existence of God is an article of faith. With Augustine, Anselm accepts the fideist position, "I believe in order that I may understand." For both Augustine and Anselm, however, once an article of faith has been accepted, it can also be supported by reason.

In the *Proslogion* Anselm attempts to provide the rational grounds for belief in the existence of God simply by meditating on the idea of God. The argument that Anselm offers is disarmingly simple and quite brief, yet through the centuries it has given rise to an enormous amount of literature. The argument is this: Everyone, even the fool, has an idea of God. The idea of God is of a being so great that no other being greater than it can be thought of; but it is impossible for this being not to exist outside our minds, since to exist outside our minds is greater than to exist only in our minds; therefore, this being, called God, must exist.

Normally, one would immediately reject as frivolous an argument that affirmed the existence of an object from the mere idea of the object. As Gaunilo (a monk about whom little is known) pointed out to Anselm in a written response to the *Proslogion*, we are not permitted to infer the existence of a lost island merely because we have the idea of a lost island in our minds. But Anselm considers the idea of God to be a very special case, since it is greater (or more perfect) than anything else that we can imagine. The idea of God, unlike the idea of a lost island, is the idea of a being so great that it cannot exist merely in the mind; to restrict it to the mind is to treat it like any other idea, which it is clearly not, since by definition it is greater than any other thing. As Anselm puts it, "If anyone finds something for me, besides "that than which none greater is conceivable," which exists either in reality or concept alone to which the logic of my argument can be applied, I will find and give him his 'Lost Island,' never to be lost again."

Faith Seeking Understanding (from Proslogion)

After I had published, at the pressing entreaties of several of my brethren, a certain short tract [the *Monologion*] as an example of meditation on the meaning of faith from the point of view of one seeking, through silent reasoning within himself, things he knows not—reflecting that this was made up of a connected chain of many arguments, I began to wonder if perhaps it might be possible to find one single argument that for its proof required no other save itself, and that by itself would suffice to prove that God really exists, that He is the supreme good needing no other and is He whom all things have need of for their being and well-being, and also to prove whatever we believe about the Divine Being. But as often and as diligently as I turned my thoughts to this, sometimes it seemed to me that I had almost reached what I was seeking, sometimes it eluded my acutest thinking completely, so that finally, in desperation, I was about to give up what I was looking for as something impossible to find. However, when I had decided to put aside this idea altogether, lest by uselessly occupying my mind it might prevent other ideas with which I could make some progress, then, in spite of my unwillingness and my resistance to it, it began to force itself upon me more and more pressingly. So it was that one day when I was quite worn out with resisting its importunacy, there came to me, in the very conflict of my thoughts, what I had despaired of finding, so that I eagerly grasped the notion which in my distraction I had been rejecting.

Judging, then, that what had given me such joy to discover would afford pleasure, if it were written down, to anyone who might read it, I have written the following short tract dealing with this question as well as several others, from the point of view of one trying to raise his mind to contemplate God and seeking to understand what he believes. In my opinion, neither this tract nor the other I mentioned before deserves to be called a book or to carry its author's name, and yet I did not think they should be sent forth without some title (by which, so to speak, they might invite those into whose hands they should come, to read them); so I have given to each its title, the first being called *An Example of Meditation on the Meaning of Faith*, and the sequel *Faith in Quest of Understanding*.

However, as both of them, under these titles, had already been copied out by several readers, a number of people (above all the reverend Archbishop of Lyons, Hugh, apostolic delegate to Gaul, who commanded me by his apostolic authority) have urged me to put my name to them. For the sake of greater convenience I have named the first book *Monologion*, that is, a soliloquy; and the other *Proslogion*, that is, an allocution.

The "Ontological Argument" for the Existence of God (from Proslogion)

Chapter II

That God Truly Exists

Well then, Lord, You who give understanding to faith, grant me that I may understand, as much as You see fit, that You exist as we believe You to exist, and that You are what we believe You to be. Now we believe that You are something than which nothing greater can be thought. Or can it be that a thing of such a nature does not exist, since 'the Fool has said in his heart, there is no God' [Ps. xiii, I, lii. I]? But surely, when this same Fool hears what I am speaking about, namely, 'something-than-which-nothing-greater-can-be-thought', he understands what he hears, and what he understands is in his mind, even if he does not understand that it actually exists. For it is one thing for an object to exist in the mind, and another thing to understand that an object actually exists. Thus, when a painter plans beforehand what he is going to execute, he has [the picture] in his mind, but he does not yet think that it actually exists because he has not yet executed it. However, when he has actually painted it, then he both has it in his mind and understands that it exists because he has now made it. Even the Fool, then, is forced to agree that something-than-which-nothing-greater-can-be-thought exists in the mind, since he understands this when he hears it, and whatever is understood is in the mind. And surely that-than-which-a-greater-cannot-be-thought cannot exist in the mind alone. For if it exists solely in the mind even, it can be thought to exist in reality also,

497

which is greater. If then that-than-which-a-greater-*cannot*-be-thought exists in the mind alone, this same that-than-which-a-greater-can-not-be-thought is that-than-which-a-greater-*can*-be-thought. But this is obviously impossible. Therefore there is absolutely no doubt that something - than - which -a - greater - cannot - be - thought exists both in the mind and in reality.

Chapter III

THAT GOD CANNOT BE THOUGHT NOT TO EXIST

And certainly this being so truly exists that it cannot be even thought not to exist. For something can be thought to exist that cannot be thought not to exist, and this is greater than that which can be thought not to exist. Hence, if that - than - which - a - greater - cannot - be - thought can be thought not to exist, then that-than-which-a-greater-cannot-be-thought is not the same as that-than-which-a-greater-cannot-be-thought, which is absurd. Something-than-which-a-greater-cannot-be-thought exists so truly then, that it cannot be even thought not to exist.

And You, Lord our God, are this being. You exist so truly, Lord my God, that You cannot even be thought not to exist. And this is as it should be, for if some intelligence could think of something better than You, the creature would be above its creator and would judge its creator—and that is completely absurd. In fact, everything else there is, except You alone, can be thought of as not existing. You alone, then, of all things most truly exist and therefore of all things possess existence to the highest degree; for anything else does not exist as truly, and so possesses existence to a lesser degree. Why then did 'the Fool say in his heart, there is no God' [Ps. xiii. I, lii. I] when it is so evident to any rational mind that You of all things exist to the highest degree? Why indeed, unless because he was stupid and a fool?

Chapter IV

HOW 'THE FOOL SAID IN HIS HEART' WHAT CANNOT BE THOUGHT

How indeed has he 'said in his heart' what he could not think; or how could he not think what he 'said in his heart', since to 'say in one's heart' and to 'think' are the same? But if he really (indeed, since he really) both thought because he 'said in his heart' and did not 'say in his heart' because he could not think, there is not only one sense in which something is 'said in one's heart' or thought. For in one sense a thing is thought when the word signifying it is thought; in another sense when the very object which the thing is understood. In the first sense, then, God can be thought not to exist, but not at all in the second sense. No one, indeed, understanding what God is can think that God does not exist, even though he may say these words in his heart either without any [objective] signification or with some peculiar signification. For God is that-than-which-nothing-greater-can-be-thought. Whoever really understands this understands clearly that this same being so exists that not even in thought can it not exist. Thus whoever understands that God exists in such a way cannot think of Him as not existing.

I give thanks, good Lord, I give thanks to You, since what I believed before through Your free gift I now so understand through Your illumination, that if I did not want to *believe* that You existed, I should nevertheless be unable not to *understand* it.

CHAPTER 48

SAINT THOMAS AQUINAS

FIVE WAYS TO PROVE GOD'S EXISTENCE

Thomas Aquinas (1224–1274), Catholic theologian and philosopher, was born in the town of Aquino, near Naples. He was educated by Benedictine and Dominican monks at the universities of Naples, Paris, and Cologne. He received a doctorate in theology at the University of Paris, where he subsequently taught until 1259. He spent the next ten years teaching at various monastaries around Rome, after which he returned to Paris to teach and write. He died in 1274 in an accident while en route to the Council of Lyons. Several months before his death Aquinas confided to a friend that he had stopped writing; having experienced an illuminating vision of God, everything he had written seemed to him like straw.

Aquinas's writings, all written in Latin, include a number of large theological treatises, disputations on various theological and philosophical topics, commentaries on the Bible, and commentaries on twelve treatises of Aristotle. For Aquinas, Aristotle was "the Philosopher"—and Aquinas did more than anyone else to bring to the attention of the Christian world the writings of the great Greek philosopher, which had been lost to the West for centuries. Aquinas's greatest works are *Summa Contra Gentiles* (1259–1264), written to aid in the conversion of the Moors in Spain, and *Summa Theologica* (1265–1273), a systematic and comprehensive synthesis of Christian theology and Aristotelian philosophy.

In 1323 Pope John XXII canonized Thomas Aquinas as a saint. The "Sacred Doctor" holds a position of special respect in the realm of Roman Catholic scholarship. Candidates for the priesthood are required to study at least two years of philosophy and four of theology, following the teachings of Saint Thomas.

Arguments for the existence of God are commonly divided into two categories: *a priori* arguments and *a posteriori* arguments. An *a priori* argument such as the ontological argument depends on a principle that can be known independently of our experience of the world; by just reflecting on the idea of God, Anselm believed, one can know that God exists. An *a posteriori* argument, on the other hand, depends on a principle or premise that can be known only through our experience of the world. The cosmological and teleological arguments, favored by Aquinas, are *a posteriori* arguments.

The first two ways of proving God's existence that Aquinas presents are "First Cause" arguments.[1] The First Way invokes the fact of change (or motion) in the world and argues that there must be an Unmoved Mover that originates all change but is itself not moved. The Second Way is from the idea of causation and argues that there must be a first cause in order to explain the existence of causality. The Third Way is from the idea of contingency: since there are dependent beings (for example, human beings), there must be an independent or necessary being on whom all the dependent beings rely for their existence. The Fourth Way is from excellence and argues that since there are degrees of excellence there must be a perfect being who is the origin of all excellences. The Fifth Way is a teleological argument stating that the harmony of nature must be explained. The only adequate explanation is that there is a divine designer who planned this harmony.

FIVE WAYS TO PROVE GOD'S EXISTENCE

The First Way: The Argument from Change

The existence of God can be shown in five ways. The first and clearest is taken from the idea of motion. (1) Now it is certain, and our senses corroborate it, that some things in this world are in motion. (2) But everything which is in motion is moved by something else. (3) For nothing is in motion except in so far as it is in potentiality in relation to that towards which it is in motion. (4) Now a thing causes movement in so far as it is in actuality. For to cause movement is nothing else than to bring something from potentiality to actuality; but a thing cannot be brought from potentiality to actuality except by something which exists in actuality, as, for example, that which is hot in actuality, like fire, makes wood, which is only hot in potentiality, to be hot in actuality, and thereby causes movement in it and alters it. (5) But it is not possible that the same thing should be at the same time in actuality and in potentiality in relation to the same thing, but only in relation to different things; for what is hot in actuality cannot at the same time be hot in potentiality, though it is at the same time cold in potentiality. (6) It is impossible, therefore, that in relation to the same thing and in the same way

[1]From Thomas Aquinas, *Summa Theologica*, Question 2. Third Article, "Whether God Exists" translated by Laurence Shapcote (London: O.P. Benziger Brothers, 1911).

anything should both cause movement and be caused, or that it should cause itself to move. (7) Everything therefore that is in motion must be moved by something else. If therefore the thing which causes it to move be in motion, this too must be moved by something else, and so on. (8) But we cannot proceed to infinity in this way, because in that case there would be no first mover, and in consequence, neither would there be any other mover; for secondary movers do not cause movement except they be moved by a first mover, as, for example, a stick cannot cause movement unless it is moved by the hand. Therefore it is necessary to stop at some first mover which is moved by nothing else. And this is what we all understand God to be.

The Second Way: The Argument from Causation

The Second Way is taken from the idea of the Efficient Cause. (1) For we find that there is among material things a regular order of efficient causes. (2) But we do not find, nor indeed is it possible, that anything is the efficient cause of itself, for in that case it would be prior to itself, which is impossible. (3) Now it is not possible to proceed to infinity in efficient causes. (4) For if we arrange in order all efficient causes, the first is the cause of the intermediate, and the intermediate the cause of the last, whether the intermediate be many or only one. (5) But if we remove a cause the effect is removed; therefore, if there is no *first* among efficient causes, neither will there be a last or an intermediate. (6) But if we proceed to infinity in efficient causes there will be no first efficient cause, and thus there will be no ultimate effect, nor any intermediate efficient causes, which is clearly false. Therefore it is necessary to suppose the existence of some first efficient cause, and this men call God.

The Third Way: The Argument from Contingency

The Third Way rests on the idea of the "contingent" and the "necessary" and is as follows: (1) Now we find that there are certain things in the Universe which are capable of existing and of not existing, for we find that some things are brought into existence and then destroyed, and consequently are capable of being or not being. (2) But it is impossible for all things which exist to be of this kind, because anything which is capable of not existing, at some time or other does not exist. (3) If therefore *all* things are capable of not existing, there was a time when nothing existed in the Universe. (4) But if this is true there would also be nothing in existence now; because anything that does not exist cannot begin to exist except by the agency of something which has existence. If therefore there was once nothing which existed, it would have been impossible for anything to begin to exist, and so nothing would exist now. (5) This is clearly false. Therefore all things are not contingent, and there must be something which is necessary in the Universe. (6) But everything which is necessary either has or has not the cause of its necessity from an outside source. Now it is not possible to proceed to infinity in necessary things which have a cause of their necessity, as has been proved in the case of efficient causes. Therefore it is necessary to suppose the existence of something which is necessary in itself, not having the cause of its necessity from any outside source, but which is the cause of necessity in others. And this "something" we call God.

The Fourth Way: The Argument from Degrees of Excellence

The Fourth Way is taken from the degrees which are found in things. (1) For among different things we find that one is more or less good or true or noble; and likewise in the case of other things of this kind. (2) But the words "more" or "less" are used of different things in proportion as they approximate in their different ways to something which has the particular quality in the highest degree—e.g., we call a thing hotter when it approximates more nearly to that which is hot in the highest degree. There is therefore something which is true in the highest degree, good in the highest degree and noble in the highest degree; (3) and consequently there must be also something which has being in the highest degree. For things which are true in the highest degree also have being in the highest degree (see Aristotle, *Metaphysics*, 2). (4) But anything which has a certain quality of any kind in the highest degree is also the cause of all the things of that kind, as, for example, fire which is hot in the highest degree is the cause of all hot things (as is said in the same book). (5) Therefore there exists something which is the cause of being, and goodness, and of every perfection in all existing things; and this we call God.

The Fifth Way: The Argument from Harmony

The Fifth Way is taken from the way in which nature is governed. (1) For we observe that certain things which lack knowledge, such as natural bodies, work for an End. This is obvious, because they always, or at any rate very frequently, operate in the same way so as to attain the best possible result. (2) Hence it is clear that they do not arrive at their goal by chance, but by purpose. (3) But those things which have no knowledge do not move towards a goal unless they are guided by someone or something which does possess knowledge and intelligence—e.g., an arrow by an archer. Therefore, there does exist something which possesses intelligence by which all natural things are directed to their goal; and this we call God.

CHAPTER 49

SØREN KIERKEGAARD

AGAINST PROOFS IN RELIGION

Søren Kierkegaard (1813–1855), a Danish religious thinker widely regarded as the founder of existentialism, was brought up in a deeply religious Lutheran household in Copenhagen. His father, a successful merchant in the city, was a moody and melancholic man with a somber view of God as a severe judge of unrighteous behavior. Young Søren, introspective and psychologically burdened with the religious melancholy of his father, sought to free himself from the demands of the religious life by adopting a playful and carefree attitude during his student years at the University of Copenhagen. Enrolling in the theological curriculum in deference to his father, he nevertheless read widely in philosophy and literature and was especially interested in the works of Plato, Shakespeare, and the Romantics. His main interests, however, were elsewhere—in the cafés and theaters of Copenhagen he pursued a bohemian life of pleasure. Gradually, however, his youthful cynicism wore off, and he came to recognize the importance of a personal commitment to ethical values and a sense of religious mission. So strong was his commitment to his newfound faith that he broke off his engagement with his fianceé, Regina Olson, feeling that married life was incompatible with the call of God in his life, which was to establish the individual as the centerpiece of philosophy against the Hegelians. His opposition to institutions led him into a prolonged conflict with the Danish state church, and every form of institutionalized religion that had corrupted the essential meaning of what it meant to be an individual before God alone.

For Kierkegaard, all philosophy must be personal, since philosophy is nothing more than a personal reflection on our own lived experience. Having himself experienced a shameful episode in which he was publicly ridiculed and made the butt of a hundred jokes by *The Corsair*, a muckraking newspaper, he knew what it was to undergo the martyrdom of laughter. From this experience he came to believe that our sense of individuality must be developed through every stage of life—we must resist the temptation of losing ourselves in the crowd. Kierkegaard was convinced that the abstract, encyclopedic philosophy of Hegel had done much to destroy the worth of the individual. Worse yet, the Danish state church had become a pale reflection of Hegelian thought. Thus Hegel and the church must be resisted.

Kierkegaard was a prolific author. In addition to his journals he is the author of *Fear and Trembling* (1843), *Either/Or* (1843), *Philosophical Fragments* (1844), and *Concluding Unscientific Postcript to the Philosophical Fragments* (1846).

"[I]f God does not exist it would of course be impossible to prove it; and if he does exist it would be folly to attempt it." Thus begins Kierkegaard's fideistic rejection of the rationalist desire for proofs of God's existence.[1] In everyday life, we do not set about to prove the existence of objects, for the existence of a thing is presupposed and is not subject to demonstration. For instance, we do not prove that a criminal exists but rather that the accused, whose existence is a given, is a criminal. Thus we always reason from existence, not toward it. Why reverse this common-sensical procedure when the subject is God?

Furthermore, there is something fundamentally misguided about trying to base religious faith on the objective evidence of reason. Not only will it not work, it is actually dangerous to faith. Kierkegaard argues passionately that faith is the highest virtue that a human can attain, higher even than reason. Genuine faith comes only when reason has "shipwrecked" in its quest for wholeness and is at the point of despair—only then will God be revealed as the Absolute Paradox, the Absurd, an offense to reason but the salvation of the soul. Faith is the soul's deepest yearnings, a hope beyond hopelessness, a *leap* into the Unknown that the rational part of us cannot comprehend. As the Apostle Paul stated, "Faith is the substance of things hoped for, the evidence of things not seen." Faith cannot be produced through academic investigations, for "The Reason has brought God as near as possible, and yet He is as far away as possible."

AGAINST PROOFS IN RELIGION[1]

But what is this unknown something with which the Reason collides when inspired by its paradoxical passion, with the result of unsettling even man's knowledge of himself? It is the Unknown. It is not a human being, in so far as we know what man is; nor is it any other known thing. So let us

[1]From Søren Kierkegaard, *Kierkegaard's Writings: VII. Philosophical Fragments/Johannes Climacus*, edited and translated by Howard V. Hong and Edna H. Hong. Copyright © 1985 by Howard V. Hong. Excerpt. pp. 49–57 reprinted with permission of Princeton University Press.

call this unknown something: *the God*. It is nothing more than a name we assign to it. The idea of demonstrating that this unknown something (the God) exists, could scarcely suggest itself to the Reason. For if the God does not exist it would of course be impossible to prove it; and if he does exist it would be folly to attempt it. For at the very outset, in beginning my proof, I would have presupposed it, not as doubtful but as certain (a presupposition is never doubtful, for the very reason that it is a presupposition), since otherwise I would not begin, readily understanding that the whole would be impossible if he did not exist. But if when I speak of proving the God's existence I mean that I propose to prove that the Unknown, which exists, is the God, then I express myself unfortunately. For in that case I do not prove anything, least of all an existence, but merely develop the content of a conception. Generally speaking, it is a difficult matter to prove that anything exists; and what is still worse for the intrepid souls who undertake the venture, the difficulty is such that fame scarcely awaits those who concern themselves with it. The entire demonstration always turns into something very different and becomes an additional development of the consequences that flow from my having assumed that the object in question exists. Thus I always reason from existence, not toward existence, whether I move in the sphere of palpable sensible fact or in the realm of thought. I do not, for example, prove that a stone exists, but that some existing thing is a stone. The procedure in a court of justice does not prove that a criminal exists, but that the accused, whose existence is given, is a criminal. Whether we call existence an *accessorium* or the eternal *prius*, it is never subject to demonstration. Let us take ample time for consideration. We have no such reason for haste as have those who from concern for themselves or for the God or for some other thing, must make haste to get existence demonstrated. Under such circumstances there may indeed be need for haste, especially if the prover sincerely seeks to appreciate the danger that he himself, or the thing in question, may be nonexistent unless the proof is finished and does not surreptitiously entertain the thought that it exists whether he succeeds in proving it or not.

If it were proposed to prove Napoleon's existence from Napoleon's deeds, would it not be a most curious proceeding? His existence does indeed explain his deeds, but the deeds do not prove *his* existence, unless I have already understood the word "his" so as thereby to have assumed his existence. But Napoleon is only an individual, and in so far there exists no absolute relationship between him and his deeds; some other person might have performed the same deeds. Perhaps this is the reason why I cannot pass from the deeds to existence. If I call these deeds the deeds of Napoleon the proof becomes superfluous, since I have already named him; if I ignore this, I can never prove from the deeds that they are Napoleon's, but only in a purely ideal manner that such deeds are the deeds of a great general, and so forth. But between the God and his works there is an absolute relationship; the God is not a name but a concept. Is this perhaps the reason that his *essentia involvit existentiam?*[1] The works of God are such that only the God can perform them. Just so, but where then are the works of the God? The works from which I would deduce his existence are not directly and immediately given. The wisdom in nature, the goodness, the wisdom in the governance of the world—are all these manifest, perhaps, upon the very face of things? Are we not here confronted with the most terrible temptations to doubt, and is it not impossible finally to dispose of all these doubts? But from such an order of things I will surely not attempt to prove God's existence; and even if I began I would never finish, and would in addition have to live constantly in suspense, lest

[1] Essence involves existence?

505

something so terrible should suddenly happen that my bit of proof would be demolished. From what works then do I propose to derive the proof? From the works as apprehended through an ideal interpretation, i.e., such as they do not immediately reveal themselves. But in that case it is not from the works that I make the proof; I merely develop the ideality I have presupposed, and because of my confidence in *this* I make so bold as to defy all objections, even those that have not yet been made. In beginning my proof I presuppose the ideal interpretation, and also that I will be successful in carrying it through; but what else is this but to presuppose that the God exists, so that I really begin by virtue of confidence in him?

And how does the God's existence emerge from the proof? Does it follow straightway, without any breach of continuity? Or have we not here an analogy to the behaviour of the little Cartesian dolls? As soon as I let go of the doll it stands on its head. As soon as I let it go—I must therefore let it go. So also with the proof. As long as I keep my hold on the proof, i.e., continue to demonstrate, the existence does not come out, if for no other reason than that I am engaged in proving it; but when I let the proof go, the existence is there. But this act of letting go is surely also something; it is indeed a contribution of mine. Must not this also be taken into the account, this little moment, brief as it may be—it need not be long, for it is a *leap.* However brief this moment, if only an instantaneous now, this "now" must be included in the reckoning. If anyone wishes to have it ignored, I will use it to tell a little anecdote, in order to show that it nevertheless does exist. Chrysippus was experimenting with a sorites to see if he could not bring about a break in its quality, either progressively or retrogressively. But Carneades could not get it in his head when the new quality actually emerged. Then Chrysippus told him to try making a little pause in the reckoning, and so—so it would be easier to understand. Carneades replied: With the greatest pleasure, please do not hesitate on my account; you may not only pause, but even lie down to sleep, and it will help you just as little; for when you awake we will begin again where you left off. Just so; it boots as little to try to get rid of something by sleeping as to try to come into the possession of something in the same manner.

Whoever therefore attempts to demonstrate the existence of God (except in the sense of clarifying the concept, and without the *reservatio finalis* noted above, that the existence emerges from the demonstration by a leap) proves in lieu thereof something else, something which at times perhaps does not need a proof, and in any case needs none better; for the fool says in his heart that there is no God, but whoever says in his heart or to men: Wait just a little and I will prove it— what a rare man of wisdom is he! If in the moment of beginning his proof it is not absolutely undetermined whether the God exists or not, he does not prove it; and if it is thus undetermined in the beginning he will never come to begin, partly from fear of failure, since the God perhaps does not exist, and partly because he has nothing with which to begin.—A project of this kind would scarcely have been undertaken by the ancients. Socrates at least, who is credited with having put forth the physico-teleological proof for God's existence, did not go about it in any such manner. He always presupposes the God's existence, and under this presupposition seeks to interpenetrate nature with the idea of purpose. Had he been asked why he pursued this method, he would doubtless have explained that he lacked the courage to venture out upon so perilous a voyage of discovery without having made sure of the God's existence behind him. At the word of the God he casts his net as if to catch the idea of purpose; for nature herself finds many means of frightening the inquirer, and distracts him by many a digression.

The paradoxical passion of the Reason thus comes repeatedly into collision with this Unknown, which does indeed exist, but is unknown, and in so far does not exist. The Reason cannot advance beyond this point, and yet it cannot refrain in its paradoxicalness from arriving at this limit and occupying itself therewith. It will not serve to dismiss its relation to it simply by asserting that the Unknown does not exist, since this itself involves a relationship. But what then is the Unknown, since the designation of it as the God merely signifies for us that it is unknown? To say that it is the Unknown because it cannot be known, and even if it were capable of being known, it could not be expressed, does not satisfy the demands of passion, though it correctly interprets the Unknown as a limit; but a limit is precisely a torment for passion, though it also serves as an incitement. And yet the Reason can come no further, whether it risks an issue *via negationis* or *via eminentia*.[2]

What then is the Unknown? It is the limit to which the Reason repeatedly comes, and in so far, substituting a static form of conception for the dynamic, it is the different, the absolutely different. But because it is absolutely different, there is no mark by which it could be distinguished. When qualified as absolutely different it seems on the verge of disclosure, but this is not the case; for the Reason cannot even conceive an absolute unlikeness. The Reason cannot negate itself absolutely, but uses itself for the purpose, and thus conceives only such an unlikeness within itself as it can conceive by means of itself; it cannot absolutely transcend itself, and hence conceives only such a superiority over itself as it can conceive by means of itself. Unless the Unknown (the God) remains a mere limiting conception, the single idea of difference will be thrown into a state of confusion, and become many ideas of many differences. The Unknown is then in a condition of dispersion ($\delta\iota\alpha\sigma\pi\rho\rho\acute{\alpha}$), and the Reason may choose at pleasure from what is at hand and the imagination may suggest (the monstrous, the ludicrous, etc.).

But it is impossible to hold fast to a difference of this nature. Every time this is done it is essentially an arbitrary act, and deepest down in the heart of piety lurks the mad caprice which knows that it has itself produced the God. If no specific determination of difference can be held fast, because there is no distinguishing mark, like and unlike finally become identified with one another, thus sharing the fate of all such dialectical opposites. The unlikeness clings to the Reason and confounds it, so that the Reason no longer knows itself and quite consistently confuses itself with the unlikeness. On this point paganism has been sufficiently prolific in fantastic inventions. As for the last named supposition, the self-irony of the Reason, I shall attempt to delineate it merely by a stroke or two, without raising any question of its being historical. There exists an individual whose appearance is precisely like that of other men; he grows up to manhood like others, he marries, he has an occupation by which he earns his livelihood, and he makes provision for the future as befits a man. For though it may be beautiful to live like the birds of the air, it is not lawful, and may lead to the sorriest of consequences: either starvation if one has enough persistence, or dependence on the bounty of others. This man is also the God. How do I know? I cannot know it, for in order to know it I would have to know the God, and the nature of the difference between the God and man; and this I cannot know, because the Reason has reduced it to likeness with that from which it was unlike. Thus the God becomes the most terrible of deceivers, because the Reason has deceived itself. The Reason has brought the God as near as possible, and yet he is as far away as ever.

[2]That is, by the method of making negative statements about God, or by the method of attributing human qualities to God. —Ed.

CHAPTER 50

ERNEST NAGEL

THE CASE FOR ATHEISM

Born in Novemesto, Czechoslovakia, Ernest Nagel (1901–1985) received his education at City College (now City University of New York) and Columbia University (Ph.D., 1931). Nagel remained at Columbia and was Professor Emeritus of Philosophy. He received honorary degrees from Bard College (L.H.D., 1964), City University of New York (L.H.D., 1972), Brandeis University (D.Sc., 1965), Rutgers (D.Litt., 1967), Case Western Reserve (D.Litt., 1970), Columbia (D.Litt., 1971), and the University of Guelph (D.Litt., 1979). A two-time Guggenheim fellow (1934–1935, 1950–1951), his writings include *Introduction to Logic and Scientific Method* (1934), *Sovereign Reason* (1954), *Goedel's Proof* (1958), *The Structure of Science* (1961), and *Teleology Revisited* (1979).

Nagel begins with two clarifications of what he means by atheism.[1] His primary concern is with *evidential atheism*, a philosophical position holding that the positive evidence for theism is insufficient to warrant belief. He examines five traditional intellectual defenses of theism—the cosmological argument, the ontological argument, the teleological argument, the moral argument, and the argument from religious experience—noting deficiencies in each. He concludes by enumerating "points of doctrine" that most philosophical atheists hold.

[1]From Ernest Nagel, "Philosophical Concepts of Atheism," in *Basic Beliefs*, edited by J.E. Fairchild (New York: Sheridan House, Inc., 1959).

The Case for Atheism

1

I must begin by stating what sense I am attaching to the word "atheism," and how I am construing the theme of this paper. I shall understand by "atheism" a critique and a denial of the major claims of all varieties of theism. And by theism I shall mean the view which holds, as one writer has expressed it, "that the heavens and the earth and all that they contain owe their existence and continuance in existence to the wisdom and will of a supreme, self-consistent, omnipotent, omniscient, righteous, and benevolent being, who is distinct from, and independent of, what he has created." Several things immediately follow from these definitions.

In the first place, atheism is not necessarily an irreligious concept, for theism is just one among many views concerning the nature and origin of the world. The denial of theism is logically compatible with a religious outlook upon life, and is in fact characteristic of some of the great historical religions. For as readers of this volume will know, early Buddhism is a religion which does not subscribe to any doctrine about a god; and there are pantheistic religions and philosophies which, because they deny that God is a being separate from and independent of the world, are not theistic in the sense of the word explained above.

The second point to note is that atheism is not to be identified with sheer unbelief, or with disbelief in some particular creed of a religious group. Thus, a child who has received no religious instruction and has never heard about God, is not an atheist—for he is not denying any theistic claims. Similarly in the case of an adult who, if he has withdrawn from the faith of his fathers without reflection or because of frank indifference to any theological issue, is also not an atheist—for such an adult is not challenging theism and is not professing any views on the subject. Moreover, though the term "atheist" has been used historically as an abusive label for those who do not happen to subscribe to some regnant orthodoxy (for example, the ancient Romans called the early Christians atheist, because the latter denied the Roman divinities), or for those who engage in conduct regarded as immoral it is not in this sense that I am discussing atheism.

One final word of preliminary explanation. I propose to examine some *philosophic* concepts of atheism, and I am not interested in the slightest in the many considerations atheists have advanced against the evidences for some particular religious and theological doctrine—for example, against the truth of the Christian story. What I mean by "philosophical" in the present context is that the views I shall consider are directed against any form of theism, and have their origin and basis in a logical analysis of the theistic position, and in a comprehensive account of the world believed to be wholly intelligible without the adoption of a theistic hypothesis.

Theism as I conceive it is a theological proposition, not a statement of a position that belongs primarily to religion. On my view, religion as a historical and social phenomenon is primarily an institutionalized *cultus* or practice, which possesses identifiable social functions and which expresses certain attitudes men take toward their world. Although it is doubtful whether men ever engage in religious practices or assume religious attitudes without some more or less explicit interpretation of their ritual or some rationale for their attitude, it is still the case that it is possible to distinguish religion as a social and personal phenomenon from the theological doctrines which may be developed as justifications for religious practices. Indeed, in some of the great religions of the world the profession of a creed plays a relatively minor role. In short, religion is a form of social communion, a participation in certain kinds of ritual (whether it be a dance, worship, prayer, or the like), and a form of experience (sometimes, though not invariably, directed to a personal confrontation with divine and holy things). Theology is an articulated and, at its best, a rational attempt at understanding these feelings and practices, in the light of their relation to other parts of human experience, and in terms of some hypothesis concerning the nature of things entire.

2

As I see it, atheistic philosophies fall into two major groups: 1) those which hold that the theistic doctrine is meaningful, but reject it either on the ground that, (a) the positive evidence for it is insufficient, or (b) the negative evidence is quite overwhelming; and 2) those who hold that the theistic thesis is not even meaningful, and reject it (a) as just nonsense or (b) as literally meaningless but interpreting it as a symbolic rendering of human ideals, thus reading the theistic thesis in a sense that most believers in theism would disavow. It will not be possible in the limited space at my disposal to discuss the second category of atheistic critiques; and in any event, most of the traditional atheistic critiques of theism belong to the first group.

But before turning to the philosophical examination of the major classical arguments for theism, it is well to note that such philosophical critiques do not quite convey the passion with which atheists have often carried on their analy-

ses of theistic views. For historically, atheism has been, and indeed continues to be, a form of social and political protest, directed as much against institutionalized religion as against theistic doctrine. Atheism has been, in effect, a moral revulsion against the undoubted abuses of the secular power exercised by religious leaders and religious institutions.

Religious authorities have opposed the correction of glaring injustices, and encouraged politically and socially reactionary policies. Religious institutions have been havens of obscurantist thought and centers for the dissemination of intolerance. Religious creeds have been used to set limits to free inquiry, to perpetuate inhumane treatment of the ill and the underprivileged, and to support moral doctrines insensitive to human suffering.

These indictments may not tell the whole story about the historical significance of religion; but they are at least an important part of the story. The refutation of theism has thus seemed to many as an indispensable step not only towards liberating men's minds from superstition, but also towards achieving a more equitable reordering of society. And no account of even the more philosophical aspects of atheistic thought is adequate, which does not give proper recognition to the powerful social motives that actuate many atheistic arguments.

But however this may be, I want now to discuss three classical arguments for the existence of God, arguments which have constituted at least a partial basis for theistic commitments. As long as theism is defended simply as a dogma, asserted as a matter of direct revelation or as the deliverance of authority, belief in the dogma is impregnable to rational argument. In fact, however, reasons are frequently advanced in support of the theistic creed, and these reasons have been the subject of acute philosophical critiques.

One of the oldest intellectual defenses of

theism is the cosmological argument, also known as the argument from a first cause. Briefly put, the argument runs as follows. Every event must have a cause. Hence an event A must have as cause some event B, which in turn must have a cause C, and so on. But if there is no end to this backward progression of causes, the progression will be infinite; and in the opinion of those who use this argument, an infinite series of actual events is unintelligible and absurd. Hence there must be a first cause, and this first cause is God, the initiator of all change in the universe.

The argument is an ancient one, and is especially effective when stated within the framework of assumptions of Aristotelian physics; and it has impressed many generations of exceptionally keen minds. The argument is nonetheless a weak reed on which to rest the theistic thesis. Let us waive any question concerning the validity of the principle that every event has a cause, for though the question is important its discussion would lead us far afield. However, if the principle is assumed, it is surely incongruous to postulate a first cause as a way of escaping from the coils of an infinite series. For if everything must have a cause, why does not God require one for His own existence? The standard answer is that He does not need any, because He is self-caused. But if God can be self-caused, why cannot the world itself be self-caused? Why do we require a God transcending the world to bring the world into existence and to initiate changes in it? On the other hand, the supposed inconceivability and absurdity of an infinite series of regressive causes will be admitted by no one who has competent familiarity with the modern mathematical analysis of infinity. The cosmological argument does not stand up under scrutiny.

The second "proof" of God's existence is usually called the ontological argument. It too has a long history going back to early Christian days, though it acquired great prominence only in medieval times. The argument can be stated in several ways, one of which is the following. Since God is conceived to be omnipotent, he is a perfect being. A perfect being is defined as one whose essence or nature lacks no attributes (or properties) whatsoever, one whose nature is complete in every respect. But it is evident that we have an idea of a perfect being, for we have just defined the idea; and since this is so, the argument continues, God who is the perfect being must exist. Why must he? Because his existence follows from his defined nature. For if God lacked the attribute of existence, he would be lacking at least one attribute, and would therefore not be perfect. To sum up, since we have an idea of God as a perfect being, God must exist.

There are several ways of approaching this argument, but I shall consider only one. The argument was exploded by the 18th century philosopher Immanuel Kant. The substance of Kant's criticism is that it is just a confusion to say that existence is an attribute, and that though the word "existence" may occur as the grammatical predicate in a sentence no attribute is being predicated of a thing when we say that the thing exists or has existence. Thus, to use Kant's example, when we think of $100 we are thinking of the nature of this sum of money; but the nature of $100 remains the same whether we have $100 in our pockets or not. Accordingly, we are confounding grammar with logic if we suppose that some characteristic is being attributed to the nature of $100 when we say that a hundred dollar bill exists in someone's pocket.

To make the point clearer, consider another example. When we say that a lion has a tawny color, we are predicating a certain attribute of the animal, and similarly when we say that the lion is fierce or is hungry. But when we say the lion exists, all that we are saying is that something is (or has the nature of) a lion; we are not specifying an attribute which belongs to the nature of anything that is a lion. In short, the word "existence" does not signify any attribute, and in consequence no attribute that belongs to the nature of anything. Accordingly, it does not follow from the assumption that we have an idea of a perfect being that such a being exists. For the idea of a perfect being does not involve the attribute of existence as a constituent of that idea, since there is no such attribute. The ontological argument thus has a serious leak, and it can hold no water.

3

The two arguments discussed thus far are purely dialectical, and attempt to establish God's existence without any appeal to empirical data. The next argument, called the argument from design, is different in character, for it is based on what purports to be empirical evidence. I wish to examine two forms of this argument.

One variant of it calls attention to the remarkable way in which different things and processes in the world are integrated with each other, and concludes that this mutual "fitness" of things can be explained only by the assumption of a divine architect who planned the world and everything in it. For example, living organisms can maintain themselves in a variety of environments, and do so in virtue of their delicate mechanisms which adapt the organisms to all sorts of environmental changes. There is thus an intricate pattern of means and ends throughout the animate world. But the existence of this pattern is unintelligible, so the argument runs, except on the hypothesis that the pattern has been deliberately instituted by a Supreme Designer. If we find a watch in some deserted spot, we do not think it came into existence by chance, and we do not hesitate to conclude that an intelligent creature

designed and made it. But the world and all its contents exhibit mechanisms and mutual adjustments that are far more complicated and subtle than are those of a watch. Must we not therefore conclude that these things too have a Creator?

The conclusion of this argument is based on an inference from analogy: the watch and the world are alike in possessing a congruence of parts and an adjustment of means to ends; the watch has a watch–maker; hence the world has a world–maker. But is the analogy a good one? Let us once more waive some important issues, in particular the issue whether the universe is the unified system such as the watch admittedly is. And let us concentrate on the question what is the ground for our assurance that watches do not come into existence except through the operations of intelligent manufacturers. The answer is plain. We have never run across a watch which has not been deliberately made by someone. But the situation is nothing like this in the case of the innumerable animate and inanimate systems with which we are familiar. Even in the case of living organisms, though they are generated by their parent organisms, the parents do not "make" their progeny in the same sense in which watch–makers make watches. And once this point is clear, the inference from the existence of living organisms to the existence of a supreme designer no longer appears credible.

Moreover, the argument loses all its force if the facts which the hypothesis of a divine designer is supposed to explain can be understood on the basis of a better supported assumption. And indeed, such an alternative explanation is one of the achievements of Darwinian biology. For Darwin showed that one can account for the variety of biological species, as well as for their adaptations to their environments, without invoking a divine creator and acts of special creation. The Darwinian theory explains the diversity of biological species in terms of chance variations in the structure of organisms, and of a mechanism of selection which retains those variant forms that possess some advantages for survival. The evidence for these assumptions is considerable; and developments subsequent to Darwin have only strengthened the case for a thoroughly naturalistic explanation of the facts of biological adaptation. In any event, this version of the argument from design has nothing to recommend it.

A second form of this argument has been recently revived in the speculations of some modern physicists. No one who is familiar with the facts, can fail to be impressed by the success with which the use of mathematical methods has enabled us to obtain intellectual mastery of many parts of nature. But some thinkers have therefore concluded that since the book of nature is ostensibly written in mathematical language, nature must be the creation of a divine mathematician. However, the argument is most dubious. For it rests, among other things, on the assumption that mathematical tools can be successfully used only if the events of nature exhibit some *special* kind of order, and on the further assumption that if the structure of things were different from what they are mathematical language would be inadequate for describing such structure. But it can be shown that no matter what the world were like—even if it impressed us as being utterly chaotic—it would still possess some order, and would in principle be amenable to a mathematical description. In point of fact, it makes no sense to say that there is absolutely *no* pattern in any conceivable subject matter. To be sure, there are differences in complexities of structure, and if the patterns of events were sufficiently complex we might not be able to unravel them. But however that may be, the success of mathematical physics in giving us some understanding of the world around us does not yield the conclusion that only a mathematician could have devised the patterns of order we have discovered in nature.

4

The inconclusiveness of the three classical arguments for the existence of God was already made evident by Kant, in a manner substantially not different from the above discussion. There are, however, other types of arguments for theism that have been influential in the history of thought, two of which I wish to consider, even if only briefly.

Indeed, though Kant destroyed the classical intellectual foundations for theism, he himself invented a fresh argument for it. Kant's attempted proof is not intended to be a purely theoretical demonstration, and is based on the supposed facts of our moral nature. It has exerted an enormous influence on subsequent theological speculation. In barest outline, the argument is as follows. According to Kant, we are subject not only to physical laws like the rest of nature, but also to moral ones. These moral laws are categorical imperatives, which we must heed not because of their utilitarian consequences, but simply because as autonomous mortal agents it is our duty to accept them as binding. However, Kant was keenly aware that though virtue may be its reward, the virtuous man (that is, the man who acts out of a sense of duty and in conformity with the moral law) does not always receive his just desserts in this world; nor did he shut his eyes to the fact that evil men frequently enjoy the best things this world has to offer. In short, virtue does not always reap happiness. Nevertheless, the highest human good is the realization of happiness commensurate with one's virtue; and Kant believed that it is a practical postulate of the moral life to promote this good. But what can guarantee that the highest good is realizable?

Such a guarantee can be found only in God, who must therefore exist if the highest good is not to be a fatuous ideal. The existence of an omnipotent, omniscient, and omnibenevolent God is thus postulated as necessary condition for the possibility of a moral life.

Despite the prestige this argument has acquired, it is difficult to grant it any force. It is easy enough to postulate God's existence. But as Bertrand Russell observed in another connection, postulation has all the advantages of theft over honest toil. No postulation carries with it any assurance that what is postulated is actually the case. And though we may postulate God's existence as a means to guaranteeing the possibility of realizing happiness together with virtue, the postulation establishes neither the actual realizability of this ideal nor the fact of his existence. Moreover, the argument is not made more cogent when we recognize that it is based squarely on the highly dubious conception that considerations of utility and human happiness must not enter into the determination of what is morally obligatory. Having built his moral theory on a radical separation of means from ends, Kant was driven to the desperate postulation of God's existence in order to relate them again. The argument is thus at best a *tour de force*, contrived to remedy a fatal flaw in Kant's initial moral assumptions. It carries no conviction to anyone who does not commit Kant's initial blunder.

One further type of argument, pervasive in much Protestant theological literature, deserves brief mention. Arguments of this type take their point of departure from the psychology of religious and mystical experience. Those who have undergone such experiences, often report that during the experience they feel themselves to be in the presence of the divine and holy, that they lose their sense of self-identity and become merged with some fundamental reality, or that

they enjoy a feeling of total dependence upon some ultimate power. The overwhelming sense of transcending one's finitude which characterizes such vivid periods of life, and of coalescing with some ultimate source of all existence, is then taken to be compelling evidence for the existence of a supreme being. In a variant form of this argument, other theologians have identified God as the object which satisfies the commonly experienced need for integrating one's scattered and conflicting impulses into a coherent unity, or as the subject which is of ultimate concern to us. In short, a proof of God's existence is found in the occurrence of certain distinctive experiences.

It would be flying in the face of well-attested facts were one to deny that such experiences frequently occur. But do these facts constitute evidence for the conclusion based on them? Does the fact, for example, that an individual experiences a profound sense of direct contact with an alleged transcendent ground of all reality, constitute competent evidence for the claim that there is such a ground and that it is the immediate cause of the experience? If well-established canons for evaluating evidence are accepted, the answer is surely negative. No one will dispute that many men do have vivid experiences in which such things as ghosts or pink elephants appear before them; but only the hopelessly credulous will without further ado count such experiences as establishing the existence of ghosts and pink elephants. To establish the existence of such things, evidence is required that is obtained under controlled conditions and that can be confirmed by independent inquirers. Again, though a man's report that he is suffering pain may be taken at face value, one cannot take at face value the claim, were he to make it, that it is the food he ate which is the cause (or a contributory cause) of his felt pain—not even if the man were to report a vivid feeling of abdominal disturbance. And similarly, an overwhelming feeling of being in the presence of the Divine is evidence enough for admitting the genuineness of such feeling; it is no evidence for the claim that a supreme being with a substantial existence independent of the experience is the cause of the experience.

5

Thus far the discussion has been concerned with noting inadequacies in various arguments widely used to support theism. However, much atheistic criticism is also directed toward exposing incoherencies in the very thesis of theism. I want therefore to consider this aspect of the atheistic critique, though I will restrict myself to the central difficulty in the theistic position which arises from the simultaneous attribution of omnipotence, omniscience, and omnibenevolence to the Deity. The difficulty is that of reconciling these attributes with the occurrence of evil in the world. Accordingly, the question to which I now turn is whether, despite the existence of evil, it is possible to construct a theodicy which will justify the ways of an infinitely powerful and just God to man.

Two main types of solutions have been proposed for this problem. One way that is frequently used is to maintain that what is commonly called evil is only an illusion, or at worst only the "privation" or absence of good. Accordingly, evil is not "really real," it is only the "negative" side of God's beneficence, it is only the product of our limited intelligence which fails to plumb the true character of God's creative bounty. A sufficient comment on this proposed solution is that facts are not altered or abolished by rebaptizing them. Evil may indeed be only an appearance and not genuine. But this does not eliminate

from the realm of appearance the tragedies, the sufferings, and the iniquities which men so frequently endure. And it raises once more, though on another level, the problem of reconciling the fact that there is evil in the realm of appearance with God's alleged omnibenevolence. In any event, it is small comfort to anyone suffering a cruel misfortune for which he is in no way responsible, to be told that what he is undergoing is only the absence of good. It is a gratuitous insult to mankind, a symptom of insensitivity and indifference to human suffering, to be assured that all the miseries and agonies men experience are only illusory.

Another gambit often played in attempting to justify the ways of God to man is to argue that the things called evil are evil only because they are viewed in isolation; they are not evil when viewed in proper perspective and in relation to the rest of creation. Thus, if one attends to but a single instrument in an orchestra, the sounds issuing from it may indeed be harsh and discordant. But if one is placed at a proper distance from the whole orchestra, the sounds of that single instrument will mingle with the sounds issuing from the other players to produce a marvellous bit of symphonic music. Analogously, experiences we call painful undoubtedly occur and are real enough. But the pain is judged to be an evil only because it is experienced in a limited perspective—the pain is there for the sake of a more inclusive good, whose reality eludes us because our intelligences are too weak to apprehend things in their entirety.

It is an appropriate retort to this argument that of course we judge things to be evil in a human perspective, but that since we are not God this is the only proper perspective in which to judge them. It may indeed be the case that what is evil for us is not evil for some other part of creation. However, we are not this other part of creation, and it is irrelevant to argue that were we something other than what we are, our evaluations of what is good and bad would be different. Moreover, the worthlessness of the argument becomes even more evident if we remind ourselves that it is unsupported speculation to suppose that whatever is evil in a finite perspective is good from the purported perspective of the totality of things. For the argument can be turned around: what we judge to be a good is a good only because it is viewed in isolation; when it is viewed in proper perspective, and in relation to the entire scheme of things, it is an evil. This is in fact a standard form of the argument for a universal pessimism. Is it any worse than the similar argument for a universal optimism? The very raising of this question is a *reductio ad absurdum* of the proposed solution to the ancient problem of evil.

I do not believe it is possible to reconcile the alleged omnipotence and omnibenevolence of God with the unvarnished facts of human existence. In point of fact, many theologians have concurred in this conclusion; for in order to escape from the difficulty which the traditional attributes of God present, they have assumed that God is not all powerful, and that there are limits as to what He can do in his efforts to establish a righteous order in the universe. But whether such a modified theology is better off, is doubtful; and in any event, the question still remains whether the facts of human life support the claim that an omnibenevolent Deity, though limited in power, is revealed in the ordering of human history. It is pertinent to note in this connection that though there have been many historians who have made the effort, no historian has yet succeeded in showing to the satisfaction of his professional colleagues that the hypothesis of a Divine Providence is capable of explaining anything which cannot be explained just as well without this hypothesis.

6

This last remark naturally leads to the question whether, apart from their polemics against theism, philosophical atheists have not shared a common set of positive views, a common set of philosophical convictions which set them off from other groups of thinkers. In one very clear sense of this query the answer is indubitably negative. For there never has been what one might call a "school of atheism," in the way in which there has been a Platonic school or even a Kantian school. In point of fact, atheistic critics of theism can be found among many of the conventional groupings of philosophical thinkers— even, I venture to add, among professional theologians in recent years who in effect preach atheism in the guise of language taken bodily from the Christian tradition.

Nevertheless, despite the variety of philosophic positions to which at one time or another in the history of thought atheists have subscribed, it seems to me that atheism is not simply a negative standpoint. At any rate, there is a certain quality of intellectual temper that has characterized, and continues to characterize, many philosophical atheists. (I am excluding from consideration the so-called "village atheist," whose primary concern is to twit and ridicule those who accept some form of theism, or for that matter those who have any religious convictions.) Moreover, their rejection of theism is based not only on the inadequacies they have found in the arguments for theism, but often also on the positive ground that atheism is a corollary to a better supported general outlook upon the nature of things. I want therefore to conclude this discussion with a brief enumeration of some points of positive doctrine to which by and large philosophical atheists seem to me to subscribe. These points fall into three major groups.

In the first place, philosophical atheists reject

the assumption that there are disembodied spirits, or that incorporeal entities of any sort can exercise a causal agency. On the contrary, atheists are generally agreed that if we wish to achieve any understanding of what takes place in the universe, we must look to the operations of organized bodies. Accordingly, the various processes taking place in nature, whether animate or inanimate, are to be explained in terms of the properties and structures of identifiable and spatio-temporally located objects. Moreover, the present variety of systems and activities found in the universe is to be accounted for on the basis of the transformations things undergo when they enter into different relations with one another—transformations which often result in the emergence of novel kinds of objects. On the other hand, though things are in flux and undergo alteration, there is no all-encompassing unitary pattern of change. Nature is ineradicably plural, both in respect to the individuals occurring in it as well as in respect to the processes in which things become involved. Accordingly, the human scene and the human perspective are not illusory; and man and his works are no less and no more "real" than are other parts or phases of the cosmos. At the risk of using a possibly misleading characterization, all of this can be summarized by saying that an atheistic view of things is a form of materialism.

In the second place, atheists generally manifest a marked empirical temper, and often take as their ideal the intellectual methods employed in the contemporaneous empirical sciences. Philosophical atheists differ considerably on important points of detail in their account of how responsible claims to knowledge are to be established. But there is substantial agreement among them that controlled sensory observation is the court of final appeal in issues concerning matters of fact. It is indeed this commitment to the use of an empirical method which is the final basis of the atheistic critique of theism. For at bottom this critique seeks to show that we can understand whatever a theistic assumption is alleged to explain, through the use of the proved methods of the positive sciences and without the introduction of empirically unsupported *ad hoc* hypotheses about a Deity. It is pertinent in this connection to recall a familiar legend about the French mathematical physicist Laplace. According to the story, Laplace made a personal presentation of a copy of his now famous book on celestial mechanics to Napoleon. Napoleon glanced through the volume, and finding no reference to the Deity asked Laplace whether God's existence played any role in the analysis. "Sire, I have no need for that hypothesis," Laplace is reported to have replied. The dismissal of sterile hypotheses characterizes not only the work of Laplace; it is the uniform rule in scientific inquiry. The sterility of the theistic assumption is one of the main burdens of the literature of atheism both ancient and modern.

And finally, atheistic thinkers have generally accepted a utilitarian basis for judging moral issues, and they have exhibited a libertarian attitude toward human needs and impulses. The conceptions of the human good they have advocated are conceptions which are commensurate with the actual capacities of mortal men, so that it is the satisfaction of the complex needs of the human creature which is the final standard for evaluating the validity of a moral ideal or moral prescription.

In consequence, the emphasis of atheistic moral reflection has been this-worldly rather than other-worldly, individualistic rather than authoritarian. The stress upon a good life that must be consummated in this world, has made atheists vigorous opponents of moral codes which seek to repress human impulses in the name of some unrealizable other-worldly ideal. The individualism that is so pronounced a strain in many philosophical atheists has made them tolerant of human limitations and sensitive to the plurality of legitimate moral goals. On the other hand, this individualism has certainly not prevented many of them from recognizing the crucial role which institutional arrangements can play in achieving desirable patterns of human living. In consequence, atheists have made important contributions to the development of a climate of opinion favorable to pursuing the values of a liberal civilization and they have played effective roles in attempts to rectify social injustices.

Atheists cannot build their moral outlook on foundations upon which so many men conduct their lives. In particular, atheism cannot offer the incentives to conduct and the consolations for misfortune which theistic religions supply to their adherents. It can offer no hope of personal immortality, no threats of Divine chastisement, no promise of eventual recompense for injustices suffered, no blueprints to sure salvation. For on its view of the place of man in nature, human excellence and human dignity must be achieved within a finite life-span, or not at all, so that the rewards of moral endeavor must come from the quality of civilized living, and not from some source of disbursement that dwells outside of time. Accordingly, atheistic moral reflection at its best does not culminate in a quiescent ideal of human perfection, but is a vigorous call to intelligent activity—activity for the sake of realizing human potentialities and for eliminating whatever stands in the way of such realization. Nevertheless, though slavish resignation to remediable ills is not characteristic of atheistic thought, responsible atheists have never pretended that human effort can invariably achieve the heart's every legitimate desire. A tragic view of life is thus an uneliminable ingredient in atheistic thought. This ingredient does not invite or generally produce lugubrious lamentation. But it does touch the atheist's view of man and his place in nature with an emotion that makes the philosophical atheist a kindred spirit to those who, within the frameworks of various religious traditions, have developed a serenely resigned attitude toward the inevitable tragedies of the human estate.

CHAPTER 51

ALVIN PLANTINGA

RELIGIOUS BELIEF WITHOUT EVIDENCE

Alvin Plantinga (1932–   ) has been the John A. O'Brien Professor of Philosophy at University of Notre Dame since 1982, after having taught at Yale University, Wayne State University, and Calvin College. Besides being an active member of the Christian Reformed Church, he has memberships in the Academy of Arts and Sciences, the Society of Christian Philosophers, and the American Philosophical Association (he acted as president of the Western division, 1981–1982). Plantinga has edited *Faith and Philosophy* (1964), *The Ontological Argument from St. Anselm to Contemporary Philosophers* (1965), and *Faith and Rationality* (with Nicholas Woltersdorff, 1983), and has authored *God and Other Minds: A Study of the Rational Justification of Belief in God* (1967), *The Nature of Necessity* (1974), and *God, Freedom and Evil* (1974). His areas of concentration include the philosophy of religion, epistemology, and metaphysics, and he has written on philosophy of science and the semantics of modal logic as well.

Plantinga contends that it is rational to believe in God even in the absence of evidence for such belief.[1] Those who believe that we must have adequate evidence for all of our beliefs (see W. K. Clifford's article in Part 2) fail to make their case, for they have not presented unambiguous criteria as to what counts for "adequate evidence" or how we can know that a belief is justified.

[1]From Alvin Plantinga, *Rationality and Religious Belief*, edited by C.F. Delaney (Notre Dame: University of Notre Dame Press, 1979), 7–12, and *Faith and Rationality*, edited by Alvin Plantinga and Nicholas Wolterstorff (Notre Dame: University of Notre Dame Press, 1983), 47–78.

Plantinga interprets the evidentialist/foundationalist position as one that claims that all justified beliefs must be either "properly basic" (by fulfilling certain criteria—for example, being self-evident, incorrigible, or evident through the senses) or be based on other beliefs. He then offers counter-examples to this position, showing that there are many beliefs that we hold to be justified that do not fit into the foundationalist framework, including memory beliefs, belief in an external world, and belief in other minds. Clearly, these beliefs are not dependent upon other beliefs, yet at the same time they are neither self-evident, incorrigible, or evident to the senses.

What then does it mean to be "properly basic?" Having demonstrated the elasticity of the concept, Plantinga argues next that John Calvin and the Protestant Reformers viewed belief in God as properly basic, summarizing their position for us. He invites us to consider this as a legitimate option, anticipating one powerful objection, which he calls "The Great Pumpkin Objection." If belief in God is called properly basic, why can't any belief be termed properly basic? Can the belief that the Great Pumpkin returns every Halloween be called properly basic? Plantinga answers, "Certainly not." Careful readers will want to ask themselves whether Plantinga's treatment of proper basicality and the Great Pumpkin objection is convincing—the philosophic community remains divided on this question.

RELIGIOUS BELIEFS WITHOUT EVIDENCE

What I mean to discuss, in this paper, is the question, Is belief in God rational? That is to say, I wish to discuss the question "Is it rational, or reasonable, or rationally acceptable, to believe in God?" I mean to *discuss* this question, not answer it. My initial aim is not to argue that religious belief *is* rational (although I think it is) but to try to understand this question.

The first thing to note is that I have stated the question misleadingly. What I really want to discuss is whether it is rational to believe that God exists—that there is such a person as God. Of course there is an important difference between believing that God exists and believing *in* God. To believe that God exists is just to accept a certain proposition—the proposition that there really is such a person as God—as true. According to the book of James (2:19) the devils

believe this proposition, and they tremble. To believe *in* God, however, is to trust him, to commit your life to him, to make his purposes your own. The devils do not do that. So there is a difference between believing in God and believing that he exists; for purposes of economy, however, I shall use the phrase 'belief in God' as a synonym for 'belief that God exists'.

Our question, therefore, is whether belief in God is rational. This question is widely asked and widely answered. Many philosophers—most prominently, those in the great tradition of natural theology—have argued that belief in God *is* rational; they have typically done so by providing what they took to be *demonstrations* or *proofs* of God's existence. Many others have argued that belief in God is *irrational*. If we call those of the first group 'natural theologians', perhaps we should call those of the second 'natural atheologians'. (That would at any rate be kinder than calling them 'unnatural theologians'.) J. L. Mackie, for example, opens his statement of the problem of evil as follows: "I think, however, that a more telling criticism can be made by way of the traditional problem of evil. Here it can be shown, not merely that religious beliefs lack rational support, but that they are positively irrational. . . ." And a very large number of philosophers take it that a central question—perhaps *the* central question—of philosophy of religion is the question whether religious belief in general and belief in God in particular is rationally acceptable.

Now an apparently straightforward and promising way to approach this question would be to take a definition of rationality and see whether belief in God conforms to it. The chief difficulty with this appealing course, however, is that no such definition of rationality seems to be available. If there *were* such a definition, it would set out some conditions for a belief's being rationally acceptable—conditions that are severally necessary and jointly sufficient. That is, each of the conditions would have to be met by a belief that is rationally acceptable; and if a belief met all the conditions, then it would follow that it is rationally acceptable. But it is monumentally difficult to find any non-trivial necessary conditions at all. Surely, for example, we cannot insist that S's belief that p is rational only if it is *true*. For consider Newton's belief that if x, y and z are moving colinearly, then the motion of z with respect to x is the sum of the motions of y with respect to x and z with respect to y. No doubt Newton was rational in accepting this belief; yet it was false, at least if contemporary physicists are to be trusted. And if they aren't—that is, if they are wrong in contradicting Newton—then *they* exemplify what I'm speaking of; they rationally believe a proposition which, as it turns out, is false.

Nor can we say that a belief is rationally acceptable only if it is possibly true, not necessarily false in the broadly logical sense. For example, I might do the sum $735 + 421 + 9{,}216$ several times and get the same answer: 10,362. I am then rational in believing that $735 + 421 + 9{,}216 = 10{,}362$, even though the fact is I've made the same error each time—failed to carry a '1' from the first column—and thus believe what is necessarily false. Or I might be a mathematical neophyte who hears from his teacher that every continuous function is differentiable. I need not be irrational in believing this, despite the fact that it is necessarily false. Examples of this sort can be multiplied.

So this question presents something of an initial enigma in that it is by no means easy to say what it is for a belief to be rational. And the fact is those philosophers who ask this question about belief in God do not typically try to answer it by giving necessary and sufficient conditions for rational belief. Instead, they typically ask whether the believer has *evidence* or *sufficient evidence* for his belief; or they may try to argue that in fact there is sufficient evidence for the proposition that there is *no* God; but in any case they try to answer this question by finding evidence for or against theistic belief. Philosophers who think there are sound arguments for the existence of God—the natural theologians— claim there is good evidence *for* this proposition; philosophers who believe that there are sound arguments for the non-existence of God naturally claim that there is evidence *against* this proposition. But they concur in holding that belief in God is rational only if there is, on balance, a preponderance of evidence for it—or less radically, only if there is not, on balance, a preponderance of evidence against it.

The nineteenth-century philosopher W. K. Clifford provides a splendid if somewhat strident example of the view that the believer in God must have evidence if he is not to be irrational. Here he does not discriminate against religious belief; he apparently holds that a belief of any sort at all is rationally acceptable only if there is sufficient evidence for it. And he goes on to insist that it is wicked, immoral, monstrous, and perhaps even impolite to accept a belief for which one does not have sufficient evidence:

> Whoso would deserve well of his fellows in this matter will guard the purity of his belief with a very fanaticism of jealous care, lest at any time it should rest on an unworthy object, and catch a stain which can never be wiped away.

He adds that if a

> belief has been accepted on insufficient evidence, the pleasure is a stolen one. Not only does it deceive ourselves by giving us a sense of power which we do not really possess, but it is sinful, because it is stolen in defiance of our duty to mankind. That duty is to guard ourselves from such beliefs as from a pestilence which may shortly master our body and spread to the rest of the town.

And finally:

> To sum up: it is wrong always, everywhere, and for anyone to believe anything upon insufficient evidence.

(It is not hard to detect, in these quotations, the "tone of robustious pathos" with which William James credits him.) Clifford finds it utterly obvious, furthermore, that those who believe in God do indeed so believe on insufficient evidence and thus deserve the above abuse. A believer in God is, on his view, at best a harmless pest and at worst a menace to society; in either case he should be discouraged.

Now there are some initial problems with Clifford's claim. For example, he doesn't tell us how *much* evidence is sufficient. More important, the notion of evidence is about as difficult as that of rationality: What is evidence? How do you know when you have some? How do you know when you have sufficient or enough? Suppose, furthermore, that a person thinks he has sufficient evidence for a proposition *p* when in fact he does not—would he then be irrational in believing *p*? Presumably a person can have sufficient evidence for what is false—else either Newton did not have sufficient evidence for his physical beliefs or contemporary physicists don't have enough for *theirs*. Suppose, then, that a person has sufficient evidence for the false proposition that he has sufficient evidence for *p*. Is he then irrational in believing *p*? Presumably not; but if not, having sufficient evidence is not, contrary to Clifford's claim, a necessary condition for believing *p* rationally.

But suppose we temporarily concede that these initial difficulties can be resolved and take a deeper look at Clifford's position. What is essential to it is the claim that we must evaluate the rationality of belief in God by examining its relation to *other* propositions. We are directed to estimate its rationality by determining whether we have *evidence* for it—whether we know, or at any rate rationally believe, some other propositions which stand in the appropriate relation to the proposition in question. And belief in God is rational, or reasonable, or rationally acceptable, on this view, only if there are other propositions with respect to which it is thus evident.

According to the Cliffordian position, then, there is a set of propositions *E* such that my belief in God is rational if and only if it is evident with respect to *E*—if and only if *E* constitutes, on balance, evidence for it. But what propositions are to be found in *E*? Do we know that belief in God is not itself in *E*? If it *is*, of course, then it is certainly evident with respect to E. How does a proposition get into E anyway? How do we decide which propositions are the ones such that my belief in God is rational if and only if it is evident with respect to them? Should we say that E contains the propositions that I *know*? But then, for our question to be interesting, we should first have to argue or agree that I don't know that God exists—that I only *believe* it, whether rationally or irrationally. This position is widely taken for granted, and indeed taken for granted by theists as well as others. But why should the latter concede that he doesn't know that God exists—that at best he rationally believes it? The Bible regularly speaks of *knowledge* in this context—not just rational or well-founded belief. Of course it is true that the believer has *faith*—faith in God, faith in what He reveals, faith that God exists— but this by no means settles the issue. The question is whether he doesn't also *know* that God exists. Indeed, according to the Heidelberg Catechism, knowledge is an essential element of faith, so that one has true faith that *p* only if he knows that *p*:

> True faith is not only a certain (i.e., sure) knowledge whereby I hold for truth all that God has revealed in His word, but also a deep-rooted assurance created in me by the Holy Spirit through the gospel that not only others but I too have had my sins forgiven, have been made forever right with God and have been granted salvation. (Q 21)

So from this point of view a man has true faith that *p* only if he knows that *p* and also meets a certain further condition: roughly (where *p* is a universal proposition) that of accepting the universal instantiation of *p* with respect to himself. Now of course the theist may be unwilling to concede that he does not have true faith that God exists; accordingly he may be unwilling to

concede—initially, at any rate—that he does not know, but only believes that God exists.

[After a discussion of others' attacks of theism from an evidentialist perspective, Plantinga turns to the foundationalist theory of knowledge, beginning with the classical version of that doctrine, held by Aquinas, Descartes, Locke, Clifford, and many others.]

Aquinas and the evidentialist objector [to theism] concur in holding that belief in God is rationally acceptable only if there is evidence for it— if, that is, it is probable with respect to some body of propositions that constitutes the evidence. And here we can get a better understanding of Aquinas and the evidentialist objector if we see them as accepting some version of *classical foundationalism*. This is a *picture* or total way of looking at faith, knowledge, justified belief, rationality, and allied topics. This picture has been enormously popular in Western thought; and despite a substantial opposing groundswell, I think it remains the dominant way of thinking about these topics. According to the foundationalist some propositions are properly basic and some are not; those that are not are rationally accepted only on the basis of *evidence*, where the evidence must trace back, ultimately, to what *is* properly basic. The existence of God, furthermore, is not among the propositions that are properly basic; hence a person is rational in accepting theistic belief only if he has evidence for it. The vast majority of those in the western world who have thought about our topic have accepted some form of classical foundationalism. The evidentialist objection to belief in God, furthermore, is obviously rooted in this way of looking at things. So suppose we try to achieve a deeper understanding of it.

Earlier I said the first thing to see about the evidentialist objection is that it is a *normative* contention or claim. The same thing must be said about foundationalism: this thesis is a normative thesis, a thesis about how a system of beliefs *ought* to be structured, a thesis about the properties of a correct, or acceptable, or rightly structured system of beliefs. According to the foundationalist there are norms, or duties, or obligations with respect to belief just as there are with respect to actions. To conform to these duties and obligations is to be rational; to fail to measure up to them is to be irrational. To be rational, then, is to exercise one's epistemic powers *properly*—to exercise them in such a way as to go contrary to none of the norms for such exercise. . . .

I think we can understand foundationalism more fully if we introduce the idea of a *noetic structure*. A person's noetic structure is the set of propositions he believes, together with certain epistemic relations that hold among him and these propositions. As we have seen, some of my beliefs may be based upon others; it may be that there are a pair of propositions A and B such that I believe B, and believe A *on the basis of B*. An account of a person's noetic structure, then, would specify which of his beliefs are basic and which nonbasic. Of course it is abstractly possible that *none* of his beliefs is basic; perhaps he holds just three beliefs, A, B, and C, and believes each of them on the basis of the other two. We might think this improper or irrational, but that is not to say it could not be done. And it is also possible that *all* of his beliefs are basic; perhaps he believes a lot of propositions but does not believe any of them on the basis of any others. In the typical case, however, a noetic structure will include both basic and nonbasic beliefs. It may be useful to give some examples of beliefs that are often basic for a person. Suppose I seem to see a tree; I have that characteristic sort of experience that goes with perceiving a tree. I may then believe the proposition that I see a tree. It is *possible* that I believe that proposition *on the basis of*

the proposition that I seem to see a tree; in the typical case, however, I will not believe the former on the basis of the latter because in the typical case I will not believe the latter at all. I will not be paying any attention to my experience but will be concentrating on the tree. Of course I *can* turn my attention to my experience, notice how things look to me, and acquire the belief that I seem to see something that looks like *that*; and if you challenge my claim that I see a tree, perhaps I *will* thus turn my attention to my experience. But in the typical case I will not believe that I see a tree on the basis of a proposition about my experience; for I believe A on the basis of B only if I believe B, and in the typical case where I perceive a tree I do not believe (or entertain) any propositions about my experience. Typically I take such a proposition as basic. Similarly, I believe I had breakfast this morning; this too is basic for me. I do not believe this proposition on the basis of some proposition about my experience—for example, that I seem to remember having had breakfast. In the typical case I will not have even considered *that* question—the question whether I *seem* to remember having had breakfast; instead I simply believe that I had breakfast; I take it as basic.

Second, an account of a noetic structure will include what we might call an index of *degree* of belief. I hold some of my beliefs much more firmly than others. I believe both that $2 + 1 = 3$ and that London, England, is north of Saskatoon, Saskatchewan; but I believe the former more resolutely than the latter. Some beliefs I hold with maximum firmness; others I do in fact accept, but in a much more tentative way. . . .

Third, a somewhat vaguer notion: an account of S's noetic structure would include something like an index of *depth of ingression*. Some of my beliefs are, we might say, on the periphery of my noetic structure. I accept them, and may even accept them firmly, but I could give them up without much change elsewhere in my noetic structure. I believe there are some large boulders on the top of the Grand Teton. If I come to give up this belief (say by climbing it and not finding any), that change need not have extensive reverberations throughout the rest of my noetic structure; it could be accommodated with minimal alteration elsewhere. So its depth of ingression into my noetic structure is not great. On the other hand, if I were to come to believe that there simply is no such thing as the Grand Teton, or no mountains at all, or no such thing as the state of Wyoming, that would have much greater reverberations. And suppose I were to come to think there had not been much of a past (that the world was created just five minutes ago, complete with all its apparent memories and traces of the past) or that there were not any other persons: these changes would have even greater reverberations; these beliefs of mine have great depth of ingression into my noetic structure. . . .

Now foundationalism is best construed, I think, as a thesis about *rational* noetic structures. A noetic structure is rational if it could be the noetic structure of a person who was completely rational. To be completely rational, as I am here using the term, is not to believe only what is true, or to believe all the logical consequences of what one believes, or to believe all necessary truths with equal firmness, or to be uninfluenced by emotion in forming belief; it is, instead, to do the right thing with respect to one's believings. It is to violate no epistemic duties. From this point of view, a rational person is one whose believings meet the appropriate standards; to criticize a person as irrational is to criticize her for failing to fulfill these duties or responsibilities, for failing to conform to the relevant norms or standards. To draw the ethical analogy, the irrational is the impermissible; the rational is the permissible. . . .

A rational noetic structure, then, is one that could be the noetic structure of a wholly rational person; and foundationalism, as I say, is a thesis about such noetic structures. We may think of the foundationalist as beginning with the observation that some of our beliefs are based upon others. According to the foundationalist a rational noetic structure will *have a foundation*—a set of beliefs not accepted on the basis of others; in a rational noetic structure some beliefs will be basic. Nonbasic beliefs, of course, will be accepted on the basis of other beliefs, which may be accepted on the basis of still other beliefs, and so on until the foundations are reached. In a rational noetic structure, therefore, every nonbasic belief is ultimately accepted on the basis of basic beliefs. . . .

According to the foundationalist, therefore, every rational noetic structure has a foundation, and all nonbasic beliefs are ultimately accepted on the basis of beliefs in the foundations. But a belief cannot properly be accepted on the basis of just *any* other belief; in a rational noetic structure, A will be accepted on the basis of B only if B *supports* A or is a member of a set of beliefs that together support A. It is not clear just what this relation—call it the "supports" relation—is; and different foundationalists propose different candidates. Presumably, however, it lies in the neighborhood of *evidence*; if A supports B, then A is evidence for B, or makes B evident; or perhaps B is likely or probable with respect to B. This relation admits of degrees. My belief that Feike can swim is supported by my knowledge that nine out of ten Frisians can swim and Feike is a Frisian; it is supported more strongly by my knowledge that the evening paper contains a picture of Feike triumphantly finishing first in the fifteen-hundred meter freestyle in the 1980 summer Olympics. And the foundationalist holds, sensibly enough, that in a rational noetic structure the strength of a nonbasic belief will depend upon the degree of support from foundational beliefs. . . .

By way of summary, then, let us say that according to foundationalism: (1) in a rational noetic structure the believed-on-the-basis-of relation is asymmetric and irreflexive, (2) a rational noetic structure has a foundation, and (3) in a rational noetic structure nonbasic belief is proportional in strength to support from the foundations.

Conditions on Proper Basicality

Next we note a further and fundamental feature of classic varieties of foundationalism: they all lay down certain conditions of proper basicality. From the foundationalist point of view not just any kind of belief can be found in the foundations of a rational noetic structure; a belief to be properly basic (that is, basic in a rational noetic structure) must meet certain conditions. It must be capable of functioning foundationally, capable of bearing its share of the weight of the whole noetic structure. Thus Thomas Aquinas, as we have seen, holds that a proposition is properly basic for a person only if it is self-evident to him or "evident to the senses."

Suppose we take a brief look at self-evidence. Under what conditions does a proposition have it? What kinds of propositions are self-evident? Examples would include very simple arithmetical truths such as

(1) $2 + 1 = 3$;

simple truths of logic such as

(2)   No man is both married and unmarried; perhaps the generalizations of simple truths of logic, such as

(3)   For any proposition p the conjunction of p with its denial is false; and certain propositions expressing identity and diversity; for example,

(4)   Redness is distinct from greenness,

(5)   The property of being prime is distinct from the property of being composite, and

(6)   The proposition *all men are mortal* is distinct from the proposition *all mortals are men.*

• • •

Still other candidates—candidates which may be less than entirely uncontroversial—come from many other areas; for example,

(7)   If p is necessarily true and p entails q, then q is necessarily true,

(8)   If e^1 occurs before e^2 and e^2 occurs before e^3, then e^1 occurs before e^3,

and

(9)   It is wrong to cause unnecessary (and unwanted) pain just for the fun of it.

What is it that characterizes these propositions? According to the tradition the outstanding characteristic of a self-evident proposition is that one simply sees it to be true upon grasping or understanding it. Understanding a self-evident proposition is sufficient for apprehending its truth. Of course this notion must be relativized to *persons;* what is self-evident to you might not be to me. Very simple arithmetical truths will be self-evident to nearly all of us, but a truth like $17 + 18 = 35$ may be self-evident only to some. And of course a proposition is self-evident to a person only if he does in fact grasp it, so a proposition will not be self-evident to those who do not apprehend the concepts it involves. As Aquinas says, some propositions are self-evident only to the learned; his example is the truth that immaterial substances do not occupy space. Among those propositions whose concepts not everyone grasps, some are such that anyone who *did* grasp them would see their truth; for example,

(10)   A model of a first-order theory T assigns truth to the axioms of T.

Others -17 + 13 = 30, for example—may be such that some but not all of those who apprehend them also see that they are true.

But how shall we understand this "seeing that they are true"? Those who speak of self-evidence explicitly turn to this visual metaphor and expressly explain self-evidence by reference to vision. There are two important aspects to the metaphor and two corresponding components to the idea of self-evidence. First, there is the *epistemic* component: a proposition p is self-evident to a person S only if S has *immediate* knowledge of p—that is, knows p, and does not know p on the basis of his knowledge of other propositions. Consider a simple arithmetic truth such as $2 + 1 = 3$ and compare it with one like $24 \times 24 = 576$. I know each of these propositions, and I know the second but not the first on the basis of computation, which is a kind of inference. So I have immediate knowledge of the first but not the second.

But there is also a phenomenological component. Consider again our two propositions; the first but not the second has about it a kind of luminous aura or glow when you bring it to mind or consider it. Locke speaks, in this connection, of an "evident luster"; a self-evident proposition, he says, displays a kind of "clarity and brightness to the attentive mind." Descartes speaks instead of "clarity and distinctness"; each, I think, is referring to the same phenomenological feature. And this feature is connected with another: upon understanding a proposition of this sort one feels a strong inclination to accept it; this luminous obviousness seems to compel or at least impel assent. Aquinas and Locke, indeed, held that a person, or at any rate a normal, well-formed human being, finds it impossible to withhold assent when considering a self-evident proposition. The phenomenological component of the idea of self-evidence, then, seems to have a double aspect: there is the luminous aura that $2 + 1 = 3$ displays, and there is also an experienced

tendency to accept or believe it. Perhaps, indeed, the luminous aura *just is* the experienced impulsion toward acceptance; perhaps these are the very same thing. In that case the phenomenological component would not have the double aspect I suggested it did have; in either case, however, we must recognize this phenomenological aspect of self-evidence.

Aquinas therefore holds that self-evident propositions are properly basic. I think he means to add that propositions "evident to the senses" are also properly basic. By this latter term I think he means to refer to *perceptual* propositions—propositions whose truth or falsehood we can determine by looking or employing some other sense. He has in mind, I think, such propositions as

(11)   There is a tree before me,
(12)   I am wearing shoes,

and

(13)   That tree's leaves are yellow.

So Aquinas holds that a proposition is properly basic if and only if it is either self-evident or evident to the senses. Other foundationalists have insisted that propositions basic in a rational noetic structure must be *certain* in some important sense. Thus it is plausible to see Descartes as holding that the foundations of a rational noetic structure include, not such propositions as (25)–(27), but more cautious claims—claims about one's own mental life; for example,

(14)   It seems to me that I see a tree,
(15)   I seem to see something green,

or, as Professor Chisholm puts it,

(16)   I am appeared greenly to.

Propositions of this latter sort seem to enjoy a kind of immunity from error not enjoyed by those of the former. I could be mistaken in think-

527

ing I see a pink rat; perhaps I am hallucinating or the victim of an illusion. But it is at the least very much harder to see that I could be mistaken in believing that I *seem* to see a pink rat, in believing that I am appeared pinkly (or pink ratly) to. Suppose we say that a proposition with respect to which I enjoy this sort of immunity from error is incorrigible for me; then perhaps Descartes means to hold that a proposition is properly basic for S only if it is either self-evident or incorrigible for S.

By way of explicit definition:

(17) p is incorrigible for S if and only if (a) it is not possible that S believe p and p be false, and (b) it is not possible that S believe $\tilde{p}$ and p be true.

• • •

Here we have a further characteristic of foundationalism: the claim that not just any proposition is properly basic. Ancient and medieval foundationalists tended to hold that a proposition is properly basic for a person only if it is either self-evident or evident to the senses; modern foundationalists—Descartes, Locke, Leibniz, and the like—tended to hold that a proposition is properly basic for S only if either self-evident or incorrigible for S. Of course this is a historical generalization and is thus perilous; but perhaps it is worth the risk. And now let us say that a *classical foundationalist* is any one who is either an ancient and medieval or a modern foundationalist.

The Collapse of Foundationalism

Now suppose we return to the main question: Why should not belief in God be among the foundations of my noetic structure? The answer, on the part of the classical foundationalist, was that even if this belief is *true*, it does not have the

characteristics a proposition must have to deserve a place in the foundations. There is no room in the foundations for a proposition that can be rationally accepted only on the basis of other propositions. The only properly basic propositions are those that are self-evident or incorrigible or evident to the senses. Since the proposition that God exists is none of the above, it is not properly basic for anyone; that is, no well-formed, rational noetic structure contains this proposition in its foundations. But now we must take a closer look at this fundamental principle of classical foundationalism:

(18)   A proposition p is properly basic for a person S if and only if p is either self-evident to S or incorrigible for S or evident to the senses for S.

(18) contains two claims: first, a proposition is properly basic *if* it is self-evident, incorrigible, or evident to the senses, and, second, a proposition is properly basic *only if* it meets this condition. The first seems true enough; suppose we concede it. But what is to be said for the second? Is there any reason to accept it? Why does the foundationalist accept it? Why does he think the theist ought to?

We should note first that if this thesis, and the correlative foundationalist thesis that a proposition is rationally acceptable only if it follows from or is probable with respect to what is properly basic—if these claims are true, then enormous quantities of what we all in fact believe are irrational. One crucial lesson to be learned from the development of modern philosophy—Descartes through Hume, roughly—is just this: relative to propositions that are self-evident and incorrigible, most of the beliefs that form the stock in trade of ordinary everyday life are not probable—at any rate there is no reason to think they are probable. Consider all those propositions that entail, say, that there are enduring physical objects, or that there are persons distinct from myself, or that the world has existed for more than five minutes: none of these propositions, I think, is more probable than not with respect to what is self-evident or incorrigible for me; at any rate no one has given good reason to think any of them is. And now suppose we add to the foundations propositions that are evident to the senses, thereby moving from modern to ancient and medieval foundationalism. Then propositions entailing the existence of material objects will of course be probable with respect to the foundations, because included therein. But the same cannot be said either for propositions about the past or for propositions entailing the existence of persons distinct from myself; as before, these will not be probable with respect to what is properly basic.

And does not this show that the thesis in question is false? The contention is that

(19)   A is properly basic for me only if A is self-evident or incorrigible or evident to the senses for me.

But many propositions that do not meet these conditions *are* properly basic for me. I believe, for example, that I had lunch this noon. I do not believe this proposition on the basis of other propositions; I take it as basic; it is in the foundations of my noetic structure. Furthermore, I am entirely rational in so taking it, even though this proposition is neither self-evident nor evident to the senses nor incorrigible for me. Of course this may not convince the foundationalist; he may think that in fact I do *not* take that proposition as basic, or perhaps he will bite the bullet and maintain that if I really *do* take it as basic, then the fact is I *am*, so far forth, irrational.

Perhaps the following will be more convincing. According to the classical foundationalist (call him *F*) a person *S* is rational in accepting (19) only if either (19) is properly basic (self-evident or incorrigible or evident to the senses) for him, or he believes (19) on the basis of propositions that are properly basic for him and support (19). Now presumably if *F* knows of some support for (19) from propositions that are self-evident or evident to the senses or incorrigible, he will be able to provide a good argument—deductive, inductive, probabilistic or whatever—whose premises are self-evident or evident to the senses or incorrigible and whose conclusion is (19). So far as I know, no foundationalist has provided such an argument. It therefore appears that the foundationalist does not know of any support for (19) from propositions that are (on his account) properly basic. So if he is to be rational in accepting (19), he must (on his own account) accept it as a basic. But according to (19) itself, (19) is properly basic for *F* only if (19) is self-evident or incorrigible or evident to the senses for him. Clearly (19) meets none of these conditions. Hence it is not properly basic for *F*. But then *F* is self-referentially inconsistent in accepting (19); he accepts (19) as basic, despite the fact that (19) does not meet the condition for proper basicality that (19) itself lays down.

Furthermore, (19) is either false or such that in accepting it the foundationalist is violating his epistemic responsibilities. For *F* does not know of any argument or evidence for (19). Hence if it is true, he will be violating his epistemic responsibilities in accepting it. So (19) is either false or such that *F* cannot rationally accept it. Still further, if the theist were to accept (19) at the foundationalist's urging but without argument, he would be adding to his noetic structure a proposition that is either false or such that in accepting it he violates his noetic responsibilities. But if there is such a thing as the ethics of belief, surely it will proscribe believing a proposition one knows to be either false or such that one ought not to believe it. Accordingly, I ought not to accept (19) in the absence of argument from premises that meet the condition it lays down. The same goes for the foundationalist: if he cannot find such an argument for (19), he ought to give it up. Furthermore, he ought not to urge and I ought not to accept any objection to theistic belief that crucially depends upon a proposition that is true only if I ought not believe it. . . .

Now we could canvass revisions of (19), and later I shall look into the proper procedure for discovering and justifying such criteria for proper basicality. It is evident, however, that classical foundationalism is bankrupt, and insofar as the evidentialist objection is rooted in classical foundationalism, it is poorly rooted indeed.

Of course the evidentialist objection *need* not presuppose classical foundationalism; someone who accepted quite a different version of foundationalism could no doubt urge this objection. But in order to evaluate it, we should have to see what criterion of proper basicality was being invoked. In the absence of such specification the objection remains at best a promissory note. So far as the present discussion goes, then, the next move is up to the evidentialist objector. He must specify a criterion for proper basicality that is free from self-referential difficulties, rules out belief in God as properly basic, and is such that there is some reason to think it is true. . . .

The Reformed Objection to Natural Theology

Suppose we think of natural theology as the attempt to prove or demonstrate the existence of God. This enterprise has a long and impressive history—a history stretching back to the dawn of Christendom and boasting among its adherents many of the truly great thinkers of the Western world. One thinks, for example, of Anselm, Aquinas, Scotus, and Ockham, of Descartes, Spinoza, and Leibniz. Recently—since

the time of Kant, perhaps—the tradition of natural theology has not been as overwhelming as it once was; yet it continues to have able defenders both within and without officially Catholic philosophy.

Many Christians, however, have been less than totally impressed. In particular Reformed or Calvinist theologians have for the most part taken a dim view of this enterprise. A few Reformed thinkers—B. B. Warfield, for example—endorse the theistic proofs, but for the most part the Reformed attitude has ranged from tepid endorsement, through indifference, to suspicion, hostility, and outright accusations of blasphemy. And this stance is initially puzzling. It looks a little like the attitude some Christians adopt toward faith healing: it can't be done, but even if it could it shouldn't be. What exactly, or even approximately, do these sons and daughters of the Reformation have against proving the existence of God? What *could* they have against it? What could be less objectionable to any but the most obdurate atheist?

THE OBJECTION INITIALLY STATED

By way of answering this question, I want to consider three representative Reformed thinkers. Let us begin with the nineteenth-century Dutch theologian Herman Bavinck:

A distinct natural theology, obtained apart from any revelation, merely through observation and study of the universe in which man lives, does not exist. . . .

Scripture urges us to behold heaven and earth, birds and ants, flowers and lilies, in order that we may see and recognize God in them. "Lift up your eyes on high, and see who hath created these." Is. 40:26. Scripture does not reason in the abstract. It does not make God the conclusion of a syllogism, leaving it to us whether we think the argument holds or not. But it speaks with authority. Both theologically and religiously it proceeds from God as the starting point.

We receive the impression that belief in the existence of God is based entirely upon these proofs. But indeed that would be "a wretched faith, which, before it invokes God, must first prove his existence." The contrary, however, is the truth. There is not a single object the existence of which we hesitate to accept until definite proofs are furnished. Of the existence of self, of the world round about us, of logical and moral laws, etc., we are so deeply convinced because of the indelible impressions which all these things make upon our consciousness that we need no arguments or demonstration. Spontaneously, altogether involuntarily: without any constraint or coercion, we accept that existence. Now the same is true in regard to the existence of God. The so-called proofs are by no means the final grounds of our most certain conviction that God exists. This certainty is established only by faith; that is, by the spontaneous testimony which forces itself upon us from every side.

According to Bavinck, then, belief in the existence of God is not based upon proofs or arguments. By "argument" here I think he means arguments in the style of natural theology—the sort given by Aquinas and Scotus and later by Descartes, Leibniz, Clarke, and others. And what he means to say, I think, is that Christians do not *need* such arguments. Do not need them for what?

Here I think Bavinck means to hold two things. First, arguments or proofs are not, in general, the source of the believer's confidence in God. Typically the believer does not believe in God on the basis of arguments; nor does he believe such truths as that God has created the world on the basis of arguments. Second, argu-

ment is not needed for *rational justification;* the believer is entirely within his epistemic right in believing, for example, that God has created the world, even if he has no argument at all for that conclusion. The believer does not need natural theology in order to achieve rationality or epistemic propriety in believing; his belief in God can be perfectly rational even if he knows of no cogent argument, deductive or inductive, for the existence of God—indeed, even if there is no such argument.

Bavinck has three further points. First he means to add, I think, that we cannot come to knowledge of God on the basis of argument; the arguments of natural theology just do not work. (And he follows this passage with a more or less traditional attempt to refute the theistic proofs, including an endorsement of some of Kant's fashionable confusions about the ontological argument.) Second, Scripture "proceeds from God as the starting point," and so should the believer. There is nothing by way of proofs or arguments for God's existence in the Bible; that is simply presupposed. The same should be true of the Christian believer then; he should *start* from belief in God rather than from the premises of some argument whose conclusion is that God exists. What is it that makes those premises a better starting point anyway? And third, Bavinck points out that belief in God relevantly resembles belief in the existence of the self and of the external world—and, we might add, belief in other minds and the past. In none of these areas do we typically *have* proof or arguments, or *need* proofs or arguments.

Suppose we turn next to John Calvin, who is as good a Calvinist as any. According to Calvin God has implanted in us all an innate tendency, or nisus, or disposition to believe in him:

'There is within the human mind, and indeed by natural instinct, an awareness of divinity.' This we take to be beyond controversy. To prevent anyone from taking refuge in the pretense of ignorance, God himself has implanted in all men a certain understanding of his divine majesty. Ever renewing its memory, he repeatedly sheds fresh drops. Since, therefore, men one and all perceive that there is a God and that he is their Maker, they are condemned by their own testimony because they have failed to honor him and to consecrate their lives to his will. If ignorance of God is to be looked for anywhere, surely one is most likely to find an example of it among the more backward folk and those more remote from civilization. Yet there is, as the eminent pagan says, no nation so barbarous, no people so savage, that they have not a deep-seated conviction that there is a God. So deeply does the common conception occupy the minds of all, so tenaciously does it inhere in the hearts of all! Therefore, since from the beginning of the world there has been no region, no city, in short, no household, that could do without religion, there lies in this a tacit confession of a sense of deity inscribed in the hearts of all.

Indeed, the perversity of the impious, who though they struggle furiously are unable to extricate themselves from the fear of God, is abundant testimony that this conviction, namely, that *there is some God,* is naturally inborn in all, and is fixed deep within, as it were in the very marrow. . . . From this we conclude *that it is not a doctrine that must first be learned in school,* but one of which each of us is master from his mother's womb and which nature itself permits no one to forget.

❙Calvin's claim, then, is that God has created us in such a way that we have a strong tendency or inclination toward belief in him.❙This tendency has been in part overlaid or suppressed by sin.

Were it not for the existence of sin in the world, human beings would believe in God to the same degree and with the same natural spontaneity that we believe in the existence of other persons, an external world, or the past. This is the natural human condition; it is because of our presently unnatural sinful condition that many of us find belief in God difficult or absurd. The fact is, Calvin thinks, one who does not believe in God is in an epistemically substandard position—rather like a man who does not believe that his wife exists, or thinks she is like a cleverly constructed robot and has no thoughts, feelings, or consciousness.

Although this disposition to believe in God is partially suppressed, it is nonetheless universally present. And it is triggered or actuated by a widely realized condition:

> Lest anyone, then, be excluded from access to happiness, he not only sowed in men's minds that seed of religion of which we have spoken, but revealed himself and daily discloses himself in the whole workmanship of the universe. As a consequence, men cannot open their eyes without being compelled to see him.

Like Kant, Calvin is especially impressed in this connection, by the marvelous compages of the starry heavens above:

> Even the common folk and the most untutored, who have been taught only by the aid of the eyes, cannot be unaware of the excellence of divine art, for it reveals itself in this innumerable and yet distinct and well-ordered variety of the heavenly host.

And Calvin's claim is that one who accedes to this tendency and in these circumstances accepts the belief that God has created the world—perhaps upon beholding the starry heavens, or the splendid majesty of the mountains, or the intricate, articulate beauty of a tiny flower—is entirely within his epistemic rights in so doing. It is not that such a person is justified or rational in so believing by virtue of having an implicit argument—some version of the teleological argument, say. No; he does not need any argument for justification or rationality. His belief need not be based on any other propositions at all; under these conditions he is perfectly rational in accepting belief in God in the utter absence of any argument, deductive or inductive. Indeed, a person in these conditions, says Calvin, *knows* that God exists.

Elsewhere Calvin speaks of "arguments from reason" or rational arguments:

> The prophets and apostles do not boast either of their keenness or of anything that obtains credit for them as they speak; nor do they dwell upon rational proofs. Rather, they bring forward God's holy name, that by it the whole world may be brought into obedience to him. Now we ought to see how apparent it is not only by plausible opinion but by clear truth that they do not call upon God's name heedlessly or falsely. If we desire to provide in the best way for our consciences—that they may not be perpetually beset by the instability of doubt or vacillation, and that they may not also boggle at the smallest quibbles—we ought to seek our conviction in a higher place than human reasons, judgments, or conjectures, that is, in the secret testimony of the Spirit. (book 1, chapter 7, p. 78)

Here the subject for discussion is not belief in the existence of God, but belief that God is the author of the Scriptures; I think it is clear, however, that Calvin would say the same thing about belief in God's existence. The Christian does not *need* natural theology, either as the source of his confidence or to justify his belief. Furthermore, the Christian *ought* not to believe on the basis of argument; if he does, his faith is likely to be "unstable and wavering," the "subject of perpetual doubt." If my belief in God is based on argument, then if I am to be properly rational, epistemically responsible, I shall have to keep checking the philosophical journals to see whether, say, Anthony Flew has finally come up with a good objection to my favorite argument. This could be bothersome and time-consuming; and what do I do if someone does find a flaw in my argument? Stop going to church? From Calvin's point of view believing in the existence of God on the basis of rational argument is like believing in the existence of your spouse on the basis of the analogical argument for other minds—whimsical at best and unlikely to delight the person concerned. . . .

Karl Barth joins Calvin and Bavinck in holding that the believer in God is entirely within his epistemic rights in believing as he does even if he does not know of any good theistic argument. They all hold that belief in God is *properly basic*—that is, such that it is rational to accept it without accepting it on the basis of any other proposition or beliefs at all. In fact, they think the Christian ought not to accept belief in God on the basis of argument; to do so is to run the risk of a faith that is unstable and wavering, subject to all the wayward whim and fancy of the latest academic fashion. What the Reformers held was that a believer is entirely rational, entirely within his epistemic rights, in *starting with* belief in God, in accepting it as basic, and in taking it as premise for argument to other conclusions.

In rejecting natural theology, therefore, these Reformed thinkers mean to say first of all that the propriety or rightness of belief in God in no way depends upon the success or availability of the sort of theistic arguments that form the natural theologian's stock in trade. I think this is their central claim here, and their central insight. As these Reformed thinkers see things, one who takes belief in God as basic in not thereby violating any epistemic duties or revealing a defect in his noetic structure; quite the reverse. The correct or proper way to believe in God, they thought, was not on the basis of arguments from natural theology or anywhere else; the correct way is to take belief in God as basic.

I spoke earlier of classical foundationalism, a view that incorporates the following three theses:

(1) In every rational noetic structure there is a set of beliefs taken as basic—that is, not accepted on the basis of any other beliefs,

(2) In a rational noetic structure nonbasic belief is proportional to support from the foundations,

and

(3) In a rational noetic structure basic beliefs will be self-evident or incorrigible or evident to the senses.

Now I think these three Reformed thinkers should be understood as rejecting classical foundationalism. They may have been inclined to accept (1); they show no objection to (2); but they were utterly at odds with the idea that the foundations of a rational noetic structure can at most include propositions that are self-evident or evident to the senses or incorrigible. In particular, they were prepared to insist that a rational noetic structure can include belief in God as basic. As Bavinck put it, "Scripture . . . does not make God the conclusion of a syllogism, leaving it to us whether we think the argument holds or not. But it speaks with authority. Both theologi-

cally and religiously it proceeds from God as the starting point." And of course Bavinck means to say that we must emulate Scripture here.

In the passages I quoted earlier, Calvin claims the believer does not need argument—does not need it, among other things, for epistemic respectability. We may understand him as holding, I think, that a rational noetic structure may very well contain belief in God among its foundations. Indeed, he means to go further, and in two separate directions. In the first place he thinks a Christian *ought* not believe in God on the basis of other propositions; a proper and well-formed Christian noetic structure will *in fact* have belief in God among its foundations. And in the second place Calvin claims that one who takes belief in God as basic can *know* that God exists. Calvin holds that one can *rationally accept* belief in God as basic; he also claims that one can *know* that God exists even if he has no argument, even if he does not believe on the basis of other propositions. A foundationalist is likely to hold that some properly basic beliefs are such that anyone who accepts them *knows* them. More exactly, he is likely to hold that among the beliefs properly basic for a person S, some are such that if S accepts them, S knows them. He could go on to say that *other* properly basic beliefs cannot be known if taken as basic, but only rationally believed; and he might think of the existence of God as a case in point. Calvin will have none of this; as he sees it, one needs no arguments to know that God exists. . . .

Is Belief in God Properly Basic?

THE GREAT PUMPKIN OBJECTION

It is tempting to raise the following sort of question. If belief in God is properly basic, why cannot *just any* belief be properly basic? Could we not say the same for any bizarre aberration we can think of? What about voodoo or astrology? What about the belief that the Great Pumpkin returns every Halloween? Could I properly take *that* as basic? Suppose I believe that if I flap my arms with sufficient vigor, I can take off and fly about the room; could I defend myself against the charge of irrationality by claiming this belief is basic? If we say that belief in God is properly basic, will we not be committed to holding that just anything, or nearly anything, can properly be taken as basic, thus throwing wide the gates to irrationalism and superstition?

[Certainly not.] According to the Reformed epistemologist certain beliefs are properly basic in certain circumstances; those same beliefs may *not* be properly basic in other circumstances. Consider the belief that I see a tree: this belief is properly basic in circumstances that are hard to describe in detail, but include my being appeared to in a certain characteristic way; that same belief is not properly basic in circumstances including, say, my knowledge that I am sitting in the living room listening to music with my eyes closed. What the Reformed epistemologist holds is that there are widely realized circumstances in which belief in God is properly basic; but why should that be thought to commit him to the idea that just about *any* belief is properly basic in any circumstances, or even to the vastly weaker claim that for any belief there are circumstances in which it is properly basic? Is it just that he rejects the criteria for proper basicality purveyed by classical foundationalism? But why should *that* be thought to commit him to such tolerance of irrationality? Consider an analogy. In the palmy days of positivism the positivists went about confidently wielding their verifiability criterion and declaring meaningless much that was clearly meaningful. Now suppose someone rejected a formulation of that criterion—the one to be found in the second edition of A. J. Ayer's *Language, Truth and Logic,* for example. Would that mean she was committed to holding that

(1)   T' was brillig; and the slithy toves did gyre and gymble in the wabe,

contrary to appearances, makes good sense? Of course not. But then the same goes for the Reformed epistemologist: the fact that he rejects the criterion of proper basicality purveyed by classical foundationalism does not mean that he is committed to supposing just anything is properly basic.

But what then is the problem? Is it that the Reformed epistemologist not only rejects those criteria for proper basicality but seems in no hurry to produce what he takes to be a better substitute? If he has no such criterion, how can he fairly reject belief in the Great Pumpkin as properly basic?

This objection betrays an important misconception. How *do* we rightly arrive at or develop criteria for meaningfulness, or justified belief, or proper basicality? Where do they come from? Must one have such a criterion before one can sensibly make any judgments—positive or negative—about proper basicality? Surely not. Suppose I do not know of a satisfactory substitute for the criteria proposed by classical foundationalism; I am nevertheless entirely within my epistemic rights in holding that certain propositions in certain conditions are not properly basic.

Some propositions seem self-evident when in fact they are not; that is the lesson of some of the Russell paradoxes. Nevertheless it would be irrational to take as basic the denial of a proposition that seems self-evident to you. Similarly, suppose it seems to you that you see a tree; you would then be irrational in taking as basic the proposition that you do not see a tree or that there are no trees. In the same way, even if I do not know of some illuminating criterion of meaning, I can quite properly declare (1) (above) meaningless.

And this raises an important question—one Roderick Chisholm has taught us to ask. What is the status of criteria for knowledge, or proper basicality, or justified belief? Typically these are universal statements. The modern foundationalist's criterion for proper basicality, for example, is doubly universal:

(2) For any proposition *A* and person *S*, *A* is properly basic for *S* if and only if *A* is incorrigible for *S* or self-evident to *S*.

But how could one know a thing like that? What are its credentials? Clearly enough, (2) is not self-evident or just obviously true. But if it is not, how does one arrive at it? What sorts of arguments would be appropriate? Of course a foundationalist might find (2) so appealing he simply takes it to be true, neither offering argument for it nor accepting it on the basis of other things he believes. If he does so, however, his noetic structure will be self-referentially incoherent. (2) itself is neither self-evident nor incorrigible; hence if he accepts (2) as basic, the modern foundationalist violates in accepting it the condition of proper basicality he himself lays down. On the other hand, perhaps the foundationalist will try to produce some argument for it from premises that are self-evident or incorrigible: it is exceeding hard to see, however, what such an argument might be like. And until he has produced such arguments, what shall the rest of us do—we who do not find (2) at all obvious or compelling? How could he use (2) to show us that belief in God, for example, is not properly basic? Why should we believe (2) or pay it any attention?

The fact is, I think, that neither (2) nor any other revealing necessary and sufficient condition for proper basicality follows from clearly self-evident premises by clearly acceptable arguments. And hence the proper way to arrive at such a criterion is, broadly speaking, *inductive*. We must assemble examples of beliefs and conditions such that the former are obviously properly basic in the latter, and examples of beliefs and conditions such that the former are obviously *not* properly basic in the latter. We must then frame hypotheses as to the necessary and sufficient conditions of proper basicality and test these hypotheses by reference to those examples. Under the right conditions, for example, it is clearly rational to believe that you see a human person before you: a being who has thoughts and feelings, who knows and believes things, who makes decisions and acts. It is clear, furthermore, that you are under no obligation to reason to this belief from others you hold; under those conditions that belief is properly basic for you. But then (2) must be mistaken; the belief in question, under those circumstances, is properly basic, though neither self-evident nor incorrigible for you. Similarly, you may seem to remember that you had breakfast this morning, and perhaps you know of no reason to suppose your memory is playing you tricks. If so, you are entirely justified in taking that belief as basic. Of course it is not properly basic on the criteria offered by classical foundationalists, but that fact counts not against you but against those criteria. . . .

Accordingly, criteria for proper basicality must be reached from below rather than above; they should not be presented *ex cathedra* but argued to and tested by a relevant set of examples. But there is no reason to assume, in advance, that everyone will agree on the examples. The Christian will of course suppose that belief in God is entirely proper and rational; if he does not accept this belief on the basis of other propositions, he will conclude that it is basic for him and quite properly so. Followers of Bertrand Russell and Madelyn Murray O'Hare may disagree; but how is that relevant? Must my criteria, or those of the Christian community, conform to their examples? Surely not. The Christian community is responsible to *its* set of examples, not to theirs. . . .

So, the Reformed epistemologist can properly hold that belief in the Great Pumpkin is not properly basic, even though he holds that belief in God is properly basic and even if he has no full-fledged criterion of proper basicality. Of course he is committed to supposing that there is a relevant *difference* between belief in God and belief in the Great Pumpkin if he holds that the former but not the latter is properly basic. But this should prove no great embarrassment; there

are plenty of candidates. These candidates are to be found in the neighborhood of the conditions that justify and ground belief in God—conditions I shall discuss in the next section. Thus, for example, the Reformed epistemologist may concur with Calvin in holding that God has implanted in us a natural tendency to see his hand in the world around us; the same cannot be said for the Great Pumpkin, there being no Great Pumpkin and no natural tendency to accept beliefs about the Great Pumpkin.

CONTEMPORARY PERSPECTIVES: THE PROBLEM OF EVIL RE-VISITED

The two selections that follow were presented at a symposium held in 1975 at the University of Lancaster in England. Richard Swinburne defends a theodicy against D. Z. Phillips, who argues that the very attempt to explain the problem of evil is a radical mistake.

In "The Problem of Evil," Swinburne distinguishes various forms of evil and shows how a theist accounts for them, offering plausible responses to each objection. He makes an important distinction between active and passive evil: Active evil is that which is directly caused by human (or rational) immoral action, while passive evil is that caused by nonmoral actions or by nature itself. To meet the objection that God should not have allowed moral evil to occur, Swinburne appeals to the free will defense: It was logically impossible for God to make a world wherein humans are free but do not practice evil. Regarding passive evil caused by humans, he argues that in order for humans to be fully responsible it is necessary for God to allow their effects upon others to be significant. Hence there must be deterministic physical laws in nature that allow reliable expectations of how human behavior will affect others.

This principle of the "uniformity of nature" also explains the presence of passive evil not due to humans. The laws of nature are such that the good is interconnected with the bad. The same rain that causes one farmer's field to germinate will ruin another farmer's field. Although there are limits to the amount of passive nonhuman evil God will allow, God cannot constantly intervene in the natural sphere without eroding either human responsibility or the laws of nature. Finite human creatures, alas, cannot hope to know where these limits of evil are.

Swinburne concludes his essay with an important insight that touches on one of the central insights of Christianity—the notion of God becoming human (the "incarnation" of God in Jesus Christ) in order to experience and empathize with the sufferings of humanity. As Swinburne puts it, "A creator is more justified in creating or permitting evils to be overcome by his creatures if he is prepared to share with them the burden of the suffering and effort."

In his critique of Swinburne's arguments, the Wittgensteinian fideist D. Z. Phillips attacks all theodicies as both futile and inappropriate. Recalling an observation made by Kierkegaard, Phillips likens Swinburne's approach to a journey that ought not to be made. Theodicists are attempting to explain what is, at bottom, a mystery. Not only are their endeavors bound to fail, more seriously, they are also an inappropriate response to the fact of evil in the world. The existence of evil need not and in fact does not prevent one from being a theist. Phillips's point is that human suffering and pain must shake us to our very core—it must be felt rather than analyzed. Attempting to treat it as some kind of logical puzzle makes the problem cold and abstract, when in fact it is anything but abstract to those who experience evil in their lives. The only proper response to evil is moral action and a sense of empathy with those who are afflicted. Phillips charges Swinburne with failing to deal with the existential nature of evil, a concrete reality that we all experience and which overwhelms many of us.

Phillips' argument raises an interesting point. Even if theists can demonstrate that there is no inconsistency in Epicurus's three premises, have they done enough? Many persons, including those who are devoutly religious, often experience psychological doubt in moments of intense suffering. Phillips would have us empathize with these individuals, sharing their pain and grief and a full sense of the agony and mystery of evil. Can we feel the agony and mystery of evil and at the same time attempt to provide philosophical explanations? Seemingly not. Perhaps we need to make a distinction between two different kinds of human contexts: one being the context of normal human activity in which people engage in social interaction, the other being the more specific context of philosophical analysis in which explanation and argument are legitimate and entirely appropriate. Confusing these two contexts would be a category mistake; hence, articulating a theodicy to an individual who has just lost a child to leukemia would be entirely inappropriate. It may well be appropriate, however, when the individual who has suffered the loss recovers sufficiently to wish to understand the reasons for what has occurred.

CHAPTER 52

RICHARD SWINBURNE

THE PROBLEM OF EVIL

Richard Swinburne (1934–   ) is Nolloth Professor of Philosophy of Religion at Oxford University. Acknowledged as one of the leading philosophers of religion in the world, he is the author of a trilogy of books on the subject, *The Coherence of Theism* (1977), *The Existence of God* (1979), and *Faith and Reason* (1981). He is also the author of *The Concept of Miracle* (1971) and *Space and Time* (1981).

THE PROBLEM OF EVIL[1]

Introduction

God is, by definition, omniscient, omnipotent, and perfectly good. By "omniscient" I understand "one who knows all true propositions." By "omnipotent" I understand "able to do anything logically possible." By "perfectly good" I understand "one who does no morally bad action," and I include among actions omissions to perform some action. The problem of evil is then often stated as the problem whether the existence of God is compatible with the existence of evil. Against the suggestion of compatibility, an atheist often suggests that the existence of evil entails the nonexistence of God. For, he argues, if God exists, then being omniscient, he knows under what circumstances evil will occur, if he does not

[1]Reprinted from Richard Swinburne, "The Problem of Evil," in *Reason and Religion*, edited by Stuart C. Brown. Copyright © 1977 by the Royal Institute of Philosophy. Used by the permission of the publisher, Cornell University Press.

act; and being omnipotent, he is able to prevent its occurrence. Hence, being perfectly good, he will prevent its occurrence and so evil will not exist. Hence the existence of God entails the nonexistence of evil. Theists have usually attacked this argument by denying the claim that necessarily a perfectly good being, foreseeing the occurrence of evil and able to prevent it, will prevent it. And indeed, if evil is understood in the very wide way in which it normally is understood in this context, to include physical pain of however slight a degree, the cited claim is somewhat implausible. For it implies that if through my neglecting frequent warnings to go to the dentist, I find myself one morning with a slight toothache, then necessarily, there does not exist a perfectly good being who foresaw the evil and was able to have prevented it. Yet it seems fairly obvious that such a being might well choose to allow me to suffer some mild consequences of my folly—as a lesson for the future which would do me real harm.

The threat to theism seems to come, not from the existence of evil as such, but rather from the existence of evil of certain kinds and degrees—severe undeserved physical pain or mental anguish, for example. I shall therefore list briefly the kinds of evil which are evident in our world, and ask whether their existence in the degrees in which we find them is compatible with the existence of God. I shall call the man who argues for compatibility the theodicist, and his opponent the antitheodicist. The theodicist will claim that it is not morally wrong for God to create or permit the various evils, normally on the grounds that doing so is providing the logically necessary conditions of greater goods. The antitheodicist denies these claims by putting forward moral principles which have as consequences that a good God would not under any circumstances create or permit the evils in question. I shall argue that these moral principles are

not, when carefully examined, at all obvious, and indeed that there is a lot to be said for their negations. Hence I shall conclude that it is plausible to suppose that the existence of these evils is compatible with the existence of God.

Since I am discussing only the compatibility of various evils with the existence of God, I am perfectly entitled to make occasionally some (non–self-contradictory) assumption, and argue that if it was true, the compatibility would hold. For if p is compatible with q, given r (where r is not self-contradictory), then p is compatible with q simpliciter. It is irrelevant to the issue of compatibility whether these assumptions are true. If, however, the assumptions which I make are clearly false, and if also it looks as if the existence of God is compatible with the existence of evil *only* given those assumptions, the formal proof of compatibility will lose much of interest. To avoid this danger, I shall make only such assumptions as are not clearly false—and also in fact the ones which I shall make will be ones to which many theists are already committed for entirely different reasons.

The Problem of Evil: Types

What then is wrong with the world? First, there are painful sensations, felt both by men, and, to a lesser extent, by animals. Second, there are painful emotions, which do not involve pain in the literal sense of this word—for example, feelings of loss and failure and frustration. Such suffering exists mainly among men, but also, I suppose, to some small extent among animals too. Third, there are evil and undesirable states of affairs, mainly states of men's minds, which do not involve suffering. For example, there are the states of mind of hatred and envy; and such states of the world as rubbish tipped over a beauty spot. And fourth, there are the evil actions of men, mainly actions having as foreseeable consequences evils of the first three types, but perhaps other actions as well—such as lying and promise breaking with no such foreseeable consequences. As before, I include among actions, omissions to perform some actions. If there are rational agents other than men and God (if he exists), such as angels or devils or strange beings on distant planets, who suffer and perform evil actions, then their evil feelings, states, and actions must be added to the list of evils.

I propose to call evil of the first type physical evil, evil of the second type mental evil, evil of the third type state evil, and evil of the fourth type moral evil. Since there is a clear contrast between evils of the first three types, which are evils that happen to men or animals or the world, and evils of the fourth type, which are evils that men do, there is an advantage in having one name for evils of any of the first three types—I shall call these passive evils. I distinguish evil from mere absence of good. Pain is not simply the absence of pleasure. A headache is a pain, whereas not having the sensation of drinking whiskey is, for many people, mere absence of pleasure. Likewise, the feeling of loss in bereavement is an evil involving suffering, to be contrasted with the mere absence of the pleasure of companionship. Some thinkers have, of course, claimed that a good God would create a "best of all (logically) possible worlds" (i.e., a world than which no better is logically possible), and for them the mere absence of good creates a problem since it looks as if a world would be a better world if it had that good. For most of us, however, the mere absence of good seems less of a threat to theism than the presence of evil, partly because it is not at all clear whether any sense can be given to the concept of a best of all possible worlds (and if it cannot then of logical necessity there will be a better world than any creatable world) and partly because even if sense can

be given to this concept it is not at all obvious that God has an obligation to create such a world—to whom would he be doing an injustice if he did not? My concern is with the threat to theism posed by the existence of evil.

Objection 1: God Ought Not to Create Evildoers

Now much of the evil in the world consists of the evil actions of men and the passive evils brought about by those actions. (These include the evils brought about intentionally by men, and also the evils which result from long years of slackness by many generations of men. Many of the evils of 1975 are in the latter category, and among them many state evils. The hatred and jealousy which many men and groups feel today result from an upbringing consequent on generations of neglected opportunities for reconciliations.) The antitheodicist suggests as a moral principle ($P1$) that a creator able to do so ought to create only creatures such that necessarily they do not do evil actions. From this it follows that God would not have made men who do evil actions. Against this suggestion the theodicist naturally deploys the free-will defense, elegantly expounded in recent years by Alvin Plantinga. This runs roughly as follows: it is not logically possible for an agent to make another agent such that necessarily he freely does only good actions. Hence if a being G creates a free agent, he gives to the agent power of choice between alternative actions, and how he will exercise that power is something which G cannot control while the agent remains free. It is a good thing that there exist free agents, but a logically necessary consequence of their existence is that their power to choose to do evil actions may sometimes be realized. The price is worth paying, however, for the existence of agents performing free actions remains a good thing even if they sometimes do evil. Hence it is not logically possible that a creator create free creatures "such that necessarily they do not do evil actions." But it is not a morally bad thing that he create free creatures, even with the possibility of their doing evil. Hence the cited moral principle is implausible.

The free-will defense as stated needs a little filling out. For surely there could be free agents who did not have the power of moral choice, agents whose only opportunities for choice were between morally indifferent alternatives—between jam and marmalade for breakfast, between watching the news on BBC 1 or the news on ITV. They might lack this power either because they lacked the power of making moral judgments (i.e., lacked moral discrimination); or because all their actions which were morally assessable were caused by factors outside their control; or because they saw with complete clarity what was right and wrong and had no temptation to do anything except the right. The free-will defense must claim, however, that it is a good thing that there exist free agents with the power and opportunity of choosing between morally good and morally evil actions, agents with sufficient moral discrimination to have some idea of the difference and some (though not overwhelming) temptation to do other than the morally good. Let us call such agents humanly free agents. The defense must then go on to claim that it is not logically possible to create humanly free agents such that necessarily they do not do morally evil actions. Unfortunately, this latter claim is highly debatable, and I have no space to debate it. I propose therefore to circumvent this issue as follows. I shall add to the definition of humanly free agents, that they are agents whose choices do not have fully deterministic precedent causes. Clearly then it will not be logically possible to create humanly free agents whose choices go one way rather than another, and so not logically

possible to create humanly free agents such that necessarily they do not do evil actions. Then the free-will defense claims that (P1) is not universally true; it is not morally wrong to create human free agents—despite the real possibility that they will do evil. Like many others who have discussed this issue, I find this a highly plausible suggestion. Surely as parents we regard it as a good thing that our children have power to do free actions of moral significance—even if the consequence is that they sometimes do evil actions. This conviction is likely to be stronger, not weaker, if we hold that the free actions with which we are concerned are ones which do not have fully deterministic precedent causes. In this way we show the existence of God to be compatible with the existence of moral evil—but only subject to a very big assumption—that men are humanly free agents. If they are not, the compatibility shown by the free-will defense is of little interest. For the agreed exception to (P1) would not then justify a creator making men who did evil actions; we should need a different exception to avoid incompatibility. The assumption seems to me not clearly false, and is also one which most theists affirm for quite other reasons. Needless to say, there is no space to discuss the assumption here.

Objection 2: Against Passive Evil

All that the free-will defense has shown so far, however (and all that Plantinga seems to show), is grounds for supposing that the existence of moral evil is compatible with the existence of God. It has not given grounds for supposing that the existence of evil consequences of moral evils is compatible with the existence of God. In an attempt to show an incompatibility, the antitheodicist may suggest instead of (P1), (P2)—that a creator able to do so ought always to ensure that any creature whom he creates does not cause passive evils, or at any rate passive evils which hurt creatures other than himself. For could not God have made a world where there are humanly free creatures, men with the power to do evil actions, but where those actions do not have evil consequences, or at any rate evil consequences which affect others—e.g., a world where men cannot cause pain and distress to other men? Men might well do actions which are evil either because they were actions which they believed would have evil consequences or because they were evil for some other reason (e.g., actions which involved promise breaking) without them in fact having any passive evils as consequences. Agents in such a world would be like men in a simulator training to be pilots. They can make mistakes, but no one suffers through those mistakes. Or men might do evil actions which did have the evil consequences which were foreseen but which damaged only themselves. . . .

I do not find (P2) a very plausible moral principle. A world in which no one except the agent was affected by his evil actions might be a world in which men had freedom but it would not be a world in which men had responsibility. The theodicist claims that it would not be wrong for God to create interdependent humanly free agents, a society of such agents responsible for each other's well-being, able to make or mar each other.

Fair enough, the antitheodicist may again say. It is not wrong to create a world where creatures have responsibilities for each other. But might not those responsibilities simply be that creatures had the opportunity to benefit or to withhold benefit from each other, not a world in which they had also the opportunity to cause each other pain? One answer to this is that if creatures have only the power to benefit and not the power to hurt each other, they obviously lack any very strong responsibility for each other. To bring out the point by a caricature—a world in which I could choose whether or not to give you sweets, but not whether or not to break your leg or make you unpopular, is not a world in which I have a very strong influence on your destiny, and so not a world in which I have a very full responsibility for you. Further, however, there is a point which will depend on an argument which I will give further on. In the actual world very often a man's withholding benefits from another is correlated with the latter's suffering some passive evil, either physical or mental. Thus if I withhold from you certain vitamins, you will suffer disease. Or if I deprive you of your wife by persuading her to live with me instead, you will suffer grief at the loss. Now it seems to me that a world in which such correlations did not hold would not necessarily be a better world than the world in which they do. The appropriateness of pain to bodily disease or deprivation, and of mental evils to various losses or lacks of a more spiritual kind, is something for which I shall argue in detail a little later.

So then the theodicist objects to (P2) on the grounds that the price of possible passive evils for other creatures is a price worth paying for agents to have great responsibilities for each other. It is a price which (logically) must be paid if they are to have those responsibilities. Here again a reasonable antitheodicist may see the point. In bringing up our own children, in order to give them responsibility, we try not to interfere too quickly in their quarrels—even at the price, sometimes, of younger children getting hurt physically. We try not to interfere, first, in order to train our children for responsibility in later life and second because responsibility here and now is a good thing in itself. True, with respect to the first reason, whatever the effects on character produced by training, God could produce without training. But if he did so by imposing a full character on a humanly free creature, this would be giving him a character which he had not in any way chosen or adopted for himself. Yet it would seem a good thing that a creator should allow humanly free creatures to influence by their own choices the sort of creatures they are to be, the kind of character they are to have. That means that the creator must create them immature, and allow them gradually to make decisions which affect the sort of beings they will be. And one of the greatest privileges which a creator can give to a creature is to allow him to help in the process of education, in putting alternatives before his fellows.

Objection 3: The Quantity of Evil

Yet though the antitheodicist may see the point, in theory, he may well react to it rather like this. "Certainly some independence is a good thing. But surely a father ought to interfere if his younger son is really getting badly hurt. The ideal of making men free and responsible is a good one, but there are limits to the amount of responsibility which it is good that men should have, and in our world men have too much responsibility. A good God would certainly have intervened long ago to stop some of the things which happen in our world." Here, I believe, lies the crux—it is simply a matter of quantity. The theodicist says that a good God could allow men to do to each other the hurt they do, in order to allow them to be free and responsible. But against him the antitheodicist puts forward as a moral principle (P3) that a creator able to do so ought to ensure that any creature whom he creates does not cause passive evils as many and as evil as those in our world. He says that in our world freedom and responsibility have gone too far—produced too much physical and mental hurt. God might well tolerate a boy hitting his younger brothers, but not Belsen.

The theodicist is in no way committed to saying that a good God will not stop things getting too bad. Indeed, if God made our world, he has clearly done so. There are limits to the amount and degree of evil which are possible in our world. Thus there are limits to the amount of pain which a person can suffer—persons live in our world only so many years and the amount which they can suffer at any given time (if mental goings-on are in any way correlated with bodily ones) is limited by their physiology. Further, theists often claim that from time to time God intervenes in the natural order which he has made to prevent evil which would otherwise occur. So the theodicist can certainly claim that a good God stops too much sufferings—it is just that he and his opponent draw the line in different places. The issue as regards the passive evils caused by men turns ultimately to the quantity of evil. To this crucial matter I shall return toward the end of the paper.

The Interconnectedness of Good and Evil

We shall have to turn next to the issue of passive evils not apparently caused by men. But, first, I must consider a further argument by the theodicist in support of the free-will defense and also an argument of the antitheodicist against it. The first is the argument that various evils are logically necessary conditions for the occurrence of actions of certain especially good kinds. Thus for a man to bear his suffering cheerfully there has to be suffering for him to bear. There have to be acts which irritate for another to show tolerance of them. Likewise, it is often said, acts of forgiveness, courage, self-sacrifice, compassion, overcoming temptation, etc., can be performed only if there are evils of various kinds. Here, however, we must be careful. One might reasonably claim that all that is necessary for some of these good acts (or acts as good as these) to be performed is belief in the existence of certain evils, not their actual existence. You can show compassion toward someone who appears to be suffering, but is not really; you can forgive someone who only appeared to insult you, but did not really. But if the world is to be populated with imaginary evils of the kind needed to enable creatures to perform acts of the above specially good kinds, it would have to be a world in which creatures are generally and systematically deceived about the feelings of their fellows—in which the behavior of creatures generally and unavoidably belies their feelings and intentions. I suggest, in the tradition of Descartes (*Meditations* 4, 5 and 6), that it would be a morally wrong act of a creator to create such a deceptive world. In that case, given a creator, then, without an immoral act on his part, for acts of courage, compassion, etc., to be acts open to men to perform, there have to be various evils. Evils give men the opportunity to perform those acts which show men at their best. A world without evils would be a world in which men could show no forgiveness, no compassion, no self-sacrifice. And men without that opportunity are deprived of the opportunity to show themselves at their noblest. For this reason God might well allow some of his creatures to perform evil acts with passive evils as consequences, since these provide the opportunity for especially noble acts.

Against the suggestion of the developed free-will defense that it would be justifiable for God to permit a creature to hurt another for the good of his or the other's soul, there is one natural objection which will surely be made. This is that it is generally supposed to be the duty of men to stop other men hurting each other badly. So why is it not God's duty to stop men hurting each other badly? Now the theodicist does not have to maintain that it is never God's duty to stop men hurting each other; but he does have to maintain that it is not God's duty in circumstances where it clearly is our duty to stop such hurt if we can—e.g., when men are torturing each other in mind or body in some of the ways in which they do this in our world and when, if God exists, he does not step in.

Now different views might be taken about the extent of our duty to interfere in the quarrels of others. But the most which could reasonably be claimed is surely this—that we have a duty to interfere in three kinds of circumstances—(1) if an oppressed person asks us to interfere and it is probable that he will suffer considerably if we do not, (2) if the participants are children or not of sane mind and it is probable that one or other will suffer considerably if we do not interfere, or (3) if it is probable that considerable harm will be done to others if we do not interfere. It is not very plausible to suppose that we have any duty to interfere in the quarrels of grown sane men who do not wish us to do so, unless it is probable that the harm will spread. Now note that in the characterization of each of the circumstances in which we would have a duty to interfere there occurs the word "probable," and it is being used in the "epistemic" sense—as "made probable by the total available evidence." But then the "probability" of an occurrence varies crucially with which community or individual is assessing it, and the amount of evidence which they have at the time in question. What is probable relative to your knowledge at t_1 may not be at all probable relative to my knowledge at t_2. Hence a person's duty to interfere in quarrels will depend on their probable consequences relative to that person's knowledge. Hence it follows that one who knows much more about the probable consequences of a quarrel may have no duty to interfere where another with less knowledge does have such a duty—and conversely. Hence a God who sees far more clearly than we do the consequences of quarrels may have duties very different from ours with respect to particular such quarrels. He may know that the suffering that A will cause B is not nearly as great as B's screams might suggest to us and will provide (unknown to us) an opportunity to C to help B recover and will thus give C a deep responsibility which he would not otherwise have. God may very well have reason for allowing particular evils which it is our bounden duty to attempt to stop at all costs simply because he knows so much more about them than we do. And this is no ad hoc hypothesis—it follows directly from the characterization of the kind of circumstances in which persons have a duty to interfere in quarrels.

We may have a duty to interfere in quarrels when God does not for a very different kind of reason. God, being our creator, the source of our beginning and continuation of existence, has rights over us which we do not have over our fellow-men. To allow a man to suffer for the good of his or someone else's soul one has to stand in some kind of parental relationship toward him. I don't have the right to let some stranger Joe Bloggs suffer for the good of his soul or of the soul of Bill Snoggs, but I do have *some* right of this kind in respect of my own children. I may let the younger son suffer *somewhat* for the good of his and his brother's soul. I have this right because in small part I am responsible for his existence, its beginning and continuance. If this is correct, then a fortiori, God who is, ex hypothesi, so much more the author of our being than are our parents, has so many more rights in this respect. God has rights to allow others to suffer, while I do not have those rights and hence have a duty to interfere instead. In these two ways the theodicist can rebut the objection that if we have a duty to stop certain particular evils which men do to others, God must have this duty too.

Objection 4: Passive Evil Not Due to Human Action

In the free-will defense, as elaborated above, the theist seems to me to have an adequate answer to the suggestion that necessarily a good God would prevent the occurrence of the evil which men cause—if we ignore the question of the quantity of evil, to which I will return at the end of my paper. But what of the passive evil apparently not due to human action? What of the pain caused to men by disease or earthquake or cyclone, and what too of animal pain which existed before there were men? There are two additional assumptions, each of which has been put forward to allow the free-will defense to show the compatibility of the existence of God and the existence of such evil. The first is that, despite appearances, men are ultimately responsible for disease, earthquake, cyclone, and much animal pain. There seem to be traces of this view in Genesis 3:16–20. One might claim that God ties the goodness of man to the well-being of the world and that a failure of one leads to a failure of the other. Lack of prayer, concern, and simple goodness lead to the evils in nature. This assumption, though it may do some service for the free-will defense, would seem unable to account for the animal pain which existed before there were men. The other assumption is that there exist humanly free creatures other than men, which we may call fallen angels, who have chosen to do evil, and have brought about the passive evils not brought about by men. These were given the care of much of the material world and have abused that care. For reasons already given, however, it is not God's moral duty to interfere to prevent the passive evils caused by such creatures. This defense has recently been used by, among others, Plantinga. This assumption, it seems to me, will do the job, and is not *clearly* false. It is also an assumption which was part of the Christian tradition long before the free-will defense was put forward in any logically rigorous form. I believe that this assumption may indeed be indispensable if the theist is to reconcile with the existence of God the existence of passive evils of certain kinds, e.g., certain animal pain. But I do not think that the theodicist need deploy it to deal with the central cases of passive evils not caused by men—mental evils and the human pain that is a sign of bodily malfunctioning. Note, however, that if he does not attribute such passive evils to the free choice of some other agent, the theodicist must attribute them to the direct action of God himself, or rather, what he must say is that God created a universe in which passive evils must necessarily occur in certain circumstances, the occurrence of which is necessary or at any rate not within the power of a humanly free agent to prevent. The antitheodicist then naturally claims, that although a creator might be justified in allowing free creatures to produce various evils, nevertheless (P4) a creator is never justified in creating a world in which evil results except by the action of a humanly free agent. Against this the theodicist tries to sketch reasons which a good creator might have for creating a world in which there is evil not brought about by humanly free agents. One reason which he produces is one which we have already considered earlier in the development of the free-will defense. This is the reason that various evils are logically necessary conditions for the occurrence of actions of certain especially noble kinds. This was adduced earlier as a reason why a creator might allow creatures to perform evil acts with passive evils as consequences. It can also be adduced as a reason why he might himself bring about passive evils—to give further opportunities for courage, patience, and tolerance. I shall consider here one further reason that, the theod-

icist may suggest, a good creator might have for creating a world in which various passive evils were implanted, which is another reason for rejecting (P4). It is, I think, a reason which is closely connected with some of the other reasons which we have been considering why a good creator might permit the existence of evil.

A creator who is going to create humanly free agents and place them in a universe has a choice of the kind of universe to create. First, he can create a finished universe in which nothing needs improving. Humanly free agents know what is right, and pursue it; and they achieve their purposes without hindrance. Second, he can create a basically evil universe, in which everything needs improving, and nothing can be improved. Or, third, he can create a basically good but half-finished universe—one in which many things need improving, humanly free agents do not altogether know what is right, and their purposes are often frustrated; but one in which agents can come to know what is right and can overcome the obstacles to the achievement of their purposes. In such a universe the bodies of creatures may work imperfectly and last only a short time; and creatures may be morally ill-educated, and set their affections on things and persons which are taken from them. The universe might be such that it requires long generations of cooperative effort between creatures to make perfect. While not wishing to deny the goodness of a universe of the first kind, I suggest that to create a universe of the third kind would be no bad thing, for it gives to creatures the privilege of making their own universe. Genesis 1 in telling of a God who tells men to "subdue" the earth pictures the creator as creating a universe of this third kind; and fairly evidently—given that men are humanly free agents—our universe is of this kind.

Now a creator who creates a half-finished

universe of this third kind has a further choice as to how he molds the humanly free agents which it contains. Clearly he will have to give them a nature of some kind, that is, certain narrow purposes which they have a natural inclination to pursue until they choose or are forced to pursue others—e.g., the immediate attainment of food, sleep, and sex. There could hardly be humanly free agents without some such initial purposes. But what is he to do about their knowledge of their duty to improve the world—e.g., to repair their bodies when they go wrong, so that they can realize long-term purposes, to help others who cannot get food to do so, etc.? He could just give them a formal hazy knowledge that they had such reasons for action without giving them any strong inclination to pursue them. Such a policy might well seem an excessively laissez-faire one. We tend to think that parents who give their children no help toward taking the right path are less than perfect parents. So a good creator might well help agents toward taking steps to improve the universe. We shall see that he can do this in one of two ways.

An action is something done for a reason. A good creator, we supposed, will give to agents some reasons for doing right actions—e.g., that they are right, that they will improve the universe. These reasons are ones of which men can be aware and then either act on or not act on. The creator could help agents toward doing right actions by making these reasons more effective causally; that is, he could make agents so that by nature they were inclined (though not perhaps compelled) to pursue what is good. But this would be to impose a moral character on agents, to give them wide general purposes which they naturally pursue, to make them naturally altruistic, tenacious of purpose, or strong-willed. But to impose a character on creatures might well seem to take away from creatures the privilege of developing their own characters and those of their fellows. We tend to think that parents who try too forcibly to impose a character, however good a character, on their children, are less than perfect parents.

The alternative way in which a creator could help creatures to perform right actions is by sometimes providing additional reasons for creatures to do what is right, reasons which by their very nature have a strong causal influence. Reasons such as improving the universe or doing one's duty do not necessarily have a strong causal influence, for as we have seen creatures may be little influenced by them. Giving a creature reasons which by their nature were strongly causally influential on a particular occasion on any creature whatever his character, would not impose a particular character on a creature. It would, however, incline him to do what is right on that occasion and maybe subsequently too. Now if a reason is by its nature to be strongly causally influential it must be something of which the agent is aware which causally inclines him (whatever his character) to perform some action, to bring about some kind of change. What kind of reason could this be except the existence of an unpleasant feeling, either a sensation such as a pain or an emotion such as a feeling of loss or deprivation? Such feelings are things of which agents are conscious, which cause them to do whatever action will get rid of those feelings, and which provide reason for performing such action. An itch causally inclines a man to do whatever will cause the itch to cease, e.g., scratch, and provides a reason for doing that action. Its causal influence is quite independent of the agent—saint or sinner, strong-willed or weak-willed, will all be strongly inclined to get rid of their pains (though some may learn to resist the inclination). Hence a creator who wished to give agents some inclination to improve the world without giving them a character, a wide set of general purposes which they naturally pursue, would tie some of the imperfections of the world to physical or mental evils.

To tie desirable states of affairs to pleasant

feelings would not have the same effect. Only an existing feeling can be causally efficacious. An agent could be moved to action by a pleasant feeling only when he had it, and the only action to which he could be moved would be to keep the world as it is, not to improve it. For men to have reasons which move men of any character to actions of perfecting the world, a creator needs to tie its imperfections to unpleasant feelings, that is, physical and mental evils.

There is to some considerable extent such tie-up in our universe. Pain normally occurs when something goes wrong with the working of our body which is going to lead to further limitation on the purposes which we can achieve; and the pain ends when the body is repaired. The existence of the pain spurs the sufferer, and others through the sympathetic suffering which arises when they learn of the sufferer's pain, to do something about the bodily malfunctioning. Yet giving men such feelings which they are inclined to end involves the imposition of no character. A man who is inclined to end his toothache by a visit to the dentist may be saint or sinner, strong-willed or weak-willed, rational or irrational. Any other way of which I can conceive of giving men an inclination to correct what goes wrong, and generally to improve the universe, would seem to involve imposing a character. A creator could, for example, have operated exclusively by threats and promises, whispering in men's ears, "unless you go to the dentist, you are going to suffer terribly," or "if you go to the dentist, you are going to feel wonderful." And if the order of nature is God's creation, he does indeed often provide us with such threats and promises—not by whispering in our ears but by providing inductive evidence. There is plenty of inductive evidence that unattended cuts and sores will lead to pain; that eating and drinking will lead to pleasure. Still, men do not always respond to threats and promises or take the trouble to notice inductive evidence (e.g., statistics showing the corre-

lation between smoking and cancer). A creator could have made men so that they naturally took more account of inductive evidence. But to do so would be to impose character. It would be to make men, apart from any choice of theirs, rational and strong-willed.

Many mental evils too are caused by things going wrong in a man's life or in the life of his fellows and often serve as a spur to a man to put things right, either to put right the cause of the particular mental evil or to put similar things right. A man's feeling of frustration at the failure of his plans spurs him either to fulfill those plans despite their initial failure or to curtail his ambitions. A man's sadness at the failure of the plans of his child will incline him to help the child more in the future. A man's grief at the absence of a loved one inclines him to do whatever will get the loved one back. As with physical pain, the spur inclines a man to do what is right but does so without imposing a character—without, say, making a man responsive to duty, or strong-willed.

Physical and mental evils may serve as spurs to long-term cooperative research leading to improvement of the universe. A feeling of sympathy for the actual and prospective suffering of many from tuberculosis or cancer leads to acquisition of knowledge and provision of cure for future sufferers. Cooperative and long-term research and cure is a very good thing, the kind of thing toward which men need a spur. A man's suffering is never in vain if it leads through sympathy to the work of others which eventually provides a long-term cure. True, there could be sympathy without a sufferer for whom the sympathy is felt. Yet in a world made by a creator, there cannot be sympathy on the large scale without a sufferer, for whom the sympathy is felt, unless the creator planned for creatures generally to be deceived about the feelings of their fellows; and that, we have claimed, would be morally wrong.

So generally many evils have a biological and psychological utility in producing spurs to right action without imposition of character, a goal which it is hard to conceive of being realized in any other way. This point provides a reason for the rejection of (P4). There are other kinds of reason which have been adduced reasons for rejecting (P4)—e.g., that a creator could be justified in bringing about evil as a punishment—but I have no space to discuss these now. I will, however, in passing, mention briefly one reason why a creator might make a world in which certain mental evils were tied to things going wrong. Mental suffering and anguish are a man's proper tribute to losses and failures, and a world in which men were immunized from such reactions to things going wrong would be a worse world than ours. By showing proper feelings a man shows his respect for himself and others. Thus a man who feels no grief at the death of his child or the seduction of his wife is rightly branded by us as insensitive, for he has failed to pay the proper tribute of feeling to others, to show in his feeling how much he values them, and thereby failed to value them properly—for valuing them properly involves having proper reactions of feeling to their loss. Again, only a world in which men feel sympathy for losses experienced by their friends, is a world in which love has full meaning.

So, I have argued, there seem to be kinds of justification for the evils which exist in the world, available to the theodicist. Although a good creator might have very different kinds of justification for producing, or allowing others to produce, various different evils, there is a central thread running through the kind of theodicy which I have made my theodicist put forward. This is that it is a good thing that a creator should make a half-finished universe and create immature creatures, who are humanly free agents, to inhabit it; and that he should allow them to exercise some choice over what kind of

creatures they are to become and what sort of universe is to be (while at the same time giving them a slight push in the direction of doing what is right); and that the creatures should have power to affect not only the development of the inanimate universe but the well-being and moral character of their fellows, and that there should be opportunities for creatures to develop noble characters and do especially noble actions. My theodicist has argued that if a creator is to make a universe of this kind, then evils of various kinds may inevitably—at any rate temporarily—belong to such a universe; and that it is not a morally bad thing to create such a universe despite the evils.

The Quantity of Evil

Now a morally sensitive antitheodicist might well in principle accept some of the above arguments. He may agree that in principle it is not wrong to create humanly free agents, despite the possible evils which might result, or to create pains as biological warnings. But where the crunch comes, it seems to me, is in the amount of evil which exists in our world. The antitheodicist says, all right, it would not be wrong to create men able to harm each other, but it would be wrong to create men able to put each other in Belsen. It would not be wrong to create backaches and headaches, even severe ones, as biological warnings, but not the long severe incurable pain of some diseases. In reply the theodicist must argue that a creator who allowed men to do little evil would be a creator who gave them little responsibility; and a creator who gave them only coughs and colds, and not cancer and cholera would be a creator who treated men as children instead of giving them real encouragement to subdue the world. The argument must go on with regard to particular cases. The antitheodicist must sketch in detail and show his adversary the horrors of particular wars and diseases. The the-odicist in reply must sketch in detail and show his adversary the good which such disasters make possible. He must show to his opponent men working together for good, men helping each other to overcome disease and famine; the hero-ism of men who choose the good in spite of temptation, who help others not merely by giv-ing them food but who teach them right and wrong, give them something to live for and something to die for. A world in which this is possible can only be a world in which there is much evil as well as great good. Interfere to stop the evil and you cut off the good.

Like all moral arguments this one can be set-tled only by each party pointing to the conse-quences of his opponent's moral position and try-ing to show that his opponent is committed to implausible consequences. They must try, too, to show that each other's moral principles do or do not fit well with other moral principles which each accepts. The exhibition of consequences is a long process, and it takes time to convince an opponent even if he is prepared to be rational, more time than is available in this paper. All that I claim to have *shown* here is that there is no *easy proof* of incompatibility between the existence of evils of the kinds we find around us and the exis-tence of God. Yet my sympathies for the out-come of any more detailed argument are proba-bly apparent, and indeed I may have said enough to convince some readers as to what that out-come would be.

My sympathies lie, of course, with the theod-icist. The theodicist's God is a god who thinks the higher goods so worthwhile that he is pre-pared to ask a lot of man in the way of enduring evil. Creatures determining in cooperation their own character and future, and that of the uni-verse in which they live, coming in the process to show charity, forgiveness, faith, and self-sacrifice is such a worthwhile thing that a creator would not be unjustified in making or permitting a cer-tain amount of evil in order that they should be realized. No doubt a good creator would put a limit on the amount of evil in the world and per-haps an end to the struggle with it after a number of years. But if he allowed creatures to struggle with evil, he would allow them a real struggle with a real enemy, not a parlor game. The anti-theodicist's mistake lies in extrapolating too quickly from *our* duties when faced with evil to the duties of a creator, while ignoring the enor-mous differences in the circumstances of each. Each of us at one time can make the existing universe better or worse only in a few particulars. A creator can choose the kind of universe and the kind of creatures there are to be. It seldom becomes us in our ignorance and weakness to do anything more than remove the evident evils—war, disease, and famine. We seldom have the power or the knowledge or the right to use such evils to forward deeper and longer-term goods. To make an analogy, the duty of the weak and ignorant is to eliminate cowpox and not to spread it, while the doctor has a duty to spread it (under carefully controlled conditions). But a creator who made or permitted his creatures to suffer much evil and asked them to suffer more is a very demanding creator, one with high ideals who expects a lot. For myself I can say that I would not be too happy to worship a creator who expected too little of his creatures. Never-theless such a God does ask a lot of creatures. A theodicist is in a better position to defend a the-odicy such as I have outlined if he is prepared also to make the further additional claim—that God knowing the worthwhileness of the con-quest of evil and the perfecting of the universe by men, shared with them this task by subjecting himself as man to the evil in the world. A creator is more justified in creating or permitting evils to be overcome by his creatures if he is prepared to share with them the burden of the suffering and effort.

CHAPTER 53

D. Z. PHILLIPS

A CRITIQUE OF SWINBURNE

Dewi Zephaniah Phillips (1934–   ), has been a Professor of Philosophy at the University College in Swansea, England, since 1971, following a four year position as Senior Lecturer. He is one of the foremost followers of Ludwig Wittgenstein, and a religious fideist. In addition to contributing a number of articles to professional journals such as *Mind* and *Philosophical Quarterly*, he has authored *Death and Immortality* (1970), *Faith and Philosophical Inquiry* (1970), *Religion Without Explanation* (1976), and *Faith After* Foundationalism (1988).

A CRITIQUE OF SWINBURNE[1]

Introduction: False Journeys

For practical purposes it would be considered unfortunate if two symposiasts agreed with each other on too many points. If disagreements are too extreme, however, there is a danger of them passing each other by. The first possibility in no way threatens the present symposium, but the

[1]Reprinted from D.Z. Phillips, "The Problem of Evil," in *Reason and Religion*, edited by Stuart C. Brown. Copyright © 1977 by the Royal Institute of Philosophy. Used by permission of the publisher, Cornell University Press.

second poses a real problem. Kierkegaard once depicted a source of confusion in philosophy as thoroughly investigating details of a road one should not have turned into in the first place. As far as I can see, Swinburne is far down such a road. Nevertheless, in my reply, I shall for the most part comment on features of the road on which he chooses to travel. My reason for doing so is that many of Swinburne's assumptions about the Great Architect must, on his own admission, pass the compatibility test with respect to what goes on in and what we know about the highways and byways of human life. If it can be shown that what Swinburne asks us to think about the roads he travels on and the people who live there distorts what we know or goes beyond the limits of what we are prepared to think, this in itself would be a reason against extrapolating possibilities of divine policy or reasoning from such dubious facts. I shall do no more than hint at some reasons why we should not turn into Swinburne's way in the first place. I fear that the extent of my disagreement makes it impossible to fulfill either task adequately, but at least I hope to indicate the various directions in which my misgivings lie.

Before we begin our travels, let us note Swinburne's terms of reference for the journey. Since various ills and misfortunes can be found in the streets where we live, religious believers are faced with difficulties which are often referred to as the problem of evil: how are evils compatible with the existence of an omnipotent, omniscient, all-good God? A theodicist is someone who seeks to answer this question by justifying God's ways to men, by showing us why things are as they are and, in particular, why that which appears to be evil to us has been sent or created by God for the general good of mankind: a little evil does no one any harm and even the greatest evil, on closer examination, turns out to be worth the price. With this context in mind, let us follow Swinburne on his travels.

The Free Will Defense

His first observation is that all men are guilty of some wrong actions. Could men have been naturally good? This is a logical and not a factual question. Does the supposition make sense? If not, it makes no sense either to blame God for not creating perfect human beings. Swinburne holds that it is "not logically possible to create humanly free agents such that necessarily they do not do morally evil actions." Let us first ask whether we could have a world in which men always make the right decisions and where no actual evil exists. If we are retaining, as this talk may be doing, a world such as ours, where deliberations and temptations are what we know them to be, these assumptions soon run into conceptual difficulties. Consider the following course of argument: Someone may say that acquiring moral conceptions entails the existence of actual evil in the world. For example, a child may be taught to condemn selfishness by being restrained from performing a selfish action. His arm may be pulled back as it reaches for a third cream bun. Moral condemnation, it may be said, develops partly by commenting on what is actually taking place. To this it may be retorted that disdain of evil could be taught by means of hypothetical inference without actual evils taking place. For example, a child may be told that if human beings were killed as animals are killed that would be a bad thing. Putting this suggestion aside for the moment, how could evil thoughts be eliminated? Someone may think that the possibility of saints whose lives are characterized by spontaneous virtues constitutes an answer to this question. Their generosity of spirit may be such that they do not entertain such thoughts. This reply, however, does not work. The impressiveness of saints cannot be explained by an attempt to isolate their characteristics in this way. We are impressed by the generosity of spirit which saints may possess, precisely because they possess it in

553

a world where it is all too easy to think otherwise of other human beings. These observations about the saints admit of wider reference. Generosity, kindness, loyalty, truth, etc., do get their identity in a world where meanness, cruelty, disloyalty and lies are also possible. We see the importance of virtues not in face of apparent or possible evils, but in face of actual evils. Swinburne himself rejects the possibility of a world where God has seen to it that people only seem to be harmed, since God would be guilty of deception if this were the case. The objection, however, is logical, not moral. When we think we ought to be generous is it in fact of apparent need or real need? How would we know the difference? The point is that we cannot, according to the argument. But this "cannot" is unintelligible, for no distinction between what can and cannot be known exists to give it any import. God, on this argument, suffers the same fate as Descartes's malignant demon. If we now look again at the question, Could there be a world where men are naturally good? we can see, for reasons already given, that such a world could not contain people we would call good. Even so, would a world of such people, whatever we call them, be a better world than the world we know? I have no idea how to answer this question.

Swinburne doubts whether the notion of the best of all logically possible worlds makes sense, but even if it did, he cannot see how God could have any obligation to create it. He does, however, think it makes sense to compare a universe without actual evil, a finished universe, with our own, a half-finished universe. Swinburne says, "While not wishing to deny the goodness of a universe of the first kind, I suggest that to create a universe of the [other] kind would be no bad thing, for it gives to creatures the privilege of making their own universe." Putting aside the dubious character of this privilege for the moment, I take it that Swinburne would also say that

God could have no obligation to create such a universe. If Swinburne's conception of God were allowed, and that, as we shall see, is to allow a great deal, what can be made of Swinburne's defense of him? Swinburne asks, ". . . . to whom would he be doing an injustice if he did not?" The suggestion seems to be that God has no obligation to create a world of any particular kind, since prior to his act of creation, there are no people to harm! But this is no defense. If God were asked why he created such a world for people to live in instead of creating a better one, should his reply be, "They wouldn't know the difference", an appropriate reply, even if it could not be uttered, would be, "No, but you did!"

Having raised some difficulties concerning the possibility of a world of naturally good men which contains no actual evil and Swinburne's claim that God could not have an obligation to create the best of all possible worlds if that notion made sense, we see that new difficulties arise in the light of Swinburne's further observations. His strategy is placed in the context of the free-will defense, a defense which "must claim that it is a good thing that there exist free agents with the power and opportunity of choosing between morally good and morally evil actions, agents with sufficient moral discrimination to have some idea of the difference and some (though not overwhelming) temptation to do other than the morally good." Objections have been made to this defense by some philosophers who ask why God has not ensured or seen to it that men as a result of their free deliberations always make the right decisions. Swinburne says that God has not done this because it would be an imposition of character on man and therefore morally wrong. My difficulty is that I have the prior problem of not knowing what it means to speak of God either ensuring or not ensuring, seeing to it or not seeing to it, where the development of human character is concerned. My difficulties can be discussed in two contexts: first, the difficulty of the metaphysical level at which the "ensuring" or "seeing to it" is supposed to take place, and second, the difficulty of knowing what it would be to see to or ensure the formation of human character.

First, then, the question of the metaphysical character of God ensuring that human beings have such-and-such characters. There is no difficulty in locating natural events or intentional acts which have influenced a person's character in specific ways. But here I can say that there may or may not have been such effects, or that some people were affected and others not or that different people were affected in different ways. Even if we say that such-and-such an event or action must have an effect of a specifiable kind, there is still a question of how such an effect is taken up into the rest of a person's life. If I want to speak of "ensuring" or "seeing to it" that a person exhibits a certain "character" then I'd think of something akin to posthypnotic suggestion. Here, although the person so influenced "obeys the command" and "gives reasons" for this conduct, we do not accept such behavior without reservation as an instance of what we would call obeying a command or giving reasons. There are features of his behavior which lead us to detect rationalization. Of course, on a given occasion, one may be taken in. A man may exhibit anger as the result of a suggestion made to him while under hypnosis in a situation where anger would have been a natural response in any case. The point to stress is not that the seeing to it or the ensuring is always detected, but that we know what it means to speak of detecting it. Add to this the possibility of our having independent knowledge of the hypnosis in the first place. Such direct knowledge is not given to us in God's case, and so we are trying to contemplate what God may or may not have done on the basis of what we already know. My difficulty is to find a discernible difference in human affairs which would confirm or refute these speculations. Those who think it makes sense to speak of God ensuring that men, after free deliberation, always make the right decisions, do not want to think of God as the divine hypnotist since (a) that is not the kind of behavior God is said to ensure and (b) God's ensuring is not something we can clearly discern as sometimes present and sometimes absent in human affairs, but as that which ensures that human affairs are what they are in the first place. My difficulty, I suppose, concerns the intelligibility of thinking of creation as an act of ensuring or seeing to things, similar in character to acts of ensuring or seeing to things that we know, different only in the resources available and the scale of operation.

Second, I find difficulty in knowing what it means to speak of someone ensuring or seeing to it that human characters are of such-and-such a kind. Swinburne does not find this difficult to imagine. He simply thinks it would be a bad thing for God to do, just as it would be a bad thing for parents to do.

The creator could help agents toward doing right actions by making these reasons more effective causally; that is, he could make agents so that by nature they were inclined (though not perhaps compelled) to pursue what is good. But this would be to impose a moral character on agents, to give them wide general purposes which they naturally pursue, to make them naturally altruistic, tenacious of purpose, or strong-willed. But to impose a character on creatures might well seem to take away from creatures the privilege of developing their own characters and those of their fellows. We tend to think that parents who try too forcibly to impose a character, however good a character, on their children, are less than perfect parents.

555

Someone might well argue from the same facts to the opposite conclusion. A parent who wants to ensure or see to it that his child has one sort of character rather than another, it may be said, is not necessarily interfering with the freedom of the child. If we do not regard such measures as an interference with freedom, despite our ignorance and all the mistakes we make, why should a logical or moral limit be drawn on God, who is not ignorant nor liable to error, seeing to it that human beings freely develop in the right way? I do not want to enter the dispute over whether either program for parental attitudes is right or wrong, since my difficulties over the intelligibility of the program remain. I am not denying that measures taken by parents may influence the development of their children in the way hoped for by the parents. I deliberately speak in the subjunctive mood and speak of hope, since I think it important to distinguish between the retrospective judgment, "I influenced the development of my child's character" or "I did what I could" with the claim, "I ensured or saw to it that my child's character developed in a certain way." Measures taken in hope recognize that such measures are taken in contexts where a great deal is outside the control of the agent, and a wise parent may recognize that this does not simply happen to be true. He would not know what it would mean if someone wanted to talk of parental influence on development of character in any other way. Greater control would recall visions of posthypnotic behavior, something we wouldn't include in developments of character at all. Thus the wise parent may say, "I thank my lucky stars that I was able to help the development of my child's character" or "I thank God that I was able to help my child." These references to God or lucky stars, here, are not references to those agents who *did* ensure the outcome. On the contrary, these utterances are themselves reactions to the fact that what is con-

tingent, in the hands of God, we might say, has gone in a certain way. It is ironic that the debate about whether God should or should not have seen to the development of human characters, uproots the language of things being in God's hands from one of its natural contexts, a context which gets much of its force from the fact that talk of ensuring or seeing to it that outcomes are of one sort or another has no place in it.

Pseudoresponsibility

Having spent a little time considering Swinburne's treatment of the question whether men could have been naturally good and whether God could have seen to it that men developed freely in this direction, I want now to consider his defense of God based on more specific evils which he has observed. This shift of attention corresponds to the first two moral principles of the antitheodicist which Swinburne wants to attack. So far he would claim to have disposed of the principle "that a creator able to do so ought to create only creatures such that necessarily they do not do evil actions." He intends next to consider the modified second principle, namely, "that a creator able to do so ought always to ensure that any creature whom he creates does not cause passive evils, or at any rate passive evils which hurt creatures other than himself." Swinburne's general theodicist strategy within which he attempts to show the implausibility of this principle is "that it is not morally wrong for God to create or permit the various evils, normally on the grounds that doing so is providing the logically necessary conditions of greater goods." What is the greater good which justifies the harm that we do to others? Swinburne replies,

A world in which no one except the agent was affected by his evil actions might be a world in which men had freedom but it would not be a world in which men had responsibility. . . . So then the theodicist objects . . . on the grounds that the price of possible passive evils for other creatures is a price worth paying for agents to have great responsibilities for each other. It is a price which (logically) must be paid if they are to have those responsibilities.

Swinburne's analysis is not an analysis of moral responsibility, but of pseudoresponsibility; it involves a vulgarization of the concept. From the truth that we could not feel responsible unless we were responsible to someone or for something, it does not follow that someone or something should be regarded as opportunities for us to feel responsible. If we remind someone of his responsibilities, we are directing his attention to concerns other than himself. Swinburne's analysis makes these concerns the servants of that self. Compare: "He recognizes the importance of his job" with "His job makes him feel important". Similarly, instead of sometimes feeling responsible for or a responsibility toward the afflictions of others, we would, in terms of Swinburne's analysis, look on those afflictions as opportunities for feeling responsible. It is as if the Parable of the Good Samaritan were thought to show that unlike the priest and the levite, the Samaritan did not pass by an opportunity of feeling responsible.

Furthermore, even if the feeling of responsibility had not been vulgarized in Swinburne's analysis, it would not follow that a responsible reaction justifies the evil or suffering which occasions it. This has been well expressed by W. Somerset Maugham:

> It may be that courage and sympathy are excellent and that they could not come into existence without danger and suffering. It is

hard to see how the Victoria Cross that rewards the soldier who has risked his life to save a blinded man is going to solace *him* for the loss of his sight. To give alms shows charity, and charity is a virtue, but does *that* good compensate for the evil of the cripple whose poverty has called it forth?

The Problem of the Quantity of Evil

Let us go further down Swinburne's road. He has noticed already that men intentionally bring evil to others, but now he also notices that there is quite a lot of evil around. Therefore he feels that a third moral principle advanced by the antitheodicist needs answering, namely, "that a creator able to do so ought to ensure that any creature whom he creates does not cause passive evils as many and as evil as those in our world." God may have laid out a moral obstacle race for mankind, but are the obstacles too difficult? A defender of the third moral principle "says that in our world freedom and responsibility have gone too far—produced too much physical and mental hurt. God might well tolerate a boy hitting his younger brother, but not Belsen." Swinburne admits that this would be a telling criticism if true, but as he looks around him he does not believe it is true. On the contrary, Swinburne believes that God has created a world where the men are sorted out from the boys. It means "that the creator must create them immature, and allow them gradually to make decisions which affect the sort of beings they will be." This is why Swinburne calls our world "a half-finished universe." The words are well chosen, since the picture is of a finishing school with God as the benevolent headmaster setting the tests. But does Swinburne's God pass the test of benevolence? It is hard to see that he does when we hear Swinburne's argument to show that in allowing evil

557

God has not gone too far:

> There are limits to the amount and degree of evil which is possible in our world. Thus there are limits to the amount of pain which a person can suffer—persons only live in our world so many years and the amount which they can suffer at any given time (if mental goings-on are in any way correlated with bodily ones) is limited by their physiology. . . . So the theodicist can certainly claim that a good God stops too much suffering—it is just that he and his opponent draw the line in different places.

Can the theodicist make such a claim on the basis of Swinburne's argument? I think not. There is an unwarrantable transition in the argument from talk of the world to talk about human beings, and, more important, from conceivable limits to actual limits. Of course, for any evils in the world we mention, more can be conceived of, but this is neither here nor there as far as the question of whether human beings are visited with greater afflictions than they can bear is concerned. Swinburne argues that since any human being can stand only so much suffering and we can conceive of more, it follows that God has not produced unlimited suffering and therefore has not gone too far. But, clearly, he has produced too much suffering for that human being and has gone too far for him. Such questions cannot be answered in an abstract or global way. What constitutes a limit or going too far for one person may not do so for another. In order to judge whether a human being has suffered more than he can bear, we need to refer to actual limits, not conceivable limits. By judging actual limits as if they were conceivable limits, Swinburne could deny that even a person's death could count as going too far in his case. "After all," he might say, "he could have died a worse death!" I find this whole defense rather perverse. God's finishing school is one where everyone is finished in one sense or another. Either they are well finished, educated to maturity by their experience in the moral obstacle race, or they are finished off completely by it. If the finishing off were done by someone who was solely the bringer of death, then, in certain circumstances, he could be described as the bringer of welcome release. But this is not true of Swinburne's God. Since the bringer of death is also the bringer of afflictions, he who devised the whole fiendish obstacle race, one cannot even attribute to him the compassion with which a dog may be put out of his misery. On the contrary, as each candidate fails to make the grade, it is surely more appropriate to say with Thomas Hardy that thus God has ended his play. Let us hurry from this scene.

As he goes further down his road, Swinburne thinks that the possibility of evil can be justified in terms of the opportunities for noble actions it provides:

> given a creator, then, without an immoral act on his part, for acts of courage, compassion, etc., to be acts open to men to perform, there have to be various evils. Evils give men the opportunity to perform those acts which show men at their best. A world without evils would be a world in which men could show no forgiveness, no compassion, no self-sacrifice. And men without that opportunity are deprived of the opportunity to show themselves at their noblest. For this reason God might well allow some of his creatures to perform evil acts with passive evils as consequences, since these provide the opportunity for especially noble acts.

This argument ignores a great deal, its main defect being its one-sided optimism. Why should evil beget good? One cannot feel remorse without having done wrong, but evil may give one an appetite for more. One cannot show forgiveness without something to forgive, but that something may destroy or prompt savage reactions. In a man's own life natural evils such as illness or social evils such as poverty may debase and destroy him. Swinburne says,

> Pain normally occurs when something goes wrong with the working of our body which is going to lead to further limitation on the purposes which we can achieve; and the pain ends when the body is repaired. The existence of the pain spurs the sufferer, and others through the sympathetic suffering which arises when they learn of the sufferer's pain, to do something about the bodily malfunctioning. Yet giving men such feelings which they are inclined to end involves the imposition of no character.

Swinburne is faced with formidable contrary testimony often expressed in art or from recollection of experience. Here are some of Settembrini's comments to Hans Castorp in Thomas Mann's *The Magic Mountain*:

> You said that the sight of dullness and disease going hand in hand must be the most melancholy in life. I grant you, I grant you that. I too prefer an intelligent ailing person to a consumptive idiot. But I take issue where you regard the combination of disease with dullness as a sort of aesthetic inconsistency, an error in taste on the part of nature, a "dilemma for the human feelings", as you were pleased to express yourself. When you professed to regard disease as something so refined, so—what did you call it?—possessing a "certain dignity"—that it doesn't "go with" stupidity. That was the expression you used. Well, I say no! Disease has nothing

refined about it, nothing dignified. Such a conception is in itself pathological, or at least tends in that direction. . . . Do not, for heaven's sake, speak to me of the ennobling effects of physical suffering! A soul without a body is as inhuman and horrible as a body without a soul—though the latter is the rule and the former the exception. It is the body, as a rule, which flourishes exceedingly, which draws everything to itself, which usurps the predominant place and lives repulsively emancipated from the soul. A human being who is first of all an invalid is *all* body; therein lies his inhumanity and his debasement. In most cases he is little better than a carcass.

Here too are W. Somerset Maugham's recollections of what he saw in hospital wards as he trained for the medical profession:

> At that time (a time to most people of sufficient ease, when peace seemed certain and prosperity secure) there was a school of writers who enlarged upon the moral value of suffering. They claimed that it was salutary. They claimed that it increased sympathy and enhanced the sensibilities. They claimed that it opened to the spirit new avenues of beauty and enables it to get into touch with the mystical kingdom of God. They claimed that it strengthened the character, purified it from its human grossness, and brought to him who did not avoid but sought it a more perfect happiness . . . I set down in my note-books, not once or twice, but in a dozen places, the facts that I had seen. I knew that suffering did not ennoble; it degraded. It made men selfish, mean, petty, and suspicious. It absorbed them in small things. It did not make them more than men; it made them less than men; and I wrote ferociously that we learn resigna-

tion not by our own suffering, but by the suffering of others.

Not only need evil not occasion goodness, but goodness itself may occasion evils. Swinburne does not consider these possibilities. The depth of a man's love may lead him to kill his wife's lover or to be destroyed when the object of his love is lost to him. A man whose love was mediocre would not have done either of these things. Love has as much to do with the terrible as with the wonderful. The presence of goodness in some may be the cause of hatred in others. Budd's goodness is more than Claggart can bear and it is the very possibility that deep love may be a reality which Iago cannot admit into his dark soul.

On his travels Swinburne has seen how human beings intervene from time to time to help each other in their troubles. Sometimes, when fortunate, they can prevent those troubles occurring, and they often try to prevent things getting worse. He realizes then that he has to answer the question why his God does not intervene in circumstances where mere mortals would not hesitate. His answers are not encouraging. Roughly, they amount to saying that just as parents know more than their children and are often right not to act when their offspring beg them to do so, so God, the Father of us all, knowing more than we know, refrains from acting despite the cries of the afflicted. Here is a sample:

> Hence a God who sees far more clearly than we do the consequences of quarrels may have duties very different from ours with respect to particular such quarrels. He may know that the suffering that A will cause B is not nearly as great as B's screams may suggest to us and will provide (unknown to us) an opportunity to C to help B recover and will thus give C a deep responsibility which he would not otherwise have.

I have already commented on the character of such a sense of responsibility, and that is not my purpose now. It is true that sometimes considering a matter further is a sign of reasonableness and maturity. But this cannot be stated absolutely, since at other times readiness to be open-minded about matters is a sign of a corrupt mind. There are screams and screams, and to ask of what use are the screams of the innocent, as Swinburne's defense would have us do, is to embark on a speculation we should not even contemplate. We have our reasons, final human reasons, for putting a moral full stop at many places. If God has other reasons, they are his reasons, not ours, and they do not overrule them. That is why, should he ask us to consider them, we, along with Ivan Karamazov, respectfully, or not so respectfully, return him the ticket. So when Swinburne says, "The argument must go on with regard to particular cases. . . . The exhibition of consequences is a long process, and it takes time to convince an opponent even if he is prepared to be rational, more time than is available in this paper," one must not be misled by apparent reasonableness. Being prepared to consider the consequences of doing something is not the hallmark of moral reasonableness. Often, when the invitation to consider consequences is made, the appropriate reply is "Get thee behind me, Satan!" And if there is a "higher" form of reasoning among God and his angels, where such matters are open for compromise and calculation, then so much the worse for God and his angels. If they reason in this way in the heavenly places, we can say with Wallace Stevens, "Alas that they should wear our colors there". . . .

The Moral Insensitivity of Theodicies

Having traveled with Swinburne to the end of the road he has chosen to go down, noting various ills and misfortunes to which human beings are subject, we are now in a position to summarize the answer to the problem of evil which he brings before us: There are doubts as to whether it makes sense to imagine men who are naturally good without actual evils in the world. It is equally doubtful to say that God ought to have seen to it that men freely reach the right decisions. Even if the notion of the best of all logically possible worlds made sense, God would have no obligation to create such a world, for whom would he harm if he did not? There are good reasons for saying that the various evils in the world are compatible with the existence of an omnipotent, omniscient, all-good God. Such evils as we bring on others give us the opportunity of feeling responsible, and that is a good thing. After all, such evils are not unlimited, since there is a limit to what anyone can stand. Evils give us an opportunity to be seen at our best in reacting to them. God does not intervene to prevent evil when any decent human being would, because he has a wider knowledge of the situations in which evils occur. In order to prompt us in the right direction without imposing characters on us, God has seen to it that physical and mental evils are linked to things going wrong. Looking back at the details of his case, Swinburne says that "a morally sensitive antitheodicist might well in principle accept some of the above arguments." This conclusion is a somewhat embarrassing one since it is evident from my comments that one of the strongest criticisms available to the antitheodicist would be the moral insensitivity of the theodicist's case. There is an example in Billie Holiday's autobiography which combines many of the circumstances to which Swinburne calls our attention but which also sums up the fragility of his optimistic analyses. She tells of a well-known jazz personality who was a drug addict:

> I can tell you about a big-name performer who had a habit and a bad one. There were times when he had it licked. And other times it licked him. It went around that way for years. He was well known, like me, which makes it worse. He had bookings to make, contracts to fulfil. In the middle of one engagement he was about to crack up and go crazy because he had run out of stuff. There was no way in God's world that he could kick cold turkey and make three shows a day. There wasn't a doctor in town who would be seen looking at him. His wife got so scared he'd kill himself that she tried to help him the only way she knew—by risking her own neck and trying to get him what he needed. She went out in the street like a pigeon, begging everyone she knew for help. Finally she found someone who sold her some stuff for an arm and a leg. It was just her luck to be carrying it back to her old man when she was arrested.

> She was as innocent and clean as the day she was born. But she knew that if she tried to tell that to the cops it would only make her a "pusher" under the law, liable for a good long time in jail. She thought if she told them she was a user, and took some of the stuff in her pocket to prove it, they might believe her, feel sorry for her, go easy on her. And she could protect her man. So that's what she did. She used junk for the first time to prove to the law she wasn't a pusher. And that's the way she got hooked. She's rotting in jail right now. Yes siree bob, life is just a bowl of cherries.

Later, Billie Holiday sums up her own attitude, "If you expect nothing but trouble, maybe a few happy days will turn up. If you expect happy days, look out."

In replying to Swinburne's arguments I have chosen in the main to comment on his reading of the fortunes and misfortunes of human life, a reading which is to serve in the construction of a theodicy. Theodicies, such as Swinburne's, are marked by their order, optimism and progress. If we want to appreciate why Swinburne should not have turned down the road on which he chooses to travel in the first place, this, above all, is what has to be put aside. Throughout Swinburne's paper, the main emphasis, with only an occasional hint of difficulties, is on the world as a God-given setting in which human beings can exercise rational choices which determine the kind of people they are to become. This is neither the world I know, nor the world in which Swinburne lives. Ours is a world where disasters of natural and moral kinds can strike without rhyme or reason. Where, if much can be done to influence character, much can also bring about such influence over which we have no control. Character has as much, and probably more, to do with reacting to the unavoidable, as with choosing between available alternatives. Commenting on a similar order, progress and optimism to Swinburne's in recent moral philosophy, I had reason to quote Hardy's comments on the limits which life placed on Tess's endeavors:

> Nature does not often say "See!" to her poor creature at a time when seeing can lead to happy doing; or reply "Here!" to a body's cry of "Where?" till the hide-and-seek has become an irksome, outworn game. We may wonder whether at the acme and summit of the human progress these anachronisms will be corrected by a finer intuition, a closer interaction of the social machinery than that which now jolts us round and along; but such completeness is not to be prophesied, or even conceived as possible.

And yet, even such poor creatures are heard to talk of God. In the context of this reply I can only hint at the import of such talk, talk which I do not claim is all of a piece or capable of being fitted into a neat theological system. I have already suggested in discussing what might be meant by someone who said the outcome was in the hands of God, that the force of the belief depends on the absence of the kind of higher level planning so essential to Swinburne's theodicy. The same is true of talk of God's grace in face of life's evils. In order even to reach the threshold of understanding what might be meant here, the sheer pointlessness of those evils has to be admitted. One has to see, for example, that there is no reason why these natural disasters should have come our way. One has to be ready to answer in face of one's cry, "Why is this happening to me?", "Why shouldn't it?" This recognition of the pointlessness of suffering in this sense can lead in various directions. It has led some to speak of the absurd, but it has led others to speak of all things as God's gifts, and of things not being one's own by right or reason, but by the grace of God. It is not my purpose to advocate these uses of language, but simply to note their existence. Again, in other contexts, a person may wonder in relation to his own character what he can do something about and what has been given by God; that is, what cannot be changed, but which he must come to terms with. On wider issues there may be much agonizing over whether something, marriage, for example, is of God, something fixed and unalterable with which we must come to terms, or whether we are confusing a human institution with God's will and erecting a barrier with no more than a nominal reality which prevents us receiving God's gifts of happiness. Such contexts as these do not imply the dismissal of those considerations which have led people to talk of the problem of evil. On the contrary, without the human cry from the midst of afflictions no sense can be made of these religious responses, and there may be constant tensions of various kinds between the responses and the evils which surround them. The responses are not, however, recognitions of a higher order, but one way of understanding the lack of such an order. Even when the response is understood in this way, it may well be regarded by those who cannot share it as an evil response.

Hardy complains ironically in face of the limits and limitations Tess had to face or fail to face, that "why so often the coarse appropriates the finer . . . the wrong man the woman, the wrong woman the man, many thousand years of analytical philosophy have failed to explain to our sense of order." In the context already mentioned I commented that Hardy, of course, was not looking for explanations. Swinburne looks for explanations. Any sense of order with which one would have been satisfied would be defective just for that reason. That must be my verdict on Swinburne's theodicy. Swinburne admits that his God does ask a lot of his creatures, but says,

A theodicist is in a better position to defend a theodicy such as I have outlined if he is prepared also to make the further additional claim—that God knowing the worthwhileness of the conquest of evil and the perfecting of the universe by men, shared with them this task by subjecting himself as man to the evil in the world. A creator is more justified in creating or permitting evils to be overcome by his creatures if he is prepared to share with them the burden of the suffering and effort.

Not so, for if the visit to our world were by a God such as Swinburne describes, those who said that there was no room at the inn would be right. We should not be at home to such callers. And if perchance we were asked to choose between this visitor and another, we should unhesitatingly demand, "Give us Prometheus!"

GLOSSARY

AGNOSTICISM   The belief that we do not have sufficient reason to either affirm or deny God's existence.

ASEITY   From the Latin, *aseitas*, meaning "being by, for, and of itself." An attribute of God expressing self-existence, unlimited being, and complete independence.

ATHEISM   The belief that there is no God; an *atheist* is a person who holds this position.

CIVIL RELIGION   State religion; in the United States, best expressed by the motto imprinted on coins, "In God we trust."

COSMOLOGICAL ARGUMENT   An argument (or family of arguments) that attempts to prove that God exists on the basis of the idea that there must have been a first cause or ultimate reason for the existence of the universe (cosmos).

CREED   From the Latin word *credo*, meaning "I believe"; a set of propositions embraced by the believing soul. Through a creed, a religion offers its picture of the world.

DEISM   A belief, popular in the seventeenth and eighteenth centuries, that affirms the existence of a God who has created the universe but who remains apart from it, permitting creation to govern itself through natural law.

DIVINE COMMAND THEORY   The view that ethical principles derive their validity from the fact that God commanded them.

HOLY   The sacred; that which is regarded with awe, reverence, and adoration.

IMMUTABLE   Absolutely unchanging.

INCORPOREAL   Not material.

INFINITE   Not finite; unlimited, inexhaustible, and endless.

MONOTHEISM   The belief that there is only one God.

MORAL ARGUMENT   The argument, advanced by Kant and others, that God must exist in order for the moral order to be intelligible.

NATURALISM   A theory that accepts the empirical world of natural science as the whole of reality; opposed to supernaturalism, which is the belief in that which is above or beyond the empirical world.

OEDIPUS COMPLEX   In psychoanalytic theory, the unconscious tendency of a child to be attracted to the parent of the opposite sex, and hostile toward the other parent; Freud believed it to be the origin of religion.

ONTOLOGICAL ARGUMENT   An *a priori* argument that attempts to prove the existence of God from the very concept of God.

ORTHODOXY   Correct belief. In Christianity, conforming to the ancient creeds; in Judaism, strictly observing all of the rites and traditions, such as *kashrut*, the Sabbath, and so on.

PANENTHEISM   All things are imbued with God's being in the sense that all things are *in* God.

PANTHEISM   The belief that God is identical with the universe; all is God and God is all.

REVELATION   A divinely inspired source of knowledge, often a holy book; in Judaism and Christianity, the Bible and in Islam, the Koran.

RITUAL   A set form or rite, publicly observed, for the sake of some higher purpose. Religious rites include prayer, meditation, sacrifice, and fasting.

SACRAMENT   In Christianity, those rituals regarded by the church as a means of grace. Protestants recognize two, Baptism and Holy Communion. Roman Catholics recognize an additional five, including marriage.

SALVATION   A transition from an unsatisfactory state of existence to a limitlessly better one.

THEISM   The belief in a personal God, the Creator and sustainer of the world, with whom we may come into relationship.

THEODICY   Justification of the ways of God to humanity; the attempt to make God's power and goodness compatible with the existence of evil in the world.

THEOLOGY   Any coherently organized body of teaching concerning the nature of God and God's relationship with humans and the universe.

TRANSCENDENCE   A state that is beyond what is given in experience; the opposite of immanence. In theology the term means that God is beyond or outside of nature.

WORSHIP   Reverence or devotion for a deity; to perform an act of religious devotion, such as prayer or meditation.

FOR FURTHER STUDY

Delaney, C. F., ed. *Rationality and Religious Belief*. Notre Dame: University of Notre Dame Press, 1978.

A very helpful collection of essays on the relation of faith and reason.

Hick, John. *Philosophy of Religion*. 4th ed. Engle-

wood Cliffs, N.J.: Prentice-Hall, 1983.
A clear, concise introduction to the central ideas in the philosophy of religion.

Lewis, C.S. *The Problem of Pain*. London: Geoffrey Bles, 1940.
A classic, clearly and cogently written.

Mackie, J.L. *The Miracle of Theism: Arguments For and Against the Existence of God*. New York: Oxford, 1983.
The best defense of atheism, taking into consideration all of the major arguments.

Macquarrie, John. *Twentieth Century Religious Thought*, rev. ed. New York: Scribners, 1981.
A useful survey of twentieth century philosophy and theology through 1980.

Phillips, D. Z. *Religion Without Explanation*. Oxford: Basil Blackwell, 1976.
An important treatment by one of the leading Wittgensteinian fideists.

Plantinga, Alvin. *God, Freedom and Evil*. New York: Harper & Row, 1974.
Develops in detail the free will defense to the problem of evil. According to Plantinga, all natural evil is reduced to moral evil, with the devil held accountable.

Plantinga, Alvin, and Nicholas Wolterstorff, eds. *Faith and Rationality*. Notre Dame: University of Notre Dame Press, 1983.
An important collection of essays on religious epistemology.

Rowe, William. *Philosophy of Religion: An Introduction*. Belmont, Calif.: Wadsworth, 1978.
A readable introduction for beginners; highly recommended.

Swinburne, Richard. *The Existence of God*. Oxford: University of Oxford Press, 1979.
Perhaps the best defense of the traditional arguments since the Middle Ages, written by a prominent British scholar.

Westphal, Merold. *God, Guilt, and Death: An Existential Phenomenology of Religion*. Bloomington: Indiana University Press, 1984.
A highly original work, exploring the thesis that guilt and death are the central problems of human existence; the meaning of religion lies in the promise of salvation from guilt and death.

PART EIGHT

◆

ETHICS

Two things fill the mind with ever new and
increasing admiration and awe. . .
the starry heavens above and the moral law within.

IMMANUEL KANT

ORIENTATION

Whether we are aware of it or not, each of us has a set of values that we live by. Life forces us constantly to make choices; when we choose, we are expressing our sense of value, rating things as better or worse, important or unimportant, right or wrong, good or bad, beautiful or ugly. Some choices are trivial: It is of little importance whether you chose to wear red rather than brown this morning. Other choices are monumental, affecting our entire life: Will we marry, join a political party, profess a religion? Since choice is inevitable (to remain undecided is itself a choice), the question is not whether we shall have preferences, loyalties, convictions, standards, or ideals—the real question is, will our choices be consistent or inconsistent, life-enhancing or life-destroying? Ignoring the role of value judgments in life leads to a lack of wholeness and perspective in our lives. If we are to choose well, we must take up the study of values, both personal and social.

Part 8 is the first of three parts dealing with axiology, the branch of philosophy dealing with values. It is concerned with ethics (the study of values in human conduct). Part 9 focuses on social and political philosophy (the study of values in society), and Part 10 with aesthetics (the study of values in art).

Our treatment of ethics is divided into the following sections: the nature of ethics, moral principles, relativism, ethical subjectivism, morality and religion, consequentialist ethical theories, nonconsequentism, and value-based ethics. The Contemporary Perspectives section is devoted to an important issue in applied ethics, abortion.

THE NATURE OF ETHICS

DEFINTIONS OF ETHICS AND MORALITY

Ethics may be defined as that branch of philosophy that seeks to analyze systematically moral concepts (such as "good," "bad," "right," "wrong," "duty," "responsibility," and so on) and to justify moral principles and theories. Ethics endeavors to establish principles of right behavior that can serve as a decision-making guide for individuals and groups. In its search for those values and virtues that are life-enhancing, ethics constructs and criticizes arguments that state valid moral principles (for example, "Kill no innocent human being," "Be a truth-teller," "Always keep promises") and the relationship between these principles (for example, are there occasions when saving a human life presents a valid reason for breaking a promise or telling a lie?).

Whereas the natural sciences are descriptive, concerned with empirical facts, ethics is prescriptive, concerned with normative values. As a normative value-based discipline, ethics is more concerned with what ought to be than what is. Ethics is a practical action-oriented discipline that seeks to effect change—from the world as it is to the world as it ought to be. Studying ethics requires a serious commitment to think honestly and soberly about how we ought to live our lives. Should we always tell the truth? Must we always keep our promises? Is it ever morally permissible to take a human life? Should a woman have an abortion? No wonder Plato could say in the *Republic*, "We are discussing no small matter, but how we ought to live."

Ethics is frequently referred to as moral philosophy. *Morality*, derived from the Latin word *moralis*, and *ethics*, derived from the Greek word *ethikos*, both mean conduct or custom. The terms *ethics* and *morality*, while frequently used interchangeably, have slightly different meanings. We shall follow the generally accepted practice of using "morality" to refer to the principles or rules of conduct that govern (or ought to govern) an individual life or society, and "ethics" to designate the systematic endeavor to understand moral concepts and justify moral principles and theories.

NORMATIVE ETHICS AND METAETHICS

Philosophers typically make a distinction between **normative ethics** and **metaethics.** Normative ethics constructs ethical theories based on valid moral principles; normative ethical statements are actual moral statements such as: "Apartheid is a glaring evil," "Abortion is always wrong," "You should honor your promise to your mother." Thus normative ethics tries systematically to establish the general principles for determining right and wrong, good and evil. By contrast, metaethics is a theoretical study centered on the analysis and meaning of the terms and language used in ethical discourse and the kind of reasoning used to justify ethical reasoning. Conceptual analysis and inquiry into the correct method for answering moral questions are two of the major concerns of metaethics. There is a close relationship between normative ethics and metaethics; by clarifying crucial moral concepts, metaethics makes normative ethics possible.

MORAL PRINCIPLES

The central feature of normative ethics is the moral principle. Principles are general guidelines for right conduct; the principles in ethical theories are intentionally general so that they may apply to every situation we are likely to encounter. The "Golden Rule" of Jesus ("Do unto others as you would have them do unto you") is a good example of a principle with the desired level of generality; from it we can work out more specific principles and rules for truth telling, giving, killing, and so on, which enables us to apply it as a useful guide to specific cases.

In his book *Ethics: Discovering Right and Wrong*, Louis P. Pojman observes that moral principles are practical guides to action possessing the following features: (1) prescriptivity, (2) universality, (3) overridingness, (4) publicity, and (5) practicability.[1]

PRESCRIPTIVITY

Prescriptivity refers to the action-guiding nature of morality. Generally, moral principles are posed as injunctions or imperatives (for example, "Do not kill," "Love your neighbor," "Do no unnecessary harm").

UNIVERSALIZABILITY

The Golden Rule exemplifies the notion of universalizability, for it prescribes that what is right for one person is right also for another, in a relevantly similar situation. From the moral point of view, there are no privileged persons; we must acknowledge that other people's welfare is just as important as our own. Justice would seem to require that we avoid partiality, the arbitrary favoring of one person over another. Henry Sidgwick formalized the Principle of Justice in this way: It cannot be right for A to treat B in a manner in which it would be wrong for B to treat A, merely on the ground they are two different individuals, and without there being any difference between the natures and circumstances of the two that can be stated as a reasonable ground for difference of treatment."[2] Universalizability, then, is at bottom the requirement of impartiality: when formulated as a principle, it functions as a rule that forbids us from treating one person differently from another when there is no good reason to do so. It is an important feature that helps us to explain what is wrong with racism and sexism.

OVERRIDINGNESS

Moral principles take precedence over other kinds of considerations, including aesthetic, prudential, and legal ones.

[1]Louis P. Pojman, *Ethics: Discovering Right and Wrong* (Belmont, Calif.: Wadsworth, 1990) 5–7.
[2]Henry Sidgwick, *The Methods of Ethics*, 7th ed. (Macmillan, 1907) 380.

Paul Gauguin may have been aesthetically justified in abandoning his family in order to devote his life to painting beautiful Pacific island pictures, but morally, or all things considered, he probably was not justified. It may be prudent to lie to save my reputation, but it probably is morally wrong to do so, in which case I should tell the truth. When the law becomes egregiously immoral, it may be my moral duty to exercise civil disobedience. There is a general moral duty to obey the law, because the law serves an overall moral purpose, and this overall purpose may give us reasons to obey laws that may not be moral or ideal; however, there may come a time when the injustice of a bad law is intolerable and hence calls for illegal but moral defiance (such as the ante-bellum laws in the South requiring citizens to return slaves to their owners). Religion is a special case, and the religious person may be morally justified in following a perceived command from God to break a normal moral rule. The Quakers' pacifist religious beliefs may cause them to renege on an obligation to fight for their country. Religious morality is morality, and ethics recognizes its legitimacy.[3]

Legal justice and moral justice do not necessarily coincide, since laws themselves may be morally unjust. Imagine a nation that had a law that unfairly discriminated against some of its inhabitants because of their sex. Suppose such a law denied that women have a legal right to life but guarantees that right to all males. In this case, legal justice would be done in this nation if this law is enforced. But it does not necessarily follow that moral justice is done. That depends not on whether there is a law in this nation but on the overriding question of whether the law recognizes and protects the moral rights of all of the nation's inhabitants. The question of civil disobedience is addressed in Part 9.

PUBLICITY

Since we use principles to play an action-guiding role in our lives, it would be self-defeating to keep them secret. To be maximally effective, moral principles must be made public.

PRACTICABILITY

A moral system must be workable; its rules must not lay too heavy a burden on moral agents. Overly idealistic principles may produce overwhelming guilt, moral despair, and ineffective action. Most ethical systems take human limitations into consideration.

[3]L. Pojman, p. 6.

RELATIVISM

Ethnocentrism, the uncritical belief of a group or a people in the superiority of their own culture, is today rightly condemned as a form of prejudice similar to racism or sexism. It is wrong, for example, to suppose that all American preferences are based on some absolute rational standard, while the preferences of other cultures are not. The rejection of ethnocentrism coupled with an increased awareness about other cultures has led many to hold a version of **ethical relativism.**

Ethical relativism is the theory that there are no universally valid principles, since all moral principles are valid relative to cultural or individual choice. It should be distinguished from **moral skepticism,** the view that there are no valid moral principles (or at least we cannot know that there are any), and from all forms of **moral absolutism** and **moral objectivism.** Moral absolutism is the theory that there is one true morality with a consistent set of moral principles that never conflict and never need to be overridden. Kant's approach to ethics is an example of this type of theory. Moral objectivism, defended by W. D. Ross and others, holds that moral principles have universal objective validity but admits that many of its principles may be overridden by other principles in certain cases.

John Ladd states the theory of ethical relativism in this way:

> Ethical relativism is the doctrine that the moral rightness and wrongness of an action varies from society to society and that there are no absolute universal moral standards binding on all men at all times. Accordingly, it holds that whether or not it is right for an individual to act in a certain way depends on or is relative to the society to which he belongs.

CULTURAL RELATIVISM

The most common expression of ethical relativism is found in **cultural relativism,** an anthropological thesis that acknowledges the fact that moral beliefs and practices differ from society to society. From this descriptive observation (which is doubtlessly correct), the cultural relativist wishes to draw a normative conclusion that is very questionable: that there is no universal or objective truth in ethics, there are only various cultural codes. Furthermore, our moral code is but one of many, and thus has no special status.

At first glance, cultural relativism seems very plausible. It is only when we examine the structure of its argumentation that we discover problems. The strategy used by cultural relativists is to argue from facts about cultural diversity to a conclusion about the nature of morality. Is there reason to believe that all moral practices are as diverse as the cultural relativist claims? In a word, no. At least two objections may be made at the level of facts and the interpretations of those facts.

In the first place, the facts really do not establish ethical relativism. Recent research in anthropology has documented universal proscriptions against incest, for example, and against wanton killing within one's social group. Even where particular moral practices and rules vary, universal areas of value related to human need have been identified: life and health, marriage and family, economic sufficiency.

In the second place, the diversity thesis fails to distinguish between diversity in particular moral practices from diversity in the principles implicit in such concerns. Practices are always guided by more general concerns. For example, how societies define property rights or how they punish wrongdoers may vary greatly, but they may still be equally concerned about both preserving property and punishing offenders, and equally concerned about having an ordered society.

Finally, we might ask the question, "What would it be like if cultural relativism were true?" James Rachels has identified three undesirable consequences of taking cultural relativism seriously.[4]

1. *We could no longer say that the customs of other countries are morally inferior to our own.* While this at first may appear to be desirable and enlightened, suppose a country waged war on its neighbors for the purpose of taking slaves? Or suppose a nation set out systematically to eliminate all Jews? Cultural relativism would preclude us from saying that either of these practices was wrong. As Rachels points out, we would not even be able to say that a society tolerant of Jews is better than the anti-Semitic society, for that would imply some sort of transcultural standard of comparison. Taking cultural relativism seriously would have the undesirable consequence of forcing us to give up our convictions that these two practices are wrong.

2. *We could decide whether actions are right or wrong just by consulting the standards of our society.* Cultural relativism is exceedingly conservative in that it endorses whatever moral views happen to be current within a society. It offers a simple test for determining what is right and wrong: an action is right if it is in accord with the code of one's society. But suppose a resident of South Africa wonders whether her country's practice of apartheid—rigid racial segregation—is morally correct. All she has to do is ask whether this policy conforms to her society's moral code. If it does, then all is well. Clearly, this is a disturbing consequence: Few of us actually believe that our society is perfect. Thus cultural relativism would not only stop us from criticizing the codes of other societies, it would stop us from criticizing our own.

3. *The idea of moral progress is called into doubt.* Throughout most of Western history, the role of women has been narrowly defined. Women could not own property, vote, or hold political office; for the most part, they were not permitted to have paying jobs; and they were under the almost absolute control of

[4]See James Rachels, *The Elements of Moral Philosophy* (New York: Random House, 1986), 17–19.

their husbands. Much of this has changed in recent times, and most people think of it as progress. But if cultural relativism is correct, can we legitimately think of this as progress? After all, progress means replacing an inferior way of doing things with an improved way. But by what standard do we judge the new way as better? If the old ways were in accordance with the social standards of their time, then cultural relativism would say it is a mistake to judge them by the standards of a different time. To say that we have made progress implies a judgment that present-day society is better, and that is precisely the sort of transcultural judgment that, according to this theory, is impermissible.

These three undesirable consequences have led many thinkers to reject cultural relativism as implausible. Faced with the choice of (a) accepting cultural relativism or (b) giving up the belief in moral progress, or the conviction that slavery and anti-Semitism are wrong, most people choose to reject (a) and embrace (b).

ETHICAL SUBJECTIVISM

Ethical subjectivism is the view that right and wrong are relative, not to the standards of culture, but to the attitudes of each individual person. Our moral opinions are based on our feelings, and nothing more. A subjectivist would claim that anyone who declares something to be right or wrong is expressing nothing more than a personal attitude. Whereas factual statements (for example, "The cat is on the mat") are either true or false, moral judgments (for example, "Abortion is wrong") are neither true nor false. They are matters of opinion, or statements expressing preference, not knowledge; hence, people can disagree about them without being mistaken.

The outstanding defender of ethical subjectivism is David Hume (1711–1776), who thought that ethics could only be accounted for on the basis of sentiment (or feeling), not on reason. Reason, he argued, could only inform us of the nature and consequences of our actions. For example, reason may tell you that if you give someone poison to drink, he will die. But after your reason has told you this, it is necessary for your sentiments to come into play—how do you feel about this person dying, do you want it, or not?—in order for you to decide what you will do. If you want the person to die, you give him the poison; if you do not want him to die, you do not poison him. All decisions are like this, in that they depend on our passions, not merely on our reason. As Hume put it, "Reason is, and ought to be, the slave of the passions."

Hume was led to this position by three persuasive arguments. In the first place, reason lacks the motivational power of moral judgments. Secondly, the origin of our moral judgments lies not in some action itself—for instance, the act of murder—but in the feeling of disapproval that we experience toward this action. Thirdly, ethical judgments are concerned with what we *ought* to do, whereas reason informs us only of what *is* the case. Because there is a logical chasm between is and ought, we can never derive ought from is; hence, ethics cannot be a deduction from reason alone.

There are problems with this theory. If ethical subjectivism is correct, then as long as a person is truly reporting how she feels, could she ever be mistaken in her moral views? Wouldn't this theory, if correct, make us all infallible? Furthermore, on this theory it is difficult to see how it is possible for people to disagree. If I say that something is right, I am merely saying that I have certain feelings on the subject; and if you say it is wrong, you are only saying that you have different feelings. Since both of us are entitled to our feelings (which, being feelings, are neither true nor false), what then could we disagree about?

MORALITY AND RELIGION

DIVINE COMMAND THEORY

Does morality depend upon religion? Do moral standards depend upon God for their validity, or is there an autonomy of ethics, such that even God is subject to the moral order? Plato raises the issue for us in the first of our reading selections when Socrates asks the pious Euthyphro, "Do the gods love holiness because it is holy, or is it holy because the gods love it?"

Divine Command Theory provides the most obvious way of connecting morality with religion. According to this theory, ethical principles are simply the commands of God. Since morality originates with God, it is argued, "moral rightness" simply means "willed by God," and "moral wrongness" means "being against the will of God." According to this theory, a moral statement such as "adultery is morally wrong" means "adultery is forbidden by God."

Divine Command Theory faces two serious problems. First, it would seem to make the attribute of the goodness of God (discussed in Part 7) redundant. When we say "God is good," we normally think that we are attributing a property to God; but if "good" simply means "what God wills or commands," then we are not attributing any property to God. Our statement "God is good" would merely translate into "God does whatever God wills to do," and the statement "God commands us to do what is good" is merely the logical tautology "God commands us to do what God commands us to do."

A second problem, equally serious, is that Divine Command Theory seems to make morality into something arbitrary. If nothing was wrong with adultery prior to God's command, then God could have no reason to forbid it; if something was wrong with it, then its wrongness is based on some standard of judgment independent of God's command. If God's fiat is the sole standard of right and wrong, it would seem logically possible for such acts as rape, murder, and incest to become morally praiseworthy if God suddenly decided to command us to do these things! If there is no independent measure or reason for moral action, this means that there are no constraints on what God can command; thus anything can become a moral duty and our moral duties can switch from moment to moment. In the Middle Ages, this position was sometimes known as **voluntarism.** For voluntarists like William Ockham (c. 1300–c. 1349) moral law, as it is revealed, is binding simply because it is God's will. Had God chosen otherwise, the law then revealed would bind us with equal force. Thus religion is prior to ethics. This is precisely the sort of situation that is recorded in Genesis 22 of the Bible, when God commands Abraham to kill his son Isaac. According to voluntarists, God's very request makes this otherwise odious act morally permissible.

A defender of Divine Command Theory may object that the will of God has been revealed in the Bible, which forbids things like rape, incest, or murder. But how is one to know that God is not lying? (You may be tempted to respond, "But God would never command us to be liars!" But why not? If God did endorse lying, it would not be commanding us to do wrong, since God's command would make lying right!) The point is, if there is no independent criterion of right and wrong except whatever God happens to will, then how can we know that God isn't willing to make lying into a duty? In such a case, believers would have no reason to believe the Bible's pronouncements on these matters. Suppose we had two sets of commands, one from God and the other from Satan. How could we ever know which set was which? Could they be identical? What exactly would make them different? Once again, if there were no independent criterion by which to judge right and wrong, it is difficult to see how we could know which was which.

There have been numerous attempts to modify the Divine Command Theory, in order to rescue it from these objections.[5] But many religious thinkers argue that it is perfectly permissible to accept the other "horn of Euthyphro's dilemma—that God commands the Good because it is good. This position accepts the notion of autonomous ethics, and argues that (1) rightness and wrongness are not based simply on God's will; and (2) there are reasons for acting one way or another that can be known independently of God's will. The autonomy of ethics means that

[5]See Robert M. Adams, "A Modified Divine Command Theory of Ethical Wrongness," in *Religion and Morality: A Collection of Essays*, edited by Gene Outka and John P. Reeder (San Angelo, TX: Anchor, 1973); and Phillip Quinn, *Divine Commands and Moral Requirements* (Oxford: Oxford University Press, 1978).

even God must obey the moral law, which exists independently, just as the laws of logic and mathematics. Just as God cannot make a four-sided triangle or commit suicide, so even God cannot make what is intrinsically good evil or make what is evil good. Since God's sovereignty and omnipotence (which the Divine Command theorist is intent on upholding at all costs) are not threatened by the fact that the laws of logic exist independently, why must it be threatened by the notion of autonomous ethics?

NATURAL LAW THEORY

In the history of Christian thought, the dominant alternative to Divine Command Theory has been **Natural Law Theory.** The most influential natural law theorist was Saint Thomas Aquinas. Aquinas argued that both natural and divine law are expressions of the one basic law established by God, namely, the eternal law. Hence, they had to be compatible with one another. Aquinas held this position, sometimes called **intellectualism,** against the voluntarism of the defenders of the Divine Command Theory.

According to Aquinas, moral judgments are "dictates of reason." In any circumstance, the best thing to do is whatever course of conduct has the best reasons on its side. The believer and the unbeliever are in exactly the same position when it comes to making moral judgments. Since both are endowed with powers of reason and conscience, both may make responsible decisions by heeding reason and remaining true to their conscience. God, who is by nature a perfectly rational being, has created the world as a rational order; men and women, in the image and likeness of God, are rational agents. Just as the realm of nature operates in conformity with natural laws discoverable by reason (such as gravity), so there are natural laws that govern how we ought to conduct ourselves. Since all people—not merely Christians—are rational creatures, even nonbelievers are able to function as rational beings. Their lack of faith prevents them from realizing that God is the ultimate source of the rational order in which they participate, yet their capacity for moral judgment is itself revelatory of God.

Drawing out the implications of Natural Law Theory, one can see that both science and morality are autonomous enterprises. Science has its own questions, its own methods, and its own standards of truth. To the scientist intent on understanding and explaining the workings of the world, religious authority is nonbinding. (There was, of course, a time when the Roman Catholic church claimed the right to judge science in the name of faith; Galileo was forced to recant his scientific findings because they were deemed incompatible with Christian doctrine. This episode has been an embarrassment to the church, and recently, Pope John Paul II exonerated Galileo completely.)

577

Like science, morality is autonomous. It too has a set of questions, its own methods of answering them, and its own standards of truth. A person facing a moral decision must ask what reason and conscience demand of her, and religious considerations are often not decisive. Thus even a person who accepts the moral authority of the Bible has much to gain from the study of philosophical ethics. Arthur Holmes, a Christian philosopher at Wheaton College in Illinois, presents this view:

> [T]he Bible gives us a vast repertoire of ethical material in different literary forms and from different historical and cultural contexts. We have a succint summary in the Ten Commandments, extended casuistry (case applications) in the Mosaic code, epigrammatic wisdom in Proverbs, reflections on life's meaning and values in Ecclesiastes, preaching of social justice in the prophets, down-to-earth homilies in the Gospels and systematic statements in Paul's letters. . . . But Christians do not claim that the Bible is exhaustive, that it tells us everything we can know or can benefit ethically from knowing. It is silent about many things, including many moral problems we face today—problems in bio- and medical ethics, for example, problems about responsibility to unborn generations and about population control. . . . We are confronted at times with moral dilemmas in which every available option is morally undesirable and a decision cannot be avoided or postponed. Suppose that in Nazi-occupied Holland you are hiding Jews in your attic and the Gestapo comes searching for them. Do you lie to save innocent lives, or do you forfeit innocent lives to save lying? Whatever you do will violate some moral rule or another. How then do you choose, and to what extent are you blame-worthy?[6]

Natural Law Theory thus leaves morality independent, in the sense that religious belief does not necessarily affect the calculation of what is morally best in a given situation. Believing souls and nonbelievers may approach moral questions in the same way, sharing common ground; if both conscientiously seek good reasons for their conduct, they may arrive at the same answers. They will part company only when theorizing about the nature of the moral choices they have made. Believing souls, of course, will regard the results of their moral inquiry as revealing God's will—the voice of God is heard in the call of conscience. Unbelievers, according to Aquinas, do not have this advantage; nevertheless, through the grace of God, they may make good moral choices. Thus, even though the believer and unbeliever may disagree about religion, the Natural Law Theory enables them to inhabit the same moral universe.

[6]Arthur F. Holmes, *Ethics: Approaching Moral Decisions* (Downers Grove, Ill.: InterVarsity Press, 1984), 12–13.

CONSEQUENTIALIST ETHICAL THEORIES

Earlier, we characterized normative ethics as the construction of ethical theories based on valid moral principles. But what are these valid principles, and how have philosophers arrived at them?

One way to think about moral principles is to imagine a situation where everyone would agree that something wrong has been done. For example, imagine that Stella has a favorite tennis racquet. She enjoys playing tennis with it, and on occasion has lent it to her friends. Ann likes the tennis racquet, too; she could purchase one, but then she could not afford to buy something else that she wants but does not need. One day, when Stella is out of town, Ann steals the tennis racquet. As a result, Stella experiences some unhappiness. Whenever she thinks about the missing racquet, she is upset and frustrated, and the enjoyment she might have received if Ann had not stolen the racquet is cancelled.

Examples such as these have led some philosophers to theorize that what makes stealing wrong is that it is the cause of bad results (or consequences)—for example, it causes such experiences as the frustration and disappointment that Stella feels. Philosophers who take this view are called **consequentialists,** since they stress the consequences or results of actions. (Consequentialist theories are sometimes known as **teleological theories.**[7]) There are many varieties of consequentialist theories in ethics. What they all have this in common is that they regard a wrong action as something that leads to bad consequences, and a good action as something that leads to good consequences. Where such theories differ, among other things, is in their assessment of the scope of consequences that must be considered—that is to say, consequences for whom? Two consequentialist theories are especially important: **ethical egoism** and **utilitarianism.** Whereas egoism asks me to consider the consequences of my actions for one person only (namely, myself), utilitarianism urges me to consider the consequences of my actions for everyone concerned, myself included.

PSYCHOLOGICAL EGOISM

Ethical egoism should be distinguished from **psychological egoism,** which is a theory that states that everyone as a matter of fact always performs that act which they perceive to be in their own best interest. Whereas psychological egoism is a theory of human nature concerned with how people *do* behave, ethical

---

[7]**Teleological** comes from the Greek word *telos*, meaning "end" or "purpose." Such theories regard actions as right or wrong if they promote or frustrate the purpose of morality, which is to bring about the greatest possible balance of good over evil.

egoism is a normative theory about how we *ought* to behave. In effect, psychological egoism defines the possibility of nonselfish behavior out of existence, since it reinterprets every piece of behavior as rooted in selfishness. There is good reason to believe that psychological egoism is counter-factual, and therefore wrong.

ETHICAL EGOISM

Ethical egoism is a theory based on an ultimate principle of self interest—everyone ought to serve his or her own self-interest. According to this theory, the only real duty we have in life is to promote our own self-interests; this we must pursue, even if it conflicts with the interests of others, or causes harm to others.

The practical implications of ethical egoism are startling. For instance, if this theory is correct, then we have no moral obligation to help others in need unless there is some benefit to be gained for us. But why should we be so exclusively preoccupied with good consequences for ourselves? In order to reject ethical egoism we need not go all the way over to **altruism**—the view that asks us to engage in only those actions that bring about good consequences for everyone except ourselves. Rather than be narrowly focused on our own welfare, to the exclusion of others (egoism), or on others, to the exclusion of ourselves (altruism), why shouldn't we be concerned with the welfare of all people? Thoughts like these lead naturally into the most popular consequentialist theory, **utilitarianism.**

UTILITARIANISM

Utilitarianism, first proposed by David Hume but worked out more systematically by Jeremy Bentham (1748–1832) and John Stuart Mill (1806–1873), is based upon an ultimate moral principle known as the "Principle of Utility." This principle has been formulated in a variety of ways. Here is one common formulation:

> Everyone ought to act so as to bring about the greatest possible balance of intrinsic good over intrinsic evil for everyone concerned.

Utilitarians, however, often do not agree on what is intrinsically good and evil. Some, like Bentham, defend **ethical hedonism** (from the Greek *hedone*, meaning pleasure)—the view that pleasure and pleasure alone is intrinsically good (or good in itself), whereas pain, the absence of pleasure, is intrinsically evil. Bentham even devised a scheme for measuring pleasure and pain that he called the "hedonic calculus." According to this system, the value of any experience could be obtained by adding up the amounts of pleasure and pain for seven aspects of the experience: its intensity, duration, certainty, nearness, fruitfulness, purity, and extent.

Bentham's version of utilitarianism was criticized by John Stuart Mill as being too simplistic. It was sometimes referred to as the "pig philosophy," since a pig enjoying its life would constitute a higher moral state than a slightly dissatisfied Socrates! Mill made a distinction between happiness and mere sensual pleasure. His version of utilitarianism, eudaimonistic utilitarianism (from the Greek word for 'happiness'), defines happiness in terms of higher order pleasures such as intellectual, aesthetic, and social enjoyments. Here is how Mill stated the Principle of Utility in his *Utilitarianism* (1861):

> According to the Greatest Happiness Principle . . . the ultimate end, end, with reference to and for the sake of which all other things are desirable (whether we are considering our own good or that of other people), is an existence exempt as far as possible from pain, and as rich as possible in enjoyments.

Three separate ideas may be identified in these formulations:

1. Actions are to be judged as right or wrong solely by virtue of their consequences.
2. When assessing consequences, the only thing that matters is the amount of happiness or unhappiness that is caused.
3. Each person's happiness is equally important; no one's happiness is to be counted as more than anyone else's. (This feature separates utilitarianism from egoism, which arbitrarily privileges the happiness of the self, violating the notion of universalizability mentioned earlier as essential to valid moral principles.)

In its own way, this is a very radical thesis; gone are all references to divine moral commands or some divinely implanted code of natural law imprinted on the world. The utilitarians were social reformers concerned with maximally promoting happiness and minimizing suffering in *this* world.

Utilitarians also disagree about how the Principle of Utility should be applied to individual actions. It is important in this regard to make a distinction between **act utilitarianism** and **rule utilitarianism.** Act utilitarianism is the view that the Principle of Utility should be applied to *individual actions*. Rule utilitarianism states that the Principle of Utility should be applied mainly to rules of action. The act utilitarian argues that whenever people must decide what to do, they ought to perform that act bringing about the greatest possible balance of intrinsic good over intrinsic evil. The rule utilitarian argues something quite different: People ought to do whatever is required by justified moral rules. These are rules that would lead to the best possible consequences, all things considered, if everyone were to abide by them. Under rule utilitarianism, a person who chooses to do what a moral rule requires might perform an act that in that particular situation might not lead to the best possible circumstances. Thus act and rule utilitarians can reach opposing moral judgments about the same action. The debate between act and rule utilitarians is one of the liveliest and most important in normative ethics. Nevertheless, there are problems with both versions.

It appears that act utilitarianism, consistently followed, could lead to a situation where an obviously wrong action might be considered right. The rightness or wrongness of an act depends only on whether or not the net consequences of the act are at least as good as the consequences that would have resulted if another act had been done. Richard Brandt criticizes act utilitarianism on precisely this point:

> It implies that if you have employed a boy to mow your lawn and he has finished the job and asks for his pay, you should pay him what you promised only if you cannot find a better use for your money. It implies that when you bring home your monthly paycheck you should use it to support your family and yourself only if it cannot be used more effectively to supply the needs of others. It implies that if your father is ill and has no prospect of good in his life, and maintaining him is a drain on the energy and enjoyment of others, then, if you can end his life without provoking any public scandal or setting a bad example, it is your positive duty to take matters into your own hands and bring his life to a close.[8]

One of the most important objections against rule utilitarianism turns on considerations about justice. It appears that rule utilitarianism could justify rules that would be manifestly unjust. For instance, suppose that there were a rule that discriminated against persons because of the color of their skin.

> Imagine this rule (R): "No one with black skin will be permitted in public after six o'clock." If we think about R, its unfairness jumps out at us. It is unjust to discriminate against people simply on the basis of skin color. However, although it is clear that R would be unjust, might not R conceivably be justified by appealing to the Principle of Utility? Certainly it seems possible that everyone's acting according to R might bring about the greatest possible balance of intrinsic good over intrinsic evil. True, black people are not likely to benefit from everyone's acting according to R. Nevertheless, their loss might be more than outweighed by nonblacks gains, especially if blacks are a small

[8]Richard Brandt, "Towards a Credible Form of Utilitarianism," in H. Castaneda and G. Nakhnikian, eds., *Morality and the Language of Conduct* (Detroit: Wayne State University Press, 1963), 109–10.

minority. Thus, if rule-utilitarianism could be used to justify flagrantly unjust rules, it is not a satisfactory theory.[9]

NONCONSEQUENTIALISM

Nonconsequentialism is a name frequently associated with normative ethical theories that are not forms of consequentialism. Hence, any theory holding that right and wrong are *not* determined solely by the relative balance of intrinsic good over intrinsic evil commonly is called nonconsequentialist. Theories answering this description are also called **deontological theories,** from the Greek *deon*, meaning "duty."

Nonconsequentialist theories may be either extreme or moderate. An extreme nonconsequentialist theory holds that the intrinsic good and evil of consequences are totally irrelevant to determining what is morally right or wrong. A moderate nonconsequentialist theory holds that the intrinsic good and evil of consequences are relevant to determining what is morally right and wrong, but they are not the only things that are relevant and may not be of greatest importance in some cases.

KANT'S CATEGORICAL IMPERATIVE: THE FORMULA OF UNIVERSAL LAW

The great German philosopher Immanuel Kant called his ultimate moral principle the **categorical imperative.** In his *Fundamental Principles of the Metaphysics of Morals* (1785) he expressed this principle in two different formulations. The first he called the **Formula of Universal Law.** Before we state it, let us define two Kantian terms: "maxim" and "law." By maxim, Kant means a general rule by which the agent intends to act. By law, he means an objective principle that passes the test of universalizability.

> Act only on that maxim whereby thou canst at the same time will that it should become a universal law.

Kant is specifying a three-step procedure here.

1. When you are thinking about performing a particular action, you are required to ask yourself what rule you would be following if you were to do that action. (This rule will be the "maxim" of the act.)

[9]*Matters of Life and Death: New Introductory Essays in Moral Philosophy*, ed. Tom Regan (New York: Random House, 1980), 19.

2. Next, you are to ask whether you are willing for that rule to be followed by everyone all of the time (that is, are you willing to universalize your maxim).

3. If you are willing for everyone to follow the rule, then the act you're contemplating is permissible; if not, then the maxim must be rejected as self-defeated, and the act is morally impermissible.

By way of example, think back to Stella and her tennis racquet. Suppose one day Stella's friend comes to her with a broken racquet and asks to borrow Stella's. If Stella refuses, then she would be following the following rule: "Don't lend out a tennis racquet to a person who has broken their tennis racquet." But would Stella wish to follow this rule all of the time? What if *Stella's* tennis racquet broke on the morning of an important match, and she desperately needed to borrow one? Would Stella want her neighbor to adopt the policy of not lending out tennis racquets? No, she wouldn't. In refusing her friend's request, Stella could not will that the maxim of her act be made into a universal law. Therefore, Stella should not refuse her friend's request.

In addition to the case of refraining from helping others, Kant applies his Formula of Universal Law to three test cases: making a lying promise, suicide, and neglecting one's talent. Unsurprisingly, lying promises, suicide, and neglecting one's talent are found to be impermissible because they are based on defective (nonuniversalizable) maxims.

KANT'S FORMULA OF THE END IN ITSELF

Kant states the **Formula of the End in Itself** as follows:

Act in such a way that you always treat humanity, whether in your own person or in the person of any other, never simply as a means but always at the same time as an end.

Let us be clear about what Kant is *not* saying. He is not saying that there is anything wrong about using someone as a means. If you order a meal in a restaurant, you are using the server as a means to accomplish your end (eating); the server in turn uses you as a means to accomplish his or her end (earning a living). In this case, each party has consented to his or her part in the transaction. To use someone as a *mere means*, however, is to involve them in a scheme of action *to which they could not in principle give consent*.

One very obvious way to use a person as a mere means is by deceiving them. For example, if we get someone involved in a business scheme or criminal activity on false pretenses, or by giving them a misleading account of what is going on, we are involving that person in something to which he or she in principle cannot consent, since the scheme requires that they be kept in the dark.

Another way of using others as a mere means is by coercing them. In her article, "The Perplexities of Famine Relief," Onora O'Neill gives the following example:

> If a rich or powerful person threatens a debtor with bankruptcy unless he or she joins in some scheme, then the creditor's intention is to coerce; and the debtor, if coerced, cannot consent to his or her part in the creditor's scheme. To make the example more specific: If a moneylender in an Indian village threatens not to renew a vital loan unless he is given the debtor's land, then he uses the debtor as a mere means. He coerces the debtor, who cannot truly consent to this "offer he cannot refuse."[10]

Are there problems and limitations to Kant's approach to ethics? Many philosophers have thought so. Particularly troublesome is Kant's insistence that moral rules are exceptionless. For example, Kant believed that the rule against lying was absolute; that is, lying under *any* circumstances is "the obliteration of one's dignity as a human being." This is an extremely strong statement. What led Kant to this view was, as we have seen, his Formula of Universal Law. We could never will that lying be made a universal law, since people would quickly learn that they could not rely on what other people said; thus, the lies would not be believed. There is certainly a compelling logic to this argument; in order for a lie to be successful, people must believe that others are telling the truth. Therefore the success of a lie depends upon there *not* being a "universal law" permitting it.

But couldn't we construct a successful counterexample to Kant's treatment of "truth-telling" as an absolute duty? Suppose a man is fleeing from a murderer and tells you that he is going home to hide. The murderer then comes to you and asks where the man went. You have reason to believe that if you tell the truth, the murderer will find his victim and kill him. Should you tell the truth or lie? (Life, unfortunately, is filled with real-life examples of this kind. During World War II, Dutch fishing boats smuggling Jewish refugees to safety would frequently be stopped by Nazi patrol boats. The Nazi captain would call out, asking who was on board the Dutch ship; the fishermen would lie and be allowed to pass. In these cases, the fishermen had only two alternatives: to lie or to allow their passengers (and possibly themselves) to be taken and shot. No third alternative, such as remaining silent, or outrunning the Nazis, existed.)

In fact, Kant has an answer to our counterexample of "The Inquiring Murderer," for the example originally is his! In an essay entitled "On a Supposed Right to Lie from Altruistic Motives," Kant has this to say:

[10]Onora O'Neill, "The Perplexities of Famine Relief," in *Matters of Life and Death: New Introductory Essays in Moral Philosophy*, ed. Tom Regan (New York: Random House, 1980), 287.

After you have honestly answered the murderer's question as to whether his intended victim is at home, it may be that he has slipped out so that he does not come in the way of the murderer, and thus that the murder may not be committed. But if you had lied and said he was not at home when he had really gone out without your knowing it, and if the murderer had then met him as he went away and murdered him, you might justly be accused as the cause of his death. For if you had told the truth as far as you knew it, perhaps the murderer might have been apprehended by the neighbors while he searched the house and thus the deed might have been prevented. Therefore, whoever tells a lie, however well intentioned he might be, must answer for the consequences, however unforeseeable they were, and pay the penalty for them. . . .

To be truthful (honest) in all deliberations, therefore, is a sacred and absolutely commanding decree of reason, limited by no expediency.

Kant's argument here is very unconvincing. He argues that since we can never know what the consequences of our actions will be—the results of lying might be unexpectedly bad—the best policy is to avoid the known evil of lying, and let the consequences come as they may. Even if the consequences are bad, they will not be our fault, for we will have done our moral duty.

The problems with Kant's argument, stated here by James Rachels, seem obvious:

In the first place, the argument depends upon an unreasonably pessimistic view of what we can know. Sometimes we can be quite confident of what the consequences of our actions will be, and justifiably so; in which case we need not hesitate because of uncertainty. Moreover . . . Kant seems to assume that although we would be morally responsible for any bad consequences of lying, we would *not* be similarly responsible for any bad consequences of telling the truth. Suppose, as a result of our telling the truth, the murderer found his victim and killed him. Kant seems to assume that we would be blameless. But can we escape responsibility so easily? After all, we aided the murderer. This argument then . . . is not very convincing.[11]

SOCIAL CONTRACT THEORY

Social Contract Theory, advocated by Thomas Hobbes (1588–1679), John Locke (1632–1704), and Jean-Jacques Rousseau (1712–1778) attempts to explain the purpose of the state as well as the nature of morality. In Part 9, we consider the

[11]James Rachels, *The Elements of Moral Philosophy* (New York: Random House, 1986), 109–10.

political implications of the theory, highlighting Locke's theories, and the work of two contemporary American contractarians, John Rawls and Robert Nozick. Chapter 56 features a selection from Hobbes' *Leviathan*.

Social Contract Theory offers a different approach to morality than any of the other approaches mentioned thus far. The basic idea is that moral rules are rules that human beings must accept if they are to live peaceably together in society. Since humans are social animals, bound to live together rather than in isolation from one another, there must be general agreement on the rules of social living; if there is no general agreement, the result is chaos and anarchy, a condition that Hobbes, Locke, and Rousseau called the **state of nature.**

The foremost British philosopher of the seventeenth century, Hobbes described how dreadful the state of nature would be in this classic passage from the *Leviathan:*

> [There would be] no place for industry, because the fruit thereof is uncertain: and consequently no culture of the earth; no navigation, nor use of the commodities that may be imported by sea; no commodious building; no instruments of moving, and removing, such things as require much force; no knowledge of the face of the earth; no account of time; no arts; no letter; no society; and which is worst of all, continual fear, and danger of violent death, and the life of man, solitary, poor, nasty, brutish, and short.[12]

To picture what life would be like in the state of nature that Hobbes depicts, imagine waking up tomorrow to a nation whose government had collapsed completely, so that there was no law, no police, no courts, and no justice. Might makes right. People would begin to hoard food and other commodities essential to life. Everyone, of necessity, would be thrown into a continual war of one against all. There would be no time for anything besides the daily war to seize what one needed for life, defending it from others. We would all be at each other's throats, armed, suspicious, afraid, and miserable.

The only way to escape the state of nature, Hobbes theorized, is to find some way for people to cooperate with one another. If people are to work together to achieve common ends, there must be guarantees that there will be no attacks, thefts, or threats of harm. More importantly, people must be able to rely on one another to keep their agreements. But in order for this to happen, Hobbes argued, there must be government. Only a strong government (with its systems of laws, police, and courts) can ensure that people can live peaceably with one another without fear of attack, and that people must keep their agreements (or contracts) with one another.

To escape the state of nature, then, people must agree to give up some of their

---

[12]Thomas Hobbes, *Leviathan* (Indianapolis: Bobbs-Merrill Educational Publishing, 1958), 107.

independence, trading it for safety. Such an agreement, to which every citizen is a party, is called the social contract.

Having established that government is needed, what about morality? James Rachels states the social contract conception of morality:

> Morality consists in the set of rules, governing how people are to treat one another, that rational people will agree to accept, for their mutual benefit, on the condition that others will follow those rules as well.[13]

On this view, morally binding rules are those that are necessary for social living. We agree to follow these rules because it is in our self-interest to do so. We agree to obey the rules only on condition that others agree as well. The state sees to it that these laws are enforced, punishing those who break them.

Like all ethical theories, social contract theory is not without its problems. The problem has to do with the issue of civil disobedience. Social contract theory requires us to obey the law. But what if the law is unjust? Are we ever justified in breaking or defying the law? The problem of civil disobedience is the subject of the Contemporary Perspectives section in Part 9.

A second problem is that the theory seems to rest on a historical fiction. Hobbes and Rousseau, for instance, both ask us to believe that people once lived in isolation from one another; finding this situation unacceptable, they eventually bonded together, agreeing to follow rules for the good of all. But there is no evidence that any of this actually happened. Was this agreement consummated in a mythical prehistory? Is so, how have we come to know of it? And even if the "contract" was agreed to by our ancestors long ago, why would it be binding on us? If it is not a real historical agreement, can it be an "implicit contract," renewed in each new generation? Is it a "useful fiction" that still provides a framework for understanding morality? John Rawls, in Chapter 67 argues that it is.

A second problem has to do with the implications of the theory for beings who are not able to participate in the contract, although they are affected by it. Non-human animals lack the capacity to enter into agreements with us; nevertheless, isn't it wrong to torture animals? Must animals be excluded from moral consideration? Hobbes thought so, as did his contemporary, René Descartes. But if animals can be excluded because they cannot enter into agreements, can't mentally retarded humans be excluded for the same reason? From a moral point of view, this is undesirable; an ethical theory that cannot extend moral considerations to these two important classes is seriously flawed.[14]

---

[13]Rachels, p. 129.

[14]In recent years, some philosophers have attempted to extend the moral point of view to include animals and the nonhuman environment. Notable in this regard are Peter Singer's pathbreaking book, *Animal Liberation: New Ethics for Our Treatment of Animals* (New York: Random House, 1975) and Tom Regan, *The Case for Animal Rights* (Berkeley: University of California Press, 1983).

VIRTUE-BASED ETHICS

Whereas most ethical theories have been either duty-based (nonconsequentialist theories) or action-based (utilitarian theories) there is a third option that goes back to Aristotle and received the support of the early Christian church. Virtue-based systems are sometimes called **aretaic ethics** (from the Greed *arete*, meaning "excellence" or "virtue"). Whereas consequentialist and nonconsequentialist theories emphasize *doing* (following moral rules), virtue ethics emphasizes *being*—it is the character of a person that lies at the heart of this approach to ethics. Whereas duty-based ethics asks "What should I do," virtue ethics asks "What sort of person should I become?" Aretaic ethics seeks to produce, very simply, good people. The focus is on the proper goal of life: living well and achieving moral excellence. According to virtue ethics, merely doing right is not enough; it is also important to have the right dispositions, motivations, and emotions when being good and doing right. We will enjoy doing good because we *are* good.

According to Aristotle, humans are social beings, made for living in community. Virtues are simply those excellences of character that enable individuals to live well in community. Humanity has an essence or function. Just as the function of a doctor is to cure the sick and the function of a knife is to cut, the function of humans is to use reason in pursuit of the good life. In order to achieve a state of well-being, or happiness (from the Greek *eudaimonia*), proper social institutions are necessary. Because moral persons cannot exist apart from a political setting, they consider ethics to be a branch of politics. The virtues, then, are the political and moral characteristics necessary for people to attain happiness.

Virtues may be classified into two types: moral and intellectual. Generally speaking, the intellectual virtues (such a rationality, skill in mathematics or philosophy) may be taught directly, while the moral ones (courage, honesty, generosity, and so on) must be lived in order to be learned. The morally virtuous life consists of living in moderation, according to what Aristotle calls the "Golden Mean." By this Aristotle means that the virtues lie midway between excess and deficiency. Courage, for instance, lies midway between cowardice and foolhardiness.

Unfortunately, Aristotle was an elitist who believed that not everyone was capable of achieving the virtues; he contended that some people (for instance, the 100,000 slaves in Athens that enabled Aristotle to have the leisure to formulate his ethical theories!) were naturally worthless and incapable of developing moral dispositions. Furthermore, he believed that the moral virtues were a necessary but not sufficient condition of happiness. In addition to being virtuous, a person also needed health, wealth, good looks, and good fortune in order to have happiness.

Critics of virtue-based ethics point out that ethical theories ought to provide some kind of guidance for decision making; Aristotle's approach is just not very helpful when facing moral dilemmas. Aristotle's advice to a person facing a moral dilemma would simply seem to be, "Do whatever a good person would do," which doesn't tell us what we need to know. What seems to be required is the translation of particular virtues into action-guiding principles. Currently, virtue theorists are at work on this very problem.

After years of neglect, virtue ethics has re-emerged as a major ethical theory, largely due to the dissatisfaction with rule and action-governed ethical systems. In his highly influential book *After Virtue*, Alasdair MacIntyre has carried on the Aristotelian project of grounding morality in the virtues, arguing that a core set of virtues is necessary for the successful functioning of society.[15]

[15] Alasdair MacIntyre, *After Virtue* (Notre Dame: Notre Dame University Press, 1981).

CHAPTER 54

PLATO

GOD AND MORALITY

Plato's irony is apparent in this selection from the *Euthyphro*[1]: the conversation on piety between Socrates and Euthyphro takes place just outside the law court where Socrates is going to stand trial for his life. The charge against Socrates? Impiety.

Although the *Euthyphro* was written long ago, the issue it raises is as relevant as ever. Many people attempt to pattern their lives on moral rules laid down in a book deemed holy and authoritative, such as the Bible. But Plato wishes us to ponder this question: Are the rules good because they appear in the holy book, or do they appear in the holy book because they are good? Or, in the words of Socrates, "Do the gods love holiness because it is holy, or is it holy because they love it?"

GOD AND MORALITY

SOCRATES: But shall we . . . say that whatever all the gods hate is unholy, and whatever they all love is holy: while whatever some of them love, and others hate, is either both or neither? Do you wish us now to define holiness and unholiness in this manner?

EUTHYPHRO: Why not, Socrates?

SOCR: There is no reason why I should not,

[1]From Plato's *Euthyphro*, translated by William Jowett (New York: Charles Scribner's Sons, 1889).

Euthyphro. It is for you to consider whether that definition will help you to instruct me as you promised.

EUTH: Well, I should say that holiness is what all the gods love, and that unholiness is what they all hate.

SOCR: Are we to examine this definition, Euthyphro, and see if it is a good one? Or are we to be content to accept the bare assertions of other men, or of ourselves, without asking any questions? Or must we examine the assertions?

EUTH: We must examine them. But for my part I think that the definition is right this time.

SOCR: We shall know that better in a little while, my good friend. Now consider this question. Do the gods love holiness because it is holy, or is it holy because they love it?

EUTH: I do not understand you, Socrates.

SOCR: I will try to explain myself: we speak of a thing being carried and carrying, and begin led and leading, and being seen and seeing; and you understand that all such expressions mean different things, and what the difference is.

EUTH: Yes, I think I understand.

SOCR: And we talk of a thing being loved, and, which is different, of a thing loving?

EUTH: Of course.

SOCR: Now tell me: is a thing which is being carried in a state of being carried, because it is carried, or for some other reason?

EUTH: No, because it is carried.

SOCR: And a thing is in a state of being led, because it is led, and of being seen, because it is seen?

EUTH: Certainly.

SOCR: Then a thing is not seen because it is in a state of being seen; it is in a state of being seen because it is seen: and a thing is not led because it is in a state of being led; it is in a state of being led because it is led: and a thing is not carried because it is in a state of being carried; it is in a state of being carried because if is carried. Is my meaning clear now, Euthyphro? I mean this: if

anything becomes, or is affected, it does not become because it is in a state of becoming; it is in a state of becoming because it becomes; and it is not affected because it is in a state of being affected: it is in a state of being affected because it is affected. Do you not agree?

EUTH: I do.

SOCR: Is not that which is being loved in a state, either of becoming, or of being affected in some way by something?

EUTH: Certainly.

SOCR: Then the same is true here as in the former cases. A thing is not loved by those who love it because it is in a state of being loved. It is in a state of being loved because they love it.

EUTH: Necessarily.

SOCR: Well, then, Euthyphro, what do we say about holiness? Is it not loved by all the gods, according to your definition?

EUTH: Yes.

SOCR: Because it is holy, or for some other reason?

EUTH: No, because it is holy.

SOCR: Then it is loved by the gods because it is holy: it is not holy because it is loved by them?

EUTH: It seems so.

SOCR: But then what is pleasing to the gods is pleasing to them, and is in a state of being loved by them, because they love it?

EUTH: Of course.

SOCR: Then holiness is not what is pleasing to the gods, and what is pleasing to the gods is not holy, as you say, Euthyphro. They are different things.

EUTH: And why, Socrates?

SOCR: Because we are agreed that the gods love holiness because it is holy: and that it is not holy because they love it. Is not this so?

EUTH: Yes.

SOCR: And that what is pleasing to the gods because they love it, is pleasing to them by reason of this same love: and that they do not love it because it is pleasing to them.

EUTH: True.

SOCR: Then, my dear Euthyphro, holiness, and what is pleasing to the gods, are different things. If the gods had loved holiness because it is holy, they would also have loved what is pleasing to them because it is pleasing to them; but if what is pleasing to them had been pleasing to them because they loved it, then holiness too would have been holiness, because they loved it. But now you see that they are opposite things, and wholly different from each other. For the one is of a sort to be loved because it is loved: while the other is loved, because it is of a sort to be loved. My question, Euthyphro, was, What is holiness? But it turns out that you have not explained to me the essence of holiness; you have been content to mention an attribute which belongs to it, namely, that all the gods love it. You have not yet told me what is its essence. Do not, if you please, keep from me what holiness is; begin again and tell me that. Never mind whether the gods love it, or whether it has other attributes: we shall not differ on that point. Do your best to make it clear to me what is holiness and what is unholiness.

CHAPTER 55

ARISTOTLE

THE ETHICS OF VIRTUE

Aristotle rejects the Platonic view that the "Good" is a transcendent concept, independent of experience, personality, and circumstances. He insists that basic moral principles are immanent in the activities of our daily lives and can be discovered only through a study of them. Accordingly, he begins his ethical inquiry with an investigation of what it is that people fundamentally desire. Finding such goals as wealth and honor insufficient, he concludes that the ultimate goal for people must be one that is self-sufficient, final, and attainable—in a word, happiness. Happiness is "an activity of the soul in accordance with virtue." In order to achieve a state of happiness, social institutions are necessary: The moral person cannot exist apart from a flourishing political setting. Thus ethics is a species of politics.

Consideration of the conditions requisite to happiness leads Aristotle into a lengthy discussion of virtue. Virtue refers to the excellence of a thing; virtues are simply those qualities and dispositions that enable individuals to live well in society. A virtuous person lives according to reason, seeking to realize his or her distinctive potential; the virtuous person wants to do virtuous acts and does them "naturally."

Aristotle identifies both moral and intellectual virtues. The intellectual virtues may be taught directly, but the moral virtues must be lived in order to be learned. The virtues, which become habitual as we live well, are the "means between extremes," our best guarantee of happiness.

594

This selection is drawn from Books I, II, and X of Aristotle's *Nichomachean Ethics*, the first systematic treatise of ethics in the Western tradition.[1]

THE ETHICS OF VIRTUE

Book 1

THE END

1. Every art and every kind of inquiry, and likewise every act and purpose, seems to aim at some good: and so it has been well said that the good is that at which everything aims.

But a difference is observable among these aims or ends. What is aimed at is sometimes the exercise of a faculty, sometimes a certain result beyond that exercise. And where there is an end beyond the act, there the result is better than the exercise of the faculty.

Now since there are may kinds of actions and many arts and sciences, it follows that there arc many ends also; e.g. health is the end of medicine, ships of shipbuilding, victory of the art of war, and wealth of economy.

But when several of these are subordinated to some one art or science—as the making of bridles and other trappings to the art of horsemanship, and this in turn, along with all else that the soldier does, to the art of war, and so on,—then the end of the master-art is always more desired than the ends of the subordinate arts, since these are pursued for its sake. And this is equally true whether the end in view be the mere exercise of a faculty or something beyond that, as in the above instances.

2. If then in what we do there be some end which we wish for on its own account, choosing all the others as means to this, but not every end without exception as a means to something else (for so we should go on *ad infinitum*, and desire would be left void and objectless),—this evidently will be the good or the best of all things.

And surely from a practical point of view it much concerns us to know this good; for then, like archers shooting at a definite mark, we shall be more likely to attain what we want.

If this be so, we must try to indicate roughly what it is, and first of all to which of the arts or sciences it belongs.

It would seem to belong to the supreme art or science, that one which most of all deserves the name of master-art or master-science.

Now Politics seems to answer to this description. For it prescribes which of the sciences a state needs, and which each man shall study, and up to what point; and to it we see subordinated even the highest arts, such as economy, rhetoric, and the art of war.

Since then it makes use of the other practical sciences, and since it further ordains what men are to do and from what to refrain, its end must include the ends of the others, and must be the proper good of man.

For though this good is the same for the individual and the state, yet the good of the state seems a grander and more perfect thing both to attain and to secure; and glad as one would be to do this service for a single individual, to do it for

[1]From Aristotle's *Nichomachean Ethics*, translated by F. H. Peters (London: Kegan Paul, Trench, Trüber & Co., 1891).

a people and for a number of states is nobler and more divine.

This then is the aim of the present inquiry, which is a sort of political inquiry.

3. We must be content if we can attain to so much precision in our statement as the subject before us admits of; for the same degree of accuracy is no more to be expected in all kinds of reasoning than in all kinds of manufacture.

Now what is noble and just (with which Politics deals) is so various and so uncertain, that some think these are merely conventional and not natural distinctions.

There is a similar uncertainty also about what is good, because good things often do people harm: men have before now been ruined by wealth, and have lost their lives through courage.

Our subject, then, and our data being of this nature, we must be content if we can indicate the truth roughly and in outline, and if, in dealing with matters that are not amenable to immutable laws, and reasoning from premises that are but probable, we can arrive at probable conclusions.

The reader, on his part, should take each of my statements in the same spirit; for it is the mark of an educated man to require, in each kind of inquiry, just so much exactness as the subject admits of: it is equally absurd to accept probable reasoning from a mathematician, and to demand scientific proof from an orator.

But each man can form a judgment about what he knows, and is called "a good judge" of that—of any special matter when he has received a special education therein, "a good judge" (without any qualifying epithet) when he has received a universal education. And hence a young man is not qualified to be a student of Politics; for he lacks experience of the affairs of life, which form the data and the subject-matter of Politics.

Further, since he is apt to be swayed by his feelings, he will derive no benefit from a study whose aim is not speculative but practical.

But in this respect young in character counts the same as young in years; for the young man's disqualification is not a matter of time, but is due to the fact that feeling rules his life and directs all his desires. Men of this character turn the knowledge they get to no account in practise, as we see with those we call incontinent; but those who direct their desires and actions by reason will gain much profit from the knowledge of these matters.

So much then by way of preface as to the student, and the spirit in which he must accept what we say, and the object which we propose to ourselves.

4. Since—to resume—all knowledge and all purpose aims at some good, what is this which we say is the aim of Politics; or, in other words, what is the highest of all realizable goods?

As to its name, I suppose nearly all men are agreed; for the masses and the men of culture alike declare that it is happiness, and hold that "to live well" or to "do well" is the same as to be "happy."

But they differ as to what this happiness is, and the masses do not give the same account of it as the philosophers.

The former take it to be something palpable and plain, as pleasure or wealth or fame; one man holds it to be this, and another that, and often the same man is of different minds at different times,—after sickness it is health, and in poverty it is wealth; while when they are impressed with the consciousness of their ignorance, they admire most those who say grand things that are above their comprehension.

Some philosophers, on the other hand, have thought that, beside these several good things, there is an "absolute" good which is the cause of their goodness.

As it would hardly be worth while to review all the opinions that have been held, we will confine ourselves to those which are most popular, or which seem to have some foundation in reason.

But we must not omit to notice the distinction that is drawn between the method of proceeding from your starting-points or principles, and the method of working up to them. Plato used with fitness to raise this question, and to ask whether the right way is from or to your starting-points, as in the race-course you may run from the judges to the boundary, or *vice versa*.

Well, we must start from what is known.

But "what is known" may mean two things: "what is known to us," which is one thing, or "what is known" simply, which is another.

I think it is safe to say that *we* must start from what is known to *us*.

And on this account nothing but a good moral training can qualify a man to study what is noble and just—in a word, to study questions of Politics. For the undemonstrated fact is here the starting-point, and if this undemonstrated fact be sufficiently evident to a man, he will not require a "reason why." Now the man who has had a good moral training either has already arrived at starting-points or principles of action, or will easily accept them when pointed out. But he who neither has them nor will accept them may hear what Hesiod says—

The best is he who of himself doth know;
Good too is he who listens to the wise;
But he who neither knows himself nor heeds
The words of others, is a useless man.

5. Let us now take up the discussion at the point from which we digressed.

As to men's notions of the good or happiness, it seems (to judge, as we reasonably may, from their lives) that the masses, who are the least refined, hold it to be pleasure, and so accept the life of enjoyment as their ideal.

For the most conspicuous kinds of life are three: this life of enjoyment, the life of the statesman, and, thirdly, the contemplative life.

The mass of men show themselves utterly slavish in their preference for the life of brute beasts, but their views receive consideration because many of those in high places have the tastes of Sardanapalus.[1]

Men of refinement with a practical turn prefer honour; for I suppose we may say that honour is the aim of the statesman's life.

But this seems too superficial to be the good we are seeking: for it appears to depend upon those who give rather than upon those who receive it; while we have a presentiment that the good is something that is peculiarly a man's own and can scarce be taken away from him.

Moreover, these men seem to pursue honour, in order that they may be assured of their own excellence,—at least, they wish to be honoured by men of sense, and by those who know them, and on the ground of their virtue or excellence. It is plain, then, that in their view, at any rate, virtue or excellence is better than honour; and perhaps we should take this to be the end of the statesman's life, rather than honour.

But virtue or excellence also appears too incomplete to be what we want; for it seems that a man might have virtue and yet be asleep or be inactive all his life, and, moreover, might meet with the greatest disasters and misfortunes; and no one would maintain that such a man is happy, except for argument's sake. But we will not dwell on these matters now, for they are sufficiently discussed in the popular treatises.

The third kind of life is the life of contemplation: we will treat of it further on.

---

[1]A legendary Assyrian king known for his sensuous lifestyle—Ed.

As for the money-making life, it is something quite contrary to nature; and wealth evidently is not the good of which we are in search, for it is merely useful as a means to something else. So we might rather take pleasure and virtue or excellence to be ends than wealth; for they are chosen on their own account. But it seems that not even they are the end, though much breath has been wasted in attempts to show that they are. . . .

7. Leaving these matters, then, let us return once more to the question, what this good can be of which we are in search.

It seems to be different in different kinds of action and in different arts,—one thing in medicine and another in war, and so on. What then is the good in each of these cases? Surely that for the sake of which all else is done. And that in medicine is health, in war is victory, in building is a house—a different thing in each different case, but always, in whatever we do and in whatever we choose, the end. For it is always for the sake of the end that all else is done.

If then there be one end of all that man does, this end will be the realizable good,—or these ends, if there be more than one.

Our argument has thus come round by a different path to the same point as before. This point we must try to explain more clearly.

We see that there are many ends. But some of these are chosen only as means, as wealth, flutes, and the whole class of instruments. And so it is plain that not all ends are final.

But the best of all things must, we conceive, be something final.

If then there be only one final end, this will be what we are seeking,—or if there be more than one, then the most final of them.

Now that which is pursued as an end in itself is more final than that which is pursued as means to something else, and that which is never chosen as means than that which is chosen both as an end in itself and as means, and that is strictly final which is always chosen as an end in itself and never as means.

Happiness seems more than anything else to answer to this description: for we always choose it for itself, and never for the sake of something else: while honour and pleasure and reason, and all virtue or excellence, we choose partly indeed for themselves (for, apart from any result, we should choose each of them), but partly also for the sake of happiness, supposing that they will help to make us happy. But no one chooses happiness for the sake of these things, or as a means to anything else at all.

We seem to be led to the same conclusion when we start from the notion of self-sufficiency.

The final good is thought to be self-sufficing. In applying this term we do not regard a man as an individual leading a solitary life, but we also take account of parents, children, wife, and, in short, friends and fellow-citizens generally, since man is naturally a social being. Some limit must indeed be set to this; for if you go on to parents and descendants and friends of friends, you will never come to a stop. But this we will consider further on: for the present we will take self-sufficing to mean what by itself makes life desirable and in want of nothing. And happiness is believed to answer to this description.

And further, happiness is believed to be the most desirable thing in the world, and that not merely as one among other good things: if it were merely one among other good things, it is plain that the addition of the least of other goods must make it more desirable; for the addition becomes a surplus of good, and of two goods the greater is always more desirable.

Thus it seems that happiness is something final and self-sufficing, and is the end of all that man does.

But perhaps the reader thinks that though no one will dispute the statement that happiness is the best thing in the world, yet a still more precise definition of it is needed.

This will best be gained, I think, by asking, What is the function of man? For as the goodness and the excellence of a piper or a sculptor, or the practiser of any art, and generally of those who have any function or business to do, lies in that function, so man's good would seem to lie in his function, if he has one.

But can we suppose that, while a carpenter and a cobbler has a function and a business of his own, man has no business and no function assigned him by nature? Nay, surely as his several members, eye and hand and foot, plainly have each his own function, so we must suppose that man also has some function over and above all these.

What then is it?

Life evidently he has in common even with the plants, but we want that which is peculiar to him. We must exclude, therefore, the life of mere nutrition and growth.

Next to this comes the life of sense; but this too he plainly shares with horses and cattle and all kinds of animals.

There remains then the life whereby he acts—the life of his rational nature, with its two sides or divisions, one rational as obeying reason, the other rational as having and exercising reason.

But as this expression is ambiguous, we must be understood to mean thereby the life that consists in the exercise of the faculties; for this seems to be more properly entitled to the name.

The function of man, then, is exercise of his vital faculties on one side in obedience to reason, and on the other side with reason.

But what is called the function of a man of any profession and the function of a man who is good in that profession are generically the same, e.g. of a harper and of a good harper; and this holds in all cases without exception, only that in the case of the latter his superior excellence at his work is added; for we say a harper's function is to harp, and a good harper's to harp well.

Man's function then being, as we say, a kind of life—that is to say, exercise of his faculties and action of various kinds with reason—the good man's function is to do this well and beautifully.

But the function of anything is done well when it is done in accordance with the proper excellence of that thing.

Putting all this together, then, we find that the good of man is exercise of his faculties in accordance with excellence or virtue, or, if there be more than one, in accordance with the best and most complete virtue.

But there must also be a full term of years for this exercise; for one swallow or one fine day does not make a spring, nor does one day or any small space of time make a blessed or happy man.

This, then, may be taken as a rough outline of the good; for this, I think, is the proper method,—first to sketch the outline, and then to fill the details. But it would seem that, the outline once fairly drawn, any one can carry on the work and fit in the several items which time reveals to us or helps us to find. And this indeed is the way in which the arts and sciences have grown; for it requires no extraordinary genius to fill up the gaps.

We must bear in mind, however, what was said above, and not demand the same degree of accuracy in all branches of study, but in each case so much as the subject-matter admits of and as is proper to that kind of inquiry. The carpenter and the geometer both look for the right angle, but in different ways: the former only wants such an approximation to it as his work requires, but the latter wants to know what constitutes a right angle, or what is its special quality; his aim is to find out the truth. And so in other cases we must

599

follow the same course, lest we spend more time on what is immaterial than on the real business in hand.

Nor must we in all cases alike demand the reasons why; sometimes it is enough if the undemonstrated fact be fairly pointed out, as in the case of the starting-points or principles of a science. Undemonstrated facts always form the first step or starting-point of a science; and these starting-points or principles are arrived at some in one way, some in another—some by induction, others by perception, others again by some kind of training. But in each case we must try to apprehend them in the proper way, and do our best to define them clearly; for they have great influence upon the subsequent course of an inquiry. A good start is more than half the race, I think, and our starting-point or principle, once found, clears up a number of our difficulties.

8. We must not be satisfied, then, with examining this starting-point or principle of ours as a conclusion from our data, but must also view it in its relation to current opinions on the subject; for all experience harmonizes with a true principle, but a false one is soon found to be incompatible with the facts.

Now, good things have been divided into three classes, external goods on the one hand, and on the other goods of the soul and goods of the body; and the goods of the soul are commonly said to be goods in the fullest sense, and more good than any other.

But "actions and exercises of the vital faculties or soul" may be said to be "of the soul." So our account is confirmed by this opinion, which is both of long standing and approved by all who busy themselves with philosophy.

But, indeed, we secure the support of this opinion by the mere statement that certain actions and exercises are the end; for this implies that it is to be ranked among the goods of the soul, and not among external goods.

Our account, again, is in harmony with the common saying that the happy man lives well and does well; for we may say that happiness, according to us, is a living well and doing well.

And, indeed, all the characteristics that men expect to find in happiness seem to belong to happiness as we define it.

Some hold it to be virtue or excellence, some prudence, others a kind of wisdom; others, again, hold it to be all or some of these, with the addition of pleasure, either as an ingredient or as a necessary accompaniment; and some even include external prosperity in their account of it.

Now, some of these views have the support of many voices and of old authority; others have few voices, but those of weight; but it is probable that neither the one side nor the other is entirely wrong, but that in some one point at least, if not in most, they are both right.

First, then, the view that happiness is excellence or a kind of excellence harmonizes with our account; for "exercise of faculties in accordance with excellence" belongs to excellence.

But I think we may say that it makes no small difference whether the good be conceived as the mere possession of something, or as its use—as a mere habit or trained faculty, or as the exercise of that faculty. For the habit or faculty may be present, and yet issue in no good result, as when a man is asleep, or in any other way hindered from his function; but with its exercise this is not possible, for it must show itself in acts and in good acts. And as at the Olympic games it is not the fairest and strongest who receive the crown, but those who contend (for among these are the victors), so in life, too, the winners are those who not only have all the excellences, but manifest these in deed.

And, further, the life of these men is in itself pleasant. For pleasure is an affection of the soul, and each man takes pleasure in that which he is said to love,—he who loves horses in horses, he who loves sight-seeing in sight-seeing, and in the same way he who loves justice in acts of justice, and generally the lover of excellence or virtue in virtuous acts or the manifestation of excellence.

And while with most men there is a perpetual conflict between the several things in which they find pleasure, since these are not naturally pleasant, those who love what is noble take pleasure in that which is naturally pleasant. For the manifestations of excellence are naturally pleasant, so that they are both pleasant to them and pleasant in themselves.

Their life, then, does not need pleasure to be added to it as an appendage, but contains pleasure in itself.

Indeed, in addition to what we have said, a man is not good at all unless he takes pleasure in noble deeds. No one would call a man just who did not take pleasure in doing justice, nor generous who took no pleasure in acts of generosity, and so on.

If this be so, the manifestations of excellence will be pleasant in themselves. But they are also both good and noble, and that in the highest degree—at least, if the good man's judgment about them is right, for this is his judgment.

Happiness, then, is at once the best and noblest and pleasantest thing in the world, and these are not separated, as the Delian inscription would have them to be:

What is most just is noblest, health is best,
Pleasantest is to get your heart's desire.

For all these characteristics are united in the best exercises of our faculties; and these, or some one of them that is better than all the others, we identify with happiness.

But nevertheless happiness plainly requires external goods too, as we said; for it is impossible, or at least not easy, to act nobly without some furniture or fortune. There are many things that can only be done through instruments, so to speak, such as friends and wealth and political influence: and there are some things whose absence takes the bloom off our happiness, as good birth, the blessing of children, personal beauty; for a man is not very likely to be happy if he is very ugly in person, or of low birth, or alone in the world, or childless, and perhaps still less if he has worthless children or friends, or has lost good ones that he had.

As we said, then, happiness seems to stand in need of this kind of prosperity; and so some identify it with good fortune, just as others identify it with excellence.

9. This has led people to ask whether happiness is attained by learning, or the formation of habits, or any other kind of training, or comes by some divine dispensation or even by chance.

Well, if the Gods do give gifts to men, happiness is likely to be among the number, more likely, indeed, than anything else, in proportion as it is better than all other human things.

This belongs more properly to another branch of inquiry; but we may say that even if it is not heaven-sent, but comes as a consequence of virtue or some kind of learning or training, still it seems to be one of the most divine things in the world; for the prize and aim of virtue would appear to be better than anything else and something divine and blessed.

Again, if it is thus acquired it will be widely accessible; for it will then be in the power of all except those who have lost the capacity for excellence to acquire it by study and diligence.

And if it be better that men should attain happiness in this way rather than by chance, it is reasonable to suppose that it is so, since in the sphere of nature all things are arranged in the best possible way, and likewise in the sphere of art, and of each mode of causation, and most of all in the sphere of the noblest mode of causation. And indeed it would be too absurd to leave what is noblest and fairest to the dispensation of chance.

But our definition itself clears up the difficulty; for happiness was defined as a certain kind of exercise of the vital faculties in accordance with excellence or virtue. And of the remaining goods, some must be present as necessary conditions, while others are aids and useful instruments to happiness. And this agrees with what we said at starting. We then laid down that the end of the art political is the best of all ends; but the chief business of that art is to make the citizens of a certain character—that is, good and apt to do what is noble. It is not without reason, then, that we do not call an ox, or a horse, or any brute happy; for none of them is able to share in this kind of activity.

For the same reason also a child is not happy; he is as yet, because of his age, unable to do such things. If we ever call a child happy, it is because we hope he will do them. For, as we said, happiness requires not only perfect excellence or virtue, but also a full term of years for its exercise. For our circumstances are liable to many changes and to all sorts of chances, and it is possible that he who is now most prosperous will in his old age meet with great disasters, as is told of Priam in the tales of the heroes; and a man who is thus used by fortune and comes to a miserable end cannot be called happy. . . .

13. Since happiness is an exercise of the vital faculties in accordance with perfect virtue or excellence, we will now inquire about virtue or excellence; for this will probably help us in our inquiry about happiness.

And indeed the true statesman seems to be especially concerned with virtue, for he wishes to make the citizens good and obedient to the laws. Of this we have an example in the Cretan and the Lacedaemonian lawgivers, and any others who have resembled them. But if the inquiry belongs to Politics or the science of the state, it is plain that it will be in accordance with our original purpose to pursue it.

The virtue or excellence that we are to consider is, of course, the excellence of man: for it is the good of man and the happiness of man that we started to seek. And by the excellence of man I mean excellence not of body, but of soul; for happiness we take to be an activity of the soul.

If this be so, then it is evident that the statesman must have some knowledge of the soul, just as the man who is to heal the eye or the whole body must have some knowledge of them, and that the more in proportion as the science of the state is higher and better than medicine. But all educated physicians take much pains to know about the body.

As statesmen, then, we must inquire into the nature of the soul, but in so doing we must keep our special purpose in view and go only so far as that requires; for to go into minuter detail would be too laborious for the present undertaking.

Now, there are certain points which are stated with sufficient precision even in the popular accounts of the soul, and these we will adopt.

For instance, they distinguish an irrational and a rational part.

Whether these are separated as are the parts of the body or any divisible thing, or whether they are only distinguishable in thought but in fact inseparable, like concave and convex in the circumference of a circle, makes no difference for our present purpose.

Of the irrational part, again, one division seems to be common to all things that live, and to be possessed by plants—I mean that which causes nutrition and growth; for we must assume that all things that take nourishment have a faculty of this kind, even when they are embryos, and have the same faculty when they are full grown; at least, this is more reasonable than to suppose that they then have a different one.

The excellence of this faculty, then, is plainly one that man shares with other beings, and not specifically human.

And this is confirmed by the fact that this part of the soul, or this faculty, is thought to be most active in sleep, while the distinction between the good and the bad man shows itself least in sleep—whence the saying that for half their lives there is no difference between the happy and the miserable. This indeed is what we should expect; for sleep is the cessation of the soul from those functions in respect of which it is called good or bad, except in so far as the motions of the body may sometimes make their way in, and give occasion to dreams which are better in the good man than in ordinary people.

However, we need not pursue this further, and may dismiss the nutritive principle, since it has no place in the excellence of man.

But there seems to be another vital principle that is irrational, and yet in some way partakes of reason. In the case of the continent and of the incontinent man alike we praise the reason or the rational part, for it exhorts them rightly and urges them to do what is best; but there is plainly present in them another principle besides the rational one, which fights and struggles against the reason. For just as a paralyzed limb, when you will to move it to the right, moves on the contrary to the left, so is it with the soul; the incontinent man's impulses run counter to his reason. Only whereas we see the refractory member in the case of the body, we do not see it in the case of the soul. But we must nevertheless, I think, hold that in the soul too there is something beside the reason, which opposes and runs counter to it (though in what sense it is distinct from the reason does not matter here).

It seems, however, to partake of reason also, as we said: at least, in the continent man it submits to the reason; while in the temperate and courageous man we may say it is still more obe-

dient; for in him it is altogether in harmony with the reason.

The irrational part, then, it appears, is twofold. There is the vegetative faculty, which has no share of reason; and the faculty of appetite or of desire in general, which partakes of reason in a manner—that is, in so far as it listens to reason and submits to its sway. But when we say "partakes of reason" or "listens to reason," we mean this in the sense in which we talk of "listening to reason" from parents or friends, not in the sense in which we talk of listening to the reasonings of mathematicians.

Further, all advice and all rebuke and exhortation testifies that the irrational part is in some way amenable to reason.

If then we like to say that this part, too, has a share of reason, the rational part also will have two divisions: one rational in the strict sense as possessing reason in itself, the other rational as listening to reason as a man listens to his father.

Now, on this division of the faculties is based the division of excellence; for we speak of intellectual excellences and of moral excellences; wisdom and understanding and prudence we call intellectual, liberality and temperance we call moral virtues or excellences. When we are speaking of a man's moral character we do not say that he is wise or intelligent, but that he is gentle or temperate. But we praise the wise man, too, for his habit of mind or trained faculty; and a habit or trained faculty that is praiseworthy is what we call an excellence or virtue.

Book II

MORAL VIRTUE

1. Excellence, then, being of these two kinds, intellectual and moral, intellectual excellence owes it birth and growth mainly to instruction, and so requires time and experience, while moral

excellence is the result of habit or custom, and has accordingly in our language received a name formed by a slight change from *ethos*.

From this it is plain that none of the moral excellences or virtues is implanted in us by nature; for that which is by nature cannot be altered by training. For instance, a stone natural-ly tends to fall downwards, and you could not train it to rise upwards, though you tried to do so by throwing it up ten thousand times, nor could you train fire to move downwards, nor accustom anything which naturally behaves in one way to behave in any other way.

The virtues, then, come neither by nature nor against nature, but nature gives the capacity for acquiring them, and this is developed by train-ing.

Again, where we do things by nature we get the power first, and put this power forth in act afterwards: as we plainly see in the case of the senses; for it is not by constantly seeing and hear-ing that we acquire those faculties, but, on the contrary, we had the power first and then used it, instead of acquiring the power by the use. But the virtues we acquire by doing the acts, as is the case with the arts too. We learn an art by doing that which we wish to do when we have learned it; we become builders by building, and harpers by harping. And so by doing just acts we become just, and by doing acts of temperance and cour-age we become temperate and courageous.

This is attested, too, by what occurs in states; for the legislators make their citizens good by training; i.e. this is the wish of all legislators, and those who do not succeed in this miss their aim, and it is this that distinguishes a good from a bad constitution.

Again, both the moral virtues and the corre-sponding vices result from and are formed by the same acts; and this is the case with the arts also. It is by harping that good harpers and bad harpers alike are produced: and so with builders and the

rest; by building well they will become good builders, and bad builders by building badly. Indeed, if it were not so, they would not want anybody to teach them, but would all be born either good or bad at their trades. And it is just the same with the virtues also. It is by our con-duct in our intercourse with other men that we become just or unjust, and by acting in circum-stances of danger, and training ourselves to feel fear or confidence, that we become courageous or cowardly. So, too, with our animal appetites and the passion of anger; for by behaving in this way or in that on the occasions with which these passions are concerned, some become temperate and gentle, and others profligate and ill-tem-pered. In a word, acts of any kind produce habits or characters of the same kind.

Hence we ought to make sure that our acts be of a certain kind; for the resulting character varies as they vary. It makes no small difference, therefore, whether a man be trained from his youth up in this way or in that, but a great dif-ference, or rather all the difference.

2. But our present inquiry has not, like the rest, a merely speculative aim; we are not inquir-ing merely in order to know what excellence or virtue is, but in order to become good; for oth-erwise it would profit us nothing. We must ask therefore about these acts, and see of what kind they are to be; for, as we said, it is they that determine our habits or character.

First of all, then, that they must be in accor-dance with right reason is a common character-istic of them, which we shall here take for grant-ed, reserving for future discussion the question what this right reason is, and how it is related to the other excellences.

But let it be understood, before we go on, that all reasoning on matters of practice must be in outline merely, and not scientifically exact: for, as we said at starting, the kind of reasoning to be demanded varies with the subject in hand;

and in practical matters and questions of expediency there are no invariable laws, any more than in questions of health.

And if our general conclusions are thus inexact, still more inexact is all reasoning about particular cases; for these fall under no system of scientifically established rules or traditional maxims, but the agent must always consider for himself what the special occasion requires, just as in medicine or navigation.

But though this is the case we must try to render what help we can.

First of all, then, we must observe that, in matters of this sort, to fall short and to exceed are alike fatal. This is plain (to illustrate what we cannot see by what we can see) in the case of strength and health. Too much and too little exercise alike destroy strength, and to take too much meat and drink, or to take too little, is equally ruinous to health, but the fitting amount produces and increases and preserves them. Just so, then, is it with temperance also, and courage, and the other virtues. The man who shuns and fears everything and never makes a stand, becomes a coward; while the man who fears nothing at all, but will face anything, becomes foolhardy. So, too, the man who takes his fill of any kind of pleasure, and abstains from none, is a profligate, but the man who shuns all (like him whom we call a "boor") is devoid of sensibility. For temperance and courage are destroyed both by excess and defect, but preserved by moderation.

But habits or types of character are not only produced and preserved and destroyed by the same occasions and the same means, but they will also manifest themselves in the same circumstances. This is the case with palpable things like strength. Strength is produced by taking plenty of nourishment and doing plenty of hard work, and the strong man, in turn, has the greatest capacity for these. And the case is the same with the virtues: by abstaining from pleasure we become temperate, and when we have become temperate we are best able to abstain. And so with courage: by habituating ourselves to despise danger, and to face it, we become courageous; and when we have become courageous, we are best able to face danger.

3. The pleasure or pain that accompanies the acts must be taken as a test of the formed habit or character.

He who abstains from the pleasures of the body and rejoices in the abstinence is temperate, while he who is vexed at having to abstain is profligate; and again, he who faces danger with pleasure, or, at any rate, without pain, is courageous, but he to whom this is painful is a coward.

For moral virtue or excellence is closely concerned with pleasure and pain. It is pleasure that moves us to do what is base, and pain that moves us to refrain from what is noble. And therefore, as Plato says, man needs to be so trained from his youth up as to find pleasure and pain in the right objects. This is what sound education means.

Another reason why virtue has to do with pleasure and pain, is that it has to do with actions and passions or affections; but every affection and every act is accompanied by pleasure or pain.

The fact is further attested by the employment of pleasure and pain in correction; they have a kind of curative property, and a cure is effected by administering the opposite of the disease.

Again, as we said before, every type of character is essentially relative to, and concerned with, those things that form it for good or for ill; but it is through pleasure and pain that bad characters are formed—that is to say, through pursuing and avoiding the wrong pleasures and pains, or pursuing and avoiding them at the wrong time, or in the wrong manner, or in any other of the various ways of going wrong that may be distinguished.

And hence some people go so far as to define the virtues as a kind of impassive or neutral state of mind. But they err in stating this absolutely, instead of qualifying it by the addition of the right and wrong manner, time, etc.

We may lay down, therefore, that this kind of excellence makes us do what is best in matters of pleasure and pain, while vice or badness has the contrary effect.

The following considerations will throw additional light on the point.

There are three kinds of things that move us to choose, and three that move us to avoid them: on the one hand, the beautiful or noble, the advantageous, the pleasant; on the other hand, the ugly or base, the hurtful, the painful. Now, the good man is apt to go right, and the bad man to go wrong, about them all, but especially about pleasure: for pleasure is not only common to man with animals, but also accompanies all pursuit or choice; since the noble, and the advantageous also, are pleasant in idea.

Again, the feeling of pleasure has been fostered in us all from our infancy by our training, and has thus become so engrained in our life that it can scarce be washed out. And, indeed, we all more or less make pleasure our test in judging of actions. For this reason too, then, our whole inquiry must be concerned with these matters; since to be pleased and pained in the right or the wrong way has great influence on our actions.

Again, to fight with pleasure is harder than to fight with wrath (which Heraclitus says is hard), and virtue, like art, is always more concerned with what is harder; for the harder the task the better is success. For this reason also, then, both virtue or excellence and the science of the state must always be concerned with pleasures and pains; for he that behaves rightly with regard to pains, for he that behaves rightly with regard to

them will be good, and he that behaves badly will be bad.

We will take it as established, then, that excellence or virtue has to do with pleasures and pains; and that the acts which produce it develop it, and also, when differently done, destroy it; and that it manifests itself in the same acts which produced it.

4. But here we may be asked what we mean by saying that men can become just and temperate only by doing what is just and temperate: surely, it may be said, if their acts are just and temperate, they themselves are already just and temperate, as they are grammarians and musicians if they do what is grammatical and musical.

We may answer, I think, firstly, that this is not quite the case even with the arts. A man may do something grammatical by chance, or at the prompting of another person: he will not be grammatical till he not only does something grammatical, but also does it grammatically, i.e., in virtue of his own knowledge of grammar.

But, secondly, the virtues are not in this point analogous to the arts. The products of art have their excellence in themselves, and so it is enough if when produced they are of a certain quality; but in the case of the virtues, a man is not said to act justly or temperately if what he does merely be of a certain sort—he must also be in a certain state of mind when he does it; i.e., first of all, he must know what he is doing; secondly, he must choose it, and choose it for itself; and, thirdly, his act must be the expression of a formed and stable character. Now, of these conditions, only one, the knowledge, is necessary for the possession of any art; but for the possession of the virtues knowledge is of little or no avail, while the other conditions that result from repeatedly doing what is just and temperate are not a little important, but all-important.

The thing that is done, therefore, is called just or temperate when it is such as the just or temperate man would do; but the man who does it is not just or temperate, unless he also does it in the spirit of the just or the temperate man.

It is right, then, to say that by doing what is just a man becomes just, and temperate by doing what is temperate, while without doing thus he has no chance of ever becoming good.

But most men, instead of doing thus, fly to theories, and fancy that they are philosophizing and that this will make them good, like a sick man who listens attentively to what the doctor says and then disobeys all his orders. This sort of philosophizing will no more produce a healthy habit of mind than this sort of treatment will produce a healthy habit of body.

5. We have next to inquire what excellence or virtue is.

A quality of the soul is either (1) a passion or emotion, or (2) a power or faculty, or (3) a habit or trained faculty; and so virtue must be one of these three. By (1) a passion or emotion we mean appetite, anger, fear, confidence, envy, joy, love, hate, longing, emulation, pity, or generally that which is accompanied by pleasure or pain; (2) a power or faculty is that in respect of which we are said to be capable of being affected in any of these ways, as, for instance, that in respect of which we are able to be angered or pained or to pity; and (3) a habit or trained faculty is that in respect of which we are well or ill regulated or disposed in the matter of our affections; as, for instance, in the matter of being angered, we are ill regulated if we are too violent or too slack, but if we are moderate in our anger we are well regulated. And so with the rest.

Now, the virtues are not emotions, nor are the vices—(1) because we are not called good or bad in respect of our emotions, but are called so in respect of our virtues or vices; (2) because we are neither praised nor blamed in respect of our emotions (a man is not praised for being afraid or angry, nor blamed for being angry simply, but for being angry in a particular way), but we are praised or blamed in respect of our virtues or vices; (3) because we may be angered or frightened without deliberate choice, but the virtues are a kind of deliberate choice, or at least are impossible without it; and (4) because in respect of our emotions we are said to be moved, but in respect of our virtues and vices we are not said to be moved, but to be regulated or disposed in this way or in that.

For these same reasons also they are not powers or faculties; for we are not called either good or bad for being merely capable of emotion, nor are we either praised or blamed for this. And further, while nature gives us our powers or faculties, she does not make us either good or bad. (This point, however, we have already treated.)

If, then, the virtues be neither emotions nor faculties, it only remains for them to be habits or trained faculties.

6. We have thus found the genus to which virtue belongs; but we want to know, not only that it is a trained faculty, but also what species of trained faculty it is.

We may safely assert that the virtue or excellence of a thing causes that thing both to be itself in good condition and to perform its function well. The excellence of the eye, for instance, makes both the eye and its work good; for it is by the excellence of the eye that we see well. So the proper excellence of the horse makes a horse what he should be, and makes him good at running, and carrying his rider, and standing a charge.

If, then, this holds good in all cases, the proper excellence or virtue of man will be a habit or trained faculty that makes a man good and makes him perform his function well.

How this is to be done we have already said, but we may exhibit the same conclusion in another way, by inquiring what the nature of this virtue is.

Now, if we have any quantity, whether continuous or discrete, it is possible to take either a larger, or a smaller, or an equal amount, and that either absolutely or relatively to our own needs.

By an equal or fair amount I understand a mean amount, or one that lies between excess and deficiency.

By the absolute mean, or mean relatively to the thing itself, I understand that which is equidistant from both extremes, and this is one and the same for all.

By the mean relatively to us I understand that which is neither too much nor too little for us; and this is not one and the same for all.

For instance, if ten be larger and two be smaller, if we take six we take the mean relatively to the thing itself; for it exceeds one extreme by the same amount by which it is exceeded by the other extreme: and this is the mean in arithmetical proportion.

But the mean relatively to us cannot be found in this way. If ten pounds of food is too much for a given man to eat, and two pounds too little, it does not follow that the trainer will order him six pounds: for that also may perhaps be too much for the man in question, or too little; too little for Milo,[2] too much for the beginner. The same holds true in running and wrestling.

And so we may say generally that a master in any art avoids what is too much and what is too little, and seeks for the mean and chooses it—not the absolute but the relative mean.

Every art or science, then, perfects its work in this way, looking to the mean and bringing its work up to this standard; so that people are wont to say of a good work that nothing could be tak-

en from it or added to it, implying that excellence is destroyed by excess or deficiency, but secured by observing the mean. And good artists, as we say, do in fact keep their eyes fixed on this in all that they do.

Virtue therefore, since like nature it is more exact and better than any art, must also aim at the mean—virtue of course meaning moral virtue or excellence; for it has to do with passions and actions, and it is these that admit of excess and deficiency and the mean. For instance, it is possible to feel fear, confidence, desire, anger, pity, and generally to be affected pleasantly and painfully, either too much or too little, in either case wrongly; but to be thus affected at the right times, and on the right occasions, and towards the right persons, and with the right object, and in the right fashion, is the mean course and the best course, and these are characteristics of virtue. And in the same way our outward acts also admit of excess and deficiency, and the mean or due amount.

Virtue, then, has to deal with feelings or passions and with outward acts, in which excess is wrong and deficiency also is blamed, but the mean amount is praised and is right—both of which are characteristics of virtue.

Virtue, then, is a kind of moderation, inasmuch as it aims at the mean or moderate amount.

Again, there are many ways of going wrong (for evil is infinite in nature, to use a Pythagorean figure, while good is finite), but only one way of going right; so that the one is easy and the other hard—easy to miss the mark and hard to hit. On this account also, then, excess and deficiency are characteristic of vice, hitting the mean is characteristic of virtue:

Goodness is simple, ill takes any shape.

Virtue, then, is a habit or trained faculty of choice, the characteristic of which lies in moder-

---

[2] A famous wrestler.—Ed.

ation or observance of the mean relatively to the persons concerned, as determined by reason, i.e., as the prudent man would determine it.

And it is a moderation, firstly, inasmuch as it comes in the middle or mean between two vices, one on the side of excess, the other on the side of defect; and, secondly, inasmuch as, while these vices fall short of or exceed the due measure in feeling and in action, it finds and chooses the mean, middling, or moderate amount.

Regarded in its essence, therefore, or according to the definition of its nature, virtue is a moderation or middle state, but viewed in its relation to what is best and right it is the extreme of perfection.

But it is not all actions nor all passions that admit of moderation; there are some whose very names imply badness, as malevolence, shamelessness, envy, and, among acts, adultery, theft, murder. These and all other like things are blamed as being bad in themselves, and not merely in their excess or deficiency. It is impossible therefore to go right in them; they are always wrong: rightness and wrongness in such things (e.g., in adultery) does not depend upon whether it is the right person and occasion and manner, but the mere doing of any one of them is wrong.

It would be equally absurd to look for moderation or excess or deficiency in unjust, cowardly or profligate conduct; for then there would be moderation in excess or deficiency, and excess in excess, and deficiency in deficiency.

The fact is that just as there can be no excess or deficiency in temperance or courage because the mean or moderate amount is, in a sense, an extreme, so in these kinds of conduct also there can be no moderation or excess or deficiency, but the acts are wrong however they be done. For, to put it generally, there cannot be moderation in excess or deficiency, nor excess or deficiency in moderation.

7. But it is not enough to make these general statements: we must go on and apply them to particulars. For in reasoning about matters of conduct general statements are too vague, and do not convey so much truth as particular propositions. It is with particulars that conduct is concerned: our statements, therefore, when applied to these particulars, should be found to hold good.

These particulars then, we will take from the following table.

Moderation in the feelings of fear and confidence is courage: of those that exceed, he that exceeds in fearlessness has no name (as often happens), but he that exceeds in confidence is foolhardy, while he that exceeds in fear, but is deficient in confidence, is cowardly.

Moderation in respect of certain pleasures and also (though to a less extent) certain pains is temperance, while excess is profligacy. But defectiveness in the matter of these pleasures is hardly ever found, and so this sort of people also have as yet received no name: let us put them down as "void of sensibility."

In the matter of giving and taking money, moderation is liberality, excess and deficiency are prodigality and illiberality. But these two vices exceed and fall short in contrary ways: the prodigal exceeds in spending, but falls short in taking; while the illiberal man exceeds in taking, but falls short in spending.

(For the present we are but giving an outline or summary, and aim at nothing more; we shall afterwards treat these points in greater detail.)

But, besides these, there are other dispositions in the matter of money: there is a moderation which is called magnificence (for the magnificent is not the same as the liberal man: the former deals with large sums, the latter with small), and an excess which is called bad taste or vulgarity, and a deficiency which is called meanness; and these vices differ from those which are opposed to liberality: how they differ will be explained later.

With respect to honour and disgrace, there is

a moderation which is high-mindedness, an excess which may be called vanity, and a deficiency which is little-mindedness.

But just as we said that liberality is related to magnificence, differing only in that it deals with small sums, so here there is a virtue related to high-mindedness, and differing only in that it is concerned with small instead of great honours. A man may have a due desire for honour, and also more or less than a due desire: he that carries this desire to excess is called ambitious, he that has not enough of it is called unambitious, but he that has the due amount has no name. There are also no abstract names for the characters, except "ambition," corresponding to ambitious. And on this account those who occupy the extremes lay claim to the middle place. And in common parlance, too, the moderate man is sometimes called ambitious and sometimes unambitious, and sometimes the ambitious man is praised and sometimes the unambitious. Why this is we will explain afterwards; for the present we will follow out our plan and enumerate the other types of character.

In the matter of anger also we find excess and deficiency and moderation. The characters themselves hardly have recognized names, but as the moderate man is here called gentle, we will call his character gentleness; of those who go into extremes, we may take the term wrathful for him who exceeds, with wrathfulness for the vice, and wrathless for him who is deficient, with wrathlessness for his character.

Besides these, there are three kinds of moderation, bearing some resemblance to one another, and yet different. They all have to do with intercourse in speech and action, but they differ in that one has to do with the truthfulness of this intercourse, while the other two have to do with its pleasantness—one of the two with pleasantness in matters of amusement, the other with pleasantness in all the relations of life. We must therefore speak of these qualities also in order that we may the more plainly see how, in all cases, moderation is praiseworthy, while the extreme courses are neither right nor praiseworthy, but blamable.

In these cases also names are for the most part wanting, but we must try, here as elsewhere, to coin names ourselves, in order to make our argument clear and easy to follow.

In the matter of truth, then, let us call him who observes the mean a true person, and observance of the mean truth: pretence, when it exaggerates, may be called boasting, and the person a boaster; when it understates, let the names be irony and ironical.

With regard to pleasantness in amusement, he who observes the mean may be called witty, and his character wittiness; excess may be called buffoonery, and the man a buffoon; while boorish may stand for the person who is deficient, and boorishness for his character.

With regard to pleasantness in the other affairs of life, he who makes himself properly pleasant may be called friendly, and his moderation friendliness; he that exceeds may be called obsequious if he have no ulterior motive, but a flatterer if he has an eye to his own advantage; he that is deficient in this respect, and always makes himself disagreeable, may be called a quarrelsome or peevish fellow.

Moreover, in mere emotions and in our conduct with regard to them, there are ways of observing the mean; for instance, shame is not a virtue, but yet the modest man is praised. For in these matters also we speak of this man as observing the mean, of that man as going beyond it (as the shamefaced man whom the least thing makes shy), while he who is deficient in the feeling, or lacks it altogether, is called shameless; but the term modest is applied to him who observes the mean.

Righteous indignation, again, hits the mean between envy and malevolence. These have to do with feelings of pleasure and pain at what happens to our neighbors. A man is called righteously indignant when he feels pain at the sight of undeserved prosperity, but your envious man goes beyond him and is pained by the sight of any one in prosperity, while the malevolent man is so far from being pained that he actually exults in the misfortunes of his neighbours.

But we shall have another opportunity of discussing these matters.

As for justice, the term is used in more senses than one; we will, therefore, after disposing of the above questions, distinguish these various senses, and show how each of these kinds of justice is a kind of moderation.

And then we will treat of the intellectual virtues in the same way.

8. There are, as we said, three classes of disposition, viz. two kinds of vice, one marked by excess, the other by deficiency, and one kind of virtue, the observance of the mean.

Now, the extreme dispositions are opposed both to the mean or moderate disposition and to one another, while the moderate disposition is opposed to both the extremes. Just as a quantity which is equal to a given quantity is also greater when compared with a less, and less when compared with a greater quantity, so the mean or moderate dispositions exceed as compared with the defective dispositions, and fall short as compared with the excessive dispositions, both in feeling and in action: e.g., the courageous man seems foolhardy as compared with the coward, and cowardly as compared with the foolhardy; and similarly the temperate man appears profligate in comparison with the insensible, and insensible in comparison with the profligate man; and the liberal man appears prodigal by the side of the illiberal man, and illiberal by the side of the prodigal man.

And so the extreme characters try to displace the mean or moderate character, and each represents him as falling into the opposite extreme, the coward calling the courageous man foolhardy, the foolhardy calling him coward, and so on in other cases.

But while the mean and the extremes are thus opposed to one another, the extremes are still more contrary to each other than to the mean; for they are further removed from one another than from the mean, as that which is greater than a given magnitude is further from that which is less, and that which is less is further from that which is greater, than either the greater of the less is from that which is equal to the given magnitude.

Sometimes, again, an extreme, when compared with the mean, has a sort of resemblance to it, as foolhardiness to courage, or prodigality to liberality; but there is the greatest possible dissimilarity between the extremes.

Again, "things that are as far as possible removed from each other" is the accepted definition of contraries, so that the further things are removed from each other the more contrary they are.

In comparison with the mean, however, it is sometimes the deficiency that is the more opposed, and sometimes the excess; e.g., foolhardiness, which is excess, is not so much opposed to courage as cowardice, which is deficiency; but insensibility, which is lack of feeling, is not so much opposed to temperance as profligacy, which is excess.

The reasons for this are two. One is the reason derived from the nature of the matter itself: since one extreme is, in fact, nearer and more similar to the mean, we naturally do not oppose it to the mean so strongly as the other; e.g., as foolhardiness seems more similar to courage and nearer to it, and cowardice more dissimilar, we speak of cowardice as the opposite rather than the other: for that which is further removed from the mean seems more opposed to it.

This, then, is one reason, derived from the nature of the thing itself. Another reason lies in ourselves: and it is this—those things to which we happen to be more prone by nature appear to be more opposed to the mean: e.g. our natural inclination is rather towards indulgence in pleasure, and so we more easily fall into profligate than into regular habits: those courses, then, in which we are more apt to run to great lengths are spoken of as more opposed to the mean; and thus profligacy, which is an excess, is more opposed to temperance than the deficiency is.

9. We have sufficiently explained, then, that moral virtue is moderation or observance of the mean, and in what sense, viz. (1) as holding a middle position between two vices, one on the side of excess, and the other on the side of deficiency, and (2) as aiming at the mean or moderate amount both in feeling and in action.

And on this account it is a hard thing to be good; for finding the middle or the mean in each case is a hard thing, just as finding the middle or centre of a circle is a thing that is not within the power of everybody, but only of him who has the requisite knowledge.

Thus any one can be angry—that is quite easy; any one can give money away or spend it: but to do these things to the right person, to the right extent, at the right time, with the right object, and in the right manner, is not what everybody can do, and is by no means easy; and that is the reason why right doing is rare and praiseworthy and noble.

He that aims at the mean, then, should first of all strive to avoid that extreme which is more opposed to it, as Calypso bids Ulysses—

Clear of these smoking breakers keep thy ship.

For of the extremes one is more dangerous, the other less. Since then it is hard to hit the mean precisely, we must "row when we cannot sail," as the proverb has it, and choose the least of two evils; and that will be best effected in the way we have described.

And secondly we must consider, each for himself, which we are most prone to—for different natures are inclined to different things—which we may learn by the pleasure or pain we feel. And then we must bend ourselves in the opposite direction; for by keeping well away from error we shall fall into the middle course, as we straighten a bent stick by bending it the other way.

But in all cases we must be especially on our guard against pleasant things, and against pleasure; for we can scarce judge her impartially. And so, in our behaviour towards her, we should imitate the behaviour of the old counselors towards Helen, and in all cases repeat their saying: if we dismiss her we shall be less likely to go wrong.

This then, in outline, is the course by which we shall best be able to hit the mean.

But it is a hard task, we must admit, especially in a particular case. It is not easy to determine, for instance, how and with whom one ought to be angry, and upon what grounds, and for how long; for public opinion sometimes praises those who fall short, and calls them gentle, and sometimes applies the term manly to those who show a harsh temper.

In fact, a slight error, whether on the side of excess or deficiency, is not blamed, but only a considerable error; for then there can be no mistake. But it is hardly possible to determine by reasoning how far or to what extent a man must err in order to incur blame; and indeed matters that fall within the scope of perception never can be so determined. Such matters lie within the region of particulars, and can only be determined by perception.

So much then is plain, that the middle character is in all cases to be praised, but that we ought to incline sometimes towards excess, sometimes towards deficiency; for in this way we shall most easily hit the mean and attain to right doing.

CHAPTER 56

THOMAS HOBBES

MORALITY AND SELF-INTEREST

Thomas Hobbes (1588–1679), the greatest English philosopher of the seventeenth century, was born prematurely when his mother heard of the approach of the Spanish Armada. Regarding the peculiar nature of his entrance into the world, he jested, "Fear and I were born twins."

Upon graduation from Oxford University in 1608, Hobbes became a private tutor to the prominent Cavendish family, allowing him to travel and make the acquaintance of such important philosophers and scientists as Galileo, Bacon, Kepler, and Descartes.

John Aubrey's *Brief Lives* records that at the age of forty, quite by accident, Hobbes became deeply interested in the deductive certainty of mathematics. "Being in a gentleman's library, Euclid's *Elements* lay open, and t'was the forty-seventh [theorem of Book I]. He read the proposition. 'By God,' he said, 'this is impossible.' So he read the demonstration of it which referred him back to such a proposition: which proposition he read. That referred him back to another, which he also read. [And so back to the self-evident axioms, when] at last he was demonstrably convinced of that truth. This made him in love with geometry."[1]

Like Galileo and Descartes, Hobbes was convinced that a systematic philosophy must be based upon the method of geometry and the newly discovered principles of physics, which viewed all change as a change in motion. Deduction

---

[1] From Thomas Hobbes's *Leviathan* (Indianapolis: Bobbs–Merrill Educational Publishing, 1958).

and materialism, then, were to be the bedrock elements of his new philosophy of human nature and society. This *mechanistic materialism*—the view that everything is ultimately reducible to material bodies in motion—determined Hobbes' view of morality as well.

His principal philosophical work, *Leviathan* (1651), expressed his views on the relationships between nature, the individual, and society. It is here that Hobbes graphically describes *the state of nature* and proposes his version of the *social contract*, attempting to justify absolutism as the only rationally defensible form of government.

In *Leviathan* Hobbes argued that morality should be viewed as the outcome of an agreement that rational, self-interested people have entered into because it is to everyone's benefit to live in a secure, peaceful commonwealth.[1] Unless there is general adherence to a basic moral code that protects basic values, society itself would be impossible. The only alternative to such a "social contract" would be the "state of nature," a "war of all against all" wherein individual life is "solitary, poor, nasty, brutish, and short."

Morality serves as an antidote to this bleak state of nature, for it allows radically self-interested individuals to fulfill their needs and desires in a social context of peace and cooperation. Morality, then, is an instrument for social control; without a general adherence to a moral point of view, society would collapse.

MORALITY AND SELF-INTEREST

Of the Interior Beginnings of Voluntary Motions Commonly Called the Passions and the Speeches by Which They Are Expressed

There be in animals, two sorts of *motions* peculiar to them: one called *vital*, begun in generation, and continued without interruption through their whole life; such as are the *course* of the *blood*, the *pulse*, the *breathing*, the *concoction, nutrition, excretion*, etc. to which motions there needs no help of imagination: the other is *animal motion*, otherwise called *voluntary motion*: as to *go*, to *speak*, to *move* any of our limbs, in such manner as is first fancied in our minds. That sense is motion in the organs and interior parts of man's body, caused by the action of the things we see, hear, etc.; and that fancy is but the relics of the same motion, remaining after sense, has been already said in the first and second chapters. And because *going, speaking*, and the like voluntary motions, depend always upon a precedent thought of *whither, which way*, and *what*; it is evident, that the imagination is the first internal beginning of all voluntary motion. And although unstudied men do not conceive any motion at all to be there, where the thing moved is invisible; or the space it is moved in is, for the shortness of it, insensible; yet that doth not hinder, but that such motions are. For let a space be never so little, that which is moved over a greater space, whereof that little one is part, must first be moved over that. These small beginnings of motion, within the body of man, before they appear in walking, speaking, striking, and other visible actions, are commonly called ENDEAVOUR.

This endeavour, when it is toward something which causes it, is called APPETITE, or DESIRE; the latter, being the general name; and the other oftentimes restrained to signify the desire of food, namely *hunger* and *thirst*. And when the endeavour is fromward something, it is generally called AVERSION. These words, *appetite* and *aversion*, we have from the Latins; and they both of them signify the motions, one of approaching, the other of retiring. So also do the Greek words for the same, which are ορμὴ and αφορμὴ. For nature itself does often press upon men those truths, which afterwards, when they look for somewhat beyond nature, they stumble at. For the Schools find in mere appetite to go, or move, no actual motion at all: but because some motion they must acknowledge, they call it metaphorical motion; which is but an absurd speech: for though words may be called metaphorical; bodies and motions can not.

That which men desire, they are also said to LOVE: and to HATE those things for which they have aversion. So that desire and love are the same thing; save that by desire, we always signify the absence of the object; by love, most commonly the presence of the same. So also by aversion, we signify the absence; and by hate, the presence of the object.

Of appetites and aversions, some are born with men; as appetite of food, appetite of excretion, and exoneration, which may also and more properly be called aversions, from somewhat they feel in their bodies; and some other appetites, not many. The rest, which are appetites of particular things, proceed from experience, and trial of their effects upon themselves or other men. For of things we know not at all, or believe not to be, we can have no further desire, than to taste and try. But aversion we have for things, not only which we know have hurt us, but also that we do not know whether they will hurt us, or not.

Those things which we neither desire, nor hate, we are said to *contemn*; CONTEMPT being nothing else but an immobility, or contumacy of the heart, in resisting the action of certain things; and proceeding from that the heart is already moved otherwise, by other more potent objects; or from want of experience of them.

And because the constitution of a man's body is in continual mutation, it is impossible that all the same things should always cause in him the same appetites, and aversions: much less can all men consent, in the desire of almost any one and the same object.

But whatsoever is the object of any man's appetite or desire, that is it which he for his part calleth *good:* and the object of his hate and aversion, *evil;* and of his contempt, *vile* and *inconsiderable*. For these words of good, evil, and contemptible, are ever used with relation to the person that useth them: there being nothing simply and absolutely so; nor any common rule of good and evil, to be taken from the nature of the objects themselves; but from the person of the man, where there is no commonwealth; or, in a commonwealth, from the person that representeth it; or from an arbitrator or judge, whom men disagreeing shall by consent set up, and make his sentence the rule thereof. . . .

Of Power, Worth, Dignity, Honour, and Worthiness

The power *of a man*, to take it universally, is his present means; to obtain some future apparent good; and is either *original* or *instrumental*.

Natural power, is the eminence of the faculties of body, or mind: as extraordinary strength, form, prudence, arts, eloquence, liberality, nobility. *Instrumental* are those powers, which acquired by these, or by fortune, are means and instruments to acquire more: as riches, reputation, friends, and the secret working of God, which men call good luck. For the nature of power, is in this point, like to fame, increasing as it proceeds; or like the motion of heavy bodies, which the further they go, make still the more haste.

The greatest of human powers, is that which is compounded of the powers of most men, united by consent, in one person, natural, or civil, that has the use of all their powers depending on his will; such as is the power of a commonwealth: or depending on the wills of each particular; such as is the power of a faction or of divers factions leagued. Therefore to have servants, is power; to have friends, is power: for they are strengths united.

Also riches joined with liberality, is power; because it procureth friends, and servants: without liberality, not so; because in this case they defend not; but expose men to envy, as a prey.

Reputation of power, is power; because it draweth with it the adherence of those that need protection.

So is reputation of love of a man's country called popularity, for the same reason.

Also, what quality soever maketh a man beloved, or feared of many; or the reputation of such quality, is power; because it is a means to have the assistance, and service of many.

Good success is power; because it maketh reputation of wisdom, or good fortune; which makes men either fear him, or rely on him.

Affability of men already in power, is increase of power; because it gaineth love.

Reputation of prudence in the conduct of peace or war, is power; because to prudent men, we commit the government of ourselves, more willingly than to others.

Nobility is power, not in all places, but only in those commonwealths, where it has privileges: for in such privileges, consisteth their power.

Eloquence is power, because it is seeming prudence.

Form is power; because being a promise of good, it recommendeth men to the favour of women and strangers.

The sciences, are small power; because not eminent; and therefore, not acknowledged in any man; nor are at all, but in a few, and in them, but of a few things. For science is of that nature, as none can understand it to be, but such as in a good measure have attained it.

Arts of public use, as fortification, making of engines, and other instruments of war; because they confer to defence, and victory, are power: and though the true mother of them, be science, namely the mathematics; yet, because they are brought into the light, by the hand of the artificer, they be esteemed, the midwife passing with the vulgar for the mother, as his issue.

The *value*, or WORTH of a man, is as of all other things, his price; that is to say, so much as would be given for the use of his power: and therefore is not absolute; but a thing dependent on the need and judgment of another. An able conductor of soldiers, is of great price in time of war present, or imminent; but in peace not so. A learned and uncorrupt judge, is much worth in time of peace; but not so much in war. And as in other things, so in men, not the seller, but the buyer determines the price. For let a man, as most men do, rate themselves at the highest value they can; yet their true value is no more than it is esteemed by others.

The manifestation of the value we set on one another, is that which is commonly called honouring, and dishonouring. To value a man at a high rate, is to *honour* him; at a low rate, is to *dishonour* him. But high, and low, in this case, is to be understood by comparison to the rate that each man setteth on himself.

The public worth of a man, which is the value set on him by the commonwealth, is that which men commonly call DIGNITY. And this value of him by the commonwealth, is understood, by offices of command, judicature, public employment; or by names and titles, introduced for distinction of such value. . . .

Of the Difference of Manners

By manners I mean not here, decency of behaviour; as how one should salute another, or how a man should wash his mouth, or pick his teeth before company, and such other points of the *small morals*; but those qualities of mankind, that concern their living together in peace, and unity. To which end we are to consider, that the felicity of this life, consisteth not in the repose of a mind satisfied. For there is no such *finis ultimus*, utmost aim, nor *summum bonum*, greatest good, as is spoken of in the books of the old moral philosophers. Nor can a man any more live, whose desires are at an end, than he, whose senses and imaginations are at a stand. Felicity is a continual progress of the desire, from one object to another; the attaining of the former, being still but the way to the latter. The cause whereof is, that the object of man's desire, is not to enjoy once only, and for one instant of time; but to assure for ever, the way of his future desire. And therefore the voluntary actions, and inclinations of all men, tend, not only to the procuring, but also to the assuring of a contented life; and differ only in the way: which ariseth partly from the diversity of passions, in divers men; and partly from the difference of the knowledge, or opinion each one has of the causes, which produce the effect desired.

So that in the first place, I put for a general inclination of all mankind, a perpetual and restless desire of power after power, that ceaseth only in death. And the cause of this, is not always that a man hopes for a more intensive delight, than he has already attained to; or that he cannot be content with a moderate power: but because he cannot assure the power and means to live well, which he hath present, without the acquisition of more. And from hence it is, that kings, whose power is greatest, turn their endeavours to the assuring it at home by laws, or abroad by wars: and when that is done, there succeedeth a new desire; in some, of fame from new conquest; in others, of ease and sensual pleasure; in others, of admiration, or being flattered for excellence in some art, or other ability of the mind.

Competition of riches, honour, command, or other power, inclineth to contention, enmity, and war: because the way of one competitor, to the attaining of his desire, is to kill, subdue, supplant, or repel the other. Particularly, competition of praise, inclineth to a reverence of antiquity. For men contend with the living, not with the dead; to these ascribing more than due, that they may obscure the glory of the other.

Desire of ease, and sensual delight, disposeth men to obey a common power: because by such desires, a man doth abandon the protection that might be hoped for from his own industry, and labour. Fear of death, and wounds, disposeth to the same; and for the same reason. On the contrary, needy men, and hardy, not contented with their present condition; as also, all men that are ambitious of military command, are inclined to continue the causes of war; and to stir up trouble and sedition: for there is no honour military but by war; nor any such hope to mend an ill game, as by causing a new shuffle.

Desire of knowledge, and arts of peace, inclineth men to obey a common power: for such desire, containeth a desire of leisure; and consequently protection from some other power than their own. . . .

Of the Natural Condition of Mankind as Concerning Their Felicity and Misery

Nature hath made men so equal, in the faculties of the body, and mind; as that though there be found one man sometimes manifestly stronger in body, or of quicker mind than another; yet when all is reckoned together, the difference between man, and man, is not so considerable, as that one man can thereupon claim to himself any benefit, to which another may not pretend, as well as he. For as to the strength of body, the weakest has strength enough to kill the strongest, either by secret machination, or by confederacy with others, that are in the same danger with himself.

And as to the faculties of the mind, setting aside the arts grounded upon words, and especially that skill of proceeding upon general, and infallible rules, called science; which very few have, and but in few things; as being not a native faculty, born with us; nor attained, as prudence, while we look after somewhat else, I find yet a greater equality amongst men, than that of strength. For prudence, is but experience; which equal time, equally bestows on all men, in those things they equally apply themselves unto. That which may perhaps make such equality incredible, is but a vain conceit of one's own wisdom, which almost all men think they have in a greater degree, than the vulgar; that is, than all men but themselves, and a few others, whom by fame, or for concurring with themselves, they approve. For such is the nature of men, that howsoever they may acknowledge many others to be more witty, or more eloquent, or more learned; yet they will hardly believe there be many so wise as themselves; for they see their own wit at hand, and other men's at a distance. For this proveth rather that men are in that point equal, than unequal. For there is not ordinarily a greater sign of the equal distribution of any thing, than that every man is contented with his share.

From this equality of ability, ariseth equality of hope in the attaining of our ends. And therefore if any two men desire the same thing, which nevertheless they cannot both enjoy, they become enemies; and in the way to their end, which is principally their own conservation, and

sometimes their delectation only, endeavour to destroy, or subdue one another. And from hence it comes to pass, that where an invader hath no more to fear, than another man's single power; if one plant, sow, build, or possess a convenient seat, others may probably be expected to come prepared with forces united, to dispossess, and deprive him, not only of the fruit of his labour, but also of his life, or liberty. And the invader again is in the like danger of another.

And from this diffidence of another, there is no way for any man to secure himself, so reasonable, as anticipation; that is, by force, or wiles, to master the persons of all men he can, so long, till he sees no other power great enough to endanger him: and this is no more than his own conservation requireth, and is generally allowed. Also because there be some, that taking pleasure in contemplating their own power in the acts of conquest, which they pursue farther than their security requires; if others, that otherwise would be glad to be at ease within modest bounds, should not by invasion increase their power, they would not be able, long time, by standing only on their defense, to subsist. And by consequence, such augmentation of dominion over men being necessary to a man's conservation, it ought to be allowed him.

Again, men have no pleasure, but on the contrary a great deal of grief, in keeping company, where there is no power able to over-awe them all. For every man looketh that his companion should value him, at the same rate he sets upon himself: and upon all signs of contempt, or undervaluing, naturally endeavours, as far as he dares, (which amongst them that have no common power to keep them in quiet, is far enough to make them destroy each other), to extort a greater value from his contemners, by damage; and from others, by the example.

So that in the nature of man, we find three principal causes of quarrel. First, competition;

secondly, diffidence; thirdly, glory.

The first, maketh men invade for gain; the second, for safety; and the third, for reputation. The first use violence, to make themselves masters of other men's persons, wives, children, and cattle; the second, to defend them; the third, for trifles, as a word, a smile, a different opinion, and any other sign of undervalue, either direct in their persons, or by reflection in their kindred, their friends, their nation, their profession, or their name.

Hereby it is manifest, that during the time men live without a common power to keep them all in awe, they are in that condition which is called war; and such a war, as is of every man, against every man. For WAR, consisteth not in battle only, or the act of fighting; but in a tract of time, wherein the will to contend by battle is sufficiently known: and therefore the notion of *time*, is to be considered in the nature of war; as it is in the nature of weather. For as the nature of foul weather, lieth not in a shower or two of rain; but in an inclination thereto of many days together: so the nature of war, consisteth not in actual fighting; but in the known disposition thereto, during all the time there is no assurance to the contrary. All other time is PEACE.

Whatsoever therefore is consequent to a time of war, where every man is enemy to every man; the same is consequent to the time, wherein men live without other security, than what their own strength, and their own invention shall furnish them withal. In such condition, there is no place for industry; because the fruit thereof is uncertain: and consequently no culture of the earth; no navigation, nor use of the commodities that may be imported by sea; no commodious building; no instruments of moving, and removing, such things as require much force; no knowledge of the face of the earth; no account of time; no arts; no letters, no society; and which is worst of all, continual fear, and danger of violent death; and the life of man, solitary, poor, nasty, brutish, and short.

It may seem strange to some man, that has not well weighed these things; that nature should thus dissociate, and render men apt to invade, and destroy one another: and he may therefore, not trusting to this inference, made from the passions, desire perhaps to have the same confirmed by experience. Let him therefore consider with himself, when taking a journey, he arms himself, and seeks to go well accompanied; when going to sleep, he locks his doors; when even in his house he locks his chests; and this when he knows there be laws, and public officers, armed, to revenge all injuries shall be done him; what opinion he has of his fellow-subjects, when he rides armed; of his fellow citizens, when he locks his doors; and of his children, and servants, when he locks his chests. Does he not there as much accuse mankind by his actions, as I do by my words? But neither of us accuse man's nature in it. The desires, and other passions of man, are in themselves no sin. No more are the actions, that proceed from those passions, till they know a law that forbids them: which till laws be made they cannot know: nor can any law be made, till they have agreed upon the person that shall make it.

It may peradventure be thought, there was never such a time, nor condition of war as this; and I believe it was never generally so, over all the world: but there are many places, where they live so now. For the savage people in many places of America, except the government of small families, the concord whereof dependeth on natural lust, have no government at all; and live at this day in that brutish manner, as I said before. Howsoever, it may be perceived what manner of life there would be, where there were no common power to fear, by the manner of life, which men that have formerly lived under a peaceful government, use to degenerate into, in a civil war.

But though there had never been any time, wherein particular men were in a condition of war one against another; yet in all times, kings, and persons of sovereign authority, because of their independency, are in continual jealousies, and in the state and posture of gladiators; having their weapons pointing, and their eyes fixed on one another; that is, their forts, garrisons, and guns upon the frontiers of their kingdoms; and continual spies upon their neighbours; which is a posture of war. But because they uphold thereby, the industry of their subjects; there does not follow from it, that misery, which accompanies the liberty of particular men.

To this war of every man, against every man, this also is consequent; that nothing can be unjust. The notions of right and wrong, justice and injustice have there no place. Where there is no common power, there is no law: where no law, no injustice. Force, and fraud, are in war the two cardinal virtues. Justice, and injustice are none of the faculties neither of the body, nor mind. If they were, they might be in a man that were alone in the world, as well as his senses, and passions. They are qualities, that relate to men in society, not in solitude. It is consequent also to the same condition, that there be no propriety, no dominion, no *mine* and *thine* distinct; but only that to be every man's, that he can get; and for so long, as he can keep it. And thus much for the ill condition, which man by mere nature is actually placed in; though with a possibility to come out of it, consisting partly in the passions, partly in his reason.

The passions that incline men to peace, are fear of death; desire of such things as are necessary to commodious living; and a hope by their industry to obtain them. And reason suggesteth convenient articles of peace, upon which men may be drawn to agreement. These articles, are they, which otherwise are called the Laws of Nature: whereof I shall speak more particularly, in the two following chapters.

Of the First and Second Natural Laws and of Contracts

The right of nature, which writers commonly call *jus naturale,* is the liberty each man hath, to use his own power, as he will himself, for the preservation of his own nature; that is to say, of his own life; and consequently, of doing any thing, which in his own judgment, and reason, he shall conceive to be the aptest means thereunto.

By liberty, is understood, according to the proper signification of the word, the absence of external impediments: which impediments, may oft take away part of a man's power to do what he would; but cannot hinder him from using the power left him, according as his judgment, and reason shall dictate to him.

A law of nature, *lex naturalis,* is a precept or general rule, found out by reason, by which a man is forbidden to do that, which is destructive of his life, or taketh away the means of preserving the same; and to omit that, by which he thinketh it may be best preserved. For though they that speak of this subject, use to confound *jus,* and *lex, right* and *law:* yet they ought to be distinguished; because RIGHT, consisteth in liberty to do, or to forbear; whereas LAW, determineth, and bindeth to one of them: so that law, and right, differ as much, as obligation, and liberty, which in one and the same matter are inconsistent.

And because the condition of man, as hath been declared in the precedent chapters, is a condition of war of every one against every one: in which case every one is governed by his own reason; and there is nothing he can make use of, that may not be a help unto him, in preserving his life against his enemies; it followeth, that in such a condition, every man has a right to every thing; even to one another's body. And therefore, as long as this natural right of every man to every thing endureth, there can be no security to any man, how strong or wise soever he be, of living out the time, which nature ordinarily alloweth men to live. And consequently it is a precept, or general rule of reason, *that every man, ought to endeavour peace, as far as he has hope of obtaining it; and when he cannot obtain it, that he may seek, and use, all helps, and advantages of war.* The first branch of which rule, containeth the first, and fundamental law of nature; which is, *to seek peace, and follow it.* The second, the sum of the right of nature; which is, *by all means we can, to defend ourselves.*

From this fundamental law of nature by which men are commanded to endeavour peace, is derived this second law; *that a man be willing, when others are so too, as far-forth, as for peace, and defence of himself he shall think it necessary, to lay down this right to all things; and be contented with so much liberty against other men, as he would allow other men against himself.* For as long as every man holdeth this right, of doing any thing he liketh; so long are all men in the condition of war. But if other men will not lay down their right, as well as he; then there is no reason for any one, to divest himself of his: for that were to expose himself to prey, which no man is bound to, rather than to dispose himself to peace. This is that law of the Gospel; *whatsoever you require that others should do to you, that do ye to them.* And that law of all men, *quod tibi fieri non vis, alteri ne feceris.*

To *lay down* a man's *right* to any thing, is to *divest* himself of the *liberty*, of hindering another of the benefit of his own right to the same. For he that renounceth, or passeth away his right, giveth not to any other man a right which he had not before; because there is nothing to which every man had not right by nature: but only standeth out of his way, that he may enjoy his own original right, without hindrance from him; not without hindrance from another. So that the effect which redoundeth to one man, by another man's defect of right, is but so much diminution of impediments to the use of his own right original.

Right is laid aside, either by simply renouncing it; or by transferring it to another. By *simply* RENOUNCING; when he cares not to whom the benefit thereof redoundeth. By TRANSFERRING; when he intendeth the benefit thereof to some certain person, or persons. And when a man hath in either manner abandoned, or granted away his right; then is he said to be OBLIGED, or BOUND, not to hinder those, to whom such right is granted, or abandoned, from the benefit of it: and that he *ought*, and it is his DUTY, not to make void that voluntary act of his own: and that such hindrance is INJUSTICE, and INJURY, as being *sine jure*, the right being before renounced, or transferred. So that *injury*, or *injustice*, in the controversies of the world, is somewhat like to that, which in the disputations of scholars is called *absurdity*. For as it is there called an absurdity, to contradict what one maintained in the beginning: so in the world, it is called injustice, and injury, voluntarily to undo that, which from the beginning he had voluntarily done. The way by which a man either simply renounceth, or transferreth his right, is a declaration, or signification, by some voluntary and sufficient sign, or signs, that he doth so renounce, or transfer; or hath so renounced, or transferred the same, to him that accepteth it. And these signs are either words only, or actions only; or, as it happeneth most often, both words, and actions. And the same are the BONDS, by which men are bound, and obliged: bonds, that have their strength, not from their own nature, for nothing is more easily broken than a man's word, but from fear of some evil consequence upon the rupture.

Whensoever a man transferreth his right, or renounceth it; it is either in consideration of some right reciprocally transferred to himself; or for some other good he hopeth for thereby. For it is a voluntary act: and of the voluntary acts of every man, the object is some *good to himself*. And therefore there be some rights, which no man can be understood by any words, or other signs, to have abandoned, or transferred. As first a man cannot lay down the right of resisting them, that assault him by force, to take away his life; because he cannot be understood to aim thereby, at any good to himself. The same may be said of wounds, and chains, and imprisonment; both because there is no benefit consequent to such patience; as there is to the patience of suffering another to be wounded, or imprisoned: as also because a man cannot tell, when he seeth men proceed against him by violence, whether they intend his death or not. And lastly the motive, and end for which this renouncing, and transferring of right is introduced, is nothing else but the security of a man's person, in his life, and in the means of so preserving life, as not to be weary of it. And therefore if a man by words, or other signs, seem to despoil himself of the end, for which those signs were intended; he is not to be understood as if he meant it, or that it was his will; but that he was ignorant of how such words and actions were to be interpreted.

CHAPTER 57

DAVID HUME

MORALITY AS SENTIMENT

David Hume (1711–1776), Scottish philosopher, historian, and man of letters, was born in Edinburgh. As a young man, he studied for a time in France at La Flèche, where Descartes had been educated some 125 years earlier. Hume enjoyed the company of the learned Jesuits at La Flèche, and it was here that he completed *A Treatise of Human Nature*, published in London in 1740. Although he had high hopes for the success of his work, the *Treatise* received little critical recognition; as Hume put it, it fell "deadborn from the press." Undaunted, Hume revised portions of the *Treatise* and published them successfully as *An Enquiry Concerning Human Understanding* and *An Enquiry Concerning the Principles of Morals*. As his reputation grew, he made a bid for an academic position in philosophy at the University of Edinburgh. Because his ideas were perceived as contrary to the religious and moral climate of the day, he was turned down. He was later appointed librarian to the Faculty of Advocates, a post that gave him an opportunity to begin his monumental *History of England*. This four-volume work established Hume as a distinguished man of letters; a master stylist, he was proclaimed by many to be the finest writer in the English language. From 1763 to 1765 he was secretary to the British embassy in Paris, where he was highly esteemed by the French *philosophes*, including Voltaire, Diderot, D'Alembert, and d'Holbach. A charming man with a winsome personality, he also befriended Jean-Jacques Rousseau; the friendship was terminated by a paranoid Rousseau, after some bizarre circumstances. Hume spent his last years in Edinburgh, where he died in 1776, the year of the American Revolution.

A thoroughgoing empiricist, Hume carried the work of Locke and Berkeley to its logical conclusions. Distrustful of philosophical speculation, Hume's skepticism led him to criticize the principle of causality as being without foundation, an idea which could not be traced back to an originating sense impression. It was Hume's attack on causality that awoke Kant from his "dogmatic slumber."

Nowhere is Hume's skepticism more evident than in his philosophy of religion. Hume was an agnostic who argued that the existence of God could not be proven nor disproven. He argued against the possibility of miracles, relentlessly criticized the teleological argument as being based on a poor analogy, and raised the problem of evil as a major issue in the philosophy of religion.

In this selection Hume raises the question of whether or not the source of morality resides in our rational nature or our passional nature.[1] Although initially he finds convincing arguments on both sides, he concludes that the case is overwhelmingly in favor of the sentiment as the source of morality, not reason. Moral distinctions have no objective rational foundation; they are purely subjective in nature.

For Hume, sentiment in morals parallels the role of custom in induction. Just as the relation between cause and effect can never be established by reason, neither can the difference between good and evil. Reason cannot stir us to action—only feelings and passions can do this. The function of moral judgments is to influence and direct conduct. "Reason is, and ought to be the slave of the passions, and can never pretend to any other office than to serve and obey them." Even so, reason still plays a role in morality; it determines that social utility is the ground of approval and disapproval, praise and blame.

MORALITY AS SENTIMENT

There has been a controversy started of late, much better worth examination, concerning the general foundation of Morals; whether they be derived from Reason, or from Sentiment; whether we attain the knowledge of them by a chain of argument and induction, or by an immediate feeling and finer internal sense; whether, like all sound judgment of truth and falsehood, they should be the same to every rational intelligent being; or whether, like the perception of beauty and deformity, they be founded entirely on the particular fabric and constitution of the human species.

The ancient philosophers, though they often affirm, that virtue is nothing but conformity to reason, yet, in general, seem to consider morals as deriving their existence from taste and sentiment. On the other hand, our modern enquirers, though they also talk much of the beauty of virtue, and deformity of vice, yet have commonly endeavored to account for these distinctions by metaphysical reasonings, and by deductions

[1]From David Hume, *An Enquiry Concerning the Principles of Morals*, 1777.

from the most abstract principles of the understanding. Such confusion reigned in these subjects, that an opposition of the greatest consequence could prevail between one system and another, and even in the parts of almost each individual system. . . .

It must be acknowledged, that both sides of the question are susceptible of specious arguments. Moral distinctions, it may be said, are discernible by pure *reasons*: else, whence the many disputes that reign in common life, as well as in philosophy, with regard to this subject: the long chain of proofs often produced on both sides; the examples cited, the authorities appealed to, the analogies employed, the fallacies detected, the inferences drawn, and the several conclusions adjusted to their proper principles. Truth is disputable; not taste: what exists in the nature of things is the standard of our judgment; what each man feels within himself is the standard of sentiment. Propositions in geometry may be proved, systems in physics may be controverted; but the harmony of verse, the tenderness of passion, the brilliancy of wit, must give immediate pleasure. No man reasons concerning another's beauty; but frequently concerning the justic or injustice of his actions. In every criminal trial the first object of the prisoner is to disprove the facts alleged, and deny the actions imputed to him: the second to prove, that, even if these actions were real, they might be justified, as innocent and lawful. It is confessedly by deductions of the understanding, that the first point is ascertained: how can we suppose that a different faculty of the mind is employed in fixing the other?

On the other hand, those who would resolve all moral determinations into *sentiment*, may endeavor to show, that it is impossible for reason ever to draw conclusions of this nature. To virtue, say they, it belongs to be *amiable*, and vice *odious*. This forms their very nature or essence. But can reason or argumentation distribute these different epithets to any subjects, and pronounce beforehand, that this must produce love, and that hatred? Or what other reason can we ever assign for these affections, but the original fabric and formation of the human mind, which is naturally adapted to receive them?

These arguments on each side (and many more might be produced) are so plausible, that I am apt to suspect, they may, the one as well as the other, be solid and satisfactory, and that *reason* and *sentiment* concur in almost all moral determinations and conclusions. The final sentence, it is probable, which pronounces characters and actions amiable or odious, praiseworthy or blameable; that which stamps on them the mark of honor or infamy, approbation or censure; that which renders morality an active principle and constitutes virtue our happiness, and vice our misery; it is probable, I say, that this final sentence depends on some internal sense or feeling, which nature has made universal in the whole species. For what else can have an influence of this nature? But in order to pave the way for such a sentiment, and give a proper discernment of its object, it is often necessary, we find, that much reasoning should precede, that nice distinctions be made, just conclusions drawn, distant comparisons formed, complicated relations examined, and general facts fixed and ascertained. Some species of beauty, especially the natural kinds, on their first appearance, command our affection and approbation; and where they fail of this effect, it is impossible for any reasoning to redress their influence, or adapt them better to our taste and sentiment. But in many orders of beauty, particularly those of the finer arts, it is requisite to employ much reasoning, in order to feel the proper sentiment; and a false relish may frequently be corrected by argument and reflection. There are just grounds to conclude, that moral beauty partakes much of this latter species, and demands the assistance of our intellectual faculties, in order to give it a suitable influence on the human mind.

The end of all moral speculations is to teach us our duty; and, by proper representations of the deformity of vice and beauty of virtue, beget correspondent habits, and engage us to avoid the one, and embrace the other. But is this ever to be expected from inferences and conclusions of the understanding, which of themselves have no hold of the affections or set in motion the active powers of men? They discover truths: but where the truths which they discover are indifferent, and beget no desire or aversion, they can have no influence on conduct and behavior. What is honorable, what is fair, what is becoming, what is noble, what is generous, takes possession of the heart, and animates us to embrace and maintain it. What is intelligible, what is evident, what is probable, what is true, procures only the cool assent of the understanding; and gratifying a speculative curiosity, puts an end to our researches.

Extinguish all the warm feelings and prepossessions in favor of virtue, and all disgust or aversion to vice: render men totally indifferent towards these distinctions; and morality is no longer a practical study, nor has any tendency to regulate our lives and actions.

Reason judges either of *matter of fact* or of *relations*. Enquire then, *first*, where is that matter of fact which we here call *crime*; point it out; determine the time of its existence; describe its essence or nature; explain the sense or faculty to which it discovers itself. It resides in the mind of the person who is ungrateful. He must, therefore, feel it, and be conscious of it. But nothing is there, except the passion of ill will or absolute indifference. You cannot say that these, of themselves, always, and in all circumstances, are crimes. No, they are only crimes when directed towards persons who have before expressed and displayed good will towards us. Consequently, we may infer, that the crime of ingratitude is not

any particular individual *fact*; but arises from a complication of circumstances, which, being presented to the spectator, excites the *sentiment* of blame, by the particular structure and fabric of his mind.

This representation, you say, is false. Crime, indeed, consists not in a particular *fact*, of whose reality we are assured by *reason*; but it consists in certain *moral relations* discovered by reason, in the same manner as we discover by reason the truths of geometry or algebra. But what are the relations, I ask, of which you here talk? In the case stated above, I see, first, goodwill and good offices in one person; then, ill will and ill offices in the other . Between these there is the relation of *contrariety*. Does the crime consist in that relation? But suppose a person bore me ill will or did me ill offices, and I, in return, were indifferent toward him, or did him good offices—here is the same relation of *contrariety*; and yet my conduct is often highly laudable. Twist and turn this matter as much as you will, you can never rest the morality on relation, but must have recourse to the decisions of sentiment.

When it is affirmed that two and three are equal to the half of ten, this relation of equality I understand perfectly. I conceive, that if ten be divided into two parts, of which one has as many units as the other; and if any of these parts be compared to two added to three, it will contain as many units as that compound number. But when you draw thence a comparison to moral relations, I own that I am altogether at a loss to understand you. A moral action, a crime, such as ingratitude, is a complicated object. Does the morality consist in the relation of its parts to each other? How? After what manner? Specify the relation: be more particular and explicit in your propositions, and you will easily see their falsehood.

No, say you, the morality consists in the relation of actions to the rule of right; and they are denominated good or ill, according as they agree or disagree with it. When then is this rule of right? In what does it consist? How is it determined? By reason, you say, which examines the moral relations of actions. So that moral relations are determined by the comparison of action to a rule. And that rule is determined by considering the moral relations of objects. Is not this fine reasoning?

The hypothesis which we embrace is plain. It maintains that morality is determined by sentiment. It defines virtue to be *whatever mental action or quality gives to a spectator the pleasing sentiment of approbation;* and vice the contrary. We then proceed to examine a plain matter of fact, to wit, what actions have this influence. We consider all the circumstances in which these actions agree, and thence endeavor to extract some general observations with regard to these sentiments.

When a man, at any time, deliberates concerning his own conduct (as, whether he had better, in a particular emergency, assist a brother or a benefactor), he must consider these separate relations, with all the circumstances and situations of the persons, in order to determine the superior duty and obligation; and in order to determine the proportion of lines in any triangle, it is necessary to examine the nature of that figure, and the relation which its several parts bear to each other. But notwithstanding this appearing similarity in the two cases, there is, at bottom, an extreme difference between them. A speculative reasoner concerning triangles or circles considers the several known and given relations of the parts of these figures; and thence infers some unknown relation, which is dependent on the former. But in moral deliberations we must be acquainted beforehand with all the objects, and all their relations to each other and from a comparison of the whole, fix our choice or approbation. No new fact to be ascertained; no new relation to be discovered. All the circum-

stances of the case are supposed to be laid before us, ere we can fix any sentence of blame or approbation. If any material circumstance be yet unknown or doubtful, we must first employ our inquiry or intellectual faculties to assure us of it; and must suspend for a time all moral decision or sentiment. While we are ignorant whether a man were aggressor or not, how can we determine whether the person who killed him be criminal or innocent? But after every circumstance, every relation is known, the understanding has no further room to operate, nor any object on which it could employ itself. The approbation or blame which then ensues, cannot be the work of the judgment, but of the heart; and is not a speculative proposition or affirmation, but an active feeling or sentiment. In the disquisitions of the understanding, from known circumstances and relations, we infer some new and unknown. In moral decisions, all the circumstances and relations must be previously known; and the mind, from the contemplation of the whole, feels some new impression of affection or disgust, esteem or contempt, approbation or blame.

Hence the great difference between a mistake of *fact* and one of *right;* and hence the reason why the one is commonly criminal and not the other. When Oedipus killed Laius, he was ignorant of the relation, and from circumstances, innocent and involuntary, formed erroneous opinions concerning the action which he committed. But when Nero killed Agrippina, all the relations between himself and the person, and all the circumstances of the fact, were previously known to him; but the motive of revenge, or fear, or interest, prevailed in his savage heart over the sentiments of duty and humanity. And when we express that detestation against him to which he himself, in a little time, became insensible, it is not that we see any relations, of which he was ignorant; but that, for the rectitude of our disposition, we feel sentiments against which he was hardened from flattery and a long perseverance in the most enormous crimes. In these sentiments then, not in a discovery of relations of any kind, do all moral determinations consist. Before we can pretend to form any decision of this kind, everything must be known and ascertained on the side of the object or action. Nothing remains but to feel, on our part, some sentiment of blame or approbation; whence we pronounce the action criminal or virtuous.

It may be esteemed, perhaps, a superfluous task to prove, that the benevolent or softer affections are estimable; and wherever they appear, engage the approbation and good will of mankind. The epithets *sociable, good-natured, humane, merciful, grateful, friendly, generous, beneficent,* or their equivalents, are known in all languages, and universally express the highest merit, which *human nature* is capable of attaining. Where these amiable qualities are attended with birth and power and eminent abilities, and display themselves in the good government or useful instruction of mankind, they seem even to raise the possessors of them above the rank of *human nature,* and make them approach in some measure to the divine. Exalted capacity, undaunted courage, prosperous success; these may only expose a hero or politician to the envy and ill will of the public: but as soon as the praises are added of humane and beneficent; when instances are displayed of lenity, tenderness or friendship; envy itself is silent, or joins the general voice of approbation and applause. . . . No qualities are more entitled to the general goodwill and approbation of mankind than beneficence and humanity, friendship and gratitude, natural affection and public spirit, or whatever proceeds from a tender sympathy with others, and a generous concern for our kind and species. These wherever they appear seem to transfuse themselves, in a manner, into each beholder, and to call forth, in their own behalf, the

same favorable and affectionate sentiments, which they exert on all around.

We may observe that, in displaying the praises of any humane, beneficent man, there is one circumstance which never fails to be amply insisted on, namely, the happiness and satisfaction, derived to society from his intercourse and good offices.

That Justice is useful to society, and consequently that *part* of its merit, at least, must arise from that consideration, it would be a superfluous undertaking to prove. That public utility is the *sole* origin of justice, and that reflections on the beneficial consequences of this virtue are the *sole* foundation of its merit; this proposition, being more curious and important, will better deserve our examination and enquiry.

Let us suppose that nature has bestowed on the human race such profuse *abundance* of all *external* conveniences, that, without any uncertainty in the event, without any care or industry on our part, every individual finds himself fully provided with whatever his most voracious appetites can want, or luxurious imagination wish or desire. His natural beauty, we shall suppose, surpasses all acquired ornaments: the perpetual clemency of the seasons renders useless all clothes or covering: the raw herbage affords him the most delicious fare; the clear fountain, the richest beverage. No laborious occupation required: no tillage: no navigation. Music, poetry, and contemplation from his sole business: conversation, mirth, and friendship his sole amusement.

It seems evident that, in such a happy state, every other social virtue would flourish and receive tenfold increase; but the cautious, jealous virtue of justice would never once have been dreamed of. For what purpose make a partition of goods, where everyone has already more than enough? Why give rise to property, where there cannot possibly be any injury? Why call this object *mine*, when upon the seizing of it by another, I need but stretch out my hand to possess myself to what is equally valuable? Justice, in that case, being totally useless, would be an idle ceremonial, and could never possibly have place in the catalogue of virtues. . . .

Again; suppose, that, though the necessities of human race continue the same as at present, yet the mind is so enlarged, and so replete with friendship and generosity, that every man has the utmost tenderness for every man, and feels no more concern for his own interest than for that of his fellows; it seems evident, that the use of justice would, in this case, be suspended by such an extensive benevolence, nor would the divisions and barriers of property and obligation have ever been thought of. Why should I bind another, by a deed or promise, to do me any good office, when I know that he is already prompted, by the strongest inclination, to seek my happiness, and would, of himself, perform the desired service; except the hurt, he thereby receives, be greater than the benefit accruing to me? in which case, he knows that, from my innate humanity and friendship, I should be the first to oppose myself to his imprudent generosity. Why raise landmarks between my neighbor's field and mine, when my heart has made no division between our interests; but shares all his joys and sorrows with the same force and vivacity as if originally my own? Every man, upon his supposition, being a second self to another, would trust all his interests to the discretion of every man; without jealousy, without partition, without distinction. And the whole human race would form only one family; where all would lie in common, and be used freely, without regard to property; but cautiously too, with as entire regard to the necessities of each individual, as if our own interests were most intimately concerned. . . .

To make this truth more evident, let us reverse the foregoing suppositions; and carrying everything to the opposite extreme, consider what would be the effect of these new situations. Suppose a society to fall into such want of all common necessaries, that the utmost frugality and industry cannot preserve the greater number from perishing, and the whole from extreme misery; it will readily, I believe, be admitted, that the strict laws of justice are suspended, in such a pressing emergency, and give place to the stronger motives of necessity and self-preservation. Is it any crime, after a shipwreck, to seize whatever means or instrument of safety one can lay hold of, without regard to former limitations of property? Or if a city besieged were perishing with hunger; can we imagine, that men will see any means of preservation before them, and lose their lives, from a scrupulous regard to what, in other situations, would be the rules of equity and justice? The use and tendency of that virtue is to procure happiness and security, by preserving order in society: but where the society is ready to perish from extreme necessity, no greater evil can be dreaded from violence and injustice; and every man may now provide for himself by all the means, which prudence can dictate, or humanity permit. The public, even in less urgent necessities, opens granaries, without the consent of proprietors, as justly supposing, that the authority or magistracy may, consistent with equity, extend so far: but were any number of men to assemble, without the tie of laws or civil jurisdiction; would an equal partition of bread in a famine, though effected by power and even violence, be regarded as criminal or injurious?

Suppose likewise, that it should be a virtuous man's fate to fall into the society of ruffians, remote from the protection of laws and government; what conduct must he embrace in that melancholy situation? He sees such a desperate rapaciousness prevail; such a desregard to equity, such contempt of order, such stupid blindness to future consequences, as must immediately have the most tragical conclusion, and must terminate in destruction to the greater number, and in a total dissolution of society to the rest. He, meanwhile, can have no other expedient than to arm himself, to whomever the sword he seizes, or the buckler, may belong: To make provision of all means of defense and security: And his particular regard to justice being no longer of use to his own safety or that of others, he must consult the dictates of self-preservation alone, without concern for those who no longer merit his care and attention.

Thus, the rules of equity or justice depend entirely on the particular state and condition in which men are placed, and owe their origin and existence to that utility, which results to the public from their strict and regular observance. Reverse, in any considerable circumstance, the condition of men: Produce extreme abundance or extreme necessity: Implant in the human breast perfect moderation and humanity, or perfect rapaciousness and malice: By rendering justice totally *useless*, you thereby totally destroy its essence, and suspend its obligation upon mankind.

The common situation of society is a medium amidst all these extremes. We are naturally partial to ourselves, and to our friends; but are capable of learning the advantage resulting from a more equitable conduct. Few enjoyments are given us from the open and liberal hand of nature; but by art, labor, and industry, we can extract them in great abundance. Hence the ideas of property become necessary in all civil society: Hence justice derives its usefulness to the public: And hence alone arises its merits and moral obligation.

It seems a happiness in the present theory; that it enters not into that vulgar dispute concerning the *degrees* of benevolence or self-love, which prevail in human nature; a dispute which is never likely to have any issue, both because men, who have taken part, are not easily convinced, and because the phenomena, which can be produced on either side, are so dispersed, so uncertain, and subject to so many interpretations, that it is scarcely possible accurately to compare them, or draw from them any determinate inference or conclusion. It is sufficient for our present purpose, if it be allowed, what surely, without the greatest absurdity cannot be disputed, that there is some benevolence, however small, infused into our bosom; some spark of friendship for humankind; some particle of the dove kneaded into our frame, along with the elements of the wolf and serpent. Let these generous sentiments be supposed ever so weak; let them be insufficient to move even a hand or finger of our body, they must still direct the determinations of our mind, and where everything else is equal, produce a cool preference of what is useful and serviceable to mankind, above what is pernicious and dangerous. A *moral distinction*, therefore, immediately arises. . . .

The notion of morals implies some sentiment common to all mankind, which recommends the same object to general approbation, and makes every man, or most men, agree in the same opinion or decision concerning it. It also implies some sentiment, so universal and comprehensive as to extend to all mankind, and render the actions and conduct, even of the persons the most remote, an object of applause or censure, according as they agree or disagree with that rule of right which is established. These two requisite circumstances belong alone to the sentiment of humanity here insisted on. The other passions produce in every breast, many strong sentiments of desire and aversion, affection and hatred; but these neither are felt so much in common, nor are so comprehensive, as to be the foundation of any general system and established theory of blame or approbation.

When a man denominates another his *enemy*, his *rival*, his *antagonist*, his *adversary*, he is understood to speak the language of self-love, and to express sentiments, peculiar to himself, and arising from his particular circumstances and situation. But when he bestows on any man the epithets of *vicious* or *odious* or *depraved*, he then speaks another language, and expresses sentiments, in which he expects all his audience are to concur with him. He must here, therefore, depart from his private and particular situation, and must choose a point of view, common to him with others; he must move some universal principle of the human frame, and touch a string to which all mankind have an accord and symphony. If he mean, therefore, to express that this man possesses qualities, whose tendency is pernicious to society, he has chosen this common point of view, and has touched the principle of humanity, in which every man, in some degree, concurs. While the human heart is compounded of the same elements as at present, it will never be wholly indifferent to public good, nor entirely unaffected with the tendency of characters and manners. And though this affection of humanity may not generally be esteemed so strong as vanity or ambition, yet, being common to all men, it can alone be the foundation of morals, or of any general system of blame or praise. One man's ambition is not another's ambition, nor will the same event or object satisfy both; but the humanity of one man is the humanity of everyone, and the same object touches this passion in all human creatures.

Whatever conduct gains my approbation, by touching my humanity, procures also the applause of all mankind, by affecting the same principle in them; but what serves my avarice or ambition pleases these passions in me alone, and affects not the avarice and ambition of the rest of mankind. There is no circumstance of conduct in any man provided it have a beneficial tendency, that is not agreeable to my humanity, however remote the person.

CHAPTER 58

IMMANUEL KANT

MORALITY AND REASON

Kant outlined his ethical system in his classic little work, *The Foundations of the Metaphysics of Morals*, published in 1785.[1] Kant set out to critique the theory of morality based on sentiment, which had been formulated by both Francis Hutcheson (1694–1746) and David Hume. According to Kant, our moral duties are unconditional, universal, and necessary; they are dependent not on feelings but on reason alone.

Kant's first formulation of the *categorical imperative* is, "Act only on that maxim whereby thou canst at the same time will that it would become a universal law." All other moral principles are subject to this one. If w cannot consciously will that everyone in the moral universe should perform the act that we contemplate, we ought to reject it as impermissible.

Kant's second formulation of the categorical imperative speaks to the issue of *respect for persons:* "So act as to treat humanity, whether in your own person or in that of any other, in every case as an end and never as a means only." Each person has individual dignity and profound worth and is not to be exploited or manipulated as a mere means to someone's ends. This formulation reveals Kant's egalitarian view of the unconditional worth and equal dignity of humanity, and it helps explain why he was enthusiastic about the French and American revolutions; it also reveals the underlying religious dimension that is present in his writings on ethics.

---

[1]From Immanuel Kant, *The Foundations of the Metaphysics of Morals*, translated by T.K. Abbott (1873).

MORALITY AND REASON

Nothing can possibly be conceived in the world, or even out of it, which can be called good without qualification, except a Good Will. Intelligence, wit, judgment, and the other *talents* of the mind, however they may be named, or courage, resolutions, perseverance, as qualities of temperament, are undoubtedly good and desirable in many respects; but these gifts of nature may also become extremely bad and mischievous if the will which is to make use of them, and which, therefore, constitutes what is called *character*, is not good. It is the same with the *gifts of fortune*. Power, riches, honor, even health, and the general well-being and contentment with one's condition which is called *happiness*, inspire pride, and often presumption, if there is not a good will to correct the influence of these on the mind, and with this also to rectify the whole principle of acting, and adapt it to its end. The sight of a being who is not adorned with a single feature of a pure and good will, enjoying unbroken prosperity, can never give pleasure to an impartial rational spectator. Thus a good will appears to constitute the indispensable condition even of being worthy of happiness.

There are even some qualities which are of service to this good will itself, and may facilitate its action, yet which have no intrinsic unconditional value, but always presuppose a good will, and this qualifies the esteem that we justly have for them, and does not permit us to regard them as absolutely good. Moderation in the affections and passions, self-control and calm deliberation are not only good in many respects, but even seem to constitute part of the intrinsic worth of the person; but they are far from deserving to be called good without qualification, although they have been so unconditionally praised by the ancients. For without the principles of a good will, they may become extremely bad, and the coolness of a villain not only makes him far more dangerous, but also directly makes him more abominable in our eyes than he would have been without it.

A good will is good not because of what it performs or effects, not by its aptness for the attainment of some proposed end, but simply by virtue of the volition, that is, it is good in itself, and considered by itself is to be esteemed much higher than all that can be brought about by it in favor of any inclination, nay, even of the sum total of all inclinations. Even if it should happen that, owing to special disfavor of fortune, or the niggardly provision of a step-motherly nature, this will should wholly lack power to accomplish its purpose, if with its greatest efforts it should yet achieve nothing, and there should remain only the good will (not, to be sure, a mere wish, but the summoning of all means in our power), then, like a jewel, it would still shine by its own light, as a thing which has its whole value in itself. Its usefulness or fruitlessness can neither add to nor take away anything from this value. It would be, as it were, only the setting to enable us to handle it the more conveniently in common commerce, or to attract to it the attention of those who are not yet connoisseurs, but not to recommend it to true connoisseurs, or to determine its value.

There is, however, something so strange in this idea of the absolute value of the mere will, in which no account is taken of its utility, that notwithstanding the thorough assent of even common reason to the idea, yet a suspicion must arise that it may perhaps really be the product of mere high-flown fancy, and that we may have misunderstood the purpose of nature in assigning reason as the governor of our will. Therefore we will examine this idea from this point of view.

In the physical constitution of an organized

being, that is, a being adapted suitably to the purposes of life, we assume it as a fundamental principle that no organ for any purpose will be found but what is also the fittest and best adapted for that purpose. Now in a being which has reason and a will, if the proper object of nature were its *conservation*, its *welfare*, in a word, its *happiness*, then nature would have hit upon a very bad arrangement in selecting the reason of the creature to carry out this purpose. For all the actions which the creature has to perform with a view to this purpose, and the whole rule of its conduct, would be far more surely prescribed to it by instinct, and that end would have been attained thereby much more certainly than it ever can be by reason. Should reason have been communicated to this favored creature over and above, it must only have served it to contemplate the happy constitution of its nature, to admire it, to congratulate itself thereon, and to feel thankful for it to the beneficent cause, but not that it should subject its desires to that weak and delusive guidance, and meddle bunglingly with the purpose of nature. In a word, nature would have taken care that reason should not break forth into *practical exercise*, nor have the presumption, with its weak insight, to think out for itself the plan of happiness, and of the means of attaining it. Nature would not only have taken on herself the choice of the ends, but also of the means, and with wise foresight would have entrusted both to instinct.

And, in fact, we find that the more a cultivated reason applies itself with deliberate purpose to the enjoyment of life and happiness, so much the more does the man fail of true satisfaction. And from this circumstance there arises in many, if they are candid enough to confess it, a certain degree of *misology*, that is, hatred of reason, especially in the case of those who are most experienced in the use of it, because after calculating all the advantages they derive, I do not say from the invention of all the arts of common luxury, but even from the sciences (which seem to them to be after all only a luxury of the understanding), they find that they have, in fact, only brought more trouble on their shoulders, rather than gained in happiness; and they end by envying, rather than despising, the more common stamp of men who keep closer to the guidance of mere instinct, and do not allow their reason much influence on their conduct. And this we must admit, that the judgment of those who would very much lower the lofty eulogies of the advantages which reason gives us in regard to the happiness and satisfaction of life, or who would even reduce them below zero, is by no means morose or ungrateful to the goodness with which the world is governed, but that there lies at the root of these judgments the idea that our existence has a different and far nobler end, for which, and not for happiness, reason is properly intended, and which must, therefore, be regarded as the supreme condition to which the private ends of man must, for the most part, be postponed.

For as reason is not competent to guide the will with certainty in regard to its objects and the satisfaction of all our wants (which it to some extent even multiplies), this being an end to which an implanted instinct would have led with much greater certainty; and since, nevertheless, reason is imparted to us as a practical faculty, *i.e.*, as one which is to have influence on the *will*, therefore, admitting that nature generally in the distribution of her capacities has adapted the means to the end, its true destination must be to produce a *will*, not merely good as a *means* to something else, but *good in itself*, for which reason was absolutely necessary. This will then, though not indeed the sole and complete good, must be the supreme good and the condition of every other, even of the desire of happiness. Under these circumstances, there is nothing inconsistent with the wisdom of nature in the fact that the cultivation of the reason, which is requisite for the first and unconditional purpose, does in many ways interfere, at least in this life, with the attainment of the second, which is always conditional, namely, happiness. Nay, it may even reduce it to nothing, without nature thereby failing of her purpose. For reason recognizes the establishment of a good will as its highest practical destination, and in attaining this purpose is capable only of a satisfaction of its own proper kind, namely, that from the attainment of an end, which end again is determined by reason only, notwithstanding that this may involve many a disappointment to the ends of inclination.

We have then to develop the notion of a will which deserves to be highly esteemed for itself, and is good without a view to anything further, a notion which exists already in the sound natural understanding, requiring rather to be cleared up than to be taught, and which in estimating the value of our actions always takes the first place, and constitutes the condition of all the rest. In order to do this we will take the notion of duty, which includes that of a good will, although implying certain subjective restrictions and hindrances. These, however, far from concealing it, or rendering it unrecognizable, rather bring it out by contrast, and make it shine forth so much the brighter.

I omit here all actions which are already recognized as inconsistent with duty, although they may be useful for this or that purpose, for with these the question whether they are done *from duty* cannot arise at all, since they even conflict with it. I also set aside those actions which really conform to duty, but to which men have *no* direct *inclination*, performing them because they are impelled thereto by some other inclination. For in this case we can readily distinguish whether the action which agrees with duty is done *from duty*, or from a selfish view. It is much harder to make this distinction when the action accords with

duty, and the subject has besides a *direct* inclination to it. For example, it is always a matter of duty that a dealer should not overcharge an inexperienced purchaser, and wherever there is much commerce the prudent tradesman does not overcharge, but keeps a fixed price for everyone, so that a child buys of him as well as any other. Men are thus *honestly* served; but this is not enough to make us believe that the tradesman has so acted from duty and from principles of honesty: his own advantage required it; it is out of the question in this case to suppose that he might besides have a direct inclination in favor of the buyers, so that as it were, from love he should give no advantage to one over another. Accordingly the action was done neither from duty nor from direct inclination, but merely with a selfish view.

On the other hand, it is a duty to maintain one's life; and, in addition, everyone has also a direct inclination to do so. But on this account the often anxious care which most men take for it has no intrinsic worth, and their maxim has no moral import. They preserve their life as *duty requires*, no doubt, but not *because duty requires*. On the other hand, if adversity and hopeless sorrow have completely taken away the relish for life; if the unfortunate one, strong in mind, indignant at his fate rather than desponding or dejected, wishes for death, and yet preserves his life without loving it—not from inclination or fear, but from duty—then his maxim has a moral worth.

To be beneficent when we can is a duty; and besides this, there are many minds so sympathetically constituted that, without any other motive of vanity or self-interest, they find a pleasure in spreading joy around them, and can take delight in the satisfaction of others so far as it is their own work. But I maintain that in such a case an action of this kind, however proper, however amiable it may be, has nevertheless no true moral worth, but is on a level with other inclinations;

e.g., the inclination to honor, which, if it is happily directed to that which is in fact of public utility and accordant with duty, and consequently honorable, deserves praise and encouragement, but not esteem. For the maxim lacks the moral import, namely, that such actions be done *from duty*, not from inclination. Put the case that the mind of that philanthropist were clouded by sorrow of his own, extinguishing all sympathy with the lot of others, and that while he still has the power to benefit others in distress, he is not touched by their trouble because he is absorbed with his own; and now suppose that he tears himself out of this dead insensibility, and performs the action without any inclination to it, but simply from duty, then first has his action its genuine moral worth. Further still; if nature has put little sympathy in the heart of this or that man; if he, supposed to be an upright man, is by temperament cold and indifferent to the sufferings of others, perhaps because in respect of his own he is provided with the special gift of patience and fortitude, and supposes, or even requires, that others should have the same—and such a man would certainly not be the meanest product of nature—but if nature had not specially framed him for a philanthropist, would he not still find in himself a source from whence to give himself a far higher worth than that of a good-natured temperament could be? Unquestionably. It is just in this that the moral worth of the character is brought out which is incomparably the highest of all, namely, that he is beneficent, not from inclination, but from duty.

The second proposition is: That an action done from duty derives its moral worth, *not from the purpose* which is to be attained by it, but from the maxim by which it is determined, and therefore does not depend on the realization of the object of the action, but merely on the *principle of volition* by which the action has taken place, without regard to any object of desire. It is clear from what precedes that the purposes which we may have in view in our actions, or their effects regarded as ends and springs of the will, cannot give to actions any unconditional or moral worth. In what, then, can their worth lie, if it is not to consist in the will and in reference to its expected effect? It cannot lie anywhere but in the *principle of the will* without regard to the ends which can be attained by the action.

The third proposition, which is a consequence of the two preceding, I would express thus: *Duty is the necessity of acting from respect for the law.* I may have *inclination* for an object as the effect of my proposed action, but I cannot have *respect* for it, just for this reason, that it is an effect and not any energy of will. Similarly, I cannot have respect for inclination, whether my own or another's; I can at most, if my own, approve it; if another's, sometimes even love it; *i.e.*, look on it as favorable to my own interest. It is only what is connected with my will as a principle, by no means as an effect—what does not subserve my inclination, but overpowers it, or at least in case of choice excludes it from its calculation—in other words, simply the law of itself, which can be an object of respect, and hence a command. Now an action done from duty must wholly exclude the influence of inclination, and with it every object of the will, so that nothing remains which can determine the will except objectively the *law*, and subjectively *pure respect* for this practical law, and consequently the maxim that I should follow this law even to the thwarting of all my inclinations.

Thus the moral worth of an action does not lie in the effect expected from it, nor in any principle of action which requires to borrow its motive from this expected effect. For all these effects—agreeableness of one's condition, and even the promotion of the happiness of others— could have been also brought about by other causes, so that for this there would have been no need of the will of a rational being; whereas it is in this alone that the supreme and unconditional good can be found. The preeminent good which we call moral can therefore consist in nothing else than *the conception of law* in itself, *which certainly is only possible in a rational being*, insofar as this conception, and not the expected effect, determines the will. This is a good which is already present in the person who acts accordingly, and we have not to wait for it to appear first in the result.

But what sort of law can that be, the conception of which must determine the will, even without paying any regard to the effect expected from it, in order that this will may be called good absolutely and without qualification? As I have deprived the will of every impulse which could arise to it from obedience to any law, there remains nothing but the universal conformity of its actions to law in general, which alone is to serve the will as a principle, *i.e.*, I am never to act otherwise than so *that I could also will that my maxim should become a universal law*. Here now, it is the simple conformity to law in general, without assuming any particular law applicable to certain actions, that serves the will as its principle, and must so serve it, if duty is not to be a vain delusion and a chimerical notion. The common reason of men in its practical judgments perfectly coincides with this, and always has in view the principle here suggested. Let the question be, for example: May I when in distress make a promise with the intention not to keep it? I readily distinguish here between the two significations which the question may have: Whether it is prudent, or whether it is right, to make a false promise. The former may undoubtedly often be the case. I see clearly indeed that it is not enough to extricate myself from a present difficulty by means of this subterfuge, but it must be well considered whether there may not hereafter spring from this lie much greater inconvenience than that from which I now free myself, and as, with all my sup-

posed *cunning*, the consequences cannot be so easily foreseen but that credit once lost may be much more injurious to me than any mischief which I seek to avoid at present, it should be considered whether it would not be more *prudent* to act herein according to a universal maxim, and to make it a habit to promise nothing except with the intention of keeping it. But it is soon clear to me that such a maxim will still only be based on the fear of consequences. Now it is a wholly different thing to be truthful from duty, and to be so from apprehension of injurious consequences. In the first case, the very notion of the action already implies a law for me; in the second case, I must first look about elsewhere to see what results may be combined with it which would affect myself. For to deviate from the principle of duty is beyond all doubt wicked; but to be unfaithful to my maxim of prudence may often be very advantageous to me, although to abide by it is certainly safer. The shortest way, however, and an unerring one, to discover the answer to this question whether a lying promise is consistent with duty, is to ask myself, Should I be content that my maxim (to extricate myself from difficulty by false promise) should hold good as a universal law, for myself as well as for others? and should I be able to say to myself, "Everyone may make a deceitful promise when he finds himself in a difficulty from which he cannot otherwise extricate himself"? Then I presently become aware that while I can will the lie, I can by no means will that lying should be a universal law. For with such a law there would be no promises at all, since it would be in vain to allege may intention in regard to my future actions to those who would not believe this allegation, or if they over-hastily did so, would pay me back in my own coin. Hence my maxim, as soon as it should be made a universal law, would necessarily destroy itself.

The conception of an objective principle,

insofar as it is obligatory for a will, is called a command (of reason), and the formula of the command is called an Imperative.

All imperatives are expressed by the word *ought* (or *shall*), and thereby indicate the relation of an objective law of reason to a will, which from its subjective constitution is not necessarily determined by it (an obligation). They say that something would be good to do or to forbear, but they say it to a will which does not always do a thing because it is conceived to be good to do it. That is practically *good*, however, which determines the will by means of the conceptions of reason, and consequently not from subjective causes, but objectively, that is on principles which are valid for every rational being as such. It is distinguished from the *pleasant*, as that which influences the will only by means of sensation from merely subjective causes, valid only for the sense of this or that one, and not as a principle of reason, which holds for everyone. . . .

Now all *imperatives* command either *hypothetically* of *categorically*. The former represent the practical necessity of a possible action as means to something else that is willed (or at least which one might possibly will). The categorical imperative would be that which represented an action as necessary of itself without reference to another end, *i.e.*, as objectively necessary.

Since every practical law represents a possible action as good, and on this account, for a subject who is practically determinable by reason, necessary, all imperatives are formulae determining an action which is necessary according to the principle of a will good in some respects. If now the action is good only as a means to *something else*, then the imperative is *hypothetical*; if it is conceived as good *in itself* and consequently as being necessarily the principle of a will which of itself conforms to reason, then it is *categorical*.

When I conceive a hypothetical imperative in general I do not know beforehand what it will

contain until I am given the condition [under which it is imperative, *viz.*, the desire which makes this imperative suitable to my purposes]. But when I conceive a categorical imperative I know at once what it contains. For as the imperative contains besides the law only the necessity that the maxims shall conform to this law, while the law contains no conditions restricting it, there remains nothing but the general statement that the maxim of the action should conform to a universal law, and it is this conformity alone that the imperative properly represents as necessary.

There is therefore but one categorical imperative, namely this: *Act only on that maxim whereby thou canst at the same time will that it should become a universal law.*

Now if all imperatives of duty can be deduced from this one imperative as from their principle, then, although it should remain undecided whether what is called duty is not merely a vain notion, yet at least we shall be able to show what we understand by it and what this notion means.

Since the universality of the law according to which effects are produced constitutes what is properly called *nature* in the most general sense (as to form), that is the existence of things as far as it is determined by general laws, the imperative of duty may be expressed thus: *Act as if the maxim of thy action were to become by thy will a Universal Law of Nature.*

1. A man reduced to despair by a series of misfortunes feels wearied of life, but is still so far in possession of his reason that he can ask himself whether it would not be contrary to his duty to himself to take his own life. Now he inquires whether the maxim of his action could become a universal law of nature. His maxim is: From self-love I adopt it as a principle to shorten my life when its longer duration is likely to bring more evil than satisfaction. It is asked then simply

whether this principle founded on self-love can become a universal law of nature. Now we see at once that a system of nature of which it should be a law to destroy life by means of the very feeling whose special nature it is to impel to the improvement of life would contradict itself, and therefore could not exist as a system of nature; hence that maxim cannot possibly exist as a universal law of nature, and consequently would be wholly inconsistent with the supreme principle of all duty.

2. Another finds himself forced by necessity to borrow money. He knows that he will not be able to repay it, but sees also that nothing will be lent to him, unless he promises stoutly to repay it in a definite time. He desires to make this promise, but he has still so much conscience as to ask himself: Is it not unlawful and inconsistent with duty to get out of a difficulty in this way? Suppose, however, that he resolves to do so, then the maxim of his action would be expressed thus: When I think myself in want of money, I will borrow money and promise to repay it, although I know that I never can do so. Now this principle of self-love or of one's own advantage may perhaps be consistent with my whole future welfare; but the question now is, Is it right? I change then the suggestion of self-love into a universal law, and state the question thus: How would it be if my maxim were a universal law? Then I see at once that it could never hold as a universal law of nature, but would necessarily contradict itself. For supposing it to be a universal law that everyone when he thinks himself in a difficulty should be able to promise whatever he pleases, with the purpose of not keeping his promise, the promise itself would become impossible, as well as the end that one might have in view in it, since no one would consider that anything was promised to him, but would ridicule all such statements as vain pretenses.

3. A third finds in himself a talent which with the help of some culture might make him a useful man in many respects. But he finds himself in comfortable circumstances, and prefers to indulge in pleasure rather than to take pains in enlarging and improving his happy natural capacities. He asks, however, whether his maxim of neglect of his natural gifts, besides agreeing with his inclination to indulgence, agrees also with what is called duty. He sees then that a system of nature could indeed subsist with such a universal law although men (like the South Sea islanders) should let their talents rust, and resolve to devote their lives merely to idleness, amusement, and propagation of their species—in a word, to enjoyment; but he cannot possibly *will* that this should be a universal law of nature, or be implanted in us as such by a natural instinct. For, as a rational being, he necessarily wills that his faculties be developed, since they serve him, and have been given him, for all sorts of possible purposes.

4. A fourth, who is in prosperity, while he sees that others have to contend with great wretchedness and that he could help them, thinks: What concern is it of mine? Let everyone be as happy as heaven pleases, or as he can make himself; I will take nothing from him nor even envy him, only I do not wish to contribute anything to his welfare or to his assistance in distress! Now no doubt if such a mode of thinking were a universal law, the human race might very well subsist, and doubtless even better than in a state in which everyone talks of sympathy and goodwill, or even takes care occasionally to put it into practice, but on the other side, also cheats when he can, betrays the rights of men, or otherwise violates them. But although it is possible that a universal law of nature might exist in accordance with that maxim, it is impossible to *will* that such a principle should have the universal validity of a law of nature. For a will which resolved this would contradict itself, inasmuch as

many cases might occur in which one would have need of the love and sympathy of others, and in which, by such a law of nature, sprung from his own will, he would deprive himself of all hope of the aid he desires.

These are a few of the many actual duties, or at least what we regard as such, which obviously fall into two classes on the one principle that we have laid down. We must be *able to will* that a maxim of our action should be a universal law. This is the canon of the moral appreciation of the action generally. Some actions are of such a character that their maxim cannot without contradiction be even *conceived* as a universal law of nature, far from it being possible that we should *will* that it *should* be so. In others this intrinsic impossibility is not found, but still it is impossible to *will* that their maxim should be raised to the universality of a law of nature, since such a will would contradict itself. It is easily seen that the former violate strict or rigorous (inflexible) duty; the latter only laxer (meritorious) duty. Thus it has been completely shown by these examples how all duties depend as regards the nature of the obligation (not the object of the action) on the same principle.

Supposing . . . that there were something *whose existence* has *in itself* an absolute worth, something which, being *an end in itself*, could be a source of definite laws, then in this and this alone would lie the source of a possible categorical imperative, *i.e.,* a practical law.

Now I say: man and generally any rational being *exists* as an end in himself, *not merely as a means* to be arbitrarily used by this or that will, but in all his actions, whether they concern himself or other rational beings, must be always regarded at the same time as an end. All objects of the inclinations have only a conditional worth, for if the inclinations and the wants founded on them did not exist, then their object would be without value. But the inclinations themselves being sources of want, are so far from having an absolute worth for which they should be desired, that on the contrary it must be the universal wish of every rational being to be wholly free from them. Thus the worth of any object which is *to be acquired* by our action is always conditional. Beings whose existence depends not on our will but on nature's, have nevertheless, if they are irrational beings, only a relative value as means, and are therefore called *things;* rational beings, on the contrary, are called *persons,* because their very nature points them out as ends in themselves, that is as something which must not be used merely as means, and so far therefore restricts freedom of action (and is an object of respect). These, therefore, are not merely subjective ends whose existence has a worth *for us* as an effect of our action, but *objective ends,* that is things whose existence is an end in itself: an end moreover for which no other can be substituted, which they should subserve *merely* as means, for otherwise nothing whatever would possess *absolute worth;* but if all worth were conditioned and therefore contingent, then there would be no supreme practical principle of reason whatever.

If then there is a supreme practical principle or, in respect of the human will, a categorical imperative, it must be one which, being drawn from the conception of that which is necessarily an end for everyone because it is *an end in itself,* constitutes an *objective* principle of will, and can therefore serve as a universal practical law. The foundation of this principle is: *rational nature exists as an end in itself.* Man necessarily conceives his own existence as being so: so far than this is a *subjective* principle of human actions. But every other rational being regards its existence similarly, just on the same rational principle that holds for me: so that it is at the same time an objective principle, from which as a supreme practical law all laws of the will must be capable of being deduced. Accordingly the practical imperative will be as follows: *So act as to treat humanity, whether in thine own person or in that of any other, in every case as an end withal, never as means only.*

The principle: So act in regard to every rational being (thyself and others), that he may always have place in thy maxim as an end in himself, is accordingly essentially identical with this other: Act upon a maxim which, at the same time, involves its own universal validity for every rational being. For that in using means for every end I should limit my maxim by the condition of its holding good as a law for every subject, this comes to the same thing as that the fundamental principle of all maxims of action must be that the subject of all ends, *i.e.,* the rational being himself, be never employed merely as means, but as the supreme condition restricting the use of all means, that is in every case as an end likewise.

We see philosophy brought to a critical position, since it has to be firmly fixed, notwithstanding that it has nothing to support it either in heaven or earth. Here it must show its purity as absolute dictator of its own laws, not the herald of those which are whispered to it by an implanted sense of who knows what tutelary nature. Although these may be better than nothing, yet they can never afford principles dictated by reason, which must have their source wholly *a priori* and thence their commanding authority, expecting everything from the supremacy of the law and the due respect for it, nothing from inclination, or else condemning the man to self-contempt and inward abhorrence.

Thus every empirical element is not only quite incapable of being an aid to principle of morality, but is even highly prejudicial to the purity of morals, for the proper and inestimable worth of an absolutely good will consists just in this, that the principle of action is free from all influence of contingent grounds, which alone experience can furnish. We cannot too much or too often repeat our warning against this lax and even mean habit of thought which seeks for its principle amongst empirical motives and laws; for human reason in its weariness is glad to rest on this pillow, and in a dream of sweet illusions (in which, instead of Juno, it embraces a cloud) it substitutes for morality a bastard patched up from limbs of various derivation, which looks like anything one chooses to see in it; only not like virtue to one who has once beheld her in her true form.

To behold virtue in her proper form is nothing else but to contemplate morality stripped of all admixture of sensible things and of every spurious ornament or reward or self-love. How much she then eclipses everything else that appears charming to the affections, everyone may readily perceive with the least exertion of his reason, if it be not wholly spoiled for abstration.

CHAPTER 59

JOHN STUART MILL

UTILITARIANISM

John Stuart Mill (1806–1873) was one of the leading figures of the Utilitarian movement in England. His life was dedicated to clarifying and continuing the teachings of his father, John Mill (himself an outstanding philosopher), and those of Jeremy Bentham. In order to realize this goal, his education was not left to chance. His father imposed on him a rigorous program of instruction from age three to fourteen. At the age of three, he studied Greek and arithmetic; at eight, Latin was added, and by the age of twelve he was reading extensively in logic, philosophy, and economics.

In 1823, following the advice of his father, Mill accepted a position with the East India Company. He held this post for thirty years, working on his books in his spare time. Upon retirement, his name was put forward as a candidate for Parliament. He was elected to office despite his refusal to campaign, and served with distinction.

Mill wrote on a wide variety of subjects. In his *System of Logic* (1843), he defended the inductive method of logic, showing how general laws may be derived from empirical facts. Other important volumes include *Principles of Political Economy* (1848), *On Liberty* (1859), and *Utilitarianism* (1861).

This selection is taken from Mill's book *Utilitarianism:*[1] it contains portions of Chapters 2 and 4. This classic volume was written against the background of a lively debate in England over the hedonistic utilitarianism of Jeremy Bentham.

[1] From John Stuart Mill, *Utilitarianism* (1861).

Mill attempts to rescue utilitarianism from its many critics (who dismiss it as a "pig philosophy") by modifying Bentham's utility principle, substituting happiness for pleasure. He argues that there are different qualities of pleasure: cultural and intellectual pleasures are superior to merely sensuous pleasures.

UTILITARIANISM

Chapter II. What Utilitarianism Is

... The creed which accepts as the foundation of morals, Utility, or the Greatest Happiness Principle, holds that actions are right in proportion as they tend to promote happiness, wrong as they tend to produce the reverse of happiness. By happiness is intended pleasure, and the absence of pain; by unhappiness, pain, and the privation of pleasure. To give a clear view of the moral standard set up by the theory, much more requires to be said; in particular, what things it includes in the ideas of pain and pleasure; and to what extent this is left an open question. But these supplementary explanations do not affect the theory of life on which this theory of morality is grounded—namely, that pleasure, and freedom from pain, are the only things desirable as ends; and that all desirable things (which are as numerous in the utilitarian as in any other scheme) are desirable either for the pleasure inherent in themselves, or as means to the promotion of pleasure and the prevention of pain.

Now, such a theory of life excites in many minds, and among them in some of the most estimable in feeling and purpose, inveterate dislike. To suppose that life has (as they express it) no higher end than pleasure—no better and nobler object of desire and pursuit—they designate as utterly mean and grovelling; as a doctrine worthy only of swine, to whom the followers of Epicurus were, at a very early period, contemptuously lik-

ened; and modern holders of the doctrine are occasionally made the subject of equally polite comparisons by its German, French, and English assailants.

When thus attacked, the Epicureans have always answered, that it is not they, but their accusers, who represent human nature in a degrading light; since the accusation supposes human beings to be capable of no pleasures except those of which swine are capable. If this supposition were true, the charge could not be gainsaid, but would then be no longer an imputation; for if the sources of pleasure were precisely the same to human beings and to swine, the rule of life which is good enough for the one would be good enough for the other. The comparison of the Epicurean life to that of beasts is felt as degrading, precisely because a beast's pleasures do not satisfy a human being's conceptions of happiness. Human beings have faculties more elevated than the animal appetites, and when once made conscious of them, do not regard anything as happiness which does not include their gratification. I do not, indeed, consider the Epicureans to have been by any means faultless in drawing out their scheme of consequences from the utilitarian principle. To do this in any sufficient manner, many Stoic, as well as Christian elements require to be included. But there is no known Epicurean theory of life which does not assign to the pleasures of the intellect, of the feelings and imagination, and of the moral sentiments, a much higher value as pleasures than to those of mere sensation. It must be admitted, however, that utilitarian writers in general have placed the superiority of mental over bodily pleasures chiefly in the greater permanency, safety, uncostliness, & c., of the former—that is, in their circumstantial advantages rather than in their intrinsic nature. And on all these points utilitarians have fully proved their case; but they might have taken the other, and, as it may be called, higher ground, with entire consistency. It is quite compatible with the principle of utility to recognise the fact, that some *kinds* of pleasure are more desirable and more valuable than others. It would be absurd that while, in estimating all other things, quality is considered as well as quantity, the estimation of pleasures should be supposed to depend on quantity alone.

If I am asked, what I mean by difference of quality in pleasures, or what makes one pleasure more valuable than another, merely as a pleasure, except its being greater in amount, there is but one possible answer. Of two pleasures, if there be one to which all or almost all who have experience of both give a decided preference, irrespective of any feeling of moral obligation to prefer it, that is the more desirable pleasure. If one of the two is, by those who are competently acquainted with both, placed so far above the other that they prefer it, even though knowing it to be attended with a greater amount of discontent, and would not resign it for any quantity of the other pleasure which their nature is capable of, we are justified in ascribing to the preferred enjoyment a superiority in quality, so far outweighing quantity as to render it, in comparison, of small account.

Now it is an unquestionable fact that those who are equally acquainted with, and equally capable of appreciating and enjoying, both, do give a most marked preference to the manner of existence which employs their higher faculties.

Few human creatures would consent to be changed into any of the lower animals, for a promise of the fullest allowance of a beast's pleasures; no intelligent human being would consent to be a fool, no instructed person would be an ignoramus, no person of feeling and conscience would be selfish and base, even though they should be persuaded that the fool, the dunce, or the rascal is better satisfied with his lot than they are with theirs. They would not resign what they possess more than he, for the most complete satisfaction of all the desires which they have in common with him. If they ever fancy they would, it is only in cases of unhappiness so extreme, that to escape from it they would exchange their lot for almost any other, however undesirable in their own eyes. A being of higher faculties requires more to make him happy, is capable probably of more acute suffering, and is certainly accessible to it at more points, than one of an inferior type; but in spite of these liabilities, he can never really wish to sink into what he feels to be a lower grade of existence. We may give what explanation we please of this unwillingness; we may attribute it to pride, a name which is given indiscriminately to some of the most and to some of the least estimable feelings of which mankind are capable; we may refer it to the love of liberty and personal independence, an appeal to which was with the Stoics one of the most effective means for the inculcation of it; to the love of power, or to the love of excitement, both of which do really enter into and contribute to it: but its most appropriate appellation is a sense of dignity, which all human beings possess in one form or other, and in some, though by no means in exact, proportion to their higher faculties, and which is so essential a part of the happiness of those in whom it is strong, that nothing which conflicts with it could be, otherwise than momentarily, an object of desire to them. Whoever supposes that this preference takes place at a sacrifice of happiness—that the superior being, in anything like the equal circumstances, is not happier than the inferior—confounds the two very different ideas, of happiness, and content. It is indisputable that the being whose capacities of enjoyment are low, has the greatest chance of having them fully satisfied; and a highly-endowed being will always feel that any happiness which he can look for, as the world is constituted, is imperfect. But he can learn to bear its imperfections, if they are at all bearable; and they will not make him envy the being who is indeed unconscious of the imperfections, but only because he feels not at all the good which those imperfections qualify. It is better to be a human being dissatisfied than a pig satisfied; better to be Socrates dissatisfied than a fool satisfied. And if the fool, or the pig, is of a different opinion, it is because they only know their own side of the question. The other party to the comparison knows both sides.

It may be objected, that many who are capable of the higher pleasures, occasionally, under the influence of temptation, postpone them to the lower. But this is quite compatible with a full appreciation of the intrinsic superiority of the higher. Men often, from infirmity of character, make their election for the nearer good, though they know it to be the less valuable; and this no less when the choice is between two bodily pleasures, than when it is between bodily and mental. They pursue sensual indulgences to the injury of health, though perfectly aware that health is the greater good. It may be further objected, that many who begin with youthful enthusiasm for everything noble, as they advance in years sink into indolence and selfishness. But I do not believe that those who undergo this very common change, voluntarily choose the lower description of pleasures in preference to the higher. I believe that before they devote themselves exclusively to the one, they have already become

incapable of the other. Capacity for the nobler feelings is in most natures a very tender plant, easily killed, not only by hostile influences, but by mere want of sustenance; and in the majority of young persons it speedily dies away if the occupations to which their position in life has devoted them, and the society into which it has thrown them, are not favourable to keeping that higher capacity in exercise. Men lose their high aspirations as they lose their intellectual tastes, because they have not time or opportunity for indulging them; and they addict themselves to inferior pleasures, not because they deliberately prefer them, but because they are either the only ones to which they have access, or the only ones which they are any longer capable of enjoying. It may be questioned whether any one who has remained equally susceptible to both classes of pleasures, ever knowingly and calmly preferred the lower, though many, in all ages, have broken down in an ineffectual attempt to combine both.

From this verdict of the only competent judges, I apprehend there can be no appeal. On a question which is the best worth having of two pleasures, or which of two modes of existence is the most grateful to the feelings, apart from its moral attributes and from its consequences, the judgment of those who are qualified by knowledge of both, or, if they differ, that of the majority among them, must be admitted as final. And there needs be the less hesitation to accept this judgment respecting the quality of pleasures, since there is no other tribunal to be referred to even on the question of quantity. What means are there of determining which is the acutest of two pains, or the intensest of two pleasurable sensations, except the general suffrage of those who are familiar with both? Neither pains nor pleasures are homogeneous, and pain is always heterogeneous with pleasure. What is there to decide whether a particular pleasure is worth purchasing at the cost of a particular pain, except the feelings and judgment of the experienced? When, therefore, those feelings and judgment declare the pleasures derived from the higher faculties to be preferable *in kind,* apart from the question of intensity, to those of which the animal nature, disjoined from the higher faculties, is susceptible, they are entitled on this subject to the same regard.

I have dwelt on this point, as being a necessary part of a perfectly just conception of Utility or Happiness, considered as the directive rule of human conduct. But it is by no means an indispensable condition to the acceptance of the utilitarian standard; for that standard is not the agent's own greatest happiness, but the greatest amount of happiness altogether; and if it may possibly be doubted whether a noble character is always the happier for its nobleness, there can be no doubt that it makes other people happier, and that the world in general is immensely a gainer by it. Utilitarianism, therefore, could only attain its end by the general cultivation of nobleness of character, even if each individual were only benefitted by the nobleness of others, and his own, so far as happiness is concerned, were a sheer deduction from the benefit. But the bare enunciation of such an absurdity as this last, renders refutation superfluous.

According to the Greatest Happiness Principle, as above explained, the ultimate end, with reference to and for the sake of which all other things are desirable (whether we are considering our own good or that of other people), is an existence exempt as far as possible from pain, and as rich as possible in enjoyments, both in point of quantity and quality; the test of quality, and the rule for measuring it against quantity, being the preference felt by those who, in their opportunities of experience, to which must be added their habits of self-consciousness and self-observation, are best furnished with the means of comparison.

This, being, according to the utilitarian opinion, the end of human action, is necessarily also the standard of morality; which may accordingly be defined, the rules and precepts for human conduct, by the observance of which an existence such as has been described might be, to the greatest extent possible, secured to all mankind; and not to them only, but, so far as the nature of things admits, to the whole sentient creation. . . .

I must again repeat, what the assailants of utilitarianism seldom have the justice to acknowledge, that the happiness which forms the utilitarian standard of what is right in conduct, is not the agent's own happiness, but that of all concerned. As between his own happiness and that of others, utilitarianism requires him to be as strictly impartial as a disinterested and benevolent spectator. In the golden rule of Jesus of Nazareth, we read the complete spirit of the ethics of utility. To do as one would be done by, and to love one's neighbour as oneself, constitute the ideal perfection of utilitarian morality. As the means of making the nearest approach to this ideal, utility would enjoin, first, that laws and social arrangements should place the happiness, or (as speaking practically it may be called) the interest, of every individual, as nearly as possible in harmony with the interest of the whole; and secondly, that education and opinion, which have so vast a power over human character, should so use that power as to establish in the mind of every individual an indissoluble association between his own happiness and the good of the whole; especially between his own happiness and the practice of such modes of conduct, negative and positive, as regard for the universal happiness prescribes: so that not only he may be unable to conceive the possibility of happiness to himself, consistently with conduct opposed to the general good, but also that a direct impulse to promote the general good may be in every individual one of the hapitual motives of action, and the sentiments connected therewith may fill a large and prominent place in every human being's sentient existence. If the impugners of the utilitarian morality represented it to their own minds in this its true character, I know not what recommendation possessed by any other morality they could possibly affirm to be wanting to it: what more beautiful or more exalted developments of human nature any other ethical system can be supposed to foster, or what springs of action, not accessible to the utilitarian, such systems rely on for giving effect to their mandates.

• • •

Chapter IV. Of What Sort of Proof the Principle of Utility is Susceptible

It has already been remarked, that questions of ultimate ends do not admit of proof, in the ordinary acceptation of the term. To be incapable of proof by reasoning is common to all first principles; to the first premises of our knowledge, as well as to those of our conduct. But the former, being matters of fact, may be the subject of a direct appeal to the faculties which judge of fact—namely, our senses, and our internal consciousness. Can an appeal be made to the same faculties on questions of practical ends? Or by what other faculty is cognizance taken of them?

Questions about ends are, in other words, questions about what things are desirable. The utilitarian doctrine is, that happiness is desirable, and the only thing desirable, as an end; all other things being only desirable as means to that end. What ought to be required of this doctrine—what conditions is it requisite that the doctrine should fulfil—to make good its claim to be believed?

The only proof capable of being given that an object is visible, is that people actually see it.

The only proof that a sound is audible, is that people hear it: and so of the other sources of our experience. In like manner, I apprehend, the sole evidence it is possible to produce that anything is desirable, is that people do actually desire it. If the end which the utilitarian doctrine proposes to itself were not, in theory and in practice, acknowledged to be an end, nothing could ever convince any person that it was so. No reason can be given why the general happiness is desirable, except that each person, so far as he believes it to be attainable, desires his own happiness. This, however, being a fact, we have not only all the proof which the case admits of, but all which it is possible to require, that happiness is a good: that each person's happiness is a good to that person, and the general happiness, therefore, a good to the aggregate of all persons. Happiness has made out its title as *one* of the ends of conduct, and consequently one of the criteria of morality.

But it has not, by this alone, proved itself to be the sole criterion. To do that, it would seem, by the same rule, necessary to show, not only that people desire happiness, but that they never desire anything else. Now it is palpable that they do desire things which, in common language, are decidedly distinguished from happiness. They desire, for example, virtue, and the absence of vice, no less really than pleasure and the absence of pain. The desire of virtue is not as universal, but it is as authentic a fact, as the desire of happiness. And hence the opponents of the utilitarian standard deem that they have a right to infer that there are other ends of human action besides happiness, and that happiness is not the standard of approbation and disapprobation.

But does the utilitarian doctrine deny that people desire virtue, or maintain that virtue is not a thing to be desired? The very reverse. It maintains not only that virtue is to be desired, but that it is to be desired disinterestedly, for itself.

647

Whatever may be the opinion of utilitarian moralists as to the original conditions by which virtue is made virtue; however they may believe (as they do) that actions and dispositions are only virtuous because they promote another end than virtue; yet this being granted, and it having been decided, from considerations of this description, what *is* virtuous, they not only place virtue at the very head of the things which are good as means to the ultimate end, but they also recognise as a psychological fact the possibility of its being, to the individual, a good in itself, without looking to any end beyond it; and hold, that the mind is not in a right state, not in a state comfortable to Utility, not in the state most conducive to the general happiness, unless it does love virtue in this manner—as a thing desirable in itself, even although, in the individual instance, it should not produce those other desirable consequences which it tends to produce, and on account of which it is held to be virtue. This opinion is not, in the smallest degree, a departure from the Happiness principle. The ingredients of happiness are very various, and each of them is desirable in itself, and not merely when considered as swelling an aggregate. The principle of utility does not mean that any given pleasure, as music, for instance, or any given exemption from pain, as for example health, are to be looked upon as a means to a collective something termed happiness, and to be desired on that account. They are desired and desirable in and for themselves; besides being means, they are a part of the end. Virtue, according to the utilitarian doctrine, is not naturally and originally part of the end, but it is capable of becoming so; and in those who love it disinterestedly it has become so, and is desired and cherished, not as a means to happiness, but as a part of their happiness.

To illustrate this farther, we may remember that virtue is not the only thing, originally a means, and which if it were not a means of any-thing else, would be and remain indifferent, but which by association with what it is a means to, comes to be desired for itself, and that too with the utmost intensity. What, for example, shall we say of the love of money? There is nothing originally more desirable about money than about any heap of glittering pebbles. Its worth is solely that of the things which it will buy; the desires for other things than itself, which it is a means of gratifying. Yet the love of money is not only one of the strongest moving forces of human life, but money is, in many cases, desired in and for itself; the desire to possess it is often stronger than the desire to use it, and goes on increasing when all the desires which point to ends beyond it, to be encompassed by it, are falling off. It may be then said truly, that money is desired not for the sake of an end, but as part of the end. From being a means to happiness, it has come to be itself a principal ingredient of the individual's conception of happiness. The same may be said of the majority of the great objects of human life—power, for example, or fame; except that to each of these there is a certain amount of immediate pleasure annexed, which has at least the semblance of being naturally inherent in them; a thing which cannot be said of money. Still, however, the strongest natural attraction, both of power and of fame, is the immense aid they give to the attainment of our other wishes; and it is the strong association thus generated between them and all our objects of desire, which gives to the direct desire of them the intensity it often assumes, so as in some characters to surpass in strength all other desires. In these cases the means have become a part of the end, and a more important part of it than any of the things which they are means to. What was once desired as an instrument for the attainment of happiness, has come to be desired for its own sake. In being desired for its own sake it is, however, desired as *part* of happiness. The person is made, or thinks he would be made, happy by its mere possession; and is made unhappy by failure to obtain it. The desire of it is not a different thing from the desire of happiness, any more than the love of music, or the desire of health. They are included in happiness. They are some of the elements of which the desire of happiness is made up. Happiness is not an abstract idea, but a concrete whole; and these are some of its parts. And the utilitarian standard sanctions and approves their being so. Life would be a poor thing, very ill provided with sources of happiness, if there were not this provision of nature, by which things originally indifferent, but conducive to, or otherwise associated with, the satisfaction of our primitive desires, become in themselves sources of pleasure more valuable than the primitive pleasures, both in permanency, in the space of human existence that they are capable of covering, and even in intensity.

Virtue, according to the utilitarian conception, is a good of this description. There was no original desire of it, or motive to it, save its conduciveness to pleasure, and especially to protection from pain. But through the association thus formed, it may be felt a good in itself, and desired as such with as great intensity as any other good; and with this difference between it and the love of money, of power, or of fame, that all of these may, and often do, render the individual noxious to the other members of the society to which he belongs, whereas there is nothing which makes him so much a blessing to them as the cultivation of the disinterested love of virtue. And consequently, the utilitarian standard, while it tolerates and approves those other acquired desires, up to the point beyond which they would be more injurious to the general happiness than promotive of it, enjoins and requires the cultivation of the love of virtue up to the greatest strength possible, as being above all things important to the general happiness.

It results from the preceding considerations, that there is in reality nothing desired except happiness. Whatever is desired otherwise than as a means to some end beyond itself, and ultimately to happiness, is desired as itself a part of happiness, and is not desired for itself until it has become so.

CHAPTER 60

FRIEDRICH NIETZSCHE

THE TRANSVALUATION OF VALUES

Convinced that philosophers must serve as "the bad conscience of their age" offering "untimely meditations," Nietzsche (see Chapter 23 for a brief biography) attacks the decadence and hypocrisy of traditional European morality—a morality that he predicts will lead inevitably to the collapse of Western culture. Nietzsche's *transvaluation of values* is intended as a "nay-saying" countermovement:

> After thousands of years of error and confusion, it is my good fortune to have rediscovered the road which leads to a Yea and to a Nay.
>
> I teach people to say Nay in the face of all that makes for weakness and exhaustion.
>
> I teach people to say Yea in the face of all that makes for strength, that preserves strength, and justifies the feeling of strength.

Nietzsche presents a corrected table of virtues to replace the traditional Judaic-Christian ones: in place of humility, he recommends pride; in place of sympathy and pity, contempt and aloofness; in place of love for one's neighbor, no more than tolerance. This transvaluation is not for the "common herd," but for the few free spirits of the age who are intellectually fit to receive it.

[1]From *The Complete Works of Friedrich Nietzsche*, vols. 12–14, edited O. Levy (New York: Macmillan, 1924).

The true morality must be built from the immediate sense of power that all people can feel within themselves. Nietzsche scorns all "slave moralities" which conceal the harshness of reality and repress the will to power. Christianity is singled out for special criticism because of its pernicious perversion of the will to power, seen in the hypocritical sermons of clergymen on meekness and the "botched and bungled" masses who are taken in by the deceptions of the priests.

Nietzsche uses the Greek gods Dionysus and Apollo to dramatize the relationship between the will and reason. The frenzied, passionate Dionysus is revered as the symbol of the undisciplined will to power. Apollo, representing rationality and order, must be the instrument by which the will to power can increase its mastery. As the Apollonian element supports rather than suppresses the Dionysian, humans can at last defy God and dominate the universe.

The Transvaluation of Values

In a tour through the many finer and coarser moralities which have hitherto prevailed or still prevail on the earth, I found certain traits recurring regularly together, and connected with one another, until finally two primary types revealed themselves to me, and a radical distinction was brought to light. There is *master-morality* and *slave-morality*,—I would at once add, however, that in all higher and mixed civilizations, there are also attempts at the reconciliation of the two moralities; but one finds still oftener the confusion and mutual misunderstanding of them, indeed, sometimes their close juxtaposition—even in the same man, within one soul. The distinctions of moral values have either originated in a ruling caste, pleasantly conscious of being different from the ruled—or among the ruled class, the slaves and dependents of all sorts. . . .

The noble type of man regards *himself* as a determiner of values; he does not require to be approved of; he passes the judgment: "What is injurious to me is injurious in itself"; he knows that it is he himself only who confers honor on things; he is a *creator of values*. He honors whatever he recognizes in himself: such morality is self-glorification. In the foreground there is the feeling of plenitude, of power, which seeks to overflow, the happiness of high tension, the consciousness of a wealth which would fain give and bestow:—the noble man also helps the unfortunate, but not—or scarcely—out of pity, but rather from an impulse generated by the superabundance of power. The noble man honors in himself the powerful one, him also who has power over himself, who knows how to speak and how to keep silence, who takes pleasure in subjecting himself to severity and hardness, and has reverence for all that is severe and hard. . . .

It is otherwise with the second type of morality, *slave morality*. Supposing that the abused, the oppressed, the suffering, the unemancipated, the weary, and those uncertain of themselves, should moralize, what will be the common element in their moral estimates? Probably a pessimistic suspicion with regard to the entire situation of man will find expression, perhaps a condemnation of man, together with his situation. The slave has an unfavorable eye for the virtues of the powerful;

he has a skepticism and distrust, a *refinement* of distrust of everything "good" that is there honored—he would fain persuade himself that the very happiness there is not genuine. On the other hand, *those* qualities which serve to alleviate the existence of sufferers are brought into prominence and flooded with light; it is here that sympathy, the kind, helping hand, the warm heart, patience, diligence, humility, and friendliness attain to honor; for here these are the most useful qualities, and almost the only means of supporting the burden of existence. Slave-morality is essentially the morality of utility. Here is the seat of the origin of the famous antithesis "good" and "evil":—power and dangerousness are assumed to reside in the evil, a certain dreadfulness, subtlety, and strength, which do not admit of being despised. According to slave-morality, therefore, the "evil" man arouses fear; according to master-morality, it is precisely the "good" man who arouses fear and seeks to arouse it, while the bad man is regarded as the despicable being.

The guidepost which first put me on the *right* track was this question—what is the true etymological significance of the various symbols for the idea "good" which have been coined in the various languages? I then found that they all led back to *the same evolution of the same idea*—that everywhere "aristocrat," "noble" (in the social sense), is the root idea, out of which have necessarily developed "good" in the sense of "with aristocratic soul," "noble," in the sense of "with a soul of high calibre," "with a privileged soul"—a development which invariably runs parallel with that other evolution by which "vulgar," "plebeian," "low," are made to change finally into "bad." . . .

The revolt of the slaves in morals begins in the very principle of *resentment* becoming creative and giving birth to values—a resentment experienced by creatures who, deprived as they are of the proper outlet of action, are forced to find their compensation in an imaginary revenge.

While every aristocratic morality springs from a triumphant affirmation of its own demands, the slave morality says "no" from the very outset to what is "outside itself," "different from itself," and "not itself": and this "no" is its creative deed. . . .

What respect for his enemies is found, forsooth, in an aristocratic man—and such a reverence is already a bridge to love! He insists on having his enemy to himself as his distinction. He tolerates no other enemy but a man in whose character there is nothing to despise and *much* to honor! On the other hand, imagine the "enemy" as the resentful man conceives him—and it is here exactly that we see his work, his creativeness; he has conceived "the evil enemy," "the evil one," and indeed that is the root idea from which he now evolves as a contrasting and corresponding figure a "good one," himself—his very self!

The method of this man is quite contrary to that of the aristocratic man, who conceives the root idea "good" spontaneously and straight away, that is to say, out of himself, and from that material then creates for himself a concept of "bad"! This "bad" of aristocratic origin and that "evil" out of the cauldron of unsatisfied hatred—the former an imitation, an "extra," an additional nuance; the latter, on the other hand, the original, the beginning, the essential act in the conception of a slave-morality—these two words "bad" and "evil," how great a difference do they mark, in spite of the fact that they have an identical contrary in the idea "good." But the idea "good" is *not* the same: much rather let the question be asked, "Who is really evil according to the meaning of the morality of resentment?" In all sternness let it be answered thus:—*just* the good man of the other morality, just the aristocrat, the powerful one, the one who rules, but who is distorted by the venomous eye of resentfulness, into a new color, a new signification, a new appearance. This particular point we would be the last to deny: the man who learned to know those "good" ones only as enemies, learned at the same time not to know them only as *"evil enemies,"* and the same men who *inter pares* [between equals] were kept so rigorously in bounds though convention, respect, custom, and gratitude, though much more through mutual vigilance and jealousy *inter pares*, these men who in their relations with each other find so many new ways of manifesting consideration, self-control, delicacy, loyalty, pride, and friendship, these men are in reference to what is outside their circle (where the foreign element, a *foreign* country, begins), not much better than beasts of prey, which have been let loose. They enjoy their freedom from all social control, they feel that in the wilderness they can give vent with impunity to that tension which is produced by enclosure and imprisonment in the peace of society, they *revert* to the innocence of the beast-of-prey conscience, like jubilant monsters, who perhaps come from a ghostly bout of murder, arson, rape, and torture, with bravado and a moral equanimity, as though merely some wild student's prank had been played, perfectly convinced that the poets have now an ample theme to sing and celebrate. It is impossible not to recognize at the core of all these aristocratic races the beast of prey, the magnificent *blond brute*, avidly rampant for spoil and victory, this hidden core needed an outlet from time to time, the beast must get loose again, must return into the wilderness.

Every elevation of the type "man," has hitherto been the work of an aristocratic society and so it will always be—a society believing in a long scale of gradations of rank and differences of worth among human beings, and requiring slavery in some form or other. Without the *pathos of distance*, such as grows out of the incarnated difference of classes, out of the constant outlooking and downlooking of the ruling caste on subordinates and instruments, and out of their equally constant practice of obeying and commanding, of keeping down and keeping at a distance—that other more mysterious pathos could never have arisen, the longing for an ever new widening of distance within the soul itself, the formation of ever higher, rarer, further, more extended, more comprehensive states, in short, just the elevation of the type "man," the continued "self-surmounting of man," to use a moral formula in a supermoral sense. To be sure, one must not resign oneself to any humanitarian illusions about the history of the origin of an aristocratic society (that is to say, of the preliminary condition for the elevation of the type "man"): the truth is hard. Let us acknowledge unprejudicedly how every higher civilization hitherto has *originated!* Men with a still natural nature, barbarians in every terrible sense of the word, men of prey, still in possession of unbroken strength of will and desire for power, threw themselves upon weaker, more moral, more peaceful races (perhaps trading or cattle-rearing communities), or upon old mellow civilizations in which the final vital force was flickering out in brilliant fireworks of wit and depravity. At the commencement, the noble caste was always the barbarian caste: their superiority did not consist first of all in their physical, but in their psychical power—they were more *complete* men (which at every point also implies the same as "more complete beasts").

The preponderance of an altruistic way of valuing is the result of a consciousness of the fact that one is botched and bungled. Upon examination, this point of view turns out to be: "I am not worth much," simply a psychological valuation; more plainly still: it is the feeling of impotence, of the lack of the great self-asserting impulses of power (in muscles, nerves, and ganglia). This valuation gets translated, according to the particular culture of these classes, into a moral or religious principle (the preeminence of religious or moral precepts is always a sign of low culture): it tries to justify itself in spheres whence, as far as it is concerned, the notion "value" hails. The interpretation by means of which the Christian sinner tries to understand himself, is an attempt at justifying his lack of power and of self-confidence: he prefers to feel himself a sinner rather than feel bad for nothing: it is in itself a symptom of decay when interpretations of this sort are used at all. In some cases the bungled and the botched do not look for the reason of their unfortunate condition in their own guilt (as the Christian does), but in society: when, however, the Socialist, the Anarchist, and the Nihilist are conscious that their existence is something for which someone must be *guilty*, they are very closely related to the Christian, who also believes that he can more easily endure his ill ease and his wretched constitution when he has found someone whom he can hold *responsible* for it. The instinct of *revenge* and *resentment* appears in both cases here as a means of enduring life, as a self-preservative measure, as is also the favor shown to *altruistic* theory and practice. The *hatred of egoism*, whether it be one's own (as in the case of the Christian), or another's (as in the case of the Socialists), thus appears as a valuation reached under the predominance of revenge; and also as an act of prudence on the part of the preservative instinct of the suffering, in the form of an increase in their feelings of cooperation and unity. . . . At bottom, as I have already suggested, the discharge of resentment which takes place in the act of judging, rejecting, and punishing egoism (one's own or that of others) is still a self-preservative measure on the part of the bungled and the botched. In short: the cult of altruism is merely a particular form of egoism, which regularly appears under certain definite physiological circumstances.

When the Socialist, with righteous indignation, cries for "justice," "rights," "equal rights," it only shows that he is oppressed by his inadequate culture, and is unable to understand why he suffers: he also finds pleasure in crying;—if he were more at ease he would take jolly good care not to cry in that way: in that case he would seek his pleasure elsewhere. The same holds good of the Christian: He curses, condemns, and slanders the "world"—and does not even except himself. But that is no reason for taking him seriously. In both cases we are in the presence of invalids who feel better for crying, and who find relief in slander.

To refrain mutually from injury, from violence, from exploitation, and put one's will on a par with that of others: this may result in a certain rough sense in good conduct among individuals when the necessary conditions are given (namely, the actual similarity of the individuals in amount of force and degree of worth, and their co-relation within one organization). As soon, however, as one wished to take this principle more generally, and if possible even as *the fundamental principle of society*, it would immediately disclose what it really is—namely, a Will to the *denial* of life, a principle of dissolution and decay. Here one must think profoundly to the very basis and resist all sentimental weakness: life itself is *essentially* appropriation, injury, conquest of the strange and weak, suppression, severity, obtrusion of peculiar forms, incorporation, and at the least, putting it mildest, exploitation;—but why should one forever use precisely these words on which for ages a disparaging purpose has been stamped? Even the organization within which, as was previously supposed, the individuals treat each other as equal—it takes place in every healthy aristocracy—must itself, if it be a living and not a dying organization, do all that towards other bodies, which the individuals within it refrain from doing to each other: it will have to be the incarnated Will to Power, it will endeavor to grow, to gain ground, attract to itself and acquire ascendency—not owing to any morality or immorality, but because it *lives,* and because life *is* precisely Will to Power. On no point, however, is the ordinary consciousness of Europeans more unwilling to be corrected than on this matter; people now rave everywhere, even under the guise of science, about coming conditions of society in which "the exploiting character" is to be absent:—that sounds to my ears as if they promised to invent a mode of life which should refrain from all organic functions. "Exploitation" does not belong to a depraved, or imperfect and primitive society: it belongs to the *nature* of the living being as a primary organic function; it is a consequence of the intrinsic Will to Power, which is precisely the Will to Life.—Granting that as a theory this is a novelty—as a reality it is the *fundamental fact* of all history: let us be so far honest towards ourselves!

I regard Christianity as the most fatal and seductive lie that has ever yet existed—as *the* greatest and most *impious lie:* I can discern the last sprouts and branches of its ideal beneath every form of disguise, I decline to enter into any compromise or false position in reference to it—I urge people to declare open war with it.

The *morality of paltry people* as the measure of all things: this is the most repugnant kind of degeneracy that civilization has ever yet brought into existence. And this *kind of ideal* is hanging still, under the name of "God," over men's heads!!

However modest one's demands may be concerning intellectual cleanliness, when one touches the New Testament one cannot help experiencing a sort of inexpressible feeling of discomfort; for the unbounded cheek with which the least qualified people will have their say in its pages, in regard to the greatest problems of existence, and claim to sit in judgment on such matters, exceeds all limits. The impudent levity with which the most unwieldy problems are spoken of

here (life, the world, God, the purpose of life), as if they were not problems at all, but the most simple things which these little bigots *know all about!!!* . . .

The *law,* which is the fundamentally realistic formula of certain self-preservative measures of a community, forbids certain actions that have a definite tendency to jeopardize the welfare of that community: it does *not* forbid the attitude of mind which gives rise to these actions—for in the pursuit of other ends the community requires these forbidden actions, namely, when it is a matter of opposing its *enemies.* The moral idealist now steps forward and says: "God sees into men's hearts: the action itself counts for nothing; the reprehensible attitude of mind from which it proceeds must be extirpated. . . ." In normal conditions men laugh at such things; it is only in exceptional cases, when a community lives *quite* beyond the need of waging war in order to maintain itself, that an ear is lent to such things. Any attitude of mind is abandoned, the utility of which cannot be conceived.

This was the case, for example, when Buddha appeared among a people that was both peaceable and afflicted with great intellectual weariness.

This was also the case in regard to the first Christian community (as also the Jewish), the primary condition of which was the absolutely *unpolitical* Jewish society. Christianity could grow only upon the soil of Judaism—that is to say, among a people that had already renounced the political life, and which led a sort of parasitic existence within the Roman sphere of government. Christianity goes a step *further:* it allows men to "emasculate" themselves even more; the circumstances actually favor their doing so.— *Nature* is *expelled* from morality when it is said, "Love ye your enemies": for *Nature's* injunction, "Ye shall *love* your neighbor and *hate* your enemy," has now become senseless in the law (in instinct); now, even *the love a man feels for his neighbor* must first be based upon something (*a sort of love of God*). *God* is introduced everywhere, and *utility* is withdrawn; the natural *origin* of morality is denied everywhere: the *veneration of Nature*, which lies in *acknowledging a natural morality*, is *destroyed* to the roots . . .

What is it I protest against? That people should regard this paltry and peaceful mediocrity, this spiritual equilibrium which knows nothing of the fine impulses of great accumulations of strength, as something high, or possibly as the standard of all things.

Among men, as among all other animals, there is a surplus of defective, diseased, degenerating, infirm, and necessarily suffering individuals; the successful cases, among men also, are always the exception; and in view of the fact that man is *the animal not yet properly adapted to his environment*, the rare exception. But worse still. The higher the type a man represents, the greater is the improbability that he will *succeed*; the accidental, the law of irrationality in the general constitution of mankind, manifests itself most terribly in its destructive effect on the higher orders of men, the conditions of whose lives are delicate, diverse, and difficult to determine. What, then, is the attitude of the two greatest religions above-mentioned to the *surplus* of failures in life? The endeavor to preserve and keep alive whatever can be preserved; in fact, as the religions for *sufferers*, they take the part of these upon principle; they are always in favor of those who suffer from life as from a disease, and they would fain treat every other experience of life as false and impossible. However highly we may esteem this indulgent and preservative care (inasmuch as in applying to others, it has applied, and applies also to the highest and usually the most suffering type of man), the hitherto *paramount* religions— to give a general appreciation of them—are

among the principal causes which have kept the type of "man" upon a lower level—they have preserved too much *that which should have perished*. One has to thank them for invaluable services; and who is sufficiently rich in gratitude not to feel poor at the contemplation of all that the "spiritual men" of Christianity have done for Europe hitherto! But when they had given comfort to the sufferers, courage to the oppressed and despairing, a staff and support to the helpless, and when they had allured from society into convents and spiritual penitentiaries the brokenhearted and distracted: what else had they to do in order to work systematically in that fashion, and with a good conscience, for the preservation of all the sick and suffering, which means, in deed and in truth, to work for *deterioration of the European race?* To *reverse* all estimates of value— *that* is what they had to do! And to shatter the strong, to spoil great hopes, to cast suspicion on the delight in beauty, to break down everything autonomous, manly, conquering, and imperious—all instincts which are natural to the highest and most successful type of "man"—into uncertainty, distress of conscience, and self-destruction; forsooth, to invert all love of the earthly and of supremacy over the earth, in hatred of the earth and earthly things.

In the whole of moral evolution, there is no sign of truth: all the conceptual elements which come into play are fictions; all the psychological tenets are false; all the forms of logic employed in this department of prevarication are sophisms. The chief feature of all moral philosophers is their total lack of intellectual cleanliness and self-control: they regard "fine feelings" as arguments: their heaving breasts seem to them the bellows of godliness. . . . Moral philosophy is the most suspicious period in the history of the human intellect . . .

Why everything resolved itself into mummery.— Rudimentary psychology, which only considered the *conscious* lapses of men (as causes), which regarded "consciousness" as an attribute of the soul, and which sought a will behind ever action (*i.e.*, an intention), could only answer *"Happiness"* to the question: *"What does man desire?"* (it was impossible to answer "Power," because that would have been *immoral*);—consequently behind all men's actions there is the intention of attaining to happiness by means of them. Secondly: if man as a matter of fact does not attain to happiness, why is it? Because he mistakes the means thereto.—*What is the unfailing means of acquiring happiness?* Answer: *virtue.*—Why virtue? Because virtue is supreme rationalness, and rationalness makes mistakes in the choice of means impossible: virtue in the form of *reason* is the way to happiness. Dialectics is the constant occupation of virtue, because it does away with passion and intellectual cloudiness.

As a matter of fact, man does *not* desire "happiness." Pleasure is a sensation of power: if the passions are excluded, those states of the mind are also excluded which afford the greatest sensation of power and therefore of pleasure. The highest rationalism is a state of cool clearness, which is very far from being able to bring about that feeling of power which every kind of *exaltation* involves. . . .

[Slave moralists] combat everything that intoxicates and exalts—everything that impairs the perfect coolness and impartiality of the mind. . . . They were consistent with their first false principle: that consciousness was the *highest*, the *supreme* state of mind, the prerequisite of perfection—whereas the reverse is true.

If one should require a proof of how deeply and thoroughly the actually *barbarous* needs of man, even in his present state of tameness and "civilization," still seek gratification, one should contemplate the "leitmotifs" of the whole of the evolution of philosophy:—a sort of revenge upon reality, a surreptitious process of destroying the values by means of which men live, a *dissatisfied* soul to which the condition of discipline is one of torture, and which takes a particular pleasure in morbidly severing all the bonds that bind it to such a condition.

The history of philosophy is the story of a *secret and mad hatred* of the prerequisites of Life, of the feelings which make for the real values of Life, and of all partisanship in favor of Life. Philosophers have never hesitated to affirm a fanciful world, provided it contradicted this world, and furnished them with a weapon wherewith they could calumniate this world. Up to the present, philosophy has been the *grand school of slander:* and its power has been so great, that even today our science, which pretends to be the advocate of Life, has *accepted* the fundamental position of slander. . . . What is the hatred which is active here?

I fear that it is still the *Circe of philosophers*—Morality, which plays them the trick of compelling them to be ever slanderers. . . . They believed in moral "truths," in these they thought they had found the highest values; what alternative had they left, save that of denying existence ever more emphatically the more they got to know about it? . . . For this life is *immoral*. . . . And it is based upon immoral first principles: and morality says *nay* to Life.

Even obvious truths, as if by the agreement of centuries, have long remained unuttered, because they have the appearance of helping the finally slain wild beast back to life again. I perhaps risk something when I allow such a truth to escape; let others capture it again and give it so much "milk of pious sentiment" to drink, that it will lie down quiet and forgotten, in its old corner.— One ought to learn anew about cruelty, and open one's eyes; one ought at last to learn impatience, in order that such immodest gross errors—as, for instance, have been fostered by ancient and modern philosophers with regard to tragedy—

may no longer wander about virtuously and boldly. Almost everything that we call "higher culture" is based upon the spiritualizing and intensifying of *cruelty*—this is my thesis; the "wild beast" has not been slain at all, it lives, it flourishes, it has only been—transfigured. That which constitutes the painful delight of tragedy is cruelty; that which operates agreeably in so-called tragic sympathy, and at the basis even of everything sublime, up to the highest and most delicate thrills of metaphysics, obtains its sweetness solely from the intermingled ingredient of cruelty. What the Roman enjoys in the arena, the Christian in the ecstasies of the cross, the Spaniard at the sight of the faggot and stake, or of the bullfight, the present-day Japanese who presses his way to the tragedy, the workman of the Parisian suburbs who has a homesickness for bloody revolutions, the Wagnerienne who, with unhinged will, "undergoes" the performance of "Tristan and Isolde"—what all these enjoy, and strive with mysterious ardor to drink in, is the philtre of the great Circe "cruelty." . . . Finally, let us consider that even the seeker of knowledge operates as an artist and glorifier of cruelty, in that he compels his spirit to perceive *against* its own inclination, and often enough against the wishes of his heart:—he forces it to say Nay, where he would like to affirm, love, and adore; indeed, every instance of taking a thing profoundly and fundamentally, is a violation, an intentional injuring of the fundamental will of the spirit, which instinctively aims at appearance and superficiality,—even in every desire for knowledge there is a drop of cruelty.

In this connection, there is the not unscrupulous readiness of the spirit to deceive other spirits and dissemble before them—the constant pressing and straining of a creating, shaping, changeable power: the spirit enjoys therein its craftiness and its variety of disguises, it enjoys also its feeling of security therein—it is precisely by its Protean arts that it is best protected and concealed!—*Counter to* this propensity for appearance, for simplification, for a disguise, for a cloak, in short, for an outside—for every outside is a cloak—there operates the sublime tendency of the man of knowledge, which takes, and *insists* on taking things profoundly, variously, and thoroughly; as a kind of cruelty of the intellectual conscience and taste, which every courageous thinker will acknowledge in himself, provided, as it ought to be, that he has sharpened and hardened his eye sufficiently long for introspection, and is accustomed to severe discipline and even severe words. He will say: "There is something cruel in the tendency of my spirit": let the virtuous and amiable try to convince him that it is not so! In fact, it would sound nicer, if instead of our cruelty, perhaps our "extravagant honesty" were talked about, whispered about and glorified—we free, *very* free spirits—and some day perhaps *such* will actually be our—posthumous glory!

What they would fain attain with all their strength, is the universal, green-meadow happiness of the herd, together with security, safety, comfort, and alleviation of life for everyone; their two most frequently chanted songs and doctrines are called "Equality of Rights" and "Sympathy with all Sufferers"—and suffering itself is looked upon by them as something which must be *done away with*. We opposite ones, however, who have opened our eye and conscience to the question how and where the plant "man" has hitherto grown most vigorously, believe that this has always taken place under the opposite conditions, that for this end the dangerousness of his situation had to be increased enormously, his inventive faculty and dissembling power (his "spirit") had to develop into subtlety and daring under long oppression and compulsion, and his Will to Life had to be increased to the unconditioned Will to Power:—we believe that severity, violence, slavery, danger in the street and in the heart, secrecy, stoicism, tempter's art and devilry of every kind,—that everything wicked, terrible, tyrannical, predatory, and serpentine in man, serves as well for the elevation of the human species as its opposite:—we do not even say enough when we only say *this much;* and in any case we find ourselves here, both with our speech and our science, at the *other* extreme of all modern ideology and gregarious desirability, as their antipodes perhaps? What wonder that we "free spirits" are not exactly the most communicative spirits? that we do not wish to betray in every respect *what* a spirit can free itself from, and *where* perhaps it will then be driven? And as to the import of the dangerous formula, "Beyond Good and Evil," with which we at least avoid confusion, we *are* something else than *"libres-penseurs," "liberi pensatori,"* "free-thinkers," and whatever these honest advocates of "modern ideas" like to call themselves. Having been at home, or at least guests, in many realms of the spirit; having escaped again and again from the gloomy, agreeable nooks in which preferences and prejudices, youth, origin, the accident of men and books, or even the weariness of travel seemed to confine us; full of malice against the seductions of dependency which lie concealed in honors, money, positions, or exaltation of the senses: grateful even for distress and the vicissitudes of illness, because they always free us from some rule, and its "prejudice," grateful to the God, devil, sheep, and worm in us; inquisitive to a fault, investigators to the point of cruelty, with unhesitating fingers for the intangible, with teeth and stomachs for the most indigestible, ready for any business that requires sagacity and acute senses, ready for every adventure, owing to an excess of "free will"; with anterior and posterior souls, into the ultimate intentions of which it is difficult to pry, with foregrounds and backgrounds to the end of which no foot may run; hidden ones under the mantles of light, appropriators, although we resemble heirs and spendthrifts, arrangers and collectors from morning till night, misers of our wealth and our full-crammed drawers, economical in learning and forgetting, inventive in scheming; sometimes proud of tables of categories, sometimes pedants, sometimes night-owls of work even in full day; yea, if necessary, even scarecrows—and it is necessary nowadays, that is to say, inasmuch as we are the born, sworn, jealous friends of *solitude,* of our own profoundest midnight and midday solitude:—such kind of men are we, we free spirits! And perhaps *ye* are also something of the same kind, ye coming ones, ye *new* philosophers?

Will they be new friends of "truth," these coming philosophers? Very probably, for all philosophers hitherto have loved their truths. But assuredly they will not be dogmatists. It must be contrary to their pride, and also contrary to their taste, that their truth should still be truth for everyone—that which has hitherto been the secret wish and ultimate purpose of all dogmatic efforts. "My opinion is *my* opinion: another person has not easily a right to it"—such a philosopher of the future will say, perhaps. One must renounce the bad taste of wishing to agree with many people. "Good" is no longer good when one's neighbor takes it into his mouth. And how could there be a "common good"! The expression contradicts itself; that which can be common is always of small value. In the end things must be as they are and have always been—the great things remain for the great, the abysses for the profound, the delicacies and thrills for the refined, and, to sum up shortly, everything rare for the rare.

Need I say expressly after all this that they will be free, *very* free spirits, these philosophers of the future—as certainly also they will not be merely free spirits, but something more, higher, greater, and fundamentally different, which does not wish to be misunderstood and mistaken? But while I say this, I feel under *obligation* almost as much to them as to ourselves (we free spirits who are their heralds and forerunners), to sweep away from ourselves altogether a stupid old prejudice and misunderstanding, which, like a fog, has too long made the conception of "free spirit" obscure. In every country of Europe, and the same in America, there is at present something which makes an abuse of this name: a very narrow, pre-possessed, enchained class of spirits, who desire almost the opposite of what our intentions and instincts prompt—not to mention that in respect to the *new* philosophers who are appearing, they must still more be closed windows and bolted doors. Briefly and regrettably, they belong to the *levelers*, these wrongly named "free spirits"—as glib-tongued and scribe-fingered slaves of the democratic taste and its "modern ideas": all of them men without solitude, without personal solitude, blunt, honest fellows to whom neither courage nor honorable conduct ought to be denied; only, they are not free, and are ludicrously superficial, especially in their innate partiality for seeing the cause of almost *all* human misery and failure in the old forms in which society has hitherto existed—a notion which happily inverts the truth entirely!

Transvalue values—what does this mean? It implies that all spontaneous motives, all new, future, and stronger motives, are still extant; but that they now appear under false names and false valuations, and have not yet become conscious of themselves.

We ought to have the courage to become conscious, and to affirm all that which has been *attained*—to get rid of the humdrum character of old valuations, which makes us unworthy of the best and strongest things that we have achieved.

Any doctrine would be superfluous for which everything is not already prepared in the way of accumulated forces and explosive material. A transvaluation of values can only be accomplished when there is a tension of new needs, and a new set of needy people who feel all old values as painful,—although they are not conscious of what is wrong.

The standpoint from which my values are determined: is abundance or desire active? . . . Is one a mere spectator, or is one's own shoulder at the wheel—is one looking away or is one turning aside? . . . Is one acting spontaneously, or is one merely reacting to a goad or to a stimulus? . . . Is one simply acting as the result of a paucity of elements, or of such an overwhelming dominion over a host of elements that this power enlists the latter into its service if it requires them? . . . Is one a *problem* one's self or is one a *solution* already? . . . Is one *perfect* through the smallness of the task, or *imperfect* owing to the extraordinary character of the aim? . . . Is one genuine or only an *actor*; is one genuine as an actor, or only the bad copy of an actor? Is one a representative or the creature represented? Is one a personality or merely a rendezvous of personalities? . . . Is one ill from a disease or from surplus health? Does one lead as a shepherd, or as an "exception" (third alternative: as a fugitive)? Is one in need of dignity, or can one play the clown? Is one in search of resistance, or is one evading it? Is one imperfect owing to one's precocity or to one's tardiness? Is it one's nature to say yea; or no, or is one a peacock's tail of garish parts? Is one proud enough not to feel ashamed even of one's vanity? Is one still able to feel a bite of conscience (this species is becoming rare; formerly conscience had to bite too often: it is as if it now no longer had enough teeth to do so)? Is one still capable of a "duty"? (there are some people who would lose the whole joy of their lives if they were *deprived* of their duty—this holds good especially of feminine creatures, who were born subjects). . . .

It is only a question of power: to have all the morbid traits of the century, but to balance them by means of overflowing, plastic, and rejuvenating power. The *strong* man.

Meanwhile—for there is plenty of time until then—we should be least inclined to deck ourselves out in such florid and fringed moral verbiage; our whole former work has just made us sick of this taste and its sprightly exuberance. They are beautiful, glistening, jingling, festive words: honesty, love of truth, love of wisdom, sacrifice for knowledge, heroism of the truthful—there is something in them that makes one's heart swell with pride. But we anchorites and marmots have long ago persuaded ourselves in all the secrecy of an anchorite's conscience, that this worthy parade of verbiage also belongs to the old false adornment, frippery, and gold dust of unconscious human vanity, and that even under

such flattering color and repainting, the terrible original text *homo natura* must again be recognized. In effect, to translate man back again into nature; to master the many vain and visionary interpretations and subordinate meanings which have hitherto been scratched and daubed over the eternal original text, *homo natura*; to bring it about that man shall henceforth stand before man as he now, hardened by the discipline of science, stands before the *other* forms of nature, with fearless Oedipus-eyes, and stopped Ulysses-ears, deaf to the enticements of old metaphysical bird-catchers, who have piped to him far too long: "Thou art more! thou art higher! thou hast a different origin!"—this may be a strange and foolish task, but that it is a *task*, who can deny!"

CONTEMPORARY PERSPECTIVES:
ABORTION

Few topics in applied ethics are more controversial than the issue of abortion. Thinking seriously about abortion forces us to assess our views about a large number of related issues of contemporary concern, including sex, equality, reproduction, privacy, constitutional law, and religion.

There are at least three reasons why abortion is a difficult issue to think clearly about: (1) Strong emotions often cloud our judgment; (2) it pits two cherished principles against each other—the "Value of Life Principle" and the "Principle of Individual Freedom" (in this case, the right of a woman over her own body, procreativity, and life); and (3) it requires the philosopher to provide not only *moral principles* (coherent guidelines for determining proper conduct with respect to women and fetuses), but also *status principles* (distinguishing such concepts as human, nonhuman, person, and nonperson in determining the status of the fetus).

What makes abortion an especially difficult moral issue is that it is all but impossible to reach consensus among opposing sides on the status of a fetus. The term fetus refers to the developing human individual from the eighth week until birth. Is the fetus a human person or not?

Most opposition to abortion centers on the claim that human life begins at conception; thus a fetus has a right to life just like any other person. Unwarranted killing of human persons is murder; hence abortion is murder. The denial of this position depends on arguments that human life does *not* begin at conception but at some later stage of pregnancy, or at birth. The question of exactly when human life, or personhood, begins is not a straightforward one. Clearly, we cannot get much help from the scientific community on this question; whether a fetal organism is a human person cannot be decided by examining a set of biological facts. Personhood is not the sort of thing that can be discovered using a microscope in a laboratory.

Joel Feinberg, in his book *The Problem of Abortion*, distinguishes three positions on the status of the fetus.[1] The *conservative* position is that human personhood begins at the moment of conception. The *liberal* position, at the other end of the spectrum, is the position that the human person does not emerge until after birth, or, more moderately, when the fetus is "viable" (somewhere between the twenty-sixth and twenty-eighth week of gestation, when the fetus is capable of living outside the womb). A *moderate* position falls between the conservative and liberal positions.

Feinberg points out that what makes the disagreement about status principles so difficult to resolve is that three common sense propositions seem to be mutually inconsistent:

1. "A newborn infant is a human person," or "Babies are people."

2. "A one-celled zygote (a cell that results from the union of sperm and egg cells) is not a human person," or "Fertilized eggs are not people."

3. "It is impossible to draw a nonarbitrary line anywhere between conception and infancy such that no beings before that line are human persons and all beings after that line are human persons."

Position 1 denies what the liberal position affirms; position 2 denies what the conservative affirms; position 3 denies what the moderate affirms. Yet all three propositions seem to have considerable common sense support!

What is even more disturbing is that even if we were to agree on the status of the fetus, considering it to be a person, it is still possible to disagree about the permissability of abortion based on divergent moral principles. Our first reading brings this out very clearly. Judith Jarvis Thomson argues that those who wish to argue for the permissibility of abortion need not become entangled in the "personhood debate" at all. For the sake of argument, she grants opponents of abortion their major point, that the fetus is a person. She then proceeds to argue that even if

[1]See Joel Feinberg, *The Problem of Abortion*, 2d. ed. (Belmont Calif.: Wadsworth, 1984), 3–4.

the fetus is a person, a woman has no moral obligation to carry it to term; a woman's right to control what is happening to her own body outweighs any rights of the fetus. Thomson draws analogies between the sacrifices pregnant women must make in order to keep fetuses alive and other situations where one person's life depends upon the willingness of another person to act on his or her behalf. By pursuing this strategy, she hopes to establish grounds for abortion that are somewhat akin to "self-defense" or "justifiable homicide" arguments. Even if abortion is homicide, she concludes, it is normally justifiable homicide. Thomson's example of the unconscious violin player who requires the use of your kidneys in order to stay alive has become legendary. You must decide how persuasive you find this and other analogies.

Our second reading selection draws us into the religious arena; this is appropriate, since much of the opposition to abortion has come from religious groups. The Roman Catholic church, for example, holds that "every unborn child must be regarded as a human person with all the rights of a human person, from the moment of conception." The Church condemns abortion as a violation of the sanctity of life, disallowing it even in cases where a woman's life may be at stake, or in cases of rape or incest.

Unlike Thomson, Stanley Hauerwas thinks that abortion is morally objectionable. Nevertheless, he thinks that Christians have so far failed to effectively communicate *why* it is morally objectionable. Shifting the issue away from the question of personhood, (which he finds "far too abstract and formal"), he attempts to explain why it is that Christians are compelled to joyfully welcome and protect new human life. He emphasizes that the Christian commitment to welcome children into the world stems from a deeply rooted political commitment to the Kingdom of God, not from any sentimental fondness for babies. The birth of a child, he states, "represents nothing less than our commitment that God will not have this world 'bettered' by destroying life. That is why there is no more profound political act for Christians than taking the time for children." Hauerwas concludes by admonishing Christians to broaden their conception of the "sanctity of life" to include all women and all children who are in need; there are, he says, political responsibilities that go beyond mere opposition to abortion.

CHAPTER 61

JUDITH JARVIS THOMSON

A DEFENSE OF ABORTION

Judith Jarvis Thomson (1929–) is professor of philosophy at the Massachusetts Institute of Technology. She has written extensively in the field of ethics, and is co-editor of an anthology entitled *Ethics*. Many of her important articles are collected in a volume entitled *Rights, Restitution, and Risk*.

A DEFENSE OF ABORTION[1]

Most opposition to abortion relies on the premise that the fetus is a human being, a person, from the moment of conception. The premise is argued for, but, as I think, not well. Take, for example, the most common argument. We are asked to notice that the development of a human being from conception through birth into childhood is continuous; then it is said that to draw a line, to choose a point in this development and say "before this point the thing is not a person, after this point it is a person" is to make an arbitrary choice, a choice for which in the nature of things no good reason can be given. It is concluded that the fetus is, or anyway that we had better say it is, a person from the moment of conception. But this conclusion does not follow. Similar things might be said about the development of an acorn into an oak tree, and it does not follow that acorns are oak trees, or that we had

[1] From Judith J. Thomson, "A Defense of Abortion." *Philosophy & Public Affairs*, Vol. 1, No. 1:47–66 (Fall 1971). Copyright © 1971 by Princeton University Press. Reprinted by permission of Princeton University Press.

better say they are. Arguments of this form are sometimes called "slippery slope arguments"—the phrase is perhaps self-explanatory—and it is dismaying that opponents of abortion rely on them so heavily and uncritically.

I am inclined to agree, however, that the prospects for "drawing a line" in the development of the fetus look dim. I am inclined to think also that we shall probably have to agree that the fetus has already become a human person well before birth. Indeed, it comes as a surprise when one first learns how early in its life it begins to acquire human characteristics. By the tenth week, for example, it already has a face, arms and legs, fingers and toes; it has internal organs, and brain activity is detectable. On the other hand, I think that the premise is false, that the fetus is not a person from the moment of conception. A newly fertilized ovum, a newly implanted clump of cells, is no more a person than an acorn is an oak tree. But I shall not discuss any of this. For it seems to me to be of great interest to ask what happens if, for the sake of argument, we allow the premise. How, precisely, are we supposed to get from there to the conclusion that abortion is morally impermissible? Opponents of abortion commonly spend most of their time establishing that the fetus is a person, and hardly any time explaining the step from there to the impermissibility of abortion. Perhaps they think the step too simple and obvious to require much comment. Or perhaps instead they are simply being economical in argument. Many of those who defend abortion rely on the premise that the fetus is not a person, but only a bit of tissue that will become a person at birth; and why pay out more arguments than you have to? Whatever the explanation, I suggest that the step they take is neither easy nor obvious, that it calls for closer examination than it is commonly given, and that when we do give it this closer examination we shall feel inclined to reject it.

I propose, then, that we grant that the fetus is a person from the moment of conception. How does the argument go from here? Something like this, I take it. Every person has a right to life. So the fetus has a right to life. No doubt the mother has a right to decide what shall happen in and to her body; everyone would grant that. But surely a person's right to life is stronger and more stringent than the mother's right to decide what happens in and to her body, and so outweighs it. So the fetus may not be killed; an abortion may not be performed.

It sounds plausible. But now let me ask you to imagine this. You wake up in the morning and find yourself back to back in bed with an unconscious violinist. A famous unconscious violinist. He has been found to have a fatal kidney ailment, and the Society of Music Lovers has canvassed all the available medical records and found that you alone have the right blood type to help. They have therefore kidnapped you, and last night the violinist's circulatory system was plugged into yours, so that your kidneys can be used to extract poisons from his blood as well as your own. The director of the hospital now tells you, "Look, we're sorry the Society of Music Lovers did this to you—we would never have permitted it if we had known. But still, they did it, and the violinist now is plugged into you. To unplug you would be to kill him. But never mind, it's only for nine months. By then he will have recovered from his ailment, and can safely be unplugged from you." Is it morally incumbent on you to accede to this situation? No doubt it would be very nice of you if you did, a great kindness, but do you *have* to accede to it? What if it were not nine months, but nine years? Or longer still? What if the director of the hospital says, "Tough luck, I agree, but you've now got to stay in bed, with the violinist plugged into you, for the rest of your life. Because remember this. All persons have a right to life, and violinists are persons. Granted you have a right to decide what happens in and to your body, but a person's right to life outweighs your right to decide what happens in and to your body. So you cannot ever be unplugged from him." I imagine you would regard this as outrageous, which suggests that something really is wrong with that plausible-sounding argument I mentioned a moment ago.

In this case, of course, you were kidnapped; you didn't volunteer for the operation that plugged the violinist into your kidneys. Can those who oppose abortion on the ground I mentioned make an exception for a pregnancy due to rape? Certainly. They can say that persons have a right to life only if they didn't come into existence because of rape; or they can say that all persons have a right to life, but that some have less of a right to life than others, in particular, that those who came into existence because of rape have less. But these statements have a rather unpleasant sound. Surely the question of whether you have a right to life at all, or how much of it you have, shouldn't turn on the question of whether or not you are the product of a rape. And in fact the people who oppose abortion on the ground I mentioned do not make this distinction, and hence do not make an exception in case of rape.

Nor do they make an exception for a case in which the mother has to spend the nine months of her pregnancy in bed. They would agree that would be a great pity, and hard on the mother; but all the same, all persons have a right to life, the fetus is a person, and so on. I suspect, in fact, that they would not make an exception for a case in which, miraculously enough, the pregnancy went on for nine years, or even the rest of the mother's life.

Some won't even make an exception for a case in which continuation of the pregnancy is likely to shorten the mother's life; they regard abortion as impermissible even to save the mother's life. Such cases are nowadays very rare, and many opponents of abortion do not accept this extreme view. All the same, it is a good place to begin: a number of points of interest come out in respect to it.

1. Let us call the view that abortion is impermissible even to save the mother's life "the extreme view." I want to suggest first that it does not issue from the argument I mentioned earlier without the addition of some fairly powerful premises. Suppose a woman has become pregnant, and now learns that she has a cardiac condition such that she will die if she carries the baby to term. What may be done for her? The fetus, being a person, has a right to life, but as the mother is a person too, so has she a right to life. Presumably they have an equal right to life. How is it supposed to come out that an abortion may not be performed? If mother and child have an equal right to life, shouldn't we perhaps flip a coin? Or should we add to the mother's right to life her right to decide what happens in and to her body, which everybody seems to be ready to grant—the sum of her rights now outweighing the fetus' right to life?

The most familiar argument here is the following. We are told that performing the abortion would be directly killing the child, whereas doing nothing would not be killing the mother, but only letting her die. Moreover in killing the child one would be killing an innocent person, for the child has committed no crime, and is not aiming at his mother's death. And then there are a variety of ways in which this might be continued. (1) But as directly killing an innocent person is always and absolutely impermissible, an abortion may not be performed. Or, (2) as directly killing an innocent person is murder, and murder is always and absolutely impermissible, an abortion may not be performed. Or, (3) as one's duty to refrain from directly killing an innocent person is more stringent than one's duty to keep a person from dying, an abortion may not be performed. Or, (4) if one's only options are directly killing an innocent person or letting a person die, one must prefer letting the person die, and thus an abortion may not be performed.

Some people seem to have thought that these are not further premises which must be added if the conclusion is to be reached, but that they follow from the very fact that an innocent person has a right to life. But this seems to me to be a mistake, and perhaps the simplest way to show this is to bring out that while we must certainly grant that innocent persons have a right to life, the theses in (1) through (4) are all false. Take (2), for example. If directly killing an innocent person is murder, and thus is impermissible, then the mother's directly killing the innocent person inside her is murder, and thus is impermissible. But it cannot seriously be thought to be murder if the mother performs an abortion on herself to save her life. It cannot seriously be said that she *must* refrain, that she *must* sit passively by and wait for her death. Let us look again at the case of you and the violinist. There you are, in bed with the violinist, and the director of the hospital says to you, "It's all most distressing, and I deeply sympathize, but you see this is putting an additional strain on your kidneys, and you'll be dead within the month. But you *have* to stay where you are all the same. Because unplugging you would be directly killing an innocent violinist, and that's murder, and that's impermissible." If anything in the world is true, it is that you do not commit murder, you do not do what is impermissible, if you reach around to your back and unplug yourself from the violinist to save your life.

The main focus of attention in writings on abortion has been on what a third party may or may not do in answer to a request from a woman for an abortion. This is in a way understandable. Things being as they are, there isn't much a woman can safely do to abort herself. So the question asked is what a third party may do, and what the mother may do, if it is mentioned at all, is deduced, almost as an afterthought, from what it is concluded that third parties may do. But it seems to me that to treat the matter in this way is to refuse to grant to the mother that very status of person which is so firmly insisted on for the fetus. For we cannot simply read off what a person may do from what a third party may do. Suppose you find yourself trapped in a tiny house with a growing child. I mean a very tiny house, and a rapidly growing child—you are already up against the wall of the house and in a few minutes you'll be crushed to death. The child on the other hand won't be crushed to death; if nothing is done to stop him from growing he'll be hurt, but in the end he'll simply burst open the house and walk out a free man. Now I could well understand it if a bystander were to say, "There's nothing we can do for you. We cannot choose between your life and his, we cannot be the ones to decide who is to live, we cannot intervene." But it cannot be concluded that you too can do nothing, that you cannot attack it to save your life. However innocent the child may be, you do not have to wait passively while it crushes you to death. Perhaps a pregnant woman is vaguely felt to have the status of house, to which we don't allow the right of self-defense. But if the woman houses the child, it should be remembered that she is a person who houses it.

I should perhaps stop to say explicitly that I am not claiming that people have a right to do anything whatever to save their lives. I think, rather, that there are drastic limits to the right of self-defense. If someone threatens you with death unless you torture someone else to death, I think you have not the right, even to save your life, to do so. But the case under consideration here is very different. In our case there are only two people involved, one whose life is threatened, and one who threatens it. Both are innocent: the one who is threatened is not threatened because of any fault, the one who threatens does not threaten because of any fault. For this reason we may feel that we bystanders cannot intervene. But the person threatened can.

In sum, a woman surely can defend her life against the threat to it posed by the unborn child, even if doing so involves its death. And this shows not merely that the theses in (1) through (4) are false; it shows also that the extreme view of abortion is false, and so we need not canvass any other possible ways of arriving at it from the argument I mentioned at the outset.

2. The extreme view could of course be weakened to say that while abortion is permissible to save the mother's life, it may not be performed by a third party, but only by the mother herself. But this cannot be right either. For what we have to keep in mind is that the mother and the unborn child are not like two tenants in a small house which has, by an unfortunate mistake, been rented to both: the mother *owns* the house. The fact that she does adds to the offensiveness of deducing that the mother can do nothing from the supposition that third parties can do nothing. But it does more than this: it casts a bright light on the supposition that third parties can do nothing. Certainly it lets us see that a third party who says "I cannot choose between you" is fooling himself if he thinks this is impartiality. If Jones has found and fastened on a certain coat, which he needs to keep him from freezing, but which Smith also needs to keep him from freezing, then it is not impartiality that says "I cannot choose between you" when Smith owns the coat. Women have said again and again "This body is *my* body!" and they have reason to feel angry, reason to feel that it has been like shouting into the wind. Smith, after all, is hardly likely to bless us if we say to him, "Of course it's your

coat, anybody would grant that it is. But no one may choose between you and Jones who is to have it."

We should really ask what it is that says "no one may choose" in the face of the fact that the body that houses the child is the mother's body. It may be simply a failure to appreciate this fact. But it may be something more interesting, namely the sense that one has a right to refuse to lay hands on people, even where it would be just and fair to do so, even where justice seems to require that somebody do so. Thus justice might call for somebody to get Smith's coat back from Jones, and yet you have a right to refuse to be the one to lay hands on Jones, a right to refuse to do physical violence to him. This, I think, must be granted. But then what should be said is not "no one may choose," but only "*I* cannot choose," and indeed not even this, but "*I* will not *act*," leaving it open that somebody else can or should, and in particular that anyone in a position of authority, with the job of securing people's rights, both can and should. So this is no difficulty. I have not been arguing that any given third party must accede to the mother's request that he perform an abortion to save her life, but only that he may.

I suppose that in some views of human life the mother's body is only on loan to her, the loan not being one which gives her any prior claim to it. One who held this view might well think it impartiality to say "I cannot choose." But I shall simply ignore this possibility. My own view is that if a human being has any just, prior claim to anything at all, he has a just, prior claim to his own body. And perhaps this needn't be argued for here anyway, since, as I mentioned, the arguments against abortion we are looking at do grant that the woman has a right to decide what happens in and to her body.

But although they do grant it, I have tried to show that they do not take seriously what is done in granting it. I suggest the same thing will reappear even more clearly when we turn away from cases in which the mother's life is at stake, and attend, as I propose we now do, to the vastly more common cases in which a woman wants an abortion for some less weighty reason than preserving her own life.

3. Where the mother's life is not at stake, the argument I mentioned at the outset seems to have a much stronger pull. "Everyone has a right to life, so the unborn person has a right to life." And isn't the child's right to life weightier than anything other than the mother's own right to life, which she might put forward as ground for an abortion?

This argument treats the right to life as if it were unproblematic. It is not, and this seems to me to be precisely the source of the mistake.

For we should now, at long last, ask what it comes to, to have a right to life. In some views having a right to life includes having a right to be given at least the bare minimum one needs for continued life. But suppose that what in fact *is* the bare minimum a man needs for continued life is something he has no right at all to be given? If I am sick unto death, and the only thing that will save my life is the touch of Henry Fonda's cool hand on my fevered brow, then all the same, I have no right to be given the touch of Henry Fonda's cool hand on my fevered brow. It would be frightfully nice of him to fly in from the West Coast to provide it. It would be less nice, though no doubt well meant, if my friends flew out to the West Coast and carried Henry Fonda back with them. But I have no right at all against anybody that he should do this for me. Or again, to return to the story I told earlier, the fact that for continued life that violinist needs the continued use of your kidneys does not establish that he has a right to be given the continued use of your kidneys. He certainly has no right against you that *you* should give him continued use of your kid-

neys. For nobody has any right to use your kidneys unless you give him such a right; and nobody has the right against you that you shall give him this right—if you do allow him to go on using your kidneys, this is a kindness on your part, and not something he can claim from you as his due. Nor has he any right against anybody else that *they* should give him continued use of your kidneys. Certainly he had no right against the Society of Music Lovers that they should plug him into you in the first place. And if you now start to unplug yourself, having learned that you will otherwise have to spend nine years in bed with him, there is nobody in the world who must try to prevent you, in order to *see* to it that he is given something he has a right to be given.

Some people are rather stricter about the right to life. In their view, it does not include the right to be given anything, but amounts to, and only to, the right not to be killed by anybody. But here a related difficulty arises. If everybody is to refrain from killing that violinist, then everybody must refrain from doing a great many different sorts of things. Everybody must refrain from slitting his throat, everybody must refrain from shooting him—and everybody must refrain from unplugging you from him. But does he have a right against everybody that they shall refrain from unplugging you from him? To refrain from doing this is to allow him to continue to use your kidneys. It could be argued that he has a right against us that *we* should allow him to continue to use your kidneys. That is, while he had no right against us that we should give him the use of your kidneys, it might be argued that he anyway has a right against us that we shall not now intervene and deprive him of the use of your kidneys. I shall come back to third-party interventions later. But certainly the violinist has no right against you that *you* shall allow him to continue to use your kidneys. As I said, if you do allow him to use

669

them, it is a kindness on your part, and not something you owe him.

This difficulty I point to here is not peculiar to the right to life. It reappears in connection with all the other natural rights; and it is something which an adequate account of rights must deal with. For present purposes it is enough just to draw attention to it. But I would stress that I am not arguing that people do not have a right to life—quite to the contrary, it seems to me that the primary control we must place on the acceptability of an account of rights is that it should turn out in that account to be a truth that all persons have a right to life. I am arguing only that having a right to life does not guarantee having either a right to be given the use of or a right to be allowed continued use of another person's body—even if one needs it for life itself. So the right to life will not serve the opponents of abortion in the very simple and clear way in which they seem to have thought it would.

4. There is another way to bring out the difficulty. In the most ordinary sort of case, to deprive someone of what he has a right to is to treat him unjustly. Suppose a boy and his small brother are jointly given a box of chocolates for Christmas. If the older boy takes the box and refuses to give his brother any of the chocolates, he is unjust to him, for the brother has been given a right to half of them. But suppose that, having learned that otherwise it means nine years in bed with that violinist, you unplug yourself from him. You surely are not being unjust to him, for you gave him no right to use your kidneys, and no one else can have given him any such right. But we have to notice that in unplugging yourself, you are killing him; and violinists, like everybody else, have a right to life, and thus in the view we were considering just now, the right not to be killed. So here you do what he supposedly has a right you shall not do, but you do not act unjustly to him in doing it.

The emendation which may be made at this point is this: the right to life consists not in the right not to be killed, but rather in the right not to be killed unjustly. This runs a risk of circularity, but never mind: it would enable us to square the fact that the violinist has a right to life with the fact that you do not act unjustly toward him in unplugging yourself, thereby killing him. For if you do not kill him unjustly, you do not violate his right to life, and so it is no wonder you do him no injustice.

But if this emendation is accepted, the gap in the argument against abortion stares us plainly in the face: it is by no means enough to show that the fetus is a person, and to remind us that all persons have a right to life—we need to be shown also that killing the fetus violates its right to life, i.e., that abortion is unjust killing. And is it?

I suppose we may take it as a datum that in a case of pregnancy due to rape the mother has not given the unborn person a right to the use of her body for food and shelter. Indeed, in what pregnancy could it be supposed that the mother has given the unborn person such a right? It is not as if there were unborn persons drifting about the world, to whom a woman who wants a child says "I invite you in."

But it might be argued that there are other ways one can have acquired a right to the use of another person's body than by having been invited to use it by that person. Suppose a woman voluntarily indulges in intercourse, knowing of the chance it will issue in pregnancy, and then she does become pregnant; is she not in part responsible for the presence, in fact the very existence, of the unborn person inside her? No doubt she did not invite it in. But doesn't her partial responsibility for its being there itself give it a right to the use of her body? If so, then her aborting it would be more like the boy's taking away the chocolates, and less like your unplugging yourself from the violinist—doing so would be depriving it of what it does have a right to, and thus would be doing it an injustice.

And then, too, it might be asked whether or not she can kill it even to save her own life: If she voluntarily called it into existence, how can she now kill it, even in self-defense?

The first thing to be said about this is that it is something new. Opponents of abortion have been so concerned to make out the independence of the fetus, in order to establish that it has a right to life, just as its mother does, that they have tended to overlook the possible support they might gain from making out that the fetus is *dependent* on the mother, in order to establish that she has a special kind of responsibility for it, a responsibility that gives it rights against her which are not possessed by an independent person—such as an ailing violinist who is a stranger to her.

On the other hand, this argument would give the unborn person a right to its mother's body only if her pregnancy resulted from a voluntary act, undertaken in full knowledge of the chance a pregnancy might result from it. It would leave out entirely the unborn person whose existence is due to rape. Pending the availability of some further argument, then, we would be left with the conclusion that unborn persons whose existence is due to rape have no right to the use of their mothers' bodies, and thus that aborting them is not depriving them of anything they have a right to and hence is not unjust killing.

And we should also notice that it is not at all plain that this argument really does go even as far as it purports to. For there are cases and cases, and the details make a difference. If the room is stuffy, and I therefore open a window to air it, and a burglar climbs in, it would be absurd to say, "Ah, now he can stay, she's given him a right to the use of her house—for she is partially responsible for his presence there, having voluntarily done what enabled him to get in, in full knowledge that there are such things as burglars, and that burglars burgle." It would be still more absurd to say this if I had had bars installed outside my windows, precisely to prevent burglars from getting in, and a burglar got in only because of a defect in the bars. It remains equally absurd if we imagine it is not a burglar who climbs in, but an innocent person who blunders or falls in. Again, suppose it were like this: people-seeds drift about in the air like pollen, and if you open your windows, one may drift in and take root in your carpets or upholstery. You don't want children, so you fix up your windows with fine mesh screens, the very best you can buy. As can happen, however, and on very, very rare occasions does happen, one of the screens is defective; and a seed drifts in and takes root. Does the person-plant who now develops have a right to the use of your house? Surely not—despite the fact that you voluntarily opened your windows, you knowingly kept carpets and upholstered furniture, and you knew that screens were sometimes defective. Someone may argue that you are responsible for its rooting, that it does have a right to your house, because after all you *could* have lived out your life with bare floors and furniture, or with sealed windows and doors. But this won't do—for by the same token anyone can avoid a pregnancy due to rape by having a hysterectomy, or anyway by never leaving home without a (reliable!) army.

It seems to me that the argument we are looking at can establish at most that there are *some* cases in which the unborn person has a right to the use of its mother's body, and therefore *some* cases in which abortion is unjust killing. There is room for much discussion and argument as to precisely which, if any. But I think we should sidestep this issue and leave it open, for at any rate the argument certainly does not establish that all abortion is unjust killing.

671

5. There is room for yet another argument here, however. We surely must all grant that there may be cases in which it would be morally indecent to detach a person from your body at the cost of his life. Suppose you learn that what the violinist needs is not nine years of your life, but only one hour: all you need do to save his life is to spend one hour in that bed with him. Suppose also that letting him use your kidneys for that one hour would not affect your health in the slightest. Admittedly you were kidnapped. Admittedly you did not give anyone permission to plug him into you. Nevertheless it seems to me plain you *ought* to allow him to use your kidneys for that hour—it would be indecent to refuse.

Again, suppose pregnancy lasted only an hour, and constituted no threat to life or health. And suppose that a woman becomes pregnant as a result of rape. Admittedly she did not voluntarily do anything to bring about the existence of a child. Admittedly she did nothing at all which would give the unborn person a right to the use of her body. All the same it might well be said, as in the newly emended violinist story, that she *ought* to allow it to remain for that hour—that it would be indecent in her to refuse.

Now some people are inclined to use the term "right" in such a way that it follows from the fact that you ought to allow a person to use your body for the hour he needs, that he has a right to use your body for the hour he needs, even though he has not been given that right by any person or act. They may say that it follows also that if you refuse, you act unjustly toward him. This use of the term is perhaps so common that it cannot be called wrong; nevertheless it seems to me to be an unfortunate loosening of what we would do better to keep a tight rein on. Suppose that box of chocolates I mentioned earlier had not been given to both boys jointly, but was given only to the older boy. There he sits, stolidly eating his way through the box, his small brother watching enviously. Here we are likely to say "You ought not to be so mean. You ought to give your brother some of those chocolates." My own view is that it just does not follow from the truth of this that the brother has any right to any of the chocolates. If the boy refuses to give his brother any, he is greedy, stingy, callous—but not unjust. I suppose that the people I have in mind will say it does follow that the brother has a right to some of the chocolates, and thus that the boy does act unjustly if he refuses to give his brother any. But the effect of saying this is to obscure what we should keep distinct, namely the difference between the boy's refusal in this case and the boy's refusal in the earlier case, in which the box was given to both boys jointly, and in which the small brother thus had what was from any point of view clear title to half.

A further objection to so using the term "right" that from the fact that A ought to do a thing for B, it follows that B has a right against A that A do it for him, is that it is going to make the question of whether or not a man has a right to a thing turn on how easy it is to provide him with it; and this seems not merely unfortunate, but morally unacceptable. Take the case of Henry Fonda again. I said earlier that I had no right to the touch of his cool hand on my fevered brow, even though I needed it to save my life. I said it would be frightfully nice of him to fly in from the West Coast to provide me with it, but that I had no right against him that he should do so. But suppose he isn't on the West Coast. Suppose he has only to walk across the room, place a hand briefly on my brow—and lo, my life is saved. Then surely he ought to do it, it would be indecent to refuse. Is it to be said "Ah, well, it follows that in this case she has a right to the touch of his hand on her brow, and so it would be an injustice in him to refuse"? So that I have a right to it when it is easy for him to provide it, though no right when it's hard? It's rather a shocking idea that anyone's rights should fade away and disappear as it gets harder and harder to accord them to him.

So my own view is that even though you ought to let the violinist use your kidneys for the one hour he needs, we should not conclude that he has a right to do so—we should say that if you refuse, you are, like the boy who owns all the chocolates and will give none away, self-centered and callous, indecent in fact, but not unjust. And similarly, that even supposing a case in which a woman pregnant due to rape ought to allow the unborn person to use her body for the hour he needs, we should not conclude that he has a right to do so; we should conclude that she is self-centered, callous, indecent, but not unjust, if she refuses. The compaints are no less grave; they are just different. However, there is no need to insist on this point. If anyone does wish to deduce "he has a right" from "you ought," then all the same he must surely grant that there are cases in which it is not morally required of you that you allow that violinist to use your kidneys, and in which he does not have a right to use them, and in which you do not do him an injustice if you refuse. And so also for mother and unborn child. Except in such cases as the unborn person has a right to demand it—and we were leaving open the possibility that there may be such cases—nobody is morally *required* to make large sacrifices, of health, of all other interests and concerns, of all other duties and commitments, for nine years, or even for nine months, in order to keep another person alive.

6. We have in fact to distinguish between two kinds of Samaritan: the Good Samaritan and what we might call the Minimally Decent Samaritan. The story of the Good Samaritan, you will remember, goes like this:

A certain man went down from Jerusalem to Jericho, and fell among theives, which stripped him of his raiment, and wounded him, and departed, leaving him half dead.

And by chance there came down a certain priest that way; and when he saw him, he passed by on the other side.

And likewise a Levite, when he was at the place, came and looked on him, and passed on the other side.

But a certain Samaritan, as he journeyed, came where he was; and when he saw him he had compassion on him.

And went to him, and bound up his wounds, pouring in oil and wine, and set him on his own beast, and brought him to an inn, and took care of him.

And on the morrow, when he departed, he took out two pence, and gave them to the host, and said unto him, "Take care of him; and whatsoever thou spendest more, when I come again, I will repay thee."

(Luke 10:30–35)

The Good Samaritan went out of his way, at some cost to himself, to help one in need of it. We are not told what the options were, that is, whether or not the priest and the Levite could have helped by doing less than the Good Samaritan did, but assuming they could have, then the fact they did nothing at all shows they were not even Minimally Decent Samaritans, not because they were not Samaritans, but because they were not even minimally decent.

These things are a matter of degree, of course, but there is a difference, and it comes out perhaps most clearly in the story of Kitty Genovese, who, as you will remember, was murdered while thirty-eight people watched or listened, and did nothing at all to help her. A Good Samaritan would have rushed out to give direct assistance against the murderer. Or perhaps we had better allow that it would have been a Splendid Samaritan who did this, on the ground that it would have involved a risk of death for himself. But the thirty-eight not only did not do this, they did not even trouble to pick up a phone to call the police. Minimally Decent Samaritanism would call for doing at least that, and their not having done it was monstrous.

After telling the story of the Good Samaritan, Jesus said "Go, and do thou likewise." Perhaps he meant that we are morally required to act as the Good Samaritan did. Perhaps he was urging people to do more than is morally required of them. At all events it seems plain that it was not morally required of any of the thirty-eight that he rush out to give direct assistance at the risk of his own life, and that it is not morally required of anyone that he give long stretches of his life— nine years or nine months—to sustaining the life of a person who has no special right (we were leaving open the possibility of this) to demand it.

Indeed, with one rather striking class of exceptions, no one in any country in the world is *legally* required to do anywhere near as much as this for anyone else. The class of exceptions is obvious. My main concern here is not the state of the law in respect to abortion, but it is worth drawing attention to the fact that in no state in this country is any man compelled by law to be even a Minimally Decent Samaritan to any person; there is no law under which charges could be brought against the thirty-eight who stood by while Kitty Genovese died. By contrast, in most states in this country women are compelled by law to be not merely Minimally Decent Samaritans, but Good Samaritans to unborn persons inside them. This doesn't by itself settle anything one way or the other, because it may well be argued that there should be laws in this country—as there are in many European countries— compelling at least Minimally Decent Samaritanism. But it does show that there is a gross injustice in the existing state of the law. And it shows also that the groups currently working against liberalization of abortion laws, in fact working toward having declared unconstitutional for a state to permit abortion, had better start working for the adoption of Good Samaritan laws generally, or earn the charge that they are acting in bad faith.

I should think, myself, that Minimally Decent Samaritan laws would be one thing. Good Samaritan laws quite another, and in fact highly improper. But we are not here concerned with the law. What we should ask is not whether anybody should be compelled by law to be a Good Samaritan, but whether we must accede to a situation in which somebody is being compelled by nature, perhaps—to be a Good Samaritan. We have, in other words, to look now at third-party interventions. I have been arguing that no person is morally required to make large sacrifices to sustain the life of another who has no right to demand them, and this even where the sacrifices do not include life itself; we are not morally required to be Good Samaritans or anyway Very Good Samaritans to one another. But what if a man cannot extricate himself from such a situation? What if he appeals to us to extricate him? It seems to me plain that there are cases in which we can, cases in which a Good Samaritan would extricate him. There you are, you were kidnapped, and nine years in bed with that violinist lie ahead of you. You have your own life to lead. You are sorry, but simply cannot see giving up so much of your life to the sustaining of his. You cannot extricate yourself, and ask us to do so. I should have thought that—in light of his having no right to the use of your body—it was obvious that we do not have to accede to your being forced to give up so much. We can do what you ask. There is no injustice to the violinist in our doing so.

7. Following the lead of the opponents of abortion, I have throughout been speaking of the

fetus merely as a person, and what I have been asking is whether or not the argument we began with, which proceeds only from the fetus' being a person, really does establish its conclusion. I have argued that it does not.

But of course there are arguments and arguments, and it may be said that I have simply fastened on the wrong one. It may be said that what is important is not merely the fact that the fetus is a person, but that it is a person for whom the woman has a special kind of responsibility issuing from the fact that she is its mother. And it might be argued that all my analogies are therefore irrelevant—for you do not have that special kind of responsibility for that violinist, Henry Fonda does not have that special kind of responsibility for me. And our attention might be drawn to the fact that men and women both *are* compelled by law to provide support for their children.

I have in effect dealth (briefly) with this argument in section 4 above; but a (still briefer) recapitulation now may be in order. Surely we do not have any such "special responsibility" for a person unless we have assumed it, explicitly or implicitly. If a set of parents do not try to prevent pregnancy, do not obtain an abortion, and then at the time of birth of the child do not put it out for adoption, but rather take it home with them, then they have assumed responsibility for it, they have given it rights, and they cannot *now* withdraw support from it at the cost of its life because they now find it difficult to go on providing for it. But if they have taken all reasonable precautions against having a child, they do not simply by virtue of their biological relationship to the child who comes into existence have a special responsibility for it. They may wish to assume responsibility for it, or they may not wish to. And I am suggesting that if assuming responsibility for it would require large sacrifices, then they may refuse. A Good Samaritan would not

refuse—or anyway, a Splendid Samaritan, if the sacrifices that had to be made were enormous. But then so would a Good Samaritan assume responsibility for that violinist; so would Henry Fonda, if he is a Good Samaritan, fly in from the West Coast and assume responsibility for me.

8. My argument will be found unsatisfactory on two counts by many of those who want to regard abortion as morally permissible. First, while I do argue that abortion is not impermissible, I do not argue that it is always permissible. There may well be cases in which carrying the child to term requires only Minimally Decent Samaritanism of the mother, and this is a standard we must not fall below. I am inclined to think it a merit of my account precisely that it does *not* give a general yes or a general no. It allows for and supports our sense that, for example, a sick and desperately frightened fourteen-year-old schoolgirl, pregnant due to rape, may *of course* choose abortion, and that any law which rules this out is an insane law. And it also allows for and supports our sense that in other cases resort to abortion is even positively indecent. It would be indecent in the woman to request an abortion, and indecent in a doctor to perform it, if she is in her seventh month, and wants the abortion just to avoid the nuisance of postponing a trip abroad. The very fact that the arguments I have been drawing attention to treat all cases of abortion, or even all cases of abortion in which the mother's life is not at stake, as morally on a par ought to have made them suspect at the outset.

Secondly, while I am arguing for the permissibility of abortion in some cases, I am not arguing for the right to secure the death of the unborn child. It is easy to confuse these two things in that up to a certain point in the life of the fetus it is not able to survive outside the mother's body; hence removing it from her body guarantees its death. But they are importantly

675

different. I have argued that you are not morally required to spend nine months in bed, sustaining the life of that violinist; but to say this is by no means to say that if, when you unplug yourself, there is a miracle and he survives, you then have a right to turn round and slit his throat. You may detach yourself even if this costs him his life; you have no right to be guaranteed his death, by some other means, if unplugging yourself does not kill him. There are some people who will feel dissatisfied by this feature of my argument. A woman may be utterly devastated by the thought of a child, a bit of herself, put out for adoption and never seen or heard of again. She may therefore want not merely that the child be detached from her, but more, that it die. Some opponents of abortion are inclined to regard this as beneath contempt—thereby showing insensitivity to what is surely a powerful source of despair. All the same, I agree that the desire for the child's death is not one which anybody may gratify, should it turn out to be possible to detach the child alive.

At this place, however, it should be remembered that we have only been pretending throughout that the fetus is a human being from the moment of conception. A very early abortion is surely not the killing of a person, and so is not dealt with by anything I have said here.

CHAPTER 62

STANLEY HAUERWAS

CHRISTIANS AND ABORTION: THE NARRATIVE CONTEXT

Stanley Hauerwas (1940–   ) is professor of religion at Duke University. A leading theological ethicist, his numerous publications include *A Community of Character: Toward a Constructive Christian Social Ethic* (1981).

After graduating cum laude in Philosophy at Southwestern University, Galveston, Texas (B.A., 1962), Hauerwas earned his Ph.D. in Christian Ethics at Yale (1968), where he was a Rockefeller Fellow. Professor Hauerwas is a member of the American Association of Religion, the American Society of Christian Ethics, and the Society for Religion and Higher Education. In addition to contributing articles and reviews to professional journals, he has authored *Vision and Virtue: Essays in Christian Ethical Reflection* (1974), *Character and the Christian Life: A Study in Theological Ethics* (1975), and *Truthfulness and Tragedy: Further Investigations in Christian Ethics* (1977), and has acted as the associate editor of the *Encyclopedia of Bioethics*, 1973–1976.

CHRISTIANS AND ABORTION: THE NARRATIVE CONTEXT[1]

. . . Christians have failed their social order by accepting too easily the terms of argument concerning abortion offered by our society. If we are to serve our society well, and on our own terms, our first task must be to address ourselves by articulating for Christians why abortion can never be regarded as morally indifferent for us. Only by doing this can we witness to our society what

[1] From Stanley Hauerwas, *A Community of Character: Toward a Constructive Christian Social Ethic* (Notre Dame: University of Notre Dame Press, 1981).

kind of people and what kind of society is required if abortion is to be excluded. . . .

To begin with, the first question is not, "Why do Christians think abortion is wrong?" To begin there already presupposes that we know and understand what abortion is. Rather, if we are to understand why Christians assume that by naming abortion they have already said something significant, we have to begin still a step back. We have to ask what it is about the kind of community, and corresponding world, that Christians create that makes them single out abortion in such a way as to exclude it.

For we must remember that "abortion" is not a description of a particular kind of behavior; rather it is a word that teaches us to see a singular kind of behavior from a particular community's moral perspective. The removal of the fetus from the mother's uterus before term can be called an "interruption of pregnancy," the child can be called "fetal matter," and the mother can be called a "patient." But from the Christian perspective, to see the situation in that way changes the self and the community in a decisive way. The christian insistence on the term "abortion" is a way to remind them that what happens in the removal of the fetus from the mother in order to destroy it strikes at the heard of their community. From this perspective the attempt of Christians to be a community where the term "abortion" remains morally intelligible is a political act.

In this respect the pro-abortionists have always been at a disadvantage. For they have had to carry out the argument in a language created by the moral presuppositions of the Jewish and Christian communities. "Abortion" still carries the connotation that this is not a good thing. Thus to be "pro-abortion" seems to put one in an embarrassing position of recommending a less than good thing. It is not without reason, therefore, that pro-abortion advocates seek to rede-

scribe both the object and act of abortion. We must remind them, however, that by doing so they not only change the description of the act, they also change themselves.

Christians insist on the significance of such a change by refusing to live in a world devoid of abortion as a moral description—a world which admittedly may, as a result, involve deep tragedy. There can be no doubt that the insistence that unjust termination of pregnancy be called "abortion" has to do with our respect for life, but this is surely too simple. Jews and Christians are taught to respect life, not as an end in itself, but as a gift created by God. Thus life is respected because all life serves God in its way. Respect for human life is but a form of our respect for all life. . . .

It is the Christian belief, nurtured by the command of Jesus, that we must learn to love one another, that we become more nearly what we were meant to be through the recognition and love of those we did not "choose" to love. Children, the weak, the ill, the dispossessed provide a particularly intense occasion for such love, as they are beings we cannot control. We must love them for what they are rather than what we want or wish them to be, and as a result we discover that we are capable of love. The existence of such love is not unique or limited to Christians. Indeed that is why we have the confidence that our Christian convictions on these matters might ring true even for those who do not share our convictions. The difference between the Christian and the non-Christian is only that what is a possibility for the non-Christian is a duty for the Christian.

But the Christian duty to welcome new life is a joyful duty, as it derives from our very being as God's people. Moreover correlative to the language of duty is the language of gift. Because children are a duty they can also be regarded as gift, for duty teaches us to accept and welcome a child into the world, not as something that is "ours," but as a gift which comes from another. As a result Christians need not resort to destructive and self-deceiving claims about the qualities they need to have, or the conditions of the world necessary to have children. Perhaps more worrisome than the moral implications of the claim "no unwanted child ought ever to be born," are the ominous assumptions about what is required for one to "want" to have a child.

Christians are thus trained to be the kind of people who are ready to receive and welcome children into the world. For they see children as a sign of the trustworthiness of God's creation and his unwillingness to abandon the world to the powers of darkness. The Christian prohibition of abortion is but the negative side of their positive commitment to welcome new life into their community: life that they know must challenge and perhaps even change their own interpretation of their tradition, but also life without which the tradition has no means to grow.

It is, of course, true that children will often be conceived and born under less than ideal conditions, but the church lives as a community which assumes that we live in an age which is always dangerous. That we live in such a time is all the more reason we must be the kind of community that can receive children into our midst. Just as we need to be virtuous, not because virtue pays but because we cannot afford to be without virtue where it does not pay, so we must learn how to be people open to new life. We can neither protect them from that suffering nor deny them the joy of participating in the adventure of God's Kingdom.

For Christians, therefore, there can be no question of whether the fetus is or is not a "human being." That way of putting the matter is far too abstract and formal. Rather, because of the kind of community we are, we see in the fetus nothing less than God's continuing creation that is destined in hope to be another citizen of his Kingdom. The question of when human life begins is of little interest to such a people, since their hope is that life will and does continue to begin time after time.

This is the form of life that brings significance to our interaction with the fetus. Our history is the basis for our "natural" sympathies, which have been trained to look forward to the joy and challenges of new life. Wertheimer may well be right that there is no corresponding "natural" welcome for life in our society that would make intelligible the recognition of the fetus as having moral status. Yet I suspect that the expectation of parents, and in particular of women, for the birth of their children remains a powerful form of life that continues to exert a force on everyone. Such an "expectation," however, in the absence of more substantive convictions about parenting, too easily becomes a destructive necessity that distorts the experience of being a parent and a child. Particularly repugnant is the assumption that women are thus primarily defined by the role of "mother," for then we forget that the role of being a parent, even for the childless, is a responsibility for everyone in the Christian community.

Nor should it be thought that the Christian commitment to welcome new life into the world stems from a sentimental fondness for babies. Rather, for Christians the having of children is one of their most significant political acts. From the world's perspective the birth of a child represents but another drain on our material and psychological resources. Children, after all, take up much of our energy that could be spent on making the world a better place and our society more just. But from the Christian perspective the birth of a child represents nothing less than our commitment that God will not have this world "bettered" by destroying life. That is why there is no more profound political act for Christians than taking the time for children. It is but an indication that God, not man, rules this existence, and we have been graciously invited to have a part in God's adventure and his Kingdom through the simple action of having children.

The Immediate Political Task

To some it may seem that I have argued Christians right out of the current controversy, for my argument has made appeal to religious convictions that are inadmissable in the court of our public ethos. But is has certainly not been my intention to make it implausible for Christians to continue to work in the public arena for the protection of all children; nor do I think that this implication follows from the position I have developed. Of course, Christians should prefer to live in societies that provide protection for children. And Christians should certainly wish to encourage those "natural" sentiments that would provide a basis for having and protecting children.

Moreover Christians must be concerned to develop forms of care and support, the absence of which seem to make abortion such a necessity in our society. In particular Christians should, in their own communities, make clear that the role of parent is one we all share. Thus the woman who is pregnant and carrying the child need not

be the one to raise it. We must be a people who stand ready to receive and care for any child, not just as if it were one of ours, but because in fact each is one of ours.

But as Christians we must not confuse our political and moral strategies designed to get the best possible care for children in our society with the substance of our convictions. Nor should we hide the latter in the interest of securing the former. For when that is done we abandon our society to its own limits. And then our arguments fall silent in the most regrettable manner, for we forget that our most fundamental political task is to be and to point to that truth which we believe to be the necessary basis for any life-enhancing and just society.

In particular, I think that we will be wise as Christians to state our opposition to abortion in a manner that makes clear our broader concerns for the kind of people we ought to be to welcome children into the world. Therefore, rather than concentrating our energies on whether the fetus is or is not a "person," we would be better advised by example and then argument to make clear why we should hope it is a child. We must show that such a hope involves more than just the question of the status of the fetus, but indeed is the very reason why being a part of God's creation is such an extraordinary and interesting adventure.

GLOSSARY

ALTRUISM   The promotion of the good of others; as a moral principle, to consider the consequences of actions for everyone except oneself.

ARETAIC ETHICS   The theory, first proposed by Aristotle, that the basis of ethical judgment

is character; focuses on the character and dispositions of the moral agent rather on actions and duties.

CATEGORICAL IMPERATIVE   Commands actions that are necessary in themselves, without reference to other ends. In Kant's nonconsequentialism, moral duties represent the injunctions of reason that command actions categorically.

CONSEQUENTIALISM Sometimes known as *teleological ethics;* the view that the correctness (rightness or wrongness) of moral conduct is judged in terms of its results (or consequences); *ethical egoism and utilitarianism* are consequentialist ethical theories.

CULTURAL RELATIVISM The descriptive thesis (sometimes known as "diversity thesis") that different cultures have different moral rules.

DIVINE COMMAND THEORY A theory holding that moral terms are defined in terms of God's commands or that moral duties are logically dependent on God's commands.

ETHICAL ABSOLUTISM The view that there is only one correct answer to every moral problem; a completely absolutist ethic is made up of absolute principles that provide an answer for every possible situation in life. It is diametrically opposed to *ethical relativism* and *ethical objectivism,* which hold that moral principles, while objective, may be overridden in certain situations.

ETHICAL EGOISM A normative theory holding that we ought to act according to self-interest; our own success and happiness should be of primary and ultimate worth and all other values should flow from this.

ETHICAL HEDONISM The theory that pleasure is the only intrinsic positive value and that pain is the only thing with negative intrinsic value; all other values are derived from these two.

ETHICAL OBJECTIVISM The view that moral principles have objective validity whether or not people recognize them as such; differs from *ethical relativism* and also from *ethical absolutism,* in that moral principles may be overridden in certain situations.

ETHICAL RELATIVISM The theory that the validity of moral judgments depends on cultural acceptance. It is opposed to *moral absolutism* and *moral objectivism.*

ETHICAL SKEPTICISM The view that we cannot know whether there is any moral truth.

ETHICAL SUBJECTIVISM The theory that moral values are expressions of human emotions, feelings, wishes, or desires, and that they have no objective referent in the world.

ETHNOCENTRISM The belief of a group or a people that their ways (values, race, religion, language, culture) are superior to all others.

FORMULA OF THE END IN ITSELF Kant's expression of the categorical imperative as Respect for Persons: Act so that you treat humanity, whether in your own person or in that of another, always as an end and never as a means only.

FORMULA OF UNIVERSAL LAW Kant's first expression of the categorical imperative in *Fundamental Principles of the Metaphysics of Morals* (1785): Act only according to that maxim by which you can at the same time will that it should become a universal law.

INTELLECTUALISM The view that God's law is the expression of God's intellect, whose object is truth; therefore the moral law is rational and the intellect superior to the will; opposed to *voluntarism.*

METAETHICS A theoretical study that inquires into logical, semantic, and epistemological issues in ethics. Metaethics is contrasted with *normative ethics,* which constructs moral theories based on moral principles.

NATURAL LAW THEORY The view, held by Thomas Aquinas, that nature is a system of God's universal prescriptions for humankind; right and wrong can be determined by rational examination of nature and the consultation of conscience.

NONCONSEQUENTIALISM Ethical theories,

such as Kant's, that deny the *consequentialist* claim that the intrinsic good and evil of consequences are the sole criterion of rightness and wrongness; sometimes called *deontological ethics*.

PSYCHOLOGICAL EGOISM   A descriptive theory about human motivation stating as fact that every person always acts to satisfy his or her self-interests.

RELATIVISM   See *Cultural relativism* and *Ethical relativism*.

SOCIAL CONTRACT THEORY   The name given to a group of related and overlapping concepts and traditions in political theory and ethics that views the origin of collective society as based on an agreement; according to Thomas Hobbes, individuals agree to limit their autonomy in exchange for the peace and security that government provides. Without such an agreement, the precollective *state of nature* prevails.

STATE OF NATURE   The condition of humanity without (or before) government. Hobbes portrays it as anarchy, with a continual war of all against all.

UTILITARIANISM   A normative consequentialist ethical theory (originally espoused by Jeremy Bentham and John Stuart Mill) that holds right action to be that which maximizes utility, bringing about good consequences for all concerned—sometimes popularized as "the greatest good for the greatest number." *Act utilitarianism* holds that the right act in a given situation is that which results in the best consequences, whereas *rule utilitarianism* holds that the right act is that conforming to the set of rules that will in turn result in the best consequences.

VOLUNTARISM   The view that moral law is binding simply because it is God's will. (In the example of Abraham, if God asked Abraham to sacrifice his son, then the very request makes it right; there is no independent standard of judgment for morality outside of God's will.)

FOR FURTHER STUDY

Feinberg, Joel, ed. *The Problem of Abortion*. Belmont, Calif.: Wadsworth, 1984.
A collection of some of the best philosophical articles on abortion.

Frankena, William K. *Ethics*. 2d. ed. Englewood Cliffs, N.J.: Prentice-Hall, 1973.
Presents the main types of ethical theory in modern philosophy.

Hardin, Russell. *Morality Within the Limits of Reason*. Chicago: University of Chicago Press, 1988.
A contemporary defense of utilitarianism.

Helm, Paul, ed. *The Divine Command Theory of Ethics*. Oxford: Oxford University Press, 1979.
A very helpful collections of essays on the subject.

Hospers, John. *Human Conduct: Problems of Ethics*. New York: Harcourt Brace Jovanovich, 1972.
Very helpful introduction for beginning students.

MacIntyre, Alasdair. *After Virtue*. Notre Dame: University of Notre Dame Press, 1981.

An important contemporary defense of virtue-based ethics.

Moore, G. E. *Principa Ethica*. Cambridge: Cambridge University Press, 1903.

The book that started the twentieth century discussion of metaethics.

Nelson, Kai. *Ethics Without God*. Pemberton Books, 1973.

A defense of secular morality; very readable.

O'Conner, D. J. *Aquinas and Natural Law*. London: Macmillan, 1968.

A good introductory treatment of natural law.

Olson, Robert G. *The Morality of Self-Interest*. New York: Harcourt, Brace, Jovanovich, 1965.

The best contemporary work by a philosopher sympathetic to ethical egoism.

Rawls, John. *A Theory of Justice*. Cambridge: Harvard University Press, 1971.

One of the most acclaimed books on moral philosophy in the past thirty years; argues for a contractarian theory of ethics.

Regan, Tom. *The Case for Animal Rights*. Berkeley: University of California Press, 1983.

A thorough defense of animal rights.

Ross, W. D. *Kant's Ethical Theory*. London: Clarendon Press, 1954.

A clear exposition of Kant's nonconsequentialism.

Smart, J. J. C. and Williams, Bernard. *Utilitarianism: For and Against*. Cambridge: Cambridge University Press, 1973.

A lively debate on the subject.

Taylor, Richard. *Good and Evil*. New York: Macmillan, 1970.

The author argues that the main role of morality is the resolution of conflicts of interest.

PART NINE

◆

SOCIAL AND POLITICAL PHILOSOPHY

The philosophers have only *interpreted* the world,
in various ways; the point is to *change* it.

KARL MARX

ORIENTATION

Social and political philosophy is the branch of philosophy that is concerned with social relationships among people, particularly those relations that exist in the nation or state. Our concept of the state and the extent of its power and authority depends upon our view of human nature. Central to the study of political philosophy is the problem of **justice:** What is the proper balance between the public interest and the need for cooperation in society on the one hand, and individual rights and private interests on the other?

When we think of justice, we tend to think of criminal cases and the problem of punishment; in other words, how to apprehend criminals and make them "pay for their crimes." This is the oldest meaning of the word justice and refers to what philosophers call **retributive justice.** But justice is much more than the problem of punishment, for it concerns the general ordering of society in daily civil matters, not merely criminal matters. Every society has a system by which individuals obtain the necessary goods for living. What are the criteria for a just distribution of goods? Should everyone in society be afforded the opportunity of education? Should there be social classes? Should all members of society, regardless of race, creed, or economic standing be given equal treatment under the law? How does a given society address the obvious inequalities that exist among people? Should a progressive income tax be used to redistribute wealth in society? As we shall see, contemporary theories of justice are very much concerned with these questions and with the problem of **distributive justice.**

There are three guiding questions of political philosophy:

1. Why does the state exist?
2. What kind of state is best?
3. What are our obligations to the state?

Since the time of Plato and Aristotle, philosophers have thought that ideally, the virtues of government are the same as the virtues of individuals. The state, like the individual, ought to be just, humane, temperate, honest, compassionate, and reasonable. It is clear then that these three questions are moral questions, and can be posed in the following way:

1. Does the state's existence have any moral justification?
2. What powers is the state morally justified in exercising?
3. Are we morally obligated to obey all the laws of the state, without exception?

This Orientation and the readings that follow are designed to highlight the importance of these questions and to show how philosophers have answered them in the history of philosophy. The Contemporary Perspectives section (as well as our first reading selection from Plato) addresses the topic of **civil disobedience,** an issue of perennial concern that arises from asking our third question.

JUSTICE AND THE STATE

Most people take the existence of the state for granted. This is odd, since no other entity has as much power and authority as the state. Consider the facts: Only the state can house an army or police force; only the state can imprison us or wage war; only the state can lawfully wield lethal force for reasons other than self-defense; only the state can levy taxes and redistribute wealth. Furthermore, the state makes an unquestioned claim on my allegience; as long as I live within its boundaries I am compelled to obey its laws on pain of punishment. Even if I disagree with the way it spends its money, I must pay my taxes. If I refuse, I will be subject to penalties imposed by the Internal Revenue Service and enforced by the legal machinery of the state. Regardless of whether they support a particular war, eighteen-year-old males are required to register for the draft; if called, they must serve. Elementary and secondary education is compulsory; if I am a certain age, I must attend school. In certain public spaces I am prohibited by the state from smoking, and so on.

Clearly, there is no other institution that exerts such power over us. If any other institution were to try to get away with these kinds of demands, we would be morally outraged. The state alone, it is claimed, has the moral right to wield this kind of power. But why? How can we justify the existence of such a coercive entity, with such a monopoly of power? What political theories of legitimation are available to us?

Some theorists have argued that the power of the state can never be legitimated. Anarchism is the view that no government has the legitimate authority to coerce people and that the public interest and individual rights can only be served without a state. Historically, anarchism has often appealed to political radicals concerned with protecting individual freedoms, but it has never had a wide following. Most people believe that the power and authority of the state can be legitimated.

It was not all that long ago that monarchs sought to justify their power by appeal to a doctrine known as the divine right of kings. In *The True Law of Free Monarchy* (1598) James I, King of England and the first of four monarchs from the Stuart family, claimed that God himself had invested the king with personal authority. Sir Robert Filmer, a defender of the divine right theory and an opponent of the contractarian view of government, wrote that, "All government is absolute monarchy; and the ground he builds on is this: That no man is born free."

To most people today, Filmer's words sound unreasonable and false. Few today accept the divine right theory as providing a sound rationale for the powers of government. Most would agree with the stirring words of Jean-Jacques Rousseau at the outset of his book, *The Social Contract:* "Man is born free, but is everywhere in chains." Because social contract theory is today widely regarded as the theory most able to justify morally the existence of the state, and because it is the theory responsible for toppling the Stuart monarchy and engendering revolutions in England, America and France, it is worthy of our study.

SOCIAL CONTRACT THEORY

Philosophers as different as Thomas Hobbes (1588–1679), John Locke, (1632–1704), Jean-Jacques Rousseau (1712–1782), and Immanuel Kant (1724–1804) have one thing in common: They all attempted to justify the existence of the state by viewing it as the product of a social contract. According to the theory of social contract, government has been established in human societies by an agreement or contract among the members of society to accomplish certain purposes. Thus the state is a human institution, voluntarily created and voluntarily joined by all who live within its boundaries. Before the contract, these individuals lived in a state of nature, a condition where there was no state, and hence, no legal limit to their freedom. When entering into a contractual relation, each individual agrees to relinquish certain freedoms and to obey the laws of the state.

Of course, the notion of a prehistorical state of nature and a subsequent social contract is widely regarded as a fiction. There is no historical evidence to suggest that states actually arose in this fashion. Still, it is a convenient or useful fiction. Social contract theory asks us to perform a thought experiment. Imagine a group of individuals having no legal constraints but possessing a sense of morality. Each of them seeks to create a society that shall conform to their natural sense of justice. What sort of society would they create if they knew that they would all have to abide by the rules that they chose? *In other words, what sort of society would they have the moral right to choose?* Wouldn't they choose to create a society in which each person was regarded as the equal of the next, where no person was to harm another person? This is exactly how John Locke formulates the state of nature where individuals are guided by the precepts of morality, or what Locke calls "natural laws:"

> The state of nature has a law of Nature to govern it, which obliges every one: And reason, which is that law, teaches all mankind who will but consult it, that being all equal and independent, no one ought to harm another in his life, health, liberty, or possessions.[1]

[1]John Locke, *The Second Treatise of Government*. para. 4 (1690).

Since social contract theory gives an account of how the state might have come about and provides a moral justification for the existence of that state, it has provided one important answer to our first question. It provides an answer to our second question as well. As Locke's quotation makes clear, social contract theory attempts to justify the existence of a particular kind of state. The best state is one that protects the **natural rights** of its citizens.

NATURAL RIGHTS

All individuals in the state of nature have certain natural rights that belong to them simply because they are human. No one can rob me of my rights, for they are basic to human life, and mine by nature. These rights, Locke believed, include the right to life, health, and property. Furthermore, I have the freedom to dispose of my property however I please—as long as I do not interfere with the rights of others to do the same. All individuals have the right to protect these rights, defending themselves from any who attempt to rob or harm them and exacting compensation from those who succeed in robbing or harming them.

Locke believed that these natural rights were given to us by God. Thomas Jefferson, who popularized Locke's thought in the Declaration of Independence, was expressing this view when he wrote these words: "All men are created equal, and are endowed by their Creator with certain unalienable rights." Contemporary contractarians have since discarded the belief that natural rights are somehow embedded by God in the natural order of things; it is sufficient, they claim, to view natural rights as agreed-upon moral rights.

There is an important disagreement along the three most prominent social contract theorists on this point. Hobbes believed that the "signers" of the social contract relinquished all of their natural rights to the state. In Part 8 we saw that Hobbes believed the state of nature to be a state of war. The only relief from such a situation is a ruler powerful enough to overawe his subjects. Hence, Hobbes advocated a nonrepublican form of government where there is no equality of rights. Locke objected to Hobbes' view of the state of nature, and the psychological egoism that undergirded it. For Locke, the state of nature is not to be viewed as a state of war; the social contract assumes a prior state of morality. Moreover, whereas Hobbes's theory was meant to justify unlimited sovereignty for an absolute monarch, Locke believed the contract to be a *limited one* between a people and its sovereign. Natural rights of life, liberty, and property (Jefferson exchanged the word "property" for "happiness" in the Declaration of Independence) are not given up, only the right to judge and punish infractions. Moreover, both Locke and Rousseau believed that because natural rights are basic moral rights they belong to us equally, regardless of whether the state recognizes them or not. If a government does not recognize or trespasses these rights, individuals as a last resort may take up and justifiably overthrow it.

Ideas have consequences. Nowhere is this more true than when studying political philosophy. It used to be thought that Locke's *Two Treatises on Government* (presented as the reading selection in Chapter 64) was written in 1689, after the "Glorious Revolution" had forced James II, the last Stuart King of England, from the throne. There is good reason to believe, however, that Locke wrote it in Holland between 1679 and 1681, under an assumed name. This remarkable treatise, written by a man out of power and out of favor with the existing monarchy, became the revolutionary document that led not only to England's bloodless revolution but the more violent revolutions in America and France at the end of the eighteenth century.

THE TRANSFER OF RIGHTS

Natural rights are of little value if they are not respected by others or if they are unenforceable. Social contract theory asks us to imagine a situation where individual freedom is threatened; where life, health, and property are in jeopardy. This is what life is like in the state of nature. What can be done?

Faced with this situation, people will join forces to ensure that their natural rights will be respected. They will agree to a system of laws that will protect their rights, outlawing murder, theft, destruction of property, and other violent acts. Next, they will devise a system for applying and enforcing these laws, creating institutions to determine when a crime has been committed, how criminals should be punished, and how to award compensation to victims of injustice. They will also need to create institutions capable of carrying out these decisions. Hence they will create a state—with legislative, judicial, and police powers.

Locke interpreted the social contract as the delegation of rights by individuals to the state. The individuals who enter into the contract agree to transfer certain natural rights to the community in order to protect other vitally important natural rights. They authorize a legislative body to pass laws to determine which actions count as infringements of their rights. They give the judicial body the right to determine who has broken these laws and how the previously prescribed punishments and compensations should be applied. They give the executive body the right to enforce these judgments.

Locke believed that ultimately these delegated rights still belong to the individual members of the community; hence the members of the community must maintain effective control over the people selected to exercise these natural rights in their name. Consequently, the state that is established must be a democratic one. For Locke, political freedom presupposes the rule of law. To be "governed by law and not by men" means that the political authorities are bound to act in accordance with general rules established by a legislative body in accordance with majority rule. The authorities are not to decide cases according to their personal whims or interests. Officials who act in our name, exercising judgment concerning our rights, must be subject to majority rule.

LIMITS ON THE STATE

The majority must have limits to its powers. The state cannot be morally free to do whatever the majority wishes it to do; its powers are limited by the original contract, and those limits, for Locke, are clear. The state has the right to protect the natural rights of its members, *and that is all.* Locke's reasoning on this point is interesting and has been a subject of much debate. In coming together to form a social contract, individuals are morally free to transfer their rightful powers, *but they cannot transfer any powers that they do not rightfully possess.* For example, they can give the state the right to pass laws forbidding murder and theft, as well as the right to imprison people who murder or steal. But the right to life, liberty, and property are **unalienable,** meaning they cannot be transferred or delegated to the state.

Locke gave two reasons for this. First, delegating these basic moral rights would destroy the entire purpose of the social contract, which is to protect these rights. Some individual rights may be transferred to protect others, but what point would there be in transferring all of them? What then would be left to protect? Locke argued that the chief purpose of the social contract is the protection of property rights; the state must not interfere with the property rights of its members. Second, no individual in the state of nature has the right to take his or her own life nor the life and property of another, except in defense of his or her own life. Since no one has these rights, no one can delegate them. Locke believed firmly that no individuals *would* delegate their property rights, and no individuals *could* delegate their rights to life and freedom.

LOCKE'S THEORY OF ORIGINAL ACQUISITION

Locke believed that the primary function of government is to protect property. As he stated in his *Two Treatises on Government*, "Government has no other end but the preservation of property." He also believed that God had created the earth for the use and enjoyment of *all* humankind. How then, does one individual acquire the right to appropriate and consume for his or her own use that which belongs to everyone? Locke's theory of original acquisition is founded on the importance of *labor:*

> Though the earth, and all inferior creatures be common to all men, yet every man has a property in his own person. This no body has any right to but

himself. The labor of his body, and the works of his hands, we may say, are properly his. Whatsoever then he removes out of the state that Nature hath provided, and left it in, he hath mixed his labor with, and joined to it something that is his own, and thereby makes it his property. . . . For this labor being the unquestionable property of the laborer, no man but he can have a right to what that was once joined to, at least where there is enough, and as good left in common for others.[2]

Labor, then, is an exception to the general rule that all things are originally, under God, held in common. No individuals in the state of nature are accountable to others for the use of their labor. Because all individuals own their own labor, whatever items are removed from the common stock belong to the individuals who removed them by their own labor.

According to the method of original acquisition, because people's appetites and their ability to consume are approximately equal, the amount of goods owned by each individual will be approximately equal. Where does inequality come from, then? How is it that some individuals have acquired more than others? Locke reasoned that inequality arose from the invention of money; unlike most goods (like food, clothing, and shelter), money is a good that does not spoil. It usually exists in the form of a metal such as gold or silver, which can last indefinitely. Furthermore, he believed that this inequality was justified because people have consented to it:

> Men have consented to disproportionate and unequal possession of the earth, they having by a tacit and voluntary consent found out a way, how a man may fairly possess more land than he himself can use the product of, by receiving in the exchange for the overplus, gold and silver, which may be hoarded up without injury to any one, these metals not spoiling or decaying in the hands of the possesser.[3]

In other words, the value of money is determined by human agreement. Locke assumes that because the value of money rests upon mutual consent, then people have also consented to all the inequalities that flow from the use of it.

This argument justifying inequality is unconvincing. It is simply untrue that individuals always agree to all of the consequences of their agreements. For instance, if after observing how a particular agreement has worked out, the participants conclude that the results have been disastrous, they may very well reconsider their original understanding. The problem with Locke's theory is that it

[2]Locke, para. 27.
[3]Locke, para. 50.

locks in inequalities forever and does not afford individuals (or resulting social classes) any means of redress. Karl Marx, as we shall see, was a notable critic of the inequalities among people. But before we turn our attention to Marx, let us examine in greater detail the political legacy of Locke's theory.

TWO CONTEMPORARY CONTRACTARIAN THEORIES

John Locke is often referred to as the father of liberal democracy. To understand what a liberal democracy is, imagine three continuums:

1. Pluralism ⸻ Totalitarianism
2. Democratic ⸻ Authoritarian
3. Capitalistic ⸻ Socialistic

The first continuum indicates the number of independent centers of power a society has. The greater the number of independent centers of power, the more **pluralistic** is the society; the fewer the independent centers of power, the more **totalitarian.** A pluralistic society places a high value on social diversity, allowing the press, religion, family, institutions of business and education, and so on, to operate independently of one another and of the state. A totalitarian state, on the other hand, seeks to control or disallow these power centers; in an attempt to exercise total control over a society, it may censor the press, restricting religious practice, restraining commerce, and the like.

The second continuum refers to the degree of democratic control that citizens exert over their government. The more citizens are allowed to participate in and direct the course of their government, the more **democratic** is their society; the more these participatory powers are denied them, the more **authoritarian** is their society.

The third continuum refers to the ownership of property. The more the means of production are owned by private citizens, the more **capitalistic** is the society; the more they are owned publicly, the more **socialistic** the society.

We may thus define a liberal democracy as a system of government that is more pluralistic than totalitarian, more democratic than authoritarian, and more capitalistic than socialistic. The society that Locke and Jefferson advocated was the prototype of liberal democracy. In recent years, a lively debate about the nature and fate of liberal democracy has been going on between two contractarian theorists, Robert Nozick and John Rawls, both of whom may be thought of as followers of Locke.

ROBERT NOZICK: JUSTICE AS ENTITLEMENT

Nozick, like Locke, is an advocate of limited government. In his book, *Anarchy, State, and Utopia,* he argues in favor of the minimal state, or a night-watchman state. Like a night watchman, the state is to be on the alert for the protection of its citizenry, organizing the military in times of war, seeing to it that its judicial system functions smoothly, and ensuring that its police force is adequate to maintain order. He contends that the state as a result of the social contract has the obligation to protect its citizens from violence, theft, and fraud, and it has the right to enforce contracts between its citizens. It also has the right to levy taxes in order to finance these functions. But that is all it has the right to do, no more. It certainly ought not to intrude into the affairs of society by, for example, establishing national goals, directing education, channeling individuals into employment most needed by society at a particular point, monitoring the numbers of minorities who get hired, and so on.

Perhaps we can get a better handle on just how minimal a state Nozick has in mind if we ask ourselves what the state does *not* have a right to do. The state cannot tell its citizens what materials they cannot read, what films they cannot see, what they cannot smoke, what they cannot drink, and what sexual acts they cannot perform. The state has no right to tell its citizens whom they should hire, fire, lease an apartment to, or admit to their places of business. It cannot force citizens to contribute to their own retirement through social security taxes, nor can it demand that they pay for schools, libraries, or parks. It cannot control prices, wages, or rents. It should not get into the business of trying to redistribute wealth or establish equality by forcing its citizens to support welfare payments, food stamps, or other programs. It has no right to use tax monies for urban renewal, mass transit, or advertising campaigns designed to discourage alcoholism and drug abuse, or to promote "safe sex."

All of the items mentioned above are infringements of individual liberties. After all, in the state of nature, I have the right to read, smoke, and drink what I wish, and to behave sexually as I please. I also have the right to refuse employment to whomever I wish, and the right to withhold giving money to the poor, *and I do not transfer these rights to the state.* Even if a majority of citizens in the state decide that it is morally correct to try to create a level playing field for minorities through affirmative action programs, they do not have the moral right to enforce that decision on me. Individual liberty severely limits what the majority can do. The purpose of the social contract is to preserve as much liberty as possible; the less government, the better.

ıgn her way to state this is to say that there are definite moral side constraints to the will of the majority; the majority simply cannot force its will on the minority. Nozick employs Kant's "Respect for Persons" moral principle (see Part 8), arguing that we have no right to treat another person as a mere means to our goals, no matter how noble those goals may be.

> Side constraints upon action reflect the underlying Kantian principle that individuals are ends and not merely means; they may not be sacrificed or used for the achieving of other ends without their consent. Individuals are inviolable.[4]

Therefore, even if the majority adopts the noble goal of eradicating racial discrimination in the workplace, they have no right to force an unwilling employer to hire a minority candidate. Similarly, the state should not have the right to coerce an unwilling employee to contribute to his or her retirement through social security paycheck deductions.

Suppose someone were to argue, against Nozick, that it is sometimes necessary to pursue such goals "for the good of society." Nozick rejects the idea (associated with utilitarianism) that it may be proper to sacrifice the interest of some persons in order to bring about a social good. There is simply no such thing as the good of society over and above the good of the individuals who make up society. To sacrifice an individual "for the good of society" is really to sacrifice that person's interests in favor of the interests of some other person or group of persons.

Nozick's position is often referred to as an **entitlement theory of justice.** Remember that for Locke, the right to private property was so basic that it preceded any social conventions or laws and existed independently of the state. What gave a person a right to a piece of property was that he had "mixed his labor with it"—in other words, he worked with it and improved it and therefore had the right to it. In today's world, where what is considered important is more typically measured in terms of salaries rather than real estate, we would say that people are *entitled* to keep what they earn as a basic moral right. Nozick's criticisms of excessive government intervention in the lives of its citizens strikes at the very heart of the mechanism that the modern state uses to redistribute wealth—taxation. Let us consider how an entitlement theorist such as Nozick would look upon a governmental policy of using taxes to support social programs.

The government that seeks to create an arrangement whereby those at the bottom end of the economic ladder can compete with those who are better off accomplishes this by taxing the earnings of all the people and then distributing the resultant benefits to those in need. Nozick claims that such practices violate individual rights, since it takes a certain number of labor hours to earn the money that is then taken away in taxes. The government's taking away of this money is the

---

[4]Rovert Nozick, *Anarchy, State, and Utopia* (New York: Basic Books, 1974), 30–31.

equivalent of forcing someone to work a number of hours for another person. As he puts it, "Taxation of earnings from labor is on a par with forced labor." The government is no more entitled to take this money than it is to force me to work for another. Of course, the government is shrewd enough not to speak of taxes as "forced labor of the rich for the sake of the poor," but that is what it amounts to all the same. In everyday language, this is the sentiment that people are expressing when they berate public officials for "spending my hard earned dollars on social programs that don't work."

JOHN RAWLS: JUSTICE AS FAIRNESS

The most serious objection to the theories of Locke and Nozick is that the "minimal state" does not seem fair. In the late nineteenth and early twentieth century, when the United States was far closer to the minimal state than it is now, extreme poverty forced young children to quit school and work long hours in dangerous workplaces for poor wages. When workers went on strike to try to improve their situation, they were quickly replaced by men and women in worse shape than they were, who were willing to work for lower wages. Workers could be fired for attempting to form labor unions, and there was no unemployment compensation to support workers who, through no fault of their own, lost their jobs. While millions of ordinary workers were living in squalid conditions, sacrificing their health and families for "the company," rich and powerful factory owners increased their wealth and power at the expense of their workers. Was this fair? Was it fair that the state protected the mines and factories from striking workers but did not see fit to protect the strikers from the often ruthless policies of the owners?

In time, the American public concluded that these practices were not fair, and ought to be changed. Politicians were elected who believed that all people have a right to a minimum standard of living—a safe job at decent wages—who believed also that the state had a moral obligation to see that the people were not deprived of these rights.

Similarly, blacks in America faced with continuing poverty and discrimination protested that they were not being given a fair chance at capturing their share of "the American dream." The vast majority of Americans decided that it was unfair that the forces of the state were used to protect businesses who discriminated against black workers and patrons, but did nothing to protect blacks from discriminatory practices (such as riding in the backs of buses and being refused access to restaurants and restrooms).

The political theory used to justify this shift from the minimal state philosophy of Locke and Nozick to an emphasis on fairness is yet another version of contractarian theory. It was formulated by one of Nozick's colleagues at Harvard, the philosopher John Rawls. In his book, *A Theory of Justice*, Rawls makes use of an important concept: the **veil of ignorance.**

THE VEIL OF IGNORANCE

The framing of a social contract in some respects resembles a game, where the goal is to devise the fairest state possible. Naturally, in formulating the rules of the game, it is in everyone's interest to adopt rules that everyone can accept. If the game is to be fair, then the choice of rules cannot arbitrarily favor one player or group of players over another. If one person knows in advance which rules will benefit him, and if he has the power to get others to agree to these rules, the game will be unfairly biased in his favor. Rawls argues that this is precisely what is wrong with Locke's version of the social contract. Although the people who draw up the social contract are theoretically supposed to be equal, in fact they are not. Some "enter the game" already wealthy, while others are poor. Some have enormous power, prestige, and influence, while others do not. In sum, the minimal state of Locke and Nozick is stacked in favor of the interests of the rich and powerful and against the interests of the poor and weak.

Imagine another scenario. Suppose that all the "players" approached the social contract as they would the creation of a fair game. To do this, they would have to be ignorant of who would have what goods, who would wield power, who would have what position in society. In other words, they would have to approach it from behind what Rawls calls a veil of ignorance. They would be forced to devise a state in such a way that they were willing to accept whatever position came to them, without any opportunity of influencing the outcome. Only then would the outcome be unbiased and fair.

TWO PRINCIPLES OF JUSTICE

Rawls argues that the framers of such a social contract would agree on two basic principles of justice. The first is known as the **equality principle:** Every person has a right to the greatest basic freedom compatible with similar freedom for all. Rawls argues that this principle has two requirements: (1) there must be equal freedom for everybody; and (2) if the extent of freedom can be increased without violating (1), then it must be increased. The second is the **difference principle,** according to which all social and economic inequalities in society must be arranged on the basis of two considerations: (1) these inequalities must be to everyone's advantage, including those on the bottom end of the social scale; and (2) these inequalities must be attached to positions that are open to all, without discrimination.

The freedoms of the first principle are analogous to Locke's natural rights and are enumerated in the U.S. Constitution and the Bill of Rights. They include rights such as freedom of assembly, freedom of speech, freedom of religion, political freedom, and so on.

The inequalities of the second principle are the kind that exist between members of society—for example, between a surgeon and an unskilled laborer. It is true that the surgeon receives greater pay and prestige than the unskilled laborer, but this inequality can be justified in the following way. Everyone, including the laborer, benefits when there are enough surgeons to serve all. But how can society ensure that enough people will endure the considerable rigors of medical school and internship, and the serious responsibilities of being a surgeon? Clearly, some additional benefits must be given to surgeons. These inequalities, then, are beneficial to all. As long as all qualified people are given an equal opportunity to become surgeons, the additional benefits can be justified.

But suppose that the inequalities become too great? What if they become larger than what is needed to benefit everyone? In the United States, we try to solve this problem through a progressive tax system that redistributes wealth, distributing it to the poorer members of society. The rich are taxed at a higher level, with revenues going to support welfare programs such as Aid to Families with Dependent Children, job training, and food stamps.

What if the most heavily rewarded positions in society are *not* open to all? For instance, suppose that blacks and other minorities are excluded from high-paying professions? In the United States, such problems are addressed through civil rights legislation.

Why would we select Rawl's two principles from behind the veil of ignorance? The answer is simple: self-interest. If we did not know in advance whether *we* would be the ones who wound up with limited freedoms, or whether *we* would suffer from a lack of equal opportunity, or whether *we* would be exploited by the rich, we would certainly not accept a system in which such unfortunate individuals would exist.

RAWLS AND NOZICK COMPARED

Both Rawls and Nozick offer us conceptions of justice that are consistent with liberal democracy. Rawls claims that a society built on his two principles is a just society because it is fair. Nozick, rejecting the conception of justice as fairness, claims that a society is just only if the state is a minimal one; the minimal state is just because it guarantees the natural rights of the individual and does not violate critically important moral side constraints. Individuals are entitled to the property they gain through honest means and are entitled to do whatever they want with their property provided they do not violate the natural rights of others.

Historically, both conceptions of justice have played important roles in the United States. The entitlement theory is evident in the thinking of the eighteenth century founders of America and can be discerned in the preamble to the Declaration of Independence. The notion of justice as fairness did not become popular until societal inequalities made worse by the Great Depression forced people to rethink their political categories. The "New Deal" of Franklin D. Roosevelt represents the maturation of this conception of justice.

It is possible to analyze much of the political debate in America in this half-century as a philosophical confrontation between these two conceptions of justice. For example, when Arizona Senator Barry Goldwater spoke out against the 1964 Civil Rights Act, he argued that all of us have the right to serve or to exclude whomever we wish in the operation of our business, regardless of the morality of our motives. He was giving voice to the entitlement conception of justice. Against this position, the supporters of the legislation (who ultimately won) argued that it was morally unjust to deny black Americans full opportunity to participate in the benefits of the American economy.

As the outcome of this pivotal debate indicates, the view of justice as fairness has prevailed. In both major political parties in America, even the most conservative politicians now admit that the government has some obligation to help the poor, create a "level playing field" for minorities, and redistribute wealth. Of course, conservatives continue to argue that social programs do not work, or are inefficient, or create a cycle of dependency—but few, if any, argue that they are inherently *unjust*. (The one exception to this generalization is in the area of affirmative action programs, where some conservatives argue that it is unjust to give preference to minorities in hiring practices and school admissions.) Today, the entitlement conception of justice is kept alive by a small American political party known as the Libertarian Party (which on several occasions has sought to elect as president one of its own, the philosopher John Hospers!)

As we shall see in the next section, the state has played an increasingly large role in the American economy. The United States today may fairly be described as a welfare state, less capitalistic than in former days.

KARL MARX: THE COMMUNIST ALTERNATIVE

Although there are serious disagreements between Nozick and Rawls, it is important to realize that there are important similarities as well. Both are contractarians who view the state as a contract between free and equal individuals. As followers of John Locke (with Nozick more faithful to Locke's original conception than Rawls), both are defenders of liberal democracy—a society that is more pluralistic than totalitarian, more democratic than authoritarian, and more capitalistic than socialistic. We turn our attention now to a conception of justice and a view of the state that is radically different than the liberal democracy of Locke, Nozick, or Rawls.

Remember that Locke wrote his *Two Treatises on Government* before the Industrial Revolution. Karl Marx (1818–1883) lived and wrote when the social dislocutions caused by that revolution were at their peak, transforming urban areas into virtual slave farms of overworked, underpaid laborers. Against the backdrop of immense human suffering and obvious exploitation of workers by capitalistic factory owners, Marx became suspicious that Lockean liberal democracy was a rationalization for a political system that concentrated wealth and power in the hands of a few. Ask yourself: If you were a wealthy capitalist factory owner, wouldn't Locke's theory of natural rights appeal to you? Wouldn't it be the perfect theory to justify your good fortune in owning nonpersonal property (such as factories and mines) as well as personal property? Isn't it a lovely theory for justifying social inequalities?

Marx certainly thought so. He uses the term "ideology" to refer to those theories (like Locke's) whose function it is to create and sustain a false consciousness of social reality. His suspicions took the form of a powerful critique of capitalist ideology—that is, the rationalization of the capitalist status quo by the rich and powerful. The notion of a "social contract" is a Lockean political fiction, designed as the perfect instrument to keep exploited workers in their place. To truly understand the nature of the state, Marx believed, one must turn from capitalist ideology to history.

MARX'S VEIW OF HISTORY

Because humans are social creatures, the history of the human race is a history of the societies in which we have lived. The most important force in society—the one that determines all morality, religion, philosophy, art, and politics—is economics. The most important questions a historian can ask of a given society are economic questions. For instance: How is labor divided? How does production of goods take place? Who performs what job? Who owns the means of production?

Divisions of property and labor in society inevitably create economic classes—separate groups with conflicting interests. In the most primitive tribal societies, class divisions were drawn within the family. Over time, the main lines of division were drawn between masters and slaves; then between landowners and serfs; then between capitalists and laborers. In each historical stage a political organization developed, designed specifically to further the interests of the ruling class. The system of political organization in a given society is inherently conservative; it is a carefully crafted apparatus designed as a means for the ruling class to remain the ruling class. The ruling class maintains its power by suppressing the other classes.

During the Middle Ages, a feudalistic economy prevailed. Economic power was in the hands of the lords of the manor, who held large tracts of land and used serfs (a class of workers attached to the land) to do the work that produced wealth. Thus whoever controlled the land controlled the labor of the serfs as well. This feudalistic economy created a feudalistic political system where the reigning monarch protected the interests of the lords and guaranteed the suppression of the serfs. The fabled Magna Carta, which the English lords forced King John to issue in 1215, was essentially the political recognition of the feudal "rights" of the lords to oppress their serfs!

Locke's liberal democracy represents the flowering of this economic and political system. As towns began to develop, so did the guild system, in which manufacturing was done in small shops, divided along trade lines. Each shop was run by a master, who trained apprentices and employed journeymen. In time, this system was replaced by a more modern manufacturing system, and a new class developed—the middle class (or **bourgeoisie**), who were the owners of the new factories. As the middle class grew in economic power, tensions developed between it and the older ruling class, the nobility. Out of this inevitable conflict came the dramatic "age of revolutions," featuring middle class revolutions most notably in France and America, but also in England and Germany. Capitalists had taken control of political power, creating a new kind of state to protect their interests and further their power. The centerpiece of the new ideology fashioned to justify the new social order was Locke's theory of natural rights, which was designed to legitimate private property ownership and capitalistic control of the means of production.

Of course, laborers were still oppressed under the new capitalistic system, just as the serfs had been under feudalism. As before, the state was the instrument of oppression by the ruling class, except this time the ruling class was the capitalistic middle class, while the oppressed class was the working class, or **proletariat.** First in England, and then in America, the new state took the form of liberal democracy. The capitalists ruled, allowing the workers the "right" to vote for governing representatives—that is, to decide every so often which members of the ruling class would oversee their oppression.

EXPLOITATION, SURPLUS VALUE, AND ALIENATION

According to Marx, capitalistic oppression takes two forms: **exploitation** and **alienation.** To understand economic exploitation, one must understand that in a capitalistic society workers are thought of as capital—that is, as a means of production, just like the machinery in a factory. Wages paid to workers are part of production costs, just like machine purchases. In wage labor, workers sell to the capitalist owner the only commodity they possess, their labor power, and receive in recompense a wage reflecting this commodity's "value." The value of the commodities that workers produce in the factory is greater than the value of the commodities that they receive to support themselves. This difference Marx calls **surplus value.** The surplus that workers create by their labor goes to the capitalist in the form of profit. Since the factory owner's main objective is profit, and since profit is calculated as earnings after expenses, the factory owner will naturally pay the worker as little as possible. Working hours and conditions will be determined by will of the owner, not by the needs of the worker. Marx, often writing as if his pen were dipped in liquid anger, was incensed by the long hours that men, women and even children were forced to labor in order to earn their subsistence:

> But in its blind unrestrainable passion, its were-wolf hunger for surplus-labor, capital oversteps not only the moral, but even the merely physical maximum bounds of the working-day. It usurps the time for growth, development, and healthy maintenance of the body. It steals the time required for the consumption of fresh air and sunlight. It niggles over meal-time, incorporating it where possible with the process of production itself, so that food is given to the laborer as to a mere means of production, as coal is supplied to the boiler, grease and oil to the machinery. . . .It produces also the premature exhaustion and death of this labour-power itself. It extends the labourer's time of production during a given period by shortening his actual lifetime.[5]

Marx thinks that the existence of surplus value is a form of exploitation, or unjust treatment. Why does he think it is unjust? For three reasons: (1) the worker creates more value than he receives; (2) a substantial portion of the work he performs is not paid for; and (3) someone who does not work in the factory receives a substantial amount of the value created by the worker in the form of profits. There is a general ethical principle underlying the theory of surplus value, a principle of formal equality, where individuals should receive the full value of what they produce by their labor.

By alienation, Marx means two things: the alienation of workers from their own labor, and their alienation from their own products. Concerning the former, consider this: Labor is more than a means of earning a living. It is also one of our primary means of fulfillment in the world. As such, it ought to be liberating and humanizing, rather than enslaving and dehumanizing. In capitalism, however, my labor is a commodity, a thing with a price tag on it, like any other commodity in the marketplace. Like a prostitute, I am forced to turn what ought to be an expres-

[5]Karl Marx, *Capital: A Critique of Political Economy*, trans. Samuel Moore and Edward Aveling (New York: International Publishers, 1967), 264–65.

sion of my love—my labor—into a item that is bought and sold. Thus capitalism transforms what ought to be an expression of my creative individuality into an extension of the machine.

Futhermore, this dehumanization is made worse by the capitalist division of labor. In preindustrialist times, workers were able to work on a product from beginning to end. Today, they are given boring, monotonous tasks. They go to work each day and take their place on the assembly line where they turn a screw or drive a rivet. Gradually, they grow to hate their work, meaning they hate and are estranged from themselves. This is what Marx means by alienation from our labor; it leads to the second form of alienation—alienation from our products.

When our labor is no longer our own but our employer's, then the products of our labor are no longer our own either. Think of modern advertising. Products are treated not as products of human labor but as independently existing objects, capable of "transforming us." Women are told they can enhance their appeal to men by wearing the right hosiery; men are told they can be virile by smoking the right cigarette; we are all told that we can have the good life if we just consume these products. Eventually, material goods are "reified"—that is, they take on a magical life of their own—as we go in debt to consume the very items that enslave us. We forget that apart from human labor these products would never have existed in the first place! But capitalism encourages such *self*-forgetfulness.

REVOLUTION

What can be done? Marx does not believe that the capitalist system can be reformed. The degradation that the worker experiences is the result of economic forces: The worker is forced to create surplus value simply to survive, and the capitalist is forced to accept surplus value as a condition of staying in business. The evils of capitalism are not accidental, nor are they the actions of evil people; they are inherent in the system. Even if the conditions of workers could be improved by shortening the work day and providing health benefits, the injustice of surplus value would remain. This injustice will disappear only with the disappearance of capitalism itself. What is needed is a revolution by the working class. After the revolution, private property will be abolished and the means of production will be publicly owned. The unjust form of capitalist distribution, which depends upon surplus value, will be replaced by the just form of communist or socialist (Marx often used the words interchangably) distribution. By **communism** Marx meant the positive abolition of private property and human self-alienation, and a socialistic economy featuring public ownership of the means of production. He believed that abolition of private property will result in the abolition of social classes. When there are no more economic classes, there will no longer be antagonism among the classes—indeed, there will be no further need for the state, since there will be no ruling class that finds it necessary to oppress and exploit any other class. Consequently, Marx believed that the state will simply "wither away." Marx's goal is a classless, stateless, utopian society in which exploitation and alienation come to an end.

THE DICTATORSHIP OF THE PROLETARIAT

The first communist revolution occurred in 1917 under the leadership of Vladimir I. Lenin (1870–1924). Lenin described the transition from capitalism to communism using a concept that he borrowed from Marx: the dictatorship of the proletariat. What he meant by this phrase was this: The coercive powers of the state will shift from capitalists to the workers, as the state takes over ownership of the factories, farms, forests, and mines, taking away the capitalists' powers of exploitation. Because the capitalists will retain influence in the state by virtue of their education, leftover wealth, and lofty positions in society, all institutions in society must be under the strict control of the Communist party. The party will control the machinery of the state *in the name of the workers.* The role of the party is to lead the workers by developing a counter-ideology to capitalism. Uniting the workers through discipline and enforced education, the party will prepare them for the final state of true communism. Under the dictatorship of the proletariat, then, everyone will work for the state. The state, under the control of the Party, will centralize all economic decision-making. Rather than following market forces, as in capitalism, the state will decide what must be produced, how it is to be produced, who will work where, and under what conditions.

In time, Lenin theorized, the workers will gain greater control. As capitalist influence is overcome and the workers learn more about the operation of the means of production, there will be less and less need for the coercive machinery of the state. As Marx predicted, it will then wither away.

Thinking back to our three continuums, we see that *Lenin's state is the exact opposite of liberal democracy.* Since all social institutions are under the control of the state, it is totalitarian; since all the means of production are in the control of the state, it is socialistic; since the party controls the machinery of the state, without opposition, it is authoritarian.

Unfortunately, since the revolution of 1917 the Soviet state has shown little evidence of withering away! On the contrary, the Soviet bureaucracy for years was deeply entrenched and self-perpetuating. Rather than leading to a free, egalitarian communist society, where, as Marx put it, "the free development of each is the condition of the free development of all," Lenin's dictatorship of the proletariat has produced an undemocratic, totalitarian, inflexible, economically ailing Soviet Union. Only with the coming to power of Mikhail Gorbachev in 1985 has the Communist Party shown any sign of openness to change or economic restructuring. As this book goes to press in 1990, historic changes have taken place in Eastern European nations formerly under the domination of the Soviet Union, and the Soviet Union itself has been forced to re-evaluate the role of Lenin's Communist party.

THE MODERN WELFARE STATE

Critics of Marx frequently point out that capitalism has proven to be capable of significant internal reform. For instance: (1) the length of the work day has been reduced; (2) child labor has been terminated; (3) health and safety measures in factories have been improved; (4) free compulsory education has been introduced; (5) unemployment insurance and welfare benefits have reduced the harm caused by losing one's job; (6) wages and living standards have increased significantly; and (7) a smaller portion of the labor force is engaged in boring, monotonous work.

Certainly we find little evidence today in the United States of the extreme class conflict that troubled Marx. Nor do we find much evidence of the extreme forms of exploitation of workers by capitalists that were common in this country only a century ago. How do we account for this transformation of capitalism? Surely this is due to the increasing role played by the state in the American economy. For example, under a pure form of capitalism, free markets are the rule. No government intervention is justifiable, even if that intervention is for the purpose of propping up an important business. Consider what happened in the 1970s when the Chrysler Corporation was in a financial state of emergency. Realizing that it could not allow this huge corporation to go bankrupt, throwing thousands of workers (and voters!) out of work and sending shock waves into the rest of the economy, the federal government intervened with a huge influx of funds (taxpayers' dollars).

Further examples of state intervention in the economy include minimum-wage laws, child-labor laws, and consumer-protection laws. Besides all this, government grudgingly came to recognize and protect the right of workers to unionize and to strike. Industry-wide labor unions, inconceivable in a pure capitalistic state, have greatly enhanced the power of workers to influence the terms of their employment, that is, how they sell their labor.

This brings up an important point. Since the time of Roosevelt's New Deal, the United States has gradually moved in the direction of a **welfare state.** By adopting social programs such as Social Security, Medicare, Medicaid, food stamps, and the like, the American state has acted to blunt the conditions that Marx thought would eventually lead to revolution here. In other words, the welfare state has neutralized class conflicts between capitalists and workers. By partially reducing the inequalities of Locke's minimal state, and by holding out the promise that these inequalities will be further reduced in the future, the welfare state has presented itself as a genuine alternative to Marxism, demonstrating the flexibility of the capitalist system. But the welfare state is a far cry from what the founders of America had in mind when they attempted to follow Locke's prescriptions for a minimal state! With the demise of communism and the abandonment of the Lockean limited state, it appears that the crucial political choice today is between welfare state capitalism and democratic socialism.

DEMOCRATIC SOCIALISM

Democratic socialists, rejecting the excesses of Marx's theory (particularly the notion of a dictatorship of the proletariat), are nevertheless critical of the welfare state, believing that it perpetuates the alienation and dehumanization of earlier forms of capitalism. Sometimes known as "Marxist humanists" (because of their emphasis on the early humanistic writings of Marx), their goal is a socialistic society that guarantees democratic freedoms and a greater degree of pluralism than has been found in communist states such as the Soviet Union and China.

Democratic socialists such as Michael Harrington point out that even though the welfare state has improved the conditions of workers somewhat, labor is still bought and sold as a commodity—that *capitalist devotion to surplus value remains unchanged.*[6] Although economic security has increased for many, life is every bit as dehumanizing as in the minimal state. Alienation continues, manifesting itself in people treating other people as commodities, exploiting them in everyday affairs. Rather than stressing the need to be a free and open person, capitalist society stresses the producing and consuming of commodities. Rather than *being*, there is *having*. Spurred on by the advertising industry (which exists in a capitalist state, of necessity, as a machine to manufacture desire where no desire previously existed, ceaselessly creating and expanding new markets for products), we reduce ourselves to acquiring, possessing, and controlling material goods.

Furthermore, welfare capitalism continues to neglect real social goods. Because businesses are governed by the necessity of maximizing profits, they continue to destroy the environment, exhaust natural resources, and waste energy. Preferring short-term profit to long-term environmental protection, they ignore the public good to pursue the private good.

Democratic socialists contend that welfare capitalism continues to leave many segments of society outside the mainstream; vast groups of people, particularly minorities and the very poor, are marginalized and voiceless. Even in times of relative economic prosperity,

---

[6]See Michael Harrington, *The Twilight of Capitalism* (New York: Simon and Schuster, 1976).

depressed areas, particularly in large urban areas, have unacceptably high rates of unemployment. In America, the richest nation on earth, the number of homeless people is staggering. Disadvantaged segments of the population remain disadvantaged, no matter what happens in the rest of society. Thus welfare state capitalism has created a permanent underclass of welfare recipients that are conveniently forgotten, bribed off by their monthly monetary allotment, which guarantees them a subsistence existence. Meanwhile, welfare capitalism often amounts to welfare for the rich in the form of tax breaks, tax "loopholes," and even direct handouts (as in the case of the Chrysler bailout).

The problem, democratic socialists maintain, is with classical capitalistic economics, dating back to Adam Smith (1723–1790). In his monumental *Wealth of Nations*, Smith argued that if producers, workers, and consumers are left free to make their own choices in the marketplace, the outcome will be a stable economy. As everyone seeks their own self-interest, producers will produce what is needed, workers will gravitate to where their labor is needed, and wages and prices will naturally arrive at their proper levels through the law of supply and demand. It was, Smith said, as if the economy was directed by an "invisible hand."

Democratic socialists argue that such a system is anarchistic and inherently selfish. Consider the problem of the environment. Clearly, clean air and water cost money. If the quality of our air and water is to be improved, then factories and automobiles (to name a few) are going to have to be re-designed. New equipment will need to be developed, bought, and installed. But these expenditures do not result in greater income to businesses, so it is unlikely that private companies will give clean air and water high priority. The capitalist frenzy for corporate profits is a counter-motivation to the need for a cleaner environment.

Furthermore, according to Smith's model, private industry has no profit incentive for redeveloping depressed areas. Its natural market choices lead it to those areas in which it can best expect to prosper. If large East Coast cities are dying, businesses can be expected to desert them for the Sunbelt (where labor costs are cheaper due to a relative absence of unions) rather than selflessly seeking to rebuild them. Capital knows no loyalty to cities or to neighborhoods.

Consequently, a "free market" economy naturally tends to neglect or ignore many significant social problems. Of course, the United States is not a pure free market economy; the government intervenes in the economy through its taxation, spending, and monetary policies, attempting to stabilize the fluctuations of the economy. But such intervention, democratic socialists maintain, will never be sufficient in a capitalistic society because of the power wielded by banks and large corporations, who make sure that all intervention is to their benefit. Consequently, we are likely to see the rich get richer while the poor get poorer and remain powerless.

To ensure that the means of production are used for the public good, and not merely the private good, they must be placed in the hands of the public. Nationalized industries would be run in accordance with a coherent national strategy, ensuring that everyone had an absolute right to employment. This would create a just society in which social goods would be distributed evenly, thus lessening alienation. With this lessening in alienation, we could expect a general improvement in the quality of life, as we learned to value social relationships with one another.

CRITICISMS OF DEMOCRATIC SOCIALISM

Critics of democratic socialism point out that there is no evidence that there would be less alienation in a socialist society. Defenders of the welfare state point out that welfare capitalism needn't continue to favor the rich and neglect the underprivileged—the system will work if voters use their ballots to turn out of office politicians who do not seek the public good.

Perhaps the most serious objection to any type of socialism, however, is economic: There is simply no evidence to suggest that centralized economic planning has been successful anywhere in the world. While the capitalist world races ahead, creating wealth on a scale unprecedented in human history, socialist nations such as the Soviet Union are mired in economic stagnation. Many argue that capitalism, unlike socialism, is a natural human force, not a contrived ideology. That is, the urge to own property and create wealth is a natural human force; socialistic attempts to tamper with it only lead to economic inefficiency and ultimately, to chaos.

CAPITALISM, SOCIALISM, AND MORALITY

What then is the solution? It appears that democratic socialism, with its vision of equality and distributive justice, is morally superior to capitalism; yet economically speaking, socialism is inferior to capitalism in its ability to create wealth. Can capitalism be made to "be moral"? Or is it more reasonable to hope that socialism can be made to be economically efficient? These are not easy questions.

It is not that capitalism is immoral. On the contrary, the trouble with capitalism lies in its moral neutrality. Capitalism and the market system is singleminded in its thrust; this is why it is so successful in creating wealth. This singlemindedness, however, is also its greatest flaw: It is blind to all other factors. It is materialistic, impersonal, and nonhuman. It responds with great speed and accuracy to market forces, *but it cannot be made to respond to moral distinctions.* To put it simply, the capitalist market system cannot (without ruining it) be made to discriminate in favor of failure. Yet the sad fact is that many humans, however fair the rules and great the opportunities in their society, will fail. Capitalist theorists who are not insensitive to the amorality of capitalism do recognize that a great many people in this country and around the world remain in deprivation, hopelessness, and great misery.[7] The very existence of these unfortunate people stands as a permanent indictment to the capitalist market system itself, highlighting its moral insensitivity.

On the other hand, the prospects for socialism are not good. The late 1980s and early 1990s have seen numerous socialist nations cast aside their ideological assumptions. In the Soviet Union under Gorbachev, *perestroika* signifies a fundamental economic reorganization, a sign that socialism and its centralized economic planning have been a dismal failure. All over Eastern Europe, formerly socialistic nations such as Poland, Czechoslovakia, Hungary, and East Germany are attempting to convert to a market economy. The most important economic and political question at the end of the twentieth century, then, appears to be this: Can this triumphant worldwide reassertion of capitalism be given a moral dimension?

[7]See Paul Johnson, "The Capitalism and Morality Debate," *First Things*, no. 1 (March 1990): 18–22.

CHAPTER 63

PLATO

WHAT DO WE OWE TO OUR COUNTRY?

One of the most famous discussions of our obligation to obey the law stems from an actual event.[1] In Plato's dialogue *Crito*, we see Socrates shortly before his death. He has just been convicted of corrupting the youth of Athens through his teachings. Having refused to leave the city, he has been condemned to death. His friend Crito wishes to arrange his escape, but Socrates refuses, insisting that acting on principle is more important than the mere prolongation of life. The verdict of the court is the law, and he believes that he has a moral obligation to obey the law.

The reasons that Socrates gives for obeying the law, even though he is convinced of his own innocence, are important. These reasons are three in number.

First, he thought that he owed a debt of gratitude to the state. The state had acted like a parent to him; under its protection, he had been born, nurtured, and educated. Thus he owed the same obedience to the state that he did to his parents.

Second, by freely consenting to live in the state, he had entered into an agreement with the state; part of that agreement is to obey its laws. (John Locke makes this same argument.)

---

[1]From Plato, *Crito*, translated by Benjamin Jowett (Oxford: Oxford University Press, 1892).

Third, if all the citizens of Athens disobeyed the law whenever they disagreed with it, the result would be chaos and anarchy. If he expected and relied on other people to obey the law, Socrates ought to do so himself.

These are all good reasons, yet they may each be questioned. Concerning the first, consider this: If your parents order you to kill yourself, are you morally obligated to do so? Concerning the second: When we consent to live in a given society, does this mean that we contract to do *anything* the state orders us to do? (Locke, Nozick, and Rawls, in the reading selections that follow, argue that the powers of the state are limited by the specific terms of the social contract.) Finally, concerning the third: When we rely upon others to keep the law, do we really rely upon them to keep *every* law? If not, does fairness require that we obey every law, even one that appears to be unjust?

WHAT DO WE OWE TO OUR COUNTRY?

Why have you come at this hour, Crito? It must be quite early?

CRITO: Yes, certainly.

SOCRATES: What is the exact time?

CRITO: The dawn is breaking.

SOCRATES: I wonder that the keeper of the prison would let you in.

CRITO: He knows me, because I often come, Socrates; moreover, I have done him a kindness.

SOCRATES: And are you only just arrived?

CRITO: No, I came some time ago.

SOCRATES: Then why did you sit and say nothing, instead of at once awakening me?

CRITO: I should not have liked myself, Socrates, to be in such great trouble and unrest as you are— indeed I should not: I have been watching with amazement your peaceful slumbers; and for that reason I did not awake you, because I wished to minimize the pain. I have always thought you to be of a happy disposition; but never did I see anything like the easy, tranquil manner in which you bear this calamity.

SOCRATES: Why, Crito, when a man has reached my age he ought not to be repining at the approach of death.

CRITO: And yet other old men find themselves in similar misfortunes, and age does not prevent them from repining.

SOCRATES: That is true. But you have not told me why you come at this early hour.

CRITO: I come to bring you a message which is sad and painful; not, as I believe, to yourself, but to all of us who are your friends, and saddest of all to me.

SOCRATES: What? Has the ship come from Delos, on the arrival of which I am to die?

CRITO: No, the ship has not actually arrived, but she will probably be here today, as persons who have come from Sunium tell me that they left her there; and therefore tomorrow, Socrates, will be the last day of your life.

SOCRATES: Very well, Crito; if such is the will of God, I am willing; but my belief is that there will be a delay of a day.

CRITO: Why do you think so?

SOCRATES: I will tell you. I am to die on the day after the arrival of the ship.

CRITO: Yes; that is what the authorities say.

SOCRATES: But I do not think that the ship will be here until tomorrow; this I infer from a vision which I had last night, or rather only just now, when you fortunately allowed me to sleep.

CRITO: And what was the nature of the vision?

SOCRATES: There appeared to me the likeness of a woman, fair and comely, clothed in bright raiment, who called to me and said: O Socrates,

The third day hence to fertile Phthia shalt thou go.[1]

CRITO: What a singular dream, Socrates!

SOCRATES: There can be no doubt about the meaning, Crito, I think.

CRITO: Yes; the meaning is only too clear. But, oh! my beloved Socrates, let me entreat you once more to take my advice and escape. For if you die I shall not only lose a friend who can never be replaced, but there is another evil: people who do not know you and me will believe that I might have saved you if I had been willing to give money, but that I did not care. Now, can there be a worse disgrace than this—that I should be thought to value money more than the life of a friend? For the many will not be persuaded that I wanted you to escape, and that you refused.

SOCRATES: But why, my dear Crito, should we care about the opinion of the many? Good men, and they are the only persons who are worth considering, will think of these things truly as they occurred.

CRITO: But you see, Socrates, that the opinion of the many must be regarded, for what is now happening shows that they can do the greatest evil to anyone who has lost their good opinion.

SOCRATES: I only wish it were so, Crito; and that the many could do the greatest evil; for then they would also be able to do the greatest good—and what a fine thing this would be! But in reality they can do neither; for they cannot make a man either wise or foolish; and whatever they do is the result of chance.

CRITO: Well, I will not dispute with you; but please to tell me, Socrates, whether you are not acting out of regard to me and your other friends: are you not afraid that if you escape from prison we may get into trouble with the informers for having stolen you away, and lose either the whole or a great part of our property; or that even a worse evil may happen to us? Now, if you fear on our account, be at ease; for in order to save you, we ought surely to run this, or even a greater risk; be persuaded, then, and do as I say.

SOCRATES: Yes, Crito, that is one fear which you mention, but by no means the only one.

CRITO: Fear not—there are persons who are willing to get you out of prison at no great cost; and as for the informers, they are far from being exorbitant in their demands—a little money will satisfy them. My means, which are certainly ample, are at your service, and if you have a scruple about spending all mine, here are strangers who will give you the use of theirs; and one of them, Simmias the Theban,[2] has brought a large sum of money for this very purpose; and Cebes and many others are prepared to spend their money in helping you to escape. I say, therefore, do not hesitate on our account, and do not say, as you did in the court, that you will have a difficulty in knowing what to do with yourself anywhere else. For men will love you in other places to which you may go, and not in Athens only; there are friends of mine in Thessaly,[3] if you like to go to them, who will value and protect you, and no Thessalian will give you any trouble. Nor can I think that you are at all justified, Socrates, in betraying your own life when you might be saved; in acting thus you are playing into the hands of your enemies, who are hurrying on your destruction. And further I should say that you are deserting your own children; for you might bring

[2]Simmias and his friend Cebes, pupils of Socrates from the nearby city of Thebes, figure largely in the next dialogue, the *Phaedo*.

[3]A province of northern Greece.

[1]*Iliad*, IX, 363.

them up and educate them; instead of which you go away and leave them, and they will have to take their chance; and if they do not meet with the usual fate of orphans, there will be small thanks to you. No man should bring children into the world who is unwilling to persevere to the end in their nurture and education. But you appear to be choosing the easier part, not the better and manlier, which would have been more becoming in one who professes to care for virtue in all his actions, like yourself. And indeed, I am ashamed not only of you, but of us who are your friends, when I reflect that the whole business will be attributed entirely to our want of courage. The trial need never have come on, or might have been managed differently; and this last act, or crowning folly, will seem to have occurred through our negligence and cowardice, who might have saved you, if we had been good for anything; and you might have saved yourself, for there was no difficulty at all. See now, Socrates, how sad and discreditable are the consequences, both to us and you. Make up your mind then, or rather have your mind already made up, for the time of deliberation is over, and there is only one thing to be done, which must be done this very night, and, if we delay at all, will be no longer practicable or possible; I beseech you therefore, Socrates, be persuaded by me, and do as I say.

SOCRATES: Dear Crito, your zeal is invaluable, if a right one; but if wrong, the greater the zeal the greater the danger; and therefore we ought to consider whether I shall or shall not do as you say. For I am and always have been one of those natures who must be guided by reason, whatever the reason may be which upon reflection appears to me to be the best; and now that this chance has befallen me, I cannot repudiate my own words: the principles which I have hitherto honored and revered I still honor, and unless we can at once find other and better principles, I am certain not to agree with you; no, not even if the power of the multitude could inflict many more

imprisonments, confiscations, deaths, frightening us like children with hobgoblin terrors. What will be the fairest way of considering the question? Shall I return to your old argument about the opinions of men?—we were saying that some of them are to be regarded, and others not. Now were we right in maintaining this before I was condemned? And has the argument which was once good now proved to be talk for the sake of talking—mere childish nonsense? That is what I want to consider with your help, Crito; whether, under my present circumstances, the argument appears to be in any way different or not; and is to be allowed by me or disallowed. That argument, which, as I believe, is maintained by many persons of authority, was to the effect, as I was saying, that the opinions of some men are to be regarded, and of other men not to be regarded. Now you, Crito, are not going to die tomorrow—at least, there is no human probability of this—and therefore you are disinterested and not liable to be deceived by the circumstances in which you are placed. Tell me then, whether I am right in saying that some opinions, and the opinions of some men only, are to be valued, and that other opinions, and the opinions of other men, are not to be valued. I ask you whether I was right in maintaining this?

CRITO: Certainly

SOCRATES: The good are to be regarded, and not the bad?

CRITO: Yes.

SOCRATES: And the opinions of the wise are good, and the opinions of the unwise are evil?

CRITO: Certainly.

SOCRATES: And what was said about another matter? Is the pupil who devotes himself to the practice of gymnastics supposed to attend to the praise and blame and opinion of every man, or of one man only—his physician or trainer, whoever he may be?

CRITO: Of one man only.

SOCRATES: And he ought to fear the censure and

welcome the praise of that one only, and not of the many?

CRITO: Clearly so.

SOCRATES: And he ought to act and train, and eat and drink in the way which seems good to his single master who has understanding, rather than according to the opinion of all other men put together?

CRITO: True.

SOCRATES: And if he disobeys and disregards the opinion and approval of the one, and regards the opinion of the many who have no understanding, will he not suffer evil?

CRITO: Certainly he will.

SOCRATES: And what will the evil be, whither tending and what affecting, in the disobedient person?

CRITO: Clearly, affecting the body; that is what is destroyed by the evil.

SOCRATES: Very good; and is not this true, Crito, of other things which we need not separately enumerate? In questions of just and unjust, fair and foul, good and evil, which are the subjects of our present consultation, ought we to follow the opinion of the many and to fear them; or the opinion of the one man who has understanding? ought we not to fear and reverence him more than all the rest of the world: and if we desert him shall we not destroy and injure that principle in us which may be assumed to be improved by justice and deteriorated by injustice—there is such a principle?

CRITO: Certainly there is, Socrates.

SOCRATES: Take a parallel instance: if, acting under the advice of those who have no understanding, we destroy that which is improved by health and is deteriorated by disease, would life be worth having? And that which has been destroyed is— the body?

CRITO: Yes.

SOCRATES: Could we live, having an evil and corrupted body?

CRITO: Certainly not.

SOCRATES: And will life be worth having, if that higher part of man be destroyed, which is improved by justice and depraved by injustice? Do we suppose that principle, whatever it may be in man, which has to do with justice and injustice, to be inferior to the body?

CRITO: Certainly not.

SOCRATES: More honorable than the body?

CRITO: Far more.

SOCRATES: Then, my friend, we must not regard what the many say of us; but what he, the one man who has understanding of just and unjust, will say, and what the truth will say. And therefore you begin in error when you advise that we should regard the opinion of the many about just and unjust, good and evil, honorable and dishonorable.— "Well," someone will say, "but the many can kill us."

CRITO: Yes, Socrates; that will clearly be the answer.

SOCRATES: And it is true: but still I find with surprise that the old argument is unshaken as ever. And I should like to know whether I may say the same of another proposition—that not life, but a good life, is to be chiefly valued?

CRITO: Yes, that also remains unshaken.

SOCRATES: And a good life is equivalent to a just and honorable one—that holds also?

CRITO: Yes, it does.

SOCRATES: From these premises I proceed to argue the question whether I ought or ought not to try and escape without the consent of the Athenians: and if I am clearly right in escaping, then I will make the attempt; but if not, I will abstain. The other considerations which you mention, of money and loss of character and the duty of educating one's children, are, I fear, only the doctrines of the multitude, who would be as ready to restore people to life, if they were able, as they are to put them to death—and with as little reason. But now, since the argument has thus far prevailed, the only question which remains to be considered is whether we shall do rightly either in escaping or in suffering others to aid in our escape and paying them in money and thanks, or whether in reality we shall not do rightly; and if the latter, then death or any other calamity which may ensue on my remaining here must not be allowed to enter into the calculation.

CRITO: I think that you are right, Socrates; how then shall we proceed?

SOCRATES: Let us consider the matter together, and do you either refute me if you can, and I will be convinced; or else cease, my dear friend, from repeating to me that I ought to escape against the wishes of the Athenians: for I highly value your attempts to persuade me to do so, but I may not be persuaded against my own better judgment. And now please to consider my first position, and try how you can best answer me.

CRITO: I will.

SOCRATES: Are we to say that we are never intentionally to do wrong, or that in one way we ought and in another way we ought not to do wrong, or is doing wrong always evil and dishonorable, as I was just now saying, and as has been already acknowledged by us? Are all our former admissions which were made within a few days to be thrown away? And have we, at our age, been earnestly discoursing with one another all our life long only to discover that we are no better than children? Or, in spite of the opinion of the many, and in spite of consequences whether better or worse, shall we insist on the truth of what was then said, that injustice is always an evil and dishonor to him who acts unjustly? Shall we say so or not?

CRITO: Yes.

SOCRATES: Then we must do no wrong?

CRITO: Certainly not.

SOCRATES: Nor, when injured, injure in return, as the many imagine; for we must injure no one at all?

CRITO: Clearly not.

SOCRATES: Again, Crito, may we do evil?

CRITO: Surely not, Socrates.

SOCRATES: And what of doing evil in return for evil, which is the morality of the many—is that just or not?

CRITO: Not just.

SOCRATES: For doing evil to another is the same as injuring him?

CRITO: Very true.

SOCRATES: Then we ought not to retaliate or render evil for evil to anyone, whatever evil we may have suffered from him. But I would have you consider, Crito, whether you really mean what you are saying. For this opinion has never been held, and never will be held, by any considerable number of persons; and those who are agreed and those who are not agreed upon this point have no common ground, and can only despise one another when they see how widely they differ. Tell me, then, whether you agree with and assent to my first principle, that neither injury nor retaliation nor warding off evil by evil is ever right. And shall that be the premise of our argument? Or do you decline and dissent from this? For so I have ever thought, and continue to think; but, if you are of another opinion, let me hear what you have to say. If, however, you remain of the same mind as formerly, I will proceed to the next step.

CRITO: You may proceed, for I have not changed my mind.

SOCRATES: Then I will go on to the next point, which may be put in the form of a question: Ought a man to do what he admits to be right, or ought he to betray the right?

CRITO: He ought to do what he thinks right.

SOCRATES: But if this is true, what is the application? In leaving the prison against the will of the Athenians, do I wrong any? or rather do I not wrong those whom I ought least to wrong? Do I not desert the principles which were acknowledged by us to be just—what do you say?

CRITO: I cannot tell, Socrates; for I do not know.

SOCRATES: Then consider the matter in this way:

715

Imagine that I am about to play truant (you may call the proceeding by any name which you like), and the laws and the government come and interrogate me: "Tell us, Socrates," they say; "what are you about? are you not going by an act of yours to overturn us—the laws, and the whole state, as far as in you lies? Do you imagine that a state can subsist and not be overthrown, in which the decisions of law have no power, but are set aside and trampled upon by individuals?"—What will be our answer, Crito, to these and the like words? Anyone, and especially a rhetorician, will have a good deal to say on behalf of the law which requires a sentence to be carried out. He will argue that this law should not be set aside; and shall we reply, "Yes; but the state has injured us and given an unjust sentence." Suppose I say that?

CRITO: Very good, Socrates.

SOCRATES: "And was that our agreement with you?" the law would answer; "or were you to abide by the sentence of the state?" And if I were to express my astonishment at their words, the law would probably add: "Answer, Socrates, instead of opening your eyes: you are in the habit of asking and answering questions. Tell us: What complaint have you to make against us which justifies you in attempting to destroy us and the state? In the first place did we not bring you into existence? Your father married your mother by our aid and begat you. Say whether you have any objection to urge against those of us who regulate marriage?" None, I should reply. "Or against those of us who after birth regulate the nurture and education of children, in which you also were trained? Were not the laws, which have the charge of education, right in commanding your father to train you in music and gymnastic?" Right, I should reply. "Well then, since you were brought into the world and nurtured and educated by us, can you deny in the first place that you are our child and slave, as your fathers were before you? And if this is true you are not on

equal terms with us; nor can you think that you have a right to do to us what we are doing to you. Would you have any right to strike or revile or do any other evil to your father or your master, if you had one, because you have been struck or reviled by him, or received some other evil at his hands? You would not say this. And because we think right to destroy you, do you think that you have any right to destroy us in return, and your country as far as in you lies? Will you, O professor of true virtue, pretend that you are justified in this? Has a philosopher like you failed to discover that our country is more to be valued and higher and holier far than mother or father or any ancestor, and more to be regarded in the eyes of the gods and of men of understanding? also to be soothed, and gently and reverently entreated when angry, even more than a father, and either to be persuaded, or if not persuaded, to be obeyed? And when we are punished by her, whether with imprisonment or stripes, the punishment is to be endured in silence; and if she lead us to wounds or death in battle, thither we follow as is right; neither may anyone yield or retreat or leave his rank, but whether in battle or in a court of law, or in any other place, he must do what his city and his country order him; or he must change their view of what is just: and if he may do no violence to his father or mother, much less may he do violence to his country." What answer shall we make to this, Crito? Do the laws speak truly, or do they not?

CRITO: I think that they do.

SOCRATES: Then the laws will say: "Consider, Socrates, if we are speaking truly that in your present attempt you are going to do us an injury. For, having brought you into the world, and nurtured and educated you, and given you and every other citizen a share in every good which we had to give, we further proclaim to any Anthenian by the liberty which we allow him, that if he does not like us when he has become of age and has seen the ways of the city, and made our acquaintance, he may go where he pleases and take his goods with him. None of us laws will forbid him or interfere with him. Anyone who does not like us and the city, and who wants to emigrate to a colony or to any other city, may go where he likes, retaining his property. But he who has experience of the manner in which we order justice and administer the state, and still remains, has entered into an implied contract that he will do as we command him. And he who disobeys us is, as we maintain, thrice wrong; first, because in disobeying us he is disobeying his parents; secondly, because we are the authors of his education; thirdly, because he has made an agreement with us that he will duly obey our commands; and he neither obeys them nor convinces us that our commands are unjust; and we do not rudely impose them, but give him the alternative of obeying or convincing us; that is what we offer, and he does neither. These are the sort of accusations to which, as we were saying, you, Socrates, will be exposed if you accomplish your intentions; you, above all other Athenians."

Suppose now I ask, why I rather than anybody else? They will justly retort upon me that I above all other men have acknowledged the agreement. "There is clear proof," they will say, "Socrates, that we and the city were not displeasing to you. Of all Athenians you have been the most constant resident in the city, which, as you never leave, you may be supposed to love. For you never went out of the city either to see the games, except once when you went to the Isthmus,[4] or to any other place unless when you were on military service; nor did you travel as other men do. Nor had you any curiosity to know other states or their laws: your affections did not go beyond us and our state; we were your special favorites, and you acquiesced in our government of you;

and here in this city you begat your children, which is a proof of your satisfaction. Moreover, you might in the course of the trial, if you had liked, have fixed the penalty at banishment; the state which refuses to let you go now would have let you go then. But you pretended that you preferred death to exile, and that you were not unwilling to die. And now you have forgotten these fine sentiments, and pay no respect to us, the laws, of whom you are the destroyer; and are doing what only a miserable slave would do, running away and turning your back upon the compacts and agreements which you made as a citizen. And, first of all, answer this very question: Are we right in saying that you agreed to be governed according to us in deed, and not in word only? Is that true or not?" How shall we answer, Crito? Must we not assent?

CRITO: We cannot help it, Socrates.

SOCRATES: Then will they not say: "You, Socrates, are breaking the covenants and agreements which you made with us at your leisure, not in any haste or under any compulsion or deception, but after you have had seventy years to think of them, during which time you were at liberty to leave the city, if we were not to your mind, or if our covenants appeared to you to be unfair. You had your choice, and might have gone either to Lacedaemon[5] or Crete, both which states are often praised by you for their good government, or to some other Hellenic or foreign state. Whereas you, above all other Athenians, seemed to be so fond of the state, or, in other words, of us, her laws (and who would care about a state which has no laws?), that you never stirred out of her; the halt, the blind, the maimed were not more stationary in her than you were. And now you run away and forsake your agreements. Not so, Socrates, if you will take our advice; do not make yourself ridiculous by escaping out of the city.

[4]The Isthmian games, held on the Isthmus of Corinth in honor of the sea god Poseidon, were almost as famous as the Olympian games in honor of Zeus.

[5]Another name for Sparta.

"For just consider, if you transgress and err in this sort of way, what good will you do either to yourself or to your friends? That your friends will be driven into exile and deprived of citizenship, or will lose their property, is tolerably certain; and you yourself, if you fly to one of the neighboring cities, as, for example, Thebes or Megara, both of which are well governed, will come to them as an enemy, Socrates, and their government will be against you, and all patriotic citizens will cast an evil eye upon you as a subverter of the laws, and you will confirm in the minds of the judges the justice of their own condemnation of you. For he who is a corrupter of the laws is more than likely to be a corrupter of the young and foolish portion of mankind. Will you then flee from well-ordered cities and virtuous men? and is existence worth having on these terms? Or will you go to them without shame, and talk to them, Socrates? And what will you say to them? What you say here about virtue and justice and institutions and laws being the best things among men? Would that be decent of you? Surely not. But if you go away from well-governed states to Crito's friends in Thessaly, where there is great disorder and license, they will be charmed to hear the tale of your escape from prison, set off with ludicrous particulars of the manner in which you were wrapped in a goatskin or some other disguise, and metamorphosed as the manner is of runaways; but will there be no one to remind you that in your old age you were not ashamed to violate the most sacred laws from a miserable desire of a little more life? Perhaps not, if you keep them in a good temper; but if they are out of temper you will hear many degrading things; you will live, but how?—as the flatterer of all men, and the servant of all men; and doing what?—eating and drinking in Thessaly, having gone abroad in order that you may get a dinner. And where will be your fine sentiments about justice and virtue? Say that you wish to live for the sake of your children—you want to bring them up and educate them—will you take them into Thessaly and deprive them of Athenian citizenship? Is this the benefit which you will confer upon them? Or are you under the impression that they will be better cared for and educated here if you are still alive, although absent from them; for your friends will take care of them? Do you fancy that if you are an inhabitant of Thessaly they will take care of them, and if you are an inhabitant of the other world that they will not take care of them? Nay; but if they who call themselves friends are good for anything, they will—to be sure they will.

"Listen, then, Socrates, to us who have brought you up. Think not of life and children first, and of justice afterwards, but of justice first, that you may be justified before the princes of the world below. For neither will you nor any that belong to you be happier or holier or juster in this life, or happier in another, if you do as Crito bids. Now you depart in innocence, a sufferer and not a doer of evil; a victim, not of the laws, but of men. But if you go forth, returning evil for evil, and injury for injury, breaking the covenants and agreements which you have made with us, and wronging those whom you ought least of all to wrong, that is to say, yourself, your friends, your country, and us, we shall be angry with you while you live, and our brethren, the laws in the world below, will receive you as an enemy; for they will know that you have done your best to destroy us. Listen, then, to us and not to Crito."

This, dear Crito, is the voice which I seem to hear murmuring in my ears, like the sound of the flute in the ears of the mystic; that voice, I say, is humming in my ears, and prevents me from hearing any other. And I know that anything more which you may say will be vain. Yet speak, if you have anything to say.

CRITO: I have nothing to say, Socrates.

SOCRATES: Leave me then, Crito, to fulfill the will of God, and to follow whither he leads.

CHAPTER 64

JOHN LOCKE

LIMITED GOVERNMENT, LABOR, AND PROPERTY

Like Thomas Hobbes, John Locke[1] believed that government exists to protect our lives and property and arises through consent of the governed. Unlike Hobbes, Locke did not believe that the "signers" of the social contract gave away *all* their "natural rights" to the government in an attempt to escape the warlike *state of nature*. Whereas Hobbes gave us a ruler whose powers are derived from his subjects but who is not answerable to his subjects in the use of that power, Locke believed that such an absolute sovereign could pose more of a threat to individuals than the state of nature itself. What is needed, then, is the rule of law, capable of restricting even the activities of our rulers. Our very enjoyment of the benefits of government is a tacit consent to obey its laws. Rulers govern only by consent of the governed, and that consent is not unconditional. If a ruler abuses his power, citizens may "appeal to heaven," and resort to force to make things right.

As far as property is concerned, everyone owns his own body and labor; additional property is acquired when people "mix their labor" with unowned objects or trade their possessions for other desired objects.

[1]From John Locke, *Two Treatises on Government* (1690).

LIMITED GOVERNMENT, LABOR, AND PROPERTY

Of the State of Nature

4. To understand political power aright, and derive it from its original, we must consider what estate all men are naturally in, and that is, a state of perfect freedom to order their actions, and dispose of their possessions and persons as they think fit, within the bounds of the law of Nature, without asking leave or depending upon the will of any other man.

A state also of equality, wherein all the power and jurisdiction is reciprocal, no one have more than another, there being nothing more evident than that creatures of the same species and rank, promiscuously born to all the same advantages of Nature, and the use of the same faculties, should also be equal one amongst another, without subordination or subjection, unless the lord and master of them all should, by any manifest declaration of his will, set one above another, and confer on him, by an evident and clear appointment, an undoubted right to dominion and sovereignty.

•   •   •

6. But though this be a state of liberty, yet it is not a state of license; though man in that state have an uncontrollable liberty to dispose of his person or possessions, yet he has not liberty to destroy himself, or so much as any creature in his possession, but where some nobler use than its bare preservation calls for it. The state of Nature has a law of Nature to govern it, which obliges everyone, and reason, which is that law, teaches all mankind who will but consult it, that being all equal and independent, no one ought to harm another in his life, health, liberty or possessions; for men being all the workmanship of one omnipotent and infinitely wise Maker; all the servants of one sovereign Master, sent into the world by His order and about His business; they are His property, whose workmanship they are made to last during His, not one another's pleasure. And, being furnished with like faculties, sharing all in one community of Nature, there cannot be supposed any such subordination among us that may authorize us to destroy one another, as if we were made for one another's uses, as the inferior ranks of creatures are for ours. Everyone as he is bound to preserve himself, and not to quit his station willfully, so by the like reason, when his own preservation comes not in competition, ought he as much as he can to preserve the rest of mankind, and not unless it be to do justice on an offender, take away or impair the life, or what tends to the preservation of the life, the liberty, health, limb, or goods of another.

7. And that all men may be restrained from invading others' rights, and from doing hurt to one another, and the law of Nature be observed, which willeth the peace and preservation of all mankind, the execution of the law of Nature is in that state put into every man's hands, whereby everyone has a right to punish the transgressors of that law to such a degree as may hinder its violation. For the law of Nature would, as all other laws that concern men in this world, be in vain if there were nobody that in the state of Nature had a power to execute that law, and thereby preserve the innocent and restrain offenders; and if anyone in the state of Nature may punish another for any evil he has done, everyone may do so. For in that state of perfect equality, where naturally there is no superiority or jurisdiction of one over another, what any may do in prosecution of that law, everyone must needs have a right to do.

8.   And thus, in the state of Nature, one man comes by a power over another, but yet no absolute or arbitrary power to use a criminal, when he has got him in his hands, according to the passionate heats of boundless extravagancy of his own will, but only to retribute to him so far as calm reason and conscience dictate, what is proportionate to his transgression, which is so much as may serve for reparation and restraint. For these two are the only reasons why one man may lawfully do harm to another, which is that we call punishment. In transgressing the law of Nature, the offender declares himself to live by another rule than that of reason and common equity, which is that measure God has set to the actions of men for their mutual security, and so he becomes dangerous to mankind; the tie which is to secure them from injury and violence being slighted and broken by him, which being a trespass against the whole species, and the peace and safety of it, provided for by the law of Nature, every man upon this score, by the right he hath to preserve mankind in general, may restrain, or where it is necessary, destroy things noxious to them, and so may bring such evil on anyone who hath transgressed that law, as may make him repent the doing of it, and thereby deter him, and, by his example, others from doing the like mischief. And in this case, and upon this ground, every man hath a right to punish the offender, and be executioner of the law of Nature.

●   ●   ●

10.   Besides the crime which consists in violating the laws, and varying from the right rule of reason, whereby a man so far becomes degenerate, and declares himself to quit the principles of human nature and to be a noxious creature, there is commonly injury done, and some person or other, some other man, receives damage by his transgression; in which case, he who hath received any damage has (besides the right of punishment common to him, with other men) a particular right to seek reparation from him that hath done it. And any other person who finds it just may also join with him that is injured, and assist him in recovering from the offender so much as may make satisfaction for the harm he hath suffered.

●   ●   ●

13.   To this strange doctrine—viz., That in the state of Nature everyone has the executive power to the law of Nature—I doubt not but it will be objected that it is unreasonable for men to be judges in their own cases, that self-love will make men partial to themselves and their friends; and, on the other side, ill-nature, passion, and revenge will carry them too far in punishing others, and hence nothing but confusion and disorder will follow, and that therefore God hath certainly appointed government to restrain the partiality and violence of men. I easily grant that civil government is the proper remedy for the inconveniences of the state of Nature, which must certainly be great where men may be judges in their own case, since it is easy to be imagined that he who was so unjust as to do his brother an injury will scarce be so just as to condemn himself for it. But I shall desire those who make this objection to remember that absolute monarchs are but men; and if government is to be the remedy of those evils which necessarily follow from men being judges in their own cases, and the state of Nature is therefore not to be endured, I desire to know what kind of government that is, and how much better it is than the state of Nature, where one man commanding a multitude has the liberty to be judge in his own case, and may do to all his subjects whatever he pleases without the least question or control of those who execute his pleasure? and in whatsoever he doth, whether led by reason, mistake, or passion, must be submitted to? which men in the state of

Nature are not bound to do one to another. And if he that judges, judges amiss in his own way or any other case, he is answerable for it to the rest of mankind.

14. It is often asked as a mighty objection, where are, or ever were, there any men in such a state of Nature? To which it may suffice as an answer at present, that since all princes and rulers of "independent" governments all through the world are in a state of Nature, it is plain the world never was, nor never will be, without numbers of men in that state. I have named all governors of "independent" communities, whether they are, or are not, in league with others; for it is not every compact that puts an end to the state of Nature between men, but only this one of agreeing together mutually to enter into one community, and make one body politic; other promises and compacts men may make one with another, and yet still be in the state of Nature. The promises and bargains for truck, etc., between the two men in Soldania, in or between a Swiss and an Indian, in the woods of America, are binding to them, though they are perfectly in a state of Nature in reference to one another for truth, and keeping of faith belongs to men as men, and not as members of society.

• • •

Of Property

• • •

25. God, who hath given the world to men in common, hath also given them reason to make use of it to the best advantage of life and convenience. The earth and all that is therein is given to men for the support and comfort of their being. And though all the fruits it naturally produces, and beasts it feeds, belong to mankind in common, as they are produced by the spontaneous hand of Nature, and nobody has originally a private dominion exclusive of the rest of mankind in any of them, as they are thus in their natural state, yet being given for the use of men, there must of necessity be a means to appropriate them some way or other before they can be of any use, or at all beneficial, to any particular men. The fruit or venison which nourishes the wild Indian, who knows no enclosure, and is still a tenant in common, must be his, and so his— i.e., a part of him, that another can no longer have any right to it before it can do him any good for the support of his life.

26. Though the earth and all inferior creatures be common to all men, yet every man has a "property" in his own "person." This nobody has any right to but himself. The "labor" of his body and the "work" of his hands, we may say, are properly his. Whatsoever, then, he removes out of the state that Nature hath provided and left it in, he hath mixed his labor with it, and joined to it something that is his own, and thereby makes it his property. It being by him removed from the common state Nature placed it in, it hath by this labor something annexed to it that excludes the common right of other men. For this "labor" being the unquestionable property of the laborer, no man but he can have a right to what that is once joined to, at least where there is enough, and as good left in common for others.

27. He that is nourished by the acorns he picked up under an oak, or the apples he gathered from the trees in the wood, has certainly appropriated them to himself. Nobody can deny but the nourishment is his. I ask, then, when did they begin to be his? when he digested? or when he ate? or when he boiled? or when he brought them home? or when he picked them up? And it is plain, if the first gathering made them not his, nothing else could. . . .

30. It will, perhaps, be objected to this, that if gathering the acorns or other fruits of the earth, etc., makes a right to them, then anyone may engross as much as he will. To which I answer, Not so. The same law of Nature that

does by this means give us property, does also bound that property too. "God has given us all things richly." Is the voice of reason confirmed by inspiration? But how far has he given it us "to enjoy"? As much as anyone can make use of to any advantage of life before it spoils, so much he may by his labor fix a property in. Whatever is beyond this is more than his share, and belongs to others. Nothing was made by God for man to spoil or destroy. And thus considering the plenty of natural provisions there was a long time in the world, and the few spenders, and to how small a part of that provision the industry of one man could extend itself and engross it to the prejudice of others, especially keeping within the bounds set by reason of what might serve for his use, there could be then little room for quarrels or contentions about property so established.

31. But the chief matter of property being now not the fruits of the earth and the beasts that subsist on it, but the earth itself, as that which takes in and carries with it all the rest, I think it is plain that property in that too is acquired as the former. As much land as a man tills, plants, improves, cultivates, and can use the product of, so much is his property. He by his labor does, as it were, enclose it from the common. . . .

32. Nor was this appropriation of any parcel of land, by improving it, any prejudice to any other man, since there was still enough and as good left, and more than the yet unprovided could use. So that, in effect, there was never the less left for others because of his enclosure for himself. For he that leaves as much as another can make use of does as good as take nothing at all. Nobody could think himself injured by the drinking of another man, though he took a good draught, who had a whole river of the same water left him to quench his thirst. And the case of land and water, where there is enough of both, is perfectly the same.

• • •

40. Nor is it so strange as, perhaps, before consideration, it may appear, that the property of labor should be able to overbalance the community of land, for it is labor indeed that puts the difference of value on everything; and let anyone consider what the difference is between an acre of land planted with tobacco or sugar, sown with wheat or barley, and an acre of the same land lying in common without any husbandry upon it, and he will find that the improvement of labor makes the far greater part of the value. I think it will be but a very modest computation to say, that of the products of the earth useful to the life of man, nine-tenths are the effects of labor. Nay, if we will rightly estimate things as they come to our use, and cast up the several expenses about them—what in them is purely owning to Nature and what to labor—we shall find that in most of them ninety-nine hundredths are wholly to be put on the account of labor.

• • •

46. The greatest part of things really useful to the life of man, and such as the necessity of subsisting made the first commoners of the world look after—as it doth the Americans now—are generally things of short duration, such as—if they are not consumed by use—will decay and perish of themselves. Gold, silver, and diamonds are things that fancy or agreement hath put the value on, more than real use and the necessary support of life. Now of those good things which Nature hath provided in common, everyone has a right (as has been said) to as much as he could use, and had a property in all he could effect with his labor; all that his industry could extend to, to alter from the state Nature had put it in, was his. He that gathered a hundred bushels of acorns or apples had thereby a property in them; they were his goods as soon as gathered. He was only to look that he used them before they spoiled, else

he took more than his share, and robbed others. And, indeed, it was a foolish thing, as well as dishonest, to hoard up more than he could make use of. If he gave away a part to anybody else, so that it perished not uselessly in his possession, these he also made use of. And if he also bartered away plums that would have rotted in a week, for nuts that would last good for his eating a whole year, he did no injury; he wasted not the common stock; destroyed no part of the portion of good that belonged to others, so long as nothing perished uselessly in his hands. Again, if he would give his nuts for a piece of metal, pleased with its color, or exchange his sheep for shells, or wool for a sparkling pebble or a diamond, and keep those by him all his life, he invaded not the right of others; he might heap up as much of these durable things as he pleased; exceeding of the bounds of his just property not lying in the largeness of his possession, but the perishing of anything uselessly in it.

47. And thus came in the use of money; some lasting thing that men might keep without spoiling, and that, by mutual consent, men would take in exchange for the truly useful but perishable supports of life.

48. And as different degrees of industry were apt to give men possessions in different proportions, so this invention of money gave them the opportunity to continue and enlarge them. For supposing an island, separate from all possible commerce with the rest of the world, wherein there were but a hundred families, but there were sheep, horses, and cows, with other useful animals, wholesome fruits, and land enough for corn for a hundred thousand times as many, but nothing in the island, either because of its commonness or perishableness, fit to supply the place of money. What reason could anyone have there to enlarge his possessions beyond the use of his family, and a plentiful supply to its consumption,

either in what their own industry produced, or they could barter for like perishable, useful commodities with others? Where there is not something both lasting and scarce, and so valuable to be hoarded up, there men will not be apt to enlarge their possessions of land, were it never so rich, never so free for them to take. For I ask, what would a man value ten thousand or a hundred thousand acres of excellent land, ready cultivated and well stocked, too, with cattle, in the middle of the inland parts of America, where he had no hopes of commerce with other parts of the world, to draw money to him by the sale of the product? It would not be worth the enclosing, and we should see him give up again to the wild common of Nature whatever was more than would supply the conveniences of life, to be had there for him and his family.

●   ●   ●

Of the Beginning of Political Societies

95. Men being, as has been said, by nature all free, equal, and independent, no one can be put out of this estate and subjected to the political power of another without his own consent, which is done by agreeing with other men, to join and unite into a community for their comfortable, safe, and peaceable living, one amongst another, in a secure enjoyment of their properties, and a greater security against any that are not of it. This any number of men may do, because it injures not the freedom of the rest; they are left, as they were, in the liberty of the state of Nature. When any number of men have so consented to make one community or government, they are thereby presently incorporated, and make one body politic, wherein the majority have a right to act and conclude the rest.

96. For, when any number of men have, by the consent of every individual, made a commu-

nity, they have thereby made that community one body, with a power to act as one body, which is only by the will and determination of the majority. For that which acts any community, being only the consent of the individuals of it, and it being one body, must move one way, it is necessary the body should move that way wither the greater force carries it, which is the consent of the majority, or else it is impossible it should act or continue one body, one community, which the consent of every individual that united into it agreed that it should; and so everyone is bound by that consent to be concluded by the majority. And therefore we see that in assemblies empowered to act by positive laws where no number is set by that positive law which empowers them, the act of the majority passes for the act of the whole, and of course determines as having, by the law of Nature and reason, the power of the whole.

•   •   •

98.   For if the consent of the majority shall not in reason be received as the act of the whole, and conclude every individual, nothing but the consent of every individual can make anything to be the act of the whole, which, considering the infirmities of health and avocations of business, which in a number though much less than that of a commonwealth, will necessarily keep many away from the public assembly; and the variety of opinions and contrariety of interests which unavoidably happen in all collections of men, it is next impossible ever to be had. And, therefore, if coming into society be upon such terms, it will be only Cato's coming into the theater, *tantum ut exiret.*[1] Such a constitution as this would make the mighty leviathan of a shorter duration than the feeblest creatures, and not let it outlast the day it was born in, which cannot be supposed till we

[1]Merely to go out again.

can think that rational creatures should desire and constitute societies only to be dissolved. For where the majority cannot conclude the rest, there they cannot act as one body, and consequently will be immediately dissolved again.

•   •   •

119.   Every man being, as has been showed, naturally free, and nothing being able to put him into subjection to any earthly power, but only his own consent, it is to be considered what shall be understood to be a sufficient declaration of a man's consent to make him subject to the laws of any government. There is a common distinction of an express and a tacit consent, which will concern our present case. Nobody doubts but an express consent of any man, entering into any society, makes him a perfect member of that society, a subject of that government. The difficulty is, what ought to be looked upon as a tacit consent, and how far it binds—i.e., how far anyone shall be looked on to have consented, and thereby submitted to any government, where he has made no expressions of it at all. And to this I say, that every man that hath any possession or enjoyment of any part of the dominions of any government doth hereby give his tacit consent, and is as far forth obliged to obedience to the laws of that government, during such enjoyment, as anyone under it, whether this his possession be of land to him and his heirs forever, or a lodging only for a week; or whether it be barely traveling freely on the highway; and, in effect, it reaches as far as the very being of anyone within the territories of that government.

•   •   •

122.   But submitting to the laws of any country, living quietly and enjoying privileges and protection under them, makes not a man a member of that society; it is only a local protection and homage due to and from all those who,

not being in a state of war, come within the territories belonging to any government, to all parts whereof the force of its law extends. But this no more makes a man a member of that society, a perpetual subject of that commonwealth, than it would make a man a subject to another in whose family he found it convenient to abide for some time, though, whilst he continued in it, he were obliged to comply with the laws and submit to the government he found there. And thus we see that foreigners, by living all their lives under another government, and enjoying the privileges and protection of it, though they are bound, even in conscience, to submit to its administration as far forth as any denizen, yet do not thereby come to be subjects or members of that commonwealth. Nothing can make any man so but his actually entering into it by positive engagement and express promise and compact. This is that which, I think, concerning the beginning of political societies, and that consent which makes anyone a member of any commonwealth.

Of the Ends of Political Society and Government

123.   If a man in the state of Nature be so free as has been said, if he be absolute lord of his own person and possessions, equal to the greatest and subject to nobody, why will he part with his freedom, this empire, and subject himself to the dominion and control of any other power? To which it is obvious to answer, that though in the state of Nature he has such a right, yet the enjoyment of it is very uncertain and constantly exposed to the invasion of others; for all being kings as much as he, every man his equal, and the greater part no strict observers of equity and justice, the enjoyment of the property he has in this state is very unsafe, very insecure. This makes him willing to quit this condition which, however free, is full of fears and continual dangers; and

it is not without reason that he seeks out and is willing to join in society with others who are already united, or have a mind to unite for the mutual preservation of their lives, liberties and estates, which I call by the general name—property.

124.   The great and chief end, therefore, of men uniting into commonwealths, and putting themselves under government, is the preservation of their property; to which in the state of Nature there are many things wanting.

Firstly, there wants an established, settled, known law, received and allowed by common consent to be the standard of right and wrong, and the common measure to decide all controversies between them. For though the law of Nature be plain and intelligible to all rational creatures, yet men, being biased by their interest, as well as ignorant for want of study of it, are not apt to allow of it as a law binding to them in the application of it to their particular cases.

125.   Secondly, in the state of Nature there wants a known and indifferent judge, with authority to determine all differences according to the established law. For everyone in that state being both judge and executioner of the law of Nature, men being partial to themselves, passion and revenge is very apt to carry them too far, and with too much heat in their own cases, as well as negligence and unconcernedness, make them too remiss in other men's.

126.   Thirdly, in the state of Nature there often wants power to back and support the sentence when right, and to give it due execution. They who by any injustice offended will seldom fail where they are able by force to make good their injustice. Such resistance many times makes the punishment dangerous, and frequently destructive to those who attempt it.

• • •

128. For in the state of Nature to omit the liberty he has of innocent delights, a man has two powers. The first is to do whatsoever he thinks fit for the preservation of himself and others within the permission of the law of Nature; by which law, common to them all, he and all the rest of mankind are one community, make up one society distinct from all other creatures, and were it not for the corruption and viciousness of degenerate men, there would be no need of any other, no necessity that men should separate from this great and natural community, and associate into lesser combinations. The other power a man has in the state of Nature is the power to punish the crimes committed against that law. Both these he gives up when he joins in a private, if I may so call it, or particular political society, and incorporates into any commonwealth separate from the rest of mankind.

129. The first power—viz., of doing whatsoever he thought fit for the preservation of himself and the rest of mankind, he gives up to be regulated by laws made by the society, so far forth as the preservation of himself and the rest of that society shall require; which laws of the society in many things confine the liberty he had by the law of Nature.

130. Secondly, the power of punishing he wholly gives up, and engages his natural force, which he might before employ in the execution of the law of Nature, by his own single authority, as he thought fit, to assist the executive power of the society as the law thereof shall require. For being now in a new state, wherein he is to enjoy many conveniences from the labor, assistance, and society of others in the same community, as well as protection from its whole strength, he is to part also with as much of his natural liberty, in providing for himself, as the good, prosperity, and safety of the society shall require, which is not only necessary but just, since the other members of the society do the like.

• • •

Of the Extent of the Legislative Power

• • •

135. Though the legislative, whether placed in one or more, whether it be always in being or only by intervals, though it be the supreme power in every commonwealth, yet, first, it is not, nor can possibly be, absolutely arbitrary over the lives and fortunes of the people. For it being but the joint power of every member of the society given up to that person or assembly which is legislator, it can be no more than those persons had in a state of Nature before they entered into society, and gave it up to the community. For nobody can transfer to another more power than he has in himself, and nobody has an absolute arbitrary power over himself, or over any other, to destroy his own life, or take away the life or property of another. A man, as has been proved, cannot subject himself to the arbitrary power of another; and having, in the state of Nature, no arbitrary power over the life, liberty, or possession of another, but only so much as the law of Nature gave him for the preservation of himself and the rest of mankind, this is all he does, or can give up to the commonwealth, and by it to the legislative power, so that the legislative can have no more than this. Their power in the utmost bounds of it is limited to the public good of the society. It is a power that has no other end but preservation, and therefore can never have a right to destroy, enslave, or designedly to impoverish the subjects; the obligations of the law of Nature cease not in society, but only in many cases are drawn closer, and have, by human laws, known penalties annexed to them to enforce their observation. Thus the law of Nature stands as an eternal rule to all men, legislators as well as others. The rules that they make for other men's actions must, as well as their own and other men's actions, be conformable to the law of Nature—

i.e., to the will of God, of which that is a declaration, and the fundamental law of Nature being the preservation of mankind, no human sanction can be good or valid against it.

136.   Secondly, the legislative or supreme authority cannot assume to itself a power to rule by extemporary arbitrary decrees, but is bound to dispense justice and decide the rights of the subject by promulgated standing laws, and known authorized judges. For the law of Nature being unwritten, and so nowhere to be found but in the minds of men, they who, through passion or interest, shall miscite or misapply it, cannot so easily be convinced of their mistake where there is no established judge; and so it serves not as it ought, to determine the rights and fence the properties of those that live under it, especially where everyone is judge, interpreter, and executioner of it too, and that in his own case; and he that has right on his side, having ordinarily but his own single strength, hath not force enough to defend himself from injuries or punish delinquents. . . .

137.   Absolute arbitrary power, or governing without settled standing laws, can neither of them consist with the ends of society and government, which men would not quit the freedom of the state of Nature for, and tie themselves up under, were it not to preserve their lives, liberties, and fortunes, and by stated rules of right and property to secure their peace and quiet. It cannot be supposed that they should intend, had they a power so to do, to give anyone or more an absolute arbitrary power over their persons and estates, and put a force into the magistrate's hand to execute his unlimited will arbitrarily upon them; this were to put themselves into a worse condition than the state of Nature, wherein they had a liberty to defend their right against the injuries of others, and were upon equal terms of force to maintain it, whether invaded by a single

man or many in combination. Whereas by supposing they have given up themselves to the absolute arbitrary power and will of a legislator, they have disarmed themselves, and armed him to make a prey of them when he pleases; he being in a much worse condition that is exposed to the arbitrary power of one man who has the command of a hundred thousand than he that is exposed to the arbitrary power of a hundred thousand single men, nobody being secure, that his will who has such a command is better than that of other men, though his force be a hundred thousand times stronger. And, therefore, whatever form the commonwealth is under, the ruling power ought to govern by declared and received laws, and not be extemporary dictates and undetermined resolutions, for then mankind will be in a far worse condition than in the state of Nature if they shall have armed one or a few men with the joint power of a multitude, to force them to obey at pleasure the exorbitant and unlimited decrees of their sudden thoughts, or unrestrained, and till that moment, unknown wills, without having any measures set down which may guide and justify their actions. For all the power the government has, being only for the good of the society, as it ought not to be arbitrary and at pleasure, so it ought to be exercised by established and promulgated laws, that both the people may know their duty, and be safe and secure within the limits of the law, and the rulers, too, kept within their due bounds, and not be tempted by the power they have in their hands to employ it to purposes, and by such measures as they would not have known, and own not willingly.

138.   Thirdly, the supreme power cannot take from any man any part of his property without his own consent. For the preservation of property being the end of government, and that for which men enter into society, it necessarily

supposes and requires that the people should have property, without which they must be supposed to lose that by entering into society which was the end for which they entered into it; too gross an absurdity for any man to own. . . .

140.   It is true governments cannot be supported without great charge, and it is fit everyone who enjoys his share of the protection should pay out of his estate his proportion for the maintenance of it. But still it must be with his own consent—i.e., the consent of the majority, giving it either by themselves or their representatives chosen by them; for if anyone shall claim a power to lay and levy taxes on the people by his own authority, and without such consent of the people, he thereby invades the fundamental law of property, and subverts the end of government. For what property have I in that which another may by right take when he pleases to himself?

141.   Fourthly, the legislative cannot transfer the power of making laws to any other hands, for it being but a delegated power from the people, they who have it cannot pass it over to others. The people alone can appoint the form of the commonwealth, which is by constituting the legislative, and appointing in whose hands that shall be. And when the people have said, "We will submit, and be governed by laws made by such men, and in such forms," nobody else can say other men shall make laws for them; nor can they be bound by any laws but such as are enacted by those whom they have chosen and authorized to make laws for them.

•   •   •

Of the Dissolution of Government

•   •   •

222.   The reason why men enter into society is the preservation of their property; and the end while they choose and authorize a legislative

is that there may be laws made, and rules set, as guards and fences to the properties of all the society, to limit the power and moderate the dominion of every part and member of the society. For since it can never be supposed to be the will of the society that the legislative should have a power to destroy that which everyone designs to secure by entering into society, and for which the people submitted themselves to legislators of their own making: whenever the legislators endeavor to take away and destroy the property of the people, or to reduce them to slavery under arbitrary power, they put themselves into a state of war with the people, who are thereupon absolved from any farther obedience, and are left to the common refuge which God hath provided for all men against force and violence. Whensoever, therefore, the legislative shall transgress this fundamental rule of society, and either by ambition, fear, folly, or corruption, endeavor to grasp themselves, or put into the hands of any other, an absolute power over the lives, liberties, and estates of the people, by this breach of trust they forfeit the power the people had put into their hands for quite contrary ends, and it devolves to the people, who have a right to resume their original liberty, and by the establishment of a new legislative (such as they shall think fit), provide for their own safety and security, which is the end for which they are in society.

•   •   •

240.   Here it is like the common question will be made: Who shall be judge whether the prince or legislative act contrary to their trust? This, perhaps, illaffected and factious men may spread amongst the people, when the prince only makes use of his due prerogative. To this I reply, The people shall be judge; for who shall be judge whether his trustee or deputy acts well and

according to the trust reposed in him, but he who deputes him and must, by having deputed him, have still a power to discard him when he fails in his trust? If this be reasonable in particular cases of private men, why should it be otherwise in that of the greatest moment, where the welfare of millions is concerned and also where the evil, if not prevented, is greater, and the redress very difficult, dear, and dangerous?

241.　But, farther, this question, Who shall be judge? cannot mean that there is no judge at all. For where there is no judicature on earth to decide controversies amongst men, God in heaven is judge. He alone, it is true, is judge of the right. But every man is judge for himself, as in all other cases so in this, whether another hath put himself into a state of war with him, and whether he should appeal to the supreme Judge, as Jephtha did.

242.　If a controversy arise betwixt a prince and some of the people in a matter where the law is silent or doubtful, and the thing be of great consequence, I should think the proper umpire in such a case should be the body of the people. For in such cases where the prince hath a trust reposed in him, and is dispensed from the common, ordinary rules of the law, there, if any men find themselves aggrieved, and think the prince acts contrary to, or beyond that trust, who so proper to judge as the body of the people (who at first lodged that trust in him) how far they meant it should extend? But if the prince, or whoever they be in the administration, decline that way of determination, the appeal then lies nowhere but to Heaven. Force between either persons who have no known superior on earth, or which permits no appeal to a judge on earth, being properly a state of war, wherein the appeal lies only to Heaven; and in that state the injured party must judge for himself when he will think fit to make use of that appeal and put himself upon it.

243.　To conclude. The power that every individual gave the society when he entered into it can never revert to the individuals again, as long as the society lasts, but will always remain in the community; because without this there can be no community—no commonwealth, which is contrary to the original agreement; so also when the society hath placed the legislative in any assembly of men, to continue in them and their successors, with direction and authority for providing such successors, the legislative can never revert to the people whilst that government lasts; because, having provided a legislative with power to continue forever, they have given up their political power to the legislative, and cannot resume it. But if they have set limits to the duration of their legislative, and made this supreme power in any person or assembly only temporary; or else when, by the miscarriages of those in authority, it is forfeited; upon the forfeiture of their rulers, or at the determination of the time set, it reverts to the society, and the people have a right to act as supreme, and continue the legislative in themselves or place it in a new form, or new hands, as they think good.

CHAPTER 65

KARL MARX AND FRIEDRICH ENGELS

THE COMMUNIST MANIFESTO

Karl Marx (1818–1883), one of the most influential philosophers in history, was born in Germany. He studied law at the University of Bonn, philosophy and history at the University of Berlin, and received his doctorate in philosophy from the University of Jena. Because of his radical political views, he was unable to teach philosophy in Germany. After a brief career in journalism, the paper which he was editing was suppressed by the authorities and he was expelled. After living for a time in Paris (where he met Friedrich Engels, with whom he would have a partnership lasting nearly forty years) and Brussels, he finally settled in 1849 in London, where he lived until his death, having found freedom to write and express his views. It was in London, in the library of the British Museum, that Marx wrote his major work, *Das Capital* (1867, 1885, 1895). Only one volume of this massive three-volume work appeared during Marx's lifetime; the last two volumes were edited by the faithful Engels. *Das Capital* contains Marx's sustained critique of capitalism and bourgeois society; it also addresses topics of general interest, such as the future of the family, education, and newly emerging forms of technology.

It is frequently argued that there are "two Marx's." The young Marx, still disentangling himself from Hegel's view of dialectic and history, wrote works that were philosophical and humanistic in tone. The views of the young Marx, frequently cited by democratic socialists and others interested in establishing distance from the Stalinist version of communism, remained largely unknown until the 1930s, when they were rediscovered, translated, and disseminated. The *Economic and Philosophical Manuscripts of 1844* and *The German Ideology* belong to this early period. The more mature Marx turned increasingly to economic history, attempting to work out a strict scientific account of economic forces.

Friedrich Engels (1820–1895), son of a wealthy German industrialist, is best known as Marx's collaborator, friend, and financial backer. As a young man, Engels had planned to be a poet; when he met Marx he abandoned his romantic view of German nationalism and all plans of succeeding his father in the family business. A forceful, eloquent writer, Engels' numerous writings include *Socialism, Utopian and Scientific* (1883), *The Origin of the Family, Private Property and the State* (1884), and *Principles of Communism* (1925). He is best known as the co-author of the stirring *Manifesto of the Communist Party*, originally published in London in 1848. The *Manifesto* has become the most widely read and influential single document of modern socialism.

In a speech given at the graveside of his friend, Engels had this to say:

> On the 14th of March, at a quarter to three in the afternoon, the greatest living thinker ceased to think. He had been left alone for scarcely two minutes, and when we came back we found him in an armchair, peacefully gone to sleep— but forever. . . .

Just as Darwin discovered the law of evolution in organic nature, so Marx discovered the law of evolution in human history; he discovered the simple fact, hitherto concealed by the overgrowth of ideology, that humankind must first eat and drink, have shelter and clothing, before it can pursue politics, science, religion, art, etc.; therefore the production of the immediate material means of subsistence and consequently the degree of economic development attained by a given people or during a given epoch, form the foundation upon which the state institutions, the legal conceptions, the art and even the religious ideas of the people concerned have been evolved, and in the light of which these things must therefore be explained, instead of vice-versa.

In the *Manifesto*[1] Marx and Engels present an overview of their interpretation of history. The economic and productive arrangements of a given society determine that society's religion, philosophy, and legal system. In the course of history, each set of economic arrangements has contained within it the seeds of its own destruction. Hence the city-states of classical antiquity gave way to the more

---

[1]Reprinted from *The Marx-Engels Reader*, second edition, edited by Robert C. Tucker, by permission of W. W. Norton & Company, Inc. Copyright © 1978, 1972 by W. W. Norton & Company, Inc.

hierarchical organization of feudal society; feudalism in turn gave rise to capitalism. Capitalism, too, contains an inner contradiction. By bringing workers together even as it forces them to compete, it fosters an ever-increasing poverty in an environment of abundance; it also generates extreme cycles of prosperity and depression. In time, capitalism will self-destruct, as workers refuse to be exploited by their capitalistic masters and refuse to accept their alienation from their own labor and its products.

THE COMMUNIST MANIFESTO

Bourgeois and Proletarians

THE HISTORY of all hitherto existing society is the history of class struggles.

Freeman and slave, patrician and plebeian, lord and serf, guild-master and journeyman, in a word, oppressor and oppressed, stood in constant opposition to one another, carried on an uninterrupted, now hidden, now open fight, a fight that each time ended, either in a revolutionary re-constitution of society at large, or in the common ruin of the contending classes.

In the earlier epochs of history, we find almost everywhere a complicated arrangement of society into various orders, a manifold gradation of social rank. In ancient Rome we have patricians, knights, plebeians, slaves; in the Middle Ages, feudal lords, vassals, guild-masters, journeymen, apprentices, serfs; in almost all of these classes, again, subordinate gradations.

The modern bourgeois society that has sprouted from the ruins of feudal society has not done away with class antagonisms. It has but established new classes, new conditions of oppression, new forms of struggle in place of the old ones.

Our epoch, the epoch of the bourgeoisie, possesses, however, this distinctive feature: it has simplified the class antagonisms: Society as a whole is more and more splitting up into two great hostile camps, into two great classes directly facing each other: Bourgeoisie and Proletariat.

*   *   *

The bourgeoisie, wherever it has got the upper hand, has put an end to all feudal, patriarchal, idyllic relations. It has pitilessly torn asunder the motley feudal ties that bound man to his "natural superiors," and has left remaining no other nexus between man and man than naked self-interest, than callous "cash payment." It has drowned the most heavenly ecstasies of religious fervour, of chivalrous enthusiasm, of philistine sentimentalism, in the icy water of egotistical calculation. It has resolved personal worth into exchange value, and in place of the numberless indefeasible chartered freedoms, has set up that single, unconscionable freedom—Free Trade. In one word, for exploitation, veiled by religious and political illusions, it has substituted naked, shameless, direct, brutal exploitation.

*   *   *

The bourgeoisie has through its exploitation of the world-market given a cosmopolitan character to production and consumption in every country. To the great chagrin of Reactionists, it has drawn from under the feet of industry the national ground on which it stood. All old-established national industries have been destroyed or are daily being destroyed. They are dislodged by new industries, whose introduction becomes a life and death question for all civilised nations, by industries that no longer work up indigenous raw material, but raw material drawn from the remotest zones; industries whose products are consumed, not only at home, but in every quarter of the globe. In place of the old wants, satisfied by the productions of the country, we find new wants, requiring for their satisfaction the products of distant lands and climes. In place of the old local and national seclusion and self-sufficiency, we have intercourse in every direction, universal inter-dependence of nations. And as in material, so also in intellectual production. The intellectual creations of individual nations become common property. National one-sidedness and narrow-mindedness become more and more impossible, and from the numerous national and local literatures, there arises a world literature.

• • •

The bourgeoisie has subjected the country to the rule of the towns. It has created enormous cities, has greatly increased the urban population as compared with the rural, and has thus rescued a considerable part of the population from the idiocy of rural life. Just as it has made the country dependent on the towns, so it has made barbarian and semi-barbarian countries dependent on the civilised ones, nations and peasants on nations of bourgeois, the East on the West.

• • •

The bourgeoisie, during its rule of scarce one hundred years, has created more massive and more colossal productive forces than have all preceding generations together. Subjection of Nature's forces to man, machinery, application of

chemistry to industry and agriculture, steam-navigation, railways, electric telegraphs, clearing of whole continents for cultivation, canalisation of rivers, whole populations conjured out of the ground—what earlier century had even a presentiment that such productive forces slumbered in the lap of social labour?

We see then: the means of production and of exchange, on whose foundation the bourgeoisie built itself up, were generated in feudal society. At a certain stage in the development of these means of production and of exchange, the conditions under which feudal society produced and exchanged, the feudal organisation of agriculture and manufacturing industry, in one word, the feudal relations of property became no longer compatible with the already developed productive forces; they became so many fetters. They had to be burst asunder; they were burst asunder.

Into their place stepped free competition, accompanied by a social and political constitution adapted to it, and by the economical and political sway of the bourgeois class.

A similar movement is going on before our own eyes. Modern bourgeois society with its relations of production, of exchange and of property, a society that has conjured up such gigantic means of production and of exchange, is like the sorcerer, who is no longer able to control the powers of the nether world whom he has called up by his spells. For many a decade past the history of industry and commerce is but the history of the revolt of modern productive forces against modern conditions of production, against the property relations that are the conditions for the existence of the bourgeoisie and of its rule. It is enough to mention the commercial crisis that by their periodical return put on its trial, each time more threateningly, the existence of the entire bourgeois society. In these crises a great part not only of the existing products, but also of the previously created productive forces, as periodically destroyed. In these crises there breaks out an epidemic that, in all earlier epochs, would have seemed an absurdity—the epidemic of over-production. Society suddenly finds itself put back into a state of momentary barbarism; it appears as if a famine, a universal war of devastation had cut off the supply of every means of subsistence; industry and commerce seem to be destroyed; and why? Because there is too much civilisation, too much means of subsistence, too much industry, too much commerce. The productive forces at the disposal of society no longer tend to further the development of the conditions of bourgeois property; on the contrary, they have become too powerful for these conditions, by which they are fettered, and so soon as they overcome these fetters, they bring disorder into the whole of bourgeois society, endanger the existence of bourgeois property. The conditions of bourgeois society are too narrow to comprise the wealth created by them. And how does the bourgeoisie get over these crises? On the one hand by enforced destruction of a mass of productive forces; on the other, by the conquest of new markets, and by the more thorough exploitation of the old ones. That is to say, by paving the way for more extensive and more destructive crises, and by diminishing the means whereby crises are prevented.

The weapons with which the bourgeoisie felled feudalism to the ground are now turned against the bourgeoisie itself.

But not only has the bourgeoisie forged the weapons that bring death to itself; it has also called into existence the men who are to wield those weapons—the modern working class—the proletarians.

In proportion as the bourgeoisie, i.e., capital, is developed, in the same proportion is the proletariat, the modern working class, developed—a class of labourers, who live only so long as they find work, and who find work only so long as their labour increases capital. These labourers, who must sell themselves piece-meal, are a commodity, like every other article of commerce, and are consequently exposed to all the vicissitudes of competition, to all the fluctuations of the market.

Owing to the extensive use of machinery and to division of labour, the work of the proletarians has lost all individual character, and consequently, all charm for the workman. He becomes an appendage of the machine, and it is only the most simple, most monotonous, and most easily acquired knack, that is required of him. Hence, the cost of production of a workman is restricted, almost entirely, to the means of subsistence that he requires for his maintenance, and for the propagation of his race. But the price of a commodity, and therefore also of labour, is equal to its cost of production. In proportion, therefore, as the repulsiveness of the work increases, the wage decreases. Nay more, in proportion as the use of machinery and division of labour increases, in the same proportion the burden of toil also increases, whether by prolongation of the working hours, by increase of the work exacted in a given time or by increased speed of the machinery, etc.

●　●　●

The lower strata of the middle class—the small tradespeople, shopkeepers, and retired tradesmen generally, the handicraftsmen and peasants—all these sink gradually into the proletariat, partly because their diminutive capital does not suffice for the scale on which Modern Industry is carried on, and is swamped in the competition with the large capitalists, partly because their specialised skill is rendered worthless by new methods of production. Thus the proletariat is recruited from all classes of the population.

• • •

All the preceding classes that got the upper hand, sought to fortify their already acquired status by subjecting society at large to their conditions of appropriation. The proletarians cannot become masters of the productive forces of society, except by abolishing their own previous mode of appropriation, and thereby also every other previous mode of appropriation. They have nothing of their own to secure and to fortify; their mission is to destroy all previous securities for, and insurances of, individual property.

All previous historical movements were movements of minorities, or in the interests of minorities. The proletarian movement is the self-conscious, independent movement of the immense majority, in the interests of the immense majority. The proletariat, the lowest stratum of our present society, cannot stir, cannot raise itself up, without the whole superincumbent strata of official society being sprung into the air.

• • •

Hitherto, every form of society has been based, as we have already seen, on the antagonism of oppressing and oppressed classes. But in order to oppress a class, certain conditions must be assured to it under which it can, at least, continue its slavish existence. The serf, in the period of serfdom, raised himself to membership in the commune, just as the petty bourgeois, under the yoke of feudal absolutism, managed to develop into a bourgeois. The modern labourer, on the contrary, instead of rising with the progress of industry, sinks deeper and deeper below the conditions of existence of his own class. He becomes a pauper, and pauperism develops more rapidly than population and wealth. And here it becomes evident, that the bourgeoisie is unfit any longer to be the ruling class in society, and to impose its conditions of existence upon society as an over-riding law. It is unfit to rule because it is incompetent to assure an existence to its slave within his slavery, because it cannot help letting him sink into such a state, that it has to feed him, instead of being fed by him. Society can no longer live under his bourgeoisie, in other words, its existence is no longer compatible with society.

The essential condition for the existence, and for the sway of the bourgeois class, is the formation and augmentation of capital; the condition for capital is wage-labour. Wage-labour rests exclusively on competition between the labourers. The advance of industry, whose involuntary promoter is the bourgeoisie, replaces the isolation of the labourers, due to competition, by their revolutionary combination, due to association. The development of Modern Industry, therefore, cuts from under its feet the very foundation on which the bourgeoisie produces and appropriates products. What the bourgeoisie, therefore, produces, above all, is its own grave-diggers. Its fall and the victory of the proletariat are equally inevitable.

Proletarians and Communists

• • •

The Communists are distinguished from the other working-class parties by this only: (1) In the national struggles of the proletarians of the different countries, they point out and bring to the front the common interests of the entire proletariat, independently of all nationality. (2) In the various stages of development which the struggle of the working class against the bourgeoisie has to pass through, they always and everywhere represent the interests of the movement as a whole.

The distinguishing feature of Communism is not the abolition of property generally, but the abolition of bourgeois property. But modern bourgeois private property is the final and most complete expression of the system of producing and appropriating products, that is based on class antagonisms, on the exploitation of the many by the few.

In this sense, the theory of the Communists may be summed up in the single sentence: Abolition of private property.

We Communists have been reproached with the desire of abolishing the right of personally acquiring property as the fruit of a man's own labour, which property is alleged to be the groundwork of all personal freedom, activity and independence.

Hard-won, self-acquired, self-earned property! Do you mean the property of the petty artisan and of the small peasant, a form of property that preceded the bourgeois form? There is no need to abolish that; the development of industry has to a great extent already destroyed it, and is still destroying it daily.

Or do you mean modern bourgeois private property?

But does wage-labour create any property for the labourer? Not a bit. It creates capital, *i.e.*, that kind of property which exploits wage-labour, and which cannot increase except upon condition of begetting a new supply of wage-labour for fresh exploitation. . . .

The average price of wage-labour is the minimum wage, *i.e.*, that quantum of the means of subsistence, which is absolutely requisite to keep the labourer in bare existence as a labourer. What, therefore, the wage-labourer appropriates by means of his labour, merely suffices to prolong and reproduce a bare existence. We by no means intend to abolish this personal appropriation of the products of labour, an appropriation that is made for the maintenance and reproduction of human life, and that leaves no surplus wherewith to command the labour of others. All that we want to do away with, is the miserable character of this appropriation, under which the labourer lives merely to increase capital, and is allowed to live only in so far as the interest of the ruling class requires it.

In bourgeois society, living labour is but a means to increase accumulated labour. In Communist society, accumulated labour is but a means to widen, to enrich, to promote the existence of the labourer.

In bourgeois society, therefore, the past dominates the present; in Communist society, the present dominates the past. In bourgeois society capital is independent and has individuality, while the living person is dependent and has no individuality.

And the abolition of this state of things is called by the bourgeois, abolition of individuality and freedom! And rightly so. The abolition of bourgeois individuality, bourgeois independence, and bourgeois freedom is undoubtedly aimed at.

● ● ●

Communism deprives no man of the power to appropriate the products of society; all that it does is to deprive him of the power to subjugate the labour of others by means of such appropriation.

It has been objected that upon the abolition of private property all work will cease, and universal laziness will overtake us.

According to this, bourgeois society ought long ago to have gone to the dogs through sheer idleness; for those of its members who work, acquire nothing, and those who acquire anything, do not work. The whole of this objection is but another expression of the tautology: that there can no longer be any wage-labour when there is no longer any capital.

All objections urged against the Communistic mode of producing and appropriating material products, have, in the same way, been urged against the Communistic modes of producing and appropriating intellectual products. Just as, to the bourgeois, the disappearance of class property is the disappearance of production itself, so the disappearance of class culture is to him identical with the disappearance of all culture.

That culture, the loss of which he laments, is, for the enormous majority, a mere training to act as a machine.

But don't wrangle with us so long as you apply, to our intended abolition of bourgeois property, the standard of your bourgeois notions of freedom, culture, law, &c. Your very ideas are but the outgrowth of the conditions of your bourgeois production and bourgeois property, just as your jurisprudence is but the will of your class made into a law for all, a will, whose essential character and direction are determined by the economical conditions of existence of your class.

The selfish misconception that induces you to transform into eternal laws of nature and of reason, the social forms springing from your present mode of production and form of property—historical relations that rise and disappear in the progress of production—this misconception you share with every ruling class that has preceded you. What you see clearly in the case of ancient property, what you admit in the case of feudal property, you are of course forbidden to admit in the case of your own bourgeois form of property.

Abolition of the family! Even the most radical flare up at this infamous proposal of the Communists.

On what foundation is the present family, the bourgeois family, based? On capital, on private gain. In its completely developed form this family exists only among the bourgeoisie. But this state of things finds its complement in the practical absence of the family among the proletarians, and in public prostitution.

The bourgeois family will vanish as a matter of course when its complement vanishes, and both will vanish with the vanishing of capital.

Do you charge us with wanting to stop the exploitation of children by their parents? To this crime we plead guilty.

But, you will say, we destroy the most hallowed of relations, when we replace home education by social.

And your education! Is not that also social, and determined by the social conditions under which you educate, by the intervention, direct or indirect, of society, by means of schools, &c.? The Communists have not invented the intervention of society in education; they do but seek to alter the character of that intervention, and to rescue education from the influence of the ruling class.

• • •

The Communists are further reproached with desiring to abolish countries and nationality.

The working men have no country. We cannot take from them what they have not got. Since the proletariat must first of all acquire political supremacy, must rise to be the leading class of the nation, must constitute itself *the* nation, it is, so far, itself national, though not in the bourgeois sense of the word.

• • •

In proportion as the exploitation of one individual by another is put an end to, the exploitation of one nation by another will also be put an end to. In proportion as the antagonism between classes within the nation vanishes, the hostility of one nation to another will come to an end.

The charges against Communism made from a religious, a philosophical, and, generally, from an ideological standpoint, are not deserving of serious examination.

Does it require deep intuition to comprehend that man's ideas, views and conceptions, in one word, man's consciousness, changes with every change in the conditions of his material existence, in his social relations and in his social life?

What else does the history of ideas prove, than that intellectual production changes its character in proportion as material production is changed? The ruling ideas of each age have ever been the ideas of its ruling class.

When people speak of ideas that revolutionise society, they do but express the fact, that within the old society, the elements of a new one have been created, and that the dissolution of the old ideas keeps even pace with the dissolution of the old conditions of existence.

When the ancient world was in its last throes, the ancient religions were overcome by Christianity. When Christian ideas succumbed in the 18th century to rationalist ideas, feudal society fought its death battle with the then revolutionary bourgeoisie. The ideas of religious liberty and freedom of conscience merely gave expression to the sway of free competition within the domain of knowledge.

"Undoubtedly," it will be said, "religious, moral, philosophical and juridical ideas have been modified in the course of historical development. But religion, morality, philosophy, political science, and law, constantly survived this change."

"There are, besides, eternal truths, such as Freedom, Justice, etc., that are common to all states of society. But Communism abolishes eternal truths, it abolishes all religion, and all morality, instead of constituting them on a new basis; it therefore acts in contradiction to all past historical experience."

What does this accusation reduce itself to? The history of all past society has consisted in the development of class antagonisms, antagonisms that assumed different forms at different epochs.

But whatever form they may have taken, one fact is common to all past ages, *viz.*, the exploitation of one part of society by the other. No wonder, then, that the social consciousness of past ages, despite all the multiplicity and variety it displays, moves within certain common forms, or general ideas, which cannot completely vanish except with the total disappearance of class antagonisms.

The Communist revolution is the most radical rupture with traditional property relations; no wonder that its development involves the most radical rupture with traditional ideas.

But let us have done with the bourgeois objections to Communism.

We have seen above, that the first step in the revolution by the working class, is to raise the proletariat to the position of ruling class, to win the battle of democracy.

The proletariat will use its political supremacy to wrest, by degrees, all capital from the bourgeoisie, to centralise all instruments of production in the hands of the State, *i.e.*, of the proletariat organised as the ruling class; and to increase the total of productive forces as rapidly as possible.

Of course, in the beginning, this cannot be effected except by means of despotic inroads on the rights of property, and on the conditions of bourgeois production; by means of measures, therefore, which appear economically insufficient and untenable, but which, in the course of the movement, outstrip themselves, necessitate further inroads upon the old social order, and are unavoidable as means of entirely revolutionising the mode of production.

These measures will of course be different in different countries.

Nevertheless in the most advanced countries, the following will be pretty generally applicable.

1. Abolition of property in land and application of all rents of land to public purposes.

2. A heavy progressive or graduated income tax.

3. Abolition of all right of inheritance.

4. Confiscation of the property of all emigrants and rebels.

5. Centralisation of credit in the hands of the State, by means of a national bank with State capital and an exclusive monopoly.

6. Centralisation of the means of communication and transport in the hands of the State.

7. Extension of factories and instruments of production owned by the State; the bringing into cultivation of wastelands, and the improvement of the soil generally in accordance with a common plan.

8. Equal liability of all to labour. Establishment of industrial armies, especially for agriculture.

9. Combination of agriculture with manufacturing industries; gradual abolition of the distinction between town and country, by a more equable distribution of the population over the country.

10. Free education for all children in public schools. Abolition of children's factory labour in its present form. Combination of education with industrial production, &c., &c.

When, in the course of development, class distinctions have disappeared, and all production has been concentrated in the hands of a vast association of the whole nation, the public power will lose its political character. Political power, properly so called, is merely the organised power of one class for oppressing another. If the proletariat during its contest with the bourgeoisie is compelled, by the force of circumstances, to organise itself as a class, if, by means of a revolution, it makes itself the ruling class, and, as such, sweeps away by force the old conditions of production, then it will, along with these conditions, have swept away the conditions for the existence of class antagonisms and of classes generally, and will thereby have abolished its own supremacy as a class.

In place of the old bourgeois society, with its classes and class antagonisms, we shall have an association, in which the free development of each is the condition for the free development of all.

CHAPTER 66

ROBERT NOZICK

AN ENTITLEMENT THEORY OF JUSTICE

Robert Nozick (1938–   ) is professor of philosophy at Harvard University and one of the most important contemporary conservative political theorists. He is the author of the influential *Anarchy, State, and Utopia* (1974), as well as *The Examined Life: Philosophical Meditations,* 1989.

In this selection from *Anarchy, State, and Utopia,* Nozick argues that any satisfactory theory of distributive justice must be historical.[1] Since goods do not magically spring into existence but are created by particular individuals, we must pay attention to the matter of how individuals came into the possession of their goods. An object may be said to belong to an individual if that person either (1) acquired it in some appropriate manner from the stock of unowned things, or (2) was voluntarily given it by another who owned it. Given the diversity of human talents and abilities, and the natural tendency to bequeath our possessions to our children, inequalities in personal holdings are inevitable. These inequalities are inevitable if we are to respect people's rights. Indeed, the attempt to redistribute holdings in order to make them equal would be a fundamental violation of individual freedom.

Nozick's *entitlement theory of justice* may seem unfair to those that are born too late to acquire holdings; past a certain point, most objects are already owned, and

---

those who are not fortunate enough to inherit goods may appear to have few opportunities to acquire property. But things are not quite so simple, Nozick contends. Following John Locke's teaching on how property is acquired, Nozick contends that one may only appropriate an unowned object if one leaves behind "enough and as good" for others to use. This requirement he calls the "Lockean Proviso." Since it is impossible for *just* appropriation to worsen the condition of others, there is a sense in which it is not unfair.

The critical question is this: Are there occasions when the productive use of unowned objects *does* worsen the condition of others? According to Nozick, this is rarely the case. As Locke pointed out, a farmer who cultivates a fallow piece of ground makes more food available and thus gives everyone new opportunities to make productive exchanges. In an analogous way, Nozick argues, the free market system greatly increases both the goods that are available and the opportunity to acquire them, thus satisfying his "Lockean Proviso."

AN ENTITLEMENT THEORY OF JUSTICE

THE MINIMAL STATE is the most extensive state that can be justified. Any state more extensive violates people's rights. Yet many persons have put forth reasons purporting to justify a more extensive state. It is impossible within the compass of this book to examine all the reasons that have been put forth. Therefore, I shall focus upon those generally acknowledged to be most weighty and influential, to see precisely wherein they fail. In this chapter we consider the claim that a more extensive state is justified, because necessary (or the best instrument) to achieve distributive justice; in the next chapter we shall take up diverse other claims.

The term "distributive justice" is not a neutral one. Hearing the term "distribution," most people presume that some thing or mechanism uses some principle or criterion to give out a supply of things. Into this process of distributing shares some error may have crept. So it is an open question, at least, whether *re*distribution should take place; whether we should do again what has already been done once, though poorly. Howev-er, we are not in the position of children who have been given portions of pie by someone who now makes last minute adjustments to rectify careless cutting. There is no *central* distribution, no person or group entitled to control all the resources, jointly deciding how they are to be doled out. What each person gets, he gets from others who give to him in exchange for something, or as a gift. In a free society, diverse persons control different resources, and new holdings arise out of the voluntary exchanges and actions of persons. There is no more a distributing or distribution of shares than there is a distributing of mates in a society in which persons choose whom they shall marry. The total result is the product of many individual decisions which the different individuals involved are entitled to make. Some uses of the term "distribution," it is true, do not imply a previous distributing appropriately judged by some criterion (for example, "probability distribution"); nevertheless, despite the title of this chapter, it would be best to use a terminology that clearly is neutral. We shall speak of people's holdings; a principle of justice in holdings describes (part of) what justice tells us (requires) about holdings. I shall state first what I take to be the correct view about justice in holdings, and then turn to the discussion of alternate views.

Section I

THE ENTITLEMENT THEORY

The subject of justice in holdings consists of three major topics. The first is the *original acquisition of holdings*, the appropriation of unheld things. This includes the issues of how unheld things may come to be held, the process, or processes, by which unheld things may come to be held, the things that may come to be held by these processes, the extent of what comes to be held by a particular process, and so on. We shall refer to the complicated truth about this topic, which we shall not formulate here, as the principle of justice in acquisition. The second topic concerns the *transfer of holdings* from one person to another. By what processes may a person transfer holdings to another? How may a person acquire a holding from another who holds it? Under this topic come general descriptions of voluntary exchange, and gift and (on the other hand) fraud, as well as reference to particular conventional details fixed upon in a given society. The complicated truth about this subject (with placeholders for conventional details) we shall call the principle of justice in transfer. (And we shall suppose it also includes principles governing how a person may divest himself of a holding, passing it into an unheld state.)

If the world were wholly just, the following inductive definition would exhaustively cover the subject of justice in holdings.

1. A person who acquires a holding in accordance with the principle of justice in acquisition is entitled to that holding.

2. A person who acquires a holding in accordance with the principle of justice in transfer, from someone else entitled to the holding, is entitled to the holding.

3. No one is entitled to a holding except by (repeated) applications of 1 and 2.

The complete principle of distributive justice would say simply that a distribution is just if everyone is entitled to the holdings they possess under the distribution.

A distribution is just if it arises from another just distribution by legitimate means. The legitimate means of moving from one distribution to another are specified by the principle of justice in transfer. The legitimate first "moves" are specified by the principle of justice in acquisition. Whatever arises from a just situation by just steps is itself just. The means of change specified by the principle of justice in transfer preserve justice. As correct rules of inference are truth-preserving, and any conclusion deduced via repeated application of such rules from only true premises is itself true, so the means of transition from one situation to another specified by the principle of justice in transfer are justice-preserving, and any situation actually arising from repeated transitions in accordance with the principle from a just situation is itself just. The parallel between justice-preserving transformations and truth-preserving transformations illuminates where it fails as well as where it holds. That a conclusion could have been deduced by truth-preserving means from premises that are true suffices to show its truth. That from a just situation a situation *could* have arisen via justice-preserving means does *not* suffice to show its justice. The fact that a thief's victims voluntarily *could* have presented him with gifts does not entitle the thief to his ill-gotten gains. Justice in holdings is historical; it depends upon what actually has happened. We shall return to this point later.

Not all actual situations are generated in accordance with the two principles of justice in holdings: the principle of justice in acquisition and the principle of justice in transfer. Some people steal from others, or defraud them, or enslave them, seizing their product and preventing them from living as they choose, or forcibly exclude others from competing in exchanges. None of these are permissible modes of transition from one situation to another. And some persons acquire holdings by means not sanctioned by the principle of justice in acquisition. The existence of past injustice (previous violations of the first two principles of justice in holdings) raises the third major topic under justice in holdings: the rectification of injustice in holdings. If past injustice has shaped present holdings in various ways, some identifiable and some not, what now, if anything, ought to be done to rectify these injustices? What obligations do the performers of injustice have toward those whose position is worse than it would have been had the injustice not been done? Or, than it would have been had compensation been paid promptly? How, if at all, do things change if the beneficiaries and those made worse off are not the direct parties in the act of injustice, but, for example, their descendants? Is an injustice done to someone whose holding was itself based upon an unrectified injustice? How far back must one go in wiping clean the historical slate of injustices? What may victims of injustice permissibly do in order to rectify the injustices being done to them, including the many injustices done by persons acting through their government? I do not know of a thorough or theoretically sophisticated treatment of such issues. Idealizing greatly, let us suppose theoretical investigation will produce a principle of rectification. This principle uses historical information about previous situations and injustices done in them (as defined by the first two principles of justice and rights against inter-

ference), and information about the actual course of events that flowed from these injustices, until the present, and it yields a description (or descriptions) of holdings in the society. The principle of rectification presumably will make use of its best estimate of subjunctive information about what would have occurred (or a probability distribution over what might have occurred, using the expected value) if the injustice had not taken place. If the actual description of holdings turns out not to be one of the descriptions yielded by the principle, then one of the descriptions yielded must be realized.

The general outlines of the theory of justice in holdings are that the holdings of a person are just if he is entitled to them by the principles of justice in acquisition and transfer, or by the principle of rectification of injustice (as specified by the first two principles). If each person's holdings are just, then the total set (distribution) of holdings is just. To turn these general outlines into a specific theory we would have to specify the details of each of the three principles of justice in holdings: the principle of acquisition of holdings, the principle of transfer of holdings, and the principle of rectification of violations of the first two principles. I shall not attempt that task here. (Locke's principle of justice in acquisition is discussed below.)

$\bullet$ $\bullet$ $\bullet$

HOW LIBERTY UPSETS PATTERNS

It is not clear how those holding alternative conceptions of distributive justice can reject the entitlement conception of justice in holdings. For suppose a distribution favored by one of these non-entitlement conceptions is realized. Let us suppose it is your favorite one and let us call this distribution D_1; perhaps everyone has an equal share, perhaps shares vary in accordance with some dimension you treasure. Now suppose that Wilt Chamberlain is greatly in demand by basketball teams, being a great gate attraction. (Also suppose contracts run only for a year, with players being free agents.) He signs the following sort of contract with a team: In each home game, twenty-five cents from the price of each ticket of admission goes to him. (We ignore the question of whether he is "gouging" the owners, letting them look out for themselves.) The season starts, and people cheerfully attend his team's games; they buy their tickets, each time dropping a separate twenty-five cents of their admission price into a special box with Chamberlain's name on it. They are excited about seeing him play; it is worth the total admission price to them. Let us suppose that in one season one million persons attend his home games, and Wilt Chamberlain winds up with $250,000, a much larger sum than the average income and larger even than anyone else has. Is he entitled to this income? Is this new distribution D_2, unjust? If so, why? There is *no* question about whether each of the people was entitled to the control over the resources they held in D_1; because that was the distribution (your favorite) that (for the purposes of argument) we assumed was acceptable. Each of these persons *chose* to give twenty-five cents of their money to Chamberlain. They could have spent it on going to the movies, or on candy bars, or on copies of *Dissent* magazine, or of *Monthly Review*. But they all, at least one million of them, converged on giving it to Wilt Chamberlain in exchange for watching him play basketball. If D_1 was a just distribution, and people voluntarily moved from it to D_2, transferring parts of their shares they were given under D_1 (what was it for if not to do something with?), isn't D_2 also just? If the people were entitled to dispose of the resources to which they were entitled (under D_1), didn't this include their being entitled to give it to, or exchange it with, Wilt Chamberlain? Can anyone else complain on grounds of justice? Each other person already has his legiti-mate share under D_1. Under D_1, there is nothing that anyone has that anyone else has a claim of justice against. After someone transfers something to Wilt Chamberlain, third parties *still* have their legitimate shares; *their* shares are not changed. By what process could such a transfer among two persons give rise to a legitimate claim of distributive justice on a portion of what was transferred, by a third party who had no claim of justice on any holding of the others *before* the transfer? To cut off objections irrelevant here, we might imagine the exchanges occurring in a socialist society, after hours. After playing whatever basketball he does in his daily work, or doing whatever other daily work he does, Wilt Chamberlain decides to put in *overtime* to earn additional money. (First his work quota is set; he works time over that.) Or imagine it is a skilled juggler people like to see, who puts on shows after hours.

Why might someone work overtime in a society in which it is assumed their needs are satisfied? Perhaps because they care about things other than needs. I like to write in books that I read, and to have easy access to books for browsing at odd hours. It would be very pleasant and convenient to have the resources of Widener Library in my back yard. No society, I assume, will provide such resources close to each person who would like them as part of his regular allotment (under D_1). Thus, persons either must do without some extra things that they want, or be allowed to do something extra to get some of these things. On what basis could the inequalities that would eventuate be forbidden? Notice also that small factories would spring up in a socialist society, unless forbidden. I melt down some of my personal possessions (under D_1) and build a machine out of the material. I offer you, and others, a philosophy lecture once a week in exchange for your cranking the handle on my machine, whose products I exchange for yet oth-

745

er things, and so on. (The raw materials used by the machine are given to me by others who possess them under D_1, in exchange for hearing lectures.) Each person might participate to gain things over and above their allotment under D_1. Some persons even might want to leave their job in socialist industry and work full time in this private sector. I shall say something more about these issues in the next chapter. Here I wish merely to note how private property even in means of production would occur in a socialist society that did not forbid people to use as they wished some of the resources they are given under the socialist distribution D_1. The socialist society would have to forbid capitalist acts between consenting adults.

The general point illustrated by the Wilt Chamberlain example and the example of the entrepreneur in a socialist society is that no end-state principle[1] or distributional patterned principle of justice[2] can be continuously realized without continuous interference with people's lives. Any favored pattern would be transformed into one unfavored by the principle, by people choosing to act in various ways; for example, by people exchanging goods and services with other people, or giving things to other people, things the transferrers are entitled to under the favored distributional pattern. To maintain a pattern one must either continually interfere to stop people from transferring resources as they wish to, or continually (or periodically) interfere to take

from some persons resources that others for some reason chose to transfer to them. (But if some time limit is to be set on how long people may keep resources others voluntarily transfer to them, why let them keep these resources for *any* period of time? Why not have immediate confiscation?) It might be objected that all persons voluntarily will choose to refrain from actions which would upset the pattern. This presupposes unrealistically (1) that all will most want to maintain the pattern (are those who don't, to be "reeducated" or forced to undergo "self-criticism"?), (2) that each can gather enough information about his own actions and the ongoing activities of others to discover which of his actions will upset the pattern, and (3) that diverse and far-flung persons can coordinate their actions to dovetail into the pattern. Compare the manner in which the market is neutral among persons' desires, as it reflects and transmits widely scattered information via prices, and coordinates persons' activities.

It puts things perhaps a bit too strongly to say that every patterned (or end-state) principle is liable to be thwarted by the voluntary actions of the individual parties transferring some of their shares they receive under the principle. For perhaps some *very* weak patterns are not so thwarted. Any distributional pattern with any egalitarian component is overturnable by the voluntary actions of individual persons over time; as is every patterned condition with sufficient content so as actually to have been proposed as presenting the central core of distributive justice. Still, given the possibility that some weak conditions or patterns may not be unstable in this way, it would be better to formulate an explicit description of the kind of interesting and contentful patterns under discussion, and to prove a theorem about their instability. Since the weaker the patterning, the more likely it is that the entitlement system itself satisfies it, a plausible con-

---

[1]According to Nozick, an "end-state principle" is one that tells us to distribute goods in a way that promotes a certain present or future structure of holdings. The principles that we should maximize utility or promote equality are end-state principles.

[2]For Nozick, "a patterned principle" is one that tells us to distribute goods in accordance with some natural feature or dimension of persons. The principles that we should distribute in accordance with need, or according to usefulness to society, or desert, are patterned principles.

jecture is that any patterning either is unstable or is satisfied by the entitlement system.

* * *

REDISTRIBUTION AND PROPERTY RIGHTS

* * *

Taxation of earnings from labor is on a par with forced labor. Some persons find this claim obviously true: taking the earnings of *n* hours labor is like taking *n* hours from the person; it is like forcing the person to work *n* hours for another's purpose. Others find the claim absurd. But even these, *if* they object to forced labor, would oppose forcing unemployed hippies to work for the benefit of the needy. And they would also object to forcing each person to work five extra hours each week for the benefit of the needy. But a system that takes five hours' wages in taxes does not seem to them like one that forces someone to work five hours, since it offers the person forced a wider range of choice in activities than does taxation in kind with the particular labor specified. (But we can imagine a gradation of systems of forced labor, from one that specifies a particular activity, to one that gives a choice among two activities, to . . . ; and so on up.) Furthermore, people envisage a system with something like a proportional tax on everything above the amount necessary for basic needs. Some think this does not force someone to work extra hours, since there is no fixed number of extra hours he is forced to work, and since he can avoid the tax entirely by earning only enough to cover his basic needs. This is a very uncharacteristic view of forcing for those who *also* think people are forced to do something *whenever* the alternatives they face are considerably worse. However, *neither* view is correct. The fact that others intentionally intervene, in violation of a side constraint against aggression, to threaten force to limit the alternatives, in this case to paying taxes or (presumably the worse alternative) bare subsistence, makes the taxation system one of forced labor and distinguishes it from other cases of limited choices which are not forcings.

The man who chooses to work longer to gain an income more than sufficient for his basic needs prefers some extra goods or services to the leisure and activities he could perform during the possible nonworking hours; whereas the man who chooses not to work the extra time prefers the leisure activities to the extra goods or services he could acquire by working more. Given this, if it would be illegitimate for a tax system to seize some of a man's leisure (forced labor) for the purpose of serving the needy, how can it be legitimate for a tax system to seize some of a man's goods for that purpose? Why should we treat the man whose happiness requires certain material goods or services differently from the man whose preferences and desires make such goods unnecessary for his happiness? Why should the man who prefers seeing a movie (and who has to earn money for a ticket) be open to the required call to aid the needy, while the person who prefers looking at a sunset (and hence need earn no extra money) is not? Indeed, isn't it surprising that redistributionists choose to ignore the man whose pleasures are so easily attainable without extra labor, while adding yet another burden to the poor unfortunate who must work for his pleasures? If anything, one would have expected the reverse. Why is the person with the nonmaterial or nonconsumption desire allowed to proceed unimpeded to his most favored feasible alternative, whereas the man whose pleasures or desires involve material things and who must work for extra money (thereby serving whomever considers his activities valuable enough to pay him) is constrained in what he can realize? . . .

LOCKE'S THEORY OF ACQUISITION

Before we turn to consider other theories of justice in detail, we must introduce an additional bit of complexity into the structure of the entitlement theory. This is best approached by considering Locke's attempt to specify a principle of justice in acquisition. Locke views property rights in an unowned object as originating through someone's mixing his labor with it. This gives rise to many questions. What are the boundaries of what labor is mixed with? If a private astronaut clears a place on Mars, has he mixed his labor with (so that he comes to own) the whole planet, the whole uninhabited universe, or just a particular plot? Which plot does an act bring under ownership? The minimal (possibly disconnected) area such that an act decreases entropy in that area, and not elsewhere? Can virgin land (for the purposes of ecological investigation by highflying airplane) come under ownership by a Lockean process? Building a fence around a territory presumably would make one the owner of only the fence (and the land immediately underneath it).

Why does mixing one's labor with something make one the owner of it? Perhaps because one owns one's labor, and so one comes to own a previously unowned thing that becomes permeated with what one owns. Ownership seeps over into the rest. But why isn't mixing what I own with what I don't own a way of losing what I own rather than a way of gaining what I don't? If I own a can of tomato juice and spill it in the sea so that its molecules (made radioactive, so I can check this) mingle evenly throughout the sea, do I thereby come to own the sea, or have I foolishly dissipated my tomato juice? Perhaps the idea, instead, is that laboring on something improves it and makes it more valuable; and anyone is entitled to own a thing whose value he has created. (Reinforcing this, perhaps, is the view that laboring is unpleasant. If some people made things effortlessly, as the cartoon characters in *The Yellow Submarine* trail flowers in their wake, would they have lesser claim to their own products

whose making didn't *cost* them anything?) Ignore the fact that laboring on something may make it less valuable (spraying pink enamel paint on a piece of driftwood that you have found). Why should one's entitlement extend to the whole object rather than just to the *added value* one's labor has produced? (Such reference to value might also serve to delimit the extent of ownership; for example, substitute "increases the value of" for "decreases entropy in" in the above entropy criterion.) No workable or coherent value-added property scheme has yet been devised, and any such scheme presumably would fall to objections (similar to those) that fell the theory of Henry George.

It will be implausible to view improving an object as giving full ownership to it, if the stock of unowned objects that might be improved is limited. For an object's coming under one person's ownership changes the situation of all others. Whereas previously they were at liberty (in Hohfeld's sense) to use the object, they now no longer are. This change in the situation of others (by removing their liberty to act on a previously unowned object) need not worsen their situation. If I appropriate a grain of sand from Coney Island, no one else may now do as they will with *that* grain of sand. But there are plenty of other grains of sand left for them to do the same with. Or if not grains of sand, then other things. Alternatively, the things I do with the grain of sand I appropriate might improve the position of others, counterbalancing their loss of the liberty to use that grain. The crucial point is whether appropriation of an unowned object worsens the situation of others.

• • •

Is the situation of persons who are unable to appropriate (there being no more accessible and useful unowned objects) worsened by a system allowing appropriation and permanent property? Here enter the various familiar social considerations favoring private property: it increases the social product by putting means of production in the hands of those who can use them most efficiently (profitably); experimentation is encouraged, because with separate persons controlling resources, there is no one person or small group whom someone with a new idea must convince to try it out; private property enables people to decide on the pattern and types of risks they wish to bear, leading to specialized types of risk bearing; private property protects future persons by leading some to hold back resources from current consumption for future markets; it provides alternate sources of employment for unpopular persons who don't have to convince any one person or small group to hire them, and so on. These considerations enter a Lockean theory to support the claim that appropriation of private property satisfies the intent behind the "enough and as good left over" proviso, *not* as a utilitarian justification of property. They enter to rebut the claim that because the proviso is violated no natural right to private property can arise by a Lockean process. The difficulty in working such an argument to show that the proviso is satisfied is in fixing the appropriate base line for comparison. Lockean appropriation makes people no worse off than they would be *how?* This question of fixing the baseline needs more detailed investigation than we are able to give it here. It would be desirable to have an estimate of the general economic importance of original appropriation in order to see how much leeway there is for differing theories of appropriation and of the location of the baseline. Perhaps this importance can be measured by the percentage of all income that is based upon untransformed raw materials and given resources (rather than upon human actions), mainly rental income representing the unimproved value of land, and the price of raw material *in situ*, and by the percentage of current wealth which represents such income in the past.

We should note that it is not only persons favoring *private* property who need a theory of how property rights legitimately originate. Those believing in collective property, for example those believing that a group of persons living in an area jointly own the territory, or its mineral resources, also must provide a theory of how such property rights arise; they must show why the persons living there have rights to determine what is done with the land and resources there that persons living elsewhere don't have (with regard to the same land and resources).

THE PROVISO

Whether or not Locke's particular theory of appropriation can be spelled out so as to handle various difficulties, I assume that any adequate theory of justice in acquisition will contain a proviso similar to the weaker of the ones we have attributed to Locke. A process normally giving rise to a permanent bequeathable property right in a previously unowned thing will not do so if the position of others no longer at liberty to use the thing is thereby worsened. It is important to specify *this* particular mode of worsening the situation of others, for the proviso does not encompass other modes. It does not include the worsening due to more limited opportunities to appropriate . . . , and it does not include how I "worsen" a seller's position if I appropriate materials to make some of what he is selling, and then enter into competition with him. Someone whose appropriation otherwise would violate the proviso still may appropriate provided he compensates the others so that their situation is not thereby worsened; unless he does compensate these others, his appropriation will violate the proviso of the principle of justice in acquisition and will be an illegitimate one. A theory of appropriation incorporating this Lockean proviso will handle correctly the cases (objections to the theory lacking the proviso) where someone appropriates the total supply of something necessary for life.

A thoery which includes this proviso in its principle of justice in acquisition must also contain a more complex principle of justice in transfer. Some reflection of the proviso about appropriation constrains later actions. If my appropriating all of a certain substance violates the Lockean proviso, then so does my appropriating some and purchasing all the rest from others who obtained it without otherwise violating the Lockean proviso. If the proviso excludes someone's appropriating all the drinkable water in the world, it also excludes his purchasing it all. (More weakly, and messily, it may exclude his charging certain prices for some of his supply.) This proviso (almost?) never will come into effect; the more someone acquires of a scarce substance which others want, the higher the price of the rest will go, and the more difficult it will become for him to acquire it all. But still, we can imagine, at least, that something like this occurs: someone makes simultaneous secret bids to the separate owners of a substance, each of whom sells assuming he can easily purchase more from the other owners; or some natural catastrophe destroys all of the supply of something except that in one person's possession. The total supply could not be permissibly appropriated by one person at the beginning. His later acquisition of it all does not show that the original appropriation violated the proviso. . . . Rather, it is the combination of the original appropriation *plus* all the later transfers and actions that violates the Lockean proviso.

Each owner's title to his holding includes the historical shadow of the Lockean proviso on appropriation. This excludes his transferring it into an agglomeration that does violate the Lockean proviso and excludes his using it in a way, in coordination with others or independently of them, so as to violate the proviso by making the situation of others worse than their baseline situation. Once it is known that someone's ownership runs afoul of the Lockean proviso, there are stringent limits on what he may do with (what it is difficult any longer unreservedly to call) "his property." Thus a person may not appropriate the only water hole in a desert and charge what he will. Nor may he charge what he will if he possesses one, and unfortunately it happens that all the water holes in the desert dry up, except for his. This unfortunate circumstance, admittedly no fault of his, brings into operation the Lockean proviso and limits his property rights. Similarly, an owner's property right in the only island in an area does not allow him to order a castaway from a shipwreck off his island as a trespasser, for this would violate the Lockean proviso.

•   •   •

The fact that someone owns the total supply of something necessary for others to stay alive does *not* entail that his (or anyone's) appropriation of anything left some people (immediately or later) in a situation worse than the baseline one. A medical researcher who synthesizes a new substance that effectively treats a certain disease and who refuses to sell except on his terms does not worsen the situation of others by depriving them of whatever he has appropriated. The others easily can possess the same materials he appropriated; the researcher's appropriation or purchase of chemicals didn't make those chemicals scarce in a way so as to violate the Lockean proviso. Nor would someone else's purchasing the total supply of the synthesized substance from the medical researcher. The fact that the medical researcher uses easily available chemicals to synthesize the drug no more violates the Lockean proviso than does the fact that the only surgeon able to perform a particular operation eats easily obtainable food in order to stay alive and to have the energy to work. This shows that the Lockean proviso is not an "end-state principle"; it focuses on a particular way that appropriative actions affect others, and not on the structure of the situation that results.

Intermediate between someone who takes all of the public supply and someone who makes the total supply out of easily obtainable substances is someone who appropriates the total supply of something in a way that does not deprive the others of it. For example, someone finds a new substance in an out-of-the-way place. He discovers that it effectively treats a certain disease and appropriates the total supply. He does not worsen the situation of others; if he did not stumble upon the substance no one else would have, and the others would remain without it. However, as time passes, the likelihood increases that others would have come across the substance; upon this fact might be based a limit to his property right in the substance so that others are not below their baseline position; for example, its bequest might be limited. The theme of someone worsening another's situation by depriving him of something he otherwise would possess may also illuminate the example of patents. An inventor's patent does not deprive others of an object which would not exist if not for the inventory. Yet patents would have this effect on others who independently invent the object. Therefore, these independent inventors, upon whom the burden of proving independent discovery may rest, should not be excluded from utilizing their own invention as they wish (including selling it to others). Furthermore, a known inventor drastically lessens the chances of actual independent invention. For persons who know of an invention usually will not try to reinvent it, and the notion of independent discovery here would be murky at best. Yet we may assume that in the absence of the original invention, sometime later someone else would have come up with it. This suggests placing a time limit on patents, as a rough rule of thumb to approximate how long it would have taken, in the absence of knowledge of the invention, for independent discovery.

I believe that the free operation of a market system will not actually run afoul of the Lockean proviso. . . .

CHAPTER 67

JOHN RAWLS

JUSTICE AS FAIRNESS

John Rawls (1921–   ) received a Ph.D. in philosophy from Princeton University in 1950. Subsequently, he taught philosophy at Cornell University and the Massachusetts Institute of Technology. He is currently professor of philosophy at Harvard University, where he has taught since 1962. His major contribution to ethics and political philosophy, *A Theory of Justice*, was published in 1971. This book, which had been eagerly awaited, was hailed as one of the most important books of the century. It has been the subject of intense study, not only by philosophers, but by economists, legal scholars, and political scientists as well.

Unlike many social contract theorists, Rawls does not suppose that there ever really was a social contract drawn up in the distant past. Instead, he considers a hypothetical situation. Suppose that a group of rational persons who each wanted to achieve their own goals came together and tried to settle on a set of rules under which they would henceforth cooperate. Any rules agreed to in this hypothetical "original position" would be worthy of general adoption because they had been freely chosen by rational individuals. The resultant rules would constitute the principles of social justice.

Such persons would surely recognize certain primary goods, such as rights and liberties, powers and opportunities, wealth and income, and the social bases of self respect. Under the "veil of ignorance," however, they would know nothing of their own specific preferences; nor would they know anything about their own race, sex, degree of wealth, or natural ability. Consequently, whatever principles they chose to structure the society that determined their fortunes—including the resulting society's political and economic system—would automatically be just.

According to Rawls, the first principle such individuals would choose is a *principle of equality*, and it can be formulated as follows: Each person is to have an equal right to the most extensive basic liberty compatible with a similar liberty for all. The second principle is the *principle of difference*: Social and economic inequalities are to be arranged so that they are both (1) to the greatest benefit of the least advantaged and (2) attached to offices and positions open to all under conditions of fair equality of opportunity.

This second principle states the essence of welfare capitalism, as we know it in the United States today. In his book, *A Theory of Justice*[1]. Rawls does not deny that some versions of socialism would also satisfy it, but he does not discuss the possibility in any detail.

JUSTICE AS FAIRNESS

My aim is to present a conception of justice which generalizes and carries to a higher level of abstraction the familiar theory of the social contract as found, say, in Locke, Rousseau, and Kant. In order to do this we are not to think of the original contract as one to enter a particular society or to set up a particular form of government. Rather, the guiding idea is that the principles of justice for the basic structure of society are the object of the original agreement. They are the principles that free and rational persons concerned to further their own interests would accept in an initial position of equality as defining the fundamental terms of their association. These principles are to regulate all further agreements: they specify the kinds of social cooperation that can be entered into and the forms of government that can be established. This way of regarding the principles of justice I shall call justice as fairness.

Thus we are to imagine that those who engage in social cooperation choose together, in one joint act, the principles which are to assign basic rights and duties and to determine the division of social benefits. Men are to decide in advance how they are to regulate their claims against one another and what is to be the foundation charter of their society. Just as each person must decide by rational reflection what constitutes his good, that is, the system of ends which it is rational for him to pursue, so a group of persons must decide once and for all what is to count among them as just and unjust. The choice which rational men would make in this hypothetical situation of equal liberty, assuming for the present that this choice problem has a solution, determines the principles of justice.

In justice as fairness the original position of equality corresponds to the state of nature in the traditional theory of the social contract. This original position is not, of course, thought of as an actual historical state of affairs, much less as a primitive condition of culture. It is understood as a purely hypothetical situation characterized so as to lead to a certain conception of justice. Among the essential features of this situation is that no one knows his place in society, his class position or social status, nor does any one know his fortune in the distribution of natural assets and abilities, his intelligence, strength, and the like. I shall even assume that the parties do not know their conceptions of the good or their special psychological propensities. The principles of justice are chosen behind a veil of ignorance. This ensures that no one is advantaged or disadvantaged in the choice of principles by the outcome of natural chance or the contingency of social circumstances. Since all are similarly situated and no one is able to design principles to favor his particular condition, the principles of justice are the result of a fair agreement or bargain. For given the circumstances of the original position, the symmetry of everyone's relations to each other, this initial situation is fair between individuals as moral persons, that is, as rational beings with their own ends and capable, I shall assume, of a sense of justice. The original position is, one might say, the appropriate initial status quo, and thus the fundamental agreements reached in it are fair. This explains the propriety of the name "justice as fairness": it conveys the idea that the principles of justice are agreed to in an initial situation that is fair. The name does not mean that the concepts of justice and fairness are the same, any more than the phrase "poetry as metaphor" means that the concepts of poetry and metaphor are the same.

Justice as fairness begins, as I have said, with one of the most general of all choices which persons might make together, namely, with the choice of the first principles of a conception of justice which is to regulate all subsequent criticism and reform of institutions. Then, having chosen a conception of justice, we can suppose that they are to choose a constitution and a legislature to enact laws, and so on, all in accordance with the principles of justice initially agreed upon. Our social situation is just if it is such that by this sequence of hypothetical agreements we would have contracted into the general system of rules which defines it.

It may be observed that once the principles of justice are thought of as arising from an original agreement in a situation of equality, it is an open question whether the principle of utility would be acknowledged. Offhand it hardly seems likely that persons who view themselves as equals, entitled to press their claims upon one another, would agree to a principle which may require lesser life prospects for some simply for the sake of a greater sum of advantages enjoyed by others. Since each desires to protect his interests, his capacity to advance his conception of the good, no one has a reason to acquiesce in an enduring loss for himself in order to bring about a greater net balance of satisfaction. In the absence of strong and lasting benevolent impulses, a rational man would not accept a basic structure merely because it maximized the algebraic sum of advantages irrespective of its permanent effects on his own basic rights and interests. Thus it seems that the principle of utility is incompatible with the conception of social cooperation among equals for mutual advantage. It appears to be inconsistent with the idea of reciprocity implicit in the notion of a well-ordered society. Or, at any rate, so I shall argue.

I shall maintain instead that the persons in the initial situation would choose two rather different principles: the first requires equality in the assignment of basic rights and duties, while the second holds that social and economic inequalities, for example inequalities of wealth and authority, are just only if they result in compensating benefits for everyone, and in particular for the least advantaged members of society. These principles rule out justifying institutions on the grounds that the hardships of some are offset by a greater good in the aggregate. It may be expedient but it is not just that some should have less in order that others may prosper. But there is no injustice in the greater benefits earned by a few provided that the situation of persons not so fortunate is thereby improved. The intuitive idea is that since everyone's well-being depends upon a scheme of cooperation without which no one could have a satisfactory life, the division of advantages should be such as to draw forth the willing cooperation of everyone taking part in it, including those less well situated. Yet this can be expected only if reasonable terms are proposed. The two principles mentioned seem to be a fair agreement on the basis of which those better endowed, or more fortunate in their social position, neither of which we can be said to deserve, could expect the willing cooperation of others when some workable scheme is a necessary condition of the welfare of all. Once we decide to look for a conception of justice that nullifies the accidents of natural endowment and the contingencies of social circumstances as counters in quest for political and economic advantage, we are led to these principles. They express the result of leaving aside those aspects of the social world that seem arbitrary from a moral point of view.

The idea of the original position is to set up a fair procedure so that any principles agreed to will be just. Somehow we must nullify the effects of specific contingencies which put men at odds and tempt them to exploit social and natural circumstances to their own advantage. Now in order to do this I assume that the parties are situated behind a veil of ignorance. They do not know how the various alternatives will affect their own particular case and they are obliged to evaluate principles solely on the basis of general considerations. The veil of ignorance enables us to make vivid to ourselves the restrictions that it seems reasonable to impose on arguments for principles of justice, and therefore on these principles themselves. Thus it seems reasonable and generally acceptable that no one should be advantaged or disadvantaged by natural fortune or social circumstances in the choice of principles. It also seems widely agreed that it should be impossible to tailor principles to the circumstances of one's own case. We should insure further that particular inclinations and aspirations, and persons' conceptions of their good do not affect the principles adopted. The aim is to rule out those principles that it would be rational to propose for acceptance, however little the chance of success, only if one knew certain things that are irrelevant from the standpoint of justice. For example, if a man knew that he was wealthy, he might find it rational to advance the principle that various taxes for welfare measures be counted unjust; if he knew that he was poor, he would most likely propose the contrary principle. To represent the desired restrictions one imagines a situation in which everyone is deprived of this sort of information. One excludes the knowledge of those contingencies which sets men at odds and allows them to be guided by their prejudices.

It is assumed, then, that the parties do not know certain kinds of particular facts. First of all, no one knows his place in society, his class position or social status; nor does he know his fortune in the distribution of natural assets and abilities, his intelligence and strength, and the like. Nor, again, does anyone know his conception of the good, the particulars of his rational plan of life, or even the special features of his psychology such as his aversion to risk or liability to optimism or pessimism. More than this, I assume that the parties do not know the particular circumstances of their own society. That is, they do not know its economic or political situation, or the level of civilization and culture it has been able to achieve. The persons in the original position have no information as to which generation they belong. These broader restrictions on knowledge are appropriate in part because questions of social justice arise between generations as well as within them, for example, the question of the appropriate rate of capital saving and of the conservation of natural resources and the environment of nature. There is also, theoretically anyway, the question of a reasonable genetic policy. In these cases too, in order to carry through the idea of the original position, the parties must not know the contingencies that set them in opposition. They must choose principles the consequences of which they are prepared to live with whatever generation they turn out to belong to. As far as possible, then, the only particular facts which the parties know is that their society is subject to the circumstances of justice and whatever this implies.

The restrictions on particular information in the original position are of fundamental importance. The veil of ignorance makes possible a unanimous choice of a particular conception of justice. Without these limitations on knowledge the bargaining problem of the original position would be hopelessly complicated. Even if theoretically a solution were to exist, we would not, at present anyway, be able to determine it. . . .

The assumption of mutually disinterested rationality . . . comes to this: the persons in the original position try to acknowledge principles which advance their system of ends as far as possible. They do this by attempting to win for themselves the highest index of primary social goods, since this enables them to promote their conception of the good most effectively whatever it turns out to be. The parties do not seek to confer benefits or to impose injuries on one

another; they are not moved by affection or rancor. Nor do they try to gain relative to each other; they are not envious or vain. Put in terms of a game, we might say: they strive for as high an absolute score as possible. They do not wish a high or a low score for their opponents, nor do they seek to maximize or minimize the difference between their successes and those of others. The idea of a game does not really apply, since the parties are not concerned to win but to get as many points as possible judged by their own system of ends.

I shall now state in a provisional form the two principles of justice that I believe would be chosen in the original position. The first statement of the two principles reads as follows.

- First: each person is to have an equal right to the most extensive basic liberty compatible with a similar liberty for others.

- Second: social and economic inequalities are to be arranged so that they are both (a) reasonably expected to be to everyone's advantage, and (b) attached to positions and offices open to all.

By way of general comment, these principles primarily apply, as I have said, to the basic structure of society. They are to govern the assignment of rights and duties and to regulate the distribution of social and economic advantages. As their formulation suggests, these principles presuppose that the social structure can be divided into two more or less distinct parts, the first principle applying to the one, the second to the other. They distinguish between those aspects of the social system that define and secure the equal liberties of citizenship and those that specify and establish social and economic inequalities. The basic liberties of citizens are, roughly speaking, political liberty (the right to vote and to be eligible for public office) together with freedom of speech and assembly; liberty of conscience and freedom of thought; freedom of the person along with the right to hold (personal) property; and freedom from arbitrary arrest and seizure as defined by the concept of the rule of law. These liberties are all required to be equal by the first principle, since citizens of a just society are to have the same basic rights.

The second principle applies, in the first approximation, to the distribution of income and wealth and to the design of organizations that makes use of differences in authority and responsibility, or chains of command. While the distribution of wealth and income need not be equal, it must be to everyone's advantage, and at the same time, positions of authority and offices of command must be accessible to all. One applies the second principle by holding positions open, and then, subject to this constraint, arranges social and economic inequalities so that everyone benefits.

These principles are to be arranged in a serial order with the first principle prior to the second. This ordering means that a departure from the institutions of equal liberty required by the first principle cannot be justified by, or compensated for, by greater social and economic advantages. The distribution of wealth and income, and the hierarchies of authority, must be consistent with both the liberties of equal citizenship and equality of opportunity.

It is clear that these principles are rather specific in their content, and their acceptance rests on certain assumptions that I must eventually try to explain and justify. For the present, it should be observed that the two principles (and this holds for all formulations) are a special case of a more general conception of justice that can be expressed as follows.

All social values—liberty and opportunity, income and wealth, and the bases of self-respect—are to be distributed equally unless an unequal distribution of any, or all, of these values is to everyone's advantage.

Injustice, then, is simply inequalities that are not be the benefit of all. Of course, this conception is extremely vague and requires interpretation.

As a first step, suppose that the basic structure of society distributes certain primary goods, that is, things that every rational man is presumed to want. These goods normally have a use whatever a person's rational plan of life. For simplicity, assume that the chief primary goods at the disposition of society are rights and liberties, powers and opportunities, income and wealth. These are the social primary goods. Other primary goods such as health and vigor, intelligence and imagination, are natural goods; although their possession is influenced by the basic structure, they are not so directly under its control. Imagine, then, a hypothetical initial arrangement in which all the social primary goods are equally distributed: everyone has similar rights and duties, and income and wealth are evenly shared. This state of affairs provides a benchmark for judging improvements. If certain inequalities of wealth and organizational powers would make everyone better off than in this hypothetical starting situation, then they accord with the general conception.

Now it is possible, at least theoretically, that by giving up some of their fundamental liberties men are sufficiently compensated by the resulting social and economic gains. The general conception of justice imposes no restrictions on what sort of inequalities are permissible; it only requires that everyone's position be improved.

The second principle insists that each person benefit from permissible inequalities in the basic structure. This means that it must be reasonable for each relevant representative man defined by this structure, when he views it as a going concern, to prefer his prospects with the inequality to his prospects without it. One is not allowed to justify differences in income or organizational powers on the ground that the disadvantages of those in one position are outweighed by the greater advantages of those in another. Much less can infringements of liberty be counterbalanced in this way. Applied to the basic structure, the principle of utility would have us maximize the sum of expectations of representative men (weighted by the number of persons they represent, on the classical view); and this would permit us to compensate for the losses of some by the gains of others. Instead, the two principles require that everyone benefit from economic and social inequalities.

The natural distribution of talents is neither just nor unjust; nor is it unjust that men are born into society at some particular position. These are simply natural facts. . . .

. . . What is just and unjust is the way that institutions deal with these facts. Aristocratic and caste societies are unjust because they make these contingencies the ascriptive basis for belonging to more or less enclosed and privileged social classes. The basic structure of these societies incorporates the arbitrariness found in nature. But there is no necessity for men to resign themselves to these contingencies. The social system is not an unchangeable order beyond human control but a pattern of human action. In justice as fairness men agree to share one another's fate. In designing institutions they undertake to avail themselves of the accidents of nature and social circumstance only when doing so is for the common benefit. The two principles are a fair way of meeting the arbitrariness of fortune; and while no doubt imperfect in other ways, the institutions which satisfy these principles are just.

There is a natural inclination to object that those better situated deserve their greater advantages whether or not they are to the benefit of others. At this point it is necessary to be clear about the notion of desert. It is perfectly true that given a just system of cooperation as a scheme of public rules and the expectations set up by it, those who, with the prospect of improving their condition, have done what the system announces that it will reward are entitled to their advantages. In this sense the more fortunate have a claim to their better situation; their claims are legitimate expectations established by social institutions, and the community is obligated to meet them. But this sense of desert presupposes the existence of the cooperative scheme; it is irrelevant to the question whether in the first place the scheme is to be designed in accordance with the difference principle or some other criterion.

Perhaps some will think that the person with greater natural endowments deserves those assets and the superior character that made their development possible. Because he is more worthy in this sense, he deserves the greater advantages that he could achieve with them. This view, however, is surely incorrect. It seems to be one of the fixed points of our considered judgments that no one deserves his place in the distribution of native endowments, any more than one deserves one's initial starting place in society. The assertion that a man deserves the superior character that enables him to make the effort to cultivate his abilities is equally problematic; for his character depends in large part upon fortunate family and social circumstances for which he can claim no credit. The notion of desert seems not to apply to these cases. Thus the more advantaged representative man cannot say that he deserves and therefore has a right to a scheme of cooperation in which he is permitted to acquire benefits in ways that do not contribute to the welfare of others. There is no basis for his making this claim. From the standpoint of common sense, then, the difference principle appears to be acceptable both to the more advantaged and to the less advantaged individual.

CONTEMPORARY PERSPECTIVES: CIVIL DISOBEDIENCE

No person can be said to be perfectly just. The same can be said of any institution or society. For this reason, occasions arise where *moral justice* and *legal justice* do not coincide. Recall the institution of slavery in the United States. In the Dred Scott decision of 1857, the Supreme Court of the United States ruled that even in a free state a slave did not have the rights of a citizen, but was to be treated as the property of his owner. Laws were enacted that made it illegal to give aid to a runaway slave; citizens who wished to be law-abiding were obligated to return runaway slaves to their masters. Ask yourself this question: Who were the heroes of this time period, the people who returned runaway slaves, or the people who worked with the underground railroad helping slaves to escape to freedom? Posing this question should give you some insight into the question of civil disobedience.

Civil disobedience may be defined as nonviolent disobedience to the law aimed at changing laws deemed unjust. The folks who worked on the underground railroad did so secretly.[1] But often, civil disobedience takes the form of public disobedience to the law. In the 1960s, public acts of civil disobedience were common in America, prompted both by segregation laws and an unpopular war in Vietnam. In the 1980s and 1990s, "Operation Rescue" protesters have engaged in this tactic in an attempt to gain the support of lawmakers to outlaw abortion.

Although people who engage in civil disobedience break particular laws because they think them unjust, this does not mean that they do not believe in the rule of law. Martin Luther King, Jr., was arrested on numerous occasions for breaking segregation laws that he deemed unjust. He was frequently asked, "How can you advocate breaking some laws and obeying others?" King responded by making a distinction between a just law and an unjust law. He made it clear that he believed he had a moral obligation to obey just laws, and a moral obligation to disobey unjust laws. One who breaks an unjust law, he said, must do so openly, lovingly, and with a willingness to accept the penalty. *Isn't this the highest respect for law?* In King's words, "I submit that an individual who breaks a law that conscience tells him is unjust, and who willingly accepts the penalty of imprisonment in order to arouse the conscience of the community over its injustice, is in reality expressing the highest respect for law."

Civil disobedience is a highly controversial issue and has been repeatedly criticized for a wide variety of reasons. Let us consider a few of the most important objections.

---

[1]For the gripping story of how one former slave escaped to freedom on the underground railroad, read Frederick Douglas's autobiography, *Narrative of the Life of Frederick Douglass, An American Slave,* Edited by Benjamin Quarles, Cambridge, MA, Belknap Press, 1960.

1. Many object that civil disobedience is inappropriate behavior in a democracy. We should all try to "work within the system." As long as we have the right to make our views known to our elected officials, there is no need for civil disobedience. Why resort to breaking the law when we have the freedom to change the law?

2. Innocent people are harmed or inconvenienced by civil disobedience. During the 1960s, service was often disrupted at "white" restaurants that refused to serve blacks. Why should someone who merely wishes to order a sandwich and coffee be penalized by demonstrators who disrupt service at a lunch counter? Why should I be late for an important job interview because demonstrators are blocking the street protesting some law?

3. Civil disobedience can lead to anarchy. When people publicly break the law in large numbers, there is an inevitable breakdown in respect for the law, even if protestors are willing to be punished.

Proponents of civil disobedience respond to the first objection by agreeing that traditional means of changing the law must first be tried. But there are occasions when laws are fundamentally unjust, and traditional means do not work. Sometimes elected representatives and the courts remain unresponsive to peaceful petitioning, and voters cannot be convinced to replace these officials. This being the case, something must be done to call attention to the injustice of the law, and civil disobedience is required.

Advocates point out that civil disobedience is a form of *moral persuasion*, not an act of coercion. When lawmakers and citizens see that decent, otherwise law-abiding members of their community are willing to face jail for their convictions, attention shifts from *the law itself* to *the moral principle behind the law*. During the height of the civil rights debate in this country, millions of television viewers were shocked to see students, ministers, and ordinary working people dragged off to jail for the "crime" of refusing to sit in the back of a bus, or the "crime" of sitting at a "white" lunch counter. Outraged Americans witnessed the police turning powerful water hoses and fierce dogs on men, women, and children, while elected officials looked on with approval and even merriment. In this way, public attitudes toward segregation laws were changed, and the way cleared for the passage of important civil rights legislation.

Concerning the second objection, civil disobedience advocates argue that some social disruption is bound to occur. But when the goal is the abolition of a fundamentally unjust institution (for example, segregation), such nonviolent disruption is morally permissible. Perhaps the innocent people whose lunch has been disturbed at the lunch counter will reflect on the ways that the existing law benefits them to the exclusion of others who are made to suffer unjustly.

What about the third objection—the threat of anarchy? Most defenders of civil disobedience deny that this is a real threat. If acts of civil disobedience are restricted to cases of fundamental injustice, and if protestors show their respect for the law by consenting peacefully to their imprisonment, anarchy will not result.

In 1849 Henry David Thoreau was arrested for refusing to pay his poll tax. His refusal to pay was his way of protesting slavery and the Mexican War. In his famous essay, "On the Duty of Civil Disobedience," Thoreau contends that if enough people follow his lead, slavery and the war would end. The government could not continue indefinitely putting decent citizens in prison. In the excerpt from the essay that follows, Thoreau states, "Under a government which imprisons any unjustly, the true place for a just man is also a prison." It was rumored that when Thoreau was imprisoned, his friend Ralph Waldo Emerson had looked in through the prison window and asked, "Henry, what are you doing in there?" Thoreau is rumored to have responded, "The question is, what are you doing out there?"

Thoreau's question was very much on Martin Luther King, Jr.'s mind on April 16, 1963. As he sat in a prison cell in Birmingham, Alabama, King was troubled by a public statement directed at him by a group of eight Birmingham clergymen. That statement, in part, reads as follows:

> [W]e are not confronted by a series of demonstrations by some of our Negro citizens, directed and led in part by outsiders. We recognize the natural impatience of people who feel that their hopes are slow in being realized. But we are convinced that these demonstrations are unwise and untimely.
>
> We . . . strongly urge our own Negro community to withdraw support from these demonstrations, and to unite in working peacefully for a better Birmingham. When rights are consistently denied, a cause should be pressed in the courts and in negotiations among local leaders, and not in the streets. We appeal to both our white and Negro citizenry to observe the principles of law and order and common sense.

King's response to the eight clergymen, "Letter From a Birmingham Jail," is a classic defense of civil disobedience and an eloquent plea for social justice in America. King begins by explaining why he is in Birmingham. Speaking with the courage and conviction of a moral prophet, King explains that, "I am in Birmingham because injustice is here." He then sets forth his theory of civil disobedience, making a distinction between just and unjust laws, and affirming his respect for the rule of law. He reminds his correspondents of some memorable cases of civil disobedience in the Bible, and expresses his regret that the Christian Church in the South, with a few notable exceptions, has not identified itself with and come to the aid of the call of justice. He concludes by expressing his desire to meet with his correspondents as fellow Christians.

We sense the importance of King's legacy and the widespread acceptance of his views on civil disobedience if we ask this question: Who today recalls the identity of these eight clergymen? History, in its inexorable march forward, has submerged their memory while elevating that of King. Nevertheless, we do well to ask other questions. Are King's criteria for distinguishing between just and unjust laws valid? What are the criteria for acts of civil disobedience? Where do we draw the line between what is acceptable and what is unacceptable? Must we be utilitarian in deciding whether the good we hope to accomplish by our actions outweighs the negative consequences of our actions? Finally, how can we be sure that our sense of what is an unjust law is not just our own sense of bigotry?

CHAPTER 68

HENRY DAVID THOREAU

ON THE DUTY OF CIVIL DISOBEDIENCE

Henry David Thoreau (1817–1862), New England transcendentalist and political anarchist, was born in Concord, Massachusetts, the son of a pencil maker. Upon his graduation from Harvard University in 1837, he attempted to teach school but soon realized that this was not his calling. Infected with the teachings of Ralph Waldo Emerson and the New England transcendentalists, Thoreau gave up all plans for a regular profession and applied himself to literature and the study of nature.

From 1841 to 1843 Thoreau lived with Emerson. During these years he became convinced that in order to simplify his existence, clarify his senses, and attain concretely what Emerson advocated abstractly as self-reliance, he ought to live alone in the wilderness. In the spring of 1845 he built a hut on the shore of Walden Pond, a small lake about one and a half miles from Concord. His mode of life during his two-year stay at the pond is eloquently described in *Walden, or Life in the Woods* (1854). For Thoreau, Walden was an exercise in anarchistic individualism, a discipline of the will and of the wild. It was his protest against acquisitive society, with its "incessant business," that kept a person from self-knowledge and self-reliance. He believed that, "to have done anything by which you earned money merely is to have been truly idle, or worse."

In 1849 Thoreau, an agitator for the abolition of slavery, refused to pay his taxes and was thrown in jail. Thoreau's 1849 essay, "Civil Disobedience" sets forth the reasons for his dramatic action. The essay has been enormously influential. In 1907 a reading of this essay helped Gandhi develop his own doctrine of passive resistance. Martin Luther King's "Letter From a Birmingham Prison" shows Thoreau's influence as well

ON THE DUTY OF CIVIL DISOBEDIENCE[1]

I heartily accept the motto—"That government is best which governs least"; and I should like to see it acted up to more readily and systematically. Carried out, it finally amounts to this, which also I believe,—"That government is best which governs not at all"; and when men are prepared for it, that will be the kind of government which they will have. Government is at best but an expedient; but most governments are usually, and all governments are sometimes, inexpedient. The objections which have been brought against a standing army, and they are many and weighty, and deserve to prevail, may also at least be brought against a standing government. The standing army is only an arm of the standing government. The government itself, which is only the mode which the people have chosen to execute their will, is equally liable to be abused and perverted before the people can act through it. Witness the present Mexican war, the work of comparatively a few individuals using the standing government as their tool; for, in the outset, the people would not have consented to this measure.

But, to speak practically and as a citizen, unlike those who call themselves no-government men, I ask for, not at once no government, but at once a better government. Let every man make known what kind of government would command his respect, and that will be one step toward obtaining it.

Must the citizen ever for a moment, or in the least degree, resign his conscience to the legislator? Why has every man a conscience, then? I think that we should be men first, and subjects afterward. It is not desirable to cultivate a respect for the law, so much as for the right. The only obligation which I have a right to assume, is to do at any time what I think right. It is truly enough said, that a corporation has no conscience; but a corporation of conscientious men is a corporation *with* a conscience. Law never made men a whit more just; and, by means of their respect for it, even the well-disposed are daily made the agents of injustice. A common and natural result of an undue respect for law is, that you may see a file of soldiers, colonel, captain, corporal, privates, powder-monkeys and all, marching in admirable order over hill and dale to the wars, against their wills, aye, against their common sense and consciences, which makes it very steep marching indeed, and produces a palpitation of the heart. They have no doubt that it is a damnable business in which they are concerned; they are all peaceably inclined. Now, what are they? Men at all? or small moveable forts and magazines, at the service of some unscrupulous man in power? Visit the Navy Yard, and behold a marine, such a man as an American government can make, or such as it can make a man with its black arts, a mere shadow and reminiscence of humanity, a man laid out alive and standing, and already, as one may say, buried under arms with funeral accompaniments.

[1]From Henry David Thoreau, *Walden and Civil Disobedience* (New York: Signet Books, 1960), 222-240.

The mass of men serve the State thus, not as men mainly, but as machines, with their bodies. They are the standing army, and the militia, jailers, constables, *posse comitatus*, etc. In most cases there is no free exercise whatever of the judgment or the moral sense; but they put themselves on a level with wood and earth and stones; and wooden men can perhaps be manufactured that will serve the purpose as well. Such command no more respect than men of straw, or a lump of dirt. They have the same sort of worth only as horses and dogs. Yet such as these even are commonly esteemed good citizens. Others, as most legislators, politicians, lawyers, ministers, and office-holders, serve the State chiefly with their heads; and, as they rarely make any moral distinctions, they are as likely to serve the devil, without intending it, as God. A very few, as heroes, patriots, martyrs, reformers in the great sense, and *men*, serve the State with their consciences also, and so necessarily resist it for the most part; and they are commonly treated by it as enemies.

How does it become a man to behave toward this American government to-day? I answer that he cannot without disgrace be associated with it. I cannot for an instant recognize that political organization as *my* government which is the *slave's* government also.

All men recognize the right of revolution; that is, the right to refuse allegiance to and to resist the government, when its tyranny or its inefficiency are great and unendurable. When a sixth of the population of a nation which has undertaken to be the refuge of liberty are slaves, and a whole country is unjustly overrun and conquered by a foreign army, and subjected to military law. I think that it is not too soon for honest men to rebel and revolutionize. What makes this duty the more urgent is the fact, that the country so overrun is not our own, but ours is the invading army.

If I have unjustly wrested a plank from a drowning man, I must restore it to him though I drown myself. This, according to Paley, would be inconvenient. But he that would save his life, in such a case, shall lose it. This people must cease to hold slaves, and to make war on Mexico, though it cost them their existence as a people.

Practically speaking, the opponents to a reform in Massachusetts are not a hundred thousand politicians at the South, but a hundred thousand merchants and farmers here, who are more interested in commerce and agriculture than they are in humanity, and are not prepared to do justice to the slaves and to Mexico, *cost what it may*. I quarrel not with far-off foes, but with those who, near at home, cooperate with, and do the bidding of those far away, and without whom the latter would be harmless.

There are thousands who are *in opinion* opposed to slavery and to the war, who yet in effect do nothing to put an end to them; who esteeming themselves children of Washington and Franklin, sit down with their hands in their pockets, and say that they know not what to do, and do nothing; who even postpone the question of freedom to the question of free-trade, and quietly read the prices-current along with the latest advices from Mexico, after dinner, and it may be, fall asleep over them both. What is the price-current on an honest man and patriot to-day? They hesitate, and they regret, and sometimes they petition; but they do nothing in earnest and with effect. They will wait, well disposed, for others to remedy the evil, that they may no longer have it to regret.

Unjust laws exist: shall we be content to obey them, or shall we endeavor to amend them, and obey them until we have succeeded, or shall we transgress them at once? Men generally, under such a government as this, think they ought to wait until they have persuaded the majority to alter them. They think that, if they should resist, the remedy would be worse than the evil. But it is the fault of the government itself that the remedy *is* worse than the evil. *It* makes it worse. Why is it not more apt to anticipate and provide for reform? Why does it not cherish its wise minority?

If the injustice is part of the necessary friction of the machine of government, let it go: perchance it will wear smooth,—certainly the machine will wear out. But if it is of such a nature that it requires you to be the agent of injustice to another, then, I say, break the law. Let your life be a counter friction to stop the machine. What I have to do is to see, at any rate, that I do not lend myself to the wrong which I condemn. As for adopting the ways which the State has provided for remedying the evil, I know not of such ways. They take too much time, and a man's life will be gone.

I do not hesitate to say, that those who call themselves abolitionists should at once effectually withdraw their support both in person and property from the government of Massachusetts.

I meet this American government, or its representative directly, and face to face, once a year, no more, in the person of its tax-gatherer; this is the only model in which a man situated as I am necessarily meets it; and it then says distinctly, Recognize me; and the simplest, the most effectual, and in the present posture of affairs, the indispensablest mode of treating with it on this head, of expressing your little satisfaction with and love for it, is to deny it then.

Under a government which imprisons any unjustly, the true place for a just man is also a prison. The proper place to-day, the only place which Massachusetts has provided for her freer and less desponding spirits, is in her prisons, to be put out and locked out of the State by her own act, as they have already put themselves out by their principles. It is there that the fugitive slave, and the Mexican prisoner on parole, and the Indian come to plead the wrongs of his race, should find them; on that separate, but more free and honorable ground, where the State places those who are not *with* her but *against* her,—the only house in a slavestate in which a free man can abide with honor. A minority is powerless while it conforms to the majority; it is not even a minority then; but it is irresistible when it clogs by its whole weight. If the alternative is to keep all just men in prison, or give up war and slavery, the State will not hesitate which to choose. If a thousand men were not to pay their taxbills this year, that would not be a violent and bloody measure, as it would be to pay them, and enable the State to commit violence and shed innocent blood. This is, in fact, the definition of a peaceable revolution if any such is possible. If the taxgatherer, or any other public officer, asks me, as one has done, "But what shall I do?" my answer is, "If you really wish to do any thing, resign your office." When the subject has refused allegiance, and the officer has resigned his office, then the revolution is accomplished. But even suppose blood should flow. Is there not a sort of blood shed when the conscience is wounded? Through this wound a man's real manhood and immortality flow out, and he bleeds to an everlasting death, I see this blood flowing now.

I have never declined paying the highway tax, because I am so desirous of being a good neighbor as I am of being a bad subject; and, as for supporting schools, I am doing my part to educate my fellow-countrymen now. It is for no particular item in the taxbill that I refuse to pay it. I simply wish to refuse allegiance to the State, to withdraw and stand aloof from it effectually. I do not care to trace the course of my dollar, if I could, till it buys a man, or a musket to shoot one with—the dollar is innocent—but I am concerned to trace the effects of my allegiance. In fact, I quietly declare war with the State, after my fashion.

I do not wish to quarrel with any man or nation. I do not wish to split hairs, to make fine distinctions, or set myelf up as better than my neighbors. I seek rather, I may say, even an excuse for conforming to the laws of the land. I am but too ready to conform to them. Indeed I have reason to suspect myself on this head; and each year, as the tax-gatherer comes round, I find myself disposed to review the acts and position of the general and state governments, and the spirit of the people, to discover a pretext for conformity. Seen from a lower point of view, the Constitution, with all its faults, is very good; the law and the courts are very respectable; even this State and this American government are, in many respects, very admirable and rare things, to be thankful for, such as a great many have described them; but seen from a point of view a little higher, they are what I have described them; seen from a higher still, and the highest who shall say what they are, or that they are worth looking at or thinking of at all?

The authority of government, even such as I am willing to submit to, for I will cheerfully obey those who know and can do better than I, and in many things even those who neither know or can do so well, is still an impure one: to be strictly just, it must have the sanction and consent of the governed. It can have no pure right over my person and property but what I concede to it. The progress from an absolute to a limited monarchy, from a limited monarchy to a democracy, is a progress toward a true respect for the individual. Is a democracy, such as we know it, the last improvement possible in government? Is it not possible to take a step further toward recognizing and organizing the rights of man? There will never be a really free and enlightened State until the State comes to recognize the individual as a higher and independent power, from which all is own power and authority derived, and treats him accordingly.

CHAPTER 69

MARTIN LUTHER KING, JR.

LETTER FROM BIRMINGHAM JAIL

Martin Luther King, Jr. (1929–1968), civil rights leader and conscience of his generation, was born in Atlanta, Georgia, the son of a Baptist minister. He graduated from Morehouse College and pursued graduate study at Crozier Theological Seminary. In 1955 he received his Ph.D. from Boston University. An ordained Baptist minister, he became pastor of the Dexter Avenue Baptist Church in Montgomery, Alabama, in 1954; his crusade for civil rights began the following year. In 1957, to coordinate the efforts of various civil rights organizations, King helped found the Southern Christian Leadership Conference.

Throughout his short life, King's eloquent pleas for racial justice, full civil rights for all people, and equality for blacks were joined to a firm commitment to nonviolent resistance. In the summer of 1963 he led a march on Washington, D.C., that will long be remembered by free people everywhere. Standing before the Lincoln Memorial, addressing 200,000 people from all over the country and millions watching on television, King shared his dream of freedom, justice, equality, and brotherhood among all God's children. He won the support and admiration of millions of people around the world. In 1964, in recognition of all his labors, he was awarded the Nobel Peace Prize.

King based his program of nonviolent resistance on the teachings of Jesus in the Bible, the social ideas of Henry David Thoreau, and the methods of Gandhi. He wrote five books: *Stride Toward Freedom* (1958), *Strength to Love* (1963), *Why We Can't Wait* (1964), *Where Do We Go From Here?* (1967), and *The Trumpet of Conscience* (1968).

An advocate of nonviolence, King was frequently, and ultimately, a victim of violence. He was stabbed in New York, stoned in Chicago, and threatened with death on numerous occasions. In April 1968, not yet forty years of age, he was assassinated in Memphis, Tennessee. The tombstone above his grave in Atlanta, Georgia, bears this inscription, taken from a Negro spiritual: "Free at last, free at last, thank God Almighty, I'm free at last."

LETTER FROM BIRMINGHAM JAIL[1]

We clergymen are among those who, in January, issued "An Appeal for Law and Order and Common Sense," in dealing with racial problems in Alabama. We expressed understanding that honest convictions in racial matters could properly be pursued in the courts, but urged that decisions of those courts should in the meantime be peacefully obeyed.

Since that time there has been some evidence of increased forbearance and a willingness to face facts. Responsible citizens have undertaken to work on various problems which cause racial friction and unrest. In Birmingham, recent public events have given indication that we all have opportunity for a new constructive and realistic approach to racial problems.

However, we are now confronted by a series of demonstrations by some of our Negro citizens, directed and led in part by outsiders. We recognize the natural impatience of people who feel that their hopes are slow in being realized. But we are convinced that these demonstrations are unwise and untimely.

We agree rather with certain local Negro leadership which has called for honest and open negotiation of racial issues in our area. And we believe this kind of facing of issues can be best accomplished by citizens of our own metropolitan area, white and negro, meeting with the knowledge and experience of the local situation. All of us need to face that responsibility and find proper channels for its accomplishment.

Just as we formerly pointed out that "hatred and violence have no sanction in our religious and political traditions," we also point out that such actions as incite to hatred and violence, however technically peaceful those actions may be, have not contributed to the resolution of our local problems. We do not believe that these days of new hope are days when extreme measures are justified in Birmingham.

We commend the community as a whole, and the local news media and law enforcement officials in particular, on the calm manner in which these demonstrations have been handled. We urge the public to continue to show restraint should the demonstrations continue, and the law enforcement officials to remain calm and continue to protect our city from violence.

We further strongly urge our own Negro community to withdraw support from these demonstrations, and to unite locally in working peacefully for a better Birmingham. When rights are consistently denied, a cause should be pressed in the courts and in negotiations among local leaders, and not in the streets. We appeal to both our white and Negro citizenry to observe the principles of law and order and common sense.

[1]From Martin Luther King, Jr. "Letter From Birmingham Jail" in *Why We Can't Wait*. Copyright © 1963, 1964 by Martin Luther King, Jr. Reprinted by permission of HarperCollins Publishers, Inc.

April 16, 1963

My Dear Fellow Clergymen:

While confined here in the Birmingham city jail, I came across your recent statement calling my present activities "unwise and untimely." Seldom do I pause to answer criticism of my work and ideas. If I sought to answer all the criticisms that cross my desk, my secretaries would have little time for anything other than such correspondence in the course of the day, and I would have no time for constructive work. But since I feel that you are men of genuine good will and that your criticisms are sincerely set forth, I want to try to answer your statement in what I hope will be patient and reasonable terms.

I think I should indicate why I am here in Birmingham, since you have been influenced by the view which argues against "outsiders coming in." I have the honor of serving as president of the Southern Christian Leadership Conference, an organization operating in every southern state, with headquarters in Atlanta, Georgia. We have some eighty-five affiliated organizations across the South, and one of them is the Alabama Christian Movement for Human Rights. Frequently we share staff, educational and financial resources with our affiliates. Several months ago the affiliate here in Birmingham asked us to be on call to engage in a nonviolent direct-action program if such were deemed necessary. We readily consented, and when the hour came we lived up to our promise. So I, along with several members of my staff, am here because I was invited here. I am here because I have organizational ties here.

But more basically, I am in Birmingham because injustice is here. Just as the prophets of the eighth century B.C. left their villages and carried their "thus saith the Lord" far beyond the boundaries of their home towns, and just as the Apostle Paul left his village of Tarsus and carried the gos-

pel of Jesus Christ to the far corners of the Greco-Roman world, so am I compelled to carry the gospel of freedom beyond my own home town. Like Paul, I must constantly respond to the Macedonian call for aid.

Moreover, I am cognizant of the interrelatedness of all communities and states. I cannot sit idly by in Atlanta and not be concerned about what happens in Birmingham. Injustice anywhere is a threat to justice everywhere. We are caught in an inescapable network of mutuality, tied in a single garment of destiny. Whatever affects one directly, affects all indirectly. Never again can we afford to live with the narrow, provincial "outside agitator" idea. Anyone who lives inside the United States can never be considered an outsider anywhere within its bounds.

You deplore the demonstrations taking place in Birmingham. But your statement, I am sorry to say, fails to express a similar concern for the conditions that brought about the demonstrations. I am sure that none of you would want to rest content with the superficial kind of social analysis that deals merely with effects and does not grapple with underlying causes. It is unfortunate that demonstrations are taking place in Birmingham, but it is even more unfortunate that the city's white power structure left the Negro community with no alternative. . . .

We know through painful experience that freedom is never voluntarily given by the oppressor; it must be demanded by the oppressed. Frankly, I have yet to engage in a direct-action campaign that was "well timed" in the view of those who have not suffered unduly from the disease of segregation. For years now I have heard the word "Wait!" It rings in the ear of every Negro with piercing familiarity. This "Wait" has almost always meant "Never." We must come to see, with one of our distinguished jurists, that "justice too long delayed is justice denied."

We have waited for more than 340 years for

our constitutional and God-given rights. The nations of Asia and Africa are moving with jetlike speed toward gaining political independence, but we still creep at horse-and-buggy pace toward gaining a cup of coffee at a lunch counter. Perhaps it is easy for those who have never felt the stinging darts of segregation to say, "Wait." But when you have seen vicious mobs lynch your mothers and fathers at will and drown your sisters and brothers at whim; when you have seen hate-filled policemen curse, kick and even kill our black brothers and sisters; when you see the vast majority of your twenty million Negro brothers smothering in an airtight cage of poverty in the midst of an affluent society; when you suddenly find your tongue twisted and your speech stammering as you seek to explain to your six-year-old daughter why she can't go to the public amusement park that has just been advertised on television, and see tears welling up in her eyes when she is told that Funtown is closed to colored children, and see ominous clouds of inferiority beginning to form in her little mental sky, and see her beginning to distort her personality by developing an unconscious bitterness toward white people; when you have to concoct an answer for a five-year-old son who is asking: "Daddy, why do white people treat colored people so mean?"; when you take a cross-country drive and find it necessary to sleep night after night in the uncomfortable corners of your automobile because no motel will accept you; when you are humiliated day in and day out by nagging signs reading "white" and "colored"; when your first name becomes "nigger," your middle name becomes "boy" (however old you are) and your last name becomes "John," and your wife and mother are never given the respected title "Mrs."; when you are harried by day and haunted by night by the fact that you are a Negro, living constantly at tiptoe stance, never quite knowing what to expect next, and are plagued with inner fears and outer resentments; when you are forever fighting a degenerating sense of "nobodiness"—then you will understand why we find it difficult to wait. There comes a time when the cup of endurance runs over, and men are no longer willing to be plunged into the abyss of despair. I hope, sirs, you can understand our legitimate and unavoidable impatience.

You express a great deal of anxiety over our willingness to break laws. This is certainly a legitimate concern. Since we so diligently urge people to obey the Supreme Court's decision of 1954 outlawing segregation in the public schools, at first glance it may seem rather paradoxical for us consciously to break laws. One may well ask: "How can you advocate breaking some laws and obeying others?" The answer lies in the fact that there are two types of laws: just and unjust. I would be the first to advocate obeying just laws. One has not only a legal but a moral responsibility to obey just laws. Conversely, one has a moral responsibility to disobey unjust laws. I would agree with St. Augustine that "an unjust law is no law at all."

Now, what is the difference between the two? How does one determine whether a law is just or unjust? A just law is a man-made code that squares with the moral law or the law of God. An unjust law is a code that is out of harmony with the moral law. To put it in the terms of St. Thomas Aquinas: An unjust law is a human law that is not rooted in eternal law and natural law. Any law that uplifts human personality is just. Any law that degrades human personality is unjust. All segregation statutes are unjust because segregation distorts the soul and damages the personality. It gives the segregator a false sense of superiority and the segregated a false sense of inferiority. Segregation, to use the terminology of the Jewish philosopher Martin Buber, substitutes an "I-it" relationship for an "I-thou" relationship and ends up relegating persons to the status of things.

771

Hence segregation is not only politically, economically and sociologically unsound, it is morally wrong and sinful. Paul Tillich has said that sin is separation. Is not segregation an existential expression of man's tragic separation, his awful estrangement, his terrible sinfulness? Thus it is that I can urge men to obey the 1954 decision of the Supreme Court, for it is morally right; and I can urge them to disobey segregation ordinances, for they are morally wrong.

Let us consider a more concrete example of just and unjust laws. An unjust law is a code that a numerical or power majority group compels a minority group to obey but does not make binding on itself. This is *difference* made legal. By the same token, a just law is a code that a majority compels a minority to follow and that it is willing to follow itself. This is *sameness* made legal.

Let me give another explanation. A law is unjust if it is inflicted on a minority that, as a result of being denied the right to vote, had no part in enacting or devising the law. Who can say that the legislature of Alabama which set up that state's segregation laws was democratically elected? Throughout Alabama all sort of devious methods are used to prevent Negros from becoming registered voters, and there are some counties in which, even though Negroes constitute a majority of the population, not a single Negro is registered. Can any law enacted under such circumstances be considered democratically structured?

Sometimes a law is just on its face and unjust in its application. For instance, I have been arrested on a charge of parading without a permit. Now, there is nothing wrong in having an ordinance which requires a permit for a parade. But such an ordinance becomes unjust when it is used to maintain segregation and to deny citizens the First-Amendment privilege of peaceful assembly and protest.

I hope you are able to see the distinction I am trying to point out. In no sense do I advocate evading or defying the law, as would the rabid segregationist. That would lead to anarchy. One who breaks an unjust law must do so openly, lovingly, and with a willingness to accept the penalty. I submit that an individual who breaks a law that conscience tells him is unjust, and who willingly accepts the penalty of imprisonment in order to arouse the conscience of the community over its injustice, is in reality expressing the highest respect for law.

Of course, there is nothing new about this kind of civil disobedience. It was evidenced sublimely in the refusal of Shadrach, Meshach and Abednego to obey the laws of Nebuchadnezzar, on the ground that a higher moral law was at stake. It was practiced superbly by the early Christians, who were willing to face hungry lions and the excruciating pain of chopping blocks rather than submit to certain unjust laws of the Roman Empire. To a degree, academic freedom is a reality today because Socrates practiced civil disobedience. In our own nation, the Boston Tea Party represented a massive act of civil disobedience.

We should never forget that everything Adolf Hitler did in Germany was "legal" and everything the Hungarian freedom fighters did in Hungary was "illegal." It was "illegal" to aid and comfort a Jew in Hitler's Germany. Even so, I am sure that, had I lived in Germany at the time, I would have aided and comforted my Jewish brothers. If today I lived in a Communist country where certain principles dear to the Christian faith are suppressed, I would openly advocate disobeying that country's antireligious laws. . . .

Oppressed people cannot remain oppressed forever. The yearning for freedom eventually manifests itself, and that is what has happened to the American Negro. Something within has reminded him of his birthright of freedom, and something without has reminded him that it can be gained. Consciously or unconsciously, he has been caught up by the *Zeitgeist,* and with his black brothers of Africa and his brown and yellow brothers of Asia, South America and the Caribbean, the United States Negro is moving with a sense of great urgency toward the promised land of racial justice. If one recognizes the vital urge that has engulfed the Negro community, one should readily understand why public demonstrations are taking place. The Negro has many pent up resentments and latent frustrations, and he must release them. So let him march; let him make prayer pilgrimages to the city hall; let him go on freedom rides—and try to understand why he must do so. If his repressed emotions are not released in nonviolent ways, they will seek expression through violence; this is not a threat but a fact of history. So I have not said to my people "Get rid of your discontent." Rather, I have tried to say that this normal and healthy discontent can be channeled into the creative outlet of nonviolent direct action. And now this approach is being termed extremist.

But though I was initially disappointed at being categorized as an extremist, as I continued to think about the matter I gradually gained a measure of satisfaction from the label. Was not Jesus an extremist for love: "Love your enemies, bless them that curse you, do good to them that hate you, and pray for them which despitefully use you, and persecute you." Was not Amos an extremist for justice: "Let justice roll down like waters and righteousness like an ever-flowing stream." Was not Paul an extremist for the Christian gospel: "I bear in my body the marks of the Lord Jesus." Was not Martin Luther an extremist: "Here I stand; I cannot do otherwise, so help me God." And John Bunyan: "I will stay in jail to the end of my days before I make a butchery of my

conscience." And Abraham Lincoln: "This nation cannot survive half slave and half free." And Thomas Jefferson: "We hold these truths to be self-evident, that all men are created equal . . ." So the question is not whether we will be extremists, but what kind of extremists we will be. Will we be extremists for hate or for love? Will we be extremists for the preservation of injustice or for the extension of justice? In that dramatic scene on Calvary's hill three men were crucified. We must never forget that all three were crucified for the same crime—the crime of extremism. Two were extremists for immorality, and thus fell below their environment. The other, Jesus Christ, was an extremist for love, truth and goodness, and thereby above his environment. Perhaps the South, the nation and the world are in dire need of creative extremists.

I had hoped that the white moderate would see this need. Perhaps I was too optimistic; perhaps I expected too much. I suppose I should have realized that few members of the oppressor race can understand the deep groans and passionate yearnings of the oppressed race, and still fewer have the vision to see that injustice must be rooted out by strong, persistent and determined action. I am thankful, however, that some of our white brothers in the South have grasped the meaning of this social revolution and committed themselves to it. They are still all too few in quantity, but they are big in quality. Some—such as Ralph McGill, Lillian Smith, Harry Golden, James McBride Dabbs, Ann Braden and Sarah Patton Boyle—have written about our struggle in eloquent and prophetic terms. Others have marched with us down nameless streets of the South. They have languished in filthy, roach-infested jails, suffering the abuse and brutality of policemen who view them as "dirty nigger-lovers." Unlike so many of their moderate brothers and sisters, they have recognized the urgency of the moment and sensed the need for powerful "action" antidotes to combat the disease of segregation. . . .

In spite of my shattered dreams, I came to Birmingham with the hope that the white religious leadership of this community would see the justice of our cause and, with deep moral concern, would serve as the channel through which our just grievances could reach the power structure. I had hoped that each of you would understand. But again I have been disappointed.

I have heard numerous southern religious leaders admonish their worshipers to comply with a desegregation decision because it is the law, but I have longed to hear white ministers declare: "Follow this decree because integration is morally right and because the Negro is your brother." In the midst of blatant injustices inflicted upon the Negro, I have watched white churchmen stand on the sideline and mouth pious irrelevancies and sanctimonious trivialities. In the midst of a mighty struggle to rid our nation of racial and economic injustice, I have heard many ministers say: "Those are social issues, with which the gospel has no real concern." And I have watched many churches commit themselves to a completely otherworldly religion which makes a strange, un-Biblical distinction between body and soul, between the sacred and the secular.

I have traveled the length and breadth of Alabama, Mississippi and all the other southern states. On sweltering summer days and crisp autumn mornings I have looked at the South's beautiful churches with their lofty spires pointing heavenward. I have beheld the impressive outlines of her massive religious-education buildings. Over and over I have found myself asking: "What kind of people worship here? Who is their God? Where were their voices when the lips of Governor Barnett dripped with words of interposition and nullification? Where were they when Governor Wallace gave a clarion call for defiance and hatred? Where were their voices of support when bruised and weary Negro men and women decided to rise from the dark dungeons of complacency to the bright hills of creative protest?"

Yes, these questions were still in my mind. In deep disappointment I have wept over the laxity of the church. But be assured that my tears have been tears of love. There can be no deep disappointment where there is not deep love. Yes, I love the church. How could I do otherwise? I am in the rather unique position of being the son, the grandson and the great-grandson of preachers. Yes, I see the church as the body of Christ. But, oh! How we have blemished and scarred that body through social neglect and through fear of being nonconformists.

There was a time when the church was very powerful—in the time when the early Christians rejoiced at being deemed worthy to suffer for what they believed. In those days the church was not merely a thermometer that recorded the ideas and principles of popular opinion; it was a thermostat that transformed the mores of society. Whenever the early Christians entered a town, the people in power became disturbed and immediately sought to convict the Christians of being "disturbers of the peace" and "outside agitators." But the Christians pressed on, in the conviction that they were "a colony of heaven," called to obey God rather than man. Small in number, they were big in commitment. They were too God-intoxicated to be "astronomically intimidated." By their effort and example they brought an end to such ancient evils as infanticide and gladiatorial contests.

Things are different now. So often the contemporary church is a weak, ineffectual voice with an uncertain sound. So often it is an arch-defender of the status quo. Far from being disturbed by the presence of the church, the power structure of the average community is consoled by the church's silent—and often even vocal—sanction of things as they are.

But the judgment of God is upon the church as never before. If today's church does not recapture the sacrificial spirit of the early church, it will lose its authenticity, forfeit the loyalty of millions, and be dismissed as an irrelevant social club with no meaning for the twentieth century. Every day I meet young people whose disappointment with the church has turned into outright disgust.

Perhaps I have once again been too optimistic. Is organized religion too inextricably bound to the status quo to save our nation and the world? Perhaps I must turn my faith to the inner spiritual church, the church within the church, as the true *ekklesia* and the hope of the world. But again I am thankful to God that some noble souls from the ranks of organized religion have broken loose from the paralyzing chains of conformity and joined us as active partners in the struggle for freedom. They have left their secure congregations and walked the streets of Albany, Georgia, with us. They have gone down the highways of the South on tortuous rides for freedom. Yes, they have gone to jail with us. Some have been dismissed from their churches, have lost the support of their bishops and fellow ministers. But they have acted in the faith that right defeated is stronger than evil triumphant. Their witness has been the spiritual salt that has preserved the true meaning of the gospel in these troubled times. They have carved a tunnel of hope through the dark mountain of disappointment.

I hope the church as a whole will meet the challenge of this decisive hour. But even if the church does not come to the aid of justice, I have no despair about the future. I have no fear about the outcome of our struggle in Birmingham, even if our motives are at present misunderstood. We will reach the goal of freedom in Birmingham and all over the nation, because the goal of America is freedom. Abused and scorned though we may be, our destiny is tied up with America's destiny. Before the pilgrims landed at Plymouth, we were here. Before the pen of Jefferson etched the majestic words of the Declaration of Independence across the pages of history, we were here. For more than two centuries our forebears labored in this country without wages; they made cotton king; they built the homes of their masters while suffering gross injustice and shameful humiliation—and yet out of a bottomless vitality they continued to thrive and develop. If the inexpressible cruelties of slavery could not stop us, the opposition we now face will surely fail. We will win our freedom because the sacred heritage of our nation and the eternal will of God are embodied in our echoing demands.

Before closing I feel impelled to mention one other point in your statement that has troubled me profoundly. You warmly commended the Birmingham police force for keeping "order" and "preventing violence." I doubt that you would have so warmly commended the police force if you had seen its dogs sinking their teeth into unarmed, nonviolent Negroes. I doubt that you would so quickly commend the policemen if you were to observe their ugly and inhumane treatment of Negroes here in the city jail; if you were to watch them push and curse old Negro women and young Negro girls; if you were to see them slap and kick old Negro men and young boys; if you were to observe them, as they did on two occasions, refuse to give us food because we wanted to sing our grace together. I cannot join you in your praise of the Birmingham police department.

It is true that the police have exercised a degree of discipline in handling the demonstrators. In this sense they have conducted themselves rather "nonviolently" in public. But for what purpose? To preserve the evil system of segregation. Over the past few years I have consistently preached that nonviolence demands that the means we use must be as pure as the ends we seek. I have tried to make clear that it is wrong to use immoral means to attain moral ends. But now I must affirm that it is just as wrong, or perhaps even more so, to use moral means to preserve immoral ends. Perhaps Mr. Connor and his policemen have been rather nonviolent in public, as was Chief Pritchett in Albany, Georgia, but they have used the moral means of nonviolence to maintain the immoral end of racial injustice. As T. S. Eliot has said: "The last temptation is the greatest treason: To do the right deed for the wrong reason."

I wish you had commended the Negro sit-inners and demonstrators of Birmingham for their sublime courage, their willingness to suffer and their amazing discipline in the midst of great provocation. One day the South will recognize its real heroes. They will be the James Merediths, with the noble sense of purpose that enables them to face jeering and hostile mobs, and with the agonizing loneliness that characterizes the life of the pioneer. They will be old, oppressed, battered Negro women, symbolized in a seventy-two-year-old woman in Montgomery, Alabama, who rose up with a sense of dignity and with her people decided not to ride segregated buses, and who responded with ungrammatical profundity to one who inquired about her weariness: "My feets is tired, but my soul is at rest." They will be the young high school and college students, the young ministers of the gospel and a host of their elders, courageously and nonviolently sitting in at lunch counters and willingly going to jail for conscience' sake. One day the South will know that when these disinherited children of God sat down at lunch counters, they were in reality standing up for what is best in the American dream and for the most sacred values in our Judaeo-Christian heritage, thereby bringing our nation back to those great wells of democracy which were dug deep by the founding fathers in their formulation of the Constitution and the Declaration of Independence.

Never before have I written so long a letter. I'm afraid it is much too long to take your precious time. I can assure you that it would have been much shorter if I had been writing from a comfortable desk, but what else can one do when he is alone in a narrow jail cell, other than write long letters, think long thoughts and pray long prayers?

If I have said anything in this letter that overstates the truth and indicates an unreasonable impatience, I beg you to forgive me. If I have said anything that understates the truth and indicates my having a patience that allows me to settle for anything less than brotherhood, I beg God to forgive me.

I hope this letter finds you strong in the faith. I also hope that circumstances will soon make it possible for me to meet each of you, not as an integrationist or a civil-rights leader but as a fellow clergyman and a Christian brother. Let us all hope that the dark clouds of racial prejudice will soon pass away and the deep fog of misunderstanding will be lifted from our fear-drenched communities, and in some not too distant tomorrow the radiant stars of love and brotherhood will shine over our great nation with all their scintillating beauty.

Yours for the cause of Peace and Brotherhood
MARTIN LUTHER KING, JR.

GLOSSARY

ALIENATION   According to Marx, a condition that affects workers in a capitalist society due to the division of labor and the market system. To be alienated from something is to be estranged from it; capitalism estranges workers from their own labor and the products of their labor.

ANARCHISM   The view that no government has the legitimate authority to coerce people, and that the public interest and individual rights can best be served without a state of any kind.

AUTHORITY   That which controls or has the right to control; for example, government has the authority to tax one's income. An authoritarian government disallows active participation in the governing process and is nondemocratic.

BOURGEOISIE   The French term for the middle class.

CAPITALISM   An economic system in which the means of production are privately owned.

CIVIL DISOBEDIENCE   Nonviolent disobedience of the law with the goal of changing laws deemed unjust.

COMMUNISM   According to Marx and Lenin, a form of society in which there is no state and no economic classes. In a communist society, workers own and operate the means of production without the need of a state.

DEMOCRACY   A form of government where policies or the makers of policies are chosen by popular mandate. A democratic government seeks participation of its citizens in the process of self-rule.

DIFFERENCE PRINCIPLE   A principle of justice advocated by John Rawls where inequalities permitted by society must be to everyone's advantage and must be attached to positions and opportunities open to all.

DISTRIBUTIVE JUSTICE   An ideal allocation to all members of society of their fair share of such things as money, property, privileges, opportunities, education, and rights.

ENTITLEMENT THEORY OF JUSTICE   A theory of justice advocated by Robert Nozick where individuals are entitled to the property they have acquired by honest means; they may do as they see fit with their property as long as they do not infringe upon the rights of others. Justice requires that they be able to keep their property and not be hindered in the lawful use of it.

EQUALITY PRINCIPLE   A principle of justice advocated by John Rawls whereby every person in society has a right to the greatest basic freedom compatible with similar freedom for all.

EXPLOITATION   According to Karl Marx, the unjust treatment of the working class by the capitalist middle class; the capitalists exploit the worker by allocating all surplus value to themselves in the form of profit.

JUSTICE   In a general sense, the virtues of an ideal society. More specifically, the balance of public interests and individual rights, the fair sharing of social goods, the proper punishment of criminals, and the fair restitution of victims of crime and misfortune in a society; See *retributive justice* and *distributive justice*.

LIBERAL DEMOCRACY   A system of government that is democratic, capitalistic, and pluralistic.

NATURAL RIGHT   According to Locke, rights that belong to persons by virtue of their being human. Natural rights may be recognized by the state, but they exist independently of it, and no one, including government, may take them away. Natural rights set the moral limits of the state.

PLURALISM   A political and social system in which there are multiple centers of power.

PROLETARIAT   The working class.

RETRIBUTIVE JUSTICE   A conception of justice where the primary aim is punishment of crime.

SOCIAL CONTRACT   A historical fiction used by some political theorists, such as Hobbes, Locke, and Rousseau, to justify the existence of the state. According to *social contract theory*, the state is the result of an agreement (tacit or explicit) among individuals that everyone shall abide by the laws of the state in order to maximize the public interest and ensure cooperation among themselves.

SOCIALISM   An economic system in which the means of production are owned by the state.

STATE OF NATURE   In social contract theory, the condition that precedes the existence of the state; the description of the state of nature differs in Hobbes, Locke, and Rousseau.

SURPLUS VALUE   The difference between the value of the commodities produced by the worker for the capitalist, and the commodities received as wages by the worker; according to Marx, the primary means of capitalist exploitation.

VEIL OF IGNORANCE   According to Rawls, the condition under which the framers of the social contract would devise a just society. Behind the veil of ignorance, none of the devisers would know how the positions in a new society would be distributed; consequently, they would agree to a society in which they would be willing to accept whatever position they end up having.

WELFARE STATE   A capitalistic society that has permitted state intervention in order to negate inequalities between individuals and to effect distributive justice.

FOR FURTHER STUDY

Bedau, H.A. *Civil Disobedience: Theory and Practice*. New York: Pegasus, 1969.
A very useful anthology.

Dworkin, Ronald. *Taking Rights Seriously*. Cambridge: Harvard University Press, 1977.
An approach to social justice that has provoked much discussion.

Harrington, Michael. *Twilight of Capitalism*. New York: Simon & Schuster, 1976.
A critique of capitalism and a defense of democratic socialism.

Lenin, V.I. *State and Revolution*. New York: International Publishers, 1943.
Lenin's major political work.

Locke, John. *Two Treatises on Civil Government*. Edited by Peter Laslett. New York: New American Library, 1965.
The classic statement of social contract theory, the basis of liberal democracy. Laslett's introduction is excellent.

Nozick, Robert. *Anarchy, State, and Utopia*. New York: Basic Books, 1974.
A stimulating contemporary defense of Locke's view of limited government; written in an engaging, witty style, although technical in places.

Plamenatz., John. *Man and Society*. London: Longmans, 1963.

An excellent history of political philosophy.

Rawls, John. *A Theory of Justice.* Cambridge: Harvard University Press, 1971.

One of the most influential works on political philosophy in our day; defends a theory of justice as fairness, based on individual rights.

Smith, Adam. *Wealth of Nations: Representative Selections,* Edited by Bruce Mazlish. Indianapolis: Bobbs-Merrill, 1961.

The classic account of liberal economic theory, in an abridged edition.

Tucker, Robert C., ed. *The Marx-Engels Reader,* 2d ed. New York: W.W. Norton, 1978.

An excellent collection of the most important writings, including the early philosophical writings.

PART TEN

◆

AESTHETICS

A thing of beauty is a joy forever.

JOHN KEATS

ORIENTATION

Quite lately, my noble friend, when I was condemning as ugly some things in certain compositions, and praising others as beautiful, somebody threw me in confusion by interrogating me in a most offensive manner, rather to this effect: "You, Socrates, pray how do you know what things are beautiful and what are ugly?" In my incompetence I was confounded, and could find no proper answer to give him—so leaving the company, I was filled with anger and reproaches against myself, and promised myself that the first time I met with one of you wise men, I would listen to him and learn, and when I had mastered my lesson thoroughly, I would go back to my questioner and join battle with him again. So you see that you have come at a beautifully appropriate moment, and I ask you to teach me properly what is beauty by itself, answering my question with the utmost precision you can attain: I do not want to be made to look a fool a second time, by another cross-examination.

Plato, *Greater Hippias*

Philosophy concerns not only the True and the Good but also the Beautiful. Our understanding of the world of values would be very limited if restricted to moral and political values. Aesthetics, from the Greek word *aisthetikos*, meaning "sensory perception," concerns the study of beauty as well as the analysis of the values, tastes, and standards involved in our experience of what we call beautiful. In recent years aesthetics has come to mean that branch of philosophy concerned with art and the nature of the work of art.

Careful readers of the above passage from Plato will not fail to notice the humility, irony, and humor of Socrates. His humility is seen in his willingness to express his ignorance and frustration at not knowing what beauty is. The irony, of course, is that he speaks of "a beautifully appropriate moment" to teach what beauty is. (How can one speak of a moment as being beautiful if one does not already know what beauty is?) The humorous element is that in the resultant conversation, Socrates is the one who demonstrates greater knowledge on the topic of beauty than his would-be "teachers"—it is they, not he, who come off as being foolish in the text.

The question of the nature of beauty continues to confound us today, just as it did Socrates in ancient Greece. Socrates believed he could justify his condemnation of some things as ugly and his praising of some things as beautiful only if he could provide an acceptable definition for those terms. And yet it is notoriously difficult to come up with a universally accepted definition of beauty. People have wildly divergent views on what the term "beauty" means, and about what objects are beautiful. This lack of consensus is what keeps alive the old saying, "Beauty is in the eye of the beholder." If you accept this maxim as true, this means that everyone uses the term "beauty" or "beautiful" differently, depending on their own individual perception. But if these words mean different things to different people, how can inter-subjective communication take place? How does this "beholder" know what that "beholder" means by "beauty" or "beautiful"? How would we be able to keep alive the conversation that Socrates has initiated on the meaning of beauty?

Because the experiences we identify as aesthetic are often connected with works of art, aesthetics is sometimes referred to as "philosophy of art." But by shifting the discussion from *beauty* to *art* we do not thereby escape the slippery ground. The question "Do you know what art is" is every bit as difficult as the question about the definition of beauty.

Contemporary works of art frequently leave us as perplexed as Socrates was long ago. If you go to a public park in downtown Hartford, Connecticut, you will see a group of thirty-six boulders. They were put there under the supervision of a man named Carl Andre, who refers to himself as an artist. Andre entitled his creation "Stone Field." In exchange for his "work," Andre received $87,000 from the National Endowment for the Arts and the Hartford Foundation for Public Giving. What shall we say? Is "Stone Field" really a work of art? Is Carl Andre really an artist?

Questions like this have led philosophers to try to formulate theories about beauty and art, aesthetic experience and aesthetic value, the properties of a work of art, the social context of art and the "art world," and the role of art and the artist in society. In general, problems in aesthetics have been approached in three different ways: (1) approaches that center on the artist; (2) approaches that center on the work of art; and (3) approaches that center on the reception of the work of art.

In tracing the philosophy of art from ancient Greece to modern times, three concepts have proven to be enormously important: Imitation, form, and expression. In this part we shall explore briefly each concept, highlighting aesthetic theories that have resulted from a consideration of each. The final Contemporary Perspectives section in this book is devoted to a discussion of the artist and society.

IMITATION

Mimesis, or imitation, as it is commonly translated from the Greek, must not be understood in any literal sense. Neither Plato nor Aristotle, as we shall see, thought of imitation as a kind of mindless, nonexpressive copying. Rather, art on this model imitates the universal Reality by expressing the eternal and divine in the guise of the temporal and human.

PLATO'S SYMPOSIUM

Plato thought of beauty as a transcendent Form. Plato's Forms (Part 3) are those eternal ideals that comprise the transcendent "World of Being." The objects that exist in our temporal "World of Becoming" are real to a lesser extent than the Forms, and only because they participate in the full reality of the Forms. The true being of any thing in this world is the ideal Form that shapes its structure. Insight into true reality occurs as we learn to recognize the ideal Form behind the imperfect representation (or appearance) of objects in this world. Just as there are Forms for the "True" and the "Good," there exists an ideal Form of Beauty. It is this ideal Form of Beauty that we recognize when we experience and fall in love with things and persons that are beautiful.

At one point in Shakespeare's *Romeo and Juliet*, Romeo thinks of Juliet and exults, "Beauty too rich for use, for earth too dear." One might say that Romeo has experienced the Platonic vision of beauty, believing that in Juliet he has found a transcendent beauty not ordinarily encountered on earth. He has come to know the Form of Beauty through one of the beautiful beings in this world. When we fall in love, we are jolted out of one plane of reality into another. This is what makes loving another person so momentous, mysterious, and profound.

For Plato, love shows us the path toward insight into the Form of Beauty. When we recognize the Form of Beauty in our love for another, we are led into further insight into the Forms in general. Because our first experience with beauty involves us in an encounter with a loftier plane of reality, we are often confused by our first experience with love. We fail to see that the beauty of our beloved is identical to the beauty of every other beautiful person or thing. Like Romeo, we are apt to think that the beauty we encounter is uniquely characteristic of our "Juliet," not realizing that such beauty is a universal Form, manifest in all that is beautiful. Only when we recognize that beauty in all its earthly manifestations is identical do we gain genuine insight into the Form of Beauty.

In our first reading selection, excerpted from **Plato's** *Symposium*, Socrates describes the several stages of insight into the Form of Beauty. Socrates recounts to his audience a conversation he had with a woman named Diotima, who taught him the mysteries of love. According to Diotima, real love begins with love of one person but reaches its highest stage of development when the lover comes to love all that is truly beautiful. In loving all that is beautiful, the lover comes to realize that he or she loves but one thing: beauty in itself. Whereas Romeo, in his initial love experience believes that he loves only Juliet, Socrates would say that what Romeo *really* loves is beauty itself—the beauty that he sees manifesting itself in Juliet.

PLATO'S ION

Whereas Plato waxed eloquent about the Form of Beauty and the way we apprehend it through beautiful things and persons, he was extremely suspicious about *works of art*. Love of another person can lead us to the Form of Beauty, but works of art are not as reliable. They tend to cause us to focus too much on the World of Appearances, distracting us from the divine World of the Forms.

In the *Ion*, we find Socrates discussing poetic talent with Ion, a poet. Ion remarks that he is able to move audiences to emotion with his renditions of Homer, but his art is insufficient to produce the same reaction when interpreting other poets. Socrates convinces Ion that his ability should not be considered an art at all. If his performances were truly an art, he would know how to apply the rules to all poetic material. Ion performs Homer well because he is divinely inspired. If he were performing with knowledge, his ability would not be limited to Homer. Because he does not possess knowledge, he cannot control and direct the art he claims to practice. Therefore, Ion is merely a vehicle employed by the gods; his soul has not gained the knowledge of the Forms.

PLATO'S REPUBLIC

Plato's ambivalence toward art is even more pronounced in *The Republic*. In this famous dialogue Socrates and his friends are discussing the qualities that make up a good state. One must keep Plato's suspicion of art in this context: He believes that art has the power to distract citizens from their proper role in the good state. For Plato, the good state is characterized by justice—by which he means a state wherein all individuals perform their own special function, thus promoting the good of the whole. The just state is perfectly harmonious; each citizen's life must therefore be harmonious. Harmony in an individual can only be achieved when reason—one of the three components of the soul—rules over the remaining two components, the appetites and the spirit.

Reason's proper role is to rule over appetite and spirit, discerning the true reality that lies behind appearances. Analogously, on the political level, the state can be harmonious only when it is ruled in accordance with reason. Art, however, directs attention to appearances and away from the divine World of the Forms. Art is imitative—it copies the appearance of material objects, which in turn copy the true reality of the Forms. Hence, art is "thrice removed from the truth!"—a copy of a copy. Instead of looking for Truth, Goodness, and Beauty, which lie beyond the material world, artists content themselves with copying the material world.

Additionally, art has the tendency to arouse passion. This in itself is not bad, for passion is the first step of the soul on the way to the Forms. But when passion is unchecked and uncontrolled by reason, it can "inspire" a person to go "against reason." The consequences of irrationalism are dire, both for the individual and the state. Consequently, Plato in *The Republic* decides that poets must be censored, since art has the power to harm even the state's best citizens.

ARISTOTLE'S POETICS

There are profound differences between Plato's metaphysics and the metaphysics of Aristotle, his most famous student. As we have seen, Plato links beauty to the transcendent World of Forms, and judges art harshly because it fails to illuminate transcendent truth. Aristotle, by contrast, is concerned with art precisely as a mode of Becoming—he wants to know how works of art come to be and the creative process that guides their formation. Thus beauty for Aristotle is very much a thing of this world. It can be studied through the careful examination of beautiful things.

Aristotle makes two important arguments against Plato. First, unlike Plato, he does not regard artistic creation as a form of divine intervention. Aristotle insists that artistic activity is a legitimate way of seeking knowledge, and hence inherently rational. Unlike history, which merely chronicles events in a disinterested fashion, art provides a rational way to understand human behavior by demonstrating what certain types of people are likely to do in certain life situations. Thus we learn from art.

Second, he argues that emotion and its expression are essential for a healthy individual and society. Tragedy, for example, provides us with the opportunity to purge ourselves of negative emotions under controlled conditions created by the artist. Tragedy, which turns on some fatal flaw in the hero's character, has a profound effect on us. It arouses our pity and fear in order to effect a **catharsis,** or cleansing, of these emotions. Central to tragedy is the plot. The aim is to arouse pity and fear through the very structure and incidents of the play so that any person who simply hears the plot recounted shall be filled with horror and pity. As we identify with the tragic hero, we sense our own human vulnerability and learn to master our feelings of vulnerability and insecurity.

In summary, Aristotle does not regard the primary task of art to be extra-artistic, a mere means of gaining access to some otherworldly realm. Rather, the arts are self-sufficient activities that give dignity to life and have more than an instrumental value. They impart to us a sense of joy that is found in contemplation for its own sake. Additionally, they provide amusement and relaxation from work. Imitative arts are no less worthy because they are imitative; the pleasures they provide are innocent and rewarding. It is through imitation, after all, that we learn. Humans take a natural delight in imitations of all sorts, as can be seen in a child's play. All humans by nature desire to learn; if we can gain pleasure through our learning, so much the better.

FORM

Although the imitative conception of art exercised a strong influence in the early Christian period (it can be seen in the writings of Saint Augustine and Saint Thomas Aquinas), the concept gradually fell into disrepute. Attention began to shift away from an artist-centered view of art to an audience-centered and object-centered point of view. Observers began to notice that aesthetic experience is permeated by formal properties—such as rhythm, harmony, design, shape, sound, color, and so on—in various combinations.

The problem is that not everyone is sufficiently educated to detect these formal characteristics apart from "formal" education. Should a person not have a special faculty—taste, for example—in order to properly understand and explain an aesthetic experience?

DAVID HUME AND THE FACULTY OF TASTE: A VIEWER-CENTERED APPROACH TO ART

Introduced in the eighteenth century as a way of explaining aesthetic experience, the concept of taste continues to be very influential today. In 1757, in an essay entitled "Of a Standard of Taste," David Hume argued that taste is a human faculty analogous to the senses of sight and hearing. Judgments of taste therefore have the same empirical foundation as do judgments about what we see or hear. Although some unfortunate people are color-blind and tone-deaf, Hume nevertheless thought that people in a "sound state of the organism" can exercise their faculty of taste in order to discern that Milton is a better poet than Ogilvie. The fact that you have probably heard of Milton, but not Ogilvie, would seem to confirm Hume's judgment that Milton is a better poet than Ogilvie. Since most people with good taste have preferred Milton to Ogilvie, the former's work has endured, while the latter's has not. Durable admiration is a good indication of the quality of an artwork. Hume proposed that standards of taste, like color charts, could be produced by studying the evaluations of competent judges (people with taste).

"There is no disputing over taste," Hume wrote, quoting some ancient writers. But doesn't this mean that everyone's taste is equally valid? If so, then how could we justifiably criticize another person's taste as deplorable? If a friend insisted that the music of the Rolling Stones is superior to Bach or Beethoven, and that Barry Manilow's music beats them all, what could we possibly say? Since there is no arguing about tastes, wouldn't we have to just throw up our hands and admit that our friend's taste in music is as good as ours? If we tried to defend Sir Laurence Olivier's film acting as superior to Sylvester Stallone's in his Rambo movies, could we do so on good grounds, or are we just being snobbish? Apart from social conventions, is there any meaning to the phrase "good taste?" Hasn't Hume made aesthetic judgment radically subjective?

Hume believed that although each of us judges subjectively, the sentiment by which we judge is a natural and human one. Hence, we can expect objective agreement among those whose sensibilities have been nurtured and educated properly. A thing is appropriately called beautiful if and only if it provokes aesthetic sentiment in competent judges. Ultimately, what matters most is not the characteristics of the object, as important as they may be, but the judgment of competent observers. The problem is that many people lack such judgment because they are uncultivated, uneducated, confused, or in poor health. The aforementioned "durable admiration"—for example, the lasting admiration for the classics and classical authors—may be a reliable indicator of great art, but it may be of little help when we are trying to judge the value of works produced in our own time. Thus Hume warned against the "caprices of mode and fashion" and the "mistakes of ignorance and envy."

Even so, there is good reason to find fault with Hume's notion of "good taste." For one thing, it is not a clear concept. Unlike vision, which is a sense faculty that can be "located" and tested, taste is elusive; there is nothing analogous to a color chart to which we could refer. Despite Hume's confidence that "laws of taste" could be discovered, much as Newton discovered the laws of physics, there is no consensus or even convergence of judgment about taste.

Furthermore, thinking of taste as a "special sensitivity" possessed by a cultivated elite has political difficulties. Hume's theory was formulated in an aristocratic age when it was quite common to equate the class of people who have good taste with the ruling elite. As Marx pointed out (see Part 9), the ruling ideas in a society are simply the ideas of the ruling class. Doesn't Hume's theory prove Marx' point that art (like everything else) is produced by historical conditions and reflects the ideology of the ruling class?

Finally, so-called "experts" with "special taste" have often turned out to be conservative dogmatists blind to the talent of budding young artists. The experts ignored Van Gogh's paintings completely. What young painter in Paris or New York is suffering the same fate today?

MONROE BEARDSLEY, CLIVE BELL, ROGER FRY: AN OBJECT-CENTERED APPROACH TO ART

There is an important alternative to Hume's viewer-centered theory—the object-centered **formalism** of Monroe Beardsley, Clive Bell, and Roger Fry. *In all art forms, formalists emphasize intrinsic qualities of the object or event itself, not what it represents or expresses.* When we observe a work of art, we should pay attention not to what it represents (or "imitates") but rather *to how it presents*. What truly matters is form, not content—hence the label "formalism."

Think back to Socrates' question: "What makes things beautiful?" Formalists respond by translating this question into another: "What things must I attend to if I am attending aesthetically?" Monroe Beardsley contends that we must attend to the features that we value aesthetically, namely **regional qualities** and **formal unity**.[1] For Beardsley, aesthetic experience is characterized by attention to and pleasure taken in an object's intrinsic qualities and the way these qualities are related to one another. Regional qualities are things such as color, pitch, or rhyme, qualities that are actually in an object that we perceive as part of the whole that we are experiencing. These qualities are regional in the sense that we can actually point them out in an object. That is, they are located in some region of the object—there is, say, a patch of green in the foreground of a painting, or a long vowel sound at the end of a line of poetry, or five ascending notes in a musical score. Formal unity has to do with the way these qualities are put together. Aesthetic objects display a pattern of organization that may be referred to as symmetry, for instance, or repetition.

Beardsley's notions of regional qualities and formal unity can be seen in most critical discussions of works of art. Here is a musical example:

> The basic sound ideal of the Renaissance was a polyphony of independent voices; the sound ideal of the Baroque was a firm bass and a florid treble, held together by unobtrusive harmony. The ideal of musical texture consisting of a single melody supported by accompanying harmonies was not in itself new.[2]

In this example, the regional qualities cited would include the "polyphony of independent voices" characteristic of Renaissance music, and the "firm bass" and "florid treble" of the Baroque period. The formal unity would be the idea of a "musical texture consisting of a single melody supported by accompanying harmonies."

In his review of the film *High Noon*, critic Bowsley Crowther provides an example of specific camera shots (regional qualities) and the way they are held together (formal unity):

> A brilliant assembly of shots . . . holds the tale in taut suspension just before the fatal hour of noon. The issues have been established, the townsfolk have fallen away and the sheriff, alone with his destiny, has sat down at his desk to wait. Over his shoulder Mr. Zimmerman [the film's director] shows us a white sheet of paper on which is scrawled "last will and testament" by a slowly

---

[1]See Monroe Beardsley, "The Aesthetic Point of View," in *Perspectives in Education*, ed. Howard E. Kiefer and Milton K. Munitz (Albany, N.Y.: Suny Press, 1970), 10.
[2]Donald Jay Gould, *A History of Western Music* (New York: Norton, 1980), 300.

moving pen. Then he gives us a shot [oft repeated] of the pendulum of the clock.[3]

The two most important figures in formalism for the visual arts were the British theorists Clive Bell and Roger Fry. They believed that what counts aesthetically cannot be the content of a work of art, for two works with the same content can be aesthetically quite different. For instance, two films—a 1940s original and a 1990s remake—can be radically different aesthetically even when dealing with the same content. The same is true of two paintings; compare a Cézanne still life with one by Rembrandt.

Form is what is directly presented to and perceived by us. Of course, each art form has its own peculiar formal qualities. Painting is concerned with colors, lines, and shapes, whereas music is characterized by pitches, rhythms, and dynamics. Dance stresses body movements, while film makes use of camera angles and lighting.

Clive Bell argues that what is peculiar to art is its "significant form"—for instance, the relations and combinations of lines and colors that evoke in us some emotional response. Bell and Fry consistently deemphasize a work's history and context, insisting that aesthetic experience has only form as its object:

> To appreciate a work of art we need bring with us nothing from life, no knowledge of its ideas and affairs, no familiarity with its emotions. Art transports us from the world of man's activity to a world of aesthetic exaltation. For a moment we are shut off from human interests; our anticipations and memories are arrested; we are lifted above the stream of life.[4]

Naturally, formalists disagree with Hume's subjective approach to aesthetic experience. In the reading selection in Chapter 74, Monroe Beardsley argues (against Hume) that we do and should dispute about tastes. We give objective reasons for our aesthetic judgments, and we expect people to change their opinions if these reasons are sufficiently good ones.

THE LIMITS OF FORMALISM

Critics of formalism usually agree that the perceptual qualities of objects are aesthetically important, but they insist that content and context matter as well. Indeed, how can we separate form from content in aesthetic experience? Can an

[3]Bowsley Crowther, review of *High Noon*, in *New York Times Film Review*, ed. George Amberg, (New York: Quadrangle Books, 1971), 271.
[4]Clive Bell, *Art* (London: Chatto & Windus, 1920), 25.

observer really see form apart from content? Do we not respond emotionally to nonformal properties of works of art?

Recently, some theorists who have been dissatisfied with formalist approaches to art have stressed the importance of the context in which the work of art is produced. Think back to Carl Andre's "Stone Field." In explaining his work Andre pointed out that his group of boulders is located next to a graveyard and, like the graveyard, uses stones taken from nearby hills. Andre claimed that he had hoped to "unite natural history with the smaller scale of human history." In other words, "Stone Field" *becomes* a work of art precisely because of its context; complex social and institutional practices combine to make it art in the twentieth century.

Marxists have been very critical of formalism. According to Marxist aesthetics, art (like everything else) is produced by historical conditions and can be understood only in terms of the ideologies that give it life. For example, Renaissance sculpture cannot be understood apart from understanding the nature of guilds; contemporary American art cannot be understood apart from the "corporate logic" of late bourgeois capitalism. Hence, social factors cannot be separated from a work of art, and it is naive to think that they can. Art objects are always situated in a certain context.

EXPRESSION

There is considerable consensus today among aestheticians that art is in some sense expressive. Vincent Van Gogh, whose paintings have captured the contemporary imagination, wrote these words about what he was doing when he created his emotional painting, *Pieta:*

> Well, I with my mental disease, I keep thinking of so many artists suffering mentally, and I tell myself that this does not prevent one from exercising the painter's profession as if nothing were amiss. When I realize that here the attacks tend to take an almost absurd religious turn, I should almost venture to think that this even *necessitates* a return to the North. Don't talk too much about this to the doctor when you see him—but I do not know if this is not caused by living in old cloisters so many months, both in the Arles hospital and here. In fact, I really must not live in such an atmosphere, one would be better in the street. I am not indifferent, and even when suffering, sometimes religious thoughts bring me great consolation. So this last time during my illness an unfortunate accident happened to me—the lithograph of Delacroix's "Pieta," along with some sheets, fell into some oil and was ruined. I was very distressed—then in the meantime I have been busy painting it, and you will see it

someday. I have made a copy of it on a size 5 or 6 canvas; I hope it has feeling.[5]

For our purposes, two things stand out in this remarkable letter. First, we seem to gain some insight into the meaning of the painting by listening to the artist describe its origin and his artistic intentions. Formalists are opposed to such an approach, citing what they call the **intentional fallacy.** The intentional fallacy is a type of genetic fallacy that makes the mistake of confusing artworks with their causes. Formalists insist that understanding the cause does not entail understanding a work of art. In the case of Van Gogh, formalists would warn against the dangers of undue attention to an artist's biography. And yet, in this case, contrary to the strictures of the formalists, understanding the causes of *Pieta* does seem to give us a deeper insight into the meaning of the work.

Second, Van Gogh's report fits with a widely held idea of what is involved in artistic production—the expression of feeling or emotion. Van Gogh's simple statement, "I hope it has feeling," is perfectly clear. The *desire* to express emotion is generally taken to be a natural and common intention of artists. The mental imagery we have is of an artist who feels an emotion deeply, and proceeds (often painfully) to create an artifact—a collection of words, shapes, movements, or sounds—that he or she believes will express the feeling. There are implications here for the viewer as well. An audience looks or listens to these artistic expressions of meaning and, if the work is successful, responds emotionally. According to this view then, artists are special on two counts: (1) they have strong feelings that they wish to communicate, and (2) they are able to embody their feelings in publicly communicable ways. In the artist there is that rare combination of deep feeling and technical skill; the art is in the feeling and the making.

Before we mention a few theorists who emphasize expression, we should point out that it was precisely this frenzied intensity of feeling (illustrated so well in the dramatic life and death of Van Gogh) that so disturbed Plato in the *Ion*. Plato, of course, wanted to create a society that was as good as possible, meaning it was to be as *rational* as possible. Thus it was clear to him that artists—whose mode of operation is emotional and hence *irrational*—should have no role in good societies! Ironically, Plato was led to this extreme position of censorship not because he valued art so little but because he valued it so much! Do not miss the point here. Art appeals to us at the deepest emotional level. Because it goes right to our hearts, it is capable of moving us to undertake actions that bypass the intellect, causing us to wholly give into our emotions. (Some have argued that, of all the arts, music is the most emotional. It is safe to say that the frenzied behavior sometimes demonstrated at rock concerts would have horrified Plato!)

[5]Vincent Van Gogh, *Further Letters of Vincent Van Gogh to His Brother,* trans. Johana van Gogh (Boston: Houghton-Mifflin, 1930), 380–81

LEO TOLSTOY

The Russian novelist Leo Tolstoy knew the tremendous power of art to produce emotion. Unlike Plato, however, he believed that its emotional energy could be harnessed for good when it was wed to religious and civic ideals. Tolstoy argued that when art is successful, artists succeed in actually making members of their audience more sensitive to the feelings and needs of others. He believed, however, that most of the art of his culture did not serve its proper function. In fact, he was convinced that art and artists in his society were becoming more and more corrupt. In the following quote, he expresses his contempt for time and energy wasted on meaningless activity:

> Not only is enormous labour spent on [art], but in it, as in war, the very lives of men are sacrificed. Hundreds of thousands of people devote their lives from childhood to learning to twirl their legs rapidly (dancers) or to touch notes and strings very rapidly (musicians), or to sketch with paint and represent what they see (artists), or to turn every phrase inside out and find a rhyme to every word. And these people, often very kind and clever and capable of all sorts of useful labour, grow savage over their specialized and stupefying occupations, and become one-sided and self-complacent specialists, dull to all the serious phenomena of life and skillful only at rapidly twisting their legs, their tongues, or their fingers.[6]

It is clear that Tolstoy views the function of art as something more than giving pleasure. In his view, art must be moral as well; it must contribute to the leading of a better life. The art of the socially elite, because it aimed only at giving pleasure, failed to serve its proper function.

JOHN DEWEY

The American pragmatist John Dewey proposed another kind of expression theory of art, one that sought to take account of the work of art as well as the artist's thoughts and feelings. He believed that the twentieth century had seen a radical dichotomy develop between the aesthetic dimension of life and the rest of life. The reason why most people today fail to discover the illumination art can bring to life is that they are blind to the presence of the aesthetic in everyday life.

Dewey based his theory of art on a theory of experience. Dewey's philosophy is of and for daily, everyday experience. Contrary to the prevailing empirical view

---

[6]Leo Tolstoy, *What is Art?*, trans. Aylmer Maude (London: Oxford University Press, 1930), 74.

of experience, which saw it primarily as a knowledge affair, Dewey saw experience as "an affair of the intercourse of a living being with its social and physical environment." Having an experience, he claimed, is different than just being alive. An experience is a coherent unit that unites the complex interactions and interventions of the human person with the chaotic jumble of things that act on him or her. In everyday experience we encounter tensions that aim at equilibrium and their ultimate resolutions. The basic rhythm of organic existence results from an organism's falling out of step with its environment and the restoration of equilibrium between the two. Art is built on the same pattern as the ceaseless rhythm of organic life. Our natural delight in artistic resolution of tensions is rooted biologically in our own being; we sense satisfaction when we reach a higher state of adjustment with our environment than we had previously.

The kind of significance that we give to meaningful experiences in our lives is an aesthetic significance. When we describe a situation from our past—say, a walk on the beach—as an "experience," we are describing it as something unified. There is some structure to the remembered event; walking on the beach *becomes a walk on the beach* when various parts are organized—for example, when there is a beginning, middle, and end to the walk. As we recall our walk, it becomes for us "an experience," a construction of elements pervaded by a unifying emotion that Dewey describes as an "aesthetic quality."

According to Dewey, experiences of this sort are the primary basis of life. When we examine our lives and consider what makes them meaningful, it is experiences of all kinds that come to mind—a high school basketball game, a kiss in the moonlight, the smile of a proud parent at graduation, even the sight of a friend stretched out on the ground in pain after an accident. We find an experience that we designate "an experience" intrinsically meaningful and satisfying, even if the contents of the experience were unpleasant at the time. The point is, these are *my* experiences, and they make me who I am.

Dewey believes that aesthetic experience presents a challenge to philosophy to attend to the artfulness of everyday life. Our aim throughout life is to reconstruct our everyday experiences so that they become more harmonious, determinate, and meaningful. Art has a way of marking out and developing what is valuable. By presenting tensions that build to culmination and resolution, art alerts us to the tensions in need of resolution in our own lives, and rewards us with a sense of aesthetic delight as they are resolved. If philosophy means to illuminate experience in general—and it does—then it must pay attention to art, which lays bare the meaning of experience and gives us back ourselves.

CHAPTER 70

PLATO

SELECTIONS FROM *THE SYMPOSIUM, THE ION,* AND *THE REPUBLIC*

In *The Symposium,* Socrates describes the stages involved in gaining insight into the Form of Beauty, relating what he has learned from Diotima of the mysteries of love.[1] True love begins with love of one person but ascends to the highest level of development when the lover comes to love all that is beautiful. In learning to love all that is beautiful, the lover has come to the realization that he loves but one thing—absolute beauty itself.

In *The Ion,* Socrates discusses poetic insight and the nature of art with Ion, a noted poetic interpreter. It is here that Plato's suspicion toward artists begins to show; it is not "mastery of knowledge" that enables Ion to move audiences but rather "divine inspiration." Although the poetry generated by divine possession is presented favorably in *The Ion,* the powers of the poet are not.

In *The Republic,* Plato's ambivalence toward art can be seen more clearly. Reason is the faculty that discerns true reality from appearances; the arts tend to distract the soul, directing its attention to appearances and away from true reality. Imitative art copies the appearance of material things, which are themselves copies of the Forms. Hence, this kind of art is "thrice removed from reality."

---

[1]The first and third selections are from Plato, *The Symposium* and *The Republic,* translated by Benjamin Jowett (Oxford: Oxford University Press, 1892); the second selection is taken from Plato, *The Ion,* translated by Paul Woodruff (Indianapolis: Hackett, 1983) and is reprinted with the permission of Hackett Publishing Company, Indianapolis, IN, and Cambridge, MA.

From *The Symposium*

[h]e who would proceed aright in this matter should begin in youth to visit beautiful forms; and first, if he be guided by his instructor aright, to love one such form only—out of that he should create fair thoughts; and soon he will of himself perceive that the beauty of one form is akin to the beauty of another; and then if beauty of form in general is his pursuit, how foolish would he be not to recognize that the beauty in every form is one and the same! And when he perceives this he will abate his violent love of the one, which he will despise and deem a small thing, and will become a lover of all beautiful forms; in the next stage he will consider that the beauty of the mind is more honourable than the beauty of the outward form. So that if a virtuous soul have but a little comeliness, he will be content to love and tend him, and will search out and bring to the birth thoughts which may improve the young, until he is compelled to contemplate and see the beauty of institutions and laws, and to understand that the beauty of them all is of one family, and that personal beauty is a trifle; and after laws and institutions he will go on to the sciences, that he may see their beauty, being not like a servant in love with the beauty of one youth or man or institution, himself a slave mean and narrow-minded, but drawing towards and contemplating the vast sea of beauty, he will create many fair and noble thoughts and notions in boundless love of wisdom; until on that shore he grows and waxes strong, and at last the vision is revealed to him of a single science, which is the science of beauty everywhere. To this I will proceed; please to give me your very best attention:

"He who has been instructed thus far in the things of love, and who has learned to see the beautiful in due order and succession, when he comes toward the end will suddenly perceive a nature of wondrous beauty (and this, Socrates, is the final cause of all our former toils)—a nature which in the first place is everlasting, not growing, and decaying, or waxing and waning; secondly, not fair in one point of view and foul in another, or at one time or in one relation or at one place fair, at another time or in another relation or at another place foul, as if fair to some and foul to others, or in the likeness of a face or hands or any other part of the bodily frame, or in any form of speech or knowledge, or existing in any other being, as for example, in an animal, or in heaven, or in earth, or in any other place; but beauty absolute, separate, simple, and everlasting, which without diminution and without increase, or any change, is imparted to the ever-growing and perishing beauties of all other things. He who from these ascending under the influence of true love, begins to perceive that beauty, is not far from the end. And the true order of going, or being led by another, to the things of love, is to begin from the beauties of earth and mount upwards for the sake of that other beauty, using these as steps only, and from one going on to two, and from two to all fair forms, and from fair forms to fair practices, and from fair practices to fair notions, until from fair notions he arrives at the notion of absolute beauty, and at last knows what the essence of beauty is. This, my dear Socrates . . . is that life above all others which man should live, in the contemplation of beauty absolute; a beauty which if you once beheld, you would see not to be after the measure of gold, and garments, and fair boys and youths, whose presence now entrances you; and you and many a one would be content to live seeing them only and conversing with them without meat or drink, if that were possible—

you only want to look at them and to be with them. But what if man had eyes to see the true beauty—the divine beauty, I mean, pure and clear and unalloyed, not clogged with the pollutions of mortality and all the colours and vanities of human life—thither looking, and holding converse with the true beauty simple and divine? Remember how in that communion only, be-

holding beauty with the eye of the mind, he will be enabled to bring forth, not images of beauty, but realities (for he has hold not of an image but of a reality), and bringing forth and nourishing true virtue to become the friend of God and be immortal, if mortal man may. Would that be an ignoble life?"

FROM THE ION

SOCRATES: I do see, Ion, and I'm going to announce to you what I think that is. As I said earlier, that's not a subject you've mastered—speaking well about Homer; it's a divine power that moves you, as a "Magnetic" stone moves iron rings. (That's what Euripides called it; most people call it "Heracleian.") This stone not only pulls those rings, if they're iron, it also puts power *in* the rings, so that they in turn can do just what the stone does—pull other rings—so that there's sometimes a very long chain of iron pieces and rings hanging from one another. And the power in all of them depends on this stone. In the same way, the Muse makes some people inspired herself, and then through those who are inspired a chain of other enthusiasts is suspended. You know, none of the epic poets, if they're good, are masters of their subject; they are inspired, possessed, and that is how they utter all those beautiful poems. The same goes for lyric poets if they're good: just as the Corybantes are not in their right minds when they dance, lyric poets, too, are not in their right minds when they make those beautiful lyrics, but as soon as they sail into harmony and rhythm they are possessed by Bacchic frenzy. Just as Bacchus worshippers when they are possessed draw honey and milk from rivers, but not when they are in their right minds—the soul of a lyric poet does this too, as

they say themselves. For of course poets tell us that they gather songs at honey-flowing springs, from glades and gardens of the Muses, and that they bear songs to us as bees carry honey, flying like bees. And what they say is true. For a poet is an airy thing, winged and holy, and he is not able to make poetry until he becomes inspired and goes out of his mind and his intellect is no longer in him. As long as a human being has his intellect in his possession he will always lack the power to make poetry or sing prophecy. Therefore because it's not by mastery that they make poems or say many lovely things about their subjects (as you do about Homer)—but because it's by a divine gift—each poet is able to compose beautifully only that for which the Muse has aroused him: one can do dithyrambs, another encomia, one can do dance songs, another, epics, and yet another, iambics; and each of them is worthless for the other types of poetry. You see, it's not mastery that enables them to speak those verses, but a divine power, since if they knew how to speak beautifully on one type of poetry by mastering the subject, they could do so for all the others also. That's why the god takes their intellect away from them when he uses them as his servants, as he does prophets and godly diviners, so that we who hear should know that *they* are not the ones who speak those verses that are of such high value, for their intellect is not in them: the god himself is the one who speaks, and he gives voice through them to us. The best evidence for this account is Tynnichus from Chalcis, who never made a poem anyone would think worth mentioning, *except* for the praise-song everyone sings, almost the most beautiful lyric-poem there is, and simply, as he says himself, "an invention of the Muses." In this more than any-thing, then, I think, the god is showing us, so that we should be in no doubt about it, that these beautiful poems are not human, not even *from* human beings, but are divine and from gods; that poets are nothing but representatives of the gods, possessed by whoever possesses them. To show *that*, the god deliberately sang the most beautiful lyric poem through the most worthless poet. Don't you think I'm right, Ion?

FROM *THE REPUBLIC*

. . . but I do not mind saying to you, that all poetical imitations are ruinous to the understanding of the hearers, and that the knowledge of their true nature is the only antidote to them.

Explain the purport of your remark.

Well, I will tell you, although I have always from my earliest youth had an awe and love of Homer, which even now makes the words falter on my lips, for he is the great captain and teacher of the whole of that charming tragic company; but a man is not to be reverenced more than the truth, and therefore I will speak out.

Very good, he said.

Listen to me then, or rather, answer me.

Put your question.

Can you tell me what imitation is? for I really do not know.

A likely thing, then, that I should know.

Why not? for the duller eye may often see a thing sooner than the keener.

Very true, he said; but in your presence, even if I had any faint notion, I could not muster courage to utter it. Will you enquire yourself?

Well then, shall we begin the enquiry in our usual manner: Whenever a number of individuals have a common name, we assume them to have also a corresponding idea or form:—do you understand me?

I do.

Let us take any common instance; there are beds and tables in the world—plenty of them, are there not?

Yes.

But there are only two ideas or forms of them—one the idea of a bed, the other of a table.

True.

And the maker of either of them makes a bed or he makes a table for our use, in accordance with the idea—that is our way of speaking in this and similar instances—but no artificer makes the ideas themselves: how could he?

Impossible.

And there is another artist,—I should like to know what you would say of him.

Who is he?

One who is the maker of all the works of all other workmen.

What an extraordinary man!

Wait a little, and there will be more reason for your saying so. For this is he who is able to make not only vessels of every kind, but plants and animals, himself and all other things—the earth and heaven, and the things which are in heaven or under the earth; he makes the gods also.

He must be a wizard and no mistake.

Oh! you are incredulous, are you? Do you

mean that there is no such maker or creator, or that in one sense there might be a maker of all these things but in another not? Do you see that there is a way in which you could make them all yourself?

What way?

An easy way enough; or rather, there are many ways in which the feat might be quickly and easily accomplished, none quicker than that of turning a mirror round and round—you would soon enough make the sun and the heavens, and the earth and yourself, and other animals and plants, and all the other things of which we were just now speaking, in the mirror.

Yes, he said; but they would be appearances only.

Very good, I said, you are coming to the point now. And the painter too is, as I conceive, just such another—a creator of appearances, is he not?

Of course.

But then I suppose you will say that what he creates is untrue. And yet there is a sense in which the painter also creates a bed?

Yes, he said, but not a real bed.

And what of the maker of the bed? were you not saying that he too makes, not the idea which, according to our view, is the essence of the bed, but only a particular bed?

Yes, I did.

Then if he does not make that which exists he cannot make true existence, but only some semblance of existence; and if any one were to say that the work of the maker of the bed, or of any other workman, has real existence, he could hardly be supposed to be speaking the truth.

At any rate, he replied, philosophers would say that he was not speaking the truth.

No wonder, then, that his work too is an indistinct expression of truth.

No wonder.

Suppose now that by the light of the exam-ples just offered we enquire who this imitator is?

If you please.

Well then, here are three beds: one existing in nature, which is made by God, as I think that we may say—for no one else can be the maker?

No.

There is another which is the work of the carpenter?

Yes.

And the work of the painter is a third?

Yes.

Beds, then, are of three kinds, and there are three artists who superintend them: God, the maker of the bed, and the painter?

Yes, there are three of them.

God, whether from choice or from necessity, made one bed in nature and one only; two or more such ideal beds neither ever have been nor ever will be made by God.

Why is that?

Because even if He had made but two, a third would still appear behind them which both of them would have for their idea, and that would be the ideal bed and not the two others.

Very true, he said.

God knew this, and He desired to be the real maker of a real bed, not a particular maker of a particular bed; and therefore He created a bed which is essentially and by nature one only.

So we believe.

Shall we, then, speak of Him as the natural author or maker of the bed?

Yes, he replied; inasmuch as by the natural process of creation He is the author of this and of all other things.

And what shall we say of the carpenter—is not he also the maker of the bed?

Yes.

But would you call the painter a creator and maker?

Certainly not.

Yet if he is not the maker, what is he in relation to the bed?

I think, he said, that we may fairly designate him as the imitator of that which the others make.

Good, I said; then you call him who is third in the descent from nature an imitator?

Certainly, he said.

And the tragic poet is an imitator, and therefore, like all other imitators, he is thrice removed from the king and from the truth?

That appears to be so.

Hear and judge: The best of us, as I conceive, when we listen to a passage of Homer, or one of the tragedians in which he represents some pitiful hero who is drawling out his sorrows in a long oration, or weeping, and smiting his breast—the best of us, you know, delight in giving way to sympathy, and are in raptures at the excellence of the poet who stirs our feelings most.

Yes, of course I know.

But when any sorrow of our own happens to us, then you may observe that we pride ourselves on the opposite quality—we would fain be quiet and patient; this is the manly part, and the other which delighted us in the recitation is now deemed to be the part of a woman.

Very true, he said.

Now can we be right in praising and admiring another who is doing that which any one of us would abominate and be ashamed of in his own person?

No, he said, that is certainly not reasonable.

Nay, I said, quite reasonable from one point of view.

What point of view?

If you consider, I said, that when in misfortune we feel a natural hunger and desire to relieve our sorrow by weeping and lamentation, and that this feeling which is kept under control in our own calamities is satisfied and delighted by the poets;—the better nature in each of us, not having been sufficiently trained by reason or habit, allows the sympathetic element to break loose because the sorrow is another's; and the spectator fancies that there can be no disgrace to himself in praising and pitying any one who comes telling him what a good man he is, and making a fuss about his troubles; he thinks that the pleasure is a gain, and why should he be supercilious and lose this and the poem too? Few persons ever reflect, as I should imagine, that from the evil of other men something of evil is communicated to themselves. And so the feeling of sorrow which has gathered strength at the sight of the misfortunes of others is with difficulty repressed in our own.

How very true!

And does not the same hold also of the ridiculous? There are jests which you would be ashamed to make yourself, and yet on the comic stage, or indeed in private, when you hear them, you are greatly amused by them, and are not at all disgusted at their unseemliness;—the case of pity is repeated;—there is a principle in human nature which is disposed to raise a laugh, and this which you once restrained by reason, because you were afraid of being thought a buffoon, is now let out again; and having stimulated the risible faculty at the theatre, you are betrayed unconsciously to yourself into playing the comic poet at home.

Quite true, he said.

And the same may be said of lust and anger and all the other affections, of desire and pain and pleasure, which are held to be inseparable from every action—in all of them poetry feeds and waters the passions instead of drying them up; she lets them rule, although they ought to be controlled, if mankind are ever to increase in happiness and virtue.

I cannot deny it.

Therefore, Glaucon, I said, whenever you meet with any of the eulogists of Homer declaring that he has been the educator of Hellas, and that he is profitable for education and for the ordering of human things, and that you should take him up again and again and get to know him and regulate your whole life according to him, we may love and honour those who say these things—they are excellent people, as far as their lights extend; and we are ready to acknowledge that Homer is the greatest of poets and first of tragedy writers; but we must remain firm in our conviction that hymns to the gods and praises of famous men are the only poetry which ought to be admitted into our State. For if you go beyond this and allow the honeyed muse to enter, either in epic or lyric verse, not law and the reason of mankind, which by common consent have ever been deemed best, but pleasure and pain will be the rulers in our State.

That is most true, he said.

And now since we have reverted to the subject of poetry, let this our defence serve to show the reasonableness of our former judgment in sending away out of our State an art having the tendencies which we have described; for reason constrained us. But that she may not impute to us any harshness or want of politeness, let us tell her that there is an ancient quarrel between philosophy and poetry; of which there are many proofs, such as the saying of "the yelping hound howling at her lord," or of one "mighty in the vain talk of fools," and "the mob of sages circumventing Zeus," and the "subtle thinkers who are beggars after all"; and there are innumerable other signs of ancient enmity between them.

. . . Notwithstanding this, let us assure our sweet friend and the sister arts of imitation, that is she will only prove her title to exist in a well-ordered State we shall be delighted to receive her—we are very conscious of her charms; but we may not on that account betray the truth. I dare say, Glaucon, that you are as much charmed by her as I am, especially when she appears in Homer?

Yes, indeed, I am greatly charmed.

Shall I propose, then, that she be allowed to return from exile, but upon this condition only—that she make a defence of herself in lyrical or some other metre?

Certainly.

And we may further grant to those of her defenders who are lovers of poetry and yet not poets the permission to speak in prose on her behalf: let them show not only that she is pleasant but also useful to States and to human life, and we will listen in a kindly spirit; for if this can be proved we shall surely be the gainers—I mean, if there is a use in poetry as well as a delight?

Certainly, he said, we shall be the gainers.

If her defence fails, then, my dear friend, like other persons who are enamoured of something, but put a restraint upon themselves when they think their desires are opposed to their interests, so too must we after the manner of lovers give her up, though not without a struggle. We too are inspired by that love of poetry which the education of noble States has implanted in us, and therefore we would have her appear at her best and truest; but so long as she is unable to make good her defence, this argument of ours shall be a charm to us, which we will repeat to ourselves while we listen to her strains; that we may not fall away into the childish love of her which captivates the many. At all events we are well aware that poetry being such as we have described is not to be regarded seriously as attaining to the truth; and he who listens to her, fearing for the safety of the city which is within him, should be on his guard against her seductions and make our words his law.

Yes, he said, I quite agree with you.

Yes, I said, my dear Glaucon, for great is the issue at stake, greater than appears, whether a man is to be good or bad. And what will any one be profited if under the influence of honour or money or power, aye, or under the excitement of poetry, he neglect justice and virtue?

CHAPTER 71

ARISTOTLE

TRAGEDY AND THE SELF-SUFFICIENCY OF ART

Unlike his teacher Plato, Aristotle viewed beauty as a notable feature of *this* world, which can be studied through an examination of beautiful things. Art is the product of human intentions; as such, an account can be given of the specific elements that comprise a good work of art. Since art is the capacity *to make*, involving a true course of reasoning, it is a kind of rational knowledge distinct from theoretical and practical ways of knowing. Art is valuable in itself, not merely valuable for the sake of something else. Thus the arts are self-sufficient activities that lend dignity to human life and give us a sense of joy and wonder that is found in any contemplation for its own sake.

Beginning with a discussion of plot, Aristotle proceeds to analyze the elements of tragedy.[1] According to his principle of *closure*, an artwork should have clear, well-defined limits; it should aim to present something that is complete in itself. Aristotle compares a tragedy to a living creature; this *organic model* has dominated the Western conception of art ever since. Each of the elements of the work of art should serve the "life" of the work as a whole, and all of these elements together should operate in harmony. Furthermore, the work should be so perfectly structured and the component elements so coordinated that any change would be a change for the worse. Thus, in a sense, the work of art has a *necessary* structure. As Aristotle wrote, "In poetry the story, as an imitation of action, must represent one

[1] From *The Works of Aristotle*, edited W. D. Ross (Oxford: Clarendon Press, 1908).

action, a complete whole, with its several incidents so closely connected that the transposal or withdrawal of any one of them will disjoin and dislocate the whole."

Tragedy aims to inspire pity and fear in its audience; but at the same time it aims to transform its audience through a *catharsis*, or cleansing. The burden of our existence is lightened as we sympathize and identify with the tragic hero—a good person who has come to a bad end.

TRAGEDY AND THE SELF-SUFFICIENCY OF ART

. . . Let us proceed now to the discussion of Tragedy; before doing so, however, we must gather up the definition resulting from what has been said. A tragedy, then is the imitation of an action that is serious and also, as having magnitude, complete in itself; in language with pleasurable accessories, each kind brought in separately in the parts of the work; in a dramatic, not in a narrative form; with incidents arousing pity and fear, wherewith to accomplish its catharsis of such emotions. Here by 'language with pleasurable accessories' I mean that with rhythm and harmony or song superadded; and by 'the kinds separately' I mean that some portions are worked out with verse only, and others in turn with song.

As they act the stories, it follows that in the first place the Spectacle (or stage-appearance of the actors) must be some part of the whole; and in the second Melody and Diction, these two being the means of their imitation. Here by 'Diction' I mean merely this, the composition of the verses; and by 'Melody', what is too completely understood to require explanation. But further: the subject represented also is an action; and the action involves agents, who must necessarily have their distinctive qualities both of character and thought, since it is from these that we ascribe certain qualities to their actions. There are in the natural order of things, therefore, two causes,

Thought and Character, of their actions, and consequently of their success or failure in their lives. Now the action (that which was done) is represented in the play by the Fable or Plot. The Fable, in our present sense of the term, is simply this, the combination of the incidents, or things done in the story; whereas Character is what makes us ascribe certain moral qualities to the agents; and Thought is shown in all they say when proving a particular point or, it may be, enunciating a general truth. There are six parts consequently of every tragedy, as a whole (that is) of such or such quality, viz. a Fable or Plot, Characters, Diction, Thought, Spectacle, and Melody; two of them arising from the means, one from the manner, and three from the objects of the dramatic imitation; and there is nothing else besides these six. Of these, its formative elements, then, not a few of the dramatists have made due use, as every play, one may say, admits of Spectacle, Character, Fable, Diction, Melody, and Thought.

The most important of the six is the combination of the incidents of the story. Tragedy is essentially an imitation not of persons but of action and life, of happiness and misery. All human happiness or misery takes the form of action; the end for which we live is a certain kind of activity, not a quality. Character gives us qualities, but it is in our actions—what we do—that

803

we are happy or the reverse. In a play accordingly they do not act in order to portray the Characters; they include the Characters for the sake of the action. So that it is the action in it, i.e. its Fable or Plot, that is the end and purpose of the tragedy; and the end is everywhere the chief thing. Besides this, a tragedy is impossible without action, but there may be one without Character. The tragedies of most of the moderns are characterless—a defect common among poets of all kinds, and with its counterpart in painting in Zeuxis as compared with Polygnotus; for whereas the latter is strong in character, the work of Zeuxis is devoid of it. And again: one may string together a series of characteristic speeches of the utmost finish as regards Diction and Thought, and yet fail to produce the true tragic effect; but one will have much better success with a tragedy which, however inferior in these respects, has a Plot, a combination of incidents, in it. And again: the most powerful elements of attraction in Tragedy, the Peripeties and Discoveries, are parts of the Plot. A further proof is in the fact that beginners succeed earlier with the Diction and Characters than with the construction of a story; and the same may be said of nearly all the early dramatists. We maintain, therefore, that the first essential, the life and soul, so to speak, of Tragedy is the Plot; and that the Characters come second—compare the parallel in painting, where the most beautiful colours laid on without order will not give one the same pleasure as a simple black-and-white sketch of a portrait. We maintain that Tragedy is primarily an imitation of action, and that it is mainly for the sake of action that it imitates the personal agents. Third comes the element of Thought, i.e. the power of saying whatever can be said, or what is appropriate to the occasion. This is what, in the speeches in Tragedy, falls under the arts of Politics and Rhetoric; for the older poets make their personages discourse like statesmen, and the modern like rhetoricians. One must not confuse it with Character. Character in a play is that which reveals the moral purpose of the agents, i.e. the sort of thing they seek or avoid, where that is not obvious—hence there is no room for Character is a speech on a purely indifferent subject. Thought, on the other hand, is shown in all they say when proving or disproving some particular point, or enunciating some universal proposition. Fourth among the literary elements is the Diction of the personages, i.e., as before explained, the expression of their thoughts in words, which is practically the same thing with verse as with prose. As for the two remaining parts, the Melody is the greatest of the pleasurable accessories of Tragedy. The Spectacle, though an attraction, is the least artistic of all the parts, and has least to do with the art of poetry. The tragic effect is quite possible without a public performance and actors; and besides, the getting-up of the Spectacle is more a matter for the costumier than the poet.

Having thus distinguished the parts, let us now consider the proper construction of the Fable or Plot, as that is at once the first and the most important thing in Tragedy. We have laid it down that a tragedy is an imitation of an action that is complete in itself, as a whole of some magnitude; for a whole may be of no magnitude to speak of. Now a whole is that which has beginning, middle, and end. A beginning is that which is not itself necessarily after anything else, and which has naturally something else after it; an end is that which is naturally after something itself, either as its necessary or usual consequent, and with nothing else after it; and a middle, that which is by nature after one thing and has also another after it. A well-constructed Plot, therefore, cannot either begin or end at any point one likes; beginning and end in it must be of the forms just described. Again: to be beautiful, a living creature, and every whole made up of parts, must not only present a certain order in its arrangement of parts, but also be of a certain definite magnitude. Beauty is a matter of size and order, and therefore impossible either (1) in a very minute creature, since our perception becomes indistinct as it approaches instantaneity; or (2) in a creature of vast size—one, say, 1,000 miles long—as in that case, instead of the object being seen all at once, the unity and wholeness of it is lost to the beholder. Just in the same way, then, as a beautiful whole made up of parts, or a beautiful living creature, must be of some size, but a size to be taken in by the eye, so a story or Plot must be of some length, but of a length to be taken in by the memory. As for the limit of its length, so far as that is relative to public performances and spectators, it does not fall within the theory of poetry. If they had to perform a hundred tragedies, they would be timed by waterclocks, as they are said to have been at one period. The limit, however, set by the actual nature of the thing is this: the longer the story, consistently with its being comprehensible as a whole, the finer it is by reason of its magnitude. As a rough general formula, 'a length which allows of the hero passing by a series of probable or necessary stages from misfortune to happiness, or from happiness to misfortune', may suffice as a limit for the magnitude of the story.

The Unity of a Plot does not consist, as some suppose, in its having one man as its subject. An infinity of things befall that one man, some of which it is impossible to reduce to unity; and in like manner there are many actions of one man which cannot be made to form one action. One sees, therefore, the mistake of all the poets who have written a *Heracleid*, a *Theseid*, or similar poems; they suppose that, because Heracles was one man, the story also of Heracles must be one story. Homer, however, evidently understood this point quite well, whether by art or instinct, just in the same way as he excels the rest in every

other respect. In writing an *Odyssey*, he did not make the poem cover all that ever befell his hero—it befell him, for instance, to get wounded on Parnassus and also to feign madness at the time of the call to arms, but the two incidents had no necessary or probable connexion with one another—instead of doing that, he took as the subject of the *Odyssey*, as also of the *Iliad*, an action with a Unity of the kind we are describing. The truth is that, just as in the other imitative arts one imitation is always one thing, so in poetry the story, as an imitation of action, must represent one action, a complete whole, with its several incidents so closely connected that the transposal or withdrawal of any one of them will disjoin and dislocate the whole. For that which makes no perceptible difference by its presence or absence is no real part of the whole.

From what we have said it will be seen that the poet's function is to describe, not the thing that has happened, but a kind of thing that might happen, i.e. what is possible as being probable or necessary. The distinction between historian and poet is not in the one writing prose and the other writing verse—you might put the work of Herodotus into verse, and it would still be a species of history; it consists really in this, that the one describes the thing that has been, and the other a kind of thing that might be. Hence poetry is something more philosophic and of graver import than history, since its statements are of the nature rather of universals, whereas those of history are singulars. By a universal statement I mean one as to what such or such a kind of man will probably or necessarily say or do—which is the aim of poetry, though it affixes proper names to the characters; by a singular statement, one as to what, say, Alcibiades did or had done to him. In Comedy this has become clear by this time; it is only when their plot is already made up of probable incidents that they give it a basis of proper names, choosing for the purpose any names that may occur to them, instead of writing like the old iambic poets about particular persons. In Tragedy, however, they still adhere to the historic names; and for this reason: what convinces is the possible; now whereas we are not yet sure as to the possibility of that which has not happened, that which has happened is manifestly possible, else it would not have come to pass. Nevertheless even in Tragedy there are some plays with but one or two known names in them, the rest being inventions; and there are some without a single known name, e.g. Agathon's *Antheus*, in which both incidents and names are of the poet's invention; and it is not less delightful on that account. So that one must not aim at a rigid adherence to the traditional stories on which tragedies are based. It would be absurd, in fact, to do so, as even the known stories are only known to a few, though they are a delight none the less to all.

It is evident from the above that the poet must be more the poet of his stories or Plots than of his verses, inasmuch as he is a poet by virtue of the imitative element in his work, and it is actions that he imitates. And if he should come to take a subject from actual history, he is none the less a poet for that; since some historic occurrences may very well be in the probable and possible order of things; and it is in that aspect of them that he is their poet.

Of simple Plots and actions the episodic are the worst. I call a Plot episodic when there is neither probability nor necessity in the sequence of its episodes. Actions of this sort bad poets construct through their own fault, and good ones on account of the players. His work being for public performance, a good poet often stretches out a Plot beyond its capabilities, and is thus obliged to twist the sequence of incident.

Tragedy, however, is an imitation not only of a complete action, but also of incidents arousing pity and fear. Such incidents have the very great-est effect on the mind when they occur unexpectedly and at the same time in consequence of one another; there is more of the marvellous in them then than if they happened of themselves or by mere chance. Even matters of chance seem most marvellous if there is an appearance of design as it were in them; as for instance the statue of Mitys at Argos killed the author of Mitys' death by falling down on him when a looker-on at a public spectacle; for incidents like that we think to be not without a meaning. A Plot, therefore, of this sort is necessarily finer than others.

Plots are either simple or complex, since the actions they represent are naturally of this twofold description. The action, proceeding in the way defined, as one continuous whole, I call simple, when the change in the hero's fortunes takes place without Peripety or Discovery; and complex, when it involves one or the other, or both. These should each of them arise out of the structure of the Plot itself, so as to be the consequence, necessary or probable, of the antecedents. There is a great difference between a thing happening *propter hoc* and *post hoc*.

A Peripety is the change of the kind described from one state of things within the play to its opposite, and that too in the way we are saying, in the probable or necessary sequence of events; as it is for instance in *Oedipus*: here the opposite state of things is produced by the Messenger, who, coming to gladden Oedipus and to remove his fears as to his mother, reveals the secret of his birth. And in *Lynceus*: just as he is being led off for execution, with Danaus at his side to put him to death, the incidents preceding this bring it about that he is saved and Danaus put to death. A Discovery is, as the very word implies, a change from ignorance to knowledge, and thus to either love or hate, in the personages marked for good or evil fortune. The finest form of Discovery is one attended by Peripeties, like that which goes with the Discovery of *Oedipus*. There are no doubt other forms of it; what we have said may happen in a way in reference to inanimate things, even things of a very casual kind; and it is also possible to discover whether some one has done or not done something. But the form most directly connected with the Plot and the action of the piece is the first-mentioned. This, with a Peripety, will arouse either pity or fear—actions of that nature being what Tragedy is assumed to represent; and it will also serve to bring about the happy or unhappy ending. The Discovery, then, being of persons, it may be that of one party only to the other, the latter being already known; or both the parties may have to discover themselves. Iphigenia, for instance, was discovered to Orestes by sending the letter; and another Discovery was required to reveal him to Iphigenia.

Two parts of the Plot, then, Peripety and Discovery, are on matters of this sort. A third part is Suffering; which we may define as an action of a destructive or painful nature, such as murders on the stage, tortures, woundings, and the like. The other two have been already explained. . . .

The next points after what we have said above will be these: (1) What is the poet to aim at, and what is he to avoid, in constructing his Plots? and (2) What are the conditions on which the tragic effect depends?

We assume that, for the finest form of Tragedy, the Plot must be not simple but complex; and further, that it must imitate actions arousing fear and pity, since that is the distinctive function of this kind of imitation. It follows, therefore, that there are three forms of Plot to be avoided. (1) A good man must not be seen passing from happiness to misery, or (2) a bad man from misery to happiness. The first situation is not fear-inspiring or piteous, but simply odious to us. The second is the most untragic that can be; it has not

one of the requisites of Tragedy; it does not appeal either to the human feeling in us, or to our pity, or to our fears. Nor, on the other hand, should (3) an extremely bad man be seen falling from happiness into misery. Such a story may arouse the human feeling in us, but it will not move us to either pity or fear; pity is occasioned by undeserved misfortune, and fear by that of one like ourselves; so that there will be nothing either piteous or fear-inspiring in the situation. There remains, then, the intermediate kind of personage, a man not preeminently virtuous and just, whose misfortune, however, is brought upon him not by vice and depravity but by some error of judgement, of the number of those in the enjoyment of great reputation and prosperity; e.g. Oedipus, Thyestes, and the men of note of similar families. The perfect Plot, accordingly, must have a single, and not (as some tell us) a double issue; the change in the hero's fortunes must be not from misery to happiness, but on the contrary from happiness to misery; and the cause of it must lie not in any depravity, but in some great error on his part; the man himself being either such as we have described, or better, not worse, than that. Fact also confirms our theory. . . .

The tragic fear and pity may be aroused by the Spectacle; but they may also be aroused by the very structure and incidents of the play—which is the better way and shows the better poet. The Plot in fact should be so framed that, even without seeing the things take place, he who simply hears the account of them shall be filled with horror and pity at the incidents; which is just the effect that the mere recital of the story in *Oedipus* would have on one. To produce this same effect by means of the Spectacle is less artistic, and requires extraneous aid. Those, however, who make use of the Spectacle to put before us that which is merely monstrous and not productive of fear, are wholly out of touch with

807

Tragedy; not every kind of pleasure should be required of a tragedy, but only its own proper pleasure. . . .

In the Characters there are four points to aim at. First and foremost, that they shall be good. There will be an element of character in the play, if (as has been observed) what a personage says or does reveals a certain moral purpose; and a good element of character, if the purpose so revealed is good. Such goodness is possible in every type of personage, even in a woman or a slave, though the one is perhaps an inferior, and the other a wholly worthless being. The second point is to make them appropriate. The Character before us may be, say, manly; but it is not appropriate in a female Character to be manly, or clever. The third is to make them like the reality, which is not the same as their being good and appropriate, in our sense of the term. The fourth is to make them consistent and the same throughout; even if inconsistency be part of the man before one for imitation as presenting that form of character, he should still be consistently inconsistent. . . .

As Tragedy is an imitation of personages better than the ordinary man, we in our way should follow the example of good portrait-painters, who reproduce the distinctive features of a man, and at the same time, without losing the likeness, make him handsomer than he is. The poet in like manner, in portraying men quick or slow to anger, or with similar infirmities of character, must know how to represent them as such, and at the same time as good men, as Agathon and Homer have represented Achilles.

CHAPTER 72

DAVID HUME

TASTES CANNOT BE DISPUTED

In this selection Hume contends that the great variety of tastes in the world confirms the maxim that "there is no disputing over tastes."[1] Aesthetic judgment is subjective. According to Hume, "We are apt to call *barbarous* whatever departs widely from our own taste and apprehension: But soon find the epithet of reproach retorted on us."

Hume argued, however, that it was possible to agree on "a Standard of Taste." Beauty, he argues, appeals to the "common sentiments" of all humankind. Although opinions may vary, the emotional response is universal, at least to every observer with sound judgment. The problem is that many people lack such judgment because they are uneducated, uncultivated, inexperienced, confused, or in poor health. So-called "durable admiration"—the lasting admiration, for instance, of the classics—may be a reliable indicator of great art, but it is of little help to us when trying to judge the value of works of art produced in our time. Hume warns against the "caprices of mode and fashion" and "the mistakes of ignorance and envy."

[1]From David Hume, "Of the Standard of Taste," in *Essays, Moral, Political, and Literary*, edited by T.H. Green (London: Longmans, Green and Co., 1882).

Tastes Cannot Be Disputed

The great variety of Taste, as well as of opinion, which prevails in the world, is too obvious not to have fallen under every one's observation. Men of the most confined knowledge are able to remark a difference of taste in the narrow circle of their acquaintance, even where the persons have been educated under the same government, and have early imbibed the same prejudices. But those, who can enlarge their view to contemplate distant nations and remote ages, are still more surprised at the great inconsistence and contrariety. We are apt to call *barbarous* whatever departs widely from our own taste and apprehension: But soon find the epithet of reproach retorted on us. And the highest arrogance and self-conceit is at last startled, on observing an equal assurance on all sides, and scruples, amidst such a contest of sentiment, to pronounce positively in its own favour.

As this variety of taste is obvious to the most careless inquirer; so will it be found, on examination, to be still greater in reality than in appearance. The sentiments of men often differ with regard to beauty and deformity of all kinds, even while their general discourse is the same. There are certain terms in every language, which import blame, and others praise; and all men, who use the same tongue, must agree in their application of them. Every voice is united in applauding elegance, propriety, simplicity, spirit in writing; and in blaming fustian, affectation, coldness, and a false brilliancy: But when critics come to particulars, this seeming unanimity vanishes; and it is found, that they had affixed a very different meaning to their expressions. In all matters of opinion and science, the case is opposite: The difference among men is there oftener found to lie in generals than in particulars; and to be less in reality than in appearance. An explanation of the terms commonly ends the controversy; and the disputants are surprised to find, that they had been quarreling, while at bottom they agreed in their judgment. . . .

It is natural for us to seek a *Standard of Taste*; a rule, by which the various sentiments of men may be reconciled; at least, a decision, afforded, confirming one sentiment, and condemning another.

There is a species of philosophy, which cuts off all hopes of success in such an attempt, and represents the impossibility of ever attaining any standard of taste. The difference, it is said, is very wide between judgment and sentiment. All sentiment is right; because sentiment has a reference to nothing beyond itself, and is always real, wherever a man is conscious of it. But all determinations of the understanding are not right; because they have a reference to something beyond themselves, to wit, real matter of fact; and are not always conformable to that standard. Among a thousand different opinions which different men may entertain of the same subject, there is one, and but one, that is just and true; and the only difficulty is to fix and ascertain it. On the contrary, a thousand different sentiments, excited by the same object, are all right: Because no sentiment represents what is really in the object. It only marks a certain conformity or relation between the object and the organs or faculties of the mind; and if that conformity did not really exist, the sentiment could never possibly have being. Beauty is no quality in things themselves: It exists merely in the mind which contemplates them; and each mind perceives a different beauty. One person may even perceive deformity, where another is sensible of beauty; and every individual ought to acquiesce in his own sentiment, without pretending to regulate those of others. To seek the real beauty, or real deformity, is as fruitless an enquiry, as to pretend to ascertain the real sweet or real bitter. According to the disposition of the organs, the same object may be both sweet and bitter; and the proverb has justly determined it to be fruitless to dispute concerning tastes. It is very natural, and even quite necessary, to extend this axiom to mental, as well as bodily taste; and thus common sense, which is so often at variance with philosophy, especially with the skeptical kind, is found, in one instance at least, to agree in pronouncing the same decision.

But though this axiom, by passing into a proverb, seems to have attained the sanction of common sense; there is certainly a species of common sense which opposes it, at least serves to modify and restrain it. Whoever would assert an equality of genius and elegance between OGILBY and MILTON, or BUNYAN and ADDISON, would be thought to defend no less an extravagance, than if he had maintained a molehill to be as high as TENERIFFE, or a pond as extensive as the ocean. Though there may be found persons, who give the preference to the former authors; no one pays attention to such a taste; and we pronounce without scruple the sentiment of these pretended critics to be absurd and ridiculous. The principle of the natural equality of tastes is then totally forgot, and while we admit it on some occasions, where the objects seem near an equality, it appears an extravagant paradox, or rather a palpable absurdity, where objects so disproportioned are compared together.

It is evident that none of the rules of composition are fixed by reasonings *a priori*, or can be esteemed abstract conclusions of the understanding, from comparing those habitudes and relations of ideas, which are eternal and immutable. Their foundation is the same with that of all the practical sciences, experience; nor are they any thing but general observations, concerning what has been universally found to please in all countries and in all ages. Many of the beauties of poetry and even of eloquence are founded on falsehood and fiction, on hyperboles, metaphors, and an abuse or perversion of terms from their natural meaning. To check the sallies of the imagination, and to reduce every expression to geometrical truth and exactness, would be the most contrary to the laws of criticism; because it would produce a work, which, by universal experience, has been found the most insipid and disagreeable. But though poetry can never submit to exact truth, it must be confined by rules of art, discovered to the author either by genius or observation. If some negligent or irregular writers have pleased, they have not pleased by their transgressions of rule or order, but in spite of these transgressions: They have possessed other beauties, which were conformable to just criticism, and the force of these beauties has been able to overpower censure, and give the mind a satisfaction superior to the disgust arising from the blemishes. . . . If they are found to please, they cannot be faults; let the pleasure, which they produce, be ever so unexpected and unaccountable.

But though all the general rules of art are founded only on experience and on the observation of the common sentiments of human nature, we must not imagine, that, on every occasion, the feelings of men will be conformable to these rules. Those finer emotions of the mind are of a very tender and delicate nature, and require the concurrence of many favourable circumstances to make them play with facility and exactness, according to their general and established principles. The least exterior hindrance to such small springs, or the least internal disorder, disturbs their motion, and confounds the operation of the whole machine. When we would make an experiment of this nature, and would try the force of any beauty or deformity, we must choose with care a proper time and place, and bring the fancy to a suitable situation and disposition. A perfect serenity of mind, a recollection of thought, a due attention to the object; if any of these circumstances be wanting, our experiment will be fallacious, and we shall be unable to judge of the catholic and universal beauty. The relation, which nature has placed between the form and the sentiment will at least be more obscure; and it will require greater accuracy to trace and discern it. We shall be able to ascertain its influence not so much from the operations of each particular beauty, as from the durable admiration, which attends those works, that have survived all the caprices of mode and fashion, all the mistakes of ignorance and envy. . . .

It appears then, that, amidst all the variety and caprice of taste, there are certain general principles of approbation or blame, whose influence a careful eye may trace in all operations of the mind. Some particular forms or qualities, from the original structure of the internal fabric, are calculated to please, and others to displease; and if they fail of their effect in any particular instance, it is from some apparent defect or imperfection in the organ. A man in a fever would not insist on his palate as able to decide concerning flavours; nor would one, affected with the jaundice, pretend to give a verdict with regard to colours. In each creature, there is a sound and a defective state; and the former alone can be supposed to afford us a true standard of taste and sentiment. If, in the sound state of the organ, there be an entire or a considerable uniformity of sentiment among men, we may thence derive an idea of the perfect beauty; in like manner as the appearance of objects in daylight, to the eye of a man in health, is denominated their true and real colour, even while colour is allowed to be merely a phantasm of the senses.

Many and frequent are the defects in the internal organs, which prevent or weaken the influence of those general principles, on which depends our sentiment of beauty or deformity. Though some objects, by the structure of the mind, be naturally calculated to give pleasure, it is not to be expected, that in every individual the pleasure will be equally felt. Particular incidents and situations occur, which either throw a false light on the objects, or hinder the true from conveying to the imagination the proper sentiment and perception.

One obvious cause, why many feel not the proper sentiment of beauty, is the want of that *delicacy* of imagination, which is requisite to convey a sensibility of those finer emotions. . . .

It is acknowledged to be the perfection of every sense or faculty, to perceive with exactness its most minute objects, and allow nothing to escape its notice and observation. The smaller the objects are, which become sensible to the eye, the finer is that organ, and the more elaborate its make and composition. A good palate is not tried by strong flavours; but by a mixture of small ingredients, where we are still sensible of each part, notwithstanding its minuteness and its confusion with the rest. In like manner, a quick and acute perception of beauty and deformity must be the perfection of our mental taste; nor can a man be satisfied with himself while he suspects, that any excellence or blemish in a discourse has passed him unobserved. In this case, the perfection of the man, and the perfection of the sense or feeling, are found to be united. A very delicate palate, on many occasions, may be a great inconvenience both to a man himself and to his friends: But a delicate taste of wit or beauty must always be a desirable quality; because it is the source of all the finest and most innocent enjoyments, of which human nature is susceptible. In this decision the sentiments of all mankind have agreed. Wherever you can ascertain a delicacy of taste, it is sure to meet with approbation; and the best way of ascertaining it is to appeal to those models and principles, which have been established by the uniform consent and experience of nations and ages.

But though there be naturally a wide difference in point of delicacy between one person and another, nothing tends further to increase and improve this talent, than *practice* in a particular art, and the frequent survey or contemplation of a particular species of beauty. When objects of any kind are first presented to the eye or imagination, the sentiment, which attends them, is obscure and confused; and the mind is, in a great measure, incapable of pronouncing concerning their merits or defects. The taste cannot perceive the several excellences of the performance; much less distinguish the particular character of each excellency, and ascertain its quality and degree. If it pronounce the whole in general to be beautiful or deformed, it is the utmost that can be expected; and even this judgment, a person, so unpractised, will be apt to deliver with great hesitation and reserve. But allow him to acquire experience in those objects, his feeling becomes more exact and nice: He not only perceives the beauties and defects of each part, but marks the distinguishing species of each quality, and assigns it suitable praise or blame. A clear and distinct sentiment attends him through the whole survey of the objects; and he discerns that very degree and kind of approbation or displeasure, which each part is naturally fitted to produce. The mist dissipates, which seemed formerly to hand over the object: The organ acquires greater perfection in its operations; and can pronounce, without danger of mistake, concerning the merits of every performance. In a word, the same address and dexterity, which practice gives to the execution of any work, is also acquired by the same means, in the judging of it. . . .

It is impossible to continue in the practice of contemplating any order of beauty, without being frequently obliged to form *comparisons* between the several species and degrees of excellence, and estimating their proportion to each other. A man, who had no opportunity of comparing the different kinds of beauty, is indeed totally unqualified to pronounce an opinion with regard to any object presented to him. By comparison alone we fix the epithets of praise or blame, and learn how to assign the due degree of each. . . .

But to enable a critic the more fully to execute this undertaking, he must preserve his mind free from all *prejudice,* and allow nothing to enter into his consideration, but the very object which is submitted to his examination. We may observe, that every work of art, in order to produce its due effect on the mind, must be surveyed in a certain point of view, and cannot be fully relished by persons, whose situation, real or imaginary, is not conformable to that which is required by the performance. . . .

It is well known, that in all questions, submitted to the understanding, prejudice is destructive of sound judgment, and perverts all operations of the intellectual faculties: It is no less contrary to good taste; nor has it less influence to corrupt our sentiment of beauty. It belongs to *good sense* to check its influence in both cases; and in this respect, as well as in many others, reason, if not an essential part of taste, is at least requisite to the operations of this latter faculty. In all the nobler productions of genius, there is a mutual relation and correspondence of parts; nor can either the beauties or blemishes be perceived by him, whose thought is not capacious enough to comprehend all those parts, and compare them with each other, in order to perceive the consistence and uniformity of the whole. Every work of art has also a certain end or purpose, for which it is calculated; and is to be deemed more or less perfect, as it is more or less fitted to attain this end. The object of eloquence is to persuade, of history to instruct, of poetry to please by means of the passions and the imagination. These ends we must carry constantly in our view, when we peruse any performance; and we must be able to judge how far the means employed are adapted to their respective purposes. Besides, every kind of composition, even the most poetical is nothing but a chain of propositions and reasonings; not always, indeed, the justest and most exact, but still plausible and specious, however disguised by the coloring of the imagination. The persons introduced in tragedy and epic poetry, must be represented as reasoning, and thinking, and concluding, and acting, suitably to their character and circumstances; and without judgment, as well as taste and invention, a poet can never hope to succeed in so delicate an undertaking. Not to mention, that the same excellence of faculties which contributes to the improvement of reason, the same clearness of conception, the same exactness of distinction, the same vivacity of apprehension, are essential to the operations of true taste, and are its infallible concomitants. It seldom, or never happens, that a man of sense, who has experience in any art, cannot judge of its beauty; and it is no less rare to meet with a man who has a just taste without a sound understanding.

Thus, though the principles of taste be universal, and, nearly, if not entirely the same in all men; yet few are qualified to give judgment on any work of art, or establish their own sentiment as the standard of beauty. The organs of internal sensation are seldom so perfect as to allow the general principles their full play, and produce a feeling correspondent to those principles. They either labour under some defect, or are vitiated by some disorder; and by that means, excite a sentiment, which may be pronounced erroneous. When the critic has no delicacy, he judges without any distinction, and is only affected by the grosser and more palpable qualities of the object: The finer touches pass unnoticed and disregarded. Where he is not aided by practice, his verdict is attended with confusion and hesitation. Where no comparison has been employed, the most frivolous beauties, such as rather merit the name of defects, are the object of his admiration. Where he lies under the influence of prejudice, all his natural sentiments are perverted. Where good sense is wanting, he is not qualified to discern the beauties of design and reasoning, which are the highest and most excellent. Under some or other of these imperfections, the generality of men labour; and hence a true judge in the finer arts is observed, even during the most polished ages, to be so rare a character: Strong sense, united to delicate sentiment, improved by practice, perfected by comparison, and cleared of all prejudice, can alone entitle critics to his valuable character; and the joint verdict of such, wherever they are to be found, is the true standard of taste and beauty.

But where are such critics to be found? By what marks are they to be known? How distinguish them from pretenders? These questions are embarrassing; and seem to throw us back into the same uncertainty, from which, during the course of this essay, we have endeavoured to extricate ourselves.

But if we consider the matter aright, these are questions of fact, not of sentiment. Whether any particular person be endowed with good sense and a delicate imagination, free from prejudice, may often be the subject of dispute, and be liable to great discussion and enquiry: But that such a character is valuable and estimable will be agreed in by all mankind. Where these doubts occur, men can do no more than in other disputable questions, which are submitted to the understanding: They must produce the best arguments, that their invention suggests to them; they must acknowledge a true and decisive standard to exist somewhere to wit, real existence and matter of fact; and they must have indulgence to such as differ from them in their appeals to this standard. It is sufficient for our present purpose, if we have proved, that the taste of all individuals is not upon an equal footing, and that some men in general, however difficult to be particularly pitched upon, will be acknowledged by universal sentiment to have a preference above others.

CHAPTER 73

LEO TOLSTOY

WHAT IS ART

Count Leo Nikolaevich Tolstoy (1828–1910), novelist, religious and moral reformer, and social critic, was born in central Russia. Orphaned at nine and raised by elderly female relatives and private tutors, he studied law and Oriental languages at the University of Kazan from 1844 to 1847, but left without completing a degree. He served in the army for a number of years, seeing duty in the Crimean War between 1853 and 1855. In 1857 and between 1860 and 1861, he traveled widely, visiting Germany, Switzerland, Italy, and England. In 1862 he married Andreyevna Bers, who worked diligently as his secretary and financial advisor, in addition to bearing the couple's thirteen children. In the remaining forty-eight years of his life, Tolstoy did not leave Russia, spending most of his time on his country estate at Yasnaya Polana.

Tolstoy's creative life is normally divided into two parts—the period during which he wrote his great novels (1852 to 1876) and that during which he was consumed with moral and social reform (1879 to 1910). The first period saw the production of *War and Peace* (1873) and *Anna Karenina* (1877), widely regarded as two of the finest novels ever written. Between 1876 and 1879 Tolstoy suffered an intense spiritual and emotional crisis. Contemplating suicide, he describes these years of crisis in *A Confession* (1879–1882). He was seeking the meaning of life; he found it in the simple Christianity of the Gospels, which he regarded as containing the basis for creating the Kingdom of God on earth, and a guide for social action. Putting his beliefs into practice, he rejected all forms of violence and coercion, became a vegetarian, renounced the life of luxury, and embraced the moral value of manual labor. His views on nonviolence made a lasting impression on Mohandas Gandhi, with whom he corresponded. He placed his own property in the hands of his wife in the 1880s, and some of it—for instance, the copyright to all his works after 1881—he renounced completely. The writings of this period include *What I Believe* (1884), *What Then Must We Do* (1886), *The Kingdom of God is Within You* (1893), and *What is Art?* (1898), an exposition of his moral views on art.

Tolstoy begins by reviewing previous attempts to define art.[1] All have failed, he contends, because they all tried to define art in terms of the pleasure that it gives rather than the necessary role it plays in human life. To say merely that art produces pleasure does not tell us what it is about art that gives it this capacity to please. Many things give us pleasure; how does art differ from all these things? Furthermore, reducing art to pleasure trivializes art. Defining art as pleasure does not give us an answer to the question of the nature of art.

For Tolstoy, art is not a pleasant luxury but rather the primary means of communication concerning the most profound and most important human emotions. The power of art lies in its *infectiousness*—its ability to produce in the minds of its audience the feelings that the artist originally had. The highest and best art is that art that produces religious feeling. A religious feeling, according to Tolstoy, is one which articulates the most universal and progressive social aspirations, such as the universal feeling of brotherhood—feelings that articulate the spirit of an age, providing a sense of cultural identity and purpose. Art tells us who and what we are and then organizes all of our different purposes around this one unifying theme, directing us towards various social goals.

WHAT IS ART?

There is no objective definition of beauty. The existing definitions . . . amount only to one and the same subjective definition, which is (strange as it seems to say so), that art is that which makes beauty manifest, and beauty is that which pleases (without exciting desire). Many estheticians have felt the insufficiency and instability of such a definition, and in order to give it a firm basis have asked themselves why a thing pleases. And they have converted the discussion on beauty into a question of taste, as did Hutcheson, Voltaire, Diderot, and others. But all attempts to define what taste is must lead to nothing, as the reader may see both from the history of esthetics and experimentally. There is and can be no explanation of why one thing pleases one man and displeases another, or *vice versa;* so that the whole existing science of esthetics fails to do what we might expect from it as a mental activity calling itself a science, namely, it does not define the

[1]From Leo Tolstoy, *What Is Art?* translated by Almyer Maude. Copyright © 1960. Reprinted with permission of Macmillan Publishing Company.

qualities and laws of art, or of the beautiful (if that be the content of art), or the nature of taste (if taste decides the question of art and its merit), and then on the basis of such definitions acknowledge as art those productions which correspond to these laws and reject those which do not come under them.

• • •

In order to define art correctly it is necessary first of all to cease to consider it as a means to pleasure, and to consider it as one of the conditions of human life. Viewing it in this way we cannot fail to observe that art is one of the means of intercourse between man and man.

Every work of art causes the receiver to enter into a certain kind of relationship both with him who produced or is producing the art, and with all those who, simultaneously, previously, or subsequently, receive the same artistic impression.

Speech transmitting the thoughts and experiences of men serves as a means of union among them, and art serves a similar purpose. The peculiarity of this latter means of intercourse, distinguishing it from intercourse by means of words, consists in this, that whereas by words a man transmits his thoughts to another, by art he transmits his feelings.

The activity of art is based on the fact that a man receiving through his sense of hearing or sight another man's expression of feeling, is capable of experiencing the emotion which moved the man who expressed it. To take the simplest example: one man laughs, and another who hears becomes merry, or a man weeps, and another who hears feels sorrow. A man is excited or irritated, and another man seeing him is brought to a similar state of mind. By his movements or by the sounds of his voice a man expresses courage and determination or sadness and calmness, and this state of mind passes on to others. A man suffers, manifesting his sufferings by groans and spasms, and this suffering transmits itself to other people; a man expresses his feelings of admiration, devotion, fear, respect, or love, to certain objects, persons, or phenomena, and others are infected by the same feelings of admiration, devotion, fear, respect, or love, to the same objects, persons, or phenomena.

And it is on this capacity of man to receive another man's expression of feeling and to experience those feelings himself, that the activity of art is based.

If a man infects another or others directly, immediately, by his appearance or by the sounds he gives vent to at the very time he experiences the feeling; if he causes another man to yawn when he himself cannot help yawning, or to laugh or cry when he himself is obliged to laugh or cry, or to suffer when he himself is suffering—that does not amount to art.

Art begins when one person with the object of joining another or others to himself in one and the same feeling, expresses that feeling by certain external indications. To take the simplest example: a boy having experienced, let us say, fear on encountering a wolf, relates that encounter, and in order to evoke in others the feeling he has experienced, describes himself, his condition before the encounter, the surroundings, the wood, his own lightheartedness, and then the wolf's appearance, its movements, the distance between himself and the wolf, and so forth. All this, if only the boy when telling the story again experiences the feelings he had lived through, and infects the hearers and compels them to feel what he had experienced—is art. Even if the boy had not seen a wolf but had frequently been afraid of one, and if wishing to evoke in others the fear he had felt, he invented an encounter with a wolf and recounted it so as to make his hearers share the feelings he experienced when he feared the wolf, that also would be art. And just in the same way it is art if a man, having experienced either the fear of suffering or the attraction of enjoyment (whether in reality or in imagination), expresses these feelings on canvas or in marble so that others are infected by them. And it is also art if a man feels, or imagines to himself, feelings of delight, gladness, sorrow, despair, courage, or despondency, and the transition from one to another of these feelings, and expresses them by sounds so that the hearers are infected by them and experience them as they were experienced by the composer.

The feelings with which the artist infects others may be most various—very strong or very weak, very important or very insignificant, very bad or very good: feelings of love of one's country, self-devotion and submission to fate or to God expressed in a drama, raptures of lovers described in a novel, feelings of voluptuousness expressed in a picture, courage expressed in a triumphal march, merriment evoked by a dance, humor evoked by a funny story, the feeling of quietness transmitted by an evening landscape or by a lullaby, or the feeling of admiration evoked by a beautiful arabesque—it is all art.

If only the spectators or auditors are infected by the feelings which the author has felt, it is art.

To evoke in oneself a feeling one has once experienced and having evoked it in oneself then by means of movements, lines, colors, sounds, or forms expressed in words, so to transmit that feeling that others experience the same feeling—this is the activity of art.

Art is a human activity consisting in this, that one man consciously by means of certain external signs, hands on to others feelings he has lived through, and that others are infected by these feelings and also experience them.

Art is not, as the metaphysicians say, the manifestation of some mysterious Idea of beauty or God; it is not, as the esthetic physiologists say, a game in which man lets off his excess of stored-up energy; it is not the expression of man's emotions by external signs; it is not the production of

pleasing objects; and, above all, it is not pleasure; but it is a means of union among men joining them together in the same feelings, and indispensable for the life and progress towards well-being of individuals and of humanity.

As every man, thanks to man's capacity to express thoughts by words, may know all that has been done for him in the realms of thought by all humanity before his day, and can in the present, thanks to this capacity to understand the thoughts of others, become a sharer in their activity and also himself hand on to his contemporaries and descendants the thoughts he has assimilated from others as well as those that have arisen in himself; so, thanks to man's capacity to be infected with the feelings of others by means of art, all that is being lived through by his contemporaries is accessible to him, as well as the feelings experienced by men thousands of years ago, and he has also the possibility of transmitting his own feelings to others.

If people lacked the capacity to receive the thoughts conceived by men who preceded them and to pass on to others their own thoughts, men would be like wild beasts, or like Kasper Hauser.

And if men lacked this other capacity of being infected by art, people might be almost more savage still, and above all more separated from, and more hostile to, one another.

And therefore the activity of art is a more important one, as important as the activity of speech itself and as generally diffused.

• • •

A few days ago I was returning home from a walk feeling depressed, as sometimes happens. On nearing the house I heard the loud singing of a large choir of peasant women. They were welcoming my daughter, celebrating her return home after her marriage. In this singing, with its cries and clanging of scythes, such a definite feeling of joy, cheerfulness, and energy, was expressed, that without noticing how it infected me I continued my way towards the house in a better mood and reached home smiling and quite in good spirits.

That same evening a visitor, an admirable musician, famed for his execution of classical music and particularly of Beethoven, played us Beethoven's sonata, Opus 101. For the benefit of those who might otherwise attribute my judgment of that sonata of Beethoven to non-comprehension of it, I should mention that whatever other people understand of that sonata and of other productions of Beethoven's later period, I, being very susceptible to music, understand equally. For a long time I used to attune myself to delight in those shapeless improvisations which form the subject-matter of the works of Beethoven's later period, but I had only to consider the question of art seriously, and to compare the impression I received from Beethoven's later works, with those pleasant, clear, and strong, musical impressions which are transmitted, for instance, by the melodies of Bach (his arias), Haydn, Mozart, Chopin (when his melodies are not overloaded with complications and ornamentation), of Beethoven himself in his earlier period, and above all, with the impressions produced by folk-songs,—Italian, Norwegian, or Russian,—by the Hungarian *csárdás*, and other such simple, clear, and powerful music, for the obscure, almost unhealthy, excitement from Beethoven's later pieces, which I had artificially evoked in myself, to be immediately destroyed.

On the completion of the performance (though it was noticeable that every one had become dull) those present warmly praised Beethoven's profound production in the accepted manner, and did not forget to add that formerly they had not been able to understand that last period of his, but that they now saw he was really then at his very best. And when I ventured to compare the impression made on me by the singing of the peasant women—an impression which had been shared by all who heard it—with the effect of this sonata, the admirers of Beethoven only smiled contemptuously, not considering it necessary to reply to such strange remarks.

But for all that, the song of the peasant women was real art transmitting a definite and strong feeling, while the 101st sonata of Beethoven was only an unsuccessful attempt at art containing no definite feeling and therefore not infectious.

For my work on art I have this winter read diligently, though with great effort, the celebrated novels and stories praised by all Europe, written by Zola, Bourget, Huysmans, and Kipling. At the same time I chanced on a story in a child's magazine, by a quite unknown writer, which told of the Easter preparations in a poor widow's family. The story tells how the mother managed with difficulty to obtain some wheat-flour, which she poured on the table ready to knead. She then went out to procure some yeast, telling the children not to leave the hut and to take care of the flour. When the mother had gone, some other children ran shouting near the window calling those in the hut to come to play. The children forgot their mother's warning, ran into the street, and were soon engrossed in the game. The mother on her return with the yeast finds a hen on the table throwing the last of the flour to her chickens, who were busily picking it out of the dust of the earthen floor. The mother, in despair, scolds the children, who cry bitterly. And the mother begins to feel pity for them—but the white flour has all gone. So to mend matters she decides to make the Easter cake with sifted rye-flour, brushing it over with white of egg and surrounding it with eggs. 'Rye-bread we bake is as good as a cake,' says the mother, using a rhyming proverb to console the children for not having an Easter cake of white flour, and the children, quickly passing from despair to rapture, repeat the proverb and await the Easter cake more merrily even than before.

Well! the reading of the novels and stories by Zola, Bourget, Huysmans, Kipling, and others, handling the most harrowing subjects, did not touch me for one moment, and I was provoked with the authors all the while as one is provoked with a man who considers you so naïve that he does not even conceal the trick by which he intends to take you in. From the first lines one sees the intention with which the book is written, the details all become superfluous, and one feels dull. Above all, one knows that the author had no other feeling all the time than a desire to write a story or a novel, and so one receives no artistic impression. On the other hand I could not tear myself away from the unknown author's tale of the children and the chickens, because I was at once infected by the feeling the author had evidently experienced, re-evoked in himself, and transmitted.

•   •   •

There is one indubitable sign distinguishing real art from its counterfeit—namely, the infectiousness of art. If a man without exercising effort and without altering his standpoint, on reading, hearing, or seeing another man's work experiences a mental condition which unites him with that man and with others who are also affected by that work, then the object evoking that condition is a work of art. And however poetic, realistic, striking, or interesting, a work may be, it is not a work of art if it does not evoke that feeling (quite distinct from all other feelings) of joy and of spiritual union with another (the author) and with others (those who are also infected by it).

The chief peculiarity of this feeling is that the recipient of a truly artistic impression is so united to the artist that he feels as if the work were his own and not some one else's—as if what it expresses were just what he had long been wishing to express. A real work of art destroys in the consciousness of the recipient the separation between himself and the artist, and not that alone, but also between himself and all whose minds receive this work of art. In this freeing of our personality from its separation and isolation, in this uniting of it with others, lies the chief characteristic and the great attractive force of art.

If a man is infected by the author's condition of soul, if he feels this emotion and this union with others, then the object which has effected this is art; but if there be no such infection, if there be not this union with the author and with others who are moved by the same work—then it is not art. And not only is infection a sure sign of art, but the degree of infectiousness is also the sole measure of excellence in art.

The stronger the infection the better is the art, as art, speaking of it now apart from its subject-matter—that is, not considering the value of the feelings it transmits.

And the degree of the infectiousness of art depends on three conditions:

(1) On the greater or lesser individuality of the feeling transmitted; (2) on the greater or lesser clearness with which the feeling is transmitted; (3) on the sincerity of the artist, that is, on the greater or lesser force with which the artist himself feels the emotion he transmits.

The more individual the feeling transmitted the more strongly does it act on the recipient; the more individual the state of soul into which he is transferred the more pleasure does the recipient obtain and therefore the more readily and strongly does he join in it.

Clearness of expression assists infection because the recipient who mingles in consciousness with the author is the better satisfied the more clearly that feeling is transmitted which, as it seems to him, he has long known and felt and for which he has only now found expression.

But most of all is the degree of infectiousness of art increased by the degree of sincerity in the artist. As soon as the spectator, hearer, or reader, feels that the artist is infected by his own production and writes, sings, or plays, for himself, and not merely to act on others, this mental condition of the artist infects the recipient; and, on the contrary, as soon as the spectator, reader, or hearer, feels that the author is not writing, singing, or playing, for his own satisfaction—does not himself feel what he wishes to express, but is doing it for him, the recipient—resistance immediately springs up, and the most individual and the newest feelings and the cleverest technique not only fail to produce any infection but actually repel.

•   •   •

The presence in various degrees of these three conditions: individuality, clearness, and sincerity, decides the merit of a work of art as art, apart from subject matter. All works of art take order of merit according to the degree in which they fulfil the first, the second, and the third, of these conditions. In one the individuality of the feeling transmitted may predominate; in another, clearness of expression; in a third, sincerity; while a fourth may have sincerity and individuality but be deficient in clearness; a fifth, individuality and clearness, but less sincerity; and so forth, in all possible degrees and combinations.

Thus is art divided from what is not art, and thus is the quality of art, as art, decided, independently of its subject matter, that is to say, apart from whether the feelings it transmits are good or bad.

•   •   •

How in the subject matter of art are we to decide what is good and what is bad?

Art like speech is a means of communication and therefore of progress, that is, of the movement of humanity forward towards perfection. Speech renders accessible to men of the latest generation all the knowledge discovered by the experience and reflection both of preceding generations and of the best and foremost men of their own times; art renders accessible to men of the latest generations all the feelings experienced by their predecessors and also those felt by their best and foremost contemporaries. And as the evolution of knowledge proceeds by truer and more necessary knowledge dislodging and replacing what was mistaken and unnecessary, so the evolution of feeling proceeds by means of art—feelings less kind and less necessary for the well-being of mankind being replaced by others kinder and more needful for that end. That is the purpose of art. And speaking now of the feelings which are its subject matter, the more art fulfils that purpose the better the art, and the less it fulfils it the worse the art.

The appraisement of feelings (that is, the recognition of one or other set of feelings as more or less good, more or less necessary for the well-being of mankind) is effected by the religious perception of the age.

In every period of history and in every human society there exists an understanding of the meaning of life, which represents the highest level to which men of that society have attained—an understanding indicating the highest good at which that society aims. This understanding is the religious perception of the given time and society. And this religious perception is always clearly expressed by a few advanced men and more or less vividly perceived by members of the society generally. Such a religious perception and its corresponding expression always exists in every society. If it appears to us that there is no religious perception in our society, this is not because there really is none, but only because we do not wish to see it. And we often wish not to see it because it exposes the fact that our life is inconsistent with that religious perception.

Religious perception in a society is like the direction of a flowing river. If the river flows at all it must have a direction. If a society lives, there must be a religious perception indicating the direction in which, more or less consciously, all its members tend.

And so there always has been, and is, a religious perception in every society. And it is by the standard of this religious perception that the feelings transmitted by art have always been appraised. It has always been only on the basis of this religious perception of their age, that men have chosen from amid the endlessly varied spheres of art that art which transmitted feelings making religious perception operative in actual life. And such art has always been highly valued and encouraged, while art transmitting feelings already outlived, flowing from the antiquated religious perceptions of a former age, has always been condemned and despised. All the rest of art transmitting those most diverse feelings by means of which people commune with one another was not condemned and was tolerated if only it did not transmit feelings contrary to religious perception.

• • •

In painting we must similarly place in the class of bad art all ecclesiastical, patriotic, and exclusive pictures; all pictures representing the amusements and allurements of a rich and idle life; all so-called symbolic pictures in which the very meaning of the symbol is comprehensible only to those of a certain circle; and above all pictures with voluptuous subjects—all that odious female nudity which fills all the exhibitions and galleries. And to this class belongs almost all

the chamber and opera music of our times,— beginning especially with Beethoven (Schumann, Berlioz, Liszt, Wagner),—by its subject-matter devoted to the expression of feelings accessible only to people who have developed in themselves an unhealthy nervous irritation evoked by this exclusive, artificial, and complex music.

'What! the *Ninth Symphony* not a good work of art!' I hear exclaimed by indignant voices.

And I reply: Most certainly it is not. All that I have written I have written with the sole purpose of finding a clear and reasonable criterion by which to judge the merits of works of art. And this criterion, coinciding with the indications of plain and sane sense, indubitably shows me that that symphony of Beethoven's is not a good work of art. Of course to people educated in the worship of certain productions and of their authors, to people whose taste has been perverted just by being educated in such a worship, the acknowledgment that such a celebrated work is bad, is amazing and strange. But how are we to escape the indications of reason and common sense?

Beethoven's *Ninth Symphony* is considered a great work of art. To verify its claim to be such I must first ask myself whether this work transmits the highest religious feeling? I reply in the negative, since music in itself cannot transmit those feelings; and therefore I ask myself next: Since this work does not belong to the highest kind of religious art, has it the other characteristic of the good art of our time—the quality of uniting all men in one common feeling—does it rank as Christian universal art? And again I have no option but to reply in the negative; for not only do I not see how the feelings transmitted by this work could unite people not specially trained to submit themselves to its complex hypnotism, but I am unable to imagine to myself a crowd of normal people who could understand anything of this long, confused, and artificial production, except short snatches which are lost in a sea of what is incomprehensible. And therefore, whether I like it or not, I am compelled to conclude that this work belongs to the rank of bad art. It is curious to note in this connexion, that attached to the end of this very symphony is a poem of Schiller's which (though somewhat obscurely) expresses this very thought, namely, that feeling (Schiller speaks only of the feeling of gladness) unites people and evokes love in them. But though this poem is sung at the end of the symphony, the music does not accord with the thought expressed in the verses; for the music is exclusive and does not unite all men, but unites only a few, dividing them off from the rest of mankind.

CHAPTER 74

MONROE BEARDSLEY

TASTES CAN BE DISPUTED

Monroe Beardsley (1915–1981) was professor of philosophy at Temple University in Philadelphia. A past president of the American Society for Aesthetics, he authored several important works in contemporary aesthetic theory, including *Aesthetics* (1958) and *Aesthetics: A Short History* (1966).[1]

Beardsley argues against Hume and others that tastes in art *can* be disputed, and they *ought* to be. In good analytic fashion, Beardsley tries to clarify the meaning of the terms 'taste' and 'dispute.' We give objective reasons for our aesthetic judgments, just as we do for our political preferences, and we naturally expect others to do the same. Likening a work of art to a tool, directly instrumental to some kind of experience, Beardsley argues that a work of art will appear to have no value to someone who is unskilled—one who does not understand its proper role. We do not claim that the value of a hammer, for instance, is a matter of taste. Similarly, the value of works of art is what they can do to and for us, "if we are capable of having it done." If a person does not have this capacity, it needs to be developed—it is in hope of remedying this unfortunate situation that we must dispute about tastes.

---

[1] From Swarthmore College Alumni Bulletin, Oct., 1958. Reprinted by permission.

TASTE IN ART

We are assured by an old and often-quoted maxim, whose authority is not diminished by its being cast in Latin, that there can be no disputing about tastes. The chief use of this maxim is in putting an end to disputes that last a long time and don't appear to be getting anywhere. And for this purpose it is very efficacious, for it has an air of profound finality, and it also seems to provide a democratic compromise of a deadlocked issue. If you can't convince someone that he is wrong, or bring yourself to admit that he is right, you can always say that neither of you is more wrong than the other, because nobody can be right.

Remarks that serve to close people's debates, however, are quite often just the remarks to start a new one among philosophers. And this maxim is no exception. It has been given a great deal of thought, some of it very illuminating; yet there is still something to be learned from further reflection upon it. Nor is it of small importance to know, if we can, whether the maxim is true or false, for if it is true we won't waste time in futile discussions, and if it is false we won't waste opportunities for fruitful discussion.

The question whether tastes are disputable is one to be approached with wariness. The first thing is to be clear about what it really means. There are two key words in it that we should pay particular attention to.

The first is the word "taste." The maxim is perhaps most readily and least doubtfully applied to taste in its primary sensory meaning: some people like ripe olives, some green; some people like turnips, others cannot abide them; some people will go long distances for pizza pies, others can hardly choke them down. And there are no disputes about olives: we don't find two schools of thought, the Ripe Olive School and the Green Olive School, publishing quarterly journals or demanding equal time on television—probably because there simply isn't much you can say about the relative merits of these comestibles.

But we apply the word "taste," of course, more broadly. We speak of a person's taste in hats and neckties; we speak of his taste in poetry and painting and music. And it is here that the *non disputandum* maxim is most significantly applied. Some people like Auden and others Swinburne, some enjoy the paintings of Jackson Pollock and others avoid them when they can, some people are panting to hear Shostakovitch's lastest symphony and others find no music since Haydn really satisfying. In these cases, unlike the olive case, people are generally not at a loss for words: there is plenty you can say about Shostakovitch, pro or con. They talk, all right; they may praise, deplore, threaten, cajole, wheedle, and scream— but, according to the maxim, they do not really dispute.

This brings us, then, to the second key word. What does it mean to say that we cannot *dispute* about tastes in literature, fine arts, and music, even though we can clearly make known our tastes? It certainly doesn't mean that we cannot disagree, or differ in taste: for obviously we do, and not only we but also the acknowledged or supposed experts in these fields. Consider James Gould Cozzens' novel, *By Love Possessed*, which appeared in August, 1957; consult the critics and reviewers to discover whether it is a good novel. Being a serious and ambitious work by a writer of standing, and also a best seller, it provoked unusually forthright judgments from a number of reviewers and critics—as may be seen in the accompanying quotations. "Masterpiece . . . brilliant . . . distinguished . . . high order . . . mediocre . . . bad;" that just about covers the spectrum of evaluation.

The International Council of the Museum of Modern Art recently took a large collection of American abstract expressionist paintings on tour in Europe. Its reception was reported in *Time*. In Spain some said, "If this is art, what was it that Goya painted?" and others cheered its "furious vitality" and "renovating spirit." In Italy one newspaper remarked, "It is not painting," but "droppings of paint, sprayings, burstings, lumps, squirts, whirls, rubs and marks, erasures, scrawls, doodles and kaleidoscope backgrounds." In Switzerland it was an "artistic event" that spoke for the genius of American art. And of course all these judgments could be found in this country too.

Not a dispute? Well, what is a dispute? Let us take first the plainest case of a disagreement (no matter what it is about): two people who say, "'Tis so!" and "'Taint so!" Let them repeat these words as often as they like, and shout them from the housetops; they still haven't got a dispute going, but merely a contradiction, or perhaps an altercation. But let one person say, "'Tis so!" and give a *reason* why 'tis so—let him say, "Jones is the best candidate for Senator because he is tactful, honest, and has had much experience in government." And let the other person say, "'Taint so!" and give a reason why 'taint so—"Jones is not the best candidate, because he is too subservient to certain interests, indecisive and wishywashy in his own views, and has no conception of the United States' international responsibilities." *Then* we have a dispute—that is, a disagreement in which the parties give reasons for their contentions. Of course this is not all there is to it; the dispute had just begun. But we see how it might continue, each side giving further reasons for its own view, and questioning whether the reasons given by the other are true, relevant, and compelling.

It is this kind of thing that counts as a dispute about the possibility of getting to the moon,

about American intervention in the Middle East, about a Supreme Court decision, or anything else. And if we can dispute about these things, why not about art?

But here is where the *non disputandum* maxim would draw the line. We do not speak (or not without irony) about people's tastes in Senatorial candidates or missile policies (if the President replied to critics by saying, "Well, your taste is for speeding up the missile program and spending money, but that's not to my taste," we would feel he ought to back up his opinion more than that). Nor do we speak of tastes in international affairs, or laws, or constitutions. And that seems to be because we believe that judgments on these matters can be, and ought to be, based on good reasons—not that they always are, of course. To prefer a democratic to a totalitarian form of government is *not* just a matter of taste, though to like green olives better than ripe olives is a matter of taste, and we don't require the green olive man to rise and give his reasons, or even to *have* reasons. What kind of reasons could he have? "Green olives are better because they are green" would not look like much of a reason to the ripe olive devotee.

The question, then, is whether a preference for Picasso or Monteverdi is more like a preference for green olives or like a preference for a Senatorial candidate: is it *arguable*? can it be *reasoned*.

When we read what critics and reviewers have to say about the things they talk about, we cannot doubt that they do not merely praise or blame, but defend their judgments by giving reasons, or what they claim to be reasons. . . . But according to the Aesthetic Skeptic—if I may choose this convenient name for the upholder of the "no disputing" doctrine—this is an illusion. The apparent reasons are not genuine reasons, or cannot be compelling reasons, like the ones we find in other fields. For in the last analysis they rest upon sheer liking or disliking, which is not susceptible of rational discussion. . . . The Aesthetic Skeptic would analyze all apparent disputes among critics in these terms: the critic can point out features of the novel, the abstract expressionist painting, the quintet for winds, but when he does this he is taking for granted, what may not be true, that you happen to like these features. You can't, says the Skeptic, argue anybody into liking something he doesn't like, and that's why there's no disputing about tastes; all disputes are in the end useless. . . .

. . . I should like to consider briefly some of the difficulties in Aesthetic Skepticism, as I see it, and point out the possibility of an alternative theory.

The Skeptical theory takes people's likes and dislikes as ultimate and unappealable facts about them; when two people finally get down to saying "I like X" and "I don't like X" (be it the flavor of turnip or subtlety of texture in music), there the discussion has to end, there the dispute vanishes. But though it is true that you can't change a disliking into a liking by arguments, that doesn't imply that you can't change it at all, or that we cannot argue whether or not it *ought* to be changed. . . . But the fact remains that one person can give reasons to another why he would be better off if he *could* enjoy music or painting that he now abhors, and sometimes the other person can set about indirectly, by study and enlarged experience, to change his own tastes, or, as we say, to improve them. There is not just your taste or mine, but better and worse taste; and this doesn't mean just that I have a taste for my taste, but not yours—I might in fact have a distaste for the limitations of my own taste (though that is a queer way to put it). It is something like a person with deep-rooted prejudices, to which he has been conditioned from an early age; perhaps he cannot quite get rid of them, no matter how he tries, and yet he may acknowledge in them a

weakness, a crippling feature of his personality, and he may resolve that he will help his children grow up free from them.

The Skeptic does not allow for the possibility that we might give reasons why a person would be better off if he liked or disliked *By Love Possessed* in the way, and to the degree, that it deserves to be liked or disliked. Sometimes, I think, he really holds that it would not be worth the trouble. After all, what does it matter whether people like green olives or ripe olives? We can obtain both in sufficient supply, and nothing much depends upon it as far as the fate of the world is concerned. That's another reason why we ordinarily don't speak of Senatorial candidates as a matter of taste—unless we want to be disparaging, as when people speak of the President's choice in Secretaries of State, to imply that he has no good reason for his choice. It does matter who is Senator, or Secretary of State—it matters a great deal. . . .

Now of course, if we are thinking of our two musical disputants about the relative merits of the two quintets, this is a dispute we may safely leave alone. Both quintets are of such a high order that it perhaps doesn't matter enormously which we decide to rank higher than the other, though there's no harm in trying to do this, if we wish. But the question about *By Love Possessed* is whether it is a "masterpiece" or "bad"; and the question about the paintings is whether they ought to be shown abroad at all. It may not matter so very much whether a person on the whole admires Mozart or Beethoven more, but what if he cannot make up his mind between Mozart and Strauss, or between Beethoven and Shostakovitch?

The fact is that the prevailing level of taste in the general public matters a great deal to me, for it has a great deal to do with determining what I shall have the chance to read, what movies will be filmed, shown, or censored, what music will be played most availably on the radio, what plays will be performed on television. And it has a great deal to do with what composers and painters and poets will do, or whether some of them will do anything at all. But more than that, even: if I am convinced that the kinds of experiences that can only be obtained by access to the greatest works is an important ingredient of the richest and most fully-developed human life, then do I not owe it to others to try to put that experience within their reach, or them within its reach? It might be as important to them as good housing, good medical and dental care, or good government.

But here is another point at which the Skeptic feels uneasy. Isn't it undemocratic to go around telling other people that they have crude tastes—wouldn't it be more in keeping with our laissez-faire spirit of tolerance, and less reminiscent of totalitarian absolutism and compulsion, to let others like and enjoy what they like and enjoy? Isn't this their natural right?

There are too many confusions in this point of view to clear them all up briefly. But some of them are worth sorting out. Of course it is a person's right to hear the music he enjoys, provided it doesn't bother other people too much. But it is no invasion of his right, if he is willing to consider the problem, to try to convince him that he should try to like other things that appear to deserve it. . . .

The distinction that many Skeptics find it hard to keep in mind is this: I may hold that there *is* a better and a worse in music and novels without at all claiming that *I know for certain* which are which. Those critics and reviewers who pronounced their judgments on *By Love Possessed* are not necessarily dogmatic because they deny that it's all a matter of taste (even though some of them were more positive than they had a right to be). They believe that some true and reasonable judgment of the novel is in principle possible,

and that objective critics, given time and discussion, could in principle agree, or come close to agreeing, on it. But they do not have to claim infallibility—people can be mistaken about novels, as they can about anything else. Works of art are complicated. There need be nothing totalitarian about literary criticism, and there is nothing especially democratic in the view that nobody is wrong because there is no good or bad to be wrong about.

It would help us all, I think, to look at the problem of judging works of art in a more direct way. These judgments, as can easily be seen in any random collection of reviews, go off in so many directions that it sometimes seems that the reviewers are talking about different things. We must keep our eye on the object—the painting, the novel, the quintet. Because the composer's love affairs were in a sorry state at the time he was composing, people think that the value of the music must somehow be connected with this circumstance. Because the painter was regarding his model while he painted, people think that the value of the painting must depend on some relation to the way she really looked, or felt. Because the novelist is known to be an anarchist or a conservative, people think that the value of the novel must consist partly in its fidelity to these attitudes. Now, of course, when we approach a work of art, there are many kinds of interest that we can take in it, as well as in its creator. But when we are trying to judge it *as* a work of art, rather than as biography or social criticism or something else, there is a central interest that ought to be kept in view.

A work of art, whatever its species, is an object of some kind—something somebody made. And the question is whether it was worth making, what it is good for, what can be done with it. In this respect it is like a tool. Tools of course are production goods, instrumental to other instruments, whereas paintings and musical

829

compositions and novels are consumption goods, directly instrumental to some sort of experience. And their own peculiar excellence consists, I believe, in their capacity to afford certain valuable kinds and degrees of aesthetic experience. Of course they do not yield this experience to those who cannot understand them, just as a tool is of no use to one who has not the skill to wield it. But we do not talk in the Skeptical way about tools: we do not say that the value of a hammer is all a matter of taste, some people having a taste for hammering nails, some not. No, the value resides in its capability to drive the nail, given a hand and arm with the right skill, and if the need should arise. And this value it would have, though unrealized, even if the skill were temporarily lost.

So with works of art, it seems to me. Their value is what they can do to and for us, if we are capable of having it done. As for those who do not, or not yet, have this capacity, it is not a simple fact that they do not, but a misfortune, and the only question is whether, or to what extent, it can be remedied. It is because this question sometimes has a hopeful answer that we dispute, and must dispute, about tastes. When the political disputant gives his reasons for supporting one Senatorial candidate over another, he cites facts about that candidate that he knows, from past experience, justify the hope of a good performance—the hope that the candidate, once elected, will do what a Senator is supposed to do, well. When the critic gives his reasons for saying that a work of art is good or bad, he is not, as the Skeptic claims, trying to guess whom it will please or displease; he is pointing out those features of the work—its qualities, structure, style, and so on—that are evidence of the work's ability or inability to provide qualified readers, listeners, or viewers, with a deep aesthetic experience.

CHAPTER 75

JOHN DEWEY

ART AS EXPERIENCE

John Dewey (1859–1952), philosopher and educator, was born in Burlington, Vermont. He was a shy youth who did not do particularly well in the formal system of schooling of his day, but his influence as an educational reformer made him known around the world. Following his graduation from the University of Vermont, he taught for a brief time in a Pennsylvania high school. He later studied at and received a Ph.D. from the newly formed Johns Hopkins University in Baltimore. He taught for ten years at the University of Michigan, for a short time at the University of Minnesota, and for ten years at the University of Chicago, where his innovative ideas about education attracted much attention. In 1904 he moved to Columbia University, remaining there until his retirement in 1930. Upon retiring, Dewey led an active life, writing and lecturing not only on philosophy but also on art, education, science, and social and political reform.

Dewey was a staunch defender of democracy and an outspoken champion of social and educational reform. As an opponent of "passive learning" and the sterility of that brand of philosophy that remains remote from real life, his goal was to make philosophy relevant to the practical problems of humanity. He lectured widely in the United States and all over the world, including China, Japan, Turkey, Mexico, and Russia. He spent two years in China, helping to reorganize the educational system there.

Dewey was a prolific writer: a complete bibliography of his works runs to more than 150 pages. Among his most influential books are *Democracy and Education* (1916), *Reconstruction in Philosophy* (1920), and *Art as Experience* (1934).[1]

Dewey's theory of art is based on a theory of experience. Having an experience, he claims, is different from just being alive. Experience is "an affair of the intercourse of a living being with its social and physical environment." The basic rhythm of organic existence results from an organism's falling out of step with its environment and the restoration of equilibrium between the two. Art is built on the same pattern as the ceaseless rhythm of organic life. Our natural delight in artistic resolution of tensions is rooted biologically in our being; we sense satisfaction when we reach a higher state of adjustment with our environment than we had previously. Not since Aristotle has a philosopher placed such stress on the "organic quality" of art.

Dewey believes that aesthetic experience presents a challenge to philosophy to attend to the artfulness of everyday life. Our aim throughout life is to reconstruct our everyday experiences so that they become more and more harmonious, determinate, and meaningful. By presenting us with tensions that build to culmination and resolution, art alerts us to the tensions in need of resolution in our lives, and rewards us with a sense of aesthetic delight as those tensions are resolved. If philosophy means to illuminate experience in general—and it does—then it must pay attention to art, which lays bare the meaning of experience and gives us back a sense of ourselves.

ART AS EXPERIENCE

The Challenge to Philosophy

Esthetic experience is imaginative. This fact, in connection with a false idea of the nature of imagination, has obscured the larger fact that all *conscious* experience has of necessity some degree of imaginative quality. For while the roots of every experience are found in the interaction of a live creature with its environment, that experience becomes conscious, a matter of perception, only when meanings enter it that are derived from prior experiences. Imagination is the only gateway through which these meanings can find their way into a present interaction; or rather, as we have just seen, the conscious adjustment of the new and the old *is* imagination. Interaction of a living being with an environment is found in vegetative and animal life. But the experience enacted is human and conscious only as that which is given here and now is extended by meanings and values drawn from what is absent in fact and present only imaginatively.[2]

[2]"Mind denotes a whole system of meanings as they are embodied in the workings of organic life. . . . Mind is a constant luminosity; consciousness is intermittent, a series of flashes of different intensities."

[1]Reprinted by permission of The Putnam Publishing Group from *Art as Experience* by John Dewey. Copyright © 1934 by John Dewey, 1962 renewed.

There is always a gap between the here and now of direct interaction and the past interactions whose funded result constitutes the meanings with which we grasp and understand what is now occurring. Because of this gap, all conscious perception involves a risk; it is a venture into the unknown, for as it assimilates the present to the past it also brings about some reconstruction of that past. When past and present fit exactly into one another, when there is only recurrence, complete uniformity, the resulting experience is routine and mechanical; it does not come to consciousness in perception. The inertia of habit overrides adaptation of the meaning of the here and now with that of experiences, without which there is no consciousness, the imaginative phase of experience.

Mind, that is the body of organized meanings by means of which events of the present have significance for us, does not always enter into the activities and undergoings that are going on here and now. Sometimes it is baffled and arrested. Then the stream of meanings aroused into activity by the present contact remain aloof. Then it forms the matter of reverie, of dream; ideas are floating, not anchored to any existence as its property, its possession of meanings. Emotions that are equally loose and floating cling to these ideas. The pleasure they afford is the reason why they are entertained and are allowed to occupy the scene; they are attached to existence only in a way that, as long as sanity abides, is felt to be only fanciful and unreal.

In every work of art, however, these meanings are actually embodied in a material which thereby becomes the medium for their expression. This fact constitutes the peculiarity of all experience that is definitely esthetic. Its imaginative quality dominates, because meanings and values that are wider and deeper than the particular here and now in which they are anchored are realized by way of *expressions* although not by way

of an object that is physically efficacious in relation to other objects. Not even a useful object is produced except by the intervention of imagination. Some existent material was perceived in the light of relations and possibilities not hitherto realized when the steam engine was invented. But when the imagined possibilities were embodied in a new assemblage of natural materials, the steam engine took its place in nature as an object that has the same physical effects as those belonging to any other physical object. Steam did the physical work and produced the consequences that attend any expanding gas under definite physical conditions. The sole difference is that the conditions under which it operates have been arranged by human contrivance.

The work of art, however, unlike the machine, is not only the outcome of imagination, but operates imaginatively rather than in the realm of physical existences. What it does is to concentrate and enlarge an immediate experience. The formed matter of esthetic experience directly *expresses*, in other words, the meanings that are imaginatively evoked; it does not, like the material brought into new relations in a machine, merely provide *means* by which purposes over and beyond the existence of the object may be executed. And yet the meanings imaginatively summoned, assembled, and integrated are embodied in material existence that here and now interacts with the self. The work of art is thus a challenge to the performance of a like act of evocation and organization, through imagination, on the part of the one who experiences it. It is not just a stimulus to and means of an overt course of action.

This fact constitutes the uniqueness of esthetic experience, and this uniqueness is in turn a challenge to thought. It is particularly a challenge to that systematic thought called philosophy. For esthetic experience is experience in its integrity. Had not the term "pure" been so often abused in philosophic literature, had it not been so often employed to suggest that there is something alloyed, impure, in the very nature of experience and to denote something beyond experience, we might say that esthetic experience is pure experience. For it is experience freed from the forces that impede and confuse its development as experience; freed, that is, from factors that subordinate an experience as it is directly had to something beyond itself. To esthetic experience, then, the philosopher must go to understand what experience is.

For this reason, while the theory of esthetics put forth by a philosopher is incidentally a test of the capacity of its author to have the experience that is the subject-matter of his analysis, it is also much more than that. It is a test of the capacity of the system he puts forth to grasp the nature of experience itself. There is no test that so surely reveals the one-sidedness of a philosophy as its treatment of art and esthetic experience. Imaginative vision is the power that unifies all the constituents of the matter of a work of art, making a whole out of them in all their variety. Yet all the elements of our being that are displayed in special emphases and partial realizations in other experiences are merged in esthetic experience. And they are so completely merged in the immediate wholeness of the experience that each is submerged:—it does not present itself in consciousness as a distinct element.

CONTEMPORARY PERSPECTIVES: THE ARTIST AND SOCIETY

Artists are special people. Nearly everyone agrees that what makes art possible and valuable is that it involves human expressiveness. Because artists have creative intentions and are able to translate those emotional intentions into works of art, they play a special role in society. The creative process is especially important. What we admire most in artists is their originality—their ability to use materials imaginatively to come up with something inventive and new. Artists do not merely hold a mirror up to nature; they dream, imagine, and create new possible worlds and present them to us for our scrutiny.

Why are artists and works of art so important to society? In a lively essay, the philosopher William Gass argues that it is not necessarily the message of a work of art that is socially important; rather, it is the uncompromising *reality* of art that is most arresting. It is not necessary for art to tell the truth (such a "truth" would be polka dot, Gass contends) but it is necessary for art to be honest, and "all there." A work of art must confront us the way few people dare to: completely, openly, at once. The aim of the artist is simply to bring into the world objects that do not already exist there—objects that are especially worthy of our love.

And what of the artist? According to Gass, we are ambivalent in our feelings toward artists. Frequently, artists are moral failures, who cannot face the world in the same way that they face their canvas, or block of stone, or printed page.

Nevertheless, Gass believes that artists possess certain virtues, which he enumerates as honesty, presence, unity, awareness, sensuality, and totality. In a controversial ending to his essay, Gass writes that artists are also revolutionaries who are necessarily the enemies of the state. The revolutionary activity of the artist operates at the level of consciousness. As Gass puts it, "[T]he torn up street is too simple for him when he sculpts or paints. He undermines everything."

William Gass is a philosopher whose fiction has won critical acclaim. Like the work of British novelist Iris Murdoch, who began her career as a philosopher, his fiction is full of philosophical themes. Elizabeth Bishop, by contrast, is one of this century's finest poets. Yet, as we have seen in the Orientation to Part 5, her poetry is deeply reflective, and, one might say, philosophical.

Bishop's poem "The Man-Moth" was inspired by a typographical error in a New York newspaper—a misprint for "mammoth." From this fortuitous error Bishop was inspired to create her surrealistic hero—the Man-Moth—whom many believe to be a representation of the artist. Emerging from the shadows, from an opening under the edge of a sidewalk, the Man-Moth pays occasional visits to the surface (conscious life), where ordinary people live. Fearful, he nevertheless climbs as high up the sides of buildings as he can, driven by his curiosity and the need to investigate. He fails, of course, in his life above the surface, and so returns to the underground existence that he calls home (a return to the *unconscious*, the realm of imagination and the source of creativity).

Bishops' depiction of the artist in the last three stanzas is uncanny. The artist in society is in many ways a misfit. Hence, Bishop speaks of the Man-Moth on the subway, *always seated facing the wrong way;* he cannot tell the rate at which he travels backward. Each night he must dream recurrent dreams and live with the constant presence of the "third rail"—a reference to the electric source of the subway, responsible for the death of countless people who have been electrified by touching it. The artist regards the third rail as "a disease he has inherited the susceptibility to." Does Bishop mean that artistic vision is a curse—that the artist must see what no one else can see, resigned to draw upon the power of the third rail, knowing full well that that power may be the source of death? With what inner demons must the artist contend in order to get a work out entire, unblemished, and pure? What is the price of this gift, of this striving with one's unconscious in order to create?

And what has the artist to offer us? One tear, like the bee's sting, his only possession. The artist offers up to us his work like a fragile human tear he has cried for us; if you're not paying attention, he'll swallow it. However, if you watch (if you give yourself over to the work of art, the artist's prized possession), he'll hand it over to you, "cool as from underground springs and pure enough to drink." The pleasure of aesthetic experience, Bishop is telling us, is the product of the artist's loving labor—it refreshes us, makes us "more nearly human", unites us with the surrealistic world of the artist. We enter the Man-Moth's underground and are blessed.

CHAPTER 76

WILLIAM H. GASS

THE ARTIST AND SOCIETY

William H. Gass (1924–   ) is David May Distinguished University Professor in the Humanities at Washington University in St. Louis. Gass is somewhat unusual in that he is a philosopher who has also written critically acclaimed works of fiction, including *Omensetter's Luck* (1966), *In the Heart of the Heart of the Country* (1968), and *Willie Master's Lonesome Wife* (1971). His philosophical writings include *Fiction and the Figures of Life* (1970), *The World Within the World* (1979), and *Habitations of the Word* (1985), all collections of critical essays.

THE ARTIST AND SOCIETY[1]

The tame bear's no better off than we are. You've seen how he sways in his cage. At first you might think him musical, but the staves are metal, and his movements are regular and even like the pulses of a pump. It's his nerves. Even when he claps his paws, rises like a man to his hind feet and full height, he looks awkward, feels strange, unsure (his private parts and underbelly are exposed); he trembles. Smiling (you remember the fawning eyeshine of the bear), he focuses his nose and waits for the marshmallow we're about to toss, alert to snap up the sweet cotton in his jaws. There's something terrible about the tame caged bear . . . all that wildness become marsh-

[1]From "The Artist in Society," in *Fiction and the Figures of Life*. New York: Alfred A. Knopf, Inc., 1970, 276–288. Reprinted by permission.

mallow, terrible for his heart, his liver, his teeth (a diet so sugary and soft and unsubstantial, the bowels seek some new employment), and terrible for us—for what we've lost. His eyes, too, are filled with a movement that's not in the things he sees, but in himself. It is the movement of his own despair, his ineffectual rage.

My subject is the artist and society, not the tamed, trained bear, but in many ways the subjects are the same. Artists are as different as men are. It would be wrong to romanticize about them. In our society, indeed, they may live in narrower and more frightened corners than most of us do. We should not imitate their ways; they're not exemplary, and set no worthy fashions. Nor does the artist bear truth dead and drooping in his arms like a lovelorn maiden or a plump goose. His mouth hasn't the proper shape for prophecies. Pot or bottle ends or words or other mouths—whole catalogs of kissing—noisy singing, the folds of funny faces he's created and erased, an excess of bugling have spoiled it for philosophy. In the ancient quarrel between the poets and philosophers, Plato was surely right to think the poets liars. They lie quite roundly, unashamedly, with glee and gusto, since lies and fancies, figments and inventions, outrageous falsehoods are frequently more real, more emotionally pure, more continuously satisfying to them than the truth, which is likely to wear a vest, fancy bucket pudding, technicolor movies, and long snoozes through Sunday.

W. H. Auden remarked quite recently, when pestered, I think it was, about Vietnam:

> Why writers should be canvassed for their opinion on controversial political issues I cannot imagine. Their views have no more authority than those of any reasonably well-educated citizen. Indeed, when read in bulk, the statements made by writers, including the greatest, would seem to indicate that literary talent and political common sense are rarely found together. . . .

Israel makes war, and there are no symposia published by prizefighters, no pronouncements from hairdressers, not a ding from the bellhops, from the dentists not even a drill's buzz, from the cabbies nary a horn beep, and from the bankers only the muffled chink of money. Composers, sculptors, painters, architects: they have no rolled-up magazine to megaphone themselves, and are, in consequence, ignored. But critics, poets, novelists, professors, journalists—those used to shooting off their mouths—they shoot (no danger, it's only their own mouth's wash they've wallowed their words in); and those used to print, they print; but neither wisdom nor goodwill nor magnanimity are the qualities which will win you your way to the rostrum . . . just plentiful friends in pushy places and a little verbal skill.

If it is pleasant to be thought an expert on croquet, imagine what bliss it is to be thought an authority on crime, on the clockwork of the human heart, the life of the city, peace and war. How hard to relinquish the certainty, which most of us have anyway, of *knowing*. How sweet it is always to be asked one's opinion. What a shame it is, when asked, not to have one.

Actually Auden's observation can be spread two ways: to include all artists, not writers merely, and to cover every topic not immediately related to their specialized and sometimes arcane talents. It's only the failed artist and his foolish public who would like to believe otherwise, for if they can honestly imagine that the purpose of art is to teach and to delight, to double the face of the world as though with a mirror, to penetrate those truths which nature is said to hold folded beneath her skirts and keeps modesty hidden from the eyes and paws of science, then they will be able to avoid art's actual impact altogether, and the artist's way of life can continue to seem outrageous, bohemian, quaint, a little sinful, irresponsible, hip, and charming, something to visit like the Breton peasants on a holiday, and not a challenge *to* and denial *of* their own manner of existence, an accusation concerning their own lack of reality.

Yet the social claims for art, and the interest normal people take in the lives of their artists, the examinations of the psychologists, the endless studies by endlessly energetic students of nearly everything, the theories of the philosophers, the deadly moral danger in which art is periodically presumed to place the young, unhappily married women, sacred institutions, tipsy souls, and unsteady parliaments, and all those nice persons in positions of power: these claims and interests are so regularly, so inevitably, so perfectly and purely irrelevant that one must begin to suspect that the tight-eyed, squeeze-eared, loin-lacking enemies of art are right; that in spite of everything that's reasonable, in spite of all the evidence, for example, that connoisseurs of yellowing marble statuary and greenish Roman coins are no more moral than the rest of us; that artists are a murky-headed, scurvy-living lot; that if art told the truth, truth must be polkadot; in spite, in short, of insuperable philosophical obstacles (and what obstacles, I ask you, could be more insuperable than those), art does tell us, in its manner, how to live, and artists are quite remarkable, even exemplary, men. We are right to keep them caged.

Thus I begin again, but this time on the other side.

Ronald Laing begins his extraordinary little book *The Politics of Experience*[2] by saying:

Few books today are forgivable. Black on the canvas, silence on the screen, an empty white sheet of paper, are perhaps feasible. There is little conjunction of truth and social "reality."

[2](New York: Pantheon, 1967).

Around us are pseudo-events, to which we adjust with a false consciousness adapted to see these events as true and real, and even as beautiful. In the society of men the truth resides now less in what things are than in what they are not. Our social realities are so ugly if seen in the light of exiled truth, and beauty is almost no longer possible if it is not a lie.

You can measure the reality of an act, a man, an institution, custom, work of art in many ways: by the constancy and quality of its effects, the depth of the response which it demands, the kinds and range of values it possesses, the actuality of its presence in space and time, the multiplicity and reliability of the sensations it provides, its particularity and uniqueness on the one hand, its abstract generality on the other—I have no desire to legislate concerning these conditions, insist on them all.

We can rob these men, these acts and objects, of their reality by refusing to acknowledge them. We pass them on the street but do not see or speak. We have no Negro problem in our small Midwestern towns. If someone has the experience of such a problem, he is mistaken. What happened to him did not happen; what he felt he did not feel; the urges he has are not the urges he has; what he wants he does not want. Automatically I reply to my son, who has expressed his desire for bubble gum: Oh, Peppy, you don't want that. Number one, then: we deny. We nullify the consciousness of others. We make their experiences unreal.

Put yourself in a public place, at a banquet—one perhaps at which awards are made. Your fork is pushing crumbs about upon your plate while someone is receiving silver in a bowler's shape amid the social warmth of clapping hands. How would you feel if at this moment a beautiful lady in a soft pink nightie should lead among the tables a handsome poodle who puddled under them, and there was a conspiracy among the rest of us not to notice? Suppose we sat quietly; our expressions did not change; we looked straight through her, herself as well as nightie, toward the fascinating figure of the speaker; suppose, leaving, we stepped heedlessly in the pools, and afterward we did not even shake our shoes. And if you gave a cry, if you warned, explained, cajoled, implored; and we regarded you then with amazement, rejected with amusement, contempt, or scorn every one of your efforts, I think you would begin to doubt your senses and your very sanity. Well, that's the idea: with the weight of our numbers, our percentile normality, we create insanities: yours, as you progressively doubt more and more of your experience, hide it from others to avoid the shame, saying "There's that woman and her damn dog again," but now saying it silently, for your experience, you think, is private; and ours, as we begin to believe our own lies, and the lady and her nightie, the lady and her poodle, the lady and the poodle's puddles, all *do* disappear, expunged from consciousness like a stenographer's mistake.

If we don't deny, we mutilate, taking a part for the whole; or we rearrange things, exaggerating some, minimizing others. There was a lady, yes, but she was wearing a cocktail dress, and there was a dog, too, very small, and very quiet, who sat primly in her lap and made no awkward demonstrations. Or we invert values, and assume strange obligations, altogether neglecting the ones which are obvious and demanding: we rob the poor to give to the rich rich gifts, to kings their kingdoms, to congressmen bribes, to companies the inexpensive purchase of our lives. We rush to buy poodles with liquid nerves—it has become, like so much else, *the rage*. Teas are fun, we say, but necking's not nice. Imagine. We still *do* say that. Or we permit events to occur for some people but not for others. Women and children have no sexual drives; men don't either, thank god, after fifty—sixty? seventy-five? We discredit events by inserting in otherwise accurate accounts outrageous lies. It was the lady who made the mess, not the poodle. In short, we do what we can to destroy experience—our own and others'. But since we can only act according to the way we see things, *"if our experience is destroyed, our behavior will be destructive."* We live in ruins, in bombed-out shells, in the basements of our buildings. In important ways, we are all mad. You don't believe it? This company, community, this state, our land, is normal? Healthy, is it? Laing has observed that normal healthy men have killed perhaps one hundred million of their fellow normal healthy men in the last fifty years.

Nudists get used to nakedness. We get used to murder.

Why are works of art so socially important? Not for the messages they may contain, not because they expose slavery or cry hurrah for the worker, although such messages in their place and time might be important, but because they insist more than most on their own reality; because of the absolute way in which they exist. Certainly, images exist, shadows and reflections, fakes exist and hypocrites, there are counterfeits (quite real) and grand illusions—but it is simply not true that the copies are as real as their originals, that they meet all of the tests which I suggested earlier. Soybean steak, by god, is soybean steak, and a pious fraud is a fraud. Reality is not a matter of fact, it is an achievement; and it is rare—rarer, let me say—than an undefeated football season. We live, most of us, amidst lies, deceits, and confusions. A work of art may not utter the truth, but it must be honest. It may champion a cause we deplore, but like Milton's Satan, it must in itself be noble; it must be *all there*. Works of art confront us the way few people dare to: completely, openly, at once. They construct,

839

they comprise, our experience; they do not deny or destroy it; and they shame us, we fall so short of the quality of their Being. We line in Lafayette or Rutland—true. We take our breaths. We fornicate and feed. But Hamlet has his history in the heart, and none of us will ever be as real, as vital, as complex and living as he is—a total creature of the stage.

This is a difficult point to make if the reality or unreality of things has not been felt. Have you met a typical nonperson lately? Then say hello, now, to your neighbor. He may be male, but his facial expressions have been put on like lipstick and eyelashes. His greeting is inevitable; so is his interest in the weather. He always smiles; he speaks only in clichés; and his opinions (as bland as Cream of Wheat, as undefined, and—when sugared—just as sweet) are drearily predictable. He has nothing but good to say to people; he collects his wisdom like dung from a Digest; he likes to share his experiences with "folks," and recite the plots of movies. He is working up this saccharine soulside manner as part of his preparation for the ministry.

These are the "good" people. "Bad" people are unreal in the same way.

Nonpersons unperson persons. They kill. For them no one is human. Like cash registers, everyone's the same, should be addressed, approached, the same: all will go ding and their cash drawers slide out when you strike the right key.

So I don't think that it's the message of a work of art that gives it any lasting social value. On the contrary, insisting on this replaces the work with its interpretation, another way of robbing it of its reality. How would you like to be replaced by your medical dossier, your analyst's notes? They take much less space in the file. The analogy, I think, is precise. The aim of the artist ought to be to bring into the world objects which do not already exist there, and objects which are especially worthy of love. We meet

people, grow to know them slowly, settle on some to companion our life. Do we value our friends for their social status, because they are burning in the public blaze? do we ask of our mistress her meaning? calculate the usefulness of our husband or wife? Only too often. Works of art are meant to be lived with and loved, and if we try to understand them, we should try to understand them as we try to understand anyone—in order to know *them* better, not in order to know something else.

Why do public officials, like those in the Soviet Union, object so strenuously to an art which has no images in it—which is wholly abstract, and says nothing? Because originals are dangerous to reproductions. For the same reason that a group of cosmetically constructed, teetotal lady-maidens is made uneasy by the addition of a boozy uncorseted madam. Because it is humiliating to be less interesting, less present, less moving, than an arrangement of enameled bedpans. Because, in a system of social relations based primarily on humbug, no real roaches must be permitted to wander. Because, though this may be simply my helpless optimism, your honest whore will outdraw, in the end, any sheaf you choose of dirty pictures.

Pornography is poor stuff, not because it promotes lascivious feelings, but because these feelings are released by and directed toward unreal things. The artist, in this sense, does not deal in dreams.

Of course there are many objects labeled works of art, I know, which are fakes—the paint, for instance, toupeed to the canvas—but I am thinking of the artist, now, as one who produces the honest article, and obviously, *he* is valuable to society if what he *produces* is valuable to it. He is presently valuable because in his shop or study he concocts amusements for our minds, foods for our souls—foods so purely spiritual and momentary they leave scarcely any stools. However, I wanted to say that despite the good reasons for wondering otherwise, the artist could be regarded an exemplary man—one whose ways are worthy of imitation. How can this be? The fellow sleeps with his models and paint jams the zipper on his trousers.

I think we can regard him as exemplary in this way: we judge it likely that a man's character will show up somewhere in his work; that if he is hot-tempered and impetuous, or reckless and gay . . . well, find somebody else to be your surgeon. And we regularly expect to see the imprint of the person in the deed, the body in the bedclothes. I think it is not unreasonable to suppose, too, that the work a man does works on him, that the brush he holds has his hand for its canvas, that the movements a man makes move the man who makes them just as much, and that the kind of ideals, dreams, perceptions, wishes his labor loves must, in him, love at least that labor

Often enough we lead split lives, the artist as often as anybody; yet it isn't Dylan Thomas or D. H. Lawrence, the drunkard or sadist, I'm suggesting we admire, but the poets they were, and the men they had to be to be such poets. It would have been better if they had been able to assume in the world the virtues they possessed when they faced the page. They were unable. It's hard. And for that the world is partly to blame. It does not *want* its artists, after all. It especially does not want the virtues which artists must employ in the act of their work lifted out of prose and paint and plaster into life.

What are some of these virtues?

Honesty is one . . . the ability to see precisely what's been done . . . the ability to face up . . . because the artist wants his every line to be lovely—that's quite natural—he wants to think well of himself, and cover himself with his own praise like the sundae with its syrup. We all know that artists are vain. But they're not vain while working. We know, too, that they're defensive, inse-

cure. But they dare not be defensive about a bad job, explain their mistakes away, substitute shouting for skill. If a runty tailor dresses himself in his dreams, he may measure for himself the suit of a wrestler. You can fill yourself with air, but will your skin hold it? They don't make balloons with the toughness and resiliency of genius.

Presence is one. The artist cannot create when out of focus. His is not another theatrical performance. There's no one to impress, no audience. He's lived with his work, doubtless, longer than he's had a wife, and it knows all about him in the thorough, hard-boiled way a wife knows. No poseur wrote "The Ballad of Reading Gaol." Presence is a state of concentration on another so complete it leaves you quite without defenses, altogether open; for walls face both ways, as do the bars of a cage. Inquire of the bears how it is. To erect bars is to be behind them. Withholding is not a requirement of poetry.

Unity is another. The artist does not create with something special called imagination which he has and you haven't. He can create with his body because that body has become a mind; he can create with his feelings because they've turned into sensations. He thinks in roughness, loudness, and in color. A painter's hands are magnified eyes. He *is* those fingers—he becomes his medium—and as many fingers close simply in a single fist, so all our faculties can close, and hold everything in one clasp as the petals close in a rose or metal edges crimp.

Awareness is another. Honesty, concentration, unity of being: these allow, in the artist, the world to be *seen*—an unimaginable thing to most of us—to fully take in a tree, a tower, a hill, a graceful arm. If you've ever had an artist's eyes fall on you, you'll know what I mean. Only through such openings may the world pass to existence.

Sensuality is another. Painting and poetry (to

name just two) are sexual acts. The artist is a lover, and he must woo his medium till she opens to him; until the richness in her rises to the surface like a blush. Could we adore one another the way the poet adores his words or the painter his colors—what would be the astonishing result?

Totality is still another. I mean that the artist dare not fail to see the whole when he sees with the whole of him. He sees the ant in the jam, yet the jam remains sweet. He must fall evenly on all sides, like a cloak. If he stops to sing a single feeling, he can do so well because he knows how feelings move; he knows the fish is offset from its shadow; knows the peck of the crow does not disturb the beauty of its beak or the dent it makes in the carrion. There is, it seems to me, in the works of the great, an inner measure, wound to beat, a balance which extends through the limbs like bones, an accurate and profound assessment of the proportion and value of things.

Naturally the artist is an enemy of the state. He cannot play politics, succumb to slogans and other simplifications, worship heroes, ally himself with any party, suck on some politician's program like a sweet. He is also an enemy of every ordinary revolution. As a man he may long for action; he may feel injustice like a burn; and certainly he may speak out. But the torn-up street is too simple for him when he sculpts or paints. He undermines everything. Even when, convinced of the rightness of a cause, he dedicates his skills to a movement, he cannot simplify, he cannot overlook, he cannot forget, omit, or falsify. In the end the movement must reject or even destroy him. The evidence of history is nearly unanimous on this point.

The artist's revolutionary activity is of a different kind. He is concerned with consciousness, and he makes his changes there. His inaction is only a blind, for his books and buildings go off under everything—not once but a thousand times. How often has Homer remade men's minds?

An uncorrupted consciousness . . . what a dangerous thing it is.

One could compile, I do not doubt, another list. These are examples, although central ones. I could so easily be wrong that no one's going to pay me any mind, and so I shall suggest most irresponsibly that we and our world might use more virtues of this kind—the artist's kind—for they are bound to the possibility of Being itself; and occasionally it strikes me as even almost tragic that there should be artists who were able, from concrete, speech, or metal, to release a brilliant life, who nevertheless could not release themselves, either from their own cage, or from ours . . . there is no difference. After all, we are— artists and society—both swaying bears *and* rigid bars. Again, it may be that the *bars* are moving, and the bears, in terror—stricken—are standing behind them . . . no, in front of them—among them—quite, quite still.

CHAPTER 77

ELIZABETH BISHOP

THE MAN-MOTH

Elizabeth Bishop (1911–1979) is regarded as one of this century's finest poets. Only months after Bishop's birth, her father died and her mother suffered a nervous breakdown, and never recovered. A shy child, Elizabeth went to live with her mother's family in Nova Scotia, then to the home of her father's parents in Worcester, Massachusetts. The memory of these traumatic early years surfaces in her poem, "In the Waiting Room" (excerpted in Part 5) and the short story "In the Village."

Bishop was educated at Vassar College. During her senior year, she met the poet Marianne Moore, with whom she developed a lifelong friendship. In her later years, Bishop taught at Harvard University along with her good friend, the Boston poet Robert Lowell.

During her lifetime Bishop published only four volumes of poetry; she was a careful, meticulous writer who often took years to complete a poem. Her first book of verse was entitled *North and South* (1946); it announced the geographical themes that were to become her trademark. In 1955 *A Cold Spring* was published, along with a reprint of *North and South*. Ten years later, in 1965, *Questions of Travel* appeared. Her final volume, published in 1976, is entitled *Geography III*. Her work has been collected and published by Farrar, Straus & Giroux in two volumes: *The Complete Poems: 1927–1979* (1983) and *The Complete Prose* (1984).

THE MAN-MOTH[1]

Here, above,
    cracks in the buildings are filled with
      battered moonlight.
    The whole shadow of Man is only as big
      as his hat.
    It lies at his feet like a circle for a doll to
      stand on,
    and he makes an inverted pin, the point
      magnetized to the moon.
    He does not see the moon; he observes
      only her vast properties,
    feeling the queer light on his hands,
      neither warm nor cold,
    of a temperature impossible to record in
      thermometers.
But when the Man-Moth
    pays his rare, although occasional, visits
      to the surface,
    the moon looks rather different to him.
      He emerges
    from an opening under the edge of one
      of the sidewalks
    and nervously begins to scale the faces of
      the buildings.
    He thinks the moon is a small hole at
      the top of the sky,
    proving the sky quite useless for
      protection.
    He trembles, but must investigate as
      high as he can climb.

Up the façades,
    his shadow dragging like a
      photographer's cloth behind him,
    he climbs fearfully, thinking that this
      time he will manage
    to push his small head through that
      round clean opening
    and be forced through, as from a tube,
      in black scrolls on the light.

(Man, standing below him, has no such
    illusions.)
But what the Man-Moth fears most he
    must do, although
he fails, of course, and falls back scared
    but quite unhurt.

Then he returns
    to the pale subways of cement he calls
      his home. He flits,
    he flutters, and cannot get aboard the
      silent trains
    fast enough to suit him. The doors close
      swiftly.
    The Man-Moth always seats himself
      facing the wrong way
    and the train starts at once at its full,
      terrible speed,
    without a shift in gears or a gradation of
      any sort.
    He cannot tell the rate at which he
      travels backwards.

Each night he must
    be carried through artificial tunnels and
      dream recurrent dreams.
    Just as the ties recur beneath his train,
      these underlie
    his rushing brain. He does not dare look
      out the window,
    for the third rail, the unbroken draught
      of poison,
    runs there beside him. He regards it as a
      disease

he has inherited the susceptibility to. He
has to keep
his hands in his pockets, as others must
wear mufflers.
If you catch him,
hold up a flashlight to his eye. It's all
dark pupil,
an entire night itself, whose haired
horizon tightens
as he stares back, and closes up the eye.

Then from the lids
one tear, his only possession, like the
bee's sting, slips.
Slyly he palms it, and if you're not
paying attention
he'll swallow it. However, if you watch,
he'll hand it over,
cool as from underground springs and
pure enough to drink.

GLOSSARY

AESTHETICS   The study of beauty and the experience of the beautiful.

CATHARSIS   According to Aristotle, the purging or purifying (cleansing) of emotion through art.

GENETIC FALLACY   The fallacy of appraising or explaining something in terms of its origin or beginning.

INTENTIONAL FALLACY   A type of *genetic fallacy* that makes the mistake of confusing artworks with their causes.

FORMAL UNITY   According to Beardsley, the way that *regional qualities* are put together in a unified way.

FORMALISM   An object-centered view of art stressing intrinsic qualities of the object or event itself, not what it represents or expresses.

REGIONAL QUALITIES   According to Beardsley, those qualities such as color, pitch, rhyme and so on that we perceive as part of the whole that we are experiencing. Qualities are regional in the sense that we can actually point them out in a work of art.

FOR FURTHER STUDY

Battcock, Gregory, ed. *The New Art*. New York: E.P. Dutton, 1966.
A critical anthology of articles written by artists and critics active since 1960 in the creation of a new aesthetic.

Bell, Clive. *Art*. New York: Capricorn Books, 1958.
A formalist approach to art, written by one of this century's most influential English theoreticians of art.

Collingwood, R. G. *The Principles of Art*. London: Oxford University Press, 1958.
Reflections on the various meanings of the term "art." An exceptionally well-written book, useful to both beginners and more advanced thinkers.

Dufrenne, Mikel. *The Phenomenology of Aesthetic Experience*. Translated by Edward S. Casey, Albert A. Anderson, Willis Domingo, Leon Jacobson. Evanston: Northwestern University Press, 1973.

A comprehensive phenomenological treatment of art.

Hausman, Carl R. *A Discourse on Novelty and Creation*. The Hague: Martinus Nijhoff, 1975.

The author argues that although creativity cannot be reduced to a system of laws, it is not to be reduced to a "mystery" that defies speech and understanding. Highly recommended.

Prall, D.W. *Aesthetic Analysis*. New York: Thomas Y. Crowell Co., 1936.

An influential book that analyzes aesthetics in terms of the data of sense perception.

NAME INDEX

GENERAL INDEX